MW00512148

k_p Cost of preferred stock

k_{RF} Rate of return on a risk-free security

k_s (1) Cost of retained earnings

(2) Required return on a stock

M   Maturity value of a bond

M/B   Market-to-book ratio

MCC   Marginal cost of capital

n   (1) Life of a project

(2) Number of shares outstanding

NPV   Net present value

P   (1) Price of a share of stock; P_0 = price of the stock today

(2) Sales price per unit of product sold

P/E   Price/earnings ratio

PMT   Periodic level payment of an annuity

PV   Present value

PVA_n Present value of an annuity for n years

PVIF   Present value interest factor for a lump sum

PVIFA   Present value interest factor for an annuity

Q   Quantity produced or sold

r   (1) Rate of return

(2) Correlation coefficient

ROA   Return on assets

ROE   Return on equity

RP   Risk premium

S   Sales

SML   Security Market Line

Σ Summation sign (capital sigma)

σ Standard deviation (lowercase sigma)

σ^2 Variance

t   (1) Tax rate

(2) Time, when used as a subscript (for example, D_t = the dividend in Year t)

TIE   Times interest earned

V   Variable cost per unit

VC   Total variable costs

WACC   Weighted average cost of capital

YTM   Yield to maturity

Introduction to Financial Management

Third Edition

Introduction to Financial Management

Third Edition

B. J. Campsey
San Jose State University

Eugene F. Brigham
University of Florida

The Dryden Press
Harcourt Brace Jovanovich College Publishers

Fort Worth   Philadelphia   San Diego   New York   Orlando   Austin   San Antonio
Toronto   Montreal   London   Sydney   Tokyo

Acquisitions Editor: Ann Heath
Developmental Editor: Kathi Erley
Project Editor: Karen Hill
Design Manager: Alan Wendt
Production Manager: Bob Lange
Permissions Editor: Cindy Lombardo
Director of Editing, Design, and Production: Jane Perkins

Text and Cover Designer: C. J. Petlick, Hunter Graphics
Copy Editor: Maureen Duffy
Compositor: The Clarinda Company
Text Type: 10/12 ITC Garamond Light

Library of Congress Cataloging-in-Publication Data
Campsey, B. J.
    Introduction to financial management / B. J. Campsey, Eugene F.
Brigham. — 3rd ed.
        p.   cm.
    Includes index.
    ISBN 0-03-051008-2
    1. Corporations — Finance.   I. Brigham, Eugene F., 1930–
II. Title.
HG4026.C23   1991
658.15 — dc20   90-43973

The paper used in this publication meets the minimum requirements
of American National Standard for Information Sciences — Permanence
of Paper for Printed Library Materials, ANSI Z39, 48–1984.

Printed in the United States of America
 23-016-9876543
Copyright © 1991, 1989, 1985 by The Dryden Press

All rights reserved. No part of this publication may be reproduced or transmitted in any
form or by any means, electronic or mechanical, including photocopy, recording, or any
information storage and retrieval system, without permission in writing from the publisher.

Requests for permission to make copies of any part of the work should be mailed to:
Permissions Department, Harcourt Brace Jovanovich, Inc., 8th Floor, Orlando, FL 32887.

Address orders:
The Dryden Press
Orlando, FL 32887

Address editorial correspondence:
The Dryden Press
301 Commerce St. Ste. 3700
Ft. Worth, TX 76107

The Dryden Press Series in Finance

Berry and Young
Managing Investments: A Case Approach

Boyet
Security Analysis for Investment Decisions: Text and Software

Brigham
Fundamentals of Financial Management
Fifth Edition

Brigham, Aberwald, and Ball
Finance with Lotus 1-2-3®: Text, Cases, and Models

Brigham and Gapenski
Cases in Financial Management

Brigham and Gapenski
Cases in Financial Management, Module A

Brigham and Gapenski
Financial Management: Theory and Practice
Sixth Edition

Brigham and Gapenski
Intermediate Financial Management
Third Edition

Campsey and Brigham
Introduction to Financial Management
Third Edition

Chance
An Introduction to Options and Futures

Cooley
Advances in Business Financial Management: A Collection of Readings

Cooley and Roden
Business Financial Management
Second Edition

Crum and Brigham
Cases in Managerial Finance
Sixth Edition with 1986 Tax Law Changes

Fama and Miller
The Theory of Finance

Gardner and Mills
Managing Financial Institutions: An Asset/ Liability Approach
Second Edition

Gitman and Joehnk
Personal Financial Planning
Fifth Edition

Goldstein Software, Inc.
Joe Spreadsheet Statistical

Harrington
Case Studies in Financial Decision Making
Second Edition

Johnson
Issues and Readings in Managerial Finance
Third Edition

Kidwell and Peterson
Financial Institutions, Markets, and Money
Fourth Edition

Koch
Bank Management

Martin, Cox, and MacMinn
The Theory of Finance: Evidence and Applications

Mayo
Finance: An Introduction
Third Edition

Mayo
Investments: An Introduction
Third Edition

Pettijohn
PROFIT+

Reilly
Investment Analysis and Portfolio Management
Third Edition

Reilly
Investments
Third Edition

Seitz
Capital Budgeting and Long-Term Financing Decisions

Siegel and Siegel
Futures Markets

Smith and Weston
PC Self-Study Manual for Finance

Tallman and Neale
Financial Analysis and Planning Package

Turnbull
Option Valuation

Weston and Brigham
Essentials of Managerial Finance
Ninth Edition

Weston and Copeland
Managerial Finance
Eighth Edition with Tax Update

Preface

The practice of financial management has changed greatly in recent years. Computers, especially personal computers, are being used increasingly to analyze financial decisions. This usage has made it imperative for financial problems to be set up in a form suitable for quantitative analysis. At the same time, the financial environment has become less predictable and more volatile. In the late 1970s and early 1980s, strong inflationary pressures pushed interest rates to unprecedented highs, and the resulting volatile cost of capital led to profound changes in corporate financial policies and practices. By the mid-1980s, however, inflationary pressures had been reduced, helping the stock market, a barometer of the country's economic health, to set a record high in the summer of 1987. Nevertheless, in October 1987, the stock market crashed, falling by 25 percent in just one day. In 1990, fears of a recession, a conflict in the oil-rich Middle East, inflation, and the huge federal and foreign trade deficits have combined to make financial decision making exceedingly difficult.

In such an uncertain environment, many in the financial world have turned to academicians for answers, and academic researchers have made a number of important contributions. Business practitioners gain insights from the use of financial theory, and in turn they provide feedback from their "real world" perspective, which has led to modifications and improvements in financial theory.

This book focuses on the practitioner, particularly one who will own or manage a small- to medium-size business. Furthermore, the book is designed for the general business student, not just for the finance major. Many so-called introductory texts seem to be designed primarily for finance and accounting majors. These may be excellent textbooks, but in their efforts to include the latest theories (some of which seem to contain little of practical use) or detailed models of financial concepts, the nonfinance major is often lost, or "turned off," to the study of finance. This is unfortunate, because financial decisions affect and in turn are affected by marketing, production, and other business decisions. Thus, all business students should have a thorough knowledge of finance. It is our hope that this book will provide that knowledge, and in a manner that is interesting and enjoyable to all business students, regardless of major.

RELATIONSHIP WITH OUR OTHER BOOKS

As the body of knowledge in finance expanded, it first became difficult, then impossible, to provide "everything one needs to know about financial management" in one text, especially in one undergraduate text. This recognition led us to limit the scope of this book and also to write other texts, with other coauthors, to deal with the materials that must necessarily be deleted from *Introduction to Financial Management.* Thus, Gene Brigham has coauthored with Lou Gapenski both an intermediate undergraduate text (*Intermediate Financial Management,* third edition) and a comprehensive book aimed primarily at MBAs (*Financial Management: Theory and Practice,* sixth edition). Brigham has also written two other introductory undergraduate texts, *Fundamentals of Financial Management,* fifth edition, and *Essentials of Managerial Finance,* ninth edition, coauthored with Fred Weston. *Essentials* and *Fundamentals* are written at the same level, but their organizational structures differ significantly. *Introduction* differs in organization and is less complex than the other undergraduate books.

INTENDED MARKET AND USE

As indicated by its title, *Introduction to Financial Management,* third edition, is intended for use in an introductory course in financial management. The main parts of the text can be covered in a one-term course, but, when supplemented with cases and some outside readings, the text can also be used over two terms.

If the book is to be used in a one-term course, instructors will probably want to cover only selected chapters, leaving the others for students to examine on their own or to use as references in conjunction with work in other courses. In our own courses, we seldom are able to complete an entire book. The material we tend to omit is contained in Chapters 22 and 23; finance majors cover these topics in subsequent courses. Other instructors have indicated that they often save material in Chapters 15, 18, 20, and 21 for an advanced course. In institutions in which a money and banking course is required, instructors may wish to omit parts of Chapters 2, 3, and 4, and in schools that do not require such a course, instructors may wish to present the material in Chapters 13, 16, and 17 earlier in the course than the chapter sequence indicates. Many other course structures are possible, and we have written the book in "modules" to make it easy to cover chapters in a sequence different from the one in the book. The Glossary and Appendix C (which summarizes the equations contained in the text) facilitate the use of alternative course outlines.

SPECIAL FEATURES OF THIS TEXT

1. Streamlined Quantitative Material. A conscious effort has been made to streamline as much of the quantitative material as possible without lowering the quality of the text. Thus, where possible, very detailed mathematical formulas or concepts have been simplified or deleted. For example, our chapter on risk analysis assumes no previous statistical knowledge. Further, the chapters on international finance, mergers, and changes in credit policy have a practical orientation.

2. Decisions in Finance. Each chapter begins with a real financial decision faced by a firm and ends with the resolution to the decision. These sections challenge students to consider how knowledge of the material contained in the chapter would help financial decision makers in the real world.

3. Industry Practice. In most chapters we present a real-world industry practice section, which highlights or expands on a key issue. These illustrations also help to enliven the material in the chapter.

4. Focus on Small Business. More than half of the chapters contain small business sections, written by Professor Christopher Barry of Texas Christian University. These sections are especially useful for giving students a view of finance from the smaller firm's standpoint.

5. Running Glossary. Brief definitions of important terms appear in the margin of the text. In addition, the key terms in each chapter are boldfaced when they are first defined.

6. Self-Test Section. After each major section in the chapter, we have inserted a set of self-test questions which students can review to test their understanding of the material they just read.

7. Bulleted Summary. Key terms in the chapter are highlighted and briefly explained in the end-of-chapter summary. This recapitulation serves as an additional review tool for students.

8. Self-Test Problems. A set of fairly rigorous self-test problems, with detailed solutions, is given at the end of the more difficult quantitative chapters. These problems serve (1) to test the student's ability to set up problems for solution and (2) to explain the solution setup for those who need help.

MAJOR CHANGES IN THE THIRD EDITION

Both the theory and practice of finance are dynamic, and as important new developments occur, they must be incorporated into a textbook such as this one. In addition, we and a team of reviewers are constantly looking for ways to improve the book's clarity and readability. As a result, we have made several important changes in this edition, including the following:

1. All sections of the book were updated to reflect 1990 interest rates, tax laws, and business developments.

2. The "Alternative Forms of Business Organization" section has been moved from Chapter 2 to Chapter 1, and the tax discussion has been combined with the discussion of the financial environment in Chapter 2.

3. A discussion of commonly used money and capital market instruments has been added to the discussion of the financial environment.

4. The chapter on the commercial banking system (Chapter 3) has been completely rewritten — it was both updated and oriented toward a broader discussion of financial institutions.

5. The discussion of interest rates (Chapter 4) has been revised to clarify the nature of the real rate of interest.

6. A balance sheet approach has been added to the discussion of financial forecasting, along with the old AFN equation approach (Chapter 7). The new approach is in many ways easier to understand, and it is much easier to use because it is ideally suited for *Lotus*® *1-2-3*® and other spreadsheet programs.

7. The time value of money chapter (Chapter 13) now includes financial calculator solutions in addition to the tabular approach. Also, time lines are used extensively throughout the chapter to enable students to visualize time value concepts.

8. The sequence of chapters in Part IV has been changed so that risk and return are covered before time value of money. This change enabled us to place the two chapters on capital budgeting (Chapters 14 and 15) adjacent to one another.

9. A new chapter on hybrid forms of financing (Chapter 18) has been added after the discussion of common stock. This new chapter contains concise discussions of leasing (which had been presented in Chapter 23 of the second edition), warrants, convertibles, and options.

10. The sections entitled "Decision in Finance" and "Industry Practice" have been updated with new examples which reflect current business practices and problems. These examples demonstrate to students that an understanding of the material in the chapter is crucial to solving real-world problems, and they also provide guides to the material in the chapter.

ANCILLARY MATERIALS

The extensive package of ancillary materials that accompanies the third edition of *Introduction to Financial Management* provides information specifically designed to enhance the text's usefulness for both students and instructors. Materials developed exclusively for the third edition include the following:

1. Instructor's Manual/Transparency Masters. A complete *Instructor's Manual* is available to instructors who adopt the book. The manual contains (1) answers to all text questions, (2) solutions to all text problems, and (3) extensive lecture notes which focus on the more difficult topics and which are keyed to special lecture transparencies.

A set of transparency masters is included in the *Instructor's Manual*. These masters highlight key material in the text and can be used as the basis for lectures to both large and small classes.

2. Test Bank. A revised and enlarged *Test Bank* with more than 1,500 class-tested questions and problems, in objective format, is available to instructors both in text form and on IBM computer diskettes (5¼"). The diskettes come in either the regular computerized test bank format or in WordPerfect®. The new questions are well suited for both quizzes and exams. Also, the questions have been arranged, within each chapter, by type (true-false questions, multiple choice conceptual questions, and multiple choice numerical problems), by topic, and by degree of difficulty.

3. Supplemental Problems. A set of additional problems, organized according to topic and level of difficulty, is also available to instructors from The Dryden Press.

4. Problem Diskette. A diskette (5¼″) containing *Lotus 1-2-3* models for the computer-related end-of-chapter problems is also available to instructors. To obtain the diskette, instructors must complete the insert card found at the front of the *Instructor's Manual.*

A number of additional items are available for purchase by students:

1. Study Guide. The *Study Guide* outlines the key sections of each chapter, provides students with self-test questions, and also provides them with a set of problems and solutions similar to those in the text.

2. Casebooks. Two new casebooks are now available: (1) *Cases in Financial Management* (Dryden Press, 1990) by Eugene F. Brigham and Louis C. Gapenski, which provides a set of 41 cases to illustrate applications of the methodologies and concepts developed in the text, and (2) a shorter version of the large casebook, *Cases in Financial Management: Module A,* which contains 12 cases and is a perfect supplement for professors who are seeking a limited number of cases at a reduced price.

3. Readings Books. A readings book, *Issues in Managerial Finance,* third edition (Dryden Press, 1987), edited by Ramon E. Johnson, provides an excellent mix of theoretical and practical articles which can be used to supplement the text. Another supplemental reader is *Advances in Business Financial Management: A Collection of Readings* (Dryden Press, 1990), edited by Philip L. Cooley, which provides a broader selection of articles from which to choose.

4. Finance with Lotus 1-2-3: Text, Cases and Models. This text by Eugene F. Brigham, Dana A. Aberwald, and Susan E. Ball (Dryden Press 1988) enables students to learn, on their own, how to use *Lotus 1-2-3,* and it explains how many commonly encountered problems in managerial finance can be analyzed with electronic spreadsheets.

5. PROFIT +. This software supplement by James Pettijohn contains 18 user-friendly programs that include the time value of money, forecasting, and capital budgeting. The supplement includes a user's manual, and it is available for the IBM PC.

ACKNOWLEDGMENTS

This book reflects the efforts of a great many people over a number of years. First, we would like to acknowledge the special critical evaluation and suggestions of Dana Aberwald of the University of Florida, Bodie Dickerson of Oregon State University, and John McDowell of Davenport College. Professor Dickerson also assisted in the selection and design of the transparency masters, and Professor McDowell made numerous helpful comments about the end-of-chapter questions and problems. Dana Aberwald helped with all phases of the revision, from designing questionnaires for reviewers to the final proofreading; without her help, the revision would never have been completed.

The following reviewers merit special thanks for their help on the third edition:

Dan Best
Craven Community College

M. P. Corrigan
Post College

Bodie Dickerson
Oregon State University

David G. Garraty
Virginia Wesleyan College

Frank Jordan
Erie Community College — South

Ambrose P. McCoy
Craven Community College

John McDowell
Davenport College

Charles W. McKinney
Whitworth College

H. R. Pickett
North Carolina Central University

Eugene Poindexter
West Georgia College

Francis C. Thomas
Stockton State College

John E. Thompson
St. Mary's College

JoAnn Vaughan
Campbell University

In addition, we would like to thank the following people, whose reviews and comments on prior editions have contributed to this edition: Frank Aleman, Bruce Berlin, Mike Binder, Joseph H. Black, Sandra Cece, Harlan Cheney, Terrence Clauretie, Bill Colclough, James Collier, Maurice Corrigan, Roy Crum, Faramarz Damanpour, Zane Dennick-Ream, Gene Dunham, Philip Fanara, Jr., Timothy Gallagher, George Granger, Damon J. Johnston, Kimberly McCollough, Joseph Moosally, Austin Murphy, Don Nast, Antonio Rodriguez, Clarence C. Rose, Dennis Schlais, George Seldat, Gary Simpson, Rodney Smith, Les Strickler, Francis Thomas, Marvin Travis, G. W. Ulseth, Paul Vanderheiden, John Wachowicz, James W. Walden, Richard Whiston, Howard R. Whitney, Sally Jo Wright, Elizabeth Yelland, and Terry Zivney.

Special thanks are due to Fred Weston, who has done much to help develop the field of financial management and who provided us with instruction and inspiration; to Ann Pierce, who authored the new "Decision in Finance" and "Industry Practice" sections in each chapter; to Christopher Barry, who authored the "Small Business" sections at the ends of several chapters; to Bruce Cochran, who helped us with the chapter on financial institutions; to Roy Crum, who helped us with the international material; to Art Herrmann, who helped us with the bankruptcy material; to Susan Ball, Mary Alice Hanebury, and Kay Mangan, who helped us develop the *Lotus 1-2-3* models; to Steve Bouchard, who helped with the ancillaries; and to Bob Karp, Carol

Stanton, and Brenda Sapp, who provided both word processing and editorial support.

Both our colleagues and our students at the University of Florida gave us many useful suggestions, and The Dryden Press staff—especially Maureen Duffy, Kathi Erley, Ann Heath, Karen Hill, Mary Jarvis, Bob Lange, Jennifer Lloyd, Cindy Lombardo, Sue Nodine, Jane Perkins, Cate Rzasa, Judy Sarwark, Bill Schoof, and Alan Wendt—helped greatly with all phases of the text development and production. We sometimes complain, but based on our many years of work on textbooks, the Dryden staff is the greatest.

Finally, to our friends and colleagues at San Jose State, the University of Florida, and around the country, thanks for your suggestions and support.

CONCLUSION

Finance is, in a real sense, the cornerstone of the free enterprise system, so good financial management is vitally important to the economic health of businesses and hence to our nation and the world. Because of its importance, finance should be widely and thoroughly understood, but this is easier said than done. The field is relatively complex, and it is undergoing constant changes in response to economic conditions. All this makes finance stimulating and exciting, but also challenging and sometimes perplexing. We hope that the third edition of *Introduction to Financial Management* will meet its own challenge by contributing to a better understanding of the financial system.

B. J. Campsey   Eugene F. Brigham
San Jose, California   Gainesville, Florida
December 1990   December 1990

About the Authors

B. J. Campsey (Ph.D., University of Texas at Austin; MBA, University of Houston) is Professor of Finance and Associate Dean at San Jose State University, San Jose, California. Professor Campsey has also taught at the University of Virginia and has been a Visiting Professor at the University of Texas at Austin and Santa Clara University. He has taught undergraduate and graduate courses in managerial finance and investments, and he has served as a consultant for financial and industrial firms as well as having been the Director of Candidate Programs for the Chartered Financial Analysts from 1979 to 1980.

A native of Fort Worth, Texas, Professor Campsey is a member of the Financial Management Association, the American Finance Association, and the Western Finance Association. His research interests are in financial management, investments, and financial education. He has written articles for several professional journals and has served as a consultant for several Silicon Valley firms.

Eugene F. Brigham (Ph.D., California, Berkeley; B.S., University of North Carolina at Chapel Hill) is Professor of Finance and Director of the Public Utility Research Center at the University of Florida. Professor Brigham has also taught at California, Berkeley, San Jose State, UCLA, Wisconsin, and Connecticut; he is Adjunct Professor at the University of Ottawa; and he has lectured in numerous executive programs in the United States and abroad. He is also past president of the Financial Management Association, and he has held offices in a number of other finance organizations.

Professor Brigham has served as a consultant to many firms and government agencies, including AT&T, Texas Power & Light, Commonwealth Edison, Shell Oil, Bank of America, and the Federal Reserve Board. He has published articles on various financial issues in *Financial Management,* the *Journal of Finance,* and other journals, and he has authored or coauthored several leading textbooks and casebooks in finance and managerial economics. Professor Brigham currently teaches graduate and undergraduate courses in financial management.

Careers in Finance

Even though some students take an introductory course in financial management because they wish to pursue a career in some area of finance, most take the course because it is required. Whatever the original motivation for taking a course, many students develop a deep enough interest in the area to warrant consideration of finance as a career.

As a result, we are often asked, "What kinds of jobs are available to finance majors?" The answer is that there are many different job opportunities in finance, ranging from banking to investments to corporate finance. If one had to categorize this book, it would be considered a corporate finance or financial management text. However, the different areas of finance are closely related, so you will study topics in this text related to the two other major sources of employment for finance students—financial institutions, especially banks, and the investment profession.

Working Capital Management. The bulk of this text is concerned with the duties of the financial staff in a corporate or business setting. Most students entering the finance department of a business are involved with some aspect of working capital management. A typical first assignment would be in the credit department, where credit analysts review initial credit applications and supervise ongoing accounts for signs of deteriorating creditworthiness. A more senior assignment might be concerned with supervision of the firm's cash account. Here the cash manager would be concerned with the rapid processing of customer payments, probably through lockbox banking arrangements, and with the timely disbursement of funds to creditors. The cash manager is also responsible for the maintenance of a positive relationship with all of the company's banks.

Capital Budgeting. As the novice financial manager gains experience, ever more challenging job opportunities will open up. For example, in the area of capital budgeting, a manager must analyze capital expenditure requests, forecast cash flows from potential capital budgeting projects, and review the progress of current projects. Such a job requires a knowledge of the entire firm (and the capital budgeting department is a good place to learn more about the business), as careful coordination with other functional areas, such as marketing for sales information, engineering for construction costs, and cost accounting for production figures. The capital budgeting staff must also project future financing needs that are associated with capital budgeting projects.

The capital budgeting staff will surely elicit the help of the treasury staff in planning a project's financing. Generally, the treaurer will be responsible for obtaining the lowest-cost funds within the parameters of the firm's target capital structure. To do this, the treasurer must be familiar with current financial market conditions, and he or she must have a close working relationship with the firm's investment bankers.

Vice President of Finance. The vice president of finance, who also has the title of chief financial officer (CFO), oversees all of the functions of the subordinate financial managers. If the company is a small one, the vice president of finance will individually perform all the functions that have been discussed. Thus, this financial manager must plan for future expenditures, evaluate past decisions, and execute the capital structure, capital budgeting, and dividend policy decisions of the firm.

Banking and Investments. Many of the topics covered in this text are also important in other areas of financial employment. For example, a banker would use the analytical tools discussed in Chapters 6 and 7 to analyze the financial statements of a loan applicant for creditworthiness. Similarly, the techniques of security valuation covered in Chapters 16 and 17 would be used by investment analysts in brokerage firms. Finally, both bankers and security analysts are concerned about the "quality of management" of companies, and a knowledge of all the topics in this book is essential for such an appraisal.

For further information of career opportunities in finance, see:

1. Jack S. Rader, *Careers in Finance* (Tampa, Fla.: Financial Management Association, 1983). Your instructor may order copies of this brochure by contacting Financial Management Association, College of Business Administration, University of South Florida, Tampa, FL 33620.

2. Frank K. Reilly, "Career Opportunities in Investments," in *Investments,* 2nd ed. (Hinsdale, Ill.: The Dryden Press, 1986).

Contents in Brief

Part I   The Financial Environment and the Firm   1

Chapter 1   Defining Financial Management   3
Chapter 2   Taxes and the Financial Environment   33
Chapter 3   Financial Institutions   85
Chapter 4   Interest Rates   117

Part II   Financial Statements and Financial Planning   147

Chapter 5   Examining a Firm's Financial Data   149
Chapter 6   Interpreting Financial Statements   179
Chapter 7   Determining Future Financial Needs   219

Part III   Short-Term Financial Management   253

Chapter 8   Short-Term Financial Planning   255
Chapter 9   Managing Cash and Marketable Securities   287
Chapter 10   Accounts Receivable and Inventories   323
Chapter 11   Financing Current Assets: Short-Term Credit   365
    Appendix 11A: The Use of Security in Short-Term Financing   395

Part IV   Capital Budgeting: Investment in Fixed Assets   403

Chapter 12   Risk and Return   405
Chapter 13   Time Value of Money   439
    Appendix 13A: Semiannual and Other Compounding Periods   482

Chapter 14   The Process of Capital Budgeting   487
    Appendix 14A: Conflicts between NPV and IRR   523
Chapter 15   Decisions in Capital Budgeting   531

Part V   Long-Term Financing   559

Chapter 16   Bonds and Preferred Stock   561
Chapter 17   Common Stock   609
Chapter 18   Hybrid Financing: Leasing and Option Securities   647

Part VI   Factors That Influence How the Firm Is Financed   685

Chapter 19   The Cost of Capital   687
Chapter 20   Leverage and the Target Capital Structure   727
    Appendix 20A: Bankruptcy   771
Chapter 21   Determining the Dividend Policy   779

Part VII   Other Topics in Financial Management   811

Chapter 22   Mergers and Acquisitions   813
Chapter 23   International Financial Management   849

Appendix A   Mathematical Tables   A-1

Appendix B   Answers to Selected End-of-Chapter Problems   B-1

Appendix C   Selected Equations   C-1

Glossary   G-1

Contents

Part I   **THE FINANCIAL ENVIRONMENT AND THE FIRM**   1

✓Chapter 1   **Defining Financial Management**   3

Decision in Finance: The Biggest Buyout — or a Sellout? *3*   The Financial Manager's Primary Activities *5*   Evolving Role of Financial Management *6* Increasing Importance of Financial Management *7*   Alternative Forms of Business Organization *10*   The Place of Finance in a Business Organization *14* The Goals of the Firm *16*   Industry Practice: The Bottom Line in Corporate Success *21*   Organization of the Book *26*   Small Business: Resources and Goals in the Small Firm *27*   Summary *29*   Resolution to Decision in Finance: The Biggest Buyout — or a Sellout? *30*

Chapter 2   **Taxes and the Financial Environment**   33

Decision in Finance: Is Wall Street Losing its Grip on Corporate America? *33* The Federal Income Tax System *34*   Depreciation *44*   The Role of Financial Markets *48*   The Role of Financial Intermediaries *54*   Industry Practice: Is It the End of an Era for Junk Bonds? *60*   The Stock Market *61*   Market Efficiency *71*   Small Business: Venture Capital: Financing and Advice *73* Summary *75*   Resolution to Decision in Finance: Is Wall Street Losing Its Grip on Corporate America? *77*

Chapter 3   **Financial Institutions**   85

Decision in Finance: Commercial Banks: The New Competitor in the Investment Banking Industry *85*   Overview of Financial Institutions *87*   The Commercial Banking System *88*   The Federal Reserve System *98*   Industry Practice: Thrift Crisis: What Happened and Who Is Going to Pay? *104*   The Savings and Loan (or Thrift) Crisis *106*   The Changing Economic Environment of Our Financial Institutions *107*   The Impact of Globalization on Our Financial Institutions *109* Small Business: Building a Banking Relationship *110*   Summary *112* Resolution to Decision in Finance: Commercial Banks: The New Competitor in the Investment Banking Industry *115*

✓Chapter 4   **Interest Rates**   117

Decision in Finance: A New Chairman for the Fed *117*   The Cost of Funds *118* Interest Rates *119*   Industry Practice: When the World Speaks . . . the Fed Listens *120*   The Determinants of Market Interest Rates *125*

The Term Structure of Interest Rates *131* Other Factors That Influence Interest Rate Levels *135* Interest Rate Levels and Stock Prices *138* Interest Rates and Business Decisions *138* Summary *140* Resolution to Decision in Finance: A New Chairman for the Fed *142*

Part II   **FINANCIAL STATEMENTS AND FINANCIAL PLANNING**   147

Chapter 5   **Examining a Firm's Financial Data**   149

Decision in Finance: Letters from Chairman Buffet *149* The Annual Report *151* The Income Statement *151* Industry Practice: Accounting Methods: The Center of a Controversy *153* The Balance Sheet *156* The Statement of Retained Earnings *159* The Cash Flow Cycle *160* The Statement of Cash Flows *163* Summary *168* Resolution to Decision in Finance: Letters from Chairman Buffet *170*

Chapter 6   **Interpreting Financial Statements**   179

Decision in Finance: Cooking the Books *179* Importance of Financial Statements *180* Ratio Analysis *180* Industry Practice: Manipulating Financial Statements *181* Sources of Comparative Ratios *199* Limitations of Ratio Analysis *201* Summary *202* Resolution to Decision in Finance: Cooking the Books *205*

Chapter 7   **Determining Future Financial Needs**   219

Decision in Finance: "Wide of Mark" Forecasts *219* Sales Forecasts *220* Forecasting Financial Requirements: The Percentage of Sales Method *221* Industry Practice: A Maverick's Forecasting Approach *222* The Relationship between Growth in Sales and Capital Requirements *229* Forecasting Financial Requirements When the Balance Sheet Ratios Are Subject to Change *232* Computerized Financial Planning Models *236* Small Business: Franchising *237* Summary *239* Resolution to Decision in Finance: "Wide of Mark" Forecasts *241*

Part III   **SHORT-TERM FINANCIAL MANAGEMENT**   253

Chapter 8   **Short-Term Financial Planning**   255

Decision in Finance: Unused Inventory . . . The Pot of Gold at the End of the Rainbow? *255* Short-Term Financial Planning Terminology *256* Overview of the Cash Conversion Cycle *258* Current Asset Investment Policies *263* Alternative Current Asset Financing Policies *266* Industry Practice: Cash Flow Problems and Bankruptcy *272* Combining Current Asset and Liability Decisions *274* Small Business: Growth and Working Capital Needs *276* Summary *277* Resolution to Decision in Finance: Unused Inventory . . . The Pot of Gold at the End of the Rainbow? *279*

Chapter 9   **Managing Cash and Marketable Securities**   287

Decision in Finance: The Buy-back Binge *287*   Cash Management *288*   The Cash Budget *290*   Increasing the Efficiency of Cash Management *295* Matching the Costs and Benefits Associated with Cash Management *302*   Bank Relationships *303*   Marketable Securities *305*   Industry Practice: Where to Stash the Cash? *313*   Summary *315*   Resolution to Decision in Finance: The Buy-back Binge *316*

Chapter 10   **Accounts Receivable and Inventories**   323

Decision in Finance: The Data Are Available, but Should Companies Use Them? *323*   Accounts Receivable *325*   Credit Policy *326*   Inventory Management *338*   Industry Practice: Just-in-Time (JIT) Inventory Method *349* Summary *352*   Resolution to Decision in Finance: The Data Are Available, but Should Companies Use Them? *354*

Chapter 11   **Financing Current Assets: Short-Term Credit**   365

Decision in Finance: A Bank That Looks at More than Numbers *365*   Accrued Wages and Taxes *366*   Accounts Payable, or Trade Credit *366*   Short-Term Bank Loans *372*   Commercial Paper *380*   Use of Security in Short-Term Financing *382*   Small Business: Financing Receivables Directly *383* Summary *385*   Resolution to Decision in Finance: A Bank That Looks at More than Numbers *388*   Appendix 11A: The Use of Security in Short-Term Financing *395*

Part IV   **CAPITAL BUDGETING: INVESTMENT IN FIXED ASSETS**   403
√Chapter 12   **Risk and Return**   405

Decision in Finance: When Money Is Not the Only Thing at Risk *405*   Defining and Measuring Risk *407*   Portfolio Risk and the Capital Asset Pricing Model *418* The Relationship between Risk and Rates of Return *425*   Summary *430* Resolution to Decision in Finance: When Money Is Not the Only Thing at Risk *432*

√Chapter 13   **Time Value of Money**   439

Decision in Finance: Can Boomers Retire? *439*   Future Value (or Compound Value) *441*   Present Value *445*   Future Value versus Present Value *449* Solving for Time and Interest Rates *451*   Future Value of an Annuity *454* Present Value of an Annuity *457*   Perpetuities *460*   Present Value of an Uneven Series of Receipts *460*   Determining Interest Rates *463*   Amortized Loans *464*   Summary *465*   Resolution to Decision in Finance: Can Boomers Retire? *472*   Appendix 13A: Semiannual and Other Compounding Periods *482*

Chapter 14   √The Process of Capital Budgeting   487

Decision in Finance: Learning from Past Errors 487   Importance of Capital
Budgeting 489   Project Proposals and Classification 490   Estimating the Cash
Flows 492   Methods Used to Evaluate Proposed Projects 498   Evaluation of
the Three Decision Rules 508   A Capital Budgeting Case 509   The Post-
Audit 512   Summary 513   Resolution to Decision in Finance: Learning from
Past Errors 515   Appendix 14A: Conflicts between NPV and IRR 523

Chapter 15   Decisions in Capital Budgeting   531

Decision in Finance: Should Government Make It Easier? 531   Risk Analysis in
Capital Budgeting 532   Introduction to Risk Assessment 532   Other Topics in
Capital Budgeting 541   Effects of Inflation on Capital Budgeting Analysis 547
Summary 549   Resolution to Decision in Finance: Should Government Make It
Easier? 551

Part V   LONG-TERM FINANCING   559
Chapter 16   Bonds and Preferred Stock   561

Decision in Finance: The Debt Crisis 561   Funded Debt 563   Term Loans 563
Bonds 564   Industry Practice: "Wall Street Raider" Has a New Definition 568
Types of Bonds 570   Recent Bond Innovations 572   Bond Ratings 577
Valuation of Bonds 583   Preferred Stock 591   Small Business: Contracting
with Providers of Risk Capital 598   Summary 600   Resolution to Decision in
Finance: The Debt Crisis 603

√Chapter 17   Common Stock   609

Decision in Finance: How to Botch a Deal 609   Legal Rights and Privileges of
the Common Stockholders 610   Common Stock Valuation 613   Evaluation of
Common Stock as a Source of Funds 624   The Decision to Go Public 626
The Investment Banking Process 629   Small Business: Going Public for Less
Than You're Worth 633   Summary 635   Resolution to Decision in Finance:
How to Botch a Deal 637

√Chapter 18   Hybrid Financing: Leasing and Option Securities   647

Decision in Finance: Sandy's Gamble 647   Leasing 648   Options 658
Warrants 663   Convertibles 665   Reporting Earnings When Warrants or
Convertibles Are Outstanding 672   Small Business: Lease Financing for Small
Businesses 673   Summary 674   Resolution to Decision in Finance: Sandy's
Gamble 676

Part VI

✓ Chapter 19

FACTORS THAT INFLUENCE HOW THE FIRM IS FINANCED   685

The Cost of Capital   687

Decision in Finance: Cost-of-Capital Punishment *687*   The Logic of the Weighted Average Cost of Capital *688*   Basic Definitions *689*   Minimum Required Return *691*   Cost of Debt, k_d $(1 - t)$ *693*   Cost of Preferred Stock, k_p *695*   Cost of Retained Earnings, k_s *696*   Finding the Basic Required Rate of Return on Common Equity *696*   Cost of Newly Issued Common Stock, or External Equity, k_e *701*   Weighted Average, or Composite, Cost of Capital, WACC $= k_a$ *702*   Changes in the Cost of Capital *703*   Combining the MCC and the Investment Opportunity Schedule (IOS) *707*   Divisional Costs of Capital *710*   Small Business: The Real Costs of Going Public *711*   Summary *713*   Resolution to Decision in Finance: Cost-of-Capital Punishment *715*

Chapter 20

Leverage and the Target Capital Structure   727

Decision in Finance: Getting the Lumps Out *727*   Types of Risk *729*   Business Risk *729*   Operating Leverage *731*   Financial Risk *738*   Degree of Financial Leverage *747*   Taxes, Bankruptcy Costs, and the Value of the Firm *750*   Additional Problems and Considerations *752*   Capital Structure and Mergers *753*   Checklist of Factors That Influence Capital Structure Decisions in Practice *755*   Variations in Capital Structures among Firms *757*   Small Business: Financing Growth Businesses in the 1990s *759*   Summary *760*   Resolution to Decision in Finance: Getting the Lumps Out *762*   Appendix 20A: Bankruptcy *771*

Chapter 21

Determining the Dividend Policy   779

Decision in Finance: To Pay or Not to Pay Dividends *779*   Residual Dividend Policy *780*   Factors That Influence Dividend Policy *785*   Dividend Payment Policies *788*   Actual Dividend Payment Procedures *792*   Industry Practice: Corporate Get-Rich-Slowly Plans *793*   Dividend Reinvestment Plans (DRIPs) *794*   Stock Repurchases *795*   Stock Dividends and Stock Splits *797*   Establishing a Dividend Policy: Some Illustrations *801*   Summary *803*   Resolution to Decision in Finance: To Pay or Not to Pay Dividends *805*

Part VII

Chapter 22

OTHER TOPICS IN FINANCIAL MANAGEMENT   811

Mergers and Acquisitions   813

Decision in Finance: Did Consolidated Freightways Take a Bad Flier? *813*   The Economic Implications of Mergers *815*   Types of Mergers *816*   Examples of Merger Activity *817*   Procedures for Combining Firms *821*   Financial Analysis of a Proposed Merger *823*   Industry Practice: High-Tech Firms Get the Urge to Merge *826*   Merger Analysis *827*   The Role of Investment Bankers *830*   Merger Defenses *830*   Fair Price *831*   Corporate Alliances *832*

Divestitures *832*   Holding Companies *835*   Leveraged Buyouts (LBOs) *838*
Small Business: Merging as a Means of Exiting a Closely Held Business *840*
Summary *841*   Resolution to Decision in Finance: Did Consolidated
Freightways Take a Bad Flier? *843*

Chapter 23   **International Financial Management**   849

Decision in Finance: Philips Has the Weight of the World on Its Shoulders *849*
Multinational versus Domestic Financial Management *852*   Industry Practice:
Learning a New Vocabulary *854*   Exchange Rates and the International
Monetary System *856*   Trading in Foreign Exchange *863*   Inflation, Interest
Rates, and Exchange Rates *865*   International Working Capital Management *866*
Procedures for Analyzing Potential Foreign Investments *870*   International
Capital Markets *872*   International Capital Structures *874*   International
Mergers *876*   Summary *877*   Resolution to Decision in Finance: Philips Has
the Weight of the World on Its Shoulders *879*

Appendix A   **Mathematical Tables**   A-1

Appendix B   **Answers to Selected End-of-Chapter Problems**   B-1

Appendix C   **Selected Equations**   C-1

                  Glossary   G-1

                  Index   I-1

Part I

THE FINANCIAL ENVIRONMENT AND THE FIRM

The goal of financial management is to maximize stockholders' wealth. It sounds like a simple goal, but this entire book is dedicated to evaluating how alternative decisions will influence the value of the firm. By maximizing the firm's value (and thereby increasing the value of its common stock), the goal of shareholder wealth maximization can be implemented.

Chapter 1 contains an overview of financial management, including the duties of a financial manager, the forms of business organization, and the role of finance in a business organization. Chapters 2, 3, and 4 describe the financial environment in which we all work. The job of financial intermediaries is to efficiently transfer funds from surplus economic units to deficit economic units. Chapter 2 briefly discusses taxes and then introduces the markets and institutions involved in successfully converting savings to productive investments. Chapter 3 describes financial institutions and the means by which the Federal Reserve System influences the economy. Both businesses and individuals are affected by interest rates, and Chapter 4 examines the factors which determine those rates.

Chapter 1

Defining Financial Management

The Biggest Buyout—or a Sellout?

Such terms as "Deal of the Decade," or even "Sale of the Century," were used in 1988 when the leveraged buyout firm Kohlberg Kravis Roberts & Co. (KKR) beat two competing bidders to acquire tobacco/food giant RJR Nabisco in the biggest acquisition ever. The total cost, including fees, was $26.4 billion, and most of this was borrowed money.

The resulting furor over the buyout's mechanics, the hostility that developed among the players, and an instinctive fear of such monumental debt led to a fundamental change in the business climate. As a result, the RJR Nabisco deal will probably be rehashed and reanalyzed for years to come.

The drama began when RJR Nabisco, the 19th-largest firm in the country, went on the auction block, after a management group headed by RJR's CEO, Ross Johnson, and their investment bankers, Shearson Lehman Hutton, made an offer to buy the company. Johnson was concerned because the trading price of RJR

See end of chapter for resolution.

stock had only recovered moderately from the 1987 stock market crash (when RJR fell from $70 to around $40 a share), despite gains in market share for many RJR products.

"We could go two ways," he said later. "We could go out and buy another food business, and pay 20 times earnings and dilute the value of our company. Or we could go into the marketplace and buy our own stock." The decision was to attempt a buyout, in which management would buy out the outside stockholders, assume full ownership, and take the firm private.

The Johnson/Shearson group offered $75 per share for the outstanding stock. As Johnson pointed out later, the stock at the time was selling for about $20 less per share, and it had never sold for as much as the bid price. Still, Johnson and Shearson were accused of trying to make a "quick buck" by grabbing the company for a price much lower than its true worth. Had either Johnson or his bankers gone through RJR's treasurer's files—as did the board of directors' investment banking advisers at a later date—they would have discovered evidence

3

that any offer under $100 a share was, by the company's own reasoning, too low.

Greed appeared to be the prime motivation for a contract discussed by Johnson and Shearson and leaked to the press by an unidentified third party. By putting up only $20 million, Johnson and six other top RJR executives expected to make $100 million in five years and to increase their equity in the firm from the 8.5 percent purchased to approximately 18.5 percent. Johnson later argued that the equity would be divided among 15,000 RJR workers, but that seems to have been an afterthought, since no such division was included in the original agreement. The directors, who were asked to approve the buyout, were shocked at this appearance of impropriety.

Meanwhile, Kohlberg Kravis Roberts & Co. stepped into the picture. Two years earlier, they had proposed a buyout to Johnson, but he had turned them down. Now KKR wanted to be part of the deal. Henry Kravis and others negotiated with Shearson to join forces, but distrust and hostility between the parties made an agree-

ment impossible, so KKR made a competing bid for RJR Nabisco at $90 a share.

This bid was topped a week later by Shearson and the RJR management group, who bid $92 a share with the help of Salomon Brothers, who had joined them. At this point, the auctioning became intense, and two other groups entered the competition. The RJR special directors' committee sent a letter to all bidders outlining some rules. One crucial concern was that any offer received should combine cash with securities that could be converted to stock at a future date. Somehow, the Shearson/Johnson group overlooked this last point, and they made their offer primarily with cash. Although their final offer of $112 was higher than KKR's final offer of $109, the directors chose KKR because they thought it was better for stockholders and because they disliked Johnson's tactics.

As you read this chapter, consider what the effects of such a buyout might be on RJR's stockholders, its bondholders, its employees, and its managers.

What are the specific tasks of a firm's financial manager? What role does the finance group, or department, play within the firm? What tools and techniques do the financial staff have at their disposal to improve the firm's performance? On a larger scale, what is the role of finance in the U.S. economy, and how can financial management be used to further our national goals as well as to help meet the goals of the firm's owners? We will attempt to answer these questions, at least in part, in this book.

The topics in finance are too diverse to cover completely in one text. Finance consists of three interrelated areas: (1) *money and capital markets,* or macro finance, which deals with many of the topics covered in macroeconomics or in "Money and Banking" courses; (2) *investments,* which focuses on the decisions of individuals and financial institutions as they choose securities for their investment portfolios; and (3) *financial management,* or business finance, which involves decisions within the firm. Each of these areas interacts with the others. For example, a financial manager must have some knowledge of money and capital markets as well as of the way in which individuals and institutions are likely to appraise the firm's securities.

THE FINANCIAL MANAGER'S PRIMARY ACTIVITIES

The financial manager's primary task is to plan for the acquisition and use of funds in order to maximize the value of the firm. Put another way, he or she makes decisions about alternative sources and uses of funds. Here are some specific activities which are involved:

1. Forecasting and planning. The financial manager must interact with other executives as they jointly look ahead and lay the plans which will shape the firm's future position.

2. Major investment and financing decisions. On the basis of long-range plans, the financial manager must raise the capital needed to support growth. A successful firm usually achieves a high rate of growth in sales, which requires increased investments in the plant, equipment, and current assets necessary to produce goods and services. The financial manager must help determine the optimal rate of sales growth, and he or she must help decide on the specific investments to be made as well as on the types of funds to be used to finance these investments. Decisions must be made about the use of internal versus external funds, the use of debt versus equity, and the use of long-term versus short-term debt.

3. Coordination and control. The financial manager must interact with the firm's other executives if the firm is to operate as efficiently as possible. All business decisions have financial implications, and all managers need to take this into account. For example, marketing decisions affect sales growth, which, in turn, changes investment requirements. Thus, marketing managers must take account of how their actions affect (and are affected by) such factors as the availability of funds, inventory policies, and plant capacity utilization.

4. Interaction with capital markets. The financial manager must deal with the money and capital markets. As we shall see in the next chapter, each firm affects and is affected by the general financial markets, where funds are raised, where the firm's securities are traded, and where its investors are either rewarded or penalized.

In general, the central responsibilities of financial managers involve decisions such as which investments their firms should make, how these projects should be financed, and how the firm can most effectively manage its existing resources. If financial managers do a good job, they can help to maximize the values of their firms, which will also maximize the long-term welfare of those who buy from or work for the firm.

Self-Test

Identify three interrelated areas of finance, and discuss the focus of each.

What is the financial manager's primary responsibility, and what are some of the specific actions involved in carrying out that responsibility?

EVOLVING ROLE OF FINANCIAL MANAGEMENT

Financial management has undergone significant changes over the years. When it first emerged as a separate field of study in the early 1900s, the emphasis was on the legal aspects of mergers, consolidations, the formation of new firms, and the various types of securities issued by corporations. Industrialization was sweeping the country, and the critical problem that firms such as Standard Oil and the Southern Pacific Railroad faced was obtaining capital for expansion. The capital markets were relatively primitive, making transfers of funds from individual savers to businesses quite difficult. The earnings and asset values reported in accounting statements were unreliable, and stock trading by insiders and manipulators caused prices to fluctuate wildly. Consequently, investors were reluctant to purchase stocks and bonds, and as a result of these environmental conditions, finance in the early 1900s focused on legal issues relating to the issuance of securities.

The emphasis remained on securities through the 1920s. However, when an unprecedented number of business failures occurred during the Great Depression of the 1930s, the study of finance began to focus on problems of corporate liquidity, bankruptcy and reorganization, and, not surprisingly, governmental regulation of the securities markets. Thus, while the study of finance was still a descriptive, legalistic subject, its emphasis changed from expansion to survival.

During the 1940s and early 1950s, finance continued to be taught as a descriptive, institutional subject, viewed from the standpoint of an outsider rather than from that of management. However, financial management techniques designed to help firms maximize their profits and stock prices were beginning to receive attention.

The evolutionary pace quickened during the late 1950s. Whereas the right-hand side of the balance sheet (liabilities and equity) had received more attention in the earlier era, the major emphasis began to shift to asset analysis. The emergence of computers made rigorous financial analysis possible, and mathematical models were developed and applied to inventories, cash, accounts receivable, and fixed assets. Increasingly, the focus of finance shifted from the outsider's to the insider's point of view, and financial decisions within the firm came to be recognized as the critical issue in managerial finance. Descriptive, institutional materials on capital markets and financing instruments were still studied, but these topics were considered in terms of their effects on a business's internal financial decisions.

The 1960s and 1970s witnessed a renewed interest in the liabilities and equity side of the balance sheet, with a focus on (1) the optimal mix of debt and equity securities, (2) the way in which individual investors make investment decisions, or *portfolio theory,* and (3) the implications of both topics for managerial finance. Financial management was redesigned to help general management take actions that would maximize the value of the firm and the wealth of its stockholders, giving recognition to the fact that the results of financial decisions depend on how investors react to them. This recognition produced a merging of investments with managerial finance.

In the 1980s four issues received emphasis: (1) inflation and its effects on interest rates, (2) deregulation of financial institutions and the accompanying trend away from specialized institutions toward broadly diversified financial service corporations, (3) a dramatic increase in the use of computers for analyzing financial decisions, and (4) a pervasive trend toward the globalization of business. Methods for combating inflation, and for understanding its widespread implications when it does increase, are being integrated into financial theories and decision processes. New financial institutions and instruments, such as money market funds and interest rate futures, have emerged as a result of the high inflation rates in the early 1980s. Older financial institutions have been compelled to make major structural concessions to the changing financial environment. These changes have been so pronounced that it is becoming more difficult to determine the differences in many financial institutions. For example, Prudential Insurance owns a stock brokerage firm; Merrill Lynch offers checking account services; and Sears, Roebuck is one of the largest U.S. financial institutions, owning such firms as Allstate Insurance and Coldwell Banker, the largest U.S. real estate brokerage company. At the same time, technological developments in the computer hardware and telecommunications areas, and the availability of software packages that make otherwise difficult numerical analyses relatively easy, are bringing about fundamental changes in the way financial managers manage. Data storage, transmittal, and retrieval techniques are reducing the judgmental aspects of management, as financial managers can often obtain relatively precise estimates of the effects of various courses of action. We predict that the two most important trends during the 1990s will be the continued globalization of business and the increased use of computer technology.

Self-Test

Briefly outline the significant changes that managerial finance has undergone from the early 1900s through the 1980s.

What financial issues have received emphasis in the 1980s?

What financial issues are likely to be most prominent in the 1990s?

INCREASING IMPORTANCE OF FINANCIAL MANAGEMENT

These evolutionary changes have greatly increased the importance of financial management. In earlier times the marketing manager would project sales, the engineering and production staffs would determine the assets necessary to meet these demands, and the financial manager's job was simply to raise the money to purchase the required plant, equipment, and inventories. This mode of operation is no longer prevalent; decisions are now made in a much more coordinated manner, and the financial manager generally has direct responsibility for the control process.

Public Service of Indiana (PSI) can be used to illustrate this change. A few years ago PSI's economic forecasters would project power demand on the basis of historical trends and then give these forecasts to the engineers, who would proceed to build the new plants necessary to meet the forecasted demand. The finance department simply had the task of raising the capital the engineers told them was needed. However, inflation, environmental regulations, and other factors combined to double or even triple plant construction costs, and this caused a corresponding increase in the need for new capital. At the same time, rising fuel costs caused dramatic increases in electricity prices, which lowered demand and made some of the new construction unnecessary. Thus, PSI found itself building a nuclear plant that it did not really need. As this situation became clear to PSI's investors, they refused to provide the utility with the capital required to complete the plant. Eventually, a $2.5 billion investment had to be written off, and the loss caused PSI's stock price to fall from $35 in the late 1970s to a low in 1985 of $6.88. The stock's price has improved from its 1985 low, but, as of early 1990, the stock had not yet returned to its high of $35. As a result of this experience, PSI (and other utilities and industrial companies) now places more emphasis on the planning and control process, and this has greatly increased the importance of the financial staff.

Certainly no business can prosper unless all functions — accounting, finance, marketing, personnel, and so forth — are fully staffed with competent individuals. In times of abundant financial resources, the role of the financial manager whose duty it is to acquire external financing may decline in importance. However, Professor Gordon Donaldson of Harvard contends that ". . . in harder times and with expensive money, the importance of the financial function grows."[1]

The direction in which business is moving, as well as the increasing importance of finance, was described in a *Fortune* article several years ago. After pointing out that well over half of the then current top executives had majored in business administration versus about 25 percent a few years earlier, the *Fortune* article continued:

> Career patterns have followed the educational trends. Like scientific and technical schooling, nuts-and-bolts business experience seems to have become less important. The proportion of executives with their primary experience in production, operations, engineering, design, and R. and D. has fallen from a third of the total to just over a quarter. And the number of top officers with legal and financial backgrounds has increased more than enough to make up the difference. Lawyers and financial people now head two out of five corporations.

---

[1]"Why the Finance Man Calls the Plays," *Business Week*, April 8, 1972, 54.

It is fair to assume the changes in training, and in the paths that led these executives to the top, reflect the shifting priorities and needs of their corporations. In fact, the expanding size and complexity of corporate organizations, coupled with their continued expansion overseas, have increased the importance of financial planning and controls. And the growth of government regulation and of obligations companies face under law has heightened the need for legal advice. The engineer and the production manager have become, in consequence, less important in management than the finance executive and the lawyer.

Today's chief executive officers have obviously perceived the shift in emphasis, and many of them wish they had personally been better prepared for it. Interestingly enough, a majority of them say they would have benefited from additional formal training, mainly in business administration, accounting, finance, and law.[2]

Although the period of high inflation and tight money of the 1980s has passed, at least temporarily, the importance of the financial manager continued as the economy moved through a very sluggish 1990. The economy's slow growth created new problems for firms and their financial managers. However, these problems can create new opportunities. As one executive noted, "The fastest way to the top in any company is to develop and implement a cure for the company's most severe problem, and then be widely recognized as the individual responsible for solving the company's toughest problem."[3] Thus, although there is no universal way to the top, in hard times, when capital is expensive and scarce, the importance of the finance function increases.

We have been emphasizing financial management, but we hasten to note that there are no unimportant functions in a business firm. Our point is simply that *there are financial implications in virtually all business decisions, and nonfinancial executives must know enough about finance to incorporate these implications into their own specialized areas.* The importance of finance to all areas of a business is reflected by the fact that most executive development programs report that their most popular course is "Financial Analysis for the Nonfinancial Executive."

Recent surveys indicate that the emphasis on finance is continuing, and it is also evident within firms of all sizes as well as in nonprofit and governmental organizations. Thus, it is becoming increasingly important for people in marketing, accounting, production, personnel, and other areas to understand finance in order to do a good job in their own fields. Marketing people, for instance, must understand how marketing decisions affect and are affected by financial decisions. When marketing efforts successfully increase sales, additional funds must be found to support increases in inventory, accounts receivable, plant capacity, and so on. Similarly, accountants must understand how accounting data are used in corporate planning and are viewed by investors.

---

[2]C. G. Burck, "A Group Profile of the Fortune 500 Chief Executive," *Fortune*, May 1976, 173.

[3]G. A. Weimer, "Finance Favored as Key to the Executive Boardroom," *Iron Age*, April 16, 1979, 35.

financial management
The acquisition and utilization of funds to maximize the efficiency and value of an enterprise.

The function of accounting is to provide quantitative financial information for use in economic decisions, whereas the main functions of **financial management** are to plan for, acquire, and utilize funds in order to maximize the efficiency and value of the enterprise.[4]

Self-Test

Explain why financial planning and controls are important to today's chief executives.

Is the trend toward more emphasis on finance continuing, and does the trend affect small firms or only large ones? Are marketing people affected?

ALTERNATIVE FORMS OF BUSINESS ORGANIZATION

There are three main forms of business organization: the sole proprietorship, the partnership, and the corporation. In terms of numbers, about 80 percent of business firms are operated as sole proprietorships, while the remainder are divided equally between partnerships and corporations. By dollar value of sales, however, about 80 percent of business is conducted by corporations, about 13 percent by sole proprietorships, and about 7 percent by partnerships. Because most business is conducted by corporations, both large and small, we shall concentrate on them in this book. Still, it is important to understand the differences among the three types of firms, as well as their advantages and disadvantages.

Sole Proprietorship

sole proprietorship
A business owned by one individual.

A **sole proprietorship** is a business owned by one individual. Going into business as a single proprietor is easy—one merely begins business operations. However, most cities require even the smallest establishments to be licensed, and occasionally state licenses are required as well.

The proprietorship has two important advantages for small operations: (1) It is easily and inexpensively formed, since no formal charter for operations is required, and it is subject to few government regulations, and (2) the business pays no corporate income taxes. However, as we shall see, the tax situation is not always a net advantage, as all earnings of the firm, whether they are reinvested in the business or withdrawn, are subject to personal income taxes at the owner's tax rate.

The proprietorship also has three important limitations: (1) It is difficult for a proprietorship to obtain large sums of capital; (2) the proprietor has unlimited personal liability for business debts, which can result in losses greater than the money invested in the company; and (3) the life of a business

---

[4]American Institute of Certified Public Accountants, *AICPA Professional Standards,* Section 100 (New York, November 1987).

organized as a proprietorship is limited to the life of the individual who created it. For these three reasons, the individual proprietorship is restricted primarily to small business operations. However, businesses are frequently started as proprietorships and then converted to corporations if and when their growth causes the disadvantages of being a proprietorship to outweigh its advantages.

Partnership

A **partnership** exists whenever two or more persons associate to conduct a noncorporate business. Partnerships may operate under different degrees of formality, ranging from informal, oral understandings to formal agreements filed with the secretary of the state in which the partnership does business. In a partnership, each partner contributes a certain amount of funding to support the business and does a certain amount of the work needed to run it. Of course, each partner then is entitled to a proportionate share of the business's profits or losses. Although partnerships are responsible for only a small fraction of the dollar volume of American business, they have long been common in small professional firms in medicine, law, and accounting, and, recently they have emerged in consulting.

> **partnership**
> An unincorporated business owned by two or more persons.

The major advantage of a partnership is its low cost and ease of formation. The disadvantages are similar to those associated with proprietorships: (1) unlimited liability, (2) limited life of the organization, (3) difficulty of transferring ownership, and (4) difficulty of raising large amounts of capital. The tax treatment of a partnership is similar to that for proprietorships, and when compared to that of a corporation, this can be either an advantage or a disadvantage, depending on the situation.

Regarding liability, normally the partners must risk all of their personal assets, even those assets not invested in the business, for under partnership law each partner is liable for the business's debts. This means that if any partner is unable to meet his or her pro rata claim in the event the partnership goes bankrupt, the remaining partners must take over the unsatisfied claims, even having to draw on their own personal assets if needed to satisfy claims.

Some of the problems of a general partnership, which we have just described, may be reduced by the formation of a **limited partnership.** In a limited partnership one or more partners are designated *general partners* and the others *limited partners.* The general partners have the same unlimited liability as with any general partnership, but the limited partners' liability extends only to the amount of their investment in the partnership. Limited partners are often termed *silent partners* because they have no active voice in management. Limited partnerships are quite common in the area of real estate investment, but they have not worked well in many other types of business ventures, hence they constitute only a small fraction of all partnership businesses.

> **limited partnership**
> An unincorporated business owned both by general partners having unlimited liability and by limited partners whose liability is limited to their investment in the firm.

The first three disadvantages of a general partnership — unlimited liability, impermanence of the organization, and difficulty of transferring ownership —

combine to cause the fourth, the difficulty partnerships have in attracting substantial amounts of capital. This is no particular problem for a slow-growing business, but if a business's products really catch on, and if it needs to raise large amounts of capital to expand and thus capitalize on its opportunities, the difficulty in attracting capital becomes a real drawback. Thus, growth companies such as Hewlett-Packard and Apple Computer generally begin life as proprietorships or partnerships, but at some point they find it necessary to convert into corporations.

Corporation

corporation

A legal entity created by a state, separate and distinct from its owners and managers, having unlimited life, easy transferability of ownership, and limited liability.

A **corporation** is a legal entity created by the state. This form of organization, which originated in Scotland in the early 1800s, is considered an important factor in the economic advancement of the West during the nineteenth and twentieth centuries. It eliminated the need for an entrepreneur to fully finance his or her ideas into productive reality, which in turn allowed managers to become separate and distinct from the capital-providing owners of the firm.

This separation gives the corporation three major advantages: (1) it has an *unlimited life* — it can continue after its original owners and managers are deceased; (2) it permits *easy transferability of ownership interest,* because ownership interests can be divided into shares of stock, which in turn can be transferred far more easily than partnership interests; and (3) it permits *limited liability.* Limited liability means that capital providers can invest in a firm with a limit on how much they can lose, but with an unlimited opportunity for profits. To illustrate, suppose you and three friends invested $25,000 each in a regular partnership, which then went bankrupt owing $1 million. Because the owners are liable for the debts of a partnership, you would lose your original investment and be liable for your share of the $1 million loss, $250,000. However, if your partners could not pay their shares of the remaining $750,000 of losses, you could be held liable for the entire $1 million. Thus, an investor in a partnership is exposed to unlimited liability. On the other hand, if you invested $25,000 in the stock of a corporation which then went bankrupt, your potential loss on the investment would be limited to your $25,000 investment.[5] These three factors — unlimited life, easy transferability of ownership interest, and limited liability — make it much easier for corporations to raise money in the general capital markets than for proprietorships or partnerships.

Although the corporate form does offer significant advantages over proprietorships and partnerships, it has two primary disadvantages: (1) Corporate earnings are subject to double taxation — the earnings of the corporation are

---

[5]In the case of small corporations, the limited liability feature is often a fiction, because bankers and credit managers frequently require personal guarantees from the stockholders of small, weak businesses.

taxed and then any earnings paid out as dividends are taxed again as income to the stockholders. (2) Setting up a corporation is more complex and time-consuming than is the case for a proprietorship or partnership.

Although a proprietorship or partnership can commence operations without much paperwork, setting up a corporation is a bit more involved. The incorporators must prepare a *charter* and a set of *bylaws*. The **charter** includes the following information: (1) name of the proposed corporation, (2) type of activities it will pursue, (3) amount of capital stock, (4) number of directors, and (5) names and addresses of directors. The charter is filed with the secretary of the state in which the firm will be incorporated, and, when it is approved, the corporation is officially in existence.

The **bylaws** are a set of rules drawn up by the founders of the corporation to aid in governing the internal management of the company. Included are such points as (1) how directors are to be elected (all elected each year or, say, one third each year for three-year terms); (2) whether the existing stockholders will have the first right to buy any new shares the firm issues; (3) what provisions there are for management committees (such as an executive committee or a finance committee) and their duties; and (4) what procedures there are for changing the bylaws themselves, should conditions require it. Attorneys have standard forms for charters and bylaws in their word processors, and they can set up a corporation with very little effort. For about $1,000 — less if you find a hungry young lawyer fresh out of law school — a business can be incorporated.

The value of any business other than a very small one will probably be maximized if it is organized as a corporation. The reasons are as follows:

1. Limited liability reduces the risks borne by investors, and, other things held constant, *the lower the firm's risk, the greater its value.*

2. A firm's value depends on its *growth opportunities,* which in turn depend on the firm's ability to attract capital. Since corporations can attract capital more easily than can unincorporated businesses, they have superior growth opportunities.

3. The value of an asset also depends on its **liquidity,** which means the ease of selling the asset and converting it to cash. Since an investment in the stock of a corporation is much more liquid than a similar investment in a proprietorship or partnership, this too means that the corporate form of organization can enhance the value of a business.

4. Corporations are taxed differently than proprietorships and partnerships, and, under certain conditions, the tax laws favor corporations. This point is discussed in detail in Chapter 2.

As we will see later in the chapter, most firms are managed with value maximization in mind, and this, in turn, has caused most large businesses to be organized as corporations.

charter
A formal legal document that describes the scope and nature of a corporation and defines the rights and duties of its stockholders and managers.

bylaws
A set of rules for governing the management of a company.

liquidity
The ability to sell an asset at a reasonable price on short notice.

Self-Test

Briefly explain the differences between a sole proprietorship, a partnership, and a corporation.

Explain why the value of any business other than a very small one will probably be maximized if it is organized as a corporation.

THE PLACE OF FINANCE IN A BUSINESS ORGANIZATION

No single organizational structure will serve for all businesses. A huge, world-wide corporation needs a large, complex finance department. For example, Du Pont's finance department contains 9 divisions with a total of 29 sections, as well as separate areas of investor relations, personnel relations, accounting policy, and international finance. A small firm, of course, would not need as much specialization as a vast, multinational corporation like Du Pont. In fact, in a small firm all the necessary financial functions may be handled by only a few persons whose other duties may include such diverse areas as market planning or production management. The smaller the organization, the more the financial duties will be shared among individual managers or perhaps between the accountant and the president.

A fairly typical picture of the role of finance in the organizational structure of a firm is presented in Figure 1-1. The chief financial officer (CFO), who has the title of vice president — finance, reports directly to the president. The controller and the treasurer are the finance vice president's key subordinates.

The dividing line between the functions of the controller and the treasurer is neither exact nor absolute. The position of the treasurer is most closely associated with the topics discussed in this text. This officer has direct responsibility for planning the capital structure and maintaining relationships with all sources of financing, such as banks, shareholders, and other suppliers of funds. The treasurer's office must also deal with the capital markets, generally through an investment banker.

The treasurer is also involved in the selection and management of the firm's assets. Financial managers must evaluate all capital projects and determine if they should be undertaken. Furthermore, existing projects must be monitored for continuing profitability. The management of working capital, which consists of short-term assets, is no less important. The treasurer must insure that enough cash is on hand to cover all checks, but he or she should invest any excess in securities. Management of accounts receivable and inventory is yet another important function of the treasurer's office (although occasionally the controller handles these tasks).

In a larger firm, the responsibilities of the treasurer remain as outlined here, but some duties are shifted to subordinates such as the credit manager, the inventory manager, and the director of capital budgeting. Additionally, employee benefits, including the pension fund and health insurance, are often handled in the treasurer's office, whereas in smaller firms, employee benefits

Figure 1-1 **Place of Finance in a Typical Business Organization**

In a typical business organization such as that shown here, most general financial management functions fall to the treasurer. The treasurer is responsible for overall financial planning, selection and management of the firm's assets, and management of cash, accounts receivable, and inventory. To plan and manage effectively, the treasurer needs constant input from the sales and manufacturing areas of the business. The controller oversees all accounting, auditing, and tax matters of the firm.

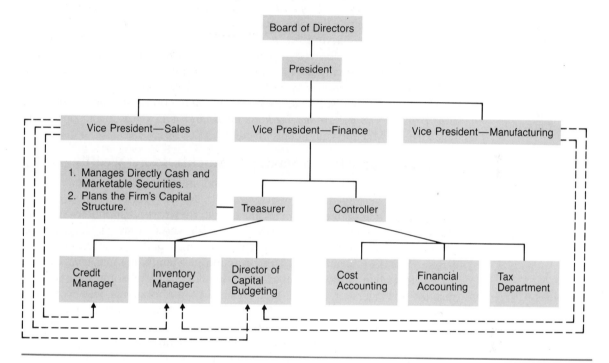

are usually assigned to an independent pension management firm and/or an insurance agency.

Thus, the traditional responsibilities assigned to the treasurer's office may be summarized as selecting and continually evaluating productive assets, forecasting financial needs, financing operations, and establishing the firm's dividend policy.

The traditional functions of the controller's office include the generation and interpretation of accounting reports, and the monitoring and control of accounts. In other words, the controller generally has responsibility for all elements of accounting and auditing. Additionally, the controller is often responsible for all tax matters, as well as for other information required by government agencies. To a large extent, we leave a discussion of the controller's function to accounting courses.

Self-Test

What are the responsibilities of a firm's treasurer, and how do these responsibilities differ from those of the controller?

THE GOALS OF THE FIRM

Decisions are not made in a vacuum, but, rather, with some objective in mind. *Throughout this book, we operate on the assumption that management's primary goal is to* **maximize the wealth of its stockholders.** As we shall see, this translates into *maximizing the price of the common stock.* Firms do, of course, have other objectives — managers, who make the actual decisions, are interested in their own personal satisfaction, in their employee's welfare, and in the good of the community and of society at large. Still, for the reasons set forth in the following sections, *stock price maximization is the most important goal of most publicly traded business firms,* and it is a reasonable operating objective on which to build decision rules.

stockholder wealth maximization

The appropriate goal for management decisions: considers the risk and timing associated with expected earnings per share in order to maximize the firm's stock price.

Why Managers Try to Maximize Stockholders' Wealth

Stockholders are the owners of the firm, and, in theory at least, control management by electing the members of the board of directors, which in turn appoints the management team. Management, therefore, is supposed to operate in the best interests of the stockholders. We know, however, that because the stock of most large firms is widely held, the managers of large corporations have a great deal of autonomy. This being the case, might not managers pursue goals other than stock price maximization? For example, some have argued that the managers of a large, well-entrenched corporation could work just enough to keep stockholder returns at a "fair" or "reasonable" level and then devote the remainder of their efforts and resources to public service activities, to employee benefits, to higher executive salaries, or to golf.

Similarly, an established, self-satisfied, and well-compensated management might avoid risky ventures, even when the possible gains to stockholders were high enough to warrant taking the gamble. The theory behind this argument is that, since stockholders are generally well diversified in the sense that they hold portfolios of many different stocks, if a company takes a chance and loses, then its stockholders lose only a small part of their wealth. Managers, on the other hand, are not so well diversified: A manager's salary generally represents his or her largest wealth asset. Thus, a potential setback, which might result in the manager's demotion or dismissal, is probably more devastating to the manager than it would be to a diversified stockholder. Accordingly, corporate managers may be less motivated to take risks that, if successful, would benefit stockholders (and to some extent managers, if they own or have options to own the firm's stock) by increasing the value of the firm's stock. Managers might also receive bonuses as part of their reward for success in a risky venture. However, if the venture is unsuccessful, it might result in the manager's rebuke, demotion, or even ouster. Therefore, some maintain that managers are not well enough compensated for their successes, and that they incur disproportionate penalties for their failures. If this is true, would a manager risk his or her job just to maximize the stockholders' wealth, or might the manager be satisfied in providing a less risky but still acceptable rate of return for the stockholder?

It is almost impossible to determine whether a particular management team is trying to maximize shareholder wealth or is merely attempting to keep stockholders satisfied while pursuing other goals. For example, how can we tell whether employee or community benefit programs are in the long-run best interests of the stockholders? Are relatively high executive salaries really necessary to attract and retain excellent managers, who, in turn, will keep the firm ahead of its competition, or are they "just another example of managers' taking advantage of stockholders"? When a risky venture is turned down, does this reflect management conservatism, or is it a correct judgment regarding the risks of the venture versus its potential rewards?

It is impossible to give definitive answers to these questions. Although several studies have suggested that managers are not completely stockholder-oriented, the evidence is cloudy. In any event, more and more firms are tying management's compensation to the company's performance, and research suggests that this motivates managers to operate in a manner consistent with stock price maximization.[6] In recent years, hostile takeovers in the form of **tender offers** and **proxy fights** have removed a number of supposedly well-entrenched management teams. A tender offer is a bid by one company to buy the stock of another company by going directly to the shareholders, while a proxy fight involves an attempt to gain control of a firm by convincing stockholders to vote a new management group into office. Since both actions are triggered by low stock prices, self-preservation will lead management to try to keep the stock values as high as possible.

Takeovers rarely present a serious threat to a well-entrenched management team if that team has succeeded in maximizing the firm's value, because raiders attempt to take over undervalued, bargain companies, not fully valued ones. While it may be true that some managers are personally more interested in their own positions than in actually maximizing shareholder wealth, the threat of losing their jobs is a great motivator. Thus, while management may have other goals, there is ample reason to view shareholder wealth maximization as the dominant goal for the management teams of most publicly traded firms.[7]

tender offer
The offer of one firm to buy the stock of another by going directly to the shareholders, frequently over the opposition of the target company's management.

proxy fight
An attempt by a person, group, or company to gain control of a firm by convincing stockholders to vote a new management team into office.

---

[6]Wilbur G. Lewellen, "Management and Ownership in the Large Firm," *Journal of Finance*, May 1969, 299–322. Lewellen concluded that managers seem to make decisions that are largely oriented toward stock price maximization. More recent studies indicate that Lewellen's conclusions are still valid.

[7]To insure that a manager acts in the best interest of the shareholders, the firm must incur agency costs to monitor management's actions. For a brief summary of the agency problem, see Eugene F. Brigham and Louis C. Gapenski, *Intermediate Financial Management*, 3rd ed. (Hinsdale, Ill: The Dryden Press, 1990), 9–16. A more complete overview of agency theory may be found in Michael C. Jensen and William H. Meckling, "Theory of the Firm: Managerial Behavior, Agency Costs, and Ownership Structure," *Journal of Financial Economics*, October 1976, 350–360.

In this public notice, ER Holdings, Inc., a wholly owned subsidiary of BTR plc, informs the Norton Company stockholders of its cash offer to purchase Norton common stock. It also informs the stockholders that if Norton's Board of Directors does not endorse the offer then BTR intends to seek majority representation on Norton's Board of Directors.

Source: Courtesy BTR plc, London.

What Can Managers Do to Maximize Stock Prices?

Assuming that the financial manager's goal is to maximize the shareholders' wealth, what decisions are important in this task? The financial manager, along with the rest of the management team, must determine the investment, financing, and dividend policies of the firm. These decisions, moreover, have many ramifications. For example, management must consider the timing and risk of the income stream from a potential investment. Also, will **profit maximization** result in stock price maximization, or should the financial manager be concerned with some other form of return, such as **earnings per share (EPS)?**

To illustrate, suppose Caprock Petroleum has one million shares outstanding and earns $2 million, or $2 per share, and you own 100 shares of the stock. Now suppose the company sells another one million shares and invests the funds received in assets that produce $1 million of income. Total income will have risen to $3 million, but earnings per share will have declined from $2 to $3,000,000/2,000,000 shares, or $1.50. Your earnings will now be only $150, down from $200. You (and the other original stockholders) will have suffered an earnings dilution, even though total corporate profits have risen. Therefore, other things held constant, *if management is interested in the well-being of its stockholders, it should concentrate on earnings per share rather than on total corporate profits.*

Will maximization of expected earnings per share always maximize stockholder welfare? The answer is *no:* other factors such as timing and risk must also be considered. Think about the *timing of the earnings.* Suppose Caprock has one project that will cause earnings per share to rise by $0.20 per year for five years, or $1.00 in total, whereas another project has no effect on earnings for four years but increases earnings by $1.25 in the fifth year. Which project is better? The answer depends on which project adds the most to the value of the stock, which in turn depends on the time value of money to investors. Thus, timing is an important reason to concentrate on wealth as measured by the price of the stock rather than on earnings alone. We consider the critical concept of the time value of money in Chapter 13.

Before going on, we should distinguish between accounting profit and economic profit. **Accounting profit** is a firm's net income as reported on its income statement. In Chapter 5, we look in detail at a firm's financial statements, including its income statement. **Economic profit** is the amount left after all factors (labor and capital) have been paid. As you will discover later, we are concerned with **cash flow,** which is the actual net cash, as opposed to accounting net income, that flows into (or out of) a firm during some specified period.

Still another issue relates to **risk.** Suppose one project is expected to increase earnings per share by $1.00, while another is expected to raise earnings by $1.20 per share. The first project is not very risky; if it is undertaken, earnings will almost certainly rise by about $1.00 per share. However, the other

profit maximization
The maximization of the firm's net income.

earnings per share (EPS)
The net income of the firm divided by the number of shares of common stock outstanding.

accounting profit
A firm's net income, as reported on its income statement.

economic profit
The amount left after all factors (labor and capital) have been paid.

cash flow
The actual net cash, as opposed to accounting net income, that flows into (or out of) a firm during some specified period.

risk
The probability that actual future earnings will be below the expected earnings.

project is quite risky, so, although our best guess is that earnings will rise by $1.20 per share, we must recognize the possibility that there may be no increase whatsoever, or that there may even be a loss. Depending on how averse stockholders are to risk, the first project may be preferable to the second.

The riskiness inherent in projected earnings per share (EPS) also depends on *how the firm is financed.* As we shall see, many firms go bankrupt every year, and the greater the use of debt, the greater the threat of bankruptcy. Consequently, *while the use of debt financing may increase expected EPS, debt also increases the riskiness of future earnings.*

Still another issue is the matter of paying dividends to stockholders versus retaining earnings and reinvesting them in the firm, thereby causing the earnings stream to grow over time. Stockholders like cash dividends, but they also like the growth in EPS that results from plowing earnings back into the business. The financial manager must decide exactly how much of the current earnings to pay out as dividends rather than to retain and to reinvest. This is called the **dividend policy decision.** The optimal dividend policy is the one that maximizes the firm's stock price.

dividend policy decision
The decision as to how much of current earnings to pay out as dividends rather than to retain for reinvestment in the firm.

We see, then, that the firm's stock price is dependent on the following factors:

1. Projected earnings per share
2. Riskiness of the projected earnings
3. Timing of the earnings stream
4. The firm's use of debt financing
5. Its dividend policy

Every significant corporate decision should be analyzed in terms of its effect on these factors, hence on the price of the firm's stock. For example, suppose the Bluefield Coal Company is considering opening a new mine. If this is done, can it be expected to increase EPS? Is there a chance that costs will exceed estimates, that prices and output will fall below projections, and that EPS will be reduced because the new mine was opened? How long will it take for the new mine to start showing a profit? How should the capital required to open the mine be raised? If debt is used, how much will this increase Bluefield's riskiness? Should Bluefield reduce its current dividends and use the cash thus saved to finance the project, or should it maintain its dividends and finance the mine with external capital? Financial management is designed to help answer questions like these, plus many more.

social responsibility
The concept that businesses should be actively concerned about the welfare of society at large, even to the detriment of their stockholders.

Social Responsibility

Another issue that deserves consideration is **social responsibility:** Should businesses operate strictly in their stockholders' best interests, or are firms also partly responsible for the welfare of society at large? In tackling this question, consider first those firms whose **profits** and **rates of return** on investment are close to **normal** (that is, close to the average for all firms). If one

normal profits/rates of return
Those profits and rates of return that are close to the average for all firms and are just sufficient to attract capital.

INDUSTRY PRACTICE

The Bottom Line in Corporate Success

Cigarette sales dropped 2 percent annually during the last decade, but Philip Morris shareholders were still happy. While earnings per share in such other large firms as IBM and Ford grew by an average of 7 percent and 16 percent, respectively, during the 1980s, the average earnings per share for Philip Morris grew roughly 20 percent. Thus, the country's largest manufacturer of cigarettes increased its sales, profits, and market share despite a shrinking customer base.

This outstanding performance, which it has sustained over several years, earned Philip Morris a ranking as one of America's most admired corporations in *Fortune* magazine's annual "Corporate Reputations Survey." The company was ranked first in "value as an investment," one of eight attributes on which corporations are judged.

Fortune has been sponsoring this survey for almost a decade, and it publishes the results every January. Approximately 8,000 financial analysts, outside directors, and high executives in 32 industry groups rank about 300 large corporations each year to determine the most admired and the least admired companies.

Philip Morris came in second overall in the 1990 report, achieving a very high "admiration quotient" in spite of the Surgeon General's report linking its product with one-sixth of all deaths in the United States. This report cited another hurdle — during the past decade, shares of tobacco companies have traded at a lower price-to-earnings multiple than the average New York Stock Exchange share. The firm has offset that, says Philip Morris's CEO, Hamish Maxwell, "by having better than average earnings growth."

Industry sales have actually increased overall, in part because of overseas expansion but also because smokers who remain addicted feel compelled to buy tobacco products even when the price goes up faster than inflation. Philip Morris has prospered more than other similar firms by increasing its market share from 28 to 40 percent. In addition, the price of its stock increased 63 percent during 1989, after the firm acquired Kraft and immediately began cutting costs in its new food unit. The result was a 30 percent increase in profits, compared with Kraft's previous average earnings gains of 12 percent.

Cigarettes and food processors were not the only industries recognized in the corporate survey. Coca-Cola also ranked near the top in financial soundness. The company's CEO, Roberto C. Goizueta, boosted the return on shareholders' equity from 21 percent in 1981, when he took charge, to 32 percent in 1989. He achieved this by lowering the dividend payout ratio from 60 percent to 41 percent and then using the savings to purchase independent bottling plants. Shareholders benefited because the strategy allowed Coca-Cola to increase sales and monitor the efficiency of the bottling process.

Coca-Cola earned a top "financial soundness" rating because of its conservative stance on debt, perhaps not unexpected in a firm that had never borrowed anything until it built a new headquarters building in 1980. Currently, Coca-Cola's $400 million in long-term debt represents only about 10 percent of its capitalization.

To insure that his managers have the same view of money as he does, Goizueta requires Coca-Cola's 19 division presidents to make 3-year projections of the economic value they will add to the corporation. This calculation involves taking a division's after-tax operating profits and subtracting the cost of the capital used to produce those profits. Goizueta says, "Adding economic value to the company is the key to rewarding shareholders in the 1990s."

Source: *Fortune,* January 29, 1990, "America's Most Admired Corporations."

One of those shareholders, Berkshire Hathaway's CEO, Warren Buffett, appreciates those rewards. He recently acquired nearly 7 percent of Coca-Cola's stock at a cost of approximately $1 billion. "There is no more heartfelt compliment," he says, "than when I sign a check."

The analysts and executives who ranked the most admired firms recognize Buffett's own abilities — they ranked Berkshire Hathaway first in use of corporate assets. This successful conglomerate comprises seven operating companies — World Book Encyclopedia, the Buffalo *News,* See's Candies, Nebraska Furniture Mart, Kirby vacuum cleaners, manufacturer Scott Fetzer, and Fechheimer Brothers, a maker of uniforms. These "sainted seven," as Buffett calls them, produce returns on equity capital averaging 67 percent.

Buffett says his real line of work is the capital allocation business — figuring out which lines of business to invest in, what companies, and at what price. Berkshire's stock market investments include, in addition to Coca-Cola, Capital Cities/ABC, Geico, and the Washington Post Company. His choices have been excellent, as shown by the fact that the book value of Berkshire Hathaway stock has grown at a rate of 23.7 percent, compounded annually, since 1964 — from $19.46 to approximately $4,300 per share. Other investors besides Buffett, who owns 42 percent of the stock, have been made rich.

In November 1988 Berkshire switched from the over-the-counter market to the New York Stock Exchange, where it opened at a price of $4,700. By the end of 1989, the stock had climbed nearly 85 percent, to more than $8,600, and most of the stock is still owned by investors who paid less than $100 per share for it in 1964.

Of course, financial health and value are not the only reasons for admiring a corporation. Other important attributes include the quality of its products or services, the quality of its management, its corporate sense of responsibility, its innovativeness, and its ability to attract and keep good people. Still, no firm that fails to meet the primary goal of maximizing its stockholders' wealth can hope for admiration.

Philip Morris, ranked second overall, provided an average total return to investors of 30.1 percent over a 10-year period, and Coca-Cola, ranked eighth overall, averaged 26.8 percent. At the other end of the spectrum, Gibraltar Financial, ranked last, provided an annual return of −35.9 percent, and LTV, also ranked near the bottom, returned −17.0 percent. Thus, the bottom line in corporate success is still the bottom line.

company attempts to exercise social responsibility, its product prices will have to increase to cover the costs of these actions. If the other businesses in the industry do not follow suit, their costs and prices will remain constant. The socially responsible firm will not be able to compete, and it will be forced to abandon its efforts. Thus, any voluntary socially responsible acts that raise costs for one firm but not for all will be difficult, if not impossible, to sustain in industries characterized by significant price competition.

What about firms with profits above normal levels — can they not devote resources to social projects? Undoubtedly they can, and many large, successful firms do engage in community projects, employee benefit programs, and the like, to a greater degree than would appear to be called for by pure profit or wealth maximization goals.[8] Still, publicly owned firms are constrained in such actions by capital market factors. To illustrate, suppose a saver who has funds to invest is considering two alternative firms. One firm devotes a substantial part of its resources to social actions, while the other concentrates on profits and stock prices. Most investors are likely to shun the socially oriented firm, thus putting it at a disadvantage in the capital market. After all, why should the stockholders of one corporation subsidize society to a greater extent than those of other businesses? For this reason, even highly profitable firms (unless they are closely held rather than publicly owned) are generally constrained against taking unilateral cost-increasing social actions.

Does all this mean that firms should not exercise social responsibility? Not at all, but it does mean that most significant cost-increasing actions will have to be put on a *mandatory* rather than a voluntary basis, at least initially, to insure that their burdens fall uniformly across all businesses. Thus, such social benefit programs as fair hiring practices, minority training, product safety, pollution abatement, and antitrust actions are most likely to be effective if realistic rules are established initially and then enforced by government agencies. Of course, it is critical that industry and government cooperate in establishing the rules of corporate behavior, and that firms follow the spirit as well as the letter of the law in their actions. In such a setting, the rules of the game become constraints. Throughout this book, we shall assume that managers are stock-price maximizers who operate subject to a set of socially imposed constraints.

Business Ethics

Related to the issue of social responsibility is the question of business ethics. Ethics are defined in Webster's Dictionary as "standards of conduct or moral behavior." Business ethics can be thought of as a company's attitude and conduct toward its employees, customers, community, and stockholders. High standards of ethical behavior demand that a firm treat each of these constituents in a fair and honest manner. A firm's commitment to business ethics can be measured by the tendency of the firm and its employees to adhere to laws and regulations relating to product safety and quality, fair employment practices, fair marketing and selling practices, the use of confidential information for personal gain, community involvement, bribery, and illegal payments to foreign governments to obtain business.

There are many examples of firms engaging in unethical behavior. For example, in 1988, employees of several prominent Wall Street investment banking houses were sentenced to prison terms for illegally using insider information on proposed mergers for their own personal gain. Additionally, E. F. Hutton, the stock brokerage firm, lost its independence through a forced

---

[8]Even firms like these often find it necessary to justify such projects at stockholder meetings by stating that these programs will contribute to long-run profit maximization.

merger after it was convicted of cheating its banks out of millions of dollars in a check kiting scheme. However, the results of a recent *Business Roundtable* study indicate that the executives of most major firms in the United States believe that their firms should, and do, try to maintain high ethical standards in all of their business dealings.[9] In fact, most executives believe that there is a positive correlation between ethics and long-term profitability. For example, Chemical Bank suggested that ethical behavior has increased its profitability by allowing the firm (1) to avoid fines and legal expenses, (2) to build public trust, (3) to gain business from customers who appreciate and support its policies, (4) to attract and keep employees of the highest caliber, and (5) to support the economic viability of the community in which it operates.

Most firms often adhere to strong codes of ethical behavior, and they conduct training programs to insure that employees understand the correct behavior in different business situations. However, it is imperative that top management — the chairman, president, and vice presidents — be openly committed to ethical behavior, and that they communicate this commitment through their own personal actions as well as through company policies, directives, and punishment/reward systems.

Stock Price Maximization and Social Welfare

If firms attempt to maximize stock prices, is this good or bad for society? In general, it is good. Aside from such illegal actions as attempting to form monopolies, violating safety codes, and failing to meet pollution control requirements — all of which are constrained by the government — *the same actions that maximize stock prices also benefit society.* First, stock price maximization requires efficient, low-cost operations that produce the desired quality and quantity of output at the lowest possible cost. Second, stock price maximization requires the development of products that consumers want and need. Additionally, the profit motive leads to new technology, to new products, and to new jobs. Finally, stock price maximization requires efficient and courteous service, adequate stocks of merchandise, and well-located business establishments — these things are all necessary to make sales, and sales are certainly necessary for profits. Therefore, the types of actions that help a firm increase the price of its stock are also directly beneficial to society at large. This is why profit-motivated, free-enterprise economies have been more successful than other types of economic systems. Since financial management plays a crucial role in the operation of successful firms, and since successful firms are absolutely necessary for a healthy, productive economy, it is easy to see why finance is important from a social standpoint.

This view is now accepted throughout most of the world. Communism and socialism were tried in Russia, China, and Eastern Europe, but it eventually became clear that the market system is a far more efficient allocator of scarce

---

[9]The Business Roundtable, *Corporate Ethics: A Prime Business Asset* (New York, February 1988).

resources than are governments. People do need to be constrained by certain laws and regulations to keep greed in check, but personal drive, spurred on by the profit motive, produces the best results for society.

The Economic Environment

Although managers can take actions which affect the values of their firms' stocks, there are additional factors that influence stock prices. Included among them are external constraints, the general level of economic activity, taxes, and conditions in the stock market. Figure 1-2 diagrams these general relationships. Working within the set of external constraints shown in the box at the extreme left, management makes a set of long-run strategic policy decisions which chart a future course for the firm. These policy decisions, along with the general level of economic activity and the level of corporate income taxes, influence the firm's expected profitability, the timing of its earnings, the eventual transfer of earnings to stockholders in the form of dividends, and the degree of uncertainty (or risk) inherent in projected earnings and dividends. Profitability, timing, and risk all affect the price of the firm's stock, but so does

Figure 1-2 **Summary of Major Factors Affecting Stock Prices**

Although managers can take actions which affect the values of their firms' stocks, additional factors influence stock prices. Working with external constraints, like environmental regulations, antitrust laws, and so forth, management makes long-term strategic policy decisions that plot the firm's future course. These policy decisions, along with the general level of economic activity and corporate income taxes, influence the firm's expected profitability, the timing of its earnings, the transfer of earnings to stockholders (dividends), and the degree of uncertainty inherent in projected earnings and dividends. Of course, stock market conditions affect a firm's stock price, because all stock prices tend to move up and down together to some extent.

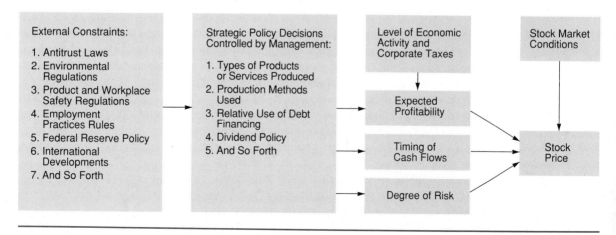

another factor, the state of the stock market as a whole, because all stock prices tend to move up and down together to some extent.

Self-Test

What should be management's primary goal in a publicly traded corporation?

What actions could be taken to oust a firm's management in a competitive market if it departed from the goal of maximizing shareholder wealth?

Will profit maximization also result in stock price maximization? Explain. Will maximization of expected earnings per share always maximize stockholder welfare? Explain.

Identify five factors within the firm's control which affect the firm's stock price.

Identify some factors beyond the firm's control which influence its stock price.

ORGANIZATION OF THE BOOK

This introductory chapter has described, in broad terms, the duties of the financial manager and the goals of the firm. Someone once said, "Any road will do if you don't know where you're going." We have therefore carefully charted our destination—the goal of shareholder wealth maximization—and attempted to indicate how this goal influences the duties and actions of the financial manager.

The remaining chapters in Part I will investigate the economic environment in which the financial manager operates. In Chapter 2 taxes are briefly discussed, and then the general purpose of financial markets—to transfer savings to firms and individuals with attractive investment opportunities—is analyzed. Chapter 3 goes on to examine the major financial institutions in our financial markets, and in Chapter 4 we explore the role of interest rates in the economy.

Part II deals with financial statements and financial planning. Both long- and short-term plans are analyzed in terms of future financial statements, so it is important to understand how these statements are developed and used by managers and other interested parties, such as creditors and investors. We first review how financial statements are constructed; we then show how they are used to analyze past operations; and, finally, we discuss how financial statements can be projected into the future to forecast profits under different strategic plans and operating conditions.

In Part III we move into the execution phase of the financial management process. Here current, ongoing operations are examined. From our study of accounting we know that assets which are expected to be converted to cash within a year, such as inventories and accounts receivable, are called *current assets* and that liabilities which must be paid off within a year are called *current liabilities.* The management of current assets and current liabilities is known as *working capital management,* and Part III deals with this topic.

In Part IV we focus on long-term assets, which produce cash flows over many years. We begin, in Chapter 13, with a discussion of the relationship between risk and return. Then, since dollars received in different years are worth different amounts, we examine "the time value of money." Finally, we apply the risk, return, and time value concepts in our discussion of *capital budgeting*, which relates to the acquisition of long-term, or fixed, assets. Since major capital expenditures take years to plan and execute, and since decisions in this area are generally not reversible and affect operations for many years, their effect on the value of the firm is obvious.

Part V focuses on raising long-term capital. Questions regarding the principal sources and forms of long-term capital, the cost of each type, and how methods of financing affect the value of the firm are all addressed in this section. Hybrid financing methods that are not strictly debt or equity are also discussed here.

Part VI describes the means by which the investor evaluates the firm's debt and equity instruments. The interrelationships among value, cost of capital, capital structure, and dividend policy serve to integrate the book and to show how the parts meld into a cohesive whole.

Finally, in Part VII, we consider some subjects that, although important, are best studied within the basic framework of the material presented earlier in the text. Included in this section are mergers and acquisitions, and international financial management.

 SMALL BUSINESS

Resources and Goals in the Small Firm

This book is about financial management, and the concepts it covers apply to small businesses as well as to large corporations. The context of financial management, however, is quite different in a small business than in a large firm, and the special characteristics of small firms must be considered. Two key characteristics of small firms are that (1) they suffer from resource poverty, and (2) their goals are quite complex.

Resource Poverty

Consider the scenario in a large firm when a decision must be made about building a new plant. The chief executive officer (CEO) calls on a financial vice president and asks her to organize the financial analysis. She turns to the manager in charge of financial analysis in the division considering the expansion, and he in turn organizes a team to conduct the analysis. The team employs 20 to 30 recent graduates with masters of business administration or bachelors of business administration to do the calculations, and they in turn depend on engineering and marketing staffs to provide them with the necessary input data. The treasurer will ask an investment banker to recommend the ways to obtain funds, such as new equity issues, new debt issues, private security sales, a large-bank relationship, and the like. The investment banker may organize a team of experienced professionals (each earning an average of more than $250,000 annually) who will work on the plan and prepare recommendations. In general, in a large corporation, there are plenty of people to share the work, and the public security markets are available to fund the projects.

That is not the case in a small firm. Suppose John Thompson, owner of 75 percent of Board Products, Inc., wishes to expand his company's production line. He considers the proposal, gets a bid on the project, and consults his banker, who says she's very busy now but she will get back to him. Meanwhile, Thompson is in the process of hiring three new laborers and a secretary, and he is preparing for a meeting with a potential client. He has spent the past three weeks trying to get the financial statements and paperwork for the quarterly tax payments completed. Thompson has little time and virtually no assistance in considering the financial aspects of the production line decision. Because he has no formal training in capital budgeting, he conducts a "seat-of-the-pants" analysis and decides to go ahead with the project. Later, it turns out that he overlooked many details which combine to make the project a bad idea.

Thompson's case is not unusual. Small businesses are characterized by resource poverty. In small firms, one or two key people frequently end up taking on far more responsibility than they can reasonably handle. Thompson, for example, may argue that other priorities in the business prevent him from spending much time putting together a budget or checking regularly to see how well the company is adhering to this budget. He might say, "I have a pretty good feel for how we're doing in terms of cash, and I really don't have time to go into more detail. Making budgets doesn't make money."

Management's lack of resources contributes to the failure of many small firms. An owner-manager deciding in a "seat-of-the-pants" fashion not to develop a detailed, accurate budget may realize too late that his cash flow is insufficient.

Not only is management "spread thin" in small firms, but small firms also frequently cannot acquire new funds needed for business expansion, or they can obtain funds only under very stringent conditions. Until Board Products achieves a fairly substantial size (say, $15 million in sales), the company will probably not be able to sell stock or bonds successfully in public markets. Furthermore, any public stock offering the firm did have would be very expensive compared with a similar stock offering by a larger firm. Thus, Board Products has only limited access to public capital markets. Banks also may be reluctant to loan money to Board Products because the firm lacks a "track record."

We see, then, that small firms are limited both in their access to managerial talent and in their ability to muster adequate financial resources. It is no wonder that small firms often fail, either because of poor (or overworked) management or because of undercapitalization.

Goals of the Small Firm

Small businesses' goals also may differ from those of big firms. Share price maximization is taken to be the goal of all publicly held firms. John Thompson, however, provides a good example of an owner whose life is tied up in his company. He depends on the firm for his livelihood, and he has staked his future on its success. His personal wealth portfolio is not at all diversified; he has put everything he owns into the company.

Thompson has a different attitude toward risk taking in his firm than would a typical investor in a public company. Such an investor would hold a number of other investments, all contributing to a well-diversified portfolio of holdings, and most of this investor's personal income comes from a job in an altogether separate industry.

The typical owner-manager of a small firm is, of course, keenly interested in the value of the company itself; after all, it is the most valuable asset the individual owns. In addition, the owner-manager may be considering "taking the firm public" or having it acquired by a larger firm some day, and he or she hopes that this will occur at the highest price possible.

Nevertheless, the owner-manager has complex motives. One of them might be the desire to continue being his or her own boss, even if this means not allowing the firm to progress as rapidly as it otherwise could. There is a value to being in control, a value that is recognized in the finance literature, but that value is extremely difficult to quantify. As a result, small business owners may be observed taking actions that make no sense when considered against a value maximization standard, but that are reasonable on the basis of other objectives.

To the extent that the goals of the small firm go beyond value maximization, some of the prescriptions in this text may not be entirely applicable. Most of the concepts will be useful for the small business, even if its objectives are different, but they may need to be modified or given different amounts of emphasis. For example, small firms may be more interested in financial statement analysis, and less interested in dividend policy, than large firms.

SUMMARY

This chapter has provided an overview of financial management. The key concepts covered are listed below:

- Finance consists of three interrelated areas: (1) **money and capital markets,** (2) **investments,** and (3) **financial management.**

- **Financial managers** are responsible for **obtaining and using funds** in a way that will **maximize the value of the firm.**

- Financial management has undergone significant changes over the years, and in the 1980s four issues have received emphasis: (1) **inflation** and its effects on interest rates, (2) **deregulation of financial institutions,** (3) a dramatic increase in the **use of computers** for analyzing financial decisions, and (4) **the trend toward the globalization of business.**

- The three main forms of business organization are the **sole proprietorship,** the **partnership,** and the **corporation.**

- Although each form of organization offers some advantages and disadvantages, **most business is conducted by corporations because this organizational form maximizes most firms' values.**

- The traditional responsibilities assigned to the **treasurer** are selecting and evaluating productive assets, forecasting financial needs arising from current and new operations, financing those operations, and establishing dividend policy for the disbursement of earnings from those operations.

- The primary goal of management should be to **maximize stockholders' wealth,** and this means **maximizing the price of the firm's stock.** Fortunately, actions which maximize stock prices also increase social welfare.

- In recent years, hostile takeovers in the form of **tender offers** and **proxy fights** have removed a number of supposedly well-entrenched managements.

- The **price of the firm's stock** depends on the firm's **projected earnings per share,** the **riskiness of projected earnings,** the **timing of earnings,** the firm's **use of debt financing,** and its **dividend policy.**

- **Small firms** suffer from resource poverty, and they have complex goals. Small businesses' goals may differ from those of larger firms. Most of the concepts in this text will be useful to small businesses, even if their goals are different from those of larger firms, but these concepts may need to be modified or given different amounts of emphasis.

 RESOLUTION TO DECISION IN FINANCE

The Biggest Buyout—or a Sellout?

There are a number of advantages and disadvantages to most leveraged buyouts (LBOs). The fact that managers and bankers involved in LBOs often make a great deal of money could fall into either category.

However, one clear advantage is the fact that companies often perform better after a buyout. When managers become owners, they tend to watch costs and monitor resources more closely, which frequently results in higher profit margins. One financier compared the difference between public and private ownership to the difference between renting and owning a house. "You take better care of your own home."

Productivity in certain types of companies may also improve because of the massive debt assumed in a buyout. When pressured to meet huge interest payments every quarter, managers

will generally tighten up and eliminate the "deadwood." Also, debt interest is tax deductible, whereas dividends are taxed twice—both as corporate earnings and as income to shareholders.

There are, of course, some disadvantages to LBOs, such as the effect on the corporation's bondholders. In the case of RJR Nabisco, when Johnson announced his buyout bid, the average price of RJR's $5 billion worth of investment-grade bonds fell 20 percent in less than a week. Another disadvantage is that R&D expenditures are often cut after a leveraged buyout.

To some observers, the buyout offer by Nabisco managers was unethical. They sold investors bonds in what they claimed was a carefully managed corporation, and then, without notice, they announced plans to turn the company into a much riskier enterprise. In the process, they decreased the value of the outstanding bonds.

As for the shareholders, do they win or lose in a leveraged buyout? Shareholders were big winners in the RJR Nabisco deal, since the bidding caused the price of RJR's stock to soar above its mediocre post-crash level. Johnson's original bid was topped within four days, and other, higher bids swiftly followed.

Sources: *Fortune,* "LBOs: Greed, Good Business or Both?," " 'They Cleaned Our Clock'," " 'Greed Really Turns Me Off," January 2, 1989, and "How Ross Johnson Blew the Buyout," April 24, 1989; *The Wall Street Journal,* "Secret Scenes from the RJR Wars," January 4, 1990, and "Cash-Rich Companies Now Rule Roost," March 9, 1990; *Newsweek,* "Going Private: A Binge That Won't Let Up," October 31, 1988; *Business Week,* "Running the Biggest LBO," October 2, 1989.

When directors finally accepted the Kohlberg Kravis Roberts bid, it was because that firm was willing to negotiate its offer. For one thing, KKR agreed to change the conversion timetable for part of its package to four years instead of two. This longer wait to convert the debentures into RJR equity would give stockholders a greater chance to benefit from higher future earnings.

Johnson and Shearson lost, in part, because they offered more cash than securities in their bids, believing the directors would consider cash a superior form of payment. This was ironic, since after that buyout, cash has become more desirable in the corporate marketplace, and the most successful buyers of corporate assets are now those who have to borrow the least.

What has happened to RJR Nabisco? Kohlberg Kravis Roberts named Louis V. Gerstner to replace Ross Johnson as CEO. Within seven months he had auctioned off more than $3.5 billion in RJR assets, selling the firm's European food units, Chun King, and Del Monte tropical fruits and canned goods. Employee cuts included more than 2,300 tobacco workers and 300 from the "overstaffed" headquarters. Returns from the reconstructed food and tobacco company should — if projections are correct — create an enormous profit for shareholders who keep their convertible securities.

As for Johnson — considered the biggest "loser" of all in this deal — he says he has no regrets. "The thing that makes me so comfortable is that I did what I was paid to do — get value for shareholders," he said.

QUESTIONS

1-1 What are the three principal forms of business organization? What are the advantages and disadvantages of each?

1-2 Would the normal rate of return on investment be the same in all industries? Would "normal" rates of return change over time? Explain.

1-3 Would the role of the financial manager be likely to increase or decrease in importance relative to other executives if the rate of inflation increased? Explain.

1-4 Should stockholder wealth maximization be thought of as a long-term or a short-term goal; that is, if one action would probably increase the stock price from a current level of $40 to $50 in 6 months and then to $60 in 5 years, but another action would probably keep the stock price at $40 for several years but then increase it to $80 in 5 years, which action would be better? Can you think of actual examples that might have these general tendencies?

1-5 What is the difference between stock price maximization and profit maximization? Under what conditions might profit maximization not lead to stock price maximization?

1-6 If you were the president of a large, publicly owned corporation, would you make decisions to maximize stockholders' welfare or your own personal interests? What are some actions stockholders could take to insure that management's interests and those of stockholders coincided? What are some other factors that might influence management's actions?

1-7 The president of NanoSecond Semiconductor Corporation made this statement in the company's annual report: "NanoSecond's primary goal is to increase the value of the common stockholders' equity over time." Later in the report, the following announcements were made:

a. The company contributed $1 million to the symphony orchestra in its home office city.

b. The company spent $300 million to open a new plant in South America. No revenues will be produced by the plant for 3 years, so earnings will be depressed during this period versus what they would have been had the decision been made not to open the new plant.

c. The company will increase its relative use of debt. Whereas assets were formerly financed with 40 percent debt and 60 percent equity, henceforth the financing mix will be 50-50.

d. The company uses a great deal of electricity in its manufacturing operations, and it generates most of this power itself. The company plans to utilize nuclear fuel rather than coal to produce electricity in the future.

e. The company has been paying out half of its earnings as dividends and retaining the other half. Henceforth, it will pay out only 20 percent as dividends.

Discuss how each of these actions might affect NanoSecond's stock price.

Chapter 2

Taxes and the Financial Environment

 RESOLUTION TO DECISION IN FINANCE

Is Wall Street Losing Its Grip on Corporate America?

Business had been booming on Wall Street. The bull market had been running for so long that it seemed as if people had forgotten what is was like for almost any deal to go sour. Wall Street was thick with young millionaires. Then came the crash. On Monday, October 19, 1987, the market took a plunge that shook Wall Street like an earthquake. The Dow Jones Industrial Average, which tracks 30 blue chip stocks and is considered to be the pulse of the stock market, did a spectacular 508-point nosedive. In one stomach-churning day, the advances of the preceding years were vaporized, along with many investors' profits. The aftershocks sent over-the-counter stocks tumbling, along with stock markets around the globe. It seemed that panic, like data, could be transmitted electronically in the blink of an eye.

The effects of the crash were immediately apparent everywhere on Wall Street. Investment firms slashed their staffs, froze salaries, abandoned marginally profitable businesses, and trimmed their expenses. E. F. Hutton, the brokerage firm, was backed into a shotgun wedding

with its former rival, Shearson Lehman Brothers, and other companies put consolidation plans into the works.

But aside from the impact of the crash on Wall Street, what was its effect on Main Street Corporate America? The years leading up to the crash had spawned a strong symbiotic relationship among the stock market, investment banks, and corporations. Although it was, at times, an antagonistic alliance, many American corporations profited from their relationship with Wall Street. Financial wizards created a dazzling assortment of innovative financing vehicles that allowed corporations to raise money in new ways. Stocks, issued at a moment's notice, provided instant cash that could be further stretched with new debt offerings. Corporate raiders made millions buying companies whether they wanted to be bought or not. Suddenly, on October 19th, all that changed. Or did it?

As you read this chapter, think about the ways that the crash might affect American corporations in the long run. How might the ways that corporations raise money be affected? What might be the effect on the market for new stocks?

See end of chapter for resolution.

A financial manager's decision to invest in new assets, or to determine the ways in which assets are to be financed, is not made in a vacuum. An understanding of financial management requires a knowledge of the environment in which financial managers operate. In this chapter, we examine the tax system under which the firm operates and the markets in which capital is raised, securities are traded, and stock prices are established, and we also examine the institutions through which these transactions are conducted.

THE FEDERAL INCOME TAX SYSTEM

The value of any financial asset, such as a share of stock, a bond, or a mortgage, as well as the values of most real assets such as plants or even entire firms, depends on the stream of cash flows produced by the asset. Cash flows from an asset consist of *usable* income plus depreciation. Usable income means income *after taxes*. Proprietorship and partnership income must be reported by the owners, and it is taxed as their personal income. Most corporations, however, must first pay taxes on the corporation's own income, and then stockholders must pay additional taxes on all corporate after-tax income distributed as dividends. Therefore, both *personal* and *corporate* income taxes are important in the determination of the cash flows produced by financial assets.

Our tax laws can be changed by Congress, and in recent years changes have occurred almost every year. Indeed, a nontrivial change has occurred, on average, every 1½ years since 1913, when our federal income tax system began. Further, certain parts of our tax system are tied to the rate of inflation, so changes automatically occur each year, depending on the rate of inflation during the previous year. Therefore, although this chapter will give you a good background on the basic nature of our tax system, you should consult current rate schedules and other data published by the Internal Revenue Service (and available in U.S. post offices) before you file your personal or business tax return!

Currently (1990), federal income tax rates for individuals go up to 33 percent, and when state and city income taxes are included, the marginal tax rate on an individual's income can exceed 40 percent. Business income is also taxed heavily. The income from partnerships and proprietorships is reported by the individual owners as personal income and, consequently, is taxed at rates going up to 40 percent or more. Corporate profits are subject to federal income tax rates of up to 39 percent, in addition to state income taxes. Because of the magnitude of the tax bite, taxes play an important role in many financial decisions.

Because the U.S. government is running a large fiscal deficit, most experts predict that tax rates will be raised in the not-too-distant future. Thus, by the time you read this chapter, rates may well be higher. Still, if you understand the chapter, you will be able to apply the new tax rates.

Taxes are so complicated that university law schools offer master's degrees in taxation to practicing lawyers, many of whom are also CPAs. In a field com-

Table 2-1 **Individual Tax Rates for 1990**

Single Individuals

If Your Taxable Income Is	You Pay This Amount on the Base of the Bracket	Plus This Percentage on the Excess over the Base	Average Tax Rate at Top of Bracket
Up to $19,450	$ 0	15%	15.0%
$19,450–$47,050	2,918	28	22.6
$47,050–$97,620	10,646	33	28.0
Over $97,620	27,334	28	28.0

Married Couples Filing Joint Returns

If Your Taxable Income Is	You Pay This Amount on the Base of the Bracket	Plus This Percentage on the Excess over the Base	Average Tax Rate at Top of Bracket
Up to $32,450	$ 0	15%	15.0%
$32,450–$78,400	4,868	28	22.6
$78,400–$162,770	17,734	33	28.0
Over $162,770	45,576	28	28.0

Notes:

a. The tax rates are for 1990 and beyond. However, the income ranges at which the 28 percent rate takes effect, as well as the ranges for the surtax discussed below, are scheduled to be indexed with inflation each year beyond 1990, so they will change from those shown in the table.

b. Technically, a surtax of 5 percent is imposed on income in the range $47,050 to $97,620 for single individuals and in the range $78,400 to $162,770 for married couples. This surtax is designed to eliminate the effects of the 15 percent rate on the first increments of income and to eliminate the benefits of the personal exemption. The surtax ceases when the personal exemption has been fully offset; thus, the dollar amount at which the marginal rate drops back to 28 percent depends on the number of exemptions claimed. The highest bracket amounts shown in this table assume one exemption for a single individual and two exemptions for a married couple. Different tables, similar to the one we present but with different numbers of exemptions, are available from the Internal Revenue Service.

plicated enough to warrant such detailed study, we can cover only the highlights. This is really enough, though, because business managers and investors should and do rely on tax specialists rather than trusting their own limited knowledge. Still, it is important to know the basic elements of the tax system as a starting point for discussions with tax experts.

Individual Income Taxes

Individuals pay taxes on wages and salaries, on investment income (dividends, interest, and profits from the sale of securities), and on the profits of proprietorships and partnerships. Our tax rates are **progressive** — that is, the higher one's income, the larger the percentage paid in taxes.[1] Table 2-1 gives the tax

progressive tax
A tax that requires a higher percentage payment on higher incomes. The personal income tax in the United States, which goes from a rate of 0 percent on the lowest increments of income to 33 percent and then back to 28 percent on the highest increments, is progressive.

---

[1]Prior to the 1986 Tax Code revisions, individual rates were more steeply progressive, going from 11 percent to 50 percent, but higher-income taxpayers were able to use a variety of tax shelters that lowered effective tax rates substantially. Indeed, many people had cash income in the millions of dollars yet were able to completely avoid taxes. The 1986 changes eliminated most tax shelters. Also, the revisions increased dramatically the tax rate on capital gains, most of which are earned by wealthy individuals. Therefore, in reality, the new law did not lower the progressivity of our tax system.

rates for single individuals and married couples filing joint returns under the rate schedules in effect in 1990.

taxable income
Gross income minus exemptions and allowable deductions as set forth in the Tax Code.

1. Taxable income is defined as gross income less a set of exemptions and deductions which are spelled out in the instructions to the tax forms individuals must file. When filing a tax return in 1991 for the tax year 1990, each taxpayer will receive an exemption of $2,050 for each dependent, including the taxpayer, which reduces taxable income. However, (1) this exemption is indexed to rise with inflation, and (2) high-income taxpayers must pay a surtax, which takes away the value of personal exemptions. Also, certain expenses, such as mortgage interest paid, state and local income taxes paid, and charitable contributions, can be deducted and thus be used to reduce taxable income.

marginal tax rate
The tax applicable to the last unit of income.

2. The **marginal tax rate** is defined as the tax on the last unit of income. Marginal rates begin at 15 percent, rise to 28 and then to 33 percent, and finally fall back to 28 percent. The average tax rate on all taxable income rises from zero to 28 percent.

average tax rate
Taxes paid divided by taxable income.

3. One can calculate **average tax rates** from the data in Table 2-1. For example, if Jill Smith, a single individual, had taxable income of $35,000, her tax bill would be $2,918 + ($35,000 − $19,450)(0.28) = $2,918 + $4,354 = $7,272. Her *average tax rate* would be $7,272/$35,000 = 20.8% versus a *marginal rate* of 28 percent. If Jill received a raise of $1,000, bringing her income to $36,000, she would have to pay $280 of it as taxes, so her after-tax raise would be $720.

bracket creep
A situation that occurs when progressive tax rates combine with inflation to cause a greater portion of each taxpayer's real income to be paid as taxes.

4. As indicated in the notes to the table, current legislation provides for tax brackets to be indexed to inflation to avoid the **bracket creep** that occurred during the 1970s and that de facto raised tax rates substantially.[2]

Taxes on Dividend and Interest Income. Dividend and interest income received by individuals from corporate securities is added to other income and thus is taxed at rates going up to 33 percent. Since corporations pay dividends out of earnings that have already been taxed, there is *double taxation* of corporate income.

---

[2]For example, if you were single and had a taxable income of $19,450, your tax bill would be $2,918. Now suppose inflation caused prices to double and your income, being tied to a cost-of-living index, rose to $38,900. Because our tax rates are progressive, if tax brackets were not indexed, your taxes would jump to $8,364. Your after-tax income would thus increase from $16,532 to $30,536, but, because prices have doubled, your real income would *decline* from $16,532 to $15,268 (calculated as one-half of $30,536). You would be in a higher tax bracket, so you would be paying a higher percentage of your real income in taxes. If this happened to everyone, and if Congress failed to change tax rates sufficiently, real disposable incomes would decline because the federal government would be taking a larger share of the national product. This is called the federal government's "inflation dividend." However, since tax brackets are now indexed, if your income doubled due to inflation, your tax bill would double, but your after-tax real income would remain constant at $16,532. Bracket creep was a real problem during the 1970s and early 1980s, but indexing — if it stays in the law — will put an end to it.

It should be noted that under U.S. tax laws, interest on most state and local government bonds, called *municipals* or *"munis,"* is not subject to federal income taxes. Thus, investors get to keep all of the interest received from most municipal bonds but only a fraction of the interest received from bonds issued by corporations or by the U.S. government. This means that a lower-yielding muni can provide the same after-tax return as a higher-yielding corporate bond. For example, a taxpayer in the 33 percent marginal tax bracket who could buy a muni that yielded 10 percent would have to receive a before-tax yield of 14.93 percent on a corporate or U.S. Treasury bond to have the same after-tax income:

$$\text{Equivalent pretax yield on taxable bond} = \frac{\text{Yield on muni}}{1 - \text{Marginal tax rate}} = \frac{10\%}{1 - 0.33} = 14.93\%.$$

If we know the yield on the taxable bond, we can use the following equation to find the equivalent yield on a muni:

$$\text{Yield on muni} = \text{Pretax yield on taxable bond} - \left(\text{Pretax yield on taxable bond}\right)\left(\text{Tax rate}\right)$$

$$= 14.93\% - (14.93\%)(0.33) = 10.0\%.$$

The exemption from federal taxes stems from the separation of federal and state powers, and its primary effect is to help state and local governments borrow at lower rates than would otherwise be available to them.

Capital Gains versus Ordinary Income. Assets such as stocks, bonds, and real estate are defined as *capital assets.* If you buy a capital asset and later sell it for more than your purchase price, the profit is called a **capital gain;** if you suffer a loss, it is called a **capital loss.** An asset sold within one year of the time it was purchased produces a *short-term gain or loss,* whereas one held for more than one year produces a *long-term gain or loss.* Thus, if you buy 100 shares of Disney stock for $70 per share and sell it for $80 per share, you make a capital gain of 100 × $10, or $1,000. However, if you sell the stock for $60 per share, you will have a $1,000 capital loss. If you hold the stock for more than one year, the gain or loss is long-term; otherwise, it is short-term. If you sell the stock for exactly $70 per share, you make neither a gain nor a loss; you simply get your $7,000 back, and no tax is due.

capital gain or loss
The profit (loss) from the sale of a capital asset for more (less) than its purchase price.

From 1921 through 1986, long-term capital gains were taxed at substantially lower rates than ordinary income. For example, in 1986 long-term capital gains were taxed at only 40 percent of the tax rate on ordinary income. However, the tax law changes which took effect in 1987 eliminated this differential, and all capital gains income (both long-term and short-term) is now taxed as if it were ordinary income.

There was a great deal of controversy over the elimination of the preferential rate for capital gains. It was argued that lower tax rates on capital

Table 2-2 **Corporate Tax Rates**

If a Corporation's Taxable Income Is	It Pays This Amount on the Base of the Bracket	Plus This Percentage on the Excess over the Base	Average Tax Rate at Top of Bracket
Up to $50,000	$ 0	15%	15.0%
$50,000 to $75,000	7,500	25	18.3
$75,000 to $100,000	13,750	34	22.3
$100,000 to $335,000	22,250	39	34.0
Over $335,000	113,900	34	34.0

Notes:

a. The rates shown here are for 1990.

b. For income in the range of $100,000 to $335,000, a surtax of 5% is added to the base rate of 34%. This surtax, which eliminates the effects of the lower rates on income below $75,000, results in a marginal tax rate of 39% for income in the $100,000 to $335,000 range.

gains (1) stimulated the flow of venture capital to new, start-up businesses (which generally provide capital gains as opposed to dividend income) and (2) caused companies to retain and reinvest a high percentage of their earnings in order to provide their stockholders with capital gains as opposed to highly taxed dividend income. Thus, it was argued that elimination of the favorable rates on capital gains would retard investment and economic growth. The proponents of preferential capital gains tax rates lost the argument in 1986, but they did succeed in keeping in the law all the language dealing with capital gains, which would make it easy to reinstate the differential if economic conditions suggest that it is indeed needed to encourage growth. The Bush administration tried to lower capital gains taxes in 1989 and 1990, and they will probably try again. Therefore, you should not be surprised if the capital gains differential is reinstated in the future.

When capital gains were taxed at lower rates, this had implications for dividend policy (it favored lower payouts and hence higher earnings retention). It also favored stock investments over bond investments, because part of the income from stock normally comes from capital gains. Thus, one can anticipate changes in corporate dividend and capital structure policy as a result of tax changes which affect capital gains tax rates.

Corporate Income Taxes

The corporate tax structure, shown in Table 2-2, is relatively simple. To illustrate, if a firm had $75,000 of taxable income, its tax bill would be

$$\text{Taxes} = \$7,500 + 0.25(\$25,000)$$

$$= \$7,500 + \$6,250$$

$$= \$13,750,$$

and its average tax rate would be $13,750/$75,000 = 18.3%. Note that for all income over $335,000 one can disregard the surtax and simply calculate the corporate tax as 34 percent of all taxable income. Thus, the corporate tax is progressive up to $335,000 of income, but it is constant thereafter.[3]

Interest and Dividend Income Received by a Corporation. Interest income received by a corporation is taxed as ordinary income at regular corporate tax rates. However, 70 percent of the dividends received by one corporation from another is excluded from taxable income, while the remaining 30 percent is taxed at the ordinary tax rate.[4] Thus, a corporation earning over $335,000 and paying a 34 percent marginal tax rate would pay only $(0.30)(0.34) = 0.102 = 10.2\%$ of its dividend income as taxes, so its effective tax rate on intercorporate dividends would be 10.2 percent. If this firm had $10,000 in pretax dividend income, its after-tax dividend income would be $8,980:

$$\frac{\text{After-tax}}{\text{income}} = \text{Before-tax income} - \text{Taxes}$$

$$= \text{Before-tax income} - (\text{Before-tax income})(\text{Effective tax rate})$$

$$= \text{Before-tax income}(1 - \text{Effective tax rate})$$

$$= \$10,000\,[1 - (0.30)(0.34)]$$

$$= \$10,000(1 - 0.102)$$

$$= \$10,000(0.898) = \$8,980.$$

---

[3]Prior to 1987, many large, profitable corporations such as General Electric and Boeing paid no income taxes. The reasons for this were as follows: (1) expenses, especially depreciation, were defined differently for calculating taxable income than for reporting earnings to stockholders, so some companies reported positive profits to stockholders but losses — hence no taxes — to the Internal Revenue Service; and (2) some companies which did have tax liabilities used various tax credits, including the investment tax credit (discussed later in the chapter) to offset taxes that would otherwise have been payable. This situation was effectively eliminated in 1987.

The principal method used to eliminate this situation is the Alternative Minimum Tax (AMT). Under the AMT, both corporate and individual taxpayers must figure their taxes in two ways, the "regular" way and the AMT way, and then pay the higher of the two. The AMT is calculated as follows: (1) Figure your regular taxes. (2) Take your taxable income under the regular method and then add back certain items, especially income on certain municipal bonds, depreciation in excess of straight line depreciation, certain research and drilling costs, itemized or standard deductions (for individuals), and a number of other items. (3) The income determined in (2) is defined as AMT income, and it must then be multiplied by the AMT tax rate (21% in 1990) to determine the tax due under the AMT system. An individual or corporation must then pay the higher of the regular tax or the AMT tax.

[4]The size of the dividend exclusion actually depends on the degree of ownership. Corporations that own less than 20 percent of the stock of the dividend-paying company can exclude 70 percent of the dividends received, firms that own over 20 percent but less than 80 percent can exclude 80 percent of the dividends, and firms that own over 80 percent can exclude the entire dividend payment. Since for investment (as opposed to control) purposes most companies own less than 20 percent of other companies, we will, in general, assume a 70 percent dividend exclusion.

If the corporation pays its own after-tax income out to its stockholders as dividends, the income is ultimately subjected to *triple taxation:* (1) The original corporation is first taxed, (2) the second corporation is then taxed on the dividends it received, and (3) the individuals who receive the final dividends are taxed again. This is the reason for the 70 percent exclusion on intercorporate dividends.

If a corporation has surplus funds that can be invested in marketable securities, the tax factor favors investment in stocks, which pay dividends, rather than in bonds, which pay interest. For example, suppose GE had $100,000 to invest, and it could buy bonds that paid interest of $8,000 per year or preferred stock that paid dividends of $7,000. GE is in the 34 percent tax bracket; therefore, its tax on the interest, if it bought bonds, would be 0.34($8,000) = $2,720 and its after-tax income would be $5,280. If it bought preferred stock, its tax would be 0.34[(0.30)($7,000)] = $714 and its after-tax income would be $6,286. Other factors might lead GE to invest in bonds, but the tax factor certainly favors stock investments when the investor is a corporation.[5]

Interest and Dividends Paid by a Corporation. A firm's operations can be financed either with debt or equity capital. If it uses debt, it must pay interest on this debt, whereas if it uses equity, it will pay dividends to the equity investors (stockholders). The interest paid by a corporation is deducted from its operating income to obtain its taxable income, but dividends paid are not deductible. Therefore, a firm needs $1 of pretax income to pay $1 of interest, but if it is in the 40 percent federal-plus-state tax bracket, it needs

$$\frac{\$1}{1 - \text{Tax rate}} = \frac{\$1}{0.60} = \$1.67$$

of pretax income to pay $1 of dividends.

To illustrate, Table 2-3 shows the situation for a firm with $1.5 million of operating income before interest and taxes. As shown in Column 1, if the firm were financed entirely by bonds, and if it made interest payments of $1.5 million, its taxable income would be zero, taxes would be zero, and its investors would receive the entire $1.5 million. (The term *investors* includes both stockholders and bondholders.) If the firm had no debt and was therefore financed only by stock, all of the $1.5 million of operating income would be taxable income to the corporation, the tax would be $1,500,000(0.40) = $600,000, and

---

[5]This illustration demonstrates why corporations favor investing in lower-yielding preferred stocks over higher-yielding bonds. When tax consequences are considered, the yield on the preferred stock, [1 − 0.34(0.30)](7.0%) = 6.286%, is higher than the yield on the bond, (1 − 0.34)(8.0%) = 5.280%. Also note that corporations are restricted in their use of borrowed funds to purchase other firms' preferred or common stocks. Without such restrictions, firms could engage in *tax arbitrage,* whereby the interest on borrowed funds reduces taxable income on a dollar-for-dollar basis, but taxable income is increased by only $0.30 per dollar of dividend income. Thus, current tax laws reduce the 70 percent dividend exclusion in proportion to the amount of borowed funds used to purchase the stock.

Table 2-3 **Cash Flows to Investors under Bond and Stock Financing**

	Use Bonds (1)	Use Stock (2)
Operating income before interest and taxes	$1,500,000	$1,500,000
Interest	1,500,000	0
Taxable income	$ 0	$1,500,000
Federal-plus-state taxes (40%)	0	600,000
After-tax income	$ 0	$ 900,000
Income to investors	$1,500,000	$ 900,000
Advantage to bonds	$ 600,000	

investors would receive only $0.9 million versus $1.5 million under debt financing.

Of course, it is generally not possible to finance exclusively with debt capital, and the risk of doing so would offset the benefits of the higher expected income. *Still, the fact that interest is a deductible expense has a profound effect on the way businesses are financed — our tax system favors debt financing over equity financing.* This point is discussed in more detail in Chapters 19 and 20.

Corporate Captal Gains. Before 1987, corporate long-term capital gains were taxed at rates lower than ordinary income, just as with individuals. Under current law, however, corporations' capital gains are taxed at the same rates as their operating income. There is a chance, though, that a favorable capital gains tax rate will be reinstated in the future.

Corporate Loss Carry-Back and Carry-Forward. Ordinary corporate operating losses can be carried back **(carry-back)** to each of the preceding 3 years and forward **(carry-forward)** for the next 15 years in the future to offset taxable income in those years. For example, an operating loss in 1991 could be carried back and used to reduce taxable income in 1988, 1989, and 1990, and forward, if necessary, and used in 1992, 1993, and so on, to the year 2006. The loss must be applied first to the earliest year, then to the next earliest year, and so on, until losses have been used up or the 15-year carry-forward limit has been reached.

To illustrate, suppose Apex Corporation had a $2 million *pretax* profit (taxable income) in 1988, 1989, and 1990, and then, in 1991, Apex lost $12 million as shown in Table 2-4. Also, assume that Apex's tax rate is 40 percent. The company would use the carry-back feature to recompute its taxes for 1988, using $2 million of the 1991 operating losses to reduce the 1988 pretax profit to zero. This would permit it to recover the amount of taxes paid in 1988. Therefore, in 1992 Apex would receive a refund of its 1988 taxes because of

tax loss carry-back and carry-forward
Losses that can be carried backward or forward in time to offset taxable income in a given year.

Table 2-4 **Apex Corporation:**
Calculation of Loss Carry-Back and Carry-Forward
for 1988–1990 Using $12 Million 1991 Loss

	1988	1989	1990
Original taxable income	$2,000,000	$2,000,000	$2,000,000
Carry-back credit	− 2,000,000	− 2,000,000	− 2,000,000
Adjusted profit	$ 0	$ 0	$ 0
Taxes previously paid (40%)	800,000	800,000	800,000
Difference = Tax refund	$ 800,000	$ 800,000	$ 800,000

Total refund check received in 1992: $800,000 + $800,000 + $800,000 = $2,400,000.
Amount of loss carry-forward available for use in 1992–2006:

1991 loss	$12,000,000
Carry-back losses used	6,000,000
Carry-forward losses still available	$ 6,000,000

the loss experienced in 1991. Because $10 million of the unrecovered losses would still be available, Apex would repeat this procedure for 1989 and 1990. Thus, in 1992 the company would pay zero taxes for 1991 and also would receive a refund for taxes paid from 1988 through 1990. Apex would still have $6 million of unrecovered losses to carry forward, subject to the 15-year limit, until the entire $12 million loss had been used to offset taxable income. The purpose of permitting this loss treatment is, of course, to avoid penalizing corporations whose incomes fluctuate substantially from year to year.

Improper Accumulation to Avoid Payment of Dividends. Corporations could refrain from paying dividends to permit their stockholders to avoid personal income taxes on dividends. To prevent this, the Tax Code contains an **improper accumulation** provision which states that earnings accumulated by a corporation are subject to penalty rates *if the purpose of the accumulation is to enable stockholders to avoid personal income taxes.* A cumulative total of $250,000 (the balance sheet item "retained earnings") is by law exempted from the improper accumulation tax for most corporations. This is a benefit primarily to small corporations.

The improper accumulation penalty applies only if the retained earnings in excess of $250,000 are *shown to be unnecessary to meet the reasonable needs of the business.* A great many companies do indeed have legitimate reasons for retaining more than $250,000 of earnings. For example, earnings may be retained and used to pay off debt, to finance growth, or to provide the corporation with a cushion against possible cash drains caused by losses. How much a firm should properly accumulate for uncertain contingencies is a matter of judgment. We shall consider this matter again in Chapter 21, which deals with corporate dividend policy.

improper accumulation

Retention of earnings by a corporation for the purpose of enabling stockholders to avoid personal income taxes.

Consolidated Corporate Tax Returns. If a corporation owns 80 percent or more of another corporation's stock, it can aggregate income and file one consolidated tax return; thus, the losses of one company can be used to offset the profits of another. (Similarly, one division's losses can be used to offset another division's profits.) No business ever wants to incur losses (you can go broke losing $1 to save 34¢ in taxes), but tax offsets do make it more feasible for large, multidivisional corporations to undertake risky new ventures or ventures that will suffer losses during a developmental period.

Taxation of Small Business: S Corporations

Subchapter S of the Internal Revenue Code provides that small businesses which meet certain restrictions as spelled out in the code may be set up as corporations and thus receive the benefits of the corporate form of organization — especially limited liability — yet still be taxed as proprietorships or partnerships rather than as corporations. These corporations are called **S corporations.**

> **S corporations**
> A small corporation which under Subchapter S of the Internal Revenue Code elects to be taxed as a proprietorship or a partnership yet retains limited liability and other benefits of the corporate form of organization.

To qualify for S corporation status, a corporation must meet the legal definition of a small business, must be a domestic corporation, must be owned by no more than 35 individuals, and must make a proper S corporation election.[6] Owners of S corporations are taxed as if they were partners in a partnership. This tax treatment is especially beneficial in the early stages of a firm's development, when it is both making heavy investments in fixed assets and incurring start-up costs, which lead to operating losses. If such firms were not corporations, the businesses' losses would be used to offset the owners' other income. *S corporation status allows the corporation to pass on those benefits as if the firm were a partnership, with the shareholders receiving the benefits on a pro rata basis in accordance with their fractional ownership of the firm's equity.*

If the firm is profitable during a year in which S corporation status is elected, the earnings are added to the individual owners' ordinary incomes. Likewise, if an S corporation has an unprofitable year, the losses reduce the owners' ordinary incomes. This feature of Subchapter S tax treatment can be either an advantage or a disadvantage. If the corporation has income in excess of $75,000, Subchapter S (1) allows the firm's income to be taxed at the maximum personal rate of 33 percent versus a corporate rate of 39 (or 34) percent, and it also (2) allows the firm to avoid double taxation when earnings are paid out as dividends. On the other hand, if the owners wish to retain all earnings in the firm to finance continued growth, and if income is less than $75,000, S corporation status may be a disadvantage. On balance, though, the new tax law has led most qualifying corporations to file for S corporation status.

---

[6]The full set of conditions that must be met to qualify for S corporation status is spelled out in the Tax Code. Because these provisions are subject to change by Congress, it is important to consult the current version of the Tax Code.

Many factors other than taxes bear on the question of whether or not a firm should be organized as a corporation. However, the provision for S corporation status makes it possible for most small businesses to enjoy the benefits of a corporation, yet avoid double taxation problems.

Self-Test

Explain what is meant by the statement, "Our tax rates are progressive."

Are tax rates progressive for all income ranges?

Explain the difference between marginal tax rates and average tax rates.

What is "bracket creep," and how has the government avoided it in the late 1980s?

What are capital gains and losses, and how are they differentiated from ordinary income?

How does the federal income tax system tax corporate dividends received by a corporation and those received by an individual? Why is this distinction made?

Briefly explain how tax loss carry-back and carry-forward procedures work.

Briefly explain what an S corporation is and why a small business would want to qualify for S corporation status.

DEPRECIATION

Suppose a firm buys a milling machine for $100,000 and uses it for 5 years, after which it is scrapped. The cost of the goods produced by the machine must include a charge for the machine, and this charge is called *depreciation*. Because depreciation reduces profits as calculated by the accountants, the higher a firm's depreciation charges, the lower its reported net income. However, depreciation is not a cash charge, so higher depreciation does not reduce cash flows. Indeed, higher depreciation *increases* cash flows, because the greater a firm's depreciation, the lower its tax bill.

Companies generally calculate depreciation one way when figuring taxes and another way when reporting income to investors: most use the *straight line* method for stockholder reporting (or "book" purposes), but they use the fastest rate permitted by law for tax purposes. Under the straight line method as used for stockholder reporting, one normally takes the cost of the asset, subtracts its estimated salvage value, and divides the net amount by the asset's useful economic life. For an asset with a 5-year life, which costs $100,000 and has a $12,500 salvage value, the annual straight line depreciation charge is ($100,000 − $12,500)/5 = $17,500.

For tax purposes, Congress changes the permissible tax depreciation methods from time to time. Prior to 1954, the straight line method was required for tax purposes, but in 1954 *accelerated* methods (double declining balance and sum-of-years'-digits) were permitted. Then, in 1981, the old accel-

Table 2-5 **Major Classes and Asset Lives for MACRS under the Tax Reform Act of 1986**

Class	Type of Property
3-year	Computers and other equipment used in research
5-year	Automobiles, tractor units, light-duty trucks, computers, and certain special manufacturing tools
7-year	Most industrial equipment, office furniture, and fixtures
10-year	Certain longer-lived types of equipment
27.5-year	Residential rental real property such as apartment buildings
31.5-year	All nonresidential real property, including commercial and industrial buildings

erated methods were replaced by a simpler procedure known as the Accelerated Cost Recovery System (ACRS). The ACRS system was changed again in 1986 as a part of the Tax Reform Act, and it is now known as the **Modified Accelerated Cost Recovery System (MACRS).**

Tax Depreciation Life

For tax purposes, the cost of an asset is expensed over its depreciable life. Historically, an asset's depreciable life was determined by its estimated useful economic life; it was intended that an asset would be fully depreciated at approximately the same time that it reached the end of its useful economic life. However, MACRS totally abandons that practice and sets simple guidelines which create several classes of assets, each with a more or less arbitrarily prescribed life called a *recovery period* or *class life.* The MACRS class life bears only a rough relationship to the expected useful economic life.

A major effect of the MACRS system has been to shorten the depreciable lives of assets, thus giving businesses larger tax deductions and thereby increasing cash flows available for reinvestment. Table 2-5 describes the types of property that fit into the different class life groups, and Table 2-6 sets forth the MACRS recovery allowances (depreciation rates) for the various classes of investment property.

Consider Table 2-5 first. The first column gives the MACRS class life, while the second column describes the types of assets which fall into each category. Property in the 27.5- and 31.5-year categories (real estate) must be depreciated by the straight line method, but 3-, 5-, 7-, and 10-year property (personal property) can be depreciated either by the accelerated method which uses the rates shown in Table 2-6 or by an alternate straight line method.[7]

Modified Accelerated Cost Recovery System (MACRS)
A depreciation system that allows businesses to write off the cost of an asset over a period much shorter than its operating life.

---

[7]As a benefit to very small companies, the Tax Code also permits companies to *expense,* which is equivalent to depreciating over one year, up to $10,000 of equipment. Thus, if a small company bought one asset worth up to $10,000, it could write the asset off in the year it was acquired. This is called "Section 179 expensing." We shall disregard this provision throughout the book.

Table 2-6 **Recovery Allowance Percentages for Personal Property**

Ownership Year	Class of Investment			
	3-Year	**5-Year**	**7-Year**	**10-Year**
1	33%	20%	14%	10%
2	45	32	25	18
3	15	19	17	14
4	7	12	13	12
5		11	9	9
6		6	9	7
7			9	7
8			4	7
9				7
10				6
11				3
	100%	100%	100%	100%

Notes:

a. We developed these recovery allowance percentages based on the 200 percent declining balance method prescribed by MACRS, with a switch to straight line depreciation at some point in the asset's life. For example, consider the 5-year recovery allowance percentages. The straight line percentage would be 20 percent per year, so the 200 percent declining balance multiplier is 2.0(20%) = 40% = 0.4. However, because the half-year convention applies, the MACRS percentage for Year 1 is 20 percent. For Year 2, there is 80 percent of the depreciable basis remaining to be depreciated, so the recovery allowance percentage is 0.4(80%) = 32%. In Year 3, 20% + 32% = 52% of the depreciation has been taken, leaving 48%, so the percentage is 0.4(48%) ≈ 19%. In Year 4, the percentage is 0.4(29%) ≈ 12%. After 4 years, straight line depreciation exceeds the declining balance depreciation, so a switch is made to straight line (this is permitted under the law). However, the half-year convention must also be applied at the end of the class life, hence the remaining 17 percent of depreciation must be taken (amortized) over 1.5 years. Thus, the percentage in Year 5 is 17%/1.5 ≈ 11%, and in Year 6, 17% − 11% = 6%. Although the tax tables carry the allowance percentages out to two decimal places, we have rounded to the nearest whole number for ease of illustration.

b. Residential rental property (apartments) is depreciated over a 27.5-year life, whereas commercial and industrial structures are depreciated over 31.5 years. In both cases, straight line depreciation must be used. The depreciation allowance for the first year is based, pro rata, on the month the asset was placed in service, with the remainder of the first year's depreciation being taken in the 28th or 32nd year.

Higher depreciation expenses result in lower taxes and hence higher cash flows. Therefore, when a firm has the option of using straight line or the MACRS rates shown in Table 2-6, it should elect to use the MACRS rates. The yearly recovery allowance, or depreciation expense, is determined by multiplying each asset's *depreciable basis* by the applicable recovery percentage shown in Table 2-6. Calculations are discussed in the following sections.

half-year convention
A feature of MACRS in which assets are assumed to be put into service at midyear and thus are allowed a half-year's depreciation regardless of when they actually go into service.

Half-Year Convention. Under MACRS, the assumption is generally made that property is placed in service in the middle of the first year. Thus, for 3-year class life property, the recovery period begins in the middle of the year the asset is placed in service and ends 3 years later. The effect of the **half-year convention** is to extend the recovery period out one more year, so 3-year class life property is depreciated over 4 calendar years, 5-year property is depreciated over 6 calendar years, and so on. This convention is incorporated into Table 2-6's recovery allowance percentages.[8]

Depreciable Basis. The **depreciable basis** is a critical element of MACRS, because each year's allowance (depreciation expense) depends jointly on the asset's depreciable basis and its MACRS class life. The depreciable basis under MACRS is equal to the purchase price of the asset plus any shipping and installation costs. The basis is *not* adjusted for *salvage value* (which is the estimated market value of the asset at the end of its useful life) regardless of whether MACRS or the straight line method is used.

Investment Tax Credit. An **investment tax credit (ITC)** provides for a direct reduction of taxes, and its purpose is to stimulate business investment. ITCs were first introduced during the Kennedy administration in 1961, and they have subsequently been put in and taken out of the tax system, depending on how Congress feels about the need to stimulate business investment versus the need for federal revenues. Immediately prior to the 1986 Tax Reform Act, ITCs applied to depreciable personal property with a life of 3 or more years, and the credit amounted to 6 percent for short-lived assets and 10 percent for longer-lived assets. The credit was determined by multiplying the cost of the asset by the applicable percentage. However, ITCs were eliminated by the 1986 tax revision. Nevertheless, you should be aware of what ITCs are, because they may be reinstated at some future date if Congress deems that they are needed to stimulate investment.

Sale of a Depreciable Asset. If a depreciable asset is sold, the sale price (actual salvage value) minus the then-existing undepreciated book value is added to operating income and taxed at the firm's marginal tax rate. For example, suppose a firm buys a 5-year class life asset for $100,000 and sells it at the end of the fourth year for $25,000. The asset's book value is equal to $100,000(0.11 + 0.06) = $100,000(0.17) = $17,000. Therefore, a profit of $25,000 − $17,000 = $8,000 is added to the firm's operating income and is taxed. Since the asset is an operating asset, not a capital asset, the profit is operating income rather than a capital gain.

MACRS Illustration. Assume that Apex Corporation buys a $150,000 computer, which falls into the MACRS 5-year class life, and places it into service on March 15, 1991. Apex must pay an additional $30,000 for delivery and in-

depreciable basis
The portion of an asset's value which can be depreciated for tax purposes. The depreciable basis under MACRS is equal to the cost of the asset, including shipping and installation charges.

investment tax credit (ITC)
A specified percentage of the cost of new assets that businesses are *sometimes* allowed by law to deduct as a credit against their income taxes. ITCs were eliminated by the 1986 Tax Reform Act.

[8]The half-year convention also applies if the straight line alternative is used, with half of one year's depreciation taken in the first year, a full year's depreciation taken in each of the remaining years of the asset's class life, and the remaining half-year's depreciation taken in the year following the end of the class life. You should recognize that virtually all companies have computerized depreciation systems. Each asset's depreciation pattern is programmed into the system at the time of its acquisition, and the computer aggregates the depreciation allowances for all assets when the accountants close the books and prepare the financial statements and tax returns.

stallation. Salvage value is not considered, so the computer's depreciable basis is $180,000. (Delivery and installation charges are included in the depreciable basis rather than expensed in the year incurred.) Each year's recovery allowance (tax depreciation expense) is determined by multiplying the depreciable basis by the applicable recovery allowance percentage. Thus, the depreciation expense for 1991 is 0.20($180,000) = $36,000, and for 1992 it is 0.32($180,000) = $57,600. Similarly, the depreciation expense is $34,200 for 1993, $21,600 for 1994, $19,800 for 1995, and $10,800 for 1996. The total depreciation expense over the 6-year recovery period is $180,000, which is equal to the depreciable basis of the machine.

Self-Test

What are the key differences between the straight line depreciation method and normal depreciation under MACRS?

What is the difference between the concept of useful economic life and the MACRS recovery period, or class life?

How do you determine the depreciable basis of an asset, and how does expected salvage value affect the depreciable basis of an asset?

How does one calculate an asset's MACRS depreciation expense?

What is the purpose of the ITC, and is it available under current tax laws?

How would you calculate the tax involved if a partially depreciated asset were sold?

THE ROLE OF FINANCIAL MARKETS

Our economy consists of many different economic units, ranging from individuals, to businesses, to the various local and state governments, to the federal government.[9] If a unit's income exceeds its spending, then the unit is a *net saver;* if its spending exceeds its income, the unit is a *borrower.* (Technically, businesses which are deficit spending units can raise funds either by borrowing or by issuing new common stock.)

In primitive societies, where financial markets do not exist, each economic unit must be self-supporting. In modern economies such as ours, *financial markets* enable us to convert savings into productive investments. For example, suppose Houston Power and Light Company forecasts an increased demand for power in their Texas Gulf Coast service area and decides to build a

---

[9]As discussed previously, the most important economic units within the domestic economy are business firms, individuals (often referred to as households), and governments (local, state, and national). Although our comments are directly concerned with business firms, the statements are valid for the other economic units as well.

new power plant. Because it will almost certainly not have the $2.5 billion necessary to pay for the plant, it will have to raise this capital in the market. Or suppose Jim Strachan, the proprietor of a Cleveland hardware store, decides to expand into appliances. Where will he get the money to buy the initial inventory of TV sets, washers, and refrigerators? Similarly, if the Martingales want to buy a home that costs $110,000, but they only have $25,000 in savings, how can they raise the additional $85,000? Also, if the City of Baltimore wants to borrow $30 million for civic improvements, and the federal government needs $125 billion to cover its projected 1993 deficit, they each need sources for raising capital.

On the other hand, some individuals and firms have incomes that exceed their current expenditures, so they have funds available to invest. For example, Susan Ashley has an income of $56,000, but her expenses are only $42,000, while Ford Motor Company has accumulated over $9 billion of excess cash which it could make available for investment.

Individuals and organizations wanting to raise capital are brought together with those having surplus funds in the *financial markets.* Note that "markets" is plural — there are a great many different financial markets, each one consisting of many institutions, in a developed economy such as ours. Within these markets, capital is allocated among firms by interest rates: Firms with the most profitable investment opportunities are willing and able to pay the most for capital, so they tend to attract it from inefficient firms or from those whose products are not in demand. Thus, in the U.S. economy most capital is allocated through the price system, with **interest rates** representing the price for borrowed capital.

Figure 2-1 shows how supply and demand interact to determine interest rates in two different markets for capital, Market A, where safe, low-risk securities are traded, and Market B, where riskier firms borrow in the "junk bond market." Naturally, savers will save more if the interest rate is higher, but borrowers will borrow more at lower interest rates, so the supply curve is upward sloping and the demand curve is downward sloping. The intersection of the supply and demand curves determines the going, or equilibrium, interest rates in each market, k_A and k_B.

The equilibrium rates in the different markets change over time, depending on conditions. For example, if the economy slips into a recession, the demand curves tend to shift to the left and interest rates fall, while the reverse holds if the economy strengthens. Similarly, if the Federal Reserve reduces the availability of credit, the supply curve shifts to the left, and interest rates rise. Note, too, that the financial markets are interrelated — savers can shift funds between markets, so if rates rise in Market A because of an increase in demand, some funds will probably be shifted from B to A, which will lower rates in Market A and raise them in B.

As we noted previously, each market deals with a somewhat different type of security, serves a different set of customers, or operates in a different part

interest rate
The price paid to borrow money.

Figure 2-1 **Interest Rates as a Function of
Supply and Demand for Funds**

The graphs below demonstrate how capital is allocated in two financial markets,
Market A, where low-risk securities are traded, and B, where riskier securities are
traded. The intersection of the supply and demand curves in each market determines
the equilibrium interest rate, where a balance between supply and demand is
reached. Because of its lower risk, Market A's interest rate is lower than that of Market
B. Market A's graph also demonstrates that interest rates will increase, and the supply
of capital will decrease, when the demand curve decreases from D_1 to D_2, as it would
during a recession.

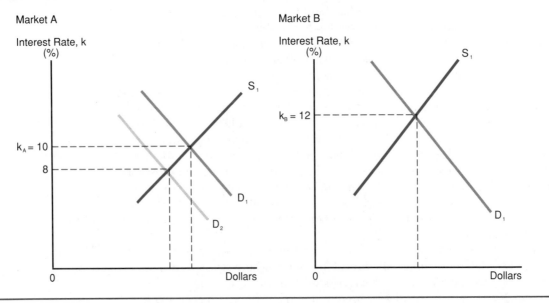

of the country. The following paragraphs discuss some of the major types of
markets:

Financial asset markets and *physical asset markets* must be distinguished.
Financial asset markets are those in which stocks, bonds, notes, mortgages, and
other *claims on assets* are traded. On the other hand, physical asset markets
are those in which real (or tangible) assets are traded. Examples of real assets
that are traded in physical asset markets are machinery, autos, computers, real
estate, or farm products such as beef and wheat.

Spot markets and *futures markets* refer to whether the assets are being
purchased or sold for "on the spot" delivery (actually, spot delivery means
within the next few days) or for delivery at some future date, such as six
months in the future. Items traded in spot markets include oil, precious metals,
textiles, and grain. The futures markets (which include the options markets)
are growing in importance. Items traded in futures markets include agricultural commodities, livestock, precious metals, and government securities. How-

ever, a detailed discussion of these specialized markets is beyond the scope of this text.

Money markets and *capital markets* are both financial markets, but they differ in the type and maturity of the securities involved. **Money markets** are for short-term (less than one year) debt securities. Major money market instruments include U.S. Treasury bills and other short-term U.S government obligations, certificates of deposit (CDs), and commercial paper, which is a financially strong company's unsecured short-term obligation. The New York money market is the world's largest, and it is dominated by the major U.S., Japanese, and European banks. London, Tokyo, and Paris are other major money market centers.

Capital markets are markets for long-term debt and corporate stocks. Major capital market instruments include U.S. Treasury bonds and other long-term U.S. government obligations, state and local government bonds, corporate bonds, preferred stocks, and common stocks. The New York Stock Exchange, which handles both the stocks and the bonds of the largest corporations, is a prime example of a capital market. The stocks and bonds of smaller corporations are handled in other segments of the capital market.

Mortgage markets deal with loans on residential, commercial, and industrial real estate, and on farmland, while *consumer credit markets* involve loans on automobiles and appliances, as well as loans for education, vacations, and so on. World, national, regional, and local markets also exist. Depending on an organization's size and scope of operations, it may be able to borrow all around the world, or it may be confined to strictly local, even neighborhood, markets.

Primary markets are markets in which newly issued securities are bought and sold for the first time. If AT&T were to sell a *new issue* of common stock to raise capital, this would be a primary market transaction. It is only through the primary markets, not the secondary markets, that firms raise funds for current operations or future projects. **Secondary markets** are those in which existing, outstanding securities are traded among investors. Thus, if Kim Cook decided to sell 100 shares of General Motors, and those shares were purchased by Matt Burak, General Motors Corporation would receive no funds from the transaction. Even though GM receives no money when its stock is traded in the secondary market, this market insures liquidity for the firm's existing stock, and an active market is highly desirable if more stock is to be issued in the primary market. The New York Stock Exchange is a secondary market, since it deals in outstanding as opposed to newly issued stocks and bonds. Secondary markets also exist for mortgages and other financial assets.

Although savings must equal investment, financial markets allow the savings and investment processes to be separated. Thus, savers do not necessarily have to have their own productive investment opportunities. Because savings and investment are rarely equal for individual economic entities, a healthy economy is dependent on efficient transfers of funds from savers to firms and individuals who need capital; that is, the economy depends on *efficient finan-*

money markets
The financial markets in which funds are borrowed or loaned for short periods (less than one year).

capital markets
The financial markets for stocks and for long-term debt (one year or longer).

primary markets
The markets in which newly issued securities are bought and sold for the first time.

secondary markets
The markets in which financial assets are traded among investors after they have been issued by corporations.

Table 2-7 **Summary of Major Market Instruments,
Market Participants, and Major Characteristics**

Instrument (1)	Market (2)	Major Participants (3)	Major Characteristics		
			Riskiness (4)	Maturity (5)	Interest rate on 3/8/90[a] (6)
U.S. Treasury bills	Money	Sold by U.S Treasury to finance federal expenditures to institutional investors	Default-free	91 days to 1 year	7.9%
Banker's acceptances	Money	Firm's promise to pay, guaranteed by bank; arises from trade	Low degree of risk if guaranteed by a strong bank	Up to 180 days	8.0
Commercial paper	Money	Issued by financially secure firms to institutional investors	Low default risk	Up to 270 days	8.2
Negotiable certificates of deposit (CDs)	Money	Issued by major money-center commercial banks to institutional investors	Riskier than Treasury bills	Up to 1 year	7.8
Money market mutual funds	Money	Includes Treasury bills, CDs, and commercial paper; held by individuals and businesses	Low degree of risk	Instant liquidity	7.6
Eurodollar market time deposits	Money	Issued by banks outside U.S.	Default risk is a function of issuing bank	Up to 1 year	8.4
U.S. Treasury notes and bonds	Capital	Issued by U.S. government to institutional investors	No default risk, but price can decline if interest rates rise	3 to 30 years	8.6
Consumer credit loans	Consumer credit	Issued by banks/ credit unions/finance companies to individuals	Risk is variable	Variable	Variable

cial markets. Without efficient transfers, the economy simply could not function. Houston Power and Light could not raise capital, so the citizens in the Texas gulf coast area would not have enough electricity; the Martingale family would not have adequate housing; Susan Ashley would have no place to invest her savings; and so on. Obviously, the level of employment and productivity, and hence our standard of living, would be much lower. It is therefore absolutely essential that financial markets function efficiently — not only quickly, but also at a low cost.[10]

[10]When organizations like the United Nations design plans to aid developing nations, just as much attention must be paid to the establishment of cost-efficient financial markets as to electrical power, transportation, communications, and other infrastructure systems. Economic efficiency is simply impossible without a good system for allocating capital within the economy.

Table 2-7 **Summary of Major Market Instruments,**
Market Participants, and Major Characteristics (*continued*)

Instrument (1)	Market (2)	Major Participants (3)	Major Characteristics		
			Riskiness (4)	Maturity (5)	Interest rate on 3/8/90[a] (6)
Mortgages	Mortgage	Issued by commercial banks and S&Ls to individuals and businesses	Risk is variable	Up to 30 years	9.7%
State and local government bonds	Capital	Issued by state and local governments to individuals and institutional investors	Riskier than U.S. government securities; exempt from most taxes	Up to 30 years	7.4
Corporate bonds	Capital	Issued by corporations to individuals and institutional investors	Riskier than U.S. government securities, but less risky than preferred and common stocks; varying degree of risk within bonds depending on strength of issuer	Up to 40 years	9.4
Leases	Capital	Similar to debt in that firms can lease assets rather than borrow and then buy the assets	Risk similar to corporate bonds	Generally 3 to 20 years	Similar to bond yields
Preferred stocks	Capital	Issued by corporations to individuals and institutional investors	Riskier than corporate bonds, but less risky than common stock	Unlimited	Variable
Common stocks	Capital	Issued by corporations to individuals and institutional investors	Risky	Unlimited	Variable

[a]Interest rates are for longest maturity securities of the type, and for the strongest securities of a given type. Thus, the 9.4% interest rate shown for corporate bonds reflects the rate on 30 year, Aaa bonds. Lower-rated bonds had higher interest rates. Also, common and preferred stock provide a "return" in the form of dividends and capital gains rather than interest.

Table 2-7 gives a listing of the most important instruments traded in the various financial markets. The instruments are arranged from top to bottom in ascending order of typical length of maturity. As we go through the book, we will look in much more detail at many of these instruments. We will see that there are actually many varieties of corporate bonds, ranging from "plain vanilla flavored" bonds, to bonds that are convertible into common stocks, and to bonds whose interest payments vary depending on the rate of inflation. Still, the table gives an idea of the characteristics and costs of the instruments traded in the major financial markets.

Self-Test

Who are the principal suppliers and demanders of capital?

Define the equilibrium interest rate in a market.

Distinguish between physical asset markets and financial asset markets, between spot and futures markets, between money and capital markets, and between primary and secondary markets.

THE ROLE OF FINANCIAL INTERMEDIARIES

financial intermediaries

Specialized financial firms that facilitate the transfer of funds from savers to demanders of capital.

The transfer of funds from savers to those who need funds is facilitated by **financial intermediaries.** Financial intermediaries include commercial banks, savings and loan associations, credit unions, pension funds, life insurance companies, and mutual funds. These intermediaries aid the capital allocation process in several ways.

By way of explanation, let us consider an economy devoid of financial intermediaries. Further, let's assume that a businesswoman, Ms. Rossi, has discovered a cure for the common cold but requires $400,000 to obtain the proper productive assets for manufacture and distribution of the product. She must find someone with savings to invest in her project.[11]

Ms. Rossi has several problems if no financial intermediaries exist. First, she must find someone with savings. Through family and friends, she finds a saver, Mr. Davis. Ms. Rossi's problems are not over, however. In persuading Mr. Davis to invest, Ms. Rossi will encounter several obstacles. First, Mr. Davis may not have enough savings to cover the entire $400,000 investment; therefore, Ms. Rossi must search for additional investors. Second, Mr. Davis realizes that by putting all of his money into a single project, he is facing more risk than he would be if he diversified by investing in several projects.[12] With this higher risk Mr. Davis may require a greater return than Ms. Rossi wishes to pay. Third, Mr. Davis may need to withdraw his funds for retirement or to meet a financial emergency before the project is completed, causing refinancing problems for Ms. Rossi. Any or all of these problems — difficulty in locating savers, savers' need to diversify, and savers' need for liquidity — may end the investment project before it begins. We see, then, that if productive investments cannot be financed, economic growth cannot be maintained.

In a developed economy such as that of the United States, many of the problems encountered by entrepreneurs like Ms. Rossi can be alleviated by a financial intermediary. Thus, transfers of capital between savers and those

---

[11]For the purposes of our example, the investment may be in the form of either an equity share or a loan.

[12]We discuss diversification and how it reduces risk in Chapter 12.

Figure 2-2 **Diagram of the Capital Formation Process**

There are three traditional ways of transferring capital between savers and those who need funds. Direct transfers without intermediaries are possible, but they are often inefficient. Investment banking houses serve as middlemen in indirect transfers, but they do not create their own financial claims. Financial intermediaries actually create new financial products such as checking and savings accounts, mutual fund shares, and insurance policies. The intermediary uses savers' funds to purchase borrowers' financial claims such as stock, bonds, and mortgages. The financial products offered by intermediaries help meet savers' needs for safety and liquidity.

1. Direct Transfers

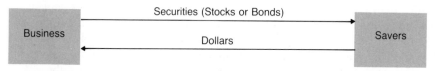

2. Indirect Transfers through Investment Bankers

3. Indirect Transfers through a Financial Intermediary

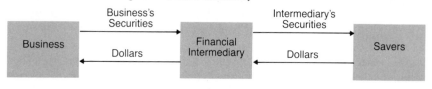

who need funds can take place in three different ways, as diagrammed in Figure 2-2:

1. *Direct transfers* of money and securities, as shown in the top section, occur when a business sells its stocks or bonds directly to savers, without going through any type of intermediary. Dollars flow from savers to the business, which then gives securities to the savers.

2. As the middle section illustrates, transfers may also go through an *investment banking house,* such as Merrill Lynch, which serves as a middleman and facilitates the issuance of securities. The company sells its stocks or bonds to the investment bank, which in turn sells these same securities to the ultimate savers. The businesses' securities and the savers' money merely "pass through" the investment banking house. Even so, the investment bank is taking a risk, since it is purchasing securities that it may not be able to resell to savers for as much or more than it paid. The company, on the other hand, is assured of getting the funds it needs whether investors buy its securities from the investment banker or not. Since the corporation receives money from the sale of the securities, this is a primary market transaction. Although they may serve as financial intermediaries in many respects, technically, investment bankers are not intermediaries because they do not create their own financial claims.

3. The bottom section of Figure 2-2 shows that transfers may occur through a *financial intermediary,* such as a bank or mutual fund, which obtains funds from savers and then issues its own securities in exchange. For example, a saver might give dollars to a bank, receiving from it a certificate of deposit, and then the bank might lend the money to a small business in the form of a mortgage loan. Thus, intermediaries literally create new forms of capital — in this case, a certificate of deposit, which is more liquid than a mortgage. This transformation of one financial claim into another that better meets the risk and return needs of the saver increases general market efficiency.

For simplicity, our example assumed that the entity which needs capital is a business, and specifically a corporation, although it is easy to visualize the demander of capital as a potential home purchaser, a government unit, and so on.

investment banking house

A financial institution that underwrites and distributes new investment securities and helps businesses obtain financing.

Direct transfers between businesses and savers are possible and do occur on occasion, but generally it is more efficient for a business to obtain the services of an **investment banking house.** Merrill Lynch and Salomon Brothers are examples of financial service corporations which offer investment banking services. Such organizations (1) help corporations design securities with the features that will be most attractive to investors, (2) buy these securities from the issuing corporation, and then (3) resell them to savers in the primary markets. Thus, the investment bankers are middlemen in the process of transferring capital from savers to businesses.

The financial intermediaries shown in the third section of Figure 2-2 do more than simply transfer money and securities between firms and savers — they literally create new financial products. For example, Mr. Davis may not have the capital or the inclination to finance Ms. Rossi's loan for assets needed to produce her common cold cure. A direct loan of this type would be quite risky, since Ms. Rossi could default and since, once the loan was made, Mr. Davis's savings could not be withdrawn and would not be repaid for many years. However, when Mr. Davis deposits his savings in a commercial bank, he is making his savings available to the bank, which can then make the loan to Ms. Rossi. So, Mr. Davis is indirectly lending the money to Ms. Rossi. By opening a savings account instead of loaning the money to Ms. Rossi directly, Mr. Davis enjoys several advantages: he does not have to evaluate Ms. Rossi's cure; the money is available on demand; and it is insured, within limits, by a government agency. Thus, intermediaries repackage the original financial claims of borrowers into financial claims on themselves. Financial obligations of intermediaries are also called "indirect securities," because they represent a rearrangement of the borrower's original promise to pay into one that is more compatible with the saver's needs for safety, return, liquidity, and maturity. These indirect claims include checking accounts, mutual fund shares, money market accounts, passbook savings, and life insurance policies.

In addition, the cost of the intermediary's funds to the borrower will be lower than if a direct loan from the original saver could be negotiated. Because intermediaries are generally large institutions, they gain economies of scale in analyzing the creditworthiness of potential borrowers, in processing and collecting loans, and in pooling risks, thus helping individual savers avoid "putting all their financial eggs into one basket." These factors allow intermediaries to lend at lower rates than can individual savers. Further, intermediaries are better able to attract funds, since a system of specialized intermediaries can enable savings to do more than just draw interest. Thus, people can put money into banks and get both interest and a convenient way of making payments (checking), put money in life insurance policies and receive both interest and financial protection in the event of early death, and so on.

In the United States and other developed nations, a large set of specialized, highly efficient financial intermediaries has evolved. The situation is changing rapidly, however, and different types of institutions are performing services that were formerly reserved for others, causing institutional distinctions to become blurred. Still, there is a degree of institutional identity, and the major types of intermediaries are discussed below:

Commercial Banks. These are the traditional financial "department stores," serving a wide variety of savers and those with needs for funds. Commercial banks are continuing to expand into an ever-widening range of services, including stock brokerage services and insurance. Historically, the commercial bank has been the major financial institution that handled checking accounts and through which the Federal Reserve System expanded or contracted the money supply. Today, however, some of the other institutions discussed here also provide checking services and significantly influence the effective money supply. Commercial banks are discussed in more detail in Chapter 3.

Savings and Loan Associations (S&Ls). S&Ls traditionally served individual savers and residential and commercial mortgage borrowers, taking the funds of many small savers, then lending the money to home buyers and other types of borrowers. The savers are provided a degree of liquidity that would be absent if they bought the mortgages or other securities directly. Therefore, one major economic function of the S&Ls is to "create liquidity" which would otherwise be lacking. Also, the S&Ls have more expertise in analyzing credit, setting up loans, and making collections than individual savers could possibly have; hence they reduce the cost and increase the availability of real estate loans. Finally, the S&Ls hold large, diversified portfolios of loans and other assets and thus spread risks in a manner that would be impossible if small savers were making mortgage loans directly. Because of these factors, savers benefit by being able to invest their savings in more liquid, better managed, and less risky accounts, whereas borrowers benefit by being able to obtain more capital, and at lower costs, than would otherwise be possible. The savings and loan industry has been going through some tough times lately. We merely present an overview of the industry here, and we discuss S&Ls in more detail in Chapter 3.

Mutual Savings Banks. Operating generally in the northeastern states, these institutions accept savings primarily from individuals, and lend mainly on a long-term basis to home buyers and consumers. Mutual savings banks are very similar to S&Ls.

Credit Unions. These are cooperative associations whose members have a common bond, such as being employees of the same firm. Members' savings are loaned only to other members, generally for automobile purchases, home improvements, and the like. Credit union loans are often the least expensive source of funds available to an individual borrower.

Pension Funds. These are retirement plans funded by corporations or government agencies for their workers and administered primarily by the trust departments of commercial banks or by life insurance companies. Pension funds invest primarily in bonds, stocks, mortgages, and real estate.

Life Insurance Companies. These institutions take savings in the form of annual premiums, then invest these funds received in stocks, bonds, real estate, and mortgages, and finally make payments to the beneficiaries of the insured parties. In recent years, life insurance companies have also offered a variety of tax-deferred savings plans designed to provide benefits to the participants when they retire.

mutual fund
A corporation that invests the pooled funds of savers, thus obtaining economies of scale in investing and reducing risk by diversification.

Mutual Funds. These are corporations which accept dollars from savers and then use those dollars to buy stocks, long-term bonds, or short-term debt instruments issued by businesses or government units. These organizations pool funds and thus reduce risks by diversification. They also gain economies of scale, which lower the costs of analyzing securities, managing portfolios, and buying and selling securities. Different **mutual funds** are designed to meet the objectives of different types of savers. Hence, there are bond funds for those who desire a fixed return; stock funds for savers who are willing to accept substantial risks in the hope of very high returns; and still other funds that are used as interest-bearing checking accounts (the **money market funds**). There are literally hundreds of different mutual funds with dozens of different goals and purposes.

> **money market fund**
> A mutual fund that invests in short-term, low-risk debt securities and allows investors to write checks against their accounts.

Commercial Finance Companies. Commercial finance companies are lending institutions that make both short- and long-term *secured* loans to businesses, but they are not permitted to hold deposits. Because borrowers turn to commercial finance companies after they have exhausted their short-term borrowing capacity from commercial banks, the interest rates on these loans tend to be higher than those on commercial bank loans. Typically, these institutions are involved in financing equipment purchases with installment loans having less than 10-year maturities.

> **commercial finance companies**
> Lending institutions that make both short- and long-term secured loans to businesses, generally at higher rates than commercial banks.

Historically, financial institutions have been heavily regulated, with the primary purpose of this regulation being to insure the safety of the institutions for the protection of their depositors. However, these regulations — which have taken the form of prohibitions on nationwide branch banking, restrictions on the types of assets the institutions can buy, ceilings on the interest rates they can pay, and limitations on the types of services they can provide — have tended to impede the free flow of capital from surplus to deficit areas, and thus have hurt the efficiency of our capital markets. Recognizing this fact, Congress has authorized some major changes, and more will be forthcoming.

The end result of the ongoing regulatory changes is a blurring of the distinctions among the different types of institutions. Indeed, the trend in the United States today is toward huge **financial service corporations,** which own banks, S&Ls, investment banking houses, insurance companies, pension plan operations, and mutual funds, and which have branches across the country and even around the world. Sears, Roebuck is, interestingly, one of the largest (if not *the* largest) financial service corporations. It owns Allstate Insurance, Dean Witter (a leading brokerage and investment banking firm), Coldwell Banker (a leading real estate brokerage firm), a huge credit card business, and a host of other related businesses. Other financial service corporations, most of which started in one area and have now diversified to cover the full financial spectrum, include Transamerica, Merrill Lynch, American Express, Citicorp, and Prudential.

> **financial service corporations**
> Institutions which offer a wide range of financial services, including investment banking, brokerage operations, insurance, and commercial banking.

Self-Test

Identify the three different ways capital is transferred between savers and borrowers.

What is the difference between a commercial bank and an investment bank?

Distinguish between investment banking houses and financial intermediaries.

List the major classes of intermediaries, and briefly describe each one's function.

INDUSTRY PRACTICE

Is It the End of an Era for Junk Bonds?

The financial marketplace of the 1990s will probably be a different world from the frenetic arena of the 1980s. Debt was the rage in the 1980s, and one firm more than any other came to symbolize the highly leveraged deal — Drexel Burnham Lambert and its "junk bond king," Michael Milken. When they self-destructed at the beginning of 1990, the event symbolized the end of an era.

Milken and Drexel created a $300 billion market by popularizing the high-risk, high-yield bonds of new companies and of corporate raiders. In just a few years, Drexel grew to be one of the top five investment bankers, earning $522 million in 1986 and becoming Wall Street's most profitable firm. Suddenly investment banking was "in," and the art of the deal became a prized skill. Drexel's activities restructured corporate America, making a torrent of takeovers possible, but also leading some companies to assume too much debt in an effort to avoid being taken over.

Milken, the "ultimate charismatic salesman," ran into trouble in 1988 when one of Drexel's bankers, Dennis Levine, pleaded guilty to insider trading. The resulting investigation led to Milken's forced departure and to his indictment for securities fraud. Drexel's CEO, Frederick H. Joseph, thought he had saved the rest of his 5,300 employees by sacrificing Milken. But, when Milken left, the company's managers found that its junk bond market was not successful without him. It was he who had changed investors' views of these bonds and persuaded insurance companies, pension funds, and thrifts (such as savings and loan associations) that the

Sources: *Business Week,* February 26, 1990, "After Drexel"; *Newsweek,* February 26, 1990, "The Downfall of Drexel"; *The Gainseville Sun,* February 17, 1990, "Drexel fires thousands in liquidation."

higher interest rates more than offset the higher risks of default. Milken made many raiders and investors rich, and he created loyalty both to himself and to Drexel by being there when needed. New companies that could not get funding elsewhere came to Milken. So did such savvy deal makers as T. Boone Pickens and Ronald O. Perleman when they mounted hostile takeover bids for such well-known companies as Gulf Oil, Revlon, and Beatrice. Implied in Milken's junk bond empire was the guarantee that he — and Drexel — would always be there to support the market.

After Milken left, Drexel was able to function — for a while. It comanaged the largest junk bond issue ever — $4 billion for the leveraged buyout of RJR Nabisco, Inc. But with competition heating up, the firm evidently lowered its standards for deals. The junk bond market began falling apart, prices dropped, and, to make matters worse, the savings and loan bailout barred thrifts from continuing to hold junk bonds.

Drexel probably made a fatal mistake when it abandoned one of its clients, Integrated Resources, Inc. Integrated, which formerly sold real estate tax shelters, had responded to changing conditions by diversifying, using funds raised with junk bonds. Its efforts failed, though, and Drexel was unable to sell $40 million of Integrated's commercial paper, or short-term IOUs. Although investors expected Drexel to support Integrated's obligation, perhaps by buying up its securities, Drexel did nothing while Integrated defaulted on $1 billion worth of debt.

Drexel's own commercial paper then became unsellable after Standard & Poor's lowered its credit rating, and Drexel began a frantic, but unsuccessful, search for a partner to inject capital. One last hope for rescue vanished on February 12, 1990, when a group of lenders, led by Citibank, turned down Drexel's plea for short-term credit because the collateral offered was junk bonds.

The next day, Drexel stopped all trading activities, and its CEO told employees that the firm had to file for Chapter 11 bankruptcy and to begin liquidating its businesses. As the Associated Press told it, just four days later, on February 16, "Drexel Burnham Lambert Inc. fired thousands of workers . . . and doled out slim severance packages as the Wall Street wonder of the 1980s headed into oblivion. The bulk of Drexel's 5,300 employees were turned loose into a slumping securities industry that already has witnessed tens of thousands of layoffs since the 1987 stock market crash."

Does all this mean, however, that junk bonds will vanish from the financial marketplace? The consensus is that they won't. A former chief economist at the Securities and Exchange Commission says the junk bond market will stabilize eventually. The vice president for investments at a major insurance company says, "We're not sitting here panicking. We think it's worthwhile to keep our hand in the pot." A major investment bank's CEO believes that now that Drexel and its problems are out of the way, the junk bond business will settle down.

It is also expected, however, that high-yield debt will lose its glamour, that credit-rating firms will be more watchful, and that the government will be tougher on Wall Street. Many companies, now heavy with debt, will probably recapitalize with more equity, and others may default on their junk bonds, forcing their bondholders to accept equity. A return to more "sober reality" in finance is widely predicted.

Meanwhile, Drexel assets are being distributed to buyers. Most of its government bond and stock holdings have been sold, as has its brokerage business with 28,000 accounts. Its stock trading and research group may be bought by a foreign bank, and Salomon Brothers bought its junk bond data base.

Reviewing the rise and fall of Drexel and Milken, analysts have reached mixed conclusions. The magnifying effect of leverage on earnings did contribute to U.S. economic growth. Some of the raids financed by Drexel shook up "musty" corporate establishments and forced executives to restructure and eliminate excesses. The company nurtured entrepreneurs like cable giant Ted Turner and William McGowan of MCI. However, it also left many weakened companies struggling with excessive debt. Milken and Drexel's originally good idea somehow went wrong in a drive for more, quicker profits.

In the 1990s, stock and traditional commercial bank financing are expected to play a bigger role in financing growth, but junk bonds will retain a place in corporate finance as a financing vehicle for innovative companies and for financiers who are locked out of traditional capital markets.

THE STOCK MARKET

As noted earlier, secondary markets are the markets in which outstanding, previously issued securities are traded. By far the most active secondary market, and the most important one to financial managers, is the *stock market*. It is here that the prices of firms' stocks are established. Since the primary goal of financial management is to maximize the firm's stock price, a knowledge of the market in which this price is established is essential for anyone involved in managing a business.

The trading floor of the New York Stock Exchange is the central location where registered members of the exchange meet to buy and sell shares for customers.

Courtesy of the New York Stock Exchange, Edward C. Topple, photographer.

The Stock Exchanges

organized security exchanges

Formal organizations having tangible, physical locations that conduct auction markets in designated ("listed") securities.

New York Stock Exchange (NYSE); American Stock Exchange (AMEX)

The two major U.S. security exchanges.

There are two basic types of stock markets. First, the **organized security exchanges,** which include the **New York Stock Exchange (NYSE),** the **American Stock Exchange (AMEX),** and several regional stock exchanges, have actual physical market locations. The second type of stock market is the less formal over-the-counter markets, which consist of brokers and dealers connected by computers and telephone networks, but which have no central location. We shall consider the organized exchanges first.

Each of the larger exchanges occupies its own building, has specifically designated members, and has an elected governing body — its board of governors. Members are said to have "seats" on the exchange, although everyone stands up on the trading floor. Memberships (or seats) are sold to the highest bidder and represent the right to trade on the exchange. The price of the 1,366 seats on the New York Stock Exchange, which is based on the volume and price levels of stock activity, can fluctuate dramatically. As recently as 1979, seats on the NYSE sold for as little as $40,000, but the highest price ever recorded for the purchase of a seat was $1,150,000 on October 8, 1987, less than two weeks before the 1987 crash. Since the price of membership fluctuates with market trends, recent prices have been much lower than their pre-crash high — in August 1990, a seat on the NYSE sold for $350,000.

Most of the larger investment banking houses operate *brokerage departments* that own seats on the exchanges, and they designate one or more of their officers as members. The exchanges are open on all normal working days, with the members meeting in a large room equipped with telephones and other electronic equipment that enable each brokerage house member to communicate with the firm's offices throughout the country.

Like other markets, security exchanges facilitate communication between buyers and sellers. For example, Merrill Lynch (the largest brokerage firm) might receive an order in its Atlanta office from a customer who wants to buy 100 shares of General Motors stock. Simultaneously, Dean Witter's Denver office might receive an order from a customer wishing to sell 100 shares of GM. Each broker communicates by wire with the firm's representative on the NYSE. Other brokers throughout the country are also communicating with their own exchange members. The exchange members with *sell orders* offer the shares for sale, and they are bid for by the members with *buy orders*. Thus, the exchanges operate as *auction markets*.

The Over-the-Counter Market

In contrast to the organized security exchanges, the **over-the-counter market** is a nebulous, intangible organization. An explanation of the term "over the counter" will help clarify exactly what this market is. The exchanges operate as auction markets; buy and sell orders come in more or less simultaneously, and exchange members match these orders. But if a stock is traded less frequently, perhaps because it is the stock of a new or a small firm, few buy and sell orders come in, and matching them within a reasonable length of time would be difficult. To avoid this problem, some brokerage firms maintain an inventory of such stocks; they buy when individual investors want to sell, and sell when investors want to buy. At one time the inventory of securities was kept in a safe, and when bought and sold, the stocks were literally passed over the counter.

Today, the over-the-counter markets are defined as the set of facilities which provides for any security transactions not conducted on the organized exchanges. These facilities consist primarily of (1) the relatively few *dealers* who hold inventories of over-the-counter securities and who are said to "make a market" in these securities, (2) the thousands of *brokers* who act as agents in bringing these dealers together with investors, and (3) the computers, terminals, and electronic networks that facilitate communications between dealers and brokers. The dealers who make a market in a particular stock continually quote a price at which they are willing to buy the stock (the **bid price**) and a price at which they will sell shares (the **asked price**). These prices, which are adjusted as supply and demand conditions change, can be

over-the-counter market
A large collection of brokers and dealers, connected electronically by telephones and computers, that provides for trading in unlisted securities.

bid price
The price a dealer in securities will pay for a stock.

asked price
The price at which a dealer in securities will sell shares of stock out of inventory.

read off computer screens all across the country. The spread between bid and asked prices represents the dealer's markup, or profit.

Brokers and dealers who make up the over-the-counter market are members of a self-regulating body known as the **National Association of Security Dealers (NASD),** which licenses both brokers and dealers and oversees trading practices. The computerized trading network used by NASD is known as the NASD Automated Quotation System (NASDAQ), and *The Wall Street Journal* and other newspapers contain information on NASDAQ transactions.

In terms of numbers of issues, the majority of stocks are traded over the counter. However, because the stocks of larger companies are listed on the exchanges, about two-thirds of the dollar volume of stock trading takes place on the organized security exchanges.

National Association of Securities Dealers (NASD)

An organization of securities dealers that works with the SEC to regulate operations in the over-the-counter market.

Some Trends in Security Trading Procedures

From the NYSE's inception in the 1800s until the 1970s, the vast majority of all stock trading occurred on the Exchange and was conducted by member firms. The NYSE established a set of minimum brokerage commission rates, and no member firm could charge a commission lower than the set rate. However, the Securities and Exchange Commission, with strong prodding from the Antitrust Division of the Justice Department, forced the NYSE to abandon its fixed commissions effective May 1, 1975. Commission rates declined dramatically, falling in some cases as much as 90 percent from former levels.

This change was a boon to the investing public, but not to the brokerage industry. A number of brokerage houses went bankrupt, and others were forced to merge with stronger firms. Many Wall Street experts predict that, once the dust settles, the number of brokerage houses will have declined from literally thousands in the 1960s to a much smaller number of large, strong, nationwide companies, many of which are units of diversified financial service corporations. Deregulation has also produced a number of small "discount brokers," some of which are affiliated with commercial banks or S&Ls; several of these are likely to be among the survivors.

Stock Market Reporting

Information on transactions both on the organized exchanges and in the over-the-counter market is contained in local newspapers, and in specialized business publications such as *Investor's Daily* and *The Wall Street Journal*. Although the details of financial reporting are covered in investment analysis, it is useful to understand now what information is available on the financial pages and how it is presented.

Table 2-8 is a section of the stock market page for stocks listed on the New York Stock Exchange taken from *The Wall Street Journal* published on Wednesday, December 6, 1989. For each listed stock the *Journal* provides specific data on the trading that took place the prior day (Tuesday, December 5th

Table 2-8 **Stock Market Transactions, December 5, 1989**

	52 weeks Hi	52 weeks Lo	Stock	Sym	Div.	Yld. (%)	PE	Vol 100s	Hi	Lo	Close	Net Chg
					—A—A—A—							
	37½	22¼	AAR	AIR	.48	1.3	23	399	36⅞	36⅜	36⅝	− ¼
n	9⅝	8⅜	ACM OppFd	AOF	1.01	10.9	...	270	9½	9¼	9¼	− ⅛
	11⅝	10¼	ACM Gvt Fd	ACG	1.26	11.2	...	524	11⅜	11¼	11¼	...
n	10⅛	8	ACM MgdIncFd	AMF	1.01	11.5	...	410	9	8⅝	8¾	− ⅛
	11½	10	ACM SecFd	GSF	1.26	11.3	...	1303	11¼	11⅛	11⅛	...
	9⅜	8⅜	ACM SpctmFd	SI	1.01	11.1	...	536	9⅜	9⅛	9⅛	− ⅛
	18	11½	AL Labs A	BMD	.12	.7	17	97	16⅝	16¼	16½	+ ¼
	4⅛	3⅛	AMCA	AIL	.12e	3.4	23	20	3½	3½	3½	+ ⅛
↓	6⅛	4¼	AM Int	AM		...	9	2605	4½	4⅛	4¼	...
	23½	19	AM Int pf		2.00	10.4	...	100	19¼	19	19¼	+ ⅛
	107¼	51½	AMR	AMR		...	8	5124	68	65½	65½	− 1
	27	25	ANR pf		2.67	10.3	...	7	25⅞	25⅝	25⅞	+ ⅛
	6½	3⅝	ARX	ARX		...	...	184	3⅞	3⅝	3⅝	− ⅛
	57½	37⅜	ASA	ASA	3.00a	5.6	...	1464	54⅝	53⅛	53¾	− ⅛
	30⅜	15½	AVX	AVX	.24	.8	29	1156	30	29⅝	29⅝	− ¼
	70⅜	46	AbbotLab	ABT	1.40	2.0	19	3059	70	69¼	69¼	− ⅝
	18¼	12¼	Abitibi	ABY	1.00	...	...	31	12⅞	12¾	12¾	...
	13	7⅝	AcmeCleve	AMT	.40	4.2	12	86	9¾	9½	9⅝	...
	9¾	5⅞	AcmeElec	ACE	.32	3.8	11	29	8½	8¼	8½	+ ⅛
	38½	22	Acuson	ACN		...	22	1087	33⅞	33⅛	33⅛	− ¾
↑	15⅝	12⅞	AdamsExp	ADX	2.06e	13.3	...	159	15¾	15½	15½	− ⅛
	12⅝	6½	AdobeRes	ADB		...	...	186	12⅛	12	12	− ⅛
	19⅜	16½	AdobeRes pf		1.84	9.8	...	1	18¾	18¾	18¾	+ ⅛
	21⅝	19⅞	AdobeRes pf		2.40	11.4	...	3	21¼	21	21	− ⅛
	10½	7⅛	AdvMicro	AMD		...	...	1282	7⅝	7½	7½	− ⅛
	35	28½	AdvMicro pf		3.00	10.1	...	81	30	29¾	29¾	...
	10⅛	6⅝	Advest	ADV	.16	1.8	13	48	9	8¾	9	...
	62½	46	AetnaLife	AET	2.76	4.5	10	3517	62	61⅝	61⅝	...
	14	11¾	AffilPub	AFP	.24	2.0	...	319	12¼	12	12	− ¼
	25	15⅛	Ahmanson	AHM	.88	4.7	9	5144	19¼	18⅝	18⅝	− ¼

Source: *The Wall Street Journal,* December 6, 1989, p.C3.

in this case), as well as other more general information. Similar information is available on stocks listed on the other organized exchanges as well as those traded over the counter.

Stocks listed on the NYSE are arranged in alphabetical order from AAR Industries to the Zwieg Fund; the data in Table 2-8 were taken from the top of the listing. We will examine the data for AAR Industries (AAR), a leading supplier of products and services for commercial, military, and general aviation, to illustrate the information that is presented in the stock listing. The two columns on the left show the highest and lowest prices at which the stock sold during the past year. AAR traded in the range of 37½ to 22¼ (that is, from a

dividend yield

A stock's current divi-
dend divided by the
current price.

high of \$37.50 to a low of \$22.25) during the preceding 52 weeks. The letters just to the right of the company's abbreviated name are its *ticker symbol,* and the following number is the dividend; AAR had a current indicated annual dividend of \$0.48 per share and a **dividend yield**[13] of 1.3 percent. Next comes the ratio of the stock's price to its annual earnings (the P/E ratio), which is 23 for AAR. Although controversy exists among analysts as to the intrinsic value of the P/E ratio as an analytical tool, its existence on the financial page allows for the computation of the firm's current earnings per share. Since the P/E is 23, we can use AAR's closing price, shown in the next to last column, to determine AAR's indicated earnings per share. Thus, AAR's indicated earnings per share is \$1.59: \$36.625/E = 23, so E = \$36.625/23 = \$1.59.

The P/E ratio is followed by the volume of trading for the day; 399,000 shares of AAR's common stock were traded on Tuesday, December 5, 1989. After the trading volume is information on the highest, lowest, and closing (last) prices paid for AAR's stock on that trading day. Thus, on December 5, 1989, AAR's common stock sold for as high as \$36.875 and as low as \$36.375, and its closing price was \$36.625. The last column indicates the net change in price from the closing price on the previous trading day. Because AAR was down by 1/4 (\$0.25), the previous close must have been \$36.875 (\$36.875 − \$0.25 = \$36.625).

The stock market page also provides other information about equity instruments. For example, the *pf* following the second AM Int indicates that this is a preferred stock issue for AM International, rather than its common stock. Notice that ANR, Advanced Micro Devices, and Adobe Resources each also have an issue (2 issues for Adobe Resources) of preferred stock. The far-left column contains other informational notes. The upward-pointing arrow indicates that Adams Express's common stock hit a 52-week high. Similarly, the downward-pointing arrow beside AM International's common stock indicates that its stock hit a 52-week low. In the same far-left column, the *n* notation means this stock is newly listed, within the last 52 weeks. Notice also that an *e* appears after the dividend amount for both AMCA and Adams Express. The *e* indicates that a dividend has been declared or paid in the preceding 12 months but that there is no regular annual dividend rate. The *a* which appears after the dividend amount for ASA indicates that this amount includes an extra dividend in addition to the regular dividend. Additional explanatory notes appear at the bottom of the first page of the transactions listing.

---

[13]To avoid confusion later, it is important to note that there is often more than one definition for certain financial terms used in finance. The term "dividend yield" is an excellent example. In the remainder of this text, we will use the terms "dividend yield" and "expected dividend yield" interchangeably; that is, we define the dividend yield to mean next year's expected dividend divided by the current market price of the common stock, D_1/P_0. In contrast, *The Wall Street Journal* defines the term "dividend yield" as the current, or indicated, dividend yield, which is calculated as the most recent dividend divided by the current market price of the common stock, D_0/P_0. Also, note that we and most others take the latest closing price as the "current" price when we calculate the dividend yield.

Table 2-9 **NYSE Bond Market Transactions, December 5, 1989**

CORPORATE BONDS
Volume, $46,500,000

Bonds	Cur Yld	Vol	Close	Net Chg
PGE 4½s93	5.1	18	88	...
PGE 8⅞s02	9.1	10	97⅝	−⅜
PGE 8s2003	8.8	6	91⅛	+⅛
PGE 7½s03	8.4	5	88⅞	+⅜
PGE 7½s04	8.5	27	88¼	+⅛
PGE 9⅛s06	9.2	7	99⅜	+¼
PGE 9⅝s06	9.6	20	100⅜	−⅜
PGE 8¼08	8.9	4	92⅜	+¼
PGE 9⅜11	9.4	35	99⅝	+⅜
PGE 10⅛12	9.8	1	103⅜	−¾

Note: *The Wall Street Journal* only lists those Pacific Gas and Electric bonds that were actually traded on the NYSE on December 5, 1989. The company has a total of 56 separate bond issues but only 10 issues traded on December 5th.
Source: *The Wall Street Journal,* December 6, 1989, p. C17.

Bond Markets

The majority of bond transactions occur in the over-the-counter market. Bond holdings are concentrated in the hands of large financial institutions, such as life insurance companies, mutual funds, and pension funds. Therefore, it is relatively easy for over-the-counter bond dealers to arrange the trade of large blocks of bonds among the comparatively few bondholders for one of their infrequent trades. It would be much more difficult to arrange similar trades in the stock market among the literally millions of large and small stockholders. Thus, most equity shares are traded on one of the organized exchanges.

Information on bond trades in the over-the-counter market is not published. However, a representative number of bonds are listed and traded on the bond division of the NYSE. Information on NYSE bond trades is published daily in *The Wall Street Journal* under the heading New York Exchange Bonds.[14] While information on the entire spectrum of bond trading is not available, the published data on NYSE bond transactions reflects reasonably well the conditions in the larger over-the-counter market. Table 2-9 is a section of the bond market page in the Wednesday, December 6, 1989, issue of *The Wall Street Journal,* reporting the bond trades of the previous trading day. A total of $46.5 million in bonds, representing 697 issues, were traded on that date, but we show only those of Pacific Gas and Electric (PGE). Bonds can have any denomination, but most have a *par* (or maturity) value of $1,000; this is how

---

[14]A limited number of bonds are also traded on the American Stock Exchange. The results of these trades are also published in *The Wall Street Journal.*

much the company borrowed and how much it must repay when the bond matures. Because other denominations are possible, however, for trading and reporting purposes bond prices are quoted as percentages of par. Looking at the last bond listed, we see that the number 10⅛ appears after the company's name; this indicates that the bond pays 10⅛ percent interest; thus it pays 0.10125($1,000) = $101.25 in interest per year.[15] The 10⅛ percent is defined as the bond's **coupon rate.** The 12, shown after the coupon rate, indicates that the bond must be repaid in the year 2012; it is not shown in the table, but this bond was issued in 1979; hence, it had a 33-year maturity when it was originally issued. The 9.8 in the second column is the bond's **current yield,** which is the annual interest payment divided by the bond's closing price: Current yield = $101.25/$1,033.75 = 9.79%, which is rounded to 9.8%. The column labeled "Vol" indicates that only one of this particular issue was traded on December 5, 1989. Bond prices, unlike equity securities, are not quoted in dollars. Bond prices are quoted as percentages of par, so the closing value of 103⅜ indicates that the bond sold for $1,033.75 (103.375% of the bond's $1,000 par value). As with common stock, the net change column refers to the change in the bond's price from the closing on the prior trading day.

Companies generally set their coupon rates at levels which reflect the "going rate of interest" on the day a bond is issued. If the rates were set lower, investors simply would not buy the bonds at the $1,000 par value, so the company could not borrow the money it needed. Thus, bonds generally sell at their par values when they are issued, but their prices fluctuate thereafter as a result of changes in either the general level of interest rates or the financial strength of the firm.

As you can see from Table 2-9, PGE's 10⅛ percent bonds maturing in 2012 were selling for approximately $1,034, while its 4½ percent bonds which mature in 1993 were selling for $880. The difference in coupon rates reflects the fact that the going rate of interest in 1961, when the 4½'s were sold, was lower than recent interest rates, so these bonds now sell at a *discount,* or an amount less than their par value. On the other hand, the 10⅛'s were originally sold in 1979, when interest rates were higher than recent rates, so these bonds sell at a *premium,* an amount greater than their par value.

Only the bonds that actually traded on a given day are listed in the newspaper (and hence in Table 2-9). Bonds are listed in alphabetical order by company and, for a company with multiple issues like PGE, in the order in which they mature. We will discuss interest rates in Chapter 4, and we will explain how investors determine the price of these debt instruments in Chapter 16.

---

coupon rate
The stated, or nominal, rate of interest on a bond.

current yield
The annual interest payment on a bond divided by its current market price.

---

[15]Pacific Gas and Electric's bonds, like most in the United States, pay interest semiannually; therefore, the company would send a check for $50.63 every six months to the holder of one of the 10⅛'s of 2012.

Regulation of Securities Markets

Sales of new securities, as well as operations in the secondary markets, are regulated by the **Securities and Exchange Commission (SEC)** and, to a lesser extent, by each of the 50 states. Certain rules apply to the issuance of new securities, while other rules apply to the trading of existing securities in the secondary markets.

1. Elements in the Regulation of New Issues by the SEC:

a. The SEC has jurisdiction over all interstate offerings to the public in amounts of $1,500,000 or more.

b. Securities must be registered with the SEC at least 20 days before they are publicly offered. The **registration statement** provides financial, legal, and technical information about the company. A **prospectus** summarizes this information for use in selling the securities. SEC lawyers and accountants analyze both the registration statement and the prospectus. If the information is inadequate or misleading, the SEC will delay or stop the public offering.

c. After the registration has become effective, the securities may be offered, but any sales solicitation must be accompanied by the prospectus. Preliminary or "red herring" prospectuses may be distributed to potential buyers during the 20-day waiting period, but no sales can be finalized during this time. The red herring prospectus contains all the key information that will appear in the final prospectus except the price.

d. If the registration statement or prospectus contains misrepresentations or omissions of material facts, any purchaser who suffers a loss may sue for damages. Severe penalties may be imposed on the issuer, its officers, directors, accountants, engineers, appraisers, underwriters, and all others who participated in the preparation of the registration statement or prospectus.

2. Elements in the Regulation of Outstanding Securities:

a. The SEC also regulates all national securities exchanges. Companies whose securities are listed on an exchange must file annual reports similar to the registration statement with both the SEC and the stock exchange, and must provide periodic reports as well.

b. The SEC has control over corporate **insiders.** Officers, directors, and major shareholders of a corporation must file monthly reports of changes in their holdings in the corporation's stock. Any short-term profits from such transactions are payable to the corporation. The prohibition against trading on information not available to the public goes beyond those directly connected to the firm; anyone who obtains information not available to the public from a corporate insider is prohibited from acting on this information to gain profits. The recent insider trading scandals prove that the SEC is very thorough in finding those who attempt to make profits by trading on inside information.

Securities and Exchange Commission (SEC)
The U.S. government agency which regulates the issuance and trading of stocks and bonds.

registration statement
A statement of facts filed with the SEC about a company planning to issue securities.

prospectus
A document describing a new security issue and the issuing company.

insiders
Officers, directors, major stockholders, or others who may have access to information not available to the public about a company's operations.

c. The SEC has the power to prohibit manipulation by such devices as pools (aggregations of funds used to affect prices artificially) or wash sales (sales between members of the same group to record artificial transaction prices).

d. The SEC has control over the form of the proxy and the way the company uses it to solicit votes.

e. Control over the flow of credit into security transactions is exercised by the Board of Governors of the Federal Reserve System. The Fed exercises this control through **margin requirements,** which stipulate the percentage of the security's purchase price that must be supplied by the purchaser. Thus, if the margin requirement is 60 percent, the purchaser must initially supply 60 percent of the security's financing, and the remaining 40 percent (1 − the margin requirement) may be borrowed. The margin requirement has been 50 percent since 1974. A decline in a stock's price can result in inadequate coverage, forcing the stockbroker to issue a *margin call,* which in turn requires investors either to put up more money or to have their margined stock sold to pay off their loans. Without a margin requirement to limit borrowing to purchase securities, such forced sales could further depress stock prices, setting off a disastrous downward spiral. Before the Great Crash of 1929, no margin was required to purchase stock, so many investors used close to 100 percent debt to obtain their securities. When prices fell, these investors were unable to cover their debts, forcing the sale of their securities at successively lower and lower values. Thus, without the stabilizing influence of a margin requirement, the spiral of lower prices and margin calls was an important contributor to the 1929 stock market crash.

margin requirement
The minimum percentage of his or her own money that a purchaser must put up when buying a security.

3. **State Regulations:**
   a. States have some control over the issuance of new securities within their boundaries. This control is usually exercised by a "corporation commissioner" or someone with a similar title.
   b. State laws relating to security sales are called **blue sky laws** because they were put into effect to keep unscrupulous promoters from selling securities that offered the "blue sky" but which actually had little or no asset backing.

blue sky laws
State laws that prevent the sale of securities having little or no asset backing.

The securities industry itself realizes the importance of stable markets, sound brokerage firms, and the absence of stock manipulation. Therefore, the various organized exchanges work closely with the SEC to police transactions on the exchanges and to maintain the integrity and credibility of the system. Similarly, the National Association of Securities Dealers (NASD) cooperates with the SEC to police trading in the OTC markets. These industry groups also cooperate with regulatory authorities to set net worth and other standards for securities firms, to develop insurance programs to protect customers of brokerage houses, and the like.

In general, government regulation of securities trading, as well as industry self-regulation, is designed to insure that investors receive information that is as accurate as possible, that no one artificially manipulates (that is, drives up or down) the market price of a given stock, and that corporate insiders do not take advantage of their position to profit in their companies' stocks at the expense of other stockholders. Neither the SEC, the state regulators, nor the industry itself can prevent investors from making foolish decisions or from having bad luck, but the regulators can and do help investors obtain the best data possible for making sound investment decisions.

Self-Test

What are the two basic types of stock markets, and how do they differ?

Briefly explain the following statement: "The exchanges operate as auction markets."

Go to Table 2-8; find Abbott Laboratories (AbbotLab); and identify (1) Abbott's December 5, 1989 closing price, (2) its P/E ratio, (3) its current dividend yield, and (4) its price range over the last 52 weeks.

Briefly explain why the majority of corporate bonds are traded on the over-the-counter market, while most common stock is traded on one of the organized exchanges.

Go to Table 2-9, find PGE's 8⅞ bond, and identify (1) its coupon rate, (2) the year in which the bond matures, (3) its current yield, and (4) the bond's closing prices on both December 4 and 5, 1989.

Differentiate among a registration statement, a prospectus, and a red herring prospectus.

MARKET EFFICIENCY

During the last decade and a half, a great deal of financial research has focused on the question of capital market efficiency. Efficiency in this context refers to the ability of stock prices to (1) react quickly to new information and (2) reflect, at any point in time, all available information about the securities. Thus, in an efficient market, prices are "fair."

Requirements for an **efficient capital market** are relatively few, and realistic, in today's investment world. First and perhaps foremost, there must be a reasonably large number of profit-seeking individuals engaged in security analysis who operate independently from one another. Second, many (but not all) investors should have quick and full access to any news about present and potential investments. Announcements of new information will be disseminated as soon as the news breaks; thus, new information will come to the market in a random fashion. Finally, the efficient markets hypothesis assumes

efficient capital market

Market in which securities are fairly priced in the sense that the price reflects all publicly available information on each security.

Figure 2-3 **Risk and Expected Returns on
Different Classes of Securities**

The risk/return tradeoff in the financial markets is illustrated in this figure. An investor willing to invest in the most risky security, common stock, has the potential to earn the highest rate of return. Investing in the least risky security, Treasury bills, will provide the lowest return. This risk/return tradeoff hypothesis has been empirically demonstrated in a study by Ibbotson Associates covering over 60 years.

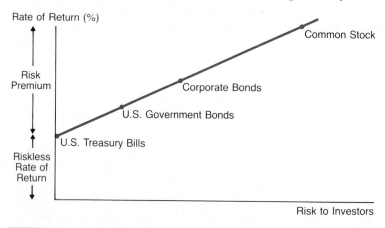

that investors are rational in that they will act (buy or sell) quickly to adjust security prices in light of new information.

One of the critical requirements for an efficient market is the free flow of reliable information to analysts and investors. The SEC and other government agencies have labored to insure that accurate information is quickly disseminated and that no special interest group is able to profit from special access to nonpublic information. The majority of academic studies, found in summary form in most textbooks on security analysis, agree that financial markets, although not perfect, are very efficient. An efficient market is therefore one in which security prices adjust rapidly to new information, reflecting all available information available on a particular security.

All financial decisions involve a tradeoff between risk and expected return. In an efficient market, securities will be priced to reflect the risks involved, with higher-risk issues providing the larger expected returns, as illustrated by Figure 2-3. If an investor is unwilling to accept financial risk, he or she should invest in low return but riskless Treasury bills. If the investor desires higher returns, however, then he or she must be willing to accept greater levels of risk. Thus, as investors move from riskless Treasury bills to riskier securities, they accept more risk, but in the expectation of receiving higher returns.

Studies of the realized returns of securities in the capital markets have supported the concept of a tradeoff between risk and return. In one such study by Ibbotson Associates, which covered the investment period from 1926 to 1989, the securities with the least risk (Treasury bills) were found to have provided the lowest rate of return, whereas the securities with the most risk (common stock) provided the highest rate of return.[16] Therefore, because of the efforts of the SEC, which insures that financial information is quickly and accurately provided, and because of the competition among many analysts, financial markets appear to be efficient in pricing securities relative to their risk.

Self-Test

Identify the requirements for an efficient capital market.

Briefly explain the following statement: "The tradeoff between risk and return should prevail in a rational economic environment."

---

[16]A word of caution is probably necessary at this point. Remember that the Ibbotson study was based on past data for many securities over long periods of time. A selected high-risk security may not provide superior returns over any time period. After all, if high-risk securities *always* provided the highest returns, there would be no risk.

 SMALL BUSINESS

Venture Capital: Financing and Advice

What Is Venture Capital?

A recent Ph.D. dissertation describes venture capital as "capital bundled with consulting." Venture capitalists provide risk capital to small businesses with the expectation of achieving high returns on their investments, but they provide more than money. When a firm and a venture capital team come to terms, several benefits should be achieved. In essence, the venture capital team becomes a part of the firm. First, it invests its money in order to receive a share of the business and a stake in future revenues or profits. Next, the venture capitalist will probably place someone on the firm's board of directors who brings expertise that the firm is lacking. Of course, the new board member will look out for the interests of the venture capitalist, but he or she also will help management find key employees, possibly including a CEO, and will serve as a consultant motivated by owning a piece of the firm.

Venture capital, then, offers more than just financing. It includes management expertise and consulting, assistance with finding key employees, assistance with planning the direction of the firm and its strategies, and assistance in avoiding the pitfalls that cause so many promising young companies to fail. It frequently also includes a commitment to provide additional financing that is commonly needed later, after a venture gets off the ground, although such agreements are subject to management's achieving targets in sales or profits.

The small business owner, therefore, must look well beyond the surface to find a good venture capital partner. Perhaps most important, the two parties must be compatible. They should get along well and be motivated by similar goals for the firm.

How Venture Capital Is Found

To attract venture capital, the company must start with a well-developed business plan. Because venture capitalists often see hundreds of business plans a year, the plan must effectively sell the company without going into excessive detail, since brevity will help insure that the plan will be read. If key factors can't be covered briefly, they should be relegated to appendices or exhibits, so that the general theme can be presented without them.

Once the business plan has been prepared and critiqued by successful business people, it can be distributed. Some venture capitalists specialize in true start-ups, but most will want to see that development has progressed at least to the market testing stage. If the firm presenting the plan has a proven record of profitable operations for several years and is ready to move ahead to the next growth level, so much the better.

It helps to have a good list of venture capital sources. There are numerous guides to sources of venture capital financing; perhaps the most comprehensive is *Pratt's Guide to Venture Capital Sources,* published by Venture Economics. *Pratt's* can usually be found in any municipal or university library. It lists more than 600 sources, and it lists them by state for easy access. *Pratt's* will also tell you whether the venture capital firm invests in start-ups, its areas of specialization, and minimum size of investment.

Many states now have venture capital fairs at which entrepreneurs can present their proposals to a room full of potential investors. If those are available in the area — or even outside the area — they are well worth attending. Contact the Chamber of Commerce or call a nearby office of the Small Business Administration for information on such fairs.

The Venture Team Must Also Sell

The venture capitalist doesn't make all the decisions about whether or not to "do a deal"; he or she must also sell the entrepreneur on the venture team. The venture capitalist should start out the first meeting with a capsule of the team's experience and with a set of references. The venture capitalist will check numerous references and other background information on the entrepreneur, and the entrepreneur should just as carefully check the venture capitalist's background. Has this individual or team been successful in helping companies grow to the public offering or acquisition stage in the past? What do former clients think about the venture capitalist's contribution to their ventures' successes? The entrepreneur may also call up others in the venture capital community for references, or may ask a banker to do some checking for him or her.

The decision to seek venture financing is an important one for the growing firm. The choice of a venture capitalist can spell the difference between success and failure. Don't accept the first offer that comes along; search for the right fit. It may mean the difference between an eventual sale of part of the firm in a public offering versus the sale of the firm's assets in a bankruptcy proceeding.

In Chapter 16, we discuss in detail the terms of a venture financing deal.

Why Proposals Fail

Venture capital proposals are rejected for many reasons. The most common is that the firm's proposal doesn't fit the capitalist's interests. Venture capital firms often specialize in certain fields and will not fund proposals outside of those fields. For example, some will fund only electronics, while others, as a matter of policy, will not consider electronics; some focus on start-ups, whereas others will not deal with start-ups.

Proposals also fail because of financial and managerial reasons. Venture deals are inherently risky; a large proportion of them fail completely, in spite of careful screening. Therefore, an agreement cannot merely allow for a healthy rate of return, it must allow for a return consistent with very high risk. Venture deals are often expected to provide rates of return of 15 to 25 percent more than safe, short-term investments. Thus, if the deal calls for a "secure" income, venture capital isn't the right source of financing.

Venture capitalists and others who study small businesses agree that poor management is one of the biggest causes of business failure. As a result, the venture capitalist will be sure to learn who is on the management team, what their experience entails, what their strengths are, how committed they are, and how well they work with others. Management factors are often pivotal in the decision on whether to fund the deal. The venture capitalist firm must be convinced that management is honest. If you are asked, for example, what problems your business has, don't answer, "None at all." Every business has problems of some kind. "None at all" reveals you to be either incompetent or a liar, and neither will impress the venture capitalist.

SUMMARY

In this chapter we discussed taxes, the nature of financial markets — where capital is raised, securities are traded, and stock prices are established — the types of instruments offered in these markets, the types of institutions that operate in these markets, and the requirements for market efficiency. The key concepts covered are listed below:

- The value of any asset depends on the stream of **after-tax cash flows** it produces. Tax rates and other aspects of our tax system are changed by Congress every year or so.

- In the United States, income tax rates are **progressive** — the higher one's income, the larger the percentage paid in taxes, up to a point.

- Corporate income is subject to **double taxation** because dividend and interest income is taxed at the recipient's tax rate.

- Assets such as stocks, bonds, and real estate are defined as **capital assets.** If a capital asset is sold for more than the purchase price, the profit is called a **capital gain.** If the capital asset is sold for a loss, it is called a **capital loss.**

- **Interest income** received by a corporation is taxed as **ordinary income;** however, 70 percent of the dividends received by one corporation from another are excluded from **taxable income.** The reason for this exclusion is that this income is ultimately subjected to **triple taxation.**

- Because interest paid by a corporation is a **deductible** expense, while dividends are not, our tax system favors debt financing over equity financing.

- Ordinary corporate operating losses can be carried back **(carry-back)** to each of the preceding 3 years and forward **(carry-forward)** for the next 15 years to offset taxable income in those years.

- Fixed assets are **depreciated** over time to reflect the decline in value of the assets. **Depreciation** is a tax-deductible, but noncash, expense. The higher the firm's depreciation, the lower its taxes and the higher its cash flows, other things held constant.

- Current tax laws permit fixed assets to be depreciated using the **Modified Accelerated Cost Recovery System (MACRS).** Tax depreciation rules have a major impact on the profitability of capital investments.

- Under MACRS, depreciation expense is calculated as the yearly **recovery allowance percentage** multiplied by the asset's depreciable basis. The asset's **depreciable basis** is equal to the purchase price of the asset plus any shipping and installation costs.

- If a depreciable asset is sold, the sale price minus the then-existing **undepreciated book value** is added to operating income and taxed at the firm's **marginal tax rate.**

- **S corporations** are small businesses that enjoy the limited-liability benefits of the corporate form of organization yet obtain the benefits of being taxed as a partnership or a proprietorship.

- There are many different types of **financial markets.** Each market serves a different set of customers or deals with a different type of security.

- Transfers of capital between borrowers and savers take place (1) by **direct transfers** of money and securities, (2) by transfers through **investment banking houses,** which act as middlemen, and (3) by transfers through **financial intermediaries,** which create new securities.

- The **stock market** is an especially important market because this is where stock prices are established.

- There are two basic types of stock markets — the **organized exchanges** and the **over-the-counter markets.**

- *The Wall Street Journal* publishes information on stock market transactions: (1) **the high and low price for the previous 52 weeks,** (2) **the current, or indicated, annual dividend,** (3) **the current dividend yield,** (4) **the P/E ratio,** (5) **trading volume,** (6) **the high, low, and closing prices for the trading day,** and (7) **the net change in price from the previous day's closing price.**

- The majority of **corporate bonds** are traded in the over-the-counter market. Bonds are (1) traded with less frequency than stocks and (2) concentrated in the hands of large financial institutions, which makes it relatively easy for over-the-counter bond dealers to arrange bond trades.

- *The Wall Street Journal* publishes information on NYSE bond trades: (1) **coupon rate,** (2) **maturity,** (3) **current yield,** (4) **volume,** (5) **closing price (expressed as a percentage),** and (6) **net change from the previous day's closing price.**

- Security markets are regulated by the **Securities and Exchange Commission (SEC).**

- The requirements for an **efficient capital market** are (1) a large number of profit-seeking individuals engaged in security analysis who operate independently from one another, (2) quick and full access by many (but not necessarily all) investors to any news about present and potential developments, and (3) quick action by investors to adjust security prices in light of new information.

- **Venture capitalists** provide risk capital to small businesses with the expectation of achieving a high return for their investment. Often, the capital investment includes consulting expertise.

RESOLUTION TO DECISION IN FINANCE

Is Wall Street Losing Its Grip on Corporate America?

Although all the ramifications may not yet be clear, the stock market crash of 1987 certainly acted to change Wall Street's relationship with thousands of companies — a relationship that had become a major force in the American economy. Some on Wall Street still eagerly assert that the crash did little to diminish their role in the financing of Corporate America. "Wall Street's relationship with Corporate America could be closer than ever," speculates Robert S. Pirie, the president of Rothschild Inc., an investment bank. "The easy-money days are behind us; corporate America will need Wall Street as never before" to find new ways of raising capital. Chrysler Corporation Treasurer Frederic Zuckerman may not share Mr. Pirie's optimism about Wall Street's vital role, but he

certainly agrees that it is going to be much more difficult for companies to raise money than it has been in the past. According to Zuckerman, the days when a financial officer, when asked to line up money for a major project, could "step up and say to his chairman, 'Piece of cake,' " are definitely over.

There are clear signs that while money is in short supply, Corporate America may be looking away from Wall Street and back to more traditional sources, such as commercial banks and insurance companies, when it comes time to raise capital.

In the 1980s, during the stock market's heyday, investment banks filled their coffers by working both sides of the street. They fueled the corporate takeover boom by helping raiders unseat managements and break up companies. But they also helped corporations defensively restructure to help ward off unwelcome takeover attempts. They counseled American companies to take on extra debt, to sell valuable as-

Source: Steve Swartz and Bryan Burrough, "The Aftermath: Crash Could Weaken Wall Street's Grip on Corporate America," *The Wall Street Journal,* December 29, 1987, 1, 4.

sets, and to concoct lucrative compensation packages, called golden parachutes, for executives facing dismissal in the course of a takeover.

The crash almost certainly marked the beginning of a slowdown in takeover activity. Says Donald G. Drapkin, vice chairman of Revlon Group Inc., the acquisitive consumer-goods concern, "The financing environment is very difficult. The initial-public-offering market is dead. . . . Investment bankers are petrified." Of course, with stock prices way down, a few cash-rich raiders may find a legion of takeover bargains.

Although investment bankers may bemoan a falloff in mergers and acquisitions, many corporate executives are hoping that takeover activity will slow way down and stay that way. They say that they would like to foster long-term growth rather than fret over next quarter's earnings. They want to worry about their bottom lines instead of whether they should restructure their companies to ward off unwelcome suitors. "Corporate America has got to get back to its knitting," asserts Texas entrepreneur H. Ross Perot. To that, many corporate executives say, "Amen."

QUESTIONS

2-1 Suppose you owned 100 shares of Disney stock, and the company earned $4 per share during the last reporting period. Suppose further that Disney could either pay all its earnings out as dividends (in which case you would receive $400) or retain the earnings in the business, buy more assets, and cause the price of the stock to go up by $4 per share (in which case the value of your stock would rise by $400).
  a. How would the tax laws influence what you, as a typical stockholder, would want the company to do?
  b. Would your choice be influenced by how much other income you had? Why might the desires of a 45-year-old physician differ with respect to corporate dividend policy from those of a pension fund manager or a retiree living on a small income?
  c. How might the corporation's decision about dividend policy influence the price of its stock?

2-2 What does *double taxation of corporate income* mean?

2-3 If you were starting a business, what tax considerations might cause you to prefer to set it up as a proprietorship or a partnership rather than as a corporation?

2-4 Explain how the federal income tax structure affects the choice of financing (use of debt versus equity) of U.S. business firms.

2-5 How can the federal government influence the level of business by adjusting the ITC?

2-6 For someone planning to start a new business, is the average or the marginal tax rate more relevant?

2-7 What would happen to the standard of living in the United States if people lost faith in the safety of our financial institutions? Explain.

2-8 How does a cost-efficient capital market hold down the prices of goods and services?

2-9 In what way does the secondary market contribute to the efficient functioning of the primary market?

2-10 What is the financial intermediary's primary role in the economy?

2-11   What are the most important services provided by financial intermediaries?

2-12   What would happen to required rates of return if no financial intermediaries existed?

SELF-TEST PROBLEMS

ST-1   Austin Sound Company had 1990 income of $200,000 from operations after all operating costs but before (1) interest charges of $5,000, (2) dividends paid of $10,000, and (3) income taxes. What is the firm's income tax liability?

ST-2   Margaret Considine earned a salary of $32,000 this year, and, in addition, she received $5,000 in dividends from some stock she owns. If Considine is a single individual and takes her $2,050 personal exemption, what is her taxable income and her tax liability for this year?

ST-3   Sections of *The Wall Street Journal* are provided for the student to use in answering the questions concerning Commonwealth Edison's (ComwEd) common stock quotation and its (CmwE) 15⅜00 bond quotation that follow.

New York Stock Exchange Composite Transactions

52 Weeks Hi	Lo	Stock	Sym	Div	Yld %	PE	Vol 100s	Hi	Lo	Close	Net Chg
40¾	32⅝	ComwEd	CWE	3.00	8.7	12	3578	35	34½	34½	−½
21½	18⅜	ComwEd pr		1.90	9.8	...	15	19⅝	19⅜	19⅜	−¾
22½	19⅝	ComwEd pr		2.00	9.7	...	5	20⅝	20⅝	20⅝	...
26¼	25	ComwEd pr		2.37	9.5	...	1	25	25	25	...
28¾	25½	ComwEd pf		2.87	10.5	...	43	27½	27⅜	27⅜	...

Source: *The Wall Street Journal,* Thursday, April 5, 1990.

New York Exchange Bonds

Quotations as of 4 p.m. Eastern Time Wednesday, April 4, 1990

Bonds	Cur Yld	Vol	Close	Net Chg
CmwE 7⅝03F	9.1	37	84	+ ⅜
CmwE 8¾05	9.7	27	90	− 1
CmwE 9⅜04	9.7	90	96⅜	+ ⅝
CmwE 8⅛07J	9.5	4	85¾	+ ¼
CmwE 8¼07	9.5	25	87	− ⅛
CmwE 15⅜00	13.9	70	110⅞	+3⅞

Source: *The Wall Street Journal,* Thursday, April 5, 1990.

I. Common Stock
a. What is the stock's dividend per share and its dividend yield?
b. What is the stock's price/earnings ratio, based on the closing price, and the firm's most recent 12 months' earnings per share?

c. How many shares were sold on the trading day you investigated?

d. How much did the stock's price rise or fall from the close of the previous day's trading?

e. Is the stock's closing price closer to the stock's high or low for the year?

II. 15⅜00 Bond

a. In what year will the bond mature?

b. How much interest will the investor receive during the year?

c. If an investor purchased the bond at the end of the trading day, what price would be paid for this bond?

d. What was the bond's price at the close of the previous day's trading?

e. Was the bond selling above, below, or at par?

PROBLEMS

Note: By the time this book is published, Congress may have changed tax rates and other provisions. Work all problems under the assumption that the information in the chapter is still current.

2-1   **Corporate tax liability.** In 1990 Nevada Industries had $150,000 in taxable income.
a. What federal income tax will the firm pay?
b. What is the firm's average tax rate?
c. What is the firm's marginal tax rate?

2-2   **Corporate tax liability.** Calais Computers had $110,000 of taxable income from operations in 1990.
a. What is the company's federal income tax bill for the year?
b. Assume Calais Computers receives an additional $30,000 of interest income from some bonds it owns. What is the tax on this interest income?
c. Now assume that the firm does *not* receive the interest income but does receive an additional $30,000 as dividends on some stock it owns. What is the tax on this dividend income?

2-3   **MACRS depreciation.** A new machine is purchased for $60,000. Another $10,000 was spend on installing the machine. The machine has a 5-year MACRS class life. What is the tax depreciation expense in Year 2?

2-4   **Individual tax liability.** Sandy Smith earned a salary of $50,000 this year, and, in addition, she received $2,500 in dividends from stock she owns. Smith is a single individual and takes $2,050 in personal exemption.
a. What is her taxable income this year?
b. What federal income tax will she pay?
c. What is her average tax rate?
d. What is her marginal tax rate?

2-5   **Loss carry-back, carry-forward.** Texas Steel has made $200,000 before taxes during each of the last 15 years, and it expects to make $200,000 a year before taxes in the future. However, this year (1990) Texas incurred a loss of $1,200,000. Texas will claim a tax credit at the time it files its 1990 income tax returns and will receive a check from the U.S. Treasury. Show how it calculates this credit, and then indicate Texas's tax liability for each of the next 5 years. To ease calculations, assume a 30 percent tax rate on *all* income.

2-6 **Personal taxes.** Carol Kiefer has the following situation for the year 1990: salary of $60,000; dividend income of $10,000; interest on GMAC bonds of $5,000; interest on state of California municipal bonds of $10,000; proceeds of $22,000 from the sale of 100 shares of IBM stock purchased in 1982 at a cost of $9,000; and proceeds of $22,000 from the November 1990 sale of 100 shares of IBM stock purchased in October 1990 at a cost of $21,000. Carol gets one exemption ($2,050), and she has allowable itemized deductions of $5,000; these amounts will be deducted from her gross income to determine her taxable income.

a. If she files an individual return, what is Carol's tax liability for 1990?

b. What are her marginal and average tax rates?

c. If she had some money to invest and was offered a choice of either California bonds with a yield of 9 percent or more GMAC bonds with a yield of 11 percent, which should she choose and why?

d. At what marginal tax rate would Carol be indifferent to the choice between California and GMAC bonds?

2-7 **Depreciation.** Riverview Industries purchased two new assets in 1990. The first is a 3-year class asset and the other is classified as a 5-year asset for MACRS depreciation (cost recovery) purposes. The assets each cost $100,000. What depreciation expense will the company report for tax purposes over the next 6 years?

2-8 **Depreciation.** Quality Systems (QS) will commence operations on January 2, 1991. It expects to have sales of $200,000 in 1991, $250,000 in 1992, and $400,000 in 1993. QS also forecasts that operating expenses excluding depreciation will total 60 percent of sales in each year during this period and that it will have interest expenses of $12,000 in 1991, $15,000 in 1992, and $20,000 in 1993. QS will make an investment in fixed assets of $100,000 on January 2, 1991. These assets will be depreciated over their 3-year class life. Use the corporate tax rates from Table 2-2.

a. What is the depreciation expense in each year (1991 through 1993) on the 3-year class life equipment?

b. What is QS's tax liability in each year from 1991 to 1993?

2-9 **Stock quotations.** Look up IBM's common stock in *The Wall Street Journal* or another appropriate financial publication.

a. On what exchange is the stock listed?

b. What is the dividend per share?

c. What is the stock's dividend yield?

d. What is the price/earnings ratio, based on the closing price, and the most recent 12 months' earnings per share?

e. How many shares were sold on the trading day you investigated?

f. How much did the stock's price rise or fall from the close of the previous day's trading?

g. Is the stock's closing price closer to the stock's high or low for the year?

2-10 **Bond quotations.** Look up General Motors Acceptance Corporation's bonds in *The Wall Street Journal* or another appropriate financial publication. The firm's bonds are identified by "GMA" in *The Wall Street Journal's* bond listings. Specifically, answer the following questions based on GMA's 12s05 bond. (*Note:* If this bond is not listed in *The Wall Street Journal* when you are working on this problem, choose another GMA bond with a similar coupon and maturity.)

a. On what exchange is the bond listed?

b. In what year will the bond mature?

c. How much interest will the investor receive during the year?

d. If an investor purchased the bond at the end of the trading day, what price would be paid?

e. What was the bond's price at the close of the previous day's trading?

f. Was the bond selling above, below, or at par?

g. If General Motors Acceptance Corporation were to sell a new issue of bonds, approximately what coupon rate would be required for the issue to sell at par?

SOLUTIONS TO SELF-TEST PROBLEMS

ST-1
Income	$200,000
Less: interest deduction	5,000
Taxable income	$195,000

Note that dividends paid are not tax deductible; therefore, they are not deducted from income to obtain taxable income.

From Table 2-2 we obtain the corporate tax rates as follows:

$$\text{Tax} = \$22,250 + 0.39(\$195,000 - \$100,000)$$
$$= \$22,250 + \$37,050$$
$$= \$59,300.$$

ST-2 Taxable income:

Salary earned	$32,000
Dividends received	5,000
Personal exemption	(2,050)
	$34,950

Tax liability:

Since Margaret Considine is a single individual, we use the tax rates for single individuals shown at the top of Table 2-1.

$$\text{Taxes} = \$2,918 + 0.28(\$34,950 - \$19,450)$$
$$= \$2,918 + \$4,340$$
$$= \$7,258.$$

ST-3   **I. Common Stock**

a. You should notice that there are 5 stock issues listed for Commonwealth Edison, only 1 of which is common stock — the first Commonwealth issue shown. (The other 4 issues are preferred stock, denoted by "pr".) Looking at the 5th column, you should see that Commonwealth's dividend per share is $3.00. The next column to the right indicates the dividend yield of 8.7 percent.

b. Looking at the 7th column, you should see that the P/E ratio is 12 times. Since the P/E ratio is 12 times, and the closing price (shown in the next-to-last column) is $34.50, the earnings per share (EPS) is calculated as follows:
P/E = 12; E = $34.50/12; E = $2.875.

c. Looking at the 8th column, you should see that 357,800 shares were sold. Notice that this column indicates volume in hundreds.

d. The last column shows the change in price from the previous trading day. For Commonwealth, the price fell by $0.50 from the previous day's close.

e. The first 2 columns give the 52-week high and low price. For the 52-week period, Commonwealth's price ranged from $32.625 to $40.75. Since Commonwealth's closing stock price is shown as $34.50, its stock was trading closer to its low than to its high price.

II. 15⅜00 Bond

a. This particular bond is the last issue shown for Commonwealth. The maturity date is indicated in the first column by the two digits 00, indicating that the bond matures in the Year 2000.

b. Again, the interest rate for this particular bond is shown in the first column after the company's ticker symbol (CmwE) by the digits 15⅜. Since a bond's par value is typically $1,000, and the interest rate is 15⅜ percent the annual interest is calculated as $0.15375 \times \$1,000 = \$153.75$.

c. The next-to-last column shows the percentage of par value at which the bond closed — 110⅞. Therefore, the price paid for the bond at the end of the day is calculated as $1.10875 \times \$1,000 = \$1,108.75$.

d. The last column shows the percentage change in par value from the previous day's close — +3⅞. Thus, the change in par value was $0.03875 \times \$1,000 = \$38.75$, so the previous day's close was $\$1,108.75 - \$38.75 = \$1,070.00$.

e. Because the next-to-last column shows a number greater than 100, the bond is selling above par.

Chapter 3

Financial Institutions

 DECISION IN FINANCE

Commercial Banks: The New Competitor in the Investment Banking Industry

When the regulations barring commercial banks from most investment-banking activities began easing in early 1989, several big banks began moving into the highly profitable securities business. Few of these banks, however, have moved very far or very fast. Citicorp and Chase Manhattan are focusing on underwriting new types of securities and junk bonds, but they've started slowly. J. P. Morgan has reorganized its new securities branch several times, apparently unable to decide exactly what to do or how to do it.

One big bank — Bankers Trust — however, has moved with speed and daring to take advantage of the Federal Reserve Board's ruling that commercial banks could underwrite corporate debt. Bankers Trust is entering the investment banking business through "merchant banking," which involves advising clients, underwriting their securities, and lending, as well as investing equity in their deals. Its approach has the poten-

tial for great profit, but it is more risky than other types of investment banking.

So far, however, the strategy has been successful. Salomon Brothers placed Bankers Trust at the top in its annual banking industry review — only the second time a major, big-city money-center bank had reached such heights. A recent coup for Bankers Trust was when the bank edged out traditional investment banker Bear, Stearns & Company for the job of adviser on a $165.89 million takeover bid. The client had used Bear, Stearns on previous takeover attempts for investment banking services and Bankers Trust for regular bank loans. By being able to offer "one-stop shopping," Bankers Trust won the day — and approximately $10 million in fees.

Bankers Trust has, however, made some mistakes. One such mistake was a $1 billion management buyout it engineered for a British kitchen-fixture manufacturer, Magnet PLC, with the bank acting as both investor and lender. Magnet's sales began to decline almost as soon as the deal was completed, and Bankers Trust

See end of chapter for resolution.

and eight other banks now share $900 million in debt that they can't, as planned, sell to other banks. Even worse, Magnet has told the banks that its debt load is too heavy, and that the debt will have to be restructured, either with lower interest rates or with a longer term.

Competing bankers suggest that Bankers Trust was too aggressive in seeking the deal, and one analyst estimates the restructuring could reduce Bankers Trust's earnings by 15 to 20 cents a share. However, the bank's co-head of corporate finance in Europe says that, in general, high interest rates and slumping retail sales are really to blame. Pointing out that other British lenders have been faced with similar restructurings, he is confident that Magnet's debt can be restructured in a satisfactory manner.

Another Bankers Trust mistake involved a highly publicized assignment to underwrite some $30 million of debt for MorningStar Foods, Inc. An announced November marketing date passed by — Bankers Trust couldn't sell the debt because of a general concern about rising junk bond defaults.

Both of those incidents, along with another aborted European buyout deal involving a conflict-of-interest charge, have detracted from Bankers Trust's image. Some bank-securities analysts worry that, in its haste to make its mark, Bankers Trust may be chasing deals too aggressively, and that it is betting too heavily that the wave of corporate restructurings will continue in the United States and spread to Europe.

The traditional investment banking firms have their own set of concerns about this new competition. They are, however, apparently resigned to legislation that would make the Fed's new policy regarding commercial banks permanent, by changing it from a policy to a law. They do still worry that banks will use loans as "loss leaders" — offering a lower interest rate on a loan to attract other business — to get investment banking assignments that would normally go to Wall Street firms. Such tie-ins are illegal, but Wall Street firms fear that banks will be able to circumvent these restrictions.

So far, however, there is no evidence that any bank has "sidestepped" the law. The only real concern for Wall Street should be that Bankers Trust, in particular, is finding more success than failure in its new strategy.

In 1989 Bankers Trust helped in the $3.65 billion LBO of NWA, Inc., the parent company of Northwest Airlines. Besides organizing a syndicate of lenders, it also invested $80 million in NWA shares. Also, Bankers Trust offered a $300 million bridge loan — temporary financing until permanent financing can be arranged — and offered to underwrite junk bonds, if those credits were needed. This willingness to go the "extra mile" caused the purchaser to name Bankers Trust a co-adviser on the deal, even though the other adviser had reportedly done most of the work.

As you read this chapter, think about the problems that may face Bankers Trust and other large commercial banks (and possibly U.S. taxpayers) as they enter new fields. What precautions do you think they must take to avoid costly mistakes?

In Chapter 2, we evaluated the role of financial intermediaries, especially those that channel long-term funds from ultimate lenders to ultimate borrowers. In this chapter, we present an overview of the major financial institutions in our economy, and we then look at two of these financial institutions in greater detail — the commercial bank and the savings and loan industry. We focus on the commercial banking system because of its importance in our economy

This chapter was co-authored by Bruce Cochran of San Jose State University.

with regard to the money supply, and we look at the savings and loan industry because of the effects its problems are having on taxpayers and the federal budget.

We will discuss ways in which the *Federal Reserve System (Fed)* regulates the economy through the banking system, and, specifically, the tools it uses to influence the availability and cost of money in the economy. We then discuss the savings and loan industry crisis, recent changes in the banking industry (both in regulation and in new products), and the globalization of our financial institutions.

OVERVIEW OF FINANCIAL INSTITUTIONS

In Table 3-1 we present a brief summary of the major financial institutions (intermediaries) in the U.S. economy. As one can see from the table, commercial banks are the largest of the U.S financial institutions in terms of asset size, further demonstrating the importance of banks in our economy.

As we learned in Chapter 2, the financial institutions listed in Table 3-1 are intermediaries — they take funds deposited by individuals and businesses, and they then lend those funds to various borrowers. Column 2 of Table 3-1, labeled "Principal Assets," shows the type of assets held by each institution, and

Table 3-1 **Financial Institutions Summary: 1990**

Type of Institution (1)	Principal Assets (2)	Principal Liabilities (3)	Total Assets (Millions) (4)	Principal Regulators (5)
Commercial banks	Business and consumer loans, mortgages, and government securities	Checking, savings, and time deposits	$3,249,600	Federal Reserve Board, Comptroller of Currency, and FDIC
Thrifts	Mortgages	Savings and time deposits	1,250,068	Office of Thrift Supervision and FDIC/ SAIF
Credit unions	Consumer loans	Savings deposits	183,688	National Credit Union Administration
Life insurance companies	Corporate bonds, mortgages, and real estate	Life insurance policies	1,303,691	State insurance commissioners
Pension funds	Government securities, corporate stocks and bonds	Pension fund reserves	2,470,000	Federal government (Employee Retirement Income Security Act of 1974)
Mutual funds	Government securities, municipal bonds, corporate stocks and bonds	Fund shares	553,871	Securities and Exchange Commission

Sources: *Federal Reserve Bulletin*, August 1990, Tables A18, A26, and A35, and "Giant Pension Funds' Explosive Growth Concentrates Economic Assets and Power," *The Wall Street Journal*, June 28, 1990.

Column 3 shows the principal types of liabilities each institution issues. Financial intermediaries increase the efficiency of our economy by bringing together individuals with surplus funds and those in need of funds. Although each institution listed is important, our major focus in this chapter is on the commercial banking and the thrift industries.

Self-Test

For each intermediary listed in Table 3-1, construct a diagram similar to Figure 2-2 ("Indirect Transfers through a Financial Intermediary") which specifically identifies the following items: the intermediary's primary assets, the savers, the users of the funds, and the types of securities the intermediary issues.

THE COMMERCIAL BANKING SYSTEM

The commercial banking system is the largest type of financial intermediary. In fact, the assets of the banking system are almost as large as the assets of all other financial intermediaries combined. Most of the deposits in the United States are in commercial banks. Banks convert these deposits into billions of dollars in loans and securities, making them the primary source of short- to intermediate-term credit for state and local governments, businesses, and consumers.

The U.S. banking system is quite different from that in other industrialized countries, as we shall see later in the chapter in our discussion of globalization. Canada, Great Britain, Germany, and Japan all have a few large banks with nationwide operations. In the United States, however, there are over 14,000 separately chartered commercial banks. We have so many banks because of our history of restricting the activities of banks to a single state and, in some states, to just one office (no branches). The early designers of our banking system were concerned over the apparent concentration of economic power in European banks. Consequently, they allowed each state to design its own banking system, and, until the 1980s, all states prohibited interstate banking. Many states, including Texas, Illinois, and Florida, would not allow any bank to operate more than one office. Such restrictive banking regulations encouraged the development of small, local institutions.

Another unique feature of U.S. banking is the dual (state and federal government) chartering system. Prior to 1863, all banks were chartered by their home states. Then, the federal government began chartering banks after the passage of the National Bank Act of 1863. This Act set up the Office of the Comptroller of the Currency (OCC) to charter, to examine, and if necessary to close national banks. National banks, however, do not operate nationwide; they are subject to the same interstate banking restrictions as state-chartered banks. Recently, however, many of the restrictions on branch and interstate banking have been eased. These changes will be discussed in greater detail later in the chapter. Many states have made regional banking pacts which allow interstate banking within the region. Such pacts exist in New England, the Southeast, and

CITICORP REDEFINES THE LIQUID LUNCH.

Citicorp Menu
Liquidity A La Carte

Commercial Paper
Served by the fastest growing dealer.

Eurocommercial Paper/Euronotes
From Citicorp who is number one in this international specialty.

Participated Loan Notes
A long-time favorite, created by Citicorp, the market leader for five years.

Foreign Currency Commercial Paper and Loan Notes
Offered by the world's number one foreign exchange dealer.

Certificates of Deposit/EuroCDs
From the first place dealer in these popular items.

Bankers Acceptances
A classic served in the manner that has made Citicorp number one.

In addition to our regular menu, we feature many other liquidity dishes, prepared to order.

For Reservations Call: John F. Ward, 212-668-3954.

Citicorp redefines the Liquid Lunch as an unrivaled buffet of short-term liquidity products.

With the variety and superb quality of our menu, it's no wonder Citicorp does over $6 billion a day in the short-term liquidity business, distributing the offerings of over 500 issuers worldwide.

We offer the most extensive global network of any investment bank. And our unique distribution capability gives the discriminating issuer access to over 7000 of the world's institutional investors, satisfying a voracious appetite for liquid products.

And remember that all of our entrees are accompanied by Citicorp's $21 billion capital base, offices in 46 countries, an active presence in every one of the world's major securities markets, and one of the largest sales forces in the world for short-term products.

Wherever you are or intend to be in the world of liquidity, let Citicorp serve you.

The products and services listed above are offered by one of the following: Citibank N.A., Citicorp Investment Bank Ltd., or Citicorp Securities, Inc.

To attract business deposits, banks are branching out from more traditional loans and offering a full "menu" of financing options to business customers.

the Midwest. Moreover, California and other states either have opened or will be opening their borders to banks from all states. The breakdown of geographic barriers is leading to a system with larger banks and more competition, as well as to innovation in the banking markets.

The banking system has changed dramatically during the past decade. During the 1980s, many banks have become virtual financial supermarkets, offering savings certificates, IRAs and other retirement plans, trust and leasing departments, discount brokerage services, and insurance products. Many of these products and services are actually offered by subsidiaries of the banks' holding companies. A **bank holding company (BHC)** is an organizational structure, which owns banks and non-bank subsidiaries. BHCs were originally designed to circumvent bank regulations, but their activities are now restricted by the Bank Holding Company Acts of 1956 and 1970, under which the Federal Reserve determines the products and services a BHC may offer. Much of the deregulation of the 1980s has resulted from Fed decrees increasing the number of permissible activities under the Bank Holding Company Acts.

During the 1980s, a number of Congressional Acts were also passed which affected banking. In 1980, Congress passed the **Depository Institutions Deregulation and Monetary Control Act (DIDMCA).** This legislation eliminated deposit rate and loan rate ceilings, removed differences between Fed member and non-member banks, and increased deposit insurance limits from $40,000 to $100,000 per account. The **Garn–St. Germain Act** of 1982, primarily a thrift bailout act, allowed banks to buy failing thrifts; the crisis surrounding the savings and loan industry will be discussed in detail later in the chapter. In 1987, Congress passed the **Competitive Equality in Banking Act (CEBA)** to stem the growth of bank-like subsidiaries of companies such as Sears, Roebuck and Merrill Lynch. Finally, in 1989 Congress voted for a major restructuring of the thrift industry in the **Financial Institutions Reform, Recovery, and Enforcement Act (FIRREA).**

Sources and Uses of Bank Funds

A review of a typical commercial bank's balance sheet provides information about the sources of bank funds and the uses to which those funds are put.[1] Look at Table 3-2 as you read this section.

Deposits are a bank's primary source of funds and a major component of the economy's money supply, so Congress has been careful to protect these accounts. In 1933, Congress created the **Federal Deposit Insurance Corporation (FDIC)** to protect depositors in insured banks from the effects of a bank failure.[2] Today, deposits of up to $100,000 are insured against bank, thrift, or credit union failures. While the explicit limit is $100,000, virtually all deposits are covered by deposit insurance. The FDIC maintains that, since its crea-

bank holding company (BHC)
A corporation which owns banks and non-bank subsidiaries, originally designed to circumvent bank regulation.

Depository Institutions Deregulation and Monetary Control Act (DIDMCA)
An act that eliminated many of the distinctions between commercial banks and other depository institutions.

Garn–St. Germain Act
A thrift bailout act which allowed banks to buy failing thrifts.

Competitive Equality in Banking Act (CEBA)
An act passed in 1987 to stem the growth of bank-like corporations.

Financial Institutions Reform, Recovery, and Enforcement Act (FIRREA)
An act passed in 1989 that restructured the thrift industry.

Federal Deposit Insurance Corporation (FDIC)
An agency created by Congress in 1933 to protect depositors in insured banks from the effects of a bank failure.

---

[1]Although this presentation of a bank's balance sheet is not technical, some readers may wish to refer to Chapter 5, "Examining a Firm's Financial Data," where balance sheets are discussed in greater detail, before continuing with this chapter.

[2]Similar programs such as the Federal Savings and Loan Insurance Corporation (FSLIC) and the National Credit Union Insurance Fund (NCUIF) were set up to protect deposits for the savings and loan and credit union industries. The FSLIC has recently been eliminated due to large losses in the thrift industry, and thrift industry deposits are now insured by the Savings Association Insurance Fund (SAIF), which is administered by the FDIC.

Table 3-2 **Banking Industry Percentage Balance Sheet**

Percentage of Total Assets	1970	1980	1987	1989
Cash	16.10%	17.90%	11.54%	8.01%
Fed funds and repos	2.80	3.80	2.55	2.33
Securities	25.50	18.00	14.65	17.72
Loans	51.80	54.30	62.05	62.23
Miscellaneous assets	3.80	6.00	9.21	9.71
Total assets	100.00%	100.00%	100.00%	100.00%
Demand deposits	42.90%	23.30%	14.96%	19.86%
Time and savings deposits	40.80	40.70	55.81	50.08
Fed funds and repos	2.90	7.20	8.61	8.24
Other short-term debt	6.40	23.00	5.51	6.06
Long-term debt	0.00	0.00	9.36	9.47
Equity	7.00	5.80	5.75	6.29
Total claims (%)	100.00%	100.00%	100.00%	100.00%

tion, 98% of all deposits in failing banks have been recovered. Because deposit insurance allows banks and thrifts to issue risk-free debt, but then to invest funds received in highly speculative ventures, this insurance has been somewhat controversial. Issues relating to deposit insurance are covered in detail later in this chapter.

There are three types of deposits — demand, savings, and time deposits. **Demand deposits,** at one time the major source of bank funds, are deposits made by individuals, businesses, or government units that are available on demand, usually through a check. Demand deposits are the major source of liquidity for all economic units. Banks attract deposits by offering transactions services and by paying interest. A bank's ability to pay interest was in the past limited in order to hold down banks' costs and thus make them safer. From 1933 through 1980, banks were prohibited from paying interest on demand deposits by **Regulation Q.** During this period, banks attracted deposits by offering such features as free checks, free services, and an occasional toaster or blender. Late in the 1970s, however, it became clear that toasters were not enough. Depositors, faced with inflation rates of 7 to 12 percent, were taking their money out of banks and placing it in money market funds. Through the lobbying efforts of banks, regulators, and consumers, Congress passed the Depository Institutions Deregulation and Monetary Control Act (DIDMCA) of 1980. This act created a new type of transaction account — one which pays interest. That account, a form of savings account that allows withdrawal by check and which is offered by banks, savings and loans, and credit unions, is referred to as a **NOW (negotiable order of withdrawal) account.** NOW accounts, however, are not available to a bank's corporate customers.

Today, as you can see from Table 3-2, the most important sources of bank funds are savings and time deposits. Savings accounts generally pay close to

demand deposits
Transaction deposits at commercial banks that are available on demand, usually through a check.

Regulation Q
A rule which, during 1933 through 1980, prohibited banks from paying interest on demand deposits.

NOW (negotiable order of withdrawal) account
A form of savings account that allows withdrawal by check.

certificate of deposit (CD)

A time deposit evidenced by a negotiable (for large-denomination CDs, generally $100,000 or more) or nonnegotiable (usually denominations under $100,000) receipt issued for funds deposited for a specified period of time; rates of interest generally depend on the amount of deposit, time to maturity, and the general level of interest rates.

Federal funds market

The market in which banks lend reserve funds among themselves for short periods of time.

Fed funds rate

The interest rate, set by market forces, at which banks borrow in the Federal funds market.

repurchase agreement (repo)

A collateralized loan by one financial institution to another.

capital account

The account that represents a bank's total assets minus its short-term liabilities.

the market interest rates and offer limited transactions services. Time deposits offer higher rates but do not allow transactions. The most common type of time deposit is a **CD,** or **certificate of deposit.** A CD is a receipt for funds deposited in an institution for a specified time which pays a specific interest rate. Generally, the interest rate on CDs increases with the term to maturity. Certificates of deposit were known but not widely used until 1961, when Citibank of New York announced that it would issue CDs in negotiable form, meaning that the funds could be used before maturity and sold in a secondary market to another investor. Because these CDs are negotiable, they attract business funds and other deposits in large denominations, beginning at $100,000. Other certificates in much smaller denominations are available to individuals and other small savers. Unlike the larger $100,000 CDs, the smaller savings certificates are not negotiable.[3]

In addition to deposits, banks may choose to finance a part of their assets with borrowed funds. The primary source of borrowed funds is the **Federal (Fed) funds market.** In the Fed funds market, banks borrow from other banks for short periods of time. A bank with excess reserves (available funds) lends funds, typically overnight, to a bank that has a temporary need for reserves. The **Fed funds rate** is the prevailing interest rate in this market. (The Fed funds rate, despite its name, is set by market forces, not by the Fed.[4]) Another source of short-term borrowings for a bank is the repo market. A **repurchase agreement,** or **repo,** is a collateralized loan (one for which security is held) by one financial institution to another financial institution. Treasury securities are generally used as collateral for these short-term loans. Finally, a small portion of a bank's short-term borrowings may be obtained from the Federal Reserve System itself. However, banks are restricted in what they can do with funds obtained as loans from the Fed, and, consequently, they prefer not to borrow from the Fed unless absolutely necessary. Finally, banks can obtain funds by selling long-term bonds.

A bank's **capital account** is similar to a business firm's net worth or common stock equity account. This account reveals the owners' contributions to the bank's financing, both through the purchase of common stock and through undistributed profits which are retained by the bank. The total assets of the bank minus liabilities equal the bank's capital. Note also that regulatory capital rules allow banks to count some portion of their long-term debt as capital.

Bank capital is important both to the bank and to its regulators. Before deposits were insured, bank capital protected depositors from losses, and, today, a bank's capital protects the deposit insurance fund and the bank's unsecured creditors from losses. Bank losses generally occur as a result of loans

---

[3]CD rates are set by the institution; however, if a saver must redeem a certificate before its maturity date, the interest rate paid is the passbook rate minus an early withdrawal penalty, generally three months' interest.

[4]The Fed explicitly sets the discount rate, which is the rate charged to banks when they borrow directly from the Fed. The Fed, however, may influence the Fed funds rate through its open-market operations, discussed later in the chapter.

that cannot be repaid or poor investments, and these losses are charged against the bank's capital. The typical commercial bank has only 5 to 10 percent of its assets financed by capital. Thus, the traditional banker's conservative attitude is well founded, because loans or investments can decline by only 5 to 10 percent before the bank becomes insolvent.

Bank Assets. Banks do more than simply act as safekeepers for depositors' funds. In fact, they keep very little of a depositor's cash on hand. According to Table 3-2, cash today accounts for only about 8 percent of a bank's total assets. This percentage is down substantially from earlier periods, signifying that banks have become more efficient cash managers. The cash account includes more than just vault cash. Part of the **cash account** includes "items in process of collection," which is the value of checks drawn on other banks but not yet collected. The cash account also includes funds that are required to be kept on deposit at the district Federal Reserve Bank.

cash account
The account that represents a bank's vault cash, checks in process of collection, and funds required to be kept on deposit with the Federal Reserve.

Of the three components of the cash account — vault cash, checks in process, and funds on deposit at the District Bank — actual cash kept at the bank for daily transactions, or vault cash, would be the smallest amount for most banks. First, banks are able to maintain relatively small amounts of vault cash because normal transactions generally result in approximately the same amount of cash deposits as cash withdrawals. Second, like other businesses, banks prefer to keep their funds invested in productive, income-producing assets. Excess cash is therefore channeled into more productive loans and investments.

Another use of funds, other than for transactions, is for the purchase of investment securities. These securities are legally required to be of the highest investment quality — highly liquid and having low risk. Typically, most of these securities are issued by the state and other political subdivisions in the bank's geographic area. U.S. Treasury securities also account for a large portion of the bank's investment portfolio. Investments provide a return for a bank, and they can also be sold quickly to raise additional cash if it is needed. The investments must be of high quality, so that they may be converted into cash quickly, and with little chance of loss.

A bank's primary purpose is to lend money in support of economic growth in its area, and loans also have a higher expected rate of return than investments. However, if there is not enough demand for loans, banks must turn to investment in securities as a source of revenue.

Banks are the major source of short-term credit for the business sector. Historically, they have preferred to make "self-liquidating loans." For example, in our agrarian past, a farmer would borrow money to buy seed and, upon harvest, would repay the loan with the proceeds of the crop's sale. A modern example of a self-liquidating loan would be a merchant's borrowing to increase inventory before Christmas. After Christmas, the merchant would repay the loan from the proceeds of the holiday sales. These short-term loans were the historical rule for banks, because their primary source of funds is short-

Table 3-3 **Banking Industry Earnings**

Percentage of Total Revenues	1970	1980	1987	1989
Loan interest income	66.20%	66.50%	65.61%	65.56%
+ Securities interest income	21.70	25.30	17.80	18.46
− Interest expense	35.80	51.60	51.72	53.01
− Provision for loan losses	2.00	2.30	16.06	5.73
Net interest income	50.10%	37.90%	15.63%	25.28%
+ Non-interest revenues	12.10	8.20	16.59	15.98
− Non-interest expenses	43.20	38.20	34.69	32.26
− Taxes	6.30	2.60	0.76	2.99
Net income	12.70%	5.30%	(3.23%)[a]	6.01%

[a]Here, and throughout the book, parentheses denote negative numbers.

term demand deposits. However, since the greater proportion of funds now comes from time and savings deposits, banks are increasingly willing to provide intermediate (3- to 7-year) term loans. Some loans, such as real estate loans, have even longer maturities.

As Table 3-3 illustrates, revenues from loans constitute approximately 66 percent of all bank revenues. The remaining revenue sources include interest on securities and non-interest revenues such as service charges and fees. Since the development of the NOW account and the elimination of Regulation Q, banks' interest expenses have grown substantially. Banks have compensated by increasing monthly fees and other service charges. Other expenses incurred by banks include the provision for loan losses, non-interest expenses (salaries and occupancy costs), and taxes. The provision for loan losses is a noncash expense which is used to prepare for expected losses in the loan portfolio. In 1987, the provision for loan losses was unusually large, and most of those expenses were in preparation for portfolio losses on loans made to Third World countries. The 1987 provisions for loan losses resulted in record losses for most of the largest U.S. banks. However, the industry recovered in 1988, and U.S. banks earned a record $10 billion, and this strong earnings performance continued into 1989. More recently, however, some of the largest institutions have again had to substantially increase their loan loss provisions, tempering the earnings gain that much of the industry made. For example, three major New England banks have set aside a total of more than $2 billion in reserves for potential loan losses in their real estate portfolios due to the sagging real estate market in that area.

Demand Deposit Creation

Banks are the most important element in our financial system, not so much because of the services they provide, but because of two other important factors. First, commercial banks are important to the economy because demand deposits are money, and the bank can create demand deposits through the extension of credit in the form of loans.[5] Second, banks are important because the Federal Reserve Board utilizes the banking system to affect the money supply and, therefore, interest rates. Thus, in the United States, demand deposits, not currency, are the most important form of money, and commercial banks are at the heart of the nation's financial system because of their ability to create money.

As we will see later in the chapter, the Fed requires a bank to maintain stated percentages of its demand, time, and savings deposits on reserve at the Fed or in vault cash, but the bank can lend the remainder of the deposited funds to others. For example, if the overall reserve requirement were 25 percent, a $1,000 deposit would result in a required reserve of $250, and the remaining $750 would be considered excess or free reserves, which could be loaned or invested by the bank. It is primarily through its loans, and, secondarily, through its investments, that the bank makes a profit.

The economy has a certain amount of productive capacity. Given our labor force, natural resources, and capital equipment, we can turn out only so many autos, hamburgers, houses, and so forth. If the economy is operating close to capacity, any increase in the money supply will simply lead to price increases, or inflation. The Federal Reserve has a primary goal of controlling inflation, and it seeks to exercise this control through the money supply. The money supply consists of two elements, currency and the far larger and more important element, bank deposits. For every $100 of deposits shown on the right side of the balance sheet, banks can have loans and investments of something less than $100, with the difference being a reserve held by a Federal Reserve bank.

If the economy slows down, as it would during a recession, and the Fed wants to expand the money supply in an effort to stimulate production, then the Fed will make additional reserves available to the banking system. The banks will then make credit available to borrowers. The way this will work is as follows: The bank will grant a loan, creating a deposit in the name of the borrower, who can then spend the money by writing checks. Those checks will, in turn, be deposited in the same or a different bank, and the money supply (bank deposits) will increase. (Of course, the Fed can reverse the process — it can reduce the supply of reserves, which will force the banking system to contract the amount of deposits, hence reduce the money supply.)

We see, then, that the banking system's ability to expand depends on the existence of **excess reserves** held with the Federal Reserve banks. By lending excess reserves, banks create money. To illustrate the process, assume that there are currently no excess reserves in the banking system and that the Fed's reserve requirement is 15 percent.[6] The Fed can increase reserves, hence the

excess reserves
Reserves held by a commercial bank with a Federal Reserve bank in excess of the bank's required reserves.

---

[5]Recently other financial intermediaries have gained the right to expand money and credit, but these efforts are *quite* limited when compared with those of the banking system.

[6]Actually, reserve requirements depend on the size and type of deposits at a commercial bank. Most banks are subject to a 12 percent reserve requirement on checking account deposits and 3 percent on CDs and passbook account deposits.

money supply, by buying Treasury securities. Assume that a commercial bank holds $1,000 of Treasury bills as an investment, which the Fed buys. The Fed pays for the bills by creating a $1,000 deposit in a Federal Reserve bank in the name of the commercial bank, and that deposit is an addition to the commercial bank's reserves.

At this point, the bank has additional reserves in the form of its own new $1,000 account in the Fed bank. Further, these reserves are all excess reserves, so they can be loaned out to borrowers.

These excess reserves will be loaned to a customer in the form of a $1,000 deposit. This is the first stage of a potentially large deposit-expansion process. At each stage in the process, both total loans and total deposits for the banking system increase by an amount equal to the excess reserves before the last loan was made. The increase in required reserves based on the initial $1,000 loan is 15 percent, or $150.

Total reserves gained from bank's sale of T-bills to Fed	$1,000
Required reserves for initial $1,000 loan	150
Excess reserves after first loan	$ 850

Now the excess reserve of $850 may be loaned to another customer seeking funds from the bank.

When the borrowed funds are used for purchases, the borrower will write a check that may be deposited in another bank. This movement of excess reserves from one bank to another will not end the expansion process in the system. Whichever bank receives the deposit also acquires an equal amount of reserves, of which all but 15 percent will be excess. In theory, this process can continue through several stages until there are no excess reserves remaining.

The process of deposit expansion is presented in Table 3-4. It is theoretically possible for the commercial banking system to expand the original $1,000 reserve addition into $5,667 in new loans, since banks need to maintain only 15 percent of each deposited dollar in reserves. We can determine the maximum possible expansion in deposits by using the following formula:

$$\text{Maximum deposit expansion} = \frac{\text{Initial reserve infusion}}{\text{Reserve requirement}}. \qquad \textbf{(3-1)}$$

In our example,

$$\text{Maximum deposit expansion} = \frac{\$1,000}{0.15} = \$6,667,$$

which includes $5,667 in new loans and the initial $1,000 deposit.

Realistically, however, two factors prevent banks from reaching the maximum deposit expansion. First, if customers decide to keep some of their newly created demand deposits as cash rather than in the bank, there will be less excess reserves available to lend. Second, the bank may decide, as a matter of

Table 3-4 **Deposit Expansion — Commercial Banking System**

	New Loans	Reserves Required	Reserves Excess	Total Demand Deposit
Initial demand deposit of $1,000		$ 150	$850	$1,000
Expansion stage				
1	$ 850	128	722	1,850
2	722	108	614	2,572
3	614	92	522	3,186
4	522	78	444	3,708
5	444	67	377	4,152
6	377	57	320	4,529
7	320	48	272	4,849
8	272	41	231	5,121
.	.	.	.	.
.	.	.	.	.
.	.	.	.	.
Final expansion stage:	$5,667	$1,000	$ 0	$6,667

policy, to keep some excess reserves in the bank in case of unexpected losses. Either of these factors creates "leakages" that reduce the deposit-expansion potential within the commercial banking system. Of course, the Fed can decrease the money supply by selling Treasury securities and thus reversing the process.

Self-Test

In terms of number of banks, how does the U.S. banking system differ from those of other industrialized nations?

How has the banking system changed during the past decade?

What is the purpose of the Federal Deposit Insurance Corporation (FDIC)?

Briefly explain the difference between demand deposits and certificates of deposit (CDs).

What are the three components of a bank's cash account?

Banks enjoy their status in our financial system, not so much because of the services they provide, but because of two other very important factors. What are these two factors?

If the Fed's reserve requirement were increased from 15 percent to 20 percent in the example given in this section, what would the maximum deposit expansion be on the $1,000 reserve increase?

THE FEDERAL RESERVE SYSTEM

Since commercial banks are at the center of the nation's financial system, a number of regulatory agencies have been developed to control the banking system and its ability to create credit. The primary bank regulators are the Office of the Comptroller of the Currency (OCC), the Federal Reserve, and the Federal Deposit Insurance Corporation (FDIC). As discussed earlier in this chapter, the OCC charters, examines, and if necessary closes nationally chartered banks, while the FDIC insures deposits and examines some state-chartered banks. The most important of the bank regulators is the **Federal Reserve (the Fed).** The Fed is involved in examinations, regulates bank holding company activities, and acts as a last-resort lender to banks, but its chief responsibility is regulating the nation's money supply. The Fed attempts to influence the ability of banks to create credit (and hence to influence the money supply), primarily by increasing or reducing the reserves available to the banking system. Later in the chapter, we will review the three major tools that the Fed uses to exercise control over reserves.

Federal Reserve (Fed)

The central banking system in the United States; the chief regulator of the banking system.

Organization and Structure

The Federal Reserve System is a decentralized central bank. The Federal Reserve Act of 1913 divided the country into 12 Federal Reserve districts. The districts' operations are conducted through a Federal Reserve Bank located in each district. These banks are located in Boston, New York, Philadelphia, Cleveland, Richmond, Atlanta, Chicago, St. Louis, Minneapolis, Kansas City, Dallas, and San Francisco. Branches of the district banks are located in 24 additional cities.

Board of Governors of the Federal Reserve System

Seven member decision-making authority of the Fed.

The real decision-making authority is given to the seven-member **Board of Governors of the Federal Reserve System,** in Washington, D.C. The seven members of the Board are appointed by the president and confirmed by the Senate. Even so, the framers of the Federal Reserve Act wished to keep the Board as free from political influence as possible, so Board members are appointed for terms of fourteen years, and their terms are arranged so that one expires every two years. Thus, it would, theoretically, take a president almost a full two terms to appoint a majority of the Board members. However, circumstances such as resignations or deaths can create a faster turnover on the Board. For example, President Carter appointed five members to the Board in just over three years. Thus, although the Fed has legal independence from the executive and legislative branches of government, great influence is still exerted on the Fed's policies by the political sector of the government.[7]

Another interesting feature of the Federal Reserve System is the organization of its member banks. All national banks are legally required to be members of the system. In addition, approximately 10 percent of all state banks are

---

[7]Even though the Fed's designers attempted to shield it from political influence, it is unlikely that the members of the Board are immune to political pressures.

voluntary members of the Federal Reserve System. One reason that more state banks did not join the system is that the Fed's reserve requirements generally were higher than the state-imposed reserve requirements. The Depository Institutions Deregulation and Monetary Control Act (DIDMCA) of 1980 eliminated many of the differences between national- and state-chartered and between Fed member and nonmember banks. For example, DIDMCA eliminated reserve requirement differences between member and nonmember banks. After an initial phase-in period, the reserve requirements became the same for all depository institutions regardless of membership in the Federal Reserve System. Reserve requirements at the present time range from 0% on nonpersonal time deposits with maturities of 1½ years or more to 12% on demand deposits in very large banks. Also, DIDMCA made the Fed's services available to all depository institutions for a fee, which has allowed development of private competition for many of these services.

Another important element of the Federal Reserve System is the **Federal Open Market Committee (FOMC),** which has responsibility for decisions relating to **open-market operations.** Open-market operations are the purchase and sale of U.S. government securities conducted through the Federal Reserve Bank of New York. As we shall see, open-market operations are the most effective monetary tool available to the Fed, so the FOMC is at the heart of the Fed's power. It consists of twelve members — the seven members of the Board of Governors and representatives from five of the twelve Federal Reserve District Banks. One of these five District Bank representatives is always the president of the Federal Reserve Bank of New York, because this bank is responsible for the transaction of the open-market operations. The other four District Bank memberships rotate among the presidents of the remaining eleven Federal Reserve Districts.

Federal Open Market Committee (FOMC)
Committee of the Federal Reserve System that makes decisions relating to open-market operations.

open-market operations
The purchase and sale of U.S. government securities by the Federal Reserve System.

Tools of Monetary Policy

The Board of Governors of the Federal Reserve System, by affecting reserves in the system, influences the money supply and hence interest rates.[8] The three principal tools of control are (1) changes in the reserve requirements, (2) changes in the discount rate, and (3) open-market operations. Reserve requirements refer to the percentage of each type of deposit that deposit institutions must hold as reserves. Discount policy refers to the terms under which deposit institutions may borrow from the Fed. Open-market operations involve the purchase or sale of U.S. government securities.

Reserve Requirements

The Federal Reserve System requires all depository institutions to hold reserves against their deposits. The amount of **required reserves** is based on the two-week average of checking account deposits ending on the second

required reserves
The minimum reserves that a bank must hold as vault cash or reserve deposits with the Federal Reserve.

---

[8]The interrelationship of reserves, money supply, and interest rates is not a simple one and is open to much debate and controversy. The interested reader should refer to any of the many excellent money and banking or economics texts for further details.

Monday of the period, and banks must settle their reserve requirements the following Wednesday.

The reserve requirement would appear to serve as a powerful, direct tool in the management of banks' reserve positions. In truth, however, the reserve requirement is seldom used. From 1963 until the time the Monetary Control Act was implemented in 1980, reserve requirements on demand deposits were changed only five times, and those on savings deposits were changed only twice. Basically, this reluctance to use reserve requirements for determining monetary policy stems from the fact that it is too powerful an instrument to be used when "fine tuning" the economy. Consider the effect of an increase in reserve requirements in a tight money period. Even a 1 percent increase in the reserve requirements would increase required reserves by hundreds of millions of dollars. Further, just as we noted with the deposit expansion example, when reserves are increased, a decrease in excess reserves reduces demand deposits by a multiple much larger than the original 1 percent decline in reserves, which would force banks to call in outstanding loans. Such a radical decline in money and credit could be damaging to the economic system. Thus, the potential impact of even a modest change in reserve requirements makes it a tool that is used cautiously by the Federal Reserve System.

The Discount Rate

discount rate
The interest rate charged by the Fed for loans of reserves to depository institutions.

The **discount rate** is the rate of interest the Fed charges to depository institutions when they borrow reserves. Institutions may find themselves temporarily short of reserves when there has been a large or unexpected shift in reserves, perhaps due to a large withdrawal, and institutions may also need to borrow from the Fed during times of tight money to relieve temporary reserve imbalances.

It is important to note that the Federal Reserve System views these loans as a temporary mechanism for the adjustment of the specific institution's reserve position, and it discourages the use of these funds for profit making. Moreover, loans from the Fed are viewed as a privilege, not as a right. Thus, the Fed can and does exert pressure on institutions to limit their borrowing. Although the borrowing privilege offers a safety valve to relieve temporary strains on reserves, there are strong incentives to repay loans quickly. For example, if a particular bank shows a borrowing pattern that is characterized by frequent or continuing indebtedness over an extended period, the Fed may press for repayment, even if it means that the bank must call in some loans or liquidate some investments. Therefore, banks are reluctant to use the Fed for other than temporary needs. In fact, some banks, particularly large banks, avoid the Fed altogether even as a source of temporary credit.

When the Federal Reserve System was established in 1913, it was thought that the discount rate would be the principal instrument of monetary control. Such has not been the case, however. As Figure 3-1 shows, the discount rate

Figure 3-1 **The Discount Rate and the Treasury Bill Rate, 1975–1990**

The Federal Reserve System makes loans to banks to correct temporary imbalances in their required reserves, charging a rate of interest known as the discount rate. First envisioned as a major instrument of monetary control, the Fed's discount rate has proven instead to lag behind other short-term rates. This figure, for example, shows how the Treasury bill rate led the discount rate from 1975 to 1990.

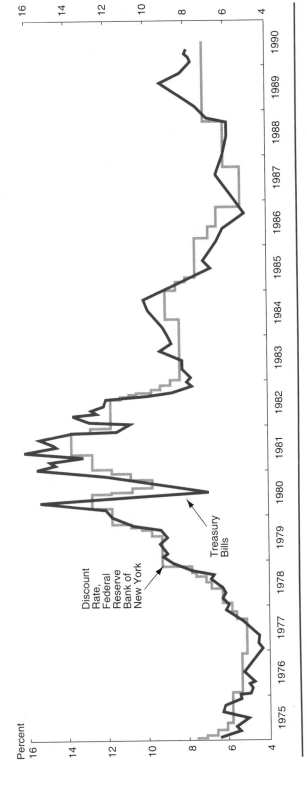

Sources: Economic Indicators, September 1989, 30, and *Federal Reserve Bulletin*.

has lagged behind other short-term rates, such as the Treasury bill rate and the prime rate. For example, the prime rate rose to 10.5 percent in November 1988 and increased to 11.5 percent by February 1989 before the discount rate was increased from 6.5 to 7 percent. The prime rate started falling in June 1989; however, the discount rate remained at 7 percent. Obviously, an effective instrument of monetary policy would lead, not follow, market rates.

Even though the discount rate is not the active tool of monetary policy that the Fed's founders envisioned, announcements of changes in the discount rate have an important psychological effect in the financial community. For example, increases in the discount rate generally signal a movement toward tight money policies. If such an announcement causes financial institutions to become more stringent in loan policies or causes businesses to reconsider expansion plans, then the discount rate, in a roundabout fashion, has done its job.

Open-Market Operations

Although the ability to change reserve requirements and the discount rate is an important element of Federal Reserve monetary policy, the infrequency of change in the reserve requirements and the lagged nature of the discount rate indicate that they are not the Fed's most important tools. *Open-market operations are the most useful instrument of monetary policy available to the Federal Reserve.* Unlike changes in the reserve requirements, which could trigger massive changes in bank reserves, securities may be bought and sold in any quantity to effect slight changes in the economy.

Assume the Federal Open Market Committee (FOMC) has determined that an expansion in the money supply and a lowering of interest rates is desirable to stimulate a depressed economy. The FOMC will direct the Federal Reserve Bank of New York to buy government securities through government securities dealers.[9] The Federal Reserve Bank pays for its purchases with a check drawn on its own account. The securities dealer deposits the check in a bank, which now has an increase in excess reserves. It is important to note that this increase in reserves does not take away from the reserves of any other bank; rather, it comes from new funds that the Fed has created by drawing a check on its own account. This action obtains the desired results in two ways. First, as the Fed purchases securities, demand will exceed supply and the price of securities will rise. The increase in price has the effect of reducing the securi-

---

[9]The Fed does not buy or sell securities directly from individuals or banks. A designated set of government securities dealers actually buys the securities from or sells them to the general public and the banks.

ties' yield.[10] This interest rate effect will spread to other sectors of the financial markets, reducing yields on other interest-bearing securities, including the rates charged for loans. Second, the bank concurrently will wish to lend the excess reserves, which were generated by the government securities dealer's deposit of the Fed's check. To stimulate borrowing, the bank will further lower the interest rate it charges on loans. Thus, the purchase of government securities by the Fed has increased the money supply and put in motion events which will serve to lower interest rates. These lower interest rates and easier credit will encourage additional borrowing and spending, providing benefits to the depressed economy.[11]

During a period of excessive expansion, or inflation, the FOMC will sell securities to reduce bank reserves. Then, as the supply of securities increases relative to demand, the securities' prices will fall, resulting in an increase in interest rates. This is, however, only the first stage in the Fed's attempt to slow economic growth. As the government securities dealers' checks for the purchased securities clear, banks will lose reserves. The effect of reserve deficiencies for individual banks will quickly spread through the banking system. Banks may attempt to replenish reserves by borrowing through the interbank Federal funds market but as the demand for excess reserves increases, the Federal funds rate will increase, and the reserves will become less easily obtained. Banks will be forced to sell securities and reduce their loan portfolios to generate needed reserves. The sale of securities by banks, along with those sold by the Fed, further increases interest rates, since an oversupply relative to demand depresses their prices. Because banks have fewer excess reserves, the availability of credit declines, further increasing interest rates. Thus, the sale of securities by the Fed reduces the ability of banks to lend and also results in higher interest rates, which discourage others from borrowing. The resulting reduction in debt-financed spending has the effect of curbing inflation.

Self-Test

Name the primary bank regulators identified in this section, and briefly explain how each of them "regulates."

What is the Federal Reserve System?

What are the three principal tools used by the Fed to conduct monetary policy? Briefly explain how each of these tools works.

---

[10]The relationship between security prices and rates of return will be discussed in Chapter 16.

[11]The Federal Reserve must take care not to overstimulate the economy through excessive creation of credit, which would lead to expectations of greater inflation.

INDUSTRY PRACTICE

Thrift Crisis: What Happened and Who Is Going to Pay?

Headlines: Thrift Crisis, Two hundred billion dollar bailout, Vernon Savings, Empire Savings, American Savings, Lincoln Savings, FIRREA

What has happened to the savings and loan industry? How could an industry created with such a noble goal — promoting home ownership — turn into such a nightmare? Where did the two hundred billion dollars go? How are we going to pay to clean up the mess?

To understand the current crisis in the S&L industry, we must examine its history. Congress, in an effort to promote affordable housing, passed the Federal Home Loan Bank Act of 1932, the Home Owners Act of 1933, and the National Housing Act of 1934. These Acts created an industry and a regulatory structure similar to that for banks, but specifically designed to provide loans to potential homeowners. The Federal Home Loan Bank System (FHLB) was set up to mimic the functions of the Federal Reserve, while the Federal Savings and Loan Insurance Corporation (FSLIC) insured deposits for the new thrift industry. S&Ls were also given favorable tax and regulatory treatment if they maintained 80 to 85 percent of their assets in mortgage-related investments. For the next 40 years, S&Ls thrived in their specially created market niche.

Unfortunately, the typical S&L portfolio mix represented a "ticking time bomb." To keep their regulatory and tax advantages, S&Ls financed 20- and 30-year fixed-rate mortgages with relatively short-term, interest-rate-sensitive deposits. Such a strategy can be profitable when interest rates remain flat or decline, but it is dangerous when rates rise, as they did in the 1970s and early 1980s. S&Ls' profits declined rapidly, and most of their owners' equity was wiped out. By 1982, many S&Ls had negative net worths.

Congress reacted to the growing crisis by partially deregulating the industry. The Depository Institutions Deregulation and Monetary Control Act of 1980 allowed S&Ls to offer checking accounts, and it expanded the deposit insurance limit to $100,000. However, these new powers did little to improve S&L profitability, and by 1982 the industry was in serious trouble. In the Garn–St. Germain Act that year, Congress changed the nature of the industry by greatly expanding the investment powers of S&Ls. They were suddenly allowed to offer a wide variety of consumer loans, to write some limited commercial loans, to invest in junk bonds, and to offer trust services. Perhaps the most important change, though, was a liberalization of rules regarding direct investment in real estate. Previously, S&Ls simply made loans, but now they were allowed to develop condominium projects, office buildings, housing subdivisions, and shopping centers through their service company subsidiaries. These new powers brought in a new breed of S&L owner.

Real estate developers saw S&L ownership as a gold mine — they could raise money through insured deposits and then use those funds to finance risky real estate projects. While thrifts did lose money on legal investments, many other losses were generated through fraudulent activities because those activities were not detected by inexperienced accountants and examiners.

These problems pointed out a fatal flaw in the nation's deposit insurance system, a flaw particularly exploited by the owners of Vernon, Empire, American, and Lincoln Savings. Under the deposit insurance system, accounts up to $100,000 are guaranteed, while those above $100,000 are not. However, in most failures, larger depositors recover most if not all of their funds. Depositors, consequently, tend to pay little attention to the management or financial condition of their institutions. Instead, they simply evaluate a thrift on the basis of its interest rates, convenience, and services offered, not on its financial strength. Therefore, an S&L could grow rapidly by simply offering the highest interest rates. Money brokers could then send millions into high-rate CD accounts. Hundreds of banks and S&Ls grew 20 to 40 percent a year by using brokered deposits. Without depositor discipline, S&L managers and owners could play a game of "heads we win, tails you lose." If high-risk real estate and junk bond investments pay off, the thrift managers and owners reap the benefits. If not, the thrift fails and deposit insurance pays the losses. Unfortunately for U.S. taxpayers, the latter situation occurred for hundreds of S&Ls. Many have been closed, and estimates are that an additional 800 to 1,000 cannot meet current capital requirements and should be closed.

As a result, Congress ordered a complete reorganization of the thrift industry in the Financial Institutions Reform, Recovery, and Enforcement Act (FIRREA) of 1989. The Federal Home Loan Bank Board has been replaced by the Office of Thrift Supervision, a new division of the Treasury. FSLIC has been replaced by the Savings Association Insurance Fund (SAIF), which is run by the FDIC. Congress also created the Resolution Trust Corporation (RTC) to sell foreclosed property, and the Resolution Financing Corporation (RFC) to raise the billions of dollars needed to pay off the depositors in failed thrifts. Deposit insurance premiums charged to banks and thrifts were increased, but the bulk of the bailout cost — perhaps as much as $500 billion — will be borne by the taxpayers.

So, we go back to our original questions. (1) What happened? Savings and loans have lost hundreds of billions of dollars; no one knows exactly how much. Hundreds of S&Ls have been closed, and hundreds more will be closed.

(2) How did this happen? Savings and loans were designed in the 1930s, in a calmer economic climate. The industry had a fatal structural defect that made it unable to survive the volatile economic conditions of the past two decades — it financed long-term assets with short-term deposits. Also, deregulation occurred at the wrong time, without a corresponding change in the deposit insurance system and without adequate controls and audits. The new thrift owners and managers were able to gamble on risky real estate deals, and many lost.

(3) What happened to the money? It did not just disappear, but it has been filtered into the economy. The media focuses on fraud, and it is true that millions were lost to fraud. However, fraudulent managers and owners did not spend or lose billions. Some of the money went to finance unnecessary construction projects, and, consequently, was paid to contractors and employees. Much of the money went to mortgage customers, who got cheap credit, and to depositors, who got high interest rates.

(4) How are we going to pay for this crisis? The money the thrift industry lost was distributed widely throughout the economy. Many of us benefited indirectly from the losses, and we are all being asked to pay for them, either directly or indirectly. Taxes will be higher than they otherwise would be. Mortgage loans will be tougher to get, and will be more expensive. Rates on deposits have already fallen, and they will fall farther as banks and thrifts pass along the increase in deposit insurance premiums. Real estate prices will drop as foreclosed properties are sold into already saturated markets. Finally, the billions of dollars that must be raised by the RFC might otherwise have been used by private companies to support economic growth. All this brings to mind some well-known advice: When you hear someone say, "I've come from Washington and I'm here to help you," run!

THE SAVINGS AND LOAN (OR THRIFT) CRISIS

Savings and loan associations, along with mutual savings banks, are known as "thrift institutions," or "thrifts." Our thrifts were modeled after England's building societies, which accepted savings from members and then made mortgage loans to help people in the community buy houses. Today, thrifts have no unique economic role (1) because of the growth of mortgage-backed securities, through which institutional investors pump money into the home loan market and (2) because other lenders are making loans directly to consumers. Despite federal subsidies, many thrifts don't make profits, and deregulation, which has forced them to diversify, has moved the thrifts farther away from their original design.

Thrifts have been in trouble for the past decade. Greed, political disputes, and extremely volatile interest rates caused major problems in the industry. In 1980, to assist the thrifts, the government lifted interest limits on deposits, but loan interest rates didn't keep up with deposit rates. In 1981, thrifts were paying depositors 11 percent, while receiving only 10 percent on their investments (30-year, fixed-rate mortgage loans). In 1981, the Federal Home Loan Bank Board (FHLBB) allowed savings and loans to offer variable-rate mortgages, which would permit their revenues to rise with their deposit rates. Then, in 1982, Congress allowed these institutions to take on nontraditional thrift investment activities like business loans and the ownership of real estate projects. Yet, by that time, 75 percent of the industry was already deeply unprofitable.

Weak thrifts advertised high interest rates to obtain cash for risky, high-interest-yielding assets. These high interest rates raised the entire industry's cost of funds. With this newly acquired cash, some savings and loans took on unfamiliar investments and loans. The institutions' deposit insurance contributed greatly to the problem — it added to the reckless way money left some of these institutions. (If the investment was bad, the government insured the depositor's money for up to $100,000.) In addition, the thrifts used their political clout to appear solvent by convincing regulators and Congress to allow accounting ploys that, in fact, hid their truly negative net worths.

In the mid-1980s, the FHLBB tried to stop these abuses, but found itself stopped by the administration and the Congress, and by the thrift industry itself. The administration and the Congress, emphasizing deregulation, denied the FHLBB money for more examiners. The thrift industry used its connections in Congress to thwart any corrections of abuses. When, in 1986, the institutions' insurance fund, the FSLIC, ran out of money, Congress did approve some aid, but it was a case of too little, too late.

Proposed Reforms

The FHLBB has tried some reforms, such as higher capital requirements, and the FSLIC has committed billions of dollars to rescuing institutions. Troubled thrifts have been turned over to developers and other nonbankers to attract investors. But these "ailing" thrifts are draining the remaining "healthy" thrifts. Special assessments have been placed on profitable thrifts for extra insurance premiums. As "ailing" thrifts pay higher yields to attract depositors, the price that savings and loans and commercial banks must pay for funds goes up.

The bailout needed for these institutions will eventually show up in the deficit and will add to pressures for an increase in taxes. In the short run, Congress will probably spread the cost among savings and loans, banks, and taxpayers.

Many experts believe the thrifts are beyond hope. In fact, every industry reform attempted over the past decade has been unsuccessful. It may ultimately be necessary to dismantle the industry. One scenario might be for healthy thrifts to buy out of the SAIF with a withdrawal fee and then either receive a bank charter and FDIC insurance or merge with existing commercial banks. Either of these actions might cause the industry to face higher capital requirements and tougher supervision. The remaining part of the industry could be liquidated, and the SAIF could use these proceeds to pay part of the cost of shutting down the insolvent thrifts. Unfortunately, the remaining cost would have to be borne by the taxpayers.

Another possible scenario is for the thrift industry not to be eliminated as a separate entity, but for its retail banking aspects to emerge as a distinct industry. These new retail financial institutions would lend to retail customers and take deposits from average citizens and small businesses — something that the thrifts are as well prepared to do as banks. The thrifts could also find profitable niches in housing, consumer, student, and small-business lending. Whatever the outcome, it is clear that this type of institution, as it exists today, will have to change in order to survive our changing economy.

Self-Test

How did deposit insurance contribute to the thrift crisis?

What was wrong with using demand deposits to invest in 30-year, fixed rate mortgages?

What alternatives exist for the industry to solve its financial problems?

THE CHANGING ECONOMIC ENVIRONMENT OF OUR FINANCIAL INSTITUTIONS

In recent years questions have surfaced about the long-term strength of the U.S. financial system. The October 1987 stock market crash led to the demise of a number of old, established investment banking concerns such as E.F. Hutton and to the loss of thousands of jobs on Wall Street and throughout the nation. Commercial banks have had to take large losses on loans to developing countries, on energy-related projects, and on real estate developments. The

S&Ls — and U.S. taxpayers — have incurred horrible losses, and the end is no-where in sight. "Crisis" and "chaos" are strong words, but they are not too strong to describe the state of many segments of our financial markets.

Reasons for the Changing Environment

It is difficult to pinpoint the reasons for all the chaos in our financial institutions system. Some analysts blame bankers for being overly ambitious in lending money to real estate developers, to "takeover artists" and to expansion-minded corporations. Some blame the soft lending controls that were characteristic of the banking industry during the 1980s. Others blame the Congress, and our huge budget and trade deficits for the problems, while still others blame regulators for letting things get out of control. All of these factors probably contributed to the turmoil, and the banking industry is now looking for a solution.

The banking industry has experienced increased competition from other financial institutions worldwide, increasing bad debts in the United States and abroad, new ways of financing based on capital markets, higher deposit insurance premiums, tougher regulation and supervision, and the prospect of more stringent capital adequacy regulations. Because of these conditions, hundreds of banks have been merged or closed; huge cutbacks in staffing have occurred; funds have been raised through low-rated bonds; and so on. There is a growing consensus that the system no longer needs 14,000 banks, and commercial banks are restructuring themselves before they become victims of unwanted takeovers.

The Outcome for Commercial Banks

In order to survive, the U.S. commercial banking system must change. Over the next few years, the following types of banks are expected to emerge: *niche banks* — specialists in a single product or market segment; *regional banks* — dominating the middle market in their part of the country; *super-regionals* — involved in the consumer and middle markets in several states and offering some services on a national scale; and *global banks* — offering full service banking to virtually everyone, everywhere.

Another development may be further deregulation of the banking industry; for example, repealing the separation of commercial and investment banking activities. This would allow for the development of financial services and products. Over the past few years, banks have been given the power to move into certain areas of the investment banking business. For example, banks can now, through subsidiaries, act as underwriters and traders in commercial paper, municipal bonds, and asset-backed securities markets. These expanded powers are needed if U.S. banks are to compete effectively with the large Japanese and European banks, but the problems the banks and S&Ls have had make Congress and regulators reluctant to expand banks' powers to offer new types of service.

Self-Test

Identify some of the factors that have contributed to the changing environment of our financial institutions.

It is difficult to pinpoint one reason for the chaos in the financial institutions system; however, give some of the reasons mentioned in this chapter.

What changes are expected to occur in the commercial banking industry?

THE IMPACT OF GLOBALIZATION ON OUR FINANCIAL INSTITUTIONS

Capital markets are becoming integrated into a global capital market. As a result, we are seeing *universal (global) banks* competing directly with *specialist banks.* **Universal (global) banks** combine in offering both commercial and investment banking services to their customers, while **specialist banks** act only as investment banks, concentrating on the origination, distribution, and trading of securities. An important question in the development of a global capital market is how successful universal banks will be relative to specialized investment banks, and whether they will dominate the capital markets. True universal banks exist only in Germany and Switzerland, while an example of a specialist bank would be the U.S. investment banking houses.

> **universal (global) banks**
> Banks that offer both commercial and investment banking services to their customers.
>
> **specialist banks**
> Banks that act only as investment banks, concentrating on the organization, distribution, and trading of securities.

The success of the universal banks will depend on their advantages and disadvantages when compared to specialist banks. The universal banks' advantages include these: (1) They can cross-sell a wider range of products, which will reduce initial marketing costs and the costs of developing and maintaining customer relationships. (2) They can cross-subsidize. This means that they can offer products in highly competitive fields at a lower cost than specialist banks and can subsidize them through higher profit margins on products in less-competitive fields. Conceivably, they could use cross subsidies to eliminate competition, then raise prices. (3) They can offer the customer the full range of products he or she may require, thus encouraging customer loyalty. (4) They have greater opportunities for smoothing income fluctuations in different areas of their business.

Their disadvantages include the following: (1) They face various conflicts of interest in different areas of their business. (2) The quality of service they offer may sometimes be lower than that offered by specialist banks. (3) Coordination becomes more difficult, and reaction time longer, the larger and more complex the organization.

The advantages appear to outweigh the disadvantages, because there is a clear trend towards universal banking throughout the world. This trend has been fueled by the commercial banks rather than by the investment banks. In the United States, development of universal banks is still constrained by the Glass Steagall Act of 1933, the Bank Holding Act of 1956, and the International Banking Act of 1978, which still enforce the strict separation of commercial and investment banking. None of this legislation has been repealed, but, as mentioned earlier, commercial banks have recently been empowered to underwrite and distribute commercial paper, municipal bonds, and mortgage-backed securities. Such activities represent a trend toward a universal banking system in the United States.

Self-Test

Differentiate between universal banks and specialist banks.

Identify the advantages and disadvantages of a universal bank.

Is there a clear trend towards universal banking throughout the world? Explain.

 SMALL BUSINESS

Building a Banking Relationship

Building a good banking relationship is important for a small business for two reasons. The most obvious reason is that the banker may lend the business money for working capital, expansion, equipment, and so on, which will allow the firm to grow. A less obvious reason is that the banker may be a valuable source of financial advice for an inexperienced small-business owner. Once the bank has loaned the business money, it is in both the bank's and the business's best interest for the company to survive. Thus, a good banker will take a genuine interest in the firm and will care about how it is doing.

Even though the bank is interested in the firm's survival, it is likely to be more risk averse than the business, because the bank shares in the firm's negative risk but not in its positive potential. If the firm fails, the entrepreneur and the bank both lose their investment. If things go well, the banker gets back only the loan money plus the interest, but the entrepreneur has the potential for huge profits. The entrepreneur, therefore, may be willing to take greater risks in the hopes of great rewards, whereas the banker will want to avoid risks.

There is a possibility, then, of a conflict of interest between the banker and the entrepreneur. Because of that potential conflict, the bank will often impose restrictions on how the firm can use its revenues or profits, on how much the firm can pay the entrepreneur in salary, and on other such matters. The bank probably will require some or all of the business's assets as collateral to safeguard the loan. The banker will be concerned about and be watchful for the one thing the entrepreneur most wants to avoid — the failure of the business. To that end, the banker will follow the firm's financial progress very closely, and that watchful eye can be of great benefit to the entrepreneur.

The 1980s saw major changes in the nature of the financial services business. As a result of innovations in financial services and of competition, a growing business today can expect to find a wider array of options than in the past. For the most part, the stereotypical image of the banker — overweight, cigar-smoking, grumpy, and stuck behind a desk — is dead. Today's bankers are viewed as aggressive, bright, involved, and probably belonging to a health club! A small business today should be able to find a knowledgeable banker who will get involved in the business and who can offer valuable advice. But, as when buying a car, always seek out more than one offer. Exert a significant effort toward finding the *right* banker.

Finding the Right Banker

Often the small business owner may not know how to go about finding the right banker. Looking for funds, he or she might go to the nearest bank and ask for money to fund an idea or proposal. If the bank is largely a retail bank with little expertise in commercial accounts, one of two negative events may occur:

1. The banker may turn down the loan, failing to see that the proposal is, in fact, a good one; or

2. The banker may make a loan that should not have been made. Then, if the project cannot return the funds, the entrepreneur might end up with worse credit than before the loan was made.

Both of these events are avoidable.

The right banker should satisfy at least three conditions: (1) The banker should understand the entrepreneur's business. (2) The banker should be interested in the business, and commit to follow it closely. (3) The banker should be experienced and understand the pitfalls that wipe out small firms. In addition, the bank itself should be adequately capitalized to offer funds at the level the business needs, and it should also provide other services (such as cash management) that the business may need.

The banker and entrepreneur must have rapport. If they can't communicate candidly and easily with each other, things may go wrong that might have been avoided.

The Approach

The first meeting between the banker and the entrepreneur should not involve a detailed discussion of the firm's financial statements. Rather, it should be a "get-acquainted" session in which the banker learns about the business and the entrepreneur learns about the bank and banker. At that first meeting, the entrepreneur should leave the business's historical financial statements with the banker for review.

By not immediately delving into problems and projections, the two parties will have an opportunity to become acquainted without pressure. Also, at such a meeting, the entrepreneur has the chance to convey the impression that he or she is in control of the business, rather than appearing excessively anxious to resolve some financial crisis.

The second meeting (if there is one) should begin with a discussion of the historical financial statements, which should then be followed by a presentation of projections. Together, the banker and entrepreneur should discuss the business's financing needs. If the banker is effective, he or she will have some suggestions for improving the projections, or perhaps he or she will anticipate some potential problems.

What the Banker Evaluates

Bankers are trained to use the following "five Cs" when evaluating a loan proposal:

- Character
- Capacity (to manage)
- Cash flow
- Collateral
- Conditions

The *character* factor considers whether the entrepreneur is a person who takes obligations seriously, is honest, and is straightforward. The second management factor, *capacity,* questions whether this manager can handle the business.

The next three Cs deal with financial issues. The banker first will ask, "Can the firm generate the cash flow to repay this loan, or, if it is a revolving line of credit, can it generate the cash flow to service the debt and keep it current?" Many loans are made to finance specific assets, such as equipment or receivables, and those are matched against collateral. Is the bank protected by the value of the collateral? Finally, many loans that are perfectly viable under one set of economic conditions may become bad debts under others. In the Oil Belt, for example, bankers have been reluctant to lend funds against oil revenues because such revenues have been especially unpredictable.

Tips from a Credit Department Manager

The credit department manager of a large commercial bank was interviewed to obtain his point of view about establishing a banking relationship with a small business. He summarized the points he teaches new officers to consider when reviewing a proposal to grant credit.

First, he tells officers to simply ask, "Why do you need the money?" He wants to know not only how the funds will be used, but also why the company cannot generate funds itself. This is not to imply that the bank is taking the arrogant view that "We only lend money to people who don't need it." Rather, the credit manager wants to be sure that the entrepreneur understands the business well enough to know the answers.

Next, the manager tells loan officers to carefully investigate how the loan will be repaid. If the funds will come from operating cash flows, how realistic are the projections? If it is a seasonal working capital loan, what is the company's track record for managing inventory and receivables? If the business is not seasonal, is the firm sufficiently profitable to meet payments on the debt from operating profits?

The manager realizes that some working capital in a growing business is essentially permanent. The next concern is whether management is truly in control of the business, and whether the financing can be supported by assets.

The final question the credit manager asks, which is the most important of all, is: "What are your biggest problems?" The loan officer should explain that he or she isn't looking for firms that have no problems, because every firm has problems. What the banker is really trying to find out is whether the entrepreneur is

1. perceptive, and in control of the business, and

2. frank and candid, and willing to talk honestly about the business's problems.

The department head explained that a good small-business owner/manager will perceive problems. If the entrepreneur isn't aware of them, they can lead to business failure. If they are recognized, the problems perhaps can be solved. It is especially important that the entrepreneur understand cash flows.

Frankness is the key to success. The business owner's willingness to share concerns is viewed by the manager as the bank's greatest protection against "surprises."

Conclusion

For a small business, a good banking relationship can mean the difference between success and failure. Establishing that relationship is important. Both sides are better off if the relationship can be an open one, where the banker and business owner understand each other and communicate honestly when dealing with the various problems of the small, but growing, firm.

SUMMARY

This chapter contained a discussion of (1) the major U.S. financial institutions, (2) the largest of all financial intermediaries—the commercial banking industry, (3) the organization of the Federal Reserve System, (4) the tools the Fed uses to conduct monetary policy, (5) the savings and loan industry and the crisis it faces, and (6) the changing economic environment of our financial institutions. The key concepts covered are listed below.

- The **U.S. banking system** is quite different from those of other industrialized countries in (1) the number of banks and (2) the dual chartering (state and federal government) system.

- The banking system has changed dramatically during the past decade. During the 1980s many banks became virtual **financial supermarkets,** offering savings certificates, IRAs and other retirement plans, trusts, leasing departments, discount brokerage services, and insurance products.

- The primary source of funds for a bank is its deposits. Deposits are either **demand, savings, or time deposits. Demand deposits** are deposits made by individuals, businesses, and government units that are available on demand, usually through checks. **Savings** (passbook) **accounts** generally pay near-market interest rates and offer limited transactions services. **Time deposits** (or **CDs**) offer higher rates but do not allow transactions.

- The **Federal Deposit Insurance Corporation (FDIC)** protects depositors in insured banks from the effects of a bank failure.

- The primary source of borrowed funds for banks is the **Federal funds market.** In this market, banks borrow for short periods of time from other banks at the **Fed funds rate.**

- Before deposit insurance was implemented, **bank capital,** which is total assets minus deposits, protected depositors from bank losses. Today, a bank's capital cushions the deposit insurance fund and unsecured creditors from losses.

- The **cash account** represents only 8 percent of a bank's total assets. The three components of the cash account are vault cash, "items in process of collection," and funds that are required by law to be kept on deposit at the district Federal Reserve Bank.

- The primary business of banks is to **lend money in support of economic growth in their area.** Loans also provide banks with a relatively high expected rate of return. If there is not enough demand for loans or if the quality of available loans is low, however, banks turn to marketable securities as a source of revenue.

- Banks enjoy their current status in our financial system not only because of the services they provide but also because (1) **banks can create demand deposits** (money) through the extension of credit in the form of loans and (2) **the Federal Reserve System works through the banking system to affect the money supply and interest rates.**

- The primary bank regulators are the **Office of the Comptroller of the Currency (OCC),** the **Federal Reserve,** and the **Federal Deposit Insurance Corporation (FDIC).**

- The **Federal Reserve** has examination responsibilities, it regulates bank holding company activities, and it acts as a last-resort lender to banks, but its chief responsibility is regulating the nation's money supply.

- The Fed's principal tools for influencing monetary policy are (1) **reserve requirements,** (2) the **discount rate,** and (3) **open-market operations.**

- Reasons given for the chaos in our financial institutions are: (1) **overly ambitious lending** to real estate developers and expansion-minded corporations, (2) **soft lending and trading controls** in the banking industry during the 1980s, (3) **regulators' overlooking the problems,** and (4) the **huge budget deficits** and **balance-of-payments shortfalls.**

- **Thrifts** were originally designed after England's building societies, to accept savings from members and then make mortgage loans to help people in the community buy houses. Today, they are left without a unique economic role, and because of deregulation they have gotten farther away from their original purpose.

- Greed, political disputes, and extremely volatile interest rates have weakened the savings and loan industry. Attempts to help the industry — the **lifting of deposit interest limits, letting it offer variable-rate mortgages,** and **allowing the industry to invest in business loans and real estate** — have failed to restore the industry to health.

- In order to survive, the U.S. commercial banking system must change. Over the next few years, the following types of banks are expected to emerge: **niche banks, regional banks, super-regionals,** and **global banks.**

- National capital markets are becoming more integrated to form a global market, and as a result, **universal (global) banks** are competing directly with **specialist (investment) banks.**

- The universal bank's **advantages** are (1) cross-selling a wider range of products, (2) cross-subsidizing products in more competitive fields with profits earned on products in less competitive fields, (3) offering customers a full range of products, and (4) being able to smooth income fluctuations in different areas of the business.

- The universal bank's **disadvantages** are (1) conflicts of interest in different areas of its business, (2) the fact that the quality of service offered at times may be lower than that of specialist banks, and (3) the difficulty of controlling and coordinating many different activities. The advantages seem to outweigh the disadvantages, as universal banks are growing rapidly.

- Building a good banking relationship is important for a small business because (1) it enables the firm to grow with the aid of bank loans, and (2) the bank can be a valuable source of financial advice.

EQUATIONS

Equation 3-1 shows the calculation for the maximum possible expansion in deposits, given the initial reserve infusion and the reserve requirement.

$$\text{Maximum deposit expansion} = \frac{\text{Initial reserve infusion}}{\text{Reserve requirement}}. \qquad (3\text{-}1)$$

 RESOLUTION TO DECISION IN FINANCE

Commercial Banks: The New Competitor in the Investment Banking Industry

Before the changing regulatory climate permitted Bankers Trust to engage in its new ventures, it had long been known as a savvy lender for leveraged buyouts. To expand into merchant banking, CEO Charles S. Sanford, Jr., and his predecessor, Alfred Brittain, moved the company from the tightly controlled, risk-fearing stance of a commercial bank to the more risky area of investment banking. The shift required that Bankers Trust strip away layers of management and titles, pay bigger bonuses, and recruit staff from Wall Street. In fact, most of Bankers Trust's successes came after mathematician Gerald Rosenfeld was hired from Wall Street to lead the merchant banking venture in the United States. One of his mandates was to build Bankers Trust's portfolio of equity investments to a value of more than $1 billion.

Poor credit decisions have been the downfall for other companies in this field. To insure that sound credit standards are not undermined by overly eager merchant bankers, Bankers Trust officials rely on their conservative, old-line chief credit officer, and on their equally conservative credit policy manager. So far the two have maintained high standards, despite complaints from some merchant bankers that "the credit guys" are turning down too many deals.

The atmosphere at one point was becoming too chaotic; executives were planning a takeover defense for one client only to find that one of their bank colleagues was on the other side. Now such conflicts are avoided, because all proposed client assignments must be entered in a log that is reviewed by senior executives.

The degree to which Sanford supports his credit staff's decisions will be crucial to Bankers Trust's merchant banking strategy, but confidence, in general, is high. The firm's head of corporate finance admits that Bankers Trust's strategy could backfire, but he doesn't think it will. "We've taken every conceivable precaution," he says. "What distinguishes Bankers Trust, we believe, is our rigorous intellectual honesty. We don't kid ourselves."

Most outside analysts agree that Bankers Trust is pursuing the correct strategy. For example, Raphael Soifer of Brown Brothers, Harriman & Co., who long has recommended Bankers Trust shares, says, "They're at the head of the pack among banks making use of securities powers. They're taking some lumps right now, but in the long run it will pay off."

Source: "Bankers Trust Leads Way for Major Banks in Investment Banking," *The Wall Street Journal,* December 5, 1989.

QUESTIONS

3-1 What are the three principal tools that the Federal Reserve System uses in affecting the nation's money supply?

3-2 When the Fed buys government securities, is it attempting to increase or decrease the money supply?

3-3 Why is the Fed reluctant to use the reserve requirement as an active tool in monetary policy?

3-4 From the standpoint of a commercial bank's balance sheet, evaluate the following statement: "One financial unit's asset is another's liability."

3-5 If the primary goal of the financial manager is to maximize shareholder wealth, what is the bank manager's primary goal?

3-6 Why do banks attempt to minimize their investments in excess reserves?

3-7 What are the characteristics of securities that banks would obtain for their investment portfolios?

3-8 Why have banks, among financial institutions, historically been the major suppliers of short-term funds to borrowers?

3-9 What is the importance of the Depository Institutions Deregulation and Monetary Control Act of 1980? (Note: This question may require investigation of sources outside this text.)

SELF-TEST PROBLEM

ST-1 What is the potential increase (decrease) in demand deposits if
  a. The Fed buys $5 million in government securities and the reserve requirement is 10 percent?
  b. The Fed sells $8 million in government securities and the reserve requirement is 12.5 percent?

PROBLEMS

3-1 **Open-market operations.** The Fed buys $9 million in government securities.
  a. Will the money supply expand or contract?
  b. If the reserve requirement is 12 percent, what is the potential increase (decrease) in demand deposits?

3-2 **Open-market operations.** The Fed sells $6 million in government securities.
  a. Will the money supply expand or contract?
  b. If the reserve requirement is 10 percent, what is the potential increase (decrease) in demand deposits?

3-3 **Comparative financial statements.** Obtain the financial statement of a local bank. Compare the bank's balance sheet with that of a manufacturer (or see Carter Chemical Company's balance sheet in Chapter 5). What major differences are apparent?

SOLUTION TO SELF-TEST PROBLEM

ST-1 **a.** Demand deposits would expand by $5,000,000/0.1 = $50,000,000.
  b. Demand deposits would decrease by $8,000,000/0.125 = $64,000,000.

Chapter 4

Interest Rates

DECISION IN FINANCE

A New Chairman for the Fed

When Paul A. Volcker reached into his pocket on June 1, 1987, and pulled out a tightly worded letter of resignation addressed to President Reagan, he ended an eight-year reign as chairman of the Federal Reserve Board. Although his decision to step down was certainly based on numerous factors, many Fed watchers believed that mounting opposition from Reagan-appointed members of the Federal Reserve Board of Governors prompted Volcker to refuse a third term of office. The five other members were fiercely independent and were not shy about voicing their economic views, which were often in opposition to the chairman's. The Board, dominated by pro-growth supply-siders, saw less inflationary threat from robust growth in the money supply than Mr. Volcker. But, having achieved his heroic stature at the Fed as an inflation fighter, Volcker was careful not to step down until he could be certain that his successor would carry on his highly effective crusade against inflation. When he and the President met to discuss possible candidates for the chair-

manship, economist Alan Greenspan's name was at the top of both their lists.

A conservative, chronically gloomy forecaster with a reputation for always putting the most pessimistic interpretation on any data, Greenspan was a rabid anti-inflationist. Not nearly as flamboyant as the 6'7", cigar-chomping Volcker, Greenspan took office in the fall of 1987, expecting to enjoy a long and quiet honeymoon period. But Greenspan was quickly put to the test. On October 19, or "black Monday" as it was quickly dubbed, the stock market plummeted a record 508 points in a single, nearly catastrophic day of trading.

As you read this chapter, think about the kinds of decisions that Alan Greenspan and the Fed's Board of Governors routinely must make. How do the Fed policies affect the country's economy, particularly interest rates? What might be the effects of a change in leadership at the Fed for American corporations, specifically as it relates to interest rates on corporate debt? What actions might the Federal Reserve Board take in the wake of a new financial crisis like "black Monday"?

See end of chapter for resolution.

117

interest rate
The price paid by borrowers to lenders for the use of funds.

Capital in a free economy is allocated through the price system. In the case of debt, the **interest rate** is the price paid to borrow capital from investors, whereas in the case of equity capital, investors' returns come in the form of dividends and capital gains. The factors which affect the supply of and demand for investment capital, and hence the cost of funds, are discussed in this chapter.

THE COST OF FUNDS

production opportunities
The returns available within an economy from investment in productive investments.

time preferences for consumption
The preferences of consumers for current consumption as opposed to saving for future consumption.

risk
In a money market context, the chance that a loan will not be repaid as promised.

inflation
The tendency of prices to increase over time.

The four most fundamental factors affecting the cost of funds are (1) **production opportunities,** (2) **time preferences for consumption,** (3) **risk,** and (4) **inflation.** To see how these factors operate, visualize an isolated island community where the people live on fish. They have a stock of fishing gear that permits them to survive reasonably well, but they would like to have more fish. Now suppose Mr. Crusoe had a bright idea for a new type of fishnet that would enable him to double his daily catch. However, it would take him a year to perfect his design, to build his net, and to learn how to use it efficiently, and Mr. Crusoe would probably starve before he could put his new net into operation. Therefore, he might suggest to Ms. Robinson, Mr. Friday, and several others that if they would give him one fish each day for a year, he would return two fish a day during all of the next year. If someone accepted the offer, then the fish which Ms. Robinson or one of the others gave to Mr. Crusoe would constitute *savings;* these savings would be *invested* in the fishnet; and the extra fish the net produced would constitute a *return on the investment.*

Obviously, the more productive Mr. Crusoe thought the new fishnet would be, the higher his expected return on the investment would be, and the more he could offer to pay Ms. Robinson, Mr. Friday, or other potential investors for their savings. In this example we assume that Mr. Crusoe thought he would be able to pay, and thus he offered, a 100 percent rate of return — he offered to give back two fish for every one he received. He might have tried to attract savings for less; for example, he might have decided to offer only 1.5 fish next year for every one he received this year, which would represent a 50 percent rate of return to Ms. Robinson and the other potential savers.

How attractive Mr. Crusoe's offer would appear to potential savers would depend in large part on their time preferences for consumption. For example, Ms. Robinson might be thinking of retirement, and she might be willing to trade fish today for fish in the future on a one-for-one basis. On the other hand, Mr. Friday might have a wife and several young children and need his current fish, so he might be unwilling to "lend" a fish today for anything less than three fish next year. Mr. Friday would be said to have a high time preference for consumption and Ms. Robinson a low time preference. Note also that if the entire population were living right at the subsistence level, time preferences for current consumption would necessarily be high, aggregate savings would be low, interest rates would be high, and capital formation would be difficult.

The risk inherent in the fishnet project, and thus in Mr. Crusoe's ability to repay the loan, would also affect the return investors would require: The higher the perceived risk, the higher the required rate of return. Also, in a more complex society there are many businesses like Mr. Crusoe's, many goods other than fish, and many savers like Ms. Robinson and Mr. Friday. Further, people use money as a medium of exchange rather than barter with fish. When money is used, rather than fish, its value in the future, which is affected by inflation, comes into play: The higher the expected rate of inflation, the larger the required return.

Thus, we see that the interest rate paid to savers depends in a basic way (1) on the rate of return producers expect to earn on invested capital, (2) on consumers'/savers' time preferences for current versus future consumption, (3) on the riskiness of the loan, and (4) on the expected rate of inflation. Producers' expected returns on their business investments set an upper limit on how much they can pay for savings, while consumers' time preferences for consumption establish how much consumption they are willing to defer and hence how much they will save at different rates of interest offered by producers.[1] Higher risk and higher inflation also lead to higher interest rates.

Self-Test

What is the price paid to borrow capital called?

What is the "price" of equity capital?

What four fundamental factors affect the cost of funds?

INTEREST RATES

As we discuss in Chapter 19, the firm's cost of capital is determined by the rate of return required by its debt and equity investors. That return is dependent, in part, on factors specific to the firm itself: its financing, product innovation, competition, and management skills, to name a few. However, the firm's cost of capital is not determined just by factors that apply exclusively to the firm; cost considerations are broader, and they include the general level of interest rates in the economy. The basis for interest rates in the economy is shaped by market forces — the supply of and demand for funds, risks such as inflation, and investor expectations about the future. The way in which various economic forces combine to determine market interest rates is analyzed in the following sections.

---

[1]The term *producers* is really too narrow. As we discussed earlier in Chapter 2, a better word might be *"borrowers,"* which would include corporations, home purchasers, people borrowing to go to college, or even people borrowing to buy autos or to pay for vacations. Also, the wealth of a society influences its people's ability to save and hence their time preferences for current versus future consumption.

INDUSTRY PRACTICE

When the World Speaks . . . the Fed Listens

When the economy slumps, as it did in early 1990, there has always been a fail-safe way to boost it back up — lower interest rates. But the traditional remedy is not automatically available anymore, and this is quite a change from the past. Then, when the Fed "spoke," the world "listened." Today, the Fed must listen to the world . . . especially to Germany and Japan.

As the world's largest debtor nation, the United States needs all the foreign funds it can get. If our interest rates start to decline, international investors will begin to pull their funds out, or, at the very least, will stop putting funds in. One major Japanese portfolio manager started cutting back on U.S. investments in his $3 billion fund in late 1989, when Japanese rates began to look better than U.S. rates. As the supply of funds to U.S. investors is cut back, U.S. interest rates can go only one way — up.

In early 1990, interest rates in Germany rose above U.S. rates, and Japanese rates reached a six-year high at about the same time. When the Treasury held a $5 billion bond auction for the savings and loan bailout funding agency, the Resolution Funding Corporation, reaction from both U.S. and foreign investors was cool, even though the Treasury and the Fed had both thought demand for the rare 40-year issue would be strong. After that, fears were widespread that foreign investors would not participate in a later $30 billion auction of Treasury bonds, which would push U.S. rates dramatically higher. As one financial analyst said, "If the Japanese suddenly cut back and buy only 10% instead of 40%" of an issue, "somebody else has to buy that 30%, and that buyer, more than

likely, is going to be looking for more of a concession (a higher rate)."

As it turned out, all U.S. auctions thus far in the 1990s have been successful, but there is anxiety among U.S. traders and investors every time the Treasury must go to the market. Foreign investors now hold nearly $400 billion of U.S. government debt, compared to less than half that amount just five years ago, and if they begin selling, or even become reluctant to add to their holdings, rates could skyrocket.

Interest rates are tied to inflation, and worries about inflation may force the Fed to keep money tight and short-term interest rates up. Even if the Fed wanted to lower rates, the situations in Frankfurt and Tokyo could make it difficult, if not impossible. In late December of 1989 the six Federal Reserve Board governors and the twelve regional Fed bank presidents met to consider the direction interest rates should take. Some were concerned about a possible recession, or at least a dangerous softening in the economy, so the Fed decided to lower short-term rates with the goal of "calming" the financial markets. That, it was hoped, would also lead to a lowering of long-term interest rates.

Rates on long-term bonds did fall slightly soon after the Fed decision, supporting the long-held dictum that long-term rates follow changes in short-term rates. However, the theory didn't hold up for long. By March, the rate on 30-year Treasury bonds was three-quarters of a percentage point *higher* than it was when the Fed acted on December 20.

Part of the rise could be accounted for by optimism that the United States would avoid a recession, hence demand for loans would remain high, but the major influence apparently came from across both oceans. Accelerating inflation caused rates to rise in Japan, while in Europe there were also fears of inflation, plus a

Sources: "Boxed in at the Fed," *Business Week,* February 5, 1990; "Fed Has Lost Much of its Power to Sway U.S. Interest Rates," *The Wall Street Journal,* March 12, 1990.

new demand for capital to modernize liberated Eastern European nations.

Lyle Gramley, who was chief economic forecaster for the Fed during the 1970s, emphasizes how things have changed. "I considered the international division more of a nuisance. The direct link from interest rates abroad to interest rates in the U.S. to the outlook for the U.S. economy — I never had to deal with that intellectually before. Who ever thought that developments in West Germany were going to be a very important influence on interest rates in the U.S.? Maybe somebody did. It wasn't me."

The new global marketplace affects not just government economists and bond traders — prospective homeowners also feel the pinch as lenders set their mortgage rates according to the latest news from Tokyo or Frankfurt rather than that from Washington or New York. Rates offered by East Coast lender Dominion Bankshares, Inc., for instance, were pushed up a full percentage point in just two months as a direct result of rising interest rates in Japan.

Wall Street economists are not immune either. David Jones, chief economist at Aubrey G. Lanston & Co., says he spent most of his time in the 1970s watching the Federal Reserve and worrying about inflation in the United States. Now, he says, "I spend 80 percent of my time worrying about the foreign side, or at least how the foreign side affects the domestic side."

Ripples in the global financial markets can spread instantaneously over the United States via an electronic network. The former Federal Reserve chairman, Paul Volcker, had to call New York to keep up with currency exchange rates, but current chairman Alan Greenspan gets instant reports via a computer terminal. Bankers and bond traders get the same reports, and as quickly, as Greenspan.

Some fear that the Fed might not be able to come through in a crunch anymore and to save our economy from either runaway inflation or a deep recession. Even Greenspan says it would be difficult, and a former president of the New York Federal Reserve Bank agrees. Noting that it is hard enough to balance economic growth and the dangers of inflation, he said, "When you add in the third thing," — the foreign factor — "it's like juggling three balls instead of two. It's very hard to do."

Figure 4-1 is a graph of the production/consumption situation in a supply/demand framework, similar to Figure 2-1 discussed in Chapter 2. As we mentioned in Chapter 2, savers will save more if producers offer higher interest rates on savings, and producers will borrow more if savers accept a lower return on their savings. There is an equilibrium rate, k, which produces a balance between the aggregate supply of and demand for capital in the economy. The equilibrium rate of return is that rate which is required to induce savers to invest and, simultaneously, it is the rate which borrowers are willing to pay. This rate, k, is not static; it changes over time, depending on conditions. For example, if a major technological breakthrough occurs and raises the rate of return on producers' investment, the investment (demand) curve in Figure 4-1 will shift to the right, causing both k and S = I to increase. Similarly, if consumers' attitudes change, and they become more thrifty, the savings curve will shift to the right, causing k to decline but S = I to increase.

Figure 4-1 **Supply of and Demand for Savings**

This figure shows how the supply/demand system works to determine the rate of interest (k) on savings. The investment (demand) curve indicates that borrowers (producers) will try to attract more savings from savers as interest rates decrease. Conversely, the savings (supply) curve shows that savers will save more only as interest rates increase. These conflicting desires of savers and borrowers come together at some equilibrium point, k, creating a balance between supply of and demand for savings. At that point, savings will equal investment (S = I).

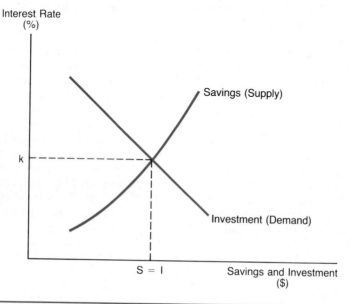

As you learned from our discussion in Chapter 2, there are many capital markets in the United States. U.S. firms also invest and raise capital throughout the world, and foreigners both borrow and lend capital in the United States. There are markets in the United States for home loans; farm loans; business loans; federal, state, and local government loans; and consumer loans. Within each category, there are regional markets as well as different types of submarkets. For example, in real estate, there are separate markets for first and second mortgages, and for loans on owner-occupied homes, apartments, office buildings, shopping centers, vacant land, and so on. Within the business sector, there are dozens of types of debt and also several sharply differentiated markets for common stocks. There is a price for each type of capital. However, even with all the differentiation in the capital markets, rates in the various capital markets are interrelated. Thus, when demand rises and causes the interest rate on business loans to increase, the interest rate on owner-occupied homes will also increase.

Figure 4-2 **Long- and Short-Term Interest Rates, 1953–1990**

This figure depicts the fluctuation of long- and short-term interest rates over the past 38 years, and it shows how these rates have responded to business recessions. Recessions have caused sharp drops in short-term rates because of Federal Reserve intervention and falling demand for money. Long-term rates are much less affected by recessions, since these rates are based on long-range expectations that are not significantly changed by relatively temporary recessions.

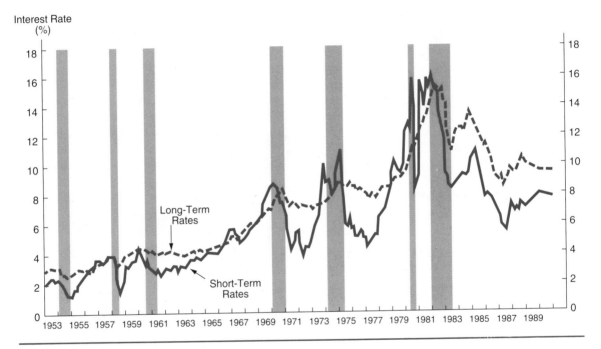

Note:
The shaded areas designate business recessions. Short-term rates are measured by four- to six-month loans to very large, strong corporations, and long-term rates are measured by Aaa corporate bonds.

Source: *Federal Reserve Bulletin,* various issues.

    The price of each type of capital changes over time as shifts occur in supply and demand conditions. Figure 4-2 shows how long- and short-term interest rates to business borrowers have varied since the 1950s. Notice that short-term interest rates are more volatile than long-term rates. This is because short-term rates are responsive to current economic conditions, while long-term rates primarily reflect long-run expectations for the economy, especially inflation. Thus, short-term rates are especially prone to rise during booms and then to fall during recessions (indicated by the shaded areas in Figure 4-2). As a result, short-term rates are sometimes above and sometimes below long-term rates. The relationship between long- and short-term rates, which is called the *term structure of interest rates,* is discussed later in this chapter.

Figure 4-3 **Relationship between Annual Inflation Rates and Long-Term Interest Rates**

There is a close, although not perfect, correlation between interest rates and rates of inflation, as shown in this figure. Over a 38-year period, the two rates tended to fluctuate together. The inflation premium built into long-term interest rates is based on expectation of future inflation, with these expectations arising largely from past and present experiences of inflation rates.

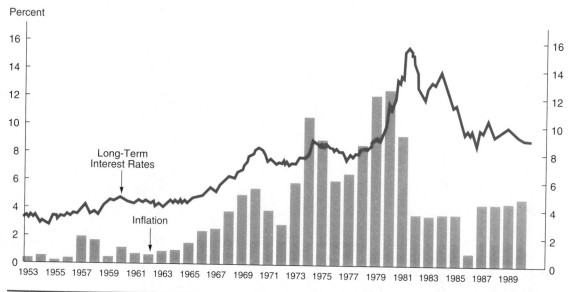

Notes:
1. Interest rates are those on Aaa long-term corporate bonds.
2. Inflation is measured as the annual rate of change in the consumer price index (CPI).

When the economy is expanding, firms need capital, and this demand for funds pushes interest rates up. Also, because inflationary pressures are strongest during business booms, the Federal Reserve tends to tighten the money supply at such times, which also exerts upward pressure on rates. Conditions are reversed during recessions: slack business reduces the demand for credit, the Fed increases the money supply, and the result is a drop in interest rates. In addition, inflationary pressures are normally weakest during recessions, and this too helps to keep interest rates down.

These tendencies do not hold exactly, and the period after 1984 is a case in point. The price of oil decreased dramatically in 1985 and 1986, reducing inflationary pressures on other prices and easing fears of serious, long-term inflation. Earlier, these fears had pushed interest rates to record levels. The economy from 1984 to 1987 was fairly strong, but the declining fears about inflation more than offset the normal tendency of interest rates to rise during good economic times, and the net result was lower interest rates.

The relationship between inflation and long-term interest rates is highlighted in Figure 4-3, which plots rates of inflation along with long-term interest rates. Prior to 1965, when the average rate of inflation was about 1 percent, interest rates on Aaa-rated bonds generally ranged from 4 to 5 percent. As the war in Vietnam accelerated in the mid-1960s, the rate of inflation increased, and interest rates began to rise. The inflation rate dropped after 1970, and so did long-term interest rates. However, the 1973 Arab oil embargo was followed by a quadrupling of oil prices in 1974, which caused a spurt in the price level, which in turn drove interest rates to new record highs in 1974 and 1975. Inflationary pressures eased in late 1975 and 1976 but then rose again after 1976. In 1980, inflation rates hit the highest level on record, and fears of continued double-digit inflation pushed interest rates up to historic highs. From 1981 through 1986, the inflation rate dropped steadily, and in 1986 inflation was only 1.1 percent, the lowest level in 25 years. Early in the period, however, investors' fears of a renewal of double-digit inflation kept long-term interest rates at relatively high levels, but as confidence built that inflation was under control, interest rates declined. Currently (1990), inflation is back up to about 5 percent, and interest rates have moved up accordingly.

Self-Test

Identify some factors which influence interest rates in the economy.

What is meant by the term "equilibrium rate of return"? Is this rate static? Explain.

Briefly explain why interest rates change during booms and recessions.

THE DETERMINANTS OF MARKET INTEREST RATES

In general, the nominal interest rate on a debt security, k, is composed of a real risk-free rate of interest, k^*, plus several premiums that reflect inflation, the riskiness of the security, and the security's marketability (or liquidity). This relationship can be expressed as follows:

$$\text{Nominal interest rate} = k = k^* + IP + DRP + LP + MRP. \quad \textbf{(4-1)}$$

If we combine $k^* + IP$ and let this sum equal k_{RF}, then we have this expression:

$$k = k_{RF} + DRP + LP + MRP. \quad \textbf{(4-2)}$$

Here,

    k = the nominal, or stated, rate of interest on a given security.[2]
        There are many different securities, hence many different stated interest rates.

---

[2]The term *nominal* as it is used here means the *stated* rate as opposed to the *real* rate, where the real rate is adjusted for inflation. If you bought a 10-year Treasury bond in January 1990, the stated or nominal rate would be about 8.3 percent, but if inflation averaged 5 percent over the next 10 years the real rate you would earn would be about 8.3% − 5.0% = 3.3%. In Chapter 13 we will use the term *nominal* in yet another way: to distinguish between stated rates and effective annual rates when compounding occurs more frequently than once a year.

k^* = the real risk-free rate of interest; k^* is pronounced "k-star," and it is the rate that would exist on a riskless security if zero inflation were expected.

k_{RF} = the nominal risk-free rate of interest. This is the stated interest rate on a security such as a U.S. Treasury bill, which is free of default risk. k_{RF} does include a premium for expected inflation, so $k_{RF} = k^* + IP$.

IP = inflation premium. IP is equal to the average expected inflation rate over the life of the security.

DRP = default risk premium. This premium reflects the possibility that the issuer will not pay interest or principal on a security at the stated time and in the stated amount. DRP is zero for U.S. Treasury securities, but it rises as the riskiness of an issuer increases.

LP = liquidity premium. This is a premium charged by lenders to reflect the fact that some securities cannot be converted to cash on short notice at a "reasonable" price. LP is very low for Treasury securities, but quite high on securities issued by very small companies.

MRP = maturity risk premium. As we explain later, longer-term bonds are exposed to a significant risk of price declines, and a maturity premium is charged by lenders to reflect this risk.

We discuss these components whose sum makes up the stated, or nominal, rate on a given security in the following sections.

The Real Risk-Free Rate of Interest, k^* *earned by government bonds*

real risk-free rate of interest, k^*
The rate of interest that would exist on short-term default-free U.S. Treasury securities if no inflation were expected.

The **real risk-free rate of interest, k^***, is defined as the interest rate that would exist on a riskless security if no inflation were expected, and it may be thought of as the rate of interest that would exist on short-term U.S. Treasury securities in an inflation-free world. The real risk-free rate is not static; it changes over time depending on economic conditions, especially (1) on the rate of return corporations and other borrowers can expect to earn on productive assets and (2) on people's time preferences for current versus future consumption. Borrowers' expected returns on real asset investments set an upper limit on how much they can afford to pay for borrowed funds, whereas savers' time preferences for consumption establish how much consumption they are willing to defer, and hence the amount of funds they will lend at different levels of interest. It is difficult to measure k^* precisely, but most experts think that in the United States it has fluctuated in the range of 1 to 4 percent in recent years.

nominal risk-free rate, k_{RF}
The rate of interest on a security that is free of all risk; k_{RF} is proxied by the T-bill rate or the T-bond rate. k_{RF} includes an inflation premium.

The Nominal Risk-Free Rate of Interest, k_{RF} — *real minus inflation*

The **nominal risk-free rate, k_{RF}**, is the real risk-free rate plus a premium for expected inflation: $k_{RF} = k^* + IP$. To be strictly correct, the risk-free rate should mean the interest rate on a totally risk-free security — one that has no risk of default, no maturity risk, no liquidity risk, and no risk of loss if inflation increases. There is no such security, and hence there is no observable truly risk-free rate. However, there is one security that is free of most risks — a U.S. Treasury bill (T-bill), which is a short-term security issued by the U.S. government. Treasury bonds (T-bonds), which are longer-term government securities, are free of default and liquidity risks, but T-bonds are exposed to some risk due to changes in the general level of interest rates.

If the term "risk-free rate" is used without either the modifier "real" or the modifier "nominal," people generally mean the nominal rate, and we will follow that convention in this book. Therefore, when we use the term risk-free rate, k_{RF}, we mean the nominal risk-free rate, which includes an inflation premium equal to the average expected inflation rate over the life of the security. In general, we use the T-bill rate to approximate the short-term risk-free rate, and the T-bond rate to approximate the long-term risk-free rate. So, whenever you see the term "risk-free rate," assume that we are referring either to the U.S. T-bill rate or to the T-bond rate.

Inflation Premium (IP)

Inflation has a major impact on interest rates because it erodes the purchasing power of the dollar and lowers the real rate of return on investments. To illustrate, suppose you save $1,000 and invest it in a Treasury bill that matures in 1 year and pays 5 percent interest. At the end of the year, you will receive $1,050 — your original $1,000 plus $50 of interest. Now suppose the rate of inflation during the year is 10 percent, and it affects all items equally. If beer had cost $1 per bottle at the beginning of the year, it would cost $1.10 at the end of the year. Therefore, your $1,000 would have bought $1,000/$1 = 1,000 bottles at the beginning of the year, but only $1,050/$1.10 = 955 bottles at the end. Thus, in *real terms,* you would be worse off; you would receive $50 of interest, but it would not be sufficient to offset inflation. You would thus be better off buying 1,000 bottles of beer (or some other storable asset such as land, timber, apartment buildings, wheat, or gold) than buying the Treasury bill.

Investors are well aware of all of this, so when they lend money, they build in an **inflation premium (IP)** equal to the expected inflation rate over the life of the security. As discussed previously, for a short-term default-free U.S. Treasury bill, the actual interest rate charged, $k_{T\text{-bill}}$, would be the real risk-free rate of interest, k^*, plus the inflation premium (IP):

inflation premium (IP)

A premium for expected inflation that investors add to the real risk-free rate of return.

$$k_{T\text{-bill}} = k_{RF} = k^* + IP. \qquad (4\text{-}3)$$

Therefore, if the real risk-free rate of interest were $k^* = 3\%$, and if inflation were expected to be 4 percent (and hence IP = 4%) during the next year, then the rate of interest on 1-year T-bills would be 7 percent. In January of 1990, the expected 1-year inflation rate was about 5 percent, and the yield on

1-year T-bills was about 7.9 percent, which implies that the real risk-free rate of interest at that time was about 2.9 percent.

It is important to note that the rate of inflation built into interest rates is the *rate of inflation expected in the future,* not the rate experienced in the past. Thus, the latest reported figures might show an annual inflation rate of 3 percent, but that is for the *past* period. If people on the average expect a 5 percent inflation rate for the future, then 5 percent would be built into the current rate of interest. Note also that the inflation rate reflected in the interest rate on any security is the *average rate of inflation expected over the security's life.* Thus, the inflation rate built into a 1-year bond is the expected inflation rate for the next year, but the inflation rate built into a 30-year bond is the average rate of inflation expected over the next 30 years.

If you turn once again to Figure 4-3, you will note the high correlation between inflation and interest rates over the years. The relationship is not perfect, however, because it is built on expectations. Studies have shown that inflation expectations for the future are closely related to recent inflation rates. In 1974–1975 and again in the late 1970s to 1980, when high inflation rates were unusual for the United States, investors' forecasts of inflation were too low and inflation was greater than interest rates. Therefore, investors' purchasing power eroded as price increases exceeded the rate of return they earned on their investments. Because of these experiences with high inflation, the rates in the early to mid-1980s remained high relative to current inflation as investors' fears of renewed high inflation kept the inflation premium (at least with hindsight) artificially high.

Inflation premiums are based on forecasts that are closely related to, although not perfectly correlated with, recent inflation experience. Therefore, if the inflation rate reported for the past few months had increased, people would tend to raise their expectations for future inflation, and this change in expectations would cause an increase in interest rates.

Default Risk Premium (DRP)

bond ratings
Ratings assigned to bonds based on the probability of their default. Those bonds with the smallest default probability are rated Aaa and carry the lowest interest rates.

The risk that a borrower will *default* on a loan, which means not to pay the interest or the principal, also affects the market interest rate on a security; the greater the default risk, the higher the interest rate lenders charge. Treasury securities have no default risk, hence they carry the lowest interest rates on taxable securities in the United States. For corporate bonds, the higher the bond's rating, the lower its default risk, and, consequently, the lower its interest rate. **Bond ratings** range from Aaa, which is the rating for the financially strongest firms, down to D, which is the rating applied to companies already in bankruptcy. The following are some representative interest rates on long-term bonds during October 1989.[3]

---

[3]*Federal Reserve Bulletin,* January 1990, p. A24.

Security	Rate	Default Risk Premium
U.S. Treasury bond	8.0%	0.0%
Aaa corporate bond	8.9	0.9
Aa corporate bond	9.2	1.2
A corporate bond	9.4	1.4
Baa corporate bond	9.8	1.8

The difference between the interest rate on a Treasury security and that of a corporate bond *with similar maturity, liquidity, and other features* is defined as the **default risk premium (DRP).** Therefore, if the previously listed bonds are otherwise similar, the default risk premium is relatively low for Aaa corporate bonds (DRP = 8.9% − 8.0% = 0.9%), but the default risk premium is higher for the higher-risk Baa corporate bonds (DRP = 9.8% − 8.0% = 1.8%). Default risk premiums vary somewhat over time, but the October 1989 figures are representative of levels in recent years.

default risk premium (DRP)
The difference between the interest rate on a U.S. Treasury bond and a corporate bond of equal maturity and marketability.

Liquidity Premium (LP)

A highly **liquid asset** is one that can be sold at a predictable price and thus can be converted to a well-specified amount of spendable cash on short notice. Active markets, which provide liquidity, exist for government bonds and for the stocks and bonds of larger corporations. Also, claims on certain financial intermediaries such as bank time deposits are highly liquid because banks will redeem them for cash. Real estate, as well as securities issued by small companies that are not known by many investors, are *illiquid* — they can be sold to raise cash, but not quickly and not at a predictable price. If a security is *not* liquid, investors will add a **liquidity premium (LP)** when they establish the market rate on the security. It is very difficult to measure liquidity premiums with precision, but a differential of at least two and probably four or five percentage points is thought to exist between the least liquid and the most liquid financial assets of similar default risk and maturity.

liquid asset
An asset that can be readily converted to spendable cash.

liquidity premium (LP)
A premium included in the equilibrium interest rate on a security if that security cannot be converted to cash on short notice.

Maturity Risk Premium (MRP)

U.S. Treasury securities are free of default risk in the sense that one can be virtually certain that the federal government will pay interest on its bonds and will also pay them off when they mature. Therefore, the default risk premium on Treasury securities is essentially zero. Further, active markets exist for Treasury securities, so their liquidity premiums are also close to zero. Thus, as a first approximation, the rate of interest on a Treasury bond should be the risk-free rate, k_{RF}, which is equal to the real risk-free rate, k^*, plus an inflation premium, IP. However, an adjustment is needed for long-term Treasury bonds. The prices of long-term bonds decline sharply whenever interest rates rise, and since interest rates can and do occasionally rise, all long-term bonds, even Treasury bonds, have an element of risk called **interest rate risk.** As a general rule, the bonds of any organization, from the U.S. government to Eastern Air-

interest rate risk
The risk of capital losses to which investors are exposed because of changing interest rates.

maturity risk premium (MRP)

A premium which compensates for interest rate risk.

lines, have more interest rate risk the longer the maturity of the bond.[4] Therefore, a **maturity risk premium (MRP),** which is higher the longer the years to maturity, must be included in the required interest rate.

The effect of maturity risk premiums is to raise interest rates on long-term bonds relative to those on short-term bonds. This premium, like the others, is extremely difficult to measure, but (1) it seems to vary over time, rising when interest rates are more volatile and uncertain and falling when they are more stable, and (2) in recent years, the maturity risk premium on 30-year T-bonds appears to have generally been in the range of one to two percentage points.

We should mention that although long-terms bonds are heavily exposed to interest rate risk, short-term bills are heavily exposed to **reinvestment rate risk.** When short-term bills mature and the funds are reinvested, or "rolled over," a decline in interest rates would result in reinvestment at a lower rate, and hence would lead to a decline in interest income. To illustrate, suppose you had $100,000 invested in 1-year T-bills, and you lived on the income. In 1981, short-term rates were about 15 percent, so your income would have been about $15,000. However, your income would have declined to about $9,000 by 1983, and to just over $8,000 by 1990. Had you invested your money in long-term bills, your income (but not the value of your principal) would have been stable. Thus, although the principal is preserved, the interest income provided by short-term T-bills varies from year to year, depending on reinvestment rates.

reinvestment rate risk

The risk that a decline in interest rates will lead to lower income when securities mature and funds are reinvested.

Self-Test

Write out the two equations for the nominal interest rate on any debt security.

Distinguish between the *real* risk-free rate of interest, k*, and the *nominal* risk-free rate of interest, k_{RF}.

The inflation rate for what period is built into the interest rate on a security?

Does the interest rate on a T-bond include a default risk premium? Explain.

Distinguish between liquid and illiquid assets, and identify some assets that are liquid and some that are illiquid.

Briefly explain the following statement: "Although long-term bonds are heavily exposed to interest rate risk, short-term bonds are heavily exposed to reinvestment rate risk."

---

[4]For example, if someone bought a 30-year Treasury bond for $1,000 in 1972, when the long-term interest rate was 7 percent, and held it until 1981, when long-term T-bond rates were about 14.5 percent, the value of the bond would have declined to about $514. That would represent a loss of almost half of the investment, and it demonstrates that long-term bonds, even U.S. Treasury bonds, are not riskless. However, had the person invested in short-term bills in 1972 and subsequently reinvested the principal each time the bills matured, he or she would still have had $1,000. This point will be discussed in detail in Chapter 16.

THE TERM STRUCTURE OF INTEREST RATES (ignore)

From Figure 4-2, we can see that at certain times, such as in 1990, short-term interest rates are lower than long-term rates, while at other times, such as in 1980 and 1981, short-term rates are higher than long-term rates. The **term structure of interest rates** is the relationship between long- and short-term rates; and it is important to both corporate treasurers and investors alike to understand (1) how long- and short-term rates are related to each other and (2) what causes shifts in their relative positions.

We can look up the interest rates on bonds of different maturities at various times in such sources as *The Wall Street Journal* or the *Federal Reserve Bulletin.* Figure 4-4 shows the graphs for interest rates for Treasury issues of different maturities on two dates. Each graph is the **yield curve** for the set of data for that date. The yield curve changes both in position and in slope over time. In March 1980, all rates were relatively high, and short-term rates were higher than long-term rates, so the yield curve on that date was *downward sloping.* However, in March 1990, all rates had fallen, and short-term rates were lower than long-term rates, so the yield curve at that time was *upward sloping.* If the yield curve had been drawn in January 1982, it would have been essentially horizontal, for long-term and short-term securities on that date had about the same rate of interest. (See Figure 4-2.)

The yield curves shown in Figure 4-4 are for U.S. Treasury securities, but yield curves could have been constructed for corporate bonds. If the corporate yield curves had been plotted on Figure 4-4, these curves would have been above those for Treasury securities on the same dates, because the corporate yields would include default risk premiums, but they would have had the same general shape as the Treasury curves. Also, the riskier the corporation, the higher its yield curve.

In a stable economy such as the United States had in the 1950s and early 1960s, in which (1) inflation fluctuated in the 1 to 3 percent range, (2) the expected future rate of inflation was about equal to the current rate, and (3) the Federal Reserve did not actively intervene in the markets, all interest rates were relatively low, and the yield curve generally had a slight upward slope to reflect maturity effects. People often define such an upward-sloping yield curve as a **normal yield curve,** and a yield curve which slopes downward as an **inverted,** or **abnormal, yield curve.** Thus, in Figure 4-4 the yield curve for March 1980 was inverted, but the one for March 1990 was normal.

term structure of interest rates
The relationship between yields and maturities of debt securities.

yield curve
A graph showing the relationship between yields and maturities of debt securities.

normal yield curve
An upward-sloping yield curve.

inverted (abnormal) yield curve
A downward-sloping yield curve.

Term Structure Theories

Several theories have been used to explain the shape of the yield curve. The three major ones are (1) the *market segmentation theory,* (2) the *liquidity preference theory,* and (3) the *expectations theory.*

Figure 4-4 U.S. Treasury Bond Interest Rates on Different Dates

This figure shows the actual yield curves for various term Treasury bonds in two recent years. In 1990 investors expected inflation to rise from the then-current 5 percent; this produced an upward-sloping yield curve, meaning that long-term bonds offered a higher interest rate than did short-term bonds. In 1980, however, inflation was expected to decline, creating a downward-sloping yield curve.

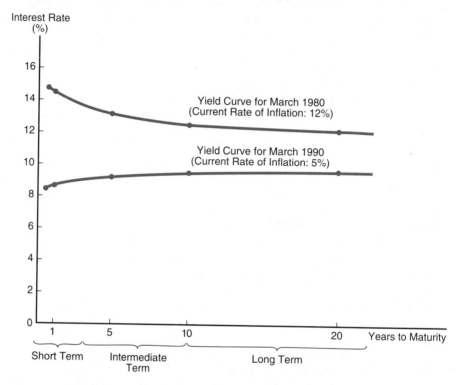

Term to Maturity	Interest Rate	
	March 1980	**March 1990**
6 months	15.0%	8.2%
1 year	14.0	8.3
5 years	13.5	8.6
10 years	12.8	8.7
20 years	12.5	8.8

market segmentation theory

The theory that each borrower and lender has a preferred maturity and that the slope of the yield curve depends on the supply of and demand for funds in the long-term market relative to the short-term market.

Market Segmentation Theory. The **market segmentation theory** states that each lender and each borrower has a preferred maturity. For example, a person borrowing to buy a long-term asset, such as a house, would want a long-term loan, while a retailer borrowing in September for Christmas inventory would prefer a short-term loan. Similarly, a person saving to take a vacation next summer would want to lend in the short-term market, but someone saving for retirement 20 years hence would probably buy long-term securities.

The main idea of this theory is that the slope of the yield curve depends on supply/demand conditions in the long- and short-term markets. According to the theory, the yield curve could at any given time be either upward or downward sloping. An upward-sloping yield curve would occur when there was a large supply of funds relative to demand in the short-term market, but a relative shortage of funds in the long-term market. Similarly, a downward-sloping curve would indicate relatively strong demand in the short-term market compared to that in the long-term market.

Liquidity Preference Theory. The **liquidity preference theory** states that long-term bonds normally yield more than short-term bonds for two reasons: (1) Investors generally prefer to hold short-term securities and will accept lower yields on them, because such securities are more liquid—they can be converted to cash with little danger of loss of principal. (2) At the same time, borrowers react in exactly the opposite way. They generally prefer long-term debt, because short-term debt exposes them to the risk of having to repay the debt under adverse conditions. Accordingly, borrowers are willing to pay a higher rate, other things held constant, for long-term funds than for short-term funds. Taken together, these preferences—and hence the liquidity preference theory—imply that under normal conditions, the maturity risk premium (MRP) is positive and increases with maturity, and that the yield curve should be upward sloping.

liquidity preference theory
The theory that lenders prefer to make short-term loans rather than long-term loans; hence, they will lend short-term funds at lower rates than long-term funds.

Expectations Theory. The **expectations theory** states that the yield curve depends on expectations about future inflation rates. Specifically, k_t, the nominal interest rate on a U.S. Treasury bond that matures in t years, is found as follows:

$$k_t = k^* + IP_t + MRP.$$

Here k^* is the real, risk-free interest rate, IP_t is an inflation premium equal to the average expected rate of inflation over the t years before the bond matures, and MRP is the maturity risk premium. Under this theory, the maturity risk premium (MRP) is assumed to be zero, so the equation reduces to

$$k_t = k^* + IP_t.$$

expectations theory
The theory that the shape of the yield curve depends primarily on investors' expectations about future inflation rates.

Note that (1) the Treasury can borrow on a short-term basis, on a long-term basis, or anywhere in between, and (2) the inflation premium built into any bond's interest rate is the *average expected inflation rate* over the bond's life, or its *term to maturity*. Therefore, it is appropriate to add a subscript, t, to the inflation premium, depending on its maturity. Thus IP_3 is the inflation premium for a 3-year bond, and it is equal to the average expected inflation rate over the next 3 years.

To illustrate, suppose that in late December 1990 the real risk-free rate of interest was k* = 2%, and expected inflation rates for the next 3 years were as follows:

	Expected Annual (1-Year) Inflation Rate	Expected Average Inflation Rate from 1990 to Indicated Year
1991	9%	9% ÷ 1 = 9.0%
1992	6%	(9% + 6%) ÷ 2 = 7.5%
1993	3%	(9% + 6% + 3%) ÷ 3 = 6.0%

Given these expectations, the following pattern of interest rates would be expected to exist:

	Real Risk-free Interest Rate (k*)		Inflation Premium, Which Is Equal to the Average Expected Inflation Rate (IP$_t$)		Interest Rate on Treasury Bond for Each Maturity (k$_{RF}$)
1-year bond	2%	+	9.0%	=	11.0%
2-year bond	2%	+	7.5%	=	9.5%
3-year bond	2%	+	6.0%	=	8.0%

Had the pattern of expected inflation rates been reversed, with inflation expected to rise from 3 percent to 6 percent and then to 9 percent, the following situation would have existed:

1-year bond	2%	+	3.0%	=	5.0%
2-year bond	2%	+	4.5%	=	6.5%
3-year bond	2%	+	6.0%	=	8.0%

These hypothetical data are plotted in Figure 4-5. The lines represent yield curves which depict the term structure of interest rates. Whenever the annual rate of inflation is expected to decline, future interest rates should also decline, and the yield curve points down. Conversely, if inflation is expected to increase, future rates should rise, and the yield curve points up.

Various tests of these theories have been conducted, and these tests indicate that all three theories have some validity. Thus, the shape of the yield curve at any given time is affected (1) by supply/demand conditions in the long- and short-term markets, (2) by liquidity preferences, and (3) by expectations about future inflation. One factor may dominate at one time, another at another time, but all three affect the structure of interest rates.

Self-Test

What is a yield curve, and what information would you need to draw this curve?

Distinguish between the following theories: (1) market segmentation theory, (2) liquidity preference theory, and (3) expectations theory.

Figure 4-5 **Hypothetical Example of the
Term Structure of Interest Rates**

The inflation premium built into the interest rate for any security is the average expected inflation rate over the life, or term to maturity, of the security. The term structure of interest rates is depicted by the hypothetical yield curves shown in this figure. If inflation is expected to decline, short-term securities will yield more than long-term securities, as shown in Yield Curve a. Conversely, if inflation is expected to increase, as in Yield Curve b, short-term securities will yield less than long-term securities.

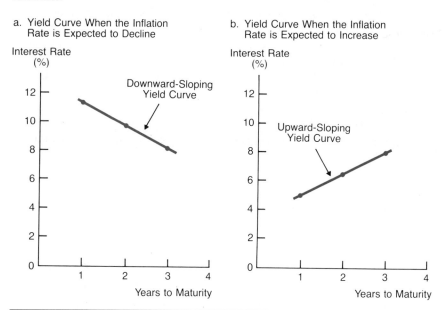

a. Yield Curve When the Inflation
   Rate is Expected to Decline

b. Yield Curve When the Inflation
   Rate is Expected to Increase

Distinguish between the shapes of a normal yield curve and an abnormal yield curve, and explain why each might exist.

OTHER FACTORS THAT INFLUENCE INTEREST RATE LEVELS

In addition to inflationary expectations, liquidity preferences, and normal supply/demand fluctuations, other factors also influence the general level of interest rates and the shape of the yield curve. The four most important ones are (1) Federal Reserve policy, (2) the level of the federal budget deficit, (3) the foreign trade balance, and (4) the level of business activity.

Federal Reserve Policy

As you learned in Chapter 3 or in your studies of economics, (1) the money supply has a major effect on both the level of economic activity and the rate of inflation, and (2) in the United States the Federal Reserve System controls the money supply. If the Fed wants to stimulate the economy, it increases growth in the money supply. The initial effect of such an action is to cause interest rates to decline, but the action also may lead to an increase in the expected rate of inflation, which in turn could push interest rates up. The reverse holds if the Fed tightens the money supply.

To illustrate, in 1981 inflation was quite high, so the Fed tightened up the money supply. The Fed deals primarily in the short-term end of the market, so this tightening had the direct effect of pushing short-term interest rates up sharply. At the same time, the very fact that the Fed was taking strong action to reduce inflation led to a decline in expectations for long-run inflation, which led to a drop in long-term bond yields. The net effect was a downward sloping, or inverted, yield curve. After the Fed's intervention ended, the yield curve resumed its normal upward slope.

We see, then, that during periods when the Fed is actively intervening in the markets, the yield curve will be distorted. Short-term rates will be temporarily "too high" if the Fed is tightening credit and "too low" if it is easing credit. Long-term rates are not affected as much by Fed intervention, except to the extent that such intervention affects expectations for long-term inflation.

Federal Deficits

If the federal government spends more than it takes in from tax revenues, it runs a deficit, and that deficit must be covered either by borrowing or by printing money. If the government borrows, this injects more demand into the market for the available supply of credit, and that pushes up interest rates. If it prints money, this increases expectations for future inflation, which also drives up interest rates. Thus, the larger the federal deficit, other things held constant, the higher the level of interest rates. Whether long- or short-term rates are more affected depends on how the deficit is financed, so we cannot state, in general, how deficits will affect the slope of the yield curve.

Foreign Trade Balance

Businesses and individuals in the United States buy from and sell to people and firms in other countries. If we buy more than we sell (that is, import more than we export), we are said to be running a *foreign trade deficit*. When trade deficits occur, they must be financed, with the main source of financing being debt. In other words, if we import $200 billion of goods but export only $100 billion, we run a trade deficit of $100 billion. We must borrow the $100 billion.[5] Therefore, the larger our trade deficit, the more we must borrow, and as we increase our borrowing, this drives up interest rates. Also, foreigners are willing to hold U.S. debt if and only if the interest rate on this debt is compet-

---

[5]The deficit could also be financed by selling assets, including gold, corporate stocks, entire companies, and real estate. The U.S. has financed its massive trade deficits by all of these means in recent years, but the primary method has been by borrowing.

itive with interest rates in other countries. Therefore, if the Federal Reserve attempts to lower interest rates in the United States, causing our rates to fall below rates abroad, then foreigners will sell U.S. bonds, those sales will depress bond prices, and the result will be higher U.S. rates.

The United States has been running annual trade deficits since the mid-1970s, and the cumulative result of these deficits is that the United States is by far the largest debtor nation of all time. As a result, interest rates are greatly influenced by the annual trade deficit situation (larger trade deficits lead to higher U.S. interest rates), and also by interest rate trends in other countries around the world (higher rates abroad lead to higher U.S. rates). Because of all this, U.S. corporate treasurers must keep up with developments in the world economy.

Business Activity

Figure 4-2, presented earlier, can be examined to see how business conditions influence interest rates. Here are the key points revealed by the graph:

1. Because inflation has generally been increasing since 1953, the tendency has been toward higher interest rates.

2. Until 1966, short-term rates were almost always below long-term rates. Thus, in those years the yield curve was almost always normal, or upward sloping, as the liquidity preference theory suggests it should be if inflation rates are stable.

3. The shaded areas in the graph represent recessions, during which both the demand for money and the rate of inflation tend to fall, and, at the same time, the Federal Reserve tends to increase the money supply in an effort to stimulate the economy. As a result, there is a tendency for interest rates to decline during recessions.

4. During recessions, short-term rates experience sharper declines than long-term rates. This occurs because (1) the Fed operates mainly in the short-term sector and hence its intervention has a major effect here, and (2) long-term rates reflect the average expected inflation rate over the next 20 to 30 years, and this expectation generally does not change much, even when the current rate of inflation is low because of a recession.

Self-Test

Other than inflationary expectations, liquidity preferences, and normal supply-demand fluctuations, name four additional factors which influence interest rates, and explain their effects.

How does the Fed stimulate the economy, and what are the effects of this action on interest rates?

INTEREST RATE LEVELS AND STOCK PRICES

Interest rates have two effects on corporate profits: (1) Because interest is a cost, the higher the rate of interest, the lower a firm's profits, other things held constant; and (2) since interest rates affect the level of economic activity, they increase or decrease business profits. Interest rates obviously affect stock prices because of their effects on profits, but, perhaps even more important, they have an effect due to competition in the marketplace between stocks and bonds. If interest rates rise sharply, investors can get higher returns on their money in the bond market, which induces them to sell stocks in order to transfer funds from the stock market to the bond market. Such transfers in response to rising interest rates obviously depress stock prices. Of course, the reverse occurs if interest rates decline. Indeed, the bull market of 1985 to 1987, when the Dow Jones Industrial Index rose from 1100 to over 2700, was caused almost entirely by the sharp drop in long-term interest rates.

The experience of Commonwealth Edison, the electric utility serving the Chicago area, can be used to illustrate the effects of interest rates on stock prices. In 1984 Commonwealth's stock sold for $21 per share, and, since the company paid a $3 dividend, the dividend yield was $3/$21 = 14.3%. Commonwealth's bonds at the time also yielded about 14.3 percent. Thus, if someone had $100,000 and invested it in either the stock or the bonds, his or her annual income would have been about $14,300. (Of course, had the investor purchased the company's stock, he or she might also have expected the stock price to grow over time, providing some capital gains.)

By 1990, all interest rates were lower, and Commonwealth's bonds were yielding only 9.3 percent. If the stock still yielded 14.3 percent, investors could switch $100,000 out of the bonds and into the stock and, in the process, increase their annual income from $9,300 to $14,300. Many people did exactly that — as interest rates dropped, orders poured in for the stock, and its price was bid up. In January 1990, Commonwealth's stock sold for $36, up over 70 percent from the 1984 level, and the dividend yield (8.3%) was slightly below the bond yield (9.3%).

Self-Test

In what two ways do changes in interest rates affect stock prices?

INTEREST RATES AND BUSINESS DECISIONS

The yield curve for March 1990, shown earlier in Figure 4-4, indicates how much the U.S. government had to pay in 1990 to borrow money for 1 year, 5 years, 10 years, and so on. A business borrower would have had to pay somewhat more, but assume for the moment that we are back in early 1990 and that the yield curve for that year also applies to your company. Now suppose your company has decided (1) to build a new plant with a 20-year life which will cost $1 million and (2) to raise the $1 million by selling an issue of debt (or borrowing) rather than by selling stock. If you borrowed in 1990 on a short-term basis — say, for one year — your interest cost for that year would be only 8.3 percent, or $83,000, whereas if you used long-term (20-year) financing, your cost would be 8.8 percent, or $88,000. Therefore, at first glance, it would seem that you should use short-term debt.

However, this could prove to be a horrible mistake. If you use short-term debt, you will have to renew your loan every year, and the rate charged on each new loan will reflect the then-current short-term rate. Interest rates could return to their March 1980 levels, so by 1992 you could be paying 14 percent, or $140,000, per year. These high interest payments would cut into and perhaps eliminate your profits. Your reduced profitability could easily increase your firm's risk to the point where your bond rating would be lowered, causing lenders to increase the risk premium built into the interest rate they charge, which in turn would force you to pay even higher rates. These very high interest rates would further reduce your profitability, worrying lenders even more, and making them reluctant to renew your loan. If your lenders refused to renew the loan and demanded payment, as they have every right to do, you might have trouble raising the cash. If you had to make price cuts to convert physical assets to cash, you might incur heavy operating losses, or even bankruptcy.

On the other hand, if you used long-term financing in 1990, your interest costs would remain constant at $88,000 per year, so an increase in interest rates in the economy would not hurt you. You might even be able to buy up some of your bankrupted competitors at bargain prices — bankruptcies increase dramatically when interest rates rise, primarily because many firms do use short-term debt.

Does all this suggest that firms should always avoid short-term debt? Not necessarily. If inflation remains low in the next few years, so will interest rates. If you had borrowed on a long-term basis for 8.8 percent in March 1990, your company would be at a major disadvantage if its debt were locked in at 8.8 percent while its competitors (who used short-term debt in 1990 and thus rode interest rates down in subsequent years) had a borrowing cost of only 6 or 7 percent. On the other hand, large federal deficits, and oil price increases resulting from Iraq's invasion of Kuwait, might drive inflation and interest rates up to new record levels. In that case, you would wish you had borrowed on a long-term basis in 1990.

Financing decisions would be easy if we could develop accurate forecasts of future interest rates. Unfortunately, predicting future interest rates with consistent accuracy is somewhere between difficult and impossible — people who make a living by selling interest rate forecasts say it is difficult, but many others say it is impossible.

Even if it is difficult to predict future interest rate *levels,* it is easy to predict that interest rates will *fluctuate* — they always have, and they always will. This being the case, sound financial policy calls for using a mix of long- and short-term debt, as well as equity, in such a manner that the firm can survive in most interest rate environments. Further, the optimal financial policy depends in an important way on the nature of the firm's assets; the easier it is to sell off assets and thus to pay off debts, the more feasible it is to use large amounts of short-term debt. This makes it more feasible to finance current assets than fixed assets with short-term debt. We will return to this issue later in the book, when we discuss working capital management.

Self-Test

If short-term interest rates are lower than long-term rates, why might a firm still choose to finance with long-term debt?

SUMMARY

In this chapter we discussed how interest rates are determined, and we explained some of the ways in which interest rates affect business decisions. The key concepts covered are listed next.

- Capital is allocated through the price system — a price is charged to "rent" money. Lenders charge **interest** on funds they lend, while equity investors receive dividends and capital gains in return for letting the firm use their money.

- Four fundamental factors affect the cost of money: (1) **production opportunities,** (2) **time preferences for consumption,** (3) **risk,** and (4) **inflation.**

- The **risk-free rate of interest (k_{RF})** is defined as the real risk-free rate (k^*) plus an inflation premium (IP): $k_{RF} = k^* + IP$.

- The **nominal interest rate** on a debt security, k, is composed of the real risk-free rate (k^*) plus premiums that reflect inflation (IP), default risk (DRP), liquidity (LP), and maturity risk (MRP): $k = k^* + IP + DRP + LP + MRP$.

- If the **real risk-free rate of interest and the various premiums were constant over time,** interest rates in the economy would be **stable.** However, the **premiums** — especially the premium for expected inflation — **do change over time, causing market interest rates to change.** Also, Federal Reserve intervention to increase or decrease the money supply leads to fluctuations in interest rates.

- The relationship between the yields on securities and securities' maturities is known as the **term structure of interest rates,** and the **yield curve** is a graph of this relationship.

- The yield curve is normally **upward sloping** — this is called a **normal yield curve** — but the curve can slope downward (an **inverted yield curve**) if the demand for short-term funds is relatively strong or if the rate of inflation is expected to decline.

- Three major theories used to explain the shape of the yield curve are (1) the **market segmentation theory,** (2) the **liquidity preference theory,** and (3) the **expectations theory.**

- **Interest rate levels have a profound effect on stock prices.** Higher interest rates (1) depress the economy, (2) increase interest expenses and thus lower corporate profits, and (3) cause investors to sell stocks and transfer funds to the bond market. Each of these factors tends to depress stock prices.

- Interest rate levels have a significant influence on corporate financial policy. Because interest rate levels are difficult if not impossible to predict, **sound financial policy** calls for using a mix of short- and long-term debt, and also for positioning the firm to survive in any future interest rate environment.

EQUATIONS

Equation 4-1 states that the nominal interest rate on a debt security, k, is composed of the real risk-free rate of interest, k^*, plus several premiums that reflect inflation, the riskiness of the security, and the security's marketability (or liquidity):

$$\text{Nominal interest rate} = k = k^* + IP + DRP + LP + MRP. \quad \textbf{(4-1)}$$

Because the nominal risk-free rate is $k_{RF} = k^* + IP$, Equation 4-2 can also be used to find k:

$$k = k_{RF} + DRP + LP + MRP. \quad \textbf{(4-2)}$$

For a default-free U.S. Treasury bill, the actual interest rate charged would be the real risk-free rate of interest plus an inflation premium:

$$k_{T\text{-bill}} = k_{RF} = k^* + IP. \quad \textbf{(4-3)}$$

Here IP would equal the expected inflation rate over the T-bill's life.

RESOLUTION TO DECISION IN FINANCE

A New Chairman for the Fed

The Federal Reserve system is the government's most important instrument for regulating the U.S. banking system. Although its mandate is to create an environment for sustained economic growth by regulating the commercial banks' ability to create credit, the effects of its policies and actions are felt well beyond the confines of the banking system. The Fed is one of the cornerstones of the U.S. economy and an important actor in international finance.

As such, much of the responsibility for cleaning up after the debacle of the October 1987 crash fell to Chairman Greenspan and the Fed. The 61-year-old Greenspan, who brought little experience in the complexities of central banking with him to the job, earned high marks for his handling of the crisis. He and other Fed officials responded quickly to the stock market collapse and used the full powers of the Fed to keep the market crash from spiraling out of control.

In this case, Greenspan's chronic pessimism paid off handsomely. Shortly after taking office,

he had quietly launched a crisis-management project to spot weaknesses in the U.S. economy and to generate alternatives to a variety of financial catastrophe scenarios ranging from bank failures to a collapse of the stock market. Therefore, officials at the Fed weren't caught unprepared by the events of October 19.

In the aftermath of the crash, the Fed acted quickly to insure that the banking system would have enough money to avoid a shortage of credit, which would cause a rise in short-term interest rates that might lead to a recession. It also countered inflationary pressures that were pressing interest rates upward.

Having weathered his first major crisis well, Chairman Greenspan still faces many challenges. An adroit politician, he has worked to garner the support of other Board members in an effort to avoid the conflicts that plagued his predecessor. But, as a political team player, he still must deal with critics who question his ability to act independently from the Reagan administration. With the onslaught of election year pressures, many observers fear that Greenspan will be compelled to push the Fed into policies that foster short-term growth versus solid progress against inflation in order to enhance the Republican's record. In any event, Greenspan is sure to be making Fed policy and headlines, at least until his term of office expires in 1991.

Sources: Blanca Riemer, "What's in Store at the Fed," *Business Week,* June 15, 1987; Mike McNamee, "Alan Greenspan is Headed for a Quiet Honeymoon,"*Business Week,* August 3, 1987; and Alan Murray, "Passing the Test: New Fed Chairman Greenspan Wins a Lot of Praise on Handling of Stock-Market Crash," *The Wall Street Journal,* November 25, 1987.

QUESTIONS

4-1 Suppose interest rates on residential mortgages of equal risk were 11 percent in California and 13 percent in New York. Could this differential persist? What forces might tend to equalize rates? Would differences in borrowing costs for businesses of equal risk located in California and New York be more or less likely than residential mortgage rate differentials? Would differentials in the cost of money for New York and

California firms be more likely to exist if the firms being compared were very large or if they were very small? What are the implications of all this for the pressure now being put on Congress to permit banks to engage in nationwide branching?

4-2   Which fluctuate more, long-term or short-term interest rates? Why?

4-3   Suppose you believe that the economy is just entering a recession. Your firm must raise capital immediately, and debt will be used. Should you borrow on a long-term or a short-term basis? Explain.

4-4   Suppose the population of Area Y is relatively young, whereas that of Area O is relatively old, but everything else about the two areas is equal.
   a. Would interest rates be the same or different in the two areas? Explain.
   b. Would trends toward nationwide branching by banks and S&Ls, and the development of diversified nationwide financial corporations, affect your answer to Part a?

4-5   Suppose a new and much more liberal Congress and administration were elected, and their first order of business was to change the Federal Reserve System and force the Fed to greatly expand the money supply. What effect would this have
   a. on the level and slope of the yield curve immediately after the announcement?
   b. on the level and slope of the yield curve that would probably exist two or three years in the future?

4-6   The federal government (1) encouraged the development of the S&L industry; (2) virtually forced the industry to make long-term, fixed interest rate mortgages; and (3) restricted the S&Ls' capital largely to deposits that were withdrawable on demand or very short notice.
   a. Would S&Ls be better off in a world with a normal or an inverted yield curve? Explain.
   b. If federal actions such as deficit spending and expansion of the money supply produced a sharp increase in inflation, why might it necessitate a federal bailout of the S&L industry?

4-7   Assume that the yield curve is horizontal. You and other investors now receive information that suggests the economy is headed into a recession. You and most other investors think that the Fed will soon relax credit and that this will lead to a decline in short-term interest rates. Over the long run (the next 5, 10, or 15 years) people expect a fairly high rate of inflation, and they expect that this will keep long-term rates fairly high. Explain what all of this will probably do to the yield curve. Use a graph to illustrate your answer.

4-8   Suppose interest rates on Treasury bonds rose from 9 percent to 14 percent. Other things held constant, what do you think would happen to the price of an average company's common stock?

4-9   Why are Treasury bills popular short-term investments for corporations and commercial banks?

4-10   Other things held constant, how would each of the following factors affect the slope and the general position of the yield curve? Indicate by a (+) if it would lead to an upward shift in the curve, a (−) if it would cause the curve to shift downward, or a (0) if it would have no effect or an indeterminate effect on the slope or position of the curve.

	Effect on the Yield Curve	
	Slope	**Position**
a. Investors perceive the risk of default to increase on securities with longer maturities; that is, they become increasingly uncertain about the more distant future.	_____	_____
b. Future interest rates are expected to fall.	_____	_____
c. The Federal Reserve pumps a large amount of money into the banking system.	_____	_____
d. Business firms begin a massive inventory build-up.	_____	_____
e. An inexpensive and efficient method of harnessing nuclear power is developed. This development leads to a decline in the expected rate of inflation.	_____	_____

SELF-TEST PROBLEM

ST-1   Assume that it is now January 1, 1991. The rate of inflation is expected to average 5 percent throughout 1991. However, increased government deficits and renewed vigor in the economy are then expected to push inflation rates higher. Investors expect the inflation rate to be 6 percent in 1992, 7 percent in 1993, and 8 percent in 1994. The real risk-free rate of interest, k^*, is currently 3 percent. Assume that no maturity or liquidity risk premiums are required on securities with 5 years or less to maturity. The current interest rate on 5-year T-bonds is 10 percent.

a. What is the average expected inflation rate over the period from 1991 through 1994?

b. What should be the prevailing interest rate on 4-year T-bonds?

c. What is the implied expected inflation rate in 1995, or Year 5, given that bonds which mature in that year yield 10 percent?

PROBLEMS

4-1   **Yield curves.** Suppose you and most other investors expect the rate of inflation to be 8 percent next year, to fall to 4 percent during a recession in the following year, and then to run at a rate of 7 percent thereafter. Assume that the real risk-free rate, k^*, is 2 percent and that maturity risk premiums on Treasury securities rise from zero on very short-term bills (those that mature in a few days) by 0.20 percentage points for each year to maturity, up to a limit of 1.0 percentage points on 5-year or longer T-bonds.

a. Calculate the interest rates on 1-, 2-, 3-, 4-, 5-, 10-, and 20-year Treasury securities, and plot the yield curve.

b. Now suppose AT&T, an Aaa-rated company, has bonds with the same maturities as the Treasury securities. As an approximation, plot an AT&T yield curve on the same graph with the Treasury yield curve. (Hint: Think about the default risk premium on AT&T's long-term versus its short-term securities.)

4-2   **Yield curves.** Look in *The Wall Street Journal* or some other newspaper which publishes interest rates on U.S. Treasury securities. Identify some Treasury securities which mature at various dates in the future, record the years to maturity and the interest rate for each, and then plot a yield curve. (Note: Some of the bonds — for example, the 3 percent issue which matures in February 1995 — will show very low yields. Disregard them — these are "flower bonds," which can be turned in and used at par value to pay estate taxes, so they always sell at close to par and have a yield which is close to the coupon yield, irrespective of the going rate of interest. Also, the yields quoted in the *Journal* are not for the same point in time for all bonds, so random variations will appear. An interest rate series that is purged of flower bonds and random variations, and hence one that provides a better picture of the true yield curve, can be obtained from the *Federal Reserve Bulletin.*)

4-3   **Risk premiums.** Look in *The Wall Street Journal.* Examine the interest rates for comparable maturity dates of U.S. Treasury securities and government agency securities.

   a. Which group of securities carries the slightly higher interest rate?

   b. Why do you think this relationship exists?

4-4   **Expected interest rates.** Assume that the real risk-free rate is 3 percent and that the maturity and liquidity risk premiums are zero. If the nominal rate of interest on 1-year Treasury securities is 9 percent and that on 2-year Treasury securities is 11 percent, what rate of inflation is expected during Year 2? What is the 1-year interest rate that is expected for Year 2? Comment on why the average interest rate during the 2-year period differs from the 1-year interest rate expected for Year 2.

4-5   **Expected rate of interest.** Suppose the annual yield on a 2-year Treasury security is 11.5 percent, while that on a 1-year Treasury security is 10 percent. k^* is 3%, and the maturity and liquidity risk premiums are zero.

   a. Using the expectations theory, forecast the interest rate on a 1-year security during the second year. (Hint: Under the expectations theory, the yield on a 2-year security is equal to the average yield on 1-year securities in Years 1 and 2.)

   b. What is the expected inflation rate in Years 1 and 2?

SOLUTION TO SELF-TEST PROBLEM

ST-1   **a.** Average = (5% + 6% + 7% + 8%)/4 = 26%/4 = 6.50%.

   b. $k_{\text{T-bond}} = k^* + IP = 0.03 + 0.065 = 0.095 = 9.50\%$.

   c. If the 5-year T-bond rate is 10 percent, the inflation rate is expected to average approximately 10% − 3% = 7% over the next 5 years. Thus, the Year 5 implied inflation rate is 9.0 percent:

$$7\% = (5\% + 6\% + 7\% + 8\% + I_5)/5$$

$$35\% = 26\% + I_5$$

$$I_5 = 9\%.$$

Part II

FINANCIAL STATEMENTS AND FINANCIAL PLANNING

A company's financial statements tell an important story about its operations, and a financial manager or financial analyst should be able to interpret these statements and understand them thoroughly. In Chapter 5 we discuss the four basic financial statements — the *income statement,* the *balance sheet,* the *statement of retained earnings,* and the *statement of cash flows.* Financial analysis, explored in Chapter 6, allows the analyst to evaluate the firm's financial strengths and weaknesses and to utilize this knowledge to develop a plan for the future. Determining future financial needs is an important requisite to effective financial management. Chapter 7 provides useful tools for making projections of future financial statements. Managers use these financial projections to evaluate future operating alternatives.

Chapter 5

Examining a Firm's Financial Data

 DECISION IN FINANCE

Letters from Chairman Buffett

Savvy readers of corporate annual reports usually check three elements: the auditor's opinion, the financial results, and the footnotes. Few give more than a glance to the chairman's letter, which they assume will be pure puffery.

But even the most jaded analysts settle back in their chairs and prepare for a good read when the Berkshire Hathaway report arrives. It invariably contains two things to which they look forward: good news about the company's financial performance and a long, insightful, and entertaining letter from Chairman Warren Buffett. In fact, the letters are so popular that Berkshire Hathaway often receives requests for reprints and, to meet demand, has assembled an anthology of the last five letters.

Most chairmen's letters try to paint a rosy corporate picture, regardless of the reality of the situation. But Buffett believes that stockholders are too smart to buy such an approach. Describing his attitude toward his readers, he says, "I assume I've got a very intelligent partner who has been away for a year and needs to be filled in on all that's happened." Conse-

quently, in his letters he often admits mistakes and emphasizes the negative. In 1979, for example, he wrote, "We continue to look for ways to expand our insurance operation, but your reaction to this intent should not be unrestrained joy. Some of our expansion efforts—largely initiated by your chairman—have been lackluster, others have been expensive failures."

Buffett also uses his letters to educate his shareholders and to help them interpret the data presented in the rest of the report. In one letter he lamented the complexities of accounting and observed, "The Yãnomamö Indians employ only three numbers: one, two, and more than two. Maybe their time will come."

As you read this chapter, think about the kinds of information that corporations provide their stockholders. Do the four basic financial statements provide adequate data for investment decisions? What other information might be helpful?

Also consider the pros and cons of Chairman Buffett's decision to include long, frank, and frequently self-critical letters in his company's annual reports. Would you suggest that other companies follow suit? Why or why not?

See end of chapter for resolution.

The theme for Pfizer Inc.'s 1988 Annual Report was "Building Shareholder Value Through Innovation" with a photograph of a chemist working. In its annual report Pfizer emphasized that its strategy is innovation, that it was entering a period with significant new products, and that R&D spending in 1989 would amount to twice the amount spent in 1984. Pfizer believes that "innovation is the soundest way to build shareholder value."

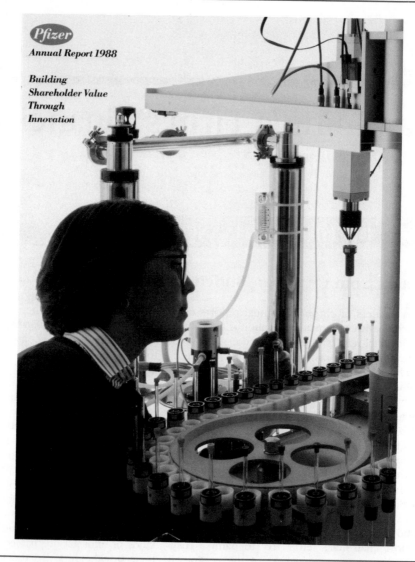

Source: Courtesy of Pfizer Inc.

Any analysis of a firm, whether by management or investors, must include an examination of the company's financial data. The most obvious and readily available source of these financial data is the company's *annual report*. In this chapter we examine the *basic financial data* included in the firm's annual report. In following chapters we discuss the *techniques of financial analysis* used to evaluate financial data in an effort to determine the firm's relative riskiness, its profit potential, and its general managerial competence.

THE ANNUAL REPORT

Of the various reports corporations issue to their stockholders, the **annual report** is by far the most important. Two types of information are given in this report. First, there is a verbal section, often presented as a letter from the president, that describes the firm's operating results during the past year and discusses new developments that will affect future operations. Second, the annual report presents four basic financial statements — the *income statement,* the *balance sheet,* the *statement of retained earnings,* and the *statement of cash flows.* Taken together, these statements give an accounting picture of the firm's operations and financial position. Detailed data are provided for the two most recent years, along with historical summaries of key operating statistics for the past five to ten years.

The quantitative and verbal information are equally important. The financial statements report *what has actually happened* to earnings and dividends over the past few years, whereas the verbal statements attempt to explain *why things turned out the way they did.* For example, suppose earnings dropped sharply last year. Management may report that the drop resulted from a strike at a key facility at the height of the busy season, but then will go on to state that the strike has now been settled and that future profits are expected to bounce back. Of course, this return to profitability may not occur, and investors and analysts should compare management's past statements with subsequent results. In any event, *the information contained in an annual report is used by investors to form expectations about future earnings and dividends, and about the riskiness of these expected cash flows.* Therefore, the annual report is obviously of great interest to investors.

For illustrative purposes, we shall use data taken from Carter Chemical Company, a major producer of industrial and consumer chemical products. The company was originally formed in 1950, it has prospered throughout the years, and it is now recognized as an industry leader. However, in recent years, the firm's earnings have started declining. Because of the competitive nature of the industry, Carter's president, Bruce Berlin, has asked the chief financial officer to conduct a careful appraisal of the firm's position and, on the basis of this analysis, to draw up a plan for future operations.

annual report
A report issued annually by a corporation to its stockholders. It contains the basic financial statements, along with management's opinion of the past year's operations and of the firm's future prospects.

Self-Test

Identify the two types of information given in the annual report. Which one is more important? Explain.

THE INCOME STATEMENT

An **income statement** summarizes a firm's revenues and expenses over an accounting period — generally a quarter or a year. Table 5-1 presents an income statement as it might appear in an annual report. This financial statement

income statement
A statement summarizing the firm's revenues and expenses over an accounting period.

Table 5-1 **Carter Chemical Company: Income Statement for Year Ending December 31 (Millions of Dollars, except per-Share Data)**

	1990	1989
Net sales	$3,000	$2,850
Costs and expenses:		
Labor and materials	$2,544	$2,413
Depreciation	100	90
Selling	22	20
General and administrative	40	35
Lease payments on buildings	28	28
Total operating costs	$2,734	$2,586
Net operating income, or earnings before interest and taxes (EBIT)	$ 266	$ 264
Less interest expense:		
Interest on notes payable	$ 8	$ 2
Interest on first mortgage bonds	40	42
Interest on debentures	18	3
Total interest	$ 66	$ 47
Earnings before taxes	$ 200	$ 217
Federal and state taxes (40%)	80	87
Net income available to common stockholders	$ 120	$ 130
Disposition of net income:		
Dividends to common stockholders	$ 100	$ 90
Addition to retained earnings	$ 20	$ 40
Per share of common stock:		
Earnings per share (EPS)[a]	$ 2.40	$ 2.60
Dividends per share (DPS)[a]	$ 2.00	$ 1.80

[a]Fifty million shares are outstanding: see Table 5-2. Calculations of EPS and DPS for 1990 are as follows:

$$\text{EPS} = \frac{\text{Net income}}{\text{Shares outstanding}} = \frac{\$120,000,000}{50,000,000} = \$2.40.$$

$$\text{DPS} = \frac{\text{Dividends paid to common stockholders}}{\text{Shares outstanding}} = \frac{\$100,000,000}{50,000,000} = \$2.00.$$

records the 1989 and 1990 profits and disbursements of Carter Chemical Company.

Reported at the top of the statement are net sales, from which various costs, including income taxes, are subtracted to obtain net income available to common shareholders. Although this is the general form for income statements, several variations exist. For example, rather than deducting all operating costs from sales, as in Table 5-1, some income statements deduct cost of goods sold from sales to arrive at gross profits. Gross profits are then reduced by all operating expenses to obtain operating profits.

The most important continuing source of revenue for a business is *sales* (or *revenues*). For a manufacturer like Carter, sales revenues are equal to total units sold multiplied by their respective prices, less any discounts offered.

INDUSTRY PRACTICE

Accounting Methods: The Center of a Controversy

Accounting standards and methods are currently at the center of controversies in two highly visible arenas — the thrift bailout and the movie business — and resolutions for the arguments in both industries have been sought in court. Suits have been filed against three major accounting firms because of the savings and loan debacle, and six of the largest accounting firms are on a federal blacklist which prevents them from doing any bailout work. The government expects to sue or otherwise act against still other accounting firms as more thrifts go under.

Investors who bought the bonds of the parent of Lincoln Savings and Loan recently brought a class-action suit against the three accounting firms. They charged that Arthur Andersen, Arthur Young, and Touche Ross were all negligent in auditing the financial statements of Lincoln Savings and Loan.

The Irvine, California, institution's demise has also led to a federal criminal investigation. Top Lincoln managers, under Chairman Charles H. Keating, Jr., were found to have made dozens of questionable deals, ranging from real estate speculation to junk bond investments. Lincoln was shut down by the federal government after its management filed for bankruptcy; the bailout is expected to cost over $2 billion. Even as the collapse became imminent, the thrift's auditors approved financial statements that now, under investigation, appear to have been seriously misleading. Keating had been trying to sell the

Sources: "For Charlie Keating, the Best Defense Is a Lawsuit," *Business Week,* May 1, 1989; "Regulators: Accounting Failed in S&L Collapse," *San Jose Mercury News,* December 28, 1989; *The Wall Street Journal,* "Big Accounting Firms Face Ban in S&L Bailouts," March 14, 1990; "Hollywood's Accounting in Spotlight" and "FDIC Sues Dallas-Area Lawyers in Vernon S&L Failure," March 21, 1990.

thrift since late 1988, after it lost $36 million in the third quarter. Although not technically insolvent, it had lost $214 million in deposits between January 1 and April 13, 1989. The thrift was reporting capital of $247 million, but the Federal Home Loan Bank Board said it actually had negative capital.

All three accounting firms deny any wrongdoing. Did they overlook obvious warning signs, or were they simply misled by Lincoln's management? Whatever the liability of the accountants, experts agree there were three main causes for the lapse:

1. deregulation of savings and loans, which brought about the need for auditing vigilance;

2. auditing procedures that didn't keep up with changes in the industry; and

3. fierce competition for big auditing accounts, which has resulted in a "give the client what he wants" attitude.

A former chief accountant of the Securities and Exchange Commission, John C. Burton, said, "We should not be surprised that this happened. Whenever you have substantial economic change in an industry such as savings and loans, you will find auditing problems. Accounting rules may no longer apply, and auditors are asked to look into things with which they are unfamiliar. And there is evidence that the competitiveness of the accounting firms does increase the risk of auditing failure."

Lawyers for the plaintiffs in the lawsuit say the accounting firms hesitated to question Lincoln's financial statements because they did not want to lose a big client — one who was paying $2.5 million for its annual audit. Competition among accountants is increasing, and many big accounting firms have merged, among them Ernst & Whinney with Arthur Young, to become Ernst & Young; Deloitte Haskins & Sells with Touche Ross, to become Deloitte & Touche. These and other mergers are causing the bigger firms to try to lure clients from smaller accounting groups.

The second-tier accounting firms, as well as some of the larger ones, will benefit from a ruling by the Federal Deposit Insurance Corporation (FDIC) banning certain accountants from work in savings and loan bailouts. Six of the largest U.S. accounting firms stand to lose out on an estimated $100 million in fees because they have been sued by the government for faulty audits of failed institutions: Coopers & Lybrand, Ernst & Young, Peat Marwick, Arthur Andersen, Grant Thornton, and Deloitte & Touche. Work to help the Resolution Trust Corporation, the new agency created to administer the thrift bailout, prepare the thrifts for receivership by assessing the collectability of their outstanding loans is bid out to accountants. "In some instances we are being forced to hire these firms because we cannot get others, but we're generally trying to keep the ban," said FDIC Chairman William L. Seidman. He also said that many more suits, resulting from questions about accounting firms' audit work, are likely. One federal suit against a banned firm involves a petition for $560 million in damages from Arthur Young for allegedly permitting a failed Texas thrift to overstate its net worth by hundreds of millions of dollars in two successive years.

Those large firms — such as Price Waterhouse and Laventhol & Horwath — which have not been sued, and, therefore, have not been banned, stand to gain a great deal of the accounting work needed to reorganize the 370 thrifts already in receivership and the 200 more that are expected to fail. Still other accounting firms, particularly regional firms, have been hired to do litigation-support work for the FDIC in its suits against the six big firms.

Accountants are not the only professionals under suspicion in the savings and loan crisis.

The FDIC has also sued a law firm and five of its former partners for misrepresentations in the failure of Vernon Savings and Loan of Dallas. The malpractice insurer for the firm has already settled for $8 million, while the suit against the former partners seeks some $1.1 billion, the amount the FDIC says Vernon's failure will cost taxpayers. The ultimate cost of the thrift industry's collapse to those who may have contributed to it through faulty audits is yet to be determined.

In addition to the financial institution industry, accounting methods were also at the center of a lawsuit in the motion picture business. Humorist Art Buchwald, who recently won a verdict against Paramount Pictures for its unacknowledged use of his story idea in Eddie Murphy's hit movie *Coming to America*, is now questioning the studio's accounting methods as he seeks to gain 19 percent of the film's net profit for himself and a co-plaintiff. The controversy stems from the formula for "net profit" that has been long accepted in Hollywood, defined as the money left after certain costs, expenses, and participation fees for the star and director are deducted. Buchwald contends that the expenses are inflated, and thus that the authors, producers, actors, and others who sign net profit contracts are usually denied their fair share.

Revenue from *Coming to America* totaled $275 million, but by the time the studio deducted distribution fees and expenses, overhead, the star/director shares, and interest on the money it spent for the movie, net "profits" turned out to be an $18 million loss. Buchwald's attorney, Pierce O'Donnell, said, "When some partners make profits and others are told they have an $18 million loss, something is rotten in Hollywood." The final accounting presented by Paramount includes detailed reviews of the 95,000 separate transactions that went into the costs of the movie.

Operating Costs and Expenses

In a typical manufacturing firm, the operating costs and expense accounts include all costs required to obtain raw materials and convert them into finished products, plus the costs of selling, and plus the costs associated with overseeing operations. *Cost of goods sold* represents costs associated with raw materials acquisition and direct production costs. Sales expenses for salaries, travel, commissions, promotion, and advertising generally are the most important items in *selling expenses*. Staff and executive salaries, and office expenses, are the major items in *general and administrative expenses*. Of course, expenses attributable to assets employed in the business must be accounted for through *depreciation,* or, if the firm leases assets, through *lease payments.*

Even though the computation of these expenses appears to be unambiguous, great discretion is allowed managers in calculating depreciation and in valuing inventory for the cost of goods sold calculation.[1]

Remaining Disbursements

The *earnings before interest and taxes,* or *operating profits,* are further reduced by interest payments on debt, which must be paid whether the company is profitable or not. Repayments of principal are not indicated on the income statement but are reported, as we shall see, on the balance sheet.

All firms have a partner, some might say an "uninvited" partner, who demands a predetermined percentage of profits. This partner is, of course, the U.S. government, which requires that a portion of the firm's profits be paid in the form of income taxes. State and local governments require tax payments as well. However, certain accounting conventions allow the firm to postpone these tax payments for a while.

The Bottom Line

Financial managers often refer to net income as "the bottom line," pointing out that of all the items on the income statement, net income draws the greatest attention. A manager once noted, "Net income is so important that we underline it twice!"

The firm's net income is either paid to the shareholders in the form of dividends or retained by the firm to support its growth. Net income and dividends paid are reported both in total dollars and on a per-share basis. Carter earned $2.40 per share in 1990, down from $2.60 in 1989, but it raised the dividend per share from $1.80 to $2.00.

---

[1]These are not the only areas of managerial discretion in financial reporting. Such items as the determination of pension fund liabilities and the decision whether to expense or capitalize certain costs also have an important effect on reported profits.

Self-Test

What does an income statement summarize?

Outline the general format for an income statement.

Differentiate among cost of goods sold, selling expenses, and general and administrative expenses.

What must be subtracted from operating profits before arriving at net income?

THE BALANCE SHEET

balance sheet
A statement of the firm's financial position at a specific point in time.

equity
Financing supplied by the firm's owners.

liabilities
All the legal claims held against the firm by non-owners.

assets
All items which the firm owns.

The income statement as discussed above reports on operations *over a period of time* — for example, during the calendar year 1990. The **balance sheet,** on the other hand, may be thought of as a snapshot of the firm's financial position *at a point in time* — for example, on December 31, 1990.

The left-hand side of Carter's balance sheet, which is shown in Table 5-2, shows the firm's assets, and the right-hand side of the statement shows claims on assets. These claims are divided into two types —claims that arise from the investment of funds by the owners of the firm, which constitutes the firm's **equity,** and claims associated with debt the firm owes the nonowners of the firm. These debts must be repaid, and they constitute the firm's **liabilities.**

Assets

The **assets** are listed in the order of their liquidity, or the length of time it typically takes to convert them to cash. The current assets, or working capital,

Table 5-2 **Carter Chemical Company: Balance Sheet as of December 31 (Millions of Dollars)**

Assets	1990	1989	Claims on Assets	1990	1989
Cash	$ 50	$ 55	Accounts payable	$ 60	$ 30
Marketable securities	0	25	Notes payable	100	60
Accounts receivable	350	315	Accrued wages	10	10
Inventories	300	215	Accrued federal income taxes	130	120
Total current assets	$ 700	$ 610	Total current liabilities	$ 300	$ 220
Gross plant and equipment	$1,800	$1,470	First mortgage bonds	$ 500	$ 520
Less depreciation	500	400	Debentures	300	60
Net plant and equipment	$1,300	$1,070	Total long-term debt	$ 800	$ 580
			Stockholders' equity:		
			Common stock (50,000,000 shares, $1 par)	$ 50	$ 50
			Additional paid-in capital	100	100
			Retained earnings	750	730
			Total stockholders' equity (common net worth)	$ 900	$ 880
Total assets	$2,000	$1,680	Total liabilities and equity	$2,000	$1,680

consist of assets that are normally converted into cash within one year. *Cash* and *marketable securities* are temporary stores of liquidity. Examples of securities included here are identified in Chapter 9. *Inventories* include raw materials used in the production process, work in process, and finished goods awaiting sale. *Accounts receivable* result when the firm sells a product on credit, and when the customer pays, the account receivable is converted to cash.

Assets with a useful life of more than one year are referred to as *fixed assets*. These assets typically include the plant, equipment, office furniture, and other assets which are used in the production process. With extended usage, these assets will eventually wear out. *Depreciation* was at one time supposed to reflect the decline in an asset's useful productive value. Depreciation is a noncash expense which postpones the firm's taxes, and today the actual relationship between an asset's productive value and its book value is low. In fact, since the introduction of the Accelerated Cost Recovery System (ACRS) method of depreciation in 1981, the economic or productive life of an asset is no longer tied to its tax life; an asset's tax life is generally shorter than its economic or productive life.

Liabilities

A liability is a claim against the assets of the firm. On the balance sheet, liabilities are listed in the order in which they mature and must be repaid. Current liabilities are those debts that mature within one year.

Accounts payable represent the amount the company owes to other businesses for purchases of goods on "open account." Each purchase is recorded on the seller's balance sheet as an account receivable. *Notes payable* represent short-term debt owed to banks or other lenders. *Accruals* are current expenses which have not yet been paid as of the date of the balance sheet. *Accrued wages* and *accrued federal income taxes* are payable on a periodic basis — weekly or monthly for wages and quarterly for income taxes. These accounts build up as the wage and tax liabilities increase during the period. Once paid, the accounts are reduced by the amounts paid, and then they begin to build again as the process continues.

Long-term liabilities are debts with more than one year remaining until maturity. The funds may have been borrowed from any source, such as from financial intermediaries or from the public in the sale of bonds. Table 5-2 indicates Carter Chemical Company has two bonds outstanding, a *first mortgage bond* issue and a *debenture* issue.[2]

The bond's principal may have to be repaid either at maturity in a lump sum or in periodic repayments. One device which helps insure the orderly repayment of a bond issue is a *sinking fund*. Carter's bonds contain a sinking fund provision which requires it to pay off $20 million each year. Accordingly, its outstanding mortgage bonds declined by $20 million from December 31,

---

[2]We discuss different types of bonds in Chapter 16.

1989, to December 31, 1990. The current portion of the long-term debt is included in notes payable here, although in a more detailed balance sheet it would be shown as a separate item.

Stockholders' Equity

stockholders' equity (net worth)

The capital supplied by stockholders — capital stock, paid-in capital, retained earnings, and, occasionally, certain reserves. *Common equity* is that part of total claims belonging to the common stockholders.

The **stockholders' equity**, or **net worth**, account represents the owners' claim against the assets of the firm. This claim differs significantly from the claims of creditors (or debtholders). For one thing, the equity claim does not mature and thus never needs to be paid off. Second, the equity is not fixed at a set amount; rather, it is a residual which can rise or fall. That is,

$$\underset{\$2,000,000,000}{\text{Assets}} \underset{-\ \$1,100,000,000}{-\ \text{Liabilities}} \underset{=\ \$900,000,000.}{=\ \text{Stockholders' equity}} \quad (5\text{-}1)$$

Suppose assets decline in value; for example, suppose some of the firm's inventory becomes obsolete and must be written off. Because liabilities remain constant, the value of the net worth declines. Therefore, the risk of asset-value fluctuations is borne entirely by the stockholders. Note, however, that if asset values rise, these benefits accrue exclusively to the stockholders. Note, too, that if the firm retains some of its earnings, this also causes the equity account to increase.

par value

The nominal or face value of a stock or bond.

The equity section of the balance sheet is divided into three accounts — *common stock, paid-in capital,* and *retained earnings.* The first two accounts arise when the firm issues new common stock to raise capital. A **par value** is generally assigned to common stock — Carter's stock has a par value of $1.[3] Now suppose Carter were to sell 1 million additional shares at a price of $30 per share. The company would raise $30 million, and the cash account would go up by this amount. On the right-hand side of the balance sheet, the transaction would be reflected by an increase of $1 per share, or a total increase of $1 million in the common stock account. The remaining $29 per share would be added to the **paid-in capital** account. This account is occasionally referred to by its more descriptive title, *capital in excess of par.* The results of a sale of new common stock are as follows:

paid-in capital

Funds received in excess of par value when a firm sells stock.

	Before Sale of Stock
Common stock (50,000,000 shares, $1 par)	$ 50,000,000
Paid-in capital	100,000,000
Retained earnings	750,000,000
Total stockholders' equity	$900,000,000

	After Sale of Stock
Common stock (51,000,000 shares, $1 par)	$ 51,000,000
Paid-in capital	129,000,000
Retained earnings	750,000,000
Total stockholders' equity	$930,000,000

[3]The par value assigned to common stock does not really mean much; there is no direct relationship between a stock's par value and its market value.

Thus, after the sale, the common stock account would show $51 million, paid-in capital would show $129 million, and there would be 51 million shares of common stock. The retained earnings account is not affected by the sale of new common stock.

The common stock and paid-in capital accounts provide information about external sources of equity funds. Self-generated, or internal, equity comes from the undistributed profits of the firm. The retained earnings account is built up over time by the firm's "saving" a part of its net income rather than paying all of its earnings out as dividends.[4] Thus, since its inception Carter has retained, or plowed back, a total of $750 million, and $20 million was added during the last year.

The breakdown of the equity accounts is important for some purposes but not for others. For example, a potential stockholder would want to know whether the company had actually earned the funds reported in its equity accounts or whether the funds had come mainly from selling stock. A potential creditor, on the other hand, would be more interested in the total amount of money the owners had put up than in the form in which they put it up. In the remainder of this chapter, we generally aggregate the three equity accounts and call this sum *common equity*, or *net worth*.

Self-Test

How does the balance sheet differ from the income statement?

Identify the two types of claims on assets shown on the right-hand side of the balance sheet.

In what order are assets and liabilities listed on the balance sheet?

Differentiate between current assets and fixed assets, and between accounts payable and accounts receivable.

How do the stockholders' claims differ from the claims of nonowners?

Into what three accounts is the equity section of the balance sheet divided? Briefly explain what information each account provides.

THE STATEMENT OF RETAINED EARNINGS

Changes in the retained earnings section of the equity account between balance sheet dates are reported in the **statement of retained earnings;** Carter's statement is shown in Table 5-3. The company earned $120 million during 1990, paid out $100 million in dividends, and plowed $20 million back into the business. Thus the balance sheet item "retained earnings" increased from $730 million at the end of 1989 to $750 million at the end of 1990.

statement of retained earnings
A statement reporting how much of the firm's earnings were not paid out in dividends. The figure for retained earnings that appears here is the sum of the annual retained earnings for each year of the firm's history.

---

[4]A word of caution is in order here. The retained earnings account does *not* represent a pool of cash from which funds may be withdrawn. The retained earnings account simply indicates the source from which some of the firm's assets were originally procured.

Table 5-3 **Carter Chemical Company: Statement of Retained Earnings for Year Ending December 31, 1990 (Millions of Dollars)**

Balance of retained earnings, December 31, 1989	$730
Add: Net income, 1990	120
Less: Dividends to stockholders	(100)
Balance of retained earnings, December 31, 1990	$750

Note that the balance sheet account "retained earnings" represents a *claim on assets,* not assets per se. Furthermore, firms retain earnings primarily to expand the business; this means investing in plant and equipment, inventories, and so on, *not* in a bank account. Thus, retained earnings as reported on the balance sheet do not represent cash, and they are not available for the payment of dividends or anything else.[5]

Self-Test

Explain the following statement: "Retained earnings as reported on the balance sheet do not represent cash, and they are not 'available' for the payment of dividends or anything else."

THE CASH FLOW CYCLE

As a company like Carter Chemical goes about its business, it makes sales, which lead (1) to a reduction of inventories, (2) to an increase in cash, and, (3) if the sales price exceeds the cost of the item sold, to a profit. If the item is sold on credit rather than for cash, the transaction is slightly more complicated. The inventory account is reduced and accounts receivable are increased; then, when the customer pays, accounts receivable are reduced and the cash account is increased. These transactions cause the balance sheet to change, and they also are reflected in the income statement.

It is important that you understand (1) that businesses deal with *physical* units like autos, computers, and chemicals; (2) that physical transactions are translated into dollar terms through the accounting system; and (3) that the purpose of financial analysis is to examine the accounting numbers in order to determine how efficient the firm is at making and selling physical goods and services. In other words, financial analysis helps determine how good the

---

[5]Recall from your accounting courses that the amount recorded in the retained earnings account is *not* an indication of the amount of cash the firm has. That amount (as of the balance sheet date) is found in the cash account — an asset account. A positive number in the retained earnings account indicates only that, in the past and according to generally accepted accounting principles, the firm has earned an income, and its dividends have been less than its reported income.

company is at taking resources in the form of labor and materials and converting them into some product or service that people want and are willing to pay for.

Several factors make financial analysis difficult. One of them is variations in accounting methods among firms. For example, different methods of inventory valuation and depreciation can lead to differences in reported profits for otherwise identical firms, and a good financial analyst must be able to adjust for these differences if he or she is to make valid comparisons among companies. Another factor involves timing. An action is taken at one point in time, but even though its full effects are not felt until some later period, the effects of the action need to be evaluated before its final results are known.

To understand how timing influences the financial statements and hence financial analysis, one must understand the **cash flow** cycle within a firm, as set forth in Figure 5-1. Here rectangles represent balance sheet accounts (assets and claims on assets) and circles represent actions taken by the firm. Each rectangle may be thought of as a reservoir, and the wavy lines designate the amount of the asset or liability in the reservoir (account) on a balance sheet date. Various transactions cause changes in the accounts. For example, the purchase of raw materials inventory increases accounts payable and eventually reduces cash, while the collection of accounts receivable increases cash. The diagram is by no means a complete representation of the cash flow cycle — to avoid undue complexity, it shows only the major flows.

The cash account is the focal point of the figure. Certain events, such as collecting accounts receivable or borrowing money from the bank, will cause the cash account to increase, while the payment of taxes, interest, dividends, and accounts payable will cause it to decline. Similar comments could be made about all the balance sheet accounts — their balances rise, fall, or remain constant depending on events that occur during the period under study, which for Carter is January 1, 1990, through December 31, 1990.

Projected sales increases may require the firm to raise cash by borrowing from its bank or selling new stock. For example, if Carter anticipates an increase in sales, it will (1) expend cash to buy or build fixed assets through the capital budgeting process, (2) step up purchases of raw materials, thereby increasing both raw materials inventories and accounts payable, (3) increase production, which will cause an increase in both accrued wages and work-in-process, and (4) eventually build up its finished goods inventory. Some cash will have been expended, decreasing the cash account, and the firm will have obligated itself to expend still more cash within a few weeks to pay off its accounts payable and its accrued wages. These events will have occurred *before* any new cash has been generated from sales. Even when the expected sales do occur, there will still be a lag in the generation of cash until receivables are collected. For example, if Carter grants credit for 30 days, it will have to wait 30 days after a sale is made before cash comes in. Depending on how much cash the firm had at the beginning of the buildup, on the length of its production-sales-collection cycle, and on how long it can delay payment of its

cash flow
The actual net cash, as opposed to accounting net income, that flows into or out of the firm during a specified period; equal to net income plus depreciation and other noncash expenses.

Figure 5-1 Cash and Materials Flows within the Firm

The focal point of a firm's cash flow cycle is its cash account, which is influenced by the firm's other accounts (rectangles) and activities (circles). The lower portion of this diagram shows how the cash account is increased through stock issues and borrowing. The cash is then used to purchase raw materials and to acquire fixed assets, both of which feed into the production of goods and eventually replenish the cash account through sales. Note that cash flows continuously through this cycle, so an action in any one portion will, after a lag, influence other portions, and will ultimately affect the cash account.

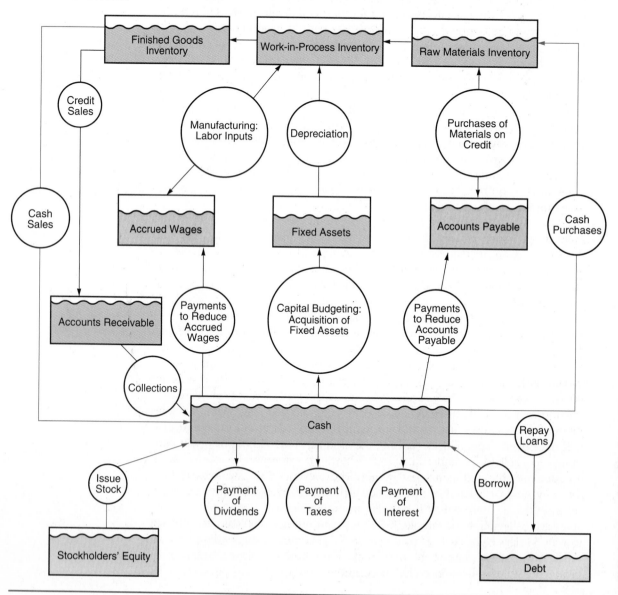

own payables and accrued wages, the company may have to obtain substantial amounts of additional cash by selling stock or bonds, or by borrowing from a bank or other financial institution.

If the firm is profitable, its sales revenues will exceed its costs, and its cash inflows will eventually exceed its cash outlays. However, even a profitable business can experience a cash shortage if it is growing rapidly. It may have to pay for plant, materials, and labor before cash from the expanded sales starts flowing in. For this reason, rapidly growing firms generally require either large bank loans or capital from other sources, or both.

An unprofitable firm, such as Eastern Airlines in recent years, will have larger cash outlays than inflows. This, in turn, will lower the cash account and also cause a slowdown in the payment of accrued wages and accounts payable, and it may also lead to heavy borrowings. Accordingly, liabilities rise to excessive levels in unprofitable firms. Similarly, an overly ambitious expansion plan will result in excessive inventories and fixed assets, while a poor credit and collection policy will result in bad debts and reduced profits that will first show up as high accounts receivable. Financial analysts are well aware of these relationships, and they use the analytical techniques discussed in the remainder of this chapter and in the next chapter to help discover problems before they become too serious.

Self-Test

Identify several factors, discussed in this section, which make financial analysis difficult.

What is the relationship between a firm's physical assets and its financial statements?

In terms of the cash flow cycle graph, what happens to unprofitable firms that have larger cash outlays than inflows, and to firms with overly ambitious expansion plans?

THE STATEMENT OF CASH FLOWS

The graphic cash flow analysis shown in Figure 5-1 is converted to numerical form and is reported in annual reports as the **statement of cash flows.** This statement is designed (1) to show how the firm's operations have affected its liquidity, as measured by its cash flows, and (2) to show the relationships among cash flows from operating, investing, and financing activities. The cash flow statement helps answer questions such as these: Is the firm generating internally the cash it needs to buy additional fixed assets for growth? Is growth so rapid that external financing is required both for maintaining operations and for investing in new fixed assets? Does the firm have enough cash flows from operations to repay financing from earlier periods or to invest in new products? This type of information is useful both for investment analysis and

statement of cash flows
A statement reporting the impact of a firm's operating, investing, and financing activities on cash flows over an accounting period.

for corporate planning, so the statement of cash flows is an important part of the annual report.

The Role of Depreciation

depreciation

An annual noncash charge against income that reflects a rough estimate of the dollar cost of equipment used up in the production process.

Before we discuss the statement of cash flows in detail, we should pause to consider one of its most important elements — **depreciation.** First, what is depreciation? In effect, it is an annual charge against income based on the estimated dollar cost of the capital equipment used up in the production process. For example, suppose a firm purchases a machine with a MACRS class life of 5 years in 1990 for $50,000. This $50,000 cost is not expensed in the purchase year but, rather, is charged against production over the machine's 6-year depreciable life. If the depreciation expense were not taken, profits would be overstated, and taxes would be too high. The annual depreciation allowance is deducted from sales revenues, along with such other costs as labor and raw materials, to determine income. However, depreciation is not a cash outlay; funds were expended back in 1990, so the depreciation charged against the income in years 1990 through 1995 is not a cash outlay, as are labor or raw materials charges. *Depreciation is a noncash charge.*

This point is illustrated with data for Carter Chemical Company in Table 5-4. Here Column 1 shows an abbreviated version of Carter's income statement, whereas Column 2 shows the statement on a cash flow basis. Assume for the moment that (1) all sales are for cash, (2) all costs except depreciation were paid during 1990, and (3) no buildups occurred in inventories or other assets. How much cash would have been generated from operations? From Column 2 we see that the answer is $220 million. The sales are all for cash, so Carter took in $3 billion in cash. Its costs, other than depreciation, were $2,634

Table 5-4 **Carter Chemical Company:**
Cash Flows versus Reported Income for 1990
(Millions of Dollars)

	Income Statement (1)	Cash Flows (2)
Sales	$3,000	$3,000
Costs and expenses		
All costs except depreciation	2,634	2,634
Depreciation (DEP)	100	—
Earnings before interest and taxes (EBIT)	$ 266	N.A.
Interest expense	66	66
Earnings before taxes	$ 200	N.A.
Taxes	80	80
Net income (NI)	$ 120	N.A.
Cash flow: CF = NI + DEP = $120 + $100 =	$ 220	$ 220

N.A. = Not Applicable

million, and these were paid in cash, leaving $366 million. Again, depreciation is *not* a cash charge — the firm does not pay out the $100 million of depreciation expenses — so $366 million of cash is still left after depreciation. Taxes and interest, however, are paid in cash, so $66 million for interest and $80 million for federal and state income taxes must be deducted from the $366 million EBIT cash flow, leaving a net cash flow from operations of $220 million. As shown in Column 1, this $220 million is, of course, exactly equal to net income plus depreciation: $120 million plus $100 million equals $220 million. Therefore, because depreciation is a noncash charge, it is added back to net income to approximate cash flows from operations, and it is included as a source of funds in the statement of cash flows, as discussed in the next section.

Before leaving the subject of depreciation, we should sound a word of caution. Depreciation does not *really provide* funds; it is simply a noncash charge. Hence, it is added back to net income to obtain an estimate of the cash flow from operations. If the firm made no sales, however, depreciation certainly would not provide cash flows. To see this point more clearly, consider the situation of Communications Satellite Corporation (Comsat), which derives its income principally from two satellites, one positioned over the Atlantic and one over the Pacific. Comsat's cash flows are approximately equal to its net income plus its depreciation charges. Yet, if its two satellites stopped working, sales would vanish, and although accountants might still calculate depreciation, this depreciation would provide no cash flows (except possibly some tax refunds).

Preparing the Statement of Cash Flows

The statement of cash flows is designed to answer at a glance these three questions: (1) What were the firm's sources of funds during the year? (2) How did the firm use its available funds? (3) Did operations during the year tend to increase or decrease the firm's liquidity as measured by its cash and marketable securities balances?[6]

The first step in preparing a statement of cash flows is to identify which balance sheet items provided cash and which used cash during the year. This is done on a "changes in balance sheet accounts," or "sources and uses of funds," statement. The change in each balance sheet account is determined, and this change is recorded as either a source or a use of funds according to the following rules:

Sources:

1. *Increase in claims* (that is, an increase in a liability or capital account). Borrowing from the bank is an example of a source of funds.

---

[6]There are several different formats for presenting the statement of cash flows, which was formerly called the statement of changes in financial position. The older format focused on net working capital (current assets minus current liabilities). The cash flow approach is now used since it provides information in the most useful way for financial analysts. Also, recall our discussion of Table 5-4, where we demonstrated that depreciation is a source of funds.

Table 5-5 **Carter Chemical Company: Changes in Balance Sheet Accounts during 1990 (Millions of Dollars)**

	Dec. 31, 1990	Jan. 1, 1990	Change Source	Change Use
Cash	$ 50	$ 55	$ 5	$
Marketable securities	0	25	25	
Accounts receivable	350	315		35
Inventories	300	215		85
Gross plant and equipment	1,800	1,470		330
Accumulated depreciation[a]	500	400	100	
Accounts payable	60	30	30	
Notes payable	100	60	40	
Accrued wages	10	10		
Accrued taxes	130	120	10	
Mortgage bonds	500	520		20
Debentures	300	60	240	
Common stock	50	50		
Paid-in capital	100	100		
Retained earnings	750	730	20	
Totals			$470	$470

[a]Depreciation is a "contra-asset," not an asset. Hence an increase in depreciation is a source of funds.

2. *Decrease in an asset account.* Selling some fixed assets or reducing inventories are also sources of funds.

Uses:

1. *Decrease in a claim on assets.* Paying off a loan is an example of a use of funds.

2. *Increase in an asset account.* Buying fixed assets or building up inventories are examples.

Thus, sources of funds include bank loans and retained earnings, as well as money generated by selling assets, by collecting receivables, and even by drawing down the cash account. Uses include acquiring fixed assets, building up receivables or inventories, and paying off debts.

Table 5-5 shows the changes in Carter Chemical Company's balance sheet accounts during the calendar year 1990, with each change designated as a source or a use. Sources and uses each total $470 million. Note that the table does not contain any summary accounts, such as total current assets or net plant and equipment. If we included summary accounts in Table 5-5 and then used these accounts to prepare the statement of cash flows, we would be "double counting."

The data contained in Table 5-5 are next used to prepare the formal statement of cash flows. The one contained in Carter's annual report is shown in

Table 5-6 **Carter Chemical Company: 1990 Statement of Cash Flows (Millions of Dollars)**

Cash Flows from Operations:

Net income	$120
Additions (sources of cash):	
Depreciation[a]	100
Increase in accounts payable	30
Increase in accrued taxes	10
Subtractions (uses of cash):	
Increase in accounts receivable[b]	(35)
Increase in inventories	(85)
Net cash flow from operations	$140

Cash Flows Associated with Long-term Investments

Acquisition of fixed assets	(330)

Cash Flows Associated with Financing Activities

Increase in notes payable	$ 40
Increase in debentures	240
Repayment of mortgage bonds	(20)
Common dividends paid	(100)
Net cash flow from financing	160
Net reduction in cash and marketable securities	($ 30)

[a]Depreciation is a noncash expense that was deducted when calculating net income. It must be added back to show the correct cash flow from operations.
[b]Recall that parentheses denote negative numbers here and throughout the book.

Table 5-6. Each balance sheet change in Table 5-6 is classified as resulting from (1) operations, (2) long-term investments, or (3) financing activities. Operating cash flows are those associated with the production and sale of goods and services. Net income is the primary operating cash flow, but changes in depreciation, accounts payable, accounts receivable, inventories, and accruals are also classified as operating cash flows. Investment cash flows arise from the purchase or sale of plant, property, and equipment. Financing cash inflows result from issuing debt or common stock, while financing outflows occur when the firm pays dividends or repays debt. The cash inflows and outflows from these three activities are totaled to determine their impact on the firm's liquidity position, which is measured by the change in the cash and marketable securities accounts.

Note that every item in the "change" columns of Table 5-5 is carried over to Table 5-6 except retained earnings. The statement of cash flows reports net income as the first line item in the "operations" section, while dividends paid are shown as a negative cash flow in the "financing activities" section, rather than netting these items out and simply reporting the increase in retained earnings. Also, note that the last line in the statement of cash flows presents the change in the cash and marketable securities account. Like most large companies, Carter Chemical regards its marketable securities as cash equivalents, so with regard to cash flows, they are treated as being equivalent to cash.

Table 5-6 shows the sources as positive numbers and the uses as negative numbers with regard to their effects on Carter's cash and marketable securities. The top part of the table shows cash flows generated by and used in operations. For Carter Chemical, operations provided net cash flows of $140 million. The major sources of operating cash flows were net income and depreciation, while the primary operating use was to increase inventories. The second section shows long-term investing activities. Carter purchased fixed assets totaling $330 million; this was its only long-term investment activity during 1990. Carter's financing activities, shown in the lower section of Table 5-6, included borrowing from banks (notes payable), selling debentures, paying off part of its mortgage bonds, and paying dividends on its common stock. Carter raised $280 million from the capital markets, but it paid $20 million on its mortgage loan and $100 million in dividends, so its net inflow of funds from financing activities during 1990 was $160 million.

When all of these sources and uses of cash are totaled, we see that Carter had a $30 million shortfall during 1990. It met that shortfall by selling its marketable securities for a total of $25 million and by reducing its cash balance by $5 million, as can be seen in Table 5-5.

Carter Chemical Company is a strong, well-managed company, and its statement of cash flows shows nothing unusual or alarming. It does show a cash drain which resulted primarily from the purchase of fixed assets, but it also shows positive cash flows from operations, so if the company were to cut back on its fixed asset expansion, it would generate positive cash flows. Thus, the cash outflow does not appear likely to continue, so it will not bleed the company to death.

Self-Test

What is depreciation, and how does it relate to cash flows from operations?

Does depreciation provide funds? Explain.

What three questions does the statement of cash flows answer?

List the rules that determine whether a change in a balance sheet item is recorded as a source or a use of funds.

Outline the general format of the statement of cash flows.

SUMMARY

The primary purpose of this chapter was to describe the basic financial statements. The key concepts covered are listed below:

- The four basic statements contained in the annual report are the **income statement,** the **balance sheet,** the **statement of retained earnings,** and the **statement of cash flows.**

- The **annual report** contains both **quantitative** and **verbal** information. The financial statements report **what has actually happened** to earnings and dividends over the past few years, while the verbal statements attempt to explain **why things turned out the way they did.**

- Investors use the information contained in these statements to form **expectations about the future levels of earnings and dividends,** and about the **riskiness of these expected values.**

- The **income statement** summarizes a firm's revenues and expenses over an accounting period — generally one year.

- The **balance sheet** may be thought of as a snapshot of the firm's financial position **at a point in time.** The balance sheet shows the firm's **assets and claims** on the assets.

- The claims on assets are divided into two types — those claims that arise from the investment of funds by the owners of the firm, which constitute the firm's **equity,** and those claims that arise from the debt the firm owes, which constitute the firm's **liabilities.**

- The **statement of retained earnings** reports changes in retained earnings between balance sheet dates.

- To understand how the timing of cash flows influences the financial statements and hence financial analysis, one must understand the **cash flow cycle** within a firm.

- The **statement of cash flows** converts the graphical cash flow analysis into numerical form. This statement is designed (1) to show how the firm's operations have affected its liquidity, as measured by its cash flows, and (2) to show the relationship among cash flows from operating, investing, and financing activities.

EQUATIONS

Calculates earnings per share given net income and the number of shares outstanding:

$$EPS = \frac{\text{Net income}}{\text{Shares outstanding}}.$$

Calculates dividends per share given dividends paid and the number of shares outstanding:

$$DPS = \frac{\text{Dividends paid to common stockholders}}{\text{Shares outstanding}}.$$

Demonstrates that stockholders' equity is a residual amount; that is, the residual of assets over claims:

$$\text{Assets} - \text{Liabilities} = \text{Stockholders' equity.} \qquad \textbf{(5-1)}$$

RESOLUTION TO DECISION IN FINANCE

Letters from Chairman Buffett

Of all the documents that large companies publish, none receives so much attention within the firm as the annual report to shareholders. At some companies top executives begin work on the report as much as six months before its publication, and most hire professional designers and writers to insure that the final product looks sharp and reads well.

Obviously, so much fuss would hardly be necessary if the only goal of an annual report were to inform shareholders about financial results. But, in fact, most big companies have turned their annual reports into flashy management showcases. In slick magazine format, using four-color photos, feature stories, and elaborate graphics, each firm tells the story its chairman would like to see told. To get the desired results, most annual reports are now produced by the director of public relations instead of the chief financial officer.

Because of their puffery, annual reports have lost credibility with serious seekers of financial information. Instead, Wall Street analysts and other sophisticated investors prefer more straightforward financial disclosure documents, such as 10-Ks, proxies, 8-Ks, and 13-Ds, all of which contain more detailed and unadorned information and must by law be filed with the Securities and Exchange Commission.

Of course, a company's philosophy and personality do count, and few other documents can offer better insight into these intangibles than an annual report. Most financial experts believe,

however, that companies owe it to their investors to distinguish between the fanfare and the facts. They want to see more annual reports that realistically examine management's conduct of business affairs and factually discuss projects that will improve corporate welfare in the future. They'd like to see annual reports become the equivalent of management report cards, detailing strengths and weaknesses and plans for improvement. Given such information, they claim, shareholders would be better equipped to make intelligent investment decisions.

Chairman Warren Buffett's letters, although probably a bit too subjective for financial reporting purists, represent a giant step in the desired direction. In fact, Berkshire Hathaway's annual reports contain no photographs, colored ink, bar charts, or graphs, freeing readers to focus on the company's financial statements and Buffett's interpretation of them. Some CEOs might contend that such a bare-bones approach is too dull for the average stockholder and, further, that some readers may actually be intimidated by the information overload. But Buffett would no doubt counter that, whatever its shortcomings, his approach shows much greater respect for shareholders' intelligence and capacity to understand than does the average annual report.

A. A. Sommer, Jr., who chaired an SEC panel which studied disclosure practices, says that his group agreed that letters like Buffett's were important. But, he says, "Warren's letters are unique. Few CEOs are as smart in as many ways as Warren. It would be awfully hard to require that kind of discussion from all CEOs." In other words, it takes a chairman with interesting ideas to write an interesting chairman's letter.

Sources: "Letters from Chairman Buffett," *Fortune,* August 22, 1983, 137–141; "Annual Reports Get an Editor in Washington," *Fortune,* May 7, 1979, 210–222; "Annual Reports: The Rites of Spring," *The Wall Street Journal,* March 12, 1984, 26.

QUESTIONS

5-1 What four statements are contained in most annual reports?

5-2 Is it true that if a "typical" firm reports $20 million of retained earnings on its balance sheet, its directors could declare a $20 million cash dividend without any qualms whatsoever?

5-3 What is the relationship between each rectangle in Figure 5-1 and each individual source and use in a statement of cash flows?

SELF-TEST PROBLEMS

ST-1 Webster Investment Services has the following net worth section reported on its balance sheet:

Common stock ($2 par)	$ 10,000,000
Paid-in capital	60,000,000
Retained earnings	50,000,000
Total shareholders' equity	$120,000,000

The company is planning to sell 1,000,000 new shares at $15.00 per share. After the sale, what will be the value of the common stock, paid-in capital, and retained earnings accounts?

ST-2 The consolidated balance sheets for the Clouse Lumber Company at the beginning and end of 1990 follow. The company bought $50 million worth of fixed assets. The charge for depreciation in 1990 was $10 million. Net income was $33 million, and the company paid out $5 million in dividends.

a. Fill in the amount of source or use in the appropriate column.

Clouse Lumber Company:
Balance Sheets at Beginning and End of 1990
(Millions of Dollars)

	Jan. 1	Dec. 31	Change Source	Use
Cash	$ 7	$ 15		
Marketable securities	0	11		
Net receivables	30	22		
Inventories	53	75		
Total current assets	$ 90	$123		
Gross fixed assets	75	125		
Less accumulated depreciation	25	35		
Net fixed assets	$ 50	$ 90		
Total assets	$140	$213		

continued

Clouse Lumber Company:
Balance Sheets at Beginning and End of 1990
(Millions of Dollars) *(continued)*

	Jan. 1	Dec. 31	Change Source	Use
Accounts payable	$ 18	$ 15	_____	_____
Notes payable	3	15	_____	_____
Other current liabilities	15	7	_____	_____
Long-term debt	8	24	_____	_____
Common stock	29	57	_____	_____
Retained earnings	67	95	_____	_____
Total liabilities and equity	$140	$213	_____	_____

Note: Total sources must equal total uses.

b. Prepare a statement of cash flows.
c. Briefly summarize your findings.

PROBLEMS

5-1   **Income statement construction.** Arrange these income statement items in their proper order:

Labor and material expense   Net income
Depreciation   Lease payments on buildings
Earnings before interest and taxes   Sales
Selling and administrative expense   Federal taxes
Earnings before taxes   Interest payments

5-2   **Income computation.** Murphy's Card Shop, Inc., sold 50,000 cards at $1.00 each this month. The cards cost 75 cents wholesale. Murphy's newspaper and radio advertising expenses are $1,250 monthly. Mr. and Mrs. Murphy work in the shop and pay themselves a combined monthly salary of $4,000. The monthly rent payment for the shop is $2,700, and the depreciation on the store fixtures is $900 per month. The tax rate is 30 percent. What is the store's profit or loss for the month?

5-3   **Income computation.** Travis Construction Company had total revenue of $300,000 last year. For the period, labor costs were $112,000; material costs were $48,000; depreciation expense was $20,000; administrative expenses were $56,000; interest on its loan was $8,000; and the principal repayment on the loan was $4,000. The firm's marginal tax rate is 35 percent.
a. What is the firm's reported net income?
b. Where does the principal repayment appear on the income statement?

5-4   **Income computation.** Ashley Resources' retained earnings account on its 1989 balance sheet was $1,500,000, and the account equaled $1,800,000 at the end of 1990.
a. If the firm paid no dividends (zero dividend payout) in 1990, what was Ashley's reported net income after dividends for 1990?
b. If, unlike Part a, Ashley paid 20 percent of net income to its shareholders in the form of common stock dividends, what was the firm's reported net income after dividends for the 1990 period?

c. If, unlike Parts a or b, Ashley retained 60 percent of earnings (net income), what was the firm's reported net income after dividends for the period?

5-5 **Categorizing balance sheet accounts.** Balance sheet items may be categorized as follows:

Current assets (CA)   Long-term debt (LTD)
Fixed assets (FA)   Common stock equity (CSE)
Current liabilities (CL)

Categorize each of the following accounts:

____ Debt maturing in less than one year   ____ Cash
____ Accounts receivable   ____ Common stock
____ Debt maturing in more than one year   ____ Short-term notes payable
____ Paid-in capital   ____ Retained earnings
____ Mortgage bond   ____ Accruals
____ Inventory   ____ Plant and equipment
____ Accounts payable   ____ Short-term marketable securities

5-6 **Net worth and per share calculations.** Bellview Corporation has the following net worth section reported on its 1990 balance sheet:

Common stock ($2 par)	$10,000
Paid-in capital	12,000
Retained earnings	28,000
Total shareholders' equity	$50,000

In addition, reported net income for 1990 was $9,000 and the company announced it would pay dividends totaling $5,000. Bellview sold no new common stock during the year.
a. What is Bellview's earnings per share for 1990?
b. What is Bellview's dividend per share for 1990?
c. What is the addition to retained earnings for 1990?

5-7 **Net worth accounts.** Arizona Gas and Electric has the following net worth section reported on its balance sheet:

Common stock ($2 par)	$ 8,000,000
Paid-in capital	9,600,000
Retained earnings	42,400,000
Total shareholders' equity	$60,000,000

The company is planning to sell an issue of $6,800,000 in equity at $6.80 per share. Fill in the following net worth section to reflect the sale of the new equity:

Common stock ($2 par)	$_____
Paid-in capital	_____
Retained earnings	_____
Total shareholders' equity	$_____

5-8 **Net worth accounts.** Shortly after the sale of the stock, Arizona Gas and Electric (from Problem 5-7) reported that net income for the year was $30,800,000. The company announced that it would pay dividends totaling $20,000,000.

a. What was the firm's earnings per share?

b. What was the firm's dividend per share?

c. Complete the following net worth section to reflect the stock sale and the effect of the firm's earnings and dividend payment:

Common stock ($2 par)	$_____
Paid-in capital	_____
Retained earnings	_____
Total shareholders' equity	$_____

5-9   **Income computation.** Romero's, Inc., had $7,875,000 in retained earnings on December 31, 1989. The firm paid $630,000 in dividends during 1990 and reported retained earnings on December 31, 1990, to be $8,426,250. What was Romero's reported net income for 1990?

5-10   **Balance sheet effects.** What effect would each of the following events have on a firm's balance sheet?

a. Purchase of a new asset for $2 million cash.

b. Purchase of a new asset for $2 million financed with 35 percent debt and 65 percent cash.

c. Sale of $100,000 in merchandise for cash.

d. Sale of $100,000 in merchandise for credit.

e. Inventory write-off of $200,000 due to obsolescence.

f. Payment of $50,000 to trade creditors.

5-11   **Balance sheet effects.** Refer to Tables 5-1 and 5-2 to answer the following questions:

a. What would Carter Chemical Company's balance sheet item "retained earnings" for 1990 have been if the firm paid $60 million in dividends for the year?

b. What would Carter's 1990 EPS have been had net income for that year been $150 million rather than $120 million?

c. Suppose that you knew that Carter's EPS was $2.40 and that net income was $120 million. Could you use this information to determine the number of shares outstanding?

d. If Carter sold inventories carried at $150 million for only $37.5 million, what effects would this have on the firm's balance sheet? (Disregard tax effects and assume cash sales.)

e. Carter's accountants find that MACRS depreciation shortens the tax life of assets. This would increase the firm's depreciation expense in the early years. How will this action affect the company's cash flows? No calculations are necessary.

5-12   **Sources and uses.** Determine last year's increase or decrease in cash for Oaksdale Manufacturing, Inc., given the following information. (Assume no other changes have occurred over the past year.)

Decrease in marketable securities	=	$ 50
Increase in accounts receivable	=	100
Increase in notes payable	=	60
Decrease in accounts payable	=	40
Increase in accrued wages and taxes	=	30
Increase in inventories	=	70
Increase in depreciation	=	10

5-13 **Sources and uses.** On its December 31, 1990, balance sheet, Albright Drugs reported gross fixed assets of $3,250,000 and net fixed assets of $2,500,000. Depreciation for the year was $250,000. Net fixed assets at December 31, 1989, had been $2,350,000. What figure for "cash flows asociated with long-term investments— fixed assets" should Albright Drugs report on its statement of cash flows for 1990?

5-14 **Sources and uses.** Determine the total sources and uses of funds for Detroit Steel, given the following information (in thousands):

	12/31/90	12/31/89
Cash	$ 20	$ 30
Marketable securities	50	0
Accounts receivable	150	90
Inventories	200	200
Gross plant and equipment	2,400	2,000 U
Depreciation	1,000	800
Accounts payable	120	100 S
Notes payable	0	30 U
Common stock	600	500 S
Paid-in capital	920	730 S
Retained earnings	180	160 S

(handwritten note: S b/c contra acc so backward)

5-15 **Statement of cash flows.** The consolidated balance sheets for Scotty's Supply Company at the beginning and end of 1990 follow. The company bought $75 million worth of fixed assets. The charge for depreciation in 1990 was $15 million. Net income was $38 million, and the company paid out $10 million in dividends.
a. Fill in the amount of source or use in the appropriate column.
b. Prepare a statement of cash flows.
c. Briefly summarize your findings.

Scotty's Supply Company:
Balance Sheet, Beginning and End of 1990
(Millions of Dollars)

			Change	
	Jan. 1	Dec. 31	Source	Use
Cash	$ 15	$ 7	_____	_____
Marketable securities	11	0	_____	_____
Net receivables	22	30	_____	_____
Inventories	53	75	_____	_____
Total current assets	$101	$112	_____	_____
Gross fixed assets	75	150	_____	_____
Less: Depreciation	(26)	(41)	_____	_____
Net fixed assets	$ 49	$109	_____	_____
Total assets	$150	$221	_____	_____

continued

Scotty's Supply Company:
Balance Sheet, Beginning and End of 1990
(Millions of Dollars) *(continued)*

	Jan. 1	Dec. 31	Change Source	Use
Accounts payable	$ 15	$18	_____	_____
Notes payable	15	3	_____	_____
Accrued wages and taxes	7	15	_____	_____
Long-term debt	8	26	_____	_____
Common stock	38	64	_____	_____
Retained earnings	67	95	_____	_____
Total liabilities and equity	$150	$221	_____	_____

SOLUTIONS TO SELF-TEST PROBLEMS

ST-1   The common stock sale results in 1,000,000 × $15 = $15,000,000 new equity. The breakdown of this money to the equity accounts is as follows:

	Before Sale	Transaction	After Sale
Common stock	$10,000,000	1,000,000 × $2 = $2,000,000	$12,000,000
Paid-in capital	60,000,000	$15,000,000 - $2,000,000 = $13,000,000	73,000,000
Retained earnings	50,000,000	-0-	50,000,000
Total shareholders' equity	$120,000,000	$15,000,000	$135,000,000

ST-2   **a.** Sources and Uses of Funds Analysis:

Clouse Lumber Company:
Balance Sheets (Millions of Dollars)

	Jan. 1	Dec. 31	Source	Use
Cash	$ 7	$ 15		$ 8
Marketable securities	0	11		11
Net receivables	30	22	$ 8	
Inventories	53	75		22
Total current assets	$ 90	$123		
Gross fixed assets	75	125		50
Less: depreciation	25	35	10	
Net fixed assets	$ 50	$ 90		
Total assets	$140	$213		
Accounts payable	$ 18	$ 15		3
Notes payable	3	15	12	
Other current liabilities	15	7		8
Long-term debt	8	24	16	
Common stock	29	57	28	
Retained earnings	67	95	28	
Total liabilities and equity	$140	$213	$102	$102

b. Clouse Lumber Company: Statement of Cash Flows, 1990 (Millions of Dollars)

Cash Flows from Operations:

Net income	$ 33	

Additions (sources of cash):

Depreciation	10	
Decrease in accounts receivable	8	

Subtractions (uses of cash):

Increase in inventories	(22)	
Decrease in accounts payable	(3)	
Decrease in other current liabilities	(8)	
Net cash flows from operations		$ 18

Long-term Investments:

Acquisition of fixed assets		(50)

Financing Activities:

Increase in notes payable	$ 12	
Sale of long-term debt	16	
Sale of common stock	28	
Dividends paid	(5)	
Net cash flows from financing		51
Net change in cash and marketable securities		$ 19

c. Investments were made in plant and inventories, and funds were also utilized to reduce accounts payable and other current liabilities. The cash and marketable securities accounts were also increased. Most funds were obtained by increasing long-term debt, selling common stock, and retaining earnings. The remainder was obtained from increasing notes payable and reducing receivables.

Chapter 6

Interpreting Financial Statements

DECISION IN FINANCE

Cooking the Books

Stories of accounting irregularities are commonplace, usually recounting how top management inflated profits or how some low-level employee tried to conceal the way he used corporate funds to line his pockets. But recently, tales of a new brand of financial finagling have made headlines, relating how middle managers faked the numbers to fool the boss. These managers weren't stealing money or taking bribes or kickbacks or anything like that. Rather, they "cooked the books" to make top management believe they were meeting their budgets and doing a good job. For some the payoff from the figure fudging was a bonus or a promotion; for others it was nothing more than keeping their jobs. According to Professor Lee Seidler of New York University, this is a completely new trend of disclosed fraud, the goal of which is to improve the manager's position rather than to steal money.

The fraud has hit some of the nation's best-known companies, among them H. J. Heinz Company, PepsiCo, McCormick & Company, and the J. Walter Thompson advertising agency. The scene of the "crime" at PepsiCo was the

company's Mexican and Philippine bottling operations. In November 1982 the company announced that officials there had falsified accounts since at least 1978. The cumulative effect—net income overstated by $92,100,000, or 6.6 percent of total net income for 1978 through the third quarter of 1982. In addition, PepsiCo said that the units' assets were overstated by $79,400,000, mainly due to overvaluing bottle and case inventories. As a result of these and other problems, PepsiCo said 1982 earnings per share would be 25 percent below 1981's restated earnings of $3.22 per share.

Tactics of the deception, which was discovered by local employees and reported to internal auditors at PepsiCo headquarters, included creating false invoices, inflating inventories and receivables, and deferring legitimate expenses to a later period—all designed to boost reported sales and earnings.

As you read this chapter, consider how falsified sales and earnings reports would affect the analysis of a company's financial statements. Since actual stealing isn't involved in cooking the books, does anyone get hurt? If so, who? What action should PepsiCo have taken when it discovered the deception?

See end of chapter for resolution.

In Chapter 5 we examined the major sources of financial information—the income statement and the balance sheet. We also discussed other statements, such as the statement of cash flows, which aid in the interpretation of the available financial data. In this chapter we continue our discussion of the techniques of financial analysis, especially ratio analysis, by which firms' relative riskiness, creditworthiness, profit potential, and general managerial competence can be appraised.

IMPORTANCE OF FINANCIAL STATEMENTS

Financial statements report both on a firm's position at a point in time and on its operations over some past period. However, their real usefulness lies in the fact that they can be used to help predict the firm's future earnings and dividends, as well as the riskiness of these cash flows. From an equity investor's viewpoint, *predicting the future* is what financial statement analysis is all about. Of course, current debtholders and others who are considering lending to the firm are also concerned with the firm's future. As we shall see, the firm's debt and equity investors are usually concerned with different aspects of the firm's prospects. From management's viewpoint, *financial statement analysis is useful both as a way to anticipate future conditions and, more important, as a starting point for planning actions that will influence the future course of events for the firm.*

Self-Test

What is the real usefulness of financial statements?

How do the viewpoints of equity investors and management differ concerning financial statement analysis?

RATIO ANALYSIS

Financial ratios are designed to show relationships among financial statement accounts. Ratios put numbers into perspective. For example, Firm A may have $5,248,760 of debt and annual interest charges of $419,900, while Firm B's debt may total $52,647,980 versus interest charges of $3,948,600. The true burden of these debts, and the companies' ability to repay them, can be ascertained only by comparing each firm's debt to its assets, and its interest charges to the income available for payment of interest. Such comparisons are made by **ratio analysis.**

ratio analysis
Analysis of the relationships among financial statement accounts.

A single ratio is relatively useless in making relevant evaluations of a firm's health. To be effectively interpreted, a ratio must be systematically compared in one of the following ways: (1) compared to several ratios in a network such as the Du Pont system of analysis[1] or other logical groupings, (2) compared to

---

[1]Discussed later in this chapter.

Manipulating Financial Statements

Annual reports are supposed to give a clear picture of a company's performance and current health. They are usually the first source to which investors trying to decide whether to buy or sell a certain stock turn. If profits as shown in the report are healthy, the company is presumably healthy too.

Annual reports, however, are not always what they seem, even though they are prepared in accordance with "generally accepted accounting principles" (GAAP), issued by the Financial Accounting Standards Board. In one of his own company's recent annual reports, respected financier Warren Buffett of Berkshire Hathaway noted, "Many managements view GAAP not as a standard to be met, but as an obstacle to be overcome." Indeed, it is possible for managers to plan transactions so that accounting principles require profits to be reported in a way that favors the company, but obscures the whole truth. Though it looks objective, auditing is actually subjective, and the only really solid number in any financial report is the one specifying cash. Everthing else is calculated according to certain assumptions. Managers and accountants can be honest and still produce annual reports that confuse and mislead rather than enlighten. They can also intentionally adjust information using aggressive, though still legal, accounting. The more the person reading an annual report knows about the figures on net income per share and shareholders' equity, the more he or she becomes aware of the assumptions that are involved and the errors that may have been introduced.

Obfuscation and accounting gimmicks abound in many annual reports issued by companies of all sizes. While smaller, fast-growing firms seem to take the most liberties, major corporations are not immune to temptation. One security analyst noted that General Motors

"found" $790 million by simply changing the depreciable life of its plants from 35 to 45 years. Another windfall of $480 million came from a change in GM's accounting for its pension plan, another $217 million from changing policies regarding the value of its inventory, and still another $270 million from a revision in assumptions about the residual value of leased cars. In total, financial adjustments accounted for about $1.8 billion of the $4.9 billion that GM reported as 1988 profits.

When the reporting standards for income taxes changed in the late 1980s to reflect the lower 34 percent corporate tax rate, General Electric reported a gain in income of $577 million, based on the new requirement that companies reduce their deferred tax provision. Other firms, which adopted a more conservative position, postponed some of the resulting gains instead of reporting them all at once.

Accounting rules regarding foreign currencies required IBM to increase shareholders' equity by $2.8 billion in 1987 when the dollar's relative value plunged. However, this gain was strictly transitional, and when the dollar subsequently strengthened, these gains quickly turned to losses. IBM followed the rules and reported truthfully, yet uninformed investors may have been misled by the reported income increase in 1987 and may have bought the stock on that basis.

How much more, then, might intentional manipulation mislead the unwary? Companies wishing to obscure the truth in their annual reports may take several routes. Among the most common abuses are these:

1. Hiding inventory. Sales may be slow, and retailers may be overstocked, but manufacturers can still record a sale every time they ship a product. By continuing to do so, whether or not the products can be sold at the other end, manufacturers can keep their own profit pictures bright — in the short run. Automobile companies have the greatest opportunity for abuse in this scenario.

Sources: "Cute Tricks on the Bottom Line," *Fortune,* April 24, 1989; *Forbes,* "Annual Obfuscation," May 2, 1988, and "Portfolio Strategy," August 8, 1988, and October 3, 1988.

2. Creating income. When companies enter into long-term contracts for development of products, they often do not receive any payment until the project is completed. Even so, accounting rules allow them to report income based on the percentage of completion that they calculate has been achieved. One biotech company annually reports $4.5 million in revenue for two long-term contracts for a developing product, even though it has not actually received nearly that much cash income. Although it is spending millions of dollars on development, it is offsetting these actual costs with *expected* income, which obviously holds profits up.

3. Storing up profits. A big gain in profits in a particular quarter may look great — until the next quarter, when profits slump badly after the one-time bonanza. To avoid investor shock, some companies create special reserves into which portions of unusual one-time profits can be moved, and they use these reserves to mask losses in later years. Another way of using big one-time gains from sales of assets is to disguise major losses, such as the cost of restructuring, by timing them to coincide with the gains. In 1988 United Technologies wrote off $149 million of inventory at the same time it gained $137 million by selling some subsidiaries. A problem occurs when the gain is truly a one-time event, but the loss is one that is likely to recur. Here the offset may delay the time when investors learn the truth.

4. Consolidating the bad news. "Taking a bath" by writing off losses all at once relieves a company of excess expenses and allows it to look good the following year. One company wrote off $1.4 billion as a loss in 1986 and managed to show a $924 million operating profit for 1987. Did it really do that much better — a $2.3 billion swing in the profit column? A partner in a New York–based regional accounting firm says, "Investors must realize that the year-to-year improvement is not comparable." The "big bath" may eventually help profits, but many of its supposed benefits are an illusion. It has, however, helped chief executives make a success of restructurings and leveraged buyouts and is especially popular with new CEOs, who can blame bad news on their predecessors. It can also help executives who get bonuses in high-profit years, but who don't have salary deductions when losses are incurred.

5. Deferring costs. A change in a company's method of deferring costs can greatly affect the figures in its annual report. In the software business, development of a new program may take years, with no income resulting until the product is actually on the market. Development expenses either can be reported as they occur or can be partially deferred until they can be offset by revenues from the product. Sequent Computer Systems' report for the 1988 fiscal year showed that profits per share increased 50 percent in nine months. The gain resulted from management's decision to start deferring software development costs.

6. Changing depreciation. The Securities and Exchange Commission stepped in when a major videocassette rental firm shortened its depreciation period for tapes from three years to only nine months. By doing so, they could understate current earnings and make later ones more impressive. The SEC ordered the company to revert to its three-year policy.

7. Buybacks. Earnings per share can be improved when companies reduce the number of shares outstanding through stock buyback programs. One firm repurchased 21 million shares in a 12-month period, reporting per-share earnings of $2. Without the stimulus of the buyback, the estimated earnings per share would have been only $1.81.

All of these methods can be used without breaking the law, but they tend to screen or distort the truth. Investors and others trying to decipher what annual reports really say would be well advised to read the "fine print" in the footnotes, where more detailed information can modify the information available in the bold-faced financial statements.

the trends of the firm's own ratios, (3) compared to management's goals for key ratios, or (4) compared to selected ratios of other firms in the same industry. When comparing a firm's ratios to those of other companies, care must be taken to select similar firms of corresponding size and industry type to insure the appropriate comparison of financial data. For example, small firms must often rely on trade credit and other short-term liabilities to finance the firm's assets, whereas larger firms have access to the capital markets for financing. This fact may lead to significant differences in liquidity and debt ratios if these firms are compared. Similarly, cross-industry comparisons often lead to incorrect conclusions. Thus an acceptable inventory turnover ratio for a retail jeweler would lead to disaster if adopted by a meat packer.

Analysts who use financial ratios extensively may be characterized as belonging to three main groups: (1) *managers,* who use ratios to help analyze, control, and thus improve the firm's operations; (2) *credit analysts,* such as bank loan officers or credit managers for industrial companies, who analyze ratios to help ascertain a company's ability to pay its debts; and (3) *security analysts,* including both stock analysts, who are interested in a company's efficiency and growth prospects, and bond analysts, who are concerned with a company's ability to pay interest on its bonds and with the assets that would be available to bondholders if the company were to go bankrupt.

Thus, each group of analysts has specific areas of interest which it wishes to investigate. A bank loan officer would concentrate on the short-term health of the firm, while a stock analyst would be more concerned with the firm's long-term prospects. Analysts, then, calculate specific groups of ratios rather than all possible ratios, as their purpose dictates. Therefore, ratios may be categorized into specific task groupings. We have categorized ratios into five groups: (1) liquidity ratios, (2) asset management ratios, (3) debt management ratios, (4) profitability ratios, and (5) market value ratios. Some of the most valuable ratios in each category are discussed and illustrated next, using Carter Chemical Company's financial data as they were presented back in Tables 5-1 and 5-2.

Liquidity Ratios

One of the first concerns of most financial analysts is liquidity: Will the firm be able to meet its maturing obligations? Carter Chemical Company has debts totaling $300 million that must be paid off within the coming year. Can these obligations be satisfied? A full liquidity analysis requires the use of cash budgets (described in Chapter 9); but, by relating the amount of cash and other current assets to the current obligations, ratio analysis provides a quick and easy-to-use measure of liquidity. Two commonly used **liquidity ratios** are presented in this section.

Current Ratio. The **current ratio** is computed by dividing current assets by current liabilities. Current assets normally include cash, marketable securities, accounts receivable, and inventories. Current liabilities consist of accounts pay-

liquidity ratios
Ratios that show the relationship of a firm's cash and other current assets to its current liabilities.

current ratio
This ratio is computed by dividing current assets by current liabilities. It indicates the extent to which the claims of short-term creditors are covered by assets expected to be converted to cash in the near future.

able, short-term notes payable, current maturities of long-term debt, accrued income taxes, and other accrued expenses (principally wages).

If a company is getting into financial difficulty, it begins paying its bills (accounts payable) more slowly, building up bank loans, and so on. If these current liabilities are rising faster than current assets, the current ratio will fall, and this could spell trouble. Accordingly, the current ratio is the most commonly used measure of short-term solvency, because it provides an indicator of the extent to which the claims of short-term creditors are covered by assets that are expected to be converted to cash in a period roughly corresponding to the maturity of the claims.

The calculation of the current ratio for Carter at year-end 1990 follows. (All dollar amounts in this section are in millions.)

$$\text{Current ratio} = \frac{\text{Current assets}}{\text{Current liabilities}} = \frac{\$700}{\$300} = 2.3 \text{ times.}$$

$$\text{Industry average} = 2.5 \text{ times.}$$

Carter's current ratio is slightly below the average for the industry, 2.5, but it is not low enough to cause concern. It appears that Carter is about in line with most other chemical firms. Since current assets are scheduled to be converted to cash in the near future, it is highly probable that they could be liquidated at close to their stated value. With a current ratio of 2.3, Carter could liquidate current assets at only 43 percent of book value and still pay off current creditors in full.[2]

Although industry average figures are discussed later in some detail, it should be stated at this point that an industry average is not a magic number that all firms should strive to maintain. In fact, some well-managed firms will be above the average, while other good firms will be below it. However, if a firm's ratios are far removed from the average for its industry, an analyst should be concerned about why this variance occurs. Thus, a deviation from the industry average should signal the analyst (or management) to check further.

We shall see shortly that Carter's current ratio declined to 2.3 in 1990 from 2.8 in 1989. Thus the *trend* is poor, and this could indicate potential future difficulties. More will be said about *trend analysis* later in the chapter.

quick, or acid test, ratio
This ratio is computed by deducting inventories from current assets and dividing the remainder by current liabilities.

Quick, or Acid Test, Ratio. The **quick, or acid test, ratio** is calculated by deducting inventories from current assets and then dividing the remainder by current liabilities. Inventories are typically the least liquid of a firm's current assets, hence they are the assets on which losses are most likely to occur in the event of liquidation. Therefore, a measure of the firm's ability to pay off short-term obligations without relying on the sale of inventories is important.

---

[2] $(1/2.3) = 0.43$, or 43 percent. Note that $(0.43)(\$700) \approx \$300$, the amount of current liabilities.

$$\text{Quick, or acid test, ratio} = \frac{\text{Current assets} - \text{Inventory}}{\text{Current liabilities}} = \frac{\$400}{\$300}$$

$$= 1.3 \text{ times.}$$

$$\text{Industry average} = 1.0 \text{ times.}$$

The industry average quick ratio is 1.0, so Carter's 1.3 quick ratio compares favorably with the quick ratios of other firms in the industry. If the accounts receivable can be collected, the company can pay off its current liabilities even without selling any inventory. Again, as we shall see, the trend is downward — 1.3 in 1990 versus 1.8 in 1989.

Asset Management Ratios

The second group of ratios, the **asset management ratios,** measures how effectively the firm is managing its assets. These ratios are designed to answer this question: Does the total amount of each type of asset as reported on the balance sheet seem reasonable, too high, or too low in view of current and projected operating levels? Carter Chemical Company and other companies must borrow or obtain capital from other sources to acquire assets. If they have too many assets, their interest expenses will be too high and hence their profits will be depressed. On the other hand, if assets are too low, profitable sales may be lost. So, having the proper level of each type of asset is important.

asset management ratios
A set of ratios which measure how effectively a firm is managing its assets.

Inventory Turnover. The **inventory turnover ratio**, also called the *inventory utilization ratio,* is defined as sales divided by inventories:

$$\text{Inventory turnover, or utilization, ratio} = \frac{\text{Sales}}{\text{Inventory}} = \frac{\$3,000}{\$300} = 10 \text{ times.}$$

$$\text{Industry average} = 9 \text{ times.}$$

inventory turnover ratio
The ratio computed by dividing sales by inventories; also called the *inventory utilization ratio.*

As a rough approximation, each item of Carter's inventory is sold out and restocked, or "turned over," 10 times per year. Its gross profit is therefore 10 times the difference between its selling prices and the cost of its inventory. Carter's ratio of 10 times compares favorably with an industry average of 9 times. This suggests that the company does not hold excessive stocks of inventory; excess stocks are, of course, unproductive and represent an investment with a low or zero rate of return. Carter's high inventory turnover ratio also reinforces our faith in the current ratio. If the turnover were low — say, 3 or 4 times — we might wonder whether the firm was holding damaged or obsolete goods not actually worth their stated value.

Two problems arise in calculating and analyzing the inventory turnover ratio. First, sales are stated at market prices, so if inventories are carried at cost, as they generally are, it would be more appropriate to use cost of goods sold in place of sales in the numerator of the formula. However, established compilers of financial ratio statistics, such as Dun & Bradstreet, use the ratio of sales to inventories carried at cost. To develop a figure that can be compared with those published by Dun & Bradstreet and similar organizations, it is necessary to measure inventory turnover with sales in the numerator, as we do here.

The second problem lies in the fact that sales occur over the entire year, while the inventory figure is for one point in time. This makes it better to use an average inventory measure.[3] If the firm's business is highly seasonal, or if there has been a strong upward or downward sales trend during the year, it is essential to make some such adjustment. To maintain comparability with industry averages, however, we did not use the average inventory figure.

days sales outstanding (DSO)
The ratio computed by dividing average *credit* sales per day into accounts receivable; indicates the average length of time the firm must wait after making a credit sale before receiving payment.

Days Sales Outstanding. Days sales outstanding (DSO)[4] is used to appraise the accounts receivable, and it is computed by dividing average daily sales into accounts receivable to find the number of days' sales tied up in receivables.[5] Thus, the DSO represents the average length of time that the firm must wait after making a sale before receiving cash. The calculations for Carter show that 42 days' sales are outstanding, slightly above the 36-day industry average:

$$\text{DSO} = \frac{\text{Days sales}}{\text{outstanding}} = \frac{\text{Receivables}}{\text{Average sales per day}} = \frac{\text{Receivables}}{\text{Annual sales/360}}$$

$$= \frac{\$350}{\$3,000/360} = \frac{\$350}{\$8.333} = 42 \text{ days.}$$

$$\text{Industry average} = 36 \text{ days.}$$

The DSO can be evaluated by comparison with the terms on which the firm sells its goods. For example, Carter's sales terms call for payment within 30 days, so the fact that 42 days' sales, not 30 days, are outstanding indicates that customers, on the average, are not paying their bills on time. If the trend in DSO over the past few years has been rising, but the credit policy has not been changed, this would be even stronger evidence that steps should be taken to expedite the collection of accounts receivable.

---

[3]Preferably, the average inventory value should be calculated by summing the monthly figures during the year and dividing by 12. If monthly data are not available, one can add the beginning and ending figures and divide by 2; this will adjust for growth but not for seasonal effects.

[4]In prior editions of this text, days sales outstanding (DSO) was referred to as average collection period (ACP). We have changed the terminology from ACP to DSO to conform to the more accepted business nomenclature. Therefore, wherever we previously used the term ACP, we now use the term DSO.

[5]Because information on the proportion of credit sales to total sales is generally unavailable, total sales may be used as a substitute in the DSO calculation. However, since all firms do not have the same percentage of credit sales, there is a good chance that the days sales outstanding will be understated if total sales are used rather than credit sales.

Fixed Assets Turnover. The **fixed assets turnover ratio,** also called the *fixed assets utilization ratio,* measures how effectively the firm uses its plant and equipment. It is the ratio of sales to net fixed assets:

$$\text{Fixed assets turnover, or utilization, ratio} = \frac{\text{Sales}}{\text{Net fixed assets}} = \frac{\$3,000}{\$1,300} = 2.3 \text{ times.}$$

$$\text{Industry average} = 3.0 \text{ times.}$$

Carter's ratio of 2.3 times compares poorly with the industry average of 3.0 times, indicating that the firm is not using its fixed assets to as high a percentage of capacity as are the other firms in the industry. The financial manager should bear this fact in mind when production people request funds for new capital investments.

A major potential problem exists when the fixed assets turnover ratio is used to compare different firms. All assets except cash and accounts receivable reflect the historical cost of the assets, and inflation has caused the value of many assets that were purchased in the past to be seriously understated. Therefore, if we were comparing an old firm which had acquired many of its fixed assets years ago at low prices with a new company which had acquired its fixed assets only recently, we probably would find that the old firm reported a higher turnover ratio. However, this would be more reflective of the inability of accountants to deal with inflation than of any inefficiency on the part of the new firm. The accounting profession is trying to devise ways of making financial statements reflect current values rather than historical values. If balance sheets were stated on a current value basis, this would eliminate the problem of comparisons, but at the moment the problem still exists. Because financial analysts typically do not have the data necessary to make adjustments, they must simply recognize that a problem may exist and deal with it judgmentally. In Carter's case, the issue is not a serious one because all firms in the industry have been expanding at about the same rate; thus, the balance sheets of the comparison firms are indeed comparable.

Total Assets Turnover. The **total assets turnover ratio** measures the turnover, or utilization, of all the firm's assets; it is calculated by dividing sales by total assets:

$$\text{Total assets turnover, or utilization, ratio} = \frac{\text{Sales}}{\text{Total assets}} = \frac{\$3,000}{\$2,000} = 1.5 \text{ times.}$$

$$\text{Industry average} = 1.8 \text{ times.}$$

Carter's ratio is somewhat below the industry average, meaning that the company is not generating a sufficient volume of business for the size of its total asset investment. Sales should be increased, some assets should be disposed of, or a combination of these steps should be taken.

fixed assets turnover ratio
The ratio of sales to net fixed assets; also called the *fixed assets utilization ratio.*

total assets turnover ratio
The ratio computed by dividing sales by total assets; also called the *total assets utilization ratio.*

Debt Management Ratios

financial leverage
The extent to which a firm uses debt financing.

The extent to which a firm uses debt financing, or **financial leverage,** has three important implications. (1) By raising funds through debt, the owners can maintain control of the firm with a limited investment. (2) Creditors look to the equity, or owner-supplied funds, to provide a margin of safety; if the owners have provided only a small proportion of the total financing, the risks of the enterprise are borne mainly by its creditors. (3) If the firm earns more on investments financed with borrowed funds than it pays in interest, the return on the owners' capital is magnified, or "leveraged."

To understand better how the use of debt, or financial leverage, affects risk and return, consider Table 6-1. Here we are analyzing two companies that are identical except for the way they are financed. Firm U (for "unleveraged")

Table 6-1 **Effect of Financial Leverage on Stockholders' Returns**

**Firm U
(Unleveraged)**

Current assets	$ 40	Debt	$ 0
Fixed assets	60	Common equity	100
Total assets	$100	Total liabilities and equity	$100

Sales	$120
Operating costs	90
Operating income (EBIT)	$ 30
Interest	0
Taxable income	$ 30
Taxes (50%)*	15
Net income (NI)	$ 15

$ROE_U = NI/Common\ equity = \$15/\$100 = 15\%.$

**Firm L
(Leveraged)**

Current assets	$ 40	Debt (16% interest rate)	$ 50
Fixed assets	60	Common equity	50
Total assets	$100	Total liabilities and equity	$100

Sales	$120
Operating costs	90
Operating income (EBIT)	$ 30
Interest	8
Taxable income	$ 22
Taxes (50%)*	11
Net income (NI)	$ 11

$ROE_L = NI/Common\ equity = \$11/\$50 = 22\%.$

*A 50% tax rate is used for ease of calculation.

has no debt, whereas Firm L (for "leveraged") is financed half with equity and half with debt which has an interest rate of 16 percent. Both companies have $100 of assets and $120 of sales. Their ratio of operating income to assets (also called earnings before interest and taxes, or EBIT), or the *basic earning power ratio,* is EBIT/Total assets = $30/$100 = 0.30 = 30%. Even though both companies' assets have the same earning power, Firm L provides its stockholders with a return on equity of 22 percent versus only 15 percent for Firm U. This difference is caused by Firm L's use of debt.

Financial leverage raises the rate of return to stockholders for two reasons: (1) Because interest is deductible, the use of debt financing lowers the tax bill and leaves more of the firm's operating income available to its investors. (2) If the firm's rate of return on assets (EBIT/Total assets) exceeds the interest rate on debt, as it generally does, then a company can use debt to finance assets, pay the interest on the debt, and have something left over as a "bonus" for its stockholders. For our hypothetical firms, these two effects have combined to push Firm L's rate of return on equity up to a level almost 50 percent higher than that of Firm U. Thus, debt can be used to "leverage up," or magnify, a firm's rate of return on equity.

However, financial leverage can cut both ways. If the return on assets declines, the leveraged firm's return on equity will fall farther and faster. Suppose, for example, that the operating costs for both firms rose to $120 because of inflation, yet competitive pressures during a recession kept the firms from increasing sales prices. Consequently, in terms of Table 6-1, operating costs would rise to $120 and EBIT would drop to zero for both firms. If we worked through the rest of the table, we would see that for Firm U, net income = $0 and ROE = 0%, while for Firm L, net income = −$8 and ROE = −16%. Firm U, because of its strong balance sheet, could ride out the recession and be ready for the next boom. Firm L, on the other hand, would be under great pressure. Because of its losses, its cash would be depleted, requiring it to raise funds. However, because it would be running a loss, Firm L would have a hard time selling stock to raise capital, and the losses would cause lenders to raise the interest rate, amplifying L's problems still further. As a result, Firm L just might not be around to enjoy the next boom.

We see, then, that firms with relatively low debt ratios are exposed to less risk of loss when the economy is in a recession, but they also have lower expected returns when the economy booms. Conversely, firms with high debt ratios are more risky, but they also have a chance of earning high profits. The prospects of high returns are desirable, but investors are averse to risk. Therefore, decisions about the use of debt require firms to balance higher expected returns against increased risk. Determining the optimal amount of debt for a given firm is a complicated process, and we defer a discussion of this topic until Chapter 20, when you will be better prepared to deal with it. For now we will simply look at two procedures analysts use to examine the firm's debt in a financial statement analysis: (1) They check balance sheet ratios to determine the extent to which borrowed funds have been used to finance assets, and (2) they review income statement ratios to determine the number of times interest and total fixed charges are covered by operating profits. These two sets of ratios are complementary, and most analysts use both types.

Total Debt to Total Assets. The ratio of total debt to total assets, generally called the **debt ratio,** measures the percentage of total funds provided by creditors. Debt includes both current liabilities and long-term debt. Creditors prefer low debt ratios, because the lower the ratio, the greater the cushion against creditors' losses in the event of liquidation. The owners, on the other hand, may seek high leverage, either to magnify earnings or because selling new stock would mean giving up some degree of control.

debt ratio
The ratio of total debt to total assets.

$$\text{Debt ratio} = \frac{\text{Total debt}}{\text{Total assets}} = \frac{\$1,100}{\$2,000} = 55.0\%.$$

$$\text{Industry average} = 40.0\%.$$

Carter's debt ratio is 55 percent; this means that its creditors have supplied more than half the firm's total financing. Since the average debt ratio for this industry — and for chemical producers generally — is about 40 percent, Carter would find it difficult to borrow additional funds without first raising more equity capital. Creditors would be reluctant to lend the firm more money, and management would probably be subjecting the firm to the risk of bankruptcy if it sought to increase the debt ratio still more by borrowing additional funds.

times-interest-earned ratio (TIE)
The ratio of earnings before interest and taxes (EBIT) to interest charges; measures the ability of the firm to meet its annual interest payments.

Times Interest Earned. The **times-interest-earned (TIE) ratio** is determined by dividing earnings before interest and taxes (EBIT) by the interest charges. The TIE ratio measures the extent to which operating income can decline before the firm is unable to meet its annual interest costs. Failure to meet this obligation can bring legal action by the firm's creditors, possibly resulting in bankruptcy. Note that the earnings before interest and taxes, rather than net income, is used in the numerator. Because income taxes are computed after interest expense is deducted, the ability to pay current interest is not affected by income taxes.

$$\text{TIE} = \frac{\text{EBIT}}{\text{Interest charges}} = \frac{\$266}{\$66} = 4.0 \text{ times.}$$

$$\text{Industry average} = 6.0 \text{ times.}$$

Carter's interest is covered 4 times, while the industry average is 6 times. Thus, the company is covering its interest charges by a relatively low margin of safety, and it deserves only a fair rating. The TIE ratio reinforces our conclusion based on the debt ratio — namely, that the company would face some difficulties if it attempted to borrow additional funds.

fixed charge coverage ratio
This ratio expands upon the TIE ratio to include the firm's annual long-term lease and sinking fund obligations.

Fixed Charge Coverage. The **fixed charge coverage ratio** is similar to the times-interest-earned ratio, but it is more inclusive because it recognizes that many firms lease assets and incur long-term obligations both under lease contracts and for sinking funds. Leasing has become widespread in certain industries in recent years, making this ratio preferable to the times-interest-earned ratio for many purposes. Note that a sinking fund payment goes toward the retirement of a bond. As discussed earlier in Chapter 5, Carter is required to pay off $20 million each year. Because sinking fund payments are not tax deductible, and interest and lease payments are deductible, the sinking fund payment is divided by (1 − Tax rate) to find the before-tax income required to pay taxes and have enough left to make the sinking fund payment.

Fixed charges include interest, annual long-term lease obligations, and sinking fund payments, and the fixed charge coverage ratio is defined as follows:

$$\text{Fixed charge coverage ratio} = \frac{\text{EBIT} + \text{Lease payments}}{\text{Interest charges} + \text{Lease payments} + \dfrac{\text{Sinking fund payments}}{(1 - \text{Tax rate})}}$$

$$= \frac{\$266 + \$28}{\$66 + \$28 + \dfrac{\$20}{(1 - 0.4)}}$$

$$= \$294/\$127 \qquad = 2.3 \text{ times.}$$

$$\text{Industry average} = 2.5 \text{ times.}$$

Carter's fixed charges are covered 2.3 times, as opposed to an industry average of 2.5 times. Again, this indicates that the firm is somewhat weaker than creditors would prefer it to be, and it points out the difficulties that Carter would probably encounter if it attempted to increase its debt.

Profitability Ratios

Profitability is the net result of a large number of policies and decisions. Although the ratios examined thus far provide some information about the way the firm is operating, the **profitability ratios** show the combined effects of liquidity, asset management, and debt management on operating results.

profitability ratios
A group of ratios showing the combined effects of liquidity, asset management, and debt management on operating results.

Profit Margin on Sales. The **profit margin on sales,** computed by dividing net income by sales, gives the profit per dollar of sales:

$$\text{Profit margin} = \frac{\text{Net income}}{\text{Sales}} = \frac{\$120}{\$3,000} = 4.0\%.$$

$$\text{Industry average} = 5.0\%.$$

profit margin on sales
This ratio measures income per dollar of sales; it is computed by dividing net income by sales.

Carter's profit margin is somewhat below the industry average of 5 percent, indicating that its sales prices are relatively low, that its costs are relatively high, or both.

basic earning power ratio
This ratio indicates the ability of the firm's assets to generate operating income; computed by dividing EBIT by total assets.

Basic Earning Power. The **basic earning power ratio,** which was discussed earlier in connection with financial leverage, is calculated by dividing earnings before interest and taxes (EBIT) by total assets:

$$\text{Basic earning power (BEP) ratio} = \frac{\text{EBIT}}{\text{Total assets}} = \frac{\$266}{\$2,000} = 13.3\%.$$

$$\text{Industry average} = 17.2\%.$$

This ratio shows the raw earning power of the firm's assets, before the influence of taxes and leverage, and it is useful for comparing firms with different tax situations and different degrees of financial leverage. Carter is not getting as high a return on its assets as is the average chemical company, because of its low turnover ratios and low operating income on sales.

return on total assets (ROA)
The ratio of net income to total assets.

Return on Total Assets. The ratio of net income to total assets measures the **return on total assets (ROA)** after interest and taxes:

$$\text{Return on total assets (ROA)} = \frac{\text{Net income}}{\text{Total assets}} = \frac{\$120}{\$2,000} = 6.0\%.$$

$$\text{Industry average} = 9.0\%.$$

Carter's 6 percent return is well below the 9 percent average for the industry. This low rate results from three primary factors: (1) the low profit margin on sales, (2) the low utilization of total assets, and (3) Carter's above-average use of debt, which causes its interest payments to be high and its profits to be reduced, thus lowering the profit margin on sales.

return on common equity (ROE)
The ratio of net income to common equity; measures the rate of return on common stockholders' investment.

Return on Common Equity. The ratio of net income to common equity (consisting of three accounts: common stock, paid-in capital, and retained earnings) measures the **return on common equity (ROE),** or the *rate of return on the stockholders' investment:*

$$\text{Return on common equity (ROE)} = \frac{\text{Net income}}{\text{Common equity}} = \frac{\$120}{\$900} = 13.3\%.$$

$$\text{Industry average} = 15.0\%.$$

Carter's 13.3 percent return is below the 15 percent industry average, but it is not as far below as the return on total assets. This results from the company's greater use of debt, a point that is analyzed in detail later in the chapter.[6]

Market Value Ratios

market value ratios
A set of ratios that relate the firm's stock price to its earnings and book value per share.

Market value ratios relate the firm's stock price to its earnings and book value per share. These ratios give management an indication of what investors think of the company's past performance and future prospects. If the firm's

---

[6]The fact that Carter's basic earning power and ROE are both 13.3 percent is a coincidence; normally, they differ. Actually, if more decimal places had been shown, the two ratios would have been different from each other.

liquidity, asset management, debt management, and profitability ratios are all good, then its market value ratios will be high, and its stock price will probably be as high as can be expected.

Price/Earnings Ratio. The **price/earnings (P/E) ratio** shows how many times earnings investors are willing to pay for the stock. Carter's stock sells for $28.50, so with an EPS of $2.40, its P/E ratio is 11.9:

$$\text{Price/earnings ratio} = \frac{\text{Market price per share}}{\text{Earnings per share}} = \frac{\$28.50}{\$2.40} = 11.9 \text{ times.}$$

$$\text{Industry average} = 12.5 \text{ times.}$$

Generally, P/E ratios are higher for firms with high growth prospects, but P/Es are lower for riskier firms. Carter's P/E ratio is slightly below those of other large chemical producers, which suggests that the company is regarded as being somewhat riskier than most, as having poorer growth prospects, or both.

Market/Book Ratio. The ratio of a stock's market price to its book value gives another indication of how investors regard the company. Companies with relatively high rates of return on assets generally sell at higher multiples of book value than those with low returns. Carter's book value per share is $18.00:

$$\text{Book value per share} = \frac{\text{Stockholders' equity}}{\text{Shares outstanding}} = \frac{\$900}{50} = \$18.00.$$

Dividing the market price per share by the book value gives a **market/book ratio (M/B)** of 1.6 times:

$$\text{Market/book ratio} = \frac{\text{Market price per share}}{\text{Book value per share}} = \frac{\$28.50}{\$18.00} = 1.6 \text{ times.}$$

$$\text{Industry average} = 1.8 \text{ times.}$$

Investors are willing to pay slightly less for Carter's book value than for that of an average chemical company.

The typical railroad, which has a very low rate of return on assets, has a market/book value ratio of less than 0.5. On the other hand, very successful firms such as IBM achieve high rates of return on their assets, and they have market values well in excess of their book values. In January 1990, IBM's book value per share was $70.80 versus a market price of $102.75, so its market/book ratio was $102.75/$70.80 = 1.5.

Summary of Ratios

The individual types of ratios, which are summarized in Table 6-2, give Carter's president, Bruce Berlin, a reasonably good idea of Carter's main strengths and weaknesses. First, the company's liquidity position is reasonably good; its

price/earnings (P/E) ratio
The ratio of the price per share to earnings per share; shows how many times earnings investors will pay for the stock.

market/book (M/B) ratio
The ratio of a stock's market price to its book value.

Table 6-2 **Summary of Carter Chemical Company's Ratios (Millions of Dollars)**

Ratio	Formula for Calculation	Calculation	Ratio	Industry Average	Comment
Liquidity					
Current	$\dfrac{\text{Current assets}}{\text{Current liabilities}}$	$\dfrac{\$\ 700}{\$\ 300}$ = 2.3 times		2.5 times	Slightly low
Quick, or acid, test	$\dfrac{\text{Current assets} - \text{Inventory}}{\text{Current liabilities}}$	$\dfrac{\$\ 400}{\$\ 300}$ = 1.3 times		1 time	OK
Asset Management					
Inventory turnover	$\dfrac{\text{Sales}}{\text{Inventory}}$	$\dfrac{\$3,000}{\$\ 300}$ = 10 times		9 times	OK
Days sales outstanding (DSO)	$\dfrac{\text{Receivables}}{\text{Sales}/360}$	$\dfrac{\$\ 350}{\$8.333}$ = 42 days		36 days	High
Fixed assets turnover	$\dfrac{\text{Sales}}{\text{Net fixed assets}}$	$\dfrac{\$3,000}{\$1,300}$ = 2.3 times		3 times	Low
Total assets turnover	$\dfrac{\text{Sales}}{\text{Total assets}}$	$\dfrac{\$3,000}{\$2,000}$ = 1.5 times		1.8 times	Low
Debt Management					
Debt to total assets	$\dfrac{\text{Total debt}}{\text{Total assets}}$	$\dfrac{\$1,100}{\$2,000}$ = 55 percent		40 percent	High
Times interest earned (TIE)	$\dfrac{\text{Earnings before interest and taxes}}{\text{Interest charges}}$	$\dfrac{\$\ 266}{\$\ 66}$ = 4 times		6 times	Low
Fixed charge coverage	$\dfrac{\text{Earnings before interest and taxes} + \text{Lease payments}}{\text{Interest charges} + \text{Lease payments} + \dfrac{\text{Sinking fund payments}}{1 - \text{Tax rate}}}$	$\dfrac{\$\ 294}{\$\ 127}$ = 2.3 times		2.5 times	Low
Profitability					
Profit margin on sales	$\dfrac{\text{Net income}}{\text{Sales}}$	$\dfrac{\$\ 120}{\$3,000}$ = 4 percent		5 percent	Low
Basic earning power (BEP)	$\dfrac{\text{Earnings before interest and taxes}}{\text{Total assets}}$	$\dfrac{\$\ 266}{\$2,000}$ = 13.3 percent		17.2 percent	Low
Return on total assets (ROA)	$\dfrac{\text{Net income}}{\text{Total assets}}$	$\dfrac{\$\ 120}{\$2,000}$ = 6 percent		9 percent	Very low
Return on common equity (ROE)	$\dfrac{\text{Net income}}{\text{Common equity}}$	$\dfrac{\$\ 120}{\$\ 900}$ = 13.3 percent		15 percent	Low
Market Value					
Price/earnings (P/E)	$\dfrac{\text{Market price per share}}{\text{Earnings per share}}$	$\dfrac{\$28.50}{\$\ 2.40}$ = 11.9 times		12.5 times	Slightly low
Market/book (M/B)	$\dfrac{\text{Market price per share}}{\text{Book value per share}}$	$\dfrac{\$28.50}{\$18.00}$ = 1.6 times		1.8 times	Slightly low

current and quick ratios appear to be satisfactory by comparison with the industry averages. Second, the inventory turnover ratio indicates that the company's inventories are in reasonable balance, but the low fixed assets turnover suggests that there has been too heavy an investment in fixed assets. This low turnover means, in effect, that the company probably could have operated with a smaller investment in fixed assets. Also, the high DSO figure suggests that the credit policy should be examined.

The debt management ratios suggest that the company is relatively indebted. With a debt ratio substantially higher than the industry average, and with coverage ratios well below the industry averages, it is doubtful that Carter could do much additional debt financing except on relatively unfavorable terms. Even if the company could borrow more, to do so would be to subject the company to the danger of default and bankruptcy in the event of a business downturn. The company could have avoided some of its debt financing, thus, lowering its interest payments, if excessive fixed asset investments had not been made. This, in turn, would have led to improved leverage and coverage ratios.

The profit margin on sales is low, indicating that costs are too high, or prices are too low, or both. When Berlin checked, he found that sales prices were in line with those of other firms, so he concluded that high costs are, in fact, the cause of the low margin. Further, he traced the high costs to high depreciation charges and high interest expenses, both of which are attributable to the excessive investment in fixed assets.

The basic earnings power ratio, and the returns on total assets and equity, are also below the industry averages. These relatively poor results are directly attributable to the firm's low profitability, which lowers the numerators of the ratios, and the excessive investment in fixed assets, which raises the denominators. Finally, Carter's market value relationships are also unfavorable—investors don't like firms with subnormal profits, and that fact is reflected in a low stock price and in low P/E and M/B ratios.

Trend Analysis

It is important to analyze trends in ratios as well as their absolute levels, for trends give clues as to whether the financial situation is improving or deteriorating. To do a **trend analysis,** one simply graphs a ratio against years, as shown in Figure 6-1. This graph shows that Carter's rate of return on common equity has been declining since 1987, even though the industry average has been relatively stable. Other ratios could be analyzed similarly.

Summary of Ratio Analysis: The Du Pont System

Table 6-2 summarizes Carter Chemical Company's ratios, and Figure 6-2, which is called a *modified Du Pont chart* because that company's managers developed the general approach, shows the relationships among return on asset investment, assets turnover, and the profit margin. The left-hand side of the chart develops the *profit margin on sales.* The various expense items are

trend analysis
An analysis of a firm's financial ratios over time; used to determine the improvement or deterioration of its financial situation.

Figure 6-1 **Rate of Return on Common Equity, 1986–1990**

In addition to comparing ratios to industry averages, it is important to analyze what trends the various ratios are taking. By simply plotting Carter's rate of return on common equity for each year, one can determine the trend that the ratio has taken from 1986 to 1990. A potential investor can quickly see that Carter's ROE has declined since 1987, whereas the industry rate as a whole has been comparatively steady. (This should not be surprising, because the industry rate is an average.)

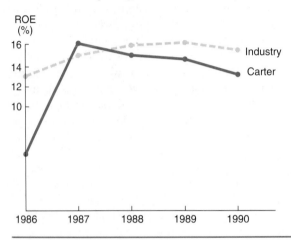

listed and then summed to obtain Carter's total costs. Subtracting costs from sales yields the company's net income. When we divide net income by sales, we find that 4 percent of each sales dollar is left over for stockholders. If the profit margin is low or trending down, one can examine the individual expense items to identify and then correct the problem.

The right-hand side of Figure 6-2 lists the various categories of assets, totals them, and then divides sales by total assets to find the number of times Carter "turns its assets over" each year. The company's total assets turnover ratio is 1.5 times.

Du Pont equation
A formula that finds the rate of return on assets by multiplying the profit margin by the total assets turnover.

The profit margin times the total assets turnover is called the **Du Pont equation,** which gives the rate of return on assets (ROA):

$$\text{ROA} = \text{Rate of return on assets} = \text{Profit margin} \times \text{Total assets turnover}$$

$$= \frac{\text{Net income}}{\text{Sales}} \times \frac{\text{Sales}}{\text{Total assets}} \tag{6-1}$$

$$= 4\% \times 1.5 = 6\%.$$

Carter made 4 percent, or 4 cents, on each dollar of sales. Assets were "turned over" 1.5 times during the year, so Carter earned a return of 6 percent on its assets.

Figure 6-2 **Modified Du Pont Chart Applied to
Carter Chemical Company (Millions of Dollars)**

The Du Pont chart was created to illustrate the relationships among key financial
ratios. The left side of the chart develops a firm's profit margin; the right side
develops its total assets turnover ratio. The profit margin is then multiplied by the
assets turnover ratio to arrive at the rate of return on assets (ROA). The use of debt is
brought into the chart by multiplying the ROA by the equity multiplier to arrive at the
rate of return on equity (ROE). The ROE could be calculated more simply, but the Du
Pont chart is useful for illustrating how debt, assets turnover, and profitability ratios
interact to determine the ROE.

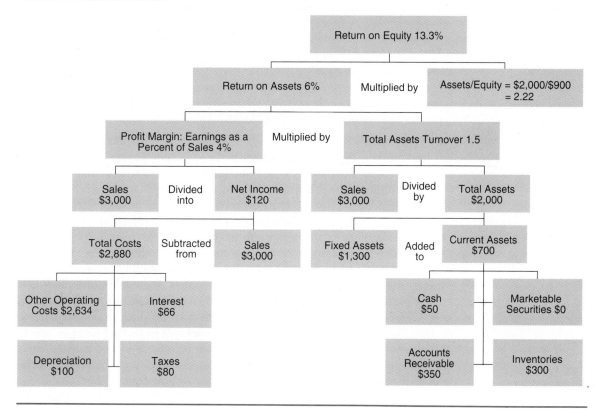

If the company had used only equity, the 6 percent rate of return on assets
would have equaled the rate of return on equity. However, 55 percent of the
firm's capital was supplied by creditors. Because the 6 percent return on *total*
assets all goes to stockholders, who put up only 45 percent of the capital, the
return on equity is higher than 6 percent. Specifically, the rate of return on
assets (ROA) must be multiplied by the *equity multiplier,* which is the ratio of
assets to common equity, to obtain the rate of return on equity (ROE):

$$\text{ROE} = \text{ROA} \times \text{Equity multiplier}$$

$$= \frac{\text{Net income}}{\text{Total assets}} \times \frac{\text{Total assets}}{\text{Common equity}} \tag{6-2}$$

$$= 6\% \times (\$2{,}000/\$900)$$

$$= 6\% \times 2.22 = 13.3\%.$$

We can also combine Equations 6-1 and 6-2 to form the extended Du Pont equation:

$$\text{ROE} = (\text{Profit margin})(\text{Total assets turnover})(\text{Equity multiplier}) \tag{6-3}$$

$$= \frac{\text{Net income}}{\text{Sales}} \times \frac{\text{Sales}}{\text{Total assets}} \times \frac{\text{Total assets}}{\text{Common equity}}.$$

Thus, for Carter, we have

$$\text{ROE} = (4\%)(1.5)(2.22)$$

$$= 13.3\%.$$

This 13.3 percent rate of return could, of course, be calculated directly: net income/common equity = $120/$900 = 13.3 percent. However, the Du Pont equation shows how the profit margin, the total assets turnover ratio, and the use of debt interact to determine the return on equity.

Du Pont chart

A chart designed to show the relationships among return on investment, assets turnover, and the profit margin.

Management can use the **Du Pont chart** to analyze ways of improving the firm's performance. On the left, or profit margin, side of Figure 6-2, Carter's marketing people can study the effects of raising sales prices (or lowering them to increase volume), of moving into new products or markets with higher margins, and so on. The company's cost accountants can study various expense items and, working with engineers, purchasing agents, and other operating personnel, seek ways of holding down costs. On the assets turnover side, Carter's financial analysts, working with both production and marketing people, can investigate ways of reducing investments in various types of assets. At the same time, the treasury staff can analyze the effects of alternative financing strategies, seeking to hold down interest expenses and the risks of debt while still using debt to increase the rate of return on equity.

As a result of this analysis, Bruce Berlin recently announced a series of moves designed to cut operating costs by more than 20 percent per year. Berlin also announced that the company intended to concentrate its capital in markets where profit margins are reasonably high, and that if competition increased in certain of its product markets, Carter would withdraw from those markets. Carter is seeking a high return on equity, and Berlin recognizes that if competition drives profit margins too low in a particular market, it then becomes impossible to earn high returns on the capital invested to serve that market. Therefore, if it is to achieve a high ROE, Carter may have to develop new products and shift capital into new areas. The company's future depends on this type of analysis, and if it succeeds in the future, then the Du Pont system will have helped it achieve that success.

Self-Test

What is ratio analysis?

A single ratio is relatively useless in making relevant evaluations of a firm's "health." How are ratios effectively interpreted?

What three main groups use ratio analysis? What types of ratios does each group emphasize?

List the five categories of financial ratios.

Identify those ratios that would be used for analyzing a firm's liquidity, and write out those equations.

Identify those ratios that would be used to measure how effectively a firm is managing its assets, and write out those equations.

Identify the debt management ratios, and write out those equations.

Identify those ratios that show the combined effects of liquidity, asset management, and debt management on operating results, and write out those equations.

Identify those ratios that relate a firm's stock price to its earnings and book value per share, and write out those equations.

Explain how the modified Du Pont system combines ratios to reveal the basic determinants of ROE.

SOURCES OF COMPARATIVE RATIOS

The preceding analysis of Carter Chemical Company pointed out the usefulness of **comparative ratio analysis** to compare firms in the same industry. Comparative ratios are available from a number of sources. One useful set of comparative data is compiled by Dun & Bradstreet, Inc. (D&B), which provides 14 ratios calculated for a large number of industries. Useful ratios can also be found in the *Annual Statement Studies* published by Robert Morris Associates, the national association of bank loan officers. The U.S. Commerce Department's *Quarterly Financial Report,* which is found in most libraries, gives a set of ratios for manufacturing firms by industry group and size of firm. Trade associations and individual firms' credit departments also compile industry average financial ratios. Finally, financial statement data are available on magnetic tapes and diskettes for thousands of publicly owned corporations, and because most of the larger brokerage houses, banks, and other financial institutions have access to these data, security analysts can and do generate comparative ratios tailored to their specific needs.

comparative ratio analysis
An analysis based on a comparison of a firm's ratios with those of other firms in the same industry.

Financial managers and investors interested in comparing a particular company's ratios with those of other firms in the same industry can find industry average data in several sources, such as the *Value Line Investment Survey,* compiled by Value Line Publishing, Inc. This excerpt from the *Value Line Survey* provides key ratios such as operating margin, net profit margin, return on equity (percent earned net worth), and the price/earnings ratio for the basic chemical industry.

						Composite Statistics: CHEMICAL (BASIC) INDUSTRY	
1985	1986	1987	1988	1989	1990		92-94E
60908	57594	66163	80684	85643	*87025*	Sales ($mill)	*104150*
16.0%	18.6%	19.9%	22.6%	21.7%	*19.5%*	Operating Margin	*20.0%*
4252.9	4429.3	4579.8	4810.0	5257.0	*5635*	Depreciation ($mill)	*6845*
2100.8	3082.1	4252.7	7641.0	7563.4	*6090*	Net Profit ($mill)	*7315*
55.3%	43.9%	45.4%	39.5%	37.7%	*39.0%*	Income Tax Rate	*40.0%*
3.4%	5.4%	6.4%	9.5%	8.8%	*7.0%*	Net Profit Margin	*7.0%*
7323.3	7426.0	9062.4	8094.4	6207.8	*9860*	Working Cap'l ($mill)	*12470*
11356	12777	12822	12847	16054	*19260*	Long-Term Debt ($mill)	*23950*
26701	26125	28325	30756	32346	*33080*	Net Worth ($mill)	*41760*
7.0%	9.4%	11.7%	18.8%	17.2%	*13.5%*	% Earned Total Cap'l	*13.0%*
7.9%	11.8%	15.0%	24.8%	23.4%	*18.5%*	% Earned Net Worth	*17.5%*
1.9%	5.9%	8.9%	17.7%	16.2%	*9.0%*	% Retained to Comm Eq	*10.0%*
77%	51%	41%	29%	32%	*46%*	% All Div'ds to Net Prof	*42%*
13.8	12.9	13.7	6.8	7.9		Avg Ann'l P/E Ratio	*10.0*
1.12	.87	.92	.56	.60		Relative P/E Ratio	*.85*
5.5%	3.9%	3.0%	4.3%	4.0%		Avg Ann'l Div'd Yield	*4.1%*

Source: *Value Line Investment Survey,* May 11, 1990, p. 1247. Copyright © 1990 by Value Line Publishing, Inc.; used by permission.

One example of industry data available to investors is the *Value Line Investment Survey. Value Line* reports are published weekly. Seventeen hundred companies are followed, and the data on each company—and its industry average—are updated four times each year. The *Survey* presents a detailed analysis of each company in the industry, plus industry average figures. Industry statistics include total industry sales data, the operating margin percentage, total depreciation dollars, total profits, the industry average income tax rate, the net profit margin percentage, total long-term debt, total net worth, the return on equity, and the average price/earnings ratio.

Each of the data-supplying organizations uses a somewhat different set of ratios, designed for its own purposes. For example, D&B deals mainly with small firms, many of which are proprietorships, and it is concerned largely with the creditors' viewpoint. Accordingly, its ratios emphasize current assets and liabilities, not market value ratios. Therefore, when you select a comparative data source, you should either be sure that your emphasis is similar to that of the agency whose ratios you use or recognize the limitations of its ratios for your purposes. In addition, there are often definitional differences in the ratios presented by different sources, so before using a source, be sure to verify the exact definitions of the ratios to insure consistency.

Self-Test

Differentiate between trend analysis and comparative ratio analysis.

LIMITATIONS OF RATIO ANALYSIS

Ratio analysis can provide useful information about a company's operations and financial condition. However, it does have some inherent problems and limitations that necessitate care and judgment. Some potential problems are listed here:

1. Many large firms operate a number of different divisions in quite different industries, making it difficult to develop a meaningful set of industry averages for comparative purposes. This tends to make ratio analysis more useful for small than for large firms.

2. Most firms want to be better than average (although half will be above and half below the median), so merely attaining average performance is not necessarily good. As a target for high-level performance, it is best to look at the industry leaders' ratios.

3. Inflation has badly distorted firms' balance sheets. Further, because inflation affects both depreciation charges and inventory costs, profits are also affected. Thus, a ratio analysis for one firm over time, or a comparative analysis of firms of different ages, must be interpreted with care and judgment.

4. The ratios can be distorted. For example, the inventory turnover ratio for a food processor will be radically different if the balance sheet figure used for inventory is the one just before versus the one just after the canning season. This problem can be minimized by using monthly averages for inventory (and receivables) when calculating some ratios.

5. Firms can employ **"window dressing" techniques** to make their financial statements look better to credit analysts. To illustrate, a Dallas manufacturer borrowed on a two-year basis on December 29, 1990, held the proceeds of the loan as cash for a few days, and then paid off the loan ahead of time on January 4, 1991. This improved the firm's current and quick ratios and made the year-end 1990 balance sheet look good. However, the improvement was strictly temporary, and a week later the balance sheet was back at the old level.

6. Different operating and accounting practices can distort comparisons. As noted earlier, inventory valuation and depreciation methods can affect the financial statements and thus distort comparisons among firms. Also, if one firm leases a substantial amount of its productive equipment, then its assets

"window dressing" techniques

Techniques employed by a firm to make its financial statements look better than they really are.

may appear low relative to sales, because leased assets often do not appear on the balance sheet. At the same time, the lease liability may not be shown as a debt. Therefore, leasing can artificially improve both the debt and turnover ratios. The accounting profession has recently taken steps that reduce this problem, and we will discuss them in Chapter 18.

7. It is difficult to generalize about whether a particular ratio is "good" or "bad." For example, a high current ratio may indicate a strong liquidity position, which is good, or excessive cash, which is bad because excess cash in the bank is a nonearning asset. Similarly, a high fixed assets turnover ratio may denote either a firm that uses assets efficiently or one that is undercapitalized and simply cannot afford to buy enough assets.

8. A firm may have some ratios which look "good" and others which look "bad," making it difficult to tell whether the company is, on balance, in a strong or a weak position. However, statistical procedures can be used to analyze the *net effects* of a set of ratios. Many banks and other lending organizations use statistical procedures to analyze firms' financial ratios and, on the basis of their analyses, classify companies according to their probability of getting into financial distress.[7]

Ratio analysis is useful in spite of these problems, but analysts should be aware of them and make adjustments as necessary. Ratio analysis conducted in a mechanical, unthinking manner is dangerous; however, used intelligently and with good judgment, ratios can provide useful insights into a firm's operations. Your judgment in interpreting a set of ratios is probably weak at this point, but it will be greatly enhanced as we go through the remainder of the book.

Self-Test

List several potential problems with ratio analysis.

SUMMARY

The primary purpose of this chapter was to discuss techniques used by investors and managers when they analyze the basic financial statements. The key concepts we covered are listed below:

- **Financial statement analysis** generally begins with the calculation of a set of **financial ratios** designed to reveal the relative strengths and weaknesses of a company as compared to other companies in the same industry, and to show whether the firm's position has been improving or deteriorating over time.

---

[7]The technique used is discriminant analysis. For a discussion, see Edward I. Altman, "Financial Ratios, Discriminant Analysis, and the Prediction of Corporate Bankruptcy," *Journal of Finance,* September 1968, 589–602, or Eugene F. Brigham and Louis C. Gapenski, *Intermediate Financial Management,* Third Edition, Appendix 20A.

- **Liquidity ratios** show the relationship of a firm's current assets to its current obligations, and thus liquidity ratios indicate the firm's ability to meet its maturing short-term debts.

- **Asset management ratios** measure how effectively a firm is managing its assets.

- **Debt management ratios** measure (1) the extent to which the firm is financed with debt and (2) the firm's ability to meet its interest and other fixed obligations.

- **Profitability ratios** show the combined effects of liquidity, asset management, and debt management on operating results.

- **Market value ratios** show what investors think of the firm by relating the stock price to earnings and book value per share.

- **Trend analysis** is important, because it reveals whether the firm's financial position is improving or deteriorating over time.

- The **Du Pont system** is designed to show how the profit margin on sales, the total assets turnover ratio, and the use of debt interact to determine the rate of return on equity.

- **Ratio analysis** has **limitations,** but used with care and judgment, it can be most helpful.

EQUATIONS

Liquidity ratios answer the question of whether the firm will be able to meet its maturing short-term obligations:

$$\text{Current ratio} = \frac{\text{Current assets}}{\text{Current liabilities}}.$$

$$\text{Quick, or acid test, ratio} = \frac{\text{Current assets} - \text{Inventory}}{\text{Current liabilities}}.$$

Asset management ratios measure how effectively the firm is managing its assets:

$$\text{Inventory turnover, or utilization, ratio} = \frac{\text{Sales}}{\text{Inventory}}.$$

$$\text{DSO} = \text{Days sales outstanding} = \frac{\text{Receivables}}{\text{Average sales per day}}.$$

$$\text{Fixed assets turnover, or utilization, ratio} = \frac{\text{Sales}}{\text{Net fixed assets}}.$$

$$\text{Total assets turnover, or utilization, ratio} = \frac{\text{Sales}}{\text{Total assets}}.$$

Debt management ratios examine the extent to which a firm uses debt financing:

$$\text{Debt ratio} = \frac{\text{Total debt}}{\text{Total assets}}.$$

$$\text{TIE} = \frac{\text{EBIT}}{\text{Interest charges}}.$$

$$\text{Fixed charge coverage ratio} = \frac{\text{EBIT} + \text{Lease payments}}{\text{Interest charges} + \text{Lease payments} + \dfrac{\text{Sinking fund payment}}{(1 - \text{Tax rate})}}.$$

Profitability ratios show the combined effects of liquidity, asset management, and debt management on operating results:

$$\text{Profit margin} = \frac{\text{Net income}}{\text{Sales}}.$$

$$\text{Basic earning power (BEP) ratio} = \frac{\text{EBIT}}{\text{Total assets}}.$$

$$\text{Return on total assets (ROA)} = \frac{\text{Net income}}{\text{Total assets}}.$$

$$\text{Return on common equity (ROE)} = \frac{\text{Net income}}{\text{Common equity}}.$$

Market value ratios give management an indication of what investors think of the company's past performance and future prospects:

$$\text{Price/earnings ratio} = \frac{\text{Market price per share}}{\text{Earnings per share}}.$$

$$\text{Book value per share} = \frac{\text{Stockholders' equity}}{\text{Shares outstanding}}.$$

$$\text{Market/book ratio} = \frac{\text{Market price per share}}{\text{Book value per share}}.$$

Du Pont system is used to analyze ways of improving the firm's performance:

$$\text{ROA} = \text{Rate of return on assets} = \text{Profit margin} \times \text{Total assets turnover}$$

$$= \frac{\text{Net income}}{\text{Sales}} \times \frac{\text{Sales}}{\text{Total assets}}. \tag{6-1}$$

$$\text{ROE} = \text{ROA} \times \text{Equity multiplier}$$

$$= \frac{\text{Net income}}{\text{Total assets}} \times \frac{\text{Total assets}}{\text{Common equity}}. \tag{6-2}$$

$$\text{Du Pont equation: ROE} = (\text{Profit margin})(\text{Total assets turnover})(\text{Equity multiplier})$$

$$= \frac{\text{Net income}}{\text{Sales}} \times \frac{\text{Sales}}{\text{Total assets}} \times \frac{\text{Total assets}}{\text{Common equity}}. \qquad (6\text{-}3)$$

RESOLUTION TO DECISION IN FINANCE

Cooking the Books

When important income and asset figures are misreported, as they were at PepsiCo, the results can be far reaching. Because such numbers are key components of many liquidity, asset management, debt management, profitability, and market value ratios, a financial analysis based on them can become badly distorted. As a result, managers, creditors, shareholders, stock analysts, and the general public may draw false conclusions and make wrong decisions.

In a highly publicized case like that of PepsiCo, the company itself pays dearly because its reputation is publicly tarnished. Such negative publicity raises questions about managerial competence and the effectiveness of corporate financial controls. Top management, whether it is a victim or an accomplice, usually gets blamed for middle-management fraud. Particularly when a number of employees are involved and when the situation continues undiscovered for several years, suspicions mount that management is either negligent or responsible.

Management is victimized in other ways, too. It may set goals based on false information, allocate investments, take out loans based on phony numbers, and pay bonuses to dishonest employees. Honest managers may actually get

punished; they may lose bonuses and promotions while their dishonest counterparts move quickly ahead.

Fraud affects shareholders as well, because they may buy or sell stock in response to erroneous information. For example, people may have bought PepsiCo's stock because they liked its healthy earnings per share and strong growth overseas. Shareholders' wealth may be further affected when the fraud comes to light. Stock prices can be expected to fall in response to such bad news, and their recovery depends on the size of the misstatement, the way that management handles the situation, and the company's overall reputation. It can take a long time for the market to regain confidence in a company that has suffered financial fraud.

In response to the falsified reports from its Mexican and Philippine operations, PepsiCo fired at least four employees, including a vice president at its corporate headquarters. At least eight other employees were replaced, although not all were fired.

In December 1982, two separate shareholder suits were filed, charging PepsiCo and its directors with filing false financial statements, but the stockholders lost the suits. The law on middle-management fraud is fuzzy, and it is hard to prove damages and management responsibility. And without proof, shareholders cannot establish either the amount of their losses or who should pay for them.

Source: Adapted from "Cooking the Books" by Arlene Hershman with Henriette Sender. Reprinted with the permission of *Dun's Business Month* (formerly *Dun's Review*), January 1983. Copyright 1983, Dun & Bradstreet Publications Corporation.

QUESTIONS

6-1 How does inflation distort ratio analysis comparisons, both for one company over time (trend analysis) and when different companies are compared? Are only balance sheet items, or both balance sheet and income statement items, affected?

6-2 If a firm's ROE is low and management wants to improve it, explain how using more debt might help.

6-3 Suppose a firm used debt to leverage up its ROE, and in the process its EPS was also boosted. Would this necessarily lead to an increase in the price of the firm's stock?

6-4 How might (a) seasonal factors and (b) different growth rates distort a comparative ratio analysis? Give some examples. How might these problems be alleviated?

6-5 Seasonal factors and differing growth rates are two problems that distort ratio analysis comparisons. What are some of the other factors that limit the effectiveness of ratio analysis?

6-6 Why would the inventory turnover ratio be more important to a grocery chain than to an insurance company?

6-7 Profit margins and turnover ratios vary from one industry to another. What differences would you expect to find between a grocery chain like Safeway and a steel company? Think particularly about the turnover ratios and the profit margin, and think about the Du Pont equation.

6-8 Indicate the effects of the transactions listed in the following table on total current assets, current ratio, and net income. Use (+) to indicate an increase, (−) to indicate a decrease, and (0) to indicate either no effect or an indeterminate effect. Be prepared to state any necessary assumptions and assume an initial current ratio of more than 1.0. (Note: As an introductory finance student, you are not expected to be familiar with all of the transactions listed. The purpose of this question is to stimulate thought about the effects of these transactions.)

	Total Current Assets	Current Ratio	Effect on Net Income
1. Cash is acquired through issuance of additional common stock.	_____	_____	_____
2. Merchandise is sold for cash.	_____	_____	_____
3. Federal income tax due for the previous year is paid.	_____	_____	_____
4. A fixed asset is sold for less than book value.	_____	_____	_____
5. A fixed asset is sold for more than book value.	_____	_____	_____
6. Merchandise is sold on credit.	_____	_____	_____
7. Payment is made to trade creditors for previous purchases.	_____	_____	_____
8. A cash dividend is declared and paid.	_____	_____	_____
9. Cash is obtained through short-term bank loans.	_____	_____	_____

	Total Current Assets	Current Ratio	Effect on Net Income
10. Short-term notes receivable are sold at a discount.	————	————	————
11. Short-term marketable securities are sold below cost.	————	————	————
12. Advances are made to employees.	————	————	————
13. Short-term promissory notes are issued to trade creditors for prior purchases.	————	————	————
14. Ten-year notes are issued to pay off accounts payable.	————	————	————
15. A fully depreciated asset is retired.	————	————	————
16. Accounts receivable are collected.	————	————	————
17. Equipment is purchased with short-term notes.	————	————	————
18. Merchandise is purchased on credit.	————	————	————
19. The estimated taxes payable are increased.	————	————	————

SELF-TEST PROBLEMS

ST-1 H. B. Jones & Co. had earnings per share of $3 last year, and it paid a $1.50 dividend. Book value per share at year-end was $30, while total retained earnings increased by $9 million during the year. Jones has no preferred stock, and no new common stock was issued during the year. If Jones's year-end debt (which equals its total liabilities) was $90 million, what was the company's year-end total debt/total assets ratio?

ST-2 The following data apply to Cavendish & Company (dollar amounts in millions):

Cash and marketable securities	$100.00
Fixed assets	$283.50
Sales	$1,000.00
Net income	$50.00
Quick ratio	2.0 ×
Current ratio	3.0 ×
Days sales outstanding (DSO)	40 days
ROE	0.12 or 12%

Cavendish has no preferred stock — only common equity, current liabilities, and long-term debt. Find Cavendish's (a) accounts receivable (A/R), (b) current liabilities, (c) current assets, (d) total assets, (e) ROA, (f) common equity, and (g) long-term debt.

ST-3 In the preceding problem you should have found that Cavendish's accounts receivable (A/R) = $111.1 million. If Cavendish could reduce its DSO from 40 days to 30 days while holding other things constant, how much cash would it generate? If this cash were used to buy back common stock (at book value) and thus reduced the amount of common equity, how would this affect (a) the ROE, (b) the ROA, and (c) the total debt/total assets ratio?

PROBLEMS

6-1   **Du Pont analysis.** Southeast Equipment's net profit margin is 4 percent, its total assets turnover ratio is 1.6 times, and its equity multiplier (assets/equity ratio) is 1.2 times. What is its rate of return on equity?

6-2   **Rate of return.** McIntire Manufacturing is 100 percent equity financed. Given the following information, calculate the firm's return on equity:

$$
\begin{aligned}
\text{Earnings before taxes (EBT)} &= \$6 \text{ million} \\
\text{Sales} &= \$30 \text{ million} \\
\text{Dividend payout ratio} = \frac{\text{DPS}}{\text{EPS}} &= 60 \text{ percent} \\
\text{Total assets turnover} &= 2.0 \text{ times} \\
\text{Combined federal and state tax rate} &= 40 \text{ percent}
\end{aligned}
$$

6-3   **Leverage ratio.** Air Express, an emerging regional airline, earns 10 percent on total assets but has a return on equity of 25 percent. What percentage of the airline's assets are financed with debt?

6-4   **Du Pont analysis.** Elizabeth Yelland, president of Quality Products, has been reviewing her firm's financial statements. She knows that the firm's return on equity is 9 percent, total debt/total assets ratio is 0.16, and total assets turnover is 2.5 times. She is sure the firm's accountant told her the profit margin before he went home, but she can't remember. Would you determine the firm's profit margin for her?

6-5   **Days sales outstanding.** Marsh's Department Store had sales of $9,000,000 this year. Of those sales, 25 percent were for cash. If the firm maintains an accounts receivable balance of $750,000, what is the firm's days sales outstanding (DSO)?

6-6   **Inventory turnover.** National Appliance Stores, Inc. had sales of $1,800,000 last year. If the firm maintains $600,000 in inventory, what is its inventory turnover? What is its inventory turnover period?

6-7   **Days sales outstanding.** Plumber's Supply House has sales of $5,760,000. Its accounts receivable balance is $688,000.
   a. If all sales are on credit, what is the company's days sales outstanding?
   b. What is the firm's days sales outstanding if 10 percent of the firm's sales are for cash?

6-8   **Liquidity ratios.** American Textile, Inc., has $2,500,000 in current assets and $1,000,000 in current liabilities. Its initial inventory level is $700,000, and it will raise funds as additional notes payable and use them to increase inventory. How much can its short-term debt (notes payable) increase without falling below a current ratio of 2 to 1? What will be the firm's quick ratio after the company has raised the maximum amount of short-term funds and purchased inventory with these funds?

6-9   **Ratio calculations.** Computer Concepts, Inc., finds itself with more debt than it would like to have. Currently, the firm has $18 million in sales, days sales outstanding

(DSO) equal to 40 days, and an inventory turnover of 6 times. Mike Binder, the firm's financial manager, is certain he can lower the DSO to 30 days and increase inventory turnover to 8 times without lowering sales. How much would be available to reduce debt if Binder succeeds in his proposed reduction of current assets?

6-10 **Ratio calculations.** Assume you are given the following relationships for The Berry Corporation:

Sales/Total assets	1.5 ×
Return on assets (ROA)	3%
Return on equity (ROE)	5%

Calculate Berry's profit margin and debt ratio.

6-11 **Ratio calculations.** Cheney Distribution Company has a quick ratio of 1.2, a current ratio of 3.6 times, an inventory turnover of 7.2 times, and current assets of $600,000. What are the firm's annual sales and, if cash and marketable securities are negligible, its days sales outstanding (DSO)?

6-12 **Pro forma statement.** Complete the balance sheet below by using the following financial information:

$$\text{Total asset turnover} = 2.0 \times$$
$$\text{Current ratio} = 2.0 \times$$
$$\text{Days sales outstanding} = 37.5 \text{ days}$$
$$\text{Inventory turnover} = 4.8 \times$$
$$\text{Debt/Total assets} = 40\%$$
$$\text{Fixed assets turnover} = 6 \times$$
$$\text{Sales} = \$2,400,000$$

Cash	$ 50,000	Current liabilities	$
Accounts receivable		Long-term debt	
Inventory	_____	Total debt	
Current assets		Common stock	100,000
Fixed assets	_____	Retained earnings	
Total assets	$_____	Total liabilities and equity	$_____

6-13 **Ratio analysis.** Data for Aspen Software Company and its industry averages follow.
a. Calculate the indicated ratios for Aspen.
b. Construct the Du Pont equation for both Aspen and the industry.
c. Outline Aspen's strengths and weaknesses as revealed by your analysis.

Aspen Software Company:
Balance Sheet as of December 31, 1990

Cash	$ 155,000	Accounts payable	$ 258,000
Receivables	672,000	Notes payable	168,000
Inventory	483,000	Other current liabilities	234,000
Total current assets	$1,310,000	Total current liabilities	$ 660,000
Net fixed assets	585,000	Long-term debt	513,000
		Common equity	722,000
Total assets	$1,895,000	Total liabilities and equity	$1,895,000

Aspen Software Company: Income Statement for Year Ended December 31, 1990

Sales		$3,215,000
Cost of goods sold:		
Materials	$1,434,000	
Labor	906,000	
Heat, light, and power	136,000	
Indirect labor	226,000	
Depreciation	83,000	2,785,000
Gross profit		430,000
Selling expenses		230,000
General and administrative expenses		60,000
Earnings before interest and taxes		$ 140,000
Interest expense		49,000
Earnings before taxes		91,000
Federal income taxes (40%)		36,400
Net income		$ 54,600

Ratio	Aspen	Industry Average
Current assets/Current liabilities	_____	2.0×
Days sales outstanding	_____	35 days
Sales/Inventories	_____	6.7×
Sales/Total assets	_____	2.9×
Net income/Sales	_____	1.2%
Net income/Total assets	_____	3.4%
Net income/Equity	_____	8.3%
Total debt/Total assets	_____	60.0%

d. Suppose that Aspen's sales as well as its inventories, accounts receivable, and common equity had doubled during 1990. How would the information about this rapid growth affect the validity of your ratio analysis? (*Hint:* Think about averages and the effects of rapid growth on ratios if averages are not used. No calculations are needed.)

6-14 **Du Pont analysis.** North Carolina Furniture Company (NCFC), a manufacturer and wholesaler of high-quality home furnishings, has been experiencing low profitability in recent years. As a result, the board of directors has replaced the president of the firm with a new president, Richard Whiston, who has asked you to make an analysis of the firm's financial position using the Du Pont chart. The most recent industry average ratios and NCFC's financial statements follow.

a. Calculate ratios to compare NCFC with the industry average ratios.

b. Construct a Du Pont equation for the firm and the industry and compare the resulting composite ratios.

c. Do the balance sheet accounts or the income statement figures seem to be primarily responsible for the low profits?

Industry Average Ratios

Current ratio	2×	Sales/Fixed assets	6×
Total debt/Total assets	30%	Sales/Total assets	3×
Times interest earned (TIE)	7×	Net profit on sales	3%
Sales/Inventory	10×	Return on total assets (ROA)	9%
Days sales outstanding (DSO)	24 days	Return on common equity (ROE)	12.8%

North Carolina Furniture Company:
Balance Sheet as of December 31, 1990 (Millions of Dollars)

	1990		1990
Cash	$ 66	Accounts payable	$ 84
Marketable securities	52	Notes payable	60
Accounts receivable	80	Other current liabilities	36
Inventories	250	Total current liabilities	$180
Total current assets	$448	Long-term debt	44
Gross fixed assets	370	Total liabilities	$224
Less: Depreciation	122	Common stock	$152
Net fixed assets	$248	Retained earnings	320
Total assets	$696	Total stockholders' equity	$472
		Total claims on assets	$696

North Carolina Furniture Company:
Income Statement for Year Ended December 31, 1990
(Millions of Dollars)

	1990
Net sales	$1,120
Cost of goods sold	930
Gross profit	$190
Operating expenses	102
Depreciation expense	26
Interest expense	10
Total expenses	$ 138
Earnings before taxes	$ 52
Taxes (50%)	26
Net income	$ 26

d. Which specific accounts seem to be most out of line in relation to other firms in the industry?

e. If NCFC had a pronounced seasonal sales pattern, or if it had grown rapidly during the year, how might this affect the validity of your ratio analysis? How might you correct for such potential problems?

6-15 **Ratio analysis.** The following data pertain to Murphy Products, Inc. (MPI):

1. MPI has outstanding debt in the form of accounts payable, notes payable, and long-term bonds. The notes carry a 14 percent interest rate, and the bonds carry a 12 percent rate. Both the notes and bonds were outstanding for the entire year.
2. Retained earnings at the beginning of the year are $7,000.
3. The dividend payout ratio (Dividends/Earnings) is 33.3 percent.
4. The debt-to-assets ratio is 60 percent.
5. The profit margin is 6 percent.
6. The return on equity (ROE) is 5 percent.
7. The inventory turnover ratio is 5 times.
8. The days sales outstanding (DSO) is 122.4 days.

a. Given this information, complete MPI's balance sheet and income statement that follow.

b. The industry average inventory turnover ratio is 6.25 times, and the industry average DSO is 72 days. Assume that at the beginning of the year MPI had been able to adjust its inventory turnover and DSO to the industry averages and that this (1) freed up capital and (2) reduced storage costs and bad debt losses. Assume that the reduction of storage costs and bad debts raised the profit margin to 10 percent. Assume further that the freed-up capital was used at the start of the year to pay an extra, one-time dividend which reduced the beginning retained earnings figure. What would have been the effect on MPI's ROE for 1990? (*Hint:* Construct a new balance sheet which will show lower inventories and accounts receivable and a different value for December 31, 1990, retained earnings. Keep common stock at the value obtained in Part a. The balance sheet will not balance; force it into balance by reducing accounts payable. Then calculate the new ROE. You can get the new net income figures directly.)

Murphy Products, Inc.:
Balance Sheet as of December 31, 1990

Cash	$ 3,750	Accounts payable	$
Inventories		Notes payable	5,000
Accounts receivable	_____		
Total current assets		Total current liabilities	_____
Net fixed assets	27,000	Bonds payable	15,000
		Total debt	
		Common stock	
		Retained earnings	_____
		Total common equity	_____
Total assets	_____	Total liabilities and equity	_____

Murphy Products, Inc.:
Income Statement for Year Ended December 31, 1990

Sales	$12,500
Cost of goods sold	_____
Gross profit	
Selling expenses	1,350
General and administrative expenses	950
EBIT	
Interest expense	
Earnings before taxes (EBT)	
Taxes	600
Net income	

6-16   Du Pont analysis. The Collier Corporation's balance sheets for 1990 and 1989 are as follows (millions of dollars):

	1990	1989
Cash	$ 21	$ 45
Marketable securities	0	33
Receivables	90	66
Inventories	225	159
Total current assets	$336	$303
Gross fixed assets	450	225
Less: Accumulated depreciation	(123)	(78)
Net fixed assets	$327	$147
Total assets	$663	$450
Accounts payable	$ 54	$ 45
Notes payable	9	45
Accruals	45	21
Total current liabilities	$108	$111
Long-term debt	78	24
Common stock	192	114
Retained earnings	285	201
Total equity	$477	$315
Total liabilities and equity	$663	$450

Additionally, Collier's 1990 income statement is as follows (millions of dollars):

Sales	$1,365
Cost of goods sold	888
General expenses	282
EBIT	$ 195
Interest	10
EBT	$ 185
Taxes (46%)	85
Net income	$ 100

a. What was Collier's dividend payout ratio in 1990?

b. The following extended Du Pont equation is the industry average for 1990:

$$\frac{\text{Profit margin} \times \text{Assets turnover} \times \text{Equity multiplier} = \text{ROE}}{6.52\% \quad \times \quad 1.82 \quad \times \quad 1.77 \quad = 21.00\%}.$$

Construct Collier's 1990 extended Du Pont equation. What does the Du Pont analysis indicate about Collier's expense control, assets utilization, and debt utilization? What is the industry's debt to assets ratio?

c. Construct Collier's 1990 statement of cash flows. What does it suggest about the company's operations?

6-17 **Ratio trend analysis.** Ameritronic Corporation's (AC) forecasted 1991 financial statements follow, along with some industry average ratios.

a. Calculate Ameritronic's 1991 forecasted ratios, compare them with the industry average data, and comment briefly on Ameritronic's projected strengths and weaknesses.

(Do Part b only if you are using the computerized problem diskette.)

b. Suppose Ameritronic is considering installing a new computer system, which would provide tighter control of inventory, accounts receivable, and accounts payable. If the new system is installed, the following data are projected rather than the data now given in certain balance sheet and income statement categories:

Cash	$ 80,000
Accounts receivable	395,000
Inventory	745,000
Other fixed assets	85,000
Accounts payable	295,000
Accruals	130,000
Retained earnings	270,710
Cost of goods sold	3,550,000
Administrative and selling expense	225,000
P/E ratio	6 ×

1. How does this affect the projected ratios and the comparison to the industry averages?

2. If the new computer system is either more efficient or less efficient and causes the cost of goods sold to decrease or increase by $200,000 from the new projections, what effect does that have on the company's position?

Ameritronic Corporation:
Pro Forma Balance Sheet as of December 31, 1991

	1991
Cash	$ 50,000
Accounts receivable	442,000
Inventory	875,000
Total current assets	$1,367,000
Land and building	238,000
Machinery	132,000
Other fixed assets	70,000
Total assets	$1,807,000
Accounts and notes payable	$ 448,000
Accruals	165,000
Total current liabilities	$ 613,000
Long-term debt	404,290
Common stock	575,000
Retained earnings	214,710
Total liabilities and equity	$1,807,000

Ameritronic Corporation:
Pro Forma Income Statement for 1991

	1991
Sales	$4,320,000
Cost of goods sold	3,650,000
Gross operating profit	$ 670,000
General administrative and selling expenses	225,270
Depreciation	144,580
Miscellaneous	143,200
Earnings before taxes	$ 156,950
Taxes (40%)	62,780
Net income	$ 94,170
Number of shares outstanding	23,000

Per-Share Data:

EPS	$4.09
Cash dividends	$0.82
P/E ratio	5×
Market price (average)	$20.47

Industry Financial Ratios (1991)[a]

Quick ratio	1.0×
Current ratio	2.7×
Inventory turnover[b]	7×
Days sales outstanding (DSO)	32 days
Fixed assets turnover[b]	13.0×
Total assets turnover[b]	2.6×
Return on total assets (ROA)	9.1%
Return on equity (ROE)	18.2%
Debt ratio	50%
Profit margin on sales	3.5%
P/E ratio	6×

[a]Industry average ratios have been constant for the past four years.
[b]Based on year-end balance sheet figures.

SOLUTIONS TO SELF-TEST PROBLEMS

ST-1 Jones paid $1.50 in dividends and retained $1.50 per share. Since total retained earnings (RE) increased by $9 million, there must be 6 million shares outstanding.

$$\Delta RE = (EPS \times \text{Number of shares}) - (DPS \times \text{Number of shares})$$

$$\Delta RE = \text{Number of shares } (EPS - DPS)$$

$$\$9,000,000 = \text{Number of shares } (\$3.00 - \$1.50)$$

$$\frac{\$9,000,000}{\$1.50} = \text{Number of shares}$$

Number of shares = 6,000,000.

With a book value of $30 per share, total common stock equity must be $30(6 million) = $180 million. Thus the debt ratio must be 33.3 percent:

$$\frac{\text{Total debt}}{\text{Total assets}} = \frac{\text{Debt}}{\text{Debt + Equity}} = \frac{\$90 \text{ million}}{\$90 \text{ million} + \$180 \text{ million}} = 33.3\%.$$

ST-2 **a.**

$$\text{DSO} = \frac{\text{Accounts receivable}}{\text{Sales}/360}$$

$$40 = \frac{\text{A/R}}{\$1,000/360}$$

$$\text{A/R} = 40(\$2.778) = \$111.1 \text{ million.}$$

b.

$$\text{Quick ratio} = \frac{\text{Current assets} - \text{Inventories}}{\text{Current liabilities}} = 2.0$$

$$= \frac{\text{Cash and marketable securities} + \text{A/R}}{\text{Current liabilities}} = 2.0.$$

$$\text{Current liabilities} = (\$100 + \$111.1)/2 = \$105.5 \text{ million.}$$

c.

$$\text{Current ratio} = \frac{\text{Current assets}}{\text{Current liabilities}} = 3.0.$$

$$\text{Current assets} = 3.0(\$105.5) = \$316.5 \text{ million.}$$

d.

$$\text{Total assets} = \text{Current assets} + \text{Fixed assets}$$

$$= \$316.5 + \$283.5 = \$600 \text{ million.}$$

e.

$$\text{ROA} = \text{Profit margin} \times \text{Total assets turnover}$$

$$= \frac{\text{Net income}}{\text{Sales}} \times \frac{\text{Sales}}{\text{Total assets}}$$

$$= \frac{\$50}{\$1,000} \times \frac{\$1,000}{\$600}$$

$$= 0.05 \times 1.667 = 0.0833 = 8.33\%.$$

f.

$$\text{ROE} = \text{ROA} \times \frac{\text{Assets}}{\text{Equity}}$$

$$12.0\% = 8.33\% \times \frac{\$600}{\text{Equity}}$$

$$\text{Equity} = \frac{(8.33\%)(\$600)}{12.0\%}$$

$$= \$416.5 \text{ million.}$$

g.

$$\text{Total assets} = \text{Total claims} = \$600$$

$$\text{Current liabilities} + \text{Long-term debt} + \text{Equity} = \$600$$

$$\$105.5 + \text{Long-term debt} + \$416.5 = \$600$$

$$\text{Long-term debt} = \$600 - \$105.5 - \$416.5 = \$78 \text{ million.}$$

Note: We could have found equity as follows:

$$\text{ROE} = \frac{\text{Net income}}{\text{Equity}}$$

$$0.12 = \frac{\$50}{\text{Equity}}$$

$$\text{Equity} = \$50/0.12$$

$$= \$416.67 \text{ million (rounding error difference).}$$

Then we could have gone on to find current liabilities and long-term debt.

ST-3 Cavendish's average sales per day were $1,000/360 = \$2.777778$ million. Its DSO was 40, so A/R $= 40(\$2,777,778) = \$111,111,111$. Its new DSO of 30 would cause A/R $= 30(\$2,777,778) = \$83,333,333$. The reduction in A/R $= \$111,111,111 - \$83,333,333 = \$27,777,778$, which would equal the amount of new cash generated.

a.
$$\text{New equity} = \text{Old equity} - \text{Stock bought back}$$
$$= \$416,500,000 - \$27,777,778$$
$$= \$388,722,222.$$

Thus

$$\text{New ROE} = \frac{\text{Net income}}{\text{New equity}}$$

$$= \frac{\$50,000,000}{\$388,722,222}$$

$$= 12.86\% \text{ (versus old ROE of 12.00\%).}$$

b.
$$\text{New ROA} = \frac{\text{Net income}}{\text{Total assets} - \text{Reduction in A/R}}$$

$$= \frac{\$50,000,000}{\$600,000,000 - \$27,777,778}$$

$$= 8.74\% \text{ (versus old ROA of 8.33\%).}$$

c. The old debt is the same as the new debt:

$$\text{New debt} = \text{Total claims} - \text{Equity}$$
$$= \$600 - \$416.5 = \$183.5 \text{ million.}$$

$$\text{Old total assets} = \$600 \text{ million.}$$

$$\text{New total assets} = \text{Old total assets} - \text{Reduction in A/R}$$
$$= \$600 - \$27.78$$
$$= \$572.22 \text{ million.}$$

Therefore

$$\frac{\text{Old debt}}{\text{Old total assets}} = \frac{\$183.5}{\$600} = 30.6\%,$$

whereas

$$\frac{\text{New debt}}{\text{New total assets}} = \frac{\$183.5}{\$572.22} = 32.1\%.$$

Chapter 7

Determining Future Financial Needs

DECISION IN FINANCE

"Wide of Mark" Forecasts

Ames Department Stores more than doubled its number of retail outlets in 1988, when it acquired 388 Zayre stores. The $800 million purchase seemed like a good idea, even though Zayre's sales had been declining for two years. Ames's management expected to turn Zayre around by applying its expertise in the operation of profitable, upscale discount stores.

A previous, flawed retail acquisition did not sway Ames's president, Peter B. Hollis, from his determination to become a major player in the retail game. In 1985, Ames had bought the G. C. Murphy Co., a variety store chain. Hollis learned only after the purchase about some serious accounting and inventory-control problems that Murphy had been experiencing. Determined not to make the same mistake twice, Hollis and his accountants pored over every detail of Zayre's operations, even shopping in its stores, before making their final decision.

Nevertheless, Ames's forecasts were wide of the mark. Because of low sales and low gross margins in its Zayre stores, Ames ended the 1989 fiscal year $228 million in the hole. Losses for the first nine months of the year had totaled $27.7 million, but analysts still predicted a profitable fourth quarter. Instead, final figures showed a disastrous fourth quarter, with a loss of about $200.3 million. Sales for 1989 totaled $5.1 billion, compared with the previous year's $3.3 billion, yet Ames still saw profits plunge from $47.2 million to a loss of $228 million.

Ames's vice president for investor relations, Douglas Ewing, said, "The size of the (1989) loss was not known until . . . we started getting details of the full fiscal year. Performance came in well below expectation."

A big part of the loss—$150 million—represented the cost of closing 74 of Zayre's least successful stores. Ames then changed the approach at the remaining stores from heavy discounting—in competition with Wal-Mart and K Mart—to "every day low prices." Ewing said,

See end of chapter for resolution.

"We were trying to re-educate the Zayre customer, but we weren't as successful as we had anticipated." In fact, they apparently alienated long-time Zayre customers by eliminating promotional sales.

In addition to the change in pricing structure, Ames gave the somewhat-dingy Zayre stores a face-lift with new paint and brighter lighting, and computerized cash registers were installed to speed up service. The parent company also rechristened the Zayre stores with the Ames name, while continuing with the redecorating efforts. Finally, to get a head start on the 1989 holiday shopping season, which was expected to be the turning point toward profitability, Ames kept all its stores open on Thanksgiving Day.

President Hollis said, "The profitability of the original Ames stores has been maintained." Indeed, sales in those 288 outlets increased 5 percent in December. For the former Zayre stores, however, sales dropped 13 percent in December, during which retailers generally achieve their highest sales of the year.

Another problem that plagued Ames, almost from the moment of the acquisition, was the overload the new stores placed on its system for tracing inventory and payments to vendors. One creditor said Ames failed to integrate its distribution network and lost control over where the merchandise was headed.

Despite the disastrous results for fiscal 1989, Ames's management remained optimistic going into 1990. They hired two investment banking firms to help restructure the company, talked of a "capital infusion," and announced that they were negotiating a new credit agreement with lending institutions.

As you read this chapter, consider the steps Ames should have taken to arrive at sales forecasts for the acquired Zayre stores. Identify possible reasons for the inaccuracies in those forecasts, and think about what might happen next as Ames struggles to get out of the "mire."

pro forma financial statement
A projected financial statement which shows how an actual statement will look if certain specified assumptions are realized.

As noted in Chapter 6, both managers and investors are deeply concerned with *future* financial statements. Therefore, managers regularly construct **pro forma,** or projected, **financial statements,** and they consider alternative courses of action in terms of how the actions will affect these projections. In this chapter we discuss how pro forma statements are constructed and then used to help estimate the need for capital.

SALES FORECASTS

sales (demand) forecast
A forecast of a firm's unit and dollar sales for some future period, generally sales based on recent trends plus forecasts of the economic prospects for the nation, region, industry, and so forth.

The most important element in financial planning is a **sales (demand) forecast.** Because such forecasts are critical for production scheduling, for plant design, for financial planning, and so on, the entire management team participates in their preparation. In fact, most larger firms have a *planning group* or *planning committee,* with its own staff of economists, which coordinates the corporation's sales forecast. A great deal of work lies behind all good sales forecasts. Companies must project the state of the national economy, economic conditions within their own geographic areas, and conditions in the product markets they serve. Further, they must consider their own pricing strategies, credit policies, advertising programs, capacity limitations, and the like. Companies also must consider the strategies and policies of their competitors, including the introduction of new products and changes in competitive pricing of key products.

If the sales forecast is off, the consequences can be serious. First, if the market expands *more* than the firm has expected and geared up for, the company will not be able to meet its customers' needs. Orders will back up, delivery times will lengthen, repairs and installations will be harder to schedule, and customer dissatisfaction will increase. Customers will end up going elsewhere, and the firm will lose market share and will have missed a major opportunity. On the other hand, if its projections are overly optimistic, the firm could end up with too much plant, equipment, and inventory. This would mean low turnover ratios, high costs for depreciation and storage, and, possibly, write-offs of obsolete inventory and equipment. All of this would result in a low rate of return on equity, which in turn would depress the company's stock price. If the company had financed the expansion with debt, its problems would, of course, be compounded.

We see, then, that an accurate sales forecast is critical to the well-being of the firm. Because sales forecasting is a rather specialized subject, we do not consider the mechanics of the forecasting process in this text. Rather, we simply take the sales forecast as given and use it to illustrate various types of financial decisions.

Self-Test

List some items which should be considered when developing the sales forecast.

Briefly explain why an accurate sales forecast is critical to the well-being of the firm.

FORECASTING FINANCIAL REQUIREMENTS: THE PERCENTAGE OF SALES METHOD

Several methods can be used to develop pro forma, or forecasted, financial statements. In this chapter we focus on the percentage of sales method, and we explain when this method can and cannot be used. Also, we discuss the growing use of computerized models for forecasting financial statements.

The **percentage of sales method** is a simple but often practical method of forecasting financial statement variables. In its simplest form, the procedure is based on two assumptions: (1) that most balance sheet accounts are tied directly to sales, and (2) that the current levels of all assets are optimal for the current sales level.

percentage of sales method
A method of forecasting financial requirements by expressing various balance sheet items as a percentage of sales and then multiplying these percentages by expected future sales to construct pro forma balance sheets.

INDUSTRY PRACTICE

A Maverick's Forecasting Approach

A public company, whose shareholders are interested primarily in quarterly profits, might not adapt well to his system, but Larry Stifler, admittedly a maverick in the art of forecasting, wonders why most other firms don't analyze their current status and future needs the way he does. Stifler is the founder and head of Health Management Resources, Inc. (HMR), a weight-loss company, and he projects and plans for impressive growth without relying on standard techniques. "It takes my accountants months to find out that I've got a problem," he says. "My system tells me immediately, and it tells me how bad things really are."

Although his system is totally quantitative, most of the numbers on which he relies are not straight dollar amounts. Instead, they are ratios, expressing relationships between one thing and another. In his two dozen locations, budgets are not drafted, and costs are not projected. But, in six years, the Stifler concept has worked well enough so that sales tripled every year, and revenues totaled $50 million in 1989. Cost controls are quite stringent, even though employees claim they don't know how much money their particular divisions spent in the past or how much they will spend in the future.

Merely knowing how much something costs and how much revenue it brings in is not enough, Stifler insists. He prefers to capture relationships within the business by building mathematical models, one of which was the catalyst for the birth of his company. Health Management Resources sprang from the founder's differences with management of the Institute for Health Maintenance (IHM), which hired him from an academic position as a behavioral psychologist to help people in the IHM program lose weight. Stifler developed a behavior modi-

Source: "The Language of Business," *Inc.,* February 1990.

fication support program which, combined with a medically supervised, very-low-calorie diet, distinguished IHM from other weight-loss firms.

Stifler agreed that IHM's program was outstanding, but he disagreed with their ideas on the future of the business and how it should be run. He worked out a mathematical model to show IHM that the company could not survive by operating free-standing, independent clinics. He tried to demonstrate that patient fees would not be enough to cover both operating costs and the big initial investment required to open a clinic. Instead, he argued, the company should cooperate with, and run its clinics in, existing hospitals, as part of physician group practices, or in other medical establishments. When IHM management couldn't be persuaded, Stifler left to found his own company, based on his own guidelines. IHM should have taken his advice, because, with its free-standing clinics, it suffered 18 months of losses before shutting them down. Meanwhile, Stifler's HMR continues to grow, relying on more of his mathematical models to keep current operations and future plans on track.

Stifler's method depends on the number of patients enrolled in his program. In a different company, the key might be the number of autos sold or clients serviced. He began building his model by estimating that a reasonable patient/staff ratio is 50 to 1. Knowing how much each employee receives in salary and benefits, he then established a direct relationship between clients and payroll. Since each staff member needs a telephone, a desk, and a chair, he also related patient enrollment directly to furniture and telephone expenses. Thus, his model shows that, for every 50 patients, he will have to spend a certain amount for payroll, telephones, and furniture. Clinic managers merely need to keep track of patient enrollment and to hire a new employee for every 50 new patients. They know the money will be avilable to pay for the additions, because each new enrollee brings in a known amount of revenue. Says a health educator at one HMR clinic, "I never write a budget or proposals. I just work with patients, and in a year of working here, there's nothing we've wanted that we couldn't get. The model tells us."

Stifler can build a model to test almost any plan by showing exactly how each facet of his business works. For instance, even though HMR offers a consumer-oriented service, the company does no consumer advertising. The model says it doesn't have to.

Patients enrolled in the weight-loss plan agree to a medically supervised fasting period followed by an 18-month maintenance program. Throughout the industry, about half of diet customers drop out after three months. From company records, Stifler learned that each patient who made it through the fast and entered maintenance brought in 2.2 new referrals to the program. If only 46 percent of the enrollees stayed on into maintenance, the program would sustain itself (since 46% × 2.2 = 100%). Management could easily project growth based on retainment of over 46 percent. Says Stifler, "Set up the business for quality care and it'll grow by itself."

In other words, the numbers say that every dollar spent providing good patient care comes back 2.2 times. Thus, a plan that would "save" $1 by changing the patient/staff ratio or otherwise reducing the costs of patient care might actually cost the company $2.20 in revenue.

This proved to be a powerful argument to use with hospital administrators, who had been accustomed to increasing profits by cutting costs.

Stifler does monitor costs, but again, by using ratios instead of dollar amounts. He keeps a running check on productivity by dividing each month's net revenue by the number of employees (figured as full-time equivalents) to get the ratio of revenues per employee. "If productivity is the same or better each month," he says, "then we're O.K." Unlike the data that accounts would provide, the number gives him an instant view of the "forest," instead of a belated "head count of the trees." If productivity does falter, he then goes a step further to try to locate the problem. Using net revenue as the constant denominator, he divides it into approximately 18 cost categories to see whether each relationship corresponds to the model. If not, he then digs further to determine the cause of the problem.

The company even uses numbers to monitor the quality of its services—not usually an easy thing to do—and to foresee problems before they cause a patient to leave. For instance, each enrollee keeps careful records and reports on such things as calories consumed and the amount worked off through exercise. Combined with other clinic records, such as the amount of weight lost, HMR not only can monitor patients' progress, but also can monitor the clinic's performance. "You can look at those numbers," says one employee, "and without even talking to patients know whether they're in trouble." Says another, "The quality-control data lets us see we have a problem before it shows up in attrition."

We illustrate the process by examining the Addison Products Company, a highly capital-intensive manufacturing company, whose December 31, 1990, balance sheet and summary income statement are given in Table 7-1. Addison operated its fixed assets at full capacity in 1990 to support its $400,000 of sales, and it had no unnecessary current assets. Its profit margin on sales was 10 percent, and it paid out 60 percent of its net income to stockholders as divi-

Table 7-1 **Addison Products Company: 1990 Financial Statements**

I. Balance Sheet, December 31, 1990 (Thousands of Dollars)

Cash	$ 10	Accounts payable	$ 40
Accounts receivable	90	Notes payable	10
Inventories	200	Accrued wages and taxes	50
Total current assets	$300	Total current liabilities	$100
Net fixed assets	300	Mortgage bonds	150
		Common stock	50
		Retained earnings	300
		Total liabilities and	
Total assets	$600	equity	$600

II. Summary Income Statement, 1990 (Thousands of Dollars)

Sales	$400
Net income	40
Dividends paid	24

dends. If Addison's sales increase to $600,000 in 1991, what will be its pro forma December 31, 1991, balance sheet, and how much additional financing will the company require during 1991?

The first step in the percentage of sales method is to identify those balance sheet items that vary directly with sales. Because Addison has been operating at full capacity, each asset item must increase if the higher level of sales is to be attained. More cash will be needed for transactions; receivables will be higher; additional inventory must be stocked; and new fixed assets must be added.[1]

If Addison's assets are to increase, its liabilities and/or equity must likewise rise: the balance sheet must balance, and any increases in assets must be financed in some manner. Some of the required funds will come spontaneously from routine business transactions, whereas other funds must be raised from outside sources. **Spontaneously generated funds** will come from such sources as accounts payable and accruals, which increase spontaneously with sales. As sales increase, so will Addison's own purchases, and larger purchases will automatically result in higher levels of accounts payable. Thus, if sales double, accounts payable will also double. Similarly, because a higher level of operations will require more labor, accrued wages will increase, and, assuming profit margins are maintained, an increase in profits will pull up accrued taxes. Retained earnings will also increase, but not in direct proportion to the

spontaneously generated funds

Funds that are obtained automatically from routine business transactions.

---

[1]Some assets, such as marketable securities, are not tied directly to operations and hence do not vary directly with sales. If anything, there will generally be an *inverse* relationship between marketable securities and growth in sales. Also, as we shall see later in this chapter, if some assets (such as fixed assets) are not being fully utilized, sales can increase without increasing those assets.

increase in sales. Other sources of financing require formal action by the firm's financial manager. For example, neither notes payable, mortgage bonds, nor common stock will increase spontaneously with sales, so management must obtain funds from these sources by taking some specific, planned action.

We can construct first approximation pro forma financial statements for December 31, 1991, proceeding as follows:

Step 1. In Table 7-2, Column 2, we multiply those balance sheet items that vary directly with sales by (1 + Sales growth rate) = 1.50. For example, since sales will grow by 50 percent, inventories must also grow by 50 percent, to $300. An item such as notes payable that does not vary directly with sales is simply carried forward from Column 1 to Column 2 to develop the first approximation balance sheet. Therefore, we carry forward figures for notes payable, for mortgage bonds, and for common stock from 1990 to 1991. One or more of these accounts will have to be changed later in the analysis, when we make our second approximation forecast.

In the lower part of Table 7-2, we multiply the income statement items by (1 + Sales growth rate) = 1.50.[2] Thus, we are assuming that each income statement item increases at the same rate as sales, which means that we are assuming constant returns to scale.

Step 2. We next add the addition to retained earnings estimated for 1991 to the December 31, 1990, balance sheet figure to obtain the December 31, 1991, projected retained earnings. Addison will have a net income of $60,000 in 1991. If the firm continues to pay out 60 percent of its income as dividends, as stated previously, the dividend payment will be $36,000, leaving $60,000 − $36,000 = $24,000 of new retained earnings. Thus, the 1991 balance sheet account retained earnings is projected to be $300,000 + $24,000 = $324,000.

Step 3. Next, we sum the balance sheet asset accounts, obtaining a projected total assets figure of $900,000, and we also sum the projected liability and equity items to obtain $669,000. At this point, the 1991 balance sheet does not balance: Assets total $900,000, but only $669,000 of liabilities and equity is projected. Thus, we have a shortfall, or **additional funds needed (AFN)** of $231,000, which will presumably be raised by bank borrowings and/or by selling securities. (For simplicity, we disregard depreciation by assuming that cash flows generated from depreciation will be used to replace worn-out fixed assets.)

additional funds needed (AFN)
Funds that a firm must acquire through borrowing or by selling new stock.

Financing the Additional Funds Needed (AFN)

Addison could use short-term bank loans (notes payable), mortgage bonds, common stock, or a combination of these securities to make up the shortfall. Ordinarily, it would make this choice on the basis of the relative costs of these

---

[2] We have simplified the process for projecting the income statement items. For example, interest expense does not vary directly with sales but will vary depending on the financing obtained to support asset growth. This refinement is dealt with in advanced finance textbooks. See Brigham and Gapenski, *Intermediate Financial Management,* third edition, Chapter 21.

Table 7-2 **Addison Products Company:**
Financial Projections (Thousands of Dollars)

	As of 12/31/90 (1)	1991 Projections First Approximation: Column 1 × 1.5 (2)	1991 Projections Second Approximation: Includes Financings (3)
Balance Sheet			
Cash	$ 10	$ 15	$ 15
Accounts receivable	90	135	135
Inventories	200	300	300
Total current assets	$300	$450	$450
Net fixed assets	300	450	450
Total assets	$600	$900	$900
Accounts payable	$ 40	$ 60	$ 60
Notes payable	10	10[a]	15[d]
Accrued wages and taxes	50	75	75
Total current liabilities	$100	$145	$150
Mortgage bonds	150	150[a]	300[e]
Common stock	50	50[a]	126[f]
Retained earnings	300	324[b]	324
Total liabilities and equity	$600	$669	$900
Additional funds needed (AFN)		$231[c]	

	For the Year Ended 12/31/90	Forecasted for 1991
Income Statement		
Sales	$400	$600
Total costs	333	500
Taxable income	$ 67	$100
Taxes (40%)	27	40
Net income	$ 40	$ 60
Dividends	24	36
Addition to retained earnings	$ 16	$ 24

[a]This account does not increase spontaneously with sales, so for the first approximation projection, the 1990 balance is carried forward. Later decisions could change the figure shown.
[b]1990 retained earnings plus 1991 addition = $300,000 + $24,000 = $324,000.
[c]AFN is a balancing item found by subtracting projected total liabilities and equity from projected total assets.
[d]$5,000 of new notes payable has been added to the first approximation balance. This is the maximum addition based on limitations on total current liabilities.
[e]$150,000 of new bonds has been added to the first approximation balance. This is the maximum additional debt due to total liability limitations.
[f]The addition to common equity is determined as a residual; it is that amount of AFN that still remains after the additon to notes payable and mortgage bonds.

different types of securities, subject to certain constraints. For example, Addison has a contractual agreement with its bondholders to keep total debt at or below 50 percent of total assets, and also to keep the current ratio at a level of 3.0 or greater. These provisions restrict the financing choices as follows:

a. *Restriction on additional debt*

Maximum debt permitted = 0.5 × Total assets

	= 0.5 × $900,000 =	$450,000

Less: Debt already projected for December 31, 1991:

Current liabilities	$145,000	
Mortgage bonds	150,000 =	295,000
Maximum additional debt		$155,000

b. *Restriction on additional current liabilities*

Maximum current liabilities = Current assets ÷ 3.0

	= $450,000 ÷ 3 =	$150,000
Current liabilities already projected		145,000
Maximum additional current liabilities		$ 5,000

c. *Common equity requirements*

Total additional funds needed (from Table 7-2)	$231,000
Maximum additional debt permitted	155,000
Common equity funds required	$ 76,000

From Table 7-2, we saw that Addison needs a total of $231,000 from external sources. Its existing debt contract limits new debt to $155,000, and of that amount, only $5,000 can be short-term debt. Thus, assuming that Addison wants to make maximum use of debt financing, it must plan to sell common stock in the amount of $76,000, in addition to its debt financing, to cover its financial requirements. Here is a summary of its projected nonspontaneous external financings:

Short-term debt (notes payable)	$ 5,000
Long-term debt	150,000
New common stock	76,000
Total	$231,000

Addison's financial manager can use the pro forma financial statements developed in Table 7-2, Column 3, to analyze the ratios implied by these statements and to construct a projected statement of cash flows. Table 7-3 shows Addison's projected statement of cash flows, and below it we show the key 1991 ratios.

These statements can be used by the financial manager to show the other executives the implications of the planned sales increase. For example, the projected rate of return on equity is 13.3 percent. Is this a reasonable target, or can it be improved? Also, the preliminary forecast calls for the sale of some common stock, but does top management really want to sell any new stock? Suppose Addison Products Company is owned entirely by Maddie Addison, who does not want to sell any stock and thereby lose her exclusive control of

Table 7-3 **Addison Products Company:
Projected Statement of Cash Flows for 1991
(Thousands of Dollars)**

Cash Flows from Operations

Net income	$60	
Additions (sources of cash):		
Increase in accounts payable	20	
Increase in accruals	25	
Subtractions (uses of cash):		
Increase in accounts receivable	(45)	
Increase in inventories	(100)	
Total cash flows from operations[a]		($40)

Cash Flows Associated with Long-Term Investments

Increase in fixed assets		(150)

Cash Flows from Financing Activities

Increase in notes payable	5	
Proceeds from sale of bonds	150	
Proceeds from sale of common stock	76	
Dividends paid	(36)	
Net cash flows from financing activities		195
Net increase in cash and equivalents		$ 5

Key Ratios Projected for December 31, 1991:

1. Current ratio	3.0×
2. Total debt/Total assets	50%
3. Rate of return on equity	13.3%
4. Sales/Inventory	2×
5. DSO	81 days

[a]*Cash flows from operations* normally includes depreciation. Here we have assumed that depreciation is reinvested in fixed assets; that is, depreciation is netted out against fixed asset additions.

the company. How then can the needed funds be raised, or what adjustments could be made? In the remainder of the chapter, we consider approaches to answering questions such as these.

Self-Test

What are the key assumptions on which the percentage of sales method is based?

Briefly explain the process you would go through to develop a percentage of sales forecast.

THE RELATIONSHIP BETWEEN GROWTH IN SALES AND CAPITAL REQUIREMENTS

The forecast of capital requirements is normally made by constructing pro forma financial statements, as described previously. However, a simple forecasting formula can be used to clarify the relationship between sales growth and financial requirements, and, under certain conditions, to calculate additional funds needed:

$$
\begin{bmatrix} \text{Additional} \\ \text{funds} \\ \text{needed} \end{bmatrix} = \begin{bmatrix} \text{Required} \\ \text{increase} \\ \text{in assets} \end{bmatrix} - \begin{bmatrix} \text{Spontaneous} \\ \text{increase in} \\ \text{liabilities} \end{bmatrix} - \begin{bmatrix} \text{Increase in} \\ \text{retained} \\ \text{earnings} \end{bmatrix} \quad \textbf{(7-1)}
$$

$$
\text{AFN} = \frac{A^*}{S}(\Delta S) - \frac{L^*}{S}(\Delta S) - MS_1(1 - d).
$$

Here,

AFN = additional funds needed.

$\frac{A^*}{S}$ = assets that increase spontaneously with sales as a percentage of sales, or required dollar increase in assets per \$1 increase in sales. $A^*/S = \$600/\$400 = 150\%$, or 1.5, for Addison from Column 1 of Table 7-2. Thus, for every \$1 increase in sales, assets must increase by \$1.50. Note that A designates total assets and A^* those assets that must increase if sales are to increase. When the firm is operating at full capacity, as is the case here, $A^* = A$.

$\frac{L^*}{S}$ = liabilities that increase spontaneously with sales as a percentage of sales, or spontaneously generated financing per \$1 increase in sales. $L^*/S = \$90/\$400 = 22.5\%$ for Addison. Thus, every \$1 increase in sales generates \$0.225 of spontaneous financing. Again, L^* represents liabilities that increase spontaneously, and L^* is normally less than L.

S_1 = total sales projected for next year. Note that $S_0 = \$400,000 =$ last year's sales. $S_1 = \$600,000$ for Addison.

ΔS = change in sales = $S_1 - S_0 = \$600,000 - \$400,000 = \$200,000$ for Addison.

M = profit margin, or rate of profit per \$1 of sales. M = 10%, or 0.10, for Addison.

d = percentage of earnings paid out in dividends, or the dividend payout ratio; d = 60%. Notice that $1 - d = 1.0 - 0.6 = 0.4$, or 40%. This is the percentage of earnings that Addison retains, and it is called the **retention rate** or *retention ratio*.

retention rate
The percentage of its earnings retained by the firm after payment of dividends, which is equal to 1 minus the dividend payout ratio.

excess capacity
Capacity that exists when
an asset is not being fully
utilized.

Because no **excess capacity** exists and ratios are constant, we can insert these values for Addison into Equation 7-1 to find the additional funds needed as follows:

$$AFN = 1.5\ (\Delta S) - 0.225(\Delta S) - 0.1(S_1)\ (1 - 0.6)$$

$$= 1.5(\$200,000) - 0.225(\$200,000) - 0.1(\$600,000)\ (0.4)$$

$$= \$300,000 - \$45,000 - \$24,000$$

$$= \$231,000.$$

To increase sales by \$200,000, Addison must increase assets by \$300,000. The \$300,000 of new assets must be financed in some manner. Of the total, \$45,000 will come from a spontaneous increase in liabilities, while another \$24,000 will be raised from retained earnings. The additional funds needed (AFN) to finance this projected growth amount to \$231,000, which must be raised over and above the internally and spontaneously generated funds. This value must, of course, agree with the number developed in Table 7-2.

Graph of the Relationship between Growth and Financial Requirements

The faster Addison's growth rate in sales, the greater its need for external financing. We can use Equation 7-1, which is plotted in Figure 7-1, to quantify this relationship. The lower section shows Addison's external financial requirements at various growth rates, and these data are plotted in the graph. Several points that can be seen from the figure are discussed below.

Financial Planning. At low growth rates, Addison needs no external financing, and it even generates surplus cash. However, if the company grows faster than 3.239 percent, it must raise capital from outside sources. If management foresees difficulties in raising the required capital — perhaps because Addison's owner does not want to sell additional stock — the company should reconsider the feasibility of its expansion plans.

Effect of Dividend Policy on Financing Needs. Dividend policy, as reflected in the payout ratio, also affects external capital requirements — the higher the payout ratio, the smaller the addition to retained earnings, and hence the greater the requirements for external capital. Therefore, if Addison foresees difficulties in raising capital, it might want to consider a reduction in the dividend payout ratio. This would lower, or shift to the right, the line in Figure 7-1, indicating lower external capital requirements at all growth rates. Before changing its dividend policy, however, management should consider the effects of such a decision on stock prices. These effects are described in Chapter 21, "Determining the Dividend Policy."

Notice that the line in Figure 7-1 does *not* pass through the origin. Thus, at low growth rates (for Addison below a growth rate of 3.239 percent), surplus funds (negative additional funds needed) will be produced, because new retained earnings plus spontaneous funds will exceed the required asset in-

Figure 7-1 **Relationship between Growth in Sales and Financial Requirements, Assuming $S_0 = \$400,000$**

External financing and a firm's sales growth rate are related. The faster a firm's growth rate in sales, the greater its need for external financing. If Addison's sales growth rate is greater than 3.239 percent, the company will need to raise capital from outside sources as shown by this graph. At growth rates less than 3.239 percent, the company will actually have surplus funds.

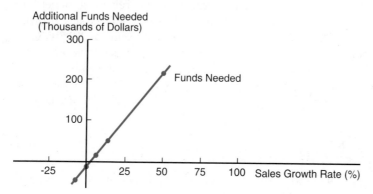

Growth Rate in Sales (1)	Increase (Decrease) in Sales, ΔS (2)	Forecasted Sales, S_1 (3)	Additional Funds Needed[a] (4)
50%	$200	$600	$231.0
10	40	440	33.4
3.239	12.956	412.956	0.0
0	0	400	(16.0)
−10	(40)	360	(65.4)

Explanation of Columns:
Column 1: Growth rate in sales, g.
Column 2: Increase (decrease) in sales, $\Delta S = g(S_0)$.
Column 3: Forecasted sales, $S_1 = S_0 + g(S_0) = S_0(1 + g)$.
Column 4: Additional funds needed $= 1.5(\Delta S) - 0.225(\Delta S) - 0.04(S_1)$.
[a]Negative additional funds required = surplus funds available.

creases. Only if the dividend payout ratio is 100 percent, meaning that the firm does not retain any of its earnings, would the "funds needed" line pass through the origin.

Capital Intensity. The amount of assets required per dollar of sales, A*/S in Equation 7-1, is often called the **capital intensity ratio.** This factor has a major effect on capital requirements per unit of sales growth. If the capital intensity ratio is low, sales can grow rapidly without much outside capital. However, if the firm is capital intensive, even a small growth in output will require a great deal of outside capital. Note that the capital intensity ratio is the reciprocal of the total assets turnover ratio only if *all* assets must grow proportionally with sales.

capital intensity ratio
The amount of assets required per dollar of sales (A*/S).

The Profit Margin and the Need for External Funds. The profit margin, M, is also an important determinant of the funds required; the higher the margin, the lower the funds requirements, other things held constant. Addison's profit margin is 10 percent. Now suppose M increased to 15 percent. This new value could be inserted into the AFN formula, and the effect would be to reduce the additional funds needed at all growth rates. In terms of the graph, an increase in the profit margin would cause the line to shift down, and its slope would also become less steep. Because of the relationship between profit margins and external capital requirements, some very rapidly growing firms do not need much external capital. For example, in the 1960s Xerox grew very rapidly with very little borrowing or stock sales. However, as the company lost patent protection and as competition intensified in the copier industry, Xerox's profit margin declined, its needs for external capital rose, and it began to borrow heavily from banks and other sources. IBM has had a similar experience.

Self-Test

Write out the formula used to show the relationship between sales growth and financial requirements, and briefly explain it.

How do each of the following affect external capital requirements:
a. Dividend policy?
b. Capital intensity?
c. Profit margin?

FORECASTING FINANCIAL REQUIREMENTS WHEN THE BALANCE SHEET RATIOS ARE SUBJECT TO CHANGE

To this point we have been assuming that the balance sheet ratios of assets and liabilities to sales (A*/S and L*/S) remain constant over time. For this to happen, each "spontaneous" asset and liability item must increase at the same rate as sales. In graph form, this assumes the type of relationship indicated in Panel a of Figure 7-2, a relationship that is linear and passes through the origin. Under these conditions, if the company's sales expand from $200 million to $400 million, accounts receivable will increase proportionately, from $100 million to $200 million.

The assumption of constant ratios is appropriate at times, but there are times when it is incorrect. Three such conditions are described in the following sections.

Economies of Scale

There are economies of scale in the use of many kinds of assets, and where economies occur, the ratios are likely to change over time as the size of the firm increases. For example, firms often need to maintain base stocks of different inventory items, even if current sales levels are quite low. Then, as sales

Figure 7-2 **Three Possible Ratio Relationships (Millions of Dollars)**

There are three possible assets/liabilities to sales relationships that can exist: Constant ratio, economies of scale, and lumpy assets. If the balance sheet ratios of assets and liabilities to sales remain constant over time (i.e, they increase at the same rate as sales), a linear relationship exists and that line passes through the origin. Panel a shows this relationship. With economies of scale, ratios are likely to change over time as the size of the firm increases. A base stock of assets is needed for even low sales levels, but the asset level grows less rapidly than the sales level. This situation is depicted in Panel b. Many industries must add fixed assets in large, discrete units; this situation is illustrated in Panel c.

a. Constant Ratios

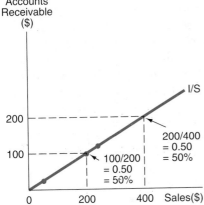

b. Economies of Scale

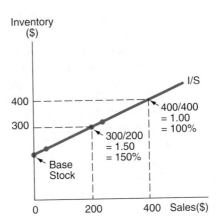

c. Lumpy Assets

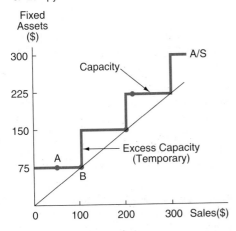

		Panel a		Panel b		Panel c	
	Sales	**AR**	**AR/Sales**	**INV**	**Inventory/Sales**	**FA**	**FA/Sales**
1988	$ 50	$ 25	0.5	$225	4.500	$ 75	1.50
1989	200	100	0.5	300	1.500	150	0.75
1990	250	125	0.5	343.75	1.375	225	0.90

expand, inventories grow less rapidly than sales, so the ratio of inventory to sales (I/S) declines. This situation is depicted in Panel b of Figure 7-2. Here we see that the inventory/sales ratio is 1.5, or 150 percent, when sales are $200 million, but it declines to 1.0 when sales climb to $400 million.

Although the relationship shown here for economies of scale is linear, this is not necessarily the case. Indeed, as we shall see in Chapter 10, if the firm uses the most popular model for establishing inventory levels, the EOQ model, then inventories will rise with the square root of sales. This means that the graph in Panel b of Figure 7-2 would tend to be a curved line whose slope decreases at higher sales levels.

Lumpy Assets

lumpy assets
Assets that cannot be acquired in small increments but must be obtained in large, discrete amounts.

In many industries, technological considerations dictate that if a firm is to be competitive, it must add fixed assets in large, discrete units; such assets are often referred to as **lumpy assets.** In the paper industry, for example, there are strong economies of scale in basic paper mill equipment, so when paper companies expand capacity, they must do so in large, or lumpy, increments. This type of situation is depicted in Panel c of Figure 7-2. Here we assume that the smallest efficient plant has a cost of $75 million, and that such a plant can produce enough output to attain a sales level of $100 million. If the firm is to be competitive, it simply must have at least $75 million of fixed assets.

This situation has a major effect on the fixed assets/sales (FA/S) ratio at different sales levels, and, consequently, on financial requirements. At Point A in Figure 7-2c, which represents a sales level of $50 million, the fixed assets are $75 million, so the ratio FA/S = $75/$50 = 1.5. However, sales can expand by $50 million, out to $100 million, with no additions to fixed assets. At that point, represented by Point B, the ratio FA/S = $75/$100 = 0.75. However, if the firm is operating at capacity (sales of $100 million), even a small increase in sales would require a doubling of plant capacity, so a small projected sales increase would bring with it very large financial requirements.

Cyclical Changes

Panels a, b, and c of Figure 7-2 all focus on target, or projected, relationships between sales and assets. Actual sales, however, are often different from projected sales, and the actual asset/sales ratio for a given period may thus be quite different from the planned ratio. To illustrate, the firm depicted in Panel b of Figure 7-2 might, when its sales are at $200 million and its inventories at $300 million, project a sales expansion to $400 million and then increase its inventories to $400 million in anticipation of the projected growth. Yet suppose an unforeseen economic downturn held sales down to only $300 million. In this case, actual inventories would be $400 million, but inventories of only $350 million would be needed to support the actual sales of $300 million. If the firm were making its forecast for the following year, it would have to recognize (1) that sales could expand by $100 million with no increase in inventories, but (2) that any sales expansion beyond $100 million would require additional financing to build inventories.

Modifying the Forecast of Additional Funds Needed

If any of the asset/sales ratios that can be calculated from data in Table 7-2 are subject to any of the conditions noted above, then it will be necessary (1) to make separate forecasts of the requirements for each type of asset, (2) to forecast spontaneously generated funds, and (3) to subtract the spontaneously generated funds and the addition to retained earnings from the forecasted asset requirements to determine the external funds needed.

To illustrate, consider again the Addison example set forth in Tables 7-1, 7-2, and 7-3. Now suppose that a ratio analysis along the lines described in Chapter 6 suggests that the cash, receivables, and inventory ratios indicated from the data in Table 7-2 are appropriate, as are the liability ratios and the retained earnings calculations, but that excess capacity exists in fixed assets. Specifically, assume that in 1990 fixed assets were being utilized at only 80 percent of capacity. To use the existing fixed assets at full capacity, 1990 sales could have been as high as $500,000:

$$\text{Full capacity sales} = \frac{\text{Current sales}}{\% \text{ fixed assets operated}} = \frac{\$400,000}{0.80} = \$500,000 \text{ sales at full capacity.}$$

This suggests that Addison's target fixed assets/sales ratio should be

$$\text{Target FA/Sales ratio} = \frac{\text{Curent level of fixed assets}}{\text{Full capacity sales}} = \frac{\$300,000}{\$500,000} = 0.6,$$

not the 0.75 that actually exists. Therefore, at the projected sales level of $600,000, Addison would need fixed assets of only 0.6($600,000) = $360,000, up only $60,000 from the $300,000 currently on hand, rather than the increase of $150,000 which was forecasted by the percentage of sales method.

We estimated earlier, in Table 7-2, that Addison would need an additional $231,000 of capital and that at least $76,000 of this amount would have to be raised by selling common stock. However, those estimates were based on the assumption that $450,000 − $300,000 = $150,000 of additional fixed assets would be required. If Addison could attain a sales level of $600,000 with only $360,000 of fixed assets, then external funds needed would decline by $90,000, to $141,000, and no new stock would have to be issued.

Self-Test

Identify and describe three conditions under which the assumption that each "spontaneous" asset and liability item increases at the same rate as sales is not correct.

Explain how one might adjust the AFN formula to calculate full capacity sales and the target FA/S ratio when excess capacity exists in fixed assets.

COMPUTERIZED FINANCIAL PLANNING MODELS

Although the type of financial forecasting described in this chapter can be done by hand, most well-managed firms with sales greater than a few million dollars employ some type of computerized financial planning model. Such models can be programmed to show the effects of different sales levels, different ratios of sales to operating assets, and different assumptions about sales prices and input costs (labor, materials, and so forth). Plans are then made regarding how financial requirements are to be met — through bank loans, thus increasing short-term notes payable; by selling long-term bonds; or by selling new common stock. Pro forma balance sheets and income statements are generated under the different financing plans, and earnings per share are projected, along with such risk measures as the current ratio, the debt/assets ratio, and the times-interest-earned ratio.

Depending on how these projections look, management may modify its initial plans. For example, the firm may conclude that its sales forecast must be cut because the requirements for external capital exceed the firm's ability to raise money. Or management may decide to reduce dividends and thus generate more funds internally. Alternatively, the company may decide to investigate production processes that require fewer fixed assets, or it may consider the possibility of buying rather than manufacturing certain components, thus eliminating raw materials and work-in-process inventories, as well as certain manufacturing facilities.

In subsequent chapters we examine in detail ways of analyzing various types of policy change. In all such considerations, the basic issue is the effect that a specific action will have on future earnings, on the riskiness of earnings, and hence on the price of the firm's stock. Because computerized planning models help management assess these effects, they are playing an ever-increasing role in corporate management.[3]

---

[3]It is becoming increasingly easy for companies to develop planning models as a result of the dramatic improvements that have been made in computer hardware and software in recent years. *Lotus 1-2-3* is one system that can be used, and a more elaborate system is the *Interactive Financial Planning System (IFPS)*. Both systems are used by literally thousands of companies, including 3M Corporation, Shell Oil, and Florida Power & Light. Increasingly, a knowledge of these or similar planning systems is becoming a requirement for getting even an entry-level job in the finance department of many corporations.

Note that in this chapter we have concentrated on long-run, or strategic, financial planning. Within the framework of the long-run strategic plan, firms also develop short-run financial plans. For example, in Table 7-2 we saw that Addison Products expects to need $231,000 by the end of 1991, and that it plans to raise this capital by using short-term debt, long-term debt, and common stock. However, we do not know when during the year the need for funds will occur, or when Addison will obtain each of its different types of capital. To address these issues, the firm must develop a short-run financial plan, the centerpiece of which is the *cash budget,* which is a projection of cash inflows and outflows on a daily, weekly, or monthly basis during the coming year (or other budget period). Although considering the cash budget here would complete our examination of the basic types of analysis done in connection with financial planning, we shall defer this discussion to Chapter 9, "Managing Cash and Marketable Securities," because cash budgets can best be understood after we have discussed the firm's target cash balance.

Self-Test

Why are computerized planning models playing an increasingly important role in corporate management?

  SMALL BUSINESS

Franchising

As was mentioned in Chapter 1, small businesses often have both limited access to capital markets and limited human resources. What can a small business owner with limited resources do to fully capitalize on a great idea? Sometimes, the owner can attract venture capital, if a lack of capital is the real impediment to developing the business. However, if developing the idea requires both substantial capital and human resources that the owner can't provide, there is another avenue to follow—franchising.

Franchising uses other people's money, energy, and desire to own their own business to promote the concept developed by the franchiser. In an ideal franchise setting, the franchiser benefits by being able to sell franchises, and the franchisees benefit from a relatively simple way of getting started in a successful business.

Nearly everyone is familiar with McDonald's, Taco Bell, and other large, fast-food franchise operations. Other, less familiar products or services offered by franchise businesses include such diverse things as automotive services, video rentals, personnel services, and even medical care.

The franchiser may provide specific benefits to franchisees, including some of the following:

- an idea
- a proprietary product
- a recognized trade name
- a volume buying service
- advertising
- training in providing a service
- plans and designs for facilities and operations
- profit planning

Typically, the franchiser will have already paid the costs of product development and will have built one or more prototypes of the business. Those prototypes give the franchiser a testing ground for working out many of the "bugs" in the business. Thus, the franchisee is spared the expense of unanticipated problems with the business. Once the prototypes are successful, the franchiser is ready to begin marketing franchises.

An Example

To illustrate, suppose you and a friend develop a recipe that allows you to make delicious cookies that bake very quickly. Also, you come up with an oven that is easy to load and unload and that fans the aroma of the cookies into the surrounding air. You open a shop and you soon learn which varieties of cookies sell well and which don't. You also begin to develop relationships with reliable suppliers, and you learn (through trial and error) which ones will provide consistently high-quality ingredients. As you operate your first cookie shop, you learn which hours have the highest volume of business and thus require more than one employee. Although your store's first location is a disaster, you learn something about choosing locations, so your second one is highly successful.

As you operate the shop, you learn a good deal about cash flow from your mother, a financial vice president with a larger firm. She helps you develop a solid, realistic cash-flow plan for timing cash inflows and outflows.

Finally, you experiment with a number of color schemes and names until you create an image for the shop that is most effective. You register the name as a trade name.

By the time you have opened your second successful shop, many of the pitfalls that could hinder such a business have been overcome. So, as you think about opening new shops, you know that these problems will not again cost you the time and money that you have already expended. The second shop is easier than the first one, and the third one is a breeze.

Why sell franchises? Perhaps the strongest motivation is that you have neither the time nor the money to get the maximum benefit from your idea on your own. You have already had to sell your Porsche and buy a bicycle to get cash, and the bank has gone about as far as it will go with your business. You no longer have a partner (she grew tired of the long hours and was unwilling to sell her BMW convertible). Time is limited. The shops you have are profitable, but they generate only enough cash to let you open a new outlet about every six months.

Further, you realize that, although selling franchises will allow others to profit from your idea, there will be more than enough profit for you to share. The franchisee benefits from your ideas and methods, your research and product development, your plans and designs, your quality control and connections with suppliers and manufacturers, and your understanding of the business. You benefit from someone's paying you a franchise fee, paying you royalties on their sales, opening shops that help increase your name recognition, and, finally, buying supplies through you so that you can take advantage of larger volume purchasing. Also, both of you benefit from the time, effort, and investment your franchisee puts into building a successful franchise.

Successful Franchises

Venture magazine recently published a survey of 50 successful franchise operations.[4] *Venture* defined success in terms of the number of franchise outlets rather than in terms of profit or market value. The survey is interesting both because of the wide range of products and services that proved successful and because of the different strategies the franchisers used.

The most successful new franchiser, by *Venture*'s standards, was a company named Novus Franchising, Inc., which sells franchises for a windshield repair and scratch removal service. The company, which sold its first franchise in October 1985, had sold 525 franchises by the end of 1986 — an average of 35 franchises per month.

A second success story was that of T. J. Cinnamons. The parent company, Signature Foods, Inc., was founded in 1983 and began selling franchises for shops selling its high-quality cinnamon rolls in September 1985. By the end of 1986, the firm owned seven units of its own and had sold franchises on another 70 units. The success of T. J. Cinnamons came only after the owners had spent several years perfecting their product and ideas. In fact, they had been asked to sell franchises long before they decided they were ready to do so — getting the details right was important to the couple that started the business.

Some Problems in Franchising

Recently, franchisers have reported problems in the field of franchising, as well as some new opportunities.[5] The problems stem from a lack of high-quality people interested in becoming franchisees, and from difficulties in the relationships between franchisers and franchisees.

---

[4]"Franchising: The Art of Reproduction," *Venture,* February 1987, 38-51.
[5]See these recent *Wall Street Journal* articles: "Franchisee Pool is Drying up for Some Firms," November 14, 1989; "Firms Try to Tighten Grip on Franchisees," January 15, 1990; and, "Overseeing Overseas: Franchisers Go Abroad," November 21, 1989.

Early in the life of a franchise operation, the franchiser attempts to establish wide distribution and recognition. The franchiser may not initially be concerned about such matters as maintenance and remodeling of franchise locations, since all of them are new. Later this can change. Kentucky Fried Chicken (KFC), for example, has 780 franchises, some dating back to the 1950s. Today, the KFC chain wants to compel its franchisees to modernize, and the franchisees want to enjoy relative autonomy. KFC's desire for a degree of control is in conflict with franchisees' desire for autonomy.

When setting up the original franchise agreement, it is difficult for a new franchiser to be far-sighted enough to anticipate all future problems. A sound agreement should, however, carefully delineate exactly who is required to do what.

The shortage of potential franchisees is a relatively recent phenomenon. It apparently stems, in part, from increased competition from well-established franchises, which makes it difficult for new franchisers to get off the ground. Finally, franchise investors themselves are getting more sophisticated and are demanding more favorable terms.

Meanwhile, overseas franchising is expanding at a rapid pace. The International Franchise Association reported that 450 U.S. franchisers were operating in foreign countries by the end of the 1980s. With the unification of the European Market in 1992, many expect Europe to be a key target for franchisers. On the other hand, franchisers expanding overseas must be prepared to deal with cultural differences, differences in consumer preferences, and difficulties in obtaining supplies.

Controlled Growth

As emphasized in this chapter, a rapidly growing firm quickly exhausts its ability to finance its growth internally. Thus, financial pressures created by growth may lead a profitable, but fast-growing, business to lose control financially. Although a franchise strategy can help a business sustain faster growth than it could otherwise achieve financially, there are still limits on growth. *Venture* reports that many successful franchisers are "intentionally keeping a tight rein on growth, recognizing that an unbridled system cannot be supervised..."[6] Even with the benefits of franchising, the franchiser will have to devote time, energy, and money to the development of the business. Quality is especially difficult to control if the number of franchises grows too rapidly.

Conclusion

Small businesses suffer from resource poverty. Franchising can offer an alternative to help the business overcome some of its capital and human resource constraints. In a well-conceived franchise operation, both the franchiser and the franchisees benefit by their agreement to work together.

----

[6]"Franchising," *Venture*, February 1987, 49.

SUMMARY

This chapter described in broad outline how firms project their financial statements and determine their capital requirements. The key concepts covered are listed below.

- **Pro forma,** or **projected, financial statements** are developed to help estimate the firm's financial requirements.

- The **percentage of sales method** for forecasting financial statements is based on the assumptions (1) that certain balance sheet accounts vary directly with sales and (2) that the firm's existing level of assets is optimum for its sales volume.

- A firm can determine the amount of **additional funds needed (AFN)** by estimating the amount of new assets necessary to support the forecasted level of sales and then subtracting from that amount the spontaneous funds that will be generated from operations and from the addition to retained earnings. The firm can then plan to raise the required AFN through bank borrowing, by issuing securities, or both.

- The **higher a firm's sales growth rate,** the **greater** will be its need for external financing. Similarly, the **larger a firm's dividend payout ratio,** the **greater** its need for external funds. On the other hand, the higher the firm's profit margin, and the greater its spontaneous sources of financing, the lower its need for external funds.

- The percentage of sales method cannot be used if **economies of scale** exist in the use of assets, if **excess capacity** exists, or if some assets must be added in **lumpy increments.** If these conditions exist, we must use a modified version of Table 7-2.

- **Franchising** permits the use of other people's money, energy, and desire to work for themselves to help expand the business concepts developed by the franchiser. In an ideal franchise operation, the franchiser benefits by being able to expand a service or product, while the franchisees benefit from the expertise developed by the franchiser.

The type of forecasting described in this chapter is important for several reasons. First, if the projected operating results are unsatisfactory, management can "go back to the drawing board," reformulate its plans, and develop more reasonable targets for the coming year. Second, it is possible that the funds required to meet the sales forecast simply cannot be obtained; if so, it is obviously better to know this in advance and to scale back the projected level of operations than to suddenly run out of cash and have operations grind to a halt. Third, even if the required funds can be raised, it is desirable to plan for their acquisition well in advance. As we shall see in later chapters, raising capital takes time, and both time and money can be saved by careful planning.

EQUATIONS

Equation 7-1 helps explain the relationship between sales growth and financial requirements. Funds required to increase assets are reduced by both the spontaneous increases in liabilities and the funds raised by retaining earnings when determining the amount of outside capital which must be raised.

$$\begin{bmatrix} \text{Additional} \\ \text{funds} \\ \text{needed} \end{bmatrix} = \begin{bmatrix} \text{Required} \\ \text{increase} \\ \text{in assets} \end{bmatrix} - \begin{bmatrix} \text{Spontaneous} \\ \text{increase in} \\ \text{liabilities} \end{bmatrix} - \begin{bmatrix} \text{Increase in} \\ \text{retained} \\ \text{earnings} \end{bmatrix} \quad \textbf{(7-1)}$$

$$\text{AFN} = \frac{A^*}{S}(\Delta S) - \frac{L^*}{S}(\Delta S) - MS_1(1 - d).$$

When there is excess capacity, the following equation is used to calculate full capacity sales, so the target fixed assets/sales ratio can be recomputed and additional funds needed can be adjusted accordingly.

$$\begin{array}{c} \text{Full} \\ \text{capacity} \\ \text{sales} \end{array} = \frac{\text{Current sales}}{\begin{array}{c} \text{\% fixed assets} \\ \text{operated} \end{array}}.$$

RESOLUTION TO DECISION IN FINANCE

"Wide of Mark" Forecasts

With the announcement in April 1990 of a $228 million loss for the 1989 fiscal year, Ames triggered speculation about a possible bankruptcy filing that sent its stock into a week-long trading turmoil. Fears were confirmed shortly thereafter when the company filed under Chapter 11 of the Federal Bankruptcy Code.

Ames officials said they had no intention of shutting down, however. Vice President Ewing insisted that there were no plans to lay off employees or close more stores, and that normal operations would continue. In fact, President Hollis called the bankruptcy a positive step. Some suppliers, saying they had not been paid for earlier deliveries, had refused to ship products to Ames for spring. "The Chapter 11 filing," said Hollis, "will give our suppliers the assur-

ance they need to resume the steady flow of merchandise into our store."

Ames stock rebounded slightly after an announcement by Chemical Bank that it would lend the company $250 million, with use of the money subject to court approval. Ewing said the financing would allow Ames to buy goods into the fall season. Nevertheless, Ames stock, which had sold at a high of 19¾ in August 1989, had dropped to just over 1 by early May 1990, and many observers believed that Ames must close many, if not most, of its remaining stores to raise the cash needed to continue operations.

That decision will be made by Stephen Pistner, who was brought in as the new CEO to try to pull the firm out of bankruptcy. Over the past 20 years, Pistner had run the Montgomery Ward, McCrory, Dayton Hudson, and Target retail chains. At Ames he will face the challenge of raising the money to pay the interest on the company's $865 million debt. It will not, however, come out of his own pocket. His salary of $2 million for his first year included a $500,000 signing bonus, to be paid in the first six months.

Sources: *Business Week,* "Ames's New CEO Had Better Be Hercules," May 14, 1990, and "'They Took Their Shot at Being a Giant'—and Missed," May 7, 1990; "Ames Stores to Report Loss for Fiscal 1990," *The Wall Street Journal,* April 10, 1990; "Ames Department Stores File in Bankruptcy Court," *Associated Press,* April 1990.

QUESTIONS

7-1 Certain liability and net worth items generally increase spontaneously with increases in sales. Put a check ($\checkmark$) by those items that typically increase spontaneously:

Accounts payable   _____

Notes payable to banks   _____

Accrued wages   _____

Accrued taxes   _____

Mortgage bonds   _____

Common stock   _____

Retained earnings   _____

7-2 The following equation can, under certain assumptions, be used to forecast financial requirements:

$$\text{Additional funds needed} = \frac{A^*}{S}(\Delta S) - \frac{L^*}{S}(\Delta S) - MS_1(1 - d).$$

Under what conditions does the equation give satisfactory predictions, and when should it not be used?

7-3 Assume that an average firm in the office supply business has a 6 percent after-tax profit margin, a 40 percent total debt/total assets ratio, a total assets turnover of 2 times, and a dividend payout ratio of 40 percent. Is it true that if such a firm is to have *any* sales growth ($g > 0$), it will be forced to sell either bonds or common stock (that is, will it need some nonspontaneous external capital, even if g is very small)?

7-4 Is it true that computerized corporate planning models were a fad during the 1970s, but, because of a need for flexibility in corporate planning, they have been dropped by most firms?

7-5 Suppose a firm makes the following policy changes. If the change means that external, nonspontaneous financial requirements for any rate of sales growth will increase, indicate this by a (+); indicate a decrease by a (−); and indicate indeterminate or no effect by a (0). Think in terms of the immediate, short-run effect on financial requirements.

a. The dividend payout ratio is increased.

b. The firm contracts to buy rather than make certain components used in its products.   _____

c. The firm decides to pay all suppliers on delivery, rather than after a 30-day delay, to take advantage of discounts for rapid payment.   _____

d. The firm begins to sell on credit; previously all sales had been on a cash basis.   _____

e. The firm's profit margin is eroded by increased competition; sales are steady.   _____

f. Advertising expenditures are stepped up.   _____

g. A decision is made to substitute long-term mortgage bonds for short-term bank loans.   _____

h. The firm begins to pay employees on a weekly basis; previously it paid them at the end of each month.   _____

SELF-TEST PROBLEMS

ST-1   J. Sarwark Productions, Inc., has the following ratios: $A^*/S = 1.6$; $L^*/S = 0.4$; profit margin $= 0.10$; and dividend payout ratio $= 0.45$, or 45 percent. Sales last year were $100 million. Assuming that these ratios will remain constant and that all liabilities increase spontaneously with increases in sales, what is the maximum growth rate Sarwark can achieve without having to employ nonspontaneous external funds?

ST-2   Suppose Sarwark's financial consultants report (1) that the inventory turnover ratio is sales/inventory = 3 times versus an industry average of 4 times, and (2) that Sarwark could raise its turnover ratio to 4 times without affecting sales, the profit margin, or the other asset turnover ratios. Under these conditions, what amount of external funds would Sarwark require during each of the next 2 years if sales grew at a rate of 20 percent per year?

PROBLEMS

7-1   **Pro forma balance sheet.** A group of investors is planning to set up a new company, Athletic Shoe, Inc., to manufacture and distribute a novel type of running shoe. To help plan the new operation's financial requirements, you have been asked to construct a pro forma balance sheet for December 31, 1991, the end of the first year of operations. Sales for 1991 are projected at $30 million, and the following are industry average ratios for athletic shoe companies:

Sales to common equity	$5\times$
Current debt to equity	50%
Total debt to equity	80%
Current ratio	$2.2\times$
Net sales to inventory	$8\times$
Accounts receivable to sales	9%
Fixed assets to equity	70%
Profit margin	3%
Dividend payout ratio	30%

Athletic Shoe, Inc.:
Pro Forma Balance Sheet, December 31, 1991 (Millions of Dollars)

Cash	$_____	Current debt	$_____
Accounts receivable	_____	Long-term debt	_____
Inventories	_____	Total debt	$_____
Total current assets	$_____	Equity	_____
Fixed assets	_____		
Total assets	$_____	Total liabilities and equity	$_____

a. Complete the preceding pro forma balance sheet, assuming that 1991 sales are $30 million.

b. If the group supplies all of the new firm's equity, how much external capital will it be required to put up by December 31, 1991?

7-2   **Long-term financing needed.** At year-end 1990, Dunham, Inc.'s total assets were $2.4 million. Sales, which were $5 million, will increase by 20 percent in 1991. The 1990 ratio of assets to sales will be maintained in 1991. Common stock amounted to

$850,000 in 1990, and retained earnings were $590,000. Accounts payable will continue to be 15 percent of sales in 1991, and the company plans to sell new common stock in the amount of $100,000. Net income is expected to be 6 percent of sales, and 60 percent of earnings will be paid out as dividends.

a. What was Dunham's total debt in 1990?

b. How much new, long-term debt financing will be needed in 1991? (*Hint:* AFN − New stock = New long-term debt.)

7-3   **Ratios and short-term financing needed.** Seldat Restaurant Supply has been growing at a rapid rate lately. As a result Mr. Seldat has been unable to devote proper attention to the management of the firm's assets. Expected sales for next year are $2.7 million with a net profit margin of 3 percent. The expected beginning of the year retained earnings are $390,000 and current liabilities are $200,000. Long-term debt and common stock have remained constant for some time. Seldat computed the following financial ratios:

$$\text{Days sales outstanding} = 40 \text{ days,}$$

$$\text{Inventory turnover} = 6 \text{ times,}$$

$$\text{Fixed assets turnover} = 4 \text{ times.}$$

Seldat anticipates no dividend payout next year. Complete the following pro forma balance sheet. Short-term debt is the appropriate balancing item. According to your projections:

a. How much will Seldat have to raise to support the expected level of sales?

b. How much of the total will be generated internally (equity); and externally (debt)?

c. What is Seldat's debt ratio?

d. What is Seldat's current ratio?

e. What is the firm's return on assets?

Seldat Restaurant Supply: Pro Forma Balance Sheet

Cash	$ 60,000		Short-term debt	$_____
Accounts receivable	_____		Long-term debt	375,000
Inventory	_____		Total debt	$_____
Total current assets	$_____		Common stock	150,000
Fixed assets	_____		Retained earnings	_____
			Total liabilities	
Total assets	$_____		and equity	$_____

7-4   **Ratios and short-term financing needed.** After making the projections in Problem 7-3, Mr. Seldat is determined to streamline his company's balance sheet. He is certain that the days sales outstanding can be reduced to 32 days and that the inventory turnover can be increased to 7.5 times. He believes that cash and fixed assets will remain at their current levels, however. Make another projection regarding Seldat's financial needs. Specifically:

a. How much will Seldat have to raise to support sales under these new conditions?

b. How much of the total will be generated internally (equity) and externally (debt)?

c. What is Seldat's debt ratio?

d. What is Seldat's current ratio?

e. What is the firm's return on assets?

7-5 **Sales growth.** Aunt Katy's Crafts, Inc., has these ratios:

$$A^*/S = 1.8$$

$$L^*/S = 0.5$$

$$\text{Profit margin, M} = 8\%$$

$$\text{Dividend payout ratio, d} = 40\%$$

Sales last year were $150 million. Assuming that these ratios remain constant, what is the maximum growth rate Aunt Katy's can achieve without having to employ nonspontaneous external funds?

7-6 **Additional funds needed.** The 1990 balance sheet for Sally Wright and Associates is shown below (in millions of dollars):

Cash	$12	Accounts payable	$ 8
Accounts receivable	12	Notes payable	6
Inventory	20	Long-term debt	12
Total current assets	$44	Total debt	$26
Fixed assets	12	Common equity	30
Total assets	$56	Total liabilities and equity	$56

Management believes that sales will increase in the next year by 25 percent over the current level of $300 million. The profit margin is expected to be 5 percent, and the dividend payout will remain at 40 percent. If the firm has no excess capacity, what additional funding is required for 1991?

7-7 **Additional funds needed — excess capacity.** Refer to Problem 7-6. Assume that all relationships hold *except* for the capacity constraint. *Now* assume that the firm has excess capacity and that no increase in fixed assets will be required to support the sales increase. Under this new condition, how much additional funding will be required for 1991?

7-8 **Additional funds needed — excess capacity.** A firm has the following balance sheet and other data (in thousands of dollars):

Cash	$ 20	Accounts payable	$ 20
Accounts receivable	20	Notes payable	40
Inventories	20	Long-term debt	80
Fixed assets	180	Common stock	80
		Retained earnings	20
Total assets	$240	Total liabilities and equity	$240

Fixed assets are being used at 80 percent of capacity; sales for the year just ended were $400,000; sales will increase $20,000 per year for the next 4 years; the profit margin is 5 percent; and the dividend payout ratio is 60 percent. What are the total outside financing requirements for the entire 4 years? (Assume that fixed assets cannot be sold.)

7-9 **AFN equation.** Calculate the total assets for Emory Suppliers given the following information: Sales this year = $1,500,000; increase in sales projected for next year = 20 percent; net income this year = $125,000; dividend payout ratio = 40 percent; projected excess funds available next year = $50,000; accounts payable = $300,000; notes payable = $50,000; accrued wages and taxes = $100,000. (Note: The company is operating at full capacity.)

7-10   **Additional funds needed — excess capacity.** Davis Corporation's December 31, 1990, balance sheet is given below (in millions of dollars):

Cash	$ 20	Accounts payable	$ 40
Accounts receivable	50	Notes payable	40
Inventory	80	Accrued wages and taxes	20
Net fixed assets	150	Long-term debt	60
		Common equity	140
Total assets	$300	Total liabilities and equity	$300

Sales during 1990 were $200 million, and they were expected to rise by 50 percent to $300 million during 1991. Also, during 1990, fixed assets were being utilized to only 80 percent of capacity; that is, Davis could have supported $200 million of sales with fixed assets that were only 80 percent of the actual 1990 fixed assets. Assuming that Davis's profit margin will remain constant at 5 percent and that the company will continue to pay out 60 percent of its earnings as dividends, what amount of nonspontaneous external funds will be needed during 1991?

7-11   **Pro forma statements and ratios.** Quality Computers makes bulk purchases of small computers, stocks them in conveniently located warehouses, and then ships them to its chain of retail stores. Quality's balance sheet as of December 31, 1990, is shown here (in millions of dollars):

Cash	$ 3.0	Accounts payable	$ 7.0
Accounts receivable	22.5	Notes payable	15.0
Inventories	49.5	Accruals	8.0
Total current assets	$ 75.0	Total current liabilities	$ 30.0
Net fixed assets	30.3	Mortgage bonds	5.1
		Common stock	12.6
		Retained earnings	57.6
Total assets	$105.3	Total liabilities and equity	$105.3

Sales for 1990 were $300 million, while net income for the year was $9 million. Quality paid dividends of $4 million to common stockholders. The firm is operating at full capacity.

a. If sales are projected to increase by $75 million, or by 25 percent, during 1991, what are Quality's projected external capital requirements?

b. Construct Quality's pro forma balance sheet for December 31, 1991. Assume that all external capital requirements are met by bank loans and are reflected in notes payable.

c. Now calculate the following ratios, based on your projected December 31, 1991, balance sheet. Quality's 1990 ratios and industry average ratios are shown here for comparison.

	Quality Computers Dec. 31, 1991	Quality Computers Dec. 31, 1990	Industry Average Dec. 31, 1990
Current ratio	_____	2.5 ×	3 ×
Total debt/total assets	_____	33.3%	30%
Return on equity	_____	12.8%	12%

d. Now assume that Quality grows by the same $75 million but that the growth is spread over 5 years; that is, sales grow by $15 million each year.

1. Calculate total external financial requirements over the 5-year period.

2. Construct a pro forma balance sheet as of December 31, 1995, using notes payable as the balancing item.

3. Calculate the current ratio, total debt/total assets ratio, and return on equity as of December 31, 1995. [*Hint:* Be sure to use *total sales,* which amount to $1,725 million, to calculate retained earnings, but use 1995 profits to calculate the return on equity — that is, (1995 profits)/(December 31, 1995, equity).]

e. Do the plans outlined in Parts c and d seem feasible to you? In other words, do you think Quality could borrow the required capital, and would the company be raising the odds on its bankruptcy to an excessive level in the event of some temporary misfortune?

7-12   **Additional funds needed.** The Corrigan Company's 1990 sales were $36 million. Each of the following balance sheet items varies directly with sales and each account can be calculated as a percentage of sales as follows:

Cash	3%
Accounts receivable	20
Inventories	25
Net fixed assets	40
Accounts payable	15
Accruals	10
Profit margin on sales	5

The dividend payout ratio is 40 percent; the December 31, 1989, balance sheet account for retained earnings was $12.3 million; and both common stock and mortgage bonds are constant and equal to the amounts shown on the following balance sheet.

a. Complete the following balance sheet.

Corrigan Company:
Balance Sheet, December 31, 1990
(Thousands of Dollars)

Cash	$____	Accounts payable	$____	
Accounts receivable	____	Notes payable	3,300	
Inventories	____	Accruals	____	
Total current assets	$____	Total current liabilities	$____	
Net fixed assets	____	Mortgage bonds	3,000	
		Common stock	3,000	
		Retained earnings	____	
Total assets	$____	Total liabilities and equity	$____	

b. Now suppose that 1991 sales increase by 10 percent over 1990 sales. How much additional external capital will be required? The company was operating at full capacity in 1990. Use both the balance sheet methodology and Equation 7-1 to answer this question.

c. Develop a finalized pro forma balance sheet for December 31, 1991, showing any required financing as notes payable.

d. What would happen to external funds requirements under each of the following conditions? Answer in words, without calculations.

1. The profit margin went (i) from 5 to 7 percent, (ii) from 5 to 3 percent.

2. The dividend payout ratio (i) was raised from 40 to 90 percent, (ii) was lowered from 40 to 20 percent.

3. Credit terms on sales were relaxed substantially, giving customers longer to pay.

4. The company had excess manufacturing capacity at December 31, 1990.

7-13 **Excess capacity.** National Business Machines' (NBM) 1990 sales were $100 million. Each of the following balance sheet items except notes payable, mortgage bonds, and common stock varies directly with sales and each account can be calculated as a percentage of sales as follows:

Cash	4%
Accounts receivable	25
Inventory	30
Net fixed assets	50
Accounts payable	15
Accruals	5
Profit margin on sales	5

The dividend payout ratio is 60 percent; the December 31, 1989, balance sheet account for retained earnings was $58 million; and both common stock and mortgage bonds are constant and equal to the amounts shown on the following balance sheet.

a. Complete the following balance sheet.

**National Business Machines:
Balance Sheet, December 31, 1990
(Millions of Dollars)**

Cash	$_____	Accounts payable	$_____
Accounts receivable	_____	Notes payable	9.5
Inventory	_____	Accruals	_____
Total current assets	$_____	Total current liabilities	$_____
Net fixed assets	_____	Mortgage bonds	13.5
		Common stock	6.0
		Retained earnings	_____
Total assets	$_____	Total liabilities and equity	$_____

b. Assume that the company was operating at full capacity in 1990 with regard to all items *except* fixed assets; had the fixed assets been used to full capacity, the fixed assets/sales ratio would have been 40 percent in 1990. By what percentage could 1991 sales increase over 1990 sales without the need for an increase in fixed assets?

c. Now suppose that 1991 sales increase by 20 percent over 1990 sales. How much additional external capital will be required? Assume the same condition as in Part b with respect to fixed assets and that NBM cannot sell any fixed assets. Assume that any required financing is borrowed as notes payable.

d. Suppose the industry averages for receivables and inventories are 20 percent and 25 percent, respectively, and that NBM matches these figures in 1991 and then uses the funds released to reduce equity. (It could pay a special dividend out of retained earnings.) What would this do to the return on year-end 1991 equity?

7-14 **Additional funds needed.** The 1990 sales of Pettit Industries, Inc., were $3 million. Common stock and notes payable are constant. The dividend payout ratio is 50 percent. Retained earnings as shown on the December 31, 1989, balance sheet were $105,000. Each of the following balance sheet items varies directly with sales and each account can be calculated as a percentage of sales as follows:

Cash	4%
Receivables	10
Inventory	20
Net fixed assets	35
Accounts payable	12
Accruals	6
Profit margin on sales	3

a. Complete the balance sheet that follows.

Pettit Industries, Inc.:
Balance Sheet, December 31, 1990

Cash	$		Accounts payable	$
Receivables			Notes payable	130,000
Inventory	————		Accruals	
Total current assets	$		Total current liabilities	$
Fixed assets	————		Common stock	1,250,000
			Retained earnings	————
Total assets	$————		Total liabilities and equity	$————

b. Suppose that in 1991 sales will increase by 10 percent over 1990 sales levels. How much additional capital will be required? Assume that the firm operated at full capacity in 1990.

c. Construct the year-end 1991 balance sheet. Assume that 50 percent of the additional capital required will be financed by selling common stock and the remainder by borrowing as notes payable.

d. If the profit margin remains at 3 percent and the dividend payout rate remains at 50 percent, at what growth rate in sales will the additional financing requirements be exactly zero?

7-15 **External financing requirements.** The 1990 balance sheet for the Duggan Company is shown next. Sales in 1990 totaled $10 million. The ratio of net profits to sales was 5 percent, and the dividend payout ratio was 60 percent of net income.

a. The firm operated at full capacity in 1990. It expects sales to increase by 25 percent during 1991. Use the percentage of sales method to determine how much outside financing is required, then develop the firm's pro forma balance sheet using AFN as the balancing item.

b. If the firm must maintain a current ratio of 2.5 and a debt ratio of 40 percent, how much financing will be obtained using notes payable, long-term debt, and common stock?

(Do Part c only if you are using the computerized problem diskette.)

c. Suppose that the firm expects sales to increase by 30 percent during 1991 and that its current ratio must be at least 2.5 but its debt ratio can be as high as 45 percent. Under this situation, how much external financing would the firm require, and how would those funds be obtained?

Duggan Company:
Balance Sheet, December 31, 1990
(Thousands of Dollars)

Assets		*Liabilities*	
Cash	$ 100	Accounts payable	$ 90
Accounts receivable	250	Accruals	50
Inventory	525	Notes payable	210
Total current assets	$ 875	Total current liabilities	$ 350
Fixed assets	2,625	Long-term debt	1,050
		Total debt	$1,400
		Common stock	1,225
		Retained earnings	875
Total assets	$3,500	Total liabilities and equity	$3,500

SOLUTIONS TO SELF-TEST PROBLEMS

ST-1   To solve this problem, we will use the three following equations:

$$\Delta S = S_0(g).$$

$$S_1 = S_0(1 + g).$$

$$AFN = (A^*/S)\Delta S - (L^*/S)\Delta S - MS_1(1 - d).$$

Set AFN = 0, substitute in known values for A^*/S, L^*/S, M, d, and S_0, and then solve for g:

$$0 = 1.6(\$100g) - 0.4(\$100g) - 0.1[\$100(1 + g)](0.55)$$

$$= \$160g - \$40g - 0.055(\$100 + \$100g)$$

$$= \$160g - \$40g - \$5.5 - \$5.5g$$

$$\$114.5g = \$5.5$$

$$g = \$5.5/\$114.5 = 0.048 = 4.8\% = \begin{array}{l}\text{Maximum growth rate} \\ \text{without external financing.}\end{array}$$

ST-2   Note that assets consist of cash, marketable securities, receivables, inventories, and fixed assets. Therefore, we can break the A^*/S ratio into its components — cash/sales, inventories/sales, and so forth. Then

$$\frac{A^*}{S} = \frac{A^* - \text{Inventories}}{S} + \frac{\text{Inventories}}{S} = 1.6.$$

We know that the inventory turnover ratio is sales/inventories = 3 times, so inventories/sales = ⅓ = 0.3333. Furthermore, if the inventory turnover ratio could be increased to 4 times, then the inventories/sales ratio would fall to ¼ = 0.25, a difference of 0.3333 − 0.2500 = 0.0833. This, in turn, would cause the A^*/S ratio to fall from A^*/S = 1.6 to A^*/S = 1.6 − 0.0833 = 1.5167.

This change would have two effects: (1) it would change the AFN equation, and (2) it would mean that Sarwark currently has excessive inventories, so there could be some sales growth without any additional inventories. Therefore, we could set up the revised AFN equation, estimate the funds needed next year, and then subtract out the excess inventories currently on hand:

Present conditions:

$$\frac{\text{Sales}}{\text{Inventories}} = \frac{\$100}{\text{Inventories}} = 3,$$

so

$$\text{Current level of inventories} = \$100/3 = \$33.3 \text{ million.}$$

New conditions:

$$\frac{\text{Sales}}{\text{Inventories}} = \frac{\$100}{\text{Inventories}} = 4,$$

so

$$\text{New level of inventories} = \$100/4 = \$25 \text{ million.}$$

Therefore,

$$\text{Excess inventories} = \$33.3 - \$25 = \$8.3 \text{ million.}$$

Forecast of funds needed, first year:

$$\Delta S \text{ in first year} = 0.2(\$100 \text{ million}) = \$20 \text{ million.}$$

$$\text{AFN} = 1.5167(\$20) - 0.4(\$20) - 0.1(\$120)(0.55) - \$8.3$$

$$= \$30.3 - \$8 - \$6.6 - \$8.3$$

$$= \$7.4 \text{ million.}$$

Forecast of funds needed, second year:

$$\Delta S \text{ in second year} = 0.2(\$120 \text{ million}) = \$24 \text{ million.}$$

$$\text{AFN} = 1.5167(\$24) - 0.4(\$24) - 0.1(\$144)(0.55)$$

$$= \$36.4 - \$9.6 - \$7.9$$

$$= \$18.9 \text{ million.}$$

Part III

SHORT-TERM FINANCIAL MANAGEMENT

If a poll were taken, financial managers would reveal that the greater part of their work day is taken up with managing and financing the firm's short-term assets. Thus, this section devotes four chapters to the important topics of curent asset management and short-term financing policy.

Chapter 8 demonstrates that the level of current assets and how those assets are financed contribute significantly to the firm's profitability and risk exposure. Then, in the next two chapters we turn to the management of four current asset accounts: Chapter 9 considers cash and marketable securities, while Chapter 10 analyzes accounts receivable and inventories. Then, in Chapter 11, we discuss the various types of short-term credit that can be used to finance current assets.

Chapter 8

Short-Term Financial Planning

 DECISION IN FINANCE

Unused Inventory . . . The Pot of Gold at the End of the Rainbow?

It may not be the pot of gold at the end of the rainbow, but there is often a treasure of sorts in the back rooms and warehouses of cash-short companies. Selling unwanted, outdated, or unused inventory may not be the most desirable way to improve profits, but it really boils down to one issue: not how much we might get from the sale, but how much less we might get if we sell nothing.

Keith Maxey, executive director of Maxey International, makes his living by raising capital for companies. He says that most unused inventory items will bring only half their original sales price, but this will still provide cash that can be invested in a company's best-selling products. "Most cash-flow shortages are primarily the result of underutilized assets," he says, "not an inherent problem with the business."

Firms who hire Maxey to help them move inventory get as much effort as necessary for their particular problems. A furniture manufacturer had a stock of a discontinued line of brass headboards, which proved fairly easy to sell (at 60% off) to one of about 50 discount retailers

---

See end of chapter for resolution.

with whom Maxey maintains a relationship. A more complicated deal involved $1 million worth of expensive garden benches, which an importer wanted sold quickly so part of a bank loan could be repaid. After compiling a list of the importer's regular customers, who could not be approached for the discount sale, Maxey compiled a list of approximately 40,000 furniture retail stores. He eliminated those he felt could not buy at least $100,000 worth of the benches and those who did not handle garden furniture. In less than two months, he managed to sell a third of the stock at 40 to 45 percent discounts. Additionally, he developed a secondary list of potential institutional buyers not likely to patronize retail furniture stores — such establishments as golf courses, restaurants, or resorts.

Occasionally, if no buyer can be found regardless of the size of the discount, Maxey recommends that the company donate the goods to a non-profit organization, or to a public institution such as a school, and simply take the tax write-off.

Companies with small lots of excess inventory might want to consider some do-it-yourself activities, including half-price sales exclusively for employees and their friends, a corporate "yard sale" for the public, or special offers pairing the excess items with some of the firm's fast-selling products. If they plan ahead, firms may also be able to negotiate buyback agreements with suppliers, or arrange a credit for the merchandise against future orders.

Regardless of how it is done, management needs to think through the risks and benefits of selling unused assets. As you read this chapter, consider the criteria firms should use in deciding to raise cash this way. Think about the price that should be offered and the potential buyers who might be targeted.

Current asset financial policy involves answering these two questions: (1) How much should we invest in each category of current assets, and (2) how should we finance that investment? Providing correct answers to these questions is vital to the firm's profitability.

Two major types of current liabilities—trade credit and accruals—are extremely convenient, flexible, and inexpensive. Thus, virtually all firms, even the most conservative ones, will show some current liabilities on their books. Also, even conservative firms will utilize borrowing to meet a temporary need for funds, provided management is sure that funds will be available to pay off the debt at its maturity. Thus, current asset financing policy is a matter of degree —the more conservative the firm, the less it will rely on short-term credit, because the greater use of such credit, the greater the firm's risk exposure. In this chapter we concentrate on short-term financial planning, or current asset investment and financing policies.

SHORT-TERM FINANCIAL PLANNING TERMINOLOGY

Short-term financial planning involves decisions that relate to current assets, including decisions the financial manager must make about the financing of current assets. *Working capital* is a term that is used frequently when discussing short-term financial planning. The term originated in the days when the old Yankee peddler would load up his wagon with goods and then go off on his route to sell his wares. The merchandise was defined as his "working capital" because it was actually sold or "turned over" to produce profits; the wagon and horse were his fixed assets. If he bought $4,000 of goods (working capital) and sold them for $5,000, he would make $1,000 per trip. If he made five trips per year, he would turn over his working capital five times and make a profit of $5 \times \$1,000 = \$5,000$ for the year.

The days of the Yankee peddler have long since passed, but the importance of working capital remains. About 40 percent of the typical firm's capital is invested in current assets, yet this doesn't tell the entire story about its importance. Financial managers probably spend more of their daily time and energy on working capital matters than on any other single function discussed in this text. In contrast, the choice of business projects and the associated fixed asset commitment occurs, for most firms, perhaps once or twice a year. As we shall see, whether the decision concerns fixed or current assets, it will affect the firm's level of risk and return.

Before taking up the topics of primary interest in this chapter, we will discuss some concepts of short-term financial planning. We begin by defining some basic terms and concepts:

1. Working capital, sometimes called *gross working capital,* simply refers to the firm's current assets (often called *short-term assets*) — commonly cash, marketable securities, inventory, and accounts receivable.

2. Net working capital is defined as current assets minus current liabilities. As we discuss later in this chapter, net working capital is therefore financed by long-term sources of funds. We shall find that working capital financing policy is extremely important in determining the firm's risk and return levels.

3. One key working capital ratio is the *current ratio,* which was defined in Chapter 6 as current assets divided by current liabilities. This ratio is intended to provide information about a firm's liquidity, or its ability to meet obligations that will come due within a year. However, a high current ratio does not insure that a firm will have the cash required to meet its needs. If inventories cannot be sold and receivables cannot be collected in a timely manner, then the apparent safety reflected in a high current ratio could be an illusion.

4. The *quick ratio,* or *acid test,* is defined as current assets minus inventories, divided by current liabilities. This ratio, which also measures liquidity, removes inventories (the least liquid current asset) from total current assets, and it thus provides an "acid test" of a company's ability to meet its current obligations.

5. Although the current and quick ratios provide an indication of the firm's ability to satisfy its maturing obligations, they do not provide a complete picture of liquidity, because they do not tell us anything about *cash flows from operations,* which can also be used to meet obligations. For example, an electric utility (or a fast-food chain, or any other business) might show $20 million of current liabilities and only $5 million of current assets, but if its cash flows from operations are sufficient, the company can have sufficient liquidity in spite of its low current ratio. Thus, to determine a firm's *effective liquidity,* it is useful to look both at its balance sheet ratios (current and quick) and at its cash flow position, as we shall do later in this chapter when we study the cash conversion cycle and in the next chapter when we study cash budgets.

6. Current asset financial policy refers to the firm's basic policies regarding (1) the target level for each category of current assets and (2) how current assets will be financed.

7. Current asset management involves the administration, within policy guidelines, of current assets, and the financing of those assets. Important elements of current asset management include cash management, credit and collections, inventory management, and short-term borrowings.

working capital
A firm's investment in short-term assets — cash, marketable securities, inventory, and accounts receivable.

net working capital
Current assets minus current liabilities.

current asset financial policy
Basic policy decisions regarding target levels for each category of current assets, and regarding how current assets will be financed.

current asset management
The administration, within policy guidelines, of current assets and the financing of those assets.

While long-term financial analysis primarily concerns strategic planning, current asset management primarily concerns day-to-day operations — making sure that production lines do not stop because the firm runs out of raw materials, that inventories do not build up because production is not slowed down when sales dip, that customers pay on time, and that enough cash is on hand to make payments when they are due. Obviously, without good current asset management, no firm can be efficient and profitable.

Self-Test

What is meant by the term "liquidity"?

Why is the quick ratio also called an acid test?

Where did the term "working capital" originate?

OVERVIEW OF THE CASH CONVERSION CYCLE

Now that we have defined working capital, we present an overview of the *cash conversion cycle* through a discussion of Figure 8-1, which is one small section of Figure 5-1, discussed in Chapter 5. Recall that Figure 5-1 showed how cash and materials flowed within the firm. Figure 8-1 shows the short-term financial operations of the firm and their effects on its current asset and current liability accounts.

For illustrative purposes, we will consider Addison Products, for which we have already presented pro forma financial statements in Chapter 7. On December 31, 1991, Addison expects to have $15,000 in cash. Addison has received information from its forecasting department about an increase in the demand for its specialized computers. Addison must accommodate this demand increase, or it will lose market share to its competitors. Thus, Addison places orders for additional materials to produce more inventory. The $15,000 is not enough to pay for the entire materials order, so Addison must purchase on credit from its suppliers, creating an account payable on Addison's balance sheet. Once Addison sells its inventory, it should be able to pay off its suppliers. Addison will sell its inventory for more than cost, creating a profit for the firm. Addison makes both cash and credit sales; however, when credit sales are made the firm does not receive cash at the time of the sale. Instead, an account receivable is created at the time of purchase, and the money is received from the customer at a later date. Then, Addison will use the cash to pay off accounts payable, and the cycle repeats itself in a continuous, ongoing manner. Of course, the amount of cash the firm has on hand at the end of each cycle will be higher than at the beginning of each cycle because of the profit made on sales.

In this illustration, we assumed that the firm would have the cash collected from its receivables in time to pay for its accounts payable. Typically, though,

Figure 8-1 **Short-Term Financial Operations**

Short-term financial operations affect the firm's current assets and current liabilities. The firm starts with some cash on hand and receives information on the demand for its product. On the basis of this forecast the firm orders materials to produce inventories of finished goods (a current asset), which it then sells to customers. When the firm orders materials, it creates an account payable (a current liability). When the firm sells inventory, it either receives cash directly from the sale or receives a promise to pay from the customer — an account receivable. When the firm collects the account receivable, it receives cash. This cycle repeats itself many times during the course of the year. (In this figure, squares represent accounts and circles represent actions.)

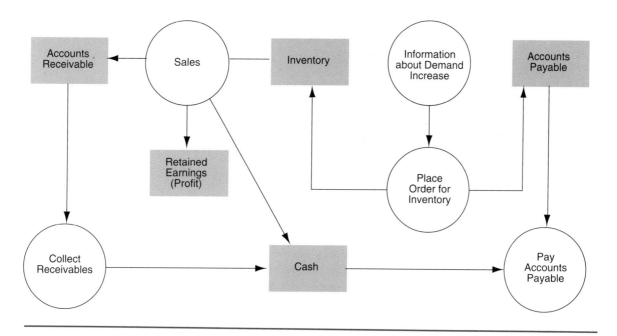

the accounts payable will have to be paid before the firm's receivables have been collected, and this will require some type of financing. The proceeds from this financing will be used to pay suppliers, so when cash is collected from receivables, it will be used to pay off the loans that were used to finance production. This concept of the cash conversion cycle is important in current asset management. In Figure 8-1 we generalize the cycle without adding numbers to the picture; however, numbers could be added to this analysis. In fact, Verlyn Richards and Eugene Laughlin developed a useful approach for analyzing the cash conversion cycle.[1] Their approach centers on the conversion of

[1]See Verlyn D. Richards and Eugene J. Laughlin, "A Cash Conversion Cycle Approach to Liquidity Analysis," *Financial Management,* Spring 1980, 32–38.

cash conversion cycle

The length of time from the payment for raw materials and labor to the collection of accounts receivable generated by the sale of the final product.

operating events to cash flows, and thus it is called the **cash conversion cycle** model. Here are some terms used in the model:

1. *Inventory conversion period,* which is the length of time required to convert raw materials into finished goods and then to sell these goods. Note that the inventory conversion period can be calculated as 360 days divided by the inventory turnover ratio (Sales/Inventory).

2. *Receivables conversion period,* which is the length of time required to convert the firm's receivables into cash — that is, to collect cash following a sale. The receivables conversion period is also called the days sales outstanding (DSO), and it was calculated in Chapter 6 as Receivables/Sales per day = Receivables/(Sales/360).

3. *Payables deferral period,* which is the length of time between the purchase of raw materials and labor and the cash payment for them.

4. *Cash conversion cycle,* which combines the three periods just defined and which equals the length of time from the firm's actual cash expenditures on productive resources (raw materials and labor) — that is, from the day labor and suppliers are paid — to the day receivables are collected. Thus, the cash conversion cycle measures the length of time the firm has funds tied up in current assets.

We can use these definitions to analyze Addison's cash conversion cycle. In Table 8-1 we give the December 31, 1991, pro forma financial statements and key ratios for Addison that were developed in Chapter 7. We will use these to generate some of the numbers for the cash conversion cycle analysis. Addison's inventory turnover is 2 times. Thus, Addison's inventory conversion period is 360/2 = 180 days. Addison's days sales outstanding (DSO) equals 81 days, so this is Addison's receivables conversion period. Because of the highly specialized nature of the materials that suppliers provide to Addison, their credit terms are more liberal than would be the case for other types of manufacturers. In Addison's case, its payables deferral period (including materials and labor) is 90 days. Now, we are ready to calculate Addison's cash conversion cycle.

The cash conversion cycle model is diagrammed in Figure 8-2. Notice that we have put the corresponding data for Addison on the diagram. Each component is given a number, and the cash conversion cycle model can be expressed by this equation:

$$
\underset{(1)}{\substack{\text{Inventory} \\ \text{conversion} \\ \text{period}}} + \underset{(2)}{\substack{\text{Receivables} \\ \text{conversion} \\ \text{period}}} - \underset{(3)}{\substack{\text{Payables} \\ \text{deferral} \\ \text{period}}} = \underset{(4)}{\substack{\text{Cash} \\ \text{conversion} \\ \text{cycle}}}. \qquad \textbf{(8-1)}
$$

Substituting Addison's numbers for each of these components, we obtain the following results:

$$180 \text{ days} + 81 \text{ days} - 90 \text{ days} = 171 \text{ days}.$$

Table 8-1 Addison Products Company:
Pro Forma Financial Statements and Key Ratios
December 31, 1991
(Thousands of Dollars)

I. Balance Sheet

Cash	$ 15	Accounts payable	$ 60
Accounts receivable	135	Notes payable	15
Inventories	300	Accrued wages and taxes	75
Total current assets	$450	Total current liabilities	$150
Net fixed assets	450	Mortgage bonds	300
		Common stock	126
		Retained earnings	324
Total assets	$900	Total liabilities and equity	$900

II. Income Statement

Sales	$600
Total costs	500
Taxable income	$100
Taxes (40%)	40
Net income	$ 60
Dividends	36
Addition to retained earnings	24

III. Key Ratios

1. Current ratio	3.0×
2. Total debt/Total assets	50%
3. Rate of return on equity	13.3%
4. Sales/Inventory	2×
5. DSO	81 days

To look at it another way,

$$\text{Delay in receipt of cash} - \text{Payment delay} = \text{Net delay}$$
$$(180 \text{ days} + 81 \text{ days}) - (90 \text{ days}) = 171 \text{ days.}$$

Given these data, Addison knows, when it decides to produce a specialized computer, that it will have to finance the computer's processing for a 171-day period. The firm's goal should be to shorten the cash conversion cycle as much as possible without hurting operations. This would improve profits, because the longer the cash conversion cycle, the greater the need for external financing—and such financing has a cost.

The cash conversion cycle can be shortened (1) by reducing the inventory conversion period, that is, by processing and selling goods more quickly; (2) by reducing the receivables conversion period (or DSO) by speeding up collections; or (3) by lengthening the payables deferral period by slowing

Figure 8-2 **The Cash Conversion Cycle Model**

The cash conversion cycle model measures the length of time it takes for cash invested in the firm's current assets to be returned. Cash invested in inventory is recaptured only when the firm collects its accounts receivable. Generally, the shorter the cash conversion cycle, the more profitable the firm will be.

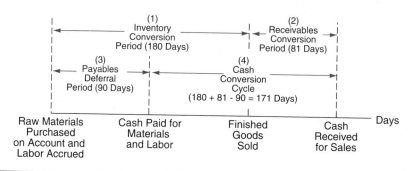

down the firm's own payments. To the extent that these actions can be taken *without increasing costs or depressing sales,* they should be carried out. You should keep the cash conversion cycle in mind as we go through the remainder of this chapter and the other chapters on short-term financial management.

Financial Statement and Ratio Effects

As noted above, the firm's goal should be to keep the cash conversion cycle as short as possible, thus freeing up cash for other uses. This cash could even be used to reduce equity through the repurchase of its common stock. This, in turn, assuming that the income statement accounts were not affected by shortening the cash conversion cycle, would increase the return on equity. Some actions which Addison could take to shorten its cash conversion cycle of 171 days are discussed below.

Inventories. Looking again at Table 8-1, we see that Addison's inventories total $300,000. If the company were to reduce its inventories by a third, or to $200,000, its inventory conversion period would decline from 180 days to 120 days. Its new inventory conversion period would be calculated as 360/(Sales/Inventory) = 360/($600/$200) = 120 days. Of course, we assume that Addison could reduce its inventory without any adverse effects on sales. As we shall see in Chapter 10, a firm needs to keep sufficient inventory to prevent stock-outs. Stock-outs create customer ill will and decrease sales. Also, in Chapter 10 we will develop a formula to calculate the optimal inventory amount to order; this optimal order quantity balances inventory carrying costs (warehousing costs) with inventory ordering costs.

Receivables. In Table 8-1 we see that Addison's receivables total $135,000. If Addison were to reduce its receivables by $35,000, or to $100,000, its receivables conversion period would decline from 81 days to 60 days. Its new receivables conversion period would be calculated as (A/R)/(Sales/360) = $100/($600/360) = 60 days. Again, we assume that Addison could reduce its receivables without affecting sales adversely. As we shall see in Chapter 10, changing the receivables balance involves the firm's credit policy. In Chapter 10, we will develop a methodology which will enable you to analyze the effect of a change in credit policy on the firm's income statement.

Payables. For purposes of this illustration, we assumed that Addison's suppliers' credit policy called for payment of bills within 90 days. What if Addison extended its payment period by 10 days, to 100 days? This action might incur the wrath of its suppliers, and such an action would be easier to pursue during times of supplier excess capacity rather than when the suppliers have no such excess capacity. In Chapter 11, we will evaluate different credit terms and their resulting cost.

For the purposes of this illustration, we will assume that Addison was able to make changes to each of the cash conversion cycle components as mentioned here. How long is Addison's new cash conversion cycle? Given the facts above, Addison's new cash conversion cycle equals:

$$120 \text{ days} + 60 \text{ days} - 100 \text{ days} = 80 \text{ days}.$$

The combined effect of each of the actions discussed would cut the cash conversion cycle by more than 50 percent, and this would have a dramatic effect on the firm. Of course, we assumed that none of the actions taken would adversely affect sales. This may not be a realistic assumption, as you will see in the remaining working capital management chapters.

Self-Test

Briefly explain the cash conversion cycle.

Briefly explain the following terms:
a. Inventory conversion period.
b. Receivables conversion period.
c. Payables deferral period.

How can the cash conversion cycle be shortened?

CURRENT ASSET INVESTMENT POLICIES

Because it is inherently difficult to quickly change the level of fixed assets, the current asset accounts are used to make initial adjustments in operations as economic conditions change. If demand begins to rise or fall, the immediate

Table 8-2 **Effect of Current Asset Investment Policies on Rates of Return on Asset Investment (Millions of Dollars)**

	Relaxed	Moderate	Restricted
Sales	$40	$40	$40
EBIT	3	3	3
Current assets	$15	$10	$ 5
Fixed assets	10	10	10
Total assets	$25	$20	$15
Basic earning power (EBIT/TA)	12%	15%	20%

response is in the current asset accounts, and the appropriateness of this response can spell success or failure for the firm.

Current asset financial policy involves two basic questions: (1) What is the appropriate level of current assets, both in total and by specific accounts? (2) How should the required level of current assets be financed? We now turn to an examination of alternative policies regarding the level of investment in current assets and the way those assets should be financed.

Effect of Current Asset Levels on Risk and Return

relaxed current asset investment policy

A policy under which relatively large amounts of cash, marketable securities, and inventories are carried and under which sales are stimulated by a liberal credit policy, resulting in a high level of receivables.

restricted current asset investment policy

A policy under which holdings of cash, securities, inventories, and receivables are minimized.

moderate current asset investment policy

A policy that is between the two extremes of current asset investment policies: relaxed and restricted policies.

Under conditions of certainty—when sales, costs, order lead times, collection periods, and so on are known with certainty—all firms within an industry would hold the same level of current assets relative to sales. Any larger amount would increase the need for external funds without a corresponding increase in profits, whereas any smaller amount would cause late payments to suppliers, lost sales, and production inefficiencies because of inventory shortages. The picture changes when uncertainty is introduced. Here the firm requires some minimum amount of cash and inventories based on expected payments, sales, order lead times, and so on, plus additional amounts, or *safety stocks,* to help it cope if events vary from their expected values. Similarly, accounts receivable levels are affected by credit terms, and the easier those terms, the higher the receivables for any given level of sales.

Table 8-2 depicts three alternative policies that a firm like Addison might have regarding the level of current assets that it carries. Under each policy, a different amount of working capital is carried to support each level of sales. A **relaxed current asset investment policy** means that the firm invests in larger amounts of cash or marketable securities, accounts receivable, and inventory than its level of sales seems to require. Conversely, with a **restricted current asset investment policy,** the levels of cash or marketable securities, inventories, and receivables are reduced to the minimum possible amount at a given level of operations. A **moderate current asset investment policy** is between these two extremes.

In general, the greater the proportion of current assets to fixed assets at any given level of output, the less risky the firm's current asset investment policy.[2] How does the "relaxed" policy reduce risk? In essence, all risk of shortages is removed. With high levels of current assets there will be ample inventory so that no stock outages will ever occur, as well as sufficient cash or near-cash marketable securities to prevent any conceivable liquidity problem. Of course, there is a price to pay for all this safety. That price, as we illustrate in Table 8-2, comes in the form of a reduced return on asset investment.

The lower return associated with the relaxed current asset investment policy stems from the fact that the firm has acquired more current assets than the minimum required to support the current level of sales. Obviously, any level of sales requires the supporting assets of inventory, accounts receivable, and cash balances for business transactions. An overabundance of these assets, however, directs resources away from more productive investments. Therefore, assuming that EBIT is constant, the rate of return will be lower as the level of current assets increases.[3] We can conclude, therefore, that an overly relaxed current asset policy misallocates resources, which lowers the overall earning power of the firm.

From this discussion, an unwary reader might conclude that the best current asset policy would be one which aggressively slashes current assets to the bare minimum. As seen in Table 8-2, the expected basic earning power return rises from 12 percent under the relaxed policy to 20 percent under the restricted policy. However, just as lower returns were the price for the safety of a relaxed current asset policy, there is a price associated with the higher *potential*[4] returns in the restricted policy — higher risk.

The probability that a given level of sales cannot be maintained is one of the risks associated with a restricted current asset policy. For example, the high rate of return resulting from the restricted policy in Table 8-2 explicitly assumes no change in sales as levels of current assets are manipulated. How could a restricted current asset policy affect sales? First, with lower levels of inventory, sales could decline as a result of stock outages. Second, other revenues might be lost because of a stringent credit policy that is designed to reduce accounts receivable. Of course, a decline in sales could result in lower returns.

---

[2] It is important to distinguish between planned and unplanned increases in current assets. Unplanned increases in inventory that cannot be sold or accounts receivable that cannot be collected are *not* examples of a "relaxed" risk-reducing current asset investment policy. Of course, such a buildup in current assets is risky and even life-threatening to the firm. The planned "relaxed" policy that we are considering here concentrates on keeping more cash and inventory on hand to insure that no shortages occur.

[3] The same principle holds true for fixed assets. Idle excess capacity bloats the asset side of the balance sheet, requiring financing to support it. Because idle assets are not producing revenues but are increasing the firm's financing charges, the profitability of the firm declines.

[4] If returns *always* were higher under the more risky current asset policy, there wouldn't be any risk, would there?

Reduced sales are not the only risk associated with a restricted policy. Since current assets provide liquidity, their reduction may lead to difficulties in paying bills or other obligations as they come due. Slow payment could lead to poor credit ratings or even to a reduction in suppliers' willingness to extend trade credit.

Therefore, an overly restricted current asset policy can lead to exactly the opposite result of that intended. As is often the case in finance, the preferred current asset policy lies somewhere between the extreme levels of restricted and relaxed policies. Even though it is difficult to prescribe an optimal level of current assets for each firm, a general guideline for current asset investment policy decisions does exist. *The level of current assets should be reduced as long as the marginal return from such an action is greater than or equal to the potential for resulting losses.* Thus, inventory should be reduced to a point where there is only an acceptably low probability of lost sales due to stock outages. Similarly, the savings resulting from lower levels of accounts receivable must be compared to the potential losses from the more stringent credit policy. Finally, the return from minimizing cash holdings, in either demand deposits or marketable securities, must be compared to the potential losses if cash were in short supply.

Self-Test

What two questions does overall current asset financial policy involve?

Differentiate among the three alternative current asset investment policies.

How could an overly restrictive current asset investment policy affect sales?

What risks are associated with a restricted current asset policy?

Identify the general guideline for current asset policy decisions.

ALTERNATIVE CURRENT ASSET FINANCING POLICIES

The concept of financing working capital originated at a time when most industries were closely related to agriculture. Farmers would borrow to buy seed in the spring and, when the crops were harvested in the fall, repay the loan with the proceeds of the crop's sale. Similarly, processors would buy crops in the fall, process them, sell the finished product, and end up just before the next harvest with relatively low inventories. Bank loans with maximum maturities of one year were used to finance both the purchase and the processing costs, and these loans were retired with the proceeds from the sale of the finished products. Thus, the loans were, in essence, self-liquidating.

This situation is depicted in Figure 8-3, in which fixed assets are shown to be growing steadily over time, while the processor's current assets jump at harvest season, decline during the year, and end at zero just before the next

Figure 8-3 **Fixed and Current Assets and Their Financing**

This figure shows an idealized model of the financing of current and fixed assets. Each season, current assets rise sharply, then gradually fall to zero. Short-term loans, used to finance these current assets, are repaid and renewed each season. Fixed assets, on the other hand, are financed with long-term debt and owners' equity.

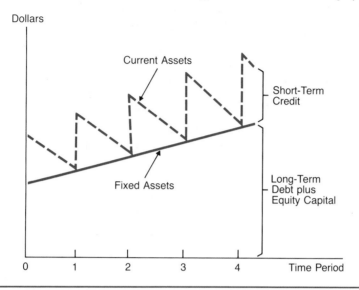

crop is harvested. Short-term credit is used to finance current assets, and long-term funds are used to finance fixed assets. Thus, the top segment of the graph deals with working capital.

The figure represents an idealized situation — actually, current assets build up gradually as crops are purchased and processed; inventories are drawn down less regularly; and ending inventory balances do not decline to zero. Nevertheless, the example does illustrate the general nature of the production and financing process, and short-term financial management consists of decisions relating to the top section of the graph — managing current assets and arranging for the short-term credit used to finance them.

Although our modern economy has become less oriented toward agriculture, seasonal and cyclical fluctuations of current assets and current liabilities still exist. For example, construction firms have peaks in the spring and summer, whereas retail sales often peak around Christmas. Consequently, manufacturers who supply either construction companies or retailers follow patterns similar to those of their customers, but with a lead time of several months. Similarly, virtually all businesses must build up current assets when the economy is moving up, but their inventories and receivables decline when the economy slacks off. Even when a business is at its seasonal or cyclical low, however, its current assets do not drop to zero, and this realization has led to

Figure 8-4 **Temporary versus Permanent Assets: Exactly Matching Maturities**

Because in the modern business world current assets rarely drop to zero, the idea of permanent current assets was developed. This figure shows these assets being financed, along with fixed assets, by long-term debt and equity capital. Those current assets that are still seasonal or cyclical continue to be financed by short-term credit. Figures 8-3 and 8-4 illustrate the traditional approach of matching asset and liability maturities.

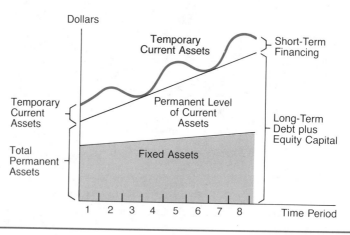

permanent current assets

Current assets that are still on hand when business activity is at seasonal or cyclical lows.

temporary current assets

Current assets that fluctuate with seasonal or cyclical sales variations.

the development of the concept of **permanent current assets.** Those current assets that rise and fall with business activity are termed **temporary current assets.** The manner in which the permanent and temporary current assets are financed constitutes the firm's *short-term financial policy.*

Maturity Matching Approach. One commonly used financing policy is to match asset and liability maturities, as shown in Figure 8-4. Here both fixed assets and permanent current assets are financed with long-term capital — equity plus long-term debt — while temporary current assets are financed with current liabilities. This strategy reduces the risk that the firm will be unable to pay off its maturing obligations. To illustrate, suppose a firm borrowed on a one-year basis and used the funds to build and equip a plant. Because cash flows from the plant (profit plus depreciation) would almost never be sufficient to pay off the loan after only one year, the loan would have to be renewed annually. Thus, the company's ability to continue operating would depend on its ability to renew the loan each year. If for some reason the lender refused to renew the loan, the firm would have serious problems. Had the plant been financed with a 20-year loan, however, the required loan payments (interest plus a small part of the principal) would have been better matched with cash flows from profits and depreciation, and the problem of renewal would arise, if at all, only once every 20 years.[5]

At the extreme, a firm could attempt to exactly match the maturity structure of its assets and liabilities. Inventory expected to be sold in 30 days would be financed with a 30-day bank loan; a machine expected to last for 5 years would be financed with a 5-year loan; a 20-year building would be financed with a 20-year mortgage; and so on. Of course, uncertainty about the lives of assets prevents this exact maturity matching. For example, a firm may finance inventories with a 30-day loan, expecting to sell the inventories and to use the cash generated to retire the loan. Yet if sales are slow, the cash will not be forthcoming, and the use of short-term credit may cause a problem.

Aggressive Approach. Figure 8-5 illustrates an aggressive current asset financing policy. Here a firm continues to finance all of its fixed assets with long-term capital, but part of its permanent current assets plus all of its temporary current assets are financed with short-term credit. Why would a firm wish to increase the amount of assets it finances with short-term credit? Basically, short-term credit is desirable because it usually is cheaper than long-term credit. Consider the sources of short-term debt. First, some sources of short-term financing are spontaneous; that is, they increase as the level of the firm's operations increases. Accounts payable and accruals are examples of spontaneous financing. As we saw in Chapter 7 and will examine in more detail in Chapter 11, when sales increase, a company obtains more raw materials from suppliers, and the increased trade credit offered by the suppliers finances the buildup in assets. Similarly, as operations increase, there is a resulting increase in accrued wages and taxes, which helps to finance the buildup in operations. Used within limits, these sources constitute "free" capital. Most other short-term debt is obtained as bank loans.

Short-term credit could be used to finance all current assets (both temporary and permanent current assets), and even to finance a portion of the fixed assets. This would be represented in Figure 8-5 by drawing the dashed line *below* the line designating fixed assets, which would indicate that all current and some fixed assets were being financed with short-term credit. This aggressive financing policy would be extremely risky because it would subject the firm to fluctuating interest rates and to the even more critical danger of loan renewal problems. Even so, since short-term debt is often cheaper than long-term debt, some firms are willing to sacrifice safety for possibly higher profits.

---

[5]Examples of maturity matching also can be found in our personal financial lives. Few of us would even think of financing a home with only a one-year note or financing a car for 30 years. In the first case, almost no one could pay for a home in one year. In the second case, the car would have turned to rust before our payments ended. Therefore, we typically finance an asset over a period that, in some manner, reflects its expected useful life.

Figure 8-5 **Temporary versus Permanent Assets: Aggressive Approach**

To take advantage of cheaper, short-term credit, a firm may finance a portion of its permanent current assets from short-term sources. The remainder of its permanent current assets, along with fixed and temporary (seasonal) current assets, are financed in the traditional way as shown in the prior two figures. A firm taking this approach sacrifices a measure of safety to lower its financing costs in hopes of increasing profits.

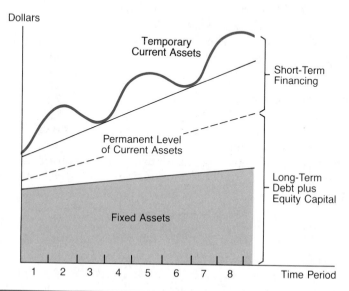

Conservative Approach. Alternatively, the firm could finance not only its fixed and permanent current assets with long-term debt and equity capital, but a portion of its temporary current assets as well. This is shown in Figure 8-6 by drawing the dashed line *above* the line designating permanent current assets, which indicates that permanent capital was being used to finance all permanent assets as well as some or all of the seasonal and cyclical demands. The humps above the dashed line in Figure 8-6 represent short-term financing; the troughs below it represent short-term security holdings. Our illustrative firm uses a small amount of short-term credit to meet its peak requirements, but it also meets a part of its seasonal needs by "storing liquidity" in the form of marketable securities during the off season. This represents a very safe, conservative current asset financing policy, but one that probably results in lower expected profits.

Advantages and Disadvantages of Short-Term Credit

The distinction among Figures 8-4, 8-5, and 8-6 is the relative amount of short-term debt financing employed. The aggressive financing policy calls for the greatest amount of short-term debt, the conservative financing policy uses the

Figure 8-6 **Temporary versus Permanent Assets: Conservative Approach**

A very conservative approach to financing current assets is illustrated in this figure. Part of the short-term financing requirement is met by using long-term capital to "store up" marketable securities during the off season. During peak seasons these securities are sold to provide needed liquidity, and they are augmented by a small amount of short-term borrowing.

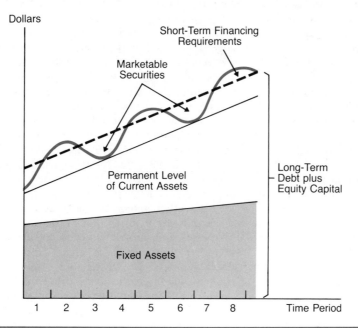

lowest amount, and the maturity matching approach falls in between. Although using short-term debt is generally more risky for the firm than using long-term debt, short-term credit does have some offsetting advantages. The pros and cons of financing with short-term debt are considered in this section.

Speed. A short-term loan can be obtained much more quickly than a long-term loan. Lenders will insist on a more thorough financial examination before granting long-term credit, and the loan agreement will have to be spelled out in considerably more detail, because a great deal can happen during the life of a 10- to 20-year loan. Therefore, if funds are needed in a hurry, the firm should look to the short-term markets.

Flexibility. If its needs for funds are seasonal or cyclical, or just hard to predict for whatever reason, a firm may not want to commit itself to long-term debt. First, loan initiation costs are generally higher for long-term debt. Sec-

INDUSTRY PRACTICE

Cash Flow Problems and Bankruptcy

Cash flow problems and increasingly cautious lenders resulted in an increase in bankruptcies, especially among small and medium-sized firms, as the 1990s began. For example, business filings for bankruptcy-law protection increased 34 percent, to over 20,000, during the fourth quarter of 1989, and the first quarter of 1990 was even worse. The clothing, retailing, real estate, and construction industries were hit hardest. "It's a result of the generally weak state of the economy," said Harvey R. Miller, co-managing partner of a New York law firm with many bankruptcy clients.

Other specialists cited other causes. Savings and loans, often in deep trouble themselves, can no longer help troubled companies. The market for junk bonds, which in the 1980s financed so many young or struggling firms, virtually disappeared in the wake of Wall Street scandals and indictments. This situation made it difficult for firms to "roll over" loans when they matured, and the rollover problem contributed to bankruptcies.

Although bankruptcy filings at the beginning of the decade are fewer than those caused by the recession in the mid-1980s, they are on the rise after declining for some time. A Los Angeles lawyer says, "I can explain the increase with three letters: LBO." The burden of debt from earlier leveraged buyouts has even sent some of the larger companies into bankruptcy court. A research firm found that 10 of the 27 largest U.S. bankruptcy filings in history took place between January 1989 and April 1990. Among them were Federated and Allied stores, retailing units of Campeau Corporation, which Campeau had bought with $7.7 billion in debt.

Sources: "Bankruptcy-Law Filings by Firms Spurt," *The Wall Street Journal,* April 6, 1990; Associated Press, May 10, 1990; "U.S. Officials Urge Bankers to Avoid Tightening Credit," *The New York Times,* May 11, 1990.

The retailers operate 260 stores, with 100,000 employees in 28 states. In early 1990, Campeau received a four-month extension of its reorganization plan deadline from the bankruptcy judge. Campeau's lawyers said a longer extension might be necessary because of the size and complexity of the case. Allied and Federated have more than 200,000 creditors, none of whom objected to the extension.

The Campeau default helped increase 1989's junk-bond default total to $11.7 billion, more than three times the $4.97 billion in defaults during 1988, and, for 1990, an increase of 28 percent, to a record $15 billion high-interest junk bond defaults, is projected.

Left with commercial banks as their only source of funds, many troubled firms are finding themselves shut out. Melvin Jaffe, president and CEO of a California-based chain of building-supply stores, said, "We ran out of cash. Our lender wouldn't give us any more. I think they were scared by what they saw happening to other retailers." Jaffe's company continued to operate under Chapter 11 of the Bankruptcy Code, while trying to work out an agreement with its creditors.

Tight credit "became a self-fulfilling prophecy" in the opinion of a New York economic consultant, A. Gary Shilling. "As lenders get more worried, they stop lending to the people who most need to borrow, forcing what they most fear, which is bankruptcy."

Delays in paying its bills signal trouble for a company, and more firms than usual are past due in meeting their obligations. While the average past-due payment in December 1989 was seven days, the time increased to nine days within the next three months. "That's a significant change," said a credit executive with the company that compiled the data. "It's a strong signal that companies are in a cash bind." For some industries, the past-due term had risen even more by March 1990 — to seventeen days for apparel shops, up from nine in December; to twenty days for savings and loans, up from twelve; and to fourteen days for general merchandise stores, up from eight.

An unexpected announcement by the nation's top banking regulators on May 10, 1990, brought some hope to troubled firms. Federal Reserve Chairman Alan Greenspan, Comptroller of the Currency Robert L. Clarke, and FDIC Chairman L. William Seidman urged American Banking Association executives to continue lending to good customers. The regulators said they wanted to clear up any misunderstandings over lending standards. While bank officers have cited increasingly tough scrutiny by bank examiners as a reason for tightening lending, the new announcement urged banks not to go too far in cutting off funds. Even though the government has repeatedly warned of the dangers of real estate lending in light of the savings and loan debacle, FDIC Chairman Seidman said, "We are not saying not to lend. We are saying they should use their judgment." One of the banking

officials said the regulators' announcement "signals that the credit crunch is biting too deep."

Some bankers say they have been forced to set aside cash to cover previously approved real estate loans in case of default and have also had to report losses on their banks' books by writing down the value of the loans. These actions have, of course, affected their willingness to make loans, which in turn has hit small businesses hard. Comptroller Clarke said that a restriction of credit when the economy slows is inevitable, but he also said, "[that] doesn't mean you should freeze up all the lending." And Fed Chairman Greenspan said, "The nature of banking is risk taking. And if you have zero loan losses, then you aren't doing your job."

Bank executives said that regulators should ease up if banks agree to do more lending. The issue, said one, is "whether the examiners are going to go by the exact numbers, or give a local banker who knows a small-business owner some latitude." If compromises between regulators and lenders occur, then the trend toward business bankruptcies may slow again.

ond, although long-term debt can be repaid early, provided the loan agreement contains a prepayment provision, prepayment penalties can be expensive. Accordingly, if a firm thinks its need for funds will diminish in the near future, it should choose short-term debt for the repayment flexibility it provides. Finally, long-term loan agreements always contain provisions, or covenants, which constrain the firm's future actions, but short-term credit agreements are generally less restrictive.

Cost of Long-Term versus Short-Term Debt. In Chapter 4, we saw that the yield curve often is upward sloping, indicating that interest rates are generally lower on short-term than on long-term debt. Thus, interest expense will generally be lower if the firm borrows on a short-term rather than a long-term basis.

Risk of Long-Term versus Short-Term Debt. Even though short-term debt is generally less expensive than long-term debt, financing with short-term debt subjects the firm to more risk for two reasons: (1) If a firm borrows on a long-term basis, its interest costs will be fixed (or if the interest rate is floating, the cost will still be relatively stable over time), but if it borrows on a short-term basis, its interest expense will fluctuate widely, at times going quite high. For example, from 1977 to 1980 the short-term rate for large corporations (the prime rate) more than *tripled,* going from 6.25 percent to 21 percent. (2) If a firm borrows on a short-term basis, there will be less time in the borrowing period to generate cash to pay the debt's principal and interest as they come due. If the firm finds itself in a weak financial position on the loan's maturity date, it is possible that the lender will not extend the loan, thereby forcing the firm into bankruptcy.

Self-Test

What is meant by the term "current asset financing policy"?

How do the three alternative current asset financing policies compare with respect to their use of short-term debt?

What are the main advantages and disadvantages of short-term credit?

COMBINING CURRENT ASSET AND LIABILITY DECISIONS

From the preceding discussion, it is obvious that a potentially profitable, yet risky, strategy would be to minimize the firm's investment in current assets and to finance a large proportion of total assets with short-term debt. Alternatively, risk could be minimized, at the expense of potential profits, by increasing current assets and financing a large proportion of total assets with long-term debt and equity.

In Table 8-3 we illustrate the effects of different current asset investment and financing policies. For these strategies, the current ratio is our measure of risk, and return on equity measures the profitability of each plan.

The conservative policy of building current assets and financing with more expensive long-term debt has reduced the firm's return, as expected. The firm's level of risk is quite low, however — its high current ratio indicates that the firm has sufficient liquidity to meet almost any emergency. In contrast, the aggressive policy of minimizing current asset investment and utilizing less costly short-term debt has led to a much higher expected return. There are dangers associated with this higher return, however. First, at this low level of current assets, it is quite possible that the firm will be unable to maintain the proposed level of sales. Second, a potentially critical problem is indicated by the firm's low level of liquidity, as measured by the current ratio and the negative net working capital.[6] With this low current ratio, the firm may find

---

[6]Note that net working capital mirrors the liquidity risk factors that are identified by the current ratio.

Table 8-3 **Combined Effects of Current Asset Levels and
Debt Maturity Mix on Risk and Return
(Thousands of Dollars)**

	Conservative	Moderate	Aggressive
Current assets	$15,000	$10,000	$ 5,000
Fixed assets	10,000	10,000	10,000
Total assets	$25,000	$20,000	$15,000
Short-term debt (10%)	$ 3,750	$ 5,000	$ 6,000
Long-term debt (14%)	8,750	5,000	1,500
Common equity	12,500	10,000	7,500
Total liabilities and equity	$25,000	$20,000	$15,000
Sales	$40,000	$40,000	$40,000
EBIT	3,000	3,000	3,000
Less: Interest	1,600	1,200	810
EBT	$ 1,400	$ 1,800	$ 2,190
Less: Taxes (40%)	560	720	876
Net income	$ 840	$ 1,080	$ 1,314
Current ratio (current assets/current liabilities)	4×	2×	0.83×
Return on equity (net income/ common equity)	6.7%	10.8%	17.5%
Net working capital (current assets − current liabilities)	$11,250	$5,000	($1,000)

future financing more difficult to obtain, and certainly it will be more expensive (due to the higher liquidity risk) if it can be obtained at all. The low current ratio also indicates that the firm may have substantial problems meeting bills and interest and principal payments as they come due. Thus, although an aggressive policy may lead to higher profits for the firm, it also increases the potential for bankruptcy. A more moderate approach, which represents a balancing of risk and return, may be preferred by many financial managers.

Procedures for evaluating the investment in each of the current asset and liability accounts are considered in the remaining chapters on short-term financial management.

Self-Test

Briefly explain why a potentially profitable, yet risky, strategy would be to minimize investment in current assets while financing a large portion of total assets with short-term debt.

SMALL BUSINESS

Growth and Working Capital Needs

Working capital is the requirement that entrepreneurs most often underestimate when seeking funds to finance a new business. The entrepreneur generally provides for research and development and for the plant and equipment required for production. Working capital, however, frequently comes as a surprise to the entrepreneur, who probably expects to develop a product the market will immediately accept and for which the market will pay a substantial premium. This premium will, he or she assumes, lead to high profit margins, which will then "finance" all of the firm's other needs. As naive as this point of view may seem, it nevertheless is common among less experienced founders of new businesses.

Ned was one of the founders of a new microcomputer software company that began seeking venture capital to support its products in early 1990. When speaking with a venture capitalist, who was concerned about the low level of funding being sought, Ned explained that the company's products had such a high profit margin that the company would be essentially self-financing.

Ned's company made and sold a computer software package. The package was shipped in the form of three diskettes and a set of manuals. The total cost of those materials was about $20, and the package sold for $500. With such a high profit margin, Ned claimed, there would be no need for financing once the marketing was under way. In fact, he said, there would be plenty of cash to pay for new product development.

Joanna, the venture capitalist, was somewhat disconcerted by Ned's reasoning. She pointed out some of the errors in Ned's "analysis": The $500 was only a suggested retail price; discounters would probably sell the package for closer to $275. This $275, in turn, was at the *end* of a marketing chain that included distributors and

dealers; Ned's firm would only receive $80 to $90 per package. This $80 to $90 would initially be added to accounts receivable — not received as cash — and probably not collected, on average, for about 60 days. Meanwhile, Ned would have to write checks to pay for overhead, for high R & D expenses, for a marketing staff, and for advertising space. Instead of $480 per package of cash flowing *in,* the firm would be, on balance, paying cash *out* for the first few years of its life.

Rapid growth consumes cash; it does not generate cash. Rapid growth may generate profits, but profits do not pay the bills — cash does. Consider what a firm must do to sustain a high growth rate. If it is a manufacturer, the components of its assets include raw materials inventory, work-in-process inventory, finished goods inventory, and accounts receivable, as well as fixed assets. With the exception of fixed assets, these items are all components of gross working capital. When the firm produces a product, it makes an investment in each of these working capital items before any cash is received from collection of receivables, assuming all sales are credit sales.

Consider a small firm that finances its activities solely through the funds it generates. Recall the financial analysis presented earlier in this chapter. Suppose the firm has an average of 120 days of sales in inventory and an average of 60 days of sales in receivables. If the firm pays cash for all of its materials and labor, it has a cash conversion cycle of 180 days; that is, between the payment for goods at the beginning of the cycle and the receipt of cash at the end, 180 days pass. Thus, the company "turns over" its cash only twice per year.

If the company earns, say, 3 percent on its sales dollar (as measured by net profit margin), it has about 3 percent more money available after a cycle than before it. With two cycles per year, about 6 percent more is available for investment at the end of the year than at the beginning. Thus, annual growth of approximately 6 percent can be supported.

If the company is growing at a rate of 20 percent per year, but it can generate only 6 percent internally, it must either obtain funds externally or face enormous pressures.

How can the company improve its ability to fund growth internally? Generally, the firm can grow by the product of the net profit margin times the number of cash conversion cycles per year.[7] Thus, it can support more rapid growth either by raising the profit margin or by shortening the cash conversion cycle (increasing the number of cycles).

To raise the profit margin, the company must raise prices, cut costs, or do both. Raising prices may reduce growth (because customers will be less eager to buy at higher prices), but it may also help bring growth and financial resources more into balance.

Shortening the cash conversion cycle requires reducing inventory, collecting receivables more efficiently, or paying suppliers more slowly. Consider the effects of these changes. Reducing inventory by 25 percent (to 90 days) and cutting receivables to 30 days (normal credit terms), reduces the cycle to 120 days. If, in addition, suppliers are willing to wait 30 days for payment, then the time cash is outstanding can be further shortened to 90 days. Cash turnover changes to four times per year from two, and internally fundable growth becomes 12 percent rather than 6 percent. Improving the cash conversion cycle by increasing the rate at which the firm can support growth internally reduces the firm's needs for outside funds to a more manageable level.

For the small business with serious constraints on obtaining outside funds, these discretionary policies can help bring the firm's rate of growth into balance with its ability to finance that growth. Furthermore, such control on the part of management may impress bankers and others who have funds and thus may help the firm get the outside financing it would have preferred to have had all along.[8]

---

[7]Several factors may mitigate the accuracy of this approximation. First, this example ignores the fact that some expenses, such as depreciation, are not cash expenses. Furthermore, no spontaneous sources of financing, discussed in Chapter 7, have been considered. Finally, the example assumes a zero payout ratio, which may not fit every situation.

[8]Limits on growth and the concept of "sustainable growth" are explored in Chapter 6 of Robert C. Higgins, *Analysis for Financial Management,* 2nd Edition (Homewood, Ill.: Irwin, 1989).

SUMMARY

This chapter examined short-term financial planning, which includes current asset investment policies and alternative ways of financing current assets. The key concepts covered are listed below.

- **Working capital** refers to current assets, and **net working capital** is defined as current assets minus current liabilities. **Current asset financing policy** refers to decisions relating to the target level and the financing of current assets.

- **Current asset management** involves the administration, within policy guidelines, of current assets, including the financing of those assets.

- The **inventory conversion period** is the length of time required to convert raw materials into finished goods and then to sell them.

- The **receivables conversion period** is the additional length of time required to convert the firm's receivables into cash, and it is equal to the days sales outstanding (DSO).

- The **payables deferral period** is the length of time between the purchase of raw materials and labor and paying for them.

- The **cash conversion cycle** is the length of time from paying for raw materials and labor to receiving cash from the sale of products. The cash conversion cycle can be calculated as follows:

$$\begin{array}{c}\text{Inventory}\\\text{conversion}\\\text{period}\end{array} + \begin{array}{c}\text{Receivables}\\\text{conversion}\\\text{period}\end{array} - \begin{array}{c}\text{Payables}\\\text{deferral}\\\text{period}\end{array} = \begin{array}{c}\text{Cash}\\\text{conversion.}\\\text{cycle}\end{array}$$

- Under a **relaxed current asset investment policy,** a firm holds relatively large amounts of each type of current asset. A **restricted current asset investment policy** entails holding minimal amounts of these items. A **moderate current asset investment policy** is between these two policies.

- **Permanent current assets** are those current assets that the firm holds even during slack times, whereas **temporary current assets** are the additional current assets that are needed during seasonal or cyclical peaks. The methods used to finance permanent and temporary current assets define the firm's **current asset financing policy.**

- A **maturity matching** approach to current asset financing involves matching the maturities of assets and liabilities in such a way that temporary current assets are financed with short-term debt and permanent current assets and fixed assets are financed with long-term debt or equity. Under an **aggressive** approach, some permanent current assets and perhaps even some fixed assets are financed with short-term debt. A **conservative** approach would be to use long-term capital to finance all fixed and permanent current assets plus some of the temporary current assets.

- The advantages of short-term credit are (1) the **speed** with which short-term loans can be arranged, (2) increased **flexibility,** and (3) the fact that **short-term interest rates** are generally **lower** than long-term rates. The principal disadvantage of short-term credit is the **extra risk** that the borrower must bear because (1) the lender can demand payment on short notice and (2) the cost of the loan will increase if interest rates rise.

- For the **small business firm** with serious constraints on obtaining outside funds, careful control of policies concerning inventories, receivables, and payables can help bring the firm's growth rate into balance with its ability to finance that growth.

EQUATIONS

The cash conversion cycle is the length of time from the firm's cash expenditures on productive resources (raw materials and labor) to its own collection of cash from the sale of products—that is, the length of time the firm has funds tied up in working capital. The cash conversion cycle can be calculated as follows:

$$\begin{array}{c} \text{Inventory} \\ \text{conversion} \\ \text{period} \end{array} + \begin{array}{c} \text{Receivables} \\ \text{conversion} \\ \text{period} \end{array} - \begin{array}{c} \text{Payables} \\ \text{deferral} \\ \text{period} \end{array} = \begin{array}{c} \text{Cash} \\ \text{conversion.} \\ \text{cycle} \end{array} \qquad \textbf{(8-1)}$$

RESOLUTION TO DECISION IN FINANCE

Unused Inventory . . . The Pot of Gold at the End of the Rainbow?

Maxey says company managers can duplicate most of what he does if they have the time to invest in the effort. The first step is the obvious one of figuring out how much it costs to hold onto the unused inventory—including warehouse rent, insurance, interest on the money invested in the unsold product, wages for warehouse workers, and the cost of additional space for storing other items that could have been housed where the unused inventory languishes.

There are also hidden costs associated with the unsold assets. For example, product improvements in the industry could make the stockpile obsolete, and changes in fashion could do the same for products dependent on consumer whims. The stock could also spoil or suffer mildew damage, destroying any chance of recovering even part of its value. An even greater liability, pointed out by Maxey, is what he calls "opportunity cost"—the cost of not being able to pursue another course of action because cash is tied up in the unused inventory.

Having made a decision to sell, to which potential buyers should the offer be made? The first rule is to avoid approaching regular customers: Offering a discount to those who willingly and regularly pay full price for a firm's products may influence them against future full-price sales. Also, if they are offered an unusual bargain, they may spend all of their available money on it, and then pass up purchases of the company's more profitable items later in the year. New customers are the best solution, because they can be offered a one-time bargain without expectation of future deals. Savvy managers can also pursue secondary accounts, developed ahead of time during the normal course of business.

Regarding price, Maxey says the normal selling price should be the basis of an offer of a 40 to 50 percent discount. Items unsold at that level should be discounted more and offered again, with this process continuing until all of the products are sold. He points out that everything has its price, but that price is not necessarily a good one. Parts of products, for instance, may be worth almost nothing. For example, he once recommended that a manufacturer donate thousands of leftover hammer handles to a school shop class, in order to obtain a tax break. Considering the costs involved in keeping them or throwing them away, this solution was the best one.

Source: "The Search for Grubby Capital," *Inc.*, March 1990.

QUESTIONS

8-1 What are the differences between permanent and temporary current assets?

8-2 What is the tradeoff between risk and return in the management of the firm's current assets?

8-3 Why do excess current assets reduce profits?

8-4 How would a period of rapidly increasing inflation affect the firm's level of current assets?

8-5 During a tight-money period, would you expect a business firm to hold higher or lower cash balances (demand deposits) than during an easy-money period? Assume the firm's volume of business remains constant over both economic periods.

8-6 How would management's ability to predict sales trends and patterns affect current asset financial policy?

8-7 From the standpoint of the borrower, is long-term or short-term credit riskier? Explain. Would it ever make sense to borrow on a short-term basis if short-term rates were above long-term rates?

8-8 If long-term credit exposes a borrower to less risk, why would people or firms ever borrow on a short-term basis?

8-9 Considering the fact that an increase in the inventory turnover and total assets turnover ratios correspond with a decrease in the cash conversion cycle, with what group of ratios would you classify the cash conversion cycle?

SELF-TEST PROBLEMS

ST-1 Vanderheiden Press, Inc., and the Herrenhouse Publishing Company had the following balance sheets as of December 31, 1990 (thousands of dollars):

	Vanderheiden Press	Herrenhouse Publishing
Current assets	$100,000	$ 80,000
Fixed assets (net)	100,000	120,000
Total assets	$200,000	$200,000
Current liabilities	$ 20,000	$ 80,000
Long-term debt	80,000	20,000
Common stock	50,000	50,000
Retained earnings	50,000	50,000
Total liabilities and equity	$200,000	$200,000

Earnings before interest and taxes (EBIT) for both firms are $30 million, and the effective federal-plus-state tax rate is 40 percent.

a. What is the return on equity for each firm if the interest rate on current liabilities is 10 percent and the rate on long-term debt is 13 percent?

b. Assume that the short-term rate rises to 20 percent. While the rate on new long-term debt rises to 16 percent, the rate on existing long-term debt remains unchanged. What would be the return on equity for Vanderheiden Press and Herrenhouse Publishing under these conditions?

c. Which company is in a riskier position? Why?

ST-2 The Calgary Company is attempting to establish a current assets policy. Fixed assets are $300,000, and the firm plans to maintain a 50 percent debt-to-assets ratio. The interest rate is 10 percent on all debt. Three alternative current asset policies are under consideration: 40, 50, and 60 percent of projected sales. The company expects to earn 15 percent before interest and taxes on sales of $1.5 million. Calgary's effective federal-plus-state tax rate is 40 percent. What is the expected return on equity under each alternative?

PROBLEMS

8-1 **Current asset policy.** Consider the following balance sheet:

Bay Harbor Industries:
Balance Sheet, December 31, 1990

Assets

Cash	$ 100,000
Marketable securities	40,000
Accounts receivable	660,000
Inventory	1,000,000
Plant and equipment (net)	1,800,000
Total assets	$3,600,000

Liabilities and Shareholders' Equity

Accounts payable	$ 160,000
Notes payable	240,000
Accrued wages	40,000
Accrued taxes	140,000
Mortgage bonds	800,000
Debentures	420,000
Common stock	200,000
Paid-in capital	400,000
Retained earnings	1,200,000
Total liabilities and shareholders' equity	$3,600,000

a. Determine Bay Harbor Industries' investment in gross working capital.

b. Determine Bay Harbor Industries' net working capital investment.

c. Does the firm's financing mix (long-term versus short-term) appear to be conservative or aggressive?

8-2 **Cash conversion cycle.** The Far East Oriental Rug Company has an inventory conversion period of 90 days, a receivables conversion period of 48 days, and a payables deferral period of 38 days.

a. What is the length of the firm's cash conversion cycle?

b. If Far East's sales are $3,240,000 and all sales are on credit, what is the firm's investment in accounts receivable?

c. How many times per year does Far East turn over its inventory?

8-3 **Current asset investment.** Southern Motors, Inc. (SMI) is a leading manufacturer of small electric motors. SMI turns out 1,000 motors a day at a cost of $9 per motor for materials and labor. It takes the firm 30 days to convert the raw materials into a motor. The motors are shipped to dealers immediately upon completion of the manufacturing process. SMI allows its customers 45 days in which to pay for the motors, and the firm generally pays its suppliers in 30 days.

a. What is the length of SMI's cash conversion cycle?

b. In a steady state in which SMI produces 1,000 motors a day, what amount of current assets must it finance?

c. By what amount could SMI reduce its current asset financing needs if it were able to stretch its payables deferral period to 35 days?

d. SMI's management is trying to analyze the effect of a proposed new manufacturing process on the firm's current asset investment. The new production process would allow SMI to decrease its inventory conversion period to 27 days and to increase its daily production to 1,200 motors. However, the new process would increase the cost of materials and labor to $10 per unit. Assuming the change does not affect the receivables conversion period (45 days) or the payables deferral period (30 days), what will be the length of the cash conversion cycle and the current asset financing requirement if the new production process is implemented? Assume finished goods inventory remains near zero.

8-4   **Current asset financing policies.** Judy Smith has been evaluating her firm's financing mix of short-term and long-term debt. She has projected the two following condensed balance sheets:

	Plan 1	**Plan 2**
Current assets	$2,500,000	$2,500,000
Fixed assets (net)	2,500,000	2,500,000
Total assets	$5,000,000	$5,000,000
Current liabilities	$ 500,000	$2,000,000
Long-term debt	2,000,000	500,000
Common stock equity	2,500,000	2,500,000
Total liabilities and equity	$5,000,000	$5,000,000

Earnings before interest and taxes (EBIT) are $750,000 and the tax rate is 40 percent under either plan.

a. If current liabilities have a 10 percent interest rate and long-term debt has a 14 percent interest rate, what is the rate of return on equity under each plan?

b. Assume that the yield curve is inverted and that the short-term rate is 18 percent while the long-term rate is still 14 percent. What is the rate of return on equity for the two plans?

c. Which plan is riskier? Explain.

8-5   **Current asset policy.** Bob Block, financial manager for Quick-Set Cement Company, has a problem. The firm's board of directors has complained about the firm's low liquidity. Bob has been ordered to raise the current ratio to at least 2.0 within a reasonable time period. One of his plans is to sell $5,000,000 in equity and invest the proceeds in Treasury bills, which yield 8 percent before taxes. The firm has a 40 percent tax rate, and, if no Treasury bills are purchased, net income is expected to be $2,000,000. Assume 100 percent payout.

Quick-Set Cement Company:
Balance Sheet, December 31, 1990

Current assets	$10,000,000	Current liabilities	$ 6,250,000
Fixed assets	15,000,000	Long-term debt	3,750,000
		Common stock equity	15,000,000
Total assets	$25,000,000	Total liabilities and equity	$25,000,000

a. Using the financial information in the accompanying balance sheet (which does not include the proposed purchase of Treasury bills), calculate the firm's current ratio, net working capital, and return on equity.

b. If Bob follows his plan and sells $5,000,000 in equity in order to purchase the 8 percent Treasury bills, what are the firm's resulting current ratio, net working capital, and return on equity?

c. What result would the plan have on the firm's liquidity?

d. Would you suggest acceptance of this plan?

8-6   **Alternate current asset financial policies.** FSA, Inc.'s management is concerned about the way in which its new firm will be financed. The three alternative plans that have been proposed are as follows:

	Plan 1	Plan 2	Plan 3
Current assets	$4,500,000	$4,500,000	$4,500,000
Fixed assets	8,000,000	8,000,000	8,000,000
Current liabilities (8.5%)	4,500,000	1,500,000	3,000,000
Long-term debt (12%)	1,500,000	4,500,000	0
Common stock equity	6,500,000	6,500,000	9,500,000

Whichever plan is chosen, sales are expected to be $20 million and operating profits (EBIT) will be $2 million. The marginal tax rate is 40 percent.

a. For each plan, calculate the following: (1) current ratio, (2) net working capital, (3) total debt/total assets ratio, and (4) return on equity.

b. Compare the risk and return associated with each plan. Which plan would you accept?

8-7   **Cash conversion cycle.** Pinto Products' balance sheet follows.

Cash	$ 200,000	Debt	$ 896,000
Accounts receivable	700,000		
Inventory	540,000	Equity	1,344,000
Fixed assets (net)	800,000		
Total assets	$2,240,000	Total liabilities and equity	$2,240,000

The company's sales are $3,600,000 annually, the payables deferral period is 35 days, and the net profit margin is 5 percent. Compute the firm's (a) inventory turnover (S/Inv), (b) inventory conversion period, (c) days sales outstanding (DSO), (d) cash conversion cycle, and (e) return on assets (ROA).

8-8 **Cash conversion cycle.** Refer to the data in Problem 8-7. The company's owner, Lee Strickler, is too busy to oversee all the financial aspects of the business. He decides to hire Elizabeth Brannigan to reduce current assets. After some study, Brannigan concludes she can reduce the firm's inventory conversion period by 14 days and the days sales outstanding (DSO) by 20 days without reducing its sales or profit margin. Under these new conditions:

a. What is the new level of inventory?

b. What is the new level of accounts receivable?

c. What is the length of the firm's cash conversion cycle after these changes are implemented?

d. If all of the savings (from the reduction in inventory and accounts receivable) are used to reduce debt, what is the firm's return on assets? (Assume the profit margin remains constant.)

8-9 **Cash conversion cycle.** The Belvedere Corporation is trying to determine the effects of its inventory turnover ratio and days sales outstanding (DSO) on its cash conversion cycle. Belvedere's 1990 sales (all on credit) were $150,000, and it earned a net profit of 6 percent, or $9,000. It turned over its inventory 6 times during the year, and its DSO was 36 days. The firm had fixed assets totaling $40,000. Belvedere's payables deferral period is 40 days.

a. Calculate Belvedere's cash conversion cycle.

b. Assuming Belvedere holds negligible amounts of cash and marketable securities, calculate its total assets turnover and ROA.

c. Suppose Belvedere's managers believe that the inventory turnover can be raised to 8 times. What would Belvedere's cash conversion cycle, total assets turnover, and ROA have been if the inventory turnover had been 8 for 1990?

8-10 **Current asset policy.** The Marshall Electric Corporation is attempting to determine the optimal level of current assets for the coming year. Management expects sales to increase to approximately $3 million as a result of an asset expansion presently being undertaken. Fixed assets total $1.5 million, and the firm wishes to maintain a 60 percent debt ratio. Marshall's interest cost is currently 9 percent on both short-term and longer-term debt (which the firm uses in its permanent structure). Three alternatives regarding the projected current asset investment are available to the firm: (1) a restricted policy requiring current assets of only 45 percent of projected sales; (2) a moderate policy of 50 percent of sales in current assets; and (3) a relaxed policy requiring current assets of 60 percent of sales. The firm expects to generate earnings before interest and taxes at a rate of 15 percent on total sales.

a. What is Marshall's expected return on equity under each current asset investment? (Assume a 40 percent federal-plus-state average tax rate.)

b. In this problem we have assumed that the level of expected sales is independent of current asset policy. Is this a valid assumption?

c. How would the overall riskiness of the firm vary under each policy?

(Do Part d only if you are using the computerized problem diskette.)

d. What would be the return on equity under each current asset investment if actual sales for the year were $3.75 million? $2.4 million? If sales were $3 million under the moderate policy but $3.75 million under the relaxed policy and $2.4 million under the restricted policy? Which current asset investment is the least risky over the range of probable sales from $2.4 million to $3.75 million? Which current asset investment do you recommend that Marshall maintain? Why?

SOLUTIONS TO SELF-TEST PROBLEMS

ST-1   **a.** and **b.**

Income Statements for Year Ended December 31, 1990 (Thousands of Dollars)

	Vanderheiden Press		Herrenhouse Publishing	
	a	b	a	b
EBIT	$ 30,000	$ 30,000	$ 30,000	$ 30,000
Interest	12,400	14,400	10,600	18,600
Taxable income	$ 17,600	$ 15,600	$ 19,400	$ 11,400
Taxes (40%)	7,040	6,240	7,760	4,560
Net income	$ 10,560	$ 9,360	$ 11,640	$ 6,840
Equity	$100,000	$100,000	$100,000	$100,000
Return on equity	10.56%	9.36%	11.64%	6.84%

The Vanderheiden Press has a higher ROE when short-term interest rates are high, whereas Herrenhouse Publishing does better when rates are lower.

c. Herrenhouse's position is riskier. First, its profits and return on equity are much more volatile than Vanderheiden's. Second, Herrenhouse must renew its large short-term loan every year, and if the renewal comes up at a time when money is very tight, when its business is depressed, or both, then Herrenhouse could be denied credit, which could put it out of business.

ST-2

The Calgary Company: Alternative Balance Sheets

	Restricted (40%)	Moderate (50%)	Relaxed (60%)
Current assets	$ 600,000	$ 750,000	$ 900,000
Fixed assets	300,000	300,000	300,000
Total assets	$ 900,000	$1,050,000	$1,200,000
Debt	$ 450,000	$ 525,000	$ 600,000
Equity	450,000	525,000	600,000
Total liabilities and equity	$ 900,000	$1,050,000	$1,200,000

The Calgary Company: Alternative Income Statements

	Restricted (40%)	Moderate (50%)	Relaxed (60%)
Sales	$1,500,000	$1,500,000	$1,500,000
EBIT	225,000	225,000	225,000
Interest (10%)	45,000	52,500	60,000
Earnings before taxes	$ 180,000	$ 172,500	$ 165,000
Taxes (40%)	72,000	69,000	66,000
Net income	$ 108,000	$ 103,500	$ 99,000
ROE	24.0%	19.7%	16.5%

Chapter 9

Managing Cash and Marketable Securities

 DECISION IN FINANCE

The Buy-back Binge

Investors usually react enthusiastically when a company announces a buy-back of its own stock. Although there can be several reasons for stock repurchases, the most common one is that management believes its stock is undervalued and thinks the purchase will push up the trading price. Several major corporations fueled a "buy-back binge" in the last weeks of 1989, including IBM, Chevron, Philip Morris, Norfolk Southern, and General Electric.

An investment strategist says that for the stock market "Share repurchases are very bullish, if only because they reduce the supply of shares on the market." Indeed, stockholders in companies that bought back their own shares after the 1987 market crash had reason to rejoice. Two weeks after announcement of the buy-backs, the repurchasing firms' shares were outperforming the market by an average of seven percentage points. This effect continued as

the market recovered over the next year, with the bought-back stocks averaging 3.1 points above the market. In a month in 1989, after their year-end buy-back announcements, GE's stock outperformed the market by 8.39 points, Chevron's by 7.22, and Coca-Cola's by 6.95.

A buy-back does not, however, always produce such good results. Dow Chemical's stock performed 4.64 percentage points below the market a month after its buy-back plan was announced, and IBM shares were 1.22 points below the market. Other companies had only marginal success.

These mixed results show that buy-backs are not always advantageous. If management has motives besides value to shareholders, the move may not be beneficial. For example, firms have used buy-backs to thwart hostile takeovers. In such cases, the repurchases may prevent an acquisition that would be good for stockholders but bad for managers.

Another hazard concerns the form of the buy-back — whether the transaction is handled

See end of chapter for resolution.

with cash or borrowed funds. If it is mostly cash, says one analyst, the buy-back "is really a tax-advantaged dividend." Investors receive and pay taxes on dividends, but the increase in stock value from a good buy-back is not taxed until the remaining investors sell their shares and report capital gains.

On the other hand, if borrowed money is used for the repurchase, a company's debt-to-equity ratio increases. The effect may not harm strong, high-quality companies, but for others, says Solomon Samson, a senior vice president at Standard & Poor's, "Buy-backs weaken the capital structure somewhat, bringing a company that could have been stronger down a peg." He notes that many firms suffer rating reductions as a direct result of repurchases. "Buy-backs use corporate assets in a way that only benefits shareholders, with no positive impact for bondholders."

Since buy-backs may also negatively affect capital spending and R&D, they may harm stockholders in the long run. One analyst notes that capital spending increased more than 11 percent for U.S. businesses between 1986 and 1988, but it only increased 2 percent for those that bought back large amounts of their own stock.

Another analyst believes that "buy-backs are turning into a low-return thing," even when cash is used. Charles Clough of Merrill Lynch recommends using corporate cash for plant and equipment enhancement instead. However, a major player in the recent "buy-back binge" disagrees. General Electric Chairman John F. Welch said on announcing the company's plans for its $10 billion repurchase, "We have looked at all the alternatives and reached the conclusion that GE stock is the best investment we can make."

As you read this chapter, think about the alternatives GE's management probably considered in reaching that decision.

Any business firm requires cash to pay for labor and materials, to buy fixed assets, to pay taxes, and so on. As we discussed in Chapter 8, the financial manager must consider the risk and return implications of working capital decisions. Because currency (and most commercial checking accounts) earns no interest, cash is generally considered a "nonearning" asset. Overinvestment in cash may reduce the firm's earning power, but underinvestment may cause the firm to be unable to meet some of its operating obligations. Thus, the goal of the cash manager is to reduce the amount of cash held to the minimum necessary to conduct business. Like cash, marketable securities provide lower yields than the firm's operating assets; however, many corporations report sizable securities balances on their financial statements. As we will learn later in this chapter, corporations do have good reasons for holding marketable securities.

CASH MANAGEMENT

cash
The total of bank demand deposits plus currency.

Approximately 1.5 percent of the average industrial firm's assets are held in the form of **cash,** which is defined as the total of bank demand deposits plus currency. In addition, sizable holdings of near-cash marketable securities such as U.S. Treasury bills (T-bills) or bank certificates of deposit (CDs) are often reported on corporate financial statements. However, cash balances vary widely both among industries and among the firms within a given industry, depending on the individual firms' specific conditions and on their owners' and managers' aversion to risk. We begin our analysis with a discussion of the reasons why firms hold cash. These same factors, incidentally, apply to the cash holdings of individuals and nonprofit organizations, including government agencies.

Reasons for Holding Cash

Firms hold cash for two primary reasons:

1. *Transactions.* Cash balances are necessary in business operations. Payments must be made in cash, and receipts are deposited in the cash account. Those cash balances associated with routine payments and collections are known as **transactions balances.**

2. *Compensation to banks for providing loans and services.* A bank makes money by lending out funds that have been deposited with it, so the larger its deposits, the better the bank's profit position. If a bank is providing services to a customer, it generally requires the customer to leave a minimum balance on deposit to help offset the costs of providing the services. This type of balance, defined as a **compensating balance,** is discussed in detail later in this chapter.

Two other reasons for holding cash that have been noted in the finance and economics literature are (1) for *precaution* and (2) for *speculation*. Cash inflows and outflows are somewhat unpredictable, with the degree of predictability varying among firms and industries. Therefore, firms need to hold some cash in reserve for random, unforeseen fluctuations in inflows and outflows. These "safety stocks" are called **precautionary balances,** and the less predictable the firm's cash flows, the larger the necessary cash balances. However, if the firm has easy access to borrowed funds—that is, if it can borrow on short notice—the need to hold its cash for precautionary purposes is reduced. Also, as we note later in this chapter, firms that would otherwise need large precautionary balances tend to hold highly liquid marketable securities rather than cash per se; marketable securities serve the same purposes as cash balances, but they provide interest income which many bank deposits do not.

Cash balances may also be held to enable the firm to take advantage of any bargain purchases that might arise; these funds are defined as **speculative balances.** As with precautionary balances, firms today are more likely to rely on reserve borrowing capacity and on marketable securities portfolios than on cash per se for speculative purposes.

Although the cash accounts of most firms can be thought of as consisting of transactions, compensating, precautionary, and speculative balances, we cannot calculate the amount needed for each purpose, add them together, and

transactions balances
Cash balances associated with payments and collections; those balances necessary to conduct day-to-day operations.

compensating balance
A checking account balance that a firm must maintain with a commercial bank to compensate the bank for services rendered.

precautionary balances
Cash balances held in reserve for random, unforeseen fluctuations in cash inflows and outflows.

speculative balances
Cash balances that are held to enable the firm to take advantage of any bargain purchases that might arise.

produce a total desired cash balance, because the same money often serves more than one purpose. For instance, precautionary and speculative balances can also be used to satisfy compensating balance requirements. Firms do, however, consider these four factors when establishing their target cash positions.

Although there are good reasons for holding *adequate* cash balances, there is a strong reason for not holding *excessive* balances — cash is a nonearning asset, so excessive cash balances simply lower the total assets turnover, thereby reducing both the firm's rate of return on equity and the value of its stock. Therefore, firms are interested in establishing procedures for increasing the efficiency of their cash management; if they can make their cash work harder, they can reduce cash balances. We now turn to a discussion of the procedures business firms use to increase cash management efficiency.

Self-Test

Why is cash management important?

What are the two primary reasons that firms hold cash?

What are the two secondary reasons for holding cash, as noted in the finance and economics literature?

THE CASH BUDGET

A firm normally estimates its needs for cash as a part of its general budgeting, or forecasting, process. First, it forecasts sales. Next, it forecasts the fixed assets and inventories that will be required to meet the forecasted sales levels. Asset purchases and the actual payments for them are then put on a time line, along with the actual timing of the sales and the timing of collections on sales. For example, the typical firm makes a 5-year sales forecast, which is then used to help plan fixed asset acquisitions (capital budgeting). Then, the firm develops an annual forecast, in which sales and inventory purchases are projected on a monthly basis, along with the times when payments for both fixed assets and inventory purchases must be made. These forecasts are combined with projections about the timing of the collection of accounts receivable, the schedule for payment of taxes, the dates when dividend and interest payments will be made, and so on. Finally, all of this information is summarized in the **cash budget,** which shows the firm's projected cash inflows and outflows over some specified period of time.

cash budget
A schedule showing cash flows (receipts, disbursements, and net cash) for a firm over a specified period.

Cash budgets can be constructed on a monthly, weekly, or even daily basis. Generally, firms use a monthly cash budget forecasted over the next 6 to 12 months, plus a more detailed daily or weekly cash budget for the coming month. The longer-term budget is used for general planning purposes, and the shorter-term one for actual cash control.

Constructing the Cash Budget

We shall illustrate the process with a monthly cash budget covering the last six months of 1991 for the Dayton Card Company, a leading producer of greeting cards. Dayton's birthday and get-well cards are sold year-round, but the bulk of the company's sales occur during September, when retailers are stocking up for Christmas. At the present time, Dayton offers no cash discount for early payment but it does offer a generous 45-day credit period to its customers. Small accounts, which compose 20 percent of its total sales, are on a "cash only" basis and pay within the month of sale. However, credit customers take full advantage of Dayton's sales terms. Thus, for 70 percent of its sales, payment is made during the month after sales. A small percentage of Dayton's customers (10 percent) pay during the second month after sales. Dayton has had virtually no problem with bad debts, so all bills are paid within 90 days of the original date of sale.

Rather than produce at a uniform rate throughout the year, Dayton prints cards immediately before they are required for delivery. Paper, ink, and other materials amount to 70 percent of sales and are bought the month before the company expects to sell the finished product. Its own purchase terms permit Dayton to delay payment on its purchases for one month. Accordingly, if July sales are forecasted at $10 million, purchases during June will amount to $7 million, and this amount will actually be paid in July.

Other cash expenditures such as wages and rent are also built into the cash budget in Table 9-1. Dayton Card Company must make tax payments of $2 million on September 15 and December 15, as well as a progress payment in October for a new plant that is under construction. Assuming that it needs to keep a **target cash balance** of $2.5 million at all times and that it will have $3 million on July 1, what are Dayton's financial requirements for the period from July through December?

The monthly cash requirements are worked out in Table 9-1. Section I of the table provides a worksheet for calculating collections on sales and payments on purchases. Line 1 gives the sales forecast for the period May through December; May and June sales are necessary to determine collections for July and August. Next, on Lines 2 through 5, cash collections are given. Line 2 shows that 20 percent of the sales during any given month are collected during that month. These sales are on a "cash only" basis, and these customers, of course, pay during the month of sale. Line 3 shows the collections on the previous month's sales, or 70 percent of sales in the preceding month; for example, in July, 70 percent of the $5,000,000 June sales, or $3,500,000, will be collected. Line 4 gives collections from sales two months earlier, or 10 percent of sales in that month; for example, the July collections for May sales are $(0.10)($5,000,000) = $500,000$. The collections during each month are summed and shown on Line 5; thus, the July collections represent 20 percent of July sales plus 70 percent of June sales plus 10 percent of May sales, or $6,000,000 in total. We assume in this example that the firm will, in fact, be

target cash balance
The cash balance that a firm plans to maintain in order to conduct business.

Table 9-1 Dayton Card Company: Worksheet and Cash Budget (Thousands of Dollars)

	May	June	July	Aug.	Sept.	Oct.	Nov.	Dec.
I. Collections and Payments								
(1) Sales[a]	$5,000	$5,000	$10,000	$15,000	$20,000	$10,000	$10,000	$5,000
Collections During:								
(2) Month of sales (20%)	1,000	1,000	2,000	3,000	4,000	2,000	2,000	1,000
(3) First month after sale month (70%)		3,500	3,500	7,000	10,500	14,000	7,000	7,000
(4) Second month after sale month (10%)			500	500	1,000	1,500	2,000	1,000
(5) Total collections	$1,000	$4,500	$ 6,000	$10,500	$15,500	$17,500	$11,000	$9,000
(6) Purchases (70% of next month's sales)	$3,500	$7,000	$10,500	$14,000	$ 7,000	$ 7,000	$ 3,500	$3,500
(7) Payments (1-month lag)		$3,500	$ 7,000	$10,500	$14,000	$ 7,000	$ 7,000	
II. Cash Gain or Loss for Month								
(8) Collections (from Line 5)			$ 6,000	$10,500	$15,500	$17,500	$11,000	$9,000
Payments (Outflows):								
(9) Purchases (from Line 7)			$ 7,000	$10,500	$14,000	$ 7,000	$ 7,000	$3,500
(10) Wages and salaries			750	1,000	1,250	750	750	500
(11) Rent			250	250	250	250	250	250)
(12) Other expenses			100	150	200	100	100	50
(13) Taxes					2,000			2,000
(14) Payment for plant construction						5,000		
(15) Total payments			$ 8,100	$11,900	$17,700	$13,100	$ 8,100	$6,300
(16) Net cash gain (loss) during month (Line 8 – Line 15)			($ 2,100)	($ 1,400)	($ 2,200)	$ 4,400	$ 2,900	$2,700
III. Cash Surplus or Loan Requirements								
(17) Cash at start of month if no borrowing is done[b]			$ 3,000	$ 900	($ 500)	($ 2,700)	$ 1,700	$4,600
(18) Cumulative cash (cash at start + gain or – loss = Line 16 + Line 17)			$ 900	($ 500)	($ 2,700)	$ 1,700	$ 4,600	$7,300
(19) Deduct target cash balance			2,500	2,500	2,500	2,500	2,500	2,500
(20) Surplus cash or total loans outstanding required to maintain $2,500 target cash balance (Line 18 – Line 19)[c]			($ 1,600)	($ 3,000)	($ 5,200)	($ 800)	$ 2,100	$4,800

[a] Although the budget period is July through December, sales and purchases data for May and June are needed to determine collections and payments during July and August.

[b] The amount shown on Line 17 for the first budget period month, the $3,000 balance on July 1, is assumed to be on hand initially. The values shown for each of the following months on Line 17 are equal to the cumulative cash as shown on Line 18 for the preceding month; for example, the $900 shown on Line 17 for August is taken from Line 18 in the July column.

[c] When the target cash balance of $2,500 (Line 19) is deducted from the cumulative cash balance (Line 18), a resulting negative figure on Line 20 represents a required loan, whereas a positive figure represents surplus cash. Loans are required from July through October, and surpluses are expected during November and December. Note also that firms can borrow or pay off loans on a daily basis, as needed, and during October the $5,200 loan that existed at the beginning of the month would be reduced daily to the $800 ending balance, which in turn would be completely paid off during November.

able to collect on all its credit sales. As we shall see in Chapter 10, credit losses are sometimes incurred.

Next, payments for purchases of raw materials are shown. July sales are forecasted at $10 million, so Dayton will purchase $7 million of materials in June (Line 6) and pay for these purchases in July (Line 7). Similarly, Dayton will purchase $10.5 million of materials in July to print cards to meet August's forecasted sales of $15 million.

With Section I completed, Section II can be constructed. Cash from collections is shown on Line 8. Lines 9 through 14 list payments made during each month, and these payments are summed on Line 15. The difference between cash receipts and cash payments (Line 8 minus Line 15) is the net cash gain or loss during the month; for July there is a net cash loss of $2,100,000, as shown on Line 16.

In Section III, we first determine Dayton's cumulative cash balance at the end of each month, assuming no borrowing is done. Then, we determine the company's forecasted cash surplus or the loan balance, if any, that is needed to force Dayton's cash balance to equal the target cash balance. The cash on hand at the beginning of the month is shown on Line 17. We assume that Dayton will have $3 million on hand on July 1, but thereafter the beginning cash balance is taken as the cumulative cash balance (Line 18) from the previous month. The beginning cash balance (Line 17) is added to the net cash gain or loss during the month (Line 16) to obtain the cumulative cash that would be on hand *if no financing were done* (Line 18); at the end of July, Dayton forecasts a cumulative cash balance of $900,000 in the absence of borrowing.

The target cash balance, $2.5 million, is then subtracted from the cumulative cash balance to determine the firm's borrowing requirements or surplus cash. Because Dayton expects to have cumulative cash, as shown on Line 18, of $900,000 in July, it will have to borrow $1,600,000 to bring the cash account up to the target balance of $2,500,000. Assuming that this amount is indeed borrowed, loans outstanding will total $1,600,000 at the end of July. (We assume that Dayton did not have any loans outstanding on July 1, because its beginning cash balance exceeded the target balance.) The cash surplus or required loan balance is given on Line 20; a positive value indicates a cash surplus, whereas a negative value indicates a loan requirement. Note that the surplus cash or loan requirement shown on Line 20 is a *cumulative amount.* Thus, Dayton must borrow $1,600,000 in July; it has a cash shortfall during August of $1,400,000 as reported on Line 16; and, therefore, its total loan requirement at the end of August is $1,600,000 + $1,400,000 = $3,000,000, as reported on Line 20. Dayton's arrangement with the bank permits it to increase its outstanding loans on a daily basis, up to a prearranged maximum, just as you could increase the amount you owe on a credit card. Dayton will use any surplus funds it generates to pay off its loans, and because the loan can be paid down at any time, Dayton will never have both a cash surplus and an outstanding loan balance.

This same procedure is used in the following months. Sales will peak in September, accompanied by increased payments for purchases, wages, and other items. Receipts from sales will also go up, but the firm will still be left with a $2,200,000 net cash outflow during the month. The total loan requirement at the end of September will be $5,200,000, the cumulative cash plus the target cash balance. This amount is also equal to the $3,000,000 needed at the end of August plus the $2,200,000 cash deficit for September. Thus, loans outstanding will hit a high of $5,200,000 at the end of September.

Sales, purchases, and payments for past purchases will fall sharply in October, and collections will be the highest of any month because they will reflect the high September sales. As a result, Dayton will enjoy a healthy $4,400,000 net cash gain during October. This net gain will be used to pay off borrowings, so loans outstanding will decline by $4,400,000, to $800,000.

Dayton will have another cash surplus in November, which will permit it to pay off all of its loans. In fact, the company is expected to have $2,100,000 in surplus cash by the month's end, and another cash surplus in December will swell the extra cash to $4,800,000. With such a large amount of unneeded funds, Dayton's treasurer will certainly want to invest in interest-bearing securities, or to put the funds to use in some other way. Various types of investments into which Dayton might put its excess funds are discussed later in this chapter.

Before concluding our discussion of the cash budget, we should make some additional points:

1. Our cash budget example does not reflect interest on loans required to maintain the target level cash balance or income from the investment of surplus cash. These refinements could easily be added.

2. If cash inflows and outflows are not uniform during the month, Dayton could be seriously understating the firm's peak financing requirements. The data in Table 9-1 show the situation expected on the last day of each month, but on any given day during the month it could be quite different. For example, if all payments must be made on the fifth of the month, but collections come in uniformly throughout the month, Dayton would need to borrow much larger amounts than those shown in Table 9-1. In this case, the company would need to prepare a cash budget on a daily basis.

3. Because depreciation is a noncash expense, it does not appear in the cash budget.

4. Because the cash budget represents a forecast, all the values in the table are *expected* values. If actual sales, purchases, and so on, are different from the forecasted levels, then the projected cash deficits and surpluses will also be incorrect. Therefore, the financial manager will wish to constantly monitor the cash budget during the period and modify it to conform to actual changes in the amount and timing of cash inflows or disbursements.

5. Computerized spreadsheet programs such as *Lotus 1-2-3* are particularly well suited for constructing and analyzing cash budgets, especially with respect to the sensitivity of cash flows to changes in sales levels, collection periods, and the like. With computerized models, one can instantly answer questions such as, "If collections slow down, what will the firm's cash needs be?"

6. Finally, we should note that the target cash balance probably will be adjusted over time, rising and falling with seasonal patterns and with long-term changes in the scale of the firm's operations. Factors that influence the target cash balance are discussed in the following sections.

Other Factors Influencing the Target Cash Balance

Any firm's target cash balance is normally set as the larger of (1) its transactions balances plus precautionary (safety stock) balances or (2) its required compensating balances as determined by its agreements with banks. Both the transactions and the precautionary balances depend on the firm's volume of business, on the degree of uncertainty inherent in its forecast of cash inflows and outflows, and on its ability to borrow on short notice to cover cash shortfalls. Recalling our cash budget for Dayton Card Company, the target cash balance could have been reduced if the firm had been able to predict its inflows and outflows with greater precision. Dayton, like most firms, does not know exactly when bills will come in or when payments will be received. Therefore, transactions balances must be sufficient to allow for a random increase in bills requiring payment at a time when receipts lag behind expectations. Most firms keep higher cash balances than absolutely necessary for transactions purposes to lower the probability that reduced inflows or unexpected outflows will cause them to run out of cash. Although we do not consider them in this book, statistical procedures are available to help improve cash flow forecasts, and the better the cash flow forecast, the lower the minimum cash balance.

Self-Test

What is done in each of the three sections of the cash budget?

Why is depreciation not included in the cash budget?

What would happen to the monthly cash budget if cash inflows and outflows were not uniform during the month? What type of analysis should be done when this situation occurs?

INCREASING THE EFFICIENCY OF CASH MANAGEMENT

Although a carefully prepared cash budget is a necessary starting point for managing the firm's cash, there are other elements of a good cash management program, some of which we describe in this section.

Cash Flow Synchronization

If you, as an individual, were to receive income on a daily basis instead of once a month, you could operate with a lower average checking account balance. If you could arrange to pay rent, tuition, and other charges on a daily basis, this would further reduce your required average cash balance. Exactly the same situation holds for business firms; by improving their forecasts and by arranging things so that cash receipts coincide with the timing of cash outflows, firms can hold their transactions balances to a minimum. Recognizing this point, utility companies, oil companies, department stores, and other firms arrange to bill customers and to pay their own bills on regular "billing cycles" throughout the month. In our cash budgeting example, if Dayton Card Company could arrange more **synchronized cash flows** and could increase the certainty of its forecasts, it would be able to reduce its cash balances, decrease its required bank loans, lower interest expenses, and boost profits.

synchronized cash flows

A situation in which inflows coincide with outflows, thereby permitting a firm to hold transactions balances to a minimum.

Speeding Collections

Another important aspect of cash management deals with processing the checks a company writes and receives. It is obviously inefficient to put checks received in a drawer and deposit them every week or so; no well-run business would follow such a practice. Similarly, cash balances are drawn down unnecessarily if bills are paid earlier than required. In fact, efficient firms go to great lengths to speed up the processing of incoming checks, thus putting the funds to work faster, and they try to stretch out their own payments as long as possible.

When a customer writes and mails a check, this does *not* mean that the funds are immediately available to the receiving firm. Most of us have deposited a check in our account and then been told that we cannot write our own checks against this deposit until the **check-clearing** process is completed. Our bank must first make sure that the check we deposited is good and receive funds itself from the customer's bank before releasing funds for us to spend.

check clearing

The process of converting a check that has been written and mailed into cash in the payee's account.

As shown on the left side of Figure 9-1, quite a bit of time may be required for a firm to process incoming checks and obtain the use of the money. A check must first be delivered through the mail and then be cleared through the banking system before the money can be put to use. Checks received from customers in distant cities are especially subject to delays because of mail time and also because more parties are involved. Possible mail delays can obviously cause problems, and clearing checks can also delay the effective use of funds received. Assume, for example, that you receive a check and deposit it in your bank. Your bank must present the check to the bank on which it was drawn. Only when this latter bank transfers funds to your bank are the funds available for your use. Checks are generally cleared through the Federal Reserve System or through a clearinghouse set up by the banks in a particular city. Of course,

Figure 9-1 **Diagram of the Check-Clearing Process**

This figure illustrates how a lockbox plan can accelerate a company's collection of receivables by two to five working days. With the regular check-clearing process, a company must wait five to eight working days for a customer's payment to pass through the mail and clear through the banks and the Federal Reserve System. When a company uses a mailing address and bank in a customer's hometown, however, the check-clearing process is expedited and the company gains quicker access to its funds. It is possible for a company to free up several million dollars in cash by using lockboxes.

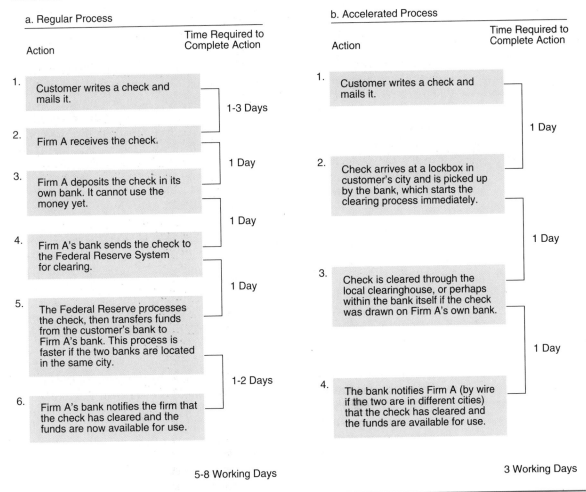

if the check is deposited in the same bank on which it was drawn, that bank merely transfers funds by bookkeeping entries from one of its depositors to another. The length of time required for checks to clear is thus a function of the distance between the payer's and the payee's banks. In the case of private clearinghouses, it can range from one to three days. The maximum time required for checks to clear through the Federal Reserve System is two days, but mail delays can slow down things on each end of the Fed's involvement in the process.

lockbox plan

A procedure used to speed up collections and reduce float through the use of post office boxes in payers' local areas.

Lockboxes. The right side of Figure 9-1 shows how the process can be speeded up. To reduce mail and clearing delays, a **lockbox plan** can be used. Suppose a New York firm makes sales to customers all across the country. It can arrange to have its customers send payments to post office boxes (lockboxes) in their own local areas. A local bank will pick up the checks, have them cleared in the local area, and then transfer the funds by wire to the company's New York bank. In this way, collection time can be reduced by several days. Examples in which this method has freed funds in the amount of $5 million or more are common. The local banks will charge the New York firm for the collection and funds-transfer services rendered. To determine whether a lockbox system is advantageous, the firm must compare the bank fees with the gains from freeing up funds.

Pre-authorized Debits. Another method of speeding collections is the use of *pre-authorized debits*. A pre-authorized debit allows funds to be automatically transferred from a customer's account to the firm's account on specified dates. These transactions are also called "checkless" or "paperless" transactions since they are accomplished without using traditional paper checks. However, a record of payment does appear on both parties' bank statements. Pre-authorized debiting accelerates the transfer of funds because mail and check-clearing times are totally eliminated, and they are used frequently for the payment of mortgages, taxes, utility bills, and payrolls. Although pre-authorized debits are efficient, and while they appear to be the trend of the future, the pace of acceptance by payers has been much slower than was originally predicted, partly because a payer who uses a pre-authorized debit system loses the use of *disbursement float* (the delay that occurs in processing checks) and partly because people like to be able to use cancelled checks as receipts.

Slowing Disbursements

Just as expediting the collection process conserves cash, slowing down disbursements accomplishes the same thing by keeping cash on hand for longer periods. One obviously could simply delay payments, but this would involve equally obvious difficulties. Firms have, in the past, devised rather ingenious methods for "legitimately" lengthening the collection periods for their own checks, primarily by writing checks on banks located in out-of-the-way places. In the past, for example, Merrill Lynch paid customers who lived east of the Mississippi River using a San Francisco bank, but to customers living west of the river, the checks were written on a New York bank. This delayed the check-clearing process, and, thus, increased the length of time during which Merrill Lynch had use of the funds. Hundreds of millions of dollars were involved, and Merrill Lynch was finally forced to stop the practice as à result of a lawsuit. Other firms use banks in southeast Missouri, North Dakota, or other hard-to-get-to spots for the same purpose. Since such practices are usually recognized for what they are, there are strict limitations on their use.

Another widely used procedure for delaying payouts is the use of *drafts*. Although a check is payable when presented to the bank on which it was drawn, a draft must be transmitted to the issuer, who approves it and then deposits funds to cover it, after which it can be collected. Insurance companies often use drafts in handling claims. For instance, Aetna can pay a claim by draft on Friday. The recipient deposits the draft at a local bank, which must then send it to Aetna's Hartford bank. It may be Wednesday or Thursday before the draft arrives. The bank then sends it to the company's accounting department, which has until 3 P.M. that day to inspect and approve it. Not until then does Aetna have to deposit funds in the bank to pay the draft.

Using Float

Suppose you have $1,000 in your bank account, and you then write a check for $600 and mail it to a company to pay for some clothes. You will immediately reduce your balance by $600, to $400. However, during the time before the company receives the check and deposits it, and until the check is cleared through the banking system, your bank will think that you still have $1,000 in your account. If your bank pays interest on checking accounts, you will continue to earn interest on the $600 until the check has cleared. The $600 is called **disbursement float,** and it is defined as the amount of checks that you (or any firm or individual) have written but that are still being processed, and thus have not yet been deducted from your checking account balance by the bank. Similarly, when you receive a check, you record it in your bank book, but then it takes time for you to deposit it, and for the bank to process it and credit your account with "good" funds. The amount of the checks which a firm or individual has received but which are in the collection process is known as **collection float.**

At any given time, a business has a number of checks that it has written but that have not been deducted by the bank from its account (disbursement float), as well as a number of checks that it has received but that have not yet

disbursement float
The amount of checks that are written but are still being processed and which have not been deducted from the account balance by the bank.

collection float
The amount of checks received but not yet credited to the account.

net float

The difference between a firm's checkbook balance and the balance shown on the bank's books, i.e., the difference between disbursement float and collection float.

been credited to its account (collection float). The difference between disbursement float and collection float is called **net float:**

$$\text{Net float} = \text{Disbursement float} - \text{Collection float}.$$

Net float can also be defined as the difference between a firm's (or an individual's) checkbook balance and the balance shown on the bank's books.

Highly efficient firms are able to operate with *positive net float;* this means that the firm is able to collect checks written to it, and thus to get the use of money paid to it, relatively rapidly. Those to whom it writes checks are relatively less efficient in clearing checks, allowing the firm to use the funds for a while after it has written checks. One large manufacturer of construction equipment has stated that although its account, according to its bank's records, shows an average cash balance of about $20 million, its *book* cash balance is *minus* $20 million. Therefore, it has $40 million of net float. Obviously, the firm must be able to forecast its positive and negative clearings accurately in order to make such a heavy use of float.

A few years ago, E.F. Hutton, a major brokerage firm, pushed cash management too far. Hutton did business with banks all across the country, and it had to keep compensating balances in these banks. The sizes of the required compensating balances were known, and any excess funds in these banks were sent, on a daily basis, to concentration banks (larger banks to which the firm channels funds from local banks operating its lockboxes), where they were invested in interest-bearing securities. However, rather than waiting to see what the end-of-day balances actually were, Hutton estimated inflows and outflows, and it transferred out for investment the *estimated* end-of-day excess. But then Hutton got greedy — it deliberately overestimated its deposits and underestimated clearings of its own checks, thereby deliberately overstating the estimated end-of-day balances. As a result, Hutton was chronically overdrawn at its local banks, and it was, in effect, earning interest on funds which really belonged to those local banks. It is entirely proper to forecast what your bank will have recorded as your balance and then to make decisions based on the estimate, even if that balance is different from the balance your own books show. However, it is illegal to forecast an overdrawn situation, and then to tell the bank that you forecast a positive balance.

Self-Test

How can a firm speed up its cash collections? How can it slow down its cash disbursements?

Is it better to have positive or negative net float? Explain your answer.

THE FINANCIAL SOURCE:

Now it's launching INTERPLEX™ to give you total control of your corporate finances automatically and earlier than ever before.

Manufacturers Hanover establishes the new standard in treasury management systems.

It's early morning as you enter your office and your financial position is waiting for you. In complete detail. Account data from all of your banks has been automatically consolidated within the integrated data base and put into a single standardized format. You're ready to perform transaction verification and account reconciliation. You know hours earlier what investment or bor-

rowing decisions to make. And you quickly realize why INTERPLEX, a fully automated treasury management system, is the industry's new standard.

INTERPLEX from Manufacturers Hanover is the microcomputer-based, multi-user, multi-task treasury management system that gives you more control. Including the ability to automatically collect data from all of your banks. Store it. Process it. Merge it. Use it. Faster.

INTERPLEX lets you conduct target balance analyses, project end of day cash posi-

tion, make cash forecasts, transfer funds, and perform many other treasury functions. Sophisticated yet simple, this system is just the beginning of a family of fully integrated financial management products from Manufacturers Hanover.

State-of-the-art leadership. Backed by a longstanding commitment to innovation. Once again, The Financial Source delivers.

Learn how you can enter the new age of INTERPLEX and gain total control. Automatically. Just contact George Chelius, Vice President, at 1-800-MHT-PLEX.

MH Financial Management Systems, Inc.

[H] MANUFACTURERS HANOVER
The Financial Source™ Worldwide.

Cash management software systems for computers, such as Interplex from Manufacturers Hanover, are available to financial managers to help them increase the efficiency of cash management.

Source: Courtesy of MH Financial Management Systems, Inc., New York.

MATCHING THE COSTS AND BENEFITS ASSOCIATED WITH CASH MANAGEMENT

Although a number of procedures may be used to hold down cash balance requirements, implementing these procedures is not a costless operation. How far should a firm go in making its cash operations more efficient? As a general rule, the firm should incur these expenses as long as marginal returns exceed marginal expenses.

For example, suppose that by establishing a lockbox system and by increasing the accuracy of cash inflow and outflow forecasts, a firm can reduce its investment in cash by $1 million without increasing the risk of running short of cash. Furthermore, suppose the firm borrows at a cost of 12 percent. The steps taken have released $1 million, which can be used to reduce bank loans and thus save $120,000 per year. If the costs of the procedures necessary to release the $1 million are less than $120,000 per year, the move is a good one; if the costs exceed $120,000, the greater efficiency is not worth the cost. It is clear that larger firms, with larger cash balances, can better afford to hire the personnel necessary to maintain tight control over their cash positions. Cash management is one element of business operations in which economies of scale are present.

Very clearly, the value of careful cash management depends on the costs of funds invested in cash, which in turn depend on the current rate of interest. Although interest rates have receded from their historic highs of the early 1980s, business firms continue to devote more care than ever to cash management.

Cash Management in the Multidivisional Firm

The concepts, techniques, and procedures described thus far in the chapter must be extended when applied to large, multidivisional, national or multinational firms. Such corporations have plants and sales offices all across the nation (or around the world), and they deal with banks in each of their operating territories. These companies must maintain compensating balances in each of their banks, and they must be sure that no bank account becomes overdrawn. Cash inflows and outflows are subject to random fluctuations, so, in the absence of close control and coordination, there would be a tendency for some accounts to have shortages while others had excess balances.

An example of such a firm is General Motors, which uses an electronic transfer system to pay its suppliers. The electronic system utilizes eight banks across the nation, and it not only speeds up the payment process but also decreases uncertainty about the timing of the payment. This system benefits both GM and its suppliers, as it reduces the required level of each firm's transactions and precautionary cash balances. GM's suppliers especially like the electronic system because overdue bills from GM have been virtually eliminated, and they take this into account when they bid for GM's business.

A sound cash management program for a multibank corporation necessarily includes provisions for keeping strict control over the level of funds in each account and for shifting funds among accounts to minimize the total corporate cash balance. Mathematical models and electronic connections between a central computer and each branch location have been developed to help with such situations; however, an in-depth discussion of these topics would go beyond the scope of this book.

Self-Test

How far should a firm go in making its cash operations more efficient?

Is cash management more important when interest rates are high or low? Explain.

BANK RELATIONSHIPS

In addition to lending firms money, banks provide many services to them — they clear checks, operate lockbox plans, supply credit information, and the like. Because these services cost the bank money, the bank must be compensated for rendering them.

Compensating Balances

Banks earn most of their income by lending money at interest, and most of the funds they lend are obtained in the form of deposits. If a firm maintains a deposit account with an average balance of $100,000, and if the bank can lend these funds at a net return of $8,000, then the account is, in a sense, worth $8,000 to the bank. Thus, it is to the bank's advantage to provide services worth up to $8,000 to attract and hold the account.

Banks first determine the costs of the services rendered to their larger customers, and then they estimate the average account balances necessary to provide enough income to compensate for these costs. Firms can make direct fee payments for these services, but they often find it more convenient to maintain compensating balances to avoid paying cash service charges to the bank.[1]

Compensating balances are also required by some bank loan agreements. During periods when the supply of credit is restricted and interest rates are high, banks frequently require that borrowers maintain accounts which average a specified percentage of the loan amount as a condition for granting a loan; 15 percent is a typical figure. If the required balance is larger than the firm would otherwise maintain, the effective cost of the loan is increased. The

---

[1]Compensating balance arrangements apply to individuals as well as to business firms. Thus, you might get "free" checking services if you maintain a minimum balance of $500, but you might be charged 10 cents per check if your balance falls below $500 during the month.

excess balance presumably "compensates" the bank for making a loan at a rate below what it could earn on the funds if they were invested elsewhere.[2]

Compensating balances can be established as either (1) an *absolute minimum* (say, $100,000) below which the actual balance must never fall, or (2) a *minimum average balance* (perhaps $100,000) during some period, generally a month. The absolute minimum is a much more restrictive requirement, because the total amount of cash held during the month must be above $100,000 by the amount of the firm's transactions balances. The $100,000 in this case is "dead money" from the firm's standpoint. With a minimum average balance, however, the account could fall to zero on one day provided it was $200,000, some other day, with the average working out to $100,000. Thus, the $100,000 in this case would be available for transactions.

Statistics on compensating balance requirements are not available, but average balances are typical and absolute minimums rare for business accounts. Discussions with bankers, however, indicate that absolute balance requirements are less rare during times of extremely tight money.

Overdraft Systems

overdraft systems
Systems whereby depositors may write checks in excess of their balances, with the banks automatically extending loans to cover the shortages.

One of the services provided by banks is an **overdraft system.** In such a system, depositors write checks in excess of their actual balances, and the bank automatically extends loans to cover the shortages. The maximum amount of such loans must, of course, be established beforehand. Although statistics are not available on the usage of overdrafts in the United States, a number of firms have worked out informal, and in some cases formal, overdraft arrangements. Also, both banks and credit card companies regularly establish cash reserve systems for individuals. In general, the use of overdrafts has been increasing in recent years, and, if this trend continues, we can anticipate a further reduction of cash balances.

Zero Balance Account

Larger corporations often set up accounts for special purposes, such as paying dividends. Suppose IBM planned to pay dividends of $1.25 per share on 600 million shares, or $750 million in total, on September 10, 1991. It could deposit $750 million in an account and then write checks to its stockholders, but because some stockholders would surely delay cashing their dividend checks, a great deal of money would be sitting idle in the account. One alternative would be for IBM to write the checks, forecast how rapidly they would be cashed and presented for payment, and then make a series of daily deposits based on those forecasts. Another procedure would be to set up a *zero balance account,* in which case (1) it would write the dividend checks, (2) each day the bank would notify IBM by 11 A.M. of the total dollar amount of checks that had been received for payment that day, and (3) IBM would have until

---

[2]The interest rate effect of compensating balances is discussed further in Chapter 11.

4 P.M. to deposit the funds to cover those checks. (Because of the nature of the clearinghouse process, all checks will have been presented by 11 A.M. for payment.) IBM could obtain the funds by transferring them to the account from its concentration account, by selling marketable securities, or by borrowing in the commercial paper market. IBM could even arrange to borrow the necessary funds from the bank itself. In any event, the account would be zeroed out at the end of each day. This type of account is being used with increasing frequency.

Self-Test

Why do firms maintain compensating balances?

Differentiate between an absolute minimum and a minimum average compensating balance.

What are overdraft systems, and how do they work?

Why would a firm use a zero balance account, and how does one work?

MARKETABLE SECURITIES

As noted at the beginning of the chapter, sizable holdings of such short-term **marketable securities** as U.S. Treasury bills or bank certificates of deposit are often reported on corporations' financial statements. The reasons for such holdings, as well as the factors that influence the choice of securities held, are discussed in this section.

marketable securities
Securities that can be sold on short notice for close to their quoted market prices.

Reasons for Holding Marketable Securities

Marketable securities typically provide much lower yields than firms' operating assets. For example, International Business Machines (IBM) holds a multi-billion-dollar portfolio of marketable securities that yields about 9 percent, whereas its operating assets have recently been providing a return of about 18 percent. Why would a company like IBM have such large holdings of low-yielding assets? There are two basic reasons for these holdings: (1) they serve as a substitute for cash balances, and (2) they are used as a temporary investment. These points are considered next.

Marketable Securities as a Substitute for Cash. Some firms hold portfolios of marketable securities in lieu of larger cash balances, then sell some securities from the portfolios whenever they need to replenish the cash account. In such situations the marketable securities could be a substitute for transactions balances, precautionary balances, speculative balances, or all three. In most cases the securities are held primarily for precautionary purposes. Most firms prefer to rely on bank credit to meet temporary transactions or speculative needs, but they may hold some liquid assets to guard against a possible shortage of bank credit.

Several years ago IBM had approximately $6 billion in marketable securities. This large liquid balance had been built up as a reserve to cover possible damage payments resulting from pending antitrust suits. When it became clear that IBM would win most of the suits, the liquidity need declined, and the company spent some of the funds on other assets, including repurchases of its own stock. This is a prime example of a firm's building up its precautionary balances to handle possible emergencies.

Marketable Securities Held as a Temporary Investment. Whenever a firm has more than 1 or 2 percent of its total assets invested in marketable securities, chances are good that these funds represent a strictly temporary investment. Such temporary investments generally occur in one of the three following situations:

1. When the firm must finance seasonal or cyclical operations. Firms engaged in seasonal operations frequently have surplus cash flows during one part of the year and deficit cash flows during another. For example, retailers such as Sears often purchase marketable securities during their surplus periods and then liquidate them when cash deficits occur. Other firms, however, choose to use bank financing to cover such shortages.

2. When the firm must meet some known financial requirements. If a major plant construction program is planned for the near future, or if a bond issue is about to mature, a firm may build up its marketable securities portfolio to provide the required funds. Furthermore, marketable securities holdings are frequently built up immediately before quarterly corporate tax payment dates.

3. When the firm has just sold long-term securities. Expanding firms generally have to sell long-term securities (stocks or bonds) periodically. The funds from such sales are often invested in marketable securities, which are then sold off to provide cash as it is needed to pay for permanent investments in operating assets.

Strategies Regarding Marketable Securities Holdings

Actually, each of the needs mentioned previously can be met either by obtaining short-term loans or by holding marketable securities. Consider a firm like Dayton Card Company, which we discussed earlier in this chapter, whose sales are growing over time but also fluctuate on a seasonal basis. As we saw from Dayton's cash budget (Table 9-1), the firm plans to borrow to meet seasonal needs. As an alternative financial strategy, Dayton could hold a portfolio of marketable securities and then liquidate these securities to meet its peak cash needs.

A firm's marketable securities policy is an integral part of its overall working capital policy. If the firm has a conservative working capital financing policy, its long-term capital will exceed its permanent assets, and it will hold mar-

Figure 9-2 **Alternative Strategies for Meeting Seasonal or Cyclical Cash Needs**

This figure shows the effects of three different approaches to the use of marketable securities to finance short-term needs for cash and other current assets. Under Plan A, a company holds no marketable securities and relies entirely on bank loans for its short-term cash. Although it may create problems in borrowing funds or repaying loans, Plan A should provide a higher return on total assets and equity because no funds are locked into low-yielding marketable securities. Under Plan B, a company accumulates a large amount of marketable securities that it then sells off to raise cash for seasonal and cyclical asset needs. This plan avoids borrowing but lowers the company's return on total assets and equity. The disadvantages of Plans A and B are moderated under Plan C, which uses a combination of marketable securities and short-term loans to finance seasonal cash and other current assets.

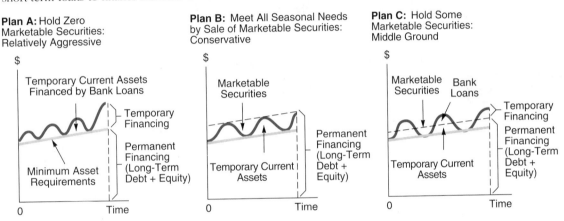

ketable securities when inventories and receivables are low. With an aggressive policy, it will never carry any securities and will borrow heavily to meet peak needs. With a moderate, or maturity matching, policy the firm will match permanent assets with long-term financing, and it will meet most seasonal increases in inventories and receivables with short-term loans, but it will also carry marketable securities at certain times.

Figure 9-2 illustrates three alternative strategies for a firm like Dayton. Under Plan A, which represents a relatively aggressive financing policy, Dayton would hold no marketable securities, relying completely on bank loans to meet seasonal peaks. Under the extremely conservative Plan B, Dayton would stockpile marketable securities during slack periods and then sell those securities to raise funds for peak needs. Plan C is a compromise; under this alternative, the company would hold some securities but not enough to meet all of its peak needs. Dayton actually follows Plan C.

There are advantages and disadvantages to each of these strategies. Plan A is clearly the most risky; the firm's current ratio is always lower than under the other plans, indicating that it might encounter difficulties either in borrowing the funds needed or in repaying the loan. On the other hand, Plan A requires no holdings of low-yielding marketable securities, and this will probably lead to a relatively high rate of return on both total assets and equity.

Factors Influencing the Choice of Securities

A wide variety of securities, differing in terms of default risk, interest rate risk, liquidity risk, and expected rate of return, are available to firms that choose to hold marketable securities. In this section we first consider the different types of risk, we then look at the extent to which each type of risk is found in different securities, and, finally, we look at specific instruments which are suitable investments for temporary excess cash. These same considerations are, incidentally, as important for individuals' investment decisions as for businesses' decisions.

default risk
The risk that a borrower will not pay the interest or principal on a loan.

Default Risk. The risk that a borrower will be unable to make interest payments, or to repay the principal amount on schedule, is known as **default risk.** If the issuer is the U.S. Treasury, the default risk is negligible, so Treasury securities are regarded as being default-free. (Treasury securities are not completely free of risk, since U.S. Government bonds are subject to risk caused by interest rate fluctuations, and they are also subject to loss of purchasing power due to inflation.) Recall that in Chapter 4 we developed this equation for determining the nominal interest rate: $k^* + IP + DRP + LP + MRP$. Here k^* is the real risk-free rate, IP is a premium for expected inflation, DRP is the default risk premium, LP is the liquidity (or marketability) risk premium, and MRP is the maturity (or interest rate) risk premium. Also, remember from Chapter 4 that the risk-free rate, k_{RF}, is equal to $k^* + IP$. As we learned in Chapter 4, a U.S. Treasury bill comes closest to the risk-free rate, while a U.S. Treasury bond has no default or liquidity risk premiums, but it is exposed to interest rate risk, so a maturity risk premium is included in its nominal interest rate. Corporate securities, as well as bonds issued by state and local governments, are subject to some degree of default risk, so these securities' returns include a default risk premium. Several organizations (for example, Moody's Investment Service and Standard & Poor's Corporation) rate bonds. They classify them on a scale that ranges from very high quality to highly speculative with a definite chance of going into default. Ratings change from time to time.

interest rate risk
The risk to which investors are exposed due to rising interest rates.

Interest Rate Risk. We will see in Chapter 16 that bond prices vary with changes in interest rates. Also, the prices of long-term bonds are much more sensitive to changes in interest rates than are prices of short-term securities — long-term bonds have more **interest rate risk.** Thus, if Dayton's treasurer purchased at par $1 million of 25-year U.S. government bonds paying 9 percent interest, and if interest rates then rose to 14.5 percent, the market value of the bonds would fall from $1 million to just below $635,000 — a loss of almost 40 percent.[3] (This actually happened from 1980 to 1982.) If 90-day Treasury bills had been held during a period of rising interest rates, however, the loss would have been negligible. From our discussion above, the Treasury bill would have a zero maturity risk premium, but the long-term Treasury bond would have a positive maturity risk premium included in its nominal interest rate.

Inflation Risk. Another type of risk is **inflation risk,** or the risk that inflation will reduce the purchasing power of a given sum of money. Inflation risk, which is important both to firms and to individual investors during times of rising prices, is lower on assets whose returns tend to rise with inflation than on assets whose returns are fixed. Thus, real estate and common stocks are generally better hedges against inflation than are bonds and other fixed-income securities. As you should recall from our discussion in Chapter 4, a security's interest rate reflects the average rate of inflation expected over the security's life. Therefore, a 90-day Treasury bill would include the average rate of inflation expected over the 90-day period, while a 30-year Treasury bond would include the average rate of inflation expected over a 30-year period. Thus, if a high rate of inflation is expected in the future, that expectation is built into interest rates. Accordingly, the real risk of inflation to bondholders is that actual inflation will exceed the expected level.

inflation risk
The risk that inflation will reduce the purchasing power of a given sum of money.

Liquidity, or Marketability, Risk. An asset that can be sold on short notice for close to its quoted market price is considered to be highly liquid. If Dayton purchased $1 million of infrequently traded bonds of a relatively obscure company like Bigham Pork Products, it would probably have to accept a price reduction in order to sell the bonds on short notice. On the other hand, if Dayton invested in U.S. Treasury bonds, or in bonds issued by AT&T, General Motors, or Exxon, it would be able to dispose of them almost instantaneously at close to the quoted market price. These latter bonds are therefore said to have very little **liquidity, or marketability, risk.** If we go back to the nominal interest rate equation discussed earlier, the bonds of Bigham Pork Products would include premiums for inflation, default, maturity, and liquidity risk in their return, while the bonds of AT&T, General Motors, and Exxon would contain inflation and maturity risk premiums, but negligible default and liquidity risk premiums.

liquidity, or marketability, risk
The risk that securities cannot be sold at close to the quoted price on short notice.

Of course, long-term bonds are exposed to interest rate risk while short-term instruments are not. There are many types of highly liquid short-term securities available in which a company can, with relative safety, invest temporary excess cash. These instruments will be discussed shortly.

---

[3]These computations are explained in detail in Chapter 16.

Table 9-2 **Securities Available for Investment of Surplus Cash**

Security	Typical Maturity at Time of Issue	Approximate Yields			Appropriate as a Near-Cash Reserve?
		6/10/77	2/10/82	3/8/90	
Suitable to Hold as Near-Cash Reserve					
U.S. Treasury bills	91 days to 1 year	4.8%	15.1%	7.9%	Yes
Banker's acceptances	Up to 180 days	—	15.0	8.0	Yes
Commercial paper	Up to 270 days	5.5	15.3	8.2	Yes
Negotiable certificates of deposit (CDs) of U.S. banks	Up to 1 year	6.0	15.5	7.8	Yes
Money market mutual funds	Instant liquidity	5.1	14.0	7.6	Yes
Eurodollar market time deposits	Up to 1 year	6.1	16.2	8.4	Questionable
Not Suitable to Hold as Near-Cash Reserve					
U.S. Treasury notes	3 to 5 years	6.8	14.8	8.6	Questionable
U.S. Treasury bonds	Up to 30 years	7.6	14.6	8.6	No
Corporate bonds (AAA)	Up to 40 years	8.2	16.0	9.4	No
State and local government bonds[a]	Up to 30 years	5.7	12.8	7.4	No
Common stocks of other corporations	Unlimited	Variable	Variable	Variable	No
Common stock of the firm in question	Unlimited	Variable	Variable	Variable	No

[a]Rates are lower on state/municipal government bonds because the interest they pay is exempt from federal income taxes.

Returns on Securities (Yields). As we know from earlier chapters, the higher a security's risk, the higher the required return on the security. Thus corporate treasurers, like other investors, must make a tradeoff between risk and return when choosing investments for their marketable securities portfolios. Because this portfolio is generally held either for a specific known need or for use in emergencies, the firm might be financially embarrassed should the portfolio decline in value. Also, most nonfinancial corporations do not have investment departments specializing in appraising securities and determining the probability of their going into default. Accordingly, the marketable securities portfolio is generally composed of highly liquid short-term securities issued either by the U.S. government or by the very strongest corporations. Given the purpose of the securities portfolio, treasurers are unwilling to sacrifice safety for higher rates of return.

Types of Marketable Securities

Although any investor wishes to minimize needless risks, a manager investing temporary excess cash must be especially aware of liquidity risk and interest rate risk. The manager has a wide variety of available securities to hold as near cash. These alternatives, both government and nongovernment securities, are discussed next, with special emphasis given to these two types of risk. Table 9-2 provides a listing of various investment alternatives, an indication of their suitability as short-term investments, and an indication of their returns.

Government Securities. The U.S. Treasury and other federal agencies issue a wide variety of securities with different maturities. Treasury bills are a popular outlet for excess funds because they have a large and active secondary market to insure liquidity and because they are free of default risk.

Treasury bills are sold at weekly auctions and have either 13-week (91-day), 26-week (182-day), or 1-year original maturities. Alternatively, they can be bought or sold in the secondary market with as little as one day remaining to maturity. Thus, the investor has a wide choice of available maturities.

Other government securities with longer maturities are available. Treasury notes are government obligations with maturities of 3 to 5 years. Treasury bonds are issued with maturities of up to 30 years. However, because of their long maturities and potentially unstable near-term prices,[4] these longer-term securities may be poor choices as investments for **near-cash reserves**, reserves that might have to be quickly converted to cash. U.S. federal agencies, such as the Federal Home Loan Bank and the Federal National Mortgage Association, also issue notes and bonds. These securities are riskier than Treasury issues, because they are not directly backed by the U.S. Treasury. Therefore, they yield a slightly higher return than Treasury issues. For example, on March 8, 1990, federal agency bonds yielded 8.9 percent versus 8.6 percent for 10-year Treasury bonds.

near-cash reserves
Reserves that can be quickly and easily converted to cash.

Nongovernment Securities. In the discussion that follows, we identify four different nongovernment securities that are appropriate as near cash reserves. The fifth security, Eurodollars, is questionable as a near-cash reserve.

Banker's Acceptance. A banker's acceptance is the promissory note of a business debtor resulting from a business transaction. A bank, by endorsing the note, assumes the obligation of payment at the due date. The instrument is widely used, especially in foreign trade. It has a low degree of risk if guaranteed by a strong bank, and there is a ready market for it, making it easy for the holder to sell the acceptance to raise immediate cash. Banker's acceptances are sold at a discount below face value and then paid off at face value when they mature, so the discount amounts to interest on the acceptance. The effective interest rate on a strong banker's acceptance is a litttle above the Treasury bill rate of interest.

Commercial Paper. Short-term unsecured promissory notes issued by the largest, most financially secure corporations in America are called **commercial paper.** Dealers in commercial paper prefer to handle the paper of firms whose net worth is $50 million or more and whose annual borrowing exceeds

commercial paper
Unsecured, short-term promissory notes of large, financially strong firms, usually issued in denominations of $100,000 or more and having an interest rate somewhat below the prime rate.

---

[4]We describe in Chapter 16 how, as interest rates rise, bond prices fall and, conversely, as interest rates fall, bond prices rise. Furthermore, the longer the term to maturity, the greater the price change for a given change in interest rates. These factors work against the use of bonds as a temporary store of value, since temporary excess cash should be invested in securities with stable and predictable returns and stable market value.

$10 million. Regular issuers include General Motors Acceptance Corporation, Ford Motor Credit Corporation, and C.I.T. Financial Corporation. Commercial paper is sold primarily to other business firms, to insurance companies, to pension funds, to money market mutual funds, and to banks. It is traded in the secondary markets, and a firm that holds the commercial paper of another firm can sell it to raise cash in a matter of hours — it is highly liquid. The amount of commercial paper has grown rapidly in recent years. At the end of February 1990, there was more than $540 billion of commercial paper outstanding, as compared to about $650 billion of bank loans to businesses.

Maturities of commercial paper generally vary from two to six months.[5] The rates on commercial paper fluctuate with supply and demand conditions; they are determined in the market place, varying daily as conditions change. However, the rates on commercial paper are low relative to other securities. The low rates reflect, among other things, the fact that default risk is low, since only the most creditworthy corporations can sell commercial paper. Recently, commercial paper rates have ranged from one to two percentage points below the stated prime rate, but slightly above the T-bill rate. For example, in March 1990 the average rate on 3-month commercial paper was 8.2 percent, whereas the stated prime rate was 10 percent and the T-bill rate was 7.9 percent.

Negotiable Certificates of Deposit. Major money-center commercial banks will issue certificates of deposit (CDs) as marketable receipts for large time deposits. Usually these deposits are over $100,000 and mature within 1 year. The interest paid on these instruments is negotiated and is paid at maturity.

A secondary market for CDs exists, but it is not as well developed as that for Treasury bills. This is one reason that the yield on CDs is generally above that on Treasury bills.

These securities should not be mistaken for the type of CDs purchased by individual small investors. The small CDs are different from the marketable securities in that their interest is established by the financial institution rather than negotiated, and smaller CDs are not marketable.

Money Market Mutual Funds. Money market mutual funds are a popular source of liquidity for both businesses and individuals. These mutual funds hold only short-term securities such as Treasury bills, CDs, and commercial paper. Shares in these funds are easily obtained — often without commissions (the so-called "no-load" funds). Because the required initial investment is small and the liquidity is comparable to lower-yielding checking and savings accounts, money market mutual funds are a popular temporary investment alternative, especially for smaller firms.

---

[5]The maximum maturity without SEC registration is 270 days. Commercial paper can be sold only to "sophisticated" investors; otherwise, SEC registration would be required even for maturities of 270 days or less.

Where to Stash the Cash?

A high level of corporate cash has been a worldwide phenomenon, dating from 1989 and fueled by a long economic expansion and relatively high interest rates. Large companies with huge stockpiles of cash can handle it in a variety of ways. Some are fairly conservative and keep it mostly untouched, while others apply a more aggressive approach. Four companies' cash management styles are presented here to illustrate some of the possibilities.

Chrysler Corporation believes in active, inventive management of its $2.5 billion in "usable" cash, according to David Chrisco, manager for corporate cash and banking administration. This total does not include "balance sheet cash" such as floats on receipts and disbursements, or cash belonging to wholly owned foreign subsidiaries. Four full-time staff members assist Chrisco, and this structure is different from the arrangement in some companies where, he says, cash management is treated "as more or less a custodial type of function, . . . as some kind of part-time job for some employee."

None of the Chrysler cash goes into bonds — Treasury or otherwise — because of the interest rate risk associated with their longer terms. However, Chrisco does work with the company's tax department on strategies for tax-advantaged securities like municipal bonds and preferred stock. He also has explored an area that most large companies avoid — loan participations, in which commercial banks pass along short-term loans to third parties. In another program, Chrysler is experimenting with the idea of outside management for the cash involved with a dividend reinvestment plan.

While Chrysler's $2.5 billion in excess cash seems like a large amount, Chrisco says it is needed as a cushion to protect the firm against unforeseen events. "If you get a wildcat strike and the plants get shut down, it doesn't take very long for the cash supply to run out the door very quickly."

At General Motors the philosophy is simple and conservative — liquidity and protection of principal. Averaging $4.5 billion, the company's cash is stashed in five types of investments — U.S. Treasury bills and notes; Ginnie Mae, Fannie Mae, and Federal Home Loan Mortgage Corporation securities; certificates of deposit and other items from domestic and foreign banks; municipal obligations; and commercial paper. Loan participations are not used, because "It takes an awful lot of manpower to review individual transactions," says Ned Case, director of corporate financing and investments.

Large amounts of available cash protect GM against such possibilities as a recession in the car business, strikes at suppliers' companies, new tax rates, and acquisitions. The last large purchases for the company — of Electronic Data Systems and Hughes Aircraft in the mid-1980s — each required more than $1 billion in cash. Case says, "We can't afford to risk principal. It's not our money to play with. If it's a choice between making a few more basis points and being comfortable with having bought a high-quality, liquid asset, we will always choose high quality and liquidity."

GM's philosophy corresponds with that of Lloyd Mistele, treasury manager of Toyota Motor Sales U.S.A., whose cash fund of between $1 and $2 billion grew by $500 million in a recent three-year period. Profitability, while desirable, is last among his priorities, after safety, liquidity, and timely availability for known expenditures. Mistele defines "cash" as a portfolio of securities, usually with maturities of a year or less. His staff needs a detailed knowledge of federal and state tax laws to manage the tax-advantaged investments in which the company stows some of its cash — included are such things as money market preferred, auction-rate preferred, municipal bonds, and tax-exempt commercial paper. Toyota U.S.A.'s taxable investments consist primarily of very short-term domestic securities and Eurodollar time deposits. Mistele and his

Source: "A Portfolio of Cash Management Strategies," *Institutional Investor,* February 1989.

staff are also conservative about transferring their funds. They review interest rates and investment guidelines regularly, but they only shift their cash a few times a year.

Not surprisingly, Mistele's policies are in line with those of his company's parent, Toyota Motor Corporation, which invests most of its 2 trillion yen cash stockpile ($13,080,000,000) in short-term bank deposits, commercial paper, or government securities. In keeping with its risk-averse approach, Toyota won't touch loan participations, stocks, or corporate bonds.

When talking about big hoards of cash, the deepest pockets in the world may belong to the German electronics firm, Siemens, jokingly known to fellow countrymen as "the bank that runs an electronics workshop on the side." Its 24 billion deutsche mark cache ($14,565,840,000) was barely affected by the $2.7 billion withdrawal for two acquisitions in 1989.

Aside from about 5 billion deutsche marks used to cover one month's costs, Siemens' money is invested in short-term time deposits, in fixed-rate bonds and notes with maturities averaging more than three years, and in an equity portfolio. The firm's money-market investments director Reinhard Warkocz's investments of choice are German federal government bonds, U.S. Treasury or government agency paper, and blue-chip German bank and insurance stocks ("safe as bonds"). Even with all that cash, Warkocz is not averse to borrowing. "In countries where we see a currency risk," he says, "we hesitate to invest our stable deutsche marks in accounts receivable and inventories, so we borrow."

The company monitors its performance by comparing it with those of outside cash managers in London and New York. Warkocz says, "From time to time, we learn from other people. But I am very proud that during the 15 years I have been at this job, we have achieved the same or even better performance than [outsiders]. It confirms that we should continue managing our own cash."

Eurodollars

Interest-bearing time deposits, denominated in U.S. dollars, placed in banks outside the United States.

Eurodollar Bank Time Deposits. Eurodollars are interest-bearing time deposits, denominated in U.S. dollars and placed in banks outside the United States. The term **Eurodollars** may be misleading because banks in Canada, Japan, and the Caribbean are important players in this market.

In many respects the Eurodollar is an international counterpart to the negotiable certificate of deposit. Interest and maturities are negotiated, but interest on these invested dollars is generally above the CD rate. Like CDs, there is a secondary market for Eurodollars, but it is still in the developmental stage, and it is not a source of certain liquidity. Default risk is a function of the issuing bank's strength.

Self-Test

What are the major reasons for a firm to hold marketable securities?

List three situations in which a firm would hold marketable securities as a temporary investment.

What are the three alternative strategies for meeting seasonal cash needs as identified in Figure 9-2? Why is one relatively aggressive and one relatively conservative?

What risks do financial managers consider when developing their marketable securities portfolios?

What government securities are suitable as near-cash reserves? What nongovernment securities are suitable as near-cash reserves?

SUMMARY

This chapter concerned cash and marketable securities management. In it we examined the motives for holding cash, the construction of the cash budget, several ways in which firms can minimize their cash holdings, cash management in the multidivisional firm, and the different types of marketable securities that can be used as substitutes for cash. The key concepts covered in the chapter are listed below:

- The primary **goal of cash management** is to reduce the amount of cash held to the minimum necessary to conduct business.

- The **transactions balance** is the cash necessary to conduct day-to-day business, whereas the **precautionary balance** is the cash reserve held to meet random, unforeseen needs. A **compensating balance** is a minimum checking account balance that a bank requires as compensation either for services provided or as part of a loan agreement. Firms also hold **speculative balances,** which allow them to take advantage of bargain purchases. Note, though, that borrowing capacity and marketable securities reduce the need for both precautionary and speculative balances.

- A **cash budget** is a statement which shows projected cash inflows and outflows over a specified period. The cash budget is used to determine when the firm will have cash surpluses and shortfalls, and thus to help management plan to invest surpluses or to cover projected shortfalls.

- A firm can lower its cash balances if it can **synchronize** its cash outflows and inflows. Also, the use of **lockboxes** can speed collections and thus reduce a firm's required cash holdings.

- **Disbursement float** is the amount of funds associated with checks written by the firm that are still in the process of clearing and hence have not yet been deducted by the bank from the firm's account.

- **Collection float** is the amount of funds associated with checks written to the firm that have not been cleared and hence are not yet available for use.

- **Net float** is the difference between disbursement float and collection float, and it also is equal to the difference between the balance in a firm's checkbook and the balance on the bank's records. The larger the net float, the smaller the cash balances the firm must maintain, so net float is good.

- Firms can reduce their cash balances by holding **marketable securities,** which can be sold on short notice at close to their quoted market values. Marketable securities serve both as a substitute for cash and as a temporary investment for funds that will be needed in the near future. Safety is the primary consideration when treasurers select marketable securities.

- In choosing a marketable securities portfolio, a financial manager must consider **default risk, interest rate risk, inflation risk,** and **liquidity (or marketability) risk.**
- Securities that are appropriate as **near-cash reserves** are U.S. Treasury bills, commercial paper, negotiable CDs, and money market mutual funds. Eurodollars and U.S. Treasury notes are questionable as near-cash reserves.

EQUATIONS

At any given time, a business has a number of checks that it has written but that have not been deducted by the bank from its account (disbursement float), as well as a number of checks that it has received but that have not yet been credited to its account (collection float). The difference between disbursement float and collection float is called net float, and it is calculated as follows:

$$\text{Net float} = \text{Disbursement float} - \text{Collection float.}$$

RESOLUTION TO DECISION IN FINANCE

The Buy-back Binge

In one of the largest buy-back proposals ever, GE announced plans to repurchase its shares over a five-year period with 60 percent cash, with the rest being financed with borrowed money. After accounting for capital expenditures, dividends, working capital, and other expenses, GE expects to generate approximately $1.2 billion in cash every year to use for the repurchase. Since debt will also be used, the company's debt-to-capital ratio will not change, and neither will its triple-A long-term debt credit rating. Standard & Poor's announced that it would maintain that rating because of expected "growth and profitability" in most GE operations that are "first or second in their worldwide markets."

Sources: *The Wall Street Journal*, "General Electric Buy-Back Plan Signals New Tack, Reflects Earnings Optimism," November 20, 1989, and "The Lowdown on Buy-Backs Isn't Upbeat," December 8, 1989.

Further, management says the repurchase will not dampen GE's capital spending, which is expected to be 7 percent higher in 1990 than it was in 1989. Annual earnings, which were about $4 billion in 1989, are projected to be more than $5 billion by 1992, while revenues are forecasted to increase from $54 billion to more than $60 billion.

Prior to the buy-back announcement, GE had spent huge sums on acquisitions as well as plant and equipment improvements — total internal and external investments amounted to about $37 billion during the 1980s. The firm acquired RCA, Borg Warner Chemicals, and Employers Reinsurance Corporation, among others. Although the new plan could be altered if circumstances warranted it, Chairman Welch says, "It would take a blockbuster acquisition to change. We don't see values out there to make acquisitions. The best bet is our own stock."

QUESTIONS

9-1   How can better methods of communication reduce the necessity for firms to hold large cash balances?

9-2   What are the two principal reasons for holding cash? Can a firm estimate its target cash balance by summing the cash held to satisfy each of these two reasons?

9-3   Explain how each of the following factors would probably affect a firm's target cash balance if all other factors were held constant.

   a. The firm institutes a new billing procedure which better synchronizes its cash inflows and outflows.

   b. The firm develops a new sales forecasting technique which improves its forecasts.

   c. The firm reduces its portfolio of U.S. Treasury bills.

   d. The firm arranges to use an overdraft system for its checking account.

   e. The firm borrows a large amount of money from its bank and also begins to pay suppliers twice as frequently as in the past; thus it must write far more checks than it did in the past even though the dollar volume of business has not changed.

   f. Interest rates on Treasury bills rise from 5 percent to 10 percent.

9-4   In the cash budget shown in Table 9-1, is the projected maximum funds requirement of $5,200,000 in September known with certainty, or should it be regarded as the expected value of a probability distribution? Consider how this peak probably would be affected by each of the following:

   a. A lengthening of the days sales outstanding (DSO).

   b. An unanticipated decline in sales that occurred when sales were supposed to peak.

   c. A sharp drop in sales prices required to meet competition.

   d. A sharp increase in interest rates for a firm with a large amount of short-term debt outstanding.

9-5   Would a lockbox plan make more sense for a firm that makes sales all over the United States or for a firm with the same volume of business, but whose business is concentrated in its home city?

9-6   Would a corporate treasurer be more tempted to invest the firm's liquidity portfolio in long-term as opposed to short-term securities when the yield curve was upward sloping or downward sloping?

9-7   What does the term *liquidity* mean? Which would be more important to a firm that held a portfolio of marketable securities as precautionary balances against the possibility of losing a major lawsuit — liquidity or rate of return? Explain.

9-8   Firm A's management is very conservative, whereas Firm B's managers are more aggressive. Is it true that, other things being equal, Firm B would probably have larger holdings of short-term marketable securities? Explain.

9-9   Is it true that *interest rate risk* refers to the risk that a firm will be unable to pay the interest on its bonds? Explain.

9-10 Corporate treasurers, when selecting securities for portfolio investments, must make a tradeoff between risk and return. Is it true that most treasurers are willing to assume a fairly high exposure to risk to gain higher expected returns?

SELF-TEST PROBLEMS

ST-1   David Banner, Limited, has grown from a small Houston firm, with customers concentrated in the Texas Gulf Coast area, to a large national firm serving customers throughout the United States. Despite its broad customer base, Banner has maintained its headquarters in the Houston area and keeps its central billing system there. Banner's management is considering an alternative collection procedure to reduce its mail time and collection float. On average, it takes 6 days from the time customers mail payments until the company receives, processes, and deposits them. Banner would like to set up a lockbox collection system, which it estimates would reduce the time lag from customer mailing to deposit by 4 days, bringing it down to 2 days. Banner receives an average of $1,000,000 in payments per day.

    a. How many days of collection float now exist (Banner's customers' disbursement float), and what would it be under the lockbox system? What reduction in cash balances would Banner achieve by initiating the lockbox system?

    b. If Banner has an opportunity cost of 10 percent, how much is the lockbox system worth on an annual basis?

    c. What should be Banner's maximum monthly cost for this lockbox system?

ST-2   The Weston Company is setting up a new checking account with Howe National Bank. Weston plans to issue checks in the amount of $1 million each day and to deduct them from its own records at the close of business on the day they are written. On average, the bank will receive and clear the checks at 5 P.M. the third day after they are written; for example, a check written on Monday will be cleared on Thursday afternoon. The firm's agreement with the bank requires it to maintain a $500,000 average compensating balance; this is $250,000 greater than the cash balance the firm would otherwise have on deposit. It makes a $500,000 deposit at the time it opens the account.

    a. Assuming that the firm makes deposits at 4 P.M. each day (and the bank includes them in that day's transactions), how much must it deposit daily in order to maintain a sufficient balance once it reaches a steady state? Indicate the required deposit on Day 1, Day 2, Day 3, if any, and each day thereafter, assuming that the company will write checks for $1 million on Day 1 and each day thereafter.

    b. How many days of float does Weston have?

    c. What ending daily balance should the firm try to maintain (1) on the bank's records and (2) on its own records?

PROBLEMS

9-1   **Net float.** The Aleman Company is setting up a new bank account with the First National Bank. Aleman plans to issue checks in the amount of $2 million each day and to deduct them from its own records at the close of business on the day they are written. On average, the bank will receive and clear (that is, deduct from the firm's bank balance) the checks at 5 P.M. the fourth day after they are written. For example, a check written on Monday will be cleared on Friday afternoon. The firm's agreement with the bank requires it to maintain a $1.5 million average compensating balance. This is $500,000 greater than the cash balance the firm would otherwise have on deposit; that is, without the compensating balance, it would carry an average deposit of $1 million. It makes a $1.5 million deposit at the time it opens the account.

a. Assuming that the firm makes deposits at 4 P.M. each day (and the bank includes the deposit in that day's transactions), how much must the firm deposit each day to maintain a sufficient balance on the day it opens the account, during the first 4 days after it opens the account, and once it reaches a "steady state"? (Ignore weekends.)

b. What ending daily balance should the firm try to maintain (1) on the bank's records and (2) on its own records?

c. Explain how net float can help increase the value of the firm's common stock.

9-2 **Lockbox system.** Doc Wilson, Inc., started 5 years ago as a small medical products firm serving customers in the Seattle area. Its reputation and market area grew quickly, however, so that today Wilson has customers throughout the United States. Despite its broad customer base, Wilson has maintained its headquarters in the Seattle area and keeps its central billing system there. Wilson's management is considering an alternative collection procedure to reduce its mail time and collection float. On average, it takes 5 days from the time customers mail payments until the company receives, processes, and deposits them. Wilson would like to set up a lockbox collection system, which it estimates would reduce the time lag from customer mailing to deposit by 3 days, bringing it down to 2 days. Wilson receives an average of $900,000 in payments per day.

a. How many days of collection float now exist (Wilson's customers' disbursement float) and what would it be under the lockbox system? What reduction in cash balances would Wilson achieve by initiating the lockbox system?

b. If Wilson has an opportunity cost of 10 percent, how much is the lockbox system worth on an annual basis?

c. What is the maximum monthly charge Wilson should pay for this lockbox system?

9-3 **Cash receipts.** United Circuits had actual sales of $50,000 during November and $75,000 during December. The company expects to have sales of $60,000 in January, $66,000 in February, and $76,000 in March. During the sales month, 20 percent of its sales are for cash, 40 percent are credit sales paid in the month following the sale, and 40 percent are credit sales paid 2 months following the sale. Prepare the firm's schedule of cash receipts for January through March.

9-4 **Cash receipts.** Crossroads Antique Store had sales of $30,000 in May, and it has forecasted sales for its peak tourist season as follows:

Actual:	April	$22,500
	May	30,000
Forecast:	June	48,750
	July	67,500
	August	56,250

From experience, management estimates that 25 percent of sales are for cash, 65 percent of sales are paid after 30 days, 8 percent of sales are paid after 60 days, and 2 percent of sales are uncollectable. Prepare a schedule of cash receipts for the firm's peak season (June through August).

9-5 **Cash disbursements.** Krogh, Inc. is scheduling the production of mopeds to be sold next summer. Orders for the next 5 months are as follows: April, 80,000 units; May, 100,000 units; June, 130,000 units; July, 80,000 units; and August, 40,000 units. Manufacturing costs for materials are $1,300 per unit, paid 1 month before manufacture. Direct labor costs equal $600 per unit, paid in the month of production.

Shipping costs are $240 per unit, paid the month after manufacture. Depreciation expense is allocated on a units-of-production basis of $100 per unit in the month of production. Advertising expense is zero for April and May but will be $400,000 in June and $1,000,000 in July. Fixed overhead is $600,000 monthly. Taxes of $16 million will be paid at the end of June.

Prepare a schedule of cash disbursements for May through July.

9-6 **Cash budgeting.** Jerry and Alice Britton recently leased space in the Appalachee Mall and opened a new business, Art Handycrafts Gallery. Business has been good, but the Brittons have frequently run out of cash. This has necessitated late payment on certain orders, which, in turn, is beginning to cause a problem with suppliers. The Brittons plan to borrow from the bank to have cash ready as needed, but first they need to determine how much they must borrow. Accordingly, they have asked you to prepare a cash budget for a critical period around Christmas, when needs will be especially high.

Sales are made on a *cash basis only.* The Britton's purchases must be paid in the month following the purchase. The Brittons pay themselves a salary of $4,800 per month, and the rent is $2,000 per month. In addition, the Brittons must make a tax payment of $12,000 in December. The current cash on hand (on December 1) is $400, but the Brittons have agreed to maintain an average bank balance of $6,000; this is their target cash balance. (Disregard till cash, which is insignificant because the Brittons keep only a small amount on hand to lessen the chances of robbery.)

The estimated sales and purchases for December, January, and February are shown in the following table. Purchases during November amounted to $140,000.

	Sales	Purchases
December	$160,000	$40,000
January	40,000	40,000
February	60,000	40,000

a. Prepare a cash budget for December, January, and February.

b. Now suppose that the Brittons were to start selling on a credit basis on December 1, giving customers 30 days to pay. All customers accept these terms, and all other facts in the problem are unchanged. What would the gallery's loan requirements be at the end of December in this case? (*Hint:* The calculations required to answer this question are minimal.)

9-7 **Cash budgeting.** Harrison, Inc., is trying to improve its cash management. You have been assigned to help in this task and are given the following data to use in your analysis:

Sales Forecasts for the Month of	Sales
December	$20,000
January	27,000
February	27,000
March	10,000
April	10,000

Collection estimates were obtained from the credit and collection department as follows: 10 percent collected within one month of sale, 80 percent collected in the month following sale, and 10 percent collected in the second month following sale.

Payments for labor and raw materials are typically made during the month following the one in which these costs are incurred.

Labor and Raw Materials Cost for the Month of	Cost
January	$15,000
February	15,000
March	7,500
April	8,500

General and administrative salaries will amount to approximately $4,080 a month; lease payments under long-term lease contracts will be $1,380 a month; depreciation charges are $5,400 a month; miscellaneous expenses will be $420 a month. Cash on hand February 1 will amount to $500, and a minimum cash balance of $7,500 should be maintained throughout the cash budget period. (Assume that the minimum cash balance policy has only recently been begun.)

Prepare a cash budget for Harrison for February through April.

9-8 **Cash budgeting.** The Silverton Corporation is planning to request a line of credit from its bank. The following sales forecasts have been made for 1991 and 1992:

May 1991	$ 75,000
June	75,000
July	150,000
August	225,000
September	300,000
October	150,000
November	150,000
December	37,500
January 1992	75,000

Collection estimates obtained from the credit and collection department are as follows: collections within the month of sale, 10 percent; collections the month following the sale, 75 percent; collections the second month following the sale, 15 percent. Payments for labor and raw materials are typically made during the month following the one in which these costs have been incurred. Total labor and raw materials costs are estimated for each month as follows:

May 1991	$37,500
June	37,500
July	52,500
August	367,500
September	127,500
October	97,500
November	67,500
December	37,500

General and administrative salaries will amount to approximately $11,250 a month; lease payments under long-term lease contracts will be $3,750 a month; depreciation charges will be $15,000 a month; miscellaneous expenses will be $1,125 a month; income tax payments of $26,250 will be due in both September and December; and a progress payment of $75,000 on a new design studio must be paid in October. Cash on hand on July 1 will amount to $35,000, and a minimum cash balance of $30,000 will be maintained throughout the cash budget period.

a. Prepare a monthly cash budget for the last six months of 1991.

b. Prepare an estimate of the required financing (or excess funds) — that is, the amount of money that Silverton will need to borrow (or will have available to invest) — for each month during that period.

c. Assume that receipts from sales come in uniformly during the month (that is, cash receipts come in at the rate of 1/30 each day) but that all outflows are paid on the fifth of the month. Will this have an effect on the cash budget? In other words, would the cash budget you have prepared be valid under these assumptions? If not, what can be done to make a valid estimate of peak financing requirements? No calculations are required, although calculations can be used to illustrate the effects.

d. Silverton produces on a seasonal basis, just ahead of sales. Without making any calculations, discuss how the company's current ratio and debt ratio would vary during the year assuming all financial requirements were met by short-term bank loans. Could changes in these ratios affect the firm's ability to obtain bank credit?

(Do Part e only if you are using the computerized problem diskette.)

e. (1) By offering a 2 percent cash discount for paying within the month of sale, the credit manager has revised the collection percentages to 50 percent, 35 percent, and 15 percent, respectively. How will this affect the loan requirements?

(2) Return the payment percentages to their base case values and the cash discount to zero. Now suppose sales fall to only 70 percent of the forecast level. Production is maintained, so cash outflows are unchanged. How does this affect Silverton's financial requirements?

(3) Return sales to the forecasted level (100%) and suppose collections slow down to 3%, 10%, and 87% for the three months, respectively. How does this affect financial requirements? If Silverton went to a cash-only sales policy, how would that affect requirements, other things held constant?

SOLUTIONS TO SELF-TEST PROBLEMS

ST-1   **a.** The collection float period is now 6 days and can be reduced by 4 days under the proposed collection system. Since Banner receives $1,000,000 daily, the 4 day reduction in float would reduce cash balances by $4,000,000.

b. $4,000,000 × 0.10 = $400,000.

c. $400,000/12 = $33,333.

ST-2   **a.** First determine the balance on the firm's checkbook and the bank's records as follows:

	Firm's Checkbook	Bank's Records
Day 1 Deposit $500,000; write checks for $1,000,000	($ 500,000)	$500,000
Day 2 Write checks for $1,000,000	($1,500,000)	$500,000
Day 3 Write checks for $1,000,000	($2,500,000)	$500,000
Day 4 Write checks for $1,000,000; deposit $1,000,000	($2,500,000)	$500,000

After Weston has reached a steady state, it must deposit $1,000,000 each day to cover the checks written 3 days earlier.

b. The firm has 3 days of float; not until Day 4 does the firm have to make any additional deposits.

c. As shown above, Weston should try to maintain a balance on the bank's records of $500,000. On its own books it will have a balance of *minus* $2,500,000.

Chapter 10

Accounts Receivable and Inventories

DECISION IN FINANCE

The Data Are Available, but Should Companies Use Them?

At least once a month, the nation's banks and retailers, among others, give credit bureaus computer tapes or electronic files detailing the purchases and payments of nearly every consumer in the United States. Twenty years ago, credit bureaus guarded this information so closely that even individual consumers could not see their own files. These files are still closely guarded, and they are virtually impossible to steal, but they are now easy to buy. "For very little cost," says the editor of *Privacy Journal,* a newsletter, "anybody can learn anything about anybody."

Credit files contain information over the entire life of an individual, literally from birth until death. Anyone who applies for credit to buy a car, a house, or any other item must submit detailed information about his or her financial status—including checking account balances, telephone bill information, payment records, family size and ages, social security numbers, medical

See end of chapter for resolution.

records, racial or ethnic background, annual income, insurance records, available credit balance on credit cards, and, of course, addresses and telephone numbers. All of this information in turn, becomes available to almost anyone who is willing to pay for it.

The "big three" credit bureaus — TRW, Trans Union, and Equifax — together generated revenues of $894,000,000 in 1988 by selling some of their more than 400,000,000 data files on 160,000,000 individuals. The stored information is becoming so detailed that marketers can distinguish the spending habits of one family from their next-door neighbors of the same age and with the same number of children.

With personal bankruptcies increasing at a rate of 25 percent a year (to 80,000 in 1989), and with about 4 percent of consumers defaulting on mortgage and credit card debts, businesses are eager to find out about their potential customers before they become uncollectible accounts receivable. To help in this regard, credit bureaus will provide forecasts on the financial soundness of individuals. Equifax, for instance, considers about 40 factors to project the probability of personal bankruptcy. Its credit division president says the projections are correct about 90 percent of the time.

Companies also spend about $2 billion a year with information providers to identify good prospects for their products, in addition to obtaining credit information. They can obtain such specific characteristics as names of Hispanics earning $500,000 a year and having $10,000 available on their credit cards, or people with $1,000,000 in the bank who live within a 50-mile radius of Dallas. According to a lawyer specializing in consumer financial services, "Consumers don't understand that for each ad stuffing their mailbox, a company without their knowledge or permission has asked a credit bureau to review their file." Besides the big three agencies, there are at least 200 more information sellers.

Legislators and consumer advocates have long been concerned about these increasing invasions of personal privacy. Ten privacy laws already exist, yet they barely affect the credit bureaus' operations. One law aimed primarily at the private sector is the Fair Credit Reporting Act of 1970. It requires that consumers be allowed to see their own credit records and that they be told of investigations for insurance or employment. It also bars credit agencies from giving information to anyone but "authorized customers." However, that definition is so broad that it includes anyone believed to have "a legitimate business need."

The Video Privacy Protection Act of 1988 forbids disclosure or sale of retailers' video rental records. Several other acts restrict government use of personal information.

Nevertheless, the computer age has made it increasingly difficult to control the flow of data. "Computers have outstripped the ability of our legal system to safeguard privacy," says a professor who chaired the 1977 U.S. Privacy Protection Commission. A researcher says few people have any idea of the kinds of information available about them, and they have no way to find out who may be using such information. Public opinion polls show that 90 percent are worried about invasion of privacy via electronic data collection, and this concern is likely to be translated into laws. For example, in late 1989, California passed a law limiting commercial use of personal records, and it allows its residents to use a post office box or business address instead of a home address on driver's license applications and in transactions with state agencies. Thus, even though people continue to fill out credit applications and to divulge information about their private lives, they seem to be increasingly concerned that it not be passed along for uses other than the original one for which they furnished it.

As you read this chapter, consider the many uses to which a business might put personal information about individuals. Then consider how those individuals might react when they learn about such uses. Finally, do you think businesses should assume a more responsible position about private information before government steps in and does it for them?

In the previous chapter, we examined the firm's investment in cash and marketable securities. To complete the analysis of current assets management, we now turn to accounts receivable and inventories. These accounts are essential for a firm's profitability and even for its existence. Inventories are needed for sales to occur, and sales are necessary for profits. Although firms would rather sell for cash than on credit, competition forces most companies to offer credit. Accounts receivable are created when the firm sells on credit.

Firms usually have large investments in accounts receivable and inventory. For example, the typical firm has about 20 percent of its total assets in accounts receivable. Inventories generally amount to another 20 percent of total assets, or more for nonmanufacturing firms. These accounts are necessary to conduct business, but a Du Pont analysis quickly reveals that ineffective management of these accounts can lead to a buildup of excess accounts receivable and inventory, resulting in a lower rate of return on invested capital. Inventory and receivables management also has an effect on the cash conversion cycle, which was discussed in Chapter 8. Remember that two of the components of the cash conversion cycle are the inventory conversion period, which is the average length of time required to convert raw materials and labor into finished goods and then to sell these goods, and the receivables conversion period, which is the length of time required to convert the firm's receivables into cash. Naturally, the larger the amount of inventories and receivables held, the longer the inventory and receivables conversion period will be, hence the longer the cash conversion cycle will be. Of course, carrying too little inventory and denying credit to potential customers can lose sales, and thus, profit opportunities. In this chapter we discuss procedures that will help the firm optimize its investment in these current assets.

ACCOUNTS RECEIVABLE

As mentioned earlier, most firms sell on credit. When goods are shipped, inventories are reduced, and an **account receivable** is created.[1] Eventually, the customer will pay the account, at which time receivables will decline and the cash account will increase. Carrying receivables is costly, but the costs involved can be offset by the fact that granting credit helps the firm by increasing its sales. The financial manager tries to balance the costs and benefits of granting credit when determining the firm's credit policy. A good receivables control system is important, for without an adequate system, receivables will build up to excessive levels, cash flows will decline, and bad debts will rise to unacceptable levels. The optimal credit policy is the one at which the marginal benefits of increased sales are exactly offset by the marginal costs of granting credit; this is the credit policy that maximizes the value of the firm.

account receivable
A balance due from a customer.

The optimal credit policy, and hence the optimal level of accounts receivable, depends on the firm's own unique operating conditions. Thus, a firm with excess capacity and low variable production costs should extend credit more liberally, and therefore should carry a higher level of accounts receiv-

---

[1]Whenever goods are sold on credit, two accounts actually are created; an asset item called an *account receivable* appears on the books of the selling firm, and a liability item called an *account payable* appears on the books of the purchaser. At this point we are analyzing the transaction from the seller's viewpoint, so we are concentrating on the variables under its control — in this case, the receivables. The transaction will be examined from the purchaser's viewpoint in Chapter 11, where we discuss accounts payable as a source of funds and consider their cost relative to the cost of funds obtained from other sources.

able, than if it were operating at full capacity or had a slim gross profit margin. Although optimal credit policies can vary among firms, or even for a single firm over time, it is still useful to analyze the effectiveness of the firm's credit policy in an aggregate sense.

Self-Test

In general terms, what credit policy maximizes the value of the firm?

Explain what is meant by the following statement: "The optimal credit policy, hence the optimal level of accounts receivable, depends on the firm's own unique operating conditions."

CREDIT POLICY

credit policy
A set of decisions that include a firm's credit period, discounts offered, credit standards, and collection policy.

The success or failure of a business depends primarily on the demand for its products; as a rule, the higher the demand, the greater its sales and profits, and the healthier the firm. Sales, in turn, depend on a number of factors, some exogenous but others controllable by the firm. The major controllable variables that affect sales are product price and quality, advertising, and the firm's credit policy. **Credit policy,** in turn, consists of these four elements:

1. The *credit period,* which is the length of time buyers have before they must pay for their purchases.

2. *Discounts* given to encourage early payment.

3. *Credit standards,* which refers to the minimum financial strength of acceptable credit customers.

4. The firm's *collection policy,* which reflects the firm's toughness or laxity in following up on slow-paying accounts.

credit terms
A statement of the credit period and any discounts offered—for example, 2/10, net 30.

The credit period and the discount allowed (if any), when combined, are called the **credit terms.** Thus, if a company allows its customers 30 days in which to pay, but then gives a 2 percent discount if payment is made within 10 days, it is said to offer credit terms of 2/10, net 30. The credit manager has the responsibility for enforcing the credit terms and administering the firm's credit policy. However, because of the pervasive importance of credit, the credit policy itself—both setting the credit terms and specifying the credit standards and collection policy—is established by the executive committee, which usually consists of the president and the vice presidents in charge of finance, marketing, and production.

Credit Period

credit period
The length of time for which credit is granted.

The **credit period** is the length of time a company gives its customers to pay; for example, credit might be extended for 30, 60, or 90 days. Several factors influence the length of time over which the firm offers credit. In part, this credit period is influenced by the terms offered by competitors. Further, there is generally a relationship between the normal inventory holding period of the producing firm's customer-stores and its credit period. For example, fresh fruits and vegetables normally are sold on very short credit terms, whereas jewelry may involve a 90-day or even a 6-month credit period.

Within these parameters there is still plenty of leeway for setting more or less generous credit terms. Lengthening the credit period may stimulate sales, but there is a cost to tying up funds in receivables. For example, if a firm changes its terms from net 30 to net 60, the average receivables for the year might rise from $100,000 to $300,000, with the increase in accounts receivable of $200,000 being caused in part by higher sales and in part by the longer credit period. Assuming that the firm's required rate of return on investment is 15 percent, the marginal return required on lengthening the credit period is $200,000 \times 15\% = $30,000$. If the incremental profit (sales price minus all direct production and selling costs, as well as any credit losses associated with the additional sales) exceeds $30,000, the change in credit policy should be made. Thus determining the optimal credit period involves many factors, but the bottom line in establishing a credit period is determining the point at which marginal profits on increased sales just offset the costs of carrying the higher amount of accounts receivable.

Cash Discounts

cash discount
A reduction in the price of goods, given to encourage early payment.

The second element in the credit policy decision, the use of **cash discounts** to encourage early payment, is analyzed by balancing the costs and benefits of different discount terms. For example, Ellen Rose Fashions might decide to change its credit terms from "net 30," which means that customers must pay within 30 days, to "2/10, net 30," which means that it will allow a 2 percent discount if payment is received within 10 days, whereas the full invoice price must otherwise be paid within 30 days. This change should produce two benefits: (1) it should attract new customers who consider discounts a type of price reduction, and (2) it should cause a reduction in the days sales outstanding (DSO), because some old customers will begin to pay within 10 days to take advantage of the discount. Offsetting these benefits is the dollar cost of the discounts taken. The optimal discount is the one at which the marginal costs and benefits are exactly offsetting. The methodology for analyzing changes in the discount is developed later in this chapter.

Offering cash discounts for prompt payment may lead to increased profits for the selling firm if its customers follow the terms of credit, but discounts can be quite costly if buyers pay late and still take the discount. One such case involved Carter Hawley Hale Stores, Inc. Arizona Wholesale Supply Company, a distributor of household products such as television sets, sold merchandise to Carter Hawley Hale on terms which allowed a 2 percent discount on invoices paid within 20 days. Arizona Wholesale filed a lawsuit charging that Carter Hawley Hale had illegally deducted $53,000 in discounts on invoices which were not paid within the stated 20-day credit period. Arizona Wholesale also charged that federal antitrust laws were being violated, because firms which allow some customers to take discounts on late payments are discriminating against other customers who are not allowed to take such discounts. Thus, Arizona Wholesale would have been guilty of antitrust violations if it had permitted Carter Hawley Hale to take discounts after the 20-day credit period but had not allowed other customers to also take such discounts. This example illustrates the fact that firms have two incentives to enforce their credit policies: profitability and the avoidance of antitrust violations.

seasonal dating

A procedure for inducing customers to buy early by not requiring payment until the customers' selling season, regardless of when the merchandise is shipped.

If sales are seasonal, a firm may use **seasonal dating** on discounts. For example, Jenson, Inc., a swimsuit manufacturer, sells on terms of 2/10, net 30, May 1 dating. This means that the effective invoice date is May 1, even if the sale was made back in January. If the discount is not taken by May 10, the full amount must be paid on May 30. If Jenson produces throughout the year, but retail sales of bathing suits are concentrated in the spring and early summer, offering seasonal datings may induce some customers to stock up early, saving Jenson storage costs and also "nailing down" sales.

Credit Standards

If a firm makes credit sales only to its strongest customers, it will never have bad debt losses, nor will it incur much in the way of expenses for its credit department. On the other hand, it will probably lose sales, and the profit forgone on these lost sales could be far larger than the costs it has avoided. Determining the optimal *credit standards* involves equating the marginal costs of credit to the marginal profits on the increased sales.

credit standards

Standards that stipulate the minimum financial strength that an applicant must demonstrate in order to be granted credit.

Credit standards refer to the strength and creditworthiness a customer must exhibit in order to qualify for credit. If a customer does not qualify for the regular credit terms, he or she can still purchase from the firm, but under more restrictive terms. For example, a firm's "regular" credit terms might call for payment after 30 days, and these terms might be extended to all qualifed customers. The firm's credit standards would be applied to determine which customers qualified for the regular credit terms and how much credit each customer should receive. The major factors considered when setting credit standards relate to the likelihood that a given customer will pay slowly, or perhaps even end up as a bad debt loss.

Setting credit standards implicitly requires a measurement of *credit quality,* which is defined in terms of the probability of a customer's default. The probability estimate for a given customer is, for the most part, a subjective judgment. Nevertheless, credit evaluation is a well-established practice, and a good credit manager can make reasonably accurate judgments of the probability of default by the different classes of customers. In this section we discuss some of the methods used by firms (and by bank loan officers) to measure credit quality.

The Five Cs System. The traditional method of measuring credit quality, where no computerized system is to be used, is to investigate potential credit customers with respect to five factors called the **five Cs of credit:**

1. *Character* refers to the probability that a customer will *try* to honor his or her obligations. This factor is of considerable importance, because every credit transaction implies a *promise* to pay. Will debtors make an honest effort to pay their debts, or are they likely to try to get away with something? Experienced credit managers frequently insist that the moral factor is the most important issue in a credit evaluation. Thus, credit reports provide background information on people's and firms' historical credit performances. Often credit analysts will seek this type of information from a firm's bankers, its other suppliers, its customers, and even its competitors.

2. *Capacity* is a subjective judgment of a customer's ability to pay. It is gauged in part by records and business methods, and it may be supplemented by physical observation of customers' plants or stores.

3. *Capital* is measured by the general financial condition of a customer firm as indicated by an analysis of its financial statements, with special emphasis on the risk ratios — the total debt/total assets ratio, the current ratio, and the times-interest-earned ratio.

4. *Collateral* refers to any assets that the customer may offer as security to obtain credit.

5. *Conditions* refers both to general economic trends and to special developments in certain geographic regions or sectors of the economy that may affect customers' ability to meet their obligations.

Information on these five factors comes from the firm's previous experience with its customers, and it is supplemented by a well-developed system of external information gatherers. Of course, once the information on the five Cs is developed, the credit manager must still make the final decision on the potential customer's overall credit quality. Because this decision is normally judgmental in nature, credit managers must rely on their background knowledge and instincts.

Sources of Credit Information. Two major sources of external information are available. The first is the work of the *credit associations,* which are local groups that meet frequently and correspond with one another to exchange information on credit customers. These local groups have also banded together to create Credit Interchange, a system developed by the National Association of Credit Management for assembling and distributing information about customers' past performances. The interchange reports show the paying records of different credit customers, the industries from which they are buying, and the trading areas in which purchases are being made.

> **five Cs of credit**
> The factors used to evaluate credit risk: character, capacity, capital, collateral, and conditions.

Credit reporting agencies (such as Dun & Bradstreet) compile and sell reports on specific companies; in this example, the information is on Gorman Manufacturing Co. Inc. These reports provide a credit rating (in top right corner) as well as factual information about the company's current financial status, public record of legal activities, banking, company history, and a brief description of the business.

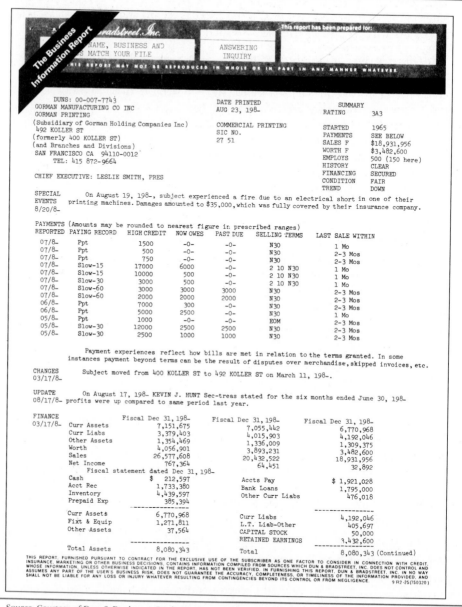

Source: Courtesy of Dun & Bradstreet Credit Services, a company of The Dun & Bradstreet Corporation.

The second source of external information is the *credit-reporting agencies*, which collect credit information and sell it for a fee. The best known of these agencies are Dun & Bradstreet (D&B) and TRW, Inc. D&B, TRW, and other agencies provide factual data that can be used in credit analysis; they also provide ratings similar to those available on corporate bonds.

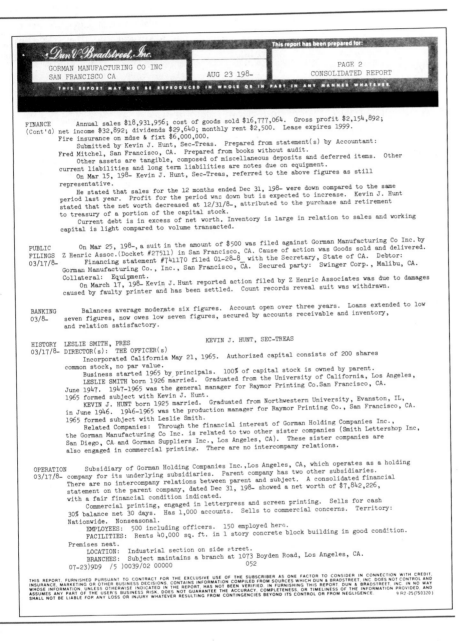

Dun & Bradstreet, Inc.

This report has been prepared for:

GORMAN MANUFACTURING CO INC
SAN FRANCISCO CA

AUG 23 198-

PAGE 2
CONSOLIDATED REPORT

THIS REPORT MAY NOT BE REPRODUCED IN WHOLE OR IN PART IN ANY MANNER WHATEVER.

FINANCE
(Cont'd)

Annual sales $18,931,956; cost of goods sold $16,777,064. Gross profit $2,154,892; net income $32,892; dividends $29,640; monthly rent $2,500. Lease expires 1999. Fire insurance on mdse & fixt $6,000,000.

Submitted by Kevin J. Hunt, Sec-Treas. Prepared from statement(s) by Accountant: Fred Mitchel, San Francisco, CA. Prepared from books without audit.

Other assets are tangible, composed of miscellaneous deposits and deferred items. Other current liabilities and long term liabilities are notes due on equipment.

On Mar 15, 198- Kevin J. Hunt, Sec-Treas, referred to the above figures as still representative.

He stated that sales for the 12 months ended Dec 31, 198- were down compared to the same period last year. Profit for the period was down but is expected to increase. Kevin J. Hunt stated that the net worth decreased at 12/31/8-, attributed to the purchase and retirement to treasury of a portion of the capital stock.

Current debt is in excess of net worth. Inventory is large in relation to sales and working capital is light compared to volume transacted.

PUBLIC FILINGS
03/17/8-

On Mar 25, 198-, a suit in the amount of $500 was filed against Gorman Manufacturing Co Inc. by Z Henric Assoc.(Docket #27511) in San Francisco. CA. Cause of action was Goods sold and delivered.

Financing statement #741170 filed 01-28-8 with the Secretary, State of CA. Debtor: Gorman Manufacturing Co., Inc., San Francisco, CA. Secured party: Swinger Corp., Malibu, CA. Collateral: Equipment.

On March 17, 198- Kevin J. Hunt reported action filed by Z Henric Associates was due to damages caused by faulty printer and has been settled. Count records reveal suit was withdrawn.

BANKING
03/8-

Balances average moderate six figures. Account open over three years. Loans extended to low seven figures, now owes low seven figures, secured by accounts receivable and inventory, and relation satisfactory.

HISTORY
03/17/8-

LESLIE SMITH, PRES   KEVIN J. HUNT, SEC-TREAS
DIRECTOR(s): THE OFFICER(s)

Incorporated California May 21, 1965. Authorized capital consists of 200 shares common stock, no par value.

Business started 1965 by principals. 100% of capital stock is owned by parent.

LESLIE SMITH born 1926 married. Graduated from the University of California, Los Angeles, June 1947. 1947-1965 was the general manager for Raymor Printing Co.San Francisco, CA. 1965 formed subject with Kevin J. Hunt.

KEVIN J. HUNT born 1925 married. Graduated from Northwestern University, Evanston, IL, in June 1946. 1946-1965 was the production manager for Raymor Printing Co., San Francisco, CA. 1965 formed subject with Leslie Smith.

Related Companies: Through the financial interest of Gorman Holding Companies Inc., the Gorman Manufacturing Co Inc. is related to two other sister companies (Smith Lettershop Inc, San Diego, CA. and Gorman Suppliers Inc., Los Angeles, CA.) These sister companies are also engaged in commercial printing. There are no intercompany relations.

OPERATION
03/17/8-

Subsidiary of Gorman Holding Companies Inc.,Los Angeles, CA, which operates as a holding company for its underlying subsidiaries. Parent company has two other subsidiaries. There are no intercompany relations between parent and subject. A consolidated financial statement on the parent company, dated Dec 31, 198- showed a net worth of $7,842,226, with a fair financial condition indicated.

Commercial printing, engaged in letterpress and screen printing. Sells for cash 30% balance net 30 days. Has 1,000 accounts. Sells to commercial concerns. Territory: Nationwide. Nonseasonal.

EMPLOYEES: 500 including officers. 150 employed here.

FACILITIES: Rents 40,000 sq. ft. in 1 story concrete block building in good condition. Premises neat.

LOCATION: Industrial section on side street.

BRANCHES: Subject maintains a branch at 1073 Boyden Road, Los Angeles, CA.

07-23)9D9 /5)0039/02 00000   052

THIS REPORT, FURNISHED PURSUANT TO CONTRACT FOR THE EXCLUSIVE USE OF THE SUBSCRIBER AS ONE FACTOR TO CONSIDER IN CONNECTION WITH CREDIT, INSURANCE, MARKETING OR OTHER BUSINESS DECISIONS. CONTAINS INFORMATION COMPILED FROM SOURCES WHICH DUN & BRADSTREET, INC DOES NOT CONTROL AND WHOSE INFORMATION, UNLESS OTHERWISE INDICATED IN THE REPORT, HAS NOT BEEN VERIFIED. IN FURNISHING THIS REPORT, DUN & BRADSTREET, INC. IN NO WAY ASSUMES ANY PART OF THE USER'S BUSINESS RISK. DOES NOT GUARANTEE THE ACCURACY, COMPLETENESS, OR TIMELINESS OF THE INFORMATION PROVIDED, AND SHALL NOT BE LIABLE FOR ANY LOSS OR INJURY WHATEVER RESULTING FROM CONTINGENCIES BEYOND ITS CONTROL OR FROM NEGLIGENCE.   9 R2-25(750320)

Managing a credit department requires fast, accurate, up-to-date information, and to help make such information available, the National Association of Credit Management (a group with 43,000 member firms) persuaded TRW, Inc., to develop a computer-based telecommunications network for the collection, storage, retrieval, and distribution of credit information. The TRW system transmits credit reports electronically, so they are available within seconds to its thousands of subscribers. Dun & Bradstreet has a similar electronic system, plus another service which provides more detailed reports through the U.S. mail.

A typical credit report would include the following pieces of information:

1. A summary balance sheet and income statement.

2. A number of key ratios, including trends in the ratios.

3. Information obtained from the firm's banks and suppliers about whether it generally pays promptly or slowly, and whether it has recently failed to make any payments.

4. A verbal description of the physical condition of the firm's facilities.

5. A verbal description of the backgrounds of the firm's owners, including any previous bankruptcies, lawsuits, fraud, and the like.

6. A summary rating, ranging from A+ for the best credit risks down to F for those judged likely to default.

Although a great deal of credit information is available, it must still be processed in a judgmental manner. Computerized information systems can assist managers in making better credit decisions, but in the final analysis credit determinations are really exercises in informed judgment.

Management by Exception. Modern credit managers often practice *management by exception.* Under such a system, statistical procedures are used to classify customers into five or six categories according to degree of risk, and the credit manager then concentrates time and attention on the customers judged most likely to cause problems. For example, the following classes might be established:

Risk Class	Percentage of Uncollectible Credit Sales	Percentage of Customers in This Class
1	0–½%	60%
2	½–2	20
3	2–5	10
4	5–10	5
5	Over 10	5

Firms in Class 1 might be extended credit automatically, and their credit status might be reviewed only once a year. Those in Class 2 might also receive credit (up to specified limits) automatically, but a ratio analysis of their financial condition would be conducted more frequently (perhaps quarterly), and they would be moved down to Class 3 if their position deteriorated. Specific approvals might be required for credit sales to Classes 3 and 4, whereas sales to Class 5 might be on a COD (cash on delivery) basis only.

Collection Policy

Collection policy refers to the procedures used to collect accounts receivable. For example, a letter might be sent to any account when the bill is 10 days past due; a more severe letter, followed by a telephone call, might be used if payment is not received within 30 days; and the account might be turned over to a collection agency after 90 days. The collection process can be expensive in terms of both out-of-pocket expenditures and lost goodwill, but some firmness is needed both to prevent an undue lengthening of the collection period and to minimize outright losses. A balance must be struck between the costs and benefits of different collection policies.

> **collection policy**
> The procedures used to collect accounts receivable.

Changes in collection policy influence the level of sales, the collection period, the bad debt loss percentage, and the percentage of customers who take discounts. The effects of a change in collection policy, along with changes in the other credit policy variables, will be analyzed later in the chapter.

Profit Potential in Carrying Accounts Receivable

Thus far we have emphasized the costs of granting credit. *However, if it is possible to sell on credit and to assess a carrying charge on the receivables that are outstanding, then credit sales can actually be more profitable than cash sales.* This is especially true for consumer durables (automobiles, appliances, clothing, and so on), but it is also true for certain types of industrial equipment. Thus, General Motors Acceptance Corporation (GMAC), which finances automobiles, is highly profitable, as is Sears, Roebuck's credit subsidiary. Some encyclopedia companies even lose money on cash sales but more than make up for these losses from the carrying charges on their credit sales; obviously, such companies would rather sell on credit than for cash!

The carrying charges on outstanding credit generally run about 18 percent on an annual interest rate basis (1½% per month, so 1.5% × 12 = 18%). Except for the early 1980s, when short-term interest rates rose to unprecedented levels, having receivables outstanding that earn 18 percent is highly profitable.

How Effective Is the Firm's Credit Policy?

As we saw in connection with the Du Pont analysis in Chapter 6, an excessive investment in any asset account will lead to a low rate of return on equity. For comparative purposes, we can examine the firm's days sales outstanding (DSO) as discussed in Chapter 6. There we saw that Carter Chemical Company's days sales outstanding was 42 days, compared to an industry average of 36 days. If Carter lowered its days sales outstanding by 6 days to 36 days, this would mean a reduction of $8,333,333 × 6 = $49,999,998 in the amount of capital tied up in receivables. Assuming that the cost of funds tied up in receivables is 10 percent, this would mean a savings of $5 million per year, other things held constant.

The DSO can also be compared to Carter's credit terms. Carter typically sells on terms of 1/10, net 30, so its customers, on average, are not paying their bills on time; the 42-day DSO is greater than the 30-day credit period. Note, however, that some of the customers are probably paying within 10 days to take advantage of the cash discount, so others must be taking much longer than 42 days to pay. One way to get a better view of the situation is to construct an **aging schedule,** which breaks down accounts receivable according to how long they have been outstanding. Carter's aging schedule is as follows:

aging schedule
A report showing how long accounts receivable have been outstanding; gives the percentage of receivables currently past due, and the percentages past due by specified periods.

Age of Accounts (Days)	Percentage of Total Value of Accounts Receivable
0–10	52%
11–30	20
31–45	13
46–60	4
Over 60	11
Total	100%

Although most of the accounts pay on schedule or after only a slight delay, a significant number are more than 1 month past due. This indicates that even though the majority of the firm's receivables are collected within the 30-day credit period, Carter has quite a bit of capital tied up in slow-paying accounts, some of which may eventually result in bad debt losses.

Management should constantly monitor the firm's days sales outstanding and aging schedule to detect trends, to see how the firm's collection experience compares with its credit terms, and to see how effectively the credit department is operating in comparison with other firms in the industry. If the DSO begins to lengthen, or if the aging schedule begins to show an increasing percentage of past-due accounts, then the firm's credit policy may have to be tightened.

Although a change in the DSO or the aging schedule should be a signal to the firm to investigate its credit policy, a deterioration in either of these measures does not *necessarily* indicate that the firm's credit policy has weakened. In fact, if a firm experiences sharp seasonal variations, or if its sales have been growing rapidly, then both the aging schedule and the DSO will be distorted. Similar problems arise with the aging schedule when sales fluctuate widely.[2]

Investors—both stockholders and bank loan officers—should pay close attention to accounts receivable management; otherwise, they could be misled by the firm's financial statements and later suffer serious losses on their investments. When a sale is made, the following events occur: (1) Inventories are reduced by the cost of the goods sold, (2) accounts receivable are increased by the sales price, and (3) the difference is recorded as a profit. If the sale is for cash, the profit is definitely earned, but if the sale is on credit, the

[2]While an overall corporate aging schedule may not be useful for a firm with fluctuating sales, individual aging schedules, that is, for individual customers, do provide useful information as to whether the customer is paying on time. See Eugene F. Brigham and Louis C. Gapenski, *Intermediate Financial Management,* 3rd ed., Chapter 19, for a more complete discussion of the problems with the DSO and aging schedules and how to deal with them.

Table 10-1 **Roark Restaurant Supply Company:**
Analysis of Credit Policy
(Millions of Dollars)

	Projected 1991 Income Statement under Current Credit Policy (1)	Effect of Credit Policy Change (2)	Projected 1991 Income Statement under New Credit Policy (3)
Gross sales	$400.0	+ $130.0	$530.0
Less: Discounts	2.0	+ 4.0	6.0
Net sales	$398.0	+ $126.0	$524.0
Production costs, including overhead	280.0	+ 91.0	371.0
Profit before credit costs and taxes	$118.0	+ $ 35.0	$153.0
Credit-related costs:			
Cost of carrying receivables	3.3	+ 1.6	4.9
Credit analysis and collection expenses	5.0	− 3.0	2.0
Bad debt losses	10.0	+ 22.0	32.0
Profit before taxes	$ 99.7	+ $ 14.4	$114.1
Taxes (40%)	39.9	+ 5.7	45.6
Net income	$ 59.8	+ $ 8.7	$ 68.5

profit is not actually earned unless and until the account is collected. Firms have been known to use credit policy to encourage "sales" to very weak customers in order to inflate reported profits. This can boost the stock price, but only until credit losses show up and begin to lower earnings, at which time the stock price will fall. An analysis along the lines suggested above will detect any such questionable practices, as well as any undetected deterioration in the quality of accounts receivable. Such early detection could help both investors and bankers avoid losses.

Analyzing Changes in the Credit Policy Variables

If a firm's credit policy is eased by such actions as lengthening the credit period, relaxing credit standards, following a less tough collection policy, or offering cash discounts, sales should increase. *Easing the credit policy normally stimulates sales.* However, if credit policy is eased and sales *do* rise, costs will also rise because (1) more labor, materials, and so on, will be required to produce the additional goods; (2) receivables outstanding will increase, which will raise carrying costs; and (3) bad debt or discount expenses may also rise. Thus, the key question when deciding on a credit policy change is this: Will sales revenues rise more than costs, causing net income to increase, or will the increase in sales revenues be more than offset by higher costs?

Table 10-1 illustrates the general idea behind credit policy analysis. Column 1 shows the projected 1991 income statement for Roark Restaurant Supply Company under the assumption that the firm's current credit policy is maintained throughout the year. In this particular case, excess capacity exists, so sales could be increased without adding either new plant or general overhead expense. Column 2 shows the expected effects of easing the credit policy by extending the credit period, offering larger discounts, relaxing credit standards, and easing collection efforts. (Firms often do not change all four variables at one time because this makes it hard to determine what caused the observed changes.) Specifically, Roark is analyzing the effects of changing its credit terms from 1/10, net 30, to 2/10, net 40, relaxing its credit standards, and putting less pressure on slow-paying customers. Column 3 shows the projected 1991 income statement incorporating the expected effects of an easing in credit policy. The generally easier policy is expected to increase sales and lower credit analysis and collection costs, but discounts and several other types of cost would rise. The overall, bottom-line effect is an $8.7 million increase in projected profits. In the following paragraphs, we explain how the numbers in the table were calculated.

Roark's annual sales are currently projected at $400 million. Under its current credit policy, 50 percent of those customers who pay do so on Day 10 and take the discount, 40 percent pay on Day 30, and 10 percent pay late, on Day 40. Thus, Roark's days sales outstanding is $(0.50)(10) + (0.40)(30) + (0.10)(40) = 21$ days.

Even though Roark spends $5 million annually to analyze accounts and to collect bad debts, 2.5 percent of sales will never be collected. Therefore, bad debt losses amount to $(0.025)($400,000,000) = 10 million. In addition, Roark's cash collections will be reduced by the amount of discounts taken. Fifty percent of the customers who pay (and 97.5 percent of all customers pay) take the 1 percent discount, so discounts equal $($400,000,000)(0.975)(0.01)(0.50) = $1,950,000 \approx 2 million. Notice that total sales are multiplied by $(1 -$ Bad debt ratio), 97.5%, to obtain collected sales, and collected sales are then multiplied by the discount percentage times the percentage of paying customers who take the discount.

The annual cost of carrying receivables is equal to the average amount of receivables times the variable cost percentage, which gives the dollars of capital invested in receivables, times the cost of money used to carry receivables:

$$\begin{pmatrix} \text{Average} \\ \text{amount of} \\ \text{receivables} \end{pmatrix} \begin{pmatrix} \text{Variable} \\ \text{cost} \\ \text{ratio} \end{pmatrix} \begin{pmatrix} \text{Cost} \\ \text{of} \\ \text{funds} \end{pmatrix} = \begin{matrix} \text{Cost of} \\ \text{carrying} \\ \text{receivables} \end{matrix}.$$

The average receivables balance, in turn, is equal to the days sales outstanding times sales per day. Roark's DSO is 21 days, its variable cost ratio is 70 percent, and its cost of funds invested in receivables is 20 percent. Therefore, its annual cost of carrying receivables is approximately $3.3 million:

$$(\text{DSO}) \begin{pmatrix} \text{Sales} \\ \text{per} \\ \text{day} \end{pmatrix} \begin{pmatrix} \text{Variable} \\ \text{cost} \\ \text{ratio} \end{pmatrix} \begin{pmatrix} \text{Cost} \\ \text{of} \\ \text{funds} \end{pmatrix} = \begin{matrix} \text{Cost of} \\ \text{carrying} \\ \text{receivables} \end{matrix}. \tag{10-1}$$

$$(21) \left(\frac{$400,000,000}{360} \right) (0.70)(0.20) = $3,266,667 \approx $3.3 \text{ million}.$$

Only variable costs enter into this calculation, because this is the only cost element that must be financed as a result of a change in the credit policy. In other words, if a new customer buys goods worth $100, Roark will have to invest only $70 (in labor and materials); therefore, it will have to finance only $70, even though accounts receivable rise by $100. Variable costs thus represent the company's investment in the goods sold.

Roark's new credit policy calls for a larger discount, a longer payment period, a relaxed collection effort, and lower credit standards. The company believes that these changes will increase sales by $130 million, to $530 million per year. Under the new credit terms, management believes that 60 percent of the customers who pay will take the 2 percent discount, and that bad debt losses will total 6 percent of sales. Therefore, discounts will increase to ($530,000,000)(0.94)(0.02)(0.60) = 5,978,400 ≈ $6 million. Half of the remaining paying customers (20 percent of the paying customers) will pay on Day 40, and the remainder on Day 50. Therefore, the new DSO is estimated to be 24 days:

$$(0.6)(10) + (0.2)(40) + (0.2)(50) = 24 \text{ days.}$$

As a result, the cost of carrying receivables will increase to $4.9 million:

$$(24)\left(\frac{\$530,000,000}{360}\right)(0.70)(0.20) = \$4,946,667 \approx \$4.9 \text{ million.}^3$$

Because it will relax credit standards, hence credit checking expenses, and also ease up on collections, the company expects to reduce its annual credit analysis and collection expenditures from $5 million to $2 million. However, the reduced credit standards and the relaxed collection effort are expected to raise bad debt losses from 2.5 percent to 6 percent of the new level of sales, or to (0.06)($530,000,000) = $32.0 million.

The combined effect of the changes in Roark's credit policy is a projected $8.7 million increase in net income. There would, of course, be corresponding changes on the projected balance sheet. The higher sales would necessitate somewhat larger cash balances, inventories, and perhaps (if the sales increase were large enough) more fixed assets. Of course, accounts receivable would also increase. Since these asset increases would have to be financed, certain liability accounts or equity would also have to be increased.

---

[3]Since the credit policy change will result in a higher DSO, Roark will have to wait longer to receive its profit on the goods it sells. Therefore, the firm will incur an opportunity cost as a result of not having the cash from these profits available for investment. The dollar amount of this opportunity cost is equal to the old sales per day times the change in DSO times the contribution margin $(1-v)$ times the cost of the funds invested in receivables:

$$\text{Opportunity cost} = (\text{Old sales}/360)(\Delta\text{DSO})(1 - v)(k)$$
$$= (\$400 \text{ million}/360)(3)(0.3)(0.20) = \$0.2 \text{ million.}$$

Here v = variable cost ratio and k = cost of funds. For simplicity, and because it is not large, we ignored opportunity costs in Table 10-1. For a more complete discussion of the analysis of changes in credit policy, see Eugene F. Brigham and Louis C. Gapenski, *Intermediate Financial Management,* 3rd ed., Chapter 19.

The $8.7 million expected increase in net income is, of course, an estimate, and the actual effects of the change could be quite different. Most important, there is uncertainty about the projected $130 million increase in sales. Conceivably, if Roark's competitors matched its credit policy changes, sales would not rise at all. Similar uncertainties must be attached to the number of customers who would take discounts, to production costs at higher or lower sales levels, to the costs of carrying additional receivables, and to the bad debt loss ratio. In view of all the uncertainties, management might deem the projected $8.7 million increase in net income insufficient to justify the change. In the final analysis, the decision to make the change will be based on judgment, but the type of quantitative analysis set forth here is essential to a good judgmental decision.

The preceding paragraphs give an overview of the way changes in credit policy are analyzed. As noted, the most important considerations have to do with changes in sales and production costs. Specific estimates of these effects are handled by the marketing and production departments within the framework set forth here. The financial manager has the responsibility for the overall analysis, plus a primary role in estimating several specific factors, including discounts taken, the cost of carrying accounts receivable, and bad debt losses. To evaluate a proposed change in credit policy, one could compare projected income statements, such as Column 1 versus Column 3 in Table 10-1. Alternatively, one could simply analyze Column 2, which shows the incremental effect (holding other things constant) of the proposed change. Of course, the two approaches are based on exactly the same data, so they must produce identical results. It is often preferable, however, to focus on the incremental approach — because firms usually change their credit policies in specific divisions or on particular products and not across the board, an analysis of complete income statements might not be feasible.

Self-Test

Identify and briefly explain the four elements of credit policy.

What is the purpose of a cash discount?

Identify and briefly explain the five Cs of credit.

What are some sources of credit information?

How do credit managers practice management by exception?

Briefly explain what the DSO and the aging schedule are, and tell how they are used to help monitor receivables.

INVENTORY MANAGEMENT

Inventories, which include (1) *raw materials,* (2) *work-in-process,* and (3) *finished goods* (or *merchandise* for a retailer), are an essential part of most business operations. Like accounts receivable, inventory levels depend heavily on sales. However, while receivables build up *after* sales have been made, inventories must be acquired *before* sales are made. This is a critical difference, and the necessity of forecasting sales before establishing target inventory levels makes **inventory management** a difficult task. Also, because errors in establishing inventory levels can lead either to lost sales and profits or to excessive costs, hence low profitability, inventory management is as important as it is difficult.

The manner in which its inventory is managed can have a direct effect on the value of a firm. Any procedure that allows a firm to achieve a given sales volume with a lower investment in inventories will increase the rate of return and, hence, increase the firm's value. However, actions to reduce inventory investment can also lead to lost sales because of stock-outs or costly production slowdowns. Managers must maintain inventories at levels which balance the benefits of reducing the level of investment against the costs associated with lowering inventories.

Inventory management focuses on three basic questions: (1) How many units of each inventory item should the firm hold in stock? (2) How many units should be ordered (or produced) at a given time? (3) At what point should inventory be ordered (or produced)? The remainder of this chapter is devoted to answering these questions.

Determining the Inventory Investment

In part, inventory policy is determined by the economics of the firm's industry; thus retailers have large stocks of finished goods but little, if any, raw materials or work-in-process. Moreover, the inventory policies of firms in a given industry can vary widely — no one inventory policy is suitable for all firms, although the policies of successful firms are often emulated by others.

No single executive establishes inventory policy. Rather, the firm's inventory policy is set by its executive committee, because production, marketing, and financial people all have a stake in inventory management. The production manager is concerned with the raw materials inventory to insure continuous production; he or she has direct control over the length of the production process (which influences work-in-process inventories) and is vitally concerned with whether the firm produces on a smooth, continuous basis throughout the year, stockpiling finished goods inventories for seasonal sales, or whether it produces irregularly in response to orders. The marketing manager wants the firm to hold large stocks of inventories to insure rapid deliveries; this will make it easier to close sales. The financial manager is concerned with the level of inventories because of the effects excessive inventories have on profitability: (1) they reduce the total assets turnover ratio, and (2) there are substantial costs of carrying inventories, so excessive inventories erode the profit margin.

Through the accounting staff, the financial manager also maintains the records relating to inventories, and in this capacity he or she is responsible for establishing information systems to monitor inventory usage and to replen-

inventory management
The balancing of a set of costs that increase with larger inventory holdings with a set of costs that decrease with larger order size.

Table 10-2 **Costs Associated with Inventories**

	Approximate Annual Percentage Cost
Carrying Costs	
Cost of capital tied up	12.0%
Storage and handling costs	0.5
Insurance	0.5
Property taxes	1.0
Depreciation and obsolescence	12.0
Total	26.0%
Ordering, Shipping, and Receiving Costs	
Cost of placing orders, including production set-up	varies
Shipping and handling costs	2.5%
Costs of Running Short (Stock-out Costs)	
Lost sales	varies
Loss of customer goodwill	varies
Disruption of production schedules	varies

Note: These costs vary from firm to firm, from item to item, and over time. The figures shown are U.S. Department of Commerce estimates for an average manufacturing firm. When costs vary so widely that no meaningful numbers can be assigned, we simply report "varies."

ish stocks as necessary. This information system is not complex in a single-product, single-plant firm, but in most modern corporations the inventory control process is as complex as it is important. Visualize an automobile or an appliance manufacturer, with thousands of dealers stocking hundreds of styles and colors of various automobiles, stoves, or refrigerators, as well as thousands of spare parts, all across the country. Production must reflect both stocks on hand and the current sales levels, and any mistake can result either in excessive stocks (which will lose value when the new models appear) or in lost sales. Grocery stores, department stores, plumbing manufacturers, textbook publishers, and most other firms are faced with similar problems.

Inventory Costs

The goal of inventory management is to provide the inventories required to sustain operations at the minimum cost. The first step is to identify all the costs involved in purchasing and maintaining inventories. Table 10-2 lists the typical costs associated with inventories, broken down into three categories: costs associated with carrying inventories, costs associated with ordering and receiving inventories, and costs associated with running short of inventories, which are called "stock-out costs."

Although they may well be the most important element, we shall at this point disregard the third category of costs — *stock-out costs* — these are dealt

Figure 10-1 **Determination of the Optimal Ordering Quantity**

To avoid the problems that may arise from carrying too much or too little inventory, a business must determine the optimal quantity of a product to purchase each time an order is placed. As this figure shows, carrying costs rise steadily as order size increases; ordering costs, on the other hand, decline with larger order sizes. The sum of these two curves is the total inventory costs curve, and the lowest point on that curve is the optimal order size, or economic ordering quantity (EOQ).

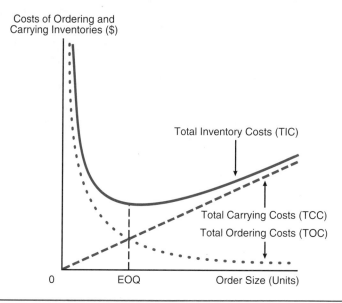

with by adding safety stocks, which we will discuss later. The costs that remain for consideration at this stage, then, are carrying costs and ordering, shipping, and receiving costs.

The Optimal Ordering Quantity

Inventories are obviously necessary, but it is equally obvious that a firm will suffer if it has too much or too little inventory. How can management determine the *optimal* inventory level? One commonly used approach is the *economic ordering quantity (EOQ) model,* which is described in this section.

Figure 10-1 illustrates the basic premise on which inventory theory is built, namely, that some costs rise with larger inventories while other costs decline, and that there is an optimal order size which minimizes the total costs associated with inventories. The average investment in inventories depends on how frequently orders are placed; if a small order is placed every day, average inventories will be much smaller than if one large order is placed annually. Further, as Figure 10-1 shows, inventory-associated **carrying costs** rise with larger orders; because larger orders mean larger average inventories, ware-

carrying costs
The costs associated with carrying inventories, including storage, capital, and depreciation costs. Carrying costs generally increase in proportion to the average amount of inventory held.

ordering costs
The costs of placing and receiving an order; this cost is fixed regardless of the average size of inventories.

economic ordering quantity (EOQ)
The optimal, or least-cost, quantity of inventory that should be ordered.

EOQ model
Formula for determining the ordering quantity that will minimize total inventory cost:

$$EOQ = \sqrt{\frac{2(F)(S)}{(C)(P)}}.$$

housing costs, interest on funds tied up in inventory, insurance costs, and obsolescence costs all will increase. At the same time, **ordering costs** decline with large orders, because the costs of placing orders, setting up production runs, and handling shipments will all decline if the firm orders infrequently and consequently holds larger quantities.

When the carrying and ordering cost curves in Figure 10-1 are added together, the sum represents the total cost of ordering and carrying inventories, the total inventory cost. The point where the total inventory cost curve is minimized represents the **economic ordering quantity (EOQ),** and this, in turn, determines the optimal average inventory level. A graph like Figure 10-1 is useful in helping the firm determine its approximate optimal ordering quantity, but to find the exact value it would be necessary to plot every possible ordering quantity. An easier method is to use the economic ordering quantity, or **EOQ, model.** It can be shown that under certain reasonable assumptions, the ordering quantity that minimizes the total cost curve in Figure 10-1 can be found by using the following formula:

$$EOQ = \sqrt{\frac{2(F)(S)}{(C)(P)}}. \qquad (10\text{-}2)$$

Here

EOQ = the economic ordering quantity, or the optimal quantity to be ordered each time an order is placed.

F = fixed costs of placing and receiving an order.

S = annual sales in units.

C = carrying cost expressed as a percentage of inventory value.

P = purchase price the firm must pay per unit of inventory.

The assumptions of the economic ordering quantity (EOQ) model include the following: (1) sales can be forecasted perfectly; (2) sales are evenly distributed throughout the year; (3) orders are received with no delays; and (4) F, C, and P are all fixed and independent of the ordering procedures.

To illustrate the EOQ model, consider the following data, supplied by Romantic Books, Inc., publisher of the classic novel *Madame Boudoir:*

S = sales = 26,000 copies per year.

C = carrying cost = 20 percent of inventory value.

P = purchase price per book to Romantic Books from a printing company = $6.1538 per copy. (The sales price Romantic Books charges is $9, but this is irrelevant for our purposes.)

F = fixed cost per order = $1,000. The bulk of this cost is the labor
cost for setting the page plates on the presses, as well as for setting up
the binding equipment for the production run. The printer bills this
cost separately from the $6.1538 cost per copy.

Substituting these data into Equation 10-2, we obtain an EOQ of 6,500 copies:

$$EOQ = \sqrt{\frac{2(F)(S)}{(C)(P)}}$$

$$= \sqrt{\frac{2(\$1,000)(26,000)}{(0.2)(\$6.1538)}}$$

$$= \sqrt{42,250,317}$$

$$= 6,500 \text{ copies.}$$

The average inventory depends directly on the EOQ; this relationship is
illustrated graphically in Figure 10-2. Immediately after an order is received,
6,500 copies are in stock. The usage rate, or sales rate, is 500 copies per week
(26,000/52 weeks), so inventories are drawn down by this amount each week,
and this determines the slope of the line. Thus, if the sales rate increases, the
line will become steeper.

The actual number of units held in inventory will vary from 6,500 books
just after an order is received to zero just before the next order arrives. On
average, the number of units held will be 6,500/2 = 3,250 books. At a cost of
$6.1538 per book, the average investment in inventories will be 3,250 ×
$6.1538 = $19,999.85 ≈ $20,000. If inventories are financed by a bank loan,
the loan will vary from a high of $40,000 to a low of $0, but the average
amount outstanding over the course of a year will be $20,000.

The EOQ, hence average inventory holdings, rises with the square root of
sales. Therefore, a given increase in sales will result in a less than proportionate increase in inventories, and the inventory turnover will thus increase as
sales grow. For example, Romantic Books' EOQ is 6,500 copies at an annual
sales level of 26,000, and the average inventory is 3,250 copies, worth $20,000.
However, if sales increase by 100 percent, to 52,000 copies per year, the EOQ
will rise to only 9,192 copies, or by 41 percent, and the average inventory will
rise by this same percentage. This suggests that there are economies of scale
in the holding of inventory.

Setting the Reorder Point

If a 2-week lead time is required for production and shipping, what is Romantic Books' **reorder point,** or the inventory level at which an order should be
placed? Romantic Books sells 26,000/52 = 500 books per week. Thus, if a

reorder point
The point at which stock
on hand must be
replenished.

Figure 10-2 **Inventory Position without Safety Stock**

This figure shows Romantic Books' average inventory position between orders. The
EOQ of 6,500 copies represents the maximum inventory and determines the average
inventory (6,500/2 = 3,250). The expected sales rate of 500 copies per week
determines the order frequency (every 13 weeks). Because a 2-week lead time is
required on orders, the reorder point is reached when inventories reach 1,000 copies.
This model assumes that both the sales rate and the required lead time on orders are
constant.

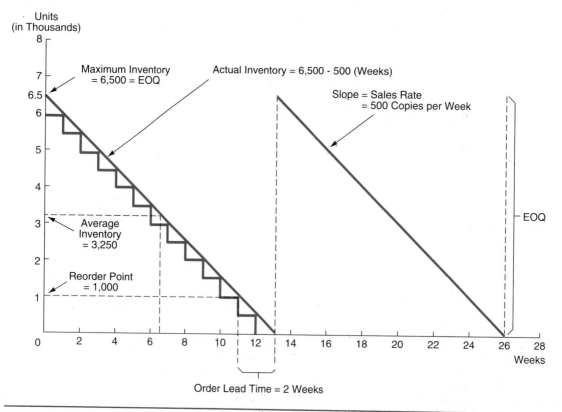

2-week lag occurs between the order and the delivery, Romantic Books must
place the order when there are 1,000 books on hand.

$$\text{Reorder point} = \text{Lead time} \times \text{Usage rate}$$

$$= 2 \times 500 = 1,000.$$

At the end of the 2-week production and shipping period, the new inventory
balance will be down to zero, but just at that time a new supply of books will
arrive.

Goods in Transit

If a new order must be placed before the previous order is received, a **goods-in-transit** inventory will build up. Goods in transit are items which have been ordered but have not yet been received. A goods-in-transit inventory will exist if the normal delivery lead time is longer than the time between orders. Although this complicates matters somewhat, the simplest solution to the problem is to deduct goods in transit when calculating the reorder point. In other words, the reorder point would be calculated as follows:

$$\text{Reorder point} = (\text{Lead time} \times \text{Usage rate}) - \text{Goods in transit}.$$

goods in transit
Goods which have been ordered but have not been received.

Goods in transit is not an issue for Romantic Books because the firm orders $26{,}000/6{,}500 = 4$ times a year, or once every 13 weeks, and the delivery lead time is 2 weeks. However, suppose that Romantic Books ordered 1,000 copies of *Madame Boudoir* every 2 weeks and the delivery lead time was 3 weeks. In that case, whenever an order was placed, another order of 1,000 books would be in transit. Therefore, Romantic Books' reorder point would be:

$$\begin{aligned}
\text{Reorder point} &= (3 \times 500) - 1{,}000 \\
&= 1{,}500 - 1{,}000 \\
&= 500.
\end{aligned}$$

Safety Stocks

If Romantic Books knew for certain that both the sales rate and the order lead time would never vary, it could operate exactly as shown in Figure 10-2. However, sales rates do change, and because production and shipping delays are frequently encountered, the company must carry additional inventories, or **safety stocks.**

The concept of a safety stock is illustrated in Figure 10-3. First, note that the slope of the sales line measures the expected rate of sales. The company *expects* to sell 500 copies each week, but let us assume a maximum likely sales rate of twice this amount, or 1,000 copies each week. Romantic Books initially orders 7,500, the EOQ plus a safety stock of 1,000 copies. Subsequently, it reorders the EOQ, 6,500 copies, whenever the inventory level falls to 2,000 copies (the safety stock of 1,000 copies plus the 1,000 copies expected to be used while awaiting delivery of the order). Notice that the company could, during the 2-week delivery period, sell 1,000 copies a week, doubling its normal expected sales. This maximum rate of sales is shown by the steeper dashed line in Figure 10-3. The condition that makes this higher maximum sales rate possible is the introduction of a safety stock of 1,000 copies; without it, the firm would run out of stock if the sales rate rose from 500 to 1,000 copies per week.

safety stocks
Additional inventories carried to guard against increases in sales rates or production/shipping delays.

Figure 10-3 **Inventory Position with Safety Stock Included**

Because sales rates and required lead times do vary, a business must carry safety stocks. In this example 1,000 copies of safety stock are initially ordered, in addition to the EOQ of 6,500 copies. The reorder point now becomes 2,000 copies. This safety stock allows the firm to handle a sales increase to 1,000 copies per week during the 2-week reorder lead time, should that occur, or if delays are encountered in receiving orders, the company could continue its average sales rate for 2 weeks beyond the usual 2-week delivery time.

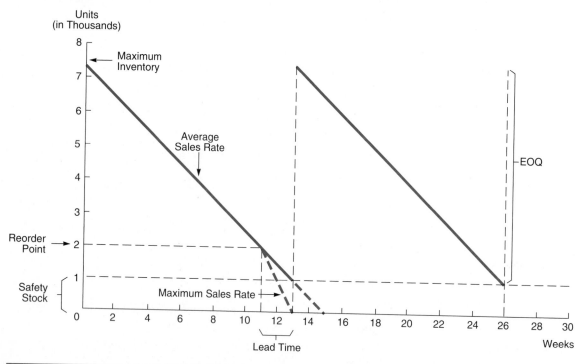

The safety stock is also useful to guard against delays in receiving orders. The expected delivery time is 2 weeks; however, with a 1,000-copy safety stock, the company could maintain sales at the expected rate of 500 copies per week for an additional 2 weeks if production or shipping delays held up an order.

Safety stocks are obviously useful, but they do have a cost. For Romantic Books, the average inventory is now EOQ/2 plus a safety stock of 1,000 units, or 6,500/2 + 1,000 = 3,250 + 1,000 = 4,250 books, and the average inventory value is (4,250)($6.1538) = $26,154. The increase in average inventory resulting from the safety stock causes an increase in inventory carrying costs.

The optimal safety stock varies from situation to situation, but in general it *increases* with (1) the uncertainty of sales forecasts, (2) the costs (in terms of lost sales and lost goodwill) that would result from inventory shortages, and (3) the probability of delays in receiving shipments. The optimal safety stock *decreases* as the cost of carrying the extra inventory increases.

Inventory Control Systems

The EOQ model, plus safety stocks, helps establish the proper inventory level, but inventory management also involves the *inventory ordering and control system.* There are various control systems that can be used — some simple and some complex. One simple control procedure is the **red-line method**. Here inventory items are stocked in a bin, a red line is drawn around the inside of the bin at the level of the reorder point, and the inventory clerk places an order when the red line shows. For the **two-bin method,** inventory items are stocked in two bins, and when the working bin is empty, an order is placed and inventory is drawn from the second bin. These procedures work well for items such as bolts in a manufacturing process and for many items in retail businesses.

Companies are increasingly employing **computerized inventory control systems.** Wal-Mart uses a computerized system called *electronic data interchange (EDI)* to help control its finished goods inventories. EDI systems allow specially formatted documents such as purchase orders to be sent from one company's computer to another's. Most items sold by Wal-Mart have bar codes which are scanned by a reader when a customer goes through the checkout stand. While the register is processing the customer's payment, information about the items that have been sold (such as color and size) is being transmitted to Wal-Mart's inventory control computers. The inventory control computers record the inventory reduction, and when the inventory level of an item falls to a specified amount, the computer automatically places an order with the manufacturer's computer through the EDI system.

A good inventory control system is dynamic. Companies like IBM and General Motors stock thousands of different types of items. The sales (or use) of these various items can rise or fall quite separately from rising or falling overall corporate sales. As the usage rate for an individual item begins to fall, the inventory manager must adjust this item's balance to avoid ending up with obsolete items — either finished goods or parts and materials for use in finished goods.

The EOQ model is useful for establishing order sizes and average inventory levels *given a correctly forecasted sales or usage rate,* and assuming that purchase prices and ordering costs are fixed. However, usage rates change over time, and both purchase prices and ordering costs may be dependent upon the buyer's arrangements with the seller, such as Wal-Mart's with its suppliers. Therefore, a good inventory management system must respond promptly to any changes in these conditions. One system that is used to monitor inventory usage rates and then to modify EOQs and inventory item levels

red-line method
An inventory control procedure in which a red line is drawn around the inside of an inventory-stocked bin to indicate the reorder point level.

two-bin method
An inventory control procedure in which the reorder point is reached when one of two inventory-stocked bins is empty.

computerized inventory control system
A system of inventory control in which computers are used to determine reorder points and to adjust inventory balances.

ABC system

A system used to categorize inventory items to insure that the most important ones are reviewed most often.

is the **ABC system.** Under this system, the firm analyzes each inventory item on the basis of its cost, frequency of usage, seriousness of a stock-out, order lead time, and other criteria related to the item's importance. Items that are expensive, are frequently used, and have long order lead times are put in the A category; somewhat less important items are put in the B category; and relatively unimportant items are designated C. Management reviews the A items' recent usage rates, stock positions, and delivery time situations quite frequently, say monthly, and adjusts the EOQ as necessary. Category B items are reviewed and adjusted less frequently, say, every quarter, and C items are reviewed perhaps annually. Thus, the inventory control group's resources are concentrated where they will do the most good.

Efficient inventory management will result in a relatively high inventory turnover ratio, low write-offs of obsolete or deteriorated inventories, and relatively few instances of work stoppages or lost sales because of stock-outs. All this, in turn, will contribute to a high profit margin, a high total assets turnover ratio, a high rate of return on investment, and a strong stock price.

Effects of Inflation on Inventory Management

Moderate inflation — say, 3 percent per year — can largely be ignored for purposes of inventory management, but the higher the rate of inflation, the more important it is to consider this factor. If the rate of inflation in the types of goods the firm stocks tends to be relatively constant, it can be dealt with quite easily — simply deduct the expected annual rate of inflation from the carrying cost percentage, C, in Equation 10-2, and use this modified version of the EOQ model to establish the working stock.

The reason for making this deduction is that inflation causes the value of the inventory to rise, thus offsetting somewhat the effects of depreciation and other carrying-cost factors. Because C will now be smaller, the calculated EOQ, and hence the average inventory, will increase. The higher the rate of inflation, however, the higher the interest rates, and this factor will increase C, thus lowering the EOQ and average inventories. On balance, there is no evidence that inflation either raises or lowers the optimal level of inventories of firms in the aggregate. Inflation should still be thoroughly considered, however, for it will raise the individual firm's optimal holdings if the rate of inflation for its own inventories is above average (and is greater than the effects of inflation on interest rates), and vice versa.

Other Inventory Issues

just-in-time (JIT) system

A system of inventory control in which a manufacturer coordinates production with suppliers so that raw materials and components arrive just as they are needed in the production process.

Two other inventory-related issues should be mentioned. The first is the **just-in-time (JIT) system,** in which a manufacturer coordinates production with suppliers so that raw materials or components arrive from suppliers just as they are needed in the production process. The primary focus of the just-in-time system is to reduce order costs and the purchase price of goods purchased. The Japanese have carried the just-in-time system to great lengths, and U.S. companies are increasingly adopting this system in their manufacturing

Just-in-Time (JIT) Inventory Method

Just-in-time (JIT) became the watchword for many U.S. manufacturers in the mid-1980s as their plants adopted a Japanese method of inventory delivery. This method involves redesigning production so parts and raw materials arrive at the factory just as they are needed, thus allowing manufacturers to save the cost of carrying inventories. As a result, at least one company, Lifeline Systems, Inc., a maker of medical-electronic equipment, was able to reverse a decline in profits even before it completed its conversion to just-in-time production.

Approximately 100 companies had converted to this system by 1986, including Campbell Soup, Motorola, Hewlett-Packard, and Intel, as well as dozens of small firms, such as Omark Industries, an Oregon manufacturer of power saw chains. General Motors switched a Lansing, Michigan, factory to just-in-time purchasing for its innovative Quad 4 engine in 1987. Under its system, purchased parts move immediately from the receiving dock to the assembly line without being inspected. When flaws are found at automated inspection stations, positioned after each of the 24 steps in the manufacturing process, the engines go back immediately to the spot where the problem occurred.

Large corporations started the just-in-time trend in the United States, but a management expert, who has written several books on the subject, says smaller companies are better positioned to adopt the method. Robert W. Hall of Indiana University points out that small firms usually have only one plant to convert, and they usually have simpler accounting and planning systems. Besides that, their management groups are smaller and can make faster decisions than can managers of larger firms. Another advantage for small firms is that smaller, nonunionized labor forces make it easier to redesign job functions.

Worker attitudes toward these changes have generally been the greatest stumbling block for companies—large or small—that convert to JIT methods. Lifeline's president, Arthur Phipps, says employee acceptance depends on management. "It's just a matter of managers getting their mind-sets correct." This can be difficult, though, since managers must give up the security of large inventories and trust their suppliers more than they ever have before. It is essential for managers to work closely with suppliers to insure that parts or materials get to the plant at the right time and in the right sequence for the assembly line. A few companies have started involving their suppliers while new products are still in the design stage, which should alleviate future problems. It is wise for management to be concerned not only with their own problems but also with those faced by their suppliers when they go to the JIT method.

Xerox, for instance, went into the new system with the idea that "this was an inventory reduction program for our benefit," according to Fred McClintock, materials manager for the copier division, "and we treated it that way, asking suppliers to hold inventories without compensation." Suppliers protested, and good relationships built over many years began to deteriorate. To improve the situation, Xerox reorganized its production and ordering schedules so suppliers could plan better. It also formed classes about the JIT system for the suppliers. One supplier, Rockford Dynatorq, reduced the time needed to make one brake part from three and a half weeks to just one day with the help of Xerox. Rockford's $1.5 million inventory dropped 10 percent in just six months.

Even one of the best JIT companies, motorcycle maker Harley Davidson, made its share of mistakes when getting started. Although it called all suppliers together to explain the system and to ask their help in implementing it, Harley's record of erratic production schedules

Sources: "Small Manufacturers Shifting to 'Just-in-Time' Techniques," *The Wall Street Journal*, December 21, 1987; "Having a Hard Time," *Fortune*, June 9, 1986; "General Motors' Little Engine That Could," *Business Week*, August 3, 1987.

and last-minute ordering made the suppliers skeptical that JIT would work. Only a few companies were willing to sign up to continue supplying the manufacturer, so Harley changed its approach. Eliminating 35-page contracts that mostly listed suppliers' obligations to them, Harley issued less complex 2-page contracts and also simplified and improved designs. Teams of engineers then helped suppliers modify their equipment to reduce the set-up time between jobs, and the company helped suppliers improve the quality of their products by teaching their employees to chart small changes in equipment performance. Harley says improvement in quality and in manufacturing techniques has reduced its expenses for reworking parts, scrap, and warranty repairs by 60 percent.

Improvement in quality control is a common by-product of JIT. Before its conversion, Lifeline Systems assembled its emergency patient-monitoring devices in lots of several hundred and tested them only when an entire lot was produced. Now each device is assembled and tested individually. "If you make them one at a time, you can't go any farther if one is bad," says a manufacturing consultant with Coopers & Lybrand. "You have to say, 'Whoops, halt!'"

Many wasteful procedures may be uncovered when manufacturers reevaluate their production processes for JIT conversion. Costs that add nothing to a product's value are incurred every time an item is moved, inspected, or stored in inventory, and JIT helps trim these costs. One company, U.S. Repeating Arms of New Haven, Connecticut, used JIT techniques to lower its minimum lot size for the manufacture of wooden gun stocks from 500 to 100, and to reduce production time from five weeks to two.

Fireplace Manufacturers, in Santa Ana, California, had sales of about $8 million in 1984, but it was having cash-flow problems because it had to keep inventory of about $1.1 million on hand. To make it economically feasible to produce parts in smaller quantities, and thus reduce inventory, the company devised ways to reduce set-up times on its machines. It also eliminated some assembly line tasks and recombined others. The firm's efforts resulted in a reduction of inventory in raw materials and work-in-process to $750,000. Its vice president of manufacturing, Don Bowker, said, "I don't think we'd be here today if it wasn't for JIT."

plants. To some extent, the just-in-time system reduces the need for the purchaser to carry inventories by passing the problem back to its suppliers; however, with a coordinated production schedule, the supplier may also benefit (1) by being able to schedule production runs better and (2) by having to carry lower finished goods inventory safety stock. In any event, coordination between suppliers and users lessens total inventory requirements and also reduces total production costs.

Toyota provides a good example of the just-in-time system. Eight of Toyota's ten factories, along with most of Toyota's suppliers, dot the countryside around Toyota City. Delivery of components is tied to the speed of the assembly line, and parts are generally delivered no more than a few hours before they are used. Not surprisingly, U.S. automobile manufacturers were among the first domestic firms to move toward just-in-time systems. Ford has been restructuring its production system with a goal of increasing its inventory turnover from 20 times a year to 30 or 40 times.

Just-in-time systems are also being adopted by smaller firms. In fact, some production experts say that small companies are better positioned than large ones to use just-in-time methods, because it is easier to redefine job functions and to educate people in small firms. Fireplace Manufacturers, Inc., a producer of prefabricated metal fireplaces, was recently experiencing serious profit and cash flow problems. It discovered that its inventory control system was inadequate, and the JIT inventory control system was recommended. The JIT system allowed Fireplace to cut its inventories by 35 percent.

Another important development related to inventories is **out-sourcing,** which is the practice of purchasing components rather than making them in-house. Thus, if General Motors arranges to buy radiators, axles, and other parts from suppliers rather than making them itself, it has increased its use of out-sourcing. Out-sourcing is often combined with just-in-time systems to reduce inventory levels. However, one important reason for out-sourcing has nothing to do with inventory policy—because of wage-rate differentials, a heavily unionized company like GM can often buy parts from a nonunionized supplier at a lower cost than it could make them.

out-sourcing
The practice of purchasing components rather than making them in-house.

A final point relating to inventory levels is the *relationship between production scheduling and inventory levels.* A firm like Dayton Card Company, whose cash budget was discussed in Chapter 9, has sales which are highly seasonal. Dayton could produce on a steady, year-round basis, or it could let production rise and fall with sales. If it established a level production schedule, its inventories would rise sharply during periods when sales were low and then would decline during peak sales periods, but the average inventory held would be substantially higher than if production were geared to rise and fall with sales.

Our discussion of just-in-time systems, out-sourcing, and production scheduling all point out the necessity of coordinating inventory policy with manufacturing/procurement policies. Companies try to minimize *total production and distribution costs,* and inventory costs are just one part of total costs. Still, they are an important cost, and financial managers should be aware of the determinants of inventory costs and how they can be minimized.

Self-Test

Into what three classifications can inventories be grouped?

Identify the three basic questions on which inventory management focuses.

What is the basic premise on which inventory theory is built?

What is the EOQ model? Give its formula.

How do you calculate the reorder point (1) when there are no goods in transit and (2) when there are goods in transit?

Identify some conditions that would normally cause the safety stock to increase and some that would cause the safety stock to decrease.

Identify and briefly explain some inventory control systems described in the text.

Explain what just-in-time and out-sourcing mean, and discuss how they affect inventory levels and costs.

SUMMARY

In this chapter we discussed accounts receivable and inventory management. Also, we presented an inventory model for helping the firm to minimize its inventory investment. The key concepts covered are listed below.

- When a firm sells goods to a customer on credit, an **account receivable** is created.

- Firms can use an **aging schedule** and the **days sales outstanding (DSO)** to help keep track of their receivables position and to help avoid the buildup of possible bad debts.

- A firm's **credit policy** consists of four elements: (1) **credit period,** (2) **discounts** given for early payment, (3) **credit standards,** and (4) **collection policy.** The first two, when combined, are called the **credit terms.**

- The traditional method of measuring credit quality, where no computerized system is to be used, is to investigate potential credit customers with respect to five factors called the **five Cs of credit.** These factors are: **character, capacity, capital, collateral,** and **conditions.**

- Two major sources of external credit information are available: **credit associations,** which are local groups that meet frequently and correspond with one another to exchange information on credit customers, and **credit reporting agencies,** which collect credit information and sell it for a fee.

- Modern credit managers often practice **management by exception.** Under this system, statistical procedures are used to classify customers into five or six categories according to degree of risk, and the credit manager then concentrates time and attention on customers judged most likely to cause problems.

- The basic objective of the credit manager is to increase profitable sales by extending credit to worthy customers and therefore to increase the firm's profits.

- If a firm **eases its credit policy,** its sales should increase. Actions which ease the credit policy include lengthening the credit period, relaxing credit standards and collection policy, and offering cash discounts. Each of these actions, however, increases costs. A firm should ease its credit policy only if the costs of doing so will be more than offset by higher sales revenues.

- **Inventory management** involves determining how much inventory to hold, when to place orders, and how many units to order at a time. Because the cost of holding inventory is high, inventory management is important.

- **Inventory** can be grouped into three categories: (1) raw materials, (2) work-in-process, and (3) finished goods.

- **Safety stocks** are held to avoid shortages (1) if demand becomes greater than expected or (2) if shipping delays are encountered.

- The **economic ordering quantity (EOQ) model** is a formula for determining the ordering quantity that will minimize total inventory costs:

$$EOQ = \sqrt{\frac{2(F)(S)}{(C)(P)}}.$$

Here F is the fixed cost per order, S is annual sales in units, C is the percentage cost of carrying inventory, and P is the purchase price per unit.

- **Reorder point** is the inventory level at which an order should be placed.

- **Goods in transit** are goods which have been ordered but have not been received.

- The **costs of running short of inventory** include lost sales and lost customer goodwill. These costs can be avoided by carrying **safety stocks.** The cost of carrying safety stocks is equal to the percentage cost of carrying inventories times the purchase price per unit times the number of units held as the safety stock. This cost is separate from those used in the EOQ model.

- Firms use inventory control systems, such as the **red-line method,** the **two-bin method,** and the **ABC method,** as well as **computerized inventory control systems,** to help them keep track of actual inventory levels and to insure that inventory levels are adjusted as sales change. *Electronic data interchange (EDI)* is a computerized inventory control system which helps the firm monitor its finished goods inventories. **Just-in-time (JIT)** systems are also used to hold down inventory costs and, simultaneously, to improve the production process. **Out-sourcing,** the practice of purchasing components rather than making them in-house, is often combined with JIT systems to reduce inventory levels.

EQUATIONS

The annual cost of carrying receivables is determined by multiplying the average amount of receivables by the variable cost percentage, which gives the dollars of capital invested in receivables, and then multiplying this amount by the cost of money used to carry receivables:

$$\begin{pmatrix} \text{Average} \\ \text{amount of} \\ \text{receivables} \end{pmatrix} \begin{pmatrix} \text{Variable} \\ \text{cost} \\ \text{ratio} \end{pmatrix} \begin{pmatrix} \text{Cost} \\ \text{of} \\ \text{funds} \end{pmatrix} = \begin{matrix} \text{Cost of} \\ \text{carrying} \\ \text{receivables} \end{matrix},$$

or

$$\text{(DSO)} \begin{pmatrix} \text{Sales} \\ \text{per} \\ \text{day} \end{pmatrix} \begin{pmatrix} \text{Variable} \\ \text{cost} \\ \text{ratio} \end{pmatrix} \begin{pmatrix} \text{Cost} \\ \text{of} \\ \text{funds} \end{pmatrix} = \begin{array}{l} \text{Cost of} \\ \text{carrying} \\ \text{receivables} \end{array} . \qquad \textbf{(10-1)}$$

The point at which the total inventory cost curve is minimized represents the economic ordering quantity (EOQ), which can be calculated as follows:

$$\text{EOQ} = \sqrt{\frac{2(F)(S)}{(C)(P)}} . \qquad \textbf{(10-2)}$$

The reorder point, or the inventory level at which an order should be placed, assuming there are no goods in transit, is calculated as follows:

$$\text{Reorder point} = \text{Lead time} \times \text{Usage rate.}$$

When there are goods in transit, the reorder point would be calculated as follows:

$$\text{Reorder point} = (\text{Lead time} \times \text{Usage rate}) - \text{Goods in transit.}$$

RESOLUTION TO DECISION IN FINANCE

The Data Are Available, but Should Companies Use Them?

A consumer advocate said, "When people find out what's going on, they are appalled." One such customer received a call urging her to switch to ITT for long-distance service. Responding that she doesn't make many out-of-town calls, she was told, "I'm surprised to hear you say that. I see from your phone records that you frequently call Newark, Delaware, and Stamford, Connecticut." The customer says, "I was shocked, scared, and paranoid. If people are able to find out who I call, what else could they find out about me?" In that case, ITT's only response was that they have very little control over the telemarketing companies who sell their services.

American Express took a different approach and salvaged an account in the process. A new customer paid his previous two months of charges in full and on time. Then, he was notified that his credit privileges were suspended, because American Express had looked at his bank records and found that there was not enough money in his checking account to pay his bill for the current month. "I felt violated," said the customer. "When I gave them my bank account number, I never thought they would use it routinely to look over my shoulder." American Express later apologized, and a spokesman said the company was wrong and should have asked permission before looking into the customer's bank balance. The customer paid his bill from his savings account, and his credit was restored.

Sources: "Is Nothing Private?" *Business Week*, September 4, 1989; "The Rising Tide of Privacy Laws," *American Demographics*, March 1990.

QUESTIONS

10-1   Is it true that when one firm sells to another on credit, the seller records the transaction as an account receivable while the buyer records it as an account payable and that, disregarding discounts, the receivable typically exceeds the payable by the amount of profit on the sale?

10-2   What are the four elements in a firm's credit policy? To what extent can firms set their own credit policies as opposed to having to accept credit policies that are dictated by "the competition"?

10-3   Suppose that a firm makes a purchase and receives the shipment on February 1. The credit terms as stated on the invoice read, "2/10, net 40, May 1 dating." What is the latest date on which payment can be made and the discount still be taken? What is the date on which payment must be made if the discount is not taken?

10-4   **a.** What is the days sales outstanding (DSO) for a firm whose sales are $2,880,000 per year and whose accounts receivable are $312,000? (Use 360 days per year.)
   b. Is it true that if this firm sells on terms of 3/10, net 40, its customers probably all pay on time?

10-5   Is it true that if a firm calculates its days sales outstanding (DSO), it has no need for an aging schedule?

10-6   Firm A had no credit losses last year, but 1 percent of Firm B's accounts receivable proved to be uncollectible and resulted in losses. Should Firm B fire its credit manager and hire A's?

10-7   Indicate by a (+), (−), or (0) whether each of the following events would probably cause accounts receivable (A/R), sales, and profits to increase, decrease, or be affected in an indeterminate manner:

	A/R	Sales	Profits
a. The firm tightens its credit standards.	___	___	___
b. The credit terms are changed from 2/10, net 30, to 3/10, net 30.	___	___	___
c. The credit terms are changed from 2/10, net 30, to 3/10, net 40.	___	___	___
d. The firm's major competitor changes its credit policy from 2/10, net 30 to 2/10, net 60.	___	___	___
e. The credit manager gets tough with past-due accounts.	___	___	___

10-8   If a firm calculates its optimal inventory of widgets to be 1,000 units when the general rate of inflation is 2 percent, is it true that the optimal inventory (in units) will almost certainly rise if the general rate of inflation climbs to 10 percent?

10-9   Indicate by a (+), (−), or (0) whether each of the following events would probably cause average annual inventories (the sum of the inventories held at the end of each month of the year divided by 12) to rise, fall, or be affected in an indeterminate manner:
   a. The firm's suppliers switch from delivering by train to air freight.   ___
   b. The firm changes from producing just in time to meet seasonal sales to steady year-round production. (Sales peak at Christmas.)   ___
   c. Competition in the markets in which the firm sells increases.   ___
   d. The rate of general inflation increases.   ___
   e. Interest rates rise; other things are constant.   ___

10-10   A firm can reduce its investment in inventory by having its suppliers hold raw materials inventories and its customers hold finished goods inventories. Explain actions a firm can take which would result in larger inventories for its suppliers and customers and smaller inventories for itself. What are the limitations of such actions?

10-11   The toy business is subject to large seasonal demand fluctuations. What effect would such fluctuations have on inventory decisions of toy manufacturers and toy retailers?

SELF-TEST PROBLEMS

ST-1   The Carson Company expects to have sales of $10 million this year under its current operating policies. Its variable costs as a percentage of sales are 80 percent, and its cost of capital is 16 percent. Currently Carson's credit policy is net 25 (no discount for early payment). However, its DSO is 30 days, and its bad debt loss percentage is 2 percent. Carson spends $50,000 per year to collect bad debts, and its effective federal-plus-state tax rate is 40 percent.

The credit manager is considering two alternative proposals (given next) for changing Carson's credit policy. Find the expected change in net income, taking into consideration anticipated changes in carrying costs for accounts receivable, the probable bad debt losses, and the discounts likely to be taken, for each proposal. Should a change in credit policy be made?

Proposal 1: Lengthen the credit period by going from net 25 to net 30. The bad debt collection expenditures will remain constant. Under this proposal, sales are expected to increase by $1 million annually, and the bad debt loss percentage on *new* sales is expected to rise to 4 percent (the loss percentage on old sales should not change). In addition, the DSO is expected to increase from 30 to 45 days on all sales.

Proposal 2: Shorten the credit period by going from net 25 to net 20. Again, collection expenses will remain constant. The anticipated effects of this change are (1) a decrease in sales of $1 million per year, (2) a decline in the DSO from 30 to 22 days, and (3) a decline in the bad debt loss percentage to 1 percent on all sales.

ST-2   The Mrs. Morris Bread Company buys and then sells (as bread) 2.6 million bushels of wheat annually. The wheat must be purchased in multiples of 2,000 bushels. Ordering costs, which include grain elevator removal charges of $3,500, are $5,000 per order. Annual carrying costs are 2 percent of the purchase price of $5 per bushel. The company maintains a safety stock of 200,000 bushels. The delivery time is 6 weeks.

   a. What is the EOQ?

   b. At what inventory level should an order be placed to prevent having to draw on the safety stock?

   c. What are the total inventory costs?

   d. The wheat processor agrees to pay the elevator removal charges if Mrs. Morris Bread Company will purchase wheat in quantities of 650,000 bushels. Would it be to Mrs. Morris Bread Company's advantage to order under this alternative?

PROBLEMS

10-1   **Receivables investment.** Alan Waters, the new credit manager for Associates International, is studying the firm's credit accounts. The company sells all its products on credit terms of 2/10, net 30. Waters's predecessor told him that the company's DSO is 40 days and that 60 percent of the customers take the discount. What is the DSO for the firm's customers who elect not to take the discount?

10-2   **Receivables investment.** Brannigan, Inc., sells on terms of 2/10, net 30. Total sales for the year are $720,000. Forty percent of Brannigan's customers pay on the tenth day and take the discount; the other 60 percent pay, on average, 45 days after their purchases.

   a. What is the days sales outstanding (DSO)?

   b. What is the average amount of receivables?

   c. What would happen to the average receivables if Brannigan toughened up on its collection policy with the result that all nondiscount customers paid on Day 30?

10-3   **Toughening credit terms.** The Welch Corporation with annual sales of $9 million, sells on terms of 2/10, net 30. Currently 45 percent of its customers pay on the tenth day and take discounts; the other 55 percent pay, on average, 40 days after their purchases. Welch plans to toughen its credit policy so that all nondiscount customers will pay on Day 30.

   a. What is the days sales outstanding both before and after the change?

   b. What is the average investment in receivables both before and after the change?

10-4   **Easing credit terms.** Ezzell Electronics, Inc., is considering changing its credit terms from 2/15, net 30, to 3/10, net 30, to speed collections. At present, 50 percent of Ezzell's customers who pay take the 2 percent discount. Under the new terms, discount customers are expected to rise to 60 percent. Regardless of the credit terms, half of the customers who do not take the discount are expected to pay on time, while the remainder will pay 10 days late. The change does not involve a relaxation of credit standards; therefore, bad debt losses are not expected to rise above their present 2 percent level. However, the more generous cash discount terms are expected to increase sales from $2 million to $2.6 million per year. Ezzell's variable cost ratio is 70 percent, its cost of capital invested in accounts receivable is 10 percent, and its average tax rate is 40 percent.

   a. What is the days sales outstanding before and after the change?

   b. Calculate the discount costs before and after the change.

   c. Calculate the dollar cost of carrying receivables before and after the change.

   d. Calculate the bad debt losses before and after the change.

   e. What is the incremental profit from the change in credit terms? Should Ezzell change its credit terms?

10-5   **Credit analysis.** University Supply makes all sales on a credit basis, selling on terms of 2/10, net 30. Once a year it evaluates the creditworthiness of all its customers. The evaluation procedure ranks customers from 1 to 5, with 1 indicating the "best" customers. Results of the ranking are as follows:

Customer Category	Percentage of Bad Debts	DSO	Credit Decision	Annual Sales Lost Due to Credit Restrictions
1	None	10	Unlimited credit	None
2	1.0	12	Unlimited credit	None
3	3.0	20	Limited credit	$365,000
4	9.0	60	Limited credit	$182,500
5	16.0	90	Limited credit	$230,000

The variable cost ratio is 75 percent, and its average tax rate is 40 percent. The cost of capital invested in receivables is 15 percent. What would be the effect on profitability of extending unlimited credit to each of the Categories 3, 4, and 5? (*Hint:* Determine separately the effect on the income statement of changing each policy. In other words, find the change in sales, change in production costs, change in receivables and the cost of carrying receivables, change in bad debt costs, and so forth, down to the change in net income. Assume that none of the customers in these three categories will take the discount.)

10-6   **Tightening credit terms.** Kate Brown, the new credit manager of the Loden Corporation, was alarmed to find that Loden sells on credit terms of net 60 days even though industry-wide credit terms have recently been lowered to net 30 days. On annual credit sales of $2.5 million, Loden currently averages 70 days' sales in accounts receivable. Brown estimates that tightening the credit terms to 30 days would reduce annual sales to $2.2 million, but accounts receivable would drop to 35 days of sales, and the savings on investment in receivables should more than overcome any loss in profit. Loden's variable cost ratio is 85 percent, and its average tax rate is 40 percent. If Loden's cost of funds invested in receivables is 18 percent, should the change in credit terms be made?

10-7   **Relaxing collection efforts.** The Zocco Corporation has annual credit sales of $5 million. Current expenses for the collection department are $100,000, bad debt losses are 3 percent of sales, and the days sales outstanding is 32 days. Zocco is considering easing its collection efforts so that collection expenses will be reduced to $75,000 per year. The change is expected to increase bad debt losses to 4 percent as well as to increase the days sales outstanding to 48 days. However, sales should increase to $5.4 million per year.

Zocco's opportunity cost of funds is 12 percent, its variable cost ratio is 80 percent, and its average tax rate is 40 percent.

a. Should Zocco relax its collection efforts?

(Do Parts b and c only if you are using the computerized problem diskette.)

b. Would the change in collection efforts be profitable if sales rose only to $5.32 million?

c. What would be Zocco's loss if it relaxed its collection efforts and sales remained at $5 million?

10-8   **Economic ordering quantity.** Buccaneer Hardware expects to sell 6,000 pounds of nails this year. Ordering costs are $30 per order, and carrying costs are $1 per pound.

a. What is the economic ordering quantity (EOQ)?

b. How many orders will be placed this year?

c. What is the average inventory under this plan, expressed in pounds?

10-9   **Inventory cost.** Compuware, Inc., must order diskettes from its supplier in lots of one dozen boxes. Given the following information, complete the table below and determine the economic ordering quantity for diskettes for Compuware.

Annual demand: 2,800 dozen
Cost per order placed: $5.25
Carrying cost: 20%
Price per dozen: $30

Order size (dozens)	35	56	70	140	200	2,800
Number of orders	——	——	——	——	——	——
Average inventory	——	——	——	——	——	——
Carrying cost	——	——	——	——	——	——
Ordering cost	——	——	——	——	——	——
Total cost	——	——	——	——	——	——

(*Hint*: Calculate carrying cost as (C)(P)(Average inventory) and calculate ordering cost as Ordering cost × Number of orders.)

10-10 **Economic ordering quantity.** Greenery Garden Centers, Inc., sells 176,400 bags of lawn fertilizer annually. The optimal safety stock (which is on hand initially) is 1,000 bags. Each bag costs Greenery $2, inventory carrying costs are 20 percent, and the cost of placing an order with its supplier is $20.

a. What is the economic ordering quantity (EOQ)?

b. What is the maximum inventory of fertilizer in both quantity and dollar value?

c. What will Greenery's average inventory be in both quantity and dollar value?

d. How often must the company order?

10-11 **Ordering discounts.** Suppose that Rich and Creamy, Inc., purchases 100,000 boxes of ice cream cones every year. Order costs are $200 per order and carrying costs are $0.40 per box. Moreover, management has determined that the EOQ is 10,000 boxes. The vendor now offers a quantity discount of $0.02 per box if the company buys cones in order sizes of 20,000 boxes. Determine the before-tax benefit or loss of accepting the quantity discount for Rich and Creamy. (Assume the carrying cost remains at $0.40 per box whether or not the discount is taken.)

10-12 **Ordering discounts.** Robinson Recreational Center (RRC) purchases 25,000 gallons of distilled water each year. Ordering costs are $20 per order, and the carrying cost, as a percentage of inventory value, is 80 percent. The purchase price to RRC is $0.20 per gallon. Management currently orders the EOQ each time an order is placed. No safety stock is carried. The supplier is now offering a quantity discount of $0.01 per gallon if RRC orders 4,000 gallons at a time. Should RRC take the discount?

10-13 **EOQ and ordering discounts.** Playtime Toys, a large manufacturer of toys and dolls, uses large quantities of flesh-colored cloth in its doll production process. Throughout the year, the firm uses 1,080,000 square yards of this cloth. The fixed costs of placing and receiving an order are $1,500, including a $1,125 set-up charge at the mill. The price of the cloth is $2.00 per square yard, and the annual cost of carrying this inventory item is 20 percent of the price. Playtime maintains 10,000 square yards of safety stock. The cloth supplier requires a 2-week lead time from order to delivery.

a. What is the EOQ for this cloth?

b. What is the average inventory dollar value, including the safety stock?

c. What is the total cost of ordering and carrying the inventory, including the safety stock? (Assume that the safety stock is on hand at the beginning of the year.)

d. Using a 52-week year, at what inventory unit level should an order be placed? (Again, assume the 10,000 unit safety stock is already on hand.)

e. Suppose the cloth supplier offers to lower the fixed cost to $1,000 if Playtime will increase its order size from 90,000 to 150,000 square yards. Would it be to Playtime's advantage to order under this alternative?

f. Now, suppose the cloth supplier offers to lower the fixed cost to $1,200 if Playtime will order 125,000 yards at a time. Should Playtime accept this alternative?

10-14 **Changes in the EOQ.** The following relationships for inventory costs have been established for the Hill Corporation:
1. Annual sales are 735,000 units.
2. The purchase price per unit is $1.00.
3. The carrying cost is 15 percent of the purchase price of goods.
4. The cost per order placed is $45.
5. Desired safety stock is 7,000 units (on hand initially).
6. One week is required for delivery.

a. What is the most economically feasible order quantity? (Round to hundreds.) What is the total cost of ordering and carrying inventories at the EOQ?
b. What is the optimal number of orders to be placed?
c. At what inventory level should Hill order?
d. If annual unit sales double, what is the percentage increase in the EOQ? What is the elasticity of EOQ with respect to sales (Percentage change in EOQ/Percentage change in sales)?
e. If the cost per order doubles, what is the elasticity of EOQ with respect to cost per order?
f. If the carrying cost declines by 50 percent, what is the elasticity of EOQ with respect to that change?
g. If purchase price declines by 50 percent, what is the elasticity of EOQ with respect to that change?

SOLUTIONS TO SELF-TEST PROBLEMS

ST-1 Under the current credit policy, the Carson Company has no discounts, has collection expenses of $50,000, has bad debt losses of $(0.02)($10,000,000) = $200,000$, and has average accounts receivable of (DSO)(Average sales per day) = $(30)($10,000,000/360) = $833,333$. The firm's cost of carrying these receivables is (Variable cost ratio) (A/R) (Cost of capital) = $(0.80)($833,333)(0.16) = $106,667$. It is necessary to multiply by the variable cost ratio because the actual *investment* in receivables is less than the dollar amount of the receivables.

Proposal 1: Lengthen the credit period to net 30 so that
1. Sales increase by $1 million.
2. Discounts = $0.
3. Bad debt losses = $(0.02)($10,000,000) + (0.04)($1,000,000)$

$$= $200,000 + $40,000$$

$$= $240,000.$$

4. DSO = 45 days on all sales.
5. New average receivables = $(45)($11,000,000/360) = $1,375,000$.
6. Cost of carrying receivables = (v)(k)(Average accounts receivable)

$$= (0.80)(0.16)($1,375,000)$$

$$= $176,000.$$

7. Collection expenses = $50,000.

Analysis of proposed change:

	Income Statement under Current Policy	Effect of Change	Income Statement under New Policy
Gross sales	$10,000,000	+ $1,000,000	$11,000,000
Less: Discounts	0	+ 0	0
Net sales	$10,000,000	+ $1,000,000	$11,000,000
Production costs (80%)	8,000,000	+ 800,000	8,800,000
Profits before credit costs and taxes	$ 2,000,000	+ $ 200,000	$ 2,200,000
Credit-related costs:			
Cost of carrying receivables	106,667	+ 69,333	176,000
Collection expenses	50,000	+ 0	50,000
Bad debt losses	200,000	+ 40,000	240,000
Profit before taxes	$ 1,643,333	+ $ 90,667	$ 1,734,000
Taxes (40%)	657,333	+ 36,267	693,600
Net income	$ 986,000	+ $ 54,400	$ 1,040,400

The proposed change appears to be a good one, assuming the assumptions are correct. We emphasize *appears* because management may deem that the projected increase may not be sufficient to justify the change, considering the uncertainties involved in the numbers used to prepare the analysis.

Proposal 2: Shorten the credit period to net 20 so that:

1. Sales decrease by $1 million.
2. Discount = $0.
3. Bad debt losses = $(0.01)($9,000,000) = $90,000$.
4. DSO = 22 days.
5. New average receivables = $(22)($9,000,000/360) = $550,000$.
6. Cost of carrying receivables = (v)(k)(Average accounts receivable)

$$= (0.80)(0.16)($550,000)$$

$$= $70,400.$$

7. Collection expenses = $50,000.

Analysis of proposed change:

	Income Statement under Current Policy	Effect of Change	Income Statement under New Policy
Gross sales	$10,000,000	− $1,000,000	$9,000,000
Less: Discounts	0	0	0
Net sales	$10,000,000	− $1,000,000	$9,000,000
Production costs (80%)	8,000,000	− 800,000	7,200,000
Profits before credit costs and taxes	$ 2,000,000	− $ 200,000	$1,800,000
Credit-related costs:			
Cost of carrying receivables	106,667	− 36,267	70,400
Collection expenses	50,000	0	50,000
Bad debt losses	200,000	− 110,000	90,000
Profit before taxes	$ 1,643,333	− $ 53,733	$1,589,600
Taxes (40%)	657,333	− 21,493	635,840
Net income	$ 986,000	− $ 32,240	$ 953,760

This change reduces net income, so it should be rejected. Carson will increase profits by accepting Proposal 1 to lengthen the credit period from 25 days to 30 days, *assuming all assumptions are correct.* This may or may not be the *optimal,* or profit-maximizing, credit policy, but it does appear to be a movement in the right direction.

ST-2   **a.**

$$EOQ = \sqrt{\frac{2(F)(S)}{(C)(P)}}$$

$$= \sqrt{\frac{(2)(\$5,000)(2,600,000)}{(0.02)(\$5.00)}}$$

$$= 509,902 \text{ bushels.}$$

Since the firm must order in multiples of 2,000 bushels, it should order in quantities of 510,000 bushels.

b.

$$\text{Average weekly sales} = 2,600,000/52$$

$$= 50,000 \text{ bushels.}$$

$$\text{Reorder point} = 6 \text{ weeks' sales} + \text{Safety stock}$$

$$= 6(50,000) + 200,000$$

$$= 300,000 + 200,000$$

$$= 500,000 \text{ bushels.}$$

c. Total inventory costs = Ordering costs + Carrying costs.

(*Note:* Ordering costs do not apply to safety stock.)

$$\frac{\text{Ordering}}{\text{costs}} = \left(\begin{array}{c}\text{Number of} \\ \text{orders}\end{array}\right)\left(\begin{array}{c}\text{Fixed order} \\ \text{cost}\end{array}\right)$$

$$= \left(\frac{2,600,000}{510,000}\right)\left(\$5,000\right)$$

$$= \$25,490.20.$$

Carrying costs apply to EOQ + Safety stock.

$$\frac{\text{Carrying}}{\text{costs}} = (\text{Average inventory})(C)(P)$$

$$= \left(\frac{510,000}{2} + 200,000\right)(0.02)(\$5)$$

$$= \$45,500.00.$$

$$\frac{\text{Total inventory}}{\text{costs}} = \$25,490.20 + \$45,500.00$$

$$= \$70,990.20.$$

d. Ordering costs would be reduced to $1,500. By ordering 650,000 bushels at a time, Mrs. Morris Bread Company can lower its total inventory costs.

$$\begin{aligned}
\frac{\text{Ordering}}{\text{costs}} &= \left(\begin{array}{c}\text{Number of}\\\text{orders}\end{array}\right)\left(\begin{array}{c}\text{Fixed order}\\\text{cost}\end{array}\right) \\[2mm]
&= \left(\frac{2,600,000}{650,000}\right)\left(\$1,500\right) \\[2mm]
&= \$6,000.
\end{aligned}$$

$$\begin{aligned}
\frac{\text{Carrying}}{\text{costs}} &= \left(\frac{650,000}{2} + 200,000\right)(0.02)(\$5) \\[2mm]
&= \$52,500.
\end{aligned}$$

$$\frac{\text{Total inventory}}{\text{costs}} = \$6,000 + \$52,500 = \$58,500.$$

Since the firm can reduce its total inventory costs by ordering 650,000 bushels at a time, it should accept the offer and place larger orders. (Incidentally, this same type of analysis is used to consider any quantity discount offer.)

Chapter 11

Financing Current Assets: Short-Term Credit

DECISION IN FINANCE

A Bank That Looks at More than Numbers

In the mid-1970s, the Northwestern National Bank of St. Paul, Minnesota, decided on a new commercial lending policy: it would lend to promising companies early, hoping thereby to develop loyal customers. Of course, even the most conservative banks want to attract new customers with great potential. But Northwestern was determined to do more than most banks: it would aggressively pursue new business, and when it found a company it believed in, it would bend traditional banking rules to sign up the company and keep it happy.

"Once a company becomes profitable and all the financial ratios are in place, then every bank

in the country wants them," says Dennis McChesney, Northwestern's senior vice president. "We try to distinguish ourselves by being aggressive and getting them early." As a result of its willingness to work with smaller and younger companies, Northwestern has gained a reputation among financial professionals as a maverick lender, willing to take risks that other banks would find unacceptable.

As you read this chapter, look for steps that Northwestern could take to attract and hold business from promising young companies. Do you agree with the bank's decision to pursue such business? Why don't more banks follow such a policy?

See end of chapter for resolution.

As we noted in Chapter 8, working capital management involves decisions relating to current assets, including decisions about how these assets are to be financed. Any statement about the flexibility, cost, and riskiness of short-term versus long-term credit depends to a large extent on the nature of the short-term credit that actually is used. The choice of the short-term credit instrument will affect both the firm's riskiness and its expected rate of return, and, hence, the market value of its stock. This chapter examines the sources and characteristics of the major types of short-term credit available to the firm. Special attention is given to the primary financial institution that specializes in short-term business loans — the commercial bank.

Short-term credit is defined as any liability originally scheduled for payment within one year. The four major sources of short-term credit are (1) accruals such as accrued wages and taxes, (2) trade credit among firms (accounts payable), (3) loans from commercial banks and finance companies, and (4) commercial paper.

ACCRUED WAGES AND TAXES

Because firms generally pay employees on a weekly, biweekly, or monthly basis, the balance sheet typically will show some accrued wages. Similarly, because the firm's own estimated income taxes, sales taxes collected, and payroll taxes are usually paid on a weekly, monthly, or quarterly basis, the balance sheet will show some accrued taxes along with accrued wages.

accruals
Continually recurring short-term liabilities, especially accrued wages and accrued taxes.

As we saw in Chapter 7, **accruals** increase automatically as a firm's operations expand, and this type of debt is "free" in the sense that no explicit interest is paid on funds raised through accruals. However, a firm cannot ordinarily control its accruals: the timing of wage payments is set by economic forces and industry custom, while tax payment dates are established by law. Thus, firms use all the accruals they can, but they have little control over the level of these accounts.

Self-Test

Define short-term credit.

What are the four major sources of short-term credit?

Why are accruals considered "free" debt?

ACCOUNTS PAYABLE, OR TRADE CREDIT

trade credit
Inter-firm debt arising from credit sales and recorded as an account receivable by the seller and as an account payable by the buyer.

Firms generally make purchases from other firms on credit, recording the debt as an *account payable*. Accounts payable, or **trade credit,** as it is commonly called, is the largest single category of short-term debt, representing about 40 percent of the current liabilities of the average nonfinancial corporation. This percentage is somewhat larger for smaller firms; because small companies often do not qualify for financing from other sources, they rely rather heavily on trade credit.[1]

Trade credit, like accruals, is a spontaneous source of financing in the sense that it arises from ordinary business transactions. For example, suppose a firm makes average purchases of $2,000 a day on terms of net 30, meaning that it must pay for goods 30 days after the invoice date. On average, it will owe 30 times $2,000, or $60,000, to its suppliers. If its sales, and consequently its purchases, doubled, its accounts payable would also double, to $120,000. Simply by growing, the firm would have *spontaneously* generated an additional $60,000 of financing. Similarly, if the terms of credit were extended from 30 to 40 days, its accounts payable would expand from $60,000 to $80,000. Therefore, lengthening the credit period, as well as expanding sales and purchases, generates additional financing.

The Cost of Trade Credit

As we saw in Chapter 10 in connection with accounts receivable management, firms that sell on credit have a *credit policy* that includes setting *credit terms*. For example, the McCue Company's textile products division sells on terms of 2/10, net 30, meaning that a 2 percent discount is given if payment is made within 10 days of the invoice date, but the full invoice amount is due and payable within 30 days if the discount is not taken.

Suppose Fall Mills, Inc., buys an average of $12 million of materials from McCue each year, minus a 2 percent discount, for net purchases of $11,760,000/360 = $32,666.67 per day. For simplicity, suppose McCue is Fall Mills's only supplier. If Fall Mills takes the discount, paying at the end of the tenth day, its payables will average (10)($32,666.67) = $326,667. Fall Mills will, on average, be receiving $326,667 of credit from its only supplier, the McCue Company.

Now suppose Fall Mills decides *not* to take the discount. What will happen? First, Fall Mills will begin paying invoices after 30 days, so its accounts payable will increase to (30)($32,666.67) = $980,000.[2] McCue will now be supplying Fall Mills with an *additional* $980,000 − $326,667 = $653,333 of credit. Fall Mills could use this additional credit to pay off bank loans, to ex-

---

[1] In a credit sale, the seller records the transaction as an account receivable, and the buyer records it as an account payable. We examined accounts receivable as an asset investment in Chapter 10. Our focus in this chapter is on accounts payable, a liability item. We may also note that if a firm's accounts payable exceed its accounts receivable, it is said to be *receiving net trade credit*, whereas if its accounts receivable exceed its accounts payable, it is *extending net trade credit*. Smaller firms frequently receive net credit; larger firms extend it.

[2] A question arises here: If a company does not plan to take discounts, should its accounts payable account reflect gross purchases or should it reflect purchases net of discounts? Although generally accepted accounting practices permit either treatment, most accountants prefer to record both inventories and payables net of discounts and then to report the higher payments that result from not taking discounts as an additional expense, called "discounts lost." Thus, *we show accounts payable net of discounts even when the company does not expect to take the discount.*

pand inventories, to increase fixed assets, to build up its cash account, or even to increase its own accounts receivable.

Fall Mills's new credit from the McCue Company has a cost — because Fall Mills is forgoing a 2 percent discount on its $12 million of gross purchases, its costs will rise by $240,000 per year. Dividing this $240,000 by the additional credit, we find the implicit percentage cost of the added trade credit as follows:

$$\text{Percentage cost} = \frac{\$240,000}{\$653,333} = 36.7\%.$$

Assuming that Fall Mills can borrow from its bank (or from other sources) at an interest rate of less than 36.7 percent, *it should not expand its payables by forgoing discounts.*

The following equation may be used to calculate the approximate percentage cost, on an annual basis, of not taking discounts:

$$\begin{matrix}\text{Approximate} \\ \text{percentage} \\ \text{cost}\end{matrix} = \frac{\text{Discount percent}}{100 - \left(\begin{matrix}\text{Discount} \\ \text{percent}\end{matrix}\right)} \times \frac{360}{\left(\begin{matrix}\text{Days credit} \\ \text{is} \\ \text{outstanding}\end{matrix}\right) - \left(\begin{matrix}\text{Discount} \\ \text{period}\end{matrix}\right)}. \qquad \textbf{(11-1)}$$

The numerator of the first term, discount percent, is the cost per dollar of credit, while the denominator (100 − Discount percent) represents the funds made available by not taking the discount. The second term shows how many times each year this cost is incurred. To illustrate the equation, the approximate cost of not taking a discount when the terms are 2/10, net 30, is computed as follows:[3]

$$\text{Cost} = \frac{2}{98} \times \frac{360}{20} = 0.0204 \times 18 = 0.367 = 36.7\%.$$

The calculated cost can be reduced by paying late. Thus, if Fall Mills pays in 60 days rather than in the specified 30, the effective credit period becomes 60 − 10 = 50 days, and the calculated cost becomes

---

[3]Equation 11-1 may be adequately (for most purposes) approximated as follows:

1. Divide the number of days in the year (360) by the difference in days between the end of the discount period and the date of payment.
2. Multiply this quotient by the forgone discount percentage.

Using the preceding illustration, there are 360/(30 − 10) = 18 20-day periods in a year. Therefore, (18)(0.02) = 36 percent is the approximate cost of forgoing the discount. However, if the payment date is delayed until the 60th day, 60 − 10 = 50 days, which is the difference between the discount period and the payment date. Then 360/50 = 7.2, and (7.2) (0.02) = 14.4 percent — a close approximation of the 14.7 percent that would be determined from Equation 11-1.

Of course, both of these methods used to determine the cost of not taking advantage of the discount are approximations of the "true" or compound interest rate to be discussed in Chapter 13. As such, Equation 11-1 and its approximation, detailed in this note, may understate the cost of trade credit in a compound interest sense.

$$\text{Cost} = \frac{2}{98} \times \frac{360}{50} = 0.0204 \times 7.2 = 0.147 = 14.7\%.$$

If their suppliers have excess capacity, firms may be able to get away with late payments, but this is an unethical practice, and it will lead to a variety of problems associated with **stretching accounts payable** and being labeled a "slow payer" account. These problems are discussed later in the chapter.

stretching accounts payable
The practice of deliberately paying accounts payable late.

The cost of the additional trade credit obtained by not taking discounts can be worked out for other purchase terms. Some illustrative costs are as follows:

Credit Terms	Cost of Additional Credit if Cash Discount Not Taken
1/10, net 20	36%
1/10, net 30	18
2/10, net 20	73
3/15, net 45	37

As these figures show, the cost of not taking discounts can be substantial. Incidentally, throughout the chapter we assume that payments are made either on the *last day* for taking discounts or on the *last day* of the credit period. It would be foolish to pay, say, on the fifth day or on the twentieth day if the credit terms were 2/10, net 30.

Effects of Trade Credit on the Financial Statements

A firm's policy with regard to taking or not taking discounts can have a significant effect on its financial statements. To illustrate, let us assume that Fall Mills is just beginning its operations. On the first day, it makes net purchases of $32,666.67. This amount is recorded on the balance sheet under accounts payable.[4] The second day it buys another $32,666.67 of goods. The first day's purchases are not yet paid for, so at the end of the second day, accounts payable total $65,333.34. Accounts payable increase by another $32,666.67 on the third day, for a total of $98,000, and after 10 days, accounts payable are up to $326,666.70.

If Fall Mills takes discounts, on the eleventh day it will have to pay for the $32,666.67 of purchases made on the first day, which will reduce accounts payable. However, it will buy another $32,666.67 of goods, which will increase payables. Thus, after the tenth day of operations, Fall Mills's balance sheet will level off, showing a balance of $326,666.70 in accounts payable, assuming the company pays on the tenth day in order to take discounts.

Now suppose Fall Mills decides not to take discounts. In this case, on the eleventh day it will add another $32,666.67 to payables, but it will not pay for

---

[4]Of course, when the financing side of the balance sheet increases, the asset side must also increase by an equal amount for the balance sheet to balance. In this case inventories will also increase by $32,666.67 daily.

Table 11-1 **Fall Mills's Balance Sheet with Different Trade Credit Policies**

A. Do Not Take Discounts; Use Maximum Trade Credit

Cash	$ 500,000	Accounts payable	$ 980,000
Accounts receivable	1,000,000	Notes payable	0
Inventories	2,000,000	Accruals	500,000
Fixed assets	2,980,000	Common equity	5,000,000
	$6,480,000		$6,480,000

B. Take Discounts; Borrow from Bank

Cash	$ 500,000	Accounts payable	$ 326,667
Accounts receivable	1,000,000	Notes payable (10%)	653,333
Inventories	2,000,000	Accruals	500,000
Fixed assets	2,980,000	Common equity	5,000,000
	$6,480,000		$6,480,000

the purchases made on the first day. Thus, the balance sheet figure for accounts payable will rise to $11 \times \$32,666.67 = \$359,333.37$. This buildup will continue through the thirtieth day, at which point payables will total $30 \times \$32,666.67 = \$980,000$. On the thirty-first day, it will buy another $32,666.67 of goods, which will increase accounts payable; but it will also pay for the purchases made on the first day, which will reduce payables. Thus, the balance sheet item "accounts payable" will stabilize at $980,000 after 30 days, assuming Fall Mills does not take discounts.

Table 11-1 shows Fall Mills's balance sheet, after it reaches a steady state, under the two trade credit policies. Total assets are unchanged by this policy decision, and we also assume that accruals and common equity are unchanged. The differences show up in accounts payable and notes payable. When Fall Mills elected to take discounts and thus gave up some of the trade credit it otherwise could have obtained, it had to raise $653,333 from some other source. It could have sold more common stock, or it could have used long-term bonds, but it chose to use bank credit, which has a 10 percent cost and is reflected in notes payable.

Table 11-2 shows Fall Mills's income statement under the two policies. If the company does not take discounts, its interest expense will be zero, but it will have a $240,000 expense for "discounts lost." On the other hand, if it does take discounts, it will incur an interest expense of $65,333, but it will avoid the cost of discounts lost. Because the cost of discounts lost would exceed the interest expense, the take-discounts policy would result in the higher net income and thus in a higher stock price.

Components of Trade Credit: Free versus Costly

Based on the preceding discussion, trade credit can be divided into two components:

**Table 11-2 Fall Mills's Income Statement with
Different Trade Credit Policies**

	Do Not Take Discounts	Take Discounts
Sales	$15,000,000	$15,000,000
Purchases	11,760,000	11,760,000
Labor and other costs	2,000,000	2,000,000
Interest	0	65,333
Discounts lost	240,000	0
Total costs	$14,000,000	$13,825,333
Earnings before taxes	1,000,000	1,174,667
Tax (40%)	400,000	469,867
Net income	$ 600,000	$ 704,800

1. Free trade credit, which involves credit received during the discount period. For Fall Mills, this amounts to ten days of net purchases, or $326,667.[5]

2. Costly trade credit, which involves credit in excess of the free credit. This credit has an implicit cost equal to the forgone discounts. Fall Mills could obtain $653,333, or 20 days' net purchases, of nonfree trade credit at a cost of approximately 37 percent.

Financial managers should always use the free component, but they should use the costly component only after analyzing the cost of this capital and determining that it is less than the costs of funds obtained from other sources. Under the terms of trade found in most industries, the costly component involves a relatively high percentage cost, so stronger firms with access to bank credit should generally use only the free component of trade credit.

It is important to note that some firms will occasionally deviate from the stated credit terms, thus altering the percentage cost figures cited previously. To illustrate, a California manufacturing firm that buys on terms of 2/10, net 30, makes a practice of paying in 15 days (rather than 10), but it still takes discounts. Its treasurer simply waits until 15 days after receipt of the goods to pay, then writes a check for the invoiced amount less the 2 percent discount. The company's suppliers want its business, so they tolerate this practice. Simi-

free trade credit
Credit received during the discount period.

costly trade credit
Credit taken in excess of free trade credit, thereby necessitating a forfeit of the discount offered.

---

[5]Accounts payable where no discount is offered, for example, where the purchase terms are net 30, is also regarded as "free." Actually, there is some question as to whether any credit is really "free," because the supplier will have a cost of carrying receivables, which must be passed on to the customer in the form of higher prices. Still, where suppliers sell on standard terms such as 2/10, net 30, and where the base price cannot be negotiated downward for early payment, for all intents and purposes the 10 days of trade credit is indeed free.

larly, a Wisconsin firm that also buys on terms of 2/10, net 30, does not take discounts, but it pays in 60 rather than in 30 days, thus "stretching" its trade credit. As we noted earlier, both practices reduce the cost of trade credit. However, neither of these firms is "loved" by its suppliers, and neither could continue these practices in times when suppliers were operating at full capacity and had order backlogs. Indeed, both firms have bad reputations in their industries, and both will have a hard time getting deliveries when their suppliers are operating at full capacity. However, these practices can and do reduce the nominal costs of trade credit during times when suppliers have excess capacity.

Self-Test

Give the equation used to calculate the approximate percentage cost, on an annual basis, of not taking discounts.

Briefly explain the difference between "free" and "costly" trade credit.

SHORT-TERM BANK LOANS

Commercial banks, whose loans generally appear on firms' balance sheets as notes payable, are second in importance to trade credit as a source of short-term financing. However, banks' influence is actually greater than it appears from the dollar amounts they lend, because banks provide *nonspontaneous* funds. As a firm's financing needs increase, it requests its bank to provide the additional funds. If the request is denied, often the firm is forced to abandon attractive growth opportunities. In this section we discuss factors that influence the choice of a bank, how to approach a bank for a business loan, and some features of bank loans.

Choosing a Bank

Individuals whose only contact with their bank is through the use of its checking services generally choose a bank for the convenience of its location and the competitive cost of its services. Businesses that borrow from banks must look at other criteria, however, and potential borrowers seeking banking relations should recognize that important differences exist among banks. Some of these differences include the following:

1. Banks often have different basic *policies toward risk*. Some banks follow relatively conservative lending practices, while others engage in what are properly termed "creative banking practices." These policies reflect both the personalities of the banks' officers and the characteristics of the banks' deposit liabilities. Thus, a bank with fluctuating deposit liabilities in a static community should be a conservative lender, whereas a bank whose deposits are growing with little interruption can more safely follow liberal credit policies. A large bank with broad diversification over geographic regions or among industries served can obtain the benefit of combining and averaging risks. Thus, specialized marginal credit risks that might be unacceptable to a small, specialized bank can be pooled by a branch banking system to reduce the overall risk of a group of marginal accounts.

2. Some bank loan officers are active in providing *advice and counsel*, and in making developmental loans to firms in their early and formative years. Certain banks have specialized departments which make loans to firms that are expected to grow and thus become more important customers. The personnel of these departments can provide valuable counseling to customers. Their experience with other firms in growth situations may enable them to spot, and then warn their customers about, developing problems.

3. Banks differ in the extent to which they will support the activities of their borrowers in bad times. This characteristic is referred to as the banks' degree of *loyalty*. Some banks may put great pressure on a business to liquidate its loans when the firm's outlook becomes clouded, while others will stand by the firm and work diligently to help it get back on its feet. An especially dramatic illustration of this point was Bank of America's bailout of Memorex Corporation. The bank could have forced Memorex into bankruptcy, but instead it loaned the company additional capital and helped it survive a bad period. Memorex's stock price subsequently rose on the New York Stock Exchange from $1.50 to $68, so Bank of America's help was indeed substantial.

4. Banks differ greatly in their degree of *loan specialization*. Larger banks have separate departments specializing in different kinds of loans — for example, real estate loans, installment loans, and commercial loans. Within these broad categories there may be a specialization by line of business, such as steel, machinery, or textiles. The banks' strengths are also likely to reflect the nature of the business environment in which they operate. For example, Seattle banks have become specialists in lending to timber and fisheries companies, whereas many Midwestern banks are agricultural specialists. A sound firm can obtain more creative cooperation and more active support by going to the bank that has the greatest experience and familiarity with its particular type of business. The financial manager should therefore choose a bank with care. A bank that is excellent for one firm may be unsatisfactory for another.

5. The *maximum loan amount* a bank can lend is determined in part by its size. Because the largest loan a bank can make to any one customer is limited to 15 percent of the bank's capital accounts (capital stock plus retained earnings), it is generally not appropriate for large firms to develop borrowing relationships with small banks.

6. Banks may also supply *other services,* such as providing lockbox systems, assisting with electronic funds transfers, helping firms obtain foreign currency, and the like. Such supplementary services should be taken into account when selecting a bank. Also, if the firm is a small business whose manager owns most of its stock, the bank's ability to provide trust and estate services should be considered.

Applying for a Bank Loan

Both large and small firms often find a temporary need for short-term funds above current resources. At such times, most business firms seek interim financing from a commercial bank.

Requests for loans take many forms. A request from a major corporation may be supported by professionally prepared and audited financial statements, complete credit analysis reports from agencies such as Dun & Bradstreet, and documentation from the company's legal counsel. On the other hand, a small firm may have only an unaudited financial statement to support the loan request.

Whatever the degree of sophistication of the data presented to support the loan request, bankers use the financial statements, both historical and pro forma, to answer questions about the term and adequacy of the loan, sources of repayment, and the certainty of those sources. The borrower therefore should anticipate the banker's questions and attempt to answer them in the loan application package. A successful application package generally would contain (1) a cover letter; (2) historical financial data; (3) projected, or pro forma, financial statements; and (4) a brief history of the firm and the resumés of its major officers.

The cover letter should indicate only the most relevant factors about the loan: the purpose of the loan, the amount requested, and the loan period. Balance sheets, income statements, and perhaps even tax records for the past three years of operation constitute an integral part of the loan application package. These data will be used by bankers to learn more about the business, and they are especially helpful in determining management's business and financial acumen. Another important factor in a banker's evaluation is the firm's capitalization. Many small businesses are undercapitalized; that is, their long-term or permanent financing is insufficient to support a larger volume of business. A bank is not the proper source for permanent capital. Additionally, bankers demand that the owner's equity investment in the business be sufficient to give the owner a considerable stake in the success or failure of the firm.

Of course, the pro forma financial statements will receive a great deal of attention from the bank's loan officer. First, the officer will consider whether the requested loan amount is sufficient for its intended purpose. Bankers note that one of the most prevalent mistakes that novice borrowers make is to underestimate the amount needed for a loan. Second, the banker will review the projected financial statements and even the firm's order book (a listing of its customers' orders) for an indication of the sources of repayment from operations and the relative certainty of those sources. If the loan is to cover only seasonal working capital requirements, a monthly or even weekly cash budget, such as the one developed in Chapter 9, is an excellent addition to the loan documentation package. Finally, if the bank's credit officers are unfamiliar with the applicants or their business, a summary of the educational and managerial backgrounds of the firm's principals and a brief history of the firm, including a review of recent company and industry trends and future prospects, should be provided.

Banks and bankers are in business to lend money, but the loan documentation package must provide the banker with enough data to support a positive response to the loan request. In addition, the loan request should indicate any security or **collateral** that is available to support the loan. Unpleasant as the prospect is, collateral is important since it indicates a source of funds available to the bank if unforeseen events cause default. Because collateral reduces the lending risk to the bank, it may reduce the cost of the loan or even be the determining factor in the decision to accept or reject the loan request. The use of collateral is discussed in more detail later in this chapter.

collateral
Assets that are pledged to secure a loan.

Some Features of Bank Loans

Maturity. Although banks do make longer-term loans, *the bulk of their lending is on a short-term basis;* about two-thirds of all bank loans mature in a year or less. Bank loans to businesses frequently are written as 90-day notes, so the loan must be repaid or renewed at the end of 90 days. Of course, if a borrower's financial position has deteriorated, the bank may refuse to renew the loan. This can mean serious trouble for the borrower.

Promissory Note. When a bank loan is approved, the agreement is executed by signing a **promissory note.** The note specifies (1) the amount borrowed; (2) the percentage interest rate; (3) the repayment schedule, which can involve either a lump sum or a series of installments; (4) any collateral that might be put up as security for the loan; and (5) any other terms and conditions to which the bank and the borrower have agreed. When the note is signed, the bank credits the borrower's checking account with the amount of the loan, so on the borrower's balance sheet, both cash and notes payable increase.

promissory note
A document specifying the terms and conditions of a loan, including the amount, interest rate, and repayment schedule.

Compensating Balances. In Chapter 9 compensating balances were discussed in connection with a firm's cash account. Banks typically require a regular borrower to maintain an average checking account balance of 10 to 20 percent of the face amount of the loan. This is called a **compensating balance (CB),** and it raises the effective interest rate on the loan. For example, if a firm needs $80,000 to pay off outstanding obligations, but it must maintain a 20 percent compensating balance, it must borrow $100,000 to obtain a usable $80,000. If the stated interest rate is 8 percent, the effective cost is actually 10 percent: $8,000 in interest divided by $80,000 of usable funds equals 10 per-

compensating balance (CB)
A minimum checking account balance that a firm must maintain with a commercial bank, generally equal to 10 to 20 percent of the amount of the loans outstanding.

cent.[6] The effective cost of a loan with a compensating balance will be discussed in more detail later in this chapter.

line of credit

An arrangement in which a financial institution commits itself to lend up to a specified maximum amount of funds during a designated period.

Line of Credit. A **line of credit** is a formal or informal understanding between the bank and the borrower indicating the maximum size loan the bank will extend to the borrower. For example, on December 31, a bank loan officer may indicate to a corporate treasurer that the bank considers the firm to be "good" for up to $80,000 for the forthcoming year. On January 10 the treasurer signs a promissory note for $15,000 for 90 days; this is called "taking down" $15,000 of the total line of credit. This amount is credited to the firm's checking account at the bank. Before repayment of the $15,000, the firm may borrow additional amounts up to a total outstanding at any one time of $80,000. Also, if the firm has surplus cash, it can pay down the loan, which will both reduce its interest expense and increase its available credit.

revolving credit agreement

A formal line of credit extended to a firm by a bank or other financial institution.

Revolving Credit Agreement. A **revolving credit agreement** is a more formal line-of-credit arrangement often used by large firms. To illustrate, Carter Chemical Company negotiated a revolving credit agreement for $100 million with a group of banks. The banks were formally committed for 4 years to lend Carter up to $100 million if the funds were needed. Carter, in turn, paid a commitment fee of one quarter of 1 percent on the unused balance of the committed funds to compensate the banks for making the funds available. Thus, if Carter did not take down any of the $100 million commitment during a given year, it would still be required to pay a $250,000 fee. If it borrowed $50 million, the unused portion of the line of credit would fall to $50 million, and the fee would fall to $125,000. Of course, interest also had to be paid on the amount of money Carter actually borrowed. As a general rule, the interest rate on "revolvers" is pegged to the T-bill rate or some other open-market rate, so the cost of the loan varies over time as interest rates vary. Carter's rate was set at the T-bill rate plus 1.5 percentage points, to be adjusted on the first of every month.

Note that a revolving credit agreement is one type of a line of credit. However, there is an important distinguishing feature between a formal revolving credit agreement and an informal line of credit. The bank has a legal obligation to honor a revolving credit agreement, and it charges a fee for this commitment. No legal obligation exists under the informal line of credit.

The Cost of Bank Loans

The cost of bank loans varies for different types of borrowers at a given point in time, and for all borrowers over time. Interest rates are higher for riskier borrowers. Rates also are higher on smaller loans because of the fixed costs

---

[6]Note, however, that the compensating balance may be set as a minimum monthly *average* or as an absolute minimum; if the firm would maintain this amount anyway, the compensating balance requirement will not raise the effective interest rate.

of making and servicing loans. If a firm can qualify as a "prime risk" because of its size and financial strength, it can borrow at the **prime rate**, which has traditionally been the lowest rate banks charge. Rates on other loans are scaled up from the prime rate, which currently (March 1990) is 10 percent.[7]

Bank lending rates vary widely over time depending on economic conditions and Federal Reserve policy. When the economy is weak, loan demand is usually slack, and the Fed also makes plenty of money available to the system. As a result, interest rates on all types of loans decline. Conversely, when the economy is booming, loan demand is typically strong, and the Fed restricts the money supply. This results in an increase in interest rates. As an indication of the kinds of fluctuations that can occur, in just five months (from August to December of 1980), the prime rate rose from 11 percent to 21 percent. Then it fell steadily until the winter of 1987, when the rate was only 7.5 percent, the lowest since 1978. From 1987 to mid-1989, the prime rate steadily rose until it reached 11.5 percent, but then it began falling to its current rate of 10 percent. Interest rates on other bank loans also vary, but generally they are kept in phase with the prime rate.

Interest rates on bank loans are calculated in three ways: as *simple* interest, as *discount* interest, and as *add-on* interest. These three methods are explained next.

prime rate
A published rate of interest charged by commercial banks to very large, strong corporations.

Regular, or Simple, Interest. Simple interest is charged on many bank loans, and is used as the basis of comparison for all other loan rates. For a loan based on **simple interest,** the borrower receives the entire amount of the loan's face value and then repays both interest and principal at maturity. For example, on a simple interest loan of $10,000 at 10 percent for 1 year, the borrower receives the $10,000 upon approval of the loan and pays back the $10,000 principal plus $10,000(0.10) = $1,000 of interest at maturity (after 1 year). In the case of a simple interest loan, the stated, or nominal, rate is also the effective rate, which is 10 percent in this example:

simple interest
Interest that is charged on the basis of the amount borrowed; it is paid when the loan matures rather than when it is taken out.

$$\text{Effective rate}_{\text{Simple}} = \frac{\text{Interest}}{\text{Borrowed amount}} \qquad \textbf{(11-2)}$$

$$= \frac{\$1,000}{\$10,000} = 10\%.$$

---

[7]Each bank sets its own prime rate, but because of competitive forces, most banks' prime rates are identical. Also, most banks follow the rate set by the large New York City banks, and they, in turn, generally follow the rate set by Citibank, New York City's largest bank. Citibank sets the prime rate each week at 1¼ to 1½ percentage points above the average rate on large certificates of deposit (CDs) during the immediately preceding three weeks. CD rates represent the price of money in the open market, and they rise and fall with the supply of and demand for money, so CD rates are "market-clearing" rates. By tying the prime rate to CD rates, the banking system insures that the prime rate will also be a market-clearing rate.

discount interest
Interest that is calculated on the face amount of a loan but is deducted in advance.

Discount Interest. When a lender makes a loan with **discount interest,** the interest is deducted from the approved loan amount before the borrower receives the proceeds of the loan. When the lender deducts the interest in advance, which is called *discounting* the loan, the effective rate of interest on the loan is increased. Thus, on a $10,000 loan with a nominal interest rate of 10 percent, the interest is $1,000. When the loan is discounted, the borrower has the use of only $9,000 of the loan's proceeds. Therefore, the effective rate of interest is 11.1 percent versus the stated 10 percent interest rate:

$$\text{Effective rate}_{\text{Discount}} = \frac{\text{Interest}}{\text{Face value} - \text{Interest}} \qquad (11\text{-}3)$$

$$= \frac{\$1,000}{\$9,000} = 11.1\%.$$

add-on interest
Interest calculated and added to funds received to determine the face amount of an installment loan.

Installment Loans: Add-On Interest. Banks (and other lenders) typically charge **add-on interest** on automobile, appliance, and other types of small installment loans. The term *add-on* means that interest is calculated and added on to the funds received to determine the face amount of the note. To illustrate, suppose the $10,000 loan is to be repaid in 12 monthly installments. At a 10 percent add-on rate, the borrower pays a total interest charge of $1,000. Thus, the signed note is for $11,000. However, because the loan is paid off in installments, the borrower has the full $10,000 only during the first month, and by the last month 11/12 of the loan will have been repaid. The borrower must pay $1,000 for the use of only about half the amount received, as the *average* amount of the original loan outstanding during the year is only about $5,000. Therefore, the effective rate on the loan is *approximately* 20 percent, calculated as follows:

$$\begin{array}{l}\text{Approximate} \\ \text{effective rate}_{\text{Add-on}}\end{array} = \frac{\text{Interest}}{(\text{Loan amount})/2} \qquad (11\text{-}4)$$

$$= \frac{\$1,000}{\$5,000} = 20\%.$$

The main point to note here is that interest is paid on the *original* amount of the loan, not on the amount actually outstanding (the declining balance), which causes the effective interest rate to be almost double the stated rate.[8]

Effective Interest Rates when Compensating Balances Apply. Compensating balances tend to raise the effective interest rate on bank loans. To illustrate, suppose a firm needs $10,000 to pay for some equipment that it recently purchased. A bank offers to lend the company money at a 10 percent simple interest rate, but the company must maintain a compensating balance

---

[8]Equation 11-4 is an approximation of the true interest rate, which is determined by utilizing the compound interest techniques described in Chapter 13.

equal to 20 percent of the loan amount. If the firm did not take the loan, it would keep no deposits with the bank. What is the effective interest rate on the loan?

First, note that although the firm needs only $10,000, it must borrow $12,500, calculated as follows:

$$\text{Amount borrowed} = \frac{\text{Funds needed}}{1.0 - \text{Compensating balance percentage}} \quad \textbf{(11-5)}$$

$$= \frac{\$10,000}{0.8} = \$12,500.$$

Even though the interest paid will be $(0.10)(\$12,500) = \$1,250$, the firm will get to use only $10,000. Therefore the effective interest rate is

$$\text{Effective rate}_{\text{Simple/CB}} = \frac{\text{Interest paid}}{\text{Funds actually used}} \quad \textbf{(11-6a)}$$

$$= \frac{\$1,250}{\$10,000} = 0.125 = 12.5\%.$$

In general, we can use this formula to find the effective interest rate when compensating balances apply:[9]

$$\text{Effective rate}_{\text{Simple/CB}} = \frac{\text{Stated interest rate } (\%)}{1.0 - \text{Compensating balance percentage}}. \quad \textbf{(11-6b)}$$

In this example,

$$\text{Effective rate}_{\text{Simple/CB}} = \frac{10\%}{1 - 0.2} = \frac{10\%}{0.8} = 12.5\%.$$

The analysis can be extended to the case where compensating balances are required and the loan is based on discounted interest:

$$\text{Effective rate}_{\text{Discount/CB}} = \frac{\text{Stated interest rate } (\%)}{1.0 - \left(\dfrac{\text{Compensating balance}}{\text{percentage}}\right) - \left(\dfrac{\text{Stated interest}}{\text{rate}}\right)}. \quad \textbf{(11-7)}$$

For example, if a firm needed $10,000 and was offered a loan with a stated interest rate of 10 percent, discount interest, with a 20 percent compensating balance, the effective interest rate would be

$$\text{Effective rate}_{\text{Discount/CB}} = \frac{10\%}{1.0 - 0.2 - 0.10} = \frac{10\%}{0.70} = 14.3\%.$$

---

[9]Note that this equation assumes a loan period of exactly one year. In Chapter 13, we discuss the calculation of an effective annual rate for time periods not equal to one year.

The amount that the firm would need to borrow would be

$$\text{Amount borrowed} = \frac{\text{Funds needed}}{1.0 - \left(\begin{array}{c}\text{Compensating}\\\text{balance}\\\text{percentage}\end{array}\right) - \left(\begin{array}{c}\text{Stated}\\\text{interest}\\\text{rate}\end{array}\right)} \qquad (11\text{-}8)$$

$$= \frac{\$10,000}{1.0 - 0.2 - 0.10} = \$14,285.71.$$

It would use this $14,285.71 as follows:

To make required payment	$10,000.00
Compensating balance (20% of $14,285.71)	2,857.14
Prepaid interest (10% of $14,285.71)	1,428.57
	$14,285.71

In this example, compensating balances and discount interest combined to push the effective rate of interest up from 10 percent to 14.3 percent. Note, however, that our analysis assumed that the compensating balance requirements forced the firm to increase its bank deposits. Had the company had transactions balances that could supply all or part of the compensating balance, the effective interest rate would have been less than 14.3 percent. Also, if the firm earned interest on its bank deposits, including the compensating balance, the effective interest rate would decrease.

Self-Test

What are some factors that should be considered when choosing a bank?

What would a successful loan application package include?

Explain how a firm that expects to need funds during the coming year might be sure that the needed funds will be available. Would there be a cost for that assurance?

Explain the difference between a regular, or simple, interest loan and a discount interest loan.

Give the formula for approximating the effective rate for an add-on interest installment loan.

How does the formula for approximating the effective rate for a simple interest loan compare to that for a simple interest loan with compensating balances?

Give the formula for calculating the amount borrowed on a discount interest loan with a compensating balance.

COMMERCIAL PAPER

In Chapter 9 we discussed the use of commercial paper as an investment medium for temporary excess cash. The present chapter would be incomplete if we did not include a discussion of commercial paper as a source of short-term financing available to the most financially secure firms. Commercial paper consists of unsecured promissory notes of large, strong firms, and it is sold primarily to other business firms, insurance companies, pension funds, money market funds, and banks in denominations of $100,000 or more. Although the amount of commercial paper outstanding is smaller than bank loans outstanding, this form of financing has grown rapidly in recent years. At the end of February 1990, there was more than $540 billion of commercial paper outstanding versus about $650 billion of bank loans to businesses.

Maturity and Cost

Maturities of commercial paper generally vary from 2 to 6 months from the original date of issue. The rates on commercial paper fluctuate with supply and demand conditions; they are determined in the marketplace and vary daily as conditions change. Recently, commercial paper rates have ranged from one to two percentage points below rates on prime business loans, and about one-half of a percentage point above the T-bill rate. For example, in March 1990 the average rate on 3-month commercial paper was 8.3 percent, while the stated prime rate was 10 percent. The T-bill rate at the time was 7.9 percent. Also, because compensating balances are not required for commercial paper, the *effective* cost differential versus the prime rate is still wider.

Use of Commercial Paper

The use of commercial paper is restricted to a comparatively small number of large firms that are exceptionally good credit risks. As we discussed in Chapter 9, purchasers of commercial paper hold it in their temporary marketable securities portfolios as liquidity reserves, and for this purpose safety is a paramount concern. Dealers prefer to handle the paper of firms whose net worth is $50 million or more and whose annual borrowing exceeds $10 million.

One potential problem with commercial paper is that a debtor who is in temporary financial difficulty may receive little help, because commercial paper dealings are generally less personal than bank relationships. Thus, banks generally are more able and willing to help a good customer weather a temporary storm than are the commercial paper dealers. On the other hand, using commercial paper permits a corporation to tap a wide range of credit sources, including banks outside its own area and industrial corporations across the country, and this can reduce interest costs. Like bonds, commercial paper is rated, and the quality of the commercial paper is reflected in the rating.

Self-Test

What types of firms use commercial paper?

Give an advantage and a disadvantage to a firm's using commercial paper.

An increasingly popular form of short-term financing among large, secure firms, *commercial paper* looks very much like a bank check, except that it is issued by a large corporation instead of a bank. Commercial paper is really just a promise to pay the bearer. It is used primarily by firms that are excellent credit risks.

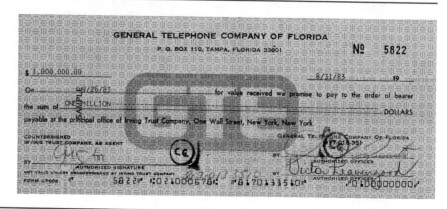

Source: Courtesy of General Telephone Company of Florida.

USE OF SECURITY IN SHORT-TERM FINANCING

secured loan
A loan backed by collateral, often inventories or receivables.

Given a choice, it is ordinarily better to borrow on an unsecured basis, as the bookkeeping costs of **secured loans** are often high. However, small or weak firms may find that they can borrow only if they put up some type of security to protect the lender, or that by using some security they can borrow at a much lower rate.

Several different kinds of collateral can be employed — marketable stocks or bonds, land or buildings, equipment, inventory, and accounts receivable. Marketable securities make excellent collateral, but few firms hold portfolios of stocks and bonds. Similarly, real property (land and buildings) and equipment are good forms of collateral, but they are generally used as security for long-term loans rather than for working capital loans. Therefore, a great deal of secured short-term business borrowing involves the use of accounts receivable and inventories as collateral.

To understand the use of security, consider the case of a San Jose hardware dealer who wanted to modernize and expand his store. He requested a $200,000 bank loan. After examining his business's financial statements, the bank indicated that it would lend him a maximum of $100,000 and that the interest rate would be 16 percent discount, or an effective rate of 19 percent. The owner had a substantial personal portfolio of stocks, and he offered to put up $300,000 of high-quality stocks to support the $200,000 loan. The bank then granted the full $200,000 loan, and at a rate of 13 percent, simple interest. The store owner also might have used his inventories or receivables as security for the loan, but processing costs would have been high.

Uniform Commercial Code
A system of standards that simplifies and standardizes procedures for establishing loan security.

In the past, state laws varied greatly with regard to the use of security in financing. Today, however, all states except Louisiana operate under the **Uniform Commercial Code,** which standardized and simplified the procedures for establishing loan security. The heart of the Uniform Commercial Code is

the *Security Agreement,* a standardized document or form on which the specific assets that are pledged are listed. The assets can be items of equipment,
accounts receivable, or inventories. Procedures for using accounts receivable
and inventories as security for short-term credit under the Uniform Commercial Code are described in Appendix 11A.

Self-Test

Why is it ordinarily better to borrow on an unsecured basis rather than on a
secured basis?

Why do firms borrow on a secured basis?

What types of collateral can be used for working capital loans? Is one type of
collateral preferred over another?

What is the Security Agreement?

 SMALL BUSINESS

Financing Receivables Directly

The growing small firm that offers its customers
credit will often find that its accounts receivable grow rapidly. As discussed in Chapter 10,
growth usually entails a growing need to finance the firm's current assets, and accounts receivable are a major portion of current assets.
Even though growth in accounts receivable
places a strain on the firm's financing ability, it
may also offer the firm special opportunities to
obtain financing.

Accounts receivable constitute important asset accounts within the firm, assets that may be
particularly liquid and thus attractive to a
lender as collateral. Two common strategies
for financing receivables that make use of these
desirable features are (1) pledging of receivables as collateral for debt and (2) factoring of
receivables.

In the case of pledged receivables, the firm
needing capital merely borrows funds and offers
its receivables as collateral for the loan. For
example, suppose Main Street Builders' Supply

sells materials wholesale to builders. To increase its sales, Main Street offers trade credit
terms of 2/10, net 60. Most of its customers
elect to delay payment. As Main Street grows, it
realizes that its cash reserves are being badly
strained, making it difficult to finance inventory
requirements. The firm arranges to pledge its
receivables to the Last Gasp National Bank. The
bank, in turn, agrees to review Main Street's major receivable accounts and to select the acceptable accounts to serve as collateral. The
bank lends Main Street about 70 percent of the
face value of the acceptable accounts, reducing
some of the financial pressure the firm had
experienced.

Pledging receivables makes sense when the
customers of the small firm have better credit
histories than the firm itself. However, the small
business still bears the credit risk if its customers do not pay, and it receives only a fraction of
the funds due from its accounts. Factoring receivables may be a better alternative.

Factoring involves the sale of receivables to a third party, called a factor, usually without recourse. The factor performs all of the credit services the firm might otherwise have to provide itself. It bears credit risk, it checks the creditworthiness of the customers, and it collects the receivable accounts themselves. Of course, it charges a price for these services.

The small firm employing a factor gets more than just credit. If Main Street Builders' Supply financed through a factor, the factor would take over Main Street's collection function almost entirely. It would be up to the factor to decide which of Main Street's customers merited credit. Also, if one of Main Street's customers, such as Reliable Homes, became unable to pay its debts, the factor rather than Main Street would absorb the loss. Of course, if Main Street wanted to sell to a customer that the factor found unacceptable, Main Street could still do so, but it would have to bear the credit risk itself.

Main Street must decide if it is worthwhile to use a comparatively high-cost factor or to maintain its own credit and collection services. The cost of funds through the factor must be compared to the direct cost of replacing all of the factor's services internally.

There is a good reason why many small firms find that using a factor's services is indeed an economical alternative; the small firm has its own special expertise (in Main Street's case, buying and selling building materials), whereas the factor has its own profession (credit services). Because managerial talent is often especially limited in small firms, it may turn out that the factors' services are a bargain in comparison with the cost of the firm's maintaining its own credit services and exposing itself to credit risks.

The fees charged by the factor normally include an interest charge for lending the funds in advance of payment, a credit fee for evaluating customers' credit, and sometimes a charge that reflects the credit risk of the customers. Also, the factor usually does not advance all of the net proceeds, making an allowance for possible returns because of disputes between the buyer and seller.

To illustrate, suppose Main Street agrees to deliver $25,000 in building supplies to Reliable Homes on terms of net 30. Main Street approaches Factor, Inc., a wholly owned subsidiary of the major local bank holding company, and Factor accepts the account. Factor charges Main Street interest at the rate of 12 percent, 2 points over prime, resulting in an interest charge of $1/12 \times 12\% \times \$25,000 = \$250$ on the $25,000 invoice amount. Factor charges an additional 2 percent as a credit fee, for another $500. Finally, Factor advances only $21,750 rather than $24,250, holding a 10 percent (or $2,500) allowance in case Reliable disputes the order or finds some problem with the merchandise.

At the end of the month, Reliable pays $24,000 directly to Factor after deducting $1,000 for defective sinks it had to return to Main Street. At that point Factor pays Main Street the remaining $1,500 due the firm on its net $24,000 sale of materials to Reliable Homes.

Considering the $750 total fee paid by Main Street to Factor for 30 days' use of $24,000, the factor seems to be an expensive source of financing. Main Street must consider, however, the cost of duplicating the additional services provided by the factor.

The firm's comparative advantage is delivering a product; the factor's advantage is in providing financial and credit services. In small firms with limited managerial resources and perhaps limited experience in monitoring and collecting credit accounts, factors may be economical sources of financing and credit services.

SUMMARY

This chapter examined (1) different types of short-term credit available to firms, (2) decisions the financial manager must make in selecting among the types of short-term credit, and (3) the use of security to obtain credit. The key concepts covered are listed below:

- **Short-term credit** is any liability originally scheduled for payment within one year. The four major sources of short-term credit are (1) accruals, (2) accounts payable, (3) loans from commercial banks and finance companies, and (4) commercial paper.

- **Accruals,** which are continually recurring short-term liabilities, represent free, spontaneous credit.

- **Accounts payable,** or **trade credit,** is the largest category of short-term debt. This credit arises spontaneously as a result of purchases on credit. Firms should use all the **free trade credit** they can obtain, but they should use **costly trade credit** only if it is less expensive than other forms of short-term debt. Suppliers often offer discounts to customers who pay within a stated discount period. The following equation may be used to calculate the approximate percentage cost, on an annual basis, of not taking discounts:

$$\begin{array}{c}\text{Approximate}\\\text{percentage}\\\text{cost}\end{array} = \frac{\text{Discount percent}}{100 - \left(\begin{array}{c}\text{Discount}\\\text{percent}\end{array}\right)} \times \frac{360}{\left(\begin{array}{c}\text{Days credit}\\\text{is outstanding}\end{array}\right) - \left(\begin{array}{c}\text{Discount}\\\text{period}\end{array}\right)}.$$

- **Bank loans** are an important source of short-term credit. Interest on bank loans may be quoted as **simple interest, discount interest,** or **add-on interest.** The effective rate on a discount or add-on loan always exceeds the stated nominal rate.

- When a bank loan is approved, a **promissory note** is signed. It specifies: (1) the amount borrowed, (2) the percentage interest rate, (3) the repayment schedule, (4) the collateral, and (5) any other conditions to which the parties have agreed.

- Banks often require borrowers to maintain **compensating balances,** which are required deposits set at between 10 and 20 percent of the loan amount. Compensating balances usually raise the effective rate of interest on bank loans.

- **Lines of credit** are formal or informal understandings between the bank and the borrower indicating the maximum amount of credit the bank will extend to the borrower.

- A **revolving credit agreement** is a formal line of credit often used by large firms; it involves a **commitment fee.**

- The **prime rate** is a published interest rate charged by banks to very large, strong corporations.

- **Simple interest** is interest charged on the basis of the amount borrowed; the effective rate on a one-year simple interest loan is calculated as follows:

$$\text{Effective rate}_{\text{Simple}} = \frac{\text{Interest}}{\text{Borrowed amount}}.$$

If compensating balances are added, the effective rate is calculated as follows:

$$\text{Effective rate}_{\text{Simple/CB}} = \frac{\text{Stated interest rate (\%)}}{1.0 - \text{Compensating balance percentage}}.$$

To calculate the loan amount with simple interest and compensating balances the following formula is used:

$$\text{Amount borrowed} = \frac{\text{Funds needed}}{1.0 - \text{Compensating balance percentage}}.$$

- **Discount interest** is interest calculated on the face amount of a loan, but it is deducted in advance; the effective rate on a one-year discount interest loan is calculated as follows:

$$\text{Effective rate}_{\text{Discount}} = \frac{\text{Interest}}{\text{Face value} - \text{Interest}}.$$

If compensating balances are added, the effective rate is calculated as follows:

$$\text{Effective rate}_{\text{Discount/CB}} = \frac{\text{Stated interest rate (\%)}}{1.0 - \text{CB} - \text{Stated interest rate}}.$$

To calculate the loan amount with discount interest and compensating balances the following formula is used:

$$\text{Amount borrowed} = \frac{\text{Funds needed}}{1.0 - \left(\begin{array}{c}\text{Compensating}\\\text{balance}\\\text{percentage}\end{array}\right) - \left(\begin{array}{c}\text{Stated}\\\text{interest}\\\text{rate}\end{array}\right)}.$$

- **Add-on interest** is interest calculated and added to funds received to determine the face amount of an installment loan; the effective rate on a one-year add-on interest loan is calculated as follows:

$$\text{Approximate effective rate}_{\text{Add-on}} = \frac{\text{Interest}}{(\text{Loan amount})/2}.$$

- **Commercial paper** is unsecured short-term debt issued by large, financially strong corporations. Although the cost of commerical paper is lower than the cost of bank loans, commercial paper's maturity is limited to 270 days, and it can be used only by large firms with exceptionally strong credit ratings.
- Sometimes a borrower will find that it is necessary to borrow on a **secured basis,** in which case the borrower pledges assets such as real estate, securities, equipment, inventories, or accounts receivable as collateral for the loan.

EQUATIONS

The following equation may be used to calculate the approximate percentage cost, on an annual basis, of not taking discounts:

$$\begin{matrix} \text{Approximate} \\ \text{percentage} \\ \text{cost} \end{matrix} = \frac{\text{Discount percent}}{100 - \left(\begin{matrix}\text{Discount}\\\text{percent}\end{matrix}\right)} \times \frac{360}{\left(\begin{matrix}\text{Days}\\\text{credit is}\\\text{outstanding}\end{matrix}\right) - \left(\begin{matrix}\text{Discount}\\\text{period}\end{matrix}\right)}. \quad \textbf{(11-1)}$$

The effective rate on a one-year simple interest loan is calculated as follows:

$$\text{Effective rate}_{\text{Simple}} = \frac{\text{Interest}}{\text{Borrowed amount}}. \quad \textbf{(11-2)}$$

One way to calculate the effective rate on a simple interest loan which includes compensating balances is

$$\text{Effective rate}_{\text{Simple/CB}} = \frac{\text{Interest paid}}{\text{Funds actually used}}. \quad \textbf{(11-6a)}$$

If compensating balances are added, the general formula to calculate the effective rate is as follows:

$$\text{Effective rate}_{\text{Simple/CB}} = \frac{\text{Stated interest (\%)}}{1.0 - \text{Compensating balance percentage}}. \quad \textbf{(11-6b)}$$

To calculate the loan amount with simple interest and compensating balances, the following formula is used:

$$\text{Amount borrowed} = \frac{\text{Funds needed}}{1.0 - \text{Compensating balance percentage}}. \quad \textbf{(11-5)}$$

The effective rate on a one-year discount interest loan is calculated as follows:

$$\text{Effective rate}_{\text{Discount}} = \frac{\text{Interest}}{\text{Face value} - \text{Interest}}. \qquad (11\text{-}3)$$

If compensating balances are added, the effective rate is calculated as follows:

$$\text{Effective rate}_{\text{Discount/CB}} = \frac{\text{Stated interest rate (\%)}}{1.0 - \left(\begin{matrix}\text{Compensating}\\ \text{balance}\\ \text{percentage}\end{matrix}\right) - \left(\begin{matrix}\text{Stated}\\ \text{interest}\\ \text{rate}\end{matrix}\right)}. \qquad (11\text{-}7)$$

To calculate the loan amount with discount interest and compensating balances, the following formula is used:

$$\text{Amount borrowed} = \frac{\text{Funds needed}}{1 - \left(\begin{matrix}\text{Compensating}\\ \text{balance}\\ \text{percentage}\end{matrix}\right) - \left(\begin{matrix}\text{Stated}\\ \text{interest}\\ \text{rate}\end{matrix}\right)}. \qquad (11\text{-}8)$$

The effective rate on a one-year add-on interest loan is calculated as follows:

$$\text{Approximate effective rate}_{\text{Add-on}} = \frac{\text{Interest}}{(\text{Loan amount})/2}. \qquad (11\text{-}4)$$

RESOLUTION TO DECISION IN FINANCE

A Bank That Looks at More than Numbers

The Northwestern National Bank of St. Paul uses a number of tactics to attract and hold business from promising young companies. The basis of its approach is its willingness to lend money to companies that other, more conservative banks would turn down. In fact, rather than putting the burden of proof on the customer, Northwestern often works hard on its own to justify making a loan. Even when a conventional credit analysis indicates that a company could be a poor risk, the bank might still lend it money if the company shows compensating strengths, such as strong management talent or solid production performance.

In support of its commitment to young businesses, in 1981 Northwestern established a special division to help identify and analyze unusual lending opportunities. The division's three lending officers concentrate primarily on companies involved in high technology and other specialized areas, such as plastics and chemicals, but Northwestern's interests aren't limited to those areas alone. And its readiness to override traditional financial criteria with good judgment dates back further than the founding of the special lending division.

Source: Adapted from "A Bank That Looks at More than Numbers," *Inc.,* March 1983, 117–118.

In fact, the bank approved its most extraordinary loan application in early 1976. At the time, the applying company had yet to generate its first dollar of revenue. Its product, a highly sophisticated supercomputer, was still in development. Based on the company's financial statements, Northwestern couldn't justify giving it a loan, so the bank decided to look instead at the product and the people. After talking to some of the company's competitors and potential customers, the bank was convinced that it could make the company a sizable loan without great risk. Thus, even though a much larger bank turned the company down, Northwestern agreed to give it a $1 million line of credit.

Ironically, the company, Cray Research, Inc., never used its new credit line. Shortly after the loan approval, the company went public, and today it is a proven performer, with annual sales in excess of $100 million.

Northwestern also believes in helping its customers survive tough financial times. For example, Detector Electronics Corporation ran into a cash crunch that threatened its ability to maintain its rapid growth. Northwestern had already given the company a fairly standard asset-based line of credit: it could borrow as needed up to 80 percent against its accounts receivable,

plus another 25 percent against the value of its inventory. But this formula wouldn't make cash available fast enough for Detector to fill all of its incoming orders.

Based on his company's assets and heavily leveraged balance sheet, Ted Larsen, Detector's president and chief executive officer, assumed that any bank would turn down his request for a larger credit line. But he hadn't taken into account Northwestern's willingness to turn aside conventional lending criteria. Because the bank believed in Detector's ability to turn its orders into sales and its sales into profits, it agreed to provide more financing for working capital by advancing cash based on a share of confirmed orders as well as on receivables and inventory. As a result, Detector was able to avert its impending financial crisis.

Of course, like any other bank, Northwestern usually charges higher rates for its riskier loans. Yet higher rates alone do not explain the bank's willingness to break with traditional lending policies. The real motivator, according to senior vice president Dennis McChesney, is the opportunity to establish ground-level relationships with newer businesses that will stay with the bank as they grow. "We think the best payoff is a loyal customer," McChesney says.

QUESTIONS

11-1 "Firms can control their accruals within fairly wide limits; depending on the cost of accruals, financing from this source will be increased or decreased." Discuss.

11-2 Is it true that both trade credit and accruals represent a spontaneous source of capital for financing growth? Explain.

11-3 Is it true that most firms are able to obtain some free trade credit and that additional trade credit is often available, but at a cost? Explain.

11-4 What is meant by the term *stretching accounts payable?*

11-5 The chapter indicated that required compensating balances usually increase the cost of a bank loan. In what situation would a compensating balance not increase the cost of a bank loan?

11-6 The availability of bank credit is often more important to a small firm than to a large one. Why?

11-7   From the standpoint of the borrower, is long-term or short-term credit riskier? Explain.

11-8   If long-term credit exposes a borrower to less risk, why would people or firms borrow on a short-term basis?

11-9   What kinds of firms use commercial paper? Could Mamma and Pappa Gus's Corner Grocery borrow using this form of credit?

11-10 Suppose a firm can obtain funds by borrowing at the prime rate or by selling commercial paper. If the prime rate is 12 percent, what is a reasonable estimate for the cost of commercial paper?

11-11 Given that commercial paper interest rates are generally lower than bank loan rates to a given borrower, why might firms which are capable of selling commercial paper also use bank credit?

SELF-TEST PROBLEM

ST-1   Kitty Burton, owner of MovieTime Rentals, is negotiating with Mechanics and Merchants Bank for a $30,000, 1-year loan. The bank has offered Burton the following alternatives. Rank the alternatives from the one with the lowest effective interest rate to the one with the highest rate. The firm will hold no balances in the bank if it does not obtain a loan from the bank.

1. A 15 percent annual rate on a simple interest loan, with no compensating balance required, interest and principal due at the end of the year.

2. A 10 percent annual rate on a simple interest loan, with a 15 percent compensating balance required and interest due at the end of the year.

3. A 9 percent annual rate on a discounted loan with a 15 percent compensating balance.

4. Interest is figured as 10 percent of the $30,000 amount, payable at the end of the year, but the $30,000 is repayable in monthly installments during the year.

PROBLEMS

11-1   **Cost of trade credit.** Calculate the implicit cost of nonfree trade credit under each of the following terms. Assume that the discount is not taken and that payment is made on the date due.
   a. 1/10, net 30
   b. 1/15, net 30
   c. 2/10, net 30
   d. 2/15, net 40
   e. 1/10, net 60
   f. 3/10, net 60
   g. 3/10, net 20

11-2   **Cost of credit.** The Lamp Gallery buys under terms of 3/15, net 60, but it actually pays on the 20th day and *still* takes the discount.
   a. What is the cost of its nonfree trade credit?
   b. Does it receive more or less trade credit than it would if it paid within 15 days?

11-3   **Cash discounts.** Suppose Rocco Fashions makes purchases of $5 million per year under terms of 2/10, net 30. It takes discounts.

    a. What is the average amount of its accounts payable, net of discounts? (Assume the $5 million purchases are net of discounts; that is, gross purchases are $5,102,041, discounts are $102,041, and net purchases are $5 million. Also, use 360 days in a year.)

    b. Is there a cost to the trade credit it uses?

    c. If it did not take discounts, what would Rocco's average payables be, and what would be the cost of this nonfree trade credit?

11-4   **Short-term financing.** Dellvoe Office Equipment, Inc., a small manufacturer of metal office equipment, has two primary sources of short-term debt: trade credit and bank loans. One supplier, which supplies Dellvoe with $50,000 of materials a year, offers Dellvoe terms of 2/10, net 50.

    a. What are Dellvoe's net daily purchases from this supplier?

    b. What is the average level of Dellvoe's accounts payable to this supplier if the discount is taken? What is the average level if the discount is not taken? What are the amounts of free credit and costly credit under both discount policies?

    c. What is the approximate cost of the costly trade credit?

11-5   **Cost of bank loan.** You plan to borrow $100,000 from the bank. The bank offers to lend you the money at a 12 percent interest rate on a 1-year loan. What is the true, or effective, rate of interest for **(a)** simple interest, **(b)** discount interest, and **(c)** add-on interest, if the loan is a 12-month installment loan?

11-6   **Cost of bank loans.** Bueso's Sporting Goods is negotiating a $500,000, 1-year current assets loan with four area banks. The banks have provided the loan opportunities listed below. What is the effective interest rate being offered by each bank? Unless otherwise required by the terms of the loan arrangement, Bueso prefers to keep cash balances as close to zero as possible.

    a. First National Bank offered a 14 percent loan with principal and interest due at the end of 1 year. No compensating balance is required.

    b. Second National Bank would lend at 11 percent stated interest if Mr. Bueso kept a 20 percent compensating balance. Mr. Bueso had not planned to keep any borrowed funds in the bank.

    c. Third National Bank suggested it would approve a loan at 11 percent if Mr. Bueso kept a 10 percent compensating balance and discounted the loan.

    d. Fourth National Bank would lend to the company at 9 percent if the principal and interest were paid in 12 equal monthly installments.

11-7   **Cost of bank loan.** Spartan Auto Parts needs to purchase $750,000 in inventory. The local bank agrees to the loan with a stated interest rate of 12 percent and a compensating balance of 20 percent. The loan will mature in 1 year.

    a. What is the loan's effective interest rate?

    b. How much interest will Spartan pay if it agrees to the loan as stated? (*Hint:* Remember that Spartan needs the loan proceeds to be $750,000.)

11-8   **Cost of bank loan.** Lapin's Card Company wishes to borrow $125,000 for one year. Its bank agrees to loan Lapin the money at 13.5 percent, on the condition that the firm keep a 20 percent compensating balance in a 5 percent savings account for the duration of the loan. If Lapin usually keeps a zero account balance, what is the effective cost of this loan? (*Hint:* Lapin only needs $100,000.)

11-9   **Trade versus bank credit.** Bob Magee of Metroplex Manufacturing is worried. Cash flow problems have prevented him from taking a 2/15, net 40, discount from his trade creditors. In fact, he has stretched payment to 55 days after purchase, and his suppliers are threatening a cutoff of credit. East Carolina National Bank has agreed to lend enough money to alleviate the firm's cash flow problems and to allow Bob to take all discounts offered. The loan provides a 13 percent stated interest rate and requires a 20 percent compensating balance.

a. What is the firm's effective cost of trade credit at the present time?

b. What is the effective cost of the bank loan offered?

c. What should Bob do?

11-10   **Cost of bank loan.** Charles Cox, owner of Cox Plumbing, is borrowing $100,000 from his local bank. Terms of the loan require a 15 percent compensating balance to qualify for a 13 percent stated interest rate. If Mr. Cox always keeps his bank cash balance as close to zero as possible, what is the effective cost of the loan? Interest and principal are due at the end of the year.

11-11   **Cost of bank loan.** Refer to Problem 11-10. Assume that rather than a zero balance, Mr. Cox, as a matter of company policy, always keeps $10,000 in the company's checking account as a cushion over expected needs. These precautionary balances may be used as part of the compensating balance. What is the effective cost of the loan under these conditions?

11-12   **Trade credit versus bank credit.** Purity Bottling Company has a cash flow problem that is preventing Purity from taking the trade discounts it is offered. The terms of sale are 3/10, net 30, but the company has been unable to pay before 70 days after purchases are made. Understandably, its suppliers are threatening to hold the company to its credit terms or withhold future credit. Purity has discussed the matter with its bank, and the bank will offer Purity a 16.5 percent discounted loan that requires a 15 percent compensating balance.

a. What is the effective cost of (1) paying payables on the 30th day; (2) continuing to pay on the 70th day; and (3) taking the bank loan?

b. What should Purity do?

11-13   **Cost of credit agreements.** Hogan Construction has entered into a revolving credit agreement with Great Southwest National Bank. Terms of the agreement allow the firm to borrow up to $30 million as the funds are needed. The firm will pay ¼ percent for the unused balance and prime plus 2 percent for the funds that are actually borrowed. The prime rate is expected to remain at 10 percent during the period covered by the loan. Determine the effective annual percentage cost of each of the following amounts borrowed under the revolving credit agreement: **(a)** no funds are used; **(b)** $9 million; **(c)** $15 million; **(d)** $24 million; **(e)** $30 million.

11-14   **Trade credit versus bank credit.** Solomon and Sons projects an increase in sales from $2.5 million to $3 million, but the company needs an additional $500,000 of assets to support this expansion. The money can be obtained from the bank at an interest rate of 10 percent discount interest. Alternatively, Solomon can finance the expansion by no longer taking discounts, thus increasing accounts payable. Solomon purchases under terms of 2/10, net 30, but it can delay payment for an additional 30 days, paying in 60 days and thus becoming 30 days past due, without penalty at this time.

a. Based strictly on an interest rate comparison, how should Solomon finance its expansion? Show your work.

b. What additional qualitative factors should Solomon consider in reaching a decision?

11-15 **Bank financing.** Sound Products, Incorporated (SPI) had sales of $2 million last year and earned a 3 percent return, after taxes, on sales. Although its terms of purchase are net 30 days, its accounts payable represent 60 days' purchases. The president of the company is seeking to increase the company's bank borrowings to become current (that is, have 30 days' payables outstanding) in meeting its trade obligations. The company's balance sheet follows.

a. How much bank financing is needed to eliminate past-due accounts payable?

b. Would you as a bank loan officer make the loan? Why?

Sound Products, Incorporated: Balance Sheet

Cash	$ 25,000	Accounts payable	$ 300,000
Accounts receivable	125,000	Bank loans	250,000
Inventory	650,000	Accruals	125,000
Current assets	$ 800,000	Current liabilities	$ 675,000
Land and buildings	250,000	Mortgage on real estate	250,000
Equipment	250,000	Common stock, par 10 cents	125,000
		Retained earnings	250,000
Total assets	$1,300,000	Total liabilities and equity	$1,300,000

11-16 **Cost of trade credit.** Price & Daughters, Inc., sells on terms of 2/10, net 40. Annual sales last year were $3.6 million. Half of Price's customers pay on the tenth day and take discounts.

a. If accounts receivable averaged $350,000, what is Price's days sales outstanding *on nondiscount sales?*

b. What rate of return is Price earning on its nondiscount receivables, where this rate of return is defined as being equal to the cost of this trade credit to the nondiscount customers?

11-17 **Short-term financing analysis.** CCM Corporation, has the following balance sheet:

CCM Corporation: Balance Sheet

Cash	$ 50,000	Accounts payable[a]	$ 500,000
Accounts receivable	450,000	Notes payable	50,000
Inventories	750,000	Accruals	50,000
Total current assets	$1,250,000	Total current liabilities	$ 600,000
		Long-term debt	150,000
Fixed assets	750,000	Common equity	1,250,000
Total assets	$2,000,000	Total liabilities and equity	$2,000,000

[a]Stated net of discounts, even though discounts may not be taken.

CCM buys on terms of 1/10, net 30, but it has not been taking discounts and has actually been paying in 70 days rather than 30 days. Now CCM's suppliers are threatening to stop shipments unless the company begins making prompt payments (that is, pays in 30 days or less). CCM can borrow on a 1-year note (call this a current liability) from its bank at a rate of 9 percent, discount interest, with a 20 percent compensating balance required. (All of the cash now on hand is needed for transactions; it cannot be used as part of the compensating balance.)

a. Determine what action CCM should take by (1) calculating the cost of nonfree trade credit and (2) calculating the cost of the bank loan.

b. Based on your decision in Part a, construct a pro forma balance sheet. (*Hint:* You will need to include an account called "prepaid interest" under current assets. Also, ignore discounts lost, if any, in your calculations.)

11-18 **Alternative financing arrangements.** Suntime Boats, Limited, estimates that because of the seasonal nature of its business, it will require an additional $1 million of cash for the month of July. Suntime Boats has the following four options available for raising the needed funds:

(1) Establish a 1-year line of credit for $1 million with a commercial bank. The commitment fee will be 0.5 percent per year on the unused portion, and the interest charge on the used funds will be 11 percent per annum. Assume that the funds are needed only in July, and that there are 30 days in July and 360 days in the year.

(2) Forgo the trade discount of 2/10, net 40, on $1 million of purchases during July.

(3) Issue $1 million of 30-day commercial paper at a 9.5 percent per annum interest rate. The total transactions fee, including the cost of a backup credit line, on using commercial paper is 0.5 percent of the amount of the issue.

(4) Issue $1 million of 60-day commercial paper at a 9 percent per annum interest rate, plus a transactions fee of 0.5 percent. Since the funds are required for only 30 days, the excess funds ($1 million) can be invested in 9.4 percent per annum marketable securities for the month of August. The total transactions cost of purchasing and selling the marketable securities is 0.4 percent of the amount of the issue.

a. What is the cost of each financing arrangement?

b. Is the source with the lowest expected cost necessarily the one to select? Why or why not?

SOLUTION TO SELF-TEST PROBLEM

ST-1 Effective rates:

1. $\dfrac{(15\%)(\$30,000)}{\$30,000} = \dfrac{\$4,500}{\$30,000} = 15\%.$

2. $\dfrac{10\%(\$30,000)}{\$30,000 - \$4,500} = \dfrac{\$3,000}{\$25,500} = 11.76\%.$

Alternative solution:

$\dfrac{10\%}{1 - 15\%} = 11.76\%.$

3. $\dfrac{(9\%)(\$30,000)}{\$30,000 - \$2,700 - \$4,500} = \dfrac{\$2,700}{\$22,800} = 11.84\%.$

Alternative solution:

$\dfrac{9\%}{1 - 9\% - 15\%} = 11.84\%.$

4. $\dfrac{(10\%)(\$30,000)}{(\$30,000/2)} = \dfrac{\$3,000}{\$15,000} = 20\%.$

Appendix 11A

The Use of Security in Short-Term Financing

Procedures under the Uniform Commercial Code for using accounts receivable and inventories as security for short-term credit are described in this appendix. As noted in this chapter, secured short-term loans involve quite a bit of paperwork and other administrative costs; hence they are relatively expensive. However, weak firms often find that they can borrow only if they put up some type of collateral to protect the lender, or they find that by using security they can borrow at a lower rate than would otherwise be possible.

Accounts Receivable Financing

Accounts receivable financing involves either the pledging of receivables or the selling of receivables (factoring). The **pledging of accounts receivable** is characterized by the fact that the lender not only has a claim against the receivables but also has **recourse** to the borrower (seller), meaning that if the person or firm that bought the goods does not pay, the selling firm (borrower) must take the loss. Therefore, the risk of default on the pledged accounts receivable remains with the borrower. Also, the buyer of the goods is not ordinarily notified about the pledging of the receivables. The financial institution that lends on the security of accounts receivable is generally either a commercial bank or one of the large industrial finance companies.

    Factoring, or *selling accounts receivable,* involves the purchase of accounts receivable by the lender, generally without recourse to the borrower (seller). Under a factoring arrangement, the buyer of the goods is typically notified of the transfer and is asked to make payments directly to the financial institution. Because the factoring firm assumes the risk of default on bad accounts, it must make the credit check. Accordingly, factors provide not only money but also a credit department for the borrower. Incidentally, the same financial institutions that make loans against pledged receivables also serve as factors. Thus, depending on the circumstances and the wishes of the borrower, a financial institution will provide either form of receivables financing.

pledging of accounts receivable
Putting accounts receivable up as security for a loan.

recourse
Situation in which the lender can require payment from the selling firm if an account receivable is uncollectible.

factoring
Outright sale of accounts receivable.

Procedure for Pledging Accounts Receivable

The financing of accounts receivable is initiated by a legally binding agreement between the seller of the goods and the financing institution. The agreement sets forth in detail the procedures to be followed and the legal obligations of both parties. Once the working relationship has been established, the seller periodically sends a batch of invoices to the financing institution. The lender reviews the invoices and makes credit appraisals of the buyers. Invoices of companies that do not meet the lender's credit standards are not accepted for pledging.

    The financial institution seeks to protect itself at every phase of the operation. First, it selects sound invoices. Second, if the buyer of the goods does not pay the invoice, the lender still has recourse against the seller of the goods. Third, additional protection is afforded the lender because the loan generally will be made for less than 100 percent of the pledged receivables; for example, the lender may advance the selling firm only 75 percent of the amount of the pledged invoices.

Procedure for Factoring Accounts Receivable

The procedure for factoring is somewhat different from that used for pledging. Again, an agreement between the seller and the factor specifies legal obligations and procedural arrangements. When the seller receives an order from a buyer, a credit approval slip is written and immediately sent to the factoring company for a credit check. If the factor approves the credit, shipment is made and the invoice is stamped to notify the buyer to make payment directly to the factoring company. If the factor does not approve the sale, the seller generally refuses to fill the order; if the sale is made anyway, the factor will not buy the account.

The factor normally performs three functions: (1) credit checking, (2) lending, and (3) risk bearing. However, the seller can select various combinations of these functions by changing provisions in the factoring agreement. For example, a small or medium-sized firm can avoid establishing a credit department by factoring receivables. The factor's charge for this service may well be less costly than maintaining a credit department that may have excess capacity for the firm's small credit volume. At the same time, if the selling firm uses an unqualified person to act as a credit analyst, then that person's lack of education, training, and experience could result in excessive losses.

The seller may use the factor to perform the credit-checking and risk-taking functions but not the lending function. The following procedure illustrates the handling of a $10,000 order under this arrangement. The factor checks and approves the invoices. The goods are shipped on terms of net 30. Payment is made to the factor, who remits to the seller. If the buyer defaults, the $10,000 must still be remitted to the seller, and if the $10,000 is never paid, the factor will sustain a $10,000 loss. Note, however, that in this situation the factor does not remit funds to the seller until either they are received from the buyer of the goods or the credit period has expired. Thus, the factor does not supply any credit.

Now consider the more typical situation in which the factor performs the lending, risk-bearing, and credit-checking functions. The goods are shipped, and even though payment is not due for 30 days, the factor immediately makes funds available to the seller. Suppose $10,000 of goods are shipped. Further, assume that the factoring commission, sometimes called a credit fee, for credit checking is 2.5 percent of the invoice price, or $250, and that the interest expense is computed at a 9 percent annual rate on the invoice balance, or $75.[1] The seller's accounting entry is as follows:

Cash	$ 9,175	
Interest expense	75	
Factoring commission	250	
Reserve due from factor on collection of account	500	
Accounts receivable		$10,000

---

[1]Because the interest is for only 1 month, we take 1/12 of the stated rate, 9 percent, and multiply this by the $10,000 invoice price:

$$(1/12)(0.09)(\$10,000) = \$75.$$

Note that the effective rate of interest is really above 9 percent, because (1) the term is for less than one year and (2) since a discounting procedure is used, the borrower does not get the full $10,000. In many instances, however, the factoring contract calls for interest to be computed on the invoice price less the factoring commission and the reserve account.

The $500 due from the factor upon collection of the account is a reserve established by the factor to cover disputes between sellers and buyers over damaged goods, goods returned by the buyers to the seller, and the failure to make an outright sale of goods. The reserve is paid to the selling firm when the factor collects on the account.

Factoring is normally a continuous process instead of the single cycle described here. The firm selling the goods receives orders; it transmits the purchase orders to the factor for approval; upon approval, the goods are shipped; the factor advances to the seller the invoice amount minus withholdings; the buyers pay the factor when payment is due; and the factor periodically remits any excess reserve to the seller of the goods. Once a routine has been established, a continuous circular flow of goods and funds takes place between the seller, the buyers of the goods, and the factor. Thus, once the factoring agreement is in force, funds from this source are *spontaneous,* in the sense that an increase in sales will automatically generate additional credit.

Cost of Receivables Financing

Accounts receivable pledging and factoring services are both convenient and advantageous, but they can be costly — especially factoring. The credit-checking and risk-bearing fee is 1 to 3 percent of the dollar amount of invoices accepted by the factor, and it may be even more if the buyers are poor credit risks. The cost of money is reflected in the interest rate (usually two to three percentage points over the prime rate) charged on the unpaid balance of the funds advanced by the factor or charged by the lender on a loan secured by pledged receivables. When risk to the factoring firm is excessive, it purchases the invoices (with or without recourse) at discounts from their face value.

Evaluation of Receivables Financing

It cannot be said categorically that accounts receivable financing is always either a good or a poor method of raising funds for an individual business. Among the advantages is, first, the flexibility of this source of financing. As the firm's sales expand, and more financing is needed, a larger volume of invoices is generated automatically. Because the dollar amounts of invoices vary directly with sales, the amount of readily available financing increases. Second, receivables provide security for a loan that a firm might otherwise be unable to obtain. Third, factoring can provide the services of a credit department that might otherwise be available to the firm only under much more expensive conditions.

Accounts receivable financing also has disadvantages. First is the cost; as discussed previously, financing charges are higher than those on unsecured credit. Second, the firm itself will incur additional administrative expenses to handle the paperwork, and if the invoices are numerous and relatively small in dollar amount, these administrative costs may be excessive. Third, some of a firm's trade creditors may refuse to sell to it on credit if it factors or pledges its receivables. This refusal is due in part to the fact that for a long time accounts receivable financing was frowned upon by most trade creditors as a sign of a firm's unsound financial position. It is no longer regarded in this light by most firms, because many financially sound firms engage in receivables factoring or pledging. Another reason for refusal is that since accounts receivables represent a firm's most liquid noncash assets (after marketable securities), factoring removes these liquid assets and accordingly weakens the position of other creditors.

Future Use of Receivables Financing

We will make a prediction at this point: in the future, accounts receivable financing will increase in relative importance. Computer technology is rapidly advancing toward the point where credit records of individuals and firms can be kept on disks and magnetic tapes. Systems are in use that allow a retailer to insert a customer's magnetic credit card into a scanner linking the store to the bank. A positive signal indicates that the credit is good and that the bank is willing to "buy" the receivable created when the store completes the sale. The cost of handling invoices is greatly reduced over older procedures because the newer systems are highly automated. This makes it possible to use accounts receivable financing for very small sales, and it reduces the cost of all receivables financing. The net result will be a marked expansion of accounts receivable financing. In fact, when consumers use credit cards like MasterCard or Visa, the seller is in effect factoring receivables. The seller normally receives the amount of the purchase, minus a percentage fee, the next working day. The buyer receives about 30 days' free credit, at which time she or he remits payment to the credit card company or sponsoring bank.

Inventory Financing

A substantial amount of credit is secured by business inventories. If a firm is a relatively good credit risk, the mere existence of the inventory may be a sufficient basis for receiving an unsecured loan. If the firm is a relatively poor risk, however, the lending institution may insist on security, which often takes the form of a *blanket lien* against the inventory. Alternatively, *trust receipts* or *warehouse receipts* can be used to secure the loan. These methods of using inventories as security are discussed in the following sections.

inventory blanket lien

A lending institution's claim on all of the borrower's inventories as security for a loan.

Inventory Blanket Lien. The **inventory blanket lien** gives the lending institution a lien against all the borrower's inventories. However, the borrower is free to sell inventories; thus the value of the collateral can be reduced below the level that existed when the loan was granted.

trust receipt

An instrument acknowledging that the borrower holds certain goods in trust for the lender.

Trust Receipts. Because of the inherent weakness of the blanket lien for inventory financing, another procedure for inventory financing has been developed — the **trust receipt.** A trust receipt is an instrument acknowledging that the borrower holds the goods in trust for the lender. When trust receipts are used, the borrowing firm, as a condition for receiving funds from the lender, signs and delivers a trust receipt for the goods. The goods can be stored in a public warehouse or be held on the borrower's premises. The trust receipt states that the goods are held in trust for the lender, or are segregated on the borrower's premises on behalf of the lender, and that any proceeds from the sale of goods held under trust receipts must be transmitted to the lender at the end of each day. Automobile dealer financing is the most common example of trust receipt financing.

One defect of trust receipt financing is the requirement that a trust receipt must be issued for specific goods. For example, if the security is autos in a dealer's inventory, the trust receipts must indicate the cars by registration number. To validate its trust receipts, the lending institution must send someone to the borrower's premises periodically to see that the auto numbers are correctly listed. Such care is necessary because borrowers who are in financial difficulty have been known to sell the assets backing the trust receipts and then use the funds obtained for other operations rather than for repaying the bank. Obviously administrative problems are compounded if borrowers have geographically diversified operations or if they are separated geographically from the lender. To offset these inconveniences, *warehousing* has come into wide use as a method of securing loans with inventory.

Warehouse Receipt Financing. Like trust receipts, **warehouse receipt financing** uses inventory as security. A *public warehouse* is an independent third-party operation engaged in the business of storing goods. Under a warehouse receipt financing arrangement, the lending institution employs the warehousing company to exercise control over the inventory and to act as its agent. Items that must age, such as tobacco and liquor, are often financed and stored in public warehouses. The value of the inventory increases as it ages, so the lender's position improves with the passage of time. However, at times a public warehouse is not practical because of the bulkiness of goods, the expense of transporting them to and from the borrower's premises, or the need for the borrower to process them on a continuous basis. In such cases, a *field warehouse* may be established on the borrower's grounds. The field warehouse arrangement is overseen by an independent third party, the field warehouse company, just as a public warehouse is run by a warehousing firm.

Field warehousing is illustrated by a simple example. Suppose a potential borrower firm has iron stacked in an open yard on its premises. A field warehouse can be established if a field warehousing concern places a temporary fence around the iron, erects a sign stating: "This is a field warehouse supervised and conducted by the Smith Field Warehousing Corporation," and assigns an employee to supervise and control the inventory. These are minimal conditions, of course.

The example illustrates the three elements in the establishment of a field warehouse: (1) public notification, (2) physical control of the inventory, and (3) supervision of the field warehouse by a custodian of the field warehousing concern. When the field warehousing operation is relatively small, the third condition is sometimes violated by hiring one of the borrower's employees to supervise the inventory. This practice is viewed as undesirable by most lending institutions, because there is no control over the collateral by a person independent of the borrowing firm.[2]

The field warehouse financing operation is best described by an actual case. A Florida vegetable cannery was interested in financing its operations by bank borrowing. The cannery had sufficient funds to finance 15 to 20 percent of its operations during the canning season. These funds were adequate to purchase and process only an initial batch of vegetables. As the cans were put into boxes and rolled into the storerooms, the cannery needed additional funds for both raw materials and labor. Because of the cannery's poor credit rating, the bank decided that a field warehousing operation would be necessary to secure its loans.

warehouse receipt financing
An arrangement under which the lending institution employs a third party to exercise control over the borrower's inventory and to act as the lender's agent.

---

[2]This absence of independent control was the main cause of the breakdown that resulted in the huge losses connected with the loans to the Allied Crude Vegetable Oil Company. American Express Field Warehousing Company hired men from Allied's staff as custodians. Their dishonesty was not discovered because of another breakdown — the fact that the American Express touring inspector did not actually take a physical inventory of the warehouses. As a consequence, the swindle was not discovered until losses running into the hundreds of millions of dollars had been suffered. See N. C. Miller, *The Great Salad Oil Swindle* (Baltimore, Md.: Penguin Books, 1965), 72–77.

The field warehouse was established, and the custodian notified the bank of the description, by number, of the boxes of canned vegetables in storage and under warehouse control. With this inventory as collateral, the bank established a line of credit for the cannery on which it could draw. From this point on, the bank financed the operations. The cannery needed only enough cash to initiate the cycle. Farmers brought more vegetables; the cannery processed them; the cans were boxed and the boxes were put into the field warehouse; field warehouse receipts were drawn up and sent to the bank; the bank increased the credit line for the cannery on the basis of additional collateral; and the cannery could draw on the credit line to continue the cycle.

Of course, the cannery's ultimate objective was to sell the canned vegetables. As the cannery received purchase orders, it transmitted them to the bank, and the bank directed the custodian to release the inventories. It was agreed that, as remittances were received by the cannery, they would be turned over to the bank. These remittances by the cannery paid off the loans made by the bank.

Typically, a seasonal pattern exists. In this example, at the beginning of the harvesting and canning season, the cannery's cash needs and loan requirements began to rise and reached a maximum at the end of the canning season. It was hoped that well before the new canning season begins, the cannery would have sold a sufficient volume to have paid off the loan completely. If for some reason the cannery had a bad year, the bank might carry part of the loan over another year to enable the company to work off its inventory.

Acceptable Products. In addition to canned foods, which account for about 17 percent of all field warehousing loans, many other types of products provide a basis for field warehouse financing. Some of these are miscellaneous groceries, which represent about 13 percent; lumber products, about 10 percent; and coal and coke, about 6 percent. These products are relatively nonperishable and are sold in well-developed, organized markets. Nonperishability protects the lender if it should have to take over the security. For this reason, a bank would not make a field warehousing loan on perishables such as fresh fish; however, frozen fish, which can be stored for a long time, can be field warehoused. An organized market aids the lender in disposing of an inventory that it takes over. Banks are not interested in going into the canning or the fish business. They want to be able to dispose of an inventory with the expenditure of a minimum of time.

Cost of Financing. The fixed costs of a field warehousing arrangement are relatively high; such financing is therefore not suitable for a very small firm. If a field warehousing company sets up the field warehouse itself, it will typically set a minimum charge of about $10,000 a year, plus about 1 to 2 percent of the amount of credit extended to the borrower. Furthermore, the financing institution will charge an interest rate of two to three percentage points over the prime rate. An efficient field warehousing operation requires a minimum inventory of about $1 million.

Appraisal. The use of inventory financing, especially field warehouse financing, as a source of funds for business firms has many advantages. First, the amount of funds available is flexible because the financing is tied to the growth of inventories, which in turn is related directly to financing needs. Second, the field warehousing arrangement increases the acceptability of inventories as loan collateral. Some inventories would not be accepted by a bank as security without a field warehousing arrangement. Third, the necessity for inventory control, safekeeping, and the use of specialists in warehousing, results in improved warehousing practices, which in turn save handling costs, insurance charges, theft losses, and so on. Thus, field warehousing companies often have saved money for firms in spite of the financing charges. The major disadvantages of a field warehousing operation are the paperwork, physical separation requirements, and, for small firms, the fixed-cost element.

PROBLEMS

11A-1 **Factoring receivables.** Muriel Industries is considering two methods of raising working capital: (1) a commercial bank loan secured by accounts receivable and (2) factoring accounts receivable. Muriel's bank has agreed to lend the firm 75 percent of its average monthly accounts receivable balance of $250,000 at an annual interest rate of 9 percent. The loan would be discounted, and a 20 percent compensating balance would also be required.

A factor has agreed to purchase Muriel's accounts receivable and to advance 85 percent of the balance to the firm. The factor would charge a 3.5 percent factoring commission and annual interest of 9 percent on the invoice price, minus both the factoring commission and the reserve account. The monthly interest payment would be deducted from the advance. If Muriel chooses the factoring arrangement, it can eliminate its credit department and reduce operating expenses by $4,000 per month. In addition, bad debt losses of 2 percent of the monthly receivables will be avoided.

a. What is the annual cost associated with each financial arrangement?

b. Discuss some considerations other than cost that might influence management's decision between factoring and a commercial bank loan.

11A-2 **Inventory financing.** Because of crop failures last year, the Midwest Valley Packing Company has no funds available to finance its canning operations during the next 6 months. It estimates that it will require $1,800,000 for inventory financing during the period. One alternative is to establish a 6-month, $2,250,000 line of credit with terms of 9 percent annual interest on the used portion, a 1 percent commitment fee on the unused portion, and a $450,000 compensating balance at all times.

Expected inventory levels to be financed are as follows:

Month	Amount
July 1991	$ 375,000
August	1,500,000
September	1,800,000
October	1,425,000
November	900,000
December	0

Calculate the cost of funds from this source, including interest charges and commitment fees. (*Hint:* Each month's borrowings will be $450,000 greater than the inventory level to be financed because of the compensating balance requirement.)

11A-3 **Field warehouse financing.** Because canned vegetables have a relatively long shelf life, field warehouse financing would also be appropriate for the Midwest Valley Packing Company in Problem 11A-2. The costs of the field warehousing alternative in this case would be a flat fee of $2,000, plus 8 percent annual interest on all outstanding credit, plus 1 percent of the maximum amount of credit extended.

a. Calculate the total cost of the field warehousing operation.

b. Compare the cost of the field warehousing arrangement to the line of credit cost in Problem 11A-2.

Which alternative should Midwest Valley choose?

11A-4   **Factoring receivables.** The Lathrop Corporation needs an additional $500,000, which it plans to obtain through a factoring arrangement. The factor would purchase Lathrop's accounts receivable and advance the invoice amount, minus a 1 percent commission, on the invoices purchased each month. Lathrop sells on terms of net 30 days. In addition, the factor charges a 13 percent annual interest rate on the total invoice amount, to be deducted in advance.

   a. What amount of accounts receivable must be factored to net $500,000?

   b. If Lathrop can reduce credit expenses by $1,000 per month and avoid bad debt losses of 2 percent on the factored amount, what is the total dollar cost of the factoring arrangement?

   (Do Parts c and d only if you are using the computerized problem diskette.)

   c. Would it be to Lathrop's advantage to offer to pay the factor a commission of 1.25 percent if it would lower the interest rate to 12 percent annually?

   d. Assume a commission of 1 percent and an interest rate of 13 percent. What would be the total cost of the factoring arrangement if the amount of funds Lathrop needed rose to $1,000,000? Would the factoring arrangement be profitable under these circumstances?

Part IV

CAPITAL BUDGETING: INVESTMENT IN FIXED ASSETS

The previous section dealt with investment decisions that concerned assets with short-term lives. In this section we present techniques for evaluating investment opportunities in long-term assets.

Chapter 12 formally introduces risk — in it we discuss ways of measuring risk, emphasizing the effect of risk on the capital budgeting decision. Because financial management often deals with situations in which we make expenditures today in exchange for future cash flows, techniques that correctly evaluate cash flows from different time periods must be developed. This important concept, the time value of money, is presented in Chapter 13, and then applied in Chapter 14, where the basic methods of capital budgeting analysis are introduced. Chapter 15 extends and refines our treatment of capital budgeting analysis, with an emphasis on how risk is handled.

Chapter 12

Risk and Return

 DECISION IN FINANCE

When Money Is Not the Only Thing at Risk

Taking big risks with no assurance of return has been, for many years, a hallmark of Canada's Reichmann brothers, former floor tile importers whose real estate enterprises now span the globe. Their firm, Olympia & York, is now the richest and most powerful real estate development company in the world. Its $25 billion in properties includes the World Financial Center in lower Manhattan; Europe's largest real estate development, Canary Wharf, which is in a depressed area near London's Thames River; First Canadian Place in Toronto, the company's home base; and more than 50 office buildings in the United States and Canada.

Paul Reichmann is the firm's leader, and his brother, Ralph, runs the building materials business. Another brother, Albert, is currently working on a project in Moscow. The company also has ambitious plans in Japan.

For the past 30 years, as it has grown into a giant in its industry, Olympia & York has been known as an innovative firm. Paul Reichmann

was among the first to realize that local government plays a pivotal role in regulating office space in an urban area. In the 1970s, he worked with Toronto officials to help design underground shopping malls for that city. "We find out what a city needs and wants, then design and develop in support of their aims," he says.

The company has participated in joint public-private projects to create whole new urban centers. One such project was the World Financial Center in lower Manhattan, constructed on inexpensive land provided by the city. The Reichmanns spent $300 million of their company's money on the center before seeking outside financing. The project helped subsidize neighboring housing and also created public spaces, changing that part of the city for the better, in much the same way Rockefeller Center changed midtown Manhattan.

The $6.6 billion Canary Wharf project is three miles from the heart of London, in a dilapidated riverside area. Plans for the 71-acre site include 24 office buildings, as well as stores, restaurants, a hotel, parks, and waterways. "We're building a whole neighborhood," says

---

See end of chapter for resolution.

405

Olympia & York's London chief. The company put up $2 billion of its own money for the first phase of the project. To persuade the government to extend a vital subway line to the development, the Reichmanns hired an expensive team of experts to plan the line, and it also agreed to help pay for the construction. Parliament approved the plan after about two years, as did Prime Minister Margaret Thatcher. With 10 million square feet of office space to fill at Canary Wharf, Paul Reichmann will undoubtedly rely on one of the innovative strategies that have worked so well in other projects: finding tenants first and financing later. As a real estate broker explains, "With no risk in the deal anymore, they borrow at the lowest possible rate."

The successful World Financial Center in New York has a 90 percent office occupancy rate. Reichmann knew that major firms had to be located there if the project was to become a prestigious business address, so he negotiated for 16 months to acquire American Express as a key tenant, along with Merrill Lynch and Dow Jones. He acquired the former offices of the first two firms in trade and allowed American Express to finish its new office tower to its own specifications. He is expected to negotiate similar deals in London to attract major tenants to Canary Wharf. However, by early 1990, only Merrill Lynch and Texaco had committed to the project (with a third large client probably planning to commit), which still left 80 percent of the project's first stage to be filled. Since the Reichmanns purchased the land for about a tenth of what similar land would have cost in central London, they can charge much lower rents than other business landlords. Nevertheless, vacancy rates have risen throughout the city because of a soft British economy, and the downturn may affect Canary Wharf as well.

Paul Reichmann justifies his firm's huge risks on the Canary Wharf project by saying that office space in most European cities is woefully inadequate compared with that in North America. He believes that the service revolution is just beginning in Europe, and he says that the growing banking, insurance, and trade industries will need modern offices. "Europe is still at a relatively early stage of renewal. London will be the business capital of Europe."

In Moscow, the firm plans to build a modern office tower for Western companies. The $210 million, 60-story structure will be the tallest in the Russian capital. Olympia & York employees demonstrated their modern construction techniques to Soviet officials by escorting them around the Canary Wharf site. In Japan, the firm is helping three Mitsubishi companies bid for contracts on a $30 billion Tokyo Bay landfill project that is so huge that it will be comparable to a second downtown Tokyo.

The Reichmanns' ability to negotiate such megaprojects has depended largely on their impeccable reputation — not only for high standards but also for keen intuition and outstanding business acumen. That reputation, however, is now threatened by one deal that did not turn out well. When fellow Canadian Robert Campeau's real estate and retailing company began to fail, the Reichmanns stepped in to help. At first they were praised as white knights, but Campeau's slide into bankruptcy also changed this praise to criticism of the Reichmanns. As you read this chapter, consider the kinds of risks Olympia & York assumed in its attempts to help Campeau, and why the Campeau deal could hurt the development company.

In this chapter, we will discuss risk and return concepts as they apply to all investors. These concepts are applicable to individual investors, when they buy stocks and bonds, and to corporations, when they invest in physical assets (capital budgeting decisions) as well as financial assets. All types of investments involve cash flows. The riskiness of those cash flows can be considered by itself, on a *stand-alone basis,* or in a *portfolio context,* where the asset is combined with other assets. In the portfolio context, we see that risk can be reduced through *diversification.* All of these topics will be discussed in the text.

Recall from our discussion in Chapter 4, on the determination of interest rates, that the interest rate on a debt security is established as the risk-free rate plus some additional premiums. The interest rate on debt depends on the riskiness of that debt. In a similar manner, stocks (which will be discussed in more detail in Chapter 17) and physical assets have an "interest rate," called the *required rate of return,* which is also dependent on risk. In this chapter, we will discuss how to measure risk.

Here, we will define the term *risk* as it applies to financial matters, discuss procedures for measuring it, and determine how risk-return characteristics may be incorporated into the investment decision process. The approach taken in this chapter is to discuss financial assets, such as stocks and bonds. However, the general approach is the same for firms investing in physical, or real, assets, as in capital budgeting, and in Chapter 15, we apply risk-return concepts to the capital budgeting decision process.

DEFINING AND MEASURING RISK

Risk is defined in *Webster's* as "a hazard; a peril; exposure to loss or injury." Thus, risk refers to the chance that some unfavorable event will occur. If you engage in skydiving, you take a chance with your life — skydiving is risky. If you bet on the horses, you risk losing your money. If you invest in speculative stocks (or, really, in *any* stock), you are taking a risk in the hope of making an appreciable return.

risk
The chance that some unfavorable event will occur.

To illustrate the riskiness of financial assets, suppose an investor buys $100,000 of short-term government bonds with an interest rate of 8 percent. In this case the rate of return on the investment, 8 percent, can be estimated quite precisely, and the investment is said to be risk-free. However, if the $100,000 were invested in the stock of a company just being organized to prospect for oil in the mid-Atlantic, then the investment's return could not be estimated precisely. One might analyze the situation and conclude that the *expected* rate of return is 20 percent. However, the *actual* rate of return could range from an extremely large positive return, say $+1,000$ percent, to a total loss of invested capital, -100 percent. Because there is a significant danger of actually earning a return considerably less than the expected return, the investment would be described as being relatively risky.

Of course, no investment would be made unless the expected rate of return was high enough to compensate the investor for taking extra risks. In fact, we could generalize by saying that the higher the perceived risk associated with an investment opportunity, the greater its expected return must be to persuade someone to accept the investment. In this example, it is clear that few, if any, investors would buy the oil company stock if its expected return were the same as that of the government bond. Naturally, the risky investment might not actually produce the higher rate of return; if the highest-risk projects always provided the highest returns, there would be no risk.

Investment risk, then, is related to the probability of earning a return less than the expected return — the greater the chances of low or negative returns, the riskier the investment. We can define risk more precisely, however, and in the following sections we will do so.

Probability Distributions

An event's *probability* is defined as the chance that the event will occur. For example, a weather forecaster may state, "There is a 40 percent chance of rain today and a 60 percent chance that it will not rain." If all possible events, or outcomes, are listed, and if a probability is assigned to each event, the listing is called a **probability distribution.** For a weather forecast, we could set up the following probability distribution:

probability distribution
A listing of all possible outcomes, or events, with a probability (chance of occurrence) assigned to each outcome.

Outcome (1)	Probability (2)
Rain	0.4 = 40%
No rain	0.6 = 60%
	1.0 = 100%

The possible outcomes are listed in Column 1, and the probabilities of these outcomes, expressed both as decimals and as percentages, are given in Column 2. Notice that the probabilities must sum to 1.0, or 100 percent.

Eastern Communications, Inc., a manufacturer and retailer of business and consumer telephones, is considering the projected rates of return on two telephones, its Standard Phone line and its new Designer Phone. Most of the firm's marketing managers believe that the Designer line should have a higher return than the Standard line in "boom" and "normal" economic periods, but in recessionary periods, when consumers typically have less to spend on luxury items, the Designer line is not expected to be profitable. Before money is invested to manufacture the phones, Eastern Communications wishes to determine the risk and return of these two products in a more direct manner.

The state of the economy and the resulting rate of return on each phone are presented in Table 12-1. Here we see that there is a 30 percent chance of a boom, in which case both products will enjoy high rates of return; a 40 percent chance of a normal economy and moderate returns; and a 30 percent probability of a recession, which will mean a low return for the Standard phone and a negative return for the Designer phone. Of course, the profits of the luxury Designer phone are more sensitive to the economic environment than the profits of the Standard phone. In fact, in recessionary periods the return on the Designer phone will drop significantly, resulting in a loss of 70 percent, while the Standard phone has no loss.

Table 12-1 **Projected Return on Each Phone Based on the State of the Economy**

Designer Phone

State of the Economy	Probability of This State Occurring	Rate of Return under This State
Boom	0.3	100%
Normal	0.4	15
Recession	0.3	$-$ 70
	1.0	

Standard Phone

State of the Economy	Probability of This State Occurring	Rate of Return under This State
Boom	0.3	20%
Normal	0.4	15
Recession	0.3	10
	1.0	

Expected Rate of Return

If we multiply each possible outcome by its probability of occurrence and then sum these products, we have a *weighted average* of outcomes. This weighted average of outcomes can be expressed in equation form as the **expected rate of return, k̂,** of a probability distribution:

$$\text{Expected rate of return} = \hat{k} = \sum_{i=1}^{n} P_i k_i. \tag{12-1}$$

Here the expected rate of return, $\hat{k}$, is the weighted average of each possible outcome, k_i, weighted by the probability of its occurrence, P_i. Using the data for the Designer line, we obtain its expected rate of return as follows:

$$\hat{k} = P_1(k_1) + P_2(k_2) + P_3(k_3)$$

$$= 0.3(100\%) + 0.4(15\%) + 0.3(-70\%)$$

$$= 15\%.$$

Similarly, we can use Equation 12-1 to determine the expected rate of return for the Standard line:

$$\hat{k} = 0.3(20\%) + 0.4(15\%) + 0.3(10\%)$$

$$= 15\%.$$

expected rate of return, k̂
The rate of return expected to be realized from an investment; the mean value of the probability distribution of possible outcomes.

Figure 12-1 **Probability Distributions of the Rates of Return for the Designer and Standard Telephone Projects: Eastern Communications, Inc.**

The expected rate of return on a project is equal to the average of all possible outcomes, with each outcome weighted by the probability of its occurrence. These bar charts show the variability of three possible outcomes for each of two projects. An average (or expected) return of 15 percent is most probable for both, but the Designer line has a much wider range of return possibilities than that for the Standard line. Thus, the Designer line is the riskier project.

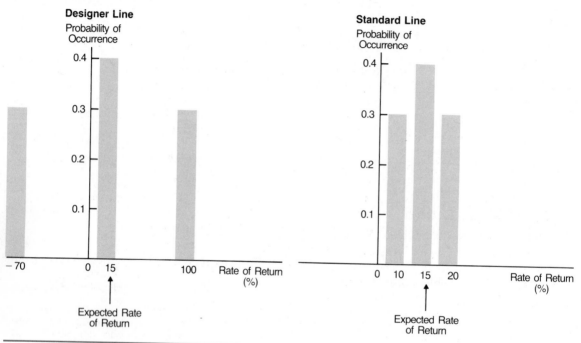

We can graph the rates of return to obtain a picture of the variability of the possible outcomes; this is shown in the bar charts in Figure 12-1. The height of each bar signifies the probability that a given outcome will occur. The range of possible returns for the Designer line is from 100 percent to −70 percent, with an average, or expected, return of 15 percent. The expected return for the Standard line is also 15 percent, but with a much narrower range of return possibilities.

Continuous Probability Distributions

Thus far, we have assumed that only three states of the economy can exist: recession, normal, and boom. Actually, of course, the state of the economy could range from a deep depression to a fantastic boom, and there are an

Figure 12-2 **Continuous Probability Distributions of the Designer and Standard Lines' Rates of Return**

Figure 12-1 graphed the probabilities of three possible outcomes for each telephone project. In reality, both projects could have numerous rates of return, which could be illustrated best by the continuous probability curves shown here. These curves indicate that the most likely rate of return for both products is 15 percent. In addition, the relative flatness of the curves indicates the extent to which returns are likely to vary from 15 percent. The height of the curve for the Standard line indicates a tight probability distribution and reflects the fact that there is a very low probability that the return will be below 10 percent or above 20 percent. The curve for the Designer line is much flatter, meaning that this project has a higher probability of returning either more or less than 15 percent, so it has the higher risk.

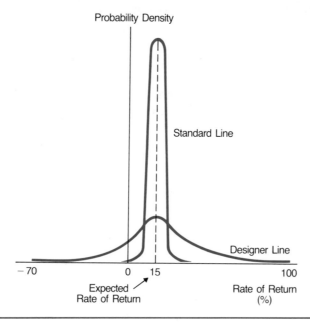

Note: The assumptions about the probabilities of various outcomes have been changed from those in Figure 12-1. There the probability of obtaining exactly 15 percent was 40 percent; here it is *much smaller*, because there are many possible outcomes instead of just three.

unlimited number of possibilities in between. Suppose we had the time and patience to assign a probability to each possible state of the economy (with the sum of the probabilities still equaling 1.0) and to assign a rate of return to each project for each state of the economy. We would have an equation similar to Equation 12-1 except that it would have many more entries. This equation could be used to calculate expected rates of return as shown previously, and the probabilities and outcomes could be approximated by the continuous curves presented in Figure 12-2. Here we have changed the assumptions so that there is a very low probability that the Designer line's return will be less than −70 percent or more than 100 percent, or that the Standard line's return will be less than 10 percent or more than 20 percent, but virtually any return within these limits is possible.

The tighter, or more peaked, the probability distribution, the more likely it is that the actual outcome will be close to the expected value, and, consequently, the less likely it is that the actual return will end up far below the expected return. Thus, the tighter the probability distribution, the lower the risk assigned to a project. Since the Standard line has a relatively tight probability distribution, its *actual return* is likely to be closer to the 15 percent *expected return* than is that of the Designer line.

Measuring Risk: The Standard Deviation

Risk is a difficult concept to grasp, and a great deal of controversy has surrounded attempts to define and measure it. However, a common definition for **measuring risk,** and one that is satisfactory for many purposes, is stated in terms of probability distributions like those presented in Figure 12-2. *The tighter the probability distribution of expected future returns, the smaller the risk of a given investment.* According to this definition, the Standard line of telephones is less risky than the Designer line, because the chances of a large loss on the Standard line are smaller than the chances of a similar loss on the Designer line.

To be most useful, any measure of risk should have a definite value; we need a measure of the tightness of the probability distribution. One such measure is the **standard deviation,** the symbol for which is **σ**, pronounced "sigma." The smaller the standard deviation, the tighter the probability distribution and, accordingly, the lower the riskiness of the project. The calculation of the standard deviation is outlined as follows:

measuring risk
A common definition is that the tighter the probability distribution of expected future returns, the smaller the risk of a given investment.

standard deviation, σ
A statistical measurement of the variability of a set of observations.

1. Calculate the expected rate of return:

$$\text{Expected rate of return} = \hat{k} = \sum_{i=1}^{n} P_i k_i. \tag{12-1}$$

For both projects, we found $\hat{k} = 15\%$.

2. Subtract the expected rate of return from each possible outcome to obtain a set of deviations about the expected rate of return, $\hat{k}$:

$$\text{Deviation}_i = k_i - \hat{k}.$$

3. Square each deviation, multiply the squared deviation by the probability of occurrence for its related outcome, and sum these products to obtain the **variance, σ²,** of the probability distribution:

variance, σ²
The square of the standard deviation.

$$\text{Variance} = \sigma^2 = \sum_{i=1}^{n} (k_i - \hat{k})^2 P_i. \tag{12-2}$$

4. Find the standard deviation by obtaining the square root of the variance:

$$\text{Standard deviation} = \sigma = \sqrt{\sum_{i=1}^{n}(k_i - \hat{k})^2 P_i.} \qquad (12\text{-}3)$$

5. We can illustrate these procedures by calculating the standard deviation for both the Designer and Standard lines:

a. Designer line:

(1) The expected rate of return, $\hat{k}$, is found, using Equation 12-1, to be 15 percent.

(2) Following the steps outlined before, we set up a table to work out the value for Equation 12-3:

(a) In Column 1, we subtract the expected return from each possible outcome to obtain Column 2, a set of deviations about $\hat{k}$.

(b) In Column 3, we square each of these deviations.

(c) In Column 4, these squared deviations are multiplied by the probability of their occurrence.

(d) In Column 5, these products are summed to obtain the variance of the probability distribution, 4,335.

(e) Below the table, we take the square root of the variance to obtain the probability distribution's standard deviation, 65.84%.

1		2	3	4	5
$k_i - \hat{k}$	=	$(k_i - \hat{k})$	$(k_i - \hat{k})^2$	$(k_i - \hat{k})^2 P_i$	
$100 - 15$		85	7,225	$(7,225)(0.3) = 2,167.5$	
$15 - 15$		0	0	$(0)(0.4) = 0.0$	
$-70 - 15$		-85	7,225	$(7,225)(0.3) = \underline{2,167.5}$	
				Variance $= \sigma_k^2 = \underline{\underline{4,335.0}}$	

$$\text{Standard deviation} = \sigma_k = \sqrt{\sigma_k^2} = \sqrt{4,335.0} = 65.84\%.$$

b. Standard line:

(1) The expected rate of return, $\hat{k}$, is 15 percent.

(2) As before, we compute the project's risk measure, the standard deviation, by utilizing the previously outlined steps to solve Equation 12-3:

1		2	3	4	5
$k_i - \hat{k}$	=	$(k_i - \hat{k})$	$(k_i - \hat{k})^2$	$(k_i - \hat{k})^2 P_i$	
$20 - 15$		5	25	$(25)(0.3) = 7.5$	
$15 - 15$		0	0	$(0)(0.4) = 0.0$	
$10 - 15$		-5	25	$(25)(0.3) = \underline{7.5}$	
				Variance $= \sigma_k^2 = \underline{\underline{15.0}}$	

$$\text{Standard deviation} = \sigma_k = \sqrt{\sigma_k^2} = \sqrt{15} = 3.87\%.$$

If a probability distribution is normal, as pictured in Figure 12-3, the actual return will lie within ± 1 standard deviation of the *expected* return about 68

Figure 12-3 **Probability Ranges for a Normal Distribution**

This figure illustrates a normal probability curve. In a normal distribution the actual value will fall within ± 1 standard deviation of the expected value about 68 percent of the time. Thus, in the Eastern Communications, Inc., example, 68 percent of the time the Standard line's actual return will be in the range of 15 percent $\pm$ 3.87 percent. Similarly, there is a 68 percent chance that the Designer line's return will fall in the range of 15 percent $\pm$ 65.84 percent. The normal curve again highlights the greater risk associated with the Designer line.

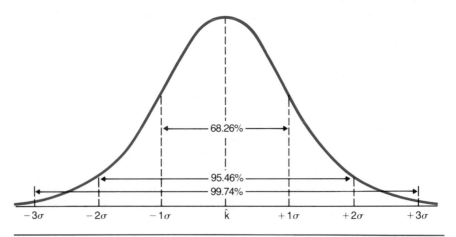

Notes:
1. The area under the normal curve equals 1.0, or 100%. *Thus, the areas under any pair of normal curves drawn on the same scale, whether they are peaked or flat, must be equal.*
2. Half of the area under a normal curve is to the left of the mean, indicating that there is a 50% probability that the actual outcome will be less than the mean, and a 50% probability that it will be greater than the mean, or to the right of it.
3. Of the area under the curve, 68.26% is within $\pm 1\sigma$ of the mean, indicating that the probability is 68.26% that the actual outcome will be within the range $\hat{k} - 1\sigma$ to $\hat{k} + 1\sigma$.
4. Procedures are available for finding the probability of other earnings ranges. These procedures are covered in statistics courses.
5. For a normal distribution, the larger the value of σ, the greater the probability that the actual outcome will vary widely from, hence perhaps be far below, the expected, or most likely, outcome. Because the probability of having the actual result turn out to be far below the expected result is one definition of risk, and because σ measures this probability, we can use σ as a measure of risk. This definition may not be a good one, however, if we are dealing with an asset held in a diversified portfolio. This point is covered later in the chapter.

percent (68.26 percent, to be exact) of the time. Figure 12-3 illustrates this point and also shows the situation for $\pm 2\sigma$ and $\pm 3\sigma$. For the Designer line, $\hat{k} = 15$ percent and $\sigma = 65.84$ percent. Thus, there is a 68.26 percent probability that the actual return will be in the range of 15 percent $\pm$ 65.84 percent, or from -50.84 percent to 80.84 percent. In a similar fashion, the expected return for the Standard line is 15 percent, but the project's standard deviation is 3.87 percent. Thus, for the Standard line there is a 68.26 percent probability that the actual return will be in the range of 15 percent $\pm$ 3.87 percent, or from 11.13 to 18.87 percent. With such a small standard deviation for the Standard line, we can conclude that there will be little chance of significant loss from investing in that product line, so the project is not very risky.[1]

Measuring Risk: The Coefficient of Variation

Another useful measure of risk, the **coefficient of variation,** is calculated by dividing the standard deviation by the expected return of the investment. The coefficient of variation (CV) shows the risk per unit of return, and it provides a more meaningful comparison when the expected returns on two alternatives are not the same. Since the Designer line and the Standard line have the same expected return, the calculation of the coefficient of variation is not really necessary in this case, because the result is obvious; the project with the larger standard deviation, the Designer line, will have the larger coefficient of variation. In fact, the coefficient of variation for the Designer line is 65.84%/15% = 4.39, whereas the CV for the Standard line is 3.87%/15% = 0.26. On the basis of this criterion, the Designer line is almost 17 times as risky as the Standard line.

coefficient of variation
Standardized measure of the risk per unit of return; calculated as the standard deviation divided by the expected return.

----

[1] In the example we described the procedure for finding the mean and standard deviation when the data are in the form of a known probability distribution. If only sample returns data over some past period are available, the standard deviation of returns can be estimated using this formula:

$$\text{Estimated } \sigma = S = \sqrt{\frac{\sum_{t=1}^{n} (\bar{k}_t - \bar{k}_{Avg})^2}{n - 1}} \qquad \text{(12-3a)}$$

Here $\bar{k}_t$ ("k bar t") denotes the past realized rate of return in Period t, and $\bar{k}_{Avg}$ is the average annual return earned during the last n years. Here is an example:

Year	$\bar{k}_t$
1988	15%
1989	−5
1990	20

$$\bar{k}_{Avg} = \frac{(15 - 5 + 20)}{3} = 10.0\%.$$

$$\text{Estimated } \sigma \text{ (or S)} = \sqrt{\frac{(15 - 10)^2 + (-5 - 10)^2 + (20 - 10)^2}{3 - 1}}$$

$$= \sqrt{\frac{350}{2}} = 13.2\%.$$

Often the historical σ is used as an estimate of the future σ. Much less often, and generally incorrectly, $\bar{k}_{Avg}$ for some past period is used as an estimate of $\hat{k}$, the expected future return. Because past variability is likely to be repeated, σ may be a good estimate of future risk, but it is much less reasonable to expect that the past *level* of return (which could have been as high as +100% or as low as −50%) is the best expectation of what investors think will happen in the future.

Now consider two other projects, A and B, which have different expected rates of return and different standard deviations. Project A has a 45 percent expected rate of return and a standard deviation of 15 percent, while Project B has an expected rate of return of 20 percent and a standard deviation of 10 percent. Is Project A riskier because it has the larger standard deviation? If we calculate the coefficients of variation for these two projects, we find that Project A has a coefficient of variation of 15%/45% = 0.33, and Project B has a coefficient of variation of 10%/20% = 0.50. Thus, we see that Project B actually has more risk per unit of return than Project A, even though Project A's standard deviation is larger. Therefore, by the coefficient of variation measure, Project B is riskier. When such differences occur, the coefficient of variation is generally the better measure of risk than the standard deviation alone.

Risk Aversion and Required Returns

Previously, we had been looking at projects as investments. Now, suppose you have worked hard and saved $100,000, which you plan to invest. You can buy a 10 percent U.S. Treasury note, and at the end of 1 year you will have a return of $110,000, which is your original investment plus $10,000 interest. The risk on this investment is quite low, and it is risk-free from the standpoint of default risk. Alternatively, you can buy stock in Genetic Innovations, Inc (GII). If GII's medical research programs are successful, you think the stock will increase in value to $220,000; however, if the research is a failure, the value of your stock will be zero, and you will lose all of your savings. You regard GII's chances of success or failure as being 50/50, so the expected value of the stock investment is 0.5($0) + 0.5($220,000) = $110,000. Subtracting the $100,000 cost of the stock leaves an expected profit of $10,000, or an expected (but risky) 10 percent rate of return:

$$\text{Expected rate of return} = (\text{Expected ending investment value} - \text{Cost})/\text{Cost}$$

$$= (\$110,000 - \$100,000)/\$100,000$$

$$= \$10,000/\$100,000$$

$$= 10 \text{ percent.}$$

Thus, you have a choice between a sure $10,000 profit (representing a 10 percent rate of return) on the Treasury note or a risky expected $10,000 profit (also representing a 10 percent expected rate of return) on the Genetic Innovations stock. Which one would you choose? *If you choose the less risky investment, you are risk averse. Most investors are indeed risk averse, and certainly the average investor is risk averse, at least with regard to his or her "serious money." Because this is a well-documented fact, we shall assume* **risk aversion** *throughout the remainder of this book.* However, the concept of risk aversion does *not* mean that investors are afraid of taking chances; rather, risk aversion indicates that individuals or businesses will take on risks only if a stock's or project's expected rate of return is sufficiently high to justify taking the risk.

risk aversion

A dislike for risk. Risk averse investors demand higher rates of return on higher-risk investments.

What are the implications of risk aversion for security prices and rates of return? The answer is that, other things held constant, the higher a security's risk, (1) the lower its price and (2) the higher its required return. To see how this works, assume that two stocks are available for investment. Suppose each stock has the same expected return and the same stock price, but they have very different risk profiles. The first, TotWear Products, a respected manufacturer of children's clothing, has little risk, and its expected rate of return is 15 percent. TotWear's common stock sells for $75. The second firm, SilTek, is involved in new technology for superconductors. SilTek's return is also expected to be 15 percent, but its returns have always been highly variable and thus risky, and they will remain so in the future due to the nature of the firm's products. SilTek's stock also sells for $75. Investors are risk averse, so with the two selling at the same price and with the same expected return, there would be a general preference for the less risky TotWear's stock. Therefore, people with money to invest would purchase TotWear's rather than SilTek's stock. Simultaneously, SilTek's stockholders would start selling shares and using the money to buy TotWear's stock. These actions would cause TotWear's price to rise and SilTek's price to decline.

These price changes, in turn, would cause changes in the expected rates of return on the two securities. Suppose, for example, that the price of TotWear's stock was bid up from $75 to $112.50, while the price of SilTek's stock declined from $75 to $56.25. Further, suppose this caused TotWear's expected rate of return to fall to 10 percent, while SilTek's expected return rose to 20 percent. The difference in returns, 20% − 10% = 10%, is a **risk premium, RP,** which represents the compensation investors require for assuming the additional risk of SilTek's stock.[2]

This example demonstrates a very important principle: *In a market dominated by risk averse investors, riskier securities must have higher expected returns as estimated by the marginal investor than less risky securities, for if this situation does not hold, actions will occur in the market to force it to come about.* We will discuss how the market prices financial assets such as bonds and common stock in subsequent chapters. Later in this chapter, we will consider the question of *how much* higher the returns of risky assets must be, after we examine in more depth how risk should be measured.

risk premium, RP
The difference between the expected rate of return on a given risky asset and that on a less risky asset.

Self-Test

Briefly explain the differences between the assumptions used in Figures 12-1 and 12-2.

Which of the two projects graphed in Figure 12-2 is less risky? Explain your answer.

---

[2]The relationship between a stock's price and its expected rate of return will be explored in greater detail in Chapters 17 and 19.

Which is a better measure of risk: (1) standard deviation or (2) coefficient of variation? Explain.

Explain what is meant by the following statement: "Most investors are risk averse."

What are the implications of risk aversion for security prices and relative rates of return?

PORTFOLIO RISK AND THE CAPITAL ASSET PRICING MODEL

In the preceding sections we considered the description and measurement of risk for an asset held in isolation or on a stand-alone basis. Now we analyze the effect of combining two or more investments into a portfolio of assets. As we shall see, investing in more than one project may actually reduce the firm's overall risk. To investigate this phenomenon, we utilize an investment in common stock such as TotWear, as opposed to an investment in capital budgeting projects like the telephones. We do this in our analysis because the risk reduction effects of combining assets were first recognized in a stock market context. Note, though, that the analysis of real and financial assets is quite similar on an analytical basis, as we shall see in our study of capital budgeting in Chapter 15.

An asset held as part of a portfolio is less risky than the same asset held in isolation. This fact has been incorporated into a generalized framework for analyzing the relationship between risk and rates of return. This framework is called the **Capital Asset Pricing Model,** or the **CAPM,** and it is an extremely important analytical tool in both financial management and investment analysis.

Capital Asset Pricing Model (CAPM)
A model based on the proposition that any stock's required rate of return is equal to the risk-free rate of return plus its risk premium, where its risk reflects the effects of diversification.

Portfolio Risk

Most financial assets are not held in isolation; rather, they are held as parts of portfolios. Banks, pension funds, insurance companies, mutual funds, and other financial institutions are required by law to hold diversified portfolios. Even individual investors — at least those individuals whose security holdings constitute a substantial part of their total wealth — generally hold stock portfolios, not just the stock of one firm. Even individuals with relatively small amounts of money to invest can obtain diversification quite easily by investing in mutual funds. Since investors can and do hold portfolios, the fact that a particular stock goes up or down is not very important; *what is important is the return of the portfolio and the portfolio's risk.* Logically, then, the risk and return of an individual security should be analyzed in terms of how that security affects the risk and return of the portfolio in which it is held.

To illustrate this point, suppose you have $100,000 to invest. You are considering two stocks. Atlas Industries and Walker Products, whose total returns (dividend yield plus capital gains or minus capital losses) over the last four years are shown in Columns 2 and 3:

Year (1)	Rate of Return		
	Atlas (2)	Walker (3)	Portfolio (4)
1987	40%	(20%)	10%
1988	(10)	50	20
1989	35	(9)	13
1990	(5)	39	17
Average return	15%	15%	15%
Standard deviation	26%	35%	4%

If you invested your entire $100,000 in either Atlas or Walker, and if returns in the future varied as they have in the past, your *expected return* on this one-stock portfolio would be $15,000, or 15 percent. However, your *actual return* could easily be negative. On the other hand, if you put half of your money into each stock, your expected return as shown in Column 4 would still be $15,000, or 15 percent, but this return would be much less risky. Thus, although the expected return of a portfolio is simply a weighted average of the expected returns on the individual stocks in the portfolio, the same is not true for the portfolio's risk. Unlike portfolio returns, the riskiness of a portfolio, σ_p, is generally *not* a weighted average of the standard deviations of the individual securities in the portfolio—the portfolio's risk will be *smaller* than the weighted average of the stock's standard deviations. These results are graphed in Figure 12-4, where we see that the ups and downs in the portfolio's returns are not nearly as pronounced as are those for the individual stocks.

What conditions are necessary for diversification to cause the riskiness of a portfolio to be less than the riskiness of the individual assets contained in the portfolio? The only condition necessary is that the returns on the stocks in the portfolio do not move together exactly. If Atlas's and Walker's returns always moved in the same direction and by the same amount, diversification using these two stocks would do no good. *In technical terms, for diversification to be effective, returns must not be perfectly positively correlated.* Since most stocks are not perfectly positively correlated, diversification generally reduces, but does not eliminate, portfolio risk.[3]

------

[3]*Correlation* is defined as the tendency of two variables to move together. The *correlation coefficient, r,* measures this tendency, and it can range from $+1.0$, denoting that the two variables move up and down in perfect synchronization, to -1.0, denoting that the variables always move in exactly opposite directions. A correlation coefficient of zero suggests that the two variables are not related to each other; that is, changes in one variable are independent of changes in the other. If stocks were negatively correlated, or if there were zero correlation, a properly constructed portfolio would have very little risk. However, stocks tend to be positively (but less than perfectly) correlated with one another, so all stock portfolios tend to be somewhat risky.

Figure 12-4 **Rates of Return on Atlas Industries, Walker Products, and a Portfolio Consisting of 50 Percent in Each Stock**

Diversification of stock holdings reduces an investor's portfolio risk. For example, both Atlas Industries and Walker Products had widely varying rates of return from 1987 through 1990, making each a risky investment if held by itself. Note, however, that the two stocks' rates of return rose and fell in opposition to each other. Thus, if the two were combined into a single portfolio, their ups and downs would tend to cancel each other out. Because the fluctuations in returns would then be less pronounced, the combined investment would be less risky. The two-stock portfolio would have a much higher probability of yielding close to the expected 15 percent rate of return.

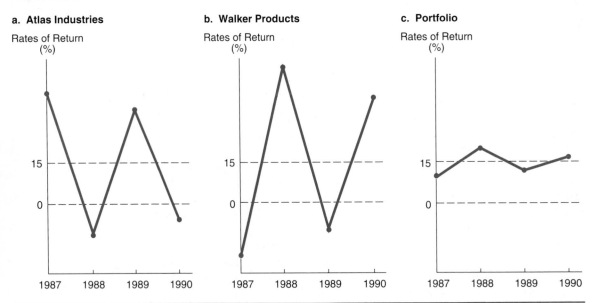

To see better how diversification affects portfolio risk, consider Figure 12-5, which shows that the riskiness of a portfolio declines as more and more randomly selected stocks are added.[4] Here risk is measured by the standard deviation of annual returns on the portfolio, σ_p. With just one stock in the portfolio, σ_p equals the standard deviation of returns on that stock, or 30 percent in this example. Notice, however, that as more stocks are added, the portfolio's risk declines and approaches a limit, 15 percent in this example. Adding more and more stocks (increasing diversification) can eliminate *some* of the riskiness of the portfolio, *but not all of it.*

---

[4]The data used in this example are adapted from W. H. Wagner and S. C. Lau, "The Effect of Diversification on Risk," *Financial Analysts' Journal,* November–December 1971, 48–53. Wagner and Lau divided a sample of 200 New York Stock Exchange stocks into 6 subgroups based on quality ratings. Then they constructed portfolios from each of the subgroups, using from 1 to 20 randomly selected securities, and applied equal weights to each security.

Figure 12-5 **Reduction of Portfolio Risk through Diversification**

Increasing diversification decreases the risk in an investor's portfolio. When an investor owns only one stock, the risk equals the standard deviation of the returns on that stock, or, in this case, 30 percent. Risk declines as more stocks are added, until the level of market risk (here, 15 percent) is reached. Market risk is related to broad swings in the stock market as a whole and cannot be eliminated through diversification. Therefore, even very large stock portfolios still contain quite a bit of risk.

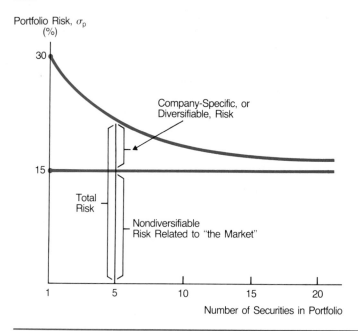

It seems quite reasonable that stocks would tend to move together, at least to some extent, because of factors in the economy. Most stocks tend to do well when the national economy is strong and to do badly when it is weak. Certain wide ranging factors affect all stocks, whereas other factors affect only individual securities. Therefore, security returns tend to be positively (but not perfectly) correlated with one another.

Risk actually consists of two parts: (1) **company-specific, or diversifiable, risk,** which can be eliminated by adding enough securities to the portfolio, and (2) **market, or nondiversifiable, risk,** which is related to broad swings in the stock market and which cannot be eliminated by diversification.[5] It is not especially important whether we call it *diversifiable, company-specific,*

company-specific (diversifiable) risk

That part of a security's risk associated with random events; it can be eliminated by proper diversification.

market (nondiversifiable) risk

That part of a security's risk that cannot be eliminated by diversification.

---

[5]Market risk is sometimes called *systematic risk,* while company-specific risk is called *unsystematic risk.* Market risk is also called *beta risk,* for reasons which we will discuss shortly.

or *unsystematic,* but the fact that part of the riskiness of any individual stock can be eliminated is vitally important.

Company-specific risk is caused by things like lawsuits, strikes, successful and unsuccessful marketing programs, the winning and losing of major contracts, and other events that are *unique to a particular firm.* Because these events are essentially random, their effects on a portfolio can be eliminated by diversification; bad events in one firm will be offset by good events in another. *Market risk,* on the other hand, stems from factors that affect all firms simultaneously, like war, inflation, recessions, and high interest rates. However, not all firms are affected equally by market risk; for example, some firms are much more sensitive to changes in interest rates than others. Later in this chapter, we discuss a means by which we can measure a firm's sensitivity to market risk. Still, because all firms are affected simultaneously by these factors, market risk cannot be eliminated by diversification.

We know that investors demand a premium for bearing risk; that is, the higher the riskiness of a security, the higher its expected return must be to induce investors to buy (or to hold) it. Investors are primarily concerned with *portfolio risk* rather than the risk of the individual securities in the portfolio. This being the case, how should the riskiness of the individual stocks be measured? The answer is this: *The relevant riskiness of an individual stock is its contribution to the riskiness of a well-diversified portfolio.* In other words, the riskiness of Apple Computer's stock to a doctor who has a portfolio of 25 stocks, or to a trust officer managing a 250-stock portfolio, or to an individual who has invested a few thousand dollars in a broadly diversified mutual fund, which in turn has invested part of that portfolio in Apple's stock, is the contribution that Apple's stock makes to the portfolio's riskiness. The stock may be quite risky if held by itself, but if most of its risk can be eliminated by diversification, then its **relevant risk,** which is its *contribution to the portfolio's risk,* may be small.

relevant risk

The risk of a security that cannot be diversified away, or market risk. This reflects a security's contribution to the risk of a portfolio.

A simple example will help make this point clear. Suppose you can flip a coin once. If a head comes up, you win $10,000, but if it comes up tails, you lose $9,500. Although this may be considered to be a good bet — the expected return is $250 — it is a highly risky proposition. Alternatively, suppose you can flip 100 coins and win $100 for each head but lose $95 for each tail. It is possible that you would hit all heads and win $10,000, and it is also possible that you would flip all tails and lose $9,500, but the chances are very high that you would actually flip about 50 heads and about 50 tails, winning a net $250. Although each individual flip is a risky bet, collectively you have a very low-risk proposition because you have diversified away most of the risk. This is the idea behind holding portfolios of stocks rather than just one stock, except that with stocks all of the risk cannot be eliminated by diversification — those risks related to broad changes in the stock market as reflected in the Dow Jones index and other stock market averages will remain.

Are all stocks equally risky in the sense that adding any one of them to a well-diversified portfolio will have the same effect on the portfolio's riskiness? The answer is no — different stocks will affect the portfolio differently, hence different securities have different degrees of relevant risk. How can the relevant risk of a stock be measured? As we mentioned before, all risk except that related to broad market movements can, and presumably will, be diversified away. After all, why accept risk that easily can be eliminated? *The risk that remains after diversifying is market risk, or risk that is inherent in the market, and this risk can be measured by the degree to which a given stock's returns tend to move up and down with the market's returns.*

The Concept of Beta

The tendency of a stock's returns to move with the market's returns is reflected in its **beta coefficient, b,** which is a measure of the stock's *volatility* relative to that of an average stock. Betas are discussed at an intuitive level in this section, then in more detail in Chapter 15.

> **beta coefficient, b**
> A measure of the extent to which the returns on a given stock move with the stock market.

An *average-risk stock* is defined as one that tends to move up and down in step with the general market as measured by some index, such as the Dow Jones Industrials, the Standard & Poor's 500, or the New York Stock Exchange Index. Such a stock will, by definition, have a beta, b, of 1.0, which indicates that, in general, if the market moves up by 10 percent, the stock will also move up by 10 percent, and that if the market falls by 10 percent, the stock will likewise fall by 10 percent. A portfolio of such b = 1.0 stocks will move up and down with the broad market averages, and it will be just as risky as the averages. If b = 0.5, the stock is only half as volatile as the market — it will rise and fall only half as much — and a portfolio of such stocks will be half as risky as a portfolio of b = 1.0 stocks. On the other hand, if b = 2.0, the stock is twice as volatile as an average stock, so a portfolio of such stocks will be twice as risky as an average portfolio.

Betas for literally thousands of companies are calculated and published by Merrill Lynch, Value Line, and numerous other organizations. The beta coefficients of some well-known companies are shown in Table 12-2. Most stocks have betas in the range of 0.50 to 1.50; the average for all stocks is 1.0, by definition.

If a high beta stock (one whose beta is greater than 1.0) is added to an average-risk (b = 1.0) portfolio, both the portfolio's beta and the riskiness of the portfolio will increase. Conversely, if a low beta stock (one whose beta is less than 1.0) is added to an average-risk portfolio, the portfolio's beta and risk will decline. *Thus, because a stock's beta measures its contribution to the riskiness of any portfolio, beta is the appropriate measure of the stock's riskiness. Therefore, a stock's market risk is measured by its beta coefficient, and we use the terms "market risk" and "beta risk" interchangeably.*

We can summarize the analysis to this point as follows:

1. A stock's risk consists of two components, market (beta) risk and company-specific risk.

2. Company-specific risk can be eliminated by diversification, and most investors do indeed diversify, either directly or indirectly by purchasing mu-

under 1% slow.
means slow.

Table 12-2 **Illustrative List of Beta Coefficients**

Stock	Beta
Albertson's, Inc.	1.00
Anheuser-Busch	0.95
Apple Computer	1.25
BellSouth Corp.	1.00
Campbell Soup Company	1.05
Delta Airlines	1.05
Du Pont	1.10
Exxon	0.80
General Motors	0.95
IBM	0.90
Kodak	0.95
Polaroid	1.25
Potomac Electric Power	0.65
Procter and Gamble	0.95
Tandem Computers	1.35
Texas Air Corporation	1.65

Source: *Value Line,* April 6, 1990.

tual funds. This leaves market (beta) risk, which is caused by general movements in the stock market and which reflects the fact that all stocks are systematically affected by certain overall economic events like war, recession, and inflation. Market (beta) risk is the only relevant risk to a rational, diversified investor, because the investor has already eliminated company-specific risk.

3. Investors must be compensated for bearing risk; the greater the riskiness of a stock, the higher its required rate of return. However, compensation is required only for risk that cannot be eliminated by diversification. If risk premiums existed for diversifiable risk, well-diversified investors would start buying these securities and bidding up their prices, and their final expected returns would reflect only nondiversifiable market (beta) risk.

4. The market (beta) risk of a stock is measured by its beta coefficient, which is an index of the stock's relative volatility. Some benchmark betas are the following:

$b = 0.5$: Stock's returns are only half as volatile, or risky, as those of an average stock.

$b = 1.0$: Stock is of average risk.

$b = 2.0$: Stock is twice as risky as the average stock.

5. *Because a stock's beta coefficient determines how it affects the riskiness of a diversified portfolio, beta is the most relevant measure of a stock's risk.*

Self-Test

Explain the following statement: "A stock held as part of a portfolio is generally less risky than the same stock held in isolation."

In general, can the riskiness of a portfolio be reduced to zero by increasing the number of stocks in the portfolio? Explain.

What is an average-risk stock?

Why is beta the theoretically correct measure of a stock's riskiness?

THE RELATIONSHIP BETWEEN RISK AND RATES OF RETURN

Now that we have established beta as the most appropriate measure of a stock's risk, the next step in the Capital Asset Pricing Model (CAPM) framework is to specify the relationship between risk and return. This relationship is known as the **Security Market Line (SML),** and it is given by this equation:

$$k = k_{RF} + (k_M - k_{RF})b_i. \tag{12-4}$$

Here:

> **Security Market Line (SML)**
> The line that shows the relationship between risk as measured by beta and the required rate of return for individual securities. SML = Equation 12-4.

k = the required rate of return on the stock in question. If the expected future return, $\hat{k}$, is less than k, you would not purchase this stock, or you would sell it if you owned it.

k_{RF} = the risk-free rate of return, generally measured by the rate of return on long-term U.S. Treasury bonds.

b_i = the beta coefficient of the stock in question.

k_M = the required rate of return on an average-risk (b = 1.0) stock. k_M is also the required rate of return on a portfolio consisting of all stocks (the "market portfolio").

$RP_M = (k_M - k_{RF})$ = the market risk premium. It is the additional return over the risk-free rate required to compensate investors for assuming an average amount of market risk.

$RP_i = (k_M - k_{RF})b_i$ = the risk premium on the stock in question. The stock's risk premium is less than, equal to, or greater than the premium on an average stock, depending on whether its beta is less than, equal to, or greater than 1.0.

**market risk
premium, RP$_M$**
The additional return
over the risk-free rate
needed to compensate
investors for assuming an
average amount of risk.

The **market risk premium, RP$_M$,** depends on the degree of aversion to risk that investors have in the aggregate. Let us assume that at the current time Treasury bonds yield $k_{RF} = 9\%$ and an average share of stock has a required return of $k_M = 13\%$. Therefore, the market risk premium is 4 percent:

$$RP_M = k_M - k_{RF} = 13\% - 9\% = 4\%.$$

The SML equation shows that the required rate of return on a given stock, k, is equal to the return required in the marketplace for securities that have no risk, k_{RF}, plus a risk premium equal to that demanded on an average stock, $k_M - k_{RF}$, scaled up or down by the relative riskiness of the firm as measured by its beta coefficient, b. Thus, if $k_{RF} = 9\%$, b = 0.5, and $k_M = 13\%$, then the RP$_M$ is 4% and the required rate of return for this low-risk stock would be

$$k = 9\% + (13\% - 9\%)0.5$$

$$= 9\% + (4\%)0.5$$

$$= 11\%.$$

An average-risk firm, with b = 1.0, would have the same return as an average stock:

$$k = 9\% + (4\%)1.0$$

$$= 13\%,$$

whereas a riskier firm, with b = 2.0, would have a required rate of return of 17 percent:

$$k = 9\% + (4\%)2.0$$

$$= 17\%.$$

Figure 12-6 shows a graph of the SML and the required rate of return for a low-risk, an average-risk, and a high-risk stock when $k_{RF} = 9\%$ and $k_M = 13\%$. Several features of the graph in Figure 12-6 are worth noting:

1. Required rates of return are shown on the vertical axis, and risk as measured by beta is shown on the horizontal axis.

2. Risk-free securities have b = 0; therefore k_{RF} appears as the vertical axis intercept, 9 percent.

3. The slope of the SML reflects the degree of risk aversion in the economy; the greater the average investor's aversion to risk, (1) the steeper the slope of the line, (2) the greater the risk premium for any risky asset, and (3) the higher the required rate of return on risky assets.[6]

---

[6]Students sometimes confuse beta with the slope of the SML. This is a mistake. The slope of any line is equal to the "rise" divided by the "run," or $(y_1 - y_0)/(x_1 - x_0)$. Consider Figure 12-6. If we let y = k and x = beta, and we go from the origin to b = 1.0, we see that the slope is $(k_M - k_{RF})/(beta_M - beta_{RF}) = (13 - 9)/(1 - 0) = 4$. Thus, the slope of the SML is equal to $(k_M - k_{RF})$, the market risk premium. To put it another way, the slope coefficient of the SML is the numerical value of the market risk premium, in this case, 4.

Figure 12-6 **The Security Market Line (SML)**

The Security Market Line reflects the relationship between a stock's riskiness and its rate of return. According to the SML equation, a stock's required rate of return equals the rate for risk-free securities (U.S. Treasury bonds) plus a risk premium. This premium is set according to whether a stock is considered to be of average risk (beta = 1.0), less than average risk (beta < 1.0), or greater than average risk (beta > 1.0). When the risk-free rate is 9 percent, a stock with a beta of 0.5 will have a 2 percent risk premium, a stock with a beta of 1.0 will have a 4 percent risk premium, and a stock with a beta of 2.0 will have an 8 percent risk premium.

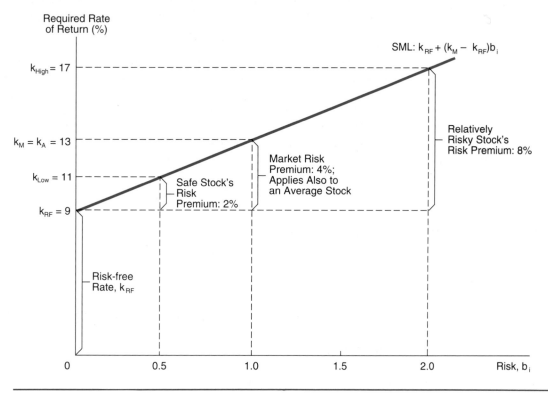

4. The values for the low-risk stock with b = 0.5, the average-risk stock with b = 1.0, and the high-risk stock with b = 2.0 are shown on the graph for k_{Low}, k_M = k_A, and k_{High}.

Both the Security Market Line and a company's position on it change over time because of changes in interest rates, investors' risk aversion, and individual companies' betas. Such changes are discussed in the following sections.

The Impact of Inflation

As we discussed in Chapter 4, interest amounts to "rent" on borrowed money, or the price of money; thus k_{RF} is the price of money to a riskless borrower. The risk-free rate as measured by the rate on U.S. Treasury securities is called the *nominal rate,* and it consists of two elements: (1) a *real, inflation-free rate of return, k*,* and (2) an *inflation premium, IP,* equal to the anticipated rate of inflation. Thus, $k_{RF} = k^* + IP$. The real rate on long-term Treasury bonds has historically ranged from 2 to 4 percent, with a mean of about 3 percent. Therefore, if no inflation were expected, long-term Treasury bonds would yield about 3 percent. As the expected rate of inflation increases, however, a premium must be added to the real risk-free rate to compensate investors for the loss of purchasing power that results from inflation. Therefore, the 9 percent k_{RF} shown in Figure 12-6 might be thought of as consisting of a 3 percent real risk-free rate of return plus a 6 percent inflation premium: $k_{RF} = k^* + IP = 3\% + 6\% = 9\%.$[7]

If the expected rate of inflation rose to 8 percent, this would cause k_{RF} to rise to 11 percent. Such a change is shown in Figure 12-7. Notice that under the CAPM, the increase in k_{RF} also causes an *equal* increase in the rate of return on all risky assets, because the inflation premium is built into the required rate of return of both risk-free and risky assets. For example, in the figure the rate of return on an average stock, k_M, increases from 13 to 15 percent. Other risky securities' returns also rise by two percentage points.

Changes in Risk Aversion

As we noted earlier, the slope of the Security Market Line reflects the extent to which investors are averse to risk; the greater the average investor's risk aversion, the steeper the slope of the SML. If investors were indifferent to risk, and if k_{RF} was 9 percent, then risky assets would also sell to provide an expected return of 9 percent. With no risk aversion, there would be no risk premium, so the SML would be horizontal. As risk aversion increases, so does the risk premium, and, thus, the slope of the SML.

Figure 12-8 illustrates an increase in risk aversion. The market risk premium rises from 4 to 6 percent, and k_M rises from 13 to 15 percent. The returns on other risky assets also rise, and the effect of this shift in risk aversion is greater for riskier securities. For example, the required return on a stock with $b_i = 0.5$ increases by only one percentage point, from 11 to 12 percent, but that on a stock with $b_i = 1.5$ increases by three percentage points, from 15 to 18 percent.

A Word of Caution

A word of caution about betas and the Capital Asset Pricing Model is in order. Although these concepts are logical, the entire theory is based on *ex ante,* or

---

[7]Remember from our discussion in Chapter 4 that long-term U.S. Treasury bonds do have interest rate risk; thus, the nominal rate on a U.S. Treasury bond is equal to $k = k^* + IP + MRP$. For purposes of this discussion we assume that MRP = 0.

Figure 12-7 **Shift in the SML Caused by an Increase in Expected Inflation**

If market participants anticipate a 2 percent increase in inflation, the return on Treasury bonds would rise from its original 9 percent to 11 percent to compensate purchasers for the expected inflation risk. This rise in k_{RF} would cause an equal rise in the rate of return for all risky assets, because the inflation risk premium is part of the required return for all assets. The change in inflationary expectations would therefore cause a parallel shift in the SML from SML_1 to SML_2, indicating a 2 percent greater required return for each investment risk level.

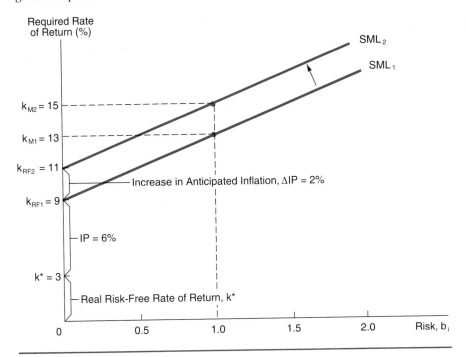

expected, conditions, yet we have available only *ex post,* or *past,* data. The betas we calculate show how volatile a stock has been in the *past,* but conditions may change, and the stock's *future volatility,* which is the item of real concern to investors, may be quite different from its past volatility. Thus, problems may arise when one attempts to measure *future* events on the basis of *past* data. Indeed, the CAPM does have some potentially serious deficiencies when applied in practice, so estimates of k found through the SML may be subject to considerable error. In spite of the potential problems in the application of the CAPM in practice, the CAPM does represent an important step forward in understanding how markets adjust for risk. Thus, abandoning the CAPM because of these potential difficulties would be like throwing the baby out with the bath water.

Figure 12-8 **Shift in the SML Caused by Increased Risk Aversion**

If market participants grow more risk averse, they will require a higher rate of return for risky investments. Therefore, the difference between the return on an average risk investment and the risk-free rate, known as the market risk premium ($k_M - k_{RF}$), will grow. In this case, the new SML (SML_2) will have a greater slope than the old one (SML_1). Note that the shift in risk aversion has no effect on either the risk-free rate or an individual stock's beta.

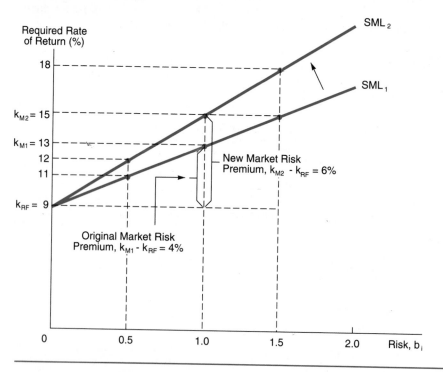

Self-Test

What happens to the SML graph when inflation increases or decreases?

What happens to the SML graph when risk aversion increases or decreases?

Does the fact that the CAPM theory is based on ex ante, or expected, conditions, while we often have only ex post, or historical, data, affect the CAPM's application in practice?

SUMMARY

The primary goals of this chapter were (1) to show how risk is measured in financial analysis and (2) to explain how risk affects rates of return. The key concepts covered are listed below:

- **Risk** can be defined as the chance that some unfavorable event will occur.

- Most rational investors hold **portfolios of stocks,** and they are more concerned with the risks of their portfolios than with the risks of individual stocks.

- The **expected return** on an investment is the mean value of the probability distribution of its possible **outcomes.**

- The **higher the probability** that the actual return will be far below the expected return, the **greater the risk** associated with owning an asset.

- The average investor is **risk averse,** which means that he or she must be compensated for holding risky securities. Therefore, riskier securities must have higher expected returns than less risky securities.

- A stock's risk consists of (1) **company-specific risk,** which can be eliminated by diversification, plus (2) **market (beta) risk,** which cannot be eliminated by diversification.

- The **relevant risk** of an individual security is its contribution to the riskiness of a well-diversified **portfolio,** which is the security's **market (beta) risk.** Since market (beta) risk cannot be eliminated by diversification, investors must be compensated for it.

- A stock's **beta coefficient, b,** is a measure of the stock's market (beta) risk. Beta measures the extent to which the stock's returns move with the market, or the stock's **relative volatility.**

- A **high-beta stock** is more volatile than an average stock, while a **low-beta stock** is less volatile than average. An **average stock** has $b = 1.0$ by definition.

- The **Security Market Line (SML)** equation shows the relationship between securities' risks and rates of return. The return required for any security i is equal to the **risk-free rate** plus the **market risk premium** times the **security's beta: $k_i = k_{RF} + (k_M - k_{RF})b_i$.**

- A number of things can happen to cause required rates of return to change: the risk-free rate can change (1) because of **changes in anticipated inflation** or (2) because of changes in **investors' aversion to risk.**

EQUATIONS

The expected rate of return is calculated by multiplying each possible return by the probability of its occurrence, and then summing the products:

$$\text{Expected rate of return} = \hat{k} = \sum_{i=1}^{n} P_i k_i. \qquad \textbf{(12-1)}$$

The variance of the probability distribution is calculated by squaring each deviation from the expected return, multiplying the squared deviation by the probability of its occurrence, and then summing the products:

$$\text{Variance} = \sigma^2 = \sum_{i=1}^{n} (k_i - \hat{k})^2 P_i. \tag{12-2}$$

The standard deviation is calculated by taking the square root of the variance:

$$\text{Standard deviation} = \sigma = \sqrt{\sum_{i=1}^{n} (k_i - \hat{k})^2 P_i}. \tag{12-3}$$

If only sample returns data over some past period are available, the standard deviation of returns can be estimated as follows:

$$\text{Estimated } \sigma = S = \sqrt{\frac{\sum_{t=1}^{n} (\bar{k}_t - \bar{k}_{Avg})^2}{n - 1}}. \tag{12-3a}$$

The relationship between risk and return can be specified by the Security Market Line (SML) equation. This equation states that the required return on a stock is equal to the risk-free rate plus a risk premium, where the risk premium is calculated by multiplying the stock's beta by the market risk premium:

$$k = k_{RF} + (k_M - k_{RF})b_i. \tag{12-4}$$

RESOLUTION TO DECISION IN FINANCE

When Money Is Not the Only Thing at Risk

The Reichmann brothers' usual attention to detail seemed to lapse when they provided money to help Campeau. They then did nothing as confidence in Campeau declined, and they were hard to reach for advice. Paul's agenda was topped by his Canary Wharf project, which kept him in London much of the time, and Albert was in Moscow for most of the month just before Campeau's crash.

Financially, Olympia & York will not suffer much from the Campeau debacle. The $250 million they loaned Campeau in September 1989 is backed by Campeau's eight office towers. The effect on their reputation is, however,

another matter. Japanese banks, among others, may be more wary as a result of this failure, and deals the Reichmanns could have negotiated in the past may not come so easily in the future. For example, in 1988 they sold $400 million of bonds secured only by leases on First Canadian Place in Toronto. Today, investors might demand part of the building as collateral as well.

In trying to help Campeau, a fellow Canadian, the Reichmanns seem to have stepped outside of familiar territory and to have lost their way. As Paul Reichmann says, what Olympia & York knows best is buildings. "The main focus for us is real estate and real estate investments internationally. The only way to succeed in the global marketplace is to strive to be the best in one area, perhaps two."

Source: "Inside the Reichmann Empire," *Business Week,* January 29, 1990.

QUESTIONS

12-1   The probability distribution of a less risky expected return is more peaked than that of a riskier return. What shape would the probability distribution have for (a) completely certain returns and (b) completely uncertain returns?

12-2   Security A has an expected return of 6 percent, a standard deviation of expected returns of 30 percent, a correlation coefficient with the market of -0.25, and a beta coefficient of -0.5. Security B has an expected return of 11 percent, a standard deviation of returns of 10 percent, a correlation with the market of 0.75, and a beta coefficient of 1.0. Which security is riskier? Why?

12-3   Suppose you owned a portfolio consisting of $500,000 worth of long-term U.S. government bonds.

    a. Would your portfolio be riskless?

    b. Now suppose you hold a portfolio consisting of $500,000 worth of 30-day Treasury bills. Every 30 days your bills mature and you reinvest the principal ($500,000) in a new batch of bills. Assume that you live on the investment income from your portfolio and that you want to maintain a constant standard of living. Is your portfolio truly riskless?

    c. You should have concluded that both long-term and short-term portfolios of government securities have some element of risk. Can you think of any asset that would be completely riskless?

12-4   A life insurance policy is a financial asset. The premiums paid represent the investment's cost.

    a. How would you calculate the expected return on a life insurance policy?

    b. Suppose the owner of the life insurance policy has no other financial assets — the person's only other asset is "human capital," or lifetime earnings capacity. What is the correlation coefficient between returns on the insurance policy and returns on the policyholder's human capital?

    c. Life insurance companies have to pay administrative costs and sales representatives' commissions; hence, the expected rate of return on insurance premiums is generally low or even negative. Use the portfolio concept to explain why people buy life insurance in spite of negative expected returns.

12-5   If investors' aversion to risk increased, would the risk premium on a high-beta stock increase more or less than that on a low-beta stock? Explain.

SELF-TEST PROBLEM

ST-1   Stocks A and B have the following historical returns:

Year	Stock A's Returns, k_A	Stock B's Returns, k_B
1986	(10.00%)	(3.00%)
1987	18.50	21.29
1988	38.67	44.25
1989	14.33	3.67
1990	33.00	28.30

    a. Calculate the average rate of return for each stock during the period 1986 through 1990. Assume that someone held a portoflio consisting of 50 percent of Stock A

and 50 percent of Stock B. What would have been the realized rate of return on
the portfolio in each year from 1986 through 1990? What would have been the
average return on the portfolio during this period?

b. Now calculate the standard deviation of returns for each stock and for the
portfolio.

c. Looking at the annual returns data on the two stocks, would you guess that the
correlation coefficient between returns on the two stocks is closer to 0.9 or to
−0.9?

d. If you added more stocks at random to the portfolio, which of the following is the
most accurate statement of what would happen to σ_p?

   1. σ_p would remain constant.

   2. σ_p would decline to somewhere in the vicinity of 15 percent.

   3. σ_p would decline to zero if enough stocks were included.

PROBLEMS

12-1   **Expected risk and return.** Analysts have determined the following probability
distribution of returns for Acorn Industries:

Probability	Returns
0.1	(5.0%)
0.2	2.5
0.4	7.5
0.2	12.5
0.1	20.0

a. Calculate the expected rate of return for Acorn. $\hat{k} = \sum\limits_{i=1}^{n} P_i k_i$

b. Calculate the standard deviation of these returns for Acorn. $\sigma \sqrt{\sum (\hat{k}-k_i)^2 \cdot P_i}$

12-2   **Expected returns.** Projects X and Y have the following probability distributions of
future rates of return:

Probability	K_i X	Y
0.1	(40%)	(25%)
0.2	0	5
0.4	20	15
0.2	40	30
0.1	70	45

$\hat{k} = (19\%)$ $SD = 17.75$

a. Calculate the expected rate of return for Project Y. The expected rate of return for
Project X is 19%.

b. Calculate the standard deviation of expected returns for Project X. The standard
deviation of expected returns for Project Y is 17.75%.

c. Calculate the coefficients of variation for Projects X and Y.

d. Is it possible that the firm's management might regard Project X as being *less* risky
than Project Y? Explain.

12-3   **Required rate of return.** Reston Corporation is evaluating three investment
opportunities. Its financial manager has forecasted the risk-free rate and the expected
market rate of return as being $k_{RF} = 9\%$ and $k_M = 13\%$, respectively. What is the
appropriate required rate of return for each stock if

$$k = k_{RF} + (k_m - k_{RF}) b_i$$

a. Stock A has a beta of 0.5?

b. Stock B has a beta of 1.0?

c. Stock C has a beta of 2.0?

12-4 **Required rate of return.** Suppose that k_{RF} = 8%, k_M = 12%, and the beta for Sierra International is 1.6.

a. What is the required rate of return for Sierra's stock?

b. Now suppose that k_{RF} (1) increases to 10 percent or (2) decreases to 6 percent. The slope of the Security Market Line (SML) remains constant (that is, [k_M − R_F] remains at 4 percent). How would each of these changes affect k_M and the required rate of return on Sierra's stock?

c. Now assume that the risk-free rate remains at 8 percent but that k_M (1) increases to 14 percent or (2) falls to 10 percent. The slope of the SML does not remain constant. How would each of these changes affect investors' required rate of return for Sierra's stock?

12-5 **Expected returns.** Suppose you were offered (1) $10,000 or (2) a gamble in which you would get $20,000 if a head was flipped but zero if a tail came up.

a. What is the expected value of the gamble?

b. Would you take the sure $10,000 or the gamble?

c. If you choose the sure $10,000, are you a risk averter or a risk seeker?

d. Suppose that you actually take the sure $10,000. You can invest it in either a U.S. Treasury bond that will return $10,900 at the end of a year or a common stock that has a 50/50 chance of being either worthless or worth $23,600 at the end of the year.

   1. What is the expected dollar profit on the stock investment? (The expected profit on the T-bond investment is $900.)

   2. What is the expected rate of return on the stock investment? (The expected rate of return on the T-bond investment is 9 percent.)

   3. Would you invest in the bond or the stock?

   4. Just how large would the expected profit (or the expected rate of return) have to be on the stock investment to make *you* invest in the stock?

   5. How might your decision be affected if, rather than buying one stock for $10,000, you could construct a portfolio consisting of 100 stocks with $100 in each? Each of these stocks has the same return characteristics as the one stock; that is, a 50/50 chance of being worth either zero or $236 at year-end. Would the correlation between returns on these stocks matter?

12-6 **Security Market Line.** The Midwest Investment Fund has a total investment of $500 million in five stocks:

Stock	Investment	Stock's Beta Coefficient
A	$150 million	0.40
B	125 million	1.20
C	75 million	1.60
D	100 million	0.80
E	50 million	1.40

The beta coefficient for a fund like Midwest Investment can be found as a weighted average of the fund's investments. The current risk-free rate is 9 percent. Market returns have the following estimated probability distribution for the next period:

Probability	Market Return
0.1	10%
0.2	12
0.4	14
0.2	16
0.1	18

a. What is the estimated equation for the Security Market Line (SML)? (*Hint:* Determine the expected market return.)

b. Compute the fund's required rate of return for the next period.

c. Suppose Midwest Investment Fund's management receives a proposal for a new stock. The investment needed to take a position in the stock is $50 million; it will have an expected return of 17 percent; and its estimated beta coefficient is 2.0. Should the new stock be purchased? At what expected rate of return should management be indifferent to purchasing the stock?

12-7 Risky cash flows. Dahl Industries is faced with two investment projects. Annual net cash flows from each project and their probability distributions are shown below:

Project A		Project B	
Probability	**Cash Flow**	**Probability**	**Cash Flow**
0.2	$4,000	0.2	$ 0
0.6	4,500	0.6	4,500
0.2	5,000	0.2	12,000

a. What is the expected value of the annual net cash flows from each project? The coefficient of variation (CV)? (*Hint:* Use Equation 12-3 to calculate the standard deviation of Project A. $\sigma_B = \$7,730$ and $CV_B = 0.76$.)

b. If it were known that Project B was negatively correlated with other cash flows of the firm whereas Project A was positively correlated, how should this knowledge affect the decision? If Project B's cash flows were negatively correlated with gross national product (GNP), would that influence your assessment of its risk?

12-8 Realized rates of return. Stocks Y and Z have the following historical returns:

Year	Stock Y's Returns, k_Y	Stock Z's Returns, k_Z
1986	(18.00%)	(14.50%)
1987	33.00	21.80
1988	15.00	30.50
1989	(0.50)	(7.60)
1990	27.00	26.30

a. Calculate the average rate of return for each stock during the period 1986 through 1990.

b. Assume that someone held a portfolio consisting of 50 percent of Stock Y and 50 percent of Stock Z. What would have been the realized rate of return on the portfolio in each year from 1986 through 1990? What would have been the average return on the portfolio during this period?

c. Calculate the standard deviation of returns for each stock and for the portfolio.

d. Calculate the coefficient of variation for each stock and for the portfolio.

e. If you are a risk averse investor, would you prefer to hold Stock Y, Stock Z, or the portfolio? Why?

SOLUTION TO SELF-TEST PROBLEM

ST-1 **a.** The average rate of return for each stock is calculated by simply averaging the returns over the five-year period. The average return for each stock is 18.90 percent, calculated for Stock A as follows:

$$k_{Avg} = (-10.00\% + 18.50\% + 38.67\% + 14.33\% + 33.00\%)/5$$

$$= 18.90\%.$$

The realized rate of return on a portfolio made up of Stock A and Stock B would be calculated by finding the average return in each year as k_A (% of Stock A) + k_B (% of Stock B) and then averaging these yearly returns:

Year	Portfolio AB's Return, k_{AB}
1986	(6.50%)
1987	19.89
1988	41.46
1989	9.00
1990	30.65
	k_{Avg} = 18.90%

b. The standard deviation of returns is estimated, using Equation 12-3a, as follows:[8]

$$\text{Estimated } \sigma = S = \sqrt{\frac{\sum\limits_{t=1}^{n} (\bar{k}_t - \bar{k}_{Avg})^2}{n - 1}}. \qquad \textbf{(12-3a)}$$

For Stock A, the estimated σ is 19.0 percent:

$$\sigma_A = \sqrt{\frac{(-10.00 - 18.9)^2 + (18.50 - 18.9)^2 + \ldots + (33.00 - 18.9)^2}{5 - 1}}$$

$$= \sqrt{\frac{1,445.92}{4}} = 19.0\%.$$

The standard deviation of returns for Stock B and for the portfolio are similarly determined, and they are as follows:

	Stock A	Stock B	Portfolio AB
Standard deviation	19.0%	19.0%	18.6%

c. Since the risk reduction from diversification is small (σ_{AB} falls only from 19.0 to 18.6 percent), the most likely value of the correlation coefficient is 0.9. If the correlation coefficient were -0.9, the risk reduction would be much larger. In fact, the correlation coefficient between Stocks A and B is 0.93.

---

[8]If only sample returns data over some past period are available, the standard deviation can be estimated using Equation 12-3a.

d. If more randomly selected stocks were added to the portfolio, σ_P would decline to somewhere in the vicinity of 15 percent, as we discussed earlier in relation to Figure 12-5. σ_P would remain constant only if the correlation coefficient were $+1.0$, which is most unlikely. σ_P would decline to zero only if the correlation coefficient, r, were less than or equal to zero, but greater than -1.0 and a large number of stocks were added to the portfolio, or if the proper proportions were held in a two-stock portfolio with $r = -1.0$.

PV = Present Value
FV = Future Value
K = Rate of Return
I = dollars of Int earned

Chapter 13

Time Value of Money

DECISION IN FINANCE

Can Boomers Retire?

"It's a lot easier to be poor when you're young than when you're in your seventies," says a pension expert who saves 15 percent of her income toward retirement. She acts on information that many young workers are aware of, but ignore — that a comfortable retirement in the 21st century requires years of planning and saving of funds, beginning in this century. The more those workers make, the more they need to save to secure the 70 percent of pre-retirement income that is recommended to maintain an accustomed standard of living when working days are over. Yet most workers under the age of 50 give little thought to retirement needs. Either they plan to keep working after age 65, or they feel that their pensions and Social Security will somehow be sufficient. Blind optimism, rather than logic, seems to rule. As Donald Kanter, coauthor of the book *The Cynical Americans: Living and Working in an Age of Discontent and Disillusion,* says, "These people have

seen inflation, layoffs, and a stock market crash. Ordinarily, looking out for 'Number One' would lead to planning for retirement. But if it seems society is going to hell, the whole effort isn't worth it."

Currently, Social Security's maximum benefit is only $10,788 a year. Jobholders making $30,000 at retirement today might, nevertheless, have enough with Social Security and a typical company pension to maintain their lifestyles. As workers' incomes climb, however, the percentage of income that will be replaced by Social Security after retirement shrinks. Those currently earning $125,000 at retirement typically need to replace 21 percent of their income with savings to maintain their standard of living.

What about retirement in the future? A 45-year-old currently earning $83,000 (*Fortune's* median subscriber) would need $1.2 million in total financial assets to be able to retire in the year 2010, at age 65, with no lowering of living standards. This figure does not even take inflation into account. Assuming an average inflation

See end of chapter for resolution.

439

rate over the next 20 years of 4.5 percent, the amount needed would be $2.8 million; to achieve it the worker would have to save 17 percent of pre-tax income every year. To retire at age 62 instead, almost 30 percent of income should be saved. "If they don't start actively planning for it," says an employee benefits expert, "the future of retirement for the baby boomers is work."

Actually, "saving" is more a generic than a descriptive term, since the income set aside should be managed more aggressively if maximum future benefits are to result. Employees who can participate in tax-deferred savings plans at work are advised by the experts to treat them not as savings accounts but as investment vehicles. Tax-deferred opportunities such as 401(k) and profit-sharing plans usually offer employees a choice of investment types—a stock mutual fund, their own company's stock, and fixed-income investments. Most employees opt for the latter, but they find their earnings seriously eroded by inflation over time. If inflation averaged a modest 4 percent a year, $70,000

would buy only $47,000 worth of goods and services after 10 years. Says one financial advisor, "Shifting from fixed-income to growth stocks could double one's account over 20 to 30 years." (Still, remember that the key word here is "could." In Chapter 12, we learned that the higher the risk of an investment, the higher its rate of return. People invest in savings accounts, money market mutual funds, and Treasury securities because the principal is relatively protected and the probability distribution of returns is tighter; thus, the risk of receiving less than the expected return is lower in fixed income securities such as bonds.)

Assume you are planning to participate in your employer's tax-deferred savings plan. As you read this chapter, consider the options that, under differing circumstances, would give you the best expected return over time. Also, suppose that your father plans to retire in 20 years, and he plans to invest $5,000 per year for the next 20 years at an average expected annual rate of 10 percent. What would his retirement nest egg be at the end of 20 years?

In Chapter 1 we stated that the firm's goal is to maximize the shareholders' wealth by maximizing the market value of its common stock. One of the variables critical to meeting that goal is the timing of the cash flows investors expect to receive. In this chapter we learn why earlier cash flows are better than later ones. This concept is then extended in later chapters.

We hesitate to claim that one chapter in this text is more important than another. Such a claim tends to start arguments, but, more important, a reader might be encouraged to think that the other chapters are not significant. Even so, because the time value of money principles, as developed in this chapter, have many applications, ranging from determining the value of stocks and bonds to making decisions about the acquisition of new equipment, we must emphasize that *of all the techniques used in finance, none is more important than the time value of money, or discounted cash flow (DCF) analysis.* A thorough understanding of the material in this chapter is vital, because this concept will be used throughout the remainder of the text to evaluate a wide array of financial topics.[1]

FUTURE VALUE (OR COMPOUND VALUE)

The first law of finance, simply stated, is: *A dollar today is worth more than a dollar tomorrow.* Why? Because today's dollar can be invested today, so that tomorrow the dollar will have earned interest, and you would end up with an amount greater than the original one dollar.[2] The process of going from present values to future values is called **compounding.** Before we begin, let us define terms that will be used throughout this chapter:

PV = the *present value* of an amount of money.

k = the **rate of return** expected on an investment opportunity.

I = dollars of interest earned during the year = k(PV).

FV_n = the **future value,** or ending amount, of an investment some number of periods, n, from now; sometimes referred to as *terminal value.* FV_n is the value n years into the *future,* after compound interest has been earned.

n = the *number of years* (or, more generally, periods) covered by an investment.

To illustrate, suppose you have $100 that you wish to invest for 1 year at a rate of 8 percent compounded annually. How much would you have at the end

compounding
The arithmetic process of determining the final value of a payment or series of payments when compound interest is applied.

rate of return (k)
The rate of interest expected on an investment.

future value (FV_n)
The amount to which a payment or series of payments will grow over a given future time period when compounded at a given interest rate.

---

[1]This chapter (indeed the entire book) is written assuming that some students do not have financial calculators. The cost of these calculators is falling rapidly, however, so most students do have them. As a result, procedures for obtaining financial calculator solutions are set forth in each of the major sections, along with procedures for obtaining solutions by using regular calculators or tables. It is highly desirable for each student to obtain a financial calculator and to learn how to use it, for calculators — and not clumsy, rounded, and incomplete tables — are used exclusively in well-run, efficient businesses.

Even though financial calculators are efficient, they do pose a danger: People sometimes learn how to use them in a "cookbook" fashion without understanding the logical processes that underlie the calculations, and then when confronted with a new type of problem, they cannot figure out how to set it up. Therefore, we urge you not only to get a good calculator and to learn how to use it but also to work through the illustrative problems "the long way" to insure that you understand the concepts involved.

[2]What about inflation? Doesn't that lower the value of tomorrow's dollar? Although we address this question in detail in later chapters, it is important to briefly answer it now. The simple answer is that the rate of return must compensate the investor for all the risks faced in the investment. Therefore, since the loss of purchasing power is one of today's largest risks, the investor must believe an investment will provide a rate of return that will be larger than the inflation rate. Otherwise, the investor would not make the investment. This need to be compensated for lost purchasing power is reflected in an inflation premium which is incorporated into nominal required interest rates, as we saw in Chapter 4.

Table 13-1 **Compound Interest Calculations**

Year	Beginning Amount, PV	× (1 + k) =	Ending Amount, FV_n	Interest Earned, PV(k)
1	$100.00	1.08	$108.00	$ 8.00
2	108.00	1.08	116.64	8.64
3	116.64	1.08	125.97	9.33
4	125.97	1.08	136.05	10.08
5	136.05	1.08	146.93	10.88
				$46.93

of 1 year? In this example, n = 1, so FV_n = FV_1 and, using our general terminology, we have

$$FV_1 = PV + I$$

$$= PV + PV(k)$$

$$= PV(1 + k). \qquad (13\text{-}1)$$

This means that the future value, FV_n, at the end of 1 period is the present value times 1 plus the interest rate.

We can now use Equation 13-1 to find how much your $100 will be worth at the end of 1 year at an 8 percent interest rate:

$$FV_1 = \$100(1 + 0.08) = \$100(1.08) = \$108.$$

Your investment will earn $8 of interest (I = $8) so you will have $108 at the end of the year.

Another way to view this problem is through a tool called a *time line*. At Time 0, you have $100. The following time line shows $100 at Year 0. You would like to know how much you will have at the end of the year, Year 1 on the time line, if the investment earns an interest rate of 8 percent. Year 1 on the time line shows a question mark and an arrow that starts at Year 0 and ends at Year 1. The interest rate of 8 percent is shown below the arrow to indicate how much your deposit will increase. From Equation 13-1 we know that the investment will increase to $108 at the end of the year, so you could replace the first question mark with $108.

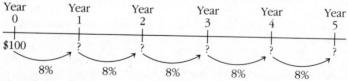

Now suppose you invest your money for 5 years; how much will you have at the end of the fifth year? The answer is $146.93; this value is worked out in Table 13-1. Notice the following points: (1) You start with $100, earn $8 of interest during the first year, and end the year with $108. (2) You start the second year with $108, earn $8.64 on this now larger amount, and end the second year with $116.64. Your second-year earnings, $8.64, were higher because you earned interest on the first year's interest. (3) This process continues, and because in each year the beginning balance is higher, your interest income increases — it is "compounding." (4) The total interest earned, $46.93, is reflected in the ending balance, $146.93, so you could replace the last question mark in the time line with $146.93.

Notice that the Table 13-1 value for FV_2, the value of the account at the end of Year 2, is equal to

$$FV_2 = FV_1(1 + k)$$
$$= PV(1 + k)(1 + k)$$
$$= PV(1 + k)^2$$
$$= \$100(1.08)^2$$
$$= \$116.64.$$

Continuing, we see that FV_3, the balance after Year 3, is

$$FV_3 = FV_2(1 + k)$$
$$= PV(1 + k)^3$$
$$= \$100(1.08)^3$$
$$= \$125.97.$$

In general, FV_n, the future value at the end of n years, is found as follows:

$$FV_n = PV(1 + k)^n. \qquad \text{(13-2)}$$

Applying Equation 13-2 to our 5-year, 8 percent case, we obtain

$$FV_5 = \$100(1.08)^5$$
$$= \$100(1.4693)$$
$$= \$146.93,$$

which is the same as the value worked out in Table 13-1.

We can solve future value problems in three ways:

1. Use a regular calculator. One can simply use a regular calculator, either by multiplying $(1 + k)$ by itself $n - 1$ times or by using the exponential function to raise $(1 + k)$ to the nth power. In our example, you would enter $1 + k = 1.08$ and multiply it by itself four times, or else enter 1.08, press 5, and then press the y^x (or exponential) function key. In either case, you would get the factor $(1.08)^5 = 1.4693$, which you would then multiply by $100 to get the final answer, $146.93.

Table 13-2 **Future Value of \$1 at the End of n Periods: $FVIF_{k,n} = (1 + k)^n$**

Period (n)	1%	2%	3%	4%	5%	6%	7%	8%	9%	10%
1	1.0100	1.0200	1.0300	1.0400	1.0500	1.0600	1.0700	1.0800	1.0900	1.1000
2	1.0201	1.0404	1.0609	1.0816	1.1025	1.1236	1.1449	1.1664	1.1881	1.2100
3	1.0303	1.0612	1.0927	1.1249	1.1576	1.1910	1.2250	1.2597	1.2950	1.3310
4	1.0406	1.0824	1.1255	1.1699	1.2155	1.2625	1.3108	1.3605	1.2950	1.3310
5	1.0510	1.1041	1.1593	1.2167	1.2763	1.3382	1.4026	1.4693	1.5386	1.6105
6	1.0615	1.1262	1.1941	1.2653	1.3401	1.4185	1.5007	1.5869	1.6771	1.7716
7	1.0721	1.1487	1.2299	1.3159	1.4071	1.5036	1.6058	1.7138	1.8280	1.9487
8	1.0829	1.1717	1.2668	1.3686	1.4775	1.5938	1.7182	1.8509	1.9926	2.1436
9	1.0937	1.1951	1.3048	1.4233	1.5513	1.6895	1.8385	1.9990	2.1719	2.3579
10	1.1046	1.2190	1.3439	1.4802	1.6289	1.7908	1.9672	2.1589	2.3674	2.5937
11	1.1157	1.2434	1.3842	1.5395	1.7103	1.8983	2.1049	2.3316	2.5804	2.8531
12	1.1268	1.2682	1.4258	1.6010	1.7959	2.0122	2.2522	2.5182	2.8127	3.1384
13	1.1381	1.2936	1.4685	1.6651	1.8856	2.1329	2.4098	2.7196	3.0658	3.4523
14	1.1495	1.3195	1.5126	1.7317	1.9799	2.2609	2.5785	2.9372	3.3417	3.7975
15	1.1610	1.3459	1.5580	1.8009	2.0789	2.3966	2.7590	3.1722	3.6425	4.1772

future value interest factor ($FVIF_{k,n}$)
The future value of \$1 left in an account for n periods paying k percent per period, which is equal to $(1 + k)^n$.

2. Use compound interest tables. The term **future value interest factor for k,n ($FVIF_{k,n}$)** is defined as being equal to $(1 + k)^n$, and tables have been constructed for values of $(1 + k)^n$ for a wide range of k and n values. Table 13-2 is illustrative, and a more complete table, with more years and more interest rates, is given in Table A-3 in Appendix A at the end of the book.[3]

Equation 13-2 can be written as $FV_n = PV(FVIF_{k,n})$. It is necessary only to go to an appropriate interest table (13-2 or A-3) to find the proper interest factor. For example, the correct interest factor for our 5-year, 8 percent illustration can be found in Table 13-2. We look down the period column to 5 and then across this row to the 8 percent column to find the interest factor, 1.4693. Then, using this interest factor, we find the value of \$100 after 5 years to be $FV_5 = PV(FVIF_{8\%,5\text{ years}}) = \$100(1.4693) = \$146.93$, which is identical to the value obtained by the long method in Table 13-1.

3. Use a financial calculator. Financial calculators have been programmed to solve most time value of money problems. In effect, the calculators first generate the $FVIF_{k,n}$ factors for a specified pair of k and n values, and then multiply the computed factor by the PV to produce the FV. In our illustrative problem, you would simply enter PV = 100, k = i = 8, and n = 5, then

[3]Notice that we have used the word *period* rather than *year* in Table 13-2. Although annual compounding will be assumed in most of the text material, compounding can occur over periods of time other than one year. Appendix 13A demonstrates how the time value of money is affected by "other than annual compounding" (semiannual, quarterly, monthly, and the like).

press the FV key, and the answer $146.93 rounded to two decimal places will appear. (The FV will appear with a minus sign on some calculators. The logic behind the negative output is that you put in the initial amount [the PV] and take out the ending amount [the FV], so one is an inflow and the other is an outflow. The negative sign reminds you of that. At this point, though, you can ignore the minus sign. Also, on some calculators you may need to press the Compute key before pressing the FV button.)

The most efficient way to solve most problems is to use a financial calculator. Therefore, you should get one and learn how to use it. However, you ought to understand how the tables are developed and used, and you should also understand the logic and the math that underlie all types of financial analysis. Otherwise, you simply will not understand stock and bond valuation, lease analysis, capital budgeting, and other critically important topics.

Graphic View of the Compounding Process: Growth

Figure 13-1 shows how $1 (or any other sum) grows over time at various rates of interest. The 5 and 10 percent curves are based on the values given in Table 13-2. Notice that the higher the rate of interest, the faster the rate of growth. The interest rate is, in fact, a growth rate. If a sum is invested at a rate of 5 percent, and interest earned is left in the account, then the investment fund will grow at a rate of 5 percent per period. Further, it should be clear that the concepts in this chapter can be applied to anything that is growing — sales, population, earnings per share, inflation, and so on. If you ever need to figure the growth rate of anything, the formulas in this chapter can be used.

Self-Test

Explain why the following statement is true: "A dollar in hand today is worth more than a dollar to be received next year."

What is compounding? What is "interest on interest"?

Explain the following equation: $FV_1 = PV + I$. (No calculations are necessary.)

Set up a time line that would show the following situation: (1) Your initial deposit is $100. (2) The account pays 8% interest annually. (3) You want to withdraw your money at the end of 3 years, and you would like to know how much you can expect to withdraw from the account.

PRESENT VALUE

Suppose you are offered the alternatives of receiving $146.93 at the end of 5 years or some currently unspecified amount today. Assume that there is no question that the $146.93 will be paid in full (perhaps the payer is the U.S. government). Further, assume that you have no current need for the money

Figure 13-1 **Relationships among Future Value
Interest Factors, Interest Rates, and Time**

This figure shows the future value interest factors for several interest rates over
various periods of time. Because of compounding, the higher the interest rate, the
faster the growth in future value. $1.00 invested at 10 percent will grow *more than*
twice as fast as $1.00 invested at 5 percent. Note, for example, that for a 10-year
period, the future value of $1.00 at 5 percent is only $1.63, but its future value at 10
percent is $2.59.

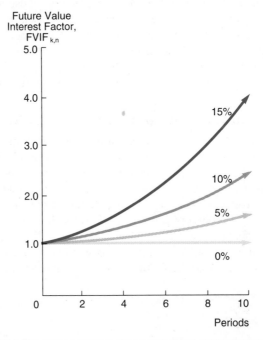

and will therefore invest it at 8 percent. (Eight percent is defined as your
opportunity cost The rate you could earn on alternative investments of equal risk.
opportunity cost, or the rate you could earn on alternative investments of
equal risk.) What amount of money today, X, would make you indifferent to
receiving $146.93 in 5 years or X today?

Table 13-1 showed that an initial investment of $100 growing at 8 percent
a year yields $146.93 at the end of 5 years. Therefore, in a financial sense, you
should be indifferent in your choice between $100 today and $146.93 at the
end of 5 years. The $100 is defined as the **present value,** or **PV,** of the future
$146.93, due in 5 years, when the opportunity cost is 8 percent. Therefore, if
the unknown present amount is anything less than $100, you should prefer the
future promised amount, $146.93. Conversely, if the amount X is greater than
$100, you should accept that amount because, when invested at 8 percent, its
value 5 years hence would be greater than $146.93.

present value (PV) The value today of a future payment or series of payments discounted at the appropriate discount rate.

The concept of present values can also be illustrated using a time line. The following one shows the future value amount of $146.93 at Year 5. A question mark appears at Year 0 — this is the value in which we are interested. Arrows begin at Year 0 and end at Year 5, and the interest rate of 8 percent appears below the arrows, indicating your opportunity cost of money.

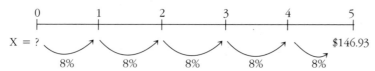

The present value of any future sum is the amount that must be invested today in order to provide that future amount. Because $100 would grow to $146.93 in 5 years at an 8 percent interest rate, the $100 amount is the *present value* of $146.93 due 5 years in the future when the appropriate interest rate is 8 percent.

Finding the present value of some future amount (or **discounting** that future value, as the process is often called) is simply the reverse of compounding. We can use Equation 13-2 to illustrate this point.

$$FV_n = PV(1 + k)^n. \tag{13-2}$$

discounting
The process of finding the present value of a payment or a series of future cash flows; the reverse of compounding.

To solve for the present value, PV, divide both sides of the equation by the interest factor, $(1 + k)^n$

$$PV = \frac{FV_n}{(1 + k)^n}. \tag{13-3}$$

Since dividing by a number and multiplying by its reciprocal give equivalent results,[4] we can rewrite Equation 13-3 as follows:

$$PV = FV_n \left[\frac{1}{(1 + k)^n} \right]. \tag{13-3a}$$

Tables have been constructed for the term in parentheses for various values of k and n; Table 13-3 is an example. (For a more complete table, see Table A-1 in Appendix A at the end of the book.) For our illustrative case, look down the 8 percent column in Table 13-3 to the fifth row. The figure shown there, 0.6806, is the **present value interest factor (PVIF$_{k,n}$)** used to determine the present value of $146.93 payable in 5 years, discounted at 8 percent:

present value interest factor (PVIF$_{k,n}$)
The present value of $1 due n periods in the future discounted at k percent per period.

$$
\begin{aligned}
PV &= FV_5(PVIF_{8\%,5\ years}) \\
&= \$146.93(0.6806) \\
&= \$100.00.
\end{aligned}
$$

---

[4]For example, dividing by 2 is the same as multiplying by ½, or dividing by 4 is equivalent to multiplying by ¼.

Table 13-3 **Present Value of $1 Due at the End of
n Periods: PVIF$_{k,n}$ = 1/(1 + k)^n**

Period (n)	1%	2%	3%	4%	5%	6%	7%	8%	9%	10%	12%	14%	15%
1	.9901	.9804	.9709	.9615	.9524	.9434	.9346	.9259	.9174	.9091	.8929	.8772	.8696
2	.9803	.9612	.9426	.9246	.9070	.8900	.8734	.8573	.8417	.8264	.7972	.7695	.7561
3	.9706	.9423	.9151	.8890	.8638	.8396	.8163	.7938	.7722	.7513	.7118	.6750	.6575
4	.9610	.9238	.8885	.8548	.8227	.7921	.7629	.7350	.7084	.6830	.6355	.5921	.5718
5	.9515	.9057	.8626	.8219	.7835	.7473	.7130	.6806	.6499	.6209	.5674	.5194	.4972
6	.9420	.8880	.8375	.7903	.7462	.7050	.6663	.6302	.5963	.5645	.5066	.4556	.4323
7	.9327	.8706	.8131	.7599	.7107	.6651	.6227	.5835	.5470	.5132	.4523	.3996	.3759
8	.9235	.8535	.7894	.7307	.6768	.6274	.5820	.5403	.5019	.4665	.4039	.3506	.3269
9	.9143	.8368	.7664	.7026	.6446	.5919	.5439	.5002	.4604	.4241	.3606	.3075	.2843
10	.9053	.8203	.7441	.6756	.6139	.5584	.5083	.4632	.4224	.3855	.3220	.2697	.2472

Again, you could use a financial calculator to find the PV of the $146.93. Just enter n = 5, k = i = 8, and FV = 146.93, and then press the PV button to find PV = $100. (Again, on some calculators, the PV will be given as −$100, and on some calculators you need to press the Compute key before pressing the PV button.)

Graphic View of the Discounting Process

Figure 13-2 shows graphically how the present value interest factors for discounting decrease as the discounting period increases. These curves, plotted with the data from Table 13-3, show that the present value of a sum to be received at some future time decreases both as the payment date is extended further into the future and as the discount rate increases. To illustrate, the present value of $1 due in 10 years is about 61 cents if the discount rate is 5 percent, but the PV is only 25 cents in 10 years if the discount rate is 15 percent. Thus, since you are investing in a project with a higher rate of return, a smaller initial payment is required to earn $1 in the future. The length of time until money is paid or received is also important. For example, $1 due in 5 years at 10 percent is worth 62 cents today, but at the same discount rate $1 due in 10 years is worth only about 39 cents today.

Thus, present values are dependent on two factors, the discount rate and the number of years until the payment will be received. If relatively high discount rates apply, funds due in the future are worth comparatively little today. Even at relatively low discount rates, the present values of funds due in the distant future are quite small. Notice that if the interest rate is zero, or if no time will lapse before the future funds will be received (n = 0), then the present and future values of a dollar are the same.

Figure 13-2 **Relationships among Present Value Interest Factors, Interest Rates, and Time**

This graph shows the discounting process at various interest rates. The longer the time until payment or the higher the interest rate, the less future payments will be worth in today's dollars. For example, if the interest rate is 10 percent, the present value of $1.00 due in 4 years is $0.68, but the value drops to about $0.39 if due in 10 years. If we vary the interest rate, we see that $1.00 received in 10 years has a present value of about $0.61 when the opportunity cost is 5 percent, whereas if the interest rate is 15 percent, its present value is about $0.25.

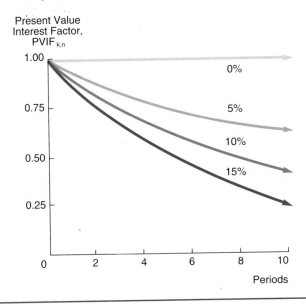

Self-Test

What is meant by the term "opportunity cost"?

What is discounting? How does it relate to compounding?

Briefly discuss how the present value of an amount to be received in the future changes as the time is extended and as the interest rate increases.

FUTURE VALUE VERSUS PRESENT VALUE

By now you have noticed that Equations 13-2 and 13-3 are really two ways of looking at the same process. People in everyday life must decide, just as financial managers do, how much to invest in order to receive future returns. Also, it should be apparent that present and future amounts cannot be directly compared: We must either compound present amounts into the future, or discount future dollars back to the present, before making comparisons.

To illustrate this point, let's use the following example. Conrad Dunn is a college student who plans to sell his car for $5,000 and to invest the money in a project that promises a 12 percent return. An uncle suggests that he would like to have the car, but he cannot pay cash for it. He does, however, have several zero coupon government bonds that mature in 15 years. Although their current value is below $5,000, they will mature in 15 years at $20,000, which is four times the car's value, Conrad's uncle notes. Should Conrad give his uncle the car in anticipation of the future $20,000 or sell it for $5,000 cash today?

Even though the value of the future sum is four times the value of the car, we cannot compare the amounts because one is a future value and the other is a present sum. To make the values comparable, we must either discount the future payment back to the present or compound the present amount into the future. The two procedures lead to the same decision (to accept or reject the uncle's offer), but we will use both methods.

If we wish to discount the future amount back to the present, we can use Equation 13-3a, employing a present value interest factor from Table A-1 in Appendix A for 12 percent, 15 years:

$$PV = FV_n \left[\frac{1}{(1 + k)^n} \right] = FV_n(PVIF_{12\%,15})$$

$$= \$20,000(0.1827)$$

$$= \$3,654.00.$$

Obviously, the offer made by Conrad's uncle is not financially attractive to Conrad, because the present value of $20,000 discounted at 12 percent for 15 years is less than the amount Conrad could receive if he sold the car today.

We come to the same conclusion if the cash value of the car if sold, $5,000, is compounded 15 years into the future. We use the future value interest factor from Table A-3 in Appendix A for 12 percent, 15 years, in Equation 13-2:

$$FV_n = PV(1 + k)^n = PV(FVIF_{12\%,15})$$

$$= \$5,000(5.4736)$$

$$= \$27,368.00.$$

As we expected, the value of $5,000 invested at a 12 percent rate of interest for 15 years exceeds the $20,000 future value of Conrad's uncle's bonds.

Figure 13-3 illustrates the point that present and future values cannot be directly compared. A present amount can be compounded into the future and then compared with a promised future amount. Conversely, a future sum can be discounted back to the present and then compared with the present value

Figure 13-3 **Discounting and Compounding Compared**

To compare a present value to a future value, we must either compound the present sum into the future or discount the future amount back to the present. Whichever method is used, the result gives a proper basis on which to compare the two values. In this figure, the future values are shown on the right ($27,368 was arrived at by compounding $5,000 at 12 percent over 15 periods), and the present values are shown on the left ($3,654 was reached by discounting $20,000 at 12 percent over 15 periods).

$3,654 $\longleftarrow$————— Discounting Using PV = $FV_n(PVIF_{k,n})$ $\longleftarrow$————— $20,000

t_0 |————————————————————————————| t_{15}

$5,000 ——————$\longrightarrow$ Compounding Using FV_n = $PV(FVIF_{k,n})$ ———$\longrightarrow$ $27,368

Time ————————————————————$\longrightarrow$

of the uncle's offer. Thus, we can compare $5,000 with $3,654, or $27,368 with $20,000, but we cannot compare $5,000 with $20,000. Conrad may still wish to give his uncle the car for the promise of $20,000 in the future, but not for financial reasons.

Self-Test

Briefly explain the following statement: "Present and future values cannot be directly compared."

If you know a future amount, the interest rate, and the number of periods, how do you convert the future amount to a present value?

If you know a present amount, the interest rate, and the number of periods, how do you convert the present amount to a future value?

SOLVING FOR TIME AND INTEREST RATES

You should recognize that we have been dealing with one equation, Equation 13-2, and its transformed version, Equation 13-3:

$$FV_n = PV(1 + k)^n = PV(FVIF_{k,n}). \qquad (13\text{-}2)$$

$$PV = \frac{FV_n}{(1 + k)^n} = FV_n(PVIF_{k,n}). \qquad (13\text{-}3)$$

Notice that there are four variables in the equations:

PV = present value.

FV_n = future value.

k = interest (or discount) rate.

n = number of periods.

If you know the values of three of the variables, you can solve for the fourth. Thus far we have always given you the interest rate (k) and the number of periods (n), as well as either the PV or the FV_n. In many situations, though, you will need to solve for either k or n. Solution procedures for these values are discussed next.

Time

Suppose you were given the following information: PV = $100, FV_n = $146.93, and k = i = 8%. Could you determine the length of time, n, involved? The answer is yes. To do this, you could set up the problem as follows:

$$FV_n = PV(FVIF_{k,n})$$

$$\$146.93 = \$100(FVIF_{8\%,n})$$

$$FVIF_{8\%,n} = \$146.93/\$100$$

$$FVIF_{8\%,n} = 1.4693.$$

Because you were given the interest rate of 8 percent, and you were solving for the future value interest factor, all you need to do is to refer to Table A-3 in Appendix A. In Table A-3, look down the 8% column until you reach the future value interest factor of 1.4693. This interest factor is in Row 5; thus, the number of time periods it takes for $100 to grow to $146.93 is equal to 5.

You could also work the problem using Equation 13-3, solving for the length of time it takes $100 to grow to $146.93 at an 8 percent interest rate:

$$PV = FV_n(PVIF_{k,n})$$

$$\$100 = \$146.93(PVIF_{8\%,n})$$

$$PVIF_{8\%,n} = \$100/\$146.93$$

$$PVIF_{8\%,n} = 0.6806.$$

Because you were given the interest rate of 8 percent, and you are solving for the present value interest factor, all you need to do is to refer to Table A-1 in Appendix A. In Table A-1, look down the 8% column until you reach the present value interest factor of 0.6806. This interest factor is in Row 5; thus, the number of time periods it takes for $100 to grow to $146.93 is equal to 5.

Finally, you could solve the problem using a financial calculator. Just input $k = i = 8$, PV = 100, FV = 146.93 (or -146.93), and then press the n button to find n = 5 periods.

Interest Rate

Suppose we were given the following facts: PV = \$100, FV_n = \$146.93, and n = 5. We need to determine the interest rate at which \$100 would grow to \$146.93 over 5 periods. We could set up the equation as follows:

$$FV_5 = PV(FVIF_{k,5})$$

$$\$146.93 = \$100(FVIF_{k,5})$$

$$FVIF_{k,5} = 1.4693.$$

Because we are given the number of time periods, 5, and we are solving for the future value interest factor, all we need to do is to refer to Table A-3 in Appendix A. We look across the Period 5 row until we reach the future value interest factor of 1.4693. We find that this interest factor is in the 8% column; thus, the interest rate at which \$100 grows to \$146.93 is equal to 8 percent.

Alternatively, we could set up this equation as follows:

$$PV = FV_5(PVIF_{k,5})$$

$$\$100 = \$146.93(PVIF_{k,5})$$

$$PVIF_{k,5} = 0.6806.$$

Because we are given the number of time periods, 5, and we are solving for the present value interest factor, all we need to do is to refer to Table A-1 in Appendix A. We look across the Period 5 row until we find the present value interest factor of 0.6806. This interest factor is in the 8% column, so the interest rate at which \$100 grows to \$146.93 is equal to 8 percent.

We could also solve the problem with a financial calculator. Simply input PV = 100, FV = 146.93 (or -146.93), and n = 5, and then press the $k = i$ button to find $k = i = 8\%$.

Self-Test

Write out the two equations that can be used to determine the time period, assuming that you are given PV, FV_n, and the interest rate, k.

Write out the two equations that can be used to determine the interest rate, assuming that you are given PV, FV_n, and the time period, n.

Figure 13-4 Time Line for an Ordinary (Deferred) Annuity: Future Value with k = 7%

This figure shows how the future value of an annuity is calculated. In this case there is a promise to pay $1,000 per year for 3 years, so a $1,000 payment is received at the end of each of three periods. Upon receipt, each payment is invested at 7 percent interest. The first payment is compounded for 2 years, the second for 1 year, and the third is not compounded at all. The sum of the three future values is the total value of the annuity.

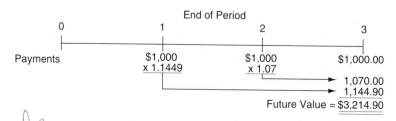

Some amt of $ ir equal time periods

FUTURE VALUE OF AN ANNUITY

annuity
A series of payments of an equal, or constant, amount for a specified number of periods.

So far we have been dealing with situations involving a single payment or receipt in the present and a single amount in the future. We now turn to a discussion of the situation where there is a series of equal annual payments or receipts, called *annuities*. An **annuity** is defined as *a series of payments of an equal, or constant, amount of money at fixed intervals for a specified number of periods.* Payments are given the symbol PMT, and if the payments are made or received at the beginning of each period, it is called an *annuity due.* However, because *ordinary (deferred) annuities* where payments occur at the end of each period are far more common in finance, when the word annuity is used in this book, you may assume that payments are received at the end of each period, unless otherwise indicated.

Ordinary (Deferred) Annuity

ordinary (deferred) annuity
An annuity the payments for which occur at the end of each period.

A promise to pay $1,000 annually for 3 years is a 3-year annuity, and if each payment is made at the end of the year, it is an **ordinary (deferred) annuity.** If you were to receive such an annuity, and if you deposited each annual payment in a savings account paying 7 percent interest, how much would you have at the end of 3 years? The answer is shown graphically on a time line in Figure 13-4. The first payment is made at the end of Year 1, the second at the end of Year 2, and the third at the end of Year 3. The last payment is not compounded at all, the second year's payment is compounded for 1 year, and the first is compounded for 2 years. When the future values of each of the $1,000 payments are added, their total is the sum of the annuity, **FVA$_n$**, which in this case is equal to $3,214.90.

FVA$_n$
The future value of an annuity over n periods.

Table 13-4 **Future Value of an Annuity of $1 per Period for n Periods:**

$$\text{FVIFA}_{k,n} = \sum_{t=1}^{n} (1 + k)^{n-t} = \frac{(1 + k)^n - 1}{k}.$$

Period (n)	1%	2%	3%	4%	5%	6%	7%	8%
1	1.0000	1.0000	1.0000	1.0000	1.0000	1.0000	1.0000	1.0000
2	2.0100	2.0200	2.0300	2.0400	2.0500	2.0600	2.0700	2.0800
3	3.0301	3.0604	3.0909	3.1216	3.1525	3.1836	3.2149	3.2464
4	4.0604	4.1216	4.1836	4.2465	4.3101	4.3746	4.4399	4.5061
5	5.1010	5.2040	5.3091	5.4163	5.5256	5.6371	5.7507	5.8666
6	6.1520	6.3081	6.4684	6.6330	6.8019	6.9753	7.1533	7.3359
7	7.2135	7.4343	7.6625	7.8983	8.1420	8.3938	8.6540	8.9228
8	8.2857	8.5830	8.8923	9.2142	9.5491	9.8975	10.2598	10.6366
9	9.3685	9.7546	10.1591	10.5828	11.0266	11.4913	11.9780	12.4876
10	10.4622	10.9497	11.4639	12.0061	12.5779	13.1808	13.8164	14.4866

Of course, you could go through the effort of calculating the interest factors yourself,[5] but the future value interest factors for an annuity, **FVIFA$_{k,n}$**, have already been calculated for various combinations of interest rates, k, and time periods, n, in Table A-4 in Appendix A. An illustrative set of these annuity factors is given in Table 13-4. To answer the preceding question, you could utilize Equation 13-4:

$$\text{FVA}_n = \text{PMT}(\text{FVIFA}_{k,n}), \qquad\qquad (13\text{-}4)$$

where

FVA$_n$ = the future compound value of an annuity,

PMT = the annuity payment or receipt, and

FVIFA$_{k,n}$ = the future value interest factor for an annuity
at k percent for n periods.

To find the future value of the 3-year, $1,000 annuity problem posed earlier, first find the future value interest factor for an annuity, FVIFA$_{k,n}$, by simply

FVIFA$_{k,n}$
The future value interest factor for an annuity of n periodic payments compounded at k percent.

---

[5]Expressed algebraically, the future value of an annuity, FVA$_n$, can be computed by multiplying the annuity, PMT, by the future value interest factor for an annuity, FVIFA$_{k,n}$:

$$\text{FVA}_n = \text{PMT}(1 + k)^{n-1} + \text{PMT}(1 + k)^{n-2} + \cdots + \text{PMT}(1 + k)^1 + \text{PMT}(1 + k)^0$$

$$= \text{PMT}[(1 + k)^{n-1} + (1 + k)^{n-2} + \cdots + (1 + k)^1 + (1 + k)^0]$$

$$= \text{PMT} \sum_{t=1}^{n} (1 + k)^{n-t}$$

$$= \text{PMT}(\text{FVIFA}_{k,n}).$$

referring to Table 13-4. Look down the 7 percent column to the Period 3 row, and then multiply the factor 3.2149 by the $1,000:

$$FVA_3 = PMT(FVIFA_{7\%, 3 \text{ years}})$$

$$= \$1,000(3.2149)$$

$$= \$3,214.90.$$

Thus, the future value of a 3-year, $1,000 annuity, received at the end of each year and invested at 7 percent annually, is $3,214.90. Notice also that Equation 13-4 is simply the summation of n values of Equation 13-2, i.e., the FV of an annuity is the sum of n individual FVs.

We can also solve annuity problems with a financial calculator. To solve our illustrative problem, merely key in n = 3, k = i = 7, and PMT = 1,000, and then press the FV button to get the answer, $3,214.90. The calculator actually calculates the future values of the three $1,000 payments and sums them to produce the answer, just as we show in Figure 13-4.

Annuity Due

annuity due
An annuity the payments for which occur at the beginning of each period.

Had the annuity in the previous example been an **annuity due,** each of the three payments would have occurred at the beginning rather than the end of the period, or at t = 0, t = 1, and t = 2. In terms of Figure 13-4, each payment would have been shifted to the left, so there would have been $1,000 under Period 0 and a zero under Period 3, meaning that each payment would be compounded for one more period.

We can modify Equation 13-4 to handle annuities due as follows:

$$FVA_n(\text{Annuity due}) = PMT(FVIFA_{k,n})(1 + k). \qquad \textbf{(13-4a)}$$

Because each payment is compounded for one extra year, multiplying the term $PMT(FVIFA_{k,n})$ by $(1 + k)$ takes care of this extra compounding. Applying Equation 13-4a to the previous example, we obtain

$$FVA_n(\text{Annuity due}) = \$1,000(3.2149)(1.07) = \$3,439.94$$

versus the $3,214.90 for the ordinary annuity.[6] Since payments on an annuity due come earlier, it will always produce a higher future value than an ordinary (deferred) annuity.

Annuity due problems can also be solved with financial calculators, most of which have a switch or key marked "Due" or "Beginning" that permits you

---

[6]Another technique can also be used to solve for the future value of an annuity due. First look up the $FVIFA_{k,n}$ for n + 1 years in the table. Then subtract 1.0 from that amount to get the $FVIFA_{k,n}$ for the annuity due. Using the previous example, the fourth period interest factor is 4.4399. This factor assumes 4 payments and 3 compounding periods, so by subtracting one payment, we will have the desired 3 payments and 3 compounding periods. Thus:

$$FVIFA_{k,n}(\text{Annuity due}) = \$1,000(4.4399 - 1.0) = \$3,439.90.$$

to convert from ordinary annuities to annuities due. Be careful, though. People sometimes change the setting to work an annuity due problem, then forget to switch the calculator back and get wrong answers to subsequent ordinary (deferred) annuity problems.

Self-Test

What is the difference between an ordinary (deferred) annuity and an annuity due?

How do you modify the equation used to determine the value of an ordinary annuity to determine the value of an annuity due?

Which annuity has the greater future value: an ordinary annuity or an annuity due?

PRESENT VALUE OF AN ANNUITY

The preceding section presented techniques that allow you to determine the *future value* of a stream of equal annual payments. You may also wish to determine the *present value* of an annuity. Suppose you were offered the alternatives of a 4-year annuity of $1,000 at the end of each year or a single (lump sum) payment today. Let's assume that you have no immediate need for the money during the next 4 years, so if you accept the annuity, you would simply deposit the annual payments in an investment that pays 9 percent interest. The lump sum payment, if you choose it, would also be deposited in an investment which pays 9 percent interest, compounded annually. How large must the lump-sum payment be to make it equivalent to the annuity?

The time line in Figure 13-5 will help you visualize the problem. Note also that, rather than multiplying each year's receipt by factors from Table 13-3 and summing the results, as suggested by Figure 13-5, a table has been constructed to facilitate the computation of the present value of an annuity, PVA_n. Table 13-5 is illustrative of the more complete set of present value interest factors for an annuity, $PVIFA_{k,n}$,[7] that is presented in Table A-2 in Appendix A. Utiliz-

PVA_n
The present value of an ordinary (deferred) annuity of n periods.

$PVIFA_{k,n}$
The present value interest factor for an annuity of n periodic payments discounted at k percent.

---

[7]The present value interest factor for an annuity, $PVIFA_{k,n}$, is computed by summing the present value interest factors for each year's receipt. The present value interest factor for the first receipt is $[1/(1 + k)]$, the second is $[1/(1 + k)^2]$, and so on. Thus:

$$PVA_n = PMT \left(\frac{1}{1+k}\right)^1 + PMT \left(\frac{1}{1+k}\right)^2 + \cdots + PMT \left(\frac{1}{1+k}\right)^n$$

$$= PMT \left[\frac{1}{(1+k)^1} + \frac{1}{(1+k)^2} + \cdots + \frac{1}{(1+k)^n}\right]$$

$$= PMT \sum_{t=1}^{n} \left(\frac{1}{1+k}\right)^t$$

$$= PMT(PVIFA_{k,n}).$$

(13-5)

Figure 13-5 **Time Line for an Ordinary (Deferred) Annuity: Present Value with k = 9%**

This figure shows how to calculate the present value of a 4-year annuity of $1,000 per year at an interest rate of 9 percent. The present value is calculated by multiplying each year's receipt by the appropriate present value interest factor from Table 13-3 and summing the resulting amounts. One can then compare this present value with any other present value to determine the wisdom of accepting this annuity.

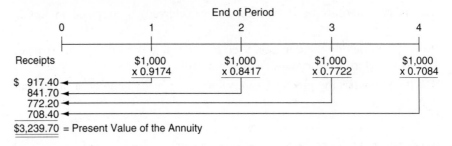

ing Equation 13-5 and the appropriate $PVIFA_{k,n}$ contained in Table 13-5, we can solve the problem in a direct fashion:

$$PVA_n = PMT(PVIFA_{k,n}) \qquad (13\text{-}5)$$

$$= \$1,000(3.2397)$$

$$= \$3,239.70.$$

Thus, the present value of an annuity, PVA_n, equals the annuity payment multiplied by the appropriate present value interest factor for an annuity, $PVIFA_{k,n}$. In the present problem, the $PVIFA_{k,n}$ for a 4-year, 9 percent annuity is found from Table 13-5 to be 3.2397. Multiplying this factor by the $1,000 annual receipt gives $3,239.70, the present value of the annuity. This figure is, of course, identical to that found by the long method suggested by Figure 13-5.

Notice that the entry for each period n in Table 13-5 is equal to the sum of the entries in Table 13-3 up to and including Period n. For example, the $PVIFA_{k,n}$ for 9 percent, 4 periods in Table 13-5 could have been calculated by summing the PVIFs for Periods 1 through 4 from Table 13-3:

$$0.9174 + 0.8417 + 0.7722 + 0.7084 = 3.2397.$$

Also, as you might expect, the easiest way to solve a PV of an annuity problem is with a financial calculator. For our illustrative problem, simply input $n = 4$, $k = i = 9$, and PMT = 1,000, and then press the PV button to find the answer, PV = $3,239.72. (Note the 2 cent rounding difference. Calculators are more accurate, as they take numbers out to 8 decimal places versus 4 places for the tables.)

Table 13-5 **Present Value of an Annuity of $1 per Period for n Periods:**

$$\text{PVIFA}_{k,n} = \sum_{t=1}^{n} \frac{1}{(1+k)^t} = \frac{1 - [1/(1+k)^n]}{k}$$

Number of Periods (n)	1%	2%	3%	4%	5%	6%	7%	8%	9%	10%
1	0.9901	0.9804	0.9709	0.9615	0.9524	0.9434	0.9346	0.9259	0.9174	0.9091
2	1.9704	1.9416	1.9135	1.8861	1.8594	1.8334	1.8080	1.7833	1.7591	1.7355
3	2.9410	2.8839	2.8286	2.7751	2.7232	2.6730	2.6243	2.5771	2.5313	2.4869
4	3.9020	3.8077	3.7171	3.6299	3.5460	3.4651	3.3872	3.3121	3.2397	3.1699
5	4.8534	4.7135	4.5797	4.4518	4.3295	4.2124	4.1002	3.9927	3.8897	3.7908
6	5.7955	5.6014	5.4172	5.2421	5.0757	4.9173	4.7665	4.6229	4.4859	4.3553
7	6.7282	6.4720	6.2303	6.0021	5.7864	5.5824	5.3893	5.2064	5.0330	4.8684
8	7.6517	7.3255	7.0197	6.7327	6.4632	6.2098	5.9713	5.7466	5.5348	5.3349
9	8.5660	8.1622	7.7861	7.4353	7.1078	6.8017	6.5152	6.2469	5.9952	5.7590
10	9.4713	8.9826	8.5302	8.1109	7.7217	7.3601	7.0236	6.7101	6.4177	6.1446

Present Value of an Annuity Due

Had the payments in the preceding example occurred at the beginning of each year, the annuity would have been an *annuity due*. In terms of Figure 13-5 each payment would have been shifted to the left, so $1,000 would have appeared under Period 0 and a zero would have appeared under Period 4. Each payment occurs one period earlier, so it has a higher PV. To account for these shifts, we multiply Equation 13-5 by $(1 + k)$ to find the present value of an annuity due:

$$\text{PVA}_n(\text{Annuity due}) = \text{PMT}(\text{PVIFA}_{k,n})(1 + k). \qquad \textbf{(13-5a)}$$

Our illustrative 9 percent, 4-year annuity, with payments made at the beginning of each year, thus has a present value of $3,531.27 versus a value of $3,239.70 on an ordinary (deferred) annuity basis:

$$\text{PVA}_3 = \$1,000(3.2397)(1.09)$$

$$= \$3,239.70(1.09)$$

$$= \$3,531.27.$$

Since each payment comes earlier, an annuity due is worth more than an ordinary (deferred) annuity.

Again, you can use a financial calculator to solve the problem. Simply set the switch to "Due" or "Begin" instead of "END" and proceed as before. When you finish, though, remember to switch back to "END."

Self-Test

Which annuity has the greater present value: an ordinary (deferred) annuity or an annuity due? Why?

PERPETUITIES

perpetuity
A stream of equal payments expected to continue forever.

Most annuities call for payments to be made over a finite time period — for example, $1,000 per year for 4 years. However, some annuities go on indefinitely; here the payments constitute an *infinite series,* and the series is called a **perpetuity.** The present value of a perpetuity is found by applying Equation 13-6:

$$PV(\text{Perpetuity}) = \frac{\text{Payment}}{\text{Interest rate}} = \frac{PMT}{k}. \qquad (13\text{-}6)$$

consol
A perpetual bond originally issued by the British government to consolidate past debts; in general, any perpetual bond.

Perpetuities can be illustrated by some British securities issued after the Napoleonic Wars. In 1815, the British government sold a huge bond issue and used the proceeds to pay off many smaller issues that had been floated in prior years to finance the wars. Because the purpose of the new bonds was to *consolidate* past debts, the bonds were called **consols.** Suppose each consol promised to pay $90 interest per year in perpetuity. (Actually, the interest was stated in pounds.) What would each bond be worth if the going rate of interest, or the discount rate, was 8 percent? The answer is $1,125:

$$\text{Value} = \$90/0.08 = \$1,125.00.$$

Perpetuities are discussed further in later chapters, where procedures for finding the values of various types of securities, particularly preferred stocks, are analyzed.

Self-Test

In what sense is a perpetuity also an annuity?

How is the present value of a perpetuity calculated?

Would it make sense to try to calculate the future value of a perpetuity? Explain.

PRESENT VALUE OF AN UNEVEN SERIES OF RECEIPTS

The definition of an annuity includes the words *constant amount;* in other words, annuities involve situations in which cash flows are *identical* in every period. Although many financial decisions do involve constant cash flows, some important decisions concern *uneven* flows of cash. In particular, common stock investments ordinarily involve uneven, hopefully increasing, dividend payments over time, and capital budgeting projects usually provide un-

Figure 13-6 Time Line for an Uneven Cash Flow Stream: Present Value with k = 6%

The method used to calculate the present value of an uneven stream of future payments is illustrated in this figure. Each payment is multiplied by the appropriate present value interest factor from Table 13-3 to arrive at its individual present value. The resulting amounts are then totaled to arrive at the present value of the stream of payments.

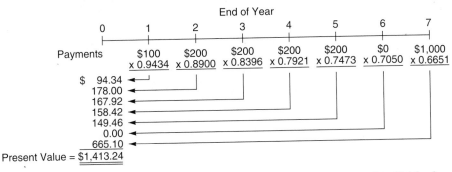

Year	Payment	×	PVIF$_{6\%,n}$	=	PV of Individual Payments
1	$ 100		0.9434		$ 94.34
2	200		0.8900		178.00
3	200		0.8396		167.92
4	200		0.7921		158.42
5	200		0.7473		149.46
6	0		0.7050		0
7	1,000		0.6651		665.10
				PV = Sum =	$1,413.24

even cash flows. Consequently, it is necessary to expand our analysis to deal with **uneven payment streams.**

The present value of an uneven stream of future payments is equal to the sum of the PVs of the individual components of the stream. For example, suppose we are trying to find the PV of the stream of payments shown in the table in Figure 13-6, discounted at 6 percent. As shown in the figure, we multiply each payment by the appropriate PVIF$_{k,n}$, then sum these products to obtain the PV of the stream, $1,413.24. The top of Figure 13-6 also gives a graphic view of the cash flow stream.

The PV of the payments shown in Figure 13-6 for Years 2 through 5 can also be found by using the annuity equation. The steps in this alternative solution process are as follows:

Step 1. Find the PV of $100 due in Year 1:

$$\$100(0.9434) = \$94.34.$$

uneven payment stream

A series of payments in which the amount varies from one period to the next.

Step 2. Recognize that a $200 annuity will be received during Years 2 through 5. Thus, we can determine the value of a 5-year annuity, subtract from it the value of a 1-year annuity, and have remaining the value of a 4-year annuity whose first payment is due in 2 years. This result is achieved by subtracting the PVIFA for a 1-year, 6 percent annuity from the PVIFA for a 5-year annuity and then multiplying the difference by $200:

$$
\begin{aligned}
\text{PV of the annuity} &= \$200(\text{PVIFA}_{6\%,5 \text{ years}}) - \$200(\text{PVIFA}_{6\%,1 \text{ year}}) \\
&= \$200[(\text{PVIFA}_{6\%,5 \text{ years}}) - (\text{PVIFA}_{6\%,1 \text{ year}})] \\
&= \$200(4.2124 - 0.9434) \\
&= \$200(3.2690) = \$653.80.
\end{aligned}
$$

Thus, the present value of the annuity component of the uneven stream is $653.80.

Step 3. Find the PV of the $1,000 due in Year 7:

$$\$1,000(0.6651) = \$665.10.$$

Step 4. Sum the components:

$$\$94.34 + \$653.80 + \$665.10 = \$1,413.24.$$

Either of the methods can be used to solve problems of this type. However, the alternative (annuity) solution is easier if the annuity component runs for many years. For example, the alternative solution would be clearly superior for finding the PV of a stream consisting of $100 in Year 1, $200 in Years 2 through 29, and $1,000 in Year 30.

The present value of a stream of future cash flows can always be found by summing the present values of each individual cash flow. However, cash flow regularities within the stream may allow the use of shortcuts, such as finding the present value of several cash flows that compose an annuity. Also, in some instances we may want to find the value of a stream of payments at some point other than the present (Year 0). In this situation, we proceed as before but compound and discount to some other point in time, say Year 2 rather than Year 0.

Problems involving unequal cash flows can be solved quite easily with most financial calculators. Most of these calculators permit you to input the separate cash flows plus the interest rate; then, when you press the PV (or NPV) button, you obtain the solution. This feature is not found on all financial calculators, but it is found on most new ones. Some of the newer financial calculators even allow you to specify annuities within the cash flow stream. For example, you could specify 1 payment of $100, 4 payments of $200, 1 payment of $0, and 1 payment of $1,000, along with an interest rate of 6 percent, to find the present value of the cash flow stream given in Figure 13-6.

We are generally more interested in the present value of a stream of payments from an asset than in the future (or terminal) value, because the PV is the value today, and hence the market value of the asset.

Self-Test

What are two types of financial decisions that typically involve uneven flows of cash?

DETERMINING INTEREST RATES

We can use the basic equations developed earlier in the chapter to determine the interest rates implicit in financial contracts.

Example 1. A bank offers to lend you $1,000 if you sign a note agreeing to repay $1,610.50 at the end of 5 years. What rate of interest would you be paying?

1. Recognize that $1,000 is the PV of $1,610.50 due in 5 years:

$$PV = \$1,000 = \$1,610.50(PVIF_{k,5 \text{ years}}).$$

2. Solve for $PVIF_{k,5 \text{ years}}$:

$$PVIF_{k,5 \text{ years}} = \frac{\$1,000}{\$1,610.50} = 0.6209.$$

3. Now turn to Table 13-3 or to Table A-1 in Appendix A. Look across the row for Period 5 until you find the value 0.6209. It is in the 10 percent column, so you would be paying a 10 percent rate of interest if you took out the loan.

Example 2. A bank offers to lend you $75,000 to buy a home. You must sign a mortgage calling for a payment of $7,635.48 at the end of each of the next 25 years. What interest rate is the bank charging you?

1. Recognize that $75,000 is the PV of a 25-year, $7,635.48 annuity:

$$PVA_{25} = \$75,000 = \sum_{t=1}^{25} \$7,635.48 \left[\frac{1}{(1 + k)^t} \right] = \$7,635.48 \, (PVIFA_{k,25 \text{ years}}).$$

2. Solve for $PVIFA_{k,25 \text{ years}}$:

$$PVIFA_{k,25 \text{ years}} = \$75,000/\$7,635.48 = 9.8226.$$

3. Turn to Table A-2 in Appendix A. Looking across the row for 25 periods, you will find 9.8226 under the column for 9 percent. Therefore, the rate of interest on this mortgage loan is 9 percent.

4. To solve this problem with a calculator, enter PV = 75,000, n = 25, and PMT = 7,635.48; then press the k = i button to determine that the interest rate the bank is charging is 9 percent. Note that this problem would be quite difficult to solve if you were using Table A-2 in Appendix A and the interest rate was not an even number. The approximate rate for the mortgage could be found by "linear interpolation," which is discussed in algebra texts, but exact solutions can be found easily with calculators.

Although the tables can be used to find the interest rate implicit in single payments and annuities, it is more difficult to find the interest rate implicit in an uneven series of payments. One can use a trial-and-error procedure, a financial calculator with an IRR feature (IRRs are discussed in Chapter 14), or a graphic procedure (which is also discussed in Chapter 14). We defer further discussion of this problem for now, but we will take it up later, in the capital budgeting chapters and again in our discussion of bond values.

Self-Test

How would one go about finding the interest rate implicit (1) in an annuity and (2) in an uneven series of payments?

AMORTIZED LOANS

amortized loan
A loan that is repaid in equal payments over its life.

One of the most important applications of compound interest involves loans that are to be paid off in installments, where the installments include both principal and interest. Examples include automobile loans, home mortgage loans, and most business debt other than very short-term debt. If a loan is to be repaid in equal periodic amounts (monthly, quarterly, or annually), it is said to be an **amortized loan.**

To illustrate, suppose a firm borrows $1,000 to be repaid in 3 equal payments at the end of each of the next 3 years. The lender is to receive 6 percent interest on the loan balance that is outstanding at the beginning of each year. The first task is to determine the amount the firm must repay each year, or the annual payment. To find this amount, recognize that the $1,000 represents the present value of an ordinary annuity of PMT dollars per year for 3 years, discounted at 6 percent:

$$\$1,000 = \text{PV of annuity} = \text{PMT}(\text{PVIFA}_{6\%,3\text{ years}}).$$

The $\text{PVIFA}_{6\%,3}$ is 2.6730, so

$$\$1,000 = \text{PMT}(2.6730).$$

Solving for PMT, we obtain

amortization schedule
A schedule showing precisely how a loan will be repaid. It gives the required payment on each specified date and a breakdown of the payment showing how much constitutes interest and how much constitutes repayment of principal.

$$\text{PMT} = \$1,000/2.6730 = \$374.11.$$

Therefore, if the firm pays the lender $374.11 at the end of each of the next 3 years, then the percentage cost to the borrower, and the rate of return to the lender, will be 6 percent.

To solve the problem with a financial calculator, simply enter n = 3, i = k = 6, and PV = 1,000, and then press PMT. The solution, PMT = 374.11 (or −374.11) will appear.

Each payment consists partly of interest and partly of a repayment of principal. This breakdown is given in the **amortization schedule** shown in

Table 13-6 **Loan Amortization Schedule**

Year	Beginning Amount (1)	Payment (2)	Interest[a] (3)	Repayment of Principal[b] (4)	Remaining Balance (5)
1	$1,000.00	$ 374.11	$ 60.00	$ 314.11	$685.89
2	685.89	374.11	41.15	332.96	352.93
3	352.93	374.11	21.18	352.93	0
		$1,122.33	$122.33	$1,000.00	

[a]Interest is calculated by multiplying the loan balance at the beginning of the year by the interest rate. Therefore, interest in Year 1 is $1,000(0.06) = $60; in Year 2 interest is $685.89(0.06) = $41.15; and in Year 3 interest is $352.93(0.06) = $21.18.
[b]Repayment of principal is equal to the payment of $374.11 minus the interest charge for each year.

Table 13-6. The interest component is largest in the first year, and it declines as the outstanding balance of the loan decreases. For tax purposes, the borrower reports the interest payments in Column 3 as a deductible cost each year, while the lender reports these same amounts as taxable income.

Self-Test

In an amortization schedule, in general terms, how do you determine the amount of the periodic payments? How do you determine the portion of the payment that goes to interest and to principal?

SUMMARY

Financial decisions often involve situations where someone pays money at one point in time and receives money at some later time. Dollars that are paid or received at two different points in time are different, and this difference is recognized and accounted for in *time value of money, or discounted cash flow (DCF), analysis.* We summarize below the types of DCF analysis and the key concepts covered in this chapter, using the data shown in Figure 13-7 to illustrate the various points. Refer to the figure constantly, and find in it an example of each point covered as you go through this section.

- **Compounding** is the process of determining the **future value (FV)** of a payment or a series of payments. The compounded amount, or future value, is equal to the beginning amount plus the interest earned.

- Future value: $FV_n = PV(1 + k)^n = PV(FVIF_{k,n})$.
  (single payment)

  Example: $961.50 compounded for 1 year at 4%.

  $$FV_1 = \$961.50(1.04)^1 = \$1,000.$$

Figure 13-7 **Illustration for Chapter Summary (k = 4%)**

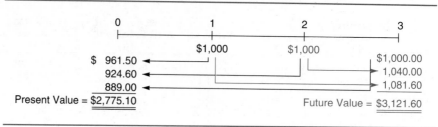

- **Discounting** is the process of finding the **present value (PV)** of a future payment or a series of payments; discounting is the reverse of compounding.
- Present value: (single payment)

$$PV = FV_n \left[\frac{1}{(1 + k)^n} \right]$$

Example: $1,000 discounted back for 2 years at 4%.

$$PV = \$1,000 \, \frac{1}{(1.04)^2} = \$1,000(0.9246) = \$924.60.$$

- An **annuity** is defined as a series of equal, periodic payments (PMT) for a specified number of periods.
- Future value: (annuity)

$$FVA_n = PMT(FVIFA_{k,n}).$$

Example: FVA of 3 payments of $1,000 when k = 4%.

$$FVA_3 = 3.1216(\$1,000) = \$3,121.60.$$

- Present value: (annuity)

$$PVA_n = PMT(PVIFA_{k,n}).$$

Example: PVA of 3 payments of $1,000 when k = 4%.

$$PVA = 2.7751(\$1,000) = \$2,775.10.$$

- An annuity that has payments occurring at the *end* of each period is called an **ordinary (deferred) annuity.** The formulas above are for ordinary (deferred) annuities.
- If each payment occurs at the beginning of the period rather than at the end, then we have an **annuity due.** In Figure 13-7, the payments would be shown at Years 0, 1, and 2 rather than at 1, 2, and 3. The PV of each payment would be larger, because each payment would be discounted back one year less, and hence the PV of the annuity would also be larger. Similarly, the FV of the annuity due would also be larger, because each

payment would be compounded for an extra year. These formulas can be used to convert the PV and FV of an ordinary (deferred) annuity to an annuity due:

$$PVA(\text{annuity due}) = PVA \text{ of an ordinary annuity} \times (1 + k).$$

$$FVA(\text{annuity due}) = FVA \text{ of an ordinary annuity} \times (1 + k).$$

- If the time line in Figure 13-7 were extended out forever, so that the $1,000 payments went on forever, we would have a **perpetuity** whose value could be found as follows:

$$\text{Value of perpetuity} = \frac{PMT}{k} = \frac{\$1,000}{0.04} = \$25,000.$$

- If the payments in Figure 13-7 were **unequal,** we could not use the annuity formulas. To find the PV or FV of the series, find the PV or FV of each individual payment and then sum them. However, if some of the payments constitute an annuity, then the annuity formula could be used to calculate the present value of that part of the payment stream.

- **Financial calculators** have built-in programs which perform all of the operations discussed in this chapter. It is very helpful to get such a calculator and to learn how to use it. However, it is essential that you also understand the logical processes involved.

- If you know the payments and the PV (or FV) of a payment stream, you can **determine the interest rate.** For example, in the Figure 13-7 illustration, if you were given the information that a loan (or bond) called for 3 payments of $1,000 each, and that the loan (or bond) had a value today of PV = $2,775.10, then you could find the interest rate that caused the sum of the PVs of the payments to equal $2,775.10. Since we are dealing with an annuity, we could proceed as follows:

  a. Recognize that $PVA = \$2,775.10 = \$1,000(PVIFA_{k,3})$.
  b. Solve for $PVIFA_{k,3}$:

$$PVIFA_{k,3} = \$2,775.10/\$1,000 = 2.7751.$$

  c. Look up 2.7751 in Table A-2 on the third row. It is in the 4% column, so the interest rate must be 4 percent. If the factor did not appear in the table, this would indicate that the interest rate was not a whole number. In this case, you could not use this procedure to find the exact rate. In practice, though, this is not a problem, because people use financial calculators to find interest rates.

- An **amortized loan** is one that is paid off in equal payments over a specified period. An **amortization schedule** shows how much of each payment constitutes interest, how much is used to reduce the principal, and the remaining balance at the end of each period.

Table 13-7 **Applications of the Time Value of Money**

Formula	Equation Number	Table	Appendix A Table Number
$FV_n = PV(FVIF_{k,n})$	13-2	13-2	A-3
$PV = FV_n(PVIF_{k,n})$	13-3	13-3	A-1
$FVA_n = PMT(FVIFA_{k,n})$	13-4	13-4	A-4
$PVA_n = PMT(PVIFA_{k,n})$	13-5	13-5	A-2

The concepts covered in this chapter will be used throughout the remainder of the book. In the next chapters, the same basic concepts are applied to corporate decisions involving both expenditures on capital assets and the types of capital that should be used to pay for assets. In later chapters we apply present value concepts to the process of valuing stocks and bonds; there we will see that the market prices of securities are established by determining the present values of the cash flows they are expected to provide.

EQUATIONS AND REVIEW OF CHAPTER CONCEPTS

In light of the large number of formulas and the importance of this chapter, a review of the equations is warranted. Actually, most problems dealing with the time value of money (compounding or discounting) can be solved by utilizing one or a combination of the four formulas listed in Table 13-7. If you have a financial calculator, you should work the problems with it as well as with the equations.

Sample Problems

Problem: Compounding a Lump Sum to a Future Period. Your aunt has given you a $3,000 tax-free gift. If you invest it in a 5-year, 8 percent certificate of deposit, how much will you have when the certificate matures?

Discussion. The variables in this problem are a present amount, PV, of $3,000; a length of time for the investment, n, of 5 years; and an investment (interest) rate, k, of 8 percent. A future amount, FV — the value of $3,000 compounded at 8 percent for 5 years — is to be found. Because a single, present amount is being compounded, we use the $FVIF_{k,n}$ found in either Table 13-2 or Table A-3 in Appendix A.

Solution.

$$FV_5 = PV(FVIF_{8\%,5 \text{ years}}) \tag{13-2}$$

$$= \$3,000(1.4693)$$

$$= \$4,407.90.$$

Problem: Present Value of a Future Lump Sum. Your friend Howard has suggested that you invest, along with him, in a real estate deal. He predicts your portion of the property in question will be worth $40,000 in 8 years. If as an alternative you can make an investment with equal risk at 10 percent, what is the maximum that you pay for the share of the venture?

Discussion. Here we are concerned with finding the present value, PV, of a future amount, FV, of $40,000 to be received in 8 years, n, with a discount rate, k, of 10 percent. With a lump-sum amount to be discounted back to the present, we use a present value interest factor, $PVIF_{k,n}$, found in Table 13-3 or in Table A-1 in Appendix A.

Solution.

$$PV = FV_8(PVIF_{10\%,8 \text{ years}})$$ (13-3)

$$= \$40,000(0.4665)$$

$$= \$18,660.00.$$

Problem: Future Value of an Ordinary (Deferred) Annuity. You are planning a great vacation to Europe in 15 years. You plan to save $500 annually, beginning next year, after you graduate. How much will you have in your vacation fund in 15 years if you invest at 9 percent?

Discussion. In this situation you need to determine the future value, FVA_n, of an annuity of $500, PMT, deposited annually for 15 years, n, at 9 percent, k. To do so you would use the interest factor for an annuity, $FVIFA_{k,n}$ where n = 15 and k = 9%, from Table A-4 in Appendix A.

Solution.

$$FVA_{15} = PMT(FVIFA_{9\%,15 \text{ years}})$$ (13-4)

$$= \$500(29.361)$$

$$= \$14,680.50.$$

Alternative Problem. Let's keep the scenario that you are saving for your vacation to Europe but change some of the elements of the problem. Now let's assume that you still want to save $500 each year for 15 years, but this time let's assume that you know the trip will cost $14,680.50. What is the rate of return you must earn to reach your goal?

Discussion. In this situation you use the same formula, Equation 13-4, but this time you solve for the future value interest factor for an annuity, $FVIFA_{k,n}$. Once you have the $FVIFA_{k,n}$, you can determine the rate of return required to meet the goal.

Solution.

$$FVA_{15} = PMT(FVIFA_{k,15 \text{ years}}) \tag{13-4}$$

$$\$14,680.50 = \$500(FVIFA_{k,15 \text{ years}})$$

$$FVIFA_{k,15 \text{ years}} = \$14,680.50/\$500$$

$$FVIFA_{k,15 \text{ years}} = 29.361.$$

Now go to Table A-4 in Appendix A and find the 15-year row. Moving to the right along the 15-year row, find the future value interest factor 29.361 in the 9 percent column. Thus 9 percent is the rate at which you must invest the annuity of $500 annually for 15 years to have a future value of $14,680.50.

Problem: Future Value of an Annuity Due. Again, let's keep the scenario that you are saving for your vacation to Europe but change the problem a bit. Now assume that you still want to save $500 each year for 15 years, but that you begin saving today by placing $500 in a money market account earning 8 percent, not 9 percent as before. If the trip will cost $14,680, will you have enough money?

Discussion. In this example we will want to find the future value of an annuity due utilizing Equation 13-4a. You will be saving $500 annually, PMT, for 15 years, n, which will be invested at 8 percent, k. The future value interest factor for an annuity is found in Table A-4 in Appendix A. Recall that in this example the annuity is an annuity due, so the $FVIFA_{k,n}$ must be multiplied by $(1+k)$ to account for this fact.

Solution.

$$FVA_n(\text{Annuity due}) = PMT(FVIFA_{8\%,15})(1+k) \tag{13-4a}$$

$$= \$500(27.152)(1.08)$$

$$= \$14,662.08.$$

Thus, you will fall short of your goal of $14,680 by $17.92.

Problem: Present Value of an Ordinary (Deferred) Annuity. Lefty Holland, star center for Central State College, has been approached by the Buffalo Bouncers of the Professional Basketball League. The Bouncers have offered Lefty a generous contract that offers him a choice in the payment of his bonus. He may choose between receiving a payment of $25,000 annually (at the end of each year) for 15 years or receiving an equivalent amount today. If Lefty can invest at 8 percent, what would be the equivalent amount if the bonus were paid today? (Ignore tax consequences for the time being.)

Discussion. Under the conditions outlined, we want to find the present value of an annuity, PVA_n, of $25,000 annually, PMT, for 15 years, n, which could be invested at 8 percent, k. The present value interest factor for an annuity, $PVIFA_{k,n}$, is found in Table A-2 of Appendix A.

Solution.

$$PVA_{15} = PMT(PVIFA_{8\%, 15 \text{ years}}) \qquad (13\text{-}5)$$

$$= \$25,000(8.5595)$$

$$= \$213,987.50.$$

Alternative Problem. To demonstrate again how a single formula (Equation 13-5) can be used to determine unknowns other than PVA_n, let's change the basketball scenario. Now assume that Lefty is given the choice of taking an immediate bonus of $213,987.50 or taking an annuity for 15 years that he could invest at 8 percent annually. What is the annual receipt from the annuity?

Discussion. We still utilize Equation 13-5, but now we solve for the annuity amount, PMT. The present value interest factor for the annuity, 8.5595, comes from Table A-2.

Solution.

$$PVA_{15} = PMT(PVIFA_{8\%, 15 \text{ years}}) \qquad (13\text{-}5)$$

$$\$213,987.50 = PMT(8.5595)$$

$$PMT = \$213,987.50/8.5595$$

$$PMT = \$25,000.00.$$

Problem: Present Value of an Annuity Due. Suppose Lefty's contract allows him to choose between receiving a payment of $25,000 annually, at the beginning of each year, for 15 years or receiving an equivalent amount today. If Lefty can invest at 8 percent, what would be the equivalent amount if the bonus were paid today? (Again, ignore tax consequences.)

Discussion. Under the conditions outlined, we want to find the present value of an annuity due of $25,000 annually, PMT, for 15 years, n, which could be invested at 8 percent, k. The formula for solving this problem is given in Equation 13-5a.

Solution.

$$PVA_n \text{ (Annuity due)} = PMT(PVIFA_{k,n})(1+k) \qquad (13\text{-}5a)$$

$$= \$25,000(8.5595)(1.08)$$

$$= \$231,106.50.$$

Problem: Present Value of a Perpetuity. Suppose you invest in a security which promises to pay you $100 forever. Assume that the going rate of interest is 10 percent. What is the value of this security?

Discussion. Here we are concerned with finding the PV of a perpetuity (because the payments go on indefinitely) with payments, PMT, of $100 at an interest rate, k, of 10 percent. The formula for solving this problem is given in Equation 13-6.

Solution.

$$PV(\text{Perpetuity}) = \frac{PMT}{k} \qquad\qquad (13\text{-}6)$$

$$= \$100/0.10$$

$$= \$1,000.00.$$

Conclusions

With a bit of practice, perhaps gained by working the end-of-chapter problems, you will find that the problems associated with the time value of money are not as difficult as they may at first appear. The tables in Appendix A can be helpful. One trick to remember is that if you wish to know a future value, you can use the formulas associated with Tables A-3 or A-4. Use Table A-3 if there is only a single, present investment; if the investment is an annuity, use Table A-4. On the other hand, if you wish to find the present value of some future amount, you can use Table A-1 or A-2. You can use Table A-1 if the future amount to be discounted is a single, lump-sum amount. If the future receipt (or payment) is an annuity, you can use Table A-2. Of course, another alternative is to use your financial calculator. When using your financial calculator, you input the data for the known variables and solve for the unknown variable.

 RESOLUTION TO DECISION IN FINANCE

Can Boomers Retire?

Regardless of a person's age or financial circumstances, experts advise a mix of growth and income securities in a retirement portfolio. The nature of this mix, however, varies with the individual. Workers in their twenties or thirties should put 70 percent or more of their retirement money into stocks, with the rest in bonds or liquid assets such as Treasury bills or money market mutual funds. Employees should not overload the stock portion of their portfolios with their own company's stock, because diversification is necessary within that portfolio.

As workers grow older, they are advised to change the mix of their retirement assets. Laurence B. Siegel, managing director of an investment research firm, says stocks alone are fine "if you're interested only in making the most money possible, and your time horizon is very long. . . ." But for people with less time to realize results he suggests "a diversified mix of

Sources: "Will You Be Able to RETIRE?" *Fortune*, July 31, 1989; *The Wall Street Journal*, "What's Wall Street's First Rule? Diversify," January 25, 1990, and "Taking Full Control of Retirement Funds," April 27, 1990.

U.S. and international stocks, bonds, and other assets—certainly including real estate."

Although bonds have traditionally been less volatile than stocks, events of the past decade have shown that an all-bond portfolio can be almost as risky as one containing all stocks. Annual returns on U.S. government and corporate bonds in the 1980s ranged from 2.29 percent to 31.09 percent.

Several formulas for long-term investment strategy have been proposed. One suggests 60 percent stocks, 35 percent bonds and 5 percent cash. Such a mix would have produced an average annual return of 9.4 percent over the last 25 years. (Of course, past returns do not necessarily indicate what future returns will be.) A more controversial formula calls for investing equally in five types of no-load mutual funds: U.S. stocks, bonds, real estate, cash, and foreign stocks. At the end of each year, investors should realign their holdings and rebalance them among the five groups. This generally involves selling some of the assets that have been performing well and using the proceeds to add to the badly performing groups. However, critics claim this "fixed mix" is a "lazy" and even dangerous strategy, since investors might be putting some of their money into areas they know little or nothing about, such as foreign stocks.

When individual employees decide about retirement fund strategies, they should select the type of plan offered by their employers which best complements their other investments. For instance, some employer plans may be invested only in guaranteed investment contracts (GICs) that pay fixed interest close to certificate of deposit rates. If so, employees in those companies should probably keep their personal IRAs (Individual Retirement Accounts) in something without a fixed return. Where companies offer a choice between a stock fund and a GIC, employees can select the one that is most different from their personal investment accounts.

One good idea is to invest, usually up to 6 percent of one's pre-tax pay, in 401(k) plans. Such an investment reduces current taxable income and also provides for the future. Also,

even if after-tax dollars must be contributed, people should always seek plans in which the employer matches employee contributions. Most (86 percent) of employers with 401(k) plans provide from 50 cents to $1 for every dollar the employee contributes. As a pension consultant points out, "Getting 50 cents on the dollar is like getting an instant 50 percent return on your money."

Let's now consider the question posed at the beginning of the chapter concerning your father's nest egg. From your reading in this chapter, you should realize that we must solve for the future value of an annuity. We know that PMT = $5,000, n = 20 years, and k = 10 percent, so we are solving for FVA_{20}. The formula is

$$FVA_{20} = PMT(FVIFA_{10\%, 20 \text{ years}})$$
$$= \$5,000(57.275)$$
$$= \$286,375.$$

Thus, your father would have $286,375 at the end of 20 years. If your father's investment had earned 12 percent rather than 10 percent, his nest egg would have been $360,260 rather than $286,375.

Suppose your father's nest egg was $286,375 when he retired, and it was earning 10 percent. How much could he withdraw each year for the next 20 years? From your reading in this chapter you should realize that we must use the present value of an annuity formula. We know that PVA_n = $286,375, k = 10 percent, and n = 20 years, so we are looking for PMT. The formula is

$$PVA_{20} = PMT(PVIFA_{10\%, 20 \text{ years}})$$
$$\$286,375 = PMT(8.5136)$$
$$PMT = \$33,637.36.$$

Thus, your father, after he retires, could withdraw $33,637.36 for each of the next 20 years if the account continues to earn 10 percent. If his nest egg had been $360,260 and had been earning 12 percent rather than 10 percent, he could have withdrawn $48,231.45 for 20 years.

From these two examples, you can see how the return on your investment determines both the amount of money in the nest egg and how much can be withdrawn from that nest egg.

However, another important concept to remember is the risk-return relationship that we learned in Chapter 12 — the higher an investment's expected return, the higher its exposure to risk.

QUESTIONS

13-1   Is it true that for all positive interest rates the following conditions hold: $FVIF_{k,n} \geq 1.0$; $PVIF_{k,n} \leq 1.0$; $FVIFA_{k,n} \geq$ number of periods the annuity lasts; $PVIFA_{k,n} \leq$ number of periods the annuity lasts?

13-2   An *annuity* is defined as a series of payments of a fixed amount for a specific number of periods. Thus, $100 a year for 10 years is an annuity, but $100 in Year 1, $200 in Year 2, and $400 a year in Years 3 through 10 does *not* constitute an annuity. However, the second series *contains* an annuity. Is this last statement true or false? Explain.

13-3   If a firm's earnings per share grew from $1 to $2 over a 10-year period, the *total growth* would be 100 percent, but the *annual growth rate* would be *less than* 10 percent. Why is this so?

13-4   To find the present value of an uneven series of payments, you must use the $PVIF_{k,n}$ tables; the $PVIFA_{k,n}$ tables can never be of use, even if some of the payments constitute an annuity (for example, $100 each year for Years 3, 4, 5, and 6), because the entire series is not an annuity. Is this statement true or false? Explain.

SELF-TEST PROBLEMS

ST-1   Assume it is now January 2, 1990. If you put $1,000 into a savings account on January 2, 1991, at an 8 percent interest rate, compounded annually:

     a. How much would you have in your account on January 2, 1994?

     b. Suppose that you deposited the $1,000 in 4 payments of $250 each on January 2 of 1991, 1992, 1993, and 1994. How much would you have in your account on January 2, 1994, based on 8 percent annual compounding?

     c. Suppose that you made 4 equal payments into your account as suggested in Part b. How large would each of your payments have to be for you to obtain the same ending balance you calculated in Part a?

ST-2   Assume that it is now January 2, 1990, and you will need $1,000 on January 2, 1994. Your bank compounds interest at an 8 percent rate annually.

     a. If only one deposit is made, how much must you place in your account today to have a balance of $1,000 on January 2, 1994?

     b. If you want to make equal payments on each January 2 from 1991 through 1994 to accumulate the $1,000 you need, how large must each of the 4 payments be?

c. If your father offered either to make the payments calculated in Part b ($221.92) or to give you a lump sum of $750 on January 2, 1991, which would you choose?

d. If you have only $750 on January 2, 1991, what interest rate, compounded annually, would you have to earn to have the necessary $1,000 on January 2, 1994?

e. Suppose that you can deposit only $186.29 each January 2 from 1991 through 1994 but you still need $1,000 on January 2, 1994. What interest rate, with annual compounding, must you seek out to achieve your goal?

ST-3 Due to unfortunate circumstances, your sister must borrow $5,000 from you. She wants to repay the loan in 3 equal annual installments that include 9 percent interest. How much should she pay for each of the next 3 years? (Note: The first payment is due one year from today.)

ST-4 Your Uncle Henry promises that if you invest $7,500 today in his latest "get rich quick" scheme, he will pay you $2,651.50 each year for the next 3 years. What rate of return is his project offering?

PROBLEMS

13-1 **Present and future values for different periods.** Find the following values *without* using the tables, then work the problems *with* the tables to check your answers. Disregard rounding errors.
a. An initial $1,000 compounded for 1 year at 6 percent.
b. An initial $1,000 compounded for 2 years at 6 percent.
c. The present value of $1,000 due in 1 year at a discount rate of 6 percent.
d. The present value of $1,000 due in 2 years at a discount rate of 6 percent.

13-2 **Present and future values for different interest rates.** Use the tables to find the following values:
a. An initial $1,000 compounded for 10 years at 5 percent.
b. An initial $1,000 compounded for 10 years at 10 percent.
c. The present value of $1,000 due in 10 years at a 5 percent discount rate.
d. The present value of $2,594 due in 10 years at a 10 percent discount rate.

13-3 **Time for a lump sum to double.** To the closest year, how long will it take $1,000 to double if it is deposited and earns the following rates?
a. 5 percent.
b. 10 percent.
c. 15 percent.
d. 100 percent.

13-4 **Future value of an ordinary annuity.** Find the *future value* of the following annuities if the first payment in each annuity is made at the end of the year; that is, it is an ordinary (deferred) annuity.
a. $1,000 per year for 10 years at 6 percent.
b. $2,000 per year for 5 years at 12 percent.
c. $1,000 per year for 5 years at zero percent.

13-5 **Future value of an annuity due.** Find the *future value* of the following annuities if the first payment is made today; that is, each one is an annuity due.
a. $1,000 per year for 10 years at 6 percent.
b. $2,000 per year for 5 years at 12 percent.
c. $1,000 per year for 5 years at zero percent.

13-6   **Present value of an ordinary annuity.** Find the *present value* of the following ordinary (deferred) annuities:

    a. $1,000 per year for 10 years at 6 percent.
    b. $2,000 per year for 5 years at 12 percent.
    c. $1,000 per year for 5 years at zero percent.

13-7   **Present value of an annuity due.** Find the *present value* of the following annuities if the first payment is made today; that is, each one is an annuity due.

    a. $1,000 per year for 10 years at 6 percent.
    b. $2,000 per year for 5 years at 12 percent.
    c. $1,000 per year for 5 years at zero percent.

13-8   **Uneven cash flows.**

    a. Find the present value of the following cash flow streams when the discount rate is 10 percent:

Year	Cash Flow Stream A	Cash Flow Stream B
1	$1,000	$5,000
2	3,000	3,000
3	3,000	3,000
4	3,000	3,000
5	5,000	1,000

    b. What is the value of each cash flow stream at a zero percent discount rate?

13-9   **Uneven cash flows.** Find the present value of the following cash flow stream, discounted at 12 percent: Year 1, $10,000; Year 2, $5,000; Years 3 to 20, $1,000.

13-10   **Growth rates.** Last year The Dickenson Company's sales were $6 million. Sales were $3 million 5 years earlier.

    a. To the nearest percentage point, at what rate have sales been growing?
    b. Suppose someone calculated the sales growth in Part a as follows: "Sales doubled in 5 years. This represents a growth of 100 percent in 5 years; so dividing 100 percent by 5, we find the growth rate to be 20 percent per year." Explain what is wrong with this calculation.

13-11   **Ordinary annuity versus annuity due.**

    a. You have decided to turn over a new leaf and begin to save money for a change. If you save $2,000 annually for the next 5 years in an 8 percent money market account, what will be the total at the end of the period? Assume that your investment will occur at the end of each year.
    b. Since the savings look so good in Part a, you want to get your savings started today. What is the future value of the $2,000 annual investment if your first payment is made today and you continue as before with 5 annual payments at an assumed rate of 8 percent?

13-12   **Effective rate of interest.** Find the interest rates, or rates of return, on each of the following:

    a. You borrow $2,000 and promise to pay back $2,200 at the end of 1 year.
    b. You lend $2,000 and receive a promise of $2,200 at the end of 1 year.
    c. You borrow $20,000 and promise to pay back $62,112 at the end of 10 years.
    d. You borrow $20,000 and promise to make payments of $5,141.78 per year for 5 years.

Annuity

√ **13-13**
A·2

Expected rate of return. Thompson Business Machines buys equipment for $1,200,000 and expects a return of $248,282.71 per year for the next 10 years. What is the expected rate of return on the equipment?

√ **13-14**
A·1

Expected rate of return. Florida Atlantic invests $1.5 million to clear a tract of land and plant some young pine trees. The trees will mature in 10 years, at which time the firm plans to sell the lumber at an expected price of $9,287,926. What is Florida Atlantic's expected rate of return?

13-15 **Effective rate of interest.** Your broker offers to sell you a note for $3,992.70 that will pay $1,000 per year for 5 years. If you buy the note, what rate of interest will you be earning?

13-16 **Effective rate of interest.** Spartan Financial Corporation offers to lend you $75,000; the loan calls for annual payments of $9,860.51 for 15 years. What interest rate is the company charging you?

13-17 **Required lump-sum payment.** To enable you to complete your last year in college and then go through law school, you need $15,000 per year for the next 4 years, starting next year (that is, you need the first payment of $15,000 one year from today). Your rich aunt has offered to provide you with a sum of money sufficient to put you through school. She plans to deposit this sum today in a bank account that is expected to yield 7 percent interest.
a. How large must the deposit be?
b. How much will be in the account immediately after you make the first withdrawal? After the last withdrawal?

13-18 **Required lump-sum investment.** Credit Finance is offering a note that matures in 5 years at $1,000. If you wish a 10 percent return on your investment, how much would you be willing to pay for this note? (Assume that no other cash flows accrue from the note other than the single lump-sum maturity payment.)

13-19 **Ordinary annuity versus annuity due.** Houston Chemicals has just purchased equipment costing $500,000. The firm can finance the equipment at 12 percent for 15 years.
a. If the annual payment is computed as an *ordinary annuity*, what is the annual payment?
b. If, however, the annual payment is computed as an *annuity due* (that is, the first payment is due today), what is the amount of the payment?

13-20 **Compound growth.** Funtime Video Centers plans to increase sales at an annual rate of 10 percent for the next 5 years from its current $5,000,000 level.
a. What is the expected level of sales each year?
b. Graph each year's sales.

13-21 **Present value of a perpetuity.** What is the present value of a perpetuity of $100 per year if the appropriate discount rate is 4 percent? If interest rates in general doubled and the appropriate discount rate rose to 8 percent, what would happen to the present value of the perpetuity?

13-22 **Amortization schedule.**
a. Set up an amortization schedule for a $10,000 loan to be repaid in equal installments at the end of each of the next 3 years. The interest rate is 9 percent.

(Do Parts b through d only if you are using the computerized problem diskette.)

    b. Set up an amortization schedule for a $20,000 loan to be repaid in equal installments at the end of each of the next 3 years. The interest is 9 percent.

    c. Set up an amortization schedule for a $100,000 loan to be repaid in equal installments at the end of each of the next 3 years. The interest rate is 10 percent.

    d. Recalculate Parts b and c using a 20-year amortization schedule.

13-23   **Finding missing cash flow.** The present value (t = 0) of the following cash flow stream is $8,972.15 when discounted at 10 percent annually. What is the value of the missing (t = 2) cash flow?

13-24   **Effect of inflation.** At an inflation rate of 9 percent, the purchasing power of $1 would be cut in half in 8.04 years. How long to the nearest year would it take the purchasing power of $1 to be cut in half if the inflation rate were only 5 percent?

13-25   **Present value of perpetuities.** You are currently at Time Period 0. At Time Period 1 you will begin to receive an annual payment of $50 in perpetuity. At Time Period 6 you will begin to receive an additional $100 in perpetuity, and at Time Period 10 you will begin to receive an additional $150 in perpetuity. If you require a 10 percent rate of return, then what is the combined present value of these 3 perpetuities?

SOLUTIONS TO SELF-TEST PROBLEMS

ST-1   **a.**

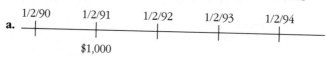

$1,000 is being compounded for 3 years, so your balance on January 2, 1994, is $1,259.71:

$$FV_n = PV(1 + k)^n$$

$$= \$1,000(1 + 0.08)^3$$

$$= \$1,259.71.$$

   b.

1/2/90	1/2/91	1/2/92	1/2/93	1/2/94
	$250	$250	$250	$250

Future value of an annuity:

$$FVA_4 = PMT(FVIFA_{8\%,4}) = \$250(4.5061)$$

$$= \$1,126.53.$$

c. $FVA_4 = \$1,259.71.$

$k = 8\%.$

$n = 4.$

$PMT = ?$

$PMT(FVIFA_{8\%,4}) = FVA_4$

$PMT(4.5061) = \$1,259.71$

$PMT = \$1,259.71/4.5061$

$= \$279.56.$

Therefore, you would have to make 4 payments of \$279.56 at the end of each year to accumulate a balance of \$1,259.71 on January 2, 1994.

ST-2   **a.** Set up a time line like those in Self-Test Problem 1 and note that your deposit will grow for 4 years at 8 percent. The deposit on January 2, 1990, is the PV, and \$1,000 = FV. The solution is as follows:

$FV_4 = \$1,000.$

$n = 4.$

$k = 8\%.$

$PV = ?$

$FV_4(PVIF_{8\%,4}) = PV$

$\$1,000(0.7350) = \$735.00$, the initial deposit
necessary to accumulate \$1,000.

b. Here we are dealing with a 4-year annuity where the first payment occurs one year from today, on January 2, 1991, and where the future value must equal \$1,000. The solution is as follows:

$FVA_4 = \$1,000.$

$n = 4.$

$k = 8\%.$

$PMT = ?$

$PMT(FVIFA_{8\%,4}) = FVA_4$

$$PMT = \frac{FVA_4}{(FVIFA_{8\%,4})}$$

$$= \frac{\$1,000}{4.5061}$$

$$= \$221.92.$$

c. This problem can be approached in several ways. Perhaps the simplest is to ask the question, "If I received $750 on January 2, 1991, and deposited it to earn 8 percent, would I have the required $1,000 on January 2, 1994?" The answer is no:

$$\$750(1.08)^3 = \$944.78.$$

This indicates that you should let your father make the payments rather than accept the lump sum of $750.

You could also compare the $750 with the PV of the payments:

$$\text{PMT} = \$221.92.$$

$$k = 8\%.$$

$$n = 4.$$

$$\text{PVA}_4 = ?$$

$$\text{PMT}(\text{PVIFA}_{8\%,4}) = \text{PVA}$$

$$\$221.92(3.3121) = \$735.02, \text{the present value of}$$
$$\text{the required payments.}$$

Because this is less than the $750 lump-sum offer, your initial reaction might be to accept the lump sum of $750. However, this would be a mistake. Note that if you deposited the $750 on January 2, 1991, at an 8 percent interest rate to be withdrawn on January 2, 1994, interest would be compounded for only 3 years, from January 2, 1991, to December 31, 1993 and the future value would be only

$$\text{PV}(\text{PVIF}_{8\%,3}) = \$750(1.2597)$$

$$= \$944.78.$$

The problem is that when you found the $735.02 present value of the annuity, you were finding the value of the annuity *today*, on January 2, 1990. You were comparing $735.02 today with the lump sum $750 one year from now. Such a comparison is, of course, invalid. What you should have done was take the $735.02, recognize that this is the present value of an annuity as of January 2, 1990, multiply $735.02 times 1.08 to get $793.82, and compare $793.82 with the lump sum of $750. You would then take your father's offer to pay off the loan rather than the lump sum on January 2, 1991.

d.
$$\text{PV} = \$750.$$

$$\text{FV}_3 = \$1,000.$$

$$n = 3.$$

$$k = ?$$

$$\text{PV}(\text{FVIF}_{k,3}) = \text{FV}_3$$

$$\text{FVIF}_{k,3} = \frac{\text{FV}_3}{\text{PV}}$$

$$= \frac{\$1,000}{\$750}$$

$$= 1.3333.$$

Use the future value of $1 (See Table A-3 in Appendix A at the end of the book) for 3 periods to find the interest rate corresponding to an FVIF of 1.3333. Look across the Period 3 row of Table A-3 until you come to 1.3333. The closest value is 1.3310 in the 10 percent column. Therefore, you would require an interest rate of approximately 10 percent to achieve your $1,000 goal. The exact rate required, found with a financial calculator, is 10.0642 percent.

e.

$$FVA_4 = \$1,000.$$

$$PMT = \$186.29.$$

$$k = ?$$

$$n = 4.$$

$$PMT(FVIFA_{k,4}) = FVA_4$$

$$\$186.29(FVIFA_{k,4}) = \$1,000$$

$$FVIFA_{k,4} = \frac{\$1,000}{\$186.29}$$

$$= 5.3680.$$

Using the future value of an annuity table for 4 periods (Table A-4 in Appendix A at the end of the book), you find that 5.3680 corresponds to a 20 percent interest rate. You might be able to find a borrower willing to offer you a 20 percent interest rate, but there would be some risk involved, and he or she might not actually pay you your $1,000!

ST-3

$$PVA_3 = \$5,000.$$

$$PMT = ?$$

$$k = 9\%.$$

$$n = 3.$$

$$PVA_3 = PMT(PVIFA_{9\%,3})$$

$$\$5,000 = PMT(2.5313)$$

$$PMT = \$5,000/2.5313$$

$$= \$1,975.27.$$

By dividing each side of the equation by the PVIFA for 3 years at 9 percent, PVIFA = 2.5313, we can solve for the annuity required to repay the loan in 3 years with a 9 percent return to the lender, which is $1,975.27.

ST-4

$$PVA_3 = \$7,500.$$

$$PMT = \$2,651.50.$$

$$k = ?$$

$$n = 3.$$

$$PVA_3 = PMT(PVIFA_{k,3})$$

$$\$7,500 = \$2,651.50(PVIFA_{k,3})$$

$$PVIFA_{k,3} = \$7,500/\$2,651.50$$

$$= 2.8286.$$

Using the present value of an annuity table (found in Table A-2 of Appendix A), go down to the third row (n = 3) and go across the row until you find the interest factor, PVIFA = 2.8286. We find that 2.8286 corresponds to only a 3 percent rate of return. Apparently this is not a very profitable investment opportunity.

Appendix 13A

Semiannual and Other Compounding Periods

In all of the examples in the chapter, we assumed that returns are received once a year, or annually. Suppose, however, that you put $1,000 in a bank which advertises that it pays 6 percent compounded *semiannually*. How much will you have at the end of 1 year? Semiannual compounding means that interest is actually paid every 6 months. The procedures for semiannual compounding are illustrated in the calculations in Table 13A-1. Here the annual interest rate is divided by 2, but twice as many compounding periods are used because interest is paid twice a year. Comparing the amount on hand at the end of the second 6-month period, $1,060.90, with what would have been on hand under annual compounding, $1,060, you see that semiannual compounding is better from your standpoint as a saver. This result occurs because you can earn *interest on interest* more frequently.

Throughout the economy, different types of investments use different compounding periods. For example, bank accounts generally pay interest monthly or daily; most bonds pay interest semiannually; stocks pay dividends quarterly; and many loans pay interest annually. Thus, if securities with different compounding periods are to be compared, one needs to put them on a common basis. This means that we must distinguish between the *nominal, or stated, interest rate* and the *effective annual rate (EAR)*.

nominal (stated) interest rate

The contracted, or stated, interest rate.

effective annual rate

The annual rate of interest actually being earned as opposed to the nominal or stated rate.

The **nominal, or stated, interest rate** is the quoted rate; thus, in this example, the nominal rate is 6 percent. The nominal interest rate is often called the *annual percentage rate (APR)* when it is reported by banks and other lending institutions.[1] The **effective annual rate** is the rate that would have produced the final compound value, $1,060.90, under annual rather than semiannual compounding. In this case, the effective annual rate is 6.09 percent, found by solving for k in the following equation:

$$\$1,000(1 + k) = \$1,060.90$$

$$k = \frac{\$1,060.90}{\$1,000} - 1 = 0.0609 = 6.09\%.$$

---

[1] In Chapter 4, we were comparing nominal interest rates to the real (inflation-adjusted) rates. In this appendix we are comparing nominal interest rates to effective annual rates.

Table 13A-1 **Future Value Calculations with Semiannual Compounding**

Period	Beginning Amount, PV	×	$(1 + k/2)$	=	Ending Amount, FV
1	$1,000.00		(1.03)		$1,030.00
2	1,030.00		(1.03)		1,060.90

Thus, if one bank offered 6 percent with semiannual compounding while another offered 6.09 percent with annual compounding, they would both be paying the same effective annual rate of interest.

In general, the effective annual rate can be determined, given the nominal rate, by solving Equation 13A-1:

$$\text{Effective annual rate} = \left(1 + \frac{k_{Nom}}{m}\right)^{m} - 1.0. \qquad (13A\text{-}1)$$

Here k_{Nom} is the nominal, or stated, interest rate, and m is the number of compounding periods per year. For example, to find the effective annual rate if the nominal rate is 6 percent, compounded semiannually, the following calculation is made:

$$\text{Effective annual rate} = \left(1 + \frac{0.06}{2}\right)^{2} - 1.0$$

$$= (1.03)^{2} - 1.0$$

$$= 1.0609 - 1.0$$

$$= 0.0609 = 6.09\%.$$

Semiannual compounding can be handled easily with a financial calculator. Simply set i = 3, n = 2, and PV = 1,000, and then press the FV button to get the solution, FV = $1,060.90.

The points made about semiannual compounding can be generalized as follows. When compounding periods are more frequent than once a year, we use a modified version of Equation 13A-2 to find the future value of a lump sum:

$$\text{Annual compounding: } FV_n = PV(1 + k)^n. \qquad (13A\text{-}2)$$

$$\text{More frequent compounding: } FV_n = PV\left(1 + \frac{k_{Nom}}{m}\right)^{mn}. \qquad (13A\text{-}2a)$$

Here m is the number of times per year compounding occurs, and n is the number of years. Therefore, if $1,000 is invested for 1 year at a nominal rate of 6 percent, compounded semiannually, the ending value can be computed using Equation 13A-2a:

$$FV_n = \$1,000[1 + (0.06/2)]^{2 \times 1}$$

$$= \$1,000(1.0609)$$

$$= \$1,060.90.$$

If the investment period is 3 years rather than 1 year, then:

$$FV_n = \$1,000[1 + (0.06/2)]^{2 \times 3}$$

$$= \$1,000(1.1941)$$

$$= \$1,194.10.$$

The interest tables often can be used when compounding occurs more than once a year. Simply divide the nominal, or stated, interest rate by the number of times compounding occurs during the year (m), then multiply the years (n) by the number of compounding periods per year (m). For example, to find the amount to which $1,000 will grow after 5 years if semiannual compounding is applied to a stated 8 percent interest rate, divide 8 percent by 2, the number of compounding periods in the year when semiannual compounding is used, and multiply the 5-year period by 2, also because of semiannual compounding. Then look in Table A-3 of Appendix A under the 4 percent column and the row for Period 10. You will find an interest factor of 1.4802. Multiplying this by the initial $1,000 gives a value of $1,480.20, the amount to which $1,000 will grow in 5 years at 8 percent, compounded semiannually. This compares to $1,469.30 for annual compounding.

The same procedure is applied in all the cases covered — compounding, discounting, single payments, and annuities. To illustrate semiannual discounting when finding the present value of an annuity, consider the case of an annuity of $1,000 a year for 3 years, discounted at 12 percent. With annual discounting, the present value interest factor is 2.4018 and the present value of the annual annuity is $2,401.80. For semiannual discounting, look under the 6 percent column and in the Period 6 row of Table A-2 in Appendix A to find the PVIFA of 4.9173. This present value interest factor for an annuity is now multiplied by half of the $1,000, or $500 received each six months, to get the present value of the annuity, PVA = $2,458.65. Because the payments come a little more rapidly (the first $500 is paid after only six months), the annuity is a little more valuable if payments are received semiannually rather than annually.

PROBLEMS

13A-1 **Future value for various compounding periods.** Find the amount to which $500 will grow under each of the following conditions:
   a. 12 percent compounded annually for 4 years.
   b. 12 percent compounded semiannually for 4 years.
   c. 12 percent compounded quarterly for 4 years.
   d. 12 percent compounded monthly for 1 year.

13A-2 **Present value for various compounding periods.** Find the present value of $500 due in the future under each of the following conditions:
   a. 12 percent nominal rate, semiannual compounding, discounted back 4 years.
   b. 12 percent nominal rate, quarterly compounding, discounted back 4 years.
   c. 12 percent nominal rate, monthly compounding, discounted back 1 year.

13A-3 **Annuity values for various compounding periods.** Find the indicated value of the following ordinary (deferred) annuities:
   a. FV of $200 each 6 months for 4 years at a nominal rate of 12 percent, compounded semiannually.
   b. PV of $200 each 3 months for 4 years at a nominal rate of 12 percent, compounded quarterly.

13A-4   **Effective versus nominal interest rates.** The First National Bank pays 11 percent interest, compounded annually, on time deposits. The Second National Bank pays 10 percent interest, compounded quarterly.

a. In which bank would you prefer to deposit your money?

b. Is your choice of banks influenced by the fact that you might want to withdraw your funds during the year rather than at the end of the year? In answering the question, assume that funds must be left on deposit during the entire compounding period for you to receive any interest.

Chapter 14

The Process of Capital Budgeting

 DECISION IN FINANCE

Learning from Past Errors

Imagine an American car dealership with Hondas, Toyotas, and Acuras displayed side by side in the showroom, along with a new domestic model designed expressly to compete with them. That's one of the marketing strategies under discussion at General Motors, where $3 billion have gone into the creation of a new compact car—the Saturn. After five years in planning, production began in the summer of 1990 on the Saturn, which comes as a two-door coupe or a four-door sedan. Originally scheduled at a 500,000-car-a-year rate, the first-year production goal was lowered to only 120,000 cars. One analyst says that number means "The car will be a marketing success but a financial flop." GM does plan to double production before the first year is over, but there are no immediate plans to do more than that. Saturn's vice president for finance admits that 500,000 cars are needed for the project to be viable, but he also says that expanding the plant is not an option at this time.

After being burned by a six-year, $40 billion capital spending spree in the early 1980s that

See end of chapter for resolution.

did not pay off, GM is trying to correct its errors, and it is using the Saturn project as a prototype. Under their previously faulty strategy, GM managers invested most of their funds in fancy technology, robots, and lasers. When the company subsequently lost rather than gained market share to Japanese automakers, Chief Financial Officer F. Alan Smith quipped ruefully that with the amount of money GM spent, it could have simply bought Nissan and Toyota instead. In their capital budgeting planning, Smith and his colleagues had failed to take into account the environment in which they operated. While they were improving their production capacity with all the new equipment, their foreign competitors were doing even more. As a result, between 1985 and 1990, U.S. companies' share of the passenger-car market shrank 11 percentage points, to 33 percent, while the Japanese companies' share climbed 7 points, to 26 percent.

Saturn is GM's hope for turning things around. The Saturn team has been set free to create a whole new company. A Ford executive observed, "They've had an opportunity to look at the entire manufacturing process with no holds barred. They may learn a lot about making cars that will have a profound effect on the way GM makes cars in the future."

The Saturn team has set a formidable goal—to sell 80 percent of its cars to drivers who otherwise would not have bought a GM product. According to one study, more than 40 percent of car shoppers won't even consider GM. In order to compete with Japanese companies, the team designed its new car to "feel" like a Honda. When the Saturn project first got under way, the company bought 70 imported cars of various makes and told the planners and engineers to drive them. They adopted the feel, as well as the look, of Japanese cars, especially in dashboard design. By enlarging the original subcompact car and by increasing its selling price from a planned $6,000 to between $10,000 and $12,000, Saturn also matched the increased size and higher costs of its chief rivals, the Honda Civic and the Toyota Corolla. Furthermore, the dealers who test-drove pre-production Saturns found them superior to Honda and Toyota in terms of handling and smoothness of ride.

Although the product itself is an imitation, the division that makes it is an original that the other GM divisions may eventually imitate. In December 1987, GM's directors approved a capital outlay of $1.9 billion for a new factory, for equipment, and for tooling. After its painful lessons of the past, however, the technology is not the expensive, superautomated, computerized, robot-in-the-dark equipment that was initially visualized. Instead, it is designed to make human workers more efficient.

Retiring GM Chairman Roger Smith created Saturn as an independent subsidiary after a team of GM managers and union laborers studied and formulated the project. Smith's goal, inspired by the earlier capital-spending debacle, was to stress good management more than expensive equipment. In keeping with that, it is the innovative relationships between people that make the Saturn team unique, particularly in the ponderous bureaucracy of GM.

As you read this chapter, consider the lesson GM learned from its mistakes in past capital budgeting projects. Decide how you might analyze plant and equipment expenditures, and how you might change the approach toward improving productivity, profits, and market share if your company faced a project similar to Saturn.

capital budgeting
The process of planning expenditures on assets whose returns extend beyond one year.

In Part III we analyzed decisions relating to the investment of funds in current assets. Now we consider investment decisions involving long-term assets, or the process of *capital budgeting*. The term *capital* refers to fixed assets used in production, and a *budget* is a plan detailing projected inflows and outflows during some future period. Thus, the *capital budget* sets forth planned expenditures on fixed assets, and **capital budgeting** is the entire process of analyzing projects, including both fixed assets and such current assets as inventory and accounts receivable which would be required to support fixed asset investment projects.

Each year businesses invest hundreds of billions of dollars in fixed assets. Capital budgeting decisions not only involve large sums of capital but also determine to a large extent the firm's future. Thus, by their very nature, such investments fundamentally affect the firm's future. A good decision can boost earnings sharply and increase the price of a firm's stock, but a bad decision can lead to bankruptcy. Capital budgeting is of fundamental importance, for a firm's long-term investment decisions chart its course for the future — indeed, these decisions *determine* the firm's future.

Our treatment of capital budgeting is divided into two parts. First, this chapter gives an overview of the process, and it explains the basic techniques used in capital budgeting analysis. Then, in Chapter 15, we go on to consider special capital budgeting situations, plus risk analysis in capital budgeting.

IMPORTANCE OF CAPITAL BUDGETING

Various factors combine to make capital budgeting decisions among the most important ones financial managers must make. Because the consequences of capital budgeting decisions continue over an extended period, after a decision the firm loses some of its flexibility. Further, the purchase of an asset with an economic life of 10 years involves an implicit 10-year sales forecast, and if the sales forecast is incorrect, the capital budgeting decision may prove to have been a mistake.

An erroneous forecast of asset requirements can have serious consequences. If the firm has invested too much in assets, it will incur unnecessarily heavy expenses, and its total assets turnover will be too low. If it has not spent enough on fixed assets, however, two problems may arise. First, the firm's equipment may not be sufficiently modern to enable it to produce competitively. Second, if it has inadequate capacity, it may lose a portion of its share of the market to rival firms, and regaining lost customers typically requires heavy selling expenses, price reductions, and product improvements, all of which are costly.

Effective capital budgeting will improve both the timing of asset acquisitions and the quality of assets purchased. A firm that forecasts its needs for capital assets in advance will have the opportunity to purchase and install the assets before its sales are at capacity. In practice, most firms do not order capital goods until their sales approach full capacity. If sales increase because of an increase in general market demand, all firms in the industry will tend to order capital goods at about the same time. This often results in backlogs, long waiting times for machinery, a deterioration in the quality of the capital goods, and an increase in their prices. The firm that foresees its needs and purchases capital assets early can avoid these problems.

Finally, capital budgeting is important because asset expansion typically involves substantial expenditures, and before a firm spends a large amount of money, it must make the proper plans — large amounts of funds are not available automatically. A firm contemplating a major capital expenditure program may need to arrange its financing several years in advance to be sure of having the funds required for the expansion.

Self-Test

Give some reasons why capital budgeting is so important.

PROJECT PROPOSALS AND CLASSIFICATION

Capital budgeting projects are created by the firm. For example, a sales representative may report that customers are asking for a particular product that the company does not now produce. The sales manager then discusses the idea with the marketing research group to determine the size of the market for the proposed product. If it appears likely that a significant market does exist, cost accountants and engineers will be asked to estimate production costs. If it appears that the product can be produced and sold to yield a sufficient profit, the project will be undertaken.

A firm's growth, development, and even its ability to remain competitive and to survive, depend on a constant flow of ideas for new products and for ways to make existing products better, or to produce them at a lower cost. Accordingly, a well-managed firm will go to great lengths to develop good capital budgeting proposals. For example, a senior executive of a major corporation recently indicated that his company takes the following steps to generate projects:

> Our R & D department is constantly searching for new products, or for ways to improve existing products. In addition, our Executive Committee, which consists of the president plus senior executives in marketing, production, and finance, identifies the products and markets in which our company will compete, and the Committee sets long-run targets for each division. These targets, which are formalized in the Corporation's strategic plan, provide a general guide to the operating executives who must meet them. The operating executives then seek new products, set expansion plans for existing products, and look for ways to reduce production and distribution costs. Since bonuses and promotions are based in large part on each unit's ability to meet or exceed its targets, these economic incentives encourage our operating executives to seek out profitable investment opportunities.
>
> While senior executives are judged and rewarded on the basis of how well their units perform, people further down the line are given bonuses for specific suggestions, including ideas that lead to profitable investments. Additionally, a percentage of our corporate profit is set aside for distribution to non-executive employees. Our objective is to encourage lower-level workers to keep on the lookout for good ideas, including those that lead to capital investments.

Not all capital project ideas come from the research and development department however. If the firm has capable and imaginative executives and employees, and if its incentive system is working properly, many ideas for capital investment will be advanced. Because some ideas will be good ones while others will not, procedures must be established for screening projects.

Although benefits may be gained from carefully screening and analyzing capital expenditure proposals, such an investigation does have a cost. For certain types of projects, a relatively refined analysis may be warranted; for others, cost/benefit studies may suggest that simpler procedures should be used.

For screening purposes, firms generally classify projects into the following categories:

1. Replacement: maintenance of business. This category includes those expenditures that are necessary to replace worn-out or damaged equipment used to produce profitable products.

2. Replacement: cost reduction. Expenditures to replace serviceable but obsolete equipment fall into this category. The purpose of these expenditures is to lower the costs of labor, materials, or other items such as electricity.

3. Expansion of existing products or markets. Included here are expenditures to increase output of existing products, or to expand outlets or distribution facilities in markets now being served.

4. Expansion into new products or markets. These are expenditures necessary to produce a new product or to expand into a geographic area not currently being served. These projects involve strategic decisions that could change the fundamental nature of the business, and they normally require the expenditure of large sums of money over long periods.

5. Safety or environmental projects. Expenditures necessary to comply with government orders, labor agreements, or insurance policy terms are listed here. These expenditures are often called *mandatory investments,* or *non-revenue-producing projects.*

6. Other. This catch-all includes home office buildings, parking lots, executive aircraft, and so on.

In general, relatively simple calculations, and only a few supporting documents, are required to support replacement decisions, especially maintenance-type investments in profitable plants. More detailed analysis is required for cost reduction replacements, for expansion of existing product lines, and especially for expansion into new products or areas. Also, within each category, projects are broken down by their dollar costs: the larger the required investment, the more detailed the analysis, and the higher the level of the officer who must authorize the expenditure. A plant manager may be authorized to approve maintenance expenditures up to $25,000 on the basis of a relatively unsophisticated analysis, but the full board of directors may have to approve decisions that involve either amounts over $1 million or expansions into new products or markets. Statistical data are generally lacking for new product decisions, so here judgments, as opposed to detailed cost data, are a key element in the decision process.

Self-Test

How does a firm get ideas for capital projects?

Identify and briefly explain how project classifications are used.

An example of a capital project in which equipment replaces human labor is robot painting in the automobile industry. This photo from Chrysler shows robots painting car interiors. The enormous capital investment in this equipment was offset by savings incurred because of the decreased cost of using equipment instead of labor.

Source: Courtesy of Chrysler Corporation.

ESTIMATING THE CASH FLOWS

cash flow

The actual net cash, as opposed to accounting net income, that flows into (or out of) a firm during some specified period.

The most important, but also the most difficult, step in the analysis of a capital expenditure proposal is estimating the **cash flows** associated with the project — the initial investment outlays that are required, and the annual net cash inflows that the project will produce after it goes into operation. Many variables are involved in the cash flow forecast, and many individuals and departments participate in developing them. For example, the market research group projects sales by means of industry analysis and test marketing of proposed products; the marketing department determines pricing policy and anticipates competitors' actions; the production and engineering departments combine to determine the necessary capital outlays and to establish production and labor requirements; and the industrial relations department determines appropriate wage and benefit packages. In addition, the accounting department estimates overhead costs for the new project. The better the forecast, the more likely it is that poor projects will be rejected and good ones accepted.

Obtaining accurate estimates of the costs and revenues associated with a large, complex project can be exceedingly difficult, and forecast errors can be quite large. For example, when several oil companies decided to build the Alaskan Pipeline, the original cost estimates were in the neighborhood of $700 million, but the final cost was closer to $7 billion. Similar (or even worse) miscalculations are common in product design cost estimates for items like new personal computers. Furthermore, as difficult as plant and equipment costs are to estimate, sales revenues and operating costs over the life of a project are even more uncertain. For example, several years ago Federal Express developed an electronic delivery system (ZapMail). It used the correct capital budgeting technique, but it incorrectly estimated the project's cash flows: Projected revenues were too high and projected costs were too low, and virtually no one was willing to pay the price required to cover the project's costs. As a result, cash flows failed to meet the forecasted levels, and Federal Express ended up losing about $200 million on the venture. This example demonstrates a basic truth — if cash flow estimates are not reasonably accurate, any analytical technique, no matter how sophisticated, can lead to poor decisions and hence to operating losses and lower stock prices. Because of its financial strength, Federal Express was able to absorb losses on the project with no problem, but the ZapMail venture could have forced a weaker firm into bankruptcy.

The major duties of the financial staff in the forecasting process are (1) coordinating the efforts of the other departments, such as engineering and marketing, (2) ensuring that everyone involved with the forecast uses a consistent set of economic assumptions, and (3) making sure that no biases are inherent in the forecasts. This last point is extremely important, because division managers often become emotionally involved with pet projects or develop empire-building complexes, which leads to cash flow forecasting biases that make bad projects look good — on paper. The ZapMail project is a good example of this problem.

It is not sufficient that the financial staff has unbiased point estimates of the key variables; data on probability distributions or other indications of the probable ranges of error are also essential. It is useful to know the relationship between each input variable and some basic economic variable, such as gross national product. If all production and sales variables can be related to such a basic variable, the financial manager can forecast how the project will do under different economic conditions.

One cannot overstate the importance of cash flow estimates — or the difficulties that are encountered in making these forecasts. However, there are certain principles that, if observed, will help to minimize forecasting errors.

Identifying the Relevant Cash Flows

An important element in cash flow estimation is the identification of **relevant cash flows,** defined as that set of cash flows which should be considered for the decision at hand. Errors are often made in specifying the relevant cash flows, but there are two cardinal rules that can help financial analysts avoid mistakes: (1) Capital budgeting decisions must be based on *cash flows,* not on accounting income; and (2) only *incremental cash flows* are relevant to the accept/reject decision. These two rules are discussed in detail in the following sections.

relevant cash flows
The specific set of cash flows that should be considered in a capital budgeting decision.

Table 14-1 **Spartan Manufacturing Company: Project X**

	Effect of Project X on	
	Reported Earnings (1)	Cash Transactions (2)
Sales	$90,000	$90,000
Less: COGS (except depreciation)	40,000	40,000
Less: Depreciation	20,000	
Gross margin	30,000	
Less: Selling and administrative expenses	15,000	15,000
Earnings before taxes	15,000	
Less: Taxes (40%)	6,000	6,000
Net income	9,000	
Net cash flow (= Net income + Depreciation)	$29,000	$29,000

Cash Flow versus Accounting Income

In capital budgeting analysis, *annual cash flows, not accounting profits,* are used. Cash flows and accounting profits can be very different. To illustrate, consider Table 14-1, which shows how accounting profits and cash flows are related to one another. To better understand the importance of cash flow in the firm's capital investment decision, let's assume that Spartan Manufacturing Company has a new project, known around the firm as "Project X," which will require $100,000 of new equipment. This equipment will be depreciated on a straight line basis for the 5-year life of the project. The effect of the project on Spartan's *reported earnings* is seen in the first column of numbers in Table 14-1.

In the second column of numbers, we show the *cash transactions* associated with the project. Costs of goods sold (COGS) is the total of all of the expenditures on the production, labor, and materials for Project X. The selling and administrative expenses are those allocated or directly attributable to the project. The taxes are those paid as a direct result of the revenues generated by the new project.

Note that each of the entries in the second column of Table 14-1 represents actual *cash* receipts or payments. In the first column, however, one expense is only a bookkeeping entry—depreciation. As discussed in Chaper 2, depreciation is a noncash allocation of the cost of a fixed asset over its useful (or IRS-determined) life. This allocation permits the company to reduce its tax burden each period, but *it involves no actual payment of cash.* Therefore, we can add the *depreciation* back to the accounting-determined *net income* attributable to the project as shown in Column 1, which in Table 14-1 equals the project's *cash flow* of $29,000.

Accounting profits are important for some purposes, but in capital budgeting, we are interested only in cash flows. Therefore, in capital budgeting, the focus must be on *net cash flow,* defined as follows:

$$\text{Net cash flow} = \text{Net income} + \text{Depreciation}, \qquad (14\text{-}1)$$

not on accounting profits per se.

An equivalent method of determining the cash flow is presented in Equation 14-1a:

$$\text{Net cash flow} = (\$REV - \$EXP)(1 - t) + (DEP)(t), \qquad (14\text{-}1a)$$

where

$REV =$ cash revenues generated by the project.

$EXP =$ cash expenses associated with the project.

$t =$ marginal tax rate.

$DEP =$ depreciation for the year on the project's fixed assets.

Using this formula and the data for Project X in Table 14-1, we obtain

$$\begin{aligned}
\text{Net cash flow} &= (\$REV - \$EXP)(1 - t) + (DEP)(t) \\
&= (\$90{,}000 - \$55{,}000)(1 - 0.4) + (\$20{,}000)(0.4) \\
&= (\$35{,}000)(0.6) + (\$20{,}000)(0.4) \\
&= \$21{,}000 + \$8{,}000 \\
&= \$29{,}000.
\end{aligned}$$

We see that Equations 14-1 and 14-1a produce exactly the same result, namely, that the cash flow is $29,000.

Note that financing expenses, such as interest and dividends, are *not deducted* in calculating cash flow. As you will learn in a subsequent chapter, the minimum acceptable rate of return for any project is the **cost of capital**, which is the weighted average of the required returns, or cost, of all sources of financing. The net cash flow for each year is *discounted,* or converted to a present value, which of course reduces it, to account for financing costs. If financing charges were *deducted* when determining the project's cash flow, and the net cash flows later were discounted by the cost of capital, then double counting of the financing costs would occur. Therefore, interest charges should *not* be dealt with explicitly in capital budgeting. In effect, we compute the project's cash flow *as if* it were financed entirely with common stock equity funding, but then we discount by the cost of capital. In essence, this approach allows the analyst to concentrate on selecting the best project available, and then, once the best project has been identified, the optimal means of financing it can be determined.

cost of capital
The discount rate that should be used in the capital budgeting process.

Incremental Cash Flows

In evaluating a capital project, we are concerned only with those cash flows that result directly from the project. These cash flows, called **incremental cash flows,** represent the changes in the firm's total cash flows that occur as

incremental cash flow
The net cash flow attributable to an investment project.

a direct result of accepting or rejecting the project. Four special problems in determining incremental cash flows are discussed below:

Sunk Costs. Sunk costs are not incremental costs, and they should not be included in the analysis. A **sunk cost** is an outlay that has already been committed or that has already occurred and hence is not affected by the accept/reject decision under consideration. To illustrate, in 1990 Northeast BankCorp was considering the establishment of a branch office in a newly developed section of Boston. To help with its evaluation, Northeast had, back in 1989, hired a consulting firm to perform a site analysis; the cost was $100,000, and this amount was paid and then expensed for tax purposes in 1989. Is this 1989 expenditure a relevant cost with respect to the 1990 capital budgeting decision? The answer is no — the $100,000 is a sunk cost, and Northeast cannot recover it regardless of whether or not the new branch is built.

Opportunity Costs. The second potential problem relates to **opportunity costs,** defined here as the cash flows that can be generated from assets the firm already owns provided they are not used for the project in question. To illustrate, Northeast BankCorp already owns a piece of land that is suitable for the branch location. When evaluating the prospective branch, should the cost of the land be disregarded because no additional cash outlay would be required? The answer is no, because there is an opportunity cost inherent in the use of the property. In this case, the land could be sold to yield $150,000 after taxes. Use of the site for the branch would require forgoing this inflow, so the $150,000 must be charged as an opportunity cost against the project. Note that the proper land cost in this example is the $150,000 market-determined value, irrespective of whether Northeast originally paid $50,000 or $500,000 for the property. (What Northeast paid would, of course, have an effect on taxes and hence on the after-tax opportunity cost.)

Effects on Other Parts of the Firm: Externalities. The third potential problem involves the effects of a project on other parts of the firm, which economists call **externalities.** For example, some of Northeast's customers who would use the new branch are already banking with Northeast's downtown office. The loans and deposits, and hence profits, attributable to these customers would not be new to the bank; rather, they would represent a transfer from the main office to the branch. Thus, the net revenues produced by these customers should not be treated as incremental income in the capital budgeting decision. On the other hand, having a suburban branch would help the bank attract new business to its downtown office, because some people like to be able to bank both close to home and close to work. In this case, the additional revenues that would actually flow to the downtown office should be attributed to the branch. Although often difficult to quantify, externalities such as these should be considered.

sunk cost
A cash outlay that has already been incurred and which cannot be recovered regardless of whether the project is accepted or rejected.

opportunity cost
The return on the best *alternative* use of an asset; the highest return that will *not* be earned if funds are invested in a particular project.

externalities
Effects of a project on cash flows in other parts of the firm.

Shipping and Installation Costs. When a firm acquires fixed assets, it often must incur substantial costs for shipping and installing the equipment. These charges are added to the invoice price of the equipment when the cost of the project is being determined. Also, the full cost of the equipment, including shipping and installation costs, is used as the depreciable basis when depreciation charges are being calculated. Thus, if Northeast BankCorp bought a computer with an invoice price of $100,000 and paid another $10,000 for shipping and installation, then the full cost of the computer, and its depreciable basis, would be $110,000.

Changes in Net Working Capital

Normally, additional inventories are required to support a new operation, and expanded sales also produce additional accounts receivable; both of these increases in assets must be financed. At the same time, however, accounts payable and accruals will increase spontaneously as a result of the expansion, and this will reduce the net cash needed to finance inventories and receivables. The difference between the required increase in current assets and the spontaneous increase in current liabilities is a required **change in net working capital.** If this change is positive, as it generally is for expansion projects, then the firm must raise this much additional capital, over and above the cost of the fixed assets, to undertake the project. This additional financing is part of the required initial cost of the project, and it is just as necessary as the investment in the project's fixed assets.

change in net working capital
The increased current assets required for a new project, minus the simultaneous increase in current liabilities.

As the end of the project's life approaches, inventories will be sold off and not replaced, and receivables will be collected and thus converted to cash. As these changes occur, the firm receives a positive end-of-project cash inflow equal to the net working capital requirement that occurred when the project began. Thus, net working capital is added when the project is begun, but those dollars are recovered at the end of the project's life.

Self-Test

What is the most important step in the analysis of a capital project?

What is the financial staff's role in the capital budgeting forecasting process?

Briefly explain the difference between accounting income and net cash flow. Which should be used in capital budgeting? Why?

Explain what these terms mean, and assess their relevance in capital budgeting: incremental cash flow, sunk cost, opportunity cost, externality, and shipping plus installation costs.

How is an increase in net working capital dealt with in the capital budgeting analysis?

Does the company get back the dollars it invests in working capital? Explain.

METHODS USED TO EVALUATE PROPOSED PROJECTS

A number of different methods are used to rank projects and to decide whether or not they should be accepted for inclusion in the capital budget. The three most commonly used **ranking methods** are payback, net present value (NPV), and internal rate of return (IRR).[1]

ranking methods

Methods used to evaluate capital expenditure proposals.

1. Payback period. This is the expected number of years required to recover the original investment.

2. Net present value (NPV). This is the present value of future cash inflows, discounted at the appropriate cost of capital, minus the cost of the investment. The NPV method is called a *discounted cash flow (DCF)* method.

3. Internal rate of return (IRR). This is the discount rate that equates the present value of future cash inflows to the initial cost of the project. The IRR is also a discounted cash flow (DCF) method.

Future cash inflows are, in all cases, defined as the incremental net cash inflows from the investments. The nature and characteristics of the three methods are illustrated and explained in the following sections, using the cash flow data shown in Table 14-2 for two projects that we call Project E and Project L. Note that the returns from Project E are much greater early in its life when compared to those of Project L, whose returns are larger late in its life. As we have discussed, these cash inflows consist of both after-tax profits and depreciation, not just profits alone. Furthermore, the **investment outlay** includes not only the cost of the fixed assets required for the project, but also any net working capital outlays caused by the project.[2]

investment outlay

Funds expended for fixed assets of a specified project (including delivery and installation) plus working capital funds expended as a result of the project's adoption.

payback period

The length of time required for the net revenues of an investment to recover the cost of the investment.

Payback Period

The **payback period** is defined as the number of years it takes a firm to recover its original investment from a project's net cash inflows. The payback method provides a measure of project *liquidity*, or the speed with which cash invested in the project will be returned. In Table 14-2 each project costs $25,000. Assuming that the cash flows come in evenly during the year, it will take 2.375 years for cash flows from Project E to equal the $25,000 cost. Therefore, the payback period for Project E is 2.375 years: $12,000 + $10,000 +

---

[1]You should be aware that there are three other ranking methods that are sometimes used: (1) the accounting rate of return, (2) the profitability index, and (3) the discounted payback period. Each of these methods can lead to incorrect rankings for projects and are thus potentially misleading. Also, a modified version of the IRR is seeing increased usage today. For a discussion of these methods, see Brigham and Gapenski, *Intermediate Financial Management,* 3rd ed., Chapter 7.

[2]Of course, only the investment in fixed assets is depreciable. When the project ends, the investment in working capital is recovered through reductions in inventory and collection of accounts receivable outstanding. This recovery is not taxable since it represents a conversion of assets without economic gain.

Table 14-2 **Cash Flows for Projects E and L**
(Investment Outlay for Each Project Is $25,000)

Year	Net Cash Flow (After-Tax Profits Plus Depreciation) Project E	Project L
1	$12,000	$ 5,400
2	10,000	8,000
3	8,000	10,000
4	5,400	12,000
Total inflows	$35,400	$35,400

($3,000/$8,000) = returns for 2 years plus 0.375 of the third year, and the payback period for Project L is 3.133 years [$5,400 + $8,000 + $10,000 + ($1,600/$12,000)]. Because Project E's largest cash flows occur early in its life, it is not surprising that it has the faster recovery of the initial investment. On the basis of payback, Project E is superior to Project L.

The payback method's principal strength is that it is easy and inexpensive to calculate and apply. This was an important consideration in the precomputer days, and prior to the 1960s, payback was the most commonly used method for screening capital expenditure proposals. However, the payback method has conceptual problems that make total reliance on this technique undesirable. Two of the major conceptual weaknesses of payback are the following:

1. It ignores returns beyond the payback period. One glaring weakness of the payback method is that it ignores any cash flow that occurs beyond the payback period. For example, if Project L had an additional return of $20,000 in Year 5, this fact would not influence the payback ranking of Projects E and L. Ignoring returns in the distant future means that the payback period is biased against long-term projects.

2. It ignores the time value of money. The timing of cash flows is obviously important (as the last chapter emphasized), yet the payback method ignores the time value of money. By this method, a dollar in Year 3 is given the same weight as a dollar in Year 1.

In spite of the conceptual drawbacks to the payback technique, this project-screening device has shown remarkable vitality over the years. Managers still use payback because it tells them something they want to know. Firms that are short of cash necessarily place a higher value on projects with a higher degree of liquidity, and a project that returns its investment quickly will allow these funds to be reinvested quickly in other projects. Such a project would be especially valuable to a small or growing firm that is unable to raise capital quickly or in large amounts. Also, the payback period is often used as an indicator of projects' relative risk. Because firms can usually forecast near-term events better than more distant ones, projects whose returns come in relatively rapidly are, other things held constant, generally less risky than longer-term projects. We see, then, that by focusing on the speed of cash inflows, the payback period provides important information to the financial manager. However, in light of payback's weaknesses, the technique should be used in conjunction with other, more technically correct project-screening methods such as net present value (NPV) and internal rate of return (IRR), which are discussed next.

Net Present Value (NPV) Method

discounted cash flow (DCF) techniques
Methods of ranking investment proposals that employ time value of money concepts; two of these are the *net present value* and *internal rate of return* methods.

net present value (NPV) method
A method of ranking investment proposals using the NPV, which is equal to the present value of future net cash flows, discounted at the cost of capital.

As the flaws in the payback method were recognized, people began to search for methods of evaluating projects which would recognize that a dollar received immediately is preferable to a dollar received at some future date. This led to the development of **discounted cash flow (DCF) techniques** to take account of the time value of money. One such DCF technique is called the *net present value (NPV) method*. To implement this approach, find the present value of the expected net cash inflows of an investment, discounted at an appropriate percentage rate, and subtract from it the initial cost outlay of the project. If its net present value is positive, the project should be accepted; if negative, it should be rejected.

The equation for the **net present value (NPV) method** is as follows:

$$NPV = \sum_{t=1}^{n} \frac{CF_t}{(1 + k)^t} - C \qquad\qquad (14\text{-}2)$$

$$= \left[\frac{CF_1}{(1 + k)^1} + \frac{CF_2}{(1 + k)^2} + \cdots + \frac{CF_n}{(1 + k)^n} \right] - C$$

$$= CF_1(PVIF_{k,1}) + CF_2(PVIF_{k,2}) + \cdots + CF_n(PVIF_{k,n}) - C.$$

Here CF_t is the expected net cash flow from the project at Period t, n is the project's expected life, and k, represented by the present value interest factor, PVIF, is the appropriate discount rate, or the cost of capital. The cost of capital, k, depends on the riskiness of the project, on the level of interest rates in the economy, and on several other factors. In this chapter we take k as a given, but it is discussed in detail in Chapter 19.

The capital outlays, C, such as the cost of buying equipment or building factories, are *negative* cash outflows and are given a minus sign. In evaluating Projects E and L, only the initial outlay (sometimes given the symbol CF_0) is negative, but for many large projects, such as General Motors' Saturn project, an electric power plant, or IBM's lap-top computer, outflows occur for several years before operations begin and positive cash inflows are generated.

Under the assumption that the two projects are equally risky, the net present values of Projects E and L are calculated in Table 14-3, based on the discounting procedures developed in Chapter 13 and used in Equation 14-2. Assuming a required rate of return of 12 percent for both projects, Project E has an NPV of $2,813 and Project L has an NPV of $944. On this basis, both projects

Table 14–3 **Calculating the Net Present Values (NPVs) of Projects E and L**

Year	Project E			Project L		
	Cash Flow	PVIF (12%)	PV of Cash Flow	Cash Flow	PVIF (12%)	PV of Cash Flow
1	$12,000	0.8929	$ 10,715	$ 5,400	0.8929	$ 4,822
2	10,000	0.7972	7,972	8,000	0.7972	6,378
3	8,000	0.7118	5,694	10,000	0.7118	7,118
4	5,400	0.6355	3,432	12,000	0.6355	7,626
		PV of inflows	$ 27,813		PV of inflows	$ 25,944
		Less: Cost	−25,000		Less: Cost	−25,000
		NPV	$ 2,813		NPV	$ 944

should be accepted if possible; however, if only one can be chosen, Project E is the better choice because it has the higher NPV.

The rationale for the NPV method is straightforward. The value of a firm is the sum of the value of its parts; that is, the value of its various projects and investments. If the firm takes on a zero-NPV project, the position of the original investors is unchanged—the firm becomes larger but its value does not change. Thus, when the NPV is zero, the project has covered all required operating and financial costs, but it has no excess returns. However, when a firm adopts a project with a positive NPV, the project's returns exceed required financial and operating costs. Therefore, the value of the firm increases by the amount of the NPV, thereby improving the position of the original investors. In this example, the value of the firm, and hence the original shareholders' wealth, increases by $2,813 if the firm chooses Project E, but by only $944 if it chooses Project L. Of course, the firm's value will increase by $3,757 if it is possible to accept both projects. *The increase in the value of the firm from its capital budget for the year is the sum of the NPVs of all accepted projects.* Thus, if Projects E and L are mutually exclusive, it is easy to see why Project E is preferable to Project L, but if they are independent, both are acceptable since each has a positive NPV. **Mutually exclusive** projects are alternative investments that serve the same purpose; if one project is taken on, the other must be rejected. The installation of a conveyor belt system in a warehouse and the purchase of a fleet of forklift trucks to do the same job for the same warehouse would be an example of mutually exclusive projects—accepting one implies rejection of the other. **Independent** projects are those whose costs and revenues are independent of one another. For example, the purchase of the company president's automobile and the purchase of a corporate jet would represent independent projects.

The Internal Rate of Return (IRR) Method

In the previous section on NPV we said that if a project's NPV is positive, the project is acceptable, and if the NPV is negative, the project is unacceptable. The **internal rate of return (IRR) method** finds the specific discount rate

mutually exclusive
If one project is accepted, the other must be rejected.

independent
Both projects can be accepted. The opposite of mutually exclusive.

internal rate of return (IRR) method
A method of ranking investment proposals using the rate of return on an asset investment, calculated by finding the discount rate that equates the present value of future cash inflows to the investment's cost.

that equates the present value of the expected future cash inflows, or receipts, to the initial cost of the project. The equation for calculating this rate is as follows:

$$\sum_{t=1}^{n} \frac{CF_t}{(1 + IRR)^t} - C = 0 \qquad \textbf{(14-3)}$$

$$\frac{CF_1}{(1 + IRR)^1} + \frac{CF_2}{(1 + IRR)^2} + \cdots \frac{CF_n}{(1 + IRR)^n} - C = 0$$

$$CF_1(PVIF_{IRR,1}) + CF_2(PVIF_{IRR,2}) + \cdots + CF_n(PVIF_{IRR,n}) - C = 0.$$

IRR

The discount rate which forces the PV of a project's cash inflows to equal the PV of its costs.

Here we know the value of the investment outlay, C, and the cash flows, CF_1, $CF_2, \cdots, CF_n$ as well, but we do not know the value of the discount rate, **IRR,** that equates the future cash flows and the present value of the investment outlays. *There is a value of IRR which will cause the sum of the discounted cash receipts to equal the initial cost of the project, making the equation equal to zero: this value is defined as the internal rate of return.*

A simple example may make this concept easier to understand. If we invest $10,000 for 6 years at 14 percent, then, by using Equation 13-2 from Chapter 13, we can determine the future (terminal) value of the investment:

$$FV_6 = PV(FVIF_{14\%,6}) \qquad \textbf{(13-2)}$$

$$= \$10,000(2.1950)$$

$$= \$21,950.$$

Now assume that we know that if we invest $10,000 today, the investment will return $21,950 in 6 years. What is the rate of return on this investment? We need to find the discount rate, or IRR, that equates the value of the investment today, $10,000, with the future value of $21,950 to be received 6 years hence. This is the same as finding the discount rate that causes the NPV of the investment to equal zero. Therefore, we solve for the present value interest factor as a step in determining the IRR:

$$PV = FV_6(PVIF_{k,6})$$

$$PVIF_{k,6} = \frac{PV}{FV_6}$$

$$= \frac{\$10,000}{\$21,950}$$

$$= 0.455581 = 0.4556.$$

Now we can find the present value interest factor of 0.4556 in Table A-1 of Appendix A by looking across the sixth-year row to the 14 percent column. A 14 percent rate equates the present cost and the PV of the future returns, so 14 percent is the internal rate of return.

Notice that the internal rate of return formula, Equation 14-3, is simply the NPV formula, Equation 14-2, solved for the particular discount rate that forces the NPV to equal zero. Thus, the same basic equation is used for both methods; in the NPV method the discount rate, k, is specified and the NPV is found, whereas in the IRR method the NPV is specified to equal zero and the discount rate that forces the NPV to equal zero is found.

The internal rate of return may be found in a number of ways. Several methods are discussed in the following sections.

Procedure 1: IRR with Constant Cash Inflows. If the cash flows from a project are constant, or equal in each year, the project's internal rate of return can be found by a relatively simple process. In essence, such a project is an annuity: the firm makes an outlay, C, and receives a stream of cash flow benefits, PMT, for a given number of years. The IRR for the project is found by applying Equation 13-5, discussed in Chapter 13.

To illustrate, suppose a project has a cost of $10,000 and is expected to produce cash flows of $1,627.45 each year for 10 years. The cost of the project, $10,000, is the present value of an annuity of $1,627.45 a year for 10 years. Applying Equation 13-5, we obtain

$$PVA_n = PMT(PVIFA_{k,10}) \qquad\qquad (13\text{-}5)$$

$$Cost = PMT(PVIFA_{k,10})$$

$$\frac{Cost}{PMT} = \frac{\$10,000}{\$1,627.45} = 6.1446 = (PVIFA_{k,10}).$$

Looking up PVIFA in Table A-2 of Appendix A (at the end of the text), across the row for Year 10, we find it located under the 10 percent column. Accordingly, 10 percent is the project's IRR. In other words, 10 percent is the discount rate that would force Equation 14-3 to be zero when PMT is constant at $1,627.45 for 10 years and C is $10,000. This procedure works only if the project has constant annual cash flows; if it does not, the IRR must be found by one of the other methods discussed below.

Procedure 2: Trial and Error. In the trial-and-error method, the present value of cash flows from an investment is first computed using a somewhat arbitrarily selected discount rate. Generally, the firm's cost of capital, in this case 12 percent, is a good starting point for most problems. Then the present value based on a 12 percent discount rate is compared with the investment's cost. Suppose the present value of the inflows is larger than the project's cost. What do we do now? We must *lower* the present value, and to do this we must *raise* the discount rate and go through the process again. Conversely, if the present value is lower than the cost, we lower the discount rate and repeat the process. This process is continued until the present value of the inflows from the investment is approximately equal to the project's cost. The discount rate that brings about this equality is the internal rate of return.

Table 14-4 **Finding the Internal Rate of Return of Project L**

Year	Cash Flows for L	12% PVIF	12% PV	14% PVIF	14% PV
1	$ 5,400	0.8929	$ 4,822	0.8772	$ 4,737
2	8,000	0.7972	6,378	0.7695	6,156
3	10,000	0.7118	7,118	0.6750	6,750
4	12,000	0.6355	7,626	0.5921	7,105
		PV of inflows $	25,944		$ 24,748
		Less: Cost	− 25,000		− 25,000
		NPV$_L$ $	944		$ (252)

Thus, *the discount rate that forces a project's NPV to equal zero is defined as the project's internal rate of return.*

This calculation process is illustrated next for the same Projects E and L that were analyzed earlier. In Table 14-4 the steps required to find the IRR for Project L are reviewed. First, the 12 percent PVIFs are obtained from Table A-1 in Appendix A at the end of the text. These factors are then multiplied by the cash flows for the corresponding years, and the present values of the cash flows are placed in the appropriate column. Next, the present values of the yearly cash flows are summed to obtain the investment's total present value. Subtracting the cost of the project from this figure gives the net present value of the project's cash flow. Because the NPV of Project L is positive at a discount rate of 12 percent, we know that the internal rate of return of this investment opportunity is *greater* than 12 percent. However, the NPV is rather small, indicating that the IRR is close to 12 percent. Thus we increase the discount rate slightly, to 14 percent. At 14 percent the NPV of Project L is a negative $252. Because the internal rate of return (IRR) causes the NPV to equal zero, we know that the internal rate of return for Project L is between 12 and 14 percent.

If we wish the IRR to be more accurate, we can interpolate between these results. To do so, we bracket the discount rate that causes the project's NPV to equal zero:

$$NPV = \$944 \text{ at } 12.0\%$$
$$NPV = \$0 \text{ at } 12.0\%$$
$$NPV = (\$252) \text{ at } \underline{14.0\%}$$
$$2.0\%$$

$$\left.\begin{array}{c} \$944 \\ (\$252) \end{array}\right\} \$1,196$$

Thus

$$IRR = 12.00\% + (\$944/\$1,196)(2.0\%)$$

$$= 12.00\% + 0.789(2.0\%)$$

$$= 13.58\%.$$

Table 14-5 **Finding the Internal Rate of Return of Project E**

Year	Cash Flow	12% PVIF	12% PV	16% PVIF	16% PV	18% PVIF	18% PV
1	$12,000	0.8929	$ 10,715	0.8621	$ 10,345	0.8475	$ 10,170
2	10,000	0.7972	7,972	0.7432	7,432	0.7182	7,182
3	8,000	0.7118	5,694	0.6407	5,126	0.6086	4,869
4	5,400	0.6355	3,432	0.5523	2,982	0.5158	2,785
		PV of inflows	$ 27,813		$ 25,885		$ 25,006
		Less: Cost	− 25,000		− 25,000		− 25,000
		NPV$_E$	$ 2,813		$ 885		$ 6

The IRR lies 944/1,196 of the way between 12 and 14 percent. Since there is a 2-percentage-point difference between 12 and 14 percent, we multiply the fraction by 2 percent before adding the quantity to 12 percent to obtain the IRR of 13.58 percent. For all practical purposes, an IRR that is accurate to within one-half of a percentage point is usually sufficient. The calculations may be carried out to several decimal places, but for most projects, when the assumptions associated with forecasting cash flows several years into the future are considered, this is spurious accuracy.

Just as we found the IRR of Project L, we now trace the steps in determining the IRR for Project E (see Table 14-5). Again, the 12 percent discount rate is employed as a starting point in the search for the project's internal rate of return. The firm's cost of capital, or the return on the best alternative investment opportunity, is usually the first discount rate used in the trial-and-error process. The NPV at 12 percent is positive, so we know the project's IRR is greater than 12 percent. Because the NPV is significantly greater than zero at 12 percent, we know the IRR is much greater than that rate. Multiplying the project's cash flows by a greater discount rate (the rate of 16 percent is chosen arbitrarily), we find that the NPV is still positive, though less than before. At 18 percent the NPV is barely larger than zero; thus, for all practical purposes the IRR of Project E is 18 percent, because at that rate the project's NPV is essentially zero.

Procedure 3: Graphic Solution. The graphic method for finding IRRs involves plotting a curve that shows the relationship between a project's NPV and the discount rate used to calculate the NPV. Such a curve is defined as the project's **net present value profile.** NPV profiles for Projects E and L are shown in Figure 14-1. To construct them, we first note that at a zero discount rate, the NPV is simply the total of the undiscounted cash flows of the project less the project's cost; thus, at a zero discount rate, the NPV of both projects is $10,400. This value is plotted as the vertical axis intercept in Figure 14-1. Next,

net present value profile
A curve showing the relationship between a project's NPV and the discount rate used.

Figure 14-1 **Net Present Value Profiles
of Projects E and L at Different Discount Rates**

A net present value profile shows a project's NPV at different discount (cost of capital) rates. In the graph below, NPV profiles are shown for Projects E and L. The Y-intercept for each curve gives the project's NPV at a 0% discount rate, while the X-intercept is the project's internal rate of return.

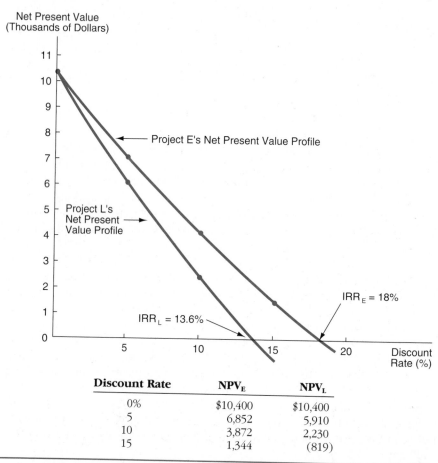

Discount Rate	NPV$_E$	NPV$_L$
0%	$10,400	$10,400
5	6,852	5,910
10	3,872	2,230
15	1,344	(819)

we calculate the projects' NPVs at three discount rates, say, 5, 10, and 15 percent, and plot these values. The data points plotted on the graph are shown at the bottom of the figure. When we connect these points, we have the net present value profiles.

Since the IRR is defined as the discount rate at which a project's NPV equals zero, *the point at which a project's net present value profile crosses the horizontal axis indicates the project's internal rate of return.* In Figure 14-1 we see that IRR$_E$ is 18 percent, whereas IRR$_L$ is 13.6 percent.

Table 14-6 **Analysis of Project E's IRR as a Loan Rate**

Year (1)	Loan Amount at Beginning of Year (2)	Cash Flow (3)	Interest on the Loan at 18% 0.18 × (2) = (4)	Repayment of Principal (3) − (4) = (5)	Ending Loan Balance (2) − (5) = (6)
1	$25,000	$12,000	$4,500	$7,500	$17,500
2	17,500	10,000	3,150	6,850	10,650
3	10,650	8,000	1,917	6,083	4,567
4	4,567	5,400	822	4,578	11[a]

[a]The exact value of IRR_E is 18.01324 percent. Had that value been used, the ending balance would have been zero. Note that the difference between this residual and that in Table 14-5 is simply the result of rounding differences.

Procedure 4: Financial Calculator and Computer Solutions. Internal rates of return can be calculated easily by financial calculators and by computers. Most larger firms have computerized their capital budgeting processes and automatically generate IRRs, NPVs, and paybacks for all projects. Also, financial calculators have built-in functions for calculating IRRs. Thus, business firms have no difficulty whatever with the mechanical side of capital budgeting.

With a financial calculator, you would input the project's cost and its cash inflows, and then press a button to obtain the IRR. You could, at the same time, specify the cost of capital and press a button marked NPV to obtain the NPV. We highly recommend that you get a good calculator and learn how to use it. You will be glad you did.

Rationale and Use of the IRR Method. What is so special about the particular discount rate that equates a project's cost with the present value of its receipts (its IRR)? To answer this question, first assume that our illustrative firm obtains the $25,000 needed to take on Project E by borrowing from a bank at an interest rate of 18 percent. Since the internal rate of return on this project was calculated to be 18 percent, the same as the cost of the bank loan, the firm can invest in the project, use the cash flows generated by the investment to pay off the principal and interest on the loan, and come out exactly even on the transaction. This point is demonstrated in Table 14-6, which shows that Project E provides cash flows that are just sufficient to pay 18 percent interest on the unpaid balance of the bank loan, retire the loan over the life of the project, and end up with a balance that differs from zero only by a rounding error of $11.

If the internal rate of return exceeds the cost of the funds used to finance a project, a surplus remains after paying for the capital. This surplus will accrue to the firm's stockholders, so taking on a project on which the IRR exceeds the firm's cost of capital increases the value of the firm's stock. If the internal rate of return is less than the cost of capital, taking on the project will impose a cost on existing stockholders, so accepting the project results in a reduction of value. It is this "breakeven" characteristic that makes us interested in the internal rate of return.[3]

Continuing with the example of Projects E and L, if both projects have a cost of capital of 12 percent, the internal rate of return rule indicates that if the projects are independent, both should be accepted — they both do better than break even. If they are mutually exclusive, E ranks higher and should be accepted whereas L should be rejected. If the cost of capital is above 18 percent, both projects should be rejected.

Self-Test

Identify the three methods that were discussed in the text for ranking capital projects.

How is the payback period of a project calculated, and what information does it provide to the firm?

Briefly explain the net present value (NPV) method.

What is the rationale behind the NPV method?

How would you calculate the IRR of a project?

What is the rationale behind the IRR method?

EVALUATION OF THE THREE DECISION RULES

We have presented three possible capital budgeting rules, all of which are used to a greater or lesser extent in practice. However, because the methods can lead to quite different accept/reject decisions, we need to answer this question: Which method is best? Obviously, the best method is the one that selects from all available projects that particular set of projects which maximizes the firm's value and hence its shareholders' wealth. If more than one method does this, then the best method would be the one that is easiest to use in practice.

There are three properties that must be exhibited by a capital budgeting method if it is to lead to consistently correct decisions:

1. The method must consider all cash flows throughout the entire life of a project.

2. The method must consider the time value of money — that is, it must reflect the fact that dollars which come in sooner are more valuable than dollars which are received in the distant future.

3. When the method is used to select from a set of mutually exclusive projects, it must signify that project which maximizes the firm's stock price.

---

[3]This example illustrates the logic of the IRR method, but for technical correctness, the capital used to finance the project should be assumed to be a mix of debt and equity, not debt alone. We will discuss this in greater detail in Chapter 19. For right now, we will continue with our earlier assumption of 100% equity financing.

How do the three decision methods compare with regard to the required properties? The payback method violates Properties 1 and 2: it does not consider all cash flows, and it ignores the time value of money. Both the NPV and IRR methods satisfy Properties 1 and 2, and both lead to identical (and correct) accept/reject decisions for independent projects. However, only the NPV method satisfies Property 3 under all conditions. As we demonstrate in Appendix 14A, there are certain conditions under which the IRR method fails to correctly identify that project, within a set of mutually exclusive projects, which maximizes the firm's stock price.

Self-Test

What are the three properties that a capital budgeting method must have in order to consistently lead to correct decisions?

Do payback period, NPV, and IRR satisfy the three properties equally well? Explain.

A CAPITAL BUDGETING CASE

An **expansion project** is one that calls for the firm to invest in new facilities in order to increase sales. For example, suppose Houston Trucking Company buys a new delivery van at a cost of $10,000. The van has a 5-year MACRS class life (see Chapter 2 for a review of MACRS depreciation); additional sales attributable to the new van will amount to $28,000 per year for 6 years; and Houston expects to be able to sell the van for $500 at the end of its 6-year service life. (Remember that a 5-year MACRS class life means that the asset is depreciated over 6 years, because only one-half year of depreciation is taken in the first year that the asset is acquired.) Operating costs (fuel, labor, and so forth) will amount to $20,000 per year. Houston's marginal federal-plus-state income tax rate is 40 percent, and its cost of capital is 12 percent. Table 14-7 works out the cash flows over the van's 6-year life.

expansion project
A project that is intended to increase sales.

Table 14-7 **Analysis of an Expansion Project:**
Houston Trucking Company

	Year 1	Year 2	Year 3	Year 4	Year 5	Year 6
Sales attributable to the project (S)	$28,000	$28,000	$28,000	$28,000	$28,000	$28,000
Operating costs (OC)	20,000	20,000	20,000	20,000	20,000	20,000
Depreciation (DEP)	2,000	3,200	1,900	1,200	1,100	600
Earnings before taxes (EBT)	$ 6,000	$ 4,800	$ 6,100	$ 6,800	$ 6,900	$ 7,400
Taxes (40%)	2,400	1,920	2,440	2,720	2,760	2,960
Net income (NI)	$ 3,600	$ 2,880	$ 3,660	$ 4,080	$ 4,140	$ 4,440
Net cash flow (CF$_t$ = NI + DEP)	$ 5,600	$ 6,080	$ 5,560	$ 5,280	$ 5,240	$ 5,040

Now we need to determine the company's initial investment, or CF_0. Houston must write a check for $10,000 to pay for the van. Also, we assume that Houston's net working capital (inventories plus accounts receivable, minus accounts payable) will rise by $3,000 if it purchases the van, but this net working capital will be recovered when the van is sold. Thus, the net investment in the van at (approximately) $t = 0$ is as follows:

Purchase price of van	$10,000
Plus investment in working capital	3,000
Net investment at $t = 0$	$13,000

When the van is disposed of at the end of 6 years, Houston expects to sell it for $500. Since the van will be fully depreciated, yet will have a value of $500, in economic terms it has been "overdepreciated." Under the tax laws, the government gets to "recapture" this depreciation by treating any salvage value in excess of the original depreciable basis as ordinary income. Therefore, the $500 will be taxed as ordinary income at a rate of 40 percent. The after-tax proceeds from the sale will be as follows:

$$\text{Salvage value after tax} = \text{Amount before tax} - \text{Tax}$$

$$= \text{Amount before tax} - \text{Amount before tax(Tax rate)}$$

$$= \text{Amount before tax}(1 - T)$$

$$= \$500(0.6)$$

$$= \$300 \text{ recovered at end of Year 6.}$$

The annual net cash flows attributable to the investment in the van are equal to net income plus depreciation. These cash flows are developed in Table 14-7. Note that depreciation under MACRS for a 5-year class life project such as the van is calculated as follows:

1. The *depreciable basis* is equal to the total cost of the van, which is $10,000. Note that any delivery, installation, and similar charges are included in the depreciable basis.

2. Annual depreciation:

Year	MACRS Allowance	×	Basis	=	Annual Depreciation
1	0.20		$10,000		$ 2,000
2	0.32		10,000		3,200
3	0.19		10,000		1,900
4	0.12		10,000		1,200
5	0.11		10,000		1,100
6	0.06		10,000		600
	1.00				$10,000

Now we have all the information necessary for calculating the project's NPV at the 12 percent cost of capital:

Year	Cash Flow	PVIF$_{12\%,t}$	PV of Cash Flow
1	$5,600	0.8929	$ 5,000
2	6,080	0.7972	4,847
3	5,560	0.7118	3,958
4	5,280	0.6355	3,355
5	5,240	0.5674	2,973
6	8,340[a]	0.5066	4,225

Total $24,358

Less: Net investment at t = 0   13,000

Net present value (NPV) $11,358

[a]$5,040 from operations + $3,000 recovery of net working capital + $300 after-tax salvage value.

Alternatively, we could set up the problem as follows:

$$NPV = \sum_{t=1}^{n} \frac{CF_t}{(1 + k)^t} - Cost$$

$$= \frac{\$5,600}{(1.12)^1} + \frac{\$6,080}{(1.12)^2} + \frac{\$5,560}{(1.12)^3} + \frac{\$5,280}{(1.12)^4} + \frac{\$5,240}{(1.12)^5} + \frac{\$8,340}{(1.12)^6} - \$13,000$$

$$= \$11,358.$$

Alternatively, we could input the cash flow data and the cost of capital into a financial calculator, press the NPV button, and obtain the NPV, $11,359. (Note the $1 rounding difference.) If the project had a fairly long life, the calculator solution would be much more efficient.

We could also solve for IRR in the following equation to find the van's IRR:

$$NPV = 0 = \frac{\$5,600}{(1 + IRR)^1} + \frac{\$6,080}{(1 + IRR)^2} + \frac{\$5,560}{(1 + IRR)^3}$$

$$+ \frac{\$5,280}{(1 + IRR)^4} + \frac{\$5,240}{(1 + IRR)^5} + \frac{\$8,340}{(1 + IRR)^6} - \$13,000.$$

The solution value is IRR = 38.30%, found with a financial calculator.

The question still remains: Should Houston Trucking invest in the delivery van? Assuming the forecasts of revenues and costs are reasonably correct, yes, the firm should invest in the van; the NPV is positive at the company's required rate of return, and the IRR is greater than the required rate of return.[4]

---

[4]As we note later, if a single project has a positive NPV, the project's IRR will always be larger than the project's required rate of return. However, complications *may* arise when comparing two or more investment opportunities. In that situation, the NPV ranking of multiple projects *may* differ from the IRR ranking.

Self-Test

What is an expansion project?

Briefly explain how you would set up an expansion project analysis.

How do you decide whether to invest in an expansion project?

THE POST-AUDIT

post-audit
A comparison of the actual and expected results for a given capital project.

The financial manager's responsibility for the purchase does not end with the acceptance of the investment opportunity. The purchase must be monitored closely by means of a *post-audit* to determine if it is living up to expectations. The **post-audit** involves (1) a comparison of actual results to those predicted in the request for funds and (2) an explanation of observed differences. For example, firms often require that the operating divisions send a monthly report for the first six months after a project goes into operation, and a quarterly report thereafter, until the project's results are up to expectations. From then on, reports on the project are handled like those on other operations.

The post-audit has several purposes, including the following:

1. Improve forecasts. When decision makers are forced to compare their projections to actual outcomes, there is a tendency for estimates to improve. Conscious or unconscious biases are observed and eliminated; new forecasting methods are sought as the need for them becomes apparent; and people simply tend to do everything better, including forecasting, if they know that their actions are being monitored.

2. Improve operations. Businesses are run by people, and people can perform at higher or lower levels of efficiency. When a divisional team has made a forecast about an investment, its members are, in a sense, putting their reputations on the line. If costs are above predicted levels, sales below expectations, and so on, executives in production, sales, and other areas will strive to improve operations and to bring results into line with forecasts. In a discussion related to this point, an IBM executive made this statement: "You academicians worry only about making good decisions. In business, we also worry about making decisions good."

The post-audit is not a simple process. There are a number of factors that can cause complications. First, one must recognize that almost every element of the cash flow forecast is subject to uncertainty, so a percentage of all projects undertaken by any reasonably venturesome firm will go awry. This fact must be considered when appraising the performances of the operating executives who submit capital expenditure requests. Second, projects sometimes fail to meet expectations for reasons beyond the control of the operating executives and for reasons that no one could realistically be expected to anticipate. For example, the increase in oil prices in 1990 adversely affected the airlines, but it helped oil producers and real estate projects in Texas and other oil-producing areas. Third, it is often difficult to separate the operating results of one investment from those of a larger system. Even though projects must stand alone to permit ready identification of costs and revenues, the actual cash flows that result from a project may be very hard to measure. Fourth, if the post-audit process is not used with care, executives may be reluctant to suggest potentially profitable but risky projects. And fifth, the executives who were actually responsible for a given decision may have moved on by the time the results of the decision are known.

Because of these difficulties, some firms tend to play down the importance of the post-audit. However, observations of both businesses and government units suggest that the best-run and most successful organizations are the ones that put the greatest emphasis on post-audits. Accordingly, the post-audit is one of the most important elements in a good capital budgeting system.

Self-Test

What is done in the post-audit?

Identify several purposes of the post-audit.

What factors can cause complications in the post-audit?

SUMMARY

This chapter discussed the capital budgeting process, and the key concepts covered are listed below:

- **Capital budgeting** is the process of analyzing potential expenditures on fixed assets and deciding whether the firm should undertake those investments.

- The capital budgeting process requires the firm (1) to determine the **cost of the project,** (2) to estimate the **expected cash flows** from the project and the riskiness of those cash flows, (3) to determine the appropriate **cost of capital** at which to discount the cash flows, and (4) to determine the **present values** of the expected cash flows and of the project. (Determining the cost of capital will be discussed in Chapter 19.)

- The most important, but also the most difficult, step in analyzing a capital budgeting project is **estimating the incremental after-tax cash flows** the project will produce.

- **Net cash flows** consist of (1) net income plus (2) depreciation.

- Capital projects often require an additional investment in **net working capital (NWC).** An increase in NWC must be included in the initial cash outlay in Year 0 and then shown as a cash inflow in the final year of the project.

- The **payback period** is defined as the expected number of years required to recover the original investment. The payback method ignores cash flows beyond the payback period, and it does not consider the time value of money. The payback does, however, provide an indication of a project's risk and liquidity, because it shows how long the original capital will be "at risk."

- The **net present value (NPV)** is the present value of all cash inflows, discounted at the project's cost of capital, minus the cost of the project. The project is accepted if the NPV is positive.

- The **internal rate of return (IRR)** is defined as the discount rate which forces the present value of the future cash inflows of a project to equal the cost of the project. The project is accepted if the IRR is greater than the project's cost of capital.

- The NPV and IRR methods make the same accept/reject decisions for **independent projects,** but if projects are **mutually exclusive,** then ranking conflicts can arise.

- The **post-audit** is a key element in the capital budgeting process. By comparing actual results with predicted results, and then determining why differences occurred, decision makers can improve both their operations and their forecasts of projects' outcomes.

Although this chapter has presented the basic elements of the capital budgeting process, there are many other aspects of this crucial topic. Some of the more important ones are discussed in the following chapter.

EQUATIONS

For determining the value of a project, we are interested only in cash flows. One method of determining cash flow is

$$\text{Net cash flow} = (\$REV - \$EXP)(1 - t) + (DEP)(t). \qquad \textbf{(14-1)}$$

This approach subtracts a project's cash expenses from its cash revenues; this result is then multiplied by one minus the tax rate. The tax effect of depreciation, which is included on the income statement, must be added into the equation. This is done by multiplying the tax rate by the depreciation amount.

Another way to calculate net cash flow is

$$\text{Net cash flow} = \text{Net income} + \text{Depreciation}.$$

The NPV method is one method used to evaluate capital budgeting projects. It includes the time value of money. The equation is

$$NPV = \sum_{t=1}^{n} \frac{CF_t}{(1 + k)^t} - C. \qquad \textbf{(14-2)}$$

The first part of the equation finds the present value of the expected net cash flows from the investment, discounted at the appropriate discount rate, and the second part subtracts the initial cost outlay of the project. The result is the NPV. If the NPV is positive, the project should be accepted; if it is negative, it should be rejected.

The internal rate of return equates the present value of the expected future net cash flows to the initial cost of the project. This equation is

$$\sum_{t=1}^{n} \frac{CF_t}{(1 + IRR)^t} - C = 0. \qquad (14\text{-}3)$$

RESOLUTION TO DECISION IN FINANCE

Learning from Past Errors

According to the agreement between GM and the United Auto Workers union, all decisions at Saturn must be made by consensus. All employees — management and labor — are on salaries, and all eat together in the company cafeteria to avoid any appearance of a "caste" system. The agreement provides that workers' starting salaries are 20 percent lower than union wages in the regular GM divisions from which they were recruited, but by meeting or exceeding productivity goals, they can earn even more than the union standard. Workers also had to give up seniority rights and resign from their former union locals. In exchange, the agreement says that the only justification for layoffs will be "unforeseen or catastrophic events or severe economic conditions."

Workers even helped decide which suppliers, dealers, and advertising agency would service Saturn. When the staff was being recruited, a panel of union members and management had to approve every new staff member — both blue- and white-collar. Expenditures on plant and equipment were made with consideration for workers. The Saturn complex is the largest single construction project in GM's history, and it incorporates body and assembly plants, paint shop, power-train factory, plastic-molding plant, and instrument/dash assembly. Incoming parts are delivered near the place where they will be used instead of to a central dock; assembly-line workers unloading them can spot defects immediately. No worker has to walk more than five minutes from his or her parked car to his workplace, and he or she will be comfortable at this workplace — the assembly-line floor is made of wood.

There is some resentment among staff in the older GM divisions about the special treatment of the Saturn project. "We could do that too, if we had all that money," some workers in other plants have allegedly said. The risk of even more hard feelings could prevent Saturn from realizing its potential. More capital won't be spent to upgrade capacity to the optimum 500,000-car-a-year level while plants in some other divisions are idled, or are operating on only one shift.

Nevertheless, the Saturn group itself is enthusiastic and certain that its innovations will result in lower production costs and a competitive product. "There are some things we're doing here that, if ever GM could do it, there'd be a ton of savings," says Saturn's finance vice president. The vice president of human resources notes that the result of the unprecedented teamwork and participatory management is that "There's a real cause here. It's been described as almost like a cult."

Sources: "GM Is Tougher Than You Think," *Fortune,* November 10, 1986; "Here Comes GM's Saturn," *Business Week,* April 9, 1990.

QUESTIONS

14-1   How is a project classification scheme (for example, replacement, expansion into new markets, and so forth) used in the capital budgeting process?

14-2   Explain how net working capital is recovered at the end of a project's life, and why it is included in a capital budgeting analysis.

14-3   Why are spontaneous liabilities such as accounts payable and accruals deducted from working capital in the analysis of capital budgeting costs?

14-4   If a firm used straight line rather than an accelerated depreciation method, how would this affect **(a)** the total amount of depreciation, net income, and net cash flows over the project's expected life; **(b)** the timing of depreciation, net income, and net cash flows; and **(c)** the project's payback and NPV?

14-5   Net cash flows rather than accounting profits are listed in Column 2 of Table 14-1. What is the basis for this emphasis on cash flows as opposed to net income?

14-6   Explain why the NPV of a long-term project, defined as one with a high percentage of its cash flows expected in the distant future, is more sensitive to changes in the cost of capital than the NPV of a short-term project.

14-7   Are there conditions under which a firm might be better off if it were to choose a project with a rapid payback rather than one with a larger NPV?

14-8   A firm has $100 million available for capital expenditures. It is considering investment in one of two projects, each costing $100 million. Project A has an IRR of 20 percent and an NPV of $9 million. It will be terminated at the end of one year at a profit of $20 million, resulting in an immediate increase in earnings per share (EPS). Project B, which cannot be postponed for one year in order to take on Project A, has an NPV of $50 million and an IRR of 30 percent. However, the firm's short-run EPS will be reduced if it accepts Project B, because no revenues will be generated by the project for several years.
     a. Should the short-run effects on EPS influence the choice between the two projects?
     b. How might situations like the one described here influence a firm's decision to use payback as a part of the capital budgeting process?

SELF-TEST PROBLEMS

ST-1   Paschal Products is considering the purchase of a new machine that will dramatically increase the firm's manufacturing capacity. The machine, if purchased today, would cost $40,550,000 and provide annual cash flows after taxes (net income plus depreciation) of $13,425,000 per year for 6 years.
     a. Determine the project's payback.
     b. Determine the project's NPV if the required return is 15 percent.
     c. Determine the project's IRR.

ST-2   Bio-Technical Engineering (BTE) is considering an investment in a gene splicing project. The investment involves acquiring land, developing a new plant, operating the plant during the project, and then disposing of the salvageable assets from the project. The following is a summary of the project's characteristics (dollars in millions):
     1. A total of $50 has been spent thus far to investigate the feasibility of the process used in the project. These funds were expensed.
     2. BTE will purchase the land immediately at a cost of $300.

3. A BTE operations building will be put up at a cost of $400. This expenditure will occur at t = 1, that is, at the end of Year 1.

4. Equipment will be installed at a cost of $200. This outlay will occur at t = 2, the end of Year 2.

5. BTE will bring in net working capital with a cost of $100. This outlay will occur at the end of Year 3, t = 3, and the working capital will be recovered at the end of the project's life, t = 8, the end of Year 8.

6. The plant will commence operations at the beginning of Year 4. The operations will continue for 5 years, until the end of Year 8. After-tax cash flows from the project (net income plus depreciation) will equal $425 annually for the 5-year operating period.

7. Even though the operating assets will be fully depreciated, management believes the building and equipment will have a combined salvage value of $150 at the end of Year 8.

8. BTE's effective tax rate is 40 percent.

9. Assume that the project is not eligible for an investment tax credit.

If the required return for a high-risk project, such as the gene splicing project at BTE, is 20 percent, should the firm invest in this project?

PROBLEMS

14-1   **Payback, NPV, and IRR calculations.** RaeTel is evaluating a project with a cost of $674,115, and expected annual cash inflows of $150,000 per year for 10 years.
   a. What is the project's payback?
   b. The firm's cost of capital is 14 percent. What is the project's NPV?
   c. What is the project's IRR? (*Hint:* Recognize that the project's cash inflows are an annuity.)

14-2   **Payback, NPV, and IRR calculations.** Florida Industries' proposed project has a cost of $3,244,320, and its expected net cash flows are $900,000 per year for 5 years.
   a. What is the payback for this project?
   b. The cost of capital is 10 percent. What is the project's NPV?
   c. What is the project's IRR? (*Hint:* Recognize that the project's net cash flows are an annuity.)

14-3   **Payback, NPV, and IRR calculations.** Sound Design is investigating a project that costs $1,392,960 and is expected to produce net cash flows of $600,000 annually for 3 years.
   a. What is the project's payback?
   b. If the cost of capital is 12 percent, what is the project's NPV?
   c. What is the project's IRR? (*Hint:* Recognize that the project's net cash flows are an annuity.)

14-4   **Payback, NPV, and IRR calculations.** The management of Hytec Electronics is evaluating the following investment opportunity, which costs $47,678.50 today but promises to return the following net cash flows:

Year	Net Cash Flow
1	$20,000
2	15,000
3	10,000
4	20,000

a. What is this project's payback?

b. What is the project's NPV if Hytec's cost of capital is 14 percent?

c. What is the project's IRR?

14-5 **Payback, NPV, and IRR calculations.** Accurex Associates is evaluating an investment opportunity that costs $100,000 today but promises to return the following net cash flows (net income plus depreciation) over the next 4 years:

Year	Net Cash Flow
1	$20,000
2	40,000
3	36,000
4	24,000

a. What is the investment's payback?

b. What is the NPV of the project if the required return is 9 percent?

c. Is the IRR of the investment greater or less than the required return?

14-6 **NPV and IRR calculations.** D. Harrington and Company is considering an investment in a new machine that will provide dramatic cost savings over the next 5 years. The cost of the machine is $72,107.10. Annual after-tax cash flows (net income plus depreciation) are projected as follows:

Year	After-Tax Cash Flow
1	$18,000
2	25,000
3	22,000
4	20,000
5	20,000

a. If the firm's required return for a project of this type is 12 percent, what is the investment's NPV?

b. What is the project's IRR?

14-7 **NPVs and IRRs for mutually exclusive projects.** Graham's Inc. is considering including two pieces of equipment, a truck and an overhead pulley system, in this year's capital budget. These projects are mutually exclusive. The cash outlay for the truck is $20,820, and that for the pulley system is $29,070. The firm's cost of capital is 15 percent. After-tax cash flows, including depreciation, are as follows:

Years	Truck	Pulley
1–5	$6,360	$9,720

Calculate the IRR and the NPV for each project, and indicate the correct accept/reject decision for each.

14-8 **NPVs and IRRs for mutually exclusive projects.** Southwest Manufacturing must choose between a gas-powered and an electric-powered forklift for moving materials in its factory. Because both forklifts perform the same function, the firm will choose only one. (They are mutually exclusive investments.) The electric-powered forklift will cost more, but it will be less expensive to operate; it will cost $27,500, whereas the gas-powered one will cost $22,000. The cost of capital that applies to both investments is 16 percent. The life for both equipment types is estimated to be 6 years, during which time the net after-tax cash flows for the electric-powered forklift will be $8,250 annually and for the gas-powered forklift will be $6,625 per year. Annual net after-tax cash flows include depreciation expenses. Calculate the NPV and IRR for each type of forklift, and decide which to recommend for purchase.

14-9   **NPVs and IRRs for independent projects.** The net cash flows for Projects X and Y follow. Each project has a cost of $40,000.

Year	Project X	Project Y
1	$26,000	$14,000
2	12,000	14,000
3	12,000	14,000
4	4,000	14,000

a. Calculate each project's payback.
b. Calculate each project's NPV at a 10 percent cost of capital.
c. Calculate each project's IRR. (*Hints:* Use the graphic approach for Project X, and notice that Project Y is an annuity.)
d. Should Project X, Project Y, or both projects be accepted if they are independent projects?
e. Which of the two projects should be accepted if they are mutually exclusive?

14-10   **Expected NPV and IRR.** McCollough Consulting has provided the following net cash flow (net income + depreciation) estimates for a proposed investment project:

Annual Net Cash Flows	
Probability	**Amount**
0.3	$30,000
0.4	45,000
0.2	56,250
0.1	67,500

This project has a life of 10 years and is expected to have a zero salvage value. An investment of $188,662.50 is required to make the project operational.
a. If the firm requires a 16 percent return, what is the project's NPV?
b. What is the project's IRR?
c. Should McCollough Consulting accept or reject the proposed project?

14-11   **Expected NPVs.** Scientific Measurement Corporation has a cost of capital that equals 12 percent. The company is choosing between two mutually exclusive projects. Alpha Project is of average risk, so its cost of capital is 12 percent, and it costs $1 million. Its expected cash flows are $220,000 annually for 8 years. The Omega Project is of above-average risk, and management estimates that its cost of capital should be 15 percent. Omega also costs $1 million, and it promises to provide a cash flow of $240,000 annually for 8 years. Each project will end with a zero salvage value at the end of its designated life. Calculate the NPV for each project and indicate which project should be accepted and which should be rejected by Scientific Measurement Corporation. What is the basis for your conclusion?

14-12   **Project evaluation.** Highlander Manufacturing Company is considering a new production line for its rapidly expanding camping equipment division. The line will have a cost of $288,000 and will be depreciated toward a zero salvage value over the next 3 years, using straight line depreciation. Other important factors are: (1) The new camping products will be responsible for new sales of $300,000 next year, $330,000 the following year, and $360,000 in the last year. (2) Cost of goods sold (excluding depreciation) is 40 percent of sales. (3) The increase in selling and administrative expenses caused by the new line is predicted to be $24,000 annually. (4) The company's cost of capital is 16 percent, and its tax rate is 40 percent.
a. What are the project's annual net cash flows?
b. What is the project's NPV?

14-13   **Project evaluation.** The director of capital budgeting for Chung Engineering is analyzing a proposal to build a new plant in Arizona. The following data have been developed thus far:

Land acquisition, cost incurred at start of Year 1 (t = 0)	$ 300,000
Plant construction, cost incurred at start of Year 2 (t = 1)	700,000
Equipment purchase, cost incurred at start of Year 3 (t = 2)	1,000,000
Net working capital, investment made at start of Year 4 (t = 3)	400,000

Operations will begin in Year 4 and will continue for 10 years, through Year 13. Sales revenues and operating costs are assumed to come at the end of each year; since the plant will be in operation for 10 years, operating costs and revenues occur at the end of Years 4 through 13 (t = 4 to 13). The following additional assumptions are made: (1) The plant and equipment will be depreciated over a 10-year life, starting in Year 4. The buildings and equipment will be worthless after 10 years' use, but Chung expects to sell the land for $300,000 when the plant is closed down. The firm's management also expects that its investment in working capital for the plant will be fully recoverable when the plant is closed. Chung uses straight line depreciation. (2) Chung uses a cost of capital of 14 percent to evaluate projects like this one. (3) Annual sales = 10,000 units at $140 per unit; annual sales revenue = $1,400,000. (4) Annual fixed operating costs *excluding* depreciation are $213,333. (5) Annual variable operating costs are $300,000, *assuming the plant operates at full capacity.* (6) Chung's marginal income tax rate is 40 percent. (7) The project is not eligible for an investment tax credit.
a. Calculate the project's NPV. Should Chung's management accept this project?
b. Assuming constant sales prices and constant variable costs per unit, what will happen to the NPV if unit sales fall 10 percent below the forecasted level?

14-14   **Cash flow estimation.** C. Barry and Company is considering the installation of a new production line for its rapidly expanding skate division. The line will have a cost of $150,000. The asset will be 5-year-class property for the purpose of MACRS depreciation. No salvage value is expected for the assets when the project ends in 6 years. Sales are expected to be $150,000 annually. Operating costs other than depreciation will be $105,000 annually. The company's required rate of return is 12 percent, and its tax rate is 40 percent.
    Determine the project's net cash flows, and then calculate the project's net present value. (The following MACRS recovery allowances are in effect: Year 1, 20%; Year 2, 32%; Year 3, 19%; Year 4, 12%; Year 5, 11%; and Year 6, 6%.)

SOLUTIONS TO SELF-TEST PROBLEMS

ST-1   **a.** The payback is defined as the length of time it takes to recover the investment in a project. For this proposed purchase, payback is determined in the following table:

Year	Cash Flow	Cumulative Cash Flow
0	($40,550,000)	
1	13,425,000	($27,125,000)
2	13,425,000	(13,700,000)
3	13,425,000	(275,000)
4	13,425,000	13,150,000
5	13,425,000	26,575,000
6	13,425,000	40,000,000

$275,000 unrecovered after 3 years.

$13,425,000/365 = $36,781 recovery per day.

$275,000/$36,781 = 7.5 days.

Therefore, the payback period is 3 years and 1 week, which would be rounded to 3 years. (Note: Since this project's cash flows are level, we could have found the payback by $40,550,000/$13,425,000 = 3.02 years, which is, of course, 3 years and 1 week.)

b. The NPV is calculated thus:

$$\text{NPV} = \text{CF}(\text{PVIFA}_{15\%,6}) - \text{Cost}$$

$$= \$13,425,000(3.7845) - \$40,550,000$$

$$= \$50,806,913 - \$40,550,000$$

$$= \$10,256,913.$$

Using a financial calculator, the solution is found through the following steps:

$$\text{PMT} = 13,425,000$$

$$n = 6$$

$$k = i = 15$$

$$\text{PV} = ?;\ \text{calculator solution gives } \$50,806,680.$$

$$\text{NPV} = \$50,806,680 - \$40,550,000 = \$10,256,680.$$

(Note: The difference between the two answers is due to rounding of the PVIFA.)

c. Since the cash flows of this project take the form of an annuity, we can solve the following equation to determine the present value interest factor for an annuity:

$$\text{PVA} = \text{PMT}(\text{PVIFA}_{k,6})$$

$$\text{PVIFA}_{k,6} = \frac{\text{PVA}}{\text{PMT}}$$

or

$$\$40{,}550{,}000 = \$13{,}425{,}000(\text{PVIFA}_{k,6})$$

$$\text{PVIFA}_{k,6} = \frac{\$40{,}550{,}000}{\$13{,}425{,}000}$$

$$= 3.0205.$$

For a 6-year annuity, the PVIFA of 3.0205 corresponds to a 24 percent rate of return.

Using a financial calculator, the solution is found through the following steps:

$$CF_0 = \$40{,}550{,}000$$

$$CF_1 - CF_6 = \$13{,}425{,}000$$

$$IRR = ?; \text{ calculator solution gives } 24.00\%.$$

ST-2 The costs associated with the gene splicing project (in millions of dollars) are as follows:

Time	Cost	Purpose
t = 0	$300	Land
t = 1	$400	Building
t = 2	$200	Equipment
t = 3	$100	Working capital

$$\begin{aligned}\text{Present value of costs} = {} & -\$300 - \$400(0.8333) \\ & - \$200(0.6944) - \$100(0.5787) \\ = {} & -\$830.07 = -\$830{,}070{,}000.\end{aligned}$$

Notice that we did not include in the cost of the project the $50 million spent on the feasibility study. This is a sunk cost and, as such, is not a relevant cash flow.

The cash flows associated with the project (in millions of dollars) are as follows:

Time	Cash Flow	Source
t = 4 - 8	$425	Cash flow from operations
t = 8	$100	Recapture of working capital
t = 8	$150	Sale of salvageable assets (taxed as ordinary income)

$$\begin{aligned}\text{Present value of cash flows} = {} & \$425(1.7307)^* + \$100(0.2326) \\ & + \$150(1 - 0.4)(0.2326) \\ = {} & \$779.7415 = \$779{,}741{,}500.\end{aligned}$$

$$\begin{aligned}\text{Net present value} = {} & \text{Discounted cash flows} - \text{Costs} \\ = {} & \$779.7415 - \$830.07 \\ = {} & -\$50.3285 = -\$50{,}328{,}500.\end{aligned}$$

$$^*\text{PVIFA}_{20\%,8} - \text{PVIFA}_{20\%,3} = 3.8372 - 2.1065 = 1.7307.$$

Because the project's NPV is negative, BTE should abandon the project. Of course, the same decision would have been reached if we had found the project's IRR. For single projects, a negative NPV indicates that the IRR of the project is less than the required return for the project. Whichever method is used, BTE should not invest in the gene splicing project.

We could also find the solution to this problem by using a financial calculator. To do this, we would begin by identifying the relevant cash flows on a time line as follows:

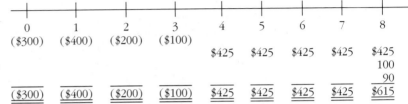

	0	1	2	3	4	5	6	7	8
Cash outflows	($300)	($400)	($200)	($100)					
Operating cash inflows					$425	$425	$425	$425	$425
Net working capital recovery									100
After-tax salvage value									90
Net cash flow	($300)	($400)	($200)	($100)	$425	$425	$425	$425	$615

Then, we would enter each cash flow in our financial calculator, discounted at the appropriate interest rate of 20 percent, to arrive at the solution of −$50.3664, or $50,366,400. (Note: The difference in values obtained is due to rounding of factors obtained from Tables A-1 through A-4 in Appendix A of the text.) Of course, the same decision would be reached, that is, BTE should not invest in the gene splicing project.

Appendix 14A

Conflicts between NPV and IRR

In Chapter 14 we indicated that the two appropriate procedures for evaluating capital budgeting projects are the NPV and the IRR methods. For single projects and for two (or more) *independent projects,* the NPV and IRR methods *always* lead to the same accept/reject decisions. As noted in Table 14A-1, if the project's internal rate of return, IRR, is greater than the company's or project's required rate of return, k, the NPV will be positive, and the project will thus be deemed acceptable. Under normal circumstances, any project that provides a return less than the required return will be rejected. In this situation the project's NPV will always be negative. Of course, where NPV = $0, the project's required and internal rates of return are equal, and the firm will be indifferent between this project and other alternatives of the same risk. (Remember that k

Table 14A-1 **Comparison of NPV and IRR Project Evaluation Rules for Independent Projects**

Method	Accept	Reject	Indifferent
NPV	Positive	Negative	Zero
IRR	Greater than k	Less than k	k = IRR

is also an opportunity cost representing the return of the best other available invest-ment opportunity.)

However, when we consider *ranking* two or more investment projects, as in the following example, these decision rules may not agree. Assume that MBI Corporation has two competing, *mutually exclusive projects*, Projects A and B. Recall that with mu-tually exclusive projects, we can choose either Project A or Project B, or we can reject both, but we cannot accept both projects. In this example, each project requires an initial investment outlay of $1,000,000. Notice in Figure 14A-1 that if the firm's cost of capital is above 7.1 percent, both the NPV and IRR methods indicate that Project A should be selected. However, if the firm's cost of capital is below 7.1 percent, a conflict between the decision methods arises. If the firm's cost of capital is 5 percent, for ex-ample, the NPV of Project A is $180,410 whereas the NPV of Project B is $206,480, as seen in Table 14A-2. We approximate the IRRs of both projects graphically in Figure 14A-1. The IRR of Project A is 14.5 percent, but the IRR of Project B, 11.8 percent, is lower. Therefore, the IRR method indicates that Project A should be selected, whereas the NPV method indicates that Project B is preferable. The critical question is, which method should we use in making capital budgeting decisions when the methods are in conflict?

Comparison of the NPV and IRR Methods

As we noted in Chapter 14, the NPV exhibits all the desired decision rule properties, and therefore it provides the best method for evaluating projects. Because the NPV method is theoretically superior to the IRR, we were tempted to explain only the NPV, state that it should be used for all capital budgeting decisions, and move on to the next topic. However, the IRR method is familiar to many corporate executives, and it is widely entrenched in industry practices. Therefore, it is important that finance students thoroughly understand the IRR method and be prepared to explain why at times a project with a lower IRR may be preferable to one with a higher IRR.

Causes of Conflicting Rankings

There are two basic conditions that cause NPV profiles to cross, as in Figure 14A-1, and thus lead to potential conflicts between the NPV and IRR methods.

1. Project size or scale differences. If the cost of one project is significantly larger than that of the other, the larger project will generally have a higher NPV than the smaller one at low discount rates. If the larger project has the higher NPV at a zero discount rate, and the smaller project has the higher IRR, the NPV profiles will cross each other. For example, Project S calls for the investment of $1.00 and yields $1.50 at the end of one year. Its IRR is 50 percent and at a 10 percent cost of capital, its NPV is 36 cents. Project L costs $1 million and yields $1.25 million at the end of the year. Its IRR is only 25 percent but its NPV at 10 percent is $136,375.

2. Timing differences. If most of the cash flows from one project come in the early years whereas most of those from the other project come in the later years, as occurred with Projects A and B, the project with the longer-term cash flows will gener-ally have a higher vertical axis intercept, so again the NPV profiles can cross each other. This situation is caused by the fact that high discount rates benefit projects that have early cash flows but impose a greater penalty on projects having cash flows that are slow to accrue. Therefore, long-term projects, like Project B, have NPV profiles that start

Figure 14A-1 **Net Present Value Profiles of Projects A and B at Different Discount Rates (Thousands of Dollars)**

Conflicting results may arise when both net present value (NPV) and internal rate of return (IRR) are used to rank mutually exclusive capital projects. In this example, at a discount rate of 5 percent, Project A has an NPV of $180.41 and an IRR of 14.5 percent, whereas Project B has an NPV of $206.48 and an IRR of 11.8 percent. Based on NPV, Project B would be preferred, but based on IRR, Project A would seem more attractive. In such cases NPV provides the least ambiguous means of ranking projects.

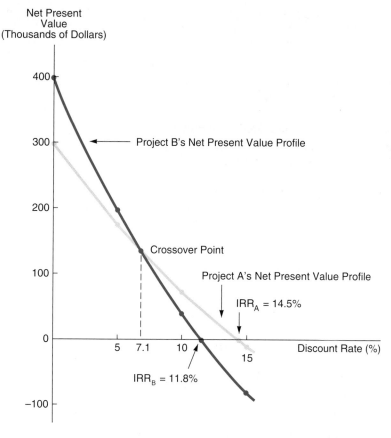

Discount Rate	NPV$_A$ (in Thousands)	NPV$_B$ (in Thousands)
0%	$300.00	$400.00
5	180.41	206.48
10	78.80	49.15
15	(8.33)	(80.13)

Note: Notice that the net present value profiles are curved — they are *not* straight lines. We should also mention that under certain conditions, the NPV profiles can cross the horizontal axis several times or never cross it.

Table 14A-2 **Calculating the NPVs of Projects A and B where k = 5%**

	Project A			Project B		
Year	Cash Flow	PVIF$_{5\%,t}$	Discounted Cash Flow	Cash Flow	PVIF$_{5\%,t}$	Discounted Cash Flow
1	$500,000	0.9524	$ 476,200	$100,000	0.9524	$ 95,240
2	400,000	0.9070	362,800	300,000	0.9070	272,100
3	300,000	0.8638	259,140	400,000	0.8638	345,520
4	100,000	0.8227	82,270	600,000	0.8227	493,620
		PV of inflows	$1,180,410			$1,206,480
		Less: Cost	1,000,000			1,000,000
		NPV	$ 180,410			$ 206,480

high on the vertical axis but that also decline quite steeply relative to those of projects like Project A, allowing the two profiles to cross.

Resolving the NPV versus IRR Conflict

When either size or timing differences occur, the methodologies that determine the desirability of capital investment projects may be in conflict. When there is a conflict in these selection methods, it should be resolved by choosing the project that has the highest NPV. The choice of the NPV method avoids three problems where the IRR criterion can provide an incorrect capital budgeting decision: (1) the problem of absolute versus relative returns, (2) the reinvestment rate assumption, and (3) the problem of multiple rates of return.[1]

Absolute versus Relative Returns

Suppose we are offered the choice between two competing one-year projects. Project Y's IRR is 10 percent, whereas Project Z's IRR is 20 percent. If we rank and select projects using the IRR criterion, we would choose the project with the larger IRR — Project Z. However, suppose that Project Z's maximum available investment was $1,000 and its NPV was equal to $200; but we could invest up to $10,000 in Project Y, which would give us an NPV of $1,000. Which would be the better project? The project that provided the higher true return — dollars — is the better one. Thus we would opt for the project that gives the higher *absolute* return, the one with the higher NPV.

Reinvestment Assumption

When either timing or size differences occur, the firm will have different amounts of funds to invest in the intervening years of the project's life, depending on which of the mutually exclusive projects it chooses. For example, if one project costs more than the other, the firm will have more money at t = 0 to invest elsewhere if it selects the less costly project. Similarly, for projects of equal cost, the one with the larger early cash inflows will provide more funds for reinvestment in the early years. Thus the rate of return at which differential cash flows can be invested is an important consideration.

---

[1]For a much more detailed and complete discussion of these factors, see Brigham and Gapenski, *Intermediate Financial Management,* 3rd ed., Chapter 7.

Although we do not prove it in this book, the fundamental reason behind the NPV/IRR conflict has to do with the **reinvestment rate assumptions** underlying the two methods.[2] The NPV method assumes that the firm can reinvest cash flows at the cost of capital, whereas the IRR method assumes that they can be reinvested at the IRR. The NPV method makes a much more conservative reinvestment assumption than the IRR method. The NPV assumes reinvestment at the cost of capital, which is the rate of return required by all suppliers of funds. Thus, the NPV reinvestment assumption is that intervening cash inflows will be reinvested at the firm's current required rate of return. On the other hand, the IRR method assumes that the intervening cash inflows from the project will be reinvested at that project's rate of return, its IRR. Thus, if a project has a *computed* IRR of 40 percent, but the best alternative for reinvesting the intervening cash flows from the project is 8 percent, the realized rate of return from the project will definitely be less than 40 percent. This does not mean that the project may not be acceptable, only that its realized return will be less than its computed IRR.

Naturally, the closer the project's IRR to the firm's opportunity cost, the less the reinvestment assumption matters. Yet, there will *never* be a problem using the NPV rule in ranking competing, or mutually exclusive, investment opportunities.

reinvestment rate assumption
The assumption that cash flows from a project can be reinvested (1) at the cost of capital, if using the NPV method, or (2) at the internal rate of return, if using the IRR method.

Multiple Rates of Return

A third reason that the NPV method provides a better criterion for ranking capital budgeting projects is that, in certain situations, there can be more than one IRR. In Figure 14A-1, Projects A and B each have only one IRR, which is found where the NPV profile crosses the X-axis — that is, where the NPV = $0. These are both normal projects in that their cash outflow (one or more cash outflows) is followed by future cash inflows. However, capital budgeting projects can have outflows followed by inflows, then by more outflows, and so on. Strip mining for coal provides an example of this nonnormal cash flow. First the land is purchased, then the coal is mined for several years, and finally the land must be returned to its natural state at the expense of the mine's owners. Oil-well drilling provides a similar example of nonnormal cash flows, as the rig must be periodically shut down and refurbished before the well can produce more cash flows.

An example of a nonnormal cash flow (in millions) is as follows:

Expected Net Cash Flow

Year 0	Year 1	Year 2
($1.6)	+ $10	($10)

If one were ranking projects based on the IRR method, this nonnormal project would create a problem, because the project's IRR is 25 percent *and* 400 percent. Both IRRs cause the NPV to equal zero, so both are correct. This situation creates confusion for firms that rely on the IRR method to select projects. However, the NPV method gives a single decision criterion, and it is thus superior to the IRR method.

---

[2]Both the NPV and the IRR methods are discounted cash flow techniques. Because both techniques utilize the time value of money, we should consider again how the present value tables are constructed. Recall that the present value of any future sum is defined as the beginning amount that, when compounded at a specified and constant rate, will grow to equal the future amount over the stated time period. From Table 13-1 we can see that the present value of $146.93 due in 5 years, when discounted at 8 percent, is $100, because $100, when reinvested and compounded at 8 percent into the future for 5 years, will grow to $146.93. Thus, compounding and discounting are reciprocal relationships, and *the very construction of the discounting and compounding tables implies a reinvestment process.*

PROBLEMS

14A-1 **NPV versus IRR ranking for mutually exclusive projects.** Two projects each involve an investment of $36,000. Cash flows (net income plus depreciation) are $24,000 a year for 2 years for Project S and $9,600 annually for 6 years for Project L.

    a. Compute the NPV for each project if the firm's cost of capital is zero percent and if it is 6 percent. NPVs for Project S at 10 and 20 percent, respectively, are $5,652.00 and $667.20, whereas NPVs for Project L at 10 and 20 percent are $5,810.88 and − $4,075.20.

    b. Graph the net present value profiles of the two projects, putting NPV on the Y-axis and the discount rate on the X-axis, and use the graph to estimate each project's IRR.

    c. Calculate the IRR for each project, using a formula.

    d. If these projects were mutually exclusive, which one would you select, assuming a cost of capital of (1) 8 percent, (2) 10.2 percent, or (3) 12 percent? Explain. For this problem, assume that the operation will terminate at the end of the project's life.

14A-2 **NPV and IRR analysis.** Each of two mutually exclusive projects involves an investment of $180,000. Net cash flows (net income plus depreciation) for the two projects have a different time pattern. Project M involves using some acreage for a mining operation. Because the expense of removing the ore is lower in the early years, when the ore will be closer to the surface, Project M will yield high returns in early years and lower returns in later years. Project O involves using the land for an orchard, and it will take a number of years for the trees to mature and become fully bearing. Thus Project O will yield lower returns in the early years and higher returns in the later years. The net cash flows from the two investments are as follows:

Year	Project M	Project O
1	$105,000	$ 15,000
2	60,000	30,000
3	45,000	45,000
4	15,000	75,000
5	15,000	120,000

    a. Calculate each project's payback period.

    b. Compute the net present value of each project when the firm's cost of capital is 0 percent, 6 percent, and 20 percent. At 10 percent, the NPV for M is $18,410 and the NPV for O is $17,975.

    c. Graph the net present value profiles of the two projects. Use the graph to estimate each project's IRR. If you have a financial calculator, use it to check your graphic estimate.

    d. Which project would you select, assuming a cost of capital of 8 percent? Of 10 percent? Of 12 percent? Explain.

    e. How might a change in the cost of capital produce a conflict between NPV and IRR results? At what value of k would this conflict exist?

    f. The company's capital budgeting manual states that no project with a payback period greater than 4 should be accepted. Discuss this rule and its effects, both in general and in this specific case.

14A-3 **NPV and IRR analysis.** Northwestern Investment Company (NIC) is considering 2 mutually exclusive investments. The projects' expected net cash flows are as follows:

	Expected Net Cash Flow	
Year	Project A	Project B
0	($275)	($405)
1	(350)	134
2	(150)	134
3	(125)	134
4	535	134
5	535	134
6	715	134
7	(100)	0

a. Construct NPV profiles for Projects A and B.

b. What is each project's IRR?

c. If you were told that each project's cost of capital was 10 percent, which project should be selected? If the cost of capital were 16 percent, what would be the proper choice?

(Do Parts d and e only if you are using the computerized problem diskette.)

d. NIC's management is confident of the projects' cash flows in Years 0 to 6 but is uncertain about what the Year 7 cash flows will be for the two projects. Under a worst case scenario, Project A's Year 7 cash flow will be − $200 and B's will be − $100, whereas under a best case scenario, the cash flows will be − $50 and + $90 for Projects A and B, respectively. Rework Parts a through c using these new cash flows. Which project should be selected under each scenario? Press the F10 function key on your computer keyboard to see the NPV profiles.

e. Change the Year 7 cash flows back to − $100 for A and zero for B. Now change the cost of capital and observe what happens to NPV, IRR, and the crossover rate at k = 0%, 5%, 20%, and 300% (input as 3). Again, press the F10 function key to see the NPV profiles.

Chapter 15

Decisions in Capital Budgeting

DECISION IN FINANCE

Should Government Make It Easier?

In the 1950s and 1960s, the United States was the "new-product laboratory" for the world. Another country now seems determined to take over that role: Japan. A major sign that this is its intention is the amount of capital spending Japan has been pouring into its economy since 1985 — 150 percent more in 1990 than five years earlier. Meanwhile, U.S. capital investment increased only 23 percent, and even the United States' total outlay of $550 billion was surpassed by Japan in 1988. Per capita, Japan outspends the United States two to one. One Japanese international trade official indicated the driving urgency behind the spending spree. "We've been developing by borrowing technology from abroad. From now on, we'll do it ourselves. We have to lead."

Nevertheless, a fifth of Japanese capital investment still goes toward adapting technologies pioneered in the United States, such as CIM, or computer integrated manufacturing. Faced with a looming labor shortage, Japanese factories are trying to eliminate the need for human workers by automating more tasks. A combination of robots and computers can monitor quality control — formerly considered a necessarily human task — via an electronic network connecting the machines at every stage of production. The factory manager receives a warning when a problem or error occurs at any point. Another priority for the Japanese is making the human workers they do have happier. Many corporations are building employee housing, recreational facilities, and dining halls. Other companies help workers buy their own homes.

Most of Japan's spending, however, is funneled into products, both new and old. Hitachi, for instance, recently brought out a washing machine with a number of new features, including an air cushion to cut noise, which is important in Japan's crowded houses. Other sluggish markets, such as those for vacuum cleaners, have been energized by new models and flashy styling. Imaginative new products recently introduced include a stamp-sized tape recorder with digital-quality sound and wireless ear-

See end of chapter for resolution.

phones that pick up stereo sound from across a room.

Japanese capital budgets are also aimed at speeding production. Although Japanese auto-makers can already bring out new models two years faster than manufacturers in the United States, they are trying to take another full year off the process.

As manufacturers forge ahead with capital spending, not everyone is pleased in Tokyo, any more than they are in Washington. As you read this chapter, consider the potential dangers to both countries that excess capital spending might pose. As a corporate financial manager, what might U.S. companies, and the U.S. govern-ment, do to meet the latest Japanese challenge?

RISK ANALYSIS IN CAPITAL BUDGETING

In Chapter 12 we explained, in general terms, how risk is defined, the proce-dures managers and security analysts use to measure risk, and the relationship between risk and return. In Chapter 13 we discussed time value of money concepts, which enabled us to cover the basic principles of capital budgeting in Chapter 14. In this chapter, we combine the topics of risk and capital budgeting to explain how managers incorporate risk measures into cap-ital budgeting decisions. In addition, we cover several special topics in capital budgeting, including the replacement decision, the comparison of projects with unequal lives, and the effect of inflation on capital budgeting decisions.

INTRODUCTION TO RISK ASSESSMENT

stand-alone risk
The risk an asset has dis-regarding the facts that it is only one asset in the firm's portfolio of assets and that stockholders are also diversified; it is mea-sured by the variability of the asset's expected returns.

within-firm risk
Risk not considering the effects of stockholders' diversification; it is mea-sured by a project's ef-fect on the firm's earn-ings variability. This risk is also called *corporate risk.*

market, or beta, risk
That part of a project's risk that cannot be elimi-nated by diversification; it is measured by the project's beta coefficient.

Risk analysis is important in all financial decisions, especially those relating to capital budgeting. Three distinct types of project risk can be identified: (1) the project's own **stand-alone risk,** or its risk disregarding the facts that it is only one asset in the firm's portfolio of assets and that the firm in question is only one stock in most investors' stock portfolios; (2) **within-firm risk,** which is the effect a project has on the company's risk without consideration for the effects of the stockholders' own personal diversification; and (3) **market,** or **beta, risk,** which is project risk assessed from the standpoint of an investor who holds a highly diversified portfolio. As we shall see, a particular project may have high stand-alone risk, yet it may not have much effect on either the firm's risk or that of its owners because of portfolio effects.

A project's stand-alone risk is measured by the variability of the project's expected returns; its within-firm risk is measured by the project's impact on the firm's earnings variability; and its market risk is measured by the project's effect on the firm's beta coefficient. Taking on a project with a high degree of either stand-alone or within-firm risk will not necessarily affect the firm's beta to any great extent, and hence the project might not appear very risky to a well diversified stockholder. To better illustrate this point, let us recall that the beta coefficient reflects only that part of an investor's risk which cannot be eliminated by forming a large portfolio of stocks. If an investor holds a portfolio consisting of 100 companies' stocks, and if each company is considering 20 equal-sized projects, then the project in question is only one of 2,000 projects from the investor's point of view. Therefore, even if the project produces a return of negative 100 percent, this would not make much difference within the overall portfolio, and the law of large numbers suggests that the loss would be offset by gains in some of the other 1,999 remaining projects.

In theory, a project's stand-alone risk should be of little or no concern. However, it is actually of great practical importance, for the following reasons:

1. It is much easier to estimate a project's stand-alone risk than its within-firm risk, and it is far easier to measure stand-alone risk than market risk.

2. In the majority of cases, all three types of risk are highly correlated — if the general economy does well, so will the firm, and if the firm does well, so will most of its projects. Thus, stand-alone risk is generally a good indicator of hard-to-measure market risk.

3. Because of Points 1 and 2, if management wants a reasonably accurate assessment of a project's riskiness, it ought to spend considerable effort on ascertaining the riskiness of the project's own cash flows — that is, its stand-alone risk. The starting point for analyzing a project's stand-alone risk involves determining the uncertainty inherent in the project's cash flows, which can be done through informal judgments or through complex economic and statistical analyses involving large-scale computer models.

Now let's consider within-firm and market (or beta) risk. To illustrate the difference between within-firm and beta risk, suppose 100 firms in the oil business each drill one wildcat well. Each company has $1 million of capital that it will invest in its well. If a firm strikes oil, it will get a return of $2.4 million and earn a profit of $1.4 million, whereas if it hits a dry hole, it will lose its $1 million investment and go bankrupt. The probability of striking oil is 50 percent. Each firm's expected rate of return is 20 percent, calculated as follows:

$$\text{Expected rate} \atop \text{of return} = \frac{\text{Expected profit}}{\text{Investment}} = \frac{0.5(-\$1 \text{ million}) + 0.5(+\$1.4 \text{ million})}{\$1 \text{ million}}$$

$$= \frac{-\$500,000 + \$700,000}{\$1,000,000} = 20\%.$$

Note, however, that even though the expected return is 20 percent, there is a 50 percent probability of each firm's being wiped out. From the standpoint of the individual firms, this is a very risky business.

Although the risk to each individual firm is high, if a stockholder constructs a portfolio consisting of a few shares of each of the 100 companies, the riskiness of this portfolio will not be high at all. Some of the firms will strike oil and do well, others will miss and go out of business, but the portfolio's return will be very close to the expected 20 percent. Therefore, because investors can diversify away the risks inherent in each of the individual companies, these risks are *not market-related;* that is, they do not affect the companies' beta coefficients. The firms remain quite risky from the standpoint of their managers and employees, however, who bear risks similar to those borne by undiversified stockholders.

With this background, *we may define the within-firm risk of a capital budgeting project as the probability that the project will incur losses which will, at a minimum, destabilize the corporation's earnings and, at the extreme, cause it to go bankrupt.* A project with a high degree of either stand-alone or within-firm risk will not necessarily affect the firm's beta to any great extent, as our hypothetical example demonstrated. On the other hand, if a project has highly uncertain returns, and if those returns are highly correlated with those of the firm's other assets and also with most other assets in the economy, the project will have a high degree of all types of risk.

For example, suppose General Motors decides to undertake a major expansion to build solar-powered automobiles. Because GM is not sure how its technology will work on a mass production basis, there are great risks in the venture — its stand-alone risk is high. Management also estimates that the project will have a higher probability of success if the economy is strong, for then people will have the money to spend on the new automobiles. This means that the project will tend to do well if GM's other divisions also do well and to do badly if other divisions do badly. This being the case, the project will also have high within-firm risk. Finally, since GM's prospects are highly correlated with those of most other firms, the project's beta coefficient will also be high. Thus, this project will be risky under all three definitions of risk.

Market, or beta, risk is important because of beta's direct effect on the value of a firm's stock. Beta affects k, and k affects the stock price. (This relationship will be explored in detail in Chapter 17.) At the same time, within-firm risk, often called *corporate risk,* is also important for three primary reasons:

1. Undiversified stockholders, including the owners of small businesses, are more concerned about corporate risk than about market risk.

2. Many financial theorists argue that investors, even those who are well diversified, consider factors other than market risk when setting required returns. Empirical studies of the determinants of required rates of return generally find that both market and corporate risk affect stock prices.

3. A firm's stability is important to its managers, workers, customers, suppliers, and creditors, as well as to the community in which it operates. Firms that are in serious danger of bankruptcy, or even of suffering low profits and reduced output, have difficulty attracting and retaining good managers and workers. Also, both suppliers and customers are reluctant to depend on weak firms, and such firms will have difficulty borrowing money except at high interest rates. These factors tend to reduce risky firms' profitability and hence the price of their stocks, and, thus, they also make corporate risk significant.[1]

Market (or Beta) Risk

The types of risk analysis discussed thus far in the chapter provide insights into projects' risks and thus help managers make better accept/reject decisions. However, these risk measures do not take into account the reduction of risk that is possible when projects are combined and evaluated as part of a portfolio of projects. In this section, we show how the Capital Asset Pricing Model (CAPM) can be used to evaluate projects as portfolios and thereby overcome the shortcomings of risk measures. Of course, the CAPM has shortcomings of its own, but it nevertheless offers useful insights into risk analysis in capital budgeting.

The CAPM provides a framework for analyzing the relationship between risk and return, and we used it in Chapter 12 to analyze the relationship between risk and return in portfolios of financial assets. The fundamental premise of this analysis is that the higher the risk associated with an investment, the higher the expected rate of return must be to compensate investors for assuming risk. This same principle holds for managers evaluating capital budgeting investment opportunities for a firm. The CAPM holds that there is a minimum required rate of return, even if there are no risks, plus a premium for all nondiversifiable risks associated with the investment. Thus

$$\text{Required rate of return} = \text{Risk-free rate} + \text{Risk premium},$$

which translates into the Security Market Line (SML) equation to express this risk/return relationship:

$$k = k_{RF} + (k_M - k_{RF})b.$$

Here the required return on an investment, k, is equal to the risk-free rate, k_{RF}, plus a risk premium that is equal to the market risk premium, $k_M - k_{RF}$, times the stock's beta coefficient, b.[2] The greater the nondiversifiable risk from a stock or project, the greater the beta and hence the larger the risk premium.

For example, consider the case of Chicago Steel Company, an integrated producer operating in the Great Lakes region. Chicago Steel's beta is 1.1, so if $k_{RF} = 8\%$ and $k_M = 12\%$, then

$$k = 8\% + (12\% - 8\%)1.1$$

$$= 8\% + (4\%)1.1$$

$$= 12.4\%.$$

---

[1] In Chapter 12, we noted that one measure of risk was the standard deviation. Other techniques for measuring corporate risk such as sensitivity analysis, scenario analysis, and simulation techniques are discussed in Brigham and Gapenski, *Intermediate Financial Management,* 3rd ed., Chapter 9.

[2] Note that both the risk-free rate, k_{RF}, and the return on a diversified portfolio of securities, k_M, are market determined and thus outside the control of the firm.

hurdle rate

The discount rate using the IRR method which determines whether a project should be accepted or rejected.

This suggests that investors would be willing to give Chicago Steel money to invest in average-risk projects if the company could earn 12.4 percent or more on this money. By average-risk projects, we mean projects having risk similar to the firm's existing assets. Therefore, as a first approximation, Chicago Steel should invest in capital projects if and only if these projects have an expected return of 12.4 percent or more.[3] In other words, Chicago Steel should use 12.4 percent as its discount rate to determine average-risk projects' NPVs or as the **hurdle rate** if the IRR method is used.

Suppose, however, that taking on a particular project would cause a change in Chicago's beta coefficient and, hence, would change the company's cost of equity capital. For example, suppose Chicago Steel is considering the construction of a fleet of barges to haul iron ore, and barge operations have betas of 1.5 rather than 1.1. Since the firm itself may be regarded as a "portfolio of assets," and since the beta of any portfolio is a weighted average of the betas of the individual assets, taking on the barge project would cause the overall corporate beta to rise to somewhere between the original beta of 1.1 and the barge project's beta of 1.5. The exact value of the new beta would depend on the relative size of the investment in barge operations versus Chicago's other assets. If 80 percent of Chicago's total funds ended up in basic steel operations with a beta of 1.1 and 20 percent in barge operations with a beta of 1.5, the new corporate beta would be 1.18:

$$\text{New beta} = 0.8(1.1) + 0.2(1.5)$$

$$= 1.18.$$

This increase in Chicago's beta coefficient would cause the stock price to decline *unless the increased beta were offset by a higher expected rate of return*. Specifically, taking on the new project would cause the overall corporate cost of capital to rise from 12.4 percent to 12.72 percent:

$$k_{(new)} = 8\% + (4\%)1.18$$

$$= 12.72\%.$$

Therefore, to keep the barge investment from lowering the value of the firm, Chicago's overall expected rate of return must also rise from 12.4 percent to 12.72 percent.

If investments in basic steel earn 12.4 percent, how much must the barge investment earn to cause the new overall rate of return to equal 12.72 percent? We know that if Chicago Steel undertakes the barge investment, it will have 80 percent of its assets invested in basic steel earning 12.4 percent and 20 percent

---

[3]To simplify things somewhat, we assume at this point that the firm uses only equity capital. If debt is used, the cost of capital used must be a weighted average of the cost of debt and equity. This point is discussed at length in Chapters 19 and 20.

in barge operations earning "X" percent, and that the average required rate of return will be 12.72 percent. Therefore,

$$0.8(12.4\%) + 0.2(X) = 12.72\%$$

$$0.2(X) = 2.8\%$$

$$X = 14.0\%.$$

Thus, we see that the barge project must have an expected rate of return of at least 14 percent if the total corporation is to earn its new cost of capital.

In summary, if Chicago Steel takes on the barge project, its corporate beta will rise from 1.1 to 1.18; its overall required rate of return will rise from 12.4 percent to 12.72 percent; and the barge investment will have to earn 14 percent if the company is to earn its new overall cost of capital. If the barge investment has an expected return of more than 14 percent, taking it on will increase the value of Chicago's stock. If the expected return is less than 14 percent, taking it on will decrease the stock's value. If its expected return is exactly 14 percent, the barge project will be a breakeven proposition in terms of its effect on the value of the stock.

This line of reasoning leads to the conclusion that, if the beta coefficient for each project could be determined, then an individual project's cost of capital could be found as follows:

$$k_{Project} = k_{RF} + (k_M - k_{RF})b_{Project}.$$

Thus, for basic steel projects with $b = 1.1$, Chicago should use 12.4 percent as the discount rate. The barge project, with $b = 1.5$, should be evaluated at a 14 percent discount rate:

$$k_{Barge} = 8\% + (4\%)1.5$$

$$= 8\% + 6\%$$

$$= 14\%.$$

On the other hand, a low-risk project such as a new steel distribution center with a beta of only 0.5 would have a cost of capital of 10 percent:

$$k_{Center} = 8\% + (4\%)0.5$$

$$= 10\%.$$

Figure 15-1 gives a graphic summary of these concepts as applied to Chicago Steel. Note the following points:

1. The SML is the same Security Market Line that we developed in Chapter 12. It shows how investors are willing to make tradeoffs between risk, as measured by beta, and expected returns. The higher the beta risk, the higher the rate of return needed to compensate investors for bearing this risk. The SML specifies the nature of this relationship.

Figure 15-1 **Using the Security Market Line Concept in Capital Budgeting**

The Security Market Line (SML) can be used in the accept/reject decision for potential projects in capital budgeting decisions. A project whose expected rate of return lies on or above the SML should be accepted. A project whose return falls below the SML should be rejected because its return will not be high enough to overcome its higher risk. In this case Project M would be accepted, whereas Project N would be rejected.

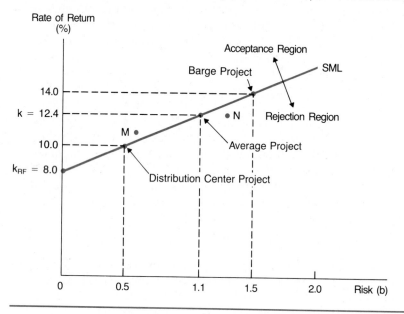

2. Chicago Steel initially had a beta of 1.1, so its required rate of return on average-risk investments is 12.4 percent.

3. High-risk investments such as the barge project require higher rates of return, whereas low-risk investments such as the distribution center require lower rates of return. It is not shown in Figure 15-1, but if Chicago makes relatively large investments in either high- or low-risk projects, as opposed to those with average risks, the corporate beta, and therefore the required rate of return on the common stock (k_s), will change.

4. If the expected rate of return on a given capital project lies *above* the SML, the expected rate of return on the project is more than enough to compensate for its risk, so the project should be accepted. Conversely, if the project's rate of return lies *below* the SML, it should be rejected. Projects that lie *on* the SML should be accepted, as their returns exactly compensate for their risk. Thus, Project M in Figure 15-1 is acceptable, whereas Project N should be rejected. Even though Project N has a higher expected rate of return than Project M, the differential is not enough to offset Project N's much higher risk.

Diversification to Reduce Risk

As we have seen, a security might be quite risky if held in isolation but not very risky if held as part of a well-diversified portfolio. The same thing is true of capital budgeting. The returns on an individual project might be highly uncertain, but if the project is small relative to the total activities of the firm, and if its returns are not highly correlated with the firm's other assets, the project may not be very risky in either the corporate or the beta sense.

Many firms do make serious efforts to diversify; often this is a specific objective of the long-run strategic plan. For example, Du Pont diversified into both coal and oil to broaden its operating base, and real estate developers have diversified geographically to lessen the effect of a slowdown in one region. The major objective of many such moves is to stabilize earnings, reduce corporate risk, and thereby raise the value of the firm's stock.

The wisdom of corporate diversification designed to reduce risk has been questioned — why should a firm diversify when stockholders can so easily diversify on their own? In other words, while it may be true that if the returns on Du Pont's and Conoco's stocks are not perfectly positively correlated then merging the companies (as happened) will reduce their risks somewhat, would it not be just as easy for investors to carry out this risk-reducing diversification directly, without all the trouble and expense of a merger?

As you might suspect, the answer is not so simple. Although stockholders could directly obtain some of the risk-reducing benefits through personal diversification, other benefits can be gained only by diversification at the corporate level. For example, a relatively stable corporation may be able to attract a better work force, and also might be able to use more low-cost debt, than could two less stable firms. And, of course, there may also be spillover effects from mergers. For example, Du Pont provided Conoco with a more stable market for its oil, while Conoco provided Du Pont with a stable supply of raw materials. Further, the two companies' research departments are reported to have gained economies of scale from combined operations.

In the previous paragraph we pointed out some benefits obtained from diversification at the corporate level. We should also mention some complications that corporations have experienced in recent years in their rush to diversify. Such negative results include (1) a corporate culture clash which hurts both firms, (2) a management which is spread "too thin," and (3) a situation in which top management of the acquiring firm has insufficient expertise in the business of the acquired firm to direct its operations. In fact, in recent years we have seen numerous thrift institutions and banks diversify themselves right into bankruptcy. Their regulators gave them the power to venture into new areas, but no one gave them the expertise to manage the acquired businesses properly.

Conclusions on Project Risk

We have discussed the three types of risk normally considered in capital budgeting analyses — stand-alone risk, within-firm (or corporate) risk, and market (or beta) risk — and we have discussed ways of assessing each. However, two important questions remain: (1) To what extent should a firm be concerned with stand-alone and within-firm risk in its capital budgeting decisions? (2) What do we do when the stand-alone or within-firm assessments and the market risk assessment lead to different conclusions?

These questions do not have easy answers. From a theoretical standpoint, well-diversified investors should be concerned only with market risk, managers should be concerned only with stock price maximization, and these two factors should lead to the conclusion that market (or beta) risk ought to be given virtually all the weight in capital budgeting decisions. However, if investors are not well diversified, if market imperfections prevent the CAPM from functioning as theory says it should, or if measurement problems keep management from implementing the CAPM approach in capital budgeting, it may be appropriate to give stand-alone and within-firm risk more weight than theory would suggest. Moreover, the CAPM does not consider bankruptcy and other costs associated with financial weakness, even though such costs are in reality often very substantial, and the probability of bankruptcy depends on a firm's corporate risk, not on its beta risk. Therefore, one could easily conclude that even well-diversified investors should want a firm's management to give at least some consideration to a project's within-firm risk instead of concentrating exclusively on market risk.

Although we would like to be able to reconcile these problems and to measure project risk on some absolute scale, the best anyone can do in practice is to determine project risk in a somewhat nebulous, relative sense. For example, the financial manager can generally say with a fair degree of confidence that a particular project has more or less stand-alone risk than the firm's average project. Then, assuming that stand-alone and within-firm, or corporate, risk are highly correlated (which is typical), the project's stand-alone risk will be a good reflection of its relative corporate risk. Finally, assuming that market risk and corporate risk are highly correlated (as studies suggest), a project with more corporate risk than average will also have a relatively high degree of market risk.

What does all this mean to the financial manager? He or she should make as good an assessment as possible of each project's relative stand-alone risk, corporate risk, and market risk. If these three types of risk are higher than average for a given project, that project's cost of capital should be increased relative to the firm's overall cost of capital. If these three types of risk are below average, the adjustment should be reversed. Unfortunately, it is impossible to specify exactly how large the adjustments should be. However, one rule-of-thumb some companies follow is to rank projects into three groups, low risk, average risk, and high risk. Then, the corporate cost of capital is used to evaluate average-risk projects, that rate is reduced by one percentage point for low-risk projects, and it is increased by one percentage point for high-risk projects. This process is arbitrary, but it does force management to address the issue of risk, and it appears to be a step in the right direction.

Self-Test

Describe the three types of project risk.

How is a project's stand-alone risk measured?

How is within-firm (or corporate) risk measured?

How is market risk measured?

List three reasons why within-firm (or corporate) risk is important.

List three reasons why, in practice, a project's stand-alone risk is important.

Explain what is meant by the term "average-risk project," and tell how one would find the cost of capital for such a project, for a "low-risk project," and for a "high-risk project."

Complete the following sentence: An increase in a company's beta coefficient would cause the stock price to decline unless . . .

Does a merger which lowers a company's risk by stabilizing earnings necessarily benefit stockholders?

Are there any good reasons why a firm might want to diversify when stockholders can just as easily diversify on their own?

In theory, is it correct for a firm to be concerned with stand-alone and within-firm risk in its capital budgeting decisions? Should the firm be concerned with these risks in practice?

If a project's stand-alone, within-firm, and market risk are highly correlated, would this make the task of measuring risk easier or harder? Explain.

OTHER TOPICS IN CAPITAL BUDGETING

In Chapter 14 we identified the techniques financial managers use to evaluate capital budgeting projects. Several important topics were omitted from that discussion, however. In the remainder of this chapter we will consider some of these special topics, including the replacement decision, the comparison of projects with unequal lives, and the effect of inflation on the evaluation of real assets.

Replacement Decisions

The example of Houston Trucking Company's decision to purchase a new van was used in Chapter 14 to illustrate how expansion projects are analyzed. Not all project analysis is for new projects, however — some investment opportunities are evaluated as part of replacement decisions, and the analysis for a **replacement decision** is somewhat different from that for expansion projects. These differences are illustrated here with a capital equipment (coffee roaster) replacement analysis for Gourmet Coffee International (GCI).

GCI of New Orleans roasts, blends, and packages coffee from imported beans for specialty shop owners in the Gulf Coast area. The company's man-

replacement decision
The decision of whether or not to replace an existing asset that is still productive with a new one. Replacement projects are by definition mutually exclusive.

agement is evaluating the purchase of a new coffee bean roaster that is quicker and more efficient than GCI's old roasting machine. This old, relatively inefficient roaster was purchased nine years ago at a cost of $300,000. The machine had an original expected life of 15 years and a zero estimated salvage value at the end of its expected life. It is being depreciated on a straight line basis and currently has a book value of $120,000.[4] The production manager reports that a new, faster machine can be purchased and installed for $325,000. Over its 6-year life, the new machine is expected to expand sales from $200,000 to $230,000 a year and, furthermore, to reduce labor usage sufficiently to cut annual operating costs from $140,000 to $100,000. The new machine, which will be depreciated using the MACRS method, has an estimated salvage value of $40,000 at the end of its 6-year life. The old machine's current market value is $20,000; the firm's marginal tax rate is 40 percent; and its cost of capital is 10 percent. Should GCI buy the new coffee roasting machine?

Table 15-1 shows the worksheet format the company uses to analyze replacement projects.[5] Each line is numbered, and a line-by-line description of the table follows.

Line 1. The top section of the table, Lines 1 through 4, sets forth the cash flows which occur at (approximately) $t = 0$, the time the investment is made. Line 1 shows the purchase price of the new machine, including installation and freight charges. Since it is an outflow, it is negative.

Line 2. Here we show the price received from the sale of the old equipment.

Line 3. Since the old equipment would be sold at less than its $120,000 book value, the sale would create a $100,000 loss, which would reduce the firm's taxable income and hence its next quarterly income tax payment. The tax savings is equal to $(Loss)(T) = ($100,000)(0.40) = $40,000$, where T is the marginal corporate tax rate. The Tax Code defines this loss as an operating loss, because it reflects the fact that inadequate depreciation was taken on the old asset. If there had been a profit on the sale (that is, if the sale price had exceeded book value), Line 3 would have shown taxes *paid,* a cash out-

---

[4]This machine was purchased prior to the Tax Act of 1981, so MACRS was not in place at the time. The company chose to depreciate the roasting machine on a straight line basis.

[5]Note that the replacement analysis shown here is more complex than the expansion example discussed in Chapter 14. Thus, we have chosen to use a worksheet approach rather than the approach based on Equation 14-1 as discussed at the beginning of Chapter 14. However, Equation 14-1 could have been used to develop any of the operating cash inflows shown in Table 15-1. For example, GCI's Year 1 operating cash inflow could have been calculated as

$$CF_1 = ($30,000 - -$40,000)(1 - 0.4) + ($65,000 - $20,000)(0.4)$$

$$= $42,000 + $18,000 = $60,000.$$

The systematic worksheet approach makes it less likely that some relevant cash flow or tax effect may be missed. Also, most firms conduct analyses like this one by using personal computers and spreadsheet programs such as *Lotus 1-2-3,* and the worksheet format we use fits perfectly into a *Lotus 1-2-3* format.

Table 15-1 **Replacement Decision Worksheet**

I. Net Cash Flows at the Time the Investment Is Made (t = 0)

1. Cost of new equipment	($325,000)
2. Price received for old equipment	20,000
3. Tax savings on sale of old equipment	40,000
4. Total net investment	($265,000)

II. Operating Inflows over the Project's Life

Year:	0	1	2	3	4	5	6
5. After-tax increase in sales and decrease in costs		$42,000	$ 42,000	$42,000	$42,000	$42,000	$42,000
6. Depreciation on new machine		$65,000	$104,000	$61,750	$39,000	$35,750	$19,500
7. Depreciation on old machine		20,000	20,000	20,000	20,000	20,000	20,000
8. Change in depreciation (6 − 7)		$45,000	$ 84,000	$41,750	$19,000	$15,750	($ 500)
9. Tax savings from change in depreciation (0.4 × 8)		18,000	33,600	16,700	7,600	6,300	(200)
10. Net operating cash flows (5 + 9)		$60,000	$ 75,600	$58,700	$49,600	$48,300	$41,800

III. Terminal Year Cash Flows

11. Estimated salvage value of new machine							$40,000
12. Tax on salvage value							16,000
13. Total termination cash flows							$24,000

IV. Net Cash Flows

	0	1	2	3	4	5	6
14. Total net cash flows	($265,000)	$60,000	$ 75,600	$58,700	$49,600	$48,300	$65,800

V. Results

Payback period: 4.4 years
IRR: 9.6% versus 10% cost of capital
NPV: − $2,862.68

flow. In the actual case, the equipment would be sold at a loss, so no taxes would be paid, and the company would realize a tax savings of $40,000.

Line 4. Here we show the total net cash outflow at the time the replacement is made. The company writes a check for $325,000 to pay for the machine; however, this outlay is partially offset by proceeds from the sale of the old equipment and by reduced taxes. Note that if additional net working capital were required as a result of the capital budgeting decision, as would generally be true for expansion investments (as opposed to cost-reducing replacement investments), this factor would have to be taken into account. The amount of net working capital (additional current assets required as a result of the expansion minus any spontaneously generated funds) would be estimated and added to the initial cash outlay. We assume that GCI will not need any additional working capital, so that factor is not relevant in this example.

Line 5. Section II of the table shows the *incremental operating cash flows,* or benefits, that are expected if the replacement is made. The first of these benefits is the increase in sales and the reduction in operating costs shown on Line 5. Cash flows increase because sales are increased (by $30,000) and operating costs are reduced (by $40,000), for a total of $70,000, but increased sales and reduced costs also mean higher taxable income and hence higher income taxes:

Increase in sales plus reduction in costs = Δ sales + Δ cost =	$70,000
Associated increase in taxes = T(Δ sales + Δ cost) = 0.4($70,000) =	28,000
Increase in net after-tax cash flows due to sales increase	
and cost reduction = Δ NCF =	$42,000
Δ NCF = (Δ sales + Δ cost)(1 − T) = ($70,000)(0.6) =	$42,000

Note that the $70,000 sales increase and cost savings is constant over Years 1 through 6; had this amount been expected to change over time, this fact would have to be built into the analysis.

Line 6. The depreciable basis of the new machine, $325,000, is multiplied by the appropriate MACRS recovery allowance for 5-year class property (see Chapter 2) to obtain the depreciation figures shown on Line 6. Note that if you summed across Line 6, the total would be $325,000, the depreciable basis.

Line 7. Line 7 shows the $20,000 per year straight line depreciation on the old machine. This is found by dividing the old machine's original life of 15 years into its purchase price of $300,000. Nine years' worth of depreciation has been taken, while 6 years' has not.

Line 8. The depreciation expense on the old machine as shown on Line 7 can no longer be taken if the replacement is made, but the new machine's depreciation will be available. Therefore, the $20,000 depreciation on the old machine is subtracted from that on the new machine to show the net change in annual depreciation. The change is positive in Years 1 through 5 but negative in Year 6. The Year 6 negative net change in annual depreciation signifies that the purchase of the replacement machine results in a *decrease* in depreciation expense during that year versus what would have occurred otherwise.

Line 9. The net change in depreciation results in a tax reduction (increase in Year 6) which is equal to the change in depreciation multiplied by the tax rate: Depreciation tax savings = T(Change in depreciation) = 0.40($45,000) = $18,000 for Year 1. Note that the relevant cash flow is the tax savings on the *net change* in depreciation, not just the depreciation on the new equipment. Capital budgeting decisions are based on *incremental* cash flows, and since GCI will lose $20,000 of depreciation if it replaces the old machine, that fact must be taken into account.

Line 10. Here we show the net operating cash flows over the project's 6-year life. These flows are found by adding the after-tax sales increase and cost decrease to the depreciation tax savings, or Line 5 + Line 9.

Line 11. Part III shows the cash flows associated with the termination of the project. To begin, Line 11 shows the estimated **salvage value** of the new machine at the end of its 6-year life, $40,000.

Line 12. Since the book value of the new machine at the end of Year 6 will be zero, the company will have to pay taxes of $40,000(0.4) = $16,000.

Line 13. Here we show the total cash flows resulting from terminating the project. Note that if additional working capital had been required and included in the initial cash outlay, that amount would have been added to the final year's cash flow, because the working capital would be recovered when the project was completed.

Line 14. Part IV shows, on Line 14, the total net cash flows in a form suitable for capital budgeting evaluation. In effect, Line 14 is a "time line." These cash flows can now be used to determine the project's NPV based on GCI's 10 percent cost of capital:

salvage value
The market price of a capital asset at the end of a specified period. In a capital budgeting decision, it is also the current market price of an asset being considered for replacement.

$$
\begin{aligned}
\text{NPV} &= \sum_{t=1}^{6} \frac{CF_t}{(1 + k)^t} - \text{Cost} \\[2mm]
&= \left(\frac{\$60,000}{(1.1)^1} + \frac{\$75,600}{(1.1)^2} + \frac{\$58,700}{(1.1)^3} \right. \\[2mm]
&\quad \left. + \frac{\$49,600}{(1.1)^4} + \frac{\$48,300}{(1.1)^5} + \frac{\$65,800}{(1.1)^6} \right) - \$265,000 \\[2mm]
&= [\$60,000(0.9091) + \$75,600(0.8264) + \$58,700(0.7513) \\[2mm]
&\quad + \$49,600(0.6830) + \$48,300(0.6209) + \$65,800(0.5645)] - \$265,000 \\[2mm]
&= \$262,133.52 - \$265,000 \\[2mm]
&= -\$2,866.48.
\end{aligned}
$$

Part V of the table, "Results," shows the replacement project's payback period, IRR, and NPV. Because the NPV is negative, GCI should not replace the old coffee bean roaster with the newer, more efficient machine. If the NPV had been positive, the decision would have been to replace the old machine. Alternatively, had we set NPV equal to zero and solved for the IRR, we would have found that the IRR = 9.6%. Since the required rate of return = 10%, and the IRR < 10%, this second method reaffirms the decision not to replace the old machine.

Comparing Projects with Unequal Lives

To simplify matters, our example of replacement decisions assumed that the new coffee roasting machine had a life equal to the remaining life of the existing one. Suppose, however, that we must choose between two mutually exclusive replacement alternatives that have *different* lives. For example, Machine S has an expected life of 10 years, whereas Machine L has a 15-year life. The most typical procedure for solving problems of this type is to set up a series of *replacement chains* extending out to the "common denominator" year — that is, the year in which both alternatives require replacement. For Machines S and L this would be Year 30, so it would be necessary to compare a 3-chain cycle for S, the 10-year machine, with a 2-chain cycle for L, the 15-year one.

replacement chain method

A method of comparing projects of unequal lives which assumes that each project can be replicated as many times as necessary to reach a common life span; the NPVs over this life span are then compared, and the project with the higher common life NPV is chosen.

To illustrate the **replacement chain method,** suppose a firm is considering the replacement of a fully depreciated printing press with a new one. The plant in which the press is used is profitable and is expected to continue in operation for many years. The old press could continue to be used indefinitely, but it is not as efficient as new presses. Two replacement machines are available. Press A has a cost of $36,100, will last for 5 years, and will produce after-tax incremental cash flows of $9,700 per year for 5 years. Press B has a cost of $57,500, will last for 10 years, and will produce net cash flows of $9,500 per year. Both the costs and performances of Presses A and B have been constant in recent years and are expected to remain constant in the future. The company's cost of capital is 10 percent.

Should the old press be replaced, and, if so, with A or with B? To answer these questions, we first calculate A's NPV as follows:

$$NPV_A = \$9,700(3.7908) - \$36,100 = \$36,771 - \$36,100 = \$671.$$

B's NPV is calculated as follows:

$$NPV_B = \$9,500(6.1446) - \$57,500 = \$58,374 - \$57,500 = \$874.$$

These calculations suggest that the old press should indeed be replaced and that Press B should be selected. However, the analysis is incomplete, and the decision to choose Press B is *incorrect.* If the company chooses Press A, it will have an opportunity to make another new investment after 5 years, and this second investment will *also* be profitable. However, if it chooses Press B, it will not have this second investment opportunity. Therefore, to make a proper comparison of Presses A and B, we must find the present value of Press A over a 10-year period and compare it with Press B over the same 10 years.

The NPV for Press B as calculated previously is correct as it stands. For Press A, however, we must take three additional steps: (1) determine the NPV of the second Press A five years hence, (2) bring this NPV back to the present, and (3) sum these two component NPVs:

1. If we assume that the cost and annual cash flows of Press A will not change if the project is repeated in 5 years and that the firm's cost of capital will remain at 10 percent, then Press A's NPV will remain the same as its first-stage NPV, $671. However, the second NPV will not accrue for five years, and hence it represents a present value at t = 5.

2. The present value (at t = 0) of the purchase of a second printing Press A is determined by discounting the second NPV (at t = 5) back five years at 10 percent to determine its present value at t = 0: $671(PVIF$_{10\%,5 \text{ years}}$) = $671(0.6209) = $417.

3. The true NPV of Press A is $671 + $417 = $1,088. This is the value that should be compared with the NPV of Press B, $874.

The value of the firm will increase more if the old press is replaced by Press A than if the firm goes with Press B; therefore Press A should be selected.

Self-Test

Briefly explain the steps involved in a replacement decision.

What are the primary differences between a replacement analysis and an expansion analysis?

Briefly explain how replacement analysis must be changed when the assets being compared have different lives.

EFFECTS OF INFLATION ON CAPITAL BUDGETING ANALYSIS

Inflation is a fact of life in the United States and most other nations, and thus it must be considered in any sound capital budgeting analysis. Several procedures are available for dealing with inflation. The two most frequently used methods are (1) to explicitly adjust the discount rate and (2) to make no explicit adjustment in the discount rate but to adjust the expected cash flows to reflect expected inflation. Both methods are discussed in this section.

To see how inflation enters the picture, suppose an investor lends $100 for 1 year at a rate of 5 percent. At the end of the year the investor will have $100(1.05) = $105. However, if prices rise by 6 percent during the year, the ending $105 will have a purchasing power, in terms of beginning-of-year values, of only $105/1.06 = $99. Thus the investor will have lost $1, or 1 percent of the original purchasing power, in spite of having earned 5 percent interest: $105 at the end of the year will buy only as much in goods as $99 would have bought at the beginning of the year.

Investors recognize this problem, and, as we learned in earlier chapters, they incorporate expectations about inflation into the required rate of return. For example, suppose investors seek a *real rate of return* (k_r) of 8 percent on an investment with a given degree of risk. Suppose further that they anticipate an *annual rate of inflation (i)* of 6 percent. Then, to end up with the 8 percent real rate of return, the *nominal rate of return (k_n)* must be a value such that

$$k_n = k_r + i$$

$$= 8\% + 6\% = 14\%.$$

Here the expected inflation rate, i, is equivalent to the inflation premium, IP, that we discussed in Chapter 4. Note also that, except for Treasury securities, k_r includes a default risk premium.

We can use these concepts to analyze capital budgeting under inflation. First, note that a project's NPV in the absence of inflation, where $k_r = k_n$ and RCF_t = the *real* net cash flow in Year t (based on t = 0 dollars), is calculated as follows:

$$NPV = \sum_{t=1}^{n} \frac{RCF_t}{(1 + k_r)^t} - \text{Cost.}$$

Next, suppose the situation changes. We now expect inflation to occur, and we expect both sales prices and input costs to rise at the rate i, the same inflation rate that is built into the estimated cost of capital. Under these conditions, the *nominal* cash flow (CF_t) will increase annually at the rate of i percent, producing this situation:

$$CF_t = \text{Actual (nominal) cash flow}_t = RCF_t(1 + i)^t.$$

For example, if a net cash flow of $100 is expected in Year 5 in the absence of inflation, then with a 5 percent rate of inflation, $CF_5 = \$100(1.05)^5 = \$127.63$.

Now if net cash flows increase at the rate of i percent per year, and if this same inflation factor is built into the cost of capital by investors seeking to protect their purchasing power, then

$$\text{Inflation-adjusted NPV} = \sum_{t=1}^{n} \frac{RCF_t(1 + i)^t}{(1 + k_n)} - \text{Cost.}$$

Remember that $k_n = k_r + i$, so the denominator in the equation has been adjusted for inflation by market forces.

This procedure is the recommended approach, but it may not be followed. People sometimes discount cash flows that have *not* been adjusted upward for inflation by the *nominal* cost of capital, which *does* include an inflation premium. This is wrong! Therefore, when the cost of capital, which usually includes an inflation risk premium, is used to discount constant dollar cash flows (not adjusted upward for expected inflation), *the resulting NPV will be downward biased.* The denominator will reflect inflation, but the numerator will not, which produces the bias. If sales prices and all costs are expected to rise at approximately the same rate, the bias can be corrected by having current cash flows increase at the inflation rate, or by using the real rate as the cost of capital.

Although it is often appropriate to assume that *variable costs* will rise at the same rate as sales prices, fixed costs (especially the depreciation associated with a project) generally increase at a lower rate. In any situation where both revenues and all costs are not expected to rise at exactly the same inflation rate as is built into the cost of capital, the best procedure is to build inflation into the basic cash flow component projections for each year. If high rates of inflation are projected, and if expected inflation rates for sales prices and input costs differ materially, such an adjustment must be made.

Self-Test

What two procedures are used to adjust the capital budgeting analysis for inflation?

What happens to the NPV when cash flows have not been adjusted for inflation, but a nominal discount rate (including an inflation premium) has been used?

SUMMARY

In this chapter, we discussed four issues in capital budgeting: risk analysis in capital budgeting, replacement decisions, replacement chains for mutually exclusive assets with unequal lives, and the effects of inflation on capital budgeting analysis.

- **Market (beta) risk** is that part of a project's risk which cannot be eliminated by diversification. It is measured by the project's beta coefficient. In theory, market risk should be the most relevant type of risk.

- **Within-firm risk (corporate risk)** reflects the effects of a project on the firm's risk, and it is measured by the project's effect on the firm's earnings variability. Stockholder diversification is not taken into account. Within-firm risk is important because it influences the firm's ability to use low-cost debt, to maintain smooth operations over time, and to avoid crises that might consume management's energy and disrupt employees, customers, suppliers, and the community.

- A project's **stand-alone risk** is the risk the project would have if it were the firm's only asset and if the firm's stockholders held only that one stock. Stand-alone risk is measured by the variability of the asset's expected returns. Stand-alone risk is often used as a proxy for both market and corporate risk, because (1) market and corporate risk are difficult to measure and (2) the three types of risk are usually highly correlated.

- Projects which are **riskier** than the firm's average project require **higher rates of return,** while **low-risk projects** require **lower rates of return.** The discount rate is increased for projects which are riskier than the firm's average project, and it is decreased for less risky projects.

- Both the **measurement of risk** and its incorporation into capital budgeting involve judgment. It is possible to use quantitative techniques as an aid to judgment, but in the final analysis the assessment of risk in capital budgeting is a subjective process.

- The analysis for a **replacement decision** is more complicated than that for an expansion decision because it is necessary to calculate the **incremental** cash flows — cash flows are produced by the new asset, but cash flows are lost from the old asset, and it is the difference between these two sets of flows which must be determined and evaluated.

- When choosing between **mutually exclusive projects** with different lives, it is necessary to adjust the NPVs using the **replacement chain method.**

- The **replacement chain method** assumes that each project being compared can be replicated as many times as is necessary to reach a common life. The NPVs are calculated for each replication, then they are discounted back to the present, and, finally, they are summed to find the total NPV of the project. The project which has the higher total NPV is chosen.

- Expected **inflation** should be accounted for in capital budgeting analysis. The most efficient way to deal with inflation is to build it into each cash flow element.

EQUATIONS

Given that the risk-free rate, the required rate of return on an average stock, and a project's beta could be determined, then an individual project's cost of capital could be found using the formula below:

$$k_{Project} = k_{RF} + (k_M - k_{RF}) \, b_{Project}.$$

The nominal rate of return consists of the real rate of return plus an inflation premium. The equation is as follows:

$$k_n = k_r + i.$$

There are two ways to account for inflation in capital budgeting analysis. One method is to discount real cash flows by a real discount rate. The equation used to find the NPV using this methodology is

$$NPV = \sum_{t=1}^{n} \frac{RCF_t}{(1 + k_r)^t} - Cost.$$

The second — and the preferred — method to adjust for inflation is to convert real cash flows to nominal cash flows by multiplying each cash flow for the time period t by $(1 + \text{inflation rate})^t$. Since the numerator includes the inflation rate, so must the denominator; therefore, the discount rate used must be a nominal discount rate (which includes an inflation premium). The equation used to find the NPV using this methodology is

$$\text{Inflation-adjusted NPV} = \sum_{t=1}^{n} \frac{RCF_t(1 + i)^t}{(1 + k_n)} - Cost.$$

RESOLUTION TO DECISION IN FINANCE

Should Government Make It Easier?

Some Japanese economists fear that so much capital spending will lead to runaway inflation and a big drop in the yen, because the capital spending binge plays such a large role in Japan's current economic expansion. At the same time, a U.S undersecretary of state expressed concern that overspending might create excessive industrial capacity and lead to worldwide price cutting. Japanese price cutting could also lead to increased imports of Japanese goods by the United States, which would further worsen our trade deficit.

A research group called Rebuild America recently warned that U.S capital budgets must include increased expenditures on new technologies or else our industrial strength will diminish. The group's report said presidential advisers should change their laissez-faire policies toward commercial ventures and give industry some assistance. The report's chief author, Lester Thurow, Dean of MIT's Sloan School of Management, pointed out in a news conference that in addition to Japan's two-to-one advantage in per capita capital spending, the United States is also behind by a third when compared with West Germany, and that both of those foreign governments pick up "50 percent of the research and development bill."

Despite these worries, growth in U.S. capital spending is forecasted to exceed growth in the gross national product during 1990 and 1991. Aircraft production should be the leading industry, with the computer industry close behind. Automobile companies, on the other hand, reported plans to cut 1990 capital spending by more than 11 percent. Spending for new buildings was also down because of an abundance of vacant office space. The general, short-term outlook, however, still calls for reasonably healthy capital investment by U.S. business.

If the government responded favorably to some of Rebuild America's suggestions, that group believes, the long-term outlook might also be less gloomy. As it is, wrote Thurow and his colleagues, "the U.S could be a second- or third-rate industrial power by the year 2000, and President Bush will be remembered as the Herbert Hoover of U.S. industrial competitiveness."

Sources: *Fortune,* "Business Spending Will Keep Contributing to Growth," June 4, 1990, and "Japan's Capital Spending Spree," April 9, 1990; Associated Press, "U.S. Must Back New Technologies," *The Gainesville Sun,* June 13, 1990.

QUESTIONS

15-1 Think about the example of GCI's coffee roasting machine purchase in Table 15-1, and answer these questions:

a. Why is the salvage value of the new machine on Line 11 reduced for taxes on Line 12?

b. Why is depreciation on the old machine deducted on Line 7 to get Line 8?

c. How would the analysis be affected if the new machine permitted a *reduction* in net working capital?

d. Why were the sales increase and cost savings figures shown on Line 5 reduced by multiplying the before-tax figure by $(1 - T)$, while the change in the depreciation figure on Line 8 was multiplied by T?

15-2   Distinguish among beta (or market) risk, within-firm (or corporate) risk, and stand-alone risk for a project being considered for inclusion in the capital budget. Which type of risk do you believe should be given the greatest weight in capital budgeting decisions? Explain.

15-3   Suppose Gonzo Technologies, which has a high beta as well as a great deal of corporate risk, merged with E-Z Patterns, Inc. E-Z Patterns' sales rise during recessions, when people are more likely to make their own clothing; consequently, its beta is negative but its corporate risk is relatively high. What would the merger do to the costs of capital in the consolidated company's technology division and in its patterns division?

15-4   Suppose a firm estimates its cost of capital for the coming year to be 10 percent. What are reasonable costs of capital for evaluating average-risk projects, high-risk projects, and low-risk projects?

SELF-TEST PROBLEMS

ST-1   You have been asked by the president of your company, Campsi Construction Company, to evaluate the proposed acquisition of a new earthmover. The earthmover's basic price is $50,000, and it will cost another $10,000 to modify it for Campsi's special use. The earthmover falls into the MACRS 3-year class. It will be sold after 3 years for $20,000. Use of the earthmover purchase will require an increase in net working capital (spare parts inventory) of $2,000. The earthmover purchase will have no effect on revenues, but it is expected to save Campsi $20,000 per year in before-tax operating costs, mainly labor. The firm's marginal tax rate is 40 percent.
   a. What is the company's net investment if it acquires the earthmover? (That is, what are the Year 0 cash flows?)
   b. What are the operating cash flows in Years 1, 2, and 3?
   c. What are the additional (nonoperating) cash flows in Year 3?
   d. If the project's cost of capital is 10 percent, should the earthmover be purchased?

ST-2   Wofford Novelty Plastics (WNP) currently uses an injection molding machine that was purchased 2 years ago. This machine is being depreciated on a straight line basis; it has 6 years of remaining life, and its current book value is $2,100. Thus, the annual depreciation expense is $2,100/6 = $350 per year. The machine currently can be sold for $2,500.
   WNP has been offered a replacement machine that has a cost of $8,000, an estimated useful life of 6 years, and an estimated salvage value of $800. This machine falls into the MACRS 5-year class. The replacement machine would permit an output expansion, so sales would rise by $1,000 per year; even so, its much greater efficiency would still cause operating expenses to decline by $1,500 per year. The new machine would require inventories to be increased by $2,000, but accounts payable would simultaneously increase by $500.
   WNP's effective tax rate is 40 percent, and its cost of capital is 15 percent. Should it replace the old machine?

PROBLEMS

15-1   **Replacement decision.** Hobbes Equipment Company is considering the purchase of a new machine to replace an obsolete one. The machine being used in current operations has both a book value and a market value of zero; it is in good working order, however, and will operate at an acceptable level for an additional 5 years. Hobbes's engineers estimate that the proposed machine will perform operations so much more efficiently that if it is installed, labor, materials, and other direct costs of the operation will decline by $42,000 annually. The proposed machine costs $112,500 delivered and installed. The asset has a tax life of 5 years and will be depreciated by the straight line method over this period (assume this is permissible). The expected salvage value of the new machine is zero. The company's cost of capital is 14 percent and its tax rate is 40 percent.

a. What is the replacement project's annual cash flow?

b. What is the project's NPV?

c. What is the project's IRR?

d. Should the old machine be replaced?

15-2 **Replacement project.** Boston Construction Company is considering replacing an old machine with a new one that will increase cash earnings before taxes by $45,000 annually. The new machine will cost $90,000 and will have an estimated life of 8 years with no salvage value. It will be depreciated over a 5-year tax life using the straight line method (assume this is permissible). The applicable corporate tax rate is 34 percent, and the firm's cost of capital is 16 percent. The old machine has been fully depreciated and has no salvage value. Calculate the net present value for the replacement project. Should the old machine be replaced by the new one?

15-3 **Replacement decision.** Nortex Manufacturing currently uses an injection molding machine that was purchased several years ago. This old machine is being depreciated on a straight line basis. It has 5 years of remaining life with zero expected salvage value. Its current book value is $4,000, and it can be sold for $4,800 at this time.

Nortex has been offered a replacement machine that has a cost of $12,800, it falls under the 5-year MACRS class life, and it has an estimated salvage value of $1,600 in Year 5. The MACRS depreciation percentages are as follows: Year 1 = 20%; Year 2 = 32%; Year 3 = 19%; Year 4 = 12%; and Year 5 = 11%. At the end of the fifth year the new machine will be sold for its salvage value. The replacement machine will permit an output expansion, so sales will rise by $1,600 annually; yet the new machine's much greater efficiency will cause operating expenses to decline by $2,400 per year. The new machine will cause inventories to increase by $3,200 and accounts payable to increase by $800.

Nortex's effective tax rate is 40 percent, and its cost of capital is 15 percent. Should it replace the old machine? *(Hint: Remember to calculate the tax on the difference between the salvage value and the book value of the replacement machine.)*

15-4 **Risk adjustment.** The risk-free rate of return is 9 percent, and the market risk premium $(k_M - k_{RF})$ is 4 percent. The beta of the project under analysis is 1.25, with the expected after-tax net cash flows estimated at $2,039 annually for 5 years. The required investment outlay for the project is $7,000.

a. What is the required risk-adjusted return on the project?

b. What is the project's NPV?

c. What is the project's IRR?

d. Should this project be accepted?

15-5 **Required rate of return.** Harrington-Wilson Technology (HWT) is considering investing in a 5-year project that has expected annual cash flows of $56,000. The project's cost is $175,000. HWT bases its required return on the Security Market Line (SML). The risk-free rate is expected to be 9 percent, and the return on an average security in the market is forecasted to be 12 percent. The firm's beta is 2.0.

a. What is the firm's required return?

b. What is the project's NPV?

c. What is the project's IRR?

d. Should the firm invest in this project?

15-6   **Risk adjustment.** The Spartan Corporation has two independent projects under consideration. Spartan's beta is 1.2. The average-risk security in the market has a return of 13 percent, and the risk-free rate is 8 percent. Project E has the same risk as Spartan's current projects, whereas Project F has a beta of 1.6. Project E has a cost of $200,000 and expected after-tax cash flows of $51,400 annually for the next 5 years. Project F also has a cost of $200,000 and expected after-tax cash flows of $58,000 annually for 5 years.

a. What is the required rate of return for each project?

b. What is the NPV for each project?

c. Which project(s) should Spartan accept?

15-7   **Risk-adjusted NPV.** Miller International is considering investing in a new capital project. The project, which has an expected productive life of 10 years, would require a $300,000 investment and promises to provide a cash flow (net income + depreciation) of $60,000 annually. Miller's cost of capital is 12 percent. However, management has determined that the project is much riskier than the firm's average projects. Miller requires an 18 percent return on high-risk projects.

a. Which rate of return, 12% or 18%, should management use in evaluating this project?

b. What is the project's NPV?

c. Should Miller invest in this project?

15-8   **Risk-adjusted NPVs.** Hinsdale Mills has an average cost of capital equaling 10 percent. The company is choosing between two mutually exclusive projects. Project B is of average risk, has a cost of $50,000, and has expected cash flows of $14,701.80 per year for 5 years. Project A is of above-average risk, and management estimates that its cost of capital would be 12 percent. Project A also costs $50,000, and it is expected to provide cash flows of $14,980.03 per year for 5 years. Calculate risk-adjusted NPVs for the two projects, and use these NPVs to choose between them.

15-9   **Replacement project.** Sierra Publishing Company is contemplating the replacement of one of its bookbinding machines with a newer and more efficient one. The old machine has a book value of $300,000 and a remaining useful life of 6 years. The firm does not expect to realize any return from scrapping the old machine in 6 years, but it can sell it now to another firm in the industry for $150,000. The old machine is being depreciated toward a zero salvage value, or by $50,000 per year, using the straight line method (assume that at the time the machine was purchased this was permissible).

The new machine has a purchase price of $1 million, a MACRS class life of 5 years, and an estimated salvage value of $75,000. It is expected to economize on electric power usage, labor, and repair costs, as well as to reduce the number of defective bindings. In total, an annual savings of $250,000 will be realized if it is installed. The company is in the 40 percent marginal tax bracket, and it has a 12 percent cost of capital.

a. What is the initial cash outlay required for the new machine?

b. Calculate the annual depreciation allowances for both machines, and compute the change in the annual depreciation expense if the replacement is made. (The appropriate MACRS depreciation percentages for a 5-year class life are these: Year 1 = 20%; Year 2 = 32%; Year 3 = 19%; Year 4 = 12%; Year 5 = 11%; and Year 6 = 6%.)

c. What are the after-tax operating cash flows in Years 1 to 6?

d. What is the after-tax cash flow from the salvage value of the new machine in Year 6?

e. Should Sierra purchase the new machine? Support your answer.

f. In general, how would each of the following factors affect the investment decision, and how should each be treated? (Give verbal answers.)

    1. The expected life of the existing machine decreases.

    2. The cost of capital is not constant but is increasing.

(Do Parts g, h, and i only if you are using the computerized problem diskette.)

g. Sierra Publishing may be able to purchase an alternative new bookbinding machine from another supplier. Its purchase price would be $850,000, but its salvage value would only be $25,000. This machine would lower annual operating costs by only $185,000. Should Sierra purchase this machine?

h. If the salvage value on the alternative new machine were $60,000 rather than $25,000, how would this affect the decision?

i. With everything as in Part h, assume that the cost of capital increased from 12 percent to 12.5 percent. How would this affect the decision?

15-10 **Unequal lives.** Modern Technology has two mutually exclusive projects code-named Gold and White. The firm must determine which of the two projects to select. The following table provides the necessary information to evaluate the projects.

	Gold	White
Cost	$30,000	$30,000
Annual after-tax cash flow	$11,000	$ 7,000
Life	4 years	8 years

If the firm's cost of capital for the projects is 14 percent, which of the two projects should be selected for investment?

15-11 **Cash flow estimate and replacement analysis.** Wonder Bakers, whose motto is, "If it's good, it's a Wonder," is considering the replacement of its oven. The old oven, with a book value of $100,000, has a useful life of 4 years and is being depreciated using the straight line method to a salvage value of zero (assume that this is permissible). If the old oven is sold today, its market value will be only $33,000. The new oven has a total cost, delivered and installed, of $120,000 and an expected salvage value of $20,000 at the end of its 4-year life. The new oven would have no effect on operating income. The firm uses the MACRS depreciation methodology and has a tax rate of 40 percent.

a. What is the initial cash outlay required for the new oven?

b. What are the after-tax operating cash flows that would result from the replacement of the old oven?

c. What is the after-tax cash flow from the salvage value of the new oven in Year 4?

d. If the firm's cost of capital is 10 percent, should Wonder replace the old oven? (The MACRS depreciation percentages for a 3-year class life are these: Year 1 = 33%; Year 2 = 45%; Year 3 = 15%; and Year 4 = 7%.)

15-12 **Cash flow estimate and replacement analysis.** Huffman Industries is considering replacing an old crane with a new one that will increase cash earnings before taxes by $120,000 per year. The new crane, which costs $240,000, will have an estimated useful life of 8 years and a salvage value of $32,000 at the end of that time. The new machine will be depreciated using a 5-year MACRS class life. The old crane, which has been in service since 1979, currently has a book value of $80,000 and a remaining life of 8 years. It is being depreciated by $10,000 per year toward a zero salvage value using the straight line method. The marginal tax rate is 40% for Huffman Industries. If replaced, the old crane can be sold now for $60,000.

a. What is the initial cash outlay required for the new crane?

b. What are the after-tax operating cash flows that occur each year as a result of the replacement decision?

c. What is the after-tax cash flow from the salvage value of the new crane in Year 6?

d. If the firm's cost of capital is 18 percent, should the replacement be made?
  (The appropriate MACRS depreciation percentages for a 5-year class life are these: Year 1 = 20%; Year 2 = 32%; Year 3 = 19%; Year 4 = 12%; Year 5 = 11%; and Year 6 = 6%.)

15-13 **CAPM approach to risk adjustments.** Toledo Rubber Company has two divisions: (1) the Tire Division, which manufactures tires for new automobiles, and (2) the Recap Division, which manufactures recapping materials that are sold to independent tire recapping shops throughout the United States. Since auto manufacturing moves up and down with the general economy, the Tire Division's earnings contribution to Toledo's stock price is highly correlated with returns on most other stocks. If the Tire Division were operated as a separate company, its beta coefficient would be about 1.60. The sales and profits of the Recap Division, on the other hand, tend to be countercyclical, as recap sales boom when people cannot afford to buy new tires. Recap's beta is estimated to be 0.40. Approximately 75 percent of Toledo's corporate assets are invested in the Tire Division and 25 percent in the Recap Division.

Currently, the rate of interest on Treasury securities is 10 percent, and the expected rate of return on an average share of stock is 15 percent. Toledo uses only common equity capital, and it has no debt outstanding.

a. What is the required rate of return on Toledo's stock?

b. What discount rate should be used to evaluate capital budgeting projects in each division? Explain your answer fully, and in the process illustrate your answer with a project that costs $104,322, has a 10-year life, and provides after-tax cash flows of $20,000 per year.

SOLUTIONS TO SELF-TEST PROBLEMS

ST-1 **a.** *Estimated Investment Requirements:*

Price	($50,000)
Modification	(10,000)
Net working capital	(2,000)
Total investment	($62,000)

b. *Operating Cash Flows:*

	Year 1	Year 2	Year 3
1. After-tax cost savings[a]	$12,000	$12,000	$12,000
2. Depreciation[b]	19,800	27,000	9,000
3. Depreciation tax savings[c]	7,920	10,800	3,600
Net cash flow (1 + 3)	$19,920	$22,800	$15,600

[a]Before-tax savings (1 − Tax rate) = $20,000(0.6) = $12,000.
[b]Depreciation in Year 1 = 0.33($60,000) = $19,800; depreciation percentages in Years 2 & 3 are 45% and 15% respectively.
[c]T(Depreciation) = Tax savings.

c. *End-of-Project Cash Flows:*

Salvage value	$20,000
Tax on salvage value[a]	(6,320)
Net working capital recovery	2,000
	$15,680

[a]Salvage value	$20,000	
Less: Book value	4,200	
Taxable income	$15,800	
Tax at 40%	$ 6,320	

d. No. Because the earthmover has a negative NPV, it should not be purchased.

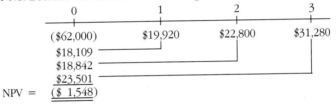

$$\begin{array}{ccccc}
0 & 1 & 2 & 3 \\
\text{($62,000)} & \text{$19,920} & \text{$22,800} & \text{$31,280} \\
\text{$18,109} & & & \\
\text{$18,842} & & & \\
\text{$23,501} & & & \\
\text{NPV} = \text{($ 1,548)} & & &
\end{array}$$

ST-2   First determine the net cash outflow at t = 0:

Purchase price	($8,000)
Sale of old machine	2,500
Tax on sale of old machine	(160[a])
Net working capital	(1,500[b])
Total investment	($7,160)

[a]The market value is $2,500 − $2,100 = $400 above the book value. Thus, there is a $400 recapture of depreciation, and WNP would have to pay 0.40($400) = $160 in taxes.
[b]The change in net working capital is a $2,000 increase in current assets minus a $500 increase in current liabilities, or $1,500.

Now examine the annual operating cash inflows:

Sales increase	$1,000
Cost decrease	1,500
Pretax operating revenue increase	$2,500

$$\text{After-tax operating revenue increase} = \$2,500(1 - T)$$
$$= \$2,500(0.60)$$
$$= \$1,500.$$

Depreciation:

	1	2	3	4	5	6
New[a]	$1,600	$2,560	$1,520	$ 960	$ 880	$480
Old	350	350	350	350	350	350
Change	$1,250	$2,210	$1,170	$ 610	$ 530	130
Depreciation tax savings[b]	$ 500	$ 884	$ 468	$ 244	$ 212	$ 52

[a]Depreciation expense each year equals depreciable basis times the MACRS factors of 0.20 for Year 1, 0.32 for Year 2, 0.19 for Year 3, 0.12 for Year 4, 0.11 for Year 5, and 0.06 for Year 6.
[b]Depreciation tax savings = Δ Depreciation(T).

Now recognize that, at the end of Year 6, WNP will recover its net working capital investment of $1,500, and it will also receive $800 from the sale of the replacement machine. However, the firm will have to pay 0.40($800) = $320 in taxes on the sale of the machine since it had been depreciated to a zero book value.

Finally, place all the cash flows on a time line:

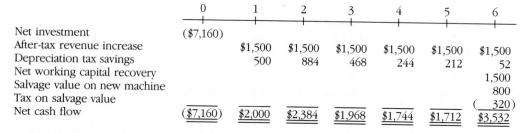

	0	1	2	3	4	5	6
Net investment	($7,160)						
After-tax revenue increase		$1,500	$1,500	$1,500	$1,500	$1,500	$1,500
Depreciation tax savings		500	884	468	244	212	52
Net working capital recovery							1,500
Salvage value on new machine							800
Tax on salvage value							(320)
Net cash flow	($7,160)	$2,000	$2,384	$1,968	$1,744	$1,712	$3,532

The net present value of this incremental cash flow stream, when discounted at 15 percent, is $1,051. Thus the replacement should be made.

Part V

LONG-TERM FINANCING

In the previous section we discussed means by which a firm can identify and evaluate investment opportunities. This section identifies the primary types of long-term capital used to finance those investments. In Chapters 16, 17, and 18 we examine the characteristics of long-term debt, preferred stock, common stock, and hybrid financing. The hybrid financing chapter includes discussions of leasing, warrants, convertibles, and options. Portions of Chapters 16 and 17 explain the determination of stock and bond values.

Chapter 16

Bonds and Preferred Stock

DECISION IN FINANCE

The Debt Crisis

A "debt crisis" looms in the 1990s over those who plunged into the acquisition binge of the 1980s and are now struggling to avoid default on interest payments on millions in debt. The best-known of these moguls is Donald Trump, ego-driven acquirer of airlines, hotels, and casinos, which he often named after himself. Trump has plenty of company in this situation. In fact, the value of corporate bonds defaulting in the first quarter of 1990 was four times that of a year earlier. In just the first three months, 13 firms defaulted on 38 bond issues totaling $5.7 billion, according to the Bond Investors Association. That organization's president said more defaults are expected "from poorly structured businesses trying to support impossible debt loads."

Trump's debt is estimated at $3.2 billion—borrowed funds easily acquired from big banks and other lenders dazzled by his "magic" name. His first two projects were profitable, and they established his reputation—the Grand Hyatt hotel, built from a run-down, older property next to Grand Central Station, and the Trump

Tower apartment/retail complex, which is still his showpiece.

Analysts say Trump's troubles began when he got involved with businesses that needed careful management to produce profits, as well as to generate large cash flows needed to meet the interest payments on money borrowed for their purchase. These properties included three Atlantic City casinos, New York's venerable Plaza Hotel, and the Shuttle airline which he bought from Eastern Airlines, all in heavily leveraged deals. One business editor blames Trump's banks (Chase, Citibank, Bankers Trust, and Manufacturers Hanover) for at least part of his woes. "All this occurred," he said, " . . . after it was clear to anyone that this same style of lending had brought ruin to the big Texas banks."

Other problems occurred that were not of Trump's own making. For one thing, the previously expanding real estate market flattened, making it harder to refinance properties whose original mortgages were based on speculative values. This situation was aggravated when regulators began to closely watch the banks' loan practices in the wake of the savings and loan

See end of chapter for resolution.

disaster. Moreover, the late 1989 plunge in the Japanese stock market caused investors, who earlier would buy anything associated with "Trump," to back off. Finally, just as his widely publicized Taj Mahal casino opened in Atlantic City, the gaming industry's growth began to slow down. The Taj has to bring in an astounding $1.3 million a day just to break even.

Trump's friends blame the economy for his problems. One said, "If we'd had two more years of the 1980s, he'd have been O.K." The same might be said for many other businesses caught in the new climate of the 1990s. Media mogul Ralph Ingersoll, for instance, has to deal with an industry-wide drop in newspaper advertising revenues as he tries to avoid default on approximately $600 million in long-term debt. The slump, hitting newspapers from small-town weeklies to major dailies, is the worst in 10 years, as classified ads and then display space purchases by troubled retailers and auto companies have been cut back.

Like Trump, Ingersoll went on a capital-spending binge in the 1980s, breaking away from the slow-paced newspaper management business founded by his father in 1958. He disliked running newspapers that were owned by other people, and he redesigned that "structural flaw" in the company by purchasing some newspapers himself. He formed two holding companies through which he owned 40 dailies and 200 weeklies, and he issued junk bonds to finance his operations. As with other junk bonds, the prices of Ingersoll's have fallen. Ordinarily this would bother only the bondholders, but in this case it is his problem too, because the bonds' indentures contain a provision that if the prices of the bonds decline, he must increase the interest payments to bring the bonds back up to par. Of course, higher interest payments increase the issuer's risk, which pushes the required yield up still more, resulting in a "vicious circle." With default appearing imminent, Ingersoll is trying to sell some of his newspapers to raise cash.

Trump has also put some of his properties on the market — his yacht and his airline, for instance. Most firms in this situation sell off some assets as a first step. The cash raised, however, is often not enough to meet their long-term interest obligations. In that case, the traditional route out from heavy debt loads has been bankruptcy court, but today, most firms are seeking alternatives. Even companies that in the past might have welcomed the Chapter 11 protection from their creditors are now avoiding it by any means possible. Restructuring the debt, says a bankruptcy lawyer, will "get you to the same place in less time and at the least expense."

Restructurings — known as "workouts" in Wall Street jargon — involve intense negotiations with lenders and bondholders to set new terms to help the company meet its obligations and survive the tough times. As you read this chapter, consider the situation of bondholders of struggling companies. Would you be willing to accept a restructuring which lowered your interest rate and par value, or which forced you to exchange some of your debt for equity just to help someone like Trump or Ingersoll survive? What alternatives would be available to you?

Most firms find it both necessary and desirable to use long-term debt financing, and some also use preferred stock. There are many types of fixed-income securities: secured and unsecured, marketable and nonmarketable, convertible and nonconvertible, and so on. Different groups of investors prefer different types of securities, and their tastes change over time. An astute financial manager knows how to package securities at a given point in time to make them appealing to the greatest possible number of potential investors, thereby keeping the firm's cost of capital to a minimum. In this chapter we analyze the three most important types of *fixed-income securities* — term loans, bonds, and preferred stocks — and discuss their valuation. Later chapters deal with other types of long-term capital.

FUNDED DEBT

Long-term debt is often called **funded debt,** and when a firm "funds" its floating debt, this means that it replaces short-term debt with securities of longer maturity. Funding does not imply that the firm places money with a trustee or other repository; it is simply part of the jargon of finance, and it means that the firm "replaces short-term debt with permanent (long-term) capital." Pacific Gas & Electric Company (PG&E) provides a good example of funding. PG&E has a continuous construction program, and it typically uses short-term debt to finance construction expenditures. Once short-term debt has built up to about $100 million, however, the company sells a stock or a bond issue, uses the proceeds to pay off (or fund) its bank loans, and starts the cycle again. There is a high fixed cost involved in selling stocks or long-term bonds, which makes it quite expensive to issue small amounts of these securities, and this makes the procedure followed by PG&E very logical.

> **funded debt**
> Long-term debt; "funding" means replacing short-term debt with longer maturity securities.

Self-Test

What is meant when it is said that a firm is funding its floating debt?

TERM LOANS

A **term loan** is a contract under which a borrower agrees to make payments of interest and principal, on specific dates, to a lender.[1] Term loans are usually negotiated directly between the borrowing firm and a financial institution — generally a bank, an insurance company, or a pension fund. Although the maturities of term loans vary from 2 to 30 years, most are for periods in the 3- to 15-year range.[2]

> **term loan**
> A loan, generally obtained from a bank or insurance company, with a maturity greater than one year.

Advantages of Term Loans

Term loans have three major advantages over publicly issued securities — *speed, flexibility,* and *low issuance costs.* Because they are negotiated directly between the lender and the borrower, formal documentation is minimized.

---

[1] If the interest and maturity payments are not met on schedule, the issuing firm is said to have *defaulted* and can then be forced into *bankruptcy*. See Appendix 20A for a discussion of bankruptcy.

[2] Term loans and private placement, which is discussed in the "Industry Practice" section later in this chapter, are both forms of so-called *direct financing*, in contrast to public financing.

The key provisions of a term loan can be worked out much more quickly than can those for a public issue, and it is not necessary for a term loan to go through the Securities and Exchange Commission (SEC) registration process. A further advantage of term loans over publicly held debt securities has to do with future flexibility: if a bond issue is held by many different bondholders, it is difficult to obtain permission to alter the terms of the agreement, even though new economic conditions may make such changes desirable. With a term loan, the borrower can generally sit down with the lender and work out mutually agreeable modifications in the contract.

Amortization

amortize
To liquidate on an installment basis; an amortized loan is one in which the principal amount of the loan is repaid in installments during the life of the loan.

Most term loans are **amortized,** or paid off, in equal installments over the life of the loan. (At this point you should review the discussion of amortization in Chapter 13.) The purpose of amortization is to have the loan repaid gradually over its life rather than fall due all at once. Amortization forces the borrower to retire the loan slowly; this protects both the lender and the borrower against the possibility that the borrower will not make adequate provisions for its retirement during the life of the loan. Amortization is especially important whenever the loan is used to purchase a specific item of equipment; here the repayment schedule should be matched to the productive life of the equipment, with the payments being made from cash flows resulting from its use.

Interest Rate

The interest rate on a term loan can either be fixed for the life of the loan or be variable. If it is fixed, the rate used will be close to the rate on long-term bonds with an equivalent maturity for companies of equivalent risk. If the rate is variable, it will usually be set at a certain number of percentage points over the prime rate, the commercial paper rate, the T-bond rate, or some other market-determined rate. Thus, when these rates go up or down, so does the rate on the outstanding balance of the term loan.

Self-Test

How are term loans usually negotiated?

What are the three major advantages that term loans have over publicly issued securities?

What is the purpose of amortizing loans?

BONDS

bond
A long-term debt instrument.

A **bond** is a long-term contract under which a borrower agrees to make payments of interest and principal, on specific dates, to the holder of the bond. Although bonds traditionally have been issued with maturities of between 20 and 30 years, in recent years shorter maturities, such as 7 to 10 years, have been used to an increasing extent. Bonds are similar to term loans, but a bond issue is generally advertised, offered to all investors (the "public"), and actually sold to many different investors. Indeed, thousands of individual and institutional investors may purchase bonds when a firm sells a bond issue, whereas there is usually only one lender in the case of a term loan. The bond is a debt contract; its **par value** represents the amount to be repaid at maturity, which typically is $1,000 for corporate bonds issued in the United States. With bonds, the interest rate, or **coupon interest rate,** is generally fixed, although in recent years there has been an increase in the use of various types of floating rate bonds. There are also a number of different types of bonds, the more important of which are discussed in this chapter.

par value
The nominal or face value of a stock or bond.

coupon interest rate
The stated annual rate of interest on a bond.

Indenture and Trustee

An **indenture** is a legal document that spells out the rights of both the bondholders and the issuing corporation. A **trustee** is an official (usually of a bank) who represents the bondholders and makes sure the terms of the indenture are carried out. The indenture may be several hundred pages in length, and it will cover such points as the conditions under which the issuer can pay off the bonds prior to maturity, the times-interest-earned ratio the issuer must maintain if it is to sell additional bonds, restrictions against the payment of dividends unless earnings meet certain specifications, and the like. The trustee monitors the situation and, in the event that the issuer violates any provision in the indenture, takes appropriate action on behalf of the bondholders. Exactly what constitutes "appropriate action" varies with the circumstances. It might be that to insist on immediate compliance would result in bankruptcy, which in turn might lead to large losses on the investors' bonds. In such a situation, the trustee may decide that the bondholders would be better served by giving the company a chance to work out its problems rather than by forcing it into bankruptcy.

indenture
A formal agreement between the issuer of a bond and the bondholders.

trustee
An official who insures that the bondholders' interests are protected and that the terms of the indenture are carried out.

The Securities and Exchange Commission approves indentures and makes sure that all indenture provisions are met before allowing a company to sell new securities to the public. It should be noted that the indentures of most larger corporations were actually written back in the 1930s or 1940s, and that many issues of new bonds, all covered by this same indenture, have been sold through the years. The interest rates on the bonds and perhaps their maturities will change from issue to issue, but bondholders' protection as spelled out in the indenture will be the same for all bonds of a given type. Some of the more important provisions contained in most indentures are discussed in the following sections.

Bond Repayment Provisions

Sinking Fund. A **sinking fund** is a provision that facilitates the orderly retirement of a bond issue (or, in some cases, an issue of preferred stock). Typically, the sinking fund provision requires the firm to retire a portion of the

sinking fund
A required annual payment designed to amortize a bond or preferred stock issue.

bond issue each year, but on rare occasions the firm may be required to deposit money with a trustee, who invests the funds and then uses the accumulated sum to retire the bonds when they mature. Sometimes the stipulated sinking fund payment is tied to sales or earnings of the current year, but usually it is a mandatory fixed amount. If it is mandatory, a failure to meet the sinking fund requirement causes the bond issue to be thrown into default, which may force the company into bankruptcy. Obviously, then, a sinking fund can constitute a dangerous cash drain on the firm.

In most cases, the firm is given the right to handle the sinking fund in either of two ways:

1. The company can call in for redemption (at par value) a certain percentage of the bonds each year; for example, it might be able to call 2 percent of the total original amount of the issue at a price of $1,000 per bond. The bonds are numbered serially, and those called for redemption are determined by a lottery administered by the trustee.

2. The company may buy the required amount of bonds on the open market.

The firm will take whichever action results in the greatest reduction of outstanding bonds for a given expenditure. Therefore, if interest rates have risen, causing bond prices to fall, the company will elect to use the option of buying bonds at a discount in the open market. If interest rates have fallen, it will call the bonds.

Although sinking funds are designed to protect bondholders by insuring that an issue is retired in an orderly fashion, it must be recognized that sinking funds will, at times, work to the detriment of bondholders. If, for example, the bond carries a 14 percent interest rate, and if similar bonds are yielding 10 percent, the bond will sell above par. A sinking fund call at par would greatly disadvantage the bondholders whose securities were called for retirement purposes, as this would require an investor to give up $140 of interest per year and then to reinvest in a bond that pays only $100.

On balance, however, securities that provide for a sinking fund and continuing redemption are likely to be offered initially on a lower-yield basis than securities without such funds. Since sinking funds provide additional protection to investors, bond issues that have them are likely to be issued with lower coupon rates than otherwise similar bonds without sinking funds.

call provision
A provision in a bond or preferred stock contract that gives the issuer the right to redeem the securities under specified terms before the normal maturity date.

Call Provision. A **call provision** gives the issuing corporation the right to call the bond for redemption. If it is used, the call provision generally states that the company must pay the bondholder an amount greater than the par value for the bond, with this additional sum being termed the *call premium*. The call premium is typically set equal to one year's interest if the bond is called during the first year, with the premium declining at a constant rate each year thereafter. For example, the call premium on a $1,000 par value, 10-year, 9 percent coupon bond would generally be $90 if it were called during the first year, $81 if it were called during the second year (calculated by reducing the $90 call premium by one-tenth annually), and so on. However, bonds are often not callable until several years (generally 5 to 10) after they are issued.

Suppose a company sold bonds when interest rates were relatively high. Provided the issue is callable, the company could sell a new issue of low-yielding securities if interest rates drop. It could then use the proceeds to retire the high-rate issue and thus reduce its interest expenses. This procedure is called a *refunding operation,* but the procedure is quite similar to a home-owner's refinancing a high-interest home loan with a lower-interest loan.

The call privilege is valuable to the firm but potentially detrimental to the investor, especially if the bond is issued in a period when interest rates are cyclically high. Accordingly, the interest rate on a new issue of callable bonds will exceed that on a new issue of noncallable bonds. For example, on June 8, 1990, Great Plains Power Company sold an issue of A-rated bonds to yield 9.625 percent. These bonds were callable immediately. On the same day Mid-west Electric sold an issue of A-rated bonds to yield 9.375 percent. Midwest's bonds were noncallable for ten years. (This is known as *deferred call.*) The two bond issues had the same original maturity and were considered to be equally liquid. Investors were apparently willing to accept a 0.25 percent lower interest rate on Midwest's bonds for the assurance that the rate of interest would be earned for at least 10 years. Great Plains, on the other hand, had to incur a 0.25 percent higher annual interest rate to obtain the option of calling the bonds in the event of a subsequent decline in interest rates.

Note that the call for refunding purposes is quite different from the call for sinking fund purposes. The call for sinking fund purposes generally has no call premium, but only a small percentage of the issue is callable each year.

Restrictive Covenants

A **restrictive covenant** is a provision in a bond indenture or term loan agreement that requires the issuer of the bond to meet certain stated conditions. Typical provisions include requiring that debt not exceed a specific percentage of total capital, that the current ratio be maintained above a specific level, that dividends not be paid on common stock unless earnings are maintained at a given level, and so on. Overall, these covenants are designed to insure, insofar as possible, that the firm does nothing to cause the bonds' quality to deteriorate after they are issued.[3] As with other provisions in the indenture, the trustee is responsible for making sure that the restrictive covenants are not violated or that violations are quickly corrected in the best interests of the bondholders or lenders.

restrictive covenant
A provision in a debt contract that constrains the actions of the borrower.

---

[3]In the decade of the 1980s, bondholders awoke to a new type of risk that often caused bond quality to deteriorate after issue. This risk was called "event risk," and it related to the negative implications for current bondholders if the firm engaged in a leveraged buyout (LBO). LBOs will be discussed in Chapter 22. The rise of LBOs has led to the inclusion of new restrictive covenants in bond indentures.

"Wall Street Raider" Has a New Definition

When the Securities and Exchange Commission passed Rule 144a in late April 1990, it created a new bull market on Wall Street. The hot commodity was not a particular corporation's stocks or bonds — rather, it was investment bankers who were skilled in the private placement of these securities. To get a piece of the $170 billion private-placement pie, investment banking firms immediately began raiding each other's staffs for top talent.

A private placement is the direct sale of a stock or bond to a big institutional investor, such as a pension fund, insurance company, or mutual fund. Rule 144a makes this process easier by allowing companies to avoid some of the registration requirements of public offerings. The new rule also makes it easy for a holder to resell privately placed securities. In essence, it exempts any U.S. or foreign institution from the registration and disclosure process in the sale of stocks and bonds to any other institution which already holds at least $100 million in securities. This resale possibility increases the liquidity of privately placed securities, hence making institutions more willing to participate in the market. As a result, Rule 144a is expected to give companies easier access to capital on somewhat better terms, and to provide somewhat higher returns to institutions which were previously shut out of the private placement market.

This rule may be the salvation of some in the securities industry, in which 45,000 workers lost their jobs in the 30 months after the October 1987 stock market crash. Revenue from investment banking activities in the first quarter of 1990 was down at least 20 percent from the first quarter figures of 1989, which had not been good.

Sources: "The Best New Stocks May Never Hit the Street," *Business Week*, December 25, 1989; *The Wall Street Journal*, "SEC Ready to Ease Private-Placement Rules," April 13, 1990, and "Street Courts Gurus in Newly Hot Private Placement," May 2, 1990.

While some, however, are reaping the benefits of the new rush to hire private-placement specialists, others are feeling some disadvantages. Merrill Lynch lost two top managers to a small investment banking company. One was a managing director, and the other had been head of Merrill's private placement division for 9 years. Two other Merrill Lynch specialists also left, but they were replaced with former employees of the now-defunct Drexel Burnham Lambert. Two Prudential-Bache vice presidents, and the head of their private-placement activities, also left, as did staffers in similar positions at Shearson Lehman Hutton. Commercial banks, too, are losing key employees in the aftermath of Rule 144a. For example, at least a dozen specialists from units of Citicorp and Bankers Trust left to start their own private-placement firm.

For former "wallflowers" in a branch of Wall Street that was never considered especially glamorous, the spotlight — and the rewards — must be dazzling. The typical private-placement specialist can annually earn from $200,000 to $600,000, helping to target potential clients and to structure deals. Says a vice-president with an executive search firm, who is helping to match up the specialists with eager new employers, "Everything relating to private placement is increasingly in demand. This is a very hot area right now."

Benefits to individuals in the industry are just a side effect of the rule, of course. Regulators believe that many businesses will benefit from a reduction in the costs of corporate financing, with a savings of perhaps half a percentage point over the interest rates companies must now pay to place debt privately. With lower costs, fewer U.S. companies will look overseas for financing, thus strengthening the domestic market. At the same time, foreign firms that have avoided this country because of the old disclosure rules may start showing a renewed interest in U.S. capital.

Though 144a has just become official, it actually represents the codification of a practice quietly allowed by the SEC for a number of years among institutions in the private market. Still, the rule should bring in many more who have feared to act without specific guidelines. Says the former head of the SEC's international corporate finance unit, "The whole character of the private-placement market will change."

Some fear it will change at the expense of the nation's public markets, and of small investors. "This is a watershed event that will shift the balance of power on Wall Street," says one executive. "It takes some of the power out of the hands of investment banks and places it in the hands of large investors." Existing public stocks cannot be traded under the new rule, but some companies which originally planned public offerings might, instead, sell them directly to big investors, rather than listing them on the exchanges. During the past decade, the private-placement market's share of all offerings grew to almost 40 percent, and at least one analyst thinks that share could rise to 75 percent because of the new rule. If so, that would mean that individual investors could be cut out of many of the best deals, and the "big boys" would enjoy even more favorable deals than they find now.

Another fear is that companies which are exempt from disclosure rules would be in a better position to push bad debt off on unsuspecting investors. If the institutional purchaser is a pension fund, this risk will ultimately fall on a large number of "little" individuals. SEC Chairman Richard Breeden is particularly concerned about banks and thrifts in this regard, and is considering a separate proposal to impose a minimum equity requirement on them, but that was not part of Rule 144a.

Some restrictions on private placement already exist. Mutual funds are usually not allowed to invest more than 10 percent of their assets in such securities. Some states also have pertinent laws, such as the New York law prohibiting insurance companies from putting more than 1 percent of their assets in foreign securities. Nevertheless, analysts predict that the firms most likely to gain the most from the new rule are those already highly visible in the international market, such as Morgan Stanley Group, First Boston, and Salomon. "The impact is already occurring," says one executive, "much like [preparations for] 1992 in Europe. Foreign issuers already are coming into the market more often. The pace has picked up."

While the changes brought about by Rule 144a may be gradual ("evolution rather than revolution"), two big foreign issues are regarded as forerunners of things to come. The State Bank of India just placed a debt offering in the private market, and the State Bank of South Australia was preparing one in mid-1990. Said Philip Bennett, capital markets director at Salomon Brothers, "These issues will be precursors of [a host of] 144a offerings."

Self-Test

Differentiate between bonds and term loans.

What points are typically covered in an indenture?

What are the two ways a sinking fund can be handled? Which method will be chosen by the firm if interest rates have risen? If interest rates have fallen?

Are securities that provide for a sinking fund regarded as being riskier than those without this type of provision? Explain.

What is the difference between a call for sinking fund purposes and a refunding call?

TYPES OF BONDS

Mortgage Bonds

mortgage bond
A bond backed by fixed assets. *First mortgage bonds* are senior in priority to claims of *second mortgage bonds.*

Under a **mortgage bond** the corporation pledges certain real assets as security for the bond. To illustrate, in 1990 Bio-tech Pharmaceuticals needed $15 million to purchase land and to build a major research and development center. Bonds in the amount of $7 million, secured by a mortgage on the property, were issued. (The remaining $8 million was financed with equity funds.) If Bio-tech defaults on the bonds, the bondholders can foreclose on the property and sell it to satisfy their claims.

If Bio-tech chooses to, it can issue *second mortgage bonds* secured by the same $15 million plant. In the event of liquidation, the holders of these second mortgage bonds would have a claim against the property only after the first mortgage bondholders had been paid off in full. Thus second mortgages are sometimes called *junior mortgages* because they are junior in priority to the claims of senior mortgages, or *first mortgage bonds.*

The first mortgage indentures of most major corporations were written 20, 30, 40, or more years ago. These indentures are generally "open-ended," meaning that new bonds may be issued from time to time under the existing indenture. However, the amount of new bonds that can be issued is almost always limited by clauses in the indenture to a specified percentage of the firm's total "bondable property," which generally includes all plant and equipment. For example, Savannah Electric can issue first mortgage bonds totaling up to 60 percent of its fixed assets. If fixed assets total $1 billion, and if it had $500 million of first mortgage bonds outstanding, it could, by the property test, issue another $100 million of first mortgage bonds (60% of $1 billion = $600 million).

At times, Savannah Electric has been unable to issue any new first mortgage bonds because of another indenture provision — its times-interest-earned (TIE) ratio was below 2.5, the minimum coverage that it must maintain to sell new bonds. Savannah Electric passed the property test but failed the coverage test; so it could not issue first mortgage bonds, and it had to finance with junior securities. Since first mortgage bonds carry lower rates of interest than junior long-term debt, this restriction was a costly one.

Savannah Electric's neighbor, Georgia Power Company, has more flexibility under its indenture; its interest coverage requirement is only 2.0. In hearings before the Georgia Public Service Commission, it was suggested that Savannah Electric change its indenture coverage to 2.0 so that it could issue more first mortgage bonds. However, this is simply not possible; the holders of the outstanding bonds would have to approve the change, and it is inconceivable that they would vote for a change that would seriously weaken their position.

Debentures

debenture
A long-term debt instrument that is not secured by a mortgage on specific property.

A **debenture** is an unsecured bond, and as such it provides no lien against specific property as security for the obligation. Debenture holders are, therefore, general creditors whose claims are protected by property not otherwise pledged. In practice, the use of debentures depends on the nature of the firm's assets and on its general credit strength. An extremely strong company, such as IBM, will tend to use debentures—it simply does not need to put up property as security for its debt. Debentures are also issued by companies in industries in which it would not be practical to provide security through a mortgage on fixed assets. Examples of such industries are the large mail-order houses and commercial banks, which characteristically hold most of their assets in the form of inventory or loans, neither of which is satisfactory security for a mortgage bond.[4]

Subordinated Debentures

The term *subordinate* means "below," or "inferior." Thus, subordinated debt has claims on assets in the event of bankruptcy only after senior debt (usually mortgage bonds) has been paid off. Debentures may be subordinated either to designated notes payable (usually bank loans) or to all other debt. In the event of liquidation or reorganization, holders of **subordinated debentures** cannot be paid until all senior debt, as named in the debentures' indenture, has been paid. Precisely how subordination works, and how it strengthens the position of senior debtholders, is explained in Appendix 20A.

subordinated debenture
A bond having a claim on assets only after the senior debt has been paid off in the event of liquidation.

Other Types of Bonds

Several other types of bonds are used sufficiently often to warrant mention. First, **convertible bonds** are securities that are convertible into shares of common stock, at a fixed price, at the option of the bondholder. Basically, convertibles provide investors with a chance to receive capital gains in exchange for a lower coupon rate, while the issuing firm gets the advantage of that lower rate. Bonds issued with warrants are similar to convertibles. **Warrants** are options that permit the holder to buy stock for a stated price, thereby providing a capital gain if the price of the stock rises. Like convertibles, bonds that are issued with warrants carry lower coupon rates than straight bonds. Warrants and convertibles are discussed in detail in Chapter 18.

convertible bond
A bond that is exchangeable, at the option of the holder, for common stock of the issuing firm.

warrant
A long-term option to buy a stated number of shares of common stock at a specified price.

　　Income bonds pay interest only when the interest is earned. This flexibility means that income bonds are similar to preferred stock in that there is no default if interest is not paid. However, unlike a preferred stock dividend, the interest payment on an income bond is a tax-deductible expense. Income bonds are often issued by companies in reorganization or by firms whose financial situation does not make it feasible to issue bonds with a fixed, mandatory interest requirement. Although these securities cannot bankrupt a company, from an investor's perspective they are riskier than regular bonds, owing to the weakness of the issuing firm and the uncertainty of interest receipts.

income bond
A bond that pays interest only if the interest is earned.

---

[4]In the late 1980s and early 1990s, as banks were getting into financial difficulty which required them to raise more nondeposit capital, they began packaging up some of their best loans, especially credit card loans, and using those loans as collateral for bonds. These "asset-based bonds" are, conceptually, exactly like mortgage bonds. Industrial companies are also increasingly issuing bonds backed by accounts receivable and other non-real-estate assets.

indexed (purchasing power) bond
A bond that has interest payments based on an inflation index so as to protect the holder from inflation.

Another type of bond that has been discussed in the United States but not yet used here to any extent is the **indexed,** or **purchasing power, bond,** which is popular in Brazil, Israel, and a few other countries plagued by high rates of inflation. The interest rate paid on these bonds is based on an inflation index such as the consumer price index (CPI), so the interest paid rises automatically when the inflation rate rises, thus protecting the bondholders against inflation. The British government has issued an indexed bond on which the interest rate is set equal to the British inflation rate plus 3 percent. Thus, these bonds provide a real rate of return of 3 percent.

Self-Test

Differentiate between mortgage bonds and debentures.

Differentiate among convertible bonds, bonds with warrants, income bonds, and indexed bonds.

Why do bonds with warrants and convertible bonds have lower coupons than bonds that do not have these features?

RECENT BOND INNOVATIONS

Zero Coupon Bonds

zeros coupon bond (zeros)
A bond that pays no annual interest but is sold at a discount below par, thus providing compensation to investors in the form of capital appreciation.

The majority of all bonds pay interest periodically, generally semiannually or annually, and then pay the principal when the bond matures. However, some bonds pay no interest but are offered at a substantial discount below their par values and hence provide capital appreciation rather than interest income. These securities are called **zero coupon bonds (zeros),** and they are unique in that they are sold at less than face value and mature at par, usually $1,000. Assume that a firm wishes to sell a 12 percent, 10-year, zero coupon bond. As found in Chapter 13, the present value of $1,000 to be received in 10 years and discounted at 12 percent would equal $322 today:

$$PV = FV_{10}(PVIF_{12\%,10})$$

$$= \$1,000(0.322)$$

$$= \$322.00.$$

(The calculator gives a solution of $321.97.)

Zeros were first used in a major way in 1981. In recent years IBM, Alcoa, J.C. Penney, ITT, Cities Service, GMAC, Martin-Marietta, and many other companies have used them to raise billions of dollars. Moreover, investment bankers have in effect created zero coupon Treasury bonds. An example will help explain zero coupon bonds. In 1990, Nast Corporation issued $100 million (par value) of zeros. They have no coupons, pay no interest, are not callable, and mature after 10 years, in the year 2000, at which time holders will be paid

$1,000 per bond. The bonds were originally issued at a discount below par, for $322 per $1,000 bond. As shown above, the compound interest rate that causes $322 to grow to $1,000 over 10 years is 12 percent. Nast received $32.2 million minus underwriting expenses for the issue, but it will have to pay back $100 million in the year 2000.

The advantages to Nast include the following: (1) no cash outlays are required for either interest or principal until the bonds mature; (2) these bonds have a relatively low yield to maturity (Nast would have had to pay approximately 12.5 percent versus the actual 12 percent had it issued regular coupon bonds at par); and (3) Nast receives an annual tax deduction equal to the yearly amortization of the discount, which means that the bonds actually provide a positive cash flow in the form of tax savings over their life. There are, however, two disadvantages to Nast: (1) the bonds simply are not callable, because they would have to be called at their $1,000 par value, and, since it is better to pay the $1,000 in the year 2000 than at some earlier date, Nast cannot refund the issue if interest rates should fall,[5] and (2) Nast will have a very large nondeductible cash outlay coming up in the year 2000.

There are two principal advantages to the purchasers of zero coupon bonds: (1) they often have no danger whatever of a call, and (2) they are guaranteed a "true" yield (12 percent in Nast's case) irrespective of what happens to interest rates. Thus, the holders of these bonds do not have to worry about having to reinvest coupons received at low rates if interest rates should fall, which would result in a true yield to maturity of less than 12 percent. This second feature is extremely important to pension funds, life insurance companies, and other institutions that make actuarial contracts based on assumed reinvestment rates; for such investors the risk of declining interest rates, hence an inability to reinvest cash inflows at the assumed rates, is greater than the risk of an increase in rates and the accompanying fall in bond values.

Because of tax considerations (the difference between the purchase price and the maturity value for individuals is treated as amortized annual interest income and not as a capital gain), these bonds are best suited for tax-exempt organizations, especially pension funds, and for tax-deferred individual savings, such as individual retirement accounts (IRAs). However, since pension funds are by far the largest purchasers of corporate bonds, the potential market for zero coupon bonds is by no means small.

Floating Rate Debt

In the early 1980s, inflation pushed interest rates up to unprecedented levels, causing sharp declines in the prices of long-term bonds. Even some supposedly "risk-free" U.S. Treasury bonds lost fully half their value, and a similar

---

[5]Some zero coupon bonds are callable at their "accreted value," calculated as the issue price compounded at the implied interest rate for the number of years since issue. For example, the accreted value of our illustrative bond after five years would be $322 (1.12)^5 = 567.47. A call premium of, say, 2 percent might also be added, making the call price $567.47(1.02) = 587.82.

situation occurred with corporate bonds, mortgages, and other fixed rate, long-term securities. (We will see how changes in interest rates affect bond values shortly.) The lenders who held the fixed rate debt were, of course, hurt very badly. Bankruptcies (or forced mergers to avoid bankruptcy) were commonplace in the banking and especially the savings and loan industries. Insurance company reserves also plummeted, causing those companies severe problems, including the bankruptcy of Baldwin-United, a $9 billion diversified insurance firm. As a result, many lenders became reluctant to lend money at fixed rates on a long-term basis, and they would do so only at extraordinarily high rates.

As we saw in Chapter 4, there is normally a *maturity risk premium* embodied in long-term interest rates; this is a risk premium designed to offset the risk of declining bond prices if interest rates rise. Prior to the 1970s, the maturity risk premium on 30-year bonds was about one percentage point, meaning that under normal conditions, a firm might expect to pay about one percentage point more to borrow on a long-term than on a short-term basis. In the early 1980s, however, the maturity risk premium is estimated to have jumped to about three percentage points, which made long-term debt very expensive relative to short-term debt. Lenders were able and willing to lend on a short-term basis, but corporations were correctly reluctant to borrow on a short-term basis to finance long-term assets — such action is, as we saw in Chapter 8, extremely dangerous. Therefore, there was a situation in which lenders did not want to lend on a long-term basis, but corporations needed long-term money. The problem was solved by the introduction of *long-term, floating rate debt.*

floating rate bond
A bond whose interest rate fluctuates with shifts in the general level of interest rates.

A typical **floating rate bond** works as follows. The coupon rate is set for, say, the initial six-month period, after which it is adjusted every six months based on some market rate. For example, Gulf Oil sold a floating rate bond that was pegged at 35 basis points (0.35%) above the going rate on 30-year Treasury bonds. Other companies' issues have been tied to short-term rates. Many additional provisions can be included in floating rate issues; for example, some are convertible to fixed rate debt, whereas others have a minimum coupon rate as well as a cap on how high the rate can go.

Floating rate debt is advantageous to lenders because the interest rate moves up if market rates rise. This, in turn, causes the market value of the debt to be stabilized, as we will see shortly, and it provides lenders such as banks with more income to meet their own obligations (for example, a bank which has bought floating rate bonds can use the interest it earns to pay interest on its own deposits). Moreover, floating rate debt is advantageous to corporations, because by using it, firms can obtain debt with a long maturity without committing themselves to paying an historically high rate of interest for the entire life of the loan. Of course, if interest rates increase after a floating rate note has been signed, the borrower would have been better off issuing conventional, fixed rate debt.

Junk Bonds

Another new type of bond is the **junk bond,** a high-risk, high-yield bond issued to finance either a leveraged buyout (LBO), a merger, or a troubled company. For example, when Ted Turner attempted to buy CBS, he planned to finance the acquisition by issuing junk bonds to CBS's stockholders in exchange for their shares. Similarly, Merrill Lynch helped Public Service of New Hampshire finance construction of its troubled Seabrook nuclear plant with junk bonds, and junk bonds were used in the RJR Nabisco LBO. In junk bond deals, the debt ratio is generally extremely high, so the bondholders must bear as much risk as stockholders normally would. The bonds' yields reflect this fact — Ted Turner's bonds would have carried a coupon rate of about 16 percent, while a coupon rate of 25 percent per annum was required to sell the Public Service of New Hampshire bonds.

The emergence of junk bonds as an important type of debt is another example of how the investment banking industry adjusts to — and facilitates — new developments in capital markets. In the 1980s, mergers and takeovers increased dramatically. People like T. Boone Pickens and Ted Turner thought that certain old-line, established companies were run inefficiently and were financed too conservatively, and they wanted to take over these companies and restructure them. To help finance these takeovers, the investment banking firm of Drexel Burnham Lambert began an active campaign to persuade certain institutions to purchase high-yield bonds. Drexel developed expertise in putting together deals that were attractive to the institutions yet feasible in the sense that cash flows were sufficient to meet the required interest payments. The fact that interest on the bonds was tax deductible, combined with the much higher debt ratios of the restructured firms, also increased after-tax cash flows and helped make the deals feasible.

Do junk bonds have a legitimate role in corporate finance aside from financing takeovers and LBOs? The development of the junk bond market has effectively extended firms' debt capacities beyond their earlier limits, and, in spite of all the publicity surrounding the use of junk bonds in mergers and acquisitions, statistics show that well over half of the junk bond issues in recent years have been used for normal expansion purposes.

The phenomenal growth of the junk bond market has been impressive but controversial. In early 1989, Drexel Burnham Lambert, the leading junk bond investment banker, agreed to pay a $650 million fine for various securities law violations. The firm also agreed to fire "junk bond king" Michael Milken, the true developer of the market, and to withhold his 1988 bonus, said to exceed $200 million. Further, a grand jury indicted Mr. Milken on charges of fraud, and in April 1990 he agreed to a settlement that included $600 million in fines and penalties. These events badly tarnished the junk bond market, which had already come under severe criticism, rightly or wrongly, for improperly fueling management takeovers. Additionally, the realization that high leverage can

junk bond
A high-risk, high-yield bond used to finance mergers, leveraged buyouts, and troubled companies.

The following table illustrates Duff & Phelps Inc.'s (one of several rating agencies) credit ratings on various securities issues for the week ending April 6, 1990, as they appeared in *The Wall Street Journal.* Credit ratings appear for new issues, and credit rating changes appear for outstanding issues. The credit ratings are assigned for first mortgage bonds (FMB), senior debt, subordinated debt, and preferred stock.

Duff & Phelps Inc.

Credit Ratings
Week Ending April 6, 1990

New Issues

Fixed Income	Rating
Arizona Public Service—Cum. Pfd. Stock (Shelf)	BB+
Associates Corp. of North America—Notes	AA−
Duke Power—F&RMB, MTN Series (Shelf)	AA−
GTE Florida—FMB	AA−
Hydro-Quebec—Debs.	AA
Louisiana Power & Light—FMB	BBB
Potomac Electric Power—FMB	AA
San Diego Gas & Electric—FMB	A+
United Telecommunications—Notes	BBB+
Washington Water Power—Pfd. Stock (Shelf)	BBB+

New Ratings

Fixed Income	Rating
Standard Credit Card Trust 1990-2—Class-A Ctfs.	AAA

New Ratings (cont'd)

Fixed Income	Rating
Standard Credit Card Trust 1990-2—Class-B Ctfs.	AA
Standard Credit Card Trust 1990-3—Class-A Ctfs.	AAA
Standard Credit Card Trust 1990-3—Class-B Ctfs.	AA

Ratings Changed

Fixed Income	From	To
Barnett Banks—Sr. Debt	AA	AA−
Barnett Banks—Sub. Debt	AA−	A+
Columbia Savings and Loan Assoc.—Long Term Deposits	B	CCC
Fleet/Norstar Financial Group—Sr. Debt	AA−	A+
Fleet/Norstar Financial Group—Sub. Debt	A+	A
Fleet/Norstar Financial Group—Pfd. Stock	A	A−
GTE California—FMB	AA−	AA
GTE California—Sinking Fund Debs.	A+	AA−

Source: *The Wall Street Journal,* April 9, 1990.

spell trouble—as when Campeau (owner of Federated and Allied Department Stores), with $3 billion in junk bond financing, filed for bankruptcy in early 1990—has slowed the growth in the junk bond market.

The final blow came when Drexel Burnham Lambert was forced into bankruptcy in 1990. The bankruptcy (1) removed the leading dealer from the market and thus drastically reduced the liquidity of junk bonds and (2) created an instant oversupply of junk as Drexel began to unload its own inventory on the market. The final verdict on junk bonds is not yet in, but it appears that junk bonds will play a much smaller role in corporate financings in the 1990s than they did in the 1980s.

Self-Test

Identify the advantages and disadvantages of zero coupon bonds to the issuer.

Identify the principal advantages of zero coupon bonds to the purchasers.

What problem was solved by the introduction of long-term floating rate debt, and how is the rate on such bonds determined?

For what purposes are junk bonds typically used?

Table 16-1 **Comparison of Bond Ratings**

| | High Quality | | Investment Grade | | "Junk" | | |
					Substandard		Speculative
Moody's	Aaa	Aa	A	Baa	Ba	B	Caa to D
S&P	AAA	AA	A	BBB	BB	B	CCC to D

Note: Both Moody's and S&P use "modifiers" for bonds rated below triple-A. S&P uses a plus and minus system; thus, A+ designates the strongest A-rated bonds and A− the weakest. Moody's uses a 1, 2, or 3 designation, with 1 denoting the strongest and 3 the weakest. Thus, within the double-A category, Aa1 is the best, Aa2 is average, and Aa3 is the weakest.

BOND RATINGS

Since the early 1900s, bonds have been assigned quality ratings that reflect their probability of going into default. The two major rating agencies are Moody's Investors Service (Moody's) and Standard & Poor's Corporation (S&P). These agencies' rating designations are shown in Table 16-1.[6]

The triple- and double-A bonds are extremely safe. The single-A and triple-B rated bonds are strong enough to be termed *investment grade,* and they are the lowest-rated bonds that many banks and other institutional investors are permitted by law to hold. Double-B and lower-rated bonds are considered speculative grade securities, or junk bonds, with increasingly higher probabilities of default as ratings decline. Many financial institutions are prohibited from buying these higher risk securities.

Although the rating assignments are judgmental, they are based on both qualitative and quantitative factors, some of which are listed below:

- **Ratio analysis:** The firm's leverage position, liquidity, and debt coverage are among the first factors considered by the bond-rating agencies. We discuss in a later section two of the more important coverage ratios—the times-interest-earned and the fixed charge coverage ratios.

- **Security provisions:** Whether the bond is backed by real assets (mortgage bond) or not (debenture), or by another firm (guaranteed bond), or whether the bonds are subordinated, are important factors in the rating scheme.

- **Sinking fund:** If the issue has a sinking fund to insure systematic repayment, this is a plus factor to the rating agencies.

---

[6]In the discussion to follow, reference to the S&P code is intended to imply the Moody code as well. Thus, for example, *triple-B bonds* means both BBB and Baa bonds, *double-B bonds* both BB and Ba bonds, and so on. Also, as a direct result of the RJR LBO, in 1989 S&P began to rate bonds with respect to the likelihood of a downgrading due to some "event" such as an LBO. The rating E-1 is best, while E-5 is the lowest rating.

- **Maturity:** Other things being the same, a bond with a shorter maturity will be judged less risky than a longer-term bond, and this will be reflected in the rating.

- **Stability:** As a general rule, the more stable the firm's sales and earnings, the stronger the rating.

- **Legal actions:** Any major legal controversies such as antitrust suits could erode the ratings.

- **Pension liabilities:** If the firm has unfunded pension liabilities that could cause a problem, this fact is reflected in its bond ratings.

- **Other:** Many other factors enter into the bond-rating scheme used by agencies. A sample of other factors includes potential for labor problems, political unrest in host countries for multinational firms, and the regulatory climate for public utilities and other regulated industries.

Analysts at the rating agencies have consistently stated that no precise formula is used to set a firm's rating; all the factors listed, plus others, are taken into account, but not in a mathematically precise manner. Statistical studies have borne out this contention; researchers who have tried to predict bond ratings on the basis of quantitative data have had only limited success, indicating that the agencies do indeed use a good deal of subjective judgment when establishing a firm's rating.[7]

Importance of Bond Ratings

Bond ratings are important both to firms and to investors. First, a bond's rating is an indicator of its default risk; hence, the rating has a direct, measurable influence on the bond's interest rate and the firm's cost of debt capital. Second, most bonds are purchased by institutional investors rather than individuals, and these institutions are generally restricted to investment-grade securities. Thus, if a firm's bonds fall below BBB, it will have a difficult time selling new bonds, as most normal purchasers will not be allowed to buy them.

Ratings also have an effect on the availability of debt capital. If an institutional investor buys BBB bonds and these bonds are subsequently downgraded to BB or lower, the institution's regulators will reprimand or perhaps impose restrictions on the institution if it continues to hold the bonds. However, since many other institutional investors cannot purchase the bonds, the institution that owns them will probably not be able to sell them except at a sizable loss. Because of this fear of downgrading, many institutions restrict their bond portfolios to at least A, or even AA, bonds. Thus, the lower a firm's bond rating, the smaller the group of available purchasers for its new issues.

As a result of their higher risk and more restricted market, lower-grade bonds have much higher required rates of return than do high-grade bonds. Figure 16-1 illustrates this point. In each of the years shown on the graph, U.S.

---

[7]See Ahmed Belkaoui, *Industrial Bonds and the Rating Process* (London: Quorum Books, 1983).

Figure 16-1 **Yields on U.S. Government Bonds, AAA Corporates, and BBB Corporates, 1953–1990**

A bond's rating is an indicator of its default risk. Because a lower-grade bond entails greater default risk, it must pay a higher interest rate to attract investors. During the 38 years shown here, U.S. government long-term bonds, which are default-free, paid the lowest interest rates. Corporate AAA bonds paid somewhat higher interest rates, while corporate BBB bonds paid the highest rates of the three shown. The spreads between the curves indicate the risk premiums that corporate bond issuers had to pay to raise capital.

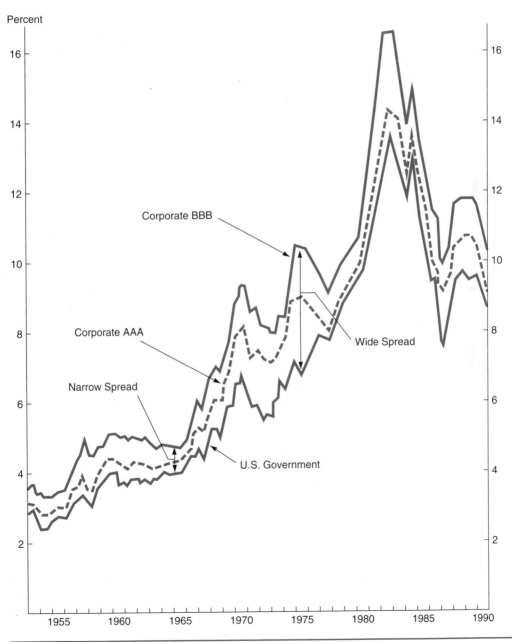

Table 16-2 **Risk Premiums in Selected Economic Periods**

	Long-Term Government Bonds (Default-Free) (1)	AAA Corporate Bonds (2)	BBB Corporate Bonds (3)	Risk Premiums	
				AAA (4) = (2) − (1)	BBB (5) = (3) − (1)
June 1963	4.00%	4.23%	4.84%	0.23%	0.84%
June 1975	6.86	8.77	10.40	1.91	3.54
April 1989	9.17	9.88	10.69	0.71	1.52
May 1990	8.73	9.47	10.41	0.74	1.68

Sources: *Federal Reserve Bulletin,* various issues; *Federal Reserve Statistical Release,* June 4, 1990.

government bonds have had the lowest yields, AAA bonds have been next, and the BBB bonds have had the highest yields of the three shown. The figure also shows that the gaps between the yields on the three types of bonds vary over time; in other words, the cost differentials, or risk premiums, fluctuate from year to year.

This point is highlighted in Table 16-2, which gives the yields on the three types of bonds, plus the risk premiums for AAA and BBB bonds, on various dates over a quarter-century. Recall from Chapter 4 that the return on financial assets is based on the real risk-free rate plus premiums for inflation and for increasing risk. Government bonds are default-risk free, but because investors in these securities still face (and must be compensated for) inflation risk and interest rate risk, the return on "risk-free" government securities must include an inflation risk premium and a maturity risk premium. The government bond rate has risen nearly 5 percentage points from 1963 to 1990, reflecting the increase in realized and anticipated inflation, and the fear of interest rate risk. While government bonds are considered to be free of default risk, corporate bonds are not. AAA bonds have little default risk, but BBB securities have a higher potential for default, so investors require a higher rate of return on these securities. Investors' risk aversion, as measured by the bonds' risk premium in Table 16-2, has increased from 1963 to the present, reflecting the economic uncertainties of the times. This increase was quite pronounced from 1963 to 1975, but it fell somewhat between 1975 and 1990. Therefore, the penalty for having a low credit rating has varied over time. Occasionally, as in 1963, this penalty is quite small, but at other times, as in 1975, it is very large. These differences reflect investors' risk aversion; in 1975 the United States was emerging from a severe recession caused by a quadrupling of oil prices in 1973 and 1974, and investors were afraid the economy would slip back into a slump. At such times people seek safety in bonds, Treasuries are in great demand, and the premium on low-quality over high-quality bonds increases.

These relationships for three selected time periods (1963, 1975, and 1989) are graphically depicted in Figure 16-2. Note that the government bond return (the default-free rate) on the vertical axis has risen since 1963, reflecting the

Figure 16-2 **Relationship between Bond Ratings and Bond Yields, 1963, 1975, and 1989**

In this figure we take a closer look at the relationship between bond ratings and bond yields. Between 1963 and 1989, the default-free rate of interest rose from 4.00 percent to 9.17 percent to reflect both realized and anticipated inflation. Corporate borrowers, of course, had to pay a default risk premium in addition. In 1963, corporate AAA bonds paid a default risk premium of 0.23 percent, and corporate BBB bonds paid a default risk premium of 0.84 percent. In 1975, this risk premium rose to 1.91 percent for AAA bonds and to 3.54 percent for BBB bonds. In 1989, this risk premium dropped to 0.71 percent for AAA bonds and to 1.52 percent for BBB bonds. The default risk premiums fluctuated to reflect changes in investors' attitudes toward assuming risk. (Note that this graph assumes that maturity risk is held constant for the three types of securities shown.)

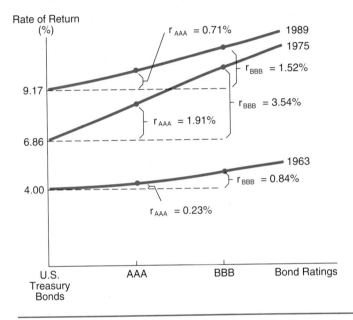

Source: Table 16-2.

r_{AAA} = risk premium on AAA bonds.
r_{BBB} = risk premium on BBB bonds.

increase in expected and realized inflation. The slope of the line reflects investors' risk aversion. The increase in risk aversion was quite pronounced from 1963 to 1975, but it fell somewhat between 1975 and 1989.

Changes in Ratings

Rating agencies review outstanding bonds on a periodic basis, occasionally upgrading or downgrading a bond as a result of its issuer's changed circumstances. For example, Dayton Hudson Corp.'s senior unsecured debt securities were placed on S&P's *Creditwatch* list in April 1990, following their announcement that they were acquiring Marshall Field's. (*Creditwatch* is S&P's weekly publication which discusses developing situations that may lead to upgradings or downgradings.) Then, in May, Dayton Hudson's senior unsecured debt securities were downgraded from A+ to A because of the heightened financial risk associated with its planned acquisition. However, on the same day as Dayton Hudson's downgrading, Western Investment Real Estate Trust's senior debt rating was raised from BBB+ to A− because of the strength of its balance sheet resulting from an infusion of equity capital and the continued strong performance of its real estate holdings.

Coverage Ratios

coverage
The measure of a firm's ability to meet interest and principal payments; times interest earned (TIE) is the most common coverage ratio.

One of the key elements in the analysis of corporate bonds is **coverage,** which measures a firm's ability to meet interest and principal payments and thus avoid default. The most commonly used coverage ratio is the *times-interest-earned (TIE) ratio.* This ratio is defined in the following formula and illustrated with data for Carter Chemical Company (see Chapters 5 and 6 for the basic data):

$$\text{Times interest earned (TIE)} = \frac{\text{Earnings before interest and taxes (EBIT)}}{\text{Interest}} = \frac{\$266}{\$66}$$

$$= 4.0 \text{ times for Carter.}$$

$$\text{Industry average} = 6 \text{ times.}$$

The times-interest-earned (TIE) ratio depends on the level of interest payments, which in turn depends on the percentage of total capital represented by debt. For example, if Carter used twice as much debt (with a corresponding reduction in equity) and if the interest rate remained constant, its interest charges would be $66 × 2 = $132. EBIT is not affected by changes in capital structure (the types of long-term financing used), so the increased use of debt would lower Carter's TIE to 2.0 times:

$$\text{TIE} = \frac{\$266}{\$132} = 2.0 \text{ times.}$$

As we will see in Chapter 20, the times-interest-earned ratio is given careful consideration when a firm establishes its *target capital structure.* The pro forma, or projected, TIE that would result under different financing plans is calculated, and care is taken to insure that the use of debt does not lower the TIE to an unacceptable level.

Another ratio that is often used to measure a company's ability to service its debt is the *fixed charge coverage ratio,* defined as follows:

$$\text{Fixed charge} \atop \text{coverage ratio} = \frac{\text{EBIT} + \text{Lease payments}}{\text{Interest} + \left(\text{Lease} \atop \text{payments}\right) + \left(\frac{\text{Sinking fund payment}}{1 - \text{Tax rate}}\right)}$$

$$= \frac{\$266 + \$28}{\$66 + \$28 + \frac{\$20}{(1 - 0.4)}}$$

$$= 2.3 \text{ times for Carter.}$$

$$\text{Industry average} = 2.5 \text{ times.}$$

Sinking funds were discussed earlier in this chapter; in essence, a sinking fund payment goes toward the retirement of the bond. Because sinking fund payments are not tax deductible, but the interest and lease payments are deductible, the sinking fund payment is divided by (1 − Tax rate) to find the before-tax income required to pay taxes and have enough left to make the sinking fund payment.

Self-Test

What are the two major rating agencies, and what are some factors that affect bond ratings?

Why are bond ratings important both to firms and to investors?

Coverage is one of the key elements in the analysis of corporate bonds. Identify two ratios commonly used, and give the equations for their calculation.

VALUATION OF BONDS

In Chapter 14 we indicated that the value of a capital budgeting project is its discounted future cash flow. What is true for the valuation of real assets is also true for financial asset valuation. In other words, the value of a financial asset — a bond, a share of preferred stock, or a share of common stock — is equal to the cash returns provided by the security discounted back to the present.

A bond is a contractual debt instrument calling for the payment of a specified amount of interest for a stated number of years, and for the repayment of the par value on the bond's maturity date.[8] Thus the bond's cash flow is represented by an annuity plus a lump sum, and its value is found as the present value of this cash flow stream.

---

[8]Actually, most bonds pay interest semiannually rather than annually, so it is necessary to modify our valuation formula, Equation 16-1, slightly. This modification is discussed in the next section.

The following equation is used to find a bond's value:

$$\text{Value} = V = \sum_{t=1}^{n} I \frac{1}{(1 + k_d)^t} + M \frac{1}{(1 + k_d)^n}$$

$$= I(\text{PVIFA}_{k_d,n}) + M(\text{PVIF}_{k_d,n}). \qquad \textbf{(16-1)}$$

Here

I = dollars of interest paid each year = coupon interest rate $\times$ par value.

M = the par value, or maturity value, which typically is $1,000.

k_d = the appropriate rate of interest on the bond, or the "going rate" on bonds with this degree of risk.[9]

n = the number of years until the bond matures; n declines each year after the bond is issued.

We can use Equation 16-1 to find the value of Carter Chemical Company's bonds. Assume that on January 2, 1991, Carter Chemical Company borrowed $50 million by selling 50,000 individual bonds for $1,000 each. Carter received the $50 million, and it promised to pay the bondholders an annual interest rate of 9 percent. Each holder of a $1,000 bond would be entitled to interest of $1,000 $\times$ 0.09 = $90. The bonds were due to mature in 15 years, at which time the maturity value of $1,000 would be paid to each bondholder. Simply substitute $90 for I, $1,000 for M, and the values for PVIFA (found in Table A-2) and for PVIF (found in Table A-1) at 9 percent, Period 15:

$$V = \$90(8.0607) + \$1,000(0.2745)$$

$$= \$725.46 + \$274.50$$

$$= \$999.96 \approx \$1,000 \text{ when } k_d = 9\% \text{ and } n = 15.$$

Figure 16-3 gives a graphic view of the bond valuation process.

If k_d remained constant at 9 percent, what would the value of the bond be 1 year after it was issued? We can find this value using the same valuation formula, but now the term to maturity is only 14 years; that is, n = 14:

$$V = \$90(7.7862) + \$1,000(0.2992)$$

$$= \$999.96 \approx \$1,000 \text{ when } k_d = 9\% \text{ and } n = 14.$$

This same result will hold for every year as long as the appropriate interest rate for the bond remains constant at 9 percent.

---

[9]The appropriate interest rate is determined by a number of factors. Most of these are reflected in the bond's rating, but they also include such factors as supply and demand in the capital markets, and the general level of interest rates at that particular point in time.

Figure 16-3 **Time Line for Carter Chemical Company Bonds**

A bond's value is equal to the sum of its future interest payments and its final lump sum payment discounted to their present value. For example, the discounted cash flows from a 15-year, 9 percent Carter Chemical bond purchased in January 1991 totaled approximately $1,000; the first interest payment of $90.00 was discounted for one year to a present value of $82.57, the second interest payment of $90.00 was discounted for two years to a present value of $75.75, and so on.

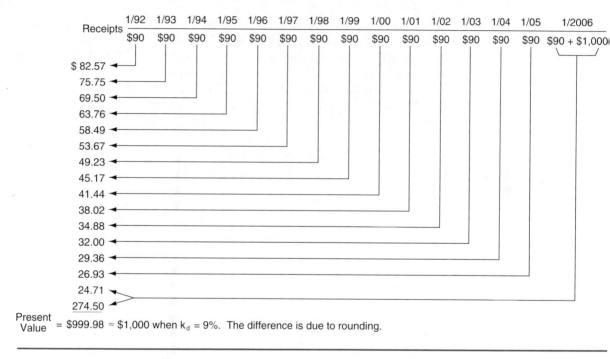

Present Value = $999.98 ≈ $1,000 when k_d = 9%. The difference is due to rounding.

Now suppose that interest rates in the economy rose immediately after Carter's 9 percent bonds were issued, and as a result k_d increased from 9 to 12 percent. Of course, the interest and principal payments on the bonds are fixed, but now 12 percent values at 15 years for PVIFA and PVIF would be used in Equation 16-1. Thus, the bond's value would be $795.68 if investors require a 12 percent return:

$$V = \$90(6.8109) + \$1,000(0.1827)$$

$$= \$612.98 + \$182.70$$

$$= \$795.68 \text{ when } k_d = 12\% \text{ and } n = 15.$$

The bond would sell at a *discount*—that is, at a price below its par value.

The arithmetic of the bond's price decrease should be clear, but what is the logic behind it? The reason for the decrease is simple. Carter Chemical's bondholders notice that other companies are issuing bonds with the same risk characteristics as Carter's but with higher rates of return. Carter's bondholders, eager to receive the higher yield, sell Carter's 9 percent bonds in order to purchase the new 12 percent bonds. The increased supply of Carter's bonds means that the price of the bonds will fall. As investors continue selling Carter's bonds, the price will be further depressed until, at the price of $795.68, Carter's bonds will yield the same rate of return to an investor as the new 12 percent bonds.

Assuming that interest rates remain constant at 12 percent for the next 15 years (which is not very likely), what would happen to the price of this Carter Chemical bond? It would rise gradually from $795.68 at present to $1,000 at maturity, when Carter Chemical must redeem each bond for $1,000. This point can be illustrated by calculating the value of the bond 1 year after issue, when it has 14 years to maturity:

$$V = \$90(6.6282) + \$1,000(0.2046)$$

$$= \$596.54 + \$204.60$$

$$= \$801.14 \text{ when } k_d = 12\% \text{ and } n = 14.$$

The value of the bond will have risen from $795.68 to $801.14, or by $5.46. If you were to calculate the value of the bond at other future dates, while holding k_d constant at 12 percent, the price would continue to rise as the maturity date approached.

Notice that if you purchased the bond at a price of $795.68 and then sold it 1 year later with k_d still at 12 percent, you would have a capital gain of $5.46, or a total return of $90 + $5.46 = $95.46. Your percentage rate of return would consist of an **interest yield** (also called a **current yield**) plus a **capital gains yield,** calculated as follows:

current (interest) yield
The annual interest payment on a bond divided by its current market price.

capital gains yield
The capital gain during any one year divided by the beginning price.

$$\text{Interest, or current, yield} = \$90.00/\$795.68 = 0.1131 = 11.31\%$$

$$\text{Capital gains yield} = \$5.46/\$795.68 = 0.0069 = \underline{0.69\%}$$

$$\text{Total rate of return, or yield} = \$95.46/\$795.68 = 0.1200 = \underline{\underline{12.00\%}}$$

If interest rates had fallen from 9 to 6 percent when Carter Chemical Company's bonds had 14 years to maturity, the value of each bond would have risen to $1,278.85

$$V = \$90(PVIFA_{6\%,14}) + \$1,000(PVIF_{6\%,14})$$

$$= \$90(9.2950) + \$1,000(0.4423)$$

$$= \$836.55 + \$442.30$$

$$= \$1,278.85 \text{ when } k_d = 6\% \text{ and } n = 14.$$

Figure 16-4 **Time Path of the Value of a 9% Coupon, $1,000 Par Value Bond when Interest Rates Are 6%, 9%, and 12%**

The value of a bond fluctuates in response to changes in market interest rates. When a bond's coupon rate is equal to the market rate of interest (the going rate), the bond sells at par. When the market rate falls below a bond's coupon rate, the bond sells above par. And when the market rate rises above a bond's coupon rate, the bond sells below par. This graph shows how the selling price of a 15-year, 9 percent bond with a par value of $1,000 will change if market interest rates rise to 12 percent or fall to 6 percent the year after issue, and remains at that level until maturity. Note that as the bond's maturity date approaches, its value fluctuates less and less until it finally reaches par.

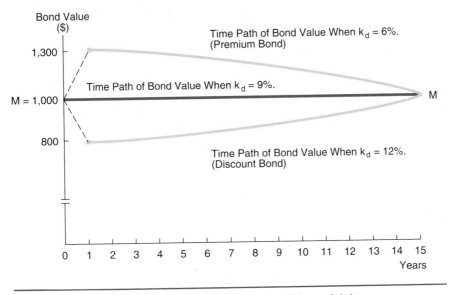

Note: The curves for 6% and 12% appear to be straight, but they actually have a slight bow.

In this case, the bond would sell at a *premium* above its par value. If interest rates remain at 6 percent for the next 14 years, the value of the bond would fall gradually from $1,278.85 to $1,000 at maturity.

Figure 16-4 graphs the value of the bond over time, assuming that interest rates in the economy either remain constant at 9 percent, rise to 12 percent, or fall to 6 percent, and, in the case of the 12 and 6 percent rates, also stay constant after the initial change. Of course, if interest rates do *not* remain constant, the price of the bond will fluctuate. Regardless of what interest rates do, however, the bond's price will approach $1,000 as the maturity date comes nearer (barring bankruptcy, in which case the bond's value might drop to zero).

Figure 16-4 illustrates the following key points:

1. Whenever the going rate of interest (k_d) is equal to the coupon rate, a bond will sell at its par value.

discount bond
A bond that sells below its par value; occurs when the going rate of interest is *higher* than the coupon rate.

premium bond
A bond that sells above its par value; occurs when the going rate of interest is *lower* than the coupon rate.

2. Whenever the going rate of interest is above the coupon rate, a bond will sell below its par value. Such a bond is called a **discount bond.**

3. Whenever the going rate of interest is below the coupon rate, a bond will sell above its par value. Such a bond is called a **premium bond.**

4. An increase in interest rates will cause the price of outstanding bonds to fall, whereas a decrease in interest rates will cause bond prices to rise.

5. The market value of a bond will approach its par value as its maturity date approaches.

These points are very important to investors, for they show that bondholders may suffer capital losses or realize capital gains depending on whether interest rates rise or fall. And, as we saw earlier in this chapter, interest rates do indeed change over time.

Semiannual Compounding for Bonds

Although some bonds do pay interest annually, most actually pay interest semi-annually. The same methodology discussed in Appendix 13A for other than annual compounding periods applies to the valuation of bonds when interest is paid more than once each year. To evaluate semiannual payment bonds, we must modify the bond valuation model (Equation 16-1) as follows:

1. Divide the annual coupon interest payment by 2 to determine the amount of interest paid each 6 months.

2. Multiply the years to maturity, n, by 2 to determine the number of periods.

3. Divide the annual interest rate, k_d, by 2 to determine the semiannual interest rate.

By making these changes, we arrive at the following equation for finding the value of a bond that pays interest semiannually:

$$V = \sum_{t=1}^{2n} \frac{I}{2} \frac{1}{\left(1 + \dfrac{k_d}{2}\right)^t} + M \frac{1}{\left(1 + \dfrac{k_d}{2}\right)^{2n}}$$

$$= I/2(\text{PVIFA}_{k_d/2,2n}) + M(\text{PVIF}_{k_d/2,2n}).$$

(16-1a)

To illustrate, assume now that a firm, Super-Natural Foods, has a bond that has a 15 percent coupon, a par value of $1,000, and 15 years to maturity. If interest is paid semiannually, the firm will pay $75 interest per bond every 6 months rather than $150 at the end of each year. Thus, each interest payment is only half as large, but there are twice as many of them. When the going rate of interest is 10 percent, the value of this 15-year bond is found as follows:

$$V = \$75(\text{PVIFA}_{5\%,30\text{ periods}}) + \$1,000(\text{PVIF}_{5\%,30\text{ periods}})$$

$$= \$75(15.3725) + \$1,000(0.2314)$$

$$= \$1,152.94 + \$231.40$$

$$= \$1,384.34.$$

If the bond had paid its interest annually, the bond's price would have been:

$$V = \$150(\text{PVIFA}_{10\%,15 \text{ periods}}) + \$1,000(\text{PVIF}_{10\%,15 \text{ periods}})$$

$$= \$150(7.6061) + \$1,000(0.2394)$$

$$= \$1,140.92 + \$239.40$$

$$= \$1,380.32.$$

The $1,384.34 value with semiannual interest payments is slightly larger than $1,380.32, the bond's value when interest is paid annually. The higher value occurs because interest payments are received somewhat faster and compounded more often under semiannual compounding.

When bonds pay interest semiannually, students sometimes want to discount the maturity value ($M = \$1,000$) at 10 percent over 15 periods, rather than at the correct 5 percent over 30 six-month periods. This is *incorrect;* logically, all cash flows in a given contract must be discounted on the same basis — semiannually in this instance. For consistency, bond traders *must* apply semiannual compounding to the maturity value, and they do.

Finding the Interest Rate on a Bond: Yield to Maturity

Suppose you were offered a 14-year, 9 percent, annual coupon, $1,000 par value bond at a price of $1,082.48. What rate of interest would you earn if you bought the bond and held it to maturity? This rate is defined as the bond's **yield to maturity,** and it is the interest rate discussed by bond traders when they talk about rates of return. To find the yield to maturity, often called the **YTM,** you could solve the following equation for k_d:

yield to maturity (YTM)
The rate of return earned on a bond if it is held to maturity.

$$V = \$1,082.48$$

$$= \frac{\$90}{(1 + k_d)^1} + \frac{\$90}{(1 + k_d)^2} + \cdots + \frac{\$90}{(1 + k_d)^{14}} + \frac{\$1,000}{(1 + k_d)^{14}}$$

$$= \$90(\text{PVIFA}_{k_d,14}) + \$1,000(\text{PVIF}_{k_d,14}).$$

Just as we did in finding the IRR for a project in Chapter 14, we can substitute values of PVIFA and PVIF in the equation until we find a rate that *just equates* the present market price of the bond with the present value of its future cash flow of interest and principal. Thus

$$\$1,082.48 = \$90(\text{PVIFA}_{k_d,14}) + \$1,000(\text{PVIF}_{k_d,14}).$$

What would be a good interest rate to use as a starting point? First, from earlier discussions, we know that since the bond is selling at a premium over its par value ($1,082.48 versus $1,000), the bond's yield is *below* the 9 percent annual coupon rate. Therefore, we might try a rate of 7 percent. Substituting interest factors for 7 percent, we obtain

$$\$90(8.7455) + \$1,000(0.3878) = \$1,174.90 \neq \$1,082.48.$$

Our calculated bond value, $1,174.90, is *above* the actual market price, so the yield to maturity is *not* 7 percent. To lower the calculated value, we must *raise* the interest rate used in the process. Inserting interest factors for 8 percent, we obtain

$$V = \$90(8.2442) + \$1,000(0.3405)$$

$$= \$741.98 + \$340.50$$

$$= \$1,082.48.$$

This calculated value is exactly equal to the market price of the bond; thus 8 percent is the bond's yield to maturity.[10]

Of course, the easiest way to find the yield to maturity (YTM) of a bond is with a financial calculator. Input the price of the bond, its term to maturity, the coupon payment, and its maturity value, and then press the $k = i$ button to find the YTM. If the bond pays interest semiannually, use 2n and I/2, and then multiply the rate shown by 2 to obtain the semiannual YTM.

The yield to maturity is the total rate of return for an investor, and this rate of return is equal to the bond's coupon rate, if the bond is selling at par. If a bond is purchased at a price other than its par value, the YTM consists of the interest yield plus either a positive capital gains yield (if the bond was purchased at a discount) or a negative capital gains yield (if the bond was purchased at a premium). Note also that a bond's yield to maturity changes whenever interest rates in the economy change, and this is almost daily. An investor who purchases a bond and holds it until maturity will receive the YTM that existed on the purchase date, but the bond's calculated YTM will change frequently between the date the bond was purchased and the time it matures.

Self-Test

Explain the following equation:

$$V = I(PVIFA_{k_d,n}) + M(PVIF_{k_d,n}).$$

Explain what happens to the price of a bond if (1) interest rates rise above the bond's coupon rate or (2) interest rates fall below the bond's coupon rate.

---

[10]A formula developed by R. J. Rodrigues can be used to find the approximate yield to maturity on a bond:

$$k_d = YTM = \frac{I + (M - V)/n}{(M + 2V)/3}.$$

In the situation where $I = \$90$, $M = \$1,000$, $V = \$1,082.48$, and $n = 14$,

$$k_d = \frac{\$90 + (\$1,000 - \$1,082.48)/14}{(\$1,000 + \$2,164.96)/3} = 0.07972 = 7.972\%.$$

This is close to the exact value, 8 percent. This formula can also be used to obtain a starting point for the trial-and-error method.

How is the general bond valuation formula changed to deal with bonds that have semiannual coupons versus bonds that have annual coupons?

Explain the following statement: "An investor who purchases a bond and holds it until maturity will receive the YTM that existed on the purchase date, but the bond's calculated YTM will change frequently between the date the bond is purchased and the time it matures."

PREFERRED STOCK

Preferred stock is a *hybrid* — it is similar to bonds in some respects and to common stock in others. The hybrid nature of preferred stock becomes apparent when we try to classify it in relation to bonds and common stock. Like bonds, preferred stock has a par value. Preferred dividends are also similar to interest payments on bonds in that they are fixed in amount and generally must be paid before common stock dividends can be paid. However, if the preferred dividend is not earned, the directors can omit (or "pass") it without throwing the company into bankruptcy. So, even though preferred stock has a fixed payment like bonds, a failure to make this payment will not lead to bankruptcy.

preferred stock
A long-term equity security which pays a fixed dividend.

Preferred stock is sometimes considered to be debt and sometimes equity, depending on the type of analysis being made. If the analysis is being made by a common stockholder considering the fixed charge that must be paid ahead of common stock dividends, the preferred stock will be viewed much like debt. Suppose, however, that the analysis is being made by a bondholder studying the firm's vulnerability to failure because of a future decline in sales and income. Since the dividends on preferred stock are not a fixed charge in the sense that failure to pay them represents a default on an obligation, preferred stock provides an additional equity base. We see, then, that common stockholders view preferred stock much like debt, while creditors view it as being like equity.

Major Provisions of Preferred Stock Issues

Preferred stock has a number of features, the most important of which are covered in the following sections.

Priority in Assets and Earnings. Preferred stockholders have priority over common stockholders with regard to earnings and assets. Thus, dividends must be paid on preferred stock before they can be paid on the common stock, and, in the event of bankruptcy, the claims of the preferred shareholders must be satisfied before the common stockholders receive anything. To reinforce these features, most preferred stock contracts have coverage requirements, similar to those on bonds, which limit the amount of preferred stock a company can use; they also require that a minimum level of retained earnings be maintained before common dividends can be paid.

Par Value. Unlike common stock, preferred stock always has a par value (or its equivalent under some other name), and this value is important. First, the par value establishes the amount due the preferred stockholders in the event of liquidation. Second, the preferred dividend is frequently stated as a percentage of the par value. For example, Duke Power has preferred stock with a par value of $100 and a stated dividend of 8.7 percent of par. It would, of course, be just as appropriate for the Duke preferred stock to simply call for an annual dividend of $8.70.

cumulative dividends

A protective feature on preferred stock that requires past preferred dividends to be paid before any common dividends can be paid.

arrearage

An omitted dividend on preferred stock.

Cumulative Dividends. Most preferred stock provides for **cumulative dividends;** that is, all preferred dividend **arrearages** must be paid before common dividends can be paid. The cumulative feature is a protective device, for if the preferred stock dividends were not cumulative, a firm could avoid paying preferred and common stock dividends for, say, 10 years and thus "save" a large amount of earnings, and then pay a large common stock dividend but pay only the stipulated annual amount to the preferred stockholders. Obviously, such an action could be used to effectively void the preferred position that the preferred stockholders are supposed to have. The cumulative feature prevents such abuses.[11]

Convertibility. Approximately 40 percent of the preferred stock that has been issued in recent years is convertible into common stock. For example, each share of Enron's $10.50 Class J preferred stock can be converted into 3.413 shares of its common stock at the option of the preferred shareholders. (Convertibility is discussed in more detail in Chapter 18.)

Some Infrequent Provisions. Some other provisions occasionally encountered in preferred stocks include the following:

1. Voting rights. Sometimes preferred stockholders are given the right to vote for directors if the company has not paid the preferred dividend for a specified period, say, four, eight, or ten quarters. This feature motivates management to make every effort to pay preferred dividends.

2. Participating. A rare type of preferred stock is one that participates with the common stock in sharing the firm's earnings. Participating preferred stocks generally work as follows: (a) the stated preferred dividend is paid—for example, $5 a share; (b) the common stock is then entitled to a dividend in an amount up to the preferred dividend—in this case, $5; and (c) if the common dividend is raised, say to $5.50, the preferred dividend must likewise be raised to $5.50.

---

[11]Note, however, that compounding is absent in most cumulative plans — in other words, the arrearages themselves earn no return. Also, many preferred issues have a limited cumulative feature; for example, arrearages might accumulate for only three years.

3. Sinking fund. In the past (before the mid-1970s), few preferred issues had sinking funds. Today, however, most newly issued preferred stocks have sinking funds which call for the purchase and retirement of a given percentage of the preferred stock each year. For example, 2 percent, which is a common amount, gives the relevant preferred issue an average life of 25 years and a maximum life of 50 years.

4. Maturity. Before the mid-1970s, most preferred stock was perpetual — it had no maturity and never needed to be paid off. However, today most new preferred stock has a sinking fund and thus an effective maturity date.

5. Call provision. A call provision gives the issuing corporation the right to call in the preferred stock for redemption, as in the case of bonds. Call provisions generally state that the company must pay an amount greater than the par value of the preferred stock, the additional sum being termed a **call premium.** For example, IBES Corporation's 12 percent, $100 par value preferred stock, issued in 1984, is noncallable for 10 years, but it may be called at a price of $112 after 1995.

call premium
The amount in excess of par value that a company must pay when it calls a security.

Evaluation of Preferred Stock

There are both advantages and disadvantages to financing with preferred stock. These are discussed in the following sections.

Issuer's Viewpoint. By using preferred stock, a firm can fix its financial costs and thus keep more of the potential future profits for its existing set of common stockholders, as with bonds, yet avoid the danger of bankruptcy if earnings are too low to meet these fixed charges. Also, by selling preferred rather than common stock, the firm avoids sharing control with new investors.

However, preferred stock does have a major disadvantage from the issuer's standpoint: It has a higher after-tax cost of capital than debt. The major reason for this higher cost is taxes: Preferred dividends are not deductible as a tax expense, while interest expense is deductible, which makes the effective cost of preferred stock much greater than that of bonds. The after-tax cost of debt is approximately two-thirds the stated coupon rate for profitable firms, whereas the cost of preferred stock is the full percentage amount of the preferred dividend. Of course, the deductibility differential is most important for issuers that are in relatively high tax brackets. If a company pays little or no taxes because it is unprofitable or because it has a great deal of accelerated depreciation, the deductibility of interest does not make much difference. Thus, the higher a company's tax bracket, the less likely it is to use preferred stock financing.

Investor's Viewpoint. In designing securities, the financial manager must also consider the investor's point of view. Frequently it is asserted that preferred stock has so many disadvantages to both the issuer and the investor that it should never be issued. Nevertheless, preferred stock is issued in substantial amounts. It provides investors with reasonably steady and assured income plus a preference over common stockholders in the event of liquidation. In addition, 70 percent of the preferred dividends received by corporations are not taxable. For this reason, most outstanding preferred stock is owned by corporations.

The principal disadvantage of preferred stock from an investor's standpoint is that although preferred stockholders bear a substantial portion of ownership risk, their returns are limited. In addition, preferred stockholders have no legally enforceable right to dividends, even if a company earns a profit. Also, companies often manage to avoid paying off all accumulated dividends when they emerge from a troubled, low-income period. Such companies frequently go through reorganization under the Bankruptcy Act, and preferred stockholders often do not fare well in these proceedings.

Recent Innovations in Preferred Stock

Because preferred dividends are not tax deductible, many companies have retired their preferred stocks and replaced them with debentures or subordinated debentures. However, as the following examples illustrate, preferred is still used to raise long-term capital when conditions are such that neither common stock nor long-term debt can be issued on reasonable terms, and a hybrid such as preferred is useful.

1. Chrysler's issue of preferred stock with warrants several years ago proved a successful means of raising capital in the face of adverse circumstances. Because of its losses, Chrysler's common stock was depressed and very much out of favor. Investors were so worried about the company's ability to survive that they were unwilling to make additional commitments without receiving some sort of senior position. Therefore, common stock was ruled out. Chrysler had already borrowed to the hilt, and it could not obtain any more debt without first building its equity base (and preferred is equity from the bondholders' viewpoint). Various incentives were offered to the brokers who handled the preferred issue, and a relatively high yield was set. As a result, the issue was so successful that its size was raised from $150 to $200 million while the underwriting was under way. Chrysler got the money it needed, and that money helped the company regain profitability. Chrysler's common stock is currently priced at over $16, up from about $3 when the preferred was issued. The preferred stock helped the company survive and achieve that gain in the common stock price.

2. Utility companies often use preferred stock to bolster the equity component of their capital structures. These companies are capital intensive, and they make heavy use of debt financing, but lenders and rating agencies require minimum equity ratios as a condition for maintaining bond ratings.

Also, the utilities have made very heavy investments in fixed assets and thus have high depreciation charges, which has held down their effective tax rates and thus has lowered the tax disadvantage of preferred stock in relation to debt.

3. In recent years there has also been a pronounced movement toward convertible preferred, which is often used in connection with mergers. For example, when Belco Petroleum was negotiating its acquisition by Enron, it was pointed out that if the buyout were for cash, Belco's stockholders (one of whom owned 40 percent of the stock and thus could block the merger) would be required to immediately pay huge capital gains taxes. However, under U.S. tax laws, if preferred stock is exchanged for the acquired company's common, this constitutes a tax-free exchange of securities. Thus, Belco's stockholders could obtain a fixed-income security yet postpone the payment of taxes on their capital gains.

Enron actually offered a choice of straight or convertible preferred to Belco's stockholders. Those stockholders who were interested primarily in income could take the straight preferred, whereas those interested in capital gains could take the convertible preferred. After the exchange, both preferred issues traded on the NYSE; the straight preferred had a yield of 11 percent, and the convertible preferred yielded 7.5 percent. However, the convertibles had a chance of gains — indeed, by October 1990 the Enron convertible preferred had risen from its initial price of $100 to $203 per share because of an increase in the price of the common into which it could be converted. Meanwhile, the price of the nonconvertible preferred remained close to its $100 par value.

4. In 1984, Alabama Power introduced a new type of security, **floating rate preferred stock.** Since this stock has a floating rate, its price stays relatively constant, making it suitable for liquidity portfolios (marketable securities held by corporations to provide funds either for planned expenditures or to meet emergencies). The combination of a floating rate, and hence a stable price, plus the 70 percent tax exemption for corporations, makes this preferred quite attractive, and it enabled Alabama Power to obtain capital at a low cost.

floating rate preferred stock
Preferred stock whose dividend rate fluctuates with changes in the general level of interest rates.

Valuation of Preferred Stock

Despite the fact that preferred stock dividends can be omitted without throwing the firm into bankruptcy, most financial managers attempt to pay these dividends without omission. Thus, these dividends may reasonably be expected to be paid on time, and, because few preferred stock dividends are participating, these dividends should not change in value from period to period.

Just as bondholders value debt instruments as the present value of the bond's future cash flows, discounted at a required rate of return, k_d, preferred stockholders also discount future cash flows (in this case dividends) to arrive at a current market price for preferred stock:[12]

$$V_{ps} = \sum_{t=1}^{\infty} \frac{D_t}{(1 + k_{ps})^t}. \qquad (16\text{-}2)$$

Here:

V_{ps} = the market price of preferred stock today.
D_t = dividend payments each period for t periods.
k_{ps} = the required rate of return on preferred stock.

Recalling that preferred stock dividends can be expected to remain at some constant amount in the future (that is, $D_1 = D_2 = D_3$ and so on), we can drop the subscripts and determine the value of preferred stock, V_{ps}:

$$V_{ps} = \frac{D}{(1 + k_{ps})^1} + \frac{D}{(1 + k_{ps})^2} + \cdots$$

$$+ \frac{D}{(1 + k_{ps})^n} + \cdots + \frac{D}{(1 + k_{ps})^\infty}. \qquad (16\text{-}2a)$$

The value of the stock, V_{ps}, can be determined by discounting each year's dividend back to the present. However, as we noted in Chapter 13, as the holding period, t, becomes infinitely large, the value of any no-growth security, a perpetuity, may be simplified from Equation 16-2 (or Equation 16-2a) to:

$$V_{ps} = \frac{D_{ps}}{k_{ps}}. \qquad (16\text{-}3)$$

Thus, if Carter Chemical Company had a $100 par value preferred stock issue with a 12 percent dividend yield and no sinking fund provision, the stock's price would be determined by the investors' required return, k_{ps}. If investors were satisfied with a 12 percent rate of return, they would pay a price equal to the stock's par value:

$$V_{ps} = \$12/0.12$$

$$= \$100.$$

---

[12]Note that previously we mentioned that more preferred stocks are being issued with sinking funds, which call for the purchase and retirement of a given percentage of the issue in each year. In this instance, the valuation of the preferred stock would involve discounting future cash flows, but these cash flows would have a *finite* life. Thus, the valuation would be similar to that for a bond.

If, however, investors desired a 14 percent rate of return, they would pay less than the preferred stock's par value:

$$V_{ps} = \$12/0.14$$

$$= \$85.71.$$

Similarly, if rates on competing investment opportunities fell to 8 percent, the price of the preferred stock would rise to $150:

$$V_{ps} = \$12/0.08$$

$$= \$150.$$

We could transpose the V_{ps} and the k_{ps} in Equation 16-3 and solve for k_{ps}. We could then look up the price of the stock and the preferred dividend in the financial section of the newspaper, and the value of D_{ps}/V_{ps} would be the rate of return we could expect to earn if we bought the stock. Thus:

$$k_{ps} = \frac{D_{ps}}{V_{ps}}. \qquad\qquad (16\text{-}4)$$

If we bought the preferred stock, which pays a constant dividend of $12, for $150, the stock's rate of return would be

$$k_{ps} = \$12/\$150 = 0.08 = 8\%.$$

However, if investors are paying only $85.71 for a preferred stock that pays a constant $12 dividend, their required rate of return would be

$$k_{ps} = \$12/\$85.71 = 0.14 = 14\%.$$

Self-Test

Explain the following statement: "Preferred stock is a hybrid."

Identify and briefly explain some of the key features of preferred stock.

What are the advantages and disadvantages of preferred stock from an issuer's viewpoint?

What are the advantages and disadvantages of preferred stock from an investor's viewpoint?

SMALL BUSINESS

Contracting with Providers of Risk Capital

Venture capitalists and others providing risk capital to support firms with high growth prospects often lose much or all of their investments. In fact, a recent study showed that more than a third of all venture capital (VC) investments lost money. In a sixth of the cases, the VC firm lost its entire investment.* That fact and other aspects of the behavior of small business investments mean that the structure of the financial contract between an entrepreneur and a venture capitalist may have a decided effect on the decision to provide capital to the business. Bill Sahlman of Harvard University argues that ". . . an effective financial design may well be the difference between a flourishing and a failed (if not a still-born) enterprise."† The points discussed below are largely based on his article.

The financial contract between a VC firm and an entrepreneur must contain a number of key points relating to the ultimate success or failure of the venture. Among the points that need to be considered are these:

- What can go wrong?
- What can go right?
- Who gets what in the case of the two above points?
- What expected return is required?
- What are the risks, and who bears them?
- What are the incentives for each of the two sides?

---

*See Linda A. Vincent, "Setting Realistic Expectations for Potential Returns — Part II," *Investing in Venture Capital* (Washington, D. C.: The Institute of Chartered Financial Analysts, 1989).

†William A. Sahlman, "Aspects of Financial Contracting in Venture Capital," *Journal of Applied Corporate Finance, VI,* No. 2 (Summer, 1988), pp. 23-36.

A deal in which the venture capitalist receives a large share and the entrepreneur receives very little will fail because the entrepreneur will have little or no incentive to make it work. So, the deal itself can destroy incentives. A good contract will insure that both sides do well if things go right.

The entrepreneur is probably optimistic about his or her project. Anyone who would devote all of his or her time and resources to a project would have to be optimistic. As a result of this optimism, the entrepreneur's viewpoint may not be realistic. The contract should delineate some conditions under which the entrepreneur is not meeting projections, and, under those conditions, the VC firm might have a greater share of the venture — perhaps also including the right to actually remove the entrepreneur from the project. To protect the VC firm, the contract must provide for the possibility that things will not work out as expected. Often, this is achieved by the VC firm's investing in the venture in the form of preferred stock (with a preference on liquidation) or convertible debt. Such an investment gives the venture capitalist's claim top priority in the event of the firm's failure and provides some "downside" protection. The security will also probably be convertible, however, so that the VC firm can convert to straight equity if the deal goes well. Convertible debt is a sort of a "have my cake and eat it too" option.

By allocating much of the risk to the entrepreneur, the venture capitalist is forcing the entrepreneur to take *actions* to confirm his or her forecasts. Any entrepreneur can produce a set of lofty forecasts, but, by agreeing to a contract under which the entrepreneur gets nothing if the venture does not meet those forecasts, the entrepreneur says, in no uncertain terms, "I believe in this deal."

Another feature of VC investment is that it does not necessarily provide all the capital a firm needs in the beginning. For example, suppose you have developed an idea for a new product, and you estimate you will need $10 million to develop a prototype, set up the manufacturing process, and begin to market the product. You will not get the $10 million in advance, and, indeed, it may be in the best interest of both the entrepreneur and the venture capitalist that you not get all of the money in advance. It makes sense to get the investment from the venture capitalist in stages, rather than all at once. The product is, at this stage, only an idea; there is at least some risk that the product will not be successful. Typically, only a small fraction of the total capital requirement is needed to develop and test a product. Once it is developed, both the entrepreneur and the investors may agree that they should not proceed with it, perhaps because by that time there is already a superior competitor on the market.

If the entrepreneur insists on the full $10 million in advance, he or she will probably get *nothing*. This is the stage at which the project faces its greatest risks, and few people would be foolish enough to invest at this stage. Accordingly, the entrepreneur would have to give up virtually all ownership rights to get the money in advance. So, he or she should accept only the money that is needed for that stage, and thus retain what he or she can of the ownership claim.

As the entrepreneur moves toward developing production facilities, he or she will want to obtain some market data to measure the need for the product, and to help determine prices. This is another source of risk, and, again, the entrepreneur is better off not insisting on capital infusions at this point, since he or she is still more willing than others to bear the risk of failure. At each stage of the project, risk is reduced, and in the later stages the entrepreneur should be able to obtain larger amounts of funding while giving up smaller fractions of ownership. Accepting money in stages, under a set of prearranged conditions, is known as "staged capital commitment."

A final suggestion for the entrepreneur designing the terms under which funds are accepted is to remain flexible. Sahlman tells of a case in which the initial investors insisted on receiving an option that permitted them to maintain 51% ownership of a venture, regardless of how much additional capital was raised from others after the initial deal. The effect of this provision was to ruin the company's chances of raising any additional capital. Potential investors felt that their investment would be diluted by the "rolling option" of the initial investors.

In a similar case, a new software firm raised funds by selling stock to investors at $5.00 per share. The CEO decided he would not let any new investors buy stock at a better price than that of the original investors. Later, when the company had problems and was in worse shape than in the beginning, it couldn't raise additional funds because the price was too steep. Thus, a provision intended to *protect* the early shareholders turned out to prevent the firm from raising capital, and, ultimately, it reduced the chances that investors would see returns on their capital. Beware of conditions that limit your options with respect to future financial needs. Even conditions created with good intentions may do more harm than good.

In summary, a good financing contract must encompass many issues. It must provide incentives for both sides in the agreement. It must lead to an appropriate sharing of both risks and returns. It must allow for raising additional funds in the future. Finally, it must be clear, as well as fair, to both sides. A deal is not good unless it is fair for all parties involved.

SUMMARY

This chapter contained a discussion of the characteristics, advantages, and disadvantages of the major types of long-term debt securities and preferred stock. The valuation of both debt and preferred stock was also discussed. The key concepts covered are listed below.

- **Term loans** and **bonds** are long-term debt contracts under which a borrower agrees to make a series of interest and principal payments on specific dates to the lender. A term loan is generally obtained from one (or a few) lenders, while a bond is typically offered to the public and sold to many different investors.

- There are many different types of bonds. They include **mortgage bonds, debentures, convertibles, bonds with warrants, income bonds,** and **purchasing power (indexed) bonds.** The return required on each type of bond is determined by the bond's riskiness.

- A bond's **indenture** is a legal document that spells out the rights of the bondholders and of the issuing corporation. A **trustee** is assigned to make sure that the terms of the indenture are carried out.

- A **call provision** gives the issuing corporation the right to redeem the bonds prior to maturity under specified terms, usually at a price greater than the maturity value (the difference is a **call premium**). A firm will typically call a bond and refund it if interest rates fall substantially.

- A **sinking fund** is a provision which requires the corporation to pay off a portion of the bond issue each year. The purpose of the sinking fund is to provide for the orderly retirement of the issue. No call premium is paid to the holders of bonds called for sinking fund purposes.

- Some recent innovations in long-term financing include **zero coupon bonds,** which pay no annual interest but which are issued at a discount; **floating rate debt,** on which interest payments fluctuate with changes in the general level of interest rates; and **junk bonds,** which are high-risk, high-yield instruments used by firms that use a great deal of financial leverage.

- Bonds are assigned **ratings** which reflect the probability of their going into default. The higher a bond's rating, the lower its interest rate.

- The **value of a bond** is found as the present value of an **annuity** (the interest payments) plus the present value of a lump sum (the **principal**). The bond is evaluated at the appropriate periodic interest rate over the number of periods for which interest payments are made.

- The equation used to find the value of an annual coupon bond is

$$V = \sum_{t=1}^{n} I \frac{1}{(1 + k_d)^t} + M \frac{1}{(1 + k_d)^n}$$

$$= I(\text{PVIFA}_{k_d,n}) + M(\text{PVIF}_{k_d,n}).$$

- An adjustment to the formula must be made if the bond pays interest **semiannually:** divide I and k_d by 2, and multiply n by 2.

- The return earned on a bond held to maturity is defined as the bond's **yield to maturity (YTM).**

- **Preferred stock** is a hybrid security having some characteristics of debt and some of equity. Equity holders view preferred stock as being similar to debt because it provides a claim on the firm's earnings ahead of the claim of the common stockholders. Bondholders, however, view preferred as equity because debtholders have a prior claim on the firm's income, and, in the event of bankruptcy, on the firm's assets.

- The primary **advantages of preferred stock** to the issuer are (1) that preferred dividends are limited and (2) that failure to pay them will not bankrupt the firm. The primary disadvantage to the issuer is that the cost of preferred is higher than that of debt because preferred dividend payments are not tax deductible.

- To the investor, preferred stock offers the advantage of **more dependable income** than common stock, and, to a corporate investor, **70 percent of such dividends are not taxable.** The principal disadvantages to the investor are that the **returns are limited** and that the investor has no **legally enforceable right to a dividend.**

- Most preferred stocks are **perpetuities,** and the value of a share of perpetual preferred stock is found as the dividend divided by the required rate of return:

$$V_{ps} = \frac{D_{ps}}{k_{ps}}.$$

EQUATIONS

The times-interest-earned (TIE) ratio is a common measure of coverage; it measures the firm's ability to meet its annual interest payments:

$$\text{Time interest earned} = \frac{\text{EBIT}}{\text{Interest}}.$$

Another ratio used to measure a company's ability to service debt is the fixed charge coverage ratio. This ratio expands upon the TIE ratio to include the firm's annual long-term lease obligations and sinking fund requirements:

$$\frac{\text{Fixed charge}}{\text{coverage ratio}} = \frac{\text{EBIT} + \text{Lease payments}}{\text{Interest} + \left(\begin{array}{c}\text{Lease}\\\text{payments}\end{array}\right) + \left(\frac{\text{Sinking fund payment}}{1 - \text{Tax rate}}\right)}.$$

The value of a bond is found as the present value of its interest payments (an annuity) plus the present value of its maturity value (a lump sum). The equation to find the value of a bond with annual interest payments is:

$$\text{Value} = V = \sum_{t=1}^{n} I\frac{1}{(1 + k_d)^t} + M\frac{1}{(1 + k_d)^n} \qquad (16\text{-}1)$$

$$= I(\text{PVIFA}_{k_d,n}) + M(\text{PVIF}_{k_d,n}).$$

For a semiannual coupon bond, modifications in the equation above are necessary. The revised equation for valuing a semiannual bond would be as follows:

$$V = \sum_{t=1}^{2n} \frac{I}{2}\frac{1}{\left(1 + \dfrac{k_d}{2}\right)^t} + M \frac{1}{\left(1 + \dfrac{k_d}{2}\right)^{2n}} \qquad (16\text{-}1a)$$

$$= I/2(\text{PVIFA}_{k_d/2,2n}) + M(\text{PVIF}_{k_d/2,2n}).$$

Preferred stockholders discount future cash flows to arrive at the current market price for perpetual preferred stock:

$$V_{ps} = \sum_{t=1}^{\infty} \frac{D_t}{(1 + k_{ps})^t} \qquad (16\text{-}2)$$

Because preferred stock dividends are expected to remain constant, the long version of Equation 16-2 is:

$$V_{ps} = \frac{D}{(1 + k_{ps})^1} + \frac{D}{(1 + k_{ps})^2} + \cdots$$

$$+ \frac{D}{(1 + k_{ps})^n} + \cdots + \frac{D}{(1 + k_{ps})^{\infty}}. \qquad (16\text{-}2a)$$

Because preferred dividends can be expected to remain constant in the future, the valuation of a preferred stock involves the perpetuity equation. The valuation equation for a preferred stock is:

$$V_{ps} = \frac{D_{ps}}{k_{ps}}. \qquad (16\text{-}3)$$

Using the equation above, we can solve for the required rate of return for a preferred stock, as follows:

$$k_{ps} = \frac{D_{ps}}{V_{ps}}. \qquad (16\text{-}4)$$

RESOLUTION TO DECISION IN FINANCE

The Debt Crisis

A friend says about Trump, "He's a good deal-maker, and this is the toughest deal of his life." Ingersoll's attempted solution involves buying back $160 million in bonds at prices well below their face value, but some bondholders announced that they will fight for a better return. Another way to raise cash may be to tap his European connections, where he owns half of Irish Press Newspapers, Ltd.

Workouts have already been successfully negotiated by a number of companies, and the deals they offered bondholders are similar to one another. The key to viability is apparently to get at least 80 to 90 percent of the creditors to agree. Seamans Furniture Company, owned by Kohlberg Kravis Roberts (KKR), got its 200 bondholders to trade in their old junk bonds paying 15 percent for new ones paying 12 percent, and with only a quarter of the face value of the originals. Bank creditors accepted lower

annual payments as well. For its part, KKR's share in the company dropped from 80 percent to just 33 percent.

Leaseway Transportation Corporation attempted a similar restructuring. It spurred bondholders with the news that liability insurance on its trucks would lapse unless they accepted a deal to take new bonds at lower rates, with some equity for senior debt holders.

Jim Walter Corporation, now Hillsborough Holdings, faces an increase in the interest rates on its junk bonds from 15 to 20 percent. It is offering new 18 percent notes to its bondholders, plus several million dollars in cash.

Bondholders are becoming more militant, and are organizing and hiring their own advisers to negotiate with management to get them the best possible terms. They gain nothing, however, if they fight too long and force the company to collapse. Taking less instead of nothing is definitely desirable. This argument will be heard often as more companies ask creditors for a break. People who buy junk bonds should recognize that they are not purchasing U.S. Treasury debt, and that the price for the chance to earn a 15 percent return could be the necessity of settling for a lot less.

Sources: "Yesterday's Bad Deals Are Today's New Business," *Business Week,* December 11, 1989; *The Wall Street Journal,* "Ralph Ingersoll Finds Newspapers Are Fun, Junk Bonds Are Not," March 26, 1990, and "Corporate Bond Defaults Rise Fourfold in Quarter," April 5, 1990; "Trump: The Fall," *Newsweek,* June 18, 1990.

QUESTIONS

16-1   What effect would each of the following items have on the interest rate a firm must pay on a new issue of long-term debt? Indicate by a plus (+), minus (−), or zero (0) whether the factor will tend to raise, lower, or have an indeterminate effect on the firm's interest rate, and then explain *why*.

	Effect on Interest Rate
a. The firm uses bonds rather than a term loan.	_____
b. The firm uses nonsubordinated debentures rather than first mortgage bonds.	_____
c. The firm makes its bonds convertible into common stock.	_____
d. The firm makes its debentures subordinated to its bank debt. What will the effect be:	
(1) On the debentures?	_____
(2) On the bank debt?	_____
(3) On the average total debt?	_____
e. The firm sells income bonds rather than debentures.	_____

f. The firm must raise $100 million, all of which will be used to construct a new plant, and is debating the sale of first mortgage bonds or debentures. If it decides to issue $50 million of each type, as opposed to $75 million of mortgage bonds and $25 million of debentures, how will this affect:

(1) The debentures?	
(2) The mortgage bonds?	_____
(3) The average cost of the $100 million?	_____

g. The firm is planning to raise $25 million of long-term capital. Its outstanding bonds yield 9 percent. If it sells preferred stock, how will this affect the yield on the outstanding debt?	_____
h. The firm puts a call provision on its new issue of bonds.	_____
i. The firm includes a sinking fund on its new issue of bonds.	_____
j. The firm's bonds are downgraded from A to BBB.	_____
k. The firm uses zero coupon bonds rather than coupon bonds.	_____

16-2   Rank the following securities from lowest (1) to highest (10) in terms of their riskiness for an investor. All securities (except the government bond) are for a given firm. If you think two or more securities are equally risky, indicate so.

	Rank (10 = Highest Risk)
a. Income bond	_____
b. Subordinated debentures — noncallable	_____
c. First mortgage bond — no sinking fund	_____
d. Preferred stock	_____
e. Common stock	_____
f. U.S. Treasury bond	_____
g. First mortgage bond — with sinking fund	_____
h. Subordinated debentures — callable	_____
i. Amortized term loan	_____
j. Nonamortized term loan	_____

16-3   A bond that pays interest forever and has no maturity date is a perpetual bond. In what respect is a perpetual bond similar to a share of preferred stock?

16-4   "The values of outstanding bonds change whenever the going rate of interest changes. In general, short-term interest rates are more volatile than long-term interest rates.

Therefore, short-term bond prices are more sensitive to interest rate changes than are long-term bond prices." Is this statement true or false? Explain.

16-5 A sinking fund can be set up in one of two ways:

  (1) The corporation makes annual payments to the trustee, who invests the proceeds in securities (frequently government bonds) and uses the accumulated total to retire the bond issue at maturity.

  (2) The trustee uses the annual payments to retire a portion of the issue each year, either calling a given percentage of the issue by a lottery and paying a specified price per bond or buying bonds on the open market, whichever is cheaper.

Discuss the advantages and disadvantages of each procedure from the viewpoints of both the firm and the bondholders.

SELF-TEST PROBLEM

ST-1 A firm issued a new series of bonds on January 2, 1973. The bonds were sold at par ($1,000), have an 8 percent annual coupon, and mature 30 years after the date of issue. Interest is paid on December 31.

  a. What was the yield to maturity (YTM) of the bonds on January 2, 1973?

  b. What was the price of the bond on January 2, 1978, five years later, assuming that the level of interest rates had risen to 10 percent?

  c. If, for this type of bond, interest rates had been 6 percent on January 2, 1978, what would investors have paid for the bond?

  d. Find the current yield and capital gains yield on the bond if interest rates as of January 2, 1978, were 6 percent, as in Part c.

  e. On January 2, 1983, the bonds sold for $525.70. What was the YTM on that date?

  f. What was the current yield and capital gains yield for the bond under the conditions described in Part e?

  g. It is now January 2, 1991. The going rate of interest is 14 percent. How large a check must you write to buy the bond?

PROBLEMS

16-1 **Preferred stock valuation.** Americal Corporation has a $100 par, $7 dividend perpetual preferred stock outstanding. Investors require a 12 percent return on investments of this type.

  a. What is the current market price of American's preferred stock?

  b. Is the price you computed in Part a the same price that you would find if you discounted each future dividend back to the present using the 12 percent discount factors?

  c. If the investment community's required return fell for American's preferred stock, what would happen to the price?

16-2 **Yield computations.** FSA Corporation sold a 20-year, 12 percent annual coupon, $1,000 par value bond issue 10 years ago. Today, with 10 years to maturity, the bond issue is selling for $849.46. What is the bond's:

  a. Current yield?

  b. Yield to maturity?

16-3 **Bond valuation.** Audiomax Corporation sold a 25-year, 15 percent annual coupon bond issue at a par value of $1,000 in September 1980. In September 1990 the bond issue's yield to maturity is 12 percent. What is the current price of the bond?

16-4 **Semiannual bond valuation.** Assume the same facts as for Problem 16-3, except that, rather than issuing annual coupon bonds, Audiomax had issued semiannual coupon bonds. What is the current price of these semiannual coupon bonds?

16-5 **Semiannual bond valuation.**
a. Olympic Industries' bonds pay $50 semiannual interest, mature in 5 years, and pay $1,000 on maturity. What will be the value of these bonds when the going annual rate of interest is: **(1)** 8 percent, **(2)** 10 percent, and **(3)** 12 percent?
b. Now suppose that Olympic has issued some other bonds that pay $50 semiannual interest, $1,000 at maturity, and mature in 1 year. What is the price of these bonds if the going annual rate of interest is: **(1)** 8 percent, **(2)** 10 percent, and **(3)** 12 percent?
c. Why do the longer-term bond prices fluctuate more when interest rates change than do the shorter-term bond prices?

16-6 **Yield to maturity.** The Barngrover Company's bonds have 5 years remaining to maturity. Interest is paid annually, the bonds have a $1,000 par value, and the annual coupon interest rate is 9 percent.
a. What is the yield to maturity at a current market price of: **(1)** $892 and **(2)** $1,126? You may wish to use the approximation formula found in Footnote 8.
b. Would you pay $892 for the bond described in Part a if you thought that the appropriate rate of interest for these bonds was 10 percent? Explain your answer.

16-7 **Bond valuation.** Suppose Southwest Publications sold an issue of bonds with a 10-year maturity, a $1,000 par value, and a 10 percent coupon rate paid annually.
a. Suppose that 4 years after the issue, the going rate of interest had risen to 14 percent. At what price would the bonds sell?
b. Suppose that the conditions in Part a continued (that is, interest rates remained at 14 percent throughout the bond's life). What would happen to the price of Southwest's bonds over time?

16-8 **Loan amortization.** Suppose that a firm is setting up an amortized term loan. What are the annual payments for a $2 million loan under the following terms:
a. 9 percent, 3 years?
b. 9 percent, 7 years?
c. 12 percent, 3 years?
d. 12 percent, 7 years?

16-9 **Amortization schedule.** Set up an amortization schedule for a $1 million, 3-year, 8 percent term loan.

16-10 **Amortization payments.** A company borrows $1 million on a 3-year, 8 percent, partially amortized term loan. The annual payments are to be set so as to amortize $700,000 over the loan's 3-year life and also to pay interest on the $300,000 nonamortized portion of the loan.
a. How large must each annual payment be? (*Hint:* Think of the loan as consisting of two loans, one fully amortized for $700,000 and one on which interest only is paid each year until the end of the third year.)
b. Suppose the firm requests a $1 million, 8 percent, 3-year loan with payments of $250,000 per year (interest plus some principal repayment) for the first 2 years and

the remainder to be paid off at the end of the third year. How large must the final payment be?

16-11   **Bond interest payments.** Potts, Inc., has 2 bond issues outstanding, and both sell for $668.84. The first issue has an annual coupon rate of 9 percent and 20 years to maturity. The second has a yield to maturity identical to the first but only 5 years until maturity. Both issues pay interest annually. What is the annual interest payment on the second issue?

16-12   **Yield to call.** (*Do this problem only if you are using the computerized problem diskette.*) It is now January 1, 1991, and you are considering the purchase of an outstanding Visscher Corporation bond that was issued on January 1, 1989. Visscher's bond has an 11.5 percent annual coupon and a 30-year original maturity (it matures in 2019). There was originally a 5-year call protection (until December 31, 1993), after which time the bond can be called at 120 (that is, at 120 percent of par, or $1,200). Interest rates have declined since the bond was issued, and the bond is now selling at 128.625 percent of par, or $1,286.25. You want to determine both the yield to maturity and the yield to call for this bond. (*Note:* The yield to call includes the impact of a call provision on the bond's probable yield. In the calculation, we assume that the bond will be outstanding until the call date, at which time it will be called. Thus, the investor will have received interest payments for the call-protected period and then will receive the call price — in this case, $1,200 — on the call date.)

a. What is the yield to maturity in 1991 for Visscher's bond? What is its yield to call?

b. If you bought this bond, which return do you think you would actually earn? Explain your reasoning.

c. Suppose that the bond had sold at a discount. Would the yield to maturity or the yield to call have been more relevant?

d. Suppose that the bond's price suddenly jumps to $1,350. What is the yield to maturity now, and what is the yield to call?

e. Suppose that the price suddenly falls to $900; now what would the YTM and the YTC be?

SOLUTION TO SELF-TEST PROBLEM

ST-1   **a.** The bonds were sold at par. Therefore, the YTM equals the coupon rate, which is 8 percent. The coupon rate is also referred to as the *nominal yield* or *stated yield.*

b. We must find the PV of the 25 remaining interest payments of $80 each and the $1,000 lump sum payment of principal to be paid when the bond matures in 25 years. Therefore

$$\text{Bond value} = \$80(\text{PVIFA}_{10\%,25 \text{ years}}) + \$1,000(\text{PVIF}_{10\%,25 \text{ years}})$$

$$= \$80(9.0770) + \$1,000(0.0923)$$

$$= \$726.16 + \$92.30$$

$$= \$818.46.$$

c. Using the 6 percent present value factors, we find

$$\text{Bond value} = \$80(12.7834) + \$1,000(0.2330)$$

$$= \$1,022.67 + \$233.00$$

$$= \$1,255.67.$$

d. If interest rates were 6 percent on January 1, 1978, the bond's price was $1,255.67, as found in Part c. Thus

$$\text{Current yield} = \frac{\text{Coupon payment}}{\text{Price}}$$

$$= \frac{\$80}{\$1,255.67}$$

$$= 0.0637 = 6.37\%.$$

$$\text{Capital gains yield} = \text{Total yield} - \text{Current yield}$$

$$= 6\% - 6.37\% = -0.37\%.$$

e. Use the approximate YTM formula to get a starting point:

$$\text{Approximate YTM} = \frac{I + (M - V)/n}{(M + 2V)/3}$$

$$= \frac{\$80 + [(\$1,000 - \$525.70)/20]}{(\$1,000 + \$1,051.40)/3}$$

$$= \frac{\$103.715}{\$683.80}$$

$$= 15.17\%.$$

Because this approximation understates the true return, we will try a higher discount rate:

$$k_d = 16\%.$$

$$V = I(\text{PVIFA}_{16\%,20}) + M(\text{PVIF}_{16\%,20})$$

$$= \$80(5.9288) + \$1,000(0.0514)$$

$$= \$474.30 + \$51.40$$

$$= \$525.70.$$

Therefore, the YTM at the beginning of January 1983 was 16 percent.

f.
$$\text{Current yield} = \$80/\$525.70$$

$$= 15.22\%.$$

$$\text{Capital gains yield} = 16\% - 15.22\%$$

$$= 0.78\%.$$

g. The bond has 12 years until it matures; at 14 percent the price would be

$$V = \$80(5.6603) + \$1,000(0.2076)$$

$$= \$452.82 + \$207.60 = \$660.42.$$

Chapter 17

Common Stock

How to Botch a Deal

Stockholders of Hilton Hotels Corporation were told by Chairman Barron Hilton, at their May 1989 annual meeting, that he might consider offers to buy the company. He said he wasn't actually looking for a buyer, but that it was a seller's market for hotels and that if a good deal came along, he might want to accept it. The announcement sent the price of Hilton stock from around $75 per share to more than $115. Among the shareholders, Barron Hilton himself stood to make a nice profit—he had just won a 10-year battle for control of a 28 percent block of stock from his father's estate.

Potential buyers started presenting themselves shortly after Hilton's announcement. Information on Hilton's four Nevada casinos was sought by Caesars World and by Donald Trump, who also expressed an interest in Hilton's Waldorf-Astoria and Chicago's landmark Palmer House. Others wanted to acquire Hilton as a whole, and analysts suggested that offers could go as high as $6 billion, or $125 a share, for the Hilton empire. With such an optimistic outlook, Barron Hilton and his board of directors felt no immediate pressure. It took them three months

to hire investment advisors Shearson Lehman Hutton and to ask Eastdil Realty to compile financial data for potential bidders who wanted information.

Both Caesars and Trump lost interest as a result of the delay (Trump said he wasn't sure Hilton really wanted to sell), but others continued to express an interest. Six of them made preliminary offers to meet a November 10 deadline and were then told to put together firmer proposals. Hotel prices began dropping in December, but, even so, the Hilton directors decided not to decide on any of the bids when they met in February. By March, one of the previous bidders for the entire company had dropped its offer from $4.4 billion to about $3.8 billion, or from $88 to $76 a share. The directors rejected both this and a similar offer as too low, and they voted to take the company off the market. Within a week, the price of Hilton stock had dropped to about $52.

What happened? Did Barron Hilton and his directors miscalculate and poorly serve their stockholders? As you read this chapter, consider some things the corporation's directors might have thought about in trying to arrange the best deal for their stockholders.

See end of chapter for resolution.

Common stock—or, for unincorporated businesses, the proprietor's or partner's capital—represents the ownership of a firm. In earlier chapters we discussed the legal and accounting aspects of common stock and the markets in which it is traded. Now we consider some of the rights and privileges of equity holders, the process by which investors establish the value of equity shares in the marketplace, and the procedures involved when firms raise new capital by issuing additional shares of stock.

LEGAL RIGHTS AND PRIVILEGES OF THE COMMON STOCKHOLDERS

The common stockholders are the *owners* of the corporation, and as such they have certain rights and privileges. The most important of these are discussed in this section.

Control of the Firm

The stockholders have the right to elect the firm's directors, who in turn select the officers who manage the business. In a small firm, the major stockholder typically assumes the positions of president and chairperson of the board of directors. In a large, publicly owned firm, the managers typically have some stock, but their personal holdings are insufficient to exercise voting control. Thus, the managements of most publicly owned firms can be removed by the stockholders if the stockholder group decides that a management team is not effective.

Various state and federal laws stipulate how stockholder control is to be exercised. First, corporations must hold an election of directors periodically, usually once a year, with the vote taken at the annual meeting. Frequently, one-third of the directors are elected each year for a three-year term. Each share of stock has one vote; thus, the owner of 1,000 shares has 1,000 votes. Stockholders can appear at the annual meeting and vote in person, but they typically transfer their right to vote to a second party by means of an instrument known as a **proxy.** Management always solicits stockholders' proxies and usually gets them. However, if earnings are poor and stockholders are dissatisfied, an outside group may solicit the proxies in an effort to overthrow management and take control of the business. This is known as a **proxy fight.**

The question of control has become a central issue in finance in recent years. The frequency of proxy fights has increased, as have attempts by one corporation to take over another by purchasing a majority of the outstanding stock. This latter action, which is called a **takeover,** is discussed in detail in Chapter 22. Some well-known examples of recent takeover battles include KKR's acquisition of RJR Nabisco, Chevron's acquisition of Gulf Oil, and CBS's successful defense against a takeover attempt by Ted Turner. (Subsequently, though, CBS's management lost control to another group headed by Lawrence Tisch.)

proxy
A document giving one person the authority to act for another, typically the power to vote shares of common stock.

proxy fight
An attempt by a person or a group of people to gain control of a firm by getting the stockholders to grant that person or group the authority to vote their shares in order to vote a new management into office.

takeover
An action whereby a person or group succeeds in ousting a firm's management and taking control of the company.

Managers who do not have majority control of their firms' stocks (over 50 percent) are very much concerned about proxy fights and takeovers, and many of them are attempting to get stockholder approval for changes in their corporate charters that would make takeovers more difficult. For example, a number of companies tried in 1990 to get their stockholders to agree (1) to elect only one-third of the directors each year (rather than to elect all directors each year), (2) to require 75 percent of the stockholders (rather than 50 percent) to approve a merger, and (3) to vote in a "poison pill" provision which would allow the stockholders of a firm that is taken over by another firm to buy shares in the second firm at a reduced price; this provision makes the acquisition unattractive and, thus, wards off hostile takeover attempts. Managements seeking such changes generally cite a fear of the firm's being picked up at a bargain price, but it often appears that managers' concern about their own positions might be an even more important consideration.

The Right to Purchase New Stock: The Preemptive Right

Common stockholders often have the right, called the **preemptive right,** to purchase, on a pro rata basis, any additional shares sold by the firm. In some states the preemptive right is automatically included in every corporate charter; in others it is necessary to specifically insert it into the charter.

The purpose of the preemptive right is twofold. First, it protects the power of control of present stockholders. If it were not for this safeguard, the management of a corporation under criticism from stockholders could prevent stockholders from removing it from office by issuing a large number of additional shares and purchasing these shares itself. Management could thereby secure control of the corporation and frustrate the will of the current stockholders.

The second, and by far the more important, reason for the preemptive right is that it protects stockholders against a dilution of value. For example, suppose 1,000 shares of common stock, each with a price of $100, were outstanding, making the total market value of the firm $100,000. If an additional 1,000 shares were sold at $50 a share, or for $50,000, this would raise the total market value of the firm to $150,000. When the total market value is divided by the new total shares outstanding, a value of $75 a share is obtained. If such an event occurred, the original stockholders would lose $25 per share whereas the new stockholders would have an instant profit of $25 per share. Thus, selling common stock at below-market values dilutes the stock's price and is detrimental to the initial stockholders and beneficial to those who purchase the new shares. The preemptive right prevents such a loss of wealth for the original stockholders.[1]

preemptive right
A provision in the corporate charter or bylaws that gives common stockholders the right to purchase on a pro rata basis new issues of common stock (or securities convertible into common stock).

---

[1] The procedure for issuing stock to existing stockholders, called a *rights offering,* is discussed in detail in Eugene F. Brigham and Louis C. Gapenski, *Intermediate Financial Management,* 3rd ed., Chapter 12.

Stock certificates, such as this sample from The Boeing Company, are issued to common stockholders as owners of the corporation. The certificate states the par value of the stock (in this case $5 each) and the number of shares purchased, which would be shown in the boxed area in the upper right corner. The intricate border design is done to make counterfeiting difficult (as with U.S. dollar bills).

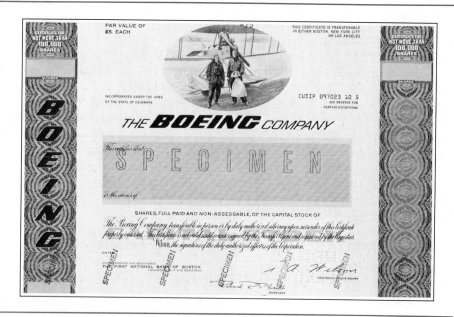

Source: Courtesy of The Boeing Company.

Types of Common Stock

classified stock

Common stock that is given special designations, such as Class A, Class B, and so forth, to meet special needs of the company.

Although most firms have only one type of common stock, in some instances **classified stock** is created to meet the special needs of the company. Generally, when different types of stock are used, one type is designated *Class A,* the second *Class B,* and so on. Small, new companies seeking to acquire funds from outside sources frequently use different types of common stock. For example, when Silicon Systems went public recently, its Class A stock was sold to the public and paid a dividend, but this stock has no voting rights until 1994. The Class B stock, which maintains all voting privileges, was retained by the organizers of the company. However, the Class B stock will not receive any dividends until the company has established its earning power by building up retained earnings to a designated level. Because of the use of classified stock, the public was able to take a position in a conservatively financed growth firm without sacrificing income, while the founders retained absolute control during the crucial early stages of the firm's development. At the same time, outside investors were protected against excessive withdrawals of funds by the original owners. The Class B stock, in similar situations, is often called **founders' shares** and is given sole voting rights in the firm's formative years.

founders' shares

Stock owned by the firm's founders that has sole voting rights but has restricted dividends for a specified number of years.

General Motors provides an example of yet another type of classification. When General Motors acquired Electronic Data Systems (EDS), it established a separate class of stock, GME, so that EDS's management would have a substantial equity stake in the business as an incentive for high-level performance. The GME shareholders have limited voting rights, but they receive dividends based on EDS's earnings rather than on those of GM. GM later acquired Hughes Aircraft and established yet another new class of stock, GMH. Currently, GM, GME, and GMH are all listed on the New York Stock Exchange.

Note that "Class A," "Class B," and so on, have no standard meanings. Most firms have no classified shares, but a firm that does could designate its Class B shares as founders' shares and its Class A shares as those sold to the public, while another firm could reverse these designations for entirely different purposes. The General Motors' GME and GMH classes discussed in the preceding paragraph are other examples.

Self-Test

Identify some approaches that corporate managements have used to make takeovers more difficult.

What are the two primary reasons for the existence of the preemptive right?

What are some reasons that a company might use classified stock?

COMMON STOCK VALUATION

As we have noted, a share of common stock represents a share in the ownership of a firm. Sometimes stockholders seek to control the firm, but most shareholders value stock for the returns that can be gained from its purchase. These returns come from two sources:

1. Cash dividends. The owner of common stock typically expects to receive dividends, but there is no guarantee that they will be paid in any given period. In order for common stock dividends to be paid, the firm must first generate earnings from which dividends can be paid, and then management must decide to pay dividends rather than retain after-tax earnings.[2] Interest payments on debt, on the other hand, are fixed legal obligations that *must* be paid. Failure to pay interest when it comes due results in bankruptcy.

2. Capital gains. When purchasers of common stock buy their securities, they generally expect the stock's price to increase in the future. If the stock is sold later at a price above its purchase price, the investor receives a *capital gain*. Of course, the investor may expect a capital gain but end up with a capital loss instead.

---

[2]We note in Chapter 21 that although most companies will make extraordinary efforts to pay dividends regularly and not let the dollar amount of those dividends decline, this effort does not guarantee the firm's ability to maintain its dividends.

Definitions of Terms Used in the Stock Valuation Models

An asset's value is determined by the benefits that the asset provides a purchaser. Financial assets provide *cash flows,* and their value is equal to the present value of those cash flows. The value of a share of common stock is determined by the present value of its expected cash flows, which consist of dividends expected in each year and the price investors expect to receive when they sell the stock. The expected final stock price includes the return of the original investment plus a capital gain.

We learned in Chapter 1 that the goal of financial management is to maximize the wealth of the owners of the firm, which means maximizing the value of the firm's stock. Through their actions, managers affect the stream of cash flows to investors as well as the riskiness of these cash flows. Therefore, financial managers need to know how alternative actions will affect stock prices. At this point we develop some models to help us understand how the value of a share of stock is determined under several different sets of conditions. We begin by defining the following terms:

D_t = dividend the stockholder expects to receive at the end of Year t. D_0 is the most recent dividend, which has already been paid; D_1 is the first dividend expected, which will be paid at the end of this year; D_2 is the dividend expected at the end of the second year; and so on. D_1 represents the first cash flow a new purchaser of the stock will receive. Note that D_0, the dividend which has just been paid, is known with certainty. However, all future dividends are expected values, so the estimate of D_t may differ among investors.

market price, P_0
The price at which a stock sells in the market.

P_0 = actual **market price** of the stock today.

$\hat{P}_t$ = price of the stock at the end of each year t. P_0 is the price of the stock today; P_1 is the price expected at the end of one year; and so on. The caret, or "hat," is used to indicate that $\hat{P}_t$ is an estimated value.

growth rate, g
The expected rate of growth in dividends per share.

g = expected annual **growth rate** in dividends. (If we assume that dividends are expected to grow at a constant rate, g is also equal to the expected rate of growth in the stock's price.)

required rate of return, k_s
The minimum expected rate of return on a common stock that a stockholder considers acceptable.

k_s = minimum acceptable, or **required, rate of return** on the stock, considering both its riskiness and the returns available on other investments. This rate was found in Chapter 12 with the SML equation; however, the subscript "s" was not used at that time.

expected rate of return, $\hat{k}_s$
The rate of return on a common stock that a stockholder expects to receive.

$\hat{k}_s$ = (pronounced "k hat s") **expected rate of return** which an investor who buys the stock should (or expects to) receive. The caret, or "hat," is used to indicate that $\hat{k}_s$ is a predicted value. $\hat{k}_s$ could be above or below k_s, but one would buy the stock only if $\hat{k}_s$ were equal to or greater than k_s.

D_1/P_0 = **expected dividend yield** on the stock during the coming year. If the stock is expected to pay a dividend of $1 during the next 12 months, and if its current price is $10, then the expected dividend yield is $1/$10 = 0.10 = 10%.

expected dividend yield
The expected dividend divided by the current price of a share of stock.

$\dfrac{\hat{P}_1 - P_0}{P_0}$ = expected **capital gains yield** on the stock during the coming year. If the stock sells for $10 today, and if it is expected to rise to $10.50 at the end of one year, the expected capital gain is $\hat{P}_1 - P_0$ = $10.50 − $10.00 = $0.50, and the expected capital gains yield is $0.50/$10 = 0.05 = 5%. If the stock price is expected to grow at a constant rate, then the growth rate, g, is equal to the capital gains yield.

capital gains yield
The capital gain (appreciation in price) during any one year divided by the beginning price.

$$\begin{array}{ccc} \text{Expected} \\ \text{total return} \end{array} = \begin{array}{ccc} \text{Expected} \\ \text{dividend yield} \end{array} + \begin{array}{ccc} \text{Expected capital} \\ \text{gains yield} \end{array}$$

$$\hat{k}_s \quad = \quad \frac{D_1}{P_0} \quad + \quad \frac{\hat{P}_1 - P_0}{P_0}.$$

In our example, the **expected total return** = $\hat{k}_s$ = 10% + 5% = 15%.

expected total return
The sum of the expected dividend yield and the expected capital gains yield on a share of stock.

Expected Dividends as the Basis for Stock Values

As we mentioned before, the value of any financial or real asset is the present value of its cash flows. For example, in our discussion of capital budgeting, the value of a project was seen to be equal to the project's cash flows (consisting of the project-related net income and depreciation), discounted back to the present:

$$NPV = \sum_{t=1}^{n} \frac{CF_t}{(1 + k)^t} - C.$$

Similarly, in Chapter 16 we found the value of a bond to be the present value of its stream of payments, in this case the present value of the interest payments over the life of the bond plus the present value of the bond's maturity or par value:

$$V = \sum_{t=1}^{n} I \frac{1}{(1 + k_d)^t} + M \frac{1}{(1 + k_d)^n} \qquad \textbf{(16-1)}$$

$$= I\,(PVIFA_{k_d,n}) + M\,(PVIF_{k_d,n}).$$

Therefore, since all other assets are valued as the present value of their future expected cash returns, one should expect the valuation model for common stock to be the same. Common stock values are determined as the present value of the stream of cash flows associated with owning the stock. But what is the stream of cash flows that a corporation provides its stockholders? As long as someone continues to own a stock, the only cash received is in the form of *dividends*. Thus, the value of a share of common stock to a permanent owner is calculated as the present value of an infinite stream of dividends:

Value of stock $= \hat{P}_0 =$ PV of expected future dividends

$$= \frac{D_1}{(1 + k_s)^1} + \frac{D_2}{(1 + k_s)^2} + \cdots + \frac{D_\infty}{(1 + k_s)^\infty}$$

$$= \sum_{t=1}^{\infty} \frac{D_t}{(1 + k_s)^t}. \tag{17-1}$$

What about a more typical case, one in which stock is purchased to be held for a shorter, finite period and then sold? Will the value of the stock change? In a word, *no*. Assume that you plan to hold a share of stock for only five years. The value of the stock will equal the present value of the dividends over the five-year period plus the present value of the stock's expected selling price in the fifth year:

$$\hat{P}_0 = \sum_{t=1}^{5} \frac{D_t}{(1 + k_s)^t} + \frac{\hat{P}_5}{(1 + k_s)^5}. \tag{17-2}$$

The next question is this: What would a rational investor pay for the stock in that future year? The rational investor would be willing to pay only the present value of the future cash flows that are expected from that point on. What are those cash flows? Dividends, of course! Therefore,

$$\hat{P}_5 = \sum_{t=6}^{\infty} \frac{D_t}{(1 + k_s)^t}. \tag{17-3}$$

If we substitute into Equation 17-2 the value of the stock in Year 5, found in Equation 17-3, it is obvious that even if the stock will be sold at some future date, *the value of the stock is still determined by the general model of discounted future cash flows presented in Equation 17-1*. To see this more clearly, recognize that for any individual investor, the expected cash flows consist of expected dividends plus the expected sale price of the stock. However, the sale price the current investor receives will be dependent upon the dividends some future investor expects to receive. Therefore, for *all* present and future investors, expected cash flows must be based on expected future dividends. To put it another way, unless a firm is liquidated or sold to another concern, the cash flows it provides to its stockholders consist only of a stream of dividends, so the value of a share of its stock must be established as the present value of that expected dividend stream.

Equation 17-1 is a generalized stock valuation model in the sense that the pattern of dividend payments can be anything; D_t can be rising, falling, or constant, or it can even be fluctuating randomly, and Equation 17-1 will still hold. However, it is difficult, even for professionals, to estimate future dividend payments beyond a few periods, so simplified models are used in the real world. In the next section we develop a simplified stock valuation model, based on the concepts from Equation 17-1, which makes only two simplifying assumptions: (1) that the growth in earnings and dividends for the firm will progress at a constant rate into the future, and (2) that k_s is greater than g.

"Normal," or Constant, Growth

As firms reach the maturity phase of their life cycles, the growth of their earnings and dividends tends to stabilize. This period of stability is not one of stagnation but rather one of moderate growth, and, in general, this growth is expected to continue into the foreseeable future at about the same rate as that of the nominal gross national product (real GNP plus inflation). On this basis, it is expected that the dividend of a "normal" or constant growth company will grow at a rate of 6 to 10 percent a year.

If we wish to determine next year's dividend, D_1, for a **normal (constant) growth** firm we need only to multiply last year's dividend, D_0, by one plus the expected growth rate. Thus, if Carter Chemical Company has just paid a dividend of $1.87, and if investors expect a 7 percent growth rate for the company throughout the foreseeable future, then next year's dividend, D_1, may be found as follows:

normal (constant) growth
Growth which is expected to continue into the foreseeable future at about the same rate as that of the economy as a whole; g = a constant.

$$D_t = D_0(1 + g)^t$$

$$D_1 = D_0(1 + g)$$

$$= \$1.87(1.07)$$

$$= \$2.00.$$

Equation 17-1 described the valuation of a share of common stock as the present value of all future cash flows, and for common stock that flow is dividends. If dividends are expected to grow *at a constant rate, g,* then Equation 17-1 can be simplified as follows.[3]

$$\hat{P}_0 = \frac{D_1}{k_s - g}. \tag{17-4}$$

If investors require a 12 percent return from an investment in Carter's common stock, k_s, the value of the firm's common stock can be determined by substituting into Equation 17-4 the values for next year's dividend, the required return on Carter's equity, and the firm's expected growth rate:

$$\hat{P}_0 = \frac{D_1}{k_s - g}$$

$$P_{\mathcal{K}} = \frac{D_1}{K - g}$$

$$= \frac{\$2.00}{0.12 - 0.07}$$

$$= \frac{\$2.00}{0.05} = \$40.00.$$

---

[3]We spare the reader the mathematical proof of our assertion. For those who are interested, the derivation of Equation 17-4 is provided in Eugene F. Brigham and Louis C. Gapenski, *Intermediate Financial Management,* 3rd ed., Appendix 3A.

Figure 17-1 **Growing Dividend Stream and
Present Value of the Stream:**
$$D_0 = \$1.87, \ g = 7\%, \ k_s = 12\%$$

This figure illustrates a constant growth stock valuation model. The value of a share of common stock equals the present value of all future dividends. This example assumes that these dividends will grow at a constant rate. At a growth rate (g) of 7 percent and a required rate of return (k_s) of 12 percent, we can plot the growing dividend stream both in actual dollar amounts and in present values into infinity. We could sum the discounted future dividends to determine the present value of the firm's stock.

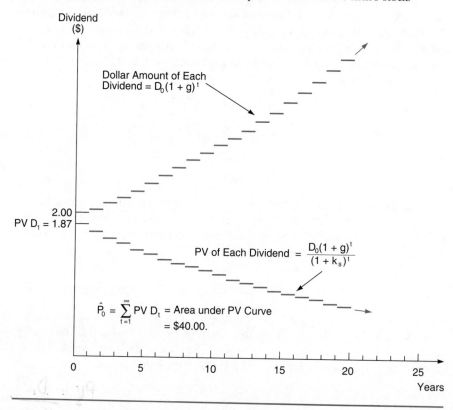

Recall that we could reach the same conclusion—that the price of Carter's common stock is $40—by utilizing the more cumbersome Equation 17-1. The **constant growth model** set forth in Equation 17-4 is often referred to as the *Gordon Model,* after Professor Myron J. Gordon, who did much to develop and popularize it.

The concept underlying the valuation process in Equation 17-4 is presented graphically in Figure 17-1. The top dashed curve represents the dollar value of Carter's dividends growing at a 7 percent rate. The bottom dashed line plots

constant growth model

Also called the Gordon Model; used to find the value of a constant growth stock.

the present value of those dividends. The value of the firm's common stock may be obtained by adding the present value of each future year's dividend, as suggested by Equation 17-1. Alternatively, because the dividends are growing at a constant rate, the value may be found by utilizing Equation 17-4. In either case, the result will be *exactly the same, $40.*

Constant growth of future dividends is a necessary condition that must be observed when utilizing Equation 17-4. For this equation to have any economic validity, the other necessary condition is that the constant growth rate, g, must always be less than the required rate of return, k_s. Although there are several excellent economic reasons to assert that k_s will never be smaller than g, the model has no rational meaning if $g \geq k_s$. For example, if Carter's $k_s = 12\%$, $D_1 = \$2.00$, but $g = 15\%$, then

$$\hat{P}_0 = \frac{\$2.00}{0.12 - 0.15}$$

$$= \frac{\$2.00}{-0.03}$$

$$= -\$66.67.$$

This result indicates that a present owner of Carter's equity would be willing to give you a share of the stock *and* $66.67 to induce you to take it. A highly unlikely scenario! Therefore, the Gordon Model, Equation 17-4, always requires a constant rate of growth, g, and it further requires that $k_s > g$.[4]

It should be made clear that the constant-growth valuation model is intended to price the equity shares of a company that has normal or constantly growing earnings and dividends. However, for a firm that is in the early stages of its life cycle or in a highly variable economic environment, Equation 17-4 may not provide an effective means of equity valuation. Equation 17-4 would be a poor choice to use in evaluating the share price of a new high-technology firm, but it would probably provide an excellent approximation of the economic value of a mature company. Therefore, the more variable the growth rate in earnings and hence dividends, the less satisfactory a job the model represented by Equation 17-4 will do in valuing a firm's common stock. We will discuss procedures for dealing with nonconstant growth in a later section.

---

[4]Note that the growth rate in Equation 17-4 can be equal to zero. If growth were equal to zero, Equation 17-4 would simplify to $\hat{P} = D/k_s$. Because the firm is not growing, there would be no difference in dividends in any period, so $D_0 = D_1 = D_2$, etc. As we will see in Chapter 21, since there are no growth opportunities for this firm, the firm would pay out all earnings as dividends, so $E_1 = D_1 = E_2$, etc. Therefore, an alternative measure of the stock price of a *no-growth* firm is $\hat{P} = E/k_s$.

Expected Rate of Return for a Constant Growth Stock

When investors purchase a stock that they expect to sell in the future, their expected rate of return is determined by the stock's expected dividend yield and expected capital gains yield. We can demonstrate this relationship by algebraically rearranging Equation 17-4 into Equation 17-5:

$$\begin{matrix} \text{Expected} \\ \text{rate of return} \end{matrix} = \begin{matrix} \text{Expected dividend} \\ \text{yield} \end{matrix} + \begin{matrix} \text{Expected growth rate,} \\ \text{or capital gains yield} \end{matrix}$$

$$\hat{k}_s = \frac{D_1}{P_0} + g. \qquad (17\text{-}5)$$

Thus, if you buy a stock for a price $P_0 = \$40.00$, and if you expect the stock to pay a dividend $D_1 = \$2.00$ one year from now and to grow at a constant rate $g = 7\%$ in the future, your expected rate of return is 12 percent:

$$\hat{k}_s = \frac{\$2.00}{\$40.00} + 7\% = 5\% + 7\% = 12\%.$$

In this form, we see that $\hat{k}_s$ is the *expected total return* and that it consists of an *expected dividend yield,* $D_1/P_0 = 5\%$, plus an *expected growth rate* or *capital gains yield,* $g = 7\%$.

Suppose the previously described analysis had been conducted on January 1, 1991, so $P_0 = \$40.00$ is the January 1, 1991, stock price and $D_1 = \$2.00$ is the dividend expected at the end of 1991 (or the beginning of 1992). What should the stock price be at the end of 1991 (or the beginning of 1992)? We would again apply Equation 17-4, but this time we would use the 1992 dividend, $D_2 = D_1(1 + g) = \$2.00(1.07) = \$2.14$:

$$\hat{P}_{1/1/1992} = \frac{D_{1992}}{k_s - g} = \frac{\$2.14}{0.12 - 0.07} = \$42.80.$$

Now notice that $42.80 is 7 percent greater than P_0, the \$40.00 price on January 1, 1991:

$$P_0 (1 + g) = \hat{P}_1$$

$$\$40.00(1.07) = \$42.80.$$

Thus, you would expect to make a capital gain of $\$42.80 - \$40.00 = \$2.80$ during the year, and to have a capital gains yield of 7 percent:

$$\text{Capital gains yield} = \frac{\text{Capital gain}}{\text{Beginning price}} = \frac{\$2.80}{\$40.00} = 0.07 = 7\%.$$

We could extend the analysis on out, and in each future year the expected capital gains yield would always equal g, the expected dividend growth rate.

The dividend yield in 1992 can be estimated as follows:

$$\text{Dividend yield}_{1992} = \frac{D_{1992}}{\hat{P}_{1992}} = \frac{\$2.14}{\$42.80} = 0.05 = 5\%.$$

The dividend yield for 1993 could also be calculated, and again it would be 5 percent. Thus, *for a constant growth stock,* these conditions must hold:

1. The dividend is expected to grow at a constant rate, g. This also requires that earnings grow at the rate g.

2. The stock price is expected to grow at this same rate.

3. The expected dividend yield is a constant.

4. The expected capital gains yield is also a constant, and it is equal to g.

5. The expected total rate of return, $\hat{k}_s$, is equal to the expected dividend yield plus the expected growth rate.

Supernormal, or Nonconstant, Growth

Firms typically go through *life cycles.* During the early part of their lives, their growth is much faster than that of the economy as a whole; then they match the economy's growth; and, if management cannot prevent it, they enter a final period when their growth is slower than that of the economy. Automobile manufacturers in the 1920s and computer software firms like Microsoft in the 1990s are examples of firms in the early part of the cycle, and these firms are called **supernormal (nonconstant) growth** firms. Figure 17-2 illustrates such nonconstant growth and compares it with normal growth, zero growth, and negative growth.

supernormal (nonconstant) growth
The part of the life cycle of a firm in which its growth is much faster than that of the economy as a whole.

In the figure, the dividends of the supernormal growth firm are expected to grow at a 30 percent rate for 3 years, after which the growth rate is expected to fall to 10 percent, the assumed norm for the economy. The value of this firm, like any other, is the present value of its expected future dividends as determined by Equation 17-1. In the case in which D_t is growing at a constant rate, we simplified Equation 17-1 to $\hat{P}_0 = D_1/(k_s - g)$. In the supernormal growth case, however, the expected growth rate is not a constant; it declines at the end of the period of supernormal growth. To find the value of such a stock, or of any nonconstant growth stock when the growth rate will eventually stabilize, we proceed in three steps:

1. Find the present value (PV) of the dividends during the period of supernormal (nonconstant) growth.

2. Find the price of the stock at the end of the supernormal (nonconstant) growth period, at which point it has become a constant growth stock, and then discount this price back to the present.

3. Add these two components to find the value of the stock, $\hat{P}_0$.

Figure 17-2 **Illustrative Dividend Growth Rates**

This figure compares dividend growth patterns for a supernormal growth firm, a normal growth firm, a zero growth firm, and a firm with declining growth. Notice that the supernormal firm's dividend growth is 30 percent per year for 3 years, and it then returns to a normal growth pattern of 10 percent per year. The normal firm's dividend growth is a steady 10 percent per year, while the zero growth firm's dividend remains at $1.82 per year. (The zero growth pattern is the same as a preferred stock dividend pattern.) Finally, the last case illustrated is that of declining dividend growth.

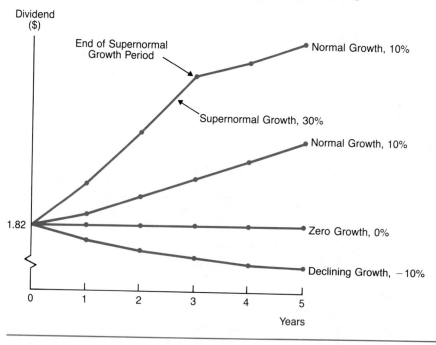

To illustrate the process for valuing nonconstant growth stocks, suppose the following facts exist:

k_s = stockholders' required rate of return = 16%.

N = years of supernormal growth = 3.

g_s = rate of growth in both earnings and dividends during the supernormal growth period = 30%.

g_n = rate of constant growth after the supernormal period = 10%.

D_0 = last dividend the company paid = $1.82.

The valuation process is graphed in Figure 17-3 and explained in the steps that follow.

Figure 17-3 **Time Line for Finding the Value of a Supernormal Growth Stock**

This figure illustrates the steps for evaluating a nonconstant, or supernormal, growth stock. The first step is to find the dividends expected during each of the supernormal (nonconstant) growth years. Each of these dividends is then discounted back to the present. The next step is to find the price of the stock at the end of the nonconstant growth period. At this point, the stock becomes a constant growth stock, so the Gordon Model can be used. This stock price is then discounted back to the present. The two values are summed to arrive at the expected current stock price.

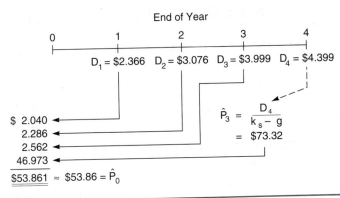

Note: $\hat{P}_3$ the stock price expected at the end of Year 3, is the sum of the PVs of dividends in Years 4 to infinity, and it is found as $\hat{P}_3 = D_4/(k_s - g_n)$.

Step 1. Find the expected dividend at the end of each of the next three years, and the PV of dividends paid (PV D_t), by using this procedure:

D_0	$\times$	$FVIF_{30\%,t}$	$=$	D_t	$\times$	$PVIF_{16\%,t}$	$=$	PV D_t
D_1: $1.82	$\times$	1.3000	$=$	$2.366	$\times$	0.8621	$=$	$2.040
D_2: 1.82	$\times$	1.6900	$=$	3.076	$\times$	0.7432	$=$	2.286
D_3: 1.82	$\times$	2.1970	$=$	3.999	$\times$	0.6407	$=$	2.562

Sum of PVs of supernormal period dividends = $\underline{\$6.888}$

Step 2. Find the PV of all the dividends expected beyond Year 3. This requires that we (a) first find the expected value of the stock at the end of Year 3 and (b) then find the present value of the Year 3 stock price:

a.
$$\hat{P}_3 = \frac{D_4}{k_s - g_n} = \frac{D_0(1 + g_s)^3(1 + g_n)}{k_s - g_n} = \frac{D_3(1 + g_n)}{0.16 - 0.10}$$

$$= \frac{\$3.999(1.10)}{0.16 - 0.10} = \frac{\$4.399}{0.06} = \$73.32.$$

b.   PV $\hat{P}_3 = \$73.32(PVIF_{16\%,3\ years}) = \$73.32(0.6407) = \$46.97.$

Step 3. Find $\hat{P}_0$, the value of the stock today:

$$\hat{P}_0 = \$6.89 + \$46.97 = \$53.86.$$

Self-Test

Explain the following statement: "Whereas a bond contains a promise to pay interest, common stock provides an expectation but no promise of dividends."

What are the two elements of a stock's expected returns?

How are the capital budgeting project valuation model, the general bond valuation model, and the general stock valuation model (Equation 17–1) similar to one another?

Write out and explain the valuation model for a constant growth stock.

How does one calculate the capital gains yield and the dividend yield of a stock?

What conditions must hold if we are to be able to use the Gordon Model (Equation 17-4)?

What three steps are involved in the valuation of a supernormal (nonconstant) growth stock?

EVALUATION OF COMMON STOCK AS A SOURCE OF FUNDS

So far this chapter has discussed the main characteristics of common stock, and we have seen how its price is determined. Now we will appraise the advantages and disadvantages of stock financing from the viewpoint of the corporation, and from a social perspective.

Advantages of Common Stock Financing

There are several advantages to the corporation associated with common stock financing:

1. Common stock does not carry a fixed obligation to pay periodic dividends to stockholders. When a firm uses debt, it incurs a legal obligation to pay interest on it, regardless of its operating conditions and its cash flows. When the company uses equity financing, however, it can pay common stock dividends if it generates earnings and has no pressing internal needs for them.

2. Common stock, unlike debt, never matures, so it never has to be repaid.

3. Common stock provides a cushion against losses from the creditors' viewpoint. Therefore, the sale of common stock increases the proportion of equity financing and thus the firm's creditworthiness. This, in turn, raises the firm's bond rating, lowers its cost of debt, and increases its future ability to use debt.

4. When a company's prospects look bright, common stock can often be sold on highly favorable terms. Stock appeals to certain groups of investors because (a) it typically carries a higher expected total return (dividends plus capital gains) than does preferred stock or debt, and (b) since stock represents the ownership of the firm, it provides the investor with a better hedge against unanticipated inflation than either preferred stock or bonds. Ordinarily, dividends rise and common stock increases in value when the firm's real asset values rise during inflationary periods.[5]

5. When a company is having operating problems, it often needs new funds to overcome its problems. However, investors are reluctant to supply capital to a troubled company, and if they do they generally require some type of security. From a practical standpoint, this often means that a firm that is experiencing problems can only obtain new capital by issuing debt, which is safer from the investor's standpoint. Corporate treasurers are well aware of this, so they often choose to finance with common stock during good times so as to maintain some **reserve borrowing capacity.** Indeed, surveys have indicated that maintenance of an adequate reserve of borrowing capacity is a primary consideration in most financing decisions.

reserve borrowing capacity
Unused debt capacity that permits borrowing if a firm needs capital in troubled times.

Disadvantages of Common Stock Financing

Disadvantages to a company that issues common stock include the following:

1. The sale of common stock extends voting rights, and perhaps even control, to new stockholders. For this reason, additional equity financing is often avoided by managers who are concerned about maintaining control. The use of classified stock or founders' shares can mitigate this problem, however.

2. Common stock gives new owners the right to share in the income of the firm. If profits soar, then new stockholders share in this bonanza, whereas if debt had been used, new investors would have received only a fixed return, no matter how profitable the company had become.

3. As we shall see, the costs of distributing common stock are usually higher than those for distributing preferred stock or debt. Issuance costs associated with the sale of common stock are characteristically higher because (a) the costs of investigating an equity security investment are higher than those for a comparable debt security, and (b) stocks are riskier than debt, meaning that investors must diversify their equity holdings, which in turn means that a given dollar amount of new stock must be sold to a larger number of purchasers than the same amount of debt.

4. As we will learn in Chapter 19, the cost of equity capital is greater than the cost of debt. Therefore, if the firm has more equity than is required for its optimal capital structure (the appropriate mix of debt and equity), the average cost of capital will be higher than necessary. Therefore, a firm will not want to sell stock beyond the point where its equity ratio exceeds this optimal level.

---

[5]For the average common stock, the rate of increase in dividends has slightly exceeded the rate of inflation since 1970.

5. Under current tax laws, common stock dividends are not deductible as an expense for calculating the corporation's taxable income, but bond interest is deductible. As we will also see in Chapter 19, the impact of this factor is reflected in an even lower effective after-tax cost of debt.

From a Social Viewpoint

From a social viewpoint, common stock is a desirable form of financing because it makes business firms less vulnerable to the consequences of declines in sales and earnings. Common stock financing involves no fixed charge payments which might force a faltering firm into reorganization or bankruptcy. From the standpoint of the economy as a whole, if too many firms used too much debt, business fluctuations would be amplified, and minor recessions could turn into major ones. Recently, when many mergers and management buyouts financed largely with debt were occurring and were raising the aggregate debt ratio (the average debt ratio of all firms), the Federal Reserve and other authorities voiced concern over the situation, and Congressional leaders debated the wisdom of social controls over corporations' use of debt. Like most important issues, this one is debatable, and the debate centers around who can better determine "appropriate" capital structures — corporate managers or government officials.

Self-Test

What are the major advantages of common stock financing to a corporation? What are the major disadvantages?

From a social viewpoint, why may common stock be considered a desirable form of financing?

THE DECISION TO GO PUBLIC

As we noted in Chapter 1, most businesses begin their lives as proprietorships or partnerships, and the more successful ones, as they grow, eventually find it desirable to convert into a corporation. The ownership of these young corporations is often kept in the hands of the founders, a few key employees, and perhaps a limited number of investors who are not actively involved in management. As the firm grows, it will probably outgrow its ability to finance its equity needs through internal sources or the increased investment of the owners. Whenever a **closely held corporation** offers stock to the public for the first time, it is said to be **going public.** The advantages and disadvantages of public ownership are discussed next.

Advantages of Going Public

Facilitates Stockholder Diversification. As a company grows and becomes more valuable, its founders often have most of their wealth tied up in the company. By selling some of their stock in a public offering, the founders can

closely held corporation
A corporation that is owned by a few individuals who are typically associated with the firm's management.

going public
The act of selling stock to the public at large by a closely held corporation or its principal stockholders.

diversify their holdings and thereby reduce somewhat the riskiness of their personal portfolios.

Increases Liquidity. The stock of a closely held firm is illiquid — it cannot be easily sold, because no ready market exists for it. If an owner wishes to sell some shares to raise cash, it is hard to find potential buyers, and even if a buyer is located, there is no established price at which to complete the transaction. These problems do not exist with **publicly owned corporations.**

publicly owned corporation
A corporation that is owned by a relatively large number of individuals who are not actively involved in its management.

Facilitates Raising New Corporate Cash. If a privately held company wants to raise cash by a sale of new stock, it must either go to its existing owners, who may neither have any money nor want to put any more eggs into this particular basket, or it must shop around for wealthy investors who are willing to make an investment in the company. However, it is usually difficult to get outsiders to put money into a closely held company, because of low diversification, low liquidity, and the disadvantages new shareholders face if they hold less than 50 percent of the stock. The inside stockholders-managers can pay or not pay dividends, pay themselves exorbitant salaries, have private deals with the company, and so on. Similarly, insiders can even keep the outsiders from knowing the company's actual earnings or its real worth. There are not many positions more vulnerable than that of an outside stockholder in a closely held company, and for this reason it is hard for closely held companies to raise new equity capital. Going public, which brings with it disclosure and regulation by the Securities and Exchange Commission (SEC), greatly reduces these problems and thus makes people more willing to invest in the company.

Establishes a Value for the Firm. For a number of reasons, it is often useful to establish a firm's value in the marketplace. For one thing, when the owner of a privately owned business dies, state and federal inheritance tax appraisers must set a value on the company for estate tax purposes. Often, these appraisers set too high a value, which creates all sorts of problems. However, a company that is publicly owned has its value established, with little room for argument. Similarly, if a company wants to give incentive stock options to key employees, it is useful to know the exact value of these options; employees much prefer to own stock, or options on stock, that is publicly traded, because public trading increases liquidity.

Disadvantages of Going Public

Cost of Reporting. A publicly owned company must file quarterly and annual reports with the SEC, with various state officials, or with both. These reports can be costly, especially for small firms.

Disclosure. Management may not like the idea of reporting operating data, because such data will then be available to competitors. Similarly, the owners of the company may not want people to know their net worth. Since publicly owned companies must disclose the number of shares owned by officers, directors, and major stockholders, it is easy enough for anyone to multiply number of shares held by price per share to estimate the insiders' net worths.

Self-dealings. The owners-managers of closely held companies have many opportunities for various types of questionable but legal self-dealings, including the payment of high salaries, nepotism, personal transactions with the business (such as leasing arrangements), excellent retirement programs, and truly unnecessary fringe benefits. Such self-dealings are much harder to arrange if a company is publicly owned; they must be disclosed, and the managers are also subject to stockholder suits.

Inactive Market/Low Price. If a firm is very small, and if its shares are not traded with much frequency, then its stock will not truly be liquid, and the market price may not be representative of the stock's real value. Security analysts and stockbrokers simply will not follow or recommend the stock, because there will not be sufficient trading activity to generate enough sales commissions to cover the analysts' or brokers' costs of keeping up with it.

Control. Because of the dramatic increase in tender offers and proxy fights in the 1980s, the managers of publicly owned firms who do not have at least 50 percent of the stock must be concerned about maintaining control. Further, there is pressure on such managers to produce annual earnings gains, even when it would be in the shareholders' best long-term interest to adopt a strategy that might penalize short-run earnings but lead to higher earnings in future years. These factors have led a number of public companies to "go private" in leveraged buyout (LBO) deals in which the managers and some related investors borrow the money to buy out the public stockholders. The RJR Nabisco deal, the largest LBO on record at about $25 billion, is an example.

Conclusions on Going Public

It should be obvious from this discussion that there are no hard-and-fast rules about whether or when a company should go public. It is an individual decision that should be made on the basis of the company's and its stockholders' unique circumstances.

If a company does decide to go public, either by the sale of newly issued stock to raise new capital for the corporation or by the sale of stock by the current owners, one key issue is that of setting the price at which shares will be offered to the public. The company and its current owners want to set the price as high as possible — the higher the offering price, the smaller the fraction of the company the current owners will have to give up to obtain any specified amount of money. On the other hand, potential buyers will want the price set as low as possible. The valuation models presented earlier in this chapter aid investment bankers in determining the initial selling price.

Self-Test

Differentiate between a closely held corporation and a publicly owned corporation.

What are the major advantages and disadvantages of going public?

THE INVESTMENT BANKING PROCESS

The role of investment bankers was discussed in general terms in Chapter 2. There we learned (1) that the major investment banking houses are often divisions of large financial service corporations engaged in a wide range of activities and (2) that investment bankers help firms issue new securities in the primary markets and also operate as brokers in the secondary markets. Sears, Roebuck is one of the largest financial services corporations — in addition to its insurance and credit card operations, it owns a large brokerage house and a major investment banking house. Similarly, Merrill Lynch has a brokerage department that operates thousands of offices, as well as an investment banking department that helps companies issue securities, take over other companies, and the like. Of course, Merrill Lynch's and Sears's brokers also sell securities that have been issued through their investment banking departments. In this section we describe how securities are issued, and we explain the role of investment bankers in this process.

Company Decisions

The firm itself makes some initial, preliminary decisions on its own, including the following:

1. Dollars to be raised. How much new capital is needed?

2. Type of securities used. Should stock, bonds, or a combination be used? Further, if stock is to be issued, should it be offered to existing stockholders or sold directly to the general public? (Of course, if the preemptive right is included in the corporate charter, the latter question need not be asked; existing stockholders must then have first option to purchase the new issue of stock.)

3. Competitive bid versus negotiated deal. Should the company simply offer a block of its securities for sale to the highest bidder, or should it sit down with an investment banker and negotiate a deal? These two procedures are called *competitive bids* and *negotiated deals.* Only about 100 of the largest firms on the NYSE, whose securities are already well known to the investment banking community, are in a position to use the competitive bid process. The investment banks would have to do a large amount of investigative work in order to bid on an issue unless they were already quite familiar with the firm, and the costs involved would be too high to make it worthwhile unless the investment bank was sure of getting the deal. Therefore, the vast majority of offerings of stock or bonds are made on a negotiated basis.

4. Selection of an investment banker. Which investment banker should the firm use? Older firms that have "been to market" before will have already established a relationship with an investment banker, although it is easy enough to change bankers if the firm is dissatisfied. A firm that is just going public will have to choose an investment banker, and different investment banking houses are better suited for different companies. Some investment banking houses specialize in new issues of firms going public for the first time, whereas others are not well suited to handle these new issues because their brokerage clients are relatively conservative.

Joint Decisions

After the firm has decided to issue new securities, there are still decisions to be made jointly by the firm and its selected investment banker, including the following:

1. Reevaluating the company's initial decisions. The firm and its investment banker will reevaluate the firm's initial decisions about the size of the issue and the type of securities to use. For example, the firm may have initially decided to raise $50 million by selling common stock, but the investment banker may convince management that it would be better off, in view of current market conditions, to limit the stock issue to $25 million and to raise the other $25 million as debt.

2. Best efforts or underwritten issues. The firm and its investment banker must decide whether the banker will work on a best efforts basis or underwrite the issue. In a **best efforts arrangement,** the banker does not guarantee that the securities will be sold or that the company will get the cash it needs. In an **underwritten arrangement,** the company does get a guarantee, so the banker bears significant risks in such an offering. For example, the same day that IBM signed an underwritten agreement to sell $1 billion of bonds in 1979, interest rates rose sharply and bond prices fell. IBM's investment bankers lost somewhere between $10 million and $20 million. Had the offering been on a best efforts basis, IBM would have been the loser.

3. Issuance costs. The investment banker's fee must be negotiated, and the firm must also estimate the other expenses it will incur in connection with the issue — lawyers' fees, accountants' costs, printing and engraving, and so on. Usually, the banker will buy the issue from the company at a discount below the price at which the securities are to be offered to the public, and this **spread** covers the banker's costs and provides a profit.

Table 17-1 gives an indication of the **flotation costs** associated with public issues of bonds, preferred stock, and common stock. As the table shows, costs as a percentage of the proceeds are higher for stocks than for bonds, and costs are also higher for small than for large issues. The relationship between size of issue and flotation costs is primarily the result of fixed costs. Certain costs must be incurred regardless of the size of the issue, so the percentage of flotation costs is quite high for small issues.

---

best efforts arrangement
Agreement for the sale of securities in which the investment bank handling the transaction gives no guarantee that the securities will be sold.

underwritten arrangement
Agreement for the sale of securities in which the investment bank guarantees the sale of the securities, thus agreeing to bear any risks involved in the transaction.

spread
The difference between the price a security dealer offers to pay for securities (the "bid" price) and the price at which the dealer offers to sell them (the "asked" price).

flotation costs
The cost of issuing new common stock, preferred stock, or bonds.

Table 17-1 Costs of Flotation for Underwritten, Nonrights Offerings (Expressed as a Percentage of Gross Proceeds)

Size of Issue (Millions of Dollars)	Bonds			Preferred Stock			Common Stock		
	Underwriting Commission	Other Expenses	Total Costs	Underwriting Commission	Other Expenses	Total Costs	Underwriting Commission	Other Expenses	Total Costs
Under 1.0	10.0%	4.0%	14.0%	—	—	—	13.0%	9.0%	22.0%
1.0–1.9	8.0	3.0	11.0	—	—	—	11.0	5.9	16.9
2.0–4.9	4.0	2.2	6.2	—	—	—	8.6	3.8	12.4
5.0–9.9	2.4	0.8	3.2	1.9%	0.7%	2.6%	6.3	1.9	8.2
10.0–19.9	1.2	0.7	1.9	1.4	0.4	1.8	5.1	0.9	6.0
20.0–49.9	1.0	0.4	1.4	1.4	0.3	1.7	4.1	0.5	4.6
50.0 and over	0.9	0.2	1.1	1.4	0.2	1.6	3.3	0.2	3.5

Notes:
1. Small issues of preferred are rare, so no data on preferred issues below $5 million are given.
2. Flotation costs tend to rise somewhat when interest rates are cyclically high; because money is in relatively tight supply, the investment bankers will have a difficult time placing issues with permanent investors. Thus, the figures shown here represent averages, and actual flotation costs vary somewhat over time.

Sources: Securities and Exchange Commission, *Cost of Flotation of Registered Equity Issues* (Washington, D.C.: U.S. Government Printing Office, December 1974); Richard H. Pettway, "A Note on the Flotation Costs of New Equity Capital Issues of Electric Companies," *Public Utilities Fortnightly,* March 18, 1982; Robert Hansen, "Evaluating the Costs of a New Equity Issue," *Midland Corporate Finance Journal,* Spring 1986; and informal surveys of common stock, preferred stock, and bond issues conducted by the authors of this book.

Also, it should be noted that when relatively small companies go public to raise new capital, the investment bankers frequently take part of their compensation in the form of options to buy stock in the firm. For example, when Data Technologies, Inc., went public with a $10 million issue in 1990 by selling 1 million shares at a price of $10, its investment bankers (1) bought the stock from the company at a price of $9.75, so the direct underwriting fee was only $1,000,000(\$10.00 - \$9.75) = \$250,000$ or 2.5 percent, and (2) received a 5-year option to buy 200,000 shares at a price of $10. If the stock goes up to $15, which the bankers expect it to do, they will make a $1 million profit on top of the $250,000 underwriting fee.

4. Setting the offering price. If the company is already publicly owned, the **offering price** will be based on the existing market price of the stock or the yield on the bonds. For common stock, the most typical arrangement calls for the investment banker to buy the securities at a prescribed number of points below the closing price on the last day of registration.

If the company is going public for the first time, there will be no established price, so the investment bankers will have to estimate the **equilibrium price,** the price that will be low enough to induce investors to buy the stock, but not so low that it will rise sharply immediately after the stock is issued. Note that if the offering price is set below the true equilibrium price, the stock will rise sharply after issue and the company and its original stockholders will have given away too much stock to raise the required capital. If

offering price
The price at which common stock is sold to the public.

equilibrium price
The price that will be low enough to induce investors to buy the stock, but not so low that it will rise sharply immediately after it is issued. At the equilibrium price, $k_s = \hat{k}_s$.

the offering price is set above the true equilibrium price, either the issue will fail or, if the bankers succeed in selling the stock, their investment clients will be unhappy when the stock subsequently falls to its equilibrium level. Therefore, it is important that the equilibrium price be approximated as closely as possible.

Selling Procedures

Once the company and its investment bankers have decided how much money to raise, the type of securities to issue, and the basis for pricing the issue, they will prepare and file an SEC registration statement and a prospectus. It generally takes about 20 days for the issue to be approved by the SEC. The final price of the stock (or the yield on a bond issue) is set at the close of business the day the issue clears the SEC, and the securities are offered to the public the following day.

Investors are not required to pay for the stock until ten days after they place their buy orders, but the investment bankers must pay the issuing firm within four days of the time the offering officially begins. Typically, the bankers sell the stock within a day or two after the offering begins, but on occasion they miscalculate, set the offering price too high, and are unable to move the issue. At still other times the market declines during the offering period, forcing the bankers to reduce the price of the stock. In either instance, on an underwritten offering the firm receives the price that was agreed upon, and the bankers must absorb any losses that are incurred.

Because they are exposed to potentially large losses, investment bankers typically do not handle the purchase and distribution of an issue singlehandedly unless it is a very small one. If the amount of money involved is large, and the risk of price fluctuations substantial, investment bankers form **underwriting syndicates** in an effort to minimize the amount of risk each one carries. The banking house that sets up the deal is called the **lead, or managing, underwriter.**

In addition to the underwriting syndicate, on larger offerings still more investment bankers are included in a **selling group,** which handles the distribution of securities to individual investors. The selling group includes all members of the underwriting syndicate plus additional dealers who take relatively small participations (or shares of the total issue) from the syndicate members. Thus the underwriters act as *wholesalers,* whereas members of the selling group act as *retailers.* The number of houses in a selling group depends partly on the size of the issue; for example, the one set up when Communications Satellite Corporation (Comsat) went public consisted of 385 members.

Shelf Registrations

The selling procedures described previously, including the 20-day minimum waiting period between registration with the SEC and sale of the issue, apply to most securities sales. However, large, well-known public companies which

underwriting syndicate
A syndicate of investment firms formed to spread the risk associated with the purchase and distribution of a new issue of securities.

lead, or managing, underwriter
The member of an underwriting syndicate that actually arranges a new securities issue.

selling group
A group of stock brokerage firms formed for the purpose of distributing a new issue of securities.

issue securities on a regular basis may file a *master registration statement* with the SEC and then update it with a *short-form statement* just prior to each individual offering. In such a case, a company that decided at 10 A.M. to sell new securities could have the sale completed before noon. This procedure is known as **shelf registration,** because in effect the company puts its new securities "on the shelf" and then sells them to investors when it thinks the market is right.

shelf registration
A procedure under which a large, well-established firm can sell new securities on very short notice.

Maintenance of the Secondary Market

In the case of a large, established firm like Carter Chemical Company, the investment banking firm's job is finished once it has disposed of the stock and turned the net proceeds over to the issuing company. However, in the case of a company going public for the first time, the investment banker is under an obligation to maintain a market for the shares after the issue has been completed. Such stocks are typically traded in the over-the-counter market, and the lead underwriter generally agrees to "make a market" in the stock so as to keep it reasonably liquid. The company wants a good market to exist for its stock, as do the stockholders. Therefore, if the banking house wants to do business with the company in the future, keep its own brokerage customers happy, and have future referral business, it will hold an inventory of the shares and help to maintain an active secondary market in the stock.

Self-Test

What is the sequence of events when a firm decides to issue new securities?

What type of firm would use a shelf registration? Explain.

 SMALL BUSINESS

Going Public for Less Than You're Worth

For many entrepreneurs, making an initial public offering (IPO) of their company's equity is a dream come true. After their years of sacrifice and hard work, the company is finally a success. The value of that offering is realized by going public. Many observers are amazed that the successful entrepreneur appears willing to sell equity in his or her firm for too little money — IPOs are "underpriced" on average.

Stocks are underpriced if they begin trading in the public markets at a price that is higher than the price in the IPO. An example would be a stock that was sold in an IPO for $12.00 which begins trading immediately after the IPO for $13.50 to $15.00 per share. Some stocks have traded for as much as twice their IPO prices in the public market.

This underpricing is a puzzle. The company

going public, and any current shareholders of the privately owned firm who are selling as part of the public offering, receive, on average, the IPO price minus a commission or "discount" of roughly 8%. Thus, shareholders selling for $12.00 per share in an IPO would typically receive about $11.00 per share. If the share price increases to $15.00 after the IPO, then the former shareholders (and the company) have received $4.00 per share less than their shares were worth. Even if the shareholders don't sell any of their own shares in the IPO, but instead sell only the company's shares, they are still hurt by underpricing, because their ownership in the firm is diluted more than it would have been had the shares been fully priced.

Underpricing is especially severe during periods known as "hot issue periods" in the market. During such periods, the *average* issue sold in an IPO has increased in price by 25% to 50% after issuance. In general, the definition of a hot issue period is one in which issue values increase after the IPO in the public market.

The large returns of IPOs in the public market are not caused by the company's performance after the IPO. They do not mean that the firm showed high earnings growth after the IPO — the higher returns generally occur on the *first trading day*. This simply means that the IPO securities were sold at a price below their value.

Why would issuers in IPOs (i.e., selling companies) willingly sell their stocks for less than their true value? There are a number of theories to explain underpricing, which are being tested by scholars, but there is no widespread consensus on the reasons for underpricing. Some possible explanations are described next.

One theory holds that issues are underpriced because the issuing companies' owners do not know everything that their underwriters know. The assumption is that there is an "information asymmetry" between issuers and underwriters, and that without this asymmetry, issues would be fully priced. This theory may explain some occurrences of underpricing, such as isolated instances in which an unethical underwriter (who presumably would not last long in the business) knowingly misinforms the issuer. How-

ever, some underwriters themselves have gone public, acting as their own underwriters, and they have also had substantial first-day returns.

A popular theory among academicians is that underpricing occurs to keep uninformed investors in the market. According to this theory, there are some well-informed investors who regularly watch the IPO market. They see new issues, and they can tell which ones are mispriced. They, therefore, buy only the underpriced issues and avoid all others. However, such informed investors do not have enough capital to buy all of the shares of any offering.

An uninformed investor may place an offer to buy some shares in every offering. This uninformed investor will get to buy a lot of stock in the overpriced or correctly priced offerings, but will obtain only a small portion of the offerings in which the informed investors are active. Unless the set of all offerings is underpriced on average, then uninformed investors would consistently lose money, they would leave the market, and the market would break down. Thus, this theory argues, the IPO market must experience general underpricing to function. Early empirical evidence is consistent with this theory. In particular, it shows that offerings about which there is great uncertainty will tend to be more underpriced, and that is observed in practice.

The most popular theory with underwriters and venture capitalists is what might be called the "good taste in the mouth" theory. According to this theory, if the company underprices its issue in an IPO, investors will be more receptive to future "seasoned" issues from the same firm. Note, too, that most IPOs involve only 10 to 20 percent of the stock, so the original owners still have 80 to 90 percent of the shares.

All of these theories have a similar implicaton: An IPO with less uncertainty concerning its value will tend to be more fully priced. This suggests some ways that firms can prepare themselves for public offerings at higher prices. For example, offerings through more prestigious underwriters are, on average, less underpriced than offerings through less reputable underwriters. Issuers that use reputable, visible accountants for their audits are also less under-priced than those with less reputable accountants, and firms that received venture capital investment from more reputable capitalists are less underpriced. In fact, even the successful application for a bank loan that is revealed in the offering prospectus is associated with less underpricing. Firms with a longer financial history and which have achieved a higher level of sales also appear to be able to obtain a better price for their shares.

The phenomenon of underpricing IPO shares remains a puzzle to finance academicians. We think we have some of the answers, but the questions are not yet settled. Meanwhile, an issuer should be aware that most IPOs are underpriced by a meaningful amount, and that this underpricing is almost certainly related to the risk and uncertainty of the business. This is important information to consider when deciding when and if the firm should make its initial public offering.

SUMMARY

This chapter describes common stock financing and the investment banking process, as well as the process for valuing common stocks. The key concepts covered are listed below:

- A **proxy** is a document which gives one person the power to act for another person, typically the power to vote shares of common stock. A proxy fight occurs when an outside group solicits stockholders' proxies in order to vote a new management team into office.

- Stockholders often have the right to purchase any additional shares sold by the firm. This right, called the **preemptive right,** protects the control of the present stockholders and prevents dilution of the value of their stock.

- The **value of a share of stock** is calculated as the **present value of the stream of dividends** to be received in the future.

- The equation used to find the **value of a constant, or normal, growth stock** is

$$\hat{P}_0 = \frac{D_1}{k_s - g}.$$

- The **expected total rate of return** from a stock consists of an **expected dividend yield** plus an **expected capital gains yield.** For a constant growth firm, both the expected dividend yield and the expected capital gains yield are constant.

- The equation for $\hat{k}_s$, **the expected rate of return on a constant growth stock,** can be expressed as follows:

$$\hat{k}_s = \frac{D_1}{P_0} + g.$$

- A **supernormal growth stock** is one for which earnings and dividends are expected to grow much faster than the economy as a whole over some specified time period.

635

- To find the **present value of a supernormal (nonconstant) growth stock,** (1) find the PV of the dividends during the supernormal growth period, (2) find the price of the stock at the end of the supernormal growth period, (3) discount this price back to the present, and (4) sum these two components.

- The major **advantages of common stock financing** are as follows: (1) there is no obligation to make fixed payments, (2) common stock never matures, (3) the use of common stock increases the creditworthiness of the firm, (4) stock can often be sold on better terms than debt, and (5) using stock helps the firm maintain its reserve borrowing capacity.

- The major **disadvantages of common stock financing** are (1) it extends voting privileges to new stockholders, (2) new stockholders share in the firm's profits, (3) the costs of stock financings are high, (4) using stock can raise the firm's cost of capital, and (5) dividends paid on common stock are not tax deductible.

- A **closely held corporation** is one that is owned by a few individuals who are typically associated with the firm's management.

- A **publicly owned corporation** is one that is owned by a relatively large number of individuals who are not actively involved in its management.

- **Going public** facilitates stockholder diversification, increases liquidity of the firm's stock, makes it easier for the firm to raise capital, and establishes a value for the firm. However, reporting costs are high, operating data must be disclosed, management self-dealings are harder to arrange, the price may sink to a low level if the stock is not traded actively, and public ownership may make it harder for management to maintain control of the firm.

- An **investment banker** assists in the issuing of securities by helping the firm determine the size of the issue and the type of securities to be used, by establishing the selling price, by selling the issue, and, in some cases, by maintaining an aftermarket for the stock.

- **Initial public offerings (IPOs)** are often underpriced (1) because of information asymmetry, (2) to keep uninformed investors in the market, and (3) to keep investors receptive to future "seasoned" issues from the same firm.

EQUATIONS

The value of a stock is the present value of its expected future dividends:

$$\hat{P}_0 = \frac{D_1}{(1 + k_s)^1} + \frac{D_2}{(1 + k_s)^2} + \ldots + \frac{D_\infty}{(1 + k_s)^\infty} \qquad \textbf{(17-1)}$$

$$= \sum_{t=1}^{\infty} \frac{D_t}{(1 + k_s)^t}.$$

If a stock's dividends are expected to grow at a constant rate, g, then Equation 17-1 can be simplified to

$$\hat{P}_0 = \frac{D_1}{k_s - g}. \qquad\qquad (17\text{-}4)$$

From Equation 17-4, the expected rate of return can be calculated as the expected dividend yield plus the expected capital gains yield, or

$$\hat{k}_s = \frac{D_1}{P_0} + g. \qquad\qquad (17\text{-}5)$$

 RESOLUTION TO DECISION IN FINANCE

How to Botch a Deal

With a casual attitude not usually typical of major corporate figures, the Hilton chairman and directors simply frittered away their options. "For almost half a year," said a real estate consultant to one of the bidders, "they had everyone waiting around, not realizing that the window of opportunity was closing."

When it took several months to select investment advisors, the board led the brokers for one prospective bidder to feel that "they weren't dealing with the highest level of professionalism." A decision on existing bids was then delayed for several more months as directors waited for the still higher ones they expected.

What they failed to do was to consider what was happening in the outside world. While they stalled, secure in their belief that they had a seller's market, the junk-bond debacle was getting worse, and bankers and investors were becoming more cautious in their dealings. Possibly worst of all, the Japanese government was discouraging its country's corporations from making any high-profile purchases in the United States, in the wake of bad feeling over Mitsubi-

shi Estate's October purchase of Rockefeller Center. At least one Japanese firm had been on the bid list for Hilton and had been expected to offer a high price.

Behaving smugly, with their "eyes closed," Hilton's board "took a little too long, and it cost them dearly," said one shareholder. A bidder said of the board, "They had expectations based on yesterday's news" when they turned down the two final $3.8 billion bids from JMB Realty of Chicago and a group led by two Los Angeles financiers.

Their mistakes cost Hilton shareholders about $2 billion, including $220 million on Barron Hilton's own stock. The firm is keeping communications open with JMB Realty in case hotel prices rise again. Donald Trump thinks the properties will be worth more at a later date, but he might not be in a position to bid at that time. Hilton could also placate its shareholders by taking on debt and then either issuing a special dividend or repurchasing some of its own outstanding shares. One long-time shareholder, George A. Foley III of Los Angeles, may have expressed the emotions of all who would have been better off with a lower-than-expected purchase price, rather than the subsequently deflated stock: "I just feel totally bagged."

Source: "Hilton: A Case Study of How to Botch a Deal," *Business Week,* March 26, 1990.

QUESTIONS

17-1 Two investors are evaluating the common stock of Multiple Basic Industries (MBI) for possible purchase. MBI is in the mature stage of its life cycle, and its earnings and dividends are growing at a constant rate. The investors agree on the expected value of D_1 and also on the expected future dividend growth rate. Furthermore, they agree on the riskiness of the stock. However, one investor normally holds stock for 2 years, while the other normally holds stock for 10 years. Based on the analysis presented in this chapter, they should both be willing to pay the same price for MBI's stock. True or false? Explain.

17-2 As we discussed in this chapter, purchasers of common stock typically expect to receive dividends plus capital gains. Would the distribution between dividends and capital gains be influenced by the firm's decision to pay more dividends rather than to retain and reinvest more of its earnings? Explain your answer.

17-3 The firm's expected dividend yield is defined as the next expected dividend, D_1, divided by the current price of the stock, P_0. What is the relationship between the dividend yield, the total yield, and the remaining years of supernormal (nonconstant) growth for a supernormal (nonconstant) growth firm?

17-4 Is it true that the following expression can be used to determine the value of a constant growth stock:

$$\hat{P}_0 = \frac{D_0}{k_s + g} \quad ?$$

Explain your answer.

17-5 Draw a Security Market Line graph. Put dots on the graph to show (approximately) where you think a particular company's **(a)** common stock and **(b)** bonds would lie. Now where would you add a dot to represent the common stock of a riskier company?

17-6 The SEC attempts to protect investors who are purchasing newly issued securities by making sure that the information put out by a company and its investment bankers is correct and is not misleading. However, the SEC *does not* provide any information about the real value of the securities; hence, an investor might pay too much for some new stock and consequently lose heavily. Do you think the SEC should, as part of every new stock or bond offering, render an opinion to investors as to the proper value of the securities being offered? Explain.

SELF-TEST PROBLEMS

ST-1 You are considering buying the stock of 2 very similar companies. Both companies are expected to earn $4.50 per share this year. However, Alliance Manufacturing (AM) is expected to pay all of its earnings out as dividends, whereas Bascombe Industries (BI) is expected to pay out only one-third of its earnings, or $1.50. AM's stock price is $30. Which of the following is most likely to be true?

a. BI will have a faster growth rate than AM. Therefore, BI's stock price should be greater than $30.

b. Although BI's growth rate should exceed AM's, AM's current dividend exceeds that of BI, and this should cause AM's price to exceed BI's.

c. An investor in AM will get his or her money back faster because AM pays out more of its earnings as dividends. Thus, in a sense, AM's stock is like a short-term bond, and BI's is like a long-term bond. Therefore, if economic shifts cause k_d and k_s to increase, and if the expected streams of dividends from AM and BI remain constant, AM's and BI's stock prices will both decline, but AM's price should decline further.

d. AM's expected and required rate of return is $\hat{k}_s = k_s = 15$ percent. BI's expected return will be higher because of its higher expected growth rate.

e. Based on the available information, the best estimate of BI's growth rate is 10 percent.

ST-2 You can buy a share of the Crown Company's stock today for 33⅛. Crown's last dividend was $2.50. In view of Crown's low risk, its required rate of return is only 14 percent. If dividends are expected to grow at a constant rate, g, in the future, and if k_s is expected to remain at 14 percent, what is Crown Company's expected stock price 5 years from now?

ST-3 TGI Group, Inc. is experiencing a period of rapid growth. Earnings and dividends are expected to grow at a rate of 18 percent during the next 2 years and 15 percent in the third year, then at a constant rate of 6 percent thereafter. TGI's last dividend was $1.15, and the required rate of return on the stock is 12 percent.

a. Calculate the price of the stock today.

b. Calculate $\hat{P}_1$ and $\hat{P}_2$.

c. Calculate the dividend yield and capital gains yield for Years 1, 2, and 3.

PROBLEMS

17-1 **Constant growth stock valuation.** Montoya Company has enjoyed many years of growth through franchising. Financial analysts now believe that the firm is moving into a mature, constant-growth phase of its life cycle. Next year's dividend is expected to be $4.50, and dividends and earnings are expected to grow at a constant 5 percent rate in the future. What price should investors pay for a share of Montoya common stock if they require a 14 percent rate of return on their investment?

17-2 **Constant growth stock valuation.** Chicago Forge and Steel's last dividend was $3.00 ($D_0 = $3.00). Chicago Forge and Steel's growth is expected to remain at a constant 6 percent. If investors demand a 12 percent rate of return, what is Chicago Forge and Steel's current market price?

17-3 **Constant growth stock valuation.** What would you expect Chicago Forge and Steel's (Problem 17-2) stock price to be in 3 years? That is, solve for $\hat{P}_3$. Assume that growth projections and investor-required returns will remain constant.

17-4 **Zero growth stock valuation.** Carolina Tobacco has been paying a $4.00 dividend for several years. Growth prospects for higher earnings are dim, but the company's treasurer is confident that the firm can continue to provide the current dividend into the foreseeable future. If investors require a 15 percent return, what is the current market price of the stock?

17-5   **Return on common stock.** Birmingham Industries' earnings and dividends have grown at a constant 7 percent rate over the past few years. This growth rate is expected to continue into the future. The firm's current dividend, D_0, is $3.00, and the current market price of the firm's stock is $32.10.

     a. What is the firm's dividend yield?

     b. What rate of return are the firm's investors expecting?

17-6   **Calculating the growth rate.** You can buy a share of Gulf and Pacific today for $60. Last year's dividend was $5.09. The required rate of return for stocks in Gulf and Pacific's risk class is 15 percent. Earnings and dividends are expected to grow at a constant rate, g, in the future, and k_s is also expected to remain at 15 percent.

     a. What rate of growth in earnings and dividends is Gulf and Pacific expecting?

     b. What is Gulf and Pacific's expected stock price 4 years from now?

17-7   **Calculating the growth rate.** Walsh-Saunders Company will pay a $2.50 dividend next year, in 1992. Seven years ago, in 1985, its dividend was $1.37. This growth in dividends is expected to remain constant in the future. If investors expect a 16 percent return, what is Walsh-Saunders's common stock price today?

17-8   **Constant growth stock valuation.** Mission Motors paid a dividend of $2.00 last year. The dividend is expected to grow at a constant rate of 5 percent into the future. You plan to buy the stock today, hold it for 3 years, and then sell it — if indeed you do decide to purchase it.

     a. What is the expected dividend for each of the next 3 years? That is, calculate D_1, D_2, and D_3. Note that $D_0 = $2.00.

     b. If the appropriate discount rate is 12 percent, and the first of these dividend payments will occur one year from today, what is the present value of the dividend stream? That is, calculate the PV of D_1, D_2, and D_3, and sum these PVs.

     c. You expect the price of the stock to be $34.73 in 3 years; that is, you expect P_3 to equal $34.73. Discounted at a 12 percent rate, what is the present value of this future stock price? In other words, calculate the PV of $34.73.

     d. If you plan to buy the stock, hold it for 3 years, and then sell it for $34.73, what is the most you should pay for it if your minimum required return is 12 percent?

     e. Use Equation 17-4 to calculate the present value of this stock. Assume that the rate of growth is a constant 5 percent.

     f. Is the value of this stock to you dependent on how long you plan to hold it? In other words, if your planned holding period were 2 years or 5 years rather than 3 years, would this affect the value of the stock today, P_0?

17-9   **Return on common stock.** Home Products Corporation's current market price is $54. Your stock broker has determined that the firm's dividends will be $5.40 next year, $5.832 in 2 years, and $6.298 in 3 years. Although your broker expects that the dividends will continue to grow at the same growth rate in the future, she recommends that you sell the stock for $68 at the end of 3 years.

     a. Calculate the growth rate in dividends.

     b. Calculate the stock's dividend yield.

     c. If the growth rate continues as expected, what is this stock's expected rate of return? Confirm your answer using Equation 17-4.

17-10   **Constant growth stock valuation.**

   a. Investors require a 12 percent rate of return on Pittsburgh Properties stock (k_s = 12%). At what price will the stock sell if the previous dividend was D_0 = $3 and investors expect dividends to grow at a constant compound rate of (1) minus 5 percent, (2) 0 percent, (3) 5 percent, (4) 9 percent, and (5) 11 percent? [*Hint:* Use D_1 = D_0 (1 + g), not D_0, in the formula.]

   b. In Part a, what is the price using Equation 17-4 for Pittsburgh Properties' stock if the required rate of return is 12 percent and the expected growth rate is **(1)** 12 percent or **(2)** 15 percent? Are these results reasonable? Explain.

17-11   **Declining growth stock valuation.** Upton Oil Company's oil and gas reserves are being depleted, and the costs of recovering a declining amount of crude petroleum products are rising each year. As a result, the company's earnings and dividends are declining at the rate of 10 percent per year. If D_0 = $5.00 and k_s = 12.5%, what is the value of Upton Oil's stock?

17-12   **Supernormal growth stock valuation.** Trinity Valley Corporation (TVC) has been growing at a rate of 20 percent per year in recent years. This same growth rate is expected to last another 3 years. After that time TVC's financial manager expects the firm's growth to slow to a constant 7 percent.

   a. Assuming that D_0 = $1.50 and that the firm's required rate of return, k_s, is 16 percent, what is TVC's stock worth today?

   b. Calculate the dividend yield and capital gains yield for Years 1, 2, and 3.

   c. Now assume that TVC's period of supernormal (20 percent) growth will last for 6 years rather than 3 years. Describe how this longer supernormal growth period will affect the stock's price, dividend yield, and capital gains yield.

17-13   **Supernormal growth stock valuation.** The earnings per share of Rakes Radiator Repair, Inc. are currently $2.00 ($E_0$ = $2.00). These earnings are expected to grow at a rate of 25 percent for the next 2 years and at 12 percent for the following 3 years, then to slow to a sustainable growth rate of 6 percent thereafter. The firm has previously had a policy of paying zero dividends because of its rapid growth. However, since its growth will be slower in the future, the payout policy will change. Payout for the next 2 years will remain at zero but will increase to 25 percent for the following 3 years. The payout will be 75 percent after Year 5. Rakes's shareholders require a 14 percent rate of return. What is the current market price for Rakes Radiator Repair, Inc.?

17-14   **Nonconstant growth stock.** A firm expects to pay dividends over each of the next 4 years of $2.00, $1.50, $2.50, and $3.50. If growth is then expected to level off at 5 percent, and if you require a 14 percent rate of return, then how much should you be willing to pay for this stock?

17-15   **Nonconstant growth stock.** Due to unfavorable economic conditions, EFB Company's earnings and dividends are expected to remain unchanged for the next 3 years. After 3 years, dividends are expected to grow at a 10 percent annual rate into the foreseeable future. The last dividend (and also the next dividend) was $1.00, and the required rate of return is 18 percent. What should be the current market value of EFB stock?

17-16   **Equilibrium stock price.** The risk-free rate of return, k_{RF}, is 9 percent; the required rate of return on the market, k_M, is 13 percent; and Concord Computer Company's (CCC's) stock has a beta coefficient of 1.5.

   a. If the dividend expected during the coming year, D_1, is $3.50, and if g = a constant 5%, at what price should CCC's stock sell?

   b. Now suppose that the Federal Reserve Board increases the money supply, causing the risk-free rate to drop to 8 percent. What would this do to the price of the stock?

   c. In addition to the change in Part b, suppose that investors' risk aversion declines; this fact, combined with the decline in k_{RF}, causes k_M to fall to 11 percent. At what price would CCC's stock sell?

   d. Assume the changes in Part c and suppose that CCC has a change in management. The new group institutes policies that increase the expected constant growth rate to 6 percent. Also, the new management stabilizes sales and profits and thus causes the beta coefficient to decline from 1.5 to 1.2. After all these changes, what is CCC's new equilibrium price? (*Note:* D_1 goes to $3.53.)

17-17   **Stock valuation.** Assume that the stock of the Perry Corporation has just paid an annual dividend of $2.50 and that this dividend is expected to grow for the next 2 years at an annual rate of 20 percent, then to grow indefinitely at an annual rate of 10 percent. If the risk-free rate is 5 percent, the expected return on the market is 15 percent, and the firm's beta is 0.80, then how much should you be willing to pay for this stock?

17-18   **Beta coefficients.** Suppose Atherton Company's management conducts a study and concludes that if Atherton expanded its consumer products division (which is less risky than its primary business, industrial chemicals), the firm's beta would decline from 1.4 to 1.1. However, consumer products have a somewhat lower profit margin, and this would cause Atherton's constant growth rate in earnings and dividends to fall from 8 to 6 percent.

   a. Should management make the change? Assume the following: k_M = 12%; k_{RF} = 9%; D_0 = $1.75.

   b. Assume all the facts as given previously except the change in the beta coefficient. What would the beta have to equal to cause the expansion to be a good one? (*Hint:* Set $\hat{P}_0$ under the new policy equal to $\hat{P}_0$ under the old one, and find the new beta that will produce this equality.)

17-19   **Stock pricing.** A. J. Krauss and Company is a small jewelry manufacturer. The company has been successful and has grown. Now Krauss is planning to sell an issue of common stock to the public for the first time, and it faces the problem of setting an appropriate price on its common stock. The company and its investment bankers believe that the proper procedure is to select firms similar to it with publicly traded common stock and to make relevant comparisons.

   Several jewelry manufacturers are reasonably similar to Krauss with respect to product mix, size, asset composition, and debt/equity proportions. Of these, Gemex and Diamond Gallery are most similar. Data are given in the following table. When analyzing these data, assume that 1985 and 1990 were reasonably normal years for all 3 companies; that is, these years were neither especially good nor bad in terms of sales, earnings, and dividends. At the time of the analysis, k_{RF} was 10 percent and k_M was 15 percent. Gemex is listed on the American Exchange and Diamond Gallery on the NYSE, whereas A. J. Krauss will be traded in the OTC market.

	Gemex (Per Share)	Diamond Gallery (Per Share)	A. J. Krauss (Totals)
Earnings			
1990	$2.25	$3.75	$600,000
1985	1.50	2.75	408,000
Price			
1990	$18.00	$32.50	———
Dividends			
1990	$1.125	$1.875	$300,000
1985	0.750	1.375	210,000
Book value			
1990	$15.00	$27.50	$4,500,000
Market/book ratio			
1990	120%	118%	———
Total assets, 1990	$14 million	$41 million	$10 million
Total debt, 1990	$6 million	$15 million	$5.5 million
Sales, 1990	$20.5 million	$70 million	$18.5 million

a. Assume that A. J. Krauss has 100 shares of stock outstanding. Use this information to calculate earnings per share (EPS), dividends per share (DPS), and book value per share for Krauss. (*Note:* Since there are only 100 shares outstanding, your results may seem a bit large.)

b. Based on your answer to Part a, do you think Krauss's stock would sell at a price in the same "ballpark" as Gemex's and Diamond Gallery's—that is, sell in the range of $25 to $100 per share?

c. Assuming that Krauss's management can split the stock so that the 100 shares could be changed to 1,000 shares, 100,000 shares, or any other number, would such an action make sense in this case? Why?

d. Now assume that Krauss did split its stock and has 400,000 shares. Calculate new values for EPS, DPS, and book value per share.

e. What can you say about the relative growth rates of the 3 companies?

f. What can you say about their dividend payout policies?

g. Return on equity (ROE) can be measured as EPS/book value per share, or as total earnings/total equity. Calculate 1990 ROEs for the 3 companies.

h. Calculate total debt/total assets ratios for the 3 companies.

i. Calculate P/E ratios for Gemex and Diamond Gallery. Are these P/Es consistent with the growth and ROE data? If not, what other factors could explain the relative P/E ratios?

j. Now determine a range of values for Krauss's stock, with 400,000 shares outstanding, by applying Gemex's and Diamond Gallery's P/E ratios, price/dividend ratios, and price/book value ratios to your data for Krauss. For example, one possible price for Krauss's stock is (P/E Gemex)(EPS Krauss) = (8)($1.5) = $12 per share. Similar calculations would produce a range of prices based on both Gemex and Diamond Gallery data.

k. Using the equation $k_s = D_1/P_0 + g$, find approximate k_s values for Gemex and Diamond Gallery. Then use these values in the constant growth stock price model to find a price for Krauss's stock.

l. At what price do you think Krauss's shares should be offered to the public? You will want to find the *equilibrium price* (i.e., a price that will be low enough to induce investors to buy the stock, but not so low that it will rise sharply immediately after it is issued). Think about relative growth rates, ROEs, dividend yields, and total returns ($k_s = D_1/P_0 + g$). Also, as you think about the appropriate price, recognize that when Howard Hughes let the Hughes Tool Company go public, different investment bankers proposed prices that ranged from $20 to $30 per share. Hughes naturally accepted the $30 price, and the stock jumped to $40 almost immediately. Nobody's perfect!

m. Would your recommended price be different if the offering was made by the Krauss family, selling some of its 400,000 shares, or if it was new stock authorized by the company? For example, another 100,000 shares could be authorized, which when issued would bring the outstanding shares up to 500,000, with 400,000 shares owned by the Krausses and 100,000 shares held by the public. If the Krausses sell their own shares, they receive the proceeds as their own personal funds. If the company sells newly issued shares, the company receives the funds and presumably uses the money to expand the business.

n. If the price you selected in Part l actually was established as the price at which the stock would be offered to the public, approximately how much money, in total, would the Krauss Company actually receive?

17-20 Supernormal growth stock valuation. The Hughes Corporation has been growing at a rate of 30 percent per year in recent years. This same growth rate is expected to last for another 2 years.

a. If $D_0 = \$2.75$, $k_s = 16\%$, and $g_n = 7\%$, what is Hughes's stock worth today? What are its current dividend yield and capital gains yield?

b. Now assume that Hughes's period of supernormal growth is 5 years rather than 2 years. How does this affect its price, dividend yield, and capital gains yield? Answer in words only.

c. What will be Hughes's dividend yield and capital gains yield the year after its period of supernormal growth ends? (*Hint:* These values will be the same regardless of whether you examine the case of 2 or 5 years of supernormal growth; the calculations are trivial.)

d. Of what interest to investors is the changing relationship between dividend yield and capital gains yield over time?

(Do Parts e and f only if you are using the computerized problem diskette.)

e. What will be Hughes's stock price, dividend yield, and capital gains yield if the supernormal growth period is 5 years?

f. What will be the price, dividend yield, and capital gains yield if the required rate of return is 18 percent and the supernormal growth period is 2 years?

SOLUTIONS TO SELF-TEST PROBLEMS

ST-1 a. This is not necessarily true. Since BI plows back two-thirds of its earnings, its growth rate should exceed that of AM, but AM pays higher dividends ($4.50 versus $1.50). We cannot say which stock should have the higher price.

b. Again, we just do not know which price would be higher.

c. This is false. The changes in k_d and k_s would have a greater effect on BI's stock—its price would decline more.

d. Once again, we just do not know which expected return would be higher. The total expected return for AM is $k_{AM} = D_1/P_0 + g = 15\% + 0\% = 15\%$. The total expected return for BI will have D_1/P_0 less than 15 percent and g greater than 0 percent, but k_{BI} could be either greater or less than AM's total expected return, 15 percent.

e. We have eliminated a, b, c, and d, so e must be correct. Based on the available information, AM's and BI's stocks should sell at about the same price, \$30.
Thus $k_s = \$4.50/\$30 = 15\%$ for both AM and BI. BI's current dividend yield is $\$1.50/\$30 = 5\%$. Therefore $g = 15\% - 5\% = 10\%$.

ST-2 The first step is to solve for g, the unknown variable, in the constant growth equation. Since D_1 is unknown, substitute $D_0(1 + g)$ as follows:

$$\hat{P}_0 = \frac{D_0(1 + g)}{k_s - g}$$

$$\$33.125 = \frac{\$2.50(1 + g)}{0.14 - g}.$$

Solving for g, we find the growth rate to be 6 percent. The next step is to use the growth rate to project the stock price 5 years hence:

$$\hat{P}_5 = \frac{D_0(1 + g)^6}{k_s - g}$$

$$= \frac{\$2.50(1.06)^6}{0.14 - 0.06}$$

$$= \$44.33.$$

[Alternatively, $\hat{P}_5 = \$33.125(1.06)^5 = \$44.33$.]

Therefore, Crown Company's expected stock price 5 years from now, $\hat{P}_5$, is \$44.33.

ST-3 **a.** *Step 1:* Calculate the PV of the dividends paid during the supernormal growth period:

$$D_1 = \$1.1500(1.18) = \$1.3570.$$

$$D_2 = \$1.3570(1.18) = \$1.6013.$$

$$D_3 = \$1.6013(1.15) = \$1.8415.$$

$$PV\ D = \$1.3570(0.8929) + \$1.6013(0.7972) + \$1.8415(0.7118)$$

$$= \$1.2117 + \$1.2766 + \$1.3108$$

$$= \$3.7991 \approx \$3.80.$$

Step 2: Find the PV of the stock's price at the end of Year 3:

$$\hat{P}_3 = \frac{D_4}{k_s - g} = \frac{D_3(1 + g_n)}{k_s - g_n}$$

$$= \frac{\$1.8415(1.06)}{0.12 - 0.06}$$

$$= \$32.53.$$

$$PV \; \hat{P}_3 = \$32.53(0.7118) = \$23.15.$$

Step 3: Sum the two components to find the price of the stock today:

$$\hat{P}_0 = \$3.80 + \$23.15 = \$26.95.$$

b.

$$\hat{P}_1 = \$1.6013(0.8929) + \$1.8415(0.7972) + \$32.53(0.7972)$$

$$= \$1.4298 + \$1.4680 + \$25.9329$$

$$= \$28.8307 \approx \$28.83.$$

$$\hat{P}_2 = \$1.8415(0.8929) + \$32.53(0.8929)$$

$$= \$1.6443 + \$29.0460$$

$$= \$30.6903 \approx \$30.69.$$

c.

Year	Dividend Yield	Capital Gains Yield	Total Return
1	$\dfrac{\$1.3570}{\$26.95} = 5.04\%$	$\dfrac{\$28.83 - \$26.95}{\$26.95} = 6.98\%$	$\approx 12\%$
2	$\dfrac{\$1.6013}{\$28.83} = 5.55\%$	$\dfrac{\$30.69 - \$28.83}{\$28.83} = 6.45\%$	12
3	$\dfrac{\$1.8415}{\$30.69} = 6.00\%$	$\dfrac{\$32.53 - \$30.69}{\$30.69} = 6.00\%$	12

Chapter 18

Hybrid Financing:
Leasing and Option Securities

 DECISION IN FINANCE

Sandy's Gamble

When McDonnell Douglas Corporation launched its DC-9-80 commercial twinjet in 1977, everyone was sure the company had a winner. Although its base price was about the same as a Boeing 727, the fuel-efficient Super 80 cost about 30 percent to 40 percent less per seat-mile to operate. In the cost-conscious airlines industry, this was expected to give McDonnell Douglas a strong competitive advantage.

By summer 1982 the promise of the Super 80 had yet to be realized, however. Total sales amounted to only 115 planes, and there were 17 airplanes built or half-built that had no buyers. The problem, realized McDonnell Douglas Chairman Sanford McDonnell, lay not in the airplanes but in the airlines industry

itself. The grim fact was that McDonnell's potential customers were simply too broke to buy airplanes on their own accounts.

Sandy McDonnell faced three tough choices. He could close down the Long Beach, California, plant where the airplanes were built, which would lay off 16,000 trained workers and leave the company holding millions of dollars' worth of useless aircraft parts. He could go on manufacturing costly airplanes without advance orders and continue trying to sell them in a depressed market. Or he could find a way to help his customers finance the airplanes they needed and wanted but couldn't afford.

As you read this chapter, consider how leasing might help solve the problems of both McDonnell Douglas and the commercial airlines. What kind of lease would be most beneficial to all parties? Why?

See end of chapter for resolution.

647

In the two preceding chapters, we examined the use of various types of debt, preferred stock, and common stock. In this chapter, we examine two other types of long-term capital: *leasing,* which is used by financial managers as an alternative to borrowing to finance fixed assets, and *option securities,* particularly warrants and convertibles, which are attractive to investors because they allow debtholders to acquire common stock at bargain prices and thus to share in the capital gains if a company is especially successful.[1]

LEASING

Firms generally own fixed assets and report them on their balance sheets, but it is the *use* of buildings and equipment that is important, not their ownership per se. One way of obtaining the use of assets is to buy them, but an alternative is to lease them. Prior to the 1950s, leasing was generally associated with real estate—land and buildings. Today, however, it is possible to lease virtually any kind of fixed asset, and in 1990 about 25 percent of all new capital equipment acquired by businesses was leased.

Types of Leases

Leasing takes three different forms: (1) *sale-and-leaseback* arrangements, (2) *operating leases,* and (3) straight *financial,* or *capital, leases.*

sale and leaseback
An operation whereby a firm sells land, buildings, or equipment and simultaneously leases the property back for a specified period under specific terms.

lessee
The party that uses, rather than the one who owns, the leased property.

lessor
The owner of the leased property.

Sale and Leaseback. Under a **sale and leaseback,** a firm that owns land, buildings, or equipment sells the property and simultaneously executes an agreement to lease the property back for a specified period under specific terms. The purchaser could be an insurance company, a commercial bank, a specialized leasing company, or even an individual investor. The sale-and-leaseback plan is an alternative to a mortgage.

The firm which is selling the property, or the **lessee,** immediately receives the purchase price put up by the buyer, or the **lessor.**[2] At the same time, the seller-lessee retains the use of the property just as if it had borrowed money and mortgaged the property to secure the loan. Note that under a mortgage loan arrangement, the financial institution would normally receive a series of equal payments just sufficient to amortize the loan while earning a specified rate of return on the outstanding balance. Under a sale-and-leaseback arrangement, the lease payments are set up in exactly the same way—the payments are set so as to return the full purchase price to the investor-lessor while providing a specified rate of return on the lessor's outstanding investment.

---

[1]Even though both topics covered in this chapter are important, time pressures may preclude a class's detailed coverage of them. Accordingly, the chapter is written in a modular form to permit instructors to cover one or both of these topics. When we are under time pressure in the basic course, we require students to read the entire chapter but to know for exam purposes only how to answer the end-of-chapter questions, not how to work the problems.

[2]The term *lessee* is pronounced "less-ee," and *lessor* is pronounced "less-or."

Operating Leases. Operating leases, sometimes called *service leases,* provide for both *financing* and *maintenance.* IBM is one of the pioneers of the operating lease contract, and computers and office copying machines, together with automobiles and trucks, are the primary types of equipment involved. Ordinarily, these leases call for the lessor to maintain and service the leased equipment, and the cost of providing maintenance is built into the lease payments.

Another important characteristic of operating leases is the fact that they are frequently *not fully amortized;* in other words, the payments required under the lease contract are not sufficient to recover the full cost of the equipment. However, the lease contract is written for a period considerably shorter than the expected economic life of the leased equipment, and the lessor expects to recover all investment costs through subsequent renewal payments, through subsequent leases to other lessees, or by selling the leased equipment.

A final feature of operating leases is that they frequently contain a *cancellation clause,* which gives the lessee the right to cancel the lease before the expiration of the basic agreement. This is an important consideration for the lessee, for it means that the equipment can be returned if it is rendered obsolete by technological developments or if it is no longer needed because of a decline in the lessee's business.

> **operating lease**
> A lease under which the lessor maintains and finances the property; also called a *service lease.*

Financial, or Capital, Leases. Financial leases, sometimes called *capital leases,* are differentiated from operating leases in three respects: (1) they do *not* provide for maintenance service, (2) they are *not* cancelable, and (3) they *are* fully amortized (that is, the lessor receives rental payments which are equal to the full price of the leased equipment plus a fair return on the investment). In a typical financial lease arrangement, the firm that will use the equipment (the lessee) selects the specific items it requires and negotiates the price and delivery terms with the manufacturer. The user firm then negotiates terms with a leasing company and, once the lease terms are set, arranges to have the lessor buy the equipment from the manufacturer or the distributor. When the equipment is purchased, the user firm simultaneously executes the lease agreement.

Financial leases are similar to sale-and-leaseback arrangements, the major difference being that the leased equipment is new and the lessor buys it from a manufacturer or a distributor instead of from the user-lessee. A sale and leaseback may thus be thought of as a special type of financial lease, and both sale and leasebacks and financial leases are analyzed in the same manner.[3]

> **financial lease**
> A lease that does not provide for maintenance services, is not cancelable, and is fully amortized over its life; also called a *capital lease.*

---

[3]For a lease transaction to qualify as a lease for tax purposes, and thus for the lessee to be able to deduct the lease payments, the life of the lease must approximate the life of the asset, and the lessee cannot be permitted to buy the asset at a nominal value when the lease expires. It is important to consult lawyers and accountants to insure that a lease is valid under IRS regulations.

Financial Statement Effects

off-balance-sheet financing
Financing in which the assets and liabilities under the contract do not appear on the firm's balance sheet.

Lease payments are shown as operating expenses on a firm's income statement, but under certain conditions, neither the leased assets nor the liabilities under the lease contract appear on the firm's balance sheet. For this reason, leasing is often called **off-balance-sheet financing.** This point is illustrated in Table 18-1 by the balance sheets of two hypothetical firms, B (for Buy) and L (for Lease). Initially, the balance sheets of both firms are identical, and both have debt ratios of 50 percent. Each firm then decides to acquire fixed assets which cost $100. Firm B borrows $100 to make the purchase, so both an asset and a liability are recorded on its balance sheet, and its debt ratio is increased to 75 percent. Firm L leases the equipment, so its balance sheet is unchanged. The lease may call for fixed charges as high as or even higher than those on the loan, and the obligations assumed under the lease may be equally or more dangerous from the standpoint of financial safety, but the firm's debt ratio remains at 50 percent.

FASB #13
The statement of the Financial Accounting Standards Board that details the conditions and procedures for capitalizing leases.

capitalizing the lease
Incorporating the lease provisions into the balance sheet by reporting the leased asset under fixed assets and reporting the present value of future lease payments as debt; required by FASB #13.

To correct this problem, the Financial Accounting Standards Board issued **FASB #13,** which requires that for an unqualified audit report, firms that enter into financial (or capital) leases must restate their balance sheets to report leased assets as fixed assets and the present value of future lease payments as a debt. This process is called **capitalizing the lease,** and its net effect is to cause Firms B and L to have similar balance sheets, both of which will in essence resemble the one shown for Firm B after the asset increase.[4]

The logic behind FASB #13 is as follows. If a firm signs a lease contract, its obligation to make lease payments is just as binding as if it had signed a loan agreement. The failure to make lease payments can bankrupt a firm just as surely as can the failure to make principal and interest payments on a loan. Therefore, for all intents and purposes, a financial lease is identical to a loan.[5] This being the case, when a firm signs a lease agreement, it has, in effect, raised its "true" debt ratio.

If a disclosure of the lease in the Table 18-1 example were not made, then investors could be deceived into thinking that Firm L's financial position is

---

[4]FASB #13, "Accounting for Leases," November 1976, spells out in detail the conditions under which leases must be capitalized, and the procedures for doing so.

[5]There are, however, certain legal differences between loans and leases. In a bankruptcy liquidation, the lessor is entitled to take possession of the leased asset, and if the value of the asset is less than the required payments under the lease, the lessor can enter a claim (as a general creditor) for one year's lease payments. In a bankruptcy reorganization, the lessor receives the asset plus three years' lease payments if needed to bring the value of the asset up to the remaining investment in the lease. Under a secured loan arrangement, on the other hand, the lender has a security interest in the asset, meaning that if it is sold, the lender will be given the proceeds, and the full unsatisfied portion of the lender's claim will be treated as a general creditor obligation (see Appendix 20A). It is not possible to state as a general rule whether a supplier of capital is in a stronger position as a secured creditor or as a lessor. Since one position is usually regarded as being about as good as the other at the time the financial arrangements are being made, a lease is about as risky as a secured term loan from both the lessor-lender's and the lessee-borrower's viewpoints.

Table 18-1 **Balance Sheet Effects of Leasing**

Before Asset Increase				After Asset Increase							
				Firm B, Which Borrows and Purchases				**Firm L, Which Leases**			
Firms B and L											
Current assets	$ 50	Debt	$ 50	Current assets	$ 50	Debt	$150	Current assets	$ 50	Debt	$ 50
Fixed assets	50	Equity	50	Fixed assets	150	Equity	50	Fixed assets	50	Equity	50
Total	$100		$100	Total	$200		$200	Total	$100		$100
	Debt ratio: 50%				Debt ratio: 75%				Debt ratio: 50%		

stronger than it actually is. Even if the existence of the lease were disclosed in a footnote, investors might not fully recognize its impact and might not see that Firms B and L are in essentially the same financial position. If this were the case, Firm L could increase its true amount of debt through a lease arrangement, but its required return on debt, k_d, its required return on equity, k_s, and consequently its average required rate of return, would increase less than those of Firm B, which borrowed directly. Thus, investors would be willing to accept a lower return from Firm L because they would view it (incorrectly) as being in a stronger financial position than Firm B. These benefits of leasing would accrue to stockholders at the expense of new investors, who were, in effect, being deceived by the fact that the firm's balance sheet did not fully reflect its true liability situation. This is why FASB #13 was issued.

A lease will be classified as a capital lease, and hence be capitalized and shown directly on the balance sheet, if any one of the following conditions exists:

1. Under the terms of the lease, ownership of the property is effectively transferred from the lessor to the lessee.

2. The lessee can purchase the property or renew the lease at less than a fair market price when the lease expires.

3. The lease runs for a period equal to or greater than 75 percent of the asset's life. Thus, if an asset has a 10-year life and if the lease is written for more than 7.5 years, the lease must be capitalized.

4. The present value of the lease payments is equal to or greater than 90 percent of the initial value of the asset.[6]

These rules, together with strong footnote disclosures for operating leases, are sufficient to insure that no one will be fooled by lease financing. Thus, leases are recognized to be essentially the same as debt, and they have the same

---

[6]The discount rate used to calculate the present value of the lease payments must be the lower of (1) the rate used by the lessor to establish the lease payments or (2) the after-tax rate of interest which the lessee would have paid for new debt with a maturity equal to that of the lease.

effects as debt on the firm's required rate of return. Therefore, leasing will not generally permit a firm to use more financial leverage than could be obtained with conventional debt.

Evaluation by the Lessee

Any prospective lease must be evaluated by both the lessee and the lessor. The lessee must determine whether leasing an asset will be less costly than buying it, and the lessor must decide whether or not the lease will provide a reasonable rate of return. Since our focus in this book is primarily on financial management as opposed to investments, we restrict our analysis to that conducted by the lessee.[7]

In the typical case, the events leading to a lease arrangement follow the sequence described in the following list. We should note that a great deal of literature exists about the theoretically correct way to evaluate lease-versus-purchase decisions, and some very complex decision models have been developed to aid in the analysis. The analysis given here, however, leads to the correct decision in every case we have ever encountered.

1. The firm decides to acquire a particular building or piece of equipment. This decision is based on regular capital budgeting procedures, and it is not an issue in the typical lease analysis. In a lease analysis, we are concerned simply with whether to finance the asset by a lease or by a loan. However, if the effective cost of the lease is substantially lower than that of debt — and this could occur for several reasons, including the situation in which the lessor is able to utilize the depreciation tax shelters but the lessee is not — then the capital budgeting decision would have to be reevaluated, and projects formerly deemed unacceptable might become acceptable.

2. Once the firm has decided to acquire the asset, the next question is how to finance it. Well-run businesses do not have excess cash lying around, so new assets must be financed in some manner.

3. Funds to purchase the asset could be obtained by borrowing, by retaining earnings, or by issuing new stock. Alternatively, the asset could be leased. Because of the FASB #13 capitalization/disclosure provision for leases, we assume that a lease would have the same capital structure effects as a loan.

As indicated earlier, a lease is comparable to a loan in the sense that the firm is required to make a specified series of payments, and a failure to make

---

[7]The lessee is typically offered a set of lease terms by the lessor, which is generally a bank, a finance company such as General Electric Capital (the largest U.S. lessor), or some other institutional lender. It can accept or reject the lease, or shop around for a better deal. In this chapter, we take the lease terms as given for purposes of our analysis. See Chapter 14 of Eugene F. Brigham and Louis C. Gapenski, *Intermediate Financial Management,* 3rd ed., for a discussion of lease analysis from the lessor's standpoint, including a discussion of how a potential lessee can use such an analysis in bargaining for better terms.

these payments can result in bankruptcy. Thus, it is most appropriate to compare the cost of lease financing with that of debt financing.[8] The lease-versus-borrow-and-purchase analysis is illustrated with data on the Mitchell Electronics Company. The following conditions are assumed:

1. Mitchell plans to acquire equipment with a 5-year life which has a cost of $10,000,000, delivered and installed.

2. Mitchell can borrow the required $10 million, using a 10 percent loan to be amortized over 5 years. Therefore, the loan will call for payments of $2,637,965.60 per year, calculated as follows:

$$\text{Payment} = \frac{\$10,000,000}{\text{PVIFA}_{10\%,5}} = \frac{\$10,000,000}{3.7908} = \$2,637,965.60.$$

With a financial calculator, input PV = 10,000,000, k = i = 10, and n = 5, and then press PMT to find the payment, $2,637,974.81. Note the rounding difference; the calculator solution is more accurate.

3. Alternatively, Mitchell can lease the equipment for 5 years at a rental charge of $2,800,000 per year, payable at the end of the year, but the lessor will own it upon the expiration of the lease.[9] (The lease payment schedule is established by the potential lessor, and Mitchell can accept it, reject it, or negotiate.)

4. The equipment will definitely be used for 5 years, at which time its estimated net salvage value will be $715,000. Mitchell plans to continue using the equipment, so (1) if it purchases the equipment, the company will keep it, and (2) if it leases the equipment, the company will exercise an option to buy it at its estimated salvage value, $715,000.

5. The lease contract stipulates that the lessor will maintain the equipment. However, if Mitchell borrows and buys, it will have to bear the cost of maintenance, which will be performed by the equipment manufacturer at a fixed contract rate of $500,000 per year, payable at year-end.

6. The equipment falls in the MACRS 5-year class life, and for this analysis we assume that Mitchell's effective tax rate is 40 percent. Also, the depreciable basis is the original cost of $10,000,000.

---

[8]The analysis should compare the cost of leasing to the cost of debt financing *regardless* of how the asset is actually financed. The asset may actually be purchased with available cash if it is not leased, but because leasing has the same effect on a firm's financial position as debt financing, a comparison between leasing and borrowing is still appropriate.

[9]Lease payments can occur at the beginning of the year or at the end of the year. In this example, we assume end-of-year payments, but we demonstrate beginning-of-year payments in Self-Test Problem ST-1.

Table 18-2 **Mitchell Electronics Company: NPV Lease Analysis (Thousands of Dollars)**

	Year				
	1	**2**	**3**	**4**	**5**
I. Borrow-and-Purchase Analysis					
a. Loan amortization schedule					
(1) Loan payment	$2,638	$2,638	$2,638	$2,638	$2,638
(2) Interest	1,000	836	656	458	240
(3) Principal payment	1,638	1,802	1,982	2,180	2,398
(4) Remaining balance	8,362	6,560	4,578	2,398	0
b. Depreciation schedule					
(5) Depreciable basis	10,000	10,000	10,000	10,000	10,000
(6) MACRS percentage	0.20	0.32	0.19	0.12	0.11
(7) Depreciation	2,000	3,200	1,900	1,200	1,100
c. Cash outflows					
(8) Loan payment	$2,638	$2,638	$2,638	$2,638	$2,638
(9) Interest tax savings	(400)	(334)	(262)	(183)	(96)
(10) Depreciation tax savings	(800)	(1,280)	(760)	(480)	(440)
(11) Maintenance (AT)	300	300	300	300	300
(12) Net cash outflows (buy)	$1,738	$1,324	$1,916	$2,275	$2,402
(13) PVIF at 6%	0.9434	0.8900	0.8396	0.7921	0.7473
(14) PV of owning cash flows	$1,640	$1,178	$1,609	$1,802	$1,795
(15) Total PV cost of owning	$8,024 = Sum of Line 14				
II. Lease Analysis					
(16) Lease cost after taxes	$1,680	$1,680	$1,680	$1,680	$1,680
(17) Purchase option payment					715
(18) Net cash outflows (lease)	$1,680	$1,680	$1,680	$1,680	$2,395
(19) PVIF at 6%	0.9434	0.8900	0.8396	0.7921	0.7473
(20) PV of leasing cash flows	$1,585	$1,495	$1,411	$1,331	$1,790
(21) Total PV cost of leasing	$7,612 = Sum of Line 20				

III. Cost Comparison

Net advantage to leasing = NAL

= Total PV cost of owning − Total PV cost of leasing

= $8,024 − $7,612

= $412.

NPV Analysis. Table 18-2 shows the outflows that would be incurred each year under the two financing plans. The table is set up to produce a time line of cash flows:

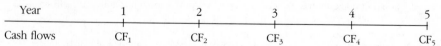

All cash flows occur at the end of the year, and the CF_t values are shown on Lines 12 and 18 of Table 18-2 for buying and leasing, respectively.

Note: a line-by-line explanation of the table follows.

Explanation of Lines

(1) Payments under the loan were determined as explained in the text.

(2) Interest is calculated as 10 percent of the prior year's remaining balance. Initially, the remaining balance (at Year 0) is $10 million, so the first year's interest is 0.1($10,000,000) = $1,000,000, written as $1,000.

(3) The principal payment is equal to the payment minus the interest component, $2,638,000 − $1,000,000 = $1,638,000 in Year 1.

(4) The remaining balance is calculated as the remaining balance from the prior year minus the principal repayment, $10,000,000 − $1,638,000 = $8,362,000 in Year 1.

(5) The depreciable basis is equal to the purchase price.

(6 and 7) Depreciation is calculated by MACRS, using rates of 0.20, 0.32, 0.19, 0.12, and 0.11. Refer back to Chapter 2 for a discussion of the MACRS depreciation system. Note that these percentages do not add to 100 percent (1.00). Because of the half-year convention, an asset with a 5-year MACRS class life would have 0.06 of the depreciable basis remaining in Year 6.

(8) The loan payment is taken from Line 1.

(9) The interest tax savings are calculated as Interest(Tax rate) = Interest(0.40). This amount is shown as a negative because it reduces outflows. To look at it another way, the after-tax cost of interest in Year 1 is $1,000,000 − $400,000 = $600,000. We included the $1,000,000 on Line 2, so we must subtract the $400,000 on Line 9.

(10) The depreciation tax savings are equal to Depreciation(Tax rate) = Depreciation(0.40). It is also shown as a negative number because it too reduces outflows. The company does not write a check to pay for depreciation, but the fact that it has depreciation does reduce its taxes, and in this sense depreciation provides a cash flow.

(11) Maintenance costs are $500,000 per year on a pre-tax basis, or $300,000 on an after-tax basis: $500,000(1 − t) = $500,000(0.6) = $300,000.

(12) Net cash outflows if Mitchell borrows and buys are calculated as follows: Line 12 = Line 8 + Line 9 + Line 10 + Line 11.

(13) PVIFs are based on the 6 percent after-tax cost of debt and are taken from Table A-1 in Appendix A. The reason that 6 percent is used is discussed later in the chapter.

(14) The PV of the cost of owning for each year is the product of Line 12 times Line 13.

(15) The total PV cost of owning is the sum of the entries on Line 14.

(16) The lease payment is given in the text as $2,800,000 before taxes and $1,680,000 after taxes. This payment includes all maintenance costs.

(17) Mitchell may purchase the machinery for $715,000 at the end of 5 years. Because it plans to continue the operation, it expects to incur this expense in Year 5. No taxes are involved.

(18) Net cash outflows if Mitchell elects to lease consist of the after-tax amount of the lease payment plus the Year 5 purchase option cost.

(19) PVIFs are the same as those shown on Line 13.

(20) PV costs of leasing are found as Line 18 times Line 19.

(21) The total PV cost of leasing is the sum of the entries on Line 20.

The top section of the table (Lines 1–15) is devoted to the costs of borrowing and buying. Lines 1–4 provide the loan amortization schedule, and on Lines 5–7 we calculate the annual depreciation charges. Lines 8–11 show the individual cash outflow items; note that the interest and depreciation tax savings are shown as negative outflows, because they are actually cash inflows resulting from the deductibility of interest and depreciation expenses. Line 12 summarizes the annual net cash outflows that Mitchell will incur if it finances the equipment with a loan. The present values of these outflows are found by multiplying each cash flow by the appropriate present value interest factor shown on Line 13.[10] The annual present values are given on Line 14, and the sum of these annual figures, which is the *present value of the cost of owning,* is shown on Line 15 in the Year 1 column.

In Section II of the table the present value cost of leasing is calculated. The lease payments are $2,800,000 per year; this rate, which in this example, but not in all cases, includes maintenance, was established by the prospective lessor and offered to Mitchell Electronics. If Mitchell accepts the lease, the full $2,800,000 will be a deductible expense, so the after-tax cost of the lease is calculated as follows:

$$\text{After-tax cost} = \text{Lease payment} - \text{Tax savings}$$

$$= \text{Lease payment} - (\text{Tax rate})(\text{Lease payment})$$

$$= \text{Lease payment}(1 - \text{Tax rate})$$

$$= \$2,800,000(1 - 0.4)$$

$$= \$1,680,000.$$

This amount is shown on Line 16.

Line 17 in the lease section shows the $715,000 which Mitchell expects to pay in Year 5 to purchase the equipment. We include this amount as a cost of leasing because Mitchell will almost certainly want to continue the operation and thus will be forced to purchase the equipment from the lessor. If we had assumed that the operation would not be continued, then no entry would have appeared on this line. However, in that case, we would have included the $715,000, minus taxes, as a Year 5 inflow (with parentheses around it) in the purchase analysis, because if the asset were purchased originally, it would be sold after 5 years. It would be subtracted because it would then be an inflow, whereas all other cash flows are outflows.

Line 20 shows the present value of the cost of leasing for each year, and Line 21 sums these costs and shows the total PV cost of leasing.

The rate used to discount the cash flows is a critical issue. In Chapter 12, we saw that the riskier a cash flow, the higher the discount rate used to find its present value. This same principle was observed in our discussion of capital budgeting, and it also applies in lease analysis. Just how risky are the cash flows under consideration here? Most of them are relatively certain, at least when compared with the types of cash flow estimates that were developed in capital budgeting. For example, the loan payment schedule is set by contract, as is the lease payment schedule. The depreciation expenses are also established by law and are not subject to change, and the $500,000 annual mainte-nance cost is fixed by contract as well. The tax savings are somewhat uncertain

---

[10]We will explain shortly that the appropriate discount rate to use in the leasing analysis is the after-tax cost of debt, or $k_d(1 - t)$, which in this case is $10\%(1 - 0.4) = 6\%$.

because tax rates may change, although tax rates do not change very often. The residual value is the least certain of the cash flows, but even here Mitchell's management is fairly confident that it will want to acquire the property and also that the cost of doing so will be close to $715,000.

Since the cash flows under both the lease and the borrow-and-purchase alternatives are all reasonably certain, they should be discounted at a relatively low rate. Most analysts recommend that the company's cost of debt be used, and this rate seems reasonable in our example. Further, since all the cash flows are on an after-tax basis, *the after-tax cost of debt, which is $k_d(1-t) = 0.10(1-0.4) = 6$ percent, should be used.* Accordingly, in Table 18-2 we multiplied the cash outflows by the 6 percent PVIFs shown below each set of cash flows, and we summed these discounted cash flows to obtain the present values of the costs of owning and leasing. The financing method that produces the smaller present value of costs is the one that should be selected. The example shown in Table 18-2 indicates that leasing has a net advantage over buying: the present value of the cost of leasing is $412,000 less than that of buying. Therefore, it is to Mitchell's advantage to lease.

Factors That Affect Leasing Decisions

The basic method of analysis set forth in Table 18-2 is sufficient to handle most situations. However, certain factors warrant additional comments.

Estimated Residual Value. It is important to note that the lessor will own the property upon the expiration of the lease. The estimated end-of-lease value of the property is called the **residual value.** Superficially, it would appear that if residual values are expected to be large, owning would have an advantage over leasing. However, if expected residual values are large — as they may be under inflation for certain types of equipment as well as if real property is involved — then competition among leasing companies will force leasing rates down to the point where potential residual values will be fully recognized in the lease contract rates. Thus, the existence of large residual values on equipment is not likely to bias the decision against leasing.

residual value
The value of leased property at the end of the lease term.

Increased Credit Availability. As noted earlier, leasing is sometimes said to have an advantage for firms that are seeking the maximum degree of financial leverage. First, it is sometimes argued that a firm can obtain more money, and for a longer period, under a lease arrangement than under a loan secured by the asset. Second, because some leases do not appear on the balance sheet, lease financing has been said to give the firm a stronger appearance in a *superficial* credit analysis, thus permitting it to use more leverage than it could if it did not lease. There may be some truth to these claims for smaller firms. However, now that larger firms are required to capitalize major leases and to report them on their balance sheets, this point is of questionable validity.

Self-Test

Define each of these terms: (1) sale-and-leaseback arrangements, (2) operating leases, and (3) financial, or capital, leases.

What is off-balance-sheet financing, what is FASB #13, and how are the two related?

List the sequence of events, for the lessee, leading to a lease arrangement.

Why is it appropriate to compare the cost of lease financing with that of debt financing? Why does the comparison *not* depend on how the asset will actually be financed if it is not leased?

OPTIONS

option

A contract that gives the option holder the right to buy or sell an asset at some predetermined price within a specified period of time.

An **option** is a contract that gives its holder the right to buy (or sell) an asset at some predetermined price within a specified period of time. "Pure options" are instruments that are created by outsiders (generally investment banking firms) rather than by the firm itself; they are bought and sold primarily by investors (or speculators). However, financial managers should understand the nature of options, because this will help them structure warrant and convertible financings.

Option Types and Markets

striking (exercise) price

The price that must be paid for a share of common stock when it is bought by exercising an option.

call option

An option to buy, or "call," a share of stock at a certain price within a specified period.

There are many types of options and option markets.[11] To understand how options work, suppose you owned 100 shares of IBM stock which on June 20, 1990, sold for $118 per share. You could sell to someone else the right to buy your 100 shares at any time during the next 3 months at a price of, say, $125 per share. The $125 is called the **striking (exercise) price.** Such options exist, and they are traded on a number of stock exchanges, with the Chicago Board Options Exchange (CBOE) being the oldest and largest. This type of option is known as a **call option,** as the purchaser has a "call" on 100 shares of stock. The seller of a call option is known as an *option writer.* An investor who writes a call option against stock held in his or her portfolio is said to be selling *covered options;* options sold without the stock to back them up are called *naked options.*

On June 20, 1990, IBM's 3-month, $125 call options sold on the CBOE for $2.875 each. Thus, for ($2.875)(100) = $287.50, you could buy an option contract that would give you the right to purchase 100 shares of IBM at a price of $125 per share at any time during the next 3 months. If the stock stayed below $125 during that period, you would lose your $287.50, but if it rose to $135, your $287.50 investment would be worth ($135 − $125)(100) = $1,000. That translates into a very healthy rate of return on your $287.50 investment. Incidentally, if the stock price did go up, you would probably not actually exercise your options and buy the stock; rather, you would sell the options, which

---

[11]For more information on options, see any standard investments textbook.

would then each have a price of at least $10 versus the $2.875 you had paid, to another option buyer.

You can also buy an option which gives you the right to *sell* a stock at a specified price at some time in the future—this is called a **put option.** For example, suppose you expect IBM's stock price to decline from its current level sometime during the next 3 months. For $150 you could buy a 3-month put option giving you the right to sell 100 shares (which you would not necessarily own) at a price of $110 per share ($110 is the put option striking price). If you bought a 100-share put contract for $150 and IBM's stock price actually fell to $100, you would make ($110 − $100)(100) = $1,000, minus the $150 you paid for the put option, for a net profit (before taxes and commissions) of $850.

Options trading is one of the hottest financial activities in the United States today. The leverage involved makes it possible for speculators with just a few dollars to make a fortune almost overnight. Also, investors with sizable portfolios can sell options against their stocks and earn the value of the options (minus brokerage commissions) even if the stocks' prices remain constant. Still, those who have profited most from the development of options trading are security firms, which earn very healthy commissions on such trades.

The corporations on whose stocks options are written, such as IBM, have nothing to do with the options market. They neither raise money in that market nor have any direct transactions in it, and option holders neither receive dividends nor vote for corporate directors (unless they exercise their options to purchase the stock, which few actually do). There have been studies by the SEC and others as to whether options trading stabilizes or destabilizes the stock market, and whether it helps or hinders corporations seeking to raise new capital. The studies have not been conclusive, but options trading is here to stay, and many regard it as the most exciting game in town.

put option
An option to sell a share of stock at a certain price, within a specified period.

Formula Value versus Option Price

How is the actual price of an option determined in the market? To begin, we define an option's **formula value** as follows:

Formula value = Current price of the stock − Striking price.

For example, if a stock sells for $50 and its options have a striking price of $20, then the formula value of the option is $30. As we shall see, options generally sell at a price greater than their formula value.

Now consider Figure 18-1, which presents some data on Space Technology, Inc. (STI), a company which recently went public and whose stock has fluctuated widely during its short history. Column 1 in the lower section shows the trading range of the stock; Column 2 shows the striking price of the option; Column 3 shows the formula values for STI's options when the stock sells at different prices; Column 4 gives the actual market prices of the option; and Column 5 shows the premium, or excess of the actual option price over its formula value. These data are plotted in the graph.

formula value
The value of an option security, calculated as the stock price minus the striking, or exercise, price.

Figure 18-1 **Space Technology, Inc.: Option Price and Formula Value**

Options have both a formula value (value if exercised today) and an actual market value, which are compared graphically in this figure. As the option's formula value increases dollar for dollar with the stock price, the premium of the market price of the option over the formula value declines. At low formula values, premiums are high because the investor has large gain and small loss potentials. As stock prices (and formula values) rise, this leverage effect is diminished, causing the premium to decrease.

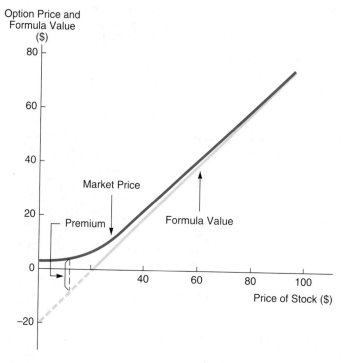

Price of Stock (1)	Striking Price (2)	Formula Value of Option (1) − (2) = (3)	Market Price of Option (4)	Premium (4) − (3) = (5)
$12.00	$20.00	($ 8.00)	$ 5.00	$13.00
20.00	20.00	0.00	9.00	9.00
21.00	20.00	1.00	9.75	8.75
22.00	20.00	2.00	10.50	8.50
35.00	20.00	15.00	21.00	6.00
42.00	20.00	22.00	26.00	4.00
50.00	20.00	30.00	32.00	2.00
73.00	20.00	53.00	54.00	1.00
98.00	20.00	78.00	78.50	0.50

In this example, for any stock price below $20, the formula value is negative; above $20, each $1 increase in the price of the stock brings with it a $1 increase in the option's formula value. Note, however, that the actual market price of the option lies above the formula value at all prices of the common stock, but that the premium declines as the price of the stock increases. For example, when the common stock sold for $20 and the option had a zero formula value, its actual price, and the premium, was $9. Then, as the price of the stock rose, the formula value matched the stock increase dollar for dollar, but the market price of the option climbed less rapidly, causing the premium to decline. Thus, the premium was $9 when the stock sold for $20 a share, but it had declined to $1 by the time the stock price reached $73 a share, and beyond that point the premium virtually disappeared.

Why does this pattern exist? Why should the option ever sell for more than its formula value, and why does the premium decline as the price of the stock increases? The answer lies in the speculative appeal of options; they provide an investor with a high degree of leverage when buying securities. To illustrate, suppose STI's stock was selling for $21, and its options sold for exactly their formula value, $1. Now suppose you were thinking of investing in the company. If you bought a share of stock and the price rose to $42, you would make a 100 percent capital gain. However, if you bought the option at its $1 formula value, your capital gain would be $21 on a $1 investment, a 2,100 percent gain! At the same time, your total loss potential with the option would be only $1, whereas the potential loss if you purchased the stock would be $21. The huge capital gains potential, combined with the loss limitation, is clearly worth something; the exact amount it is worth to investors is the amount of the premium.

Why does the premium decline as the price of the stock rises? Part of the answer is that both the leverage effect and the loss protection feature decline at high stock prices. For example, if you were thinking of buying the stock when its price was $73 a share, the formula value of the option would be $53. If the stock price doubled to $146, the formula value of STI's option would go from $53 to $126, an increase of 138 percent versus the 2,100 percent gain when the stock price doubled from $21. Notice also that the potential loss on the option is much greater when the option is selling at high prices. These two factors—the declining leverage effect and the increasing danger of losses—help explain why the premium diminishes as the price of the common stock rises.

In addition to the stock price and the striking price, the value of an option also depends on (1) the option's time to maturity and (2) the variability of the underlying stock's price, as explained below:

1. The longer an option has to run, the greater its value, and the larger its premium. If an option expires at 4 P.M. today, there is not much chance that the stock price will go way up. Therefore, the option will sell at close to its formula value, and its premium will be small. On the other hand, if it has a year to go, the stock price could rise sharply, pulling the option's value up with it.

2. An option on an extremely volatile stock will be worth more than one on a very stable stock. We know that an option on a stock whose price rarely moves will not offer much chance for a large gain. On the other hand, an option on a stock that is highly volatile could provide a large gain, so such an option will be valuable. Note also that because losses on options are limited, large declines in a stock's price do not have a corresponding bad effect on option holders. Therefore, stock price volatility can only enhance the value of an option.[12]

If everything else were held constant, then in a graph like Figure 18-1, the longer an option's life, the higher its market price line would be above the formula value line. Also, the more volatile the price of the underlying stock, the higher the market price line would be.

Self-Test

Differentiate between a call option and a put option.

Do the corporations on which options are written raise money in the options market? Explain.

How does one calculate the formula value of an option? How is the premium on the option calculated?

Why does the premium on the option decline as the price of the stock increases?

Explain how these factors affect the premium on an option: (1) the time remaining before the option expires, and (2) the volatility of the underlying stock.

---

[12]To illustrate this point, suppose that for $2 you could buy an option on a stock now selling for $20. The striking price is also $20. Now suppose the stock is highly volatile, and you think it has a 50 percent probability of selling for either $10 or $30 when the option expires in one month. What is the expected value of the option? If the stock sells for $30, the option will be worth $30 − $20 = $10. Since there is a 50-50 chance that the stock will be worth $10 or $30, the expected value of the option is $5:

$$\text{Expected value of option} = 0.5(0) + 0.5(\$10) = \$5.$$

To be exactly correct, we would have to discount the $5 back for one month.

Now suppose the stock was more volatile, with a 50-50 chance of being worth zero or $40. Here the option would be worth

$$\text{Expected value of option} = 0.5(0) + 0.5(\$20) = \$10.$$

This demonstrates that the higher the volatility of the stock, the greater the value of the option. The reason this result occurs is that the large loss on the stock ($20) had no more of an adverse effect on the option holder than the small loss ($10). Thus, option holders benefit greatly if a stock goes way up, but they do not lose too badly if it drops all the way to zero. These concepts have been used to develop formulas for pricing options, with the most widely used formula being the Black-Scholes model, which is discussed in most investments texts.

WARRANTS

A **warrant** is an option issued by a company which gives the holder the right to buy a stated number of shares of the company's stock at a specified price. Generally, warrants are distributed along with debt, and they are used to induce investors to buy a firm's long-term debt at a lower interest rate than would otherwise be required.

warrant
A long-term option to buy a stated number of shares of common stock at a specified price.

For example, when Pan-Pacific Airlines (PPA) wanted to sell $50 million of 20-year bonds in 1990, the company's investment bankers informed the financial vice president that straight bonds would be difficult to sell, and that an interest rate of 14 percent would be required. However, the bankers suggested as an alternative that investors would be willing to buy bonds with a coupon rate as low as 10⅜ percent if the company would offer 30 warrants with each $1,000 bond, where each warrant entitled the holder to buy one share of common stock at a price of $22 per share. The stock was selling for $20 per share at the time, and the warrants would expire in 1997 if they had not been exercised previously.

Why would investors be willing to buy Pan-Pacific's bonds at a yield of only 10⅜ percent in a 14 percent market just because warrants were offered as part of the package? The answer is that warrants are long-term *options,* and they have a value for the reasons set forth in the previous section. In the PPA case, the option value offset the low interest rate on the bonds and made the entire package of low-interest bonds plus warrants attractive to investors.

Initial Market Price of Bond with Warrants

If the PPA bonds had been issued as straight debt, they would have carried a 14 percent interest rate. With warrants attached, however, the bonds were sold to yield 10⅜ percent. Someone buying one of the bonds at its $1,000 initial offering price would thus be receiving a package consisting of a 10⅜ percent, 20-year bond plus 30 warrants. Since the going interest rate on bonds as risky as those of PPA was 14 percent, we can find the pure-debt value of the bonds, assuming an annual coupon, as follows:

$$\text{Pure-debt value of bonds} = \sum_{t=1}^{n} \frac{I}{(1 + k_s)^t} + \frac{M}{(1 + k_s)^n}$$

$$= \sum_{t=1}^{20} \frac{\$103.75}{(1.14)^t} + \frac{\$1,000}{(1.14)^{20}}$$

$$= \$103.75(\text{PVIFA}_{14\%,20}) + \$1,000(\text{PVIF}_{14\%,20})$$

$$= \$687.15 + \$72.80$$

$$= \$759.95 \approx \$760.$$

Thus, a person buying the bonds in the initial underwriting would pay $1,000 and receive in exchange a pure bond worth about $760 plus warrants presumably worth about $1,000 − $760 = $240:

$$\begin{array}{ccc} \text{Price paid for} \\ \text{bond with warrants} \end{array} = \begin{array}{c} \text{Straight-bond} \\ \text{value} \end{array} + \begin{array}{c} \text{Value of} \\ \text{warrants} \end{array}$$

$$\$1,000 \qquad = \qquad \$760 \quad + \quad \$240.$$

Because investors receive 30 warrants with each bond, each warrant has an implied value of $240/30 = $8.

The key issue in setting the terms of a bond-with-warrants offering is finding the value of the warrants. The pure-debt value of the bond can be estimated quite accurately. However, it is much more difficult to estimate the value of the warrants. If their value is overestimated relative to their true market value, it will be difficult to sell the issue at its par value. Conversely, if the warrants' value is underestimated, investors in the issue will receive a windfall profit, because they can sell the warrants in the market for more than they implicitly paid for them, and this windfall profit would come out of the pockets of PPA's current stockholders.

Use of Warrants in Financing

Warrants are generally used by small, rapidly growing firms as "sweeteners" to help sell either debt or preferred stock. Such firms are frequently regarded as being highly risky, and their bonds can be sold only if the firms are willing to pay extremely high rates of interest and to accept very restrictive indenture provisions. To avoid this, firms such as Pan-Pacific often offer warrants along with their bonds. However, some strong firms also have used warrants. In one of the largest financings of any type ever undertaken by a business firm, AT&T raised $1.75 billion by selling bonds with warrants. This marked the first use ever of warrants by a large, strong corporation.

Getting warrants along with bonds enables investors to share in a company's growth if that firm does in fact grow and prosper; therefore, investors are willing to accept a lower bond interest rate and less restrictive indenture provisions. A bond with warrants has some characteristics of debt and some of equity. It is a hybrid security that provides the financial manager with an opportunity to expand the firm's mix of securities and thus to appeal to a broader group of investors, hence lowering the firm's cost of capital.

detachable warrant
A warrant that can be detached from a bond and traded separately.

Virtually all warrants today are **detachable warrants,** meaning that after a bond with attached warrants has been sold, the warrants can be detached and traded separately from the bond. Further, when these warrants are exercised, the bonds themselves (with their low coupon rate) will remain outstanding. Thus, the warrants will bring in additional equity while leaving low interest rate debt on the books.

The warrants' exercise price is generally set at from 10 to 30 percent above the market price of the stock on the date the bond is issued. For example, if the stock sells for $10, the exercise price will probably be set in the $11 to $13 range. If the firm does grow and prosper, and if its stock price rises above the exercise price at which shares may be purchased, warrant holders will turn in their warrants, along with cash equal to the stated exercise price, in exchange for stock. Without some incentive, however, many warrants would never be exercised prior to maturity. Their value in the market would be greater than their formula, or exercise, value; hence holders would sell warrants rather than exercise them.

There are three conditions which encourage holders to exercise their warrants: (1) Warrant holders will *surely* exercise warrants and buy stock if the warrants are about to expire with the market price of the stock above the exercise price. This means that if a firm wants its warrants exercised soon in order to raise additional capital, it should set a relatively short expiration date. (2) Warrant holders will tend to exercise *voluntarily* and buy stock if the company raises the dividend on the common stock by a sufficient amount. Since no dividend is paid on the warrant, it provides no current income. However, if the common stock pays a high dividend, it provides an attractive dividend yield. Therefore, the higher the stock's dividend, the greater the opportunity cost of holding the warrant rather than exercising it. Thus, if a firm wants its warrants exercised, it can raise the common stock's dividend. (3) Warrants sometimes have **stepped-up exercise prices,** which prod owners into exercising them. For example, the Billingham Instrument Company has warrants outstanding with an exercise price of $25 until December 31, 1992, at which time the exercise price will rise to $30. If the price of the common stock is over $25 just before December 31, 1992, many warrant holders will exercise their options before the stepped-up price takes effect.

stepped-up exercise price
An exercise price that is specified to be higher if a warrant is exercised after a designated date.

Another useful feature of warrants is that they generally bring in funds only if such funds are needed. If the company grows, it will probably need new equity capital. At the same time, this growth will cause the price of the stock to rise and the warrants to be exercised, thereby allowing the firm to obtain additional cash. If the company is not successful and cannot profitably employ additional money, the price of its stock will probably not rise sufficiently to induce exercise of the options.

Self-Test

Explain (showing two formulas, but without doing any calculations) how you would determine the value of warrants attached to bonds.

Why can bonds with warrants be expected to bring in additional capital?

What three conditions would encourage holders to exercise their warrants?

Do warrants bring in additional funds to the firm when exercised? Explain.

CONVERTIBLES

Convertible securities are bonds or preferred stocks that can be exchanged for common stock at the option of the holder. Unlike the exercise of warrants, which provides the firm with additional funds, conversion does not bring in

convertible security
A security, usually a bond or preferred stock, that is exchangeable at the option of the holder into shares of common stock.

additional capital—debt (or preferred stock) is simply replaced by common equity. Of course, this reduction of debt or preferred stock will strengthen the firm's balance sheet and will make it easier to raise additional capital, but this is a separate action.

Conversion Ratio and Conversion Price

conversion ratio, CR
The number of shares that are received when converting a convertible bond or share of convertible preferred stock.

conversion price, P_c
The effective price paid for common stock obtained by converting a convertible security.

One of the most important provisions of a convertible security is the **conversion ratio, CR,** defined as the number of shares of stock the convertible holder receives upon conversion. Related to the conversion ratio is the **conversion price, P_c,** which is the effective price the company receives for its common stock when conversion occurs. The relationship between the conversion ratio and the conversion price can be illustrated by the Jackson Electronics Company's convertible debentures, issued at their $1,000 par value in 1990. At any time prior to maturity on July 1, 2010, a debenture holder can exchange a bond for 20 shares of common stock; therefore, CR = 20. The bond has a par value of $1,000, so the holder would be relinquishing that amount upon conversion. Dividing the $1,000 par value by the 20 shares received gives a conversion price of P_c = $50 a share:

$$\text{Conversion price} = P_c = \frac{\text{Par value of bond}}{\text{CR}}$$

$$= \frac{\$1,000}{20} = \$50.$$

Similarly, if we know the conversion price, we can find CR:

$$\text{CR} = \frac{\text{Par value of bond}}{P_c} = \frac{\$1,000}{\$50} = 20 \text{ shares.}$$

Once CR is set, the value of P_c is established, and vice versa.

Like a warrant's exercise price, the conversion price is characteristically set at from 10 to 30 percent above the prevailing market price of the common stock at the time the convertible issue is sold. Generally, the conversion price and ratio are fixed for the life of the bond, although sometimes a stepped-up conversion price is used. For example, Arden Industries' convertible debentures, issued in 1985, are convertible into 12.5 shares until 1993; into 11.76 shares from 1993 until 1998; and into 11.11 shares from 1998 until maturity in 2004. The conversion price thus started at $80, will rise to $85 in 1993, and then will go to $90 in 1998. Arden's convertibles, like most, became callable at the option of the company after a 3-year call protection period.

Another factor that may cause a change in the conversion price and ratio is a standard feature of almost all convertibles — the clause protecting the convertible against dilution from stock splits, stock dividends, and the sale of common stock at prices below the conversion price. The typical provision states

In this convertible subordinated debenture issued by Deere & Company, Deere agrees to make semiannual interest payments to bondholders. The *convertible* feature gives bondholders the option of converting it into shares of common stock, while the *subordinated* feature means that, in the event of bankruptcy, bondholders would not be paid until senior debt has been paid off.

Source: Courtesy of Deere & Company.

that if common stock is sold at a price below the conversion price, the conversion price must be lowered (and the conversion ratio raised) to the price at which the new stock was issued. Also, if the stock is split (or if a stock dividend is declared), the conversion price must be lowered by the percentage amount of the stock dividend or split.[13] For example, if Jackson Electronics were to have a two-for-one stock split, the conversion ratio would automatically be adjusted from 20 to 40, and the conversion price lowered from $50 to $25. If this protection were not contained in the contract, a company could completely thwart conversion by the use of stock splits. Warrants are similarly protected against such dilution.

The standard protection against dilution from selling new stock at prices below the conversion price can, however, get a company into trouble. For example, Arden Industries' stock was selling for only $64 in 1990 versus the conversion price of $80. Thus, Arden would have had to give its bondholders a tremendous break if it wanted to sell new common stock. Problems like this must be kept in mind by firms considering the use of convertibles or bonds with warrants.[14]

---

[13]Stock splits and stock dividends will be discussed in Chapter 21.

[14]For a more complete discussion of how the terms are set on a convertible offering, see M. Wayne Marr and G. Rodney Thompson, "The Pricing of New Convertible Bond Issues," *Financial Management,* Summer 1984, 31–37.

Convertible Bond Analysis

In 1990 Jackson Electronics Company was thinking of issuing 20-year convertible bonds at a price of $1,000 each. Each bond would pay a 10 percent annual coupon interest rate, or $100 per year, and each would be convertible into 20 shares of stock. Thus, the conversion price would be $1,000/20 = $50. If the bonds did not have the conversion feature, investors would require a yield of 12 percent, because k_d = 12%. Knowing k_d, the coupon rate, and the maturity, we can find the pure-bond value of the convertibles at the time of issue, B_0, using the bond valuation model developed back in Chapter 16. The bonds would initally sell at a price of $851, were it not for the conversion feature:

$$\text{Pure-bond value at} \atop \text{time of issue} = B_0 = \sum_{t=1}^{20} \frac{\$100}{(1.12)^t} + \frac{\$1,000}{(1.12)^{20}} = \$851.$$

Jackson's stock is expected to pay a dividend of $2.80 in the coming year; it currently sells at $35 per share, and this price is expected to grow at a constant rate of 8 percent per year. Thus, the stock price expected in each future Year t is $P_t = P_0(1 + g)^t = \$35(1.08)^t$. Further, since Jackson's convertibles would allow their holders to convert them into 20 shares of stock, the value a bondholder would expect to receive if he or she converted, defined as C_t, would be $C_t = \$35(1.08)^t(20)$.

The convertible bonds would not be callable for 10 years, after which they could be called at a price of $1,000. If after 10 years the conversion value exceeded the call price by at least 20 percent, management has indicated that it would call the bonds.

Figure 18-2 shows the expectations of both an average investor and the company. Here are the key features of the figure:

1. The horizontal line at M = $1,000 represents the par (and maturity) value. Also, $1,000 is the price at which the bond would initially be offered to the public.

2. The pure-bond value of the convertible would initially be $851, but it would rise to $1,000 over the 20-year life of the bond. The bond's pure-debt value is shown by the line B_t in Figure 18-2.

conversion value, C_t
The value of common stock obtained by converting a convertible security.

3. The bond's initial **conversion value, C_t**, or the value of the stock the investor would receive if the bond were converted at t = 0, is $700: Conversion value = $P_0(CR)$ = $35(20 shares) = $700. As indicated previously, the stock's price is expected to grow at an 8 percent rate, so $P_t = \$35(1.08)^t$. If the price of the stock rises over time, so will the conversion value of the bond. For example, in Year 3 the conversion value would be $C_3 = P_3(CR)$ = $35(1.08)^3(20) = $882. The expected conversion value over time is given by the line C_t in Figure 18-2.

4. The actual market price of the bond must always be equal to or greater than the *higher* of its pure-bond value or its conversion value. Therefore, the higher of the bond value or the conversion value curves in Figure 18-2

Figure 18-2 **Model of a Convertible Bond, Jackson Electronics Company**

This graph compares the pure-bond value, the "floor" value, the conversion value, and the market value lines for the Jackson Electronics Company's 20-year convertible bond. As this graph illustrates, the market value of a convertible will exceed the floor price because investors are willing to pay a premium over the pure-bond value for the possibility of earning large capital gains if the stock price shoots up. The gap between the market price of the convertible and the floor, or the premium investors are willing to pay, declines over time, and it is zero in Year 10.

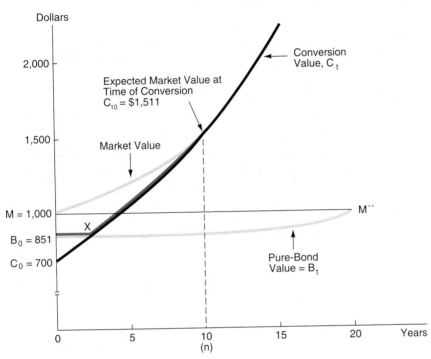

Year	Pure-Bond Value, B_t	Conversion Value, C_t	Maturity Value, M	Market Value
0	$ 851	$ 700	$1,000	$1,000
1	853	756	1,000	1,042
2	855	816	1,000	1,086
3	858	882	1,000	1,132
4	861	952	1,000	1,180
5	864	1,029	1,000	1,229
6	867	1,111	1,000	1,281
7	872	1,200	1,000	1,335
8	876	1,296	1,000	1,391
9	881	1,399	1,000	1,450
10	887	1,511	1,000	1,511
11	893	1,632	1,000	1,632
.	.	.	.	.
.	.	.	.	.
.	.	.	.	.
20	1,000	3,263	1,000	3,263

represents a "floor price" for the bond; this is indicated by the heavy line B_0XC_t.

5. The market value of a convertible generally will exceed the floor price for the same reasons that an option's or a warrant's price will exceed its formula value. Investors are willing to pay a premium over the pure-bond value (which establishes the initial floor) because of the possibility of earning large capital gains if the stock price shoots up. After Year 3, when the conversion value exceeds the pure-bond value and thus establishes the floor, the market price will still exceed the floor. This is because the convertible is safer than the stock, for even if profits decline and the stock price drops, the bond's value will never fall below its pure-bond value.[15]

6. The gap between the market price of the convertible and the floor, or the premium investors are willing to pay, declines over time and is zero in Year 10. This decline occurs for two reasons. First, the dividends received on the stock presumably are growing at 8 percent a year, whereas the interest on the bond is fixed at $100 annually. After 8 years, the dividends which would be received from 20 shares of stock, $2.80(1.08)^8(20) = \$103.65$, would exceed the $100 of interest paid on the bond; beyond that point the opportunity cost of holding the bond rather than converting it would become increasingly high. Second, after 10 years the bond would become callable at a price of $1,000. If Jackson called the issue, the bondholder could either convert the bond to common stock worth $C_{10} = \$1,511$ or receive $1,000 in cash. The holder would, of course, choose the $1,511 of stock. Note, however, that if the convertible were selling at a price greater than $C_{10} = \$1,511$ when the call occurred, the holder would suffer an immediate loss equal to the difference between the bond's price and $1,511. Therefore, because of the call provision, the market value of the bond cannot logically exceed the higher of the call price or the conversion price after the bond becomes callable.

7. If investors purchased Jackson's stock, they would expect a return of $\hat{k}_s = D_1/P_0 + g = \$2.80/\$35 + 8\% = 16\%$. If they bought a pure bond, they would earn 12 percent. The convertible has some guaranteed interest plus the expectation of some capital gains, so its risk and therefore its expected rate of return should lie between $k_d = 12\%$ and $\hat{k}_s = 16\%$. We can find the expected return on the convertible by solving for k_c in the following equation:

$$\text{Initial price} = \sum_{t=1}^{n} \frac{\text{Interest}}{(1 + k_c)^t} + \frac{\text{Conversion value}}{(1 + k_c)^n}$$

$$\$1,000 = \sum_{t=1}^{10} \frac{\$100}{(1 + k_c)^t} + \frac{\$1,511}{(1 + k_c)^{10}}.$$

---

[15]Note, however, that the bond value line B_0M'' would fall if interest rates rose in the economy or if the company's credit risk deteriorated, both of which would cause k_d to rise.

Using a financial calculator, we find $\hat{k}_c$ = 12.8%. Therefore, under the assumptions of this example, an investor who purchased the convertible at its initial $1,000 offering price should expect to earn a rate of return of 12.8 percent.

Use of Convertibles in Financing

Convertibles offer two important advantages from the issuer's standpoint. First, convertibles, like bonds with warrants, permit a company to sell debt with a lower interest rate and with less restrictive covenants than straight bonds. Second, convertibles provide a way of selling common stock at prices higher than those currently prevailing. Many companies actually want to sell common stock and not debt, but they believe that the price of their stock is temporarily depressed. The financial manager may know, for example, that earnings are depressed because of start-up costs associated with a new project, but he or she may expect earnings to rise sharply during the next year or so, pulling the price of the stock along. In this case, if the company sold stock now it would be giving up too many shares to raise a given amount of money. However, if it sets the conversion price at 20 to 30 percent above the present market price of the stock, then 20 to 30 percent fewer shares will have to be given up when the bonds are converted. Notice, however, that management is counting on the stock price's rising sufficiently above the conversion price to make the bonds attractive in conversion. If earnings do not rise and pull the stock price up, and hence if conversion does not occur, the company could be saddled with debt in the face of low earnings, which could be disastrous.

How can the company be sure that conversion will occur if the price of the stock rises above the conversion price? Typically, convertibles contain a call provision that enables the issuing firm to force bondholders to convert. Suppose the conversion price is $50, the conversion ratio is 20, the market price of the common stock has risen to $60, and the call price on the convertible bond is $1,050. If the company calls the bond, bondholders can either convert into common stock with a market value of $1,200 or allow the company to redeem the bond for $1,050. Naturally, bondholders prefer $1,200 to $1,050, so conversion will occur. The call provision therefore gives the company a means of forcing conversion, but only if the market price of the stock is greater than the conversion price.

Convertibles are useful, but they do have three important disadvantages. (1) The use of a convertible security may in effect give the issuer the opportunity to sell common stock at a higher price than it could otherwise sell stock. However, if the common stock increases greatly in price, the company would probably have been better off if it had used straight debt in spite of its higher interest rate and then later sold common stock to refund the debt. (2) If the company truly wants to raise equity capital, and if the price of the stock does not rise sufficiently after the bond is issued, then the firm will be stuck with debt. (3) Convertibles typically have a low coupon interest rate, an advantage that will be lost when conversion occurs. Warrrant financings, on the other hand, permit the company to continue to use the low-coupon debt for a longer period.

Self-Test

Does the exchange of convertible securities for common stock bring in additional funds to the firm? Explain.

How do you calculate (1) the conversion price, P_c, and (2) the conversion ratio, CR?

How is a convertible bond's initial conversion value, C_t, calculated? How does this value change over time?

Why does the premium (the excess of the market value of a convertible over either the conversion value or the straight bond value) decline over time and eventually go to zero?

What are the key advantages and disadvantages of convertibles?

REPORTING EARNINGS WHEN WARRANTS OR CONVERTIBLES ARE OUTSTANDING

If warrants or convertibles are outstanding, a firm can theoretically report earnings per share in one of three ways:

1. Simple EPS. The earnings available to common stockholders are divided by the average number of shares actually outstanding during the period.

2. Primary EPS. The earnings available are divided by the average number of shares that would have been outstanding if warrants and convertibles likely to be converted in the near future had actually been exercised or converted.

3. Fully diluted EPS. This is similar to primary EPS except that *all* warrants and convertibles are assumed to be exercised or converted, regardless of the likelihood of either occurring.

Simple EPS is virtually never reported by firms which have warrants or convertibles likely to be exercised or converted; the SEC prohibits use of this figure, and it requires that primary and fully diluted earnings be shown on the financial statements.

Self-Test

Differentiate among simple EPS, primary EPS, and fully diluted EPS.

SMALL BUSINESS

Lease Financing for Small Businesses

In this chapter we saw that, under certain conditions, leasing an asset can be less costly than borrowing to purchase the asset. For the small firm, leasing often offers three additional advantages: (1) conserves cash, (2) makes better use of managers' time, and (3) provides financing quickly.

Conserving Cash

Small firms often have limited cash resources. Because many leasing companies do not require the lessee to make even a small down payment, and because leases are often for longer terms and thus require lower payments than bank loans, leasing can help the small firm conserve its cash. Leasing companies also may be willing to work with a company to design a flexible leasing package that will help the lessee preserve its cash during critical times. For example, when Surgicare of Central Jersey opened its first surgical center, the firm did not have sufficient cash to pay for the necessary equipment. Surgicare's options were to borrow at a high interest rate, to sell stock to the public (which is difficult for a start-up firm), or to lease the equipment. Surgicare's financial vice president, John Rutzel, decided to lease the needed equipment from Copelco Financial Services, a leasing company which specializes in health care equipment. Copelco allowed Surgicare to make very low payments for the first 6 months, slightly higher payments during the second 6 months, and level payments thereafter. These unique lease terms "got Surgicare through the start-up phase, when cash flow was the critical consideration."

Freeing Managers for Other Tasks

Most small business owners find that they never have enough time to get everything done — they are simply spread too thin, being in charge of sales, operations, budgeting, and everything else. If an asset is owned, the firm must maintain it in good working condition and also keep records on its use for tax depreciation purposes. However, leasing assets frees the business's owner of these duties. First, paperwork is reduced, because maintenance records, depreciation schedules, and other records do not have to be maintained on leased assets. Second, less time may have to be spent "shopping around" for the right equipment, because leasing companies, which generally specialize in a particular industry, can often provide the manager with the information necessary to select the best assets for the job at hand. Third, since the assets can be traded in if they become obsolete, the initial choice of equipment is less critical. Fourth, the burden of servicing and repairing the equipment can be passed on to the lessor.

Obtaining Assets More Quickly and at a Lower Cost

Many new, small firms find that banks are unwilling to lend them money at a reasonable cost. Because leasing companies retain the ownership of the equipment, they may be more willing to take chances with start-up firms. When Ed Lavin started Offset Printing Company, his bank would not lend him the money to purchase the necessary printing presses — the bank wanted to lend only to firms with proven track records. Lavin arranged to lease the needed presses from Eaton Financial Corporation, which also advised him on the best type of equipment to meet his needs. Recently, Lavin's firm achieved sales of $250,000, and, as his company grew, he expanded by leasing additional equipment. Thus, (1) leasing allowed Lavin to go into business when his bank was unwilling to help, (2) his leasing company provided him with help in selecting equipment, and (3) the leasing company also provided additional capital to meet his expansion needs.

SUMMARY

This chapter discussed hybrid forms of long-term financing: leasing and option securities. The key concepts covered are listed below:

- **Leasing** is a means of obtaining the use of an asset without purchasing that asset. The three most important forms of leasing are: (1) **sale-and-leaseback** arrangements, under which a firm sells an asset to another party and leases the asset back for a specified period under specific terms, (2) **operating leases,** under which the lessor both maintains and finances the asset, and (3) **financial leases,** under which the asset is fully amortized over the life of the lease, the lessor does not provide maintenance, and the lease is not cancelable.

- The **decision whether to lease or to buy an asset** is made by comparing the financing costs of the two alternatives and choosing the financing method with the lower present value cost. All cash flows should be discounted at the **after-tax cost of debt,** because lease analysis cash flows are relatively certain and are on an after-tax basis.

- An **option** is a contract that gives its holder the right to buy (or sell) an asset at some predetermined price within a specified period of time. Options features are used by firms to "sweeten" debt offerings.

- A **warrant** is an option issued along with a bond which gives the holder the right to purchase a stated number of shares of stock at a specified price within a specified period. A warrant will be exercised if it is about to expire and the stock price is above the exercise price.

- A **convertible security** is a bond or preferred stock which can be exchanged for common stock at the option of the holder. When a security is converted, debt or preferred stock is replaced with common stock, and no money changes hands.

- The **conversion of bonds or preferred stock** by their holders **does not provide additional funds** to the company, but it does lower the firm's fixed obligations. The conversion of bonds also lowers the debt ratio. The **exercise of warrants does provide additional funds,** which strengthens the firm's equity position, but it still leaves the debt or preferred stock on the balance sheet. Low interest rate debt remains outstanding when warrants are exercised, but the firm loses this advantage when convertibles are converted.

- For the small firm, leasing offers three advantages: (1) **cash is conserved,** (2) **managers' time is freed** for other tasks, and (3) **financing can often be obtained** more **quickly** and at a **lower cost.**

EQUATIONS

The after-tax cost of the lease payment is calculated as follows:

$$\text{After-tax cost} = \text{Lease payment} - \text{Tax savings}$$

$$= \text{Lease payment} - (\text{Tax rate})(\text{Lease payment})$$

$$= \text{Lease payment}(1 - \text{Tax rate}).$$

An option's formula value is calculated as the stock price minus the striking, or exercise, price:

$$\text{Formula value} = \text{Current price of the stock} - \text{Striking price}.$$

The price paid for a bond issued with warrants is equal to its straight-bond value plus the value of the warrants:

$$\begin{array}{c}\text{Price paid for} \\ \text{bond with warrants}\end{array} = \begin{array}{c}\text{Straight-bond} \\ \text{value}\end{array} + \begin{array}{c}\text{Value of} \\ \text{warrants}\end{array}.$$

The effective price paid for common stock obtained by converting a convertible security is calculated by dividing the par value of the bond by the number of shares of stock the holder receives upon conversion:

$$\text{Conversion price} = P_c = \frac{\text{Par value of bond}}{\text{CR}}.$$

From the above equation, if we know the conversion price, we can find the conversion ratio, the number of shares of stock the convertible holder receives upon conversion:

$$\text{CR} = \frac{\text{Par value of bond}}{P_c}.$$

To find the expected rate of return on a convertible, $\hat{k}_c$, we solve for k_c in the following formula:

$$\text{Initial price} = \sum_{t=1}^{n} \frac{\text{Interest}}{(1 + k_c)^t} + \frac{\text{Conversion value}}{(1 + k_c)^n}.$$

RESOLUTION TO DECISION IN FINANCE

Sandy's Gamble

By tradition, airplane manufacturers have always insisted on selling their products either directly to the airlines or to leasing companies which then lease to the carriers for 15 years or longer. But Sandy McDonnell decided to break that tradition with short-term, fly-before-buy leasing deals that he hoped would convert to sales when the economy improved.

McDonnell's first customer, in October 1982, was American Airlines, which took a 5-year lease on 20 DC-9-80s, with the option of a 13-year extension. The plan called for American to make lease payments of about $180,000 per plane per month—roughly what the loan payment would have been on the original price. To sweeten the deal, the airline would run virtually no risk: it would have no cash tied up in down payments, and, on 30 days' notice, it could return the planes for a penalty of less than $2 million per plane. McDonnell worked out similar deals with TWA and Alitalia shortly thereafter.

Leasing was a daring route for Sandy McDonnell to take. He had to raise around $450 million to fund production and finance ownership on the American and TWA deals. McDonnell Douglas itself put up about 75 percent of the money, while its suppliers, including engine maker Pratt & Whitney, put up the rest.

Sources: Adapted from "Sandy's Gamble," *Forbes*, December 20, 1982, 79–85; and "A Leasing Plan to Keep Jet Production Rolling," *Business Week*, October 11, 1982, 34–35.

The net effect of the leasing deals was expected to depress McDonnell Douglas's earnings for at least 3 years, but from Sandy McDonnell's point of view, that was a necessary price to pay for all the benefits the company would receive.

The most important benefit was the fact that the leasing deals filled the production lines and averted the plant shutdown that everyone had dreaded. In addition, they attracted new interest in the company's products, squelched rumors that McDonnell Douglas might abandon the commercial airplane market, and instilled confidence that the DC-9-80 would not become obsolete for at least 5 years. The leases also created goodwill because they enabled airlines to acquire the efficient planes they needed but couldn't afford to buy or lease conventionally.

Of course, the biggest risk to McDonnell Douglas was that the planes might be returned. But the company was sure that once the airlines flew the planes, they would like them and keep them. Even if American had returned its planes after 5 years, it would have paid between 25 percent and 40 percent of their cost, and McDonnell Douglas would have depreciated them to less than market value. "We're strong enough financially to take them all back," said a company official.

Although the leases penalized McDonnell Douglas's short-term profits, they helped ensure the viability of the company that Sandy McDonnell's uncle founded more than 45 years ago. We have to give him and his board credit for courage, innovativeness, and farsightedness.

QUESTIONS

18-1   Distinguish between operating leases and financial leases. Would a firm be more likely to finance a fleet of trucks or a manufacturing plant with an operating lease?

18-2   One alleged advantage of leasing voiced in the past was that it kept liabilities off the balance sheet, thus making it possible for a firm to obtain more leverage than it otherwise could have. This raised the question of whether or not both the lease obligation and the asset involved should be capitalized and shown on the balance sheet. Discuss the pros and cons of capitalizing leases and related assets.

18-3 Suppose there were no IRS restrictions on what constitutes a valid lease. Explain in a manner that a legislator might understand why some restrictions should be imposed.

18-4 Suppose Congress changed the tax laws in a way that (1) permitted equipment to be depreciated over a shorter period, (2) lowered corporate tax rates, and (3) reinstated the investment tax credit. Discuss how each of these changes would affect the relative use of leasing versus conventional debt in the U.S. economy.

18-5 Why do options typically sell at prices higher than their formula values?

18-6 What effect does the expected growth rate of a firm's stock price (subsequent to issue) have on its ability to raise additional funds through (a) convertibles and (b) warrants?

18-7 **a.** How would a firm's decision to pay out a higher percentage of its earnings as dividends affect each of the following?
   (1) The value of its long-term warrants.
   (2) The likelihood that its convertible bonds will be converted.
   (3) The likelihood that its warrants will be exercised.
b. If you owned the warrants or convertibles of a company, would you be pleased or displeased if it raised its payout rate from 20 percent to 80 percent? Why?

18-8 Evaluate the following statement: "Issuing convertible securities represents a means by which a firm can sell common stock at a price above the existing market price."

18-9 Suppose a company simultaneously issues $50 million of convertible bonds with a coupon rate of 9 percent and $50 million of pure bonds with a coupon rate of 12 percent. Both bonds have the same maturity. Does the fact that the convertible issue has the lower coupon rate suggest that it is less risky than the pure bond? Would you regard its cost of capital as being lower on the convertible than on the pure bond? Explain. (*Hint:* Although it might appear at first glance that the convertible's cost of capital is lower, this is not necessarily the case, because the interest rate on the convertible understates its cost. Think about this.)

SELF-TEST PROBLEM

ST-1 **Lease analysis.** The Olsen Company has decided to acquire a new truck. One alternative is to lease the truck on a 4-year contract for a lease payment of $10,000 per year, with payments to be made at the *beginning* of each year. The lease would include maintenance. Alternatively, Olsen could purchase the truck outright for $40,000, financing with a bank loan for the net purchase price, amortized over a 4-year period at an interest rate of 10 percent per year, payments to be made at the *end* of each year. Under the borrow-to-purchase arrangement, Olsen would have to maintain the truck at a cost of $1,000 per year, payable at year-end. The truck falls into the MACRS 3-year class. It has a salvage value of $10,000, which is the expected market value after 4 years, at which time Olsen plans to replace the truck irrespective of whether it leases or buys. Olsen has a tax rate of 40 percent.
a. What is Olsen's PV cost of leasing?
b. What is Olsen's PV cost of owning? Should the truck be leased or purchased?

c. The appropriate discount rate for use in Olsen's analysis is the firm's after-tax cost of debt. Why?

d. The salvage value is the least certain cash flow in the analysis. How might Olsen incorporate the higher riskiness of this cash flow into the analysis?

PROBLEMS

18-1   Establishing lease payments. Sav-U-Lease specializes in leasing trucks and equipment to construction firms in the metropolitan Atlanta area. Nelson-Long Construction wishes to lease $3 million in equipment from Sav-U-Lease for a 5-year period. What is the annual lease payment Nelson-Long would pay if the lease is based on a 14 percent lease rate? The lease payments are to be made at the end of each year. (Note that the 14 percent rate is simply the rate used to establish the lease payments; it is not Sav-U-Lease's rate of return.)

18-2   Establishing lease payments. Refer to Problem 18-1. What would the annual lease payments be if Sav-U-Lease required lease payments to be made at the beginning of the year rather than at the end of the year? Note that 5 payments will be made, with the first due immediately.

18-3   Balance sheet effects of leasing. Two textile companies, Adams Manufacturing and Porter Mills, began operations with identical balance sheets. A year later, both required additional manufacturing capacity at a cost of $150,000. Adams obtained a 5-year, $150,000 loan at a 9 percent interest rate from its bank. Porter, on the other hand, decided to lease the required $150,000 capacity from American Leasing for 5 years; a 9 percent return was built into the lease. The balance sheet for each company, before the asset increases, is as follows:

		Debt	$150,000
		Equity	150,000
Total assets	$300,000	Total liabilities and equity	$300,000

a. Show the balance sheet of each firm after the asset increase, and calculate each firm's new debt ratio. (*Hint:* Assume off-balance-sheet financing for the lease.)

b. Show how Porter's balance sheet would have looked immediately after the financing if it had capitalized the lease.

c. Would the rate of return (1) on assets and (2) on equity be affected by the choice of financing? How?

18-4   Lease versus buy. Condor Air Service, a small commuter airline, is negotiating a lease of a small airplane with Capital Leasing. The airplane can be purchased by Capital from Airway Engineering for $4 million. Capital's lease terms call for 4 annual end-of-year payments of $1,125,000 each. As an alternative to leasing, the firm can borrow from a regional bank and buy the airplane. The $4 million would be borrowed on an amortized term loan at a 10 percent interest rate for 4 years. Airplanes of this type fall into the MACRS 3-year class and have an expected after-tax residual value of $400,000. Maintenance costs would be included in the lease. If the airplane is purchased, a maintenance contract can be obtained that calls for $50,000 payments made at the end of each year. Condor will sell the fully depreciated airplane at the end of 4 years, or if the airplane is leased, it will not renew the lease. Condor's marginal tax rate is 30 percent. Should Condor lease the airplane from Capital Leasing? Assume the MACRS percentages in effect during the lease period are: Year 1, 33%; Year 2, 45%; Year 3, 15%; and Year 4, 7%. (*Hint:* Include the after-tax residual value as an inflow in Year 4 in the cost of owning analysis.)

18-5 **Lease versus buy.** Kanawha Coal Company must install $2 million of new machinery in its West Virginia mine. It can obtain a bank loan for 100 percent of the required amount. Alternatively, a West Virginia investment banking firm which represents a group of investors believes that it can arrange for a lease financing plan. Assume that the following facts apply:

(1) The equipment falls in the MACRS 3-year class. MACRS allowances are 33%, 45%, 15%, and 7%.

(2) Estimated maintenance expenses are $100,000 per year.

(3) Kanawha's tax rate is 40 percent.

(4) If the money is borrowed, the bank loan will be at a rate of 15 percent, amortized in 3 equal installments to be paid at the end of each year.

(5) The tentative lease terms call for payments of $640,000 per year for 3 years.

(6) Under the proposed lease terms, the lessee must pay for insurance, property taxes, and maintenance.

(7) Kanawha must use the equipment if it is to continue in business, so it will almost certainly want to acquire the property at the end of the lease. If it does, then under the lease terms it can purchase the machinery at its fair market value at that time. The best estimate of this market value is the $433,000 salvage value, but it could be much higher or lower under certain circumstances.

To assist management in making the proper lease-versus-buy decision, you are asked to answer the following questions:

a. Assuming that the lease can be arranged, should Kanawha lease or should it borrow and buy the equipment? Explain. (*Hint:* PV cost of owning = $1,362,137 versus $1,306,383 for leasing; use these as check figures.)

b. Consider the $433,000 estimated salvage value. Is it appropriate to discount it at the same rate as the other cash flows? What about the other cash flows — are they all equally risky? (*Hint:* Riskier cash flows are normally discounted at higher rates, but when the cash flows are *costs* rather than *inflows,* the normal procedure must be reversed.)

(Do Parts c and d only if you are using the computerized problem diskette.)

c. Determine the lease payment at which Kanawha Coal would be indifferent to buying or leasing — that is, the lease payment that equates the NPV of leasing to that of buying. (*Hint:* Use trial-and-error.)

d. Using the $640,000 lease payment, what would be the effect if Kanawha's tax rate fell to 20 percent? What would be the effect if the tax rate fell to zero percent? What do those results suggest?

18-6 **Warrants.** Brooks Industries, Inc., has warrants outstanding that permit its holders to purchase one share of stock per warrant at a price of $14.

a. Calculate the formula value of Brooks's warrants if the common stock sells at each of the following prices: $12, $14, $17, and $47.

b. At what approximate price do you think the warrants would actually sell under each condition indicated in Part a? What premium is implied in your price? Your answer will be a guess, but your prices and premiums should bear reasonable relationships to each other.

c. How would each of the following factors affect your estimates of the warrants' prices and premiums in Part b?

(1) The life of the warrant is lengthened.

(2) The expected variability (as measured by σ_p) in the stock's price decreases.

(3) The expected growth rate in the stock's EPS increases.

(4) The company announces the following change in dividend policy: Whereas it formerly paid no dividends, henceforth it will pay out *all* earnings as dividends.

d. Assume Brooks's stock now sells for $12 per share. The company wants to sell some 20-year, annual interest, $1,000 par value bonds. Each bond will have 75 warrants, each exercisable into one share of stock at an exercise price of $14. Brooks's pure bonds yield 10 percent. Regardless of your answer to Part b, assume that the warrants will have a market value of $1.00 when the stock sells at $12. What coupon interest rate and dollar coupon must the company set on the bonds with warrants if they are to clear the market? Round to the nearest dollar or percentage point.

18-7 **Convertibles.** The Microchip Computer Company was planning to finance an expansion in the summer of 1991. The principal executives of the company agreed that an industrial company like theirs should finance growth by means of common stock rather than by debt. However, they believed that the price of the company's common stock did not reflect its true worth, so they decided to sell a convertible security. They considered a convertible debenture but feared the burden of fixed interest charges if the common stock did not rise enough to make conversion attractive. They decided on an issue of convertible preferred stock, which would pay a dividend of $2.10 per share.

The common stock was selling for $42 a share at the time. Management projected earnings for 1991 at $3.00 a share and an expected annual future growth rate of 10 percent in 1992 and beyond. It was agreed by the investment bankers and management that the common stock would continue to sell at 14 times earnings, the current price/earnings ratio.

a. What conversion price should be set by the issuer? The conversion rate will be 1.0; that is, each share of convertible preferred can be converted into one share of common. Therefore, the convertible's par value (as well as the issue price) will be equal to the conversion price, which in turn will be determined as a percentage over the current market price of the common. Your answer will be a guess, but make it a reasonable one.

b. Should the preferred stock include a call provision? Why or why not?

18-8 **Financing alternatives.** The Boca Grande Company has grown rapidly during the past 5 years. Recently its commercial bank urged the company to consider increasing its permanent financing. Its bank loan under a line of credit has risen to $150,000, carrying a 10 percent interest rate, and Boca Grande has been 30 to 60 days late in paying trade creditors.

Discussions with an investment banker have resulted in the decision to raise $250,000 at this time. Investment bankers have assured Boca Grande that the following alternatives are feasible (flotation costs will be ignored):

- *Alternative 1:* Sell common stock at $10 per share.

- *Alternative 2:* Sell convertible bonds at a 10 percent coupon, convertible into 80 shares of common stock for each $1,000 bond (that is, the conversion price is $12.50 per share).

- *Alternative 3:* Sell debentures with a 10 percent coupon; each $1,000 bond will have 80 warrants to buy a share of common stock at $12.50.

Brenda Sapp, the president, owns 80 percent of Boca Grande's common stock and wishes to maintain control of the company; 50,000 shares are outstanding. The following are summaries of Boca Grande's latest financial statements:

Balance Sheet

		Current liabilities	$200,000
		Common stock, $1 par	50,000
		Retained earnings	25,000
Total assets	$275,000	Total liabilities and equity	$275,000

Income Statement

Sales	$550,000
All costs except interest	495,000
EBIT	$ 55,000
Interest	15,000
EBT	$ 40,000
Taxes at 40%	16,000
Net income	$ 24,000

Shares outstanding	50,000
Earnings per share	$0.48
Price/earnings ratio	18×
Market price of stock	$8.64

a. Show the new balance sheet under each alternative. For Alternatives 2 and 3, show the balance sheet after conversion of the debentures or exercise of the warrants. Assume that $150,000 of the funds raised will be used to pay off the bank loan and the rest to increase total assets.

b. Show Sapp's control position under each alternative, assuming that she does not purchase additional shares.

c. What is the effect on earnings per share of each alternative if it is assumed that profits before interest and taxes will be 20 percent of total assets?

d. What will be the debt ratio under each alternative?

e. Which of the three alternatives would you recommend to Sapp and why?

18-9 **Convertibles.** Flint Computers, Inc., needs to raise $35 million to begin producing a new microcomputer. Flint's straight, nonconvertible debentures currently yield 12 percent. Its stock sells for $38 per share; the last dividend was $2.46; and the expected growth rate is a constant 8 percent. Investment bankers have tentatively proposed that Flint raise the $35 million by issuing convertible debentures. These convertibles would have a $1,000 par value, carry a coupon rate of 10 percent, have a 20-year maturity, and be convertible into 20 shares of stock. The bonds would be noncallable for 5 years, after which they would be callable at a price of $1,075; this call price would decline by $5 per year in Year 6 and each year thereafter. Management has called convertibles in the past (and presumably will call them again in the future), once they were eligible for call, as soon as their conversion value was about 20 percent above their par value (not their call price).

a. Draw an accurate graph similar to Figure 18-2 representing the expectations set forth in the problem.

b. Suppose the previously outlined projects work out on schedule for 2 years, but then Flint begins to experience extremely strong competition from Japanese firms. As a result, Flint's expected growth rate drops from 8 percent to zero. Assume that the dividend at the time of the drop is $2.87. The company's credit strength is not impaired, and its value of k_s is also unchanged. What would happen (1) to the stock price and (2) to the convertible bond's price? Be as precise as you can.

SOLUTION TO SELF-TEST PROBLEM

ST-1   **a.** *Cost of leasing:*

	Beginning of Year			
	0	**1**	**2**	**3**
Lease payment (AT)[a]	$ 6,000	$6,000	$6,000	$6,000
PVIFs (6%)[b]	1.000	0.9434	0.8900	0.8396
PV of leasing	$ 6,000	$5,660	$5,340	$5,038
Total PV cost of leasing =	$22,038			

[a]After-tax payment = $10,000(1 − t) = $10,000(0.60) = $6,000.
[b]This is the after-tax cost of debt: 10%(1 − t) = 10%(0.60) = 6.0%.

b. *Cost of owning:*

$$\text{Purchase price} = \$40,000.$$

$$\text{Loan payment} = \$40,000/(\text{PVIFA}_{10\%,4})$$

$$= \$40,000/(3.1699)$$

$$= \$12,619.$$

$$\text{Depreciable basis} = \$40,000.$$

Here are the cash flows under the borrow-and-buy alternative:

	End of Year			
	1	**2**	**3**	**4**
1. Amortization schedule				
(a) Loan payment	$12,619	$12,619	$12,619	$12,619
(b) Interest	4,000	3,138	2,190	1,147
(c) Principal payment	8,619	9,481	10,429	11,472
(d) Remaining balance	31,381	21,900	11,472	0
2. Depreciation schedule				
(e) Depreciable basis	$40,000	$40,000	$40,000	$40,000
(f) MACRS percentage	0.33	0.45	0.15	0.07
(g) Depreciation	13,200	18,000	6,000	2,800
3. Cash outflows				
(h) Loan payment	$12,619	$12,619	$12,619	$12,619
(i) Interest tax savings	(1,600)[a]	(1,255)	(876)	(459)
(j) Depreciation tax savings	(5,280)[b]	(7,200)	(2,400)	(1,120)
(k) Maintenance (AT)	600	600	600	600
(l) Salvage value (AT)				(6,000)
(m) Total cash outflows	$ 6,339	$ 4,764	$ 9,943	$ 5,640
PVIFs	0.9434	0.8900	0.8396	0.7921
PV of owning	$ 5,980	$ 4,240	$ 8,348	$ 4,467
Total PV cost of owning =	$23,035			

[a]Interest(t) = $4,000(0.40) = $1,600.
[b]Deprecitation(t) = $13,200(0.40) = $5,280.

Because the present value of the cost of leasing is less than that of owning, the truck should be leased: $23,035 − $22,038 = $997, net advantage to leasing.

c. The discount rate is based on the cost of debt because most cash flows are fixed by contract and, consequently, are relatively certain. Thus, the lease cash flows have about the same risk as the firm's debt. Also, leasing is considered to be a substitute for debt. We use an after-tax cost rate because the cash flows are stated net of taxes.

d. Olsen could increase the discount rate on the salvage value cash flow. This would increase the PV cost of owning and make leasing even more advantageous.

PART VI

FACTORS THAT INFLUENCE HOW THE FIRM IS FINANCED

In the previous section, we examined the characteristics and valuation of long-term debt, preferred stock, and common stock. We also looked at hybrid forms of financing, such as leasing, warrants, and convertibles. The values of stocks and bonds are determined, in part, by the rate of return required by investors. In Chapter 19, we see how the investors' required returns are combined to determine the firm's weighted average cost of capital. In Chapter 20 we explain how the concepts of business and financial risk are used to determine the optimal capital structure, defined as that mix of debt and equity which maximizes the value of the firm. Finally, in Chapter 21 we explain how the interaction of financing and investment decisions determines the firm's dividend policy.

Chapter 19

The Cost of Capital

 DECISION IN FINANCE

Cost-of-Capital Punishment

Citicorp, the U.S. bank with the largest overseas branch network, is starting to look like a lonely island in an increasingly empty sea. Most U.S. banks are dropping out of the foreign marketplace, both in Europe and in Asia, where they can no longer compete because of their higher cost of capital.

The price they must pay shareholders and creditors to raise money is about twice that paid by their competitors in Japan and West Germany. A vice president with Bankers Trust says, "It is a little discouraging looking at this as an American. The serious competitors in global finance are shrinking to a very small number. Only three or four American banks are active and effective enough to be included." The share of U.S. banks in the international market dropped from 27 percent to 15 percent between 1983 and 1988, while Japanese banks almost doubled their share to 40 percent.

One reason U.S. banks must pay more to raise capital is their size. None are in the world's top 20 in terms of market value, and

investors expect the largest Japanese banks to keep growing faster than the largest U.S. banks, so they are willing to accept a lower current return on their money. Fuji, for instance, is valued at more than $50 billion, compared to Citicorp's approximately $8 billion, while Sumitomo and Dai-Ichi Kangyo are valued at well over $40 billion. The Japanese giants' price-to-earnings ratios (ranging from about 30 to 44 times) also greatly exceed Citicorp's 20 times.

Major U.S. institutions, such as Manufacturers Hanover, BankAmerica, Chemical Bank, First Interstate, and First Chicago have all closed offices around the world — the latter shutting down in seven countries, including Singapore, the financial capital of Southeast Asia. Also, three of the four U.S. giants which still expect to maintain high visibility overseas are changing their tactics. For example, Chase Manhattan is focusing on wealthy private customers around the world, financing leveraged buyouts in Europe, and generally changing its strategy. "We'll advise clients on investments and cross-border acquisitions," says vice-chairman Richard J. Boyle. Bankers Trust and J. P. Morgan are merging their traditional commercial banking with investment

See end of chapter for resolution.

banking, advising on mergers and acquisitions, and trading securities and foreign exchange. Even with all its closings around the world, First Chicago Corporation has added more people to its London and Tokyo offices. The new staff, however, has little to do with traditional loans. "We're doing things with relatively modest capital requirements," says a senior vice president. The bank has cut its syndicated loans to governments in half—from $8 billion in 1983 to $4 billion in 1990.

Citicorp alone plans to maintain a full range of banking services around the world. Citicorp's executive vice president, Thomas Jones, says,

"In no way are we retreating at all. We're committed to growing overseas. Over the past four years we have significantly expanded our branches in Italy, Japan, Korea, and Spain." Some observers doubt that they can succeed. One international banker said, "I really don't see how any bank can make money in Europe."

As you read this chapter, consider the steps Citicorp might take to maintain a profitable international presence. Aside from its corporate strategy, is there a broader solution to the high-cost-of-capital problem faced by U.S. banks? And what does the banks' problem suggest about the U.S. economy as a whole?

The cost of capital is critically important in finance for several reasons. First, capital budgeting decisions have a major impact on a firm, and correct capital budgeting decisions require an estimate of the cost of capital. Second, many other types of decisions, including those related to leasing, to bond refunding, and to working capital policy, require estimates of the cost of capital. Finally, maximizing the value of a firm requires that the costs of all inputs, including capital, be minimized, and to minimize the cost of capital managers must be able to measure it.[1]

We begin this chapter with an explanation of the logic of the weighted average cost of capital. Next, we consider the costs of the major types of capital. Third, the costs of the individual components of the capital structure are brought together to form a weighted average cost of capital. Finally, the relationship between capital budgeting and the cost of capital is discussed.

THE LOGIC OF THE WEIGHTED AVERAGE COST OF CAPITAL

When we discussed capital budgeting, we assumed that equity was the only source of financing used by the firm. We made this assumption so we could concentrate on the investment decision without being concerned about how the project was to be financed. Of course, few firms are financed entirely with

---

[1]The cost of capital is also vitally important in regulated industries, including electric, gas, telephone, and water companies. In essence, regulatory commissions first seek to measure a utility's cost of capital, and then set prices so that the company will earn just this rate of return. If the cost of capital estimate is too low, the company will not be able to attract sufficient capital to meet long-term demands for service, and the public will suffer. If the estimate of capital costs is too high, customers will pay too much for service.

equity — most firms finance a substantial portion of their new assets with debt, and some use preferred stock as well. For these firms, the cost of capital must reflect the average cost of the various sources of long-term funds used, not just the cost of equity.

Assume that Precision Associates (PA), a subcontractor of engineering systems to many of the nation's largest aerospace firms, has a cost of debt of 11 percent, a 13 percent cost of preferred stock, and a cost of equity of 16 percent. Suppose the firm decides to finance all of next year's projects with debt. The argument is sometimes made that the cost of capital for a project financed exclusively with debt is equal to the cost of debt. However, this position is *incorrect*. To finance a particular set of projects exclusively with debt implies that the firm will be using up some of its potential for obtaining new low-cost debt in the future. As the firm continues to expand in subsequent years, PA will at some point find it necessary to use additional equity financing to prevent the debt ratio from becoming too large.

To illustrate, suppose PA borrows heavily at 11 percent during 1991 to finance projects yielding 12 percent, using up its debt capacity in the process. Now assume that in 1992 it has new projects available that yield 15 percent, well above the return on the 1991 projects, but PA cannot accept them because they would have to be financed with 16 percent equity money. *To avoid this problem, PA should be viewed as an ongoing concern, and the cost of capital used in capital budgeting should be calculated as a weighted average, or composite, of the various types of funds it generally uses, regardless of the specific financing used to fund a particular project.*

Self-Test

Why should the cost of capital used in capital budgeting be calculated as a weighted average of the various types of funds the firm generally uses, regardless of the specific financing used to fund a particular project?

BASIC DEFINITIONS

Capital components are the long-term items on the right-hand side of a firm's balance sheet: various types of debt, preferred stock, and common equity. Any increase in total assets must be financed by an increase in one or more of these capital components. *Capital* is a necessary factor of production, and, like any other factor, it has a cost. The cost of each component is defined as the *component cost* of that particular type of capital. For example, if Precision Associates can borrow money at 11 percent, its component cost of debt is defined as 11 percent.[2] Throughout most of this chapter we concentrate on

capital component
One of the types of capital used by firms to raise money.

---

[2] As we saw in Chapter 18, firms have both a before-tax and an after-tax cost of debt. Eleven percent is PA's before-tax component cost of debt.

debt, preferred stock, retained earnings, and new issues of common stock. These are the major capital structure components; their component costs are identified by the following symbols:

k_d = interest rate on the firm's new debt = before-tax component cost of debt. For Precision Associates (PA), $k_d = 11\%$.

$k_d(1 - t)$ = after-tax component cost of debt, where t is the firm's marginal tax rate. The term $k_d(1 - t)$ is the debt cost used to calculate the weighted average cost of capital. For PA, $t = 40\%$, so $k_d(1 - t) = 11\%(1 - 0.4) = 11\%(0.6) = 6.6\%$.

k_p = component cost of preferred stock. For PA, $k_p = 13\%$.

k_s = component cost of retained earnings (or internal equity). This k_s is identical to the k_s developed in Chapters 12 and 17 and defined there as the required rate of return on common stock. It is quite difficult to estimate k_s, but, as we shall see shortly, for PA, $k_s = 16\%$.

k_e = component cost of external equity obtained by issuing new common stock as opposed to retained earnings. As we shall see, it is necessary to distinguish between equity raised by retained earnings and that raised by selling new stock. This is why we distinguish between internal and external equity, k_s and k_e. Further, k_e is always greater than k_s. For PA, $k_e = 17\%$.

k_a = WACC = the weighted average cost of capital. If PA raises new capital to finance asset expansion, and if it is to keep its capital structure in balance (that is, if it is to keep the same percentage of debt, preferred stock, and common equity funds), then it must raise part of its new funds as debt, part as preferred stock, and part as common equity (with equity coming either from retained earnings or from the issuance of new common stock).[3] The terms k_a and WACC are used interchangeably. We will calculate WACC for Precision Associates shortly.

These definitions and concepts are explained in detail in the remainder of the chapter, where we develop a marginal cost of capital (MCC) schedule that can be used in capital budgeting. Then, in Chapter 20, we extend the analysis to

_____

[3]Firms try to keep their debt, preferred stock, and common equity in optimal proportions; we will see how they establish these proportions in Chapter 20. However, firms do not try to maintain any proportional relationship between the common stock and retained earnings accounts as shown on the balance sheet — common equity is common equity, whether it is represented by common stock or by retained earnings.

determine the mix of types of capital that will minimize the firm's cost of capital and thereby maximize its value.

Self-Test

Identify the firm's four major capital structure components, and give their respective component cost symbols.

MINIMUM REQUIRED RETURN

Any source of funds that the company uses has an implicit cost associated with it. As we learned in the chapters on capital budgeting, the firm raises money to invest in productive assets, which provide a cash flow to the firm. The cash flow must cover not only the project's *operating expenses* but the *financial costs* of the funds used to finance the project as well. With debt financing, the project's cash flow must cover the periodic interest payments plus repayments of principal. If the company is financed in part with preferred stock, preferred dividends must be paid. Finally, the required return on common equity financing must also be met through the project's cash flow. The firm will also determine the portion of after-tax earnings that will be paid in the form of dividends to shareholders and the portion that will be reinvested to insure the firm's future growth. Remember, even if one particular project is financed entirely with debt, the appropriate required return for the project is still the firm's weighted average cost of capital. Therefore, the project's cash flow must be large enough to cover all explicit financial costs (interest, repayment of principal, and dividends) as well as implicit financial costs (earnings retention for growth).

The minimum acceptable rate of return a project must earn is that rate which just satisfies all sources of financing. Perhaps a simple example with a company other than PA will clarify this point. Heath Publishing Company is planning to begin operations by purchasing a new printing press plus other necessary operating assets for $5 million. The company will raise funds for the new machine in proportion to the industry's average capital structure, 40 percent debt and 60 percent common equity. Heath does not plan to use any preferred stock. The lenders will require a 13 percent return, whereas equity investors, including the firm's founders, expect to receive a 16 percent return on their investment. Let us also suppose, for simplicity's sake, that the after-tax cash returns from the firm will continue at their current planned level forever and that all earnings will be paid out as dividends. If the company's marginal tax rate is 40 percent, what minimum cash flow *after* operating expenses (net income plus depreciation) must be produced to justify the creation of the firm? In essence, the question becomes this: What return must the firm produce to satisfy all sources of financing?

In Chapter 5, we discussed the expenses that a firm must cover if it is to make a profit. However, satisfying only the claims arising from operations (labor and materials costs, for example) and the claims of the government for taxes still leaves one group, the firm's capital suppliers, without their rightful return. Therefore, the successful firm must cover interest payments plus dividends and capital gains required by equity investors, as well as operating costs and taxes. Hence, the project's required cash flow, after operating expenses, is equal to the amount of financing times the required return of each financing source:

$$
\begin{aligned}
\text{Required} \\
\text{cash} \\
\text{flow}
\end{aligned}
=
\begin{aligned}
&\text{Required after-tax return on debt} \times \text{Amount of debt} \\
+\ &\text{Required return on preferred} \times \text{Amount of preferred} \\
+\ &\text{Required return on common equity} \\
&\times \text{Amount of common equity}
\end{aligned}
$$

$$= (0.13)(1 - t)(\$2{,}000{,}000) + \$0 + (0.16)(\$3{,}000{,}000)$$

$$= (0.13)(1 - 0.4)(\$2{,}000{,}000) + \$0 + (0.16)(\$3{,}000{,}000)$$

$$= \$156{,}000 + \$480{,}000$$

$$= \$636{,}000.$$

Thus,

$$\frac{\text{Minimum acceptable}}{\text{rate of return}} = \frac{\text{Required cash flow}}{\text{Investment}}$$

$$= \frac{\$636{,}000}{\$5{,}000{,}000}$$

$$= 12.72\%.$$

As we shall demonstrate later in the chapter, a company's cost of capital is the weighted average of the component costs of each source of capital. In the present example, with a capital structure composed of 40 percent debt and 60 percent common equity,

$$
\begin{aligned}
\text{Cost of capital} =\ &\text{After-tax cost of debt} \times \text{Proportion of debt in} \\
&\text{the capital structure} + \text{Cost of equity} \times \\
&\text{Proportion of equity in the capital structure}
\end{aligned}
$$

$$= (0.13)(1 - 0.4)(0.4) + (0.16)(0.6)$$

$$= 0.0312 + 0.096$$

$$= 0.1272, \text{ or } 12.72\%.$$

Thus, it should be clear that for either a project or a firm (which is a combination of projects), the minimum acceptable cash flow is the one that just satisfies each of the suppliers of capital. Therefore, the minimum acceptable rate of return for a project of average risk, or for the firm as a whole, is the cost of capital. In Chapter 14, we found this to be the point where the project's net present value (NPV) equaled zero, for if NPV = $0, then the claims of all contributors to the project's success have been exactly satisfied. Operating costs for labor, materials, and so on, have been paid, taxes have been paid, and the required rates of return for each of the various suppliers of capital have been met. Thus, the true breakeven point for the firm is where all of its projects' NPVs = $0.[4] Recall from Chapter 14 that firms do not seek projects whose NPV = $0, but, rather, firms actively seek projects that have positive NPVs. This reflects the fact that once all claims from operations have been satisfied, the owners of the firm — its common stockholders — receive a return in excess of their required return. Naturally, a firm would reject any project with an anticipated NPV that is negative, since the cash flows from the project would not be sufficient to cover operating expenses, tax obligations, and financing costs.

Now that we have analyzed the basic concept behind the cost of capital and its use as the minimum acceptable rate of return for investment proposals, we will turn to a more complete definition of how the component cost of each source of capital is computed.

Self-Test

What must a successful firm's cash flow cover?

Give the equation for determining a firm's required cash flow, assuming the firm has no preferred stock.

Give the equation for a firm's minimum acceptable rate of return.

COST OF DEBT, $k_d(1 - t)$

The component cost used to calculate the weighted cost of capital is the interest rate on debt, k_d, less the tax savings that result because interest is deductible. This is the same as k_d multiplied by $(1 - t)$, where t is the firm's marginal tax rate:[5]

$$\text{After-tax component cost of debt} = \text{Interest rate} - \text{Tax savings}$$

$$= k_d - k_d t$$

$$= k_d(1 - t). \qquad (19\text{-}1)$$

---

[4]In Chapter 20 we will introduce an operating breakeven point where EBIT = $0, that is, where all operating costs are just satisfied. As we will explain there, this breakeven point can be expanded to include the payment of fixed financial charges such as interest (that is, where EBT = $0). Yet these definitions of breakeven are incomplete because they do not contain a provision for providing the return required by the firm's owners, its common stockholders.

[5]In our discussion of the required return on equity, flotation costs (or the cost of selling equity through an investment banker) will be an integral part of the *cost of equity*. This is also the case when we examine the cost of preferred stock. However, when we evaluate the *cost of debt*, flotation costs will be ignored. The flotation cost for a debt issue, sold through investment bankers in the capital markets, is usually quite low as a percentage of the issue. In fact, most debt is placed directly with banks, insurance companies, pension funds, and the like, and therefore has virtually no flotation cost. Thus, although the costs associated with the sale of debt, preferred, and common equity by investment bankers are real, only the costs of selling preferred stock and common equity will be considered in this chapter.

after-tax cost of debt, $k_d(1 - t)$
The relevant cost of new debt financing, taking into account the tax deductibility of interest; used to calculate the WACC.

In effect, the government pays part of the cost of debt because interest is deductible. Therefore, if Precision Associates can borrow at a rate of 11 percent, and if it has a marginal federal-plus-state tax rate of 40 percent, then its **after-tax cost of debt** is

$$k_d(1 - t) = 11\%(0.6) = 6.6\%.$$

The reason for using the after-tax cost of debt is as follows. The value of the firm's stock, which we want to maximize, depends on *after-tax* cash flows. Because interest is a deductible expense, it produces tax savings which reduce the net cost of debt, so the after-tax cost of debt is less than the before-tax cost. Since cash flows and rates of return should be on a comparable basis, we adjust the interest rate downward to account for the preferential tax treatment of debt.[6]

The importance of the tax deductibility of interest may be observed in the following example. Suppose a firm with a 50 percent tax rate has the choice of financing with debt or preferred stock. Interest is paid before taxes (thus it is tax deductible), whereas dividends are paid after taxes and therefore are not tax deductible. If we assume the interest *or* the preferred dividend payment is equal to $1,000, the result is as follows:

	Debt Option	Preferred Stock Option
EBIT	$5,000	$5,000
−I	−1,000	− 0
EBT	$4,000	$5,000
−T	−2,000	−2,500
EAIT	$2,000	$2,500
−PFD DIV	− 0	−1,000
NI	$2,000	$1,500

Note that because of the tax deductibility of interest, the preferred dividend would have to fall by the amount of the tax subsidy on interest — by 50 percent, or to $500 in this example — for the net income under the preferred-stock-financed income stream to equal the debt-financed stream's net income. Therefore, the effective cost of debt capital to a firm is not the interest rate on debt but, rather, the after-tax cost determined by Equation 19-1.

Our primary concern with the cost of capital is to use it in a decision-making process — to determine the minimum acceptable return on new capital budgeting projects. Thus, the appropriate cost of debt is the cost for new borrowing, not the historical interest rates on old, previously outstanding debt. In other words, we are interested in the cost of the next dollar borrowed, or

---

[6]The tax rate is *zero* for a firm with losses. Therefore, for a company that does not pay taxes, the cost of debt is not reduced; that is, in Equation 19-1 the tax rate equals zero, so the after-tax cost of debt is equal to the interest rate.

the *marginal* cost of debt. The rate at which the firm has borrowed in the past is a *sunk cost*, and it is irrelevant for cost of capital purposes.

Self-Test

Why is the after-tax rather than the before-tax cost of debt used to calculate the weighted average cost of capital?

Is the relevant cost of debt the interest rate on already *outstanding* debt or that on *new* debt? Explain why this cost is used.

COST OF PREFERRED STOCK, k_p

The component **cost of preferred stock, k_p,** used to calculate the weighted cost of capital is the preferred dividend, D_p, divided by the net issuing price, P_n, or the price the firm receives after deducting flotation costs:

$$\text{Component cost of preferred stock} = k_p = D_p/P_n. \qquad (19\text{-}2)$$

In Equation 19-2, we assume that the dividend from the preferred stock remains constant — that is, that the dividend will always be paid, that the preferred stock is not a participating preferred issue, and that it does not have a sinking fund.

For example, Precision Associates has preferred stock that pays a $12.68 dividend per share and which sells for $100 per share in the market. If it issues new shares of preferred, it will incur an underwriting (or flotation) cost of 2.5 percent, or $2.50 per share, so it will net $97.50 per share. Therefore, PA's cost of preferred stock is approximately 13 percent:

$$k_p = \$12.68/\$97.50 \approx 13\%.$$

Equation 19-2 can also be used to determine the cost of preferred stock if an issue is already outstanding. Suppose the price of PA's preferred stock falls to $84.50 per share. This is a signal to the firm that investors will no longer accept a return of 13 percent; now they will require a 15 percent return:

$$k_p = \$12.68/\$84.50 \approx 15\%.$$

Note that no tax adjustments are made when calculating k_p because, unlike interest on debt, dividends are not tax deductible; hence there are no tax savings associated with the use of preferred stock.

Self-Test

Does the component cost of preferred stock include or exclude flotation costs? Explain.

Is a tax adjustment made to the cost of preferred stock? Why or why not?

> **cost of preferred stock, k_p**
> The preferred dividend, D_p, divided by the net issuing price, P_n.

COST OF RETAINED EARNINGS, k_s

cost of retained earnings, k_s
The rate of return required by stockholders on a firm's common stock.

The costs of debt and preferred stock are based on the returns investors require on these securities. Similarly, the **cost of retained earnings, k_s,** is the rate of return stockholders require on equity capital obtained by retaining earnings.[7]

opportunity cost
The return on the best alternative investment available; the highest return that will *not* be earned if funds are reinvested in the firm.

At one time many managers believed that retained earnings were a costless source of funds. Now, however, managers realize that retained earnings are not free. The reason that a cost of capital must be assigned to retained earnings can be explained by the **opportunity cost** principle. The firm's after-tax earnings literally belong to its stockholders. Bondholders are compensated by interest payments, and preferred stockholders by preferred dividends, but the earnings remaining after interest and preferred dividends have been paid belong to the common stockholders and serve to compensate them for the use of their capital. Management may either pay out earnings in the form of dividends or retain earnings and reinvest them in the business. If management decides to retain earnings, there is an opportunity cost involved — stockholders could have received the earnings as dividends and then invested this money in other stocks, in bonds, in real estate, or in anything else. Thus, the firm should earn on its retained earnings at least as much as its stockholders could earn on alternative investments of comparable risk.

What rate of return can stockholders expect to earn on equivalent-risk investments? For example, assume that PA's stockholders expect to earn a return of $k_s = 16\%$ on their money. If a stockholder received $10,000 from any source — from savings, from dividends paid by Precision, or from anywhere else — he or she could buy more stock in Precision or in some other company with similar risk and expect to earn $k_s = 16\%$. *Therefore, if the firm cannot invest retained earnings and earn at least k_s, it should pay these funds to its stockholders and let them invest directly in other stocks that do provide this return.*

Self-Test

Why must a cost be assigned to retained earnings?

FINDING THE BASIC REQUIRED RATE OF RETURN ON COMMON EQUITY

The majority of U.S. business firms have debt-to-total-assets ratios that are less than 50 percent. Thus, common stock equity provides the largest proportion of financing in the average firm's capital structure.

---

[7]The term *retained earnings* can be interpreted to mean either the balance sheet item "retained earnings," consisting of all the earnings retained in the business throughout its history, or the income statement item "additions to retained earnings." The latter definition is used in this chapter. For our purpose, *retained earnings* refers to the company's *change in retained earnings* or, in other words, to that part of the year's earnings not paid out in dividends and hence available for reinvestment in the business during the year.

Unfortunately, the cost of equity is the most difficult of the cost of capital components to determine. Other sources of capital have periodic fixed payment schedules, such as debt's interest and principal payments, which are contractual obligations, and preferred stock's dividends, which are not contractually guaranteed but are generally treated as fixed obligations by financial managers. The amount and timing of cash flows from these securities can be forecasted with a high degree of certainty, making investors' required returns (and hence the costs of capital from these sources) easy to determine. Unlike debt and preferred stock, however, the cash flows resulting from the purchase of common stock are difficult to forecast. Still, although it is not easy to measure k_s, we can employ the principles developed in Chapters 12 and 17 to produce reasonably good estimates of the cost of equity.

It is obvious by now that the basic rate of return investors require on a firm's common equity, k_s, is a most important quantity. This required rate of return is the cost of retained earnings, and it forms the basis for the cost of capital obtained from new stock issues. How is this all-important quantity estimated? To begin, we know that for stocks in equilibrium (which is the typical situation), the required rate of return, k_s, is also equal to the expected rate of return, $\hat{k}_s$. Further, the required return is equal to a risk-free rate, k_{RF}, plus a premium for all risks, RP, and the expected return on a constant growth stock is equal to a dividend yield, D_1/P_0, plus an expected growth rate, g:

$$\text{Required rate of return} = \text{Expected rate of return}$$

$$k_s = k_{RF} + RP = D_1/P_0 + g = \hat{k}_s.$$

Therefore, k_s can be estimated either directly as $k_s = k_{RF} + RP$ or indirectly as $k_s = \hat{k}_s = D_1/P_0 + g$. Actually, we can use three methods for finding the cost of retained earnings: (1) the discounted cash flow (DCF) approach, which was introduced in Chapter 17, (2) the CAPM approach, which was introduced in Chapter 12, and (3) the bond-yield-plus-risk-premium approach, which we will discuss shortly. These three approaches are discussed in the following sections.

Discounted Cash Flow (DCF) Approach

In Chapter 17 we saw that

$$\hat{k}_s = \frac{D_1}{P_0} + \text{Expected g.} \qquad \textbf{(17-5)}$$

Note, however, that if a firm's growth rate is not expected to remain constant, Equation 17-5 cannot be used. Thus, investors expect to receive a dividend yield, D_1/P_0, plus a capital gains yield (a measure of the expected growth in the firm's value), g, for a total expected return of $\hat{k}_s$.

To illustrate, suppose Precision Associates begins to retain some earnings rather than paying them all out as dividends. The stock is in equilibrium, it sells for $30.00, the next expected dividend is $2.70, and the expected growth rate is now 7 percent. Therefore, the firm's expected and required rate of return, and hence its cost of retained earnings, is

$$\hat{k}_s = k_s = \frac{\$2.70}{\$30.00} + 7\% = 9\% + 7\% = 16\%.$$

Thus, 16 percent is the minimum rate of return that PA's management must expect to earn on the equity-financed projects to justify retaining earnings and plowing them back into the business rather than paying them out to stockholders as dividends. Henceforth in this chapter, we assume that equilibrium exists, so k_s and $\hat{k}_s$ are equal. Therefore, we use the terms k_s and $\hat{k}_s$ interchangeably.

It is relatively easy to determine the dividend yield, but it is difficult to establish the proper growth rate. If past growth rates in earnings and dividends have been relatively stable, and if investors appear to be projecting a continuation of past trends, then g may be based on the firm's historical growth rate. *However, if the company's past growth rate has been abnormally high or low, either because of its own unique situation or because of general economic conditions, investors will not blindly project the past growth rate into the future.* Remember, an investor is purchasing the firm's *future, not its past,* cash flows.

In practice, security analysts regularly make forecasts of the growth in both dividends and earnings, looking at such factors as projected sales, profit margins, and competitive factors. An individual making a cost of capital estimate can obtain some analysts' forecasts, average them, use the average as a proxy for the growth expectations of investors in general, and then combine the forecasted growth with the current dividend yield to estimate the cost of equity capital, as follows:

$$k_s = D_1/P_0 + \text{growth rate, g, as projected by security analysts.}$$

Again, note that this estimate of k_s is based on the assumption that g is expected to remain constant in the future.[8]

CAPM Approach

The Capital Asset Pricing Model (CAPM) as developed in Chapter 12 can be used to help estimate k_s as follows:

Step 1. Estimate the risk-free rate, k_{RF}, generally taken to be either the U.S. Treasury bond rate or the 30-day Treasury bill rate.

---

[8]Analysts' growth rate forecasts are usually for 5 years into the future, and the rates provided represent the average growth rate over that 5-year horizon. Studies have shown that analysts' forecasts represent the best source of growth data for DCF cost of capital estimates. See Robert Harris, "Using Analysts' Growth Rate Forecasts to Estimate Shareholder Required Rates of Return," *Financial Management,* Spring 1986, pp. 58–67.

Another method for estimating g involves first forecasting the firm's average future dividend payout ratio and its complement, the *retention rate,* and then multiplying the retention rate by the company's average future projected rate of return on equity (ROE):

$$g = (\text{Retention rate})(\text{ROE}) = (1.0 - \text{Payout rate})(\text{ROE}).$$

Security analysts often use this procedure when they estimate growth rates.

Step 2. Estimate the stock's beta coefficient, b_i, and use this as an index of the stock's market risk. The i signifies the i'th company's beta.

Step 3. Estimate the required rate of return on the market or on an "average" stock. Designate this return k_M.

Step 4. Substitute the preceding values into the CAPM equation to estimate the required rate of return on a firm's stock:

$$k_s = k_{RF} + (k_M - k_{RF})b_i.$$

This equation shows that the CAPM estimate of k_s begins with the risk-free rate, k_{RF}, to which is added a risk premium set equal to the premium on an average stock, $k_M - k_{RF}$, scaled up or down to reflect the particular stock's relative risk as measured by its beta coefficient. Note that this is the Security Market Line (SML) equation which we discussed in Chapter 12.

To illustrate the CAPM approach, assume that $k_{RF} = 8\%$, $k_M = 14\%$, and $b_i = 1.25$ for PA's stock. PA's k_s is calculated as follows:

$$k_s = 8\% + (14\% - 8\%)1.25 = 8\% + 7.5\% = 15.5\%.$$

Had b_i been 0.7, indicating that the stock was less risky than average, its k_s would have been

$$k_s = 8\% + (6\%)0.7 = 8\% + 4.2\% = 12.2\%.$$

For an average stock,

$$k_s = k_M = 8\% + (6\%)1.0 = 8\% + 6\% = 14\%.$$

It should be noted that although the CAPM approach appears to yield accurate, precise estimates of k_s, there are actually several problems with this approach. First, as we saw in Chapter 12, if a firm's stockholders are not well diversified, they may be concerned with *total risk* rather than market risk only; in this case the firm's true investment risk will not be measured by its beta, and the CAPM procedure will understate the correct value of k_s. Further, even if the CAPM method is valid, it is hard to obtain correct estimates of the inputs required to make it operational because (1) there is uncertainty about whether to use long-term or short-term Treasury bonds for k_{RF}; (2) it is hard to estimate the beta that investors expect the company to have in the future; and (3) it is difficult to estimate the market risk premium.

Bond-Yield-plus-Risk-Premium Approach

Although it is essentially an ad hoc, subjective procedure, analysts often estimate a firm's cost of common equity by adding a risk premium of from three to five percentage points to the interest rate on the firm's own long-term debt. It is logical to think that firms with risky, low-rated, and consequently high-interest-rate debt will also have risky, high-cost equity, and the procedure of basing the cost of equity on a readily observable debt cost utilizes this precept.

For example, if PA's bonds, which are rated A, yield 11 percent, its cost of equity might be estimated as follows:

$$k_s = \text{Bond rate} + \text{Risk premium} = 11\% + 4\% = 15\%.$$

This 4 percent risk premium is a judgmental estimate, so the estimated value of k_s is also judgmental.[9] A judgmental estimate is not likely to result in a precise measure of the cost of equity capital — about all that it can do is "get us into the right ballpark." Low premiums occur when interest rates are quite high and people are reluctant to invest in long-term bonds for fear of runaway inflation, further increases in interest rates, and losses on bond investments. High premiums occur when interest rates are relatively low.

Conclusions on the Cost of Equity Capital

Which of the methods used to determine the cost of equity is most correct? The answer depends on the data that are available — for which method, in a specific instance, do we have the most reasonable data? Many business firms use all of these methods or more to approximate the cost of equity. In fact, the Du Pont Corporation uses five different methods to evaluate and approximate its cost of equity capital. Therefore, we suggest that in practical work it is best to use all three of the methods discussed here and then apply judgment when the methods produce differing results. Managers experienced in estimating equity capital costs recognize that both careful analysis and some good judgment are required. *It would be nice to pretend that the judgment is unnecessary and to specify an easy, precise way of determining the exact cost of equity capital. Unfortunately, this is not possible. Finance is in large part a matter of judgment, and we simply must face this fact.*

Precision Associates' financial managers used the three methods discussed above and obtained a range for PA's common equity from 15% to 16%. After much discussion, they decided to use 16 percent as the firm's cost of common equity.

Self-Test

What are the three methods for estimating the cost of retained earnings?

Which of the components of the constant growth DCF formula — dividend yield or growth rate — is more difficult to estimate? Explain your answer.

Identify some potential problems with the CAPM approach.

What is the reasoning behind the bond-yield-plus-risk-premium approach?

---

[9]Analysts who use this procedure often cite studies of historical returns on stocks and bonds and use the difference between the average yield (dividends plus capital gains) on stocks and the average yield on bonds as the risk premium of stocks over bonds. The most frequently cited study is R. G. Ibbotson and R. A. Sinquefield, "Stocks, Bonds, Bills, and Inflation: Year-By-Year Historical Returns (1926–1974)," *Journal of Business,* January 1976, pp. 11–47.

COST OF NEWLY ISSUED COMMON STOCK, OR EXTERNAL EQUITY, k_e

The **cost of new common equity, k_e,** *or external equity capital, is higher than the cost of retained earnings, k_s, because of flotation costs involved in selling new common stock.* What rate of return must be earned on funds raised by selling stock in order to make issuing new stock worthwhile? To put it another way, what is the cost of new common stock?

For a firm with a constant growth rate, the answer is found by applying the following formula:

$$k_e = \frac{D_1}{P_0(1 - F)} + g. \qquad (19\text{-}3)$$

Here **F** is the percentage **flotation cost** incurred in selling the new stock issue, so $P_0(1 - F)$ is the net price per share received by the company when it sells new shares.

Recall that Precision Associates has a required return of 16 percent on its common equity from retained earnings. If the firm wishes to issue new stock, however, there will be a flotation cost charged by the investment banker, and that will affect the cost of equity. If the flotation charge for PA's new issue is 10 percent, the cost of new outside equity is computed as follows:

$$k_e = \frac{\$2.70}{\$30(1 - 0.10)} + 7\%$$

$$= \frac{\$2.70}{\$27} + 7\%$$

$$= 10\% + 7\%$$

$$= 17\%.$$

Investors require a return on equity capital that consists of a current dividend yield, D_1/P_0, and a growth or capital gains component, g. For PA this required return, k_s, was 16 percent. However, because of flotation costs, the company *must earn more* than 16 percent on funds obtained by selling common stock if it is to provide a return of 16 percent to its stockholders. What causes this seeming contradiction? Specifically, the firm will have to provide the $2.70 in dividends next year and maintain a 7 percent growth based on $27 of assets, even though stockholders put up $30. The firm must meet these investor expectations with only 90 percent of the share price, because 10 percent goes to the investment banker for services in selling the stock. Therefore, if Precision earns less than 17 percent on the new equity-financed project, the investment will be unable to provide the required dividend of $2.70 and the anticipated 7 percent growth. Such a decline in either dividends, growth, or both would cause the value of the stock to decline below the $30 price investors paid. Conversely, if the project earns more than 17 percent, the firm's dividend and/ or growth will be larger than required, and the price of PA's stock will rise.

cost of new common equity, k_e
The cost of external equity; based on the cost of retained earnings, but increased for flotation costs.

flotation cost, F
The percentage cost of issuing new common stock.

Self-Test

Why is the cost of external equity capital higher than the cost of retained earnings?

How can the DCF model be modified to incorporate flotation costs?

WEIGHTED AVERAGE, OR COMPOSITE, COST OF CAPITAL, WACC = k_a

target (optimal) capital structure
The percentages of debt, preferred stock, and common equity that will minimize the firm's weighted average cost of capital (WACC) and therefore maximize the price of the firm's stock.

As we shall see in Chapter 20, each firm has a **target (optimal) capital structure,** which is that mix of debt, preferred stock, and common equity that minimizes the firm's *weighted average cost of capital (WACC)* and therefore causes the firm's stock price to be maximized. A rational, value-maximizing firm will establish its optimal capital structure and then raise new capital in a manner that will keep the actual capital structure on target over time. In this chapter we assume that the firm has identified its optimal capital structure, that it uses this optimum as the target, and that it finances so as to remain constantly on target. How the target is established will be examined in Chapter 20.

weighted average cost of capital, WACC = k_a
A weighted average of the component costs of debt, preferred stock, and common equity.

The target proportions of debt, preferred stock, and common equity, along with the component costs of capital, are used to calculate the firm's **weighted average cost of capital, WACC = k_a.** To illustrate, suppose Precision Associates has a target capital structure calling for 30 percent debt, 10 percent preferred stock, and 60 percent common equity (retained earnings plus common stock). Its before-tax cost of debt, k_d, is 11 percent; its after-tax cost of debt = $k_d(1 - t)$ = 11%(0.6) = 6.6%; its cost of preferred stock, k_p, is 13 percent; its cost of common equity from retained earnings, k_s, is 16 percent; and its marginal tax rate is 40 percent. Now we can calculate Precision's weighted average cost of capital, WACC, as follows:

$$WACC = k_a = w_d k_d (1 - t) + w_p k_p + w_s k_s \qquad \textbf{(19-4)}$$

$$= 0.3(11\%)(0.6) + 0.1(13\%) + 0.6(16\%) = 12.88\%.$$

Here w_d, w_p, and w_s are the weights used for debt, preferred, and common equity, respectively.

Every dollar of new capital that Precision obtains consists of 30 cents of debt with an after-tax cost of 6.6 percent, 10 cents of preferred stock with a cost of 13 percent, and 60 cents of common equity (all from additions to retained earnings) with a cost of 16 percent. The average cost of each whole dollar, WACC, is 12.88 percent.

The weights could be based either on the accounting values shown on the firm's balance sheet (book values) or on the market values of the different securities, where one would determine the market value of the debt using bond valuation techniques and the value of the common equity (common stock plus retained earnings) by multiplying the stock price times the shares outstanding. Theoretically, the weights should be based on market values, but if a firm's book value weights are reasonably close to its market value weights, book value weights can be used as a proxy for market value weights. This point is discussed further in Chapter 20, but in the remainder of this chapter we shall assume that the firm's market values are approximately equal to its book values, and we will use book value capital structure weights.

Self-Test

How does one calculate the weighted average cost of capital?

CHANGES IN THE COST OF CAPITAL

The *marginal cost* of any item is the cost of another unit of that item; for example, the marginal cost of labor is the cost of adding one additional worker. The marginal cost of labor may be $25 per person if 10 workers are added but $35 per person if the firm tries to hire 100 new workers, because it will be harder to find 100 people willing and able to do the work. The same concept applies to capital. As the firm tries to attract more new dollars, the cost of each dollar will at some point rise. *Thus, the* **marginal cost of capital (MCC)** *is defined as the cost of the last dollar of new capital that the firm raises, and the marginal cost rises as more and more capital is raised during a given period.*

> **marginal cost of capital (MCC)**
> The cost of obtaining another dollar of new capital; the weighted average cost of the last dollar of new capital raised.

The cost of capital changes as the proportion of debt and equity in the capital structure changes. As a general rule, a different marginal cost of capital (MCC) will exist for every possible capital structure; *the optimal capital structure is the one that produces the lowest MCC.* Could Precision raise an unlimited amount of new capital at the 12.88 percent cost as long as its capital structure is maintained at 30 percent debt, 10 percent preferred, and 60 percent common equity? The answer is *no*. As companies raise larger and larger sums during a given time period, the costs of the debt, preferred, and common equity components begin to rise, and as this occurs, the weighted average cost of obtaining new capital rises.

This increase in the cost of capital occurs for several reasons. First, even if the proportions of debt, preferred, and common equity remain the same, the level of interest payments must increase as the debt increases. As the fixed interest payments increase, coverage ratios decline, financial risk increases, and the suppliers of debt capital will require higher interest rates to offset the greater risk. As the amount of preferred stock increases, the level of preferred dividends increases too. Finally, generating larger amounts of common equity means that the firm will exhaust its internal equity and will have to turn to more expensive new common equity. Another factor that would affect the cost of capital is that the firm's risk profile may change with rapid growth, because the company's management may be pressed beyond its capabilities, or the firm may take on more risky projects than before.

marginal cost of capital (MCC) schedule
A graph that relates the firm's weighted average cost of each dollar of capital to the total amount of new capital raised.

Where will these cost increases, or breaks in the **MCC schedule,** occur? Although it is difficult to tell in practice, we can provide some insights into the determination of these points by utilizing the data for Precision Associates. Additionally, we need to assume the following:

1. The firm wishes to maintain the same 30%/10%/60% debt/preferred/common equity capital structure under all financing plans.

2. The company's new projects will be about as risky as its current projects.

3. PA can borrow up to $45,000 at the current 11 percent interest rate, but additional debt will cost 12.5 percent.

4. The firm expects to retain $72,000 of its earnings for the current year. If it needs additional common equity, above this $72,000, a 10 percent flotation charge will be incurred if new common stock is sold.

5. $k_s = D_1/P_0 + g = \$2.70/\$30 + 7\% = 16\%.$

$k_e = D_1/P_0(1 - F) + g = \$2.70/[\$30(1 - 0.10)] + 7\% = 17\%,$

where

D_1 = next year's dividend,

P_0 = current common stock price for PA's shares,

F = percentage flotation cost for new equity shares, and

g = expected growth rate.

6. The marginal tax rate will remain constant at 40 percent.

PA's weighted average cost of capital (which was calculated in the previous section) is shown in Table 19-1, where the firm first uses retained earnings and then new common stock. We see that the weighted average cost of each dollar, or the marginal cost of capital, is 12.88 percent as long as retained earnings are used, but the average cost jumps to 13.48 percent as soon as the firm exhausts its internal financing and is forced to sell new common stock.

break, or jump, in the MCC schedule
A change in the weighted average cost of capital that occurs when there is a change in a component cost of capital.

break point (BP)
The dollar value of total new capital that can be raised before an increase occurs in the firm's weighted average cost of capital.

How much new capital can Precision raise before it exhausts its retained earnings and is forced to sell new common stock; that is, where will the **break, or jump, in the MCC schedule** occur? The question becomes one of how much *total financing* — debt, preferred stock, and the $72,000 in retained earnings — can be done before retained earnings are exhausted and the firm is forced to sell new common stock. Sixty percent of the total financing will consist of retained earnings, which amount to $72,000, so

$$0.6(\text{Total financing}) = \text{Retained earnings} = \$72,000.$$

Solving for Total financing, we obtain the **break point (BP):**

$$\text{Break point} = \text{Total financing} = \frac{\text{Retained earnings}}{0.6} = \frac{\$72,000}{0.6} = \$120,000.$$

Table 19-1 **PA's Marginal Cost of Capital Using**
(1) Retained Earnings and (2) New Common Stock

Source	Weight	×	Component Cost	=	Product
(1) MCC When Equity Is Obtained Internally (from Retained Earnings):					
Debt	0.3		6.6%[a]		1.98%
Preferred stock	0.1		13.0		1.3
Common equity (Retained earnings)	0.6		16.0		9.6
	1.0				12.88%
(2) MCC When Equity Is Obtained Externally (from Sale of New Common Stock):					
Debt	0.3		6.6%		1.98%
Preferred stock	0.1		13.0		1.3
Common equity (New common stock)	0.6		17.0		10.2
	1.0				13.48%

[a]Recall that the cost of debt = $k_d(1 - t) = 11\%(0.6) = 6.6\%$.

Thus, PA can raise a total of $120,000, consisting of $72,000 of retained earnings, $12,000 of preferred stock (0.1 × $120,000), and $36,000 [$120,000 − ($72,000 + $12,000) = $36,000] of new debt supported by these new retained earnings, without altering its capital structure:

30% — new debt supported by retained earnings	$ 36,000
10% — preferred stock	12,000
60% — retained earnings	72,000
Total financing supported by retained earnings, or break point for retained earnings in the MCC schedule	$120,000

There can be other breaks in the MCC schedule — in fact, a break occurs when the cost of any component changes. One such possible change for PA would be the increase in the cost of debt if more than $45,000 is needed. If more than $45,000 of new debt is required, it can be raised, but at a cost of 12.5 percent. This will result in a second break point in the MCC schedule, at the point where the $45,000 of cheaper, 11 percent debt is exhausted. At what amount of *total financing* will the 11 percent debt be used up? Since 30 percent of this total financing will be $45,000 of 11 percent debt, we can find the debt-caused break point as follows:

$$0.3(\text{Total financing}) = \$45,000,$$

and, solving for Total financing, we obtain

$$\frac{\text{Total}}{\text{financing}} = \frac{11\% \text{ debt}}{0.3} = \frac{\$45,000}{0.3} = \$150,000 = \text{Break point for debt.}$$

A general break point formula can be written as

$$\text{Break point} = \frac{\text{Total amount of lower-cost capital of a given type}}{\text{Fraction of this type of capital in the capital structure}}. \quad (19\text{-}5)$$

Thus, there will be another break in the MCC schedule after PA has raised a total of $150,000. As we demonstrated previously, up to $120,000 the MCC is 12.88 percent, but beyond $120,000 the MCC rises to 13.48 percent. Now we see that the MCC rises again, at $150,000, to 13.75 percent:

Source	Weight	×	Component Cost	=	Product
Debt	0.3		7.50%[a]		2.25%
Preferred stock	0.1		13.00		1.30
Common equity	0.6		17.00		10.20
	1.0				13.75%

[a]The cost of debt = $k_d(1 - t) = 12.5\% \ (1 - 0.4) = 7.5\%$.

In other words, the next dollar beyond $150,000 will consist of 30 cents of 12.5 percent debt (7.5 percent after taxes), 10 cents of 13 percent preferred stock, and 60 cents of new common stock (retained earnings were used up much earlier), and this marginal dollar will have an average cost of 13.75 percent.

The effect of this new MCC increase is shown in Figure 19-1. PA now has two breaks, one caused by using up all of the retained earnings and the other caused by using up all of the 11 percent debt. With the two breaks, there are three different MCCs: $MCC_1 = 12.88\%$ for the first $120,000 of new capital; $MCC_2 = 13.48\%$ in the interval between $120,000 and $150,000; and $MCC_3 = 13.75\%$ for all new capital beyond $150,000.

There could, of course, be still more break points. For example, debt costs could continue to rise, or the flotation costs on new common stock could increase above 10 percent as larger amounts of stock are sold. Preferred stock costs could rise due to higher flotation costs as well. These changes would cause more breaks in the MCC.

The easiest sequence for calculating MCC schedules is as follows:

1. Identify the points where breaks occur. A break will occur any time the cost of one of the capital components rises. (However, it is possible that two capital components could both increase at the same point.)

2. Determine the cost of capital for each component in the intervals between breaks.

3. Calculate the weighted averages of these costs; the weighted averages are the MCCs in each interval.

Notice that if there are n separate breaks, there will be n + 1 different MCCs. For example, in Figure 19-1 we see two breaks and three different MCCs.

Before concluding this section, we should note again that a different MCC schedule would result if a different capital structure, with different fractions of debt, preferred stock, and common equity, were used. The optimal capital structure produces the lowest MCC.

Figure 19-1 **Marginal Cost of Capital Schedule for PA Using
Retained Earnings, New Common Stock, Preferred Stock, and Debt**

Even though a business may always finance at its optimal capital structure, it cannot
count on raising an unlimited amount of new capital at a constant cost. For example,
PA can expect to encounter two breaks, or increases, in its marginal cost of capital
(MCC) if it raises more than $150,000. The first occurs at $120,000 in total financing,
when retained earnings are exhausted and the firm issues new common stock. The
second break comes at $150,000, when the cost of debt increases, bringing the MCC
to 13.75 percent. A break will occur whenever costs of debt, preferred stock, or
common equity increase.

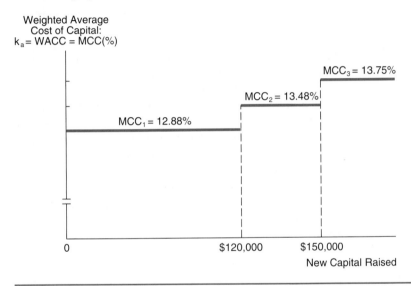

Self-Test

What are break points, and why do they occur in MCC schedules?

How can a break point be determined?

How does one calculate a firm's MCC schedule?

If there are n breaks in the MCC schedule, how many different MCCs are there?

COMBINING THE MCC AND THE INVESTMENT OPPORTUNITY SCHEDULE (IOS)

Now that we have calculated the MCC schedule, we can use it to determine
the discount rate used in the capital budgeting process; that is, *we can use the
MCC schedule to find the cost of capital for determining projects' net present
values (NPVs) as discussed in Chapter 14.*

Table 19-2 **Potential Capital Budgeting Projects Available to PA**

Project	Cost	Annual Inflows	Project Life (Years)	IRR (or Discount Rate at Which NPV = $0)
A	$30,000	$ 8,530	5	13.0%
B	23,000	5,530	7	15.0
C	35,000	6,195	10	12.0
D	52,000	14,490	6	17.0
E	30,000	6,470	8	14.0
F	35,000	15,585	3	16.0

To understand how the MCC is used in capital budgeting, assume that Precision has three financial executives: a financial vice president (VP), a treasurer, and a director of capital budgeting (DCB). Of course, if the firm were smaller, the steps we will outline would still be carried out, but by the financial officer rather than by a staff as in the case of a larger firm.

For PA, the financial VP asks the treasurer to develop the firm's MCC schedule, as we have done in Figure 19-1. At the same time, the financial vice president asks the director of capital budgeting to determine the dollar amounts of potentially acceptable projects. The DCB has a listing of all the firm's potential projects, including the cost of each project, its projected annual net cash inflows, its life, and its IRR. This listing is shown in Table 19-2. For simplicity, we assume now that all projects are independent as opposed to mutually exclusive, that they are equally risky, and that their risks are all equal to those of the firm's average existing assets.

investment opportunity schedule (IOS)
A graph of the firm's investment opportunities ranked in order of the projects' internal rates of return.

The DCB then plots the data in Table 19-2 as the **investment opportunity schedule (IOS)** shown in Figure 19-2. The figure also reproduces Precision's MCC schedule as plotted in Figure 19-1. The IOS shows how much money PA could invest at different rates of return. If the cost of capital were above 17 percent, none of the available projects would have a positive NPV, and hence none of them should be accepted. In that case, Precision would simply not expand. If the cost of capital were 17 percent, PA should take on only Project D, and its capital budget would call for the company to raise and invest $52,000. If the cost of capital were 16 percent, the firm should take on Projects D and F, raising a total of $87,000. Successively lower costs of capital call for larger and larger investment outlays.

Just how far down its IOS curve should the firm go? In other words, which of its available projects should it accept? The answer is that the firm should accept the four projects (D, F, B, and E) that have rates of return which equal or exceed the cost of capital that would be required to finance them. Projects A and C should be rejected, because they would have to be financed with capital that has a cost of 13.75 percent, and at that cost of capital, A and C have negative NPVs and IRRs that are below their costs of capital. Therefore, Precision Associates should have a capital budget of $140,000.

Figure 19-2 **Combining PA's MCC and IOS Curves to Determine Its Optimal Capital Budget**

This figure shows how the MCC schedule is used in capital budgeting. The investment opportunity schedule (IOS) indicates how much PA can invest at different rates of return. The two schedules intersect at an MCC of 13.48 percent, which is the cost of capital that should be used in evaluating projects in capital budgeting. Projects D, F, B, and E, which have returns in excess of the cost of capital, would thus be accepted, making the total optimal capital budget $140,000. Because Projects A and C would have to be financed with 13.75 percent money, they should be rejected.

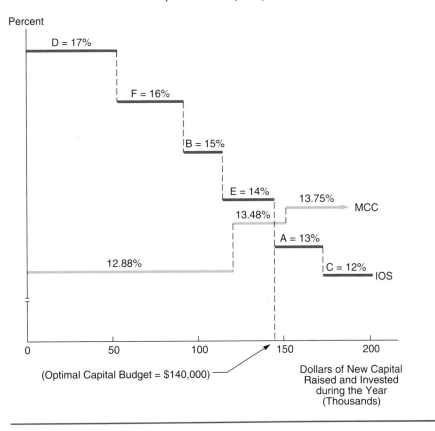

The intersection of the IOS and MCC schedules should be noted — in our example the MCC is 13.48 percent at that point. If the firm uses 13.48 percent to evaluate all projects, then Projects D, F, B, and E will be accepted, whereas A and C will be rejected. *Thus, the cost of capital used in the capital budgeting process as discussed in Chapter 14 is actually determined at the intersection of the IOS and MCC schedules.* If this intersection rate is used, the firm will make correct accept/reject decisions, and its level of financing and investment will be optimal. If it uses any other rate, its capital budget will not be optimal. A lower rate will cause too many projects to be accepted (by the NPV or IRR methods), while a higher rate will cause too few projects to be accepted.

Self-Test

Explain what the MCC and the IOS schedules are and how they are used to determine a firm's cost of capital.

How is the firm's cost of capital used in the capital budgeting process?

DIVISIONAL COSTS OF CAPITAL

In Chapter 15 we learned that capital budgeting can affect a firm's beta risk, its within-firm risk, or both. We also saw that it is exceedingly difficult to quantify either effect. In other words, although it may be possible to reach the general conclusion that one project is riskier than another (in either the beta or the within-firm sense), it is difficult to develop a really good measure of project risk. Further, this lack of precision in measuring project risk makes it difficult to specify risk-adjusted rates of return, or project costs of capital, with which to evaluate individual projects. It is generally agreed, however, that riskier projects should be evaluated with a higher cost of capital than the overall corporate cost, whereas for lower-risk projects a lower cost of capital should be used. Unfortunately, there is no good way of specifying exactly how much higher or lower these cost rates should be; given the present state of the art, risk adjustments are necessarily judgmental, and somewhat arbitrary.

Debt effects must also be taken into account. For example, one division may own a substantial amount of real estate, which is well suited as collateral for loans, whereas another division may have most of its capital tied up in special-purpose machinery, which is not good collateral. As a result, the division with the real estate may have a higher *debt capacity* than the machinery division. In this case, the first division might calculate its overall, or weighted average, cost of capital using a higher debt ratio than the second division.

risk-adjusted discount rate
The discount rate that applies to a particular risky stream of cash flows; the firm's or division's cost of capital, WACC, plus a risk premium appropriate to the level of risk attached to a particular project's income stream.

Although the process is not exact, Precision Associates (and many other companies) develops **risk-adjusted discount rates** for use in capital budgeting in a two-step process: (1) divisional costs of capital are established for each of the major operating divisions on the basis of the divisions' estimated risk and capital structures, and (2) within each division, all projects are classified into three categories — high risk, average risk, and low risk. Each of PA's divisions then uses its basic divisional cost of capital as the discount rate for average-risk projects, reduces the discount rate by one percentage point when evaluating low-risk projects, and raises the rate by two percentage points for high-risk projects.

For example, if a division's basic cost of capital is estimated to be 10 percent, a 12 percent discount rate would be used for high-risk projects and a 9 percent rate for low-risk ones. Average-risk projects, which constitute about 80 percent of most of its divisions' capital budgets, would be evaluated at the 10 percent divisional cost of capital. This procedure is not very elegant, but at least it recognizes that different divisions have different characteristics and hence different costs of capital, and it acknowledges differential project riskiness within divisions. PA's financial staff believes that these adjustments are in the right direction and that they result in better decisions than would be obtained if no adjustments were made.

Self-Test

How are risk-adjusted discount rates used to incorporate project risk into the capital budgeting decision process?

Briefly explain the two-step process many companies use to develop risk-adjusted discount rates for use in capital budgeting.

 SMALL BUSINESS

The Real Costs of Going Public

In Chapter 17, we discussed some of the costs of going public, including the underwriter's discount (or commission) and the other cash expenses in public offerings. As we explained in Chapter 17's Small Business section, initial public offerings (IPOs) of common stock are generally underpriced, and that underpricing is an additional cost of going public. Furthermore, some underwriters ask for and obtain warrants allowing them to buy, at a future date, some of the issuer's shares at a lower price than the stock's initial market price. Such warrants represent another cost. Finally, some nonquantifiable costs are involved in going public. In this section, we will describe these additional costs of the public offering.

IPOs are typically underpriced, and Professor Jay Ritter has argued that such underpricing is itself a cost of going public.[10] Consider this example: Suppose your firm sold shares to the public at a price of $10 and those shares rose to $15 in the immediate aftermarket. You have sold shares worth $15 for only $10, so, in es-

sence, you have discounted your shares by one-third. If you only counted the underwriter's commission and other cash expenses, you would be severely understating the cost of your public offering. Ritter's analysis takes this into account.

Ritter examines underpricing, underwriters' commissions, and other cash expenses, and he calculates the total cost of going public, including these three sources of cost. However, rather than looking at these costs as a fraction of gross proceeds (as in Chapter 17), he looks at costs as a fraction of the realized market values of the equities. To explain, consider again the example of the $10 IPO stock that rose to a market value of $15. If the underwriter's commission was 10% (of the $10 offered price) and cash expenses were 6% (again, of this $10), then the total costs were: $5.00 Underpricing + $1.00 Commission + $0.60 Cash expenses = $6.60. Since the stock had a market value of $15, then the total costs of going public were $6.60/$15 = 44% of the market value. Ignoring underpricing, and computing cost only on the basis of the offered price, the cost would have been calculated as just 16% instead of the more realistic 44%.

[10]Jay R. Ritter, "The Costs of Going Public," *Journal of Financial Economics,* 19(2) (December 1987), pp. 269–283.

By computing the costs of going public in his own way, Ritter found that the average total cost of going public was 21.22% for firm commitment offers and 31.87% for best-efforts offers. It was not surprising that the costs of the best-efforts offers were higher (on a percentage basis), because they involved smaller offers by riskier, less-established firms. As indicated in Chapter 17, the costs were much higher for smaller offerings than for larger offerings.

The breakdown into best-efforts versus firm commitment offerings was useful in Ritter's analysis in another way as well. He argued that an additional factor to consider is the possibility that an offer might fail entirely. Underwritten offers are in essence guaranteed against failure. In a best-efforts offering, however, the offering is "called off" if the offering does not achieve a minimum number of sales as stated in the prospectus. Ritter found that nearly half (47%) of the best-efforts offerings in a sample failed entirely. An additional cost to consider, therefore, is that the firm may not receive any funds, in spite of having invested considerable effort in preparing for an offering. If the funds to be raised in the offering are necessary for the business's survival, then using a best-efforts offering presents a serious risk to the firm.

Barry, Muscarella, and Vetsuypens (BMV) examined public offerings in which the underwriter was paid, in part, through the receipt of warrants to buy the issuer's stock.[11] Such warrants, called underwriter warrants (UWs), enable the underwriter to buy a fixed number of shares of the issuer's stock at a fixed price over a number of years, usually five. (Chapter 18 provided some details about warrants.) BMV found that these warrants themselves have values almost as high as the explicit commissions paid to the underwriters. These warrants also present a problem for the issuer. If the underwriter underprices the issue by a large amount, then the warrants the underwriter holds will be more valuable. There is, therefore, an incentive for the underwriter to price the issue too low. Evidence from the sample examined by BMV, for example, shows that among offerings through the lowest tier of underwriters, issues with UWs had average underpricing (measured by initial returns) of nearly 65%, while offerings through the lowest tier of underwriters without UWs had an average underpricing (measured by initial returns) of only 5%. Thus, the issuer should be careful about the decision to use UWs in a public offering.

Some additional costs of going public also exist. One obvious cost involves the issuer's requirement to do a "road show" before the offering. In this road show, the CEO and/or some other key representatives of the issuing company spend six weeks or more traveling and talking with investor groups and telling the company's story. This road show, therefore, represents a real loss of productive time for the company.

Also, the public company has a serious reporting responsibility, since it must file quarterly and annual reports with the Securities and Exchange Commission and provide material information to investors. Any failure to report, or reporting incorrect information, exposes the officers, directors, and the corporation to possible securities litigation. In fact, some authors contend that a motivation for underpricing an IPO is to make sure that the stock price doesn't fall in the aftermarket and trigger investor lawsuits against the firm. Such drops in stock price often trigger investor or lawyer searches to try to ascertain whether the company failed to report or reported inaccurately. Such information could then serve as the basis for a lawsuit. Directors' and officers' insurance against such lawsuits is, consequently, becoming very expensive.

In general, the cost of going public includes many elements, and it is much greater than it would appear from an evaluation of only the commissions paid to underwriters and the other cash expenses of the offering. For many firms, the costs of going public at an early stage in their existence, when there are still many risks, are simply too high in relation to other alternative sources of financing.

[11]Christopher B. Barry, Chris J. Muscarella, and Michael R. Vetsuypens, "Underwriter Warrants, Underwriter Compensation and the Costs of Going Public," Working paper, Texas Christian University and Southern Methodist University, 1990.

SUMMARY

This chapter showed how the MCC schedule is developed and then used in the capital budgeting process. The key concepts covered are listed below:

- The cost of capital to be used in capital budgeting decisions is the **weighted average** of the various types of capital the firm uses, typically debt, preferred stock, and common equity.

- The **component cost of debt** is the **after-tax** cost of new debt. It is found by multiplying the cost of new debt by $(1 - t)$, where t is the firm's marginal tax rate: $k_d(1 - t)$.

- The **component cost of preferred stock** is calculated as the preferred dividend divided by the net issuing price, where the net issuing price is the price the firm receives after deducting flotation costs: $k_p = D_p/P_n$.

- The **cost of common equity** is the cost of retained earnings as long as the firm has retained earnings, but the cost of equity becomes the cost of new common stock once the firm has exhausted its retained earnings.

- The **cost of retained earnings** is the rate of return required by stockholders on the firm's common stock, and it can be estimated using one (or all) of three methods: (1) the **dividend-yield-plus-growth-rate,** or **DCF, approach,** (2) the **CAPM approach,** and (3) the **bond-yield-plus-risk-premium approach.**

- To use the **dividend-yield-plus-growth-rate approach,** also called the **DCF approach,** one adds the firm's expected growth rate to its expected dividend yield: $k_s = D_1/P_0 + g$.

- To use the **CAPM approach,** one (1) estimates the firm's beta, (2) multiplies this beta by the market risk premium to determine the firm's risk premium, and (3) adds the firm's risk premium to the risk-free rate to obtain the firm's cost of retained earnings: $k_s = k_{RF} + (k_M - k_{RF})b_i$.

- The **bond-yield-plus-risk-premium approach** requires one to add a risk premium of from 3 to 5 percentage points to the firm's interest rate on long-term debt: $k_s = $ Bond rate $+ RP$.

- The **cost of new common equity** is higher than the cost of retained earnings because the firm must incur **flotation expenses** to sell stock. To find the cost of new common equity, the stock price is first reduced by the flotation expense, next the dividend yield is calculated on the basis of the price the firm will actually receive, and then the expected growth rate is added to this **adjusted dividend yield:** $k_e = D_1/[P_0(1 - F)] + g$.

- Each firm has an **optimal capital structure,** defined as that mix of debt, preferred stock, and common equity which minimizes the firm's **weighted average cost of capital (WACC):**

$$k_a = WACC = w_dk_d(1- t) + w_pk_p + w_s(k_s \text{ or } k_e).$$

- The **marginal cost of capital (MCC)** is defined as the cost of the last dollar of new capital that the firm raises. The MCC increases as the firm raises more and more capital during a given period. A graph of the MCC plotted against dollars raised is the **MCC schedule.**
- A **break point** will occur in the MCC schedule each time the cost of one of the capital components increases.
- The **investment opportunity schedule (IOS)** is a graph of the firm's investment opportunities, with the projects having the highest internal rates of return plotted first.
- The MCC schedule is combined with the IOS schedule, and the intersection defines the **firm's cost of capital,** which is used to evaluate average-risk capital budgeting projects.

The concepts developed in this chapter are extended in Chapter 20, where we consider the effect of the capital structure on the cost of capital.

EQUATIONS

A project's required cash flow after operating expenses is equal to the amount of financing times the required return of each financing source:

$$\text{Required cash flow} = \text{Required after-tax return on debt} \times \text{Amount of debt} + \text{Required return on preferred} \times \text{Amount of preferred}$$
$$+ \text{Required return on common equity} \times \text{Amount of common equity} \,.$$

The minimum acceptable rate of return on a project can be determined as follows:

$$\text{Minimum acceptable rate of return} = \frac{\text{Required cash flow}}{\text{Investment}} \,.$$

The after-tax component cost of debt used in the WACC is calculated as

$$k_d(1 - t) \tag{19-1}$$

The component cost of preferrred stock used in the WACC is calculated as

$$k_p = D_p/P_n. \tag{19-2}$$

In this chapter we used three approaches for measuring k_s, the cost of equity:

DCF Approach. $\hat{k}_s = D_1/P_0 + g.$

CAPM Approach. $k_s = k_{RF} + (k_M - k_{RF})b_i.$

Bond-Yield-plus-Risk-Premium Approach. $k_s = \text{Bond rate} + \text{Risk premium}.$

The component cost of newly issued common stock, or external equity, k_e, used in the WACC, is calculated as

$$k_e = \frac{D_1}{P_0(1 - F)} + g. \qquad (19\text{-}3)$$

The weighted average cost of capital, which should be used in evaluating capital budgeting projects, is calculated as follows:

$$\text{WACC} = w_d k_d(1 - t) + w_p k_p + w_s k_s. \qquad (19\text{-}4)$$

The general formula for calculating a jump, or break, in the MCC schedule can be written in the following form:

$$\text{Break point} = \frac{\text{Total amount of lower-cost capital of a given type}}{\text{Fraction of this type of capital in the capital structure}}. \qquad (19\text{-}5)$$

 RESOLUTION TO DECISION IN FINANCE

Cost-of-Capital Punishment

Citicorp believes its road to foreign success will be paved with consumer loans. Throughout the 1980s, the bank's foreign loans to individuals increased from 14 percent to 45 percent, while its overseas corporate loans declined by 8 percent. Returns on loans to big corporate borrowers are minimal, so Citicorp has restricted its efforts in this market. Citicorp's consumer push is particularly strong in Asia and the Pacific, where it currently has 83 deposit-taking branches. It hopes to add five more annually in Japan to the nine it already has (five in Tokyo and one each in Kobe, Nagoya, Osaka, and Yokohama). Twenty more branches are planned in South Korea, where it currently has five. Although China continues to bar foreign banks from accepting local deposits, Citicorp has expressed its willingness to enter that market. Finally, the bank plans to invest heavily in automated teller machines around the world, and in regional computer centers to process transactions faster.

Sources: Gary Hector, "Why U.S. Banks Are in Retreat" and Ford S. Worthy, "No Pullback for Citicorp," *Fortune,* May 7, 1990.

In addition to recruiting "mom-and-pop" borrowers, Citicorp plans to appeal to Asian businesses with fee services, such as arranging debt-for-equity trades in parts of the world, like Latin America, where Asian banks are not yet established. The bank is also using technology to gain an edge. One project is a new program that allows corporate treasurers anywhere in Asia to manage cash from their desktop computers — they can open letters of credit, monitor account balances around the region, and even shift surplus cash into different currencies.

Some competitors call Citicorp's foreign policy, at least in Japan, suicidal, primarily because of the high costs of doing business in that country ($4 million a year in rent per branch is not unusual). The bank's consumer services head in Japan responds, "Sure, it's expensive to do business here, but it's like the oil business. You go where oil is, and Japan is where money is."

Even if Citicorp does hold on (and it *is* attracting new overseas business), what effect will the retreat of most big banks from overseas have on the U.S. economy? For one thing, the expertise of U.S. banks in some areas of international lending will decline, making it hard for small U.S. companies to get advice on planned foreign expansions. Also, with loans to foreign governments now virtually eliminated because of the low returns and big risks, U.S. banks will not be able to help finance the United States' economic policies in other countries — an embarrassment for U.S. officials and policymakers.

The only solution seems to involve changing behavior in both the United States and Japan. The Japanese have to open their markets, and the United States has to become more competitive in world markets to boost exports and reduce imports, and thus reduce the huge foreign trade deficit which puts so much money in the hands of foreign banks. At the same time, such action would help boost the U.S. savings rate, so the cost of loans could be lowered. Short of that, banks are lobbying for broader powers — for instance, the power to sell insurance and securities at home as well as abroad. "We can't change the fact that foreigners can raise capital more cheaply," says a former Citicorp vice chairman, "but at least we can give U.S. banks equal flexibility in how they use their capital." Note, though, that the savings and loans made similar statements in the 1960s and 1970s, and that their broader powers contributed to the S&L debacle of the 1980s. Clearly, it is better to "cure the disease" than to "treat the symptoms."

QUESTIONS

19-1 In what sense does the marginal cost of capital (MCC) schedule represent a series of average costs?

19-2 How would each of the following affect a firm's cost of debt, $k_d(1 - t)$; its cost of equity, k_s; and its weighted average cost of capital, WACC? Indicate by a plus ($+$), a minus ($-$), or a zero (0) if the factor would raise, lower, or have an indeterminate effect on the items in question. Assume other things are held constant. Be prepared to justify your answer, but recognize that several of the parts probably have no single correct answer; these questions are designed to stimulate thought and discussion.

	Effect on		
	$k_d(1 - t)$	k_s	WACC
a. The corporate tax rate is lowered.	____	____	____
b. The Federal Reserve tightens credit.	____	____	____
c. The dividend payout ratio is increased.	____	____	____
d. The firm doubles the amount of capital it raises during the year.	____	____	____
e. The firm expands into a risky new area.	____	____	____
f. The firm merges with another firm whose earnings are countercyclical both to those of the first firm and to the stock market.	____	____	____
g. The stock market falls drastically, and the firm's stock falls along with the rest.	____	____	____
h. Investors become more risk averse.	____	____	____
i. The firm is an electric utility with a large investment in nuclear plants. Several states propose a ban on nuclear power generation.	____	____	____

19-3 Suppose a firm estimates its MCC and IOS schedules for the coming year and finds that they intersect at the point 10%, $10 million. What cost of capital should be used to evaluate average-risk projects, high-risk projects, and low-risk projects?

SELF-TEST PROBLEM

ST-1 L. H. Clore, Inc., has the following capital structure, which it considers to be optimal:

Debt	25%
Preferred stock	15
Common equity	60
	100%

Clore's expected net income this year is $171,428.60; its established dividend payout ratio is 30 percent; its federal-plus-state tax rate is 40 percent; and investors expect earnings and dividends to grow at a constant rate of 9 percent in the future. Clore paid a dividend of $3.60 per share last year. Its stock currently sells at a price of $60 per share.

Clore can obtain new capital in the following ways:

- *Common:* New common stock would have a flotation cost of 10 percent for up to $60,000 of new stock and of 20 percent for all common over $60,000.

- *Preferred:* New preferred can be sold to the public at a price of $100 per share, with a dividend of $11. However, flotation costs of $5 per share will be incurred for up to $37,500 of preferred, rising to $10, or 10 percent, on all preferred over $37,500.

- *Debt:* Up to $25,000 of debt can be sold at an interest rate of 12 percent; debt in the range of $25,001 to $50,000 must carry an interest rate of 14 percent; and all debt over $50,000 will have an interest rate of 16 percent.

Clore has the following investment opportunities:

Project	Cost at t = 0	Annual Net Cash Flow	Project Life (Years)	IRR
A	$ 50,000	$10,956	7	12.0%
B	50,000	15,772	5	17.4
C	50,000	10,851	8	14.2
D	100,000	18,947	10	13.7
E	100,000	27,139	6	

a. Find the break points in the MCC schedule.
b. Determine the cost of each capital structure component.
c. Calculate the weighted average cost of capital in the interval between each break in the MCC schedule.
d. Calculate the IRR for Project E.
e. Construct a graph showing the MCC and IOS schedules.
f. Which projects should L. H. Clore accept?

PROBLEMS

19-1   **After-tax cost of debt.** Calculate the after-tax cost of debt under each of the following conditions:
  a. Interest rate = 11%; tax rate = 0 percent.
  b. Interest rate = 11%; tax rate = 34 percent.
  c. Interest rate = 11%; tax rate = 40 percent.
  d. Interest rate = 11%; tax rate = 60 percent.

19-2   **After-tax cost of debt.** Juarez Enterprises can sell a bond with a 12.5 percent coupon. Analysts believe the company can sell the bond at a price that will provide a yield to maturity of 12.5 percent. If the tax rate is 40 percent, what is the firm's after-tax cost of debt?

19-3   **Cost of debt.** Wachowicz Corporation has a 10 percent, $1,000 par bond issue outstanding with 15 years left to maturity.
  a. If investors require a 12 percent return (yield to maturity), what is the current market price of the bond?
  b. If the company wishes to sell a new issue of equal-risk bonds at par, what coupon rate will the investors require?

19-4   **Cost of preferred stock.** Midwest Electric & Gas plans to issue some $50 par value preferred stock with a 13 percent dividend. To issue the stock, the utility must pay flotation costs of 8 percent to the investment bankers. What is the cost of capital for this preferred stock?

19-5   **Cost of preferred stock.** Fanara Group, Inc., plans to issue some $100 par preferred stock with a 12 percent dividend. The stock is selling on the market for $97.00, and Fanara must pay flotation costs of 10 percent of the market price.
  a. What is the cost of preferred stock to Fanara?
  b. If the firm's tax rate is 40 percent, what is the after-tax component cost of preferred stock to Fanara?

19-6   **Cost of debt.** Austin-Murphy Publishing has a bond issue outstanding with the following financial characteristics: 14 percent coupon; 5 years to maturity; $1,000 par value; and $1,200 current market price.
  a. Using the formula found in Footnote 10 of Chapter 16, calculate the bond's approximate yield to maturity.
  b. With the information obtained in Part a, determine the bond's exact yield to maturity.
  c. What is the relationship between the yield to maturity on outstanding bonds and the cost of debt for new debt securities the firm wishes to issue?

19-7   **Cost of retained earnings.** E. F. Dunham and Associates paid a dividend of $5.00 per share recently; that is, $D_0 = \$5.00$. The company's stock sells for $71.42 per share. The expected growth rate is 10 percent. Calculate Dunham's cost of retained earnings.

19-8   **Cost of retained earnings.** Ohio Athleticwear's EPS 5 years ago was $2.60; its EPS today is $4.00. The company pays out 35 percent of its earnings as dividends, and the firm's stock sells for $19.12.
  a. Calculate the firm's growth rate. (Assume that the growth rate and payout rate have been constant over the 5-year period.)
  b. Calculate the expected dividend, D_1. (Note: $D_0 = 0.35(\$4.00) = \$1.40$.) Assume that the payout rate and past growth rate will continue into the foreseeable future.
  c. What is the cost of retained earnings for the firm?

19-9 **Cost of retained earnings.** The risk-free rate is 9 percent and the required return on an average-risk security in the market is 13 percent. Calculate the firm's cost of retained earnings if the following conditions occur:

a. Beta = 1.5.

b. Beta = 0.6.

c. Beta = 1.0.

19-10 **Cost of retained earnings.** The earnings, dividends, and stock price of Sunshine State, Inc., are expected to grow at a rate of 5 percent into the foreseeable future. Sunshine's common stock sells for $28.00 per share, and its last dividend, D_0, was $2.40.

a. Using the discounted cash flow (DCF) approach, what is the firm's cost of retained earnings?

b. The firm's beta is 1.4, the risk-free rate is 8 percent, and the average return in the market is 12 percent. What is the firm's cost of retained earnings as computed by the CAPM approach?

c. If Sunshine State's bonds yield 10.5 percent, what is k_s, according to the bond-yield-plus-risk-premium approach?

d. Based on the results in Parts a through c, what would you estimate Sunshine State's cost of retained earnings to be?

19-11 **Cost of equity.** Rodriguez Industries' last dividend was $2.00, its growth rate is 6 percent (which is expected to continue at a constant rate), and the stock now sells for $23.56. New stock can be sold to net the firm $21.91 after flotation costs.

a. What is Rodriguez Industries' cost of retained earnings?

b. What is Rodriguez Industries' percentage flotation cost, F?

c. What is Rodriguez Industries' cost of new common stock, k_e?

19-12 **Return on common stock.** Detroit Motors' common stock is currently selling for $41.25 per share. The firm is expected to earn $7.50 and to pay a year-end dividend of $4.125. The firm's return on assets is 6 percent, but 60 percent of its assets are financed with debt.

a. What is the firm's return on equity (ROE)?

b. What is the firm's expected growth rate? (*Hint:* g = b(ROE), where b = the fraction of earnings that are retained. See Footnote 8.)

c. What is the firm's cost of equity capital?

19-13 **Cost of equity.** You have been hired as the treasurer of Stendardi Resources. The firm's president has asked you to compute the firm's cost of capital. You have gathered all pertinent financial data to make the calculations. Stendardi's EPS this year will be $5.00, whereas 7 years ago EPS was $1.40. The firm's expected dividend, D_1, will be $2.75, and Stendardi's market price is $30.50. The risk-free rate is 7 percent, and the return on an average security is 13 percent. Stendardi's beta is 1.5. Its bond issue is currently selling to yield investors 11 percent to maturity.

a. Using all three approaches, calculate the firm's cost of equity capital.

b. What conclusions can be drawn from your calculations? What is your best estimate of Stendardi Resources' cost of equity capital? Explain your findings to the firm's president, Ed Stendardi.

19-14 **Break point calculations.** Pier 39 Imports, Inc., expects earnings of $10 million next year. Its dividend payout ratio is 30 percent, and its debt/assets ratio is 40 percent. The firm uses no preferred stock.

a. How much will the firm pay in dividends next year?

b. What amount of additional retained earnings does the firm expect next year?

c. At what amount of total equity financing will there be a break point in the MCC schedule because of an increase in the component cost of equity?

d. The firm can borrow $7.5 million at an interest rate of 10 percent, but additional borrowing up to $12.5 million will require a rate of 12 percent, and above $12.5 million, additional debt will cost 15 percent. At what points will rising debt costs cause breaks in the MCC schedule?

19-15   **Required cash flow.** Barenbaum Electronics is making final calculations on the purchase of a new production assembler. The equipment is valued at $1,000,000. It will be in service for 5 years and will be depreciated at $200,000 annually. (Assume straight-line depreciation is allowed.) There is no salvage value. Additional annual costs include the following:

Labor	$125,000
Materials	166,667
Building lease	100,000
Overhead	41,667

If all costs are constant during the 5-year period, what is the minimum level of sales that will allow Barenbaum to earn at least its 14 percent cost of capital? Barenbaum's marginal tax rate is 40 percent.

19-16   **Weighted average cost of capital.** The Dorfman Company has the following capital structure, which is considered optimal:

Debt	$120,000
Preferred stock	45,000
Common stock equity	135,000
Total liabilities and equity	$300,000

The cost of debt is 11 percent, the cost of preferred stock is 13 percent, and the cost of equity is 16 percent. The firm's marginal tax rate is 34 percent. What is Dorfman's cost of capital?

19-17   **Optimal capital budget.** Silvers Inc., has a debt ratio of 25 percent. Management has concluded that this capital structure is optimal. Silvers has analyzed its investment opportunities for the coming year and has identified 4 possible additions to assets which generate IRRs greater than zero.

Investment	Size	IRR
A	$ 6 million	16.2%
B	12 million	15.3
C	12 million	14.1
D	6 million	13.0

Silvers is forecasting net income for the coming year of $15 million and expects to pay out 40 percent in dividends to the 1 million outstanding shares of common stock. The earnings have been growing at a constant rate of 8 percent over the past few years, and this rate is expected to continue indefinitely. If Silvers has to sell new common stock, it will be faced with flotation costs of 15 percent (current market price = $75 per share). Any debt that is raised, up to $7.5 million, will require a coupon rate of 8 percent. However, if the total debt required is greater than $7.5 million, the coupon rate will have to be 10 percent. The marginal tax rate is 34 percent. How large will the capital budget be if all investments with IRR > MCC are accepted?

19-18 **Optimal capital budget.** Hettenhouse Publishers has the following (independent) investment opportunities:

	Annual Cost	Cash Inflows	Life (Years)
Project A	$ 5,000	$1,456	5
Project B	12,000	2,252	9
Project C	10,000	1,874	8

The optimal capital structure calls for financing all projects with 60 percent common equity and 40 percent debt. If the following information applies to the future financial position of Hettenhouse Publishers, in which of the projects (if any) should it invest and what is the firm's capital budget? The last dividend (D_0) was $3.50. The growth rate of earnings and dividends is 6 percent. The current price per share of common stock is $46. If new common stock is issued, a flotation cost of 5 percent will be incurred. The company can raise as much debt as it wants at a coupon rate of 12 percent. The firm's dividend payout ratio is 30 percent, and it is in a 40 percent tax bracket. Hettenhouse Publishers earned $15,000 last year after taxes.

19-19 **Optimal capital budget.** Walker Corporation expects to earn $50,000 before taxes this year. Its tax rate is 35 percent and the dividend payout ratio is 40 percent. The company can raise debt at a 12 percent (before-tax) cost for any amount of debt up to $10,000. However, a 15 percent rate will apply to all debt if the company raises more than $10,000. The cost of retained earnings has been calculated to be 13 percent, and the cost of new common stock is 13.5 percent. Walker has the opportunity to invest in the following projects:

Project	Cost	Annual Cash Inflows	Life (Years)
A	$10,000	$ 2,774	5
B	14,000	3,264	7
C	50,000	10,346	10

The company will finance all capital expenditures with 30 percent debt and 70 percent common equity. In which projects should Walker invest? What is Walker's capital budget?

19-20 **Marginal cost of capital.** Grunewald Manufacturing's earnings per share have been growing at a steady 7 percent during the last 10 years. The firm's stock, 500,000 shares outstanding, is now selling for $80 a share, and the expected dividend for next year, D_1, is $7.20. The firm pays out 48 percent of its earnings in dividends. The current interest rate on new debt is 12 percent. The firm's marginal tax rate is 40 percent. The firm's capital structure, considered to be optimal, is as follows:

Debt	$ 5,000,000
Common equity	5,000,000
Total liabilities and equity	$10,000,000

a. Calculate the after-tax cost of new debt and the cost of common equity, assuming that new equity comes only from retained earnings. Because the historical growth rate is expected to continue, we may calculate the cost of equity as $\hat{k}_s = D_1/P_0 + g$.

b. Find the marginal cost of capital, again assuming that no new common stock is to be sold.

c. If this year's addition to retained earnings is $3.9 million, how much can be spent for capital investments before external equity must be sold? (*Hint:* Calculate the retained earnings break point.)

d. What is the marginal cost of capital (cost of funds raised in excess of the amount calculated in Part c) if new common stock can be sold to the public at $80 a share to net the firm $72 a share after flotation costs? The cost of debt is constant.

19-21   **Optimal capital budget.** On January 1 the total assets of Visscher Printing were $35 million. During the year the company plans to raise and invest $15 million. The firm's present capital structure, shown below (in thousands), is considered to be optimal. Assume that there is no short-term debt.

Debt	$14,000
Common equity	21,000
Total liabilities and equity	$35,000

New bonds will have an 11 percent coupon rate and will be sold at par. Common stock, currently selling at $50 a share, can be sold to net the company $42.50 a share. The stockholders' required rate of return is estimated to be 15 percent, consisting of a dividend yield of 6 percent and an expected growth rate of 9 percent. (The next expected dividend is $3, so $3/$50 = 6%.) Retained earnings for the year are estimated to be $3 million (ignore depreciation). The marginal corporate tax rate is 40 percent.

a. Assuming that all asset expansion (gross expenditures for fixed assets plus related working capital) is included in the capital budget, what is the dollar amount of the capital budget? (Ignore depreciation.)

b. To maintain the present capital structure, how much of the capital budget must be financed by common equity?

c. How much of the needed new common equity funds will be generated internally? Externally?

d. Calculate the cost of each of the common equity components.

e. At what level of capital expenditures will there be a break in the MCC schedule?

f. Calculate the MCC **(1)** below and **(2)** above the break in the schedule.

g. Plot the MCC schedule. Also, draw in an investment opportunity schedule that is consistent with both the MCC schedule and the projected capital budget. Any IOS that is consistent will do.

■ 19-22   **Optimal capital budget.** EFB Group has the following capital structure, which it considers to be optimal under present and forecasted conditions:

Debt (long-term only)	40%
Common equity	60
Total liabilities and equity	100%

For the coming year, management expects after-tax earnings of $2.4 million. EFB's past dividend policy of paying out 60 percent of earnings will continue. Present commitments from its banker will allow EFB to borrow according to the following schedule:

Loan Amount	Interest Rate
$0 to $750,000	9% on this increment of debt
$750,001 to $1,350,000	11% on this increment of debt
$1,350,001 and above	13% on this increment of debt

The company's average tax rate is 40 percent, the current market price of its stock is $48 per share, its *last* dividend was $4.57 per share, and the expected growth rate is 5 percent. External equity (new common) can be sold at a flotation cost of 10 percent.
EFB has the following investment opportunities for the next year:

Project	Cost	Annual Cash Flows	Project Life (Years)	IRR
1	$ 900,000	$186,210	10	
2	1,200,000	316,904	6	15.0%
3	500,000	303,644	2	
4	750,000	246,926	4	12.0
5	1,000,000	194,322	8	11.0

Management asks you to help determine which projects (if any) should be undertaken. You proceed with this analysis by answering the following questions as posed in a logical sequence:

a. How many breaks are there in the MCC schedule?

b. At what dollar amounts do the breaks occur, and what causes them?

c. What is the weighted average cost of capital, WACC, in each of the intervals between the breaks?

d. What are the IRR values for Projects 1 and 3?

e. Graph the IOS and MCC schedules.

f. Which projects should EFB's management accept?

g. What assumptions about project risk are implicit in this problem? If you learned that Projects 1, 2, and 3 were of above-average risk, yet EFB chose the projects that you indicated in Part f, how would this affect the situation?

h. The problem stated that EFB pays out 60 percent of its earnings as dividends. In words, how would the analysis change if the payout ratio were changed to zero, to 100 percent, or somewhere in between? If you are using the computerized problem diskette, reanalyze the firm's capital budgeting decision using dividend payout ratios of zero, 100 percent, and 40 percent.

(Do Parts i through l only if you are using the computerized problem diskette.)

i. Suppose EFB's tax rate fell to zero, with other variables remaining constant. How would that affect the MCC schedule and the capital budget?

j. Return the tax rate to 40 percent. Now assume that the debt ratio is increased to 65 percent, causing all interest rates to rise by 1 percentage point, to 10 percent, 12 percent, and 14 percent, and causing g to increase from 5 percent to 6 percent. What happens to the MCC schedule and the capital budget?

k. New information becomes available. Change the Part j scenario to assume earnings of only $1,000,000 but a growth rate of 9 percent. How does that affect the capital budget?

l. Would it be reasonable to use the model to analyze the effects of a change in the payout ratio without changing other variables?

SOLUTION TO SELF-TEST PROBLEM

ST-1   **a.** A break point will occur each time a low-cost type of capital is used up. We establish the break points as follows, after first noting that Clore has $120,000 of retained earnings:

$$\text{Retained earnings} = (\text{Total earnings})(1.0 - \text{Payout})$$

$$= \$171{,}428.60(0.7)$$

$$= \$120{,}000.$$

$$\text{Break point} = \frac{\text{Total amount of low-cost capital of a given type}}{\text{Fraction of this type of capital in the capital structure (weight)}}.$$

Capital Used Up	Break Point Calculation		Break Number
Retained earnings	$BP_{RE} = \dfrac{\$120{,}000}{0.60}$	$= \$200{,}000$	2
10% flotation common	$BP_{10\%E} = \dfrac{\$120{,}000 + \$60{,}000}{0.60}$	$= \$300{,}000$	4
5% flotation preferred	$BP_{5\%P} = \dfrac{\$37{,}500}{0.15}$	$= \$250{,}000$	3
12% debt	$BP_{12\%D} = \dfrac{\$25{,}000}{0.25}$	$= \$100{,}000$	1
14% debt	$BP_{14\%D} = \dfrac{\$25{,}000 + \$25{,}000}{0.25}$	$= \$200{,}000$	2

A summary of the break points follows:

1. There are three common equity costs, and hence two changes, and, therefore, two equity-induced breaks in the MCC. There are two preferred costs and hence one preferred break. There are three debt costs and hence two debt breaks.

2. The numbers in the third column of the table above designate the sequential order of the breaks, determined after all the break points were calculated. Note that the second debt break and the break for retained earnings both occur at $200,000.

3. The first break point occurs at $100,000, when the 12 percent debt is used up. The second break point, $200,000, results from using up both retained earnings and the 14 percent debt. The MCC curve also rises at $250,000 and $300,000 as preferred stock with a 5 percent flotation cost and common stock with a 10 percent flotation cost, respectively, are used up.

b. Component costs within indicated total capital intervals are as follows: Retained earnings (used in interval $0 to $200,000):

$$\hat{k}_s = \frac{D_1}{P_0} + g = \frac{D_0(1 + g)}{P_0} + g$$

$$= \frac{\$3.60(1.09)}{\$60} + 0.09$$

$$= 0.0654 + 0.09 = 15.54\%.$$

Common with F = 10% ($200,001 to $300,000):

$$k_e = \frac{D_1}{P_0(1.0 - F)} + g = \frac{\$3.924}{\$60(0.9)} + 9\% = 16.27\%.$$

Common with F = 20% (over $300,000):

$$k_e = \frac{\$3.924}{\$60(0.8)} + 9\% = 17.18\%.$$

Preferred with F = 5% ($0 to $250,000):

$$k_p = \frac{D_p}{P_n} = \frac{\$11}{\$100(0.95)} = 11.58\%.$$

Preferred with F = 10% (over $250,000):

$$k_p = \frac{\$11}{\$100(0.90)} = 12.22\%.$$

Debt at k_d = 12% ($0 to $100,000):

$$k_d(1 - t) = 12\%(0.6) = 7.20\%.$$

Debt at k_d = 14% ($100,001 to $200,000):

$$k_d(1 - t) = 14\%(0.6) = 8.40\%.$$

Debt at k_d = 16% (over $200,000):

$$k_d(1 - t) = 16\%(0.6) = 9.60\%.$$

c. WACC calculations within indicated total capital intervals:
  1. $0 to $100,000 (debt = 7.2%, preferred = 11.58%, and RE = 15.54%):

$$WACC_1 = w_d k_d(1 - t) + w_p k_p + w_s k_s$$

$$= 0.25(7.2\%) + 0.15(11.58\%) + 0.60(15.54\%) = 12.86\%.$$

  2. $100,001 to $200,000 (debt = 8.4%, preferred = 11.58%, and RE = 15.54%):

$$WACC_2 = 0.25(8.4\%) + 0.15(11.58\%) + 0.60(15.54\%) = 13.16\%.$$

  3. $200,001 to $250,000 (debt = 9.6%, preferred = 11.58%, and equity = 16.27%):

$$WACC_3 = 0.25(9.6\%) + 0.15(11.58\%) + 0.60(16.27\%) = 13.90\%.$$

  4. $250,001 to $300,000 (debt = 9.6%, preferred = 12.22%, and equity = 16.27%):

$$WACC_4 = 0.25(9.6\%) + 0.15(12.22\%) + 0.60(16.27\%) = 14.00\%.$$

  5. Over $300,000 (debt = 9.6%, preferred = 12.22%, and equity = 17.18%):

$$WACC_5 = 0.25(9.6\%) + 0.15(12.22\%) + 0.60(17.18\%) = 14.54\%.$$

d. IRR calculation for Project E:

$$PVIFA_{k,6} = \frac{\$100,000}{\$27,139} = 3.6847.$$

This is the factor for 16 percent, so IRR_E = 16%.

MCC and IOS Schedules for L. H. Clore, Inc.

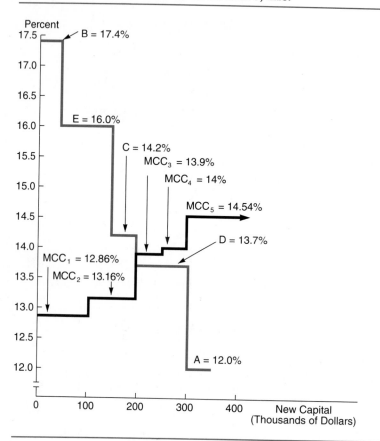

e. See the graph of the MCC and IOS schedules for Clore shown above.

f. Clore clearly should accept Projects B, E, and C. It should reject Projects A and D, because their IRRs do not exceed the marginal costs of funds needed to finance them. The firm's capital budget would total $200,000.

Chapter 20

Leverage and the Target Capital Structure

DECISION IN FINANCE

Getting the Lumps Out

An "aggressive price" is what Gibbons Green van Amerongen, a New York leveraged buyout firm, called its May 1989 payment that beat out five other bidders for acquisition of Ohio Mattress Company, maker of Sealy mattresses. Just three months later, it found that the "bed it had made for itself" was, in fact, not very comfortable.

The deal totaled almost $1 billion, which was one-and-a-half times the manufacturer's sales. Analysts contended at the time that the price was much too high. Edward W. Gibbons, a partner in the buyout firm, responded by saying they expected to recover the cost through improvements in Ohio Mattress and quick expansion overseas. To finance the deal, Gibbons Green planned to sell $475 million in junk bonds. Unfortunately, Gibbons's timing was bad. The economy was slipping, leverage was losing its magic, and investors were suddenly starting to turn away from new issues of junk bonds unless they provided huge yields. Bond defaults

See end of chapter for resolution.

for 1989 were up to $4 billion by August 11, the date when Gibbons Green put the Ohio Mattress bonds on the market. No buyers were interested in the offered yield, which was as high as the company could afford, given its cash flows.

Ohio Mattress had become the largest mattress manufacturer in the United States, under the guidance of long-time CEO Ernest Wuliger, who helped the firm grow, mainly through acquisitions. Wuliger, the largest shareholder, was paid $60 million in the buyout, and the new owners selected Malcolm Candlish, formerly with Samsonite, to replace him.

The company operated for almost a year on a "bridge loan" (a short-term, temporary loan) from First Boston Corporation. The loan was supposed to be paid back from proceeds of (1) the sale of $250 million of bonds, which paid 14.5 percent cash interest, and (2) $225 million of payment-in-kind (PIK) bonds, which were to pay interest of 15.5 percent, but in additional bonds rather than in cash. When no buyers were found for the initial offering, the company patiently waited six months, hoping for a rebound in the junk-bond market. Although many junk offerings had been successful in the past — by one count they have totaled 2,000 issues valued at $200 billion — investors today are wary of these offerings. Although Ohio Mattress was well respected, its cash flow did not cover its interest expense, and its required debt amortization schedule was daunting, so investors bypassed it.

When the bridge loan matured on April 20, 1990, Ohio Mattress (renamed Sealy Corporation, after its major brand) had to pay or face the agreed-upon alternative of exchanging the loan for notes with astronomical 18 and 20 percent interest rates. Giving up on junk bonds, Sealy had to contemplate defaulting and declaring bankruptcy, as so many other highly leveraged companies had been forced to do.

As you read this chapter, consider the problems Sealy and its lenders faced. Was bankruptcy the only viable solution? If not, what alternative financial arrangements might help the firm to avoid it?

In Chapter 19, when we calculated the weighted average cost of capital for capital budgeting purposes, we took the proportions of debt and equity in the capital structure as given. However, changing the proportion of debt and equity in the capital structure influences the firm's risk and thus its cost of capital. Naturally, as the firm's cost of capital changes, the set of acceptable projects will change as well. A lower cost of capital would increase the number of acceptable projects, whereas a higher cost of capital would reduce the set of acceptable projects. The firm's cost of capital is determined by investors' required rates of return, and a change in the riskiness of the firm affects the value of its securities and thereby its value. Therefore, the choice of a capital structure, or the mix of securities the firm uses to finance its assets, has important ramifications for shareholders' wealth.

target capital structure
The mix of debt, preferred stock, and common equity that the firm would like to have in its capital structure.

As we will see, a number of factors must be considered in determining the **target capital structure.** This target may change over time as conditions vary, but at any given moment the firm's management has a specific capital structure in mind, and individual financing decisions should be consistent with this target. If the actual debt ratio is below the target level, expansion capital will probably be raised by issuing debt, whereas if the debt ratio is currently above the target, stock will probably be sold.

Capital structure policy involves a tradeoff between risk and return. Using more debt raises the riskiness of the firm's earnings stream, but a higher debt ratio generally leads to a higher expected rate of return. Higher risk associated with greater debt tends to lower the stock's price, but a higher expected rate of return raises it. *The optimal capital structure strikes a balance between risk and return, such that the price of the stock is maximized, and, simultaneously, the firm's overall cost of capital is minimized.* Because stock price maximization and capital cost minimization occur simultaneously, finding the optimal capital structure can be approached as either a value maximization or a cost minimization problem.

TYPES OF RISK

Throughout this text we have emphasized many different facets of risk. In Chapter 4, we introduced the concept of risk and return, and we indicated that a security's returns are determined by the real risk-free rate of interest plus appropriate risk premiums, which include a *default risk premium*. Then, in Chapter 12, we examined risk from the viewpoint of the individual investor, and we distinguished between *market risk*, which cannot be diversified away and is measured by the beta coefficient, and *total risk*, which includes both market risk *and* an element of risk that can be eliminated by diversification. In Chapter 15 we viewed risk from the firm's viewpoint, considering how capital budgeting decisions affect the riskiness of the firm. There we distinguished between *beta (or market) risk* (the effect of a project on the firm's beta risk) and *within-firm risk* (the effect of the project on the firm's total risk).

Now we introduce two other dimensions of risk: (1) **business risk,** which is the riskiness of the firm's operations that would exist even if the firm used no debt, and (2) **financial risk,** which is the additional risk placed on the common shareholders as a result of the firm's decision to use debt. Conceptually, the firm has a certain amount of risk inherent in its operations; this is its business risk. In the absence of debt in the capital structure, business risk equals total risk. When debt is used, total risk is apportioned, with most risk being allotted to one class of investors — the common stockholders.[1] However, the common stockholders must be compensated by a higher *expected* rate of return.

> **business risk**
> The risk associated with future operating income; the risk that would exist even if the firm's operations were all equity-financed.

> **financial risk**
> The portion of stockholders' risk, over and above the firm's basic business risk, that results from the use of financial leverage.

Self-Test

If the actual debt ratio is below the target capital structure level, how should expansion capital be raised? How should it be raised if the actual debt ratio is above the target level?

In what sense does capital structure policy involve a tradeoff between risk and return?

BUSINESS RISK

The uncertainty associated with forecasting and realizing future **operating income** — earnings before interest and taxes (EBIT) — has been termed *business risk*. The element of uncertainty associated with business risk includes both the chance of not reaching a positive level of operating profits and the

> **operating income**
> Earnings before interest and taxes (EBIT).

---

[1]Using preferred stock also adds to financial risk. To simplify matters somewhat, in this chapter we shall consider only debt and common equity. Also, if a firm uses an especially large amount of debt in a leveraged buyout (LBO), as RJR Nabisco did, then its debt will be classified as junk bonds, and the bondholders will also be exposed to financial risk. Some junk bonds practically amount to equity.

problems associated with fluctuating returns. Year-to-year fluctuations can be caused by many factors — booms or recessions in the national economy, successful new products introduced either by the firm or by its competitors, labor strikes, price controls, changes in the prices of raw materials, or disasters such as fires, floods, and the like.[2]

Business risk varies not only from industry to industry but also among firms within a given industry. Furthermore, business risk can change over time. For example, electric utilities, regarded for years as having little business risk, were affected by a combination of events in the 1970s and 1980s that drastically altered their situation, producing sharp declines in operating income and ROE for some companies, and greatly increasing the industry's business risk. Two examples of "safe" industries that turned out to be risky are the railroads just before automobiles, airplanes, and trucks took away most of their business, and the telegraph business just before telephones came on the scene. Also, numerous individual companies have been hurt, if not destroyed, by antitrust actions, fraud, or just plain bad management. Today food processors and grocery retailers are frequently given as examples of industries with low business risk, whereas cyclical manufacturing industries, such as steel, are regarded as having especially high business risk. Factors other than industry affiliation also play a role in determining business risk. For example, smaller companies, or companies dependent on a single product or customer, are often regarded as having a high degree of business risk.[3]

Business risk depends on a number of factors, the most important of which are the following:

1. Demand variability. The more stable the demand for a firm's products, other things held constant, the lower its business risk.

2. Sales price variability. Firms whose products are sold in highly volatile markets are exposed to more business risk than similar firms whose sales prices are more stable.

3. Input price variability. Firms whose input prices are highly uncertain are exposed to a high degree of business risk.

4. Ability to adjust sales prices for changes in input prices. Some firms are better able to raise their own sales prices when input costs rise than others. The greater the ability to adjust sales prices, the lower the degree of business risk, other things held constant. This factor is especially important during periods of high inflation.

---

[2]The variability in EBIT will be equal to the variability in ROE (and EPS) if the firm uses *no* financial leverage. However, if financial leverage is used, then ROE and EPS are more volatile than EBIT, and the greater the use of leverage, the greater the volatility difference.

[3]Any action which increases business risk will generally increase a firm's beta coefficient, but a part of business risk, as we define it, will generally be company-specific and, hence, subject to elimination through diversification by the firm's stockholders.

5. Changing technology. If a company operates in an industry where technology is changing rapidly, and new products are constantly being brought out, then it will be exposed to a high degree of business risk.

6. The extent to which operating costs are fixed — operating leverage. If a high percentage of a firm's operating costs are fixed, and hence do not decline when demand falls off, this increases the company's business risk. This factor is called *operating leverage,* and it is discussed at length in the next section.

Each of these factors is determined in part by the firm's industry characteristics, but most of them are also controllable to some extent by management. For example, most firms can, through their marketing policies, take actions to stabilize both unit sales and sales prices. However, this stabilization may require firms to make large expenditures on advertising or offer price concessions to induce customers to commit to purchasing fixed quantities at fixed prices in the future. Similarly, firms can reduce the volatility of future input costs by negotiating long-term labor and materials supply contracts, but they may have to agree to pay prices above the current spot price level to obtain these contracts.

Self-Test

Does business risk vary from one industry to another? Explain.

Business risk depends on a number of factors. Briefly identify and explain the most important ones. Can management control these factors? Explain.

OPERATING LEVERAGE

As noted previously, business risk exists even if the firm has no **fixed operating costs.** However, when the firm has some fixed operating expenses, as the majority of firms do, a change in sales results in a greater than proportional change in operating profits and ROE. Business risk is intensified to the extent that a firm builds fixed costs into its operations. If fixed costs are high, even a small decline in sales can lead to a large decline in EBIT and ROE; thus, other things held constant, the higher a firm's fixed operating costs, the greater its business risk. Higher fixed operating costs are generally associated with more highly automated, capital intensive firms and industries. Also, businesses that employ highly skilled workers who must be retained and paid even during business recessions have relatively high fixed costs.

If a high percentage of a firm's total operating costs are fixed, the firm is said to have a high degree of **operating leverage.** In physics, leverage implies the use of a lever to raise a heavy object with a small amount of force. In politics, if individuals have leverage, their smallest word or action can accom-

fixed operating costs
Operating costs that do not vary directly with sales, that is, costs that would exist even if no sales were made. Examples include depreciation and lease payments.

operating leverage
The extent to which fixed costs are used in a firm's operation.

plish a great deal. *In business terminology, a high degree of operating leverage, other things held constant, implies that a relatively small change in sales will result in a large change in operating income and ROE.* The common element in all of these examples is that a small initiating change is followed by a proportionally greater effect.

Figure 20-1 illustrates this concept by comparing the results that All-Technology Manufacturing (ATM) can expect if it uses different degrees of operating leverage. Option 1 calls for a relatively small amount of fixed operating charges, which will be accomplished by using less automated equipment. Depreciation, maintenance, property taxes, and so on, will be lower than in the case of the other operating option. Note, however, that under Option 1 the total cost line in Figure 20-1 has a relatively steep slope, indicating that **variable operating costs** are higher per unit than if the firm were to use more operating leverage. Option 2 calls for a higher level of fixed operating costs in order to reduce variable costs per unit. Here the firm uses more automated equipment, thereby requiring fewer workers to make its product. Automation allows an operator to turn out few or many products at the same labor cost. Therefore, to reduce variable cost per unit, Option 2 employs more fixed operating costs.

variable operating costs
Operating coss that vary directly with sales. For example, selling and labor expenses.

The differences in the way fixed and variable operating costs are apportioned between Option 1 and Option 2 result in a **breakeven point** that is higher under Option 2; breakeven occurs at 40,000 units under Option 1 versus 60,000 units under Option 2.

breakeven point
The volume of sales at which total operating costs equal total revenues, and operating profits (EBIT) equal zero.

The breakeven point is the level of sales that just covers all operating costs, both fixed and variable. Therefore,

$$\text{Total revenues} = \text{Total costs}$$

$$QP = QV + F,$$

where

Q = number of units produced and sold,

P = selling price per unit,

$QP = Q \times P$ = level of sales in dollars,

V = variable cost per unit produced,

$QV = Q \times V$ = variable operating costs in dollars, and

F = fixed operating costs.

If we combine terms,

$$QP - QV = F.$$

Factoring out Q leads to

$$Q(P - V) = F.$$

Figure 20-1 **Effect of Operating Leverage on All-Technology Manufacturing**

This figure demonstrates that higher operating leverage (i.e., higher fixed operating costs) will create higher business risk and greater potential for large swings in EBIT and ROE. Both plans project sales of 100,000 units at $2.00 each, but Option 1 has one-third the fixed operating costs of Option 2. As a result, Option 2 has a higher breakeven point. As both the graphs and tables show, the further sales move away from the breakeven point, the more profits or losses under Option 2 outstrip those under Option 1.

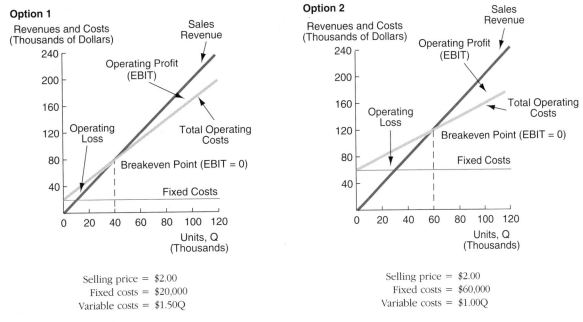

Selling price = $2.00
Fixed costs = $20,000
Variable costs = $1.50Q

Selling price = $2.00
Fixed costs = $60,000
Variable costs = $1.00Q

Expected level of sales under either production plan is 100,000 units.

Units Sold, Q	Sales Revenue	Option 1 Total Operating Costs	Option 1 Operating Profit (EBIT)	NI	ROE	Option 2 Total Operating Costs	Option 2 Operating Profit (EBIT)	NI	ROE
0	$ 0	$ 20,000	($20,000)	($12,000)	(6.0%)	$ 60,000	($60,000)	($36,000)	(18.0%)
40,000	80,000	80,000	0	0	0.0	100,000	(20,000)	(12,000)	(6.0)
60,000	120,000	110,000	10,000	6,000	3.0	120,000	0	0	0.0
80,000	160,000	140,000	20,000	12,000	6.0	140,000	20,000	12,000	6.0
100,000	200,000	170,000	30,000	18,000	9.0	160,000	40,000	24,000	12.0
110,000	220,000	185,000	35,000	21,000	10.5	170,000	50,000	30,000	15.0
160,000	320,000	260,000	60,000	36,000	18.0	220,000	100,000	60,000	30.0
180,000	360,000	290,000	70,000	42,000	21.0	240,000	120,000	72,000	36.0
200,000	400,000	320,000	80,000	48,000	24.0	260,000	140,000	84,000	42.0
Expected value			$30,000	$18,000	9.0%		$40,000	$24,000	12.0%

Notes:
a. ATM has a 40 percent federal-plus-state tax rate.
b. The firm has no debt, so Assets = Equity = $200,000.

Dividing both sides of the equation by (P − V), we have

$$Q_{BE} = \frac{F}{(P - V)}.$$ (20-1)

Equation 20-1 defines the breakeven point, stated in terms of units of the company's product that must be sold to exactly break even. We can solve Equation 20-1 for the breakeven quantity, Q_{BE} for ATM under both options:

For Option 1,

$$Q_1 = \$20,000/(\$2.00 - \$1.50)$$

$$= 40,000 \text{ units.}$$

For Option 2,

$$Q_2 = \$60,000/(\$2.00 - \$1.00)$$

$$= 60,000 \text{ units.}$$

We have seen that changing the level of fixed and variable operating costs changes the breakeven point. But how does operating leverage affect business risk? Other things held constant, *the higher a firm's operating leverage, the higher its business risk.* Since Option 2 requires a higher proportion of fixed to total operating costs, we can conclude that ATM will have more business risk if it adopts that plan. This point is demonstrated numerically in the lower part of Figure 20-1 and graphically in Figure 20-2.

The top section of Figure 20-2 gives the probability distribution of sales. This distribution depends on how demand for the product varies, not on whether the product is manufactured under Option 1 or Option 2. Therefore, the same sales probability distribution applies to both production plans, and expected sales for the next period are $200,000, with a range from zero to about $400,000, under either plan.

If we had actually specified the sales probability distribution, we could have used this information, together with the EBIT and ROE at each sales level as shown in the lower part of Figure 20-1, to develop probability distributions for ROE under Options 1 and 2. Typical ROE distributions are shown in the lower part of Figure 20-2. At the expected sales level of $200,000, Option 2's EBIT and ROE are higher than Option 1's EBIT and ROE. Unfortunately, chances for losses are also greater for Option 2 than for Option 1. Therefore, Option 2, the one with more fixed operating costs and higher operating leverage, is riskier. *Holding other things constant, the higher the degree of operating leverage, the greater the degree of business risk as measured by the variability of EBIT or ROE.*

We can describe the risk associated with operating leverage in a different fashion, utilizing the sales and operating profit levels from Figure 20-1. Note that if ATM had no fixed operating costs, an increase of 25 percent in sales would lead to a proportional 25 percent increase in operating profits. With fixed operating costs, however, there would be a larger than proportional change in operating profits, given a change in sales. For example, if current sales were $160,000, and if they then increased by 25 percent, to $200,000,

Figure 20-2 **Analysis of Business Risk**

Under both Option 1 and Option 2, expected sales are 100,000 units, as shown in the top probability curve. Taking the information from such a curve together with the EBIT and ROE at each level from the lower part of Figure 20-1, it is possible to create probability distributions for EBIT or ROE under Options 1 and 2, as shown in the lower curve of this figure. Again the greater volatility of Option 2 is evident.

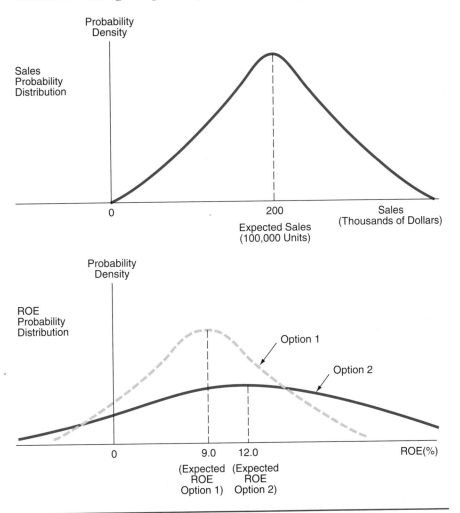

Note: We are using continuous distributions to approximate the discrete distributions contained in Figure 20-1.

profits under Option 1 would increase by 50 percent, from $20,000 to $30,000. On the other hand, because of the larger operating leverage inherent in Option 2, the same 25 percent increase in sales would result in a 100 percent increase in operating profits. Operating leverage causes problems when sales decline, however. Just as operating profits increase at a greater rate when sales are increasing, when sales decline operating lossses are also magnified by the existence of fixed operating costs. For example, a 25 percent decline in sales from $160,000 to $120,000 would result in a 50 percent decline in operating profits under Option 1, but a much larger loss of 100 percent under Option 2!

The degree of operating leverage can be quantified so as to measure the reaction of operating profits to changes in the volume of sales. The **degree of operating leverage (DOL)** can be defined as the ratio of the percentage change in EBIT to the percentage change in sales, and Equation 20-2 can be used to calculate the degree of operating leverage:

degree of operating leverage (DOL)

The percentage change in EBIT resulting from a given percentage change in sales.

$$\text{Degree of operating leverage} = \text{DOL} = \frac{Q(P - V)}{Q(P - V) - F}. \qquad (20\text{-}2)$$

The symbols are the same as those developed earlier in this chapter, so

Q = units of output,

P = sales price per unit,

V = variable operating cost per unit, and

F = fixed operating cost.

Alternatively, we could have reached the same conclusion regarding DOL based on dollar sales rather than on units,

$$\text{DOL} = \frac{S - VC}{S - VC - F}. \qquad (20\text{-}2a)$$

Here, QP, the number of units sold times the sales price, equals sales, S, and QV, the number of units times the variable cost per unit, equals the amount of variable cost, VC.

Applying Equation 20-2a for ATM's operating leverage for Options 1 and 2 at $160,000 in sales, we arrive at the same degrees of operating leverage calculated in Table 20-1:

Option 1 (S = $160,000, VC = $120,000, F = $20,000):

$$\text{DOL} = \frac{\$160,000 - \$120,000}{\$160,000 - \$120,000 - \$20,000}$$

$$= \frac{\$40,000}{\$20,000}$$

$$= 2.0.$$

Option 2 (S = $160,000, VC = $80,000, F = $60,000):

$$\text{DOL} = \frac{\$160,000 - \$80,000}{\$160,000 - \$80,000 - \$60,000}$$

$$= \frac{\$80,000}{\$20,000}$$

$$= 4.0.$$

Table 20-1 Degree of Operating Leverage at $160,000 in Sales for ATM

$$DOL_1 = \frac{Q(P - V)}{Q(P - V) - F}$$

$$DOL_2 = \frac{Q(P - V)}{Q(P - V) - F}$$

$$= \frac{80,000(\$2.00 - \$1.50)}{80,000(\$2.00 - \$1.50) - \$20,000}$$

$$= \frac{80,000(\$2.00 - \$1.00)}{80,000(\$2.00 - \$1.00) - \$60,000}$$

$$= \frac{\$40,000}{\$20,000}$$

$$= \frac{\$80,000}{\$20,000}$$

$$= 2.0.$$

$$= 4.0.$$

Notice that these are the same answers for DOL that were calculated in Table 20-1, indicating that either equation can be used to arrive at a firm's DOL at a specific sales level.

Using Equation 20-2, we determined in Table 20-1 the degree of operating leverage for Option 1 (DOL_1) and Option 2 (DOL_2) *at a particular level of sales* — in this case $160,000 in sales.[4] (The DOL changes as the level of sales changes, so we stress the phrase "at a particular level of sales.") A DOL of 2 means that with a given percentage change in sales, a doubled percentage change in EBIT will result under the operating leverage provided by Option 1. Thus a 10 percent increase in sales will result in twice as large (20 percent) an increase in operating profits. As we already saw for Option 1, a 25 percent change in sales was doubled to a 50 percent change in operating profits. For Option 2, the DOL of 4 means that a percentage change in sales will result in a quadrupled change in EBIT. A 5 percent decline in sales will result in a four times larger (20 percent) decline in operating profits. Thus, before adopting Option 2, the financial planners at ATM should consider the probability of future sales fluctuations.[5]

To what extent can firms control their operating leverage? For the most part, operating leverage is determined by technology. Electric utilities, telephone companies, airlines, steel mills, and chemical companies simply *must* have heavy investments in fixed assets; this results in high fixed operating costs and high operating leverage. Grocery stores, on the other hand, generally have substantially lower fixed operating costs, and hence lower operating leverage. Still, although industry factors do exert a major influence, all firms have some

---

[4]A word of caution: the degree of operating leverage changes as the level of sales changes. For example, in Table 20-1 we found that at sales of $160,000 $DOL_1 = 2$ and $DOL_2 = 4$. However, at the expected sales level of $200,000 $DOL_1 = 1.67$ and $DOL_2 = 2.5$.

[5]It is interesting to note that ATM chose neither Option 1 nor Option 2 for its operating leverage. Rather, as is often the case, the firm reached a compromise between the two options. Recall that Option 1 had the higher variable-cost ratio (75 percent of sales) but a lower level of fixed costs, $20,000, and Option 2 had lower variable costs (50 percent of sales) but higher fixed costs, $60,000. The compromise option selected a mid-level for both costs, with variable operating costs at 60 percent of sales and fixed operating costs of $40,000, as we shall see in the next section.

control over their operating leverage. For example, an electric utility can expand its generating capacity by building either a nuclear reactor or a coal-fired plant. The nuclear plant would require a larger investment in fixed assets, which would involve higher fixed operating costs, but its variable operating costs would be relatively low. The coal plant, on the other hand, would require a smaller investment in fixed assets and would have lower fixed operating costs, but the variable operating costs (for coal) would be high. Thus, by its capital budgeting decisions a utility (or any other company) can influence its operating leverage and, hence, its basic business risk.

The concept of operating leverage was, in fact, originally developed for use in capital budgeting. Alternative methods for producing a given product often have different degrees of operating leverage and, therefore, different breakeven points and different degrees of risk. Companies regularly undertake some type of breakeven analysis as part of their evaluation of proposed new projects. Still, once established, the degree of operating leverage, and hence the degree to which future operating profits will be uncertain, is an important factor in determining the firm's capital structure, as we demonstrate in a later section.

Self-Test

What is the equation used to calculate the breakeven point?

What does a "high degree of operating leverage" mean, and what are some implications of having a high degree of operating leverage?

Give the two equations used to calculate the degree of operating leverage (DOL), and explain what DOL is.

To what extent can firms control their operating leverage?

FINANCIAL RISK

financial leverage
The extent to which fixed-income securities (debt and preferred stock) are used in a firm's capital structure.

Financial risk is the additional risk placed on the common shareholders as a result of **financial leverage.** Whereas operating leverage refers to the use of fixed operating costs, financial leverage refers to the use of fixed-income securities — debt and preferred stock. In this section we show how financial leverage affects a firm's expected earnings per share, the riskiness of earnings, and consequently the price of the firm's stock. As we will see, the value of a firm that has no debt first rises as it substitutes debt for equity, then hits a peak, and finally declines as the use of debt becomes excessive. The objective of our analysis is to determine the capital structure at which value is maximized; this structure is then used as the *target capital structure.*

Determining the Optimal Capital Structure

At the present time All-Technology Manufacturing has no debt and is thus 100 percent equity financed (as shown in Table 20-2). Should ATM continue this

Table 20-2 **Data on All-Technology Manufacturing**

I. Balance Sheet on 12/31/90

Current assets	$100,000	Debt	$	0
Net fixed assets	100,000	Common equity (10,000 shares		
		outstanding)		200,000
Total assets	$200,000	Total liabilities and equity		$200,000

II. Income Statement for 1990

Sales		$200,000
Fixed operating costs	$ 40,000	
Variable operating costs	120,000	160,000
Earnings before interest and taxes (EBIT)		$ 40,000
Interest		0
Taxable income		$ 40,000
Taxes (40%)		16,000
Net income		$ 24,000

III. Other Data

1. Earnings per share = EPS = $24,000/10,000 shares = $2.40.
2. Dividends per share = DPS = $24,000/10,000 shares = $2.40.
   (Thus ATM pays all of its earnings out as dividends. Alternatively stated, ATM has a 100 percent payout ratio.)
3. Book value per share = $200,000/10,000 shares = $20.
4. Market price per share = P_0 = $20. Thus the stock sells at its book value.
5. Price/earnings ratio = P/E = $20/$2.40 = 8.33 times.
6. Variable operating costs equal 60 percent of sales.

policy of using no debt, or should it start using financial leverage? And if ATM does decide to substitute debt for equity, how far should it go? As in all such decisions, the correct answer is that *it should choose the capital structure that maximizes the price of its stock.*

Because the price of a share of stock is the present value of the stock's expected future dividends, if the use of financial leverage is to affect the stock's price, it must do so by changing either the expected dividend stream or the required rate of return on equity, k_s, or both. We first consider the effect of capital structure on earnings and dividends; then we examine its effect on k_s.

The Effect of Financial Leverage on Expected EPS

Changes in the use of debt will cause changes in earnings per share (EPS) and consequently in the stock price. To understand the relationship between financial leverage and EPS, consider first Table 20-3, which shows how ATM's cost of debt would vary if it used different percentages of debt in its capital structure. Naturally, the higher the percentage of debt, the riskier the debt, and hence the higher the interest rate lenders will charge.

Table 20-3 **Interest Rates for ATM with Different Debt/Assets Ratios**

Amount Borrowed	Debt/Assets Ratio[a]	Interest Rate, k_d, on All Debt
$ 20,000	10%	8.0%
40,000	20	8.3
60,000	30	9.0
80,000	40	10.0
100,000	50	12.0
120,000	60	15.0

[a]We assume that the firm must borrow in increments of $20,000. We also assume that ATM is unable to borrow more than $120,000, or 60 percent of assets, because of restrictions in its corporate charter.

Table 20-4 goes on to show how expected EPS varies with changes in financial leverage. Section I of the table shows EBIT at sales of $100,000, $200,000, and $300,000. We assume for simplicity that sales can take on only these three values. EBIT is independent of financial leverage — although it does depend on operating leverage, *EBIT does not depend on financial leverage*.

Section II of Table 20-4 goes on to show the situation if ATM continues to use no debt. Net income is divided by the 10,000 shares outstanding to calculate EPS. If sales are as low as $100,000, EPS will be zero, but at sales of $300,000, EPS will rise to $4.80.

The EPS at each sales level is next multiplied by the probability of that sales level to calculate the expected EPS, which is $2.40 if ATM uses no debt. We also calculate the standard deviation of EPS and the coefficient of variation as indicators of the firm's risk at a zero debt ratio: $\sigma_{EPS} = \$1.52$, and $CV_{EPS} = 0.63.$[6]

Section III of the table shows the financial results that would occur if the company financed with a debt/assets ratio of 50 percent. In this situation, $100,000 of the $200,000 total capital would be debt. The interest rate on the debt, 12 percent, is taken from Table 20-3. With $100,000 of 12 percent debt outstanding, the company's interest expense is shown in Table 20-4 to be $12,000 per year. This is a fixed financing cost, and it is deducted from EBIT as calculated in the top section. Next, taxes are taken out, to derive net income. Then we calculate EPS as net income divided by shares outstanding. With debt = $0, there are 10,000 shares outstanding. However, if half the equity were replaced by debt (debt = $100,000), there would be only 5,000 shares outstanding, and this fact is used to determine the EPS figures that would result at each sales level in Section III. With a debt/assets ratio of 50 percent, EPS

[6]The procedures for calculating the standard deviation and the coefficient of variation were explained in Chapter 12. The coefficient of variation is simply the standard deviation divided by the expected EPS.

Table 20-4 ATM: EPS with Different Amounts of Financial Leverage (Thousands of Dollars except Per-Share Figures)

I. Calculation of EBIT

Probability of Indicated Sales	0.2	0.6	0.2
Sales	$100.0	$200.0	$300.0
Fixed operating costs	40.0	40.0	40.0
Variable operating costs (60% of sales)	60.0	120.0	180.0
Total operating costs (except interest)	$100.0	$160.0	$220.0
Earnings before interest and taxes (EBIT)	$ 0.0	$ 40.0	$ 80.0

II. Situation if Debt/Assets (D/A) = 0%

Less: Interest	0.0	0.0	0.0
Earnings before taxes	$ 0.0	$ 40.0	$ 80.0
Taxes (40%)	0.0	16.0	32.0
Net income	$ 0.0	$ 24.0	$ 48.0
Earnings per share on 10,000 shares (EPS)	$ 0.0	$ 2.40	$ 4.80
Expected EPS		$ 2.40	
Standard deviation of EPS		$ 1.52	
Coefficient of variation		0.63	

III. Situation if Debt/Assets (D/A) = 50%

EBIT (from Section I)	$ 0.0	$ 40.0	$ 80.0
Less: Interest (0.12 × $100,000)	12.0	12.0	12.0
Earnings before taxes	($ 12.0)	$ 28.0	$ 68.0
Taxes (40%)	(4.8)[a]	11.2	27.2
Net income	($ 7.2)	$ 16.8	$ 40.8
Earnings per share on 5,000 shares (EPS)	($ 1.44)	$ 3.36	$ 8.16
Expected EPS		$ 3.36	
Standard deviation of EPS		$ 3.04	
Coefficient of variation		0.90	

[a]Assumes tax credit on losses.

would be a negative $1.44 if sales were as low as $100,000; it would rise to $3.36 if sales were $200,000; and it would soar to $8.16 if sales were as high as $300,000.

The EPS distributions under the two financial structures are graphed in Figure 20-3, where we use continuous distributions to approximate the discrete distributions contained in Table 20-4. Although expected EPS would be much higher if financial leverage were employed, the graph makes it clear that the risk of low or even negative EPS would also be higher if debt were used.

The relationships among expected EPS, risk, and financial leverage are extended in Table 20-5, and the Table 20-5 data are plotted in Figure 20-4. Here we see that expected EPS rises for a while as the use of debt increases—interest charges rise, but a smaller number of shares outstanding (as debt is substituted for equity) still causes EPS to increase. However, in this particular

Figure 20-3 **ATM: Probability Distribution of EPS with Different Amounts of Financial Leverage**

Financial leverage (debt or other fixed-income securities) affects a firm's expected earnings per share and thus the price of its stock. With zero financial leverage, expected EPS is lower than expected EPS with 50 percent debt ($2.40 versus $3.36). However, with greater leverage, the probability of lower or even negative earnings is increased. Clearly, increased financial leverage carries with it both higher expected earnings and greater risk.

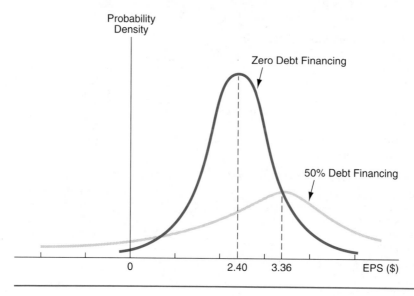

Table 20-5 **ATM: Expected EPS, Standard Deviation, and Coefficient of Variation with Different Degrees of Financial Leverage**

Debt/Assets Ratio	Expected EPS	Standard Deviation of EPS	Coefficient of Variation
0%	$2.40[a]	$1.52[a]	0.63[a]
10	2.56	1.69	0.66
20	2.75	1.90	0.69
30	2.97	2.17	0.73
40	3.20	2.53	0.79
50	3.36[a]	3.04[a]	0.90[a]
60	3.30	3.79	1.15

[a]Values for D/A = 0 and 50 percent were taken from Table 20-4. Values for other D/A ratios were calculated similarly.

Figure 20-4 **ATM: Relationships among Expected EPS, Risk, and Financial Leverage**

As shown on the right side of this figure, financial risk rises at an increasing rate with each addition of financial leverage. Earnings per share, on the other hand, rise only to a certain point, as shown on the left. Beyond this peak, interest rates become prohibitively high and EPS begins to fall.

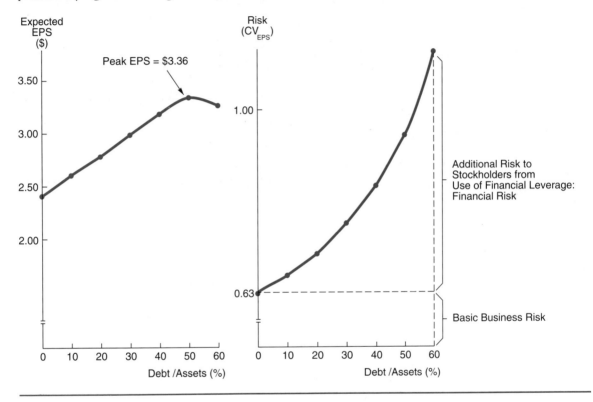

case EPS peaks at a debt ratio of 50 percent. Beyond this ratio, interest rates rise so fast that EPS is depressed in spite of the decreasing number of shares outstanding. The right panel of Figure 20-4 shows that risk, as measured by the coefficient of variation of EPS, rises continuously and at an increasing rate as debt is substituted for equity.

We see, then, that using leverage involves a risk-return tradeoff; higher leverage increases expected earnings per share (at least for a while — in this example, until the D/A ratio equals 50 percent), but greater leverage also increases the firm's risk. Clearly, the debt ratio for ATM should not exceed 50 percent, but where, in the range of 0 to 50 percent, should it be set? Exactly how this tradeoff should be resolved is discussed in the next section.

Table 20-6 **ATM: Stock Price Estimates with Different Debt/Assets Ratios**

Debt/ Assets (1)	k_d (2)	Expected EPS (and DPS)[a] (3)	Estimated Beta (4)	k_s[b] (5)	Estimated Price[c] (6)	Resulting P/E Ratio (7)	Weighted Average Cost of Capital (8)[d]
0%	—	$2.40	1.50	12.0%	$20.00	8.33	12.00%
10	8.0%	2.56	1.55	12.2	20.98	8.20	11.46
20	8.3	2.75	1.65	12.6	21.83	7.94	11.08
30	9.0	2.97	1.80	13.2	22.50	7.58	10.86
40	**10.0**	**3.20**	**2.00**	**14.0**	**22.86**	**7.14**	**10.80**
50	12.0	3.36	2.30	15.2	22.11	6.58	11.20
60	15.0	3.30	2.70	16.8	19.64	5.95	12.12

[a]We assume that ATM pays all of its earnings out as dividends; hence EPS = DPS.
[b]The cost of equity in Column 5 is based on the CAPM: $k_s = k_{RF} + (k_M - k_{RF})b$. We assume that $k_{RF} = 6\%$ and $k_M = 10\%$. Therefore, at debt/assets = 0, $k_s = 6\% + (10\% - 6\%)1.5 = 6\% + 6\% = 12\%$. Other values of k_s are calculated similarly.
[c]In Chapter 17 we learned that under certain conditions the value of a share of stock is equal to $\hat{P}_0 = D_1/(k_s - g)$. We have already noted that ATM's payout is 100 percent; thus dividends and earnings are equivalent. If all earnings are paid out as dividends, no retained earnings will be plowed back into the firm, and growth in earnings and dividends will be zero. Thus, in this special case, D = E and g = 0. Therefore, at debt/assets = 0,

$$\hat{P}_0 = \frac{E}{k_s}$$

$$= \frac{\$2.40}{0.12} = \$20.$$

Other prices are calculated similarly.
[d]Column 8 is found by using the weighted average cost of capital (WACC) equation developed in Chapter 19:

$$WACC = w_d k_d (1 - t) + w_s k_s$$

$$= (D/A)(k_d)(1 - t) + (1 - D/A)k_s.$$

For example, at D/A = 40%,

$$k_a = 0.4(10\%)(0.6) + 0.6(14\%) = 10.8\%.$$

The Effect of Financial Leverage on Stock Prices

As we saw in the preceding section, ATM's EPS is maximized at a debt/assets ratio of 50 percent. Does this mean that ATM's optimal capital structure is 50 percent debt, 50 percent equity? The answer is a resounding no — *the optimal capital structure is the one that maximizes the price of the firm's stock, and this always calls for a debt ratio which is lower than the one that maximizes expected EPS.*

This statement is demonstrated in Table 20-6, where we develop ATM's estimated stock price and weighted average cost of capital at different debt/assets ratios. The data in Columns 1, 2, and 3 are taken from Tables 20-3 and 20-5. The beta coefficients shown in Column 4 were estimated. Recall from Chapter 12 that a stock's beta measures its relative volatility as compared with that of an average stock. It has been demonstrated both theoretically and empirically that a firm's beta increases with its degree of financial leverage. The exact nature of this relationship for a given firm like ATM is difficult to estimate, but the values given in Column 4 do show the approximate nature of the relationship for ATM.

Assuming that the risk-free rate of return, k_{RF}, is 6 percent and that the required return on an average stock, k_M, is 10 percent, we use the CAPM equation to develop estimates of the required rates of return for ATM as shown in Column 5. Here we see that k_s is 12 percent if no financial leverage is used, but k_s rises to 16.8 percent if the company finances with 60 percent debt, the maximum permitted by its charter.

The "zero growth" stock valuation model in Footnote c of Table 20-6 is used, along with the Column 3 values of dividends and earnings per share and the Column 5 values of k_s, to develop the estimated stock prices shown in Column 6. Here we see that the expected stock price first rises with financial leverage, hits a peak of $22.86 at a debt/assets ratio of 40 percent, and then begins to decline. *Thus, ATM's optimal capital structure calls for 40 percent debt.*

The price/earnings ratios shown in Column 7 were calculated by dividing the estimated price in Column 6 by the expected earnings given in Column 3. We use the pattern of P/E ratios as a check on the "reasonableness" of the other data. As a rule, P/E ratios should decline as the riskiness of a firm increases. Also, at the time ATM's data were being analyzed, the P/Es shown here were generally consistent with those of zero growth companies with varying amounts of financial leverage. Thus, the data in Column 7 reinforce our confidence in the reasonableness of the estimated prices shown in Column 6.

Finally, Column 8 shows ATM's weighted average cost of capital, WACC, calculated as described in Chapter 19, at the different capital structures. If the firm continues to use zero debt, its assets are all equity financed, and in that case ATM's WACC $= k_s = 12\%$. As the firm begins to employ lower-cost debt, its weighted average cost of capital declines. As the debt ratio increases, however, the costs of both debt and equity rise, and the increasing costs of the two components begin to offset the fact that a larger proportion of the lower-cost debt component is being used. At 40 percent debt, WACC reaches a minimum, and it rises after that as the debt ratio is increased.

The debt/assets ratio, EPS, cost of capital, and stock price data in Table 20-6 are plotted in Figure 20-5. As the graph shows, the debt/assets ratio that maximizes ATM's expected EPS is 50 percent. However, the expected stock price is maximized, and the cost of capital is minimized, at a 40 percent debt ratio. *Thus, the optimal capital structure calls for 40 percent debt and 60 percent equity.* Management should set its target capital structure at these ratios, and if the present ratios are off target, it should move toward the target when new security offerings are made.

Figure 20-5 **ATM: Relationships among Debt/Assets Ratio, Expected EPS, Cost of Capital, and Estimated Stock Prices**

The amount of financial leverage that maximizes a firm's earnings per share is not necessarily the amount that will maximize its stock price. In this example, with data plotted from Table 20-6, the stock price is maximized and the cost of capital is minimized at a debt/assets ratio of 40 percent, even though expected EPS would be higher at 50 percent debt. This firm will thus seek to target its capital structure at 40 percent debt, 60 percent equity.

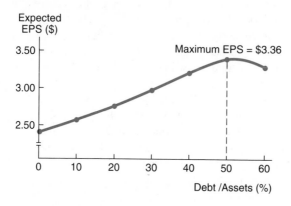

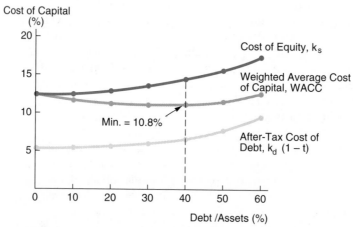

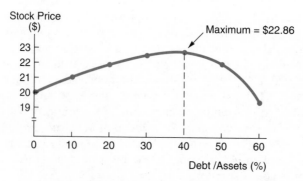

Self-Test

Explain the following statement: "Using leverage involves a risk-return tradeoff."

Is the optimal capital structure the one that maximizes expected EPS? Explain.

DEGREE OF FINANCIAL LEVERAGE

Earlier in this chapter, we investigated the effect of fixed operating charges on ATM's operating profits under two proposed plans. At that time we made no mention of financial leverage, and when we discussed financial leverage, we assumed operating leverage was given. Actually the two types of leverage are interrelated. For example, firms with high operating leverage often choose low levels of debt to reduce the overall variability of their cash flows. For firms with little operating leverage, however, the optimal capital structure might contain more debt.

Unfortunately, the theory of finance has not been developed to the point where we can actually specify simultaneously the optimal levels of operating and financial leverage. Even so, we can gain a better understanding of how operating and financial leverage interact through an analysis of the degrees of financial and total leverage.

Operating leverage affects earnings before interest and taxes (EBIT), whereas financial leverage affects earnings after interest and taxes, or the earnings available to common stockholders. In terms of Table 20-4, operating leverage affects Section I of the table, whereas financial leverage affects Sections II and III. Thus, if ATM decided to use more operating leverage, its fixed operating costs would be higher than $40,000, its variable cost ratio would be lower than 60 percent of sales, and its earnings before interest and taxes would be more sensitive to changes in sales. Financial leverage takes over where operating leverage leaves off, further magnifying the effects on earnings per share of changes in the level of sales. For this reason, operating leverage is sometimes referred to as *first-stage leverage* and financial leverage as *second-stage leverage*.

The **degree of financial leverage (DFL)** is defined as the percentage change in earnings available to common shareholders that is associated with a given percentage change in earnings before interest and taxes (EBIT). Where fixed financial charges exist, a change in EBIT will result in a greater than proportional change in earnings per share, net income, and ROE. Equation 20-3[7]

degree of financial leverage (DFL)
The percentage change in earnings available to common shareholders associated with a given percentage change in earnings before interest and taxes.

---

[7]Equation 20-3 is developed as follows, utilizing the same symbols as those used earlier in the chapter:

$$DFL = \frac{Q(P - V) - F}{Q(P - V) - F - I}.$$

However, since EBIT = Q(P − V) − F, Equation 20-3 represents a less cumbersome statement of DFL. Even though we have ignored preferred stock, its presence in the firm's financial structure also will increase the firm's financial leverage and hence the DFL.

has been developed as an aid in calculating the degree of financial leverage for any given level of EBIT and financing charges, I:

$$\text{Degree of financial leverage} = \frac{\text{EBIT}}{\text{EBIT} - \text{I}}. \qquad (20\text{-}3)$$

For ATM at sales of \$200,000 and EBIT of \$40,000, the degree of financial leverage with a 50 percent debt ratio is

$$\text{DFL at 50\% debt} = \frac{\$40,000}{\$40,000 - \$12,000}$$

$$= 1.43.$$

Therefore, a 20 percent increase in EBIT would result in a 20%(1.43) = 28.6% increase in earnings per share. If no debt were used, I in Equation 20-3 would equal zero, and the DFL would equal 1.0. Thus, in the absence of fixed financial charges, a 20 percent increase in EBIT would produce a proportional 20 percent increase in EPS. This can be confirmed from the data in Section II of Table 20-4.

Degree of Total Leverage (DTL)

We have seen that the greater the degree of operating leverage (or fixed operating costs), the more sensitive EBIT will be to changes in sales, and that the greater the degree of financial leverage, the more sensitive net income, EPS, and ROE will be to changes in EBIT. Therefore, if a firm uses a considerable amount of both operating and financial leverage, then even small changes in sales will produce wide fluctuations in EPS.

Equation 20-2 (for the degree of operating leverage) can be combined with Equation 20-3 (for the degree of financial leverage) to produce the equation for the **degree of total leverage (DTL),** which shows how a given change in sales will affect earnings per share.[8]

degree of total leverage (DTL)
The percentage change in net income, EPS, and ROE brought about by a given percentage change in sales; DTL shows the effects of both operating leverage and financial leverage.

$$\text{Degree of total leverage (DTL)} = \frac{Q(P - V)}{Q(P - V) - F - I}. \qquad (20\text{-}4)$$

---

[8]The degree of total leverage, DTL, is equal to the product of the DOL and DFL:

$$\text{DTL} = \frac{Q(P - V)}{Q(P - V) - F} \times \frac{Q(P - V) - F}{Q(P - V) - F - I} = \frac{Q(P - V)}{Q(P - V) - F - I},$$

and, thus, DTL = DOL × DFL.

Table 20-7 Operating, Financial, and Total Leverage Effects for ATM with a 20 Percent Increase in Sales from a Sales Level of $200,000

Income Statement	Original Status	Percentage Increase	Resulting Status
QP = Sales	$200,000	20%	$240,000
QV = Variable operating costs (60% of sales)	120,000	20	144,000
F = Fixed operating costs	40,000	0	40,000
EBIT = Operating profits	$ 40,000	40	$ 56,000
−I = Fixed financing charges[a]	12,000	0	12,000
EBT = Earnings before taxes	$ 28,000	57[b]	$ 44,000
−T = Taxes (40%)	11,200	57[b]	17,600
NI = Net income	$ 16,800	57[b]	$ 26,400
Common stock equity shares outstanding	5,000	0	5,000
Earnings per share	$3.36	57[c]	$5.28

[a]Fixed financing charges include interest or a tax-adjusted preferred dividend equivalent or both. Since preferred dividends are paid after taxes and since interest is a pretax expense, preferred dividends must be modified for the tax effect. Thus,

$$\text{Pretax equivalent preferred dividend} = \text{Preferred dividend}/(1 - \text{Tax rate}).$$

In this case all fixed financing costs result from interest charges.
[b]Note that EBT also increases by the same 57 percent. Since taxes are a variable cost in this example, they do not affect the degree of leverage.
[c]Note that because of operating leverage (DOL = 2.0), a 20 percent increase in sales will result in twice as large a change in operating profits. Similarly, the effects of the combination of operating and financial leverage cause a change in sales to be magnified by 2.86×. Recall that DOL = 2.0 and DFL = 1.43; therefore 2.0 × 1.43 = 2.86, and if sales increase by 20 percent then the result would be a 0.20(2.86) = 57 percent increase in EBT, NI, EPS, and ROE. Unfortunately, a 20 percent decrease in sales will likewise be magnified into a 57 percent decline in EBT, NI, EPS, and ROE!

For ATM at sales of $200,000, the degree of total leverage, using 50 percent debt, is

$$\text{DTL} = \frac{\$200,000 - \$120,000}{\$200,000 - \$120,000 - \$40,000 - \$12,000}$$

$$= \frac{\$80,000}{\$28,000}$$

$$= 2.86.$$

Therefore, a 20 percent increase in sales would lead to a 2.86 times larger increase in earnings, or a 20%(2.86) = 57.2 percent increase in ATM's net income. Table 20-7 provides more detail on this effect.

The usefulness of the degree of leverage concept lies in the facts first, that it enables us to specify the precise effect of a change in sales volume on earnings available to common stock, and, second, that it permits us to show the interrelationship between operating and financial leverage. For example, if

ATM could *reduce* its degree of operating leverage, it probably could *increase* its use of financial leverage. On the other hand, if the company decided to use more operating leverage, its optimal capital structure would probably call for a lower debt ratio. As we noted earlier, there is a tradeoff between operating risk and financial risk.

Self-Test

Give the formula for calculating the degree of financial leverage (DFL), and explain what this calculation means.

Give the formula for calculating the degree of total leverage (DTL), and explain what DTL is.

Why is the degree of leverage concept useful?

TAXES, BANKRUPTCY COSTS, AND THE VALUE OF THE FIRM

Why does the expected stock price first rise as the firm begins to use financial leverage, then hit a peak, and finally decline when leverage becomes excessive? This pattern occurs primarily as a result of *corporate income taxes* and *bankruptcy costs*. Because interest on debt is tax deductible, the more debt a firm has, the greater the proportion of its operating income that escapes taxation and flows through to investors, and hence the higher the value of the firm. At the same time, though, the more debt used, the greater the risk of bankruptcy. At very high levels of debt, the odds are very great that bankruptcy will occur, and if this happens, lawyers may end up with as much of the firm's assets as the investors.[9]

In addition, if its suppliers think that a firm is in danger of going bankrupt, they will cut it off and thus produce a bankruptcy, which may eliminate all operating income. This happened to Robert Campeau's retailing empire in 1989 and 1990. Similarly, if its customers think a company is in danger of bankruptcy, they will avoid it. For example, would you rather hold a ticket for your Caribbean vacation on Eastern Airlines, which may not be in existence next summer, or on Delta, which almost certainly will still exist? Thus, the operating effects of excessive leverage and possible bankruptcy can represent high implicit costs.

Figure 20-6 illustrates how taxes and potential bankruptcy costs interact with financial leverage to affect the firm's value. When ATM has zero debt, the value of its stock is $20 per share. As it begins to use debt, the stock price begins to rise because of the tax shelter benefits of debt. Prior to D_1, potential bankruptcy costs are insignificant. However, at D_1 investors begin to worry about the effects of debt, so *potential* bankruptcy costs begin to offset the

---

[9]See Appendix 20A for a discussion of bankruptcy costs.

Figure 20-6 **ATM: Effects of Tax Deductions and Bankruptcy Costs on Stock Value**

When a firm uses financial leverage, its expected stock price first rises and then falls. The initial rise occurs because the interest payments on corporate debt are tax deductible. Thus, as a firm's debt load increases, more of its operating income escapes taxation and flows through to investors. As levels of debt increase, however, so does the risk of bankruptcy. Consequently, at Point D_1, when investors begin to worry about the effects of debt, the potential risk of bankruptcy begins to offset the benefits of the tax-deductible interest. At Point D_2 the balance between the benefits of leverage and the potential cost of bankruptcy is reached and the firm's capital structure is optimized. Beyond Point D_2 the potential cost of bankruptcy overshadows the benefits of leverage and the stock's price falls.

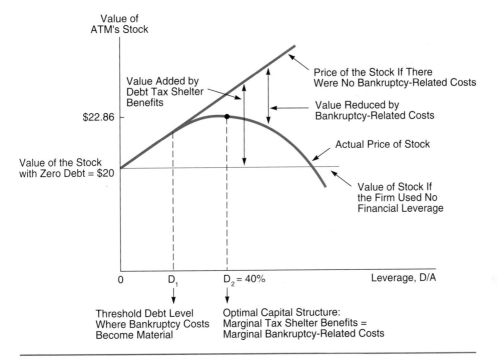

debt's tax shelter benefits. At D_2 the marginal tax shelter benefits are equal to the marginal potential bankruptcy costs, and the value of the stock is maximized. Beyond D_2 potential bankruptcy costs more than offset the benefits of additional debt, so further increases in leverage reduce the price of the stock. Thus D_2 represents the optimal capital structure.[10]

---

[10]This entire concept — including (1) the reasons the tax shelter benefits cause a linear increase in value, (2) the specific elements that make up bankruptcy-related costs, and (3) the effects of personal income taxes on capital structure decisions — is discussed in Eugene F. Brigham and Louis Gapenski, *Intermediate Financial Management,* 3rd ed., Chapter 5.

Self-Test

Why does the expected stock price first rise as the firm begins to use financial leverage, then hit a peak, and finally decline when leverage becomes excessive?

ADDITIONAL PROBLEMS AND CONSIDERATIONS

There are some difficult problems with the type of analysis described thus far in the chapter, including the following:

1. Because of the difficulties in determining exactly how P/E ratios and k_s values are affected by different degrees of financial leverage, management rarely, if ever, has sufficient confidence in the type of analysis set forth in Table 20-6 to use it as the sole determinant of the target capital structure.

2. A firm's managers may be more or less conservative than the average stockholder; hence, management may set a somewhat different target capital structure than the one that would maximize the stock price. The managers of a publicly owned firm would never admit this, for unless they owned voting control, they would quickly be removed from office. However, in view of the uncertainties about what constitutes the value-maximizing capital structure, management could always say that the target capital structure employed is, in its judgment, the value-maximizing structure, and it would be difficult to prove otherwise. Still, if management is far off target, especially on the low side, then chances are very good that some other firm or management group will take over the company, increase its leverage, and thereby raise its value. This point is discussed in more detail later in the chapter.

3. Managers of firms which provide vital services such as electricity or telephones have a responsibility to provide *continuous* service; therefore, they must refrain from using leverage to the point where the firm's long-term viability is endangered. Long-term viability may conflict with short-term stock price maximization and short-term capital cost minimization.

For all of these reasons, managers are very much concerned about the effects of financial leverage on the risk of bankruptcy, so an analysis of this factor is an important input in all capital structure decisions. Accordingly, managements give considerable weight to financial strength indicators such as the *times-interest-earned ratio (TIE)*. The lower this ratio, the higher the probability that a firm will default on its debt and be forced into bankruptcy.

Table 20-8 shows how ATM's expected TIE ratio declines as the debt/assets ratio increases. When the debt/assets ratio is only 10 percent, the expected TIE is a high 25 times, but the interest coverage ratio declines rapidly as debt rises. Note, however, that these coverages are the expected values; the actual TIE will be higher if sales exceed the expected $200,000 level but lower if sales fall below $200,000. The variability of the TIE ratios is highlighted in Figure 20-7, which shows the probability distributions of these ratios at debt/assets

Table 20-8 **ATM: Expected Times-Interest-Earned Ratio at Different Debt/Assets Ratios**

Debt/Assets	TIE[a]
0%	Undefined
10	25.0
20	12.0
30	7.4
40	5.0
50	3.3
60	2.2

[a]TIE = EBIT/Interest. For example, if debt/assets = 50%, then TIE = $40,000/$12,000 = 3.3. Data are from Tables 20-3 and 20-4.

ratios of 40 percent and 60 percent. The expected TIE is much higher if only 40 percent debt is used. Even more important, with less debt there is a much lower probability of a TIE of less than 1.0, the level at which the firm is not earning enough to meet its required interest payments and is seriously exposed to the threat of bankruptcy.

Self-Test

Why do managers give considerable weight to the TIE ratio when they make capital structure decisions? Why might they not use the capital structure that maximizes the stock price?

CAPITAL STRUCTURE AND MERGERS

One of the more exciting developments in the financial world during the 1980s has been the high level of merger activity, especially hostile takeovers, and leveraged buyouts. A *hostile takeover* occurs when one firm buys out another over the opposition of the acquired firm's management. Because the acquired firm's stock is considered to be undervalued, the acquiring firm is willing to pay a premium of perhaps 50 percent to gain control. For example, General Electric offered $66.50 per share for RCA (which owns the NBC television network, among other things) versus RCA's preannouncement price of $45 per share, and Kohlberg Kravis Roberts (KKR) paid $106 for RJR Nabisco's stock versus RJR's preannouncement price of $55 in its LBO. Mergers are discussed at length in Chapter 22, but it is useful to mention these points now: (1) very often the acquiring firm issues debt and uses it to buy the target firm's stock; (2) this action effectively raises the enterprise's debt ratio; and (3) if the acquired firm was operating below its optimal capital structure, the value enhancement resulting from the use of debt may be sufficient to cover the premium offered for the stock and still leave a profit for the acquiring company.

Figure 20-7 **ATM: Probability Distributions of Times-Interest-Earned Ratios with Different Capital Structures**

The times-interest-earned ratio is an important indicator of bankruptcy risk. The lower the TIE, the greater the potential for bankruptcy. Management will be especially concerned about keeping TIE above 1.0, the point below which a firm's earnings will not cover its required interest payments. This figure shows that a 60 percent debt/assets ratio not only creates an overall lower expected TIE than a 40 percent debt/assets ratio but also results in a much higher probability of an expected TIE below 1.0.

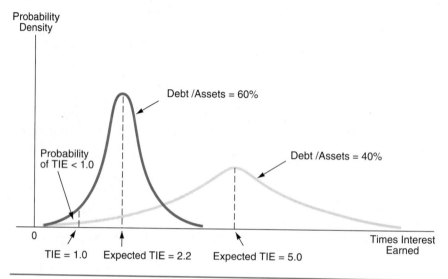

The recognition of the points made in this chapter has led to the creation of companies such as Kohlberg Kravis Roberts whose major function is to acquire other companies through debt-financed takeovers. The managers of these acquiring companies frequently have made huge personal fortunes. Shrewd individual investors, including a few finance professors, have selected stock portfolios heavily weighted with prime acquisition targets and have done well in the market. Of course, the managements of firms with low leverage ratios who do not want to be taken over can be expected to react by attempting to find their optimal debt levels and then issuing debt and repurchasing stock. By doing so they would raise the price of their firms' stocks and thus make their companies less attractive acquisition targets. This is called *restructuring,* and a great deal of it has been going on lately. CBS, for example, did this when it was fighting off an acquisition attempt by Ted Turner, and Phillips Petroleum did likewise to fend off T. Boone Pickens.

The game is far from over — indeed, it can never end, because economic shifts lead to continuing changes in optimal capital structures. This makes it especially important that the lessons to be learned from this chapter are thoroughly understood by everyone actively involved in financial management.

Self-Test

Why do capital structure considerations sometimes cause one firm to take over another?

What is meant by the term "restructuring"?

CHECKLIST OF FACTORS THAT INFLUENCE CAPITAL STRUCTURE DECISIONS IN PRACTICE

The factors listed and briefly discussed in this section all have an important, though hard to measure, bearing on a firm's choice of a target capital structure.

1. Sales stability. If its sales are relatively stable, a firm can safely take on more debt and incur higher fixed charges than can a company with unstable sales. For example, utility companies, because of their stable demand, are able to carry higher debt ratios than the average industrial firm.

2. Asset structure. Firms whose assets are suitable as security for loans tend to use debt rather heavily. General-purpose assets which can be used by many businesses make good collateral, whereas special-purpose assets do not. Thus, real estate companies tend to be highly leveraged, whereas manufacturers with heavy investments in specialized machinery and work-in-process inventories should employ less debt.

3. Operating leverage. Other things held constant, a firm with less operating leverage is better able to employ financial leverage. Earlier in this chapter we discussed how operating and financial leverage interact to determine the overall effect of a decline in sales on operating income and earnings per share.

4. Growth rate. Other things held constant, faster-growing firms must rely more heavily on external capital (see Chapter 7). Furthermore, the flotation costs involved in selling common stock exceed those incurred when selling debt. Thus, to minimize financing costs, rapidly growing firms tend to use somewhat more debt than slower-growing companies do. This is especially true of small, privately owned companies.

5. Profitability. One often observes that firms with very high rates of return on investment use relatively little debt. Although there is no theoretical justification for this fact, one practical explanation seems to be that very profitable firms like IBM, 3M, and Microsoft simply do not need to do much debt financing. Their high profit margins enable them to do most of their financing with retained earnings.

6. Taxes. Interest is a deductible expense, whereas dividends are not deductible. Therefore, the higher a firm's corporate tax rate, the greater the advantage of using debt. This point was discussed in Chapter 19.

7. Control. The effect that debt or stock financing might have on a management's control position may influence its capital structure decision. If management has voting control (over 50 percent of the stock) but is not in a position to buy any more stock, debt may be the choice for new financings. On the other hand, a management group that is not concerned about voting control may decide to use equity rather than debt if the firm's financial situation is so weak that the use of debt might subject the firm to serious risk of default; if the firm goes into default, the managers will almost surely lose their jobs. If too little debt is used, however, management runs the risk of a takeover attempt. In general, control considerations do not necessarily suggest the use of debt or equity, but if management is at all insecure, the effects of capital structure on control will certainly be taken into account.

8. Management attitudes. In the absence of proof that one capital structure will lead to higher stock prices than another, management can exercise its own judgment about the proper capital structure. Some managements tend to be more conservative than others and thus use less debt than the average firm in their industry, while other managers do the reverse.

9. Lender and rating agency attitudes. Regardless of managers' own analyses of the proper leverage factors for their firms, there is no question that lenders' and rating agencies' attitudes frequently influence financial structure decisions. In the majority of cases, the corporation discusses its financial structure with lenders and rating agencies and gives much weight to their advice. For example, one large utility was recently told by Moody and Standard & Poor that its bonds would be downgraded if it issued more bonds. This influenced its decision to finance its expansion with common equity.

10. Market conditions. Conditions in the stock and bond markets undergo both long- and short-term changes, which can have an important bearing on a firm's optimal capital structure. For example, during the credit crunch in the fall of 1990, there was simply no market at any "reasonable" interest rate for new long-term bonds rated below A, and the stock market was also weak. Therefore, low-rated companies that needed capital were forced to go to the short-term debt market. Thus, stock and bond market conditions at a point in time do influence the type of securities used for a given financing.

11. The firm's internal conditions. A firm's own internal conditions also have a bearing on its target capital structure. For example, suppose a firm has just successfully completed a research and development program, and it projects higher earnings in the immediate future. However, the new earnings are not yet anticipated by investors and hence are not reflected in the price of the stock. This company would not want to issue stock; it would prefer to finance with debt until the higher earnings materialize and are reflected in the stock price, at which time it could sell an issue of common stock, retire the debt, and return to its target capital structure.

12. Financial flexibility. Astute observers have noted that firms can earn a great deal more money from good capital budgeting and operating decisions than they can from good financing decisions. Indeed, we cannot tell for sure how much financing decisions affect stock prices, but we do know that having to turn down a large order because funds are not available for buying the raw materials or equipment needed to fill it will adversely affect profits. For this reason, most treasurers' primary goal is to always have the ability to raise *the capital needed to support operations.* We also know that when times are good, firms can raise capital with either stock or bonds, but when times are bad, suppliers of capital are much more willing to make funds available if they are given a secured position, and this means *secured debt.*

Putting these two thoughts together gives rise to the goal of *maintaining financial flexibility,* which from an operational viewpoint means *maintaining adequate reserve borrowing capacity.* What constitutes "adequate" reserve borrowing capacity is judgmental, but it clearly depends on the factors mentioned previously in the chapter, including the firm's forecasted need for funds, predicted capital market conditions, management's confidence in its forecasts, and the consequences of a capital shortage.

Self-Test

How does sales stability affect capital structure?

How does asset structure affect capital structure?

How does growth rate affect capital structure?

How do taxes affect capital structure?

How do lender and rating agency attitudes affect capital structure?

How might the firm's internal condition affect capital structure?

What is "financial flexibility," and is it increased or decreased by having a high debt ratio?

VARIATIONS IN CAPITAL STRUCTURES AMONG FIRMS

As might be expected, wide variations in the use of financial leverage occur both among industries and among the individual firms in each industry. Table 20-9 illustrates this point for four industries, ranked in descending order of common equity ratios, as shown in Column 1.

The drug and steel companies do not use much debt (their common equity ratios are high); the uncertainties inherent in industries that are cyclical, oriented toward research, or subject to huge product liability suits render the heavy use of leverage unwise. Retailers and utility companies, on the other

Table 20-9 **Capital Structure Percentages, 1989:**
Four Industries Ranked by Common Equity Ratios

Industry	Common Equity (1)	Preferred Stock (2)	Total Debt (3)	Long-Term Debt (4)	Short-Term Debt (5)	Times-Interest-Earned Ratio (6)	Return on Equity (7)
Drugs	71.8%	1.5%	26.7%	16.0%	10.7%	10.5 ×	24.5%
Steel	63.2	0.0	36.8	32.2	4.6	4.0	10.7
Retailing	48.1	1.3	50.6	36.1	14.5	3.8	15.7
Utilities	43.3	6.0	50.7	46.9	3.8	2.4	9.2
Composite (average of all industries, not just those listed above)	40.3%	1.7%	58.0%	35.4%	22.6%	2.2 ×	13.7%

Note: These ratios are based on accounting (or book) values. Stated on a market value basis, the results would be somewhat different. Most important, the equity percentage would rise, because most stocks sell at prices that are much higher than their book values.
Source: *Compustat* Industrial Data Tape, 1990.

hand, use debt relatively heavily, but for unrelated reasons. Retailers use short-term debt to finance inventories and long-term debt secured by mortgages on their stores. The utility companies have traditionally used large amounts of debt, particularly long-term debt because their fixed assets make good security for mortgage bonds, and their relatively stable sales make it safe for them to carry more debt than can firms with more business risk.

Particular attention should be given to the times-interest-earned (TIE) ratio, because it gives a measure of how safe the debt is and how vulnerable the company is to financial disasters. The TIE ratio depends on three factors: (1) the percentage of debt, (2) the interest rate on the debt, and (3) the company's profitability. Interest rates paid are fairly similar among the firms in the four industries, but their ROEs are quite different. Thus, the retailing industry, which uses much more debt than the steel industry (50.6 percent versus 36.8 percent), still has a TIE ratio close to that of the steel industry because of retailing's much higher profitability.

Wide variations in capital structures also exist among firms within given industries — for example, although the average common equity ratio in 1989 for the drug industry was 71.8 percent, ICN Pharmaceuticals' equity ratio was less than 40 percent, while Bristol-Myers's ratio was over 90 percent. Thus, factors unique to individual firms, including managerial attitudes, do play an important role in setting target capital structures.

Self-Test

Is it true that wide variations in the use of financial leverage occur both among industries and among the individual firms in each industry? Why do these variations occur?

Financing Growth Businesses in the 1990s

Growth requires cash. The financing needs of small but rapidly growing firms are often greater than the firms can meet from internal sources. So, small businesses that hope to become more substantial have to look to financial markets for capital. Where should they look?

In the early to mid-1980s, firms were looking increasingly at the use of venture capital. As a result of the many successful high-tech start-ups in the late 1970s and early 1980s, money poured into venture capital funds. New venture capital firms continued to be formed, often by people who were less experienced than those associated with venture capital in the past. Then, because so much money was available for investment and so many entrepreneurs were trying to get financing, rates of return went way down in the venture capital industry during the mid-to-late 1980s. The "euphoria" over venture capital investment disappeared — some venture capitalists left the business and others became more discriminating when choosing projects in which to invest. Thus, venture capital has become somewhat less available than in the past.

Where will financing for growth be found in the future? *The Wall Street Journal* published figures from the Innovation Development Institute that provided some estimates about sources of growth capital in the 1990s:[11]

Venture capital funds	10%
Individual investors	35%
Large corporations	35%
Federal small business innovation research grants	10%
State, local, and other economic development agencies	10%

Source: Innovation Development Institute as reported by *The Wall Street Journal*, January 24, 1990.

These estimates differ from earlier sources because they include a reduction in venture capital, a reduction in federal sources, and a substantial increase in funds from large corporations. Larger companies are increasingly aware of the need to identify and share in the ownership of flexible and innovative small firms that are developing new products and technologies. Interestingly, one of the most rapidly increasing sources of funds is from foreign-owned corporations, particularly Japanese firms. The United States has always been especially good at creating innovations, and foreign companies are recognizing this fact and taking advantage of it.

Large corporations are especially likely to finance smaller firms that are developing products which might be useful to the larger firms at some point. Often, a large firm will make an equity investment in a small firm and later acquire the smaller firm if it succeeds. The smaller firm's innovations, in the meantime, have not been stifled in the earlier phases of development by being part of the larger firm's bureaucratic structure.

The role of venture capitalists is also changing. In the past, venture capitalists often identified a promising investment and invested some of their own funds in that project. They would then find other venture capitalists and encourage them to invest in the same project. Today, the changing nature of funding opportunities means that the venture capitalists may enlist "the resources of large U.S. corporations and overseas investors" to invest in the venture rather than enlisting other venture capital investors.[12]

Individuals are providing increasing amounts of capital, often in concert with local or state agencies. For example, the city of San Antonio has benefited from the Texas Research and Technology Foundation, which received sub-

[11]Udayan Gupta, "Venture Capital Dims for Start-ups, but Not to Worry," *The Wall Street Journal*, January 24, 1990. Also see Gupta's earlier article, "Home-Grown Businesses Help Revive Local Economies," *The Wall Street Journal*, January 4, 1990.

[12]Glenn Mueller, managing partner of Mayfield Fund, as quoted in Gupta, "Venture Capital," *The Wall Street Journal*, January 24, 1990.

stantial donations from the billionaire Ross Perot (founder of Electronic Data Systems [EDS]) and Trammel Crow, the Dallas-based real estate developer. The San Antonio foundation is just one example of a large number of organizations sponsored all over the United States by state and local governments to stimulate economic development.

While the sources of equity investment are changing, a banker can still be a vital source of funds for the small but growing business. There are advantages to dealing with bankers, particularly for the growing small business that may go public one day. When a small business goes public, it develops a prospectus that must disclose a great deal of information. This might require revealing vital plans to competitors. Once these plans are revealed, competitors could act on them, destroying the very opportunity that was the small firm's greatest asset. One way to circumvent that problem is to deal privately with a bank or a venture capitalist, and to obtain funds from such a source. When it is time for a public offering, the relationship with a banker or venture capitalist sends two favorable signals: (1) that the firm has been able to secure financing (and probably revealed some favor-able inside information, legally, to do so), and (2) that someone has been actively monitoring management's actions. Two recent empirical studies have found that initial public offerings are not as underpriced when bank loans are disclosed or when high-quality venture capitalists have invested in the companies going public.[13]

Entrepreneurial companies with high-growth prospects will continue to need financing to support their growth in the future. The sources of that financing will increasingly include larger corporations, foreign investors, and new sources of funds from state and local governments. However, banks and venture capitalists will continue to be important sources both of funds and of strategic advice for small businesses.

---

[13]Christopher James and Peggy Wier, "Borrowing Relationships, Intermediation, and the Cost of Issuing Public Securities," Working paper, University of Florida and University of Oregon, January 1990; and Christopher Barry, Chris Muscarella, John Peavy, and Michael Vetsuypens, "The Role of Venture Capital in the Creation of Public Corporations: Evidence from the Going Public Process," Working paper, Texas Christian University and Southern Methodist University, February 1990.

SUMMARY

In this chapter we examined the effects of financial leverage on stock prices, earnings per share, and the cost of capital. The key concepts covered are summarized below:

- A firm's **optimal capital structure** is that mix of debt, preferred stock, and common equity which maximizes the price of the firm's stock. At any point in time, the firm's management has a specific **target capital structure** in mind, presumably the optimal one, although this target may change over time.

- **Business risk** is the uncertainty associated with a firm's future operating income (EBIT). A firm will tend to have low business risk if the demand for its products is stable, if the prices of its inputs and products remain relatively constant, if it can adjust its prices freely as its costs increase, and if a high percentage of its costs are variable and hence decrease if its output and sales decrease. Other things the same, the lower a firm's business risk, the higher its optimal debt ratio.

- **Financial leverage** is the extent to which fixed-income securities (debt and preferred stock) are used in a firm's capital structure. **Financial risk** is the added risk to stockholders which results from financial leverage.

- The **degree of operating leverage (DOL)** shows how changes in sales affect operating income, whereas the **degree of financial leverage (DFL)** shows how changes in operating income affect earnings per share. The **degree of total leverage (DTL)** shows the percentage change in EPS resulting from a given percentage change in sales: DTL = DOL × DFL.

- Several factors influence a firm's capital structure decisions. These factors include (1) the firm's **business risk,** (2) its **tax position,** and (3) its need for **financial flexibility.**

- **Entrepreneurial companies** with high-growth prospects need **financing** to support future growth. Financing sources will include larger corporations, foreign investors, and funds from state and local governments. Banks and **venture capitalists,** however, will continue to be important sources of funds and advice for these firms.

Although it is theoretically possible to determine a firm's optimal capital structure, as a practical matter we cannot estimate this structure with precision. Accordingly, financial executives generally treat the optimal capital structure as a range — for example, 40 to 50 percent debt — rather than as a precise point, such as 45 percent. The concepts discussed in this chapter help managers understand the factors they should consider when they set the optimal capital structure ranges for their firms.

EQUATIONS

The breakeven point is the level of sales that just covers all operating costs, and is calculated as

$$Q_{BE} = \frac{F}{(P - V)}.$$ (20-1)

The degree of operating leverage (DOL) measures the reaction of operating profits to changes in the volume of sales, and it can be calculated in one of two ways:

$$DOL = \frac{Q(P - V)}{Q(P - V) - F}.$$ (20-2)

$$DOL = \frac{S - VC}{S - VC - F}.$$ (20-2a)

RESOLUTION TO DECISION IN FINANCE

Getting the Lumps Out

Deciding that bankruptcy would benefit no one, Sealy and its bridge lender, First Boston, worked out a new agreement. First, to ease its own debt burden, First Boston passed along $250 million of the debt to its Swiss parent company, Credit-Suisse Holdings. Then, First Boston and Gibbons Green agreed to forfeit approximately $17 million in fees, further reducing the original bridge loan. With $200 million remaining to be refinanced, First Boston exchanged part of the debt for a 40 percent equity stake in Sealy. This reduced the equity of Gibbons Green, its partners, and its investors to 60 percent. To refinance the rest of the bridge loan, First Boston planned a private placement of zero coupon bonds coming due in 1999. David M. Malcolm, an executive at First Boston, said the investment bank will "probably sell this remaining piece in fairly short order." He said interest levels would be set to "look, act, walk, and talk like the levels in 1989" and that bond buyers might have to be given some common stock "depend[ing] on what we think of the market when we put it [the issue] together."

Commercial banks carrying Gibbons's debt also made concessions. A syndicate of banks led by First National Bank of Chicago agreed to accept a single $40 million repayment in 1996 instead of two $20 million repayments due in 1991 and 1992. In return, Gibbons will reduce its revolving credit by $30 million.

Meanwhile, CEO Candlish has not been lying down on the job in the "burning bed," as Sealy was facetiously dubbed. He trimmed costs as well as increasing revenues 6.2 percent in his first year. Sealy had $76.4 million in operating cash flows, up 20 percent over the previous year. Candlish announced plans to close 13 of Sealy's 38 plants, to sell off a subsidiary and excess real estate, and to use the proceeds to help pay off the debt. Revenues increased, in part because of an agreement he negotiated with Sears, and he says that meeting all his cash requirements is "eminently doable."

Even so, the debt restructuring plans are not pleasing everyone. Some specialists cautioned that the zero coupon bonds aren't sure sellers, even when sweetened with equity. And Edward Gibbons of Gibbons Green ruefully discussed his firm's investors and partners who had to give up 40 percent of their equity, saying, "They're unhappy, we're unhappy." Nevertheless, the changes had to be made; Sealy had to establish a solid financial foundation before it could go on with its strategic operating plans.

Sources: Christopher Farrell and Leah J. Nathans, "The Bills Are Coming Due," *Business Week,* September 11, 1989; Maria Mallory, "Ohio Mattress Gets the Lumps Out at Last," *Business Week,* May 7, 1990; Reed Abelson, "Out of the Burning Bed," *Forbes,* April 30, 1990.

The degree of financial leverage (DFL) shows how changes in operating income affect earnings per share, and it can be calculated as

$$DFL = \frac{EBIT}{EBIT - I}. \tag{20-3}$$

The degree of operating leverage (DOL) measures the reaction of operating profits to changes in the volume of sales, and it can be calculated in one of two ways:

$$DTL = \frac{Q(P - V)}{Q(P - V) - F - I}. \qquad \textbf{(20-4)}$$

$$DTL = DOL \times DFL. \qquad \text{(Footnote 8.)}$$

QUESTIONS

20-1 "One type of leverage affects both EBIT and EPS. The other type affects only EPS." Explain what this statement means.

20-2 What is the relationship between market (or beta) risk and leverage?

20-3 Explain why the following statement is true: "Other things the same, firms with relatively stable sales are able to carry relatively high debt ratios."

20-4 Why do public utility companies usually pursue a different financial policy than retail firms?

20-5 Some economists believe that swings in business cycles will not be as wide in the future as they have been in the past. Assuming that they are correct in their analysis, what effect might this added stability have on the types of financing used by firms in the United States? Would your answer be true for all firms?

20-6 Why is EBIT generally considered to be independent of financial leverage? Why might EBIT actually be influenced by financial leverage at high debt levels?

20-7 How might increasingly volatile inflation rates, interest rates, and bond prices affect the optimal capital structure for corporations?

20-8 If a firm went from zero debt to successively higher levels of debt, why would you expect its stock price to first rise, then hit a peak, and then begin to decline?

20-9 Why is the debt level that maximizes a firm's expected EPS always higher than the debt level that maximizes its stock price?

20-10 In public utility rate cases, a utility's riskiness is a key issue, as utilities are supposed to be allowed to earn the same rate of return on common equity as unregulated firms of comparable risk. The difficulty is in specifying in quantitative terms the riskiness of utilities and nonutilities. Describe how the degree of leverage concepts (DOL, DFL, and DTL) might be used as indicators of risk in a rate case.

20-11 The Bell System was broken up, with the old AT&T being split into a new AT&T plus 7 regional telephone companies. The specific reason for forcing the breakup was to increase the degree of competition in the telephone industry. AT&T had had a monopoly on local service, long distance, and the manufacture of all the equipment used by telephone companies, and the breakup was expected to open most of these markets to competition. In the court order that laid out the terms of the breakup, the capital structures of the surviving companies were specified, and much attention was given to the increased competition telephone companies could expect in the future. Do you think the optimal capital structure after the breakup was the same as the prebreakup optimal capital structure? Do you think competition could force companies to use more debt in order to reduce taxes? Explain your position.

20-12   Assume that you are advising the management of a firm that is about to double its assets to serve its rapidly growing market. It must choose between a highly automated production process and a less automated one, and it must also choose a capital structure for financing the expansion. Should the asset investment and financing decisions be jointly determined, or should each decision be made separately? How would these decisions affect one another? How could the degree of leverage concept be used to help management analyze the situation?

20-13   Your firm's R&D department has been working on a new process which, if it works, can produce oil from coal at a cost of about $5 per barrel versus a current market price of $20 per barrel. The company needs $10 million of external funds at this time to complete the research. The results of the research will be known in about a year, and there is about a 50-50 chance of success. If the research is successful, your company will need to raise a substantial amount of new money to put the idea into production. Your economists forecast that although the economy will be depressed next year, interest rates will be high because of international monetary problems. You must recommend how the currently needed $10 million should be raised — as debt or as equity. How would the potential impact of your project influence your financing decision?

SELF-TEST PROBLEMS

ST-1   Visical, Inc., produces medical test equipment for ophthalmologists, which sells for $500 per unit. Visical's fixed operating costs are $1 million; 5,000 units are produced and sold each year; operating profits total $250,000; and the firm's assets (all equity financed) are $2,500,000. Visical estimates that it can change its production process, thereby adding $2 million to investment and $250,000 to fixed operating costs. This change will reduce variable operating costs per unit by $50 and increase output by 2,000 units, but the sales price on all units will have to be lowered to $475 to permit sales of the additional output. Visical has tax loss carry-forwards that cause its tax rate to be zero. It uses no debt, and its average cost of capital is 10 percent.

a. Should Visical make the change?

b. Would Visical's operating leverage as measured by DOL increase or decrease if it made the change? What about its breakeven point?

c. Suppose the investment totaled $4 million, and Visical had to borrow $2 million at an interest rate of 7 percent. Find the ROE on the $2 million incremental equity investment. Should Visical make the change if debt financing must be used?

ST-2   Brosky Production's situation is as follows: (1) EBIT = $2.86 million; (2) tax rate = $t = 40\%$; (3) debt outstanding = D = $4 million; (4) k_d = 9%; (5) k_s = 12%; and (6) shares of stock outstanding = 500,000. Since Brosky's product market is stable and the company expects no growth, all earnings are paid out as dividends. The debt consists of perpetual bonds.

a. What are Brosky's earnings per share (EPS) and its price per share (P_0)?

b. What is Brosky's weighted average cost of capital (WACC)?

c. Brosky can increase its debt by $4 million, to a total of $8 million, using the new debt to buy back and retire some of its shares at the current price. Its interest rate on debt will be 12 percent (it will have to call and refund the old debt), and its cost of equity will rise from 12 percent to 15 percent. EBIT will remain constant. Should Brosky change its capital structure?

    d. What is Brosky's TIE coverage ratio under the original situation and under the conditions in Part c?

PROBLEMS

20-1   **Combined leverage effects.** Clouse, Inc., has a DOL of 2.0 and a DFL of 3.0. If sales increase by 10 percent, what will happen to net income?

20-2   **Operating leverage effects.** The Delano Company has a single product, which sells for $45 and has a variable cost of $30 per unit. Fixed operating costs are $750,000.

    a. What is the firm's breakeven point in units?

    b. What is the firm's breakeven point in sales dollars?

    c. What is the firm's DOL if sales are 15,000 units above the breakeven point?

    d. What is the firm's EBIT if Delano's sales are 7,500 units below the breakeven point for the period?

20-3   **Operating leverage effects.** Now assume that The Delano Company (Problem 20-2) has begun an impressive modernization program. To reduce its per-unit variable costs to $15 per unit, the company's fixed operating costs have been allowed to rise to $2.1 million annually. Under these new conditions:

    a. What is the firm's breakeven point in units?

    b. What is the firm's breakeven point in sales dollars?

    c. What is the firm's DOL if sales are 15,000 units above the breakeven point?

    d. What is the firm's EBIT if Delano's sales are 7,500 units below the breakeven point for the period?

    e. What are the financial implications of the new level of operating leverage as compared to Delano's operating leverage before modernization?

20-4   **Operating leverage.** Wei Manufacturing is selling 300,000 units of its only product at $100 per unit. Variable costs are $40 per unit, whereas annual fixed operating costs are $15 million.

    a. What is the firm's operating profit?

    b. What is the firm's DOL?

    c. If sales increase by 5 percent, what is the resulting operating profit? Use the DOL to answer this question.

    d. Confirm your answer in Part c by preparing an income statement showing the dollar level of sales, fixed and variable operating costs, and operating profit after the 5 percent growth in sales.

    e. What would happen to operating profits if sales decline by 5 percent? Confirm your answer with a pro forma income statement.

20-5   **Operating leverage.** Refer back to Figure 20-1.

    a. Calculate the degree of operating leverage for Options 1 and 2 at sales of $40,000, $120,000, and $360,000. The degree of operating leverage for other levels of sales are as follows:

Sales	DOL$_1$	DOL$_2$
$ 80,000	Undefined (or ∞)	(2.0)
160,000	2.0	4.0
200,000	1.67	2.5

b. Is it true that the DOL is approximately equal to infinity just above the breakeven point, implying that a very small increase in sales will produce a huge percentage increase in EBIT, but that the DOL declines when calculated at higher levels of sales?

c. Is it true for both options for all sales levels where DOL > 0 that $DOL_2 < DOL_1$? Explain.

20-6   **Breakeven analysis.** O'Connor Industries will produce 200,000 outdoor gas grills this year. Variable costs are $24 per unit and fixed operating costs are $5,700,000. What selling price is required for O'Connor to obtain operating profits of $300,000 if all 200,000 units are sold?

20-7   **Breakeven point.** Romantic Books sells paperback books for $5.60 each. The variable cost per book is $4. At current annual sales of 150,000 books, the publisher is just breaking even. It is estimated that if the authors' royalties are reduced, the variable cost per book will drop by $1. Assume the authors' royalties are reduced and sales remain constant; how much more money can the publisher put into advertising (a fixed operating cost) and still break even?

20-8   **Combined leverage effects.** Annie's Sweet Shop has sales of $9.6 million, and variable cost is 65 percent of sales. Fixed operating costs are $1.8 million. The firm just received an $8.4 million loan with an interest rate of 11 percent. Assume that this loan is the firm's only debt.
a. What is the firm's DOL?
b. What is the firm's DFL?
c. What is the firm's DTL?

20-9   **Combined leverage effects.** Nachman Novelty has a single product, which it sells for $50. Variable costs per unit are $35 and total fixed operating costs are $600,000, which include interest payments of $120,000. The firm plans to produce and sell 48,000 units this year.
a. What is the firm's DOL?
b. What is the firm's DFL?
c. What is the firm's DTL?

20-10   **Combined leverage effects.** Muscarella Vineyards expects sales of $15 million this year. Variable costs are 45 percent of sales, and fixed operating costs are $7.5 million. The firm has debt of $10 million on which it pays 9 percent interest.
a. What is the firm's DOL?
b. What is the firm's DFL?
c. What is the firm's DTL?

20-11   **Financial leverage.** Puckett's Playtime Store has annual sales of $7.4 million, variable costs are 40 percent of sales, and fixed operating costs are $4 million. The firm's DFL = 4.0. How much interest does the firm pay annually?

20-12   **Degree of financial leverage.** A company currently sells 150,000 units annually. At this sales level, its EBIT is $8 million, and its degree of total leverage is 2.0. The firm's debt consists of $20 million in bonds with a 12 percent coupon. The company is considering a new production method which will entail an increase in fixed operating costs, resulting in a degree of operating leverage of 1.8. Being concerned about the total risk of the firm, the president wants to keep the degree of total leverage at 2.0. If EBIT remains at $8 million, what amount of bonds must be retired to accomplish this?

20-13 **Combined leverage effects.** Enholm Engineering has the following financial characteristics:

$$\text{Sales in units} = 50{,}000.$$
$$\text{Unit sales price} = \$140.$$
$$\text{Variable cost per unit} = \$77.$$
$$\text{Fixed operating costs} = \$2.1 \text{ million.}$$
$$\text{Annual interest charges} = \$350{,}000.$$
$$\text{Tax rate} = 40\%.$$
$$\text{Shares outstanding} = 200{,}000.$$

a. Determine the firm's EPS if sales increase by 20 percent next year. Use the DTL equation as the basis for your computations.
b. Confirm your answer in Part a by preparing a projected income statement.

20-14 **Combined leverage effects.** Southwest Manufacturing Incorporated (SMI) is a new firm that will manufacture and sell replacement parts for equipment to construction firms. The firm must determine the operating and financial leverage under which it will operate. SMI can use a low operating leverage (LOL) plan under which variable costs are $15 per unit (75 percent of sales) and fixed operating costs are $200,000. Alternatively, SMI can use high operating leverage (called the HOL plan) under which the variable costs are $10 per unit (50 percent of sales) and fixed operating costs are $600,000. Whichever production plan is implemented, the firm's product will sell for $20 per unit.
a. Calculate the degree of operating leverage (DOL) for the LOL and HOL production plans at sales of $1.2 million and $1.6 million.
b. Assume that the LOL and HOL plans can be financed in either of the following ways: (1) no debt, or (2) $900,000 of debt at 10 percent interest. Calculate the degree of financial leverage (DFL) for the LOL plan at sales levels of both $1.2 and $1.6 million. The DFLs for the HOL plan at $900,000 of debt and these same sales levels are 0 and 1.82, respectively.
c. Calculate the degree of total leverage (DTL) under the LOL plan with $900,000 of debt at sales of $1.2 and $1.6 million. The DTLs for the HOL plan at these same sales levels are −6.67 and 7.27, respectively.
d. At the sales level of $1.2 million, the DTL for the HOL plan was negative (DTL$_{HOL}$ = −6.67). Does a negative degree of operating leverage imply that an increase in sales will *lower* profits?

20-15 **Changing capital structure.** Parrish Paper Company is an all-equity firm that is considering changing its capital structure to include debt. The return on an average security in the market, k_M, is 14 percent, and the risk-free rate, k_{RF}, is 9 percent. Parrish's beta is 1.1. If Parrish borrows to the extent that 30 percent of its total financing is debt financed, its beta will rise to 1.4. What is the cost of equity for Parrish Paper Company before and after the proposed change?

20-16 **Financing alternatives.** Chang, Inc., plans to raise a net amount of $360 million to finance new equipment and working capital in early 1991. Two alternatives are being considered: Common stock may be sold to net $40 per share, or debentures yielding

10 percent may be issued. Chang's balance sheet and income statement prior to financing are as follows:

Chang, Inc.:
Balance Sheet as of December 31, 1990
(Millions of Dollars)

Current assets	$1,200	Accounts payable	$ 230
Net fixed assets	600	Notes payable to bank	370
		Other current liabilities	300
		Total current liabilities	$ 900
		Long-term debt	370
		Common stock, $2 par	80
		Retained earnings	450
Total assets	$1,800	Total liabilities and equity	$1,800

Chang, Inc.:
Income Statement for Year Ended December 31, 1990
(Millions of Dollars)

Sales	$3,300
Operating costs	2,970
Earnings before interest and taxes (10%)	$ 330
Interest on debt	60
Earnings before taxes	$ 270
Federal-plus-state taxes (40%)	108
Net income	$ 162

The probability distribution for annual sales is as follows:

Probability	Annual Sales (Millions of Dollars)
0.30	$3,000
0.40	3,600
0.30	4,200

a. Assuming that EBIT is equal to 10 percent of sales, calculate earnings per share under both the debt financing and the stock financing alternatives at each possible level of sales. Then calculate expected earnings per share and σ_{EPS} under both debt and stock financing. Also calculate the debt ratio and the times-interest-earned (TIE) ratio at the expected sales level under each alternative. The old debt will remain outstanding. Which financing method would you recommend?

(Do Part b only if you are using the computerized problem diskette.)

b. Suppose each of the following happens, with other values held at Part a levels:
   (1) The interest rate on new debt falls to 5 percent.
   (2) The interest rate on new debt rises to 20 percent.
   (3) The stock price falls to $20 (return k_d to 0.10 = 10%).
   (4) The stock price rises to $70.
   (5) With P_0 = $40 and k_d = 0.10 = 10%, now change the sales probability distribution to the following:

	Sales	Probability		Sales	Probability
(a)	$3,000	0	(b) $	0	0.3
	3,600	1.0		3,600	0.4
	4,200	0		10,000	0.3

What are the implications of these changes?

SOLUTIONS TO SELF-TEST PROBLEMS

ST-1   **a. 1.** Determine the variable cost per unit at present, using the following definitions and equations:

P = average sales price per unit of output = $500.

F = fixed operating costs = $1 million.

Q = units of output (sales) = 5,000.

V = variable costs per unit, found as follows:

Operating profit = QP − QV − F

$$\$250,000 = 5,000(\$500) - 5,000(V) - \$1,000,000$$

$$5,000V = \$1,250,000$$

$$V = \$250.$$

2. Determine the new operating profit level if the change is made:

New operating profit = $Q_2(P_2) - Q_2(V_2) - F_2$

$$= 7,000(\$475) - 7,000(\$200) - \$1,250,000$$

$$= \$675,000.$$

3. Determine the incremental operating profit:

$$\Delta\text{Operating profit} = \$675,000 - \$250,000 = \$425,000.$$

4. Estimate the approximate rate of return on the new investment:

$$\text{ROI} = \frac{\Delta\text{Profit}}{\text{Investment}} = \frac{\$425,000}{\$2,000,000} = 21.25\%.$$

Since the ROI exceeds Visical's average cost of capital, this analysis suggests that Visical should go ahead and make the investment.

b.

$$\text{DOL} = \frac{Q(P - V)}{Q(P - V) - F}$$

$$\text{DOL}_{\text{Old}} = \frac{5,000(\$500 - \$250)}{5,000(\$500 - \$250) - \$1,000,000} = 5.00.$$

$$\text{DOL}_{\text{New}} = \frac{7,000(\$475 - \$200)}{7,000(\$475 - \$200) - \$1,250,000} = 2.85.$$

This indicates that operating income will be less sensitive to changes in sales if the production process is changed, thus suggesting that the change would reduce risks. However, the change also would increase the breakeven point. Still, with a lower sales price, it might be easier to achieve the higher new breakeven volume:

$$Old: Q_{BE} = \frac{F}{P - V} = \frac{\$1,000,000}{\$500 - \$250} = 4,000 \text{ units.}$$

$$New: Q_{BE} = \frac{F_2}{P_2 - V_2} = \frac{\$1,250,000}{\$475 - \$200} = 4,545 \text{ units.}$$

c. The incremental ROE is

$$ROE = \frac{\Delta Profit}{\Delta Equity}.$$

Using debt financing, the incremental profit associated with the equity investment is equal to that found in Part a minus the interest expense incurred as a result of the investment:

$$\Delta \text{Operating profit} = \text{New profit} - \text{Old profit} - \text{Interest}$$

$$= \$675,000 - \$250,000 - 0.07(\$2,000,000)$$

$$= \$285,000.$$

$$ROE = \frac{\$285,000}{\$2,000,000}$$

$$= 14.25\%.$$

The return on the new equity investment still exceeds the average cost of capital, so Visical should make the investment.

ST-2   **a.**

EBIT	$2,860,000
Interest ($4,000,000 × 0.09)	360,000
Earnings before taxes (EBT)	2,500,000
Taxes (40%)	1,000,000
Net income	$1,500,000

$$EPS = \$1,500,000/500,000 = \$3.00.$$

$$P_0 = \$3.00/0.12 = \$25.00.$$

b. $\text{Equity} = 500,000 \times \$25 = \$12,500,000.$

$\text{Debt} = \$4,000,000.$

$\text{Total capital} = \$16,500,000.$

$WACC = w_d k_d(1 - t) + w_s k_s$

$= (\$4,000,000/\$16,500,000)(9\%)(1 - 0.4) + (\$12,500,000/\$16,500,000)(12\%)$

$= 1.31\% + 9.09\%$

$= 10.40\%.$

c. EBIT $2,860,000
    Interest ($8,000,000 × 0.12)   960,000
    Earnings before taxes (EBT) $1,900,000
    Taxes (40%)   760,000
    Net income $1,140,000

Shares bought and retired:

$$\Delta N = \Delta Debt/P_0 = \$4,000,000/\$25 = 160,000.$$

New outstanding shares:

$$N_1 = N_0 - \Delta N = 500,000 - 160,000 = 340,000.$$

New EPS:

$$EPS = \$1,140,000/340,000 = \$3.35.$$

New price per share:

$$P_0 = \$3.35/0.15 = \$22.33 \text{ versus } \$25.00.$$

Therefore, Brosky should not change its capital structure.

d.
$$TIE = \frac{EBIT}{I}.$$

$$\text{Original TIE} = \frac{\$2,860,000}{\$360,000} = 7.94.$$

$$\text{New TIE} = \frac{\$2,860,000}{\$960,000} = 2.98.$$

Appendix 20A[1]

Bankruptcy

In the event of bankruptcy, debtholders have a prior claim to a firm's income and assets over common and preferred stockholders. Because different classes of debtholders are accorded different treatments in bankruptcy settlements, it is important for one to know who gets what if the firm fails. These topics are discussed in this appendix.[2]

Federal Bankruptcy Laws

Bankruptcy actually begins when a debtor is unable to meet scheduled payments to creditors or when the firm's cash flow projections indicate that it will soon be unable

---

[1]This appendix was coauthored by Arthur L. Hermann of the University of Hartford.
[2]Much of the current work in this area is based on writings of Edward I. Altman. For a summary of his work and that of others, see Edward I. Altman, "Bankruptcy and Reorganization," in *Financial Handbook,* ed. Edward I. Altman (New York: Wiley, 1986), Chapter 19.

to meet payments. As the bankruptcy proceedings go forward, the following central issues arise:

1. Is the inability to meet scheduled debt payments a temporary cash flow problem, or does it represent a permanent problem caused by asset values' having fallen below debt obligations?

2. If the problem is a temporary one, an extension that gives the firm time to recover and to satisfy creditors will be worked out. If basic long-run asset values have truly declined, economic losses have occurred. In this event, who should bear the losses?

3. Is the company "worth more dead than alive"? In other words, would the business be more valuable if it were maintained and continued in operation, or if it were liquidated and sold off in pieces?

4. Who should control the firm while it is being liquidated or rehabilitated? Should the existing management be left in control, or should a *trustee* be placed in charge of operations?

These primary issues are addressed in the federal bankruptcy statutes.

The U.S. bankruptcy laws were first enacted in 1898, modified substantially in 1938, changed again in 1978, and further fine-tuned in 1984. The 1978 act, which provides the basic laws that govern bankruptcy today, was a major revision designed to streamline and expedite proceedings, and it consists of eight odd-numbered chapters, the even-numbered chapters of the earlier act having been deleted. Chapters 1, 3, and 5 of the 1978 act contain general provisions applicable to the other chapters; Chapter 7 details the procedures to be followed when liquidating a firm; Chapter 9 provides for financially distressed municipalities; Chapter 11 is the business reorganization chapter; Chapter 13 covers the adjustment of debts for "individuals with regular income"; and Chapter 15 sets up a system of trustees who help administer proceedings under the act.

Chapters 11 and 7 are the most important ones for financial management purposes. When you read in the paper that Eastern Airlines or some other company has "filed for **Chapter 11,**" this means that the company is bankrupt and is trying to reorganize under Chapter 11 of the act. If a reorganization plan cannot be worked out, then the company will be liquidated as prescribed in **Chapter 7** of the act.

The 1978 act is quite flexible, and it provides a great deal of scope for informal negotiations between a company and its creditors. Under this act, a case is opened by filing a petition with a federal district bankruptcy court. The petition may be either voluntary or involuntary; that is, it may be filed either by the firm's management or by its creditors. A committee of unsecured creditors is then appointed by the court to negotiate with management for a *reorganization,* which may include the restructuring of debt and other claims against the firm. (A restructuring could involve lengthening the maturity of debt, lowering the interest rate on it, reducing the principal amount owed, exchanging common or preferred stock for debt, or some combination of these actions.) A trustee may be appointed by the court if it is in the best interests of the creditors and stockholders; otherwise, the existing management will retain control. Under Chapter 11, if no fair and feasible reorganization can be worked out, the firm will be liquidated under the procedures spelled out in Chapter 7.

Financial Decisions in Bankruptcy

When a business becomes insolvent, a decision must be made whether to dissolve the firm through **liquidation** or to keep it alive through **reorganization.** Fundamentally, this decision depends on a determination of the value of the firm if it is rehabilitated

Chapter 11
A chapter of the Bankruptcy Reform Act that governs reorganizations, or restructurings, due to bankruptcy.

Chapter 7
A chapter of the Bankruptcy Reform Act that governs liquidations, or selling of the firm's assets, due to bankruptcy.

liquidation
The dissolution of a firm by selling off its assets.

reorganization
The restructuring of debt and other claims against the firm.

as compared with the value of the assets if they are sold off individually. The procedure that promises higher returns to the creditors and owners will be adopted. Often the greater indicated value of the firm in reorganization versus its value in liquidation is used to force a compromise agreement among the claimants in a reorganization, even when each group believes that its relative position has not been treated fairly in the reorganization plan. Both the SEC and the courts are called upon to determine the *fairness* and the *feasibility* of proposed plans of reorganization.

Standard of Fairness. The basic doctrine of fairness states that claims must be recognized in the order of their legal and contractual priority. Carrying out this concept of fairness in a reorganization (as opposed to a liquidation) involves the following steps:

1. Future sales must be estimated.

2. Operating conditions must be analyzed so that the future earnings and cash flows can be predicted.

3. The capitalization (or discount) rate to be applied to these future cash flows must be determined.

4. This capitalization rate must be applied to the estimated cash flows to obtain a present value figure, which is the indicated value for the reorganized company.

5. Provisions for the distribution of the restructured firm's securities to its claimants must be made.

Standard of Feasibility. The primary test of *feasibility* in a reorganization is whether the fixed charges after reorganization can be adequately covered by cash flows. Adequate coverage generally requires an improvement in operating earnings, a reduction of fixed charges, or both. Among the actions that must generally be taken are the following:

1. Debt maturities are usually lengthened, interest rates may be scaled back, and some debt may be converted into equity.

2. When the quality of management has been substandard, a new team must be given control of the company.

3. If inventories have become obsolete or depleted, they must be replaced.

4. Sometimes the plant and the equipment must be modernized before the firm can operate on a competitive basis.

Liquidation Procedures

If a company is too far gone to be reorganized, it must be liquidated. Liquidation should occur if the business is worth more dead than alive, or if the possibility of restoring it to financial health is so remote that the creditors would face a high risk of even greater losses if operations were continued.

Chapter 7 of the Bankruptcy Reform Act is designed to do three things: (1) provide safeguards against the withdrawal of assets by the owners of the bankrupt firm; (2) provide for an equitable distribution of the assets among the creditors; and (3) allow insolvent debtors to discharge all their obligations and to start new businesses unhampered by a burden of prior debt. Liquidation is time-consuming, it can be costly, and it results in the loss of the business.

The distribution of assets in a liquidation under Chapter 7 of the Bankruptcy Act is governed by the following priority of claims:

1. *Secured creditors, who are entitled to the proceeds of the sale of specific property pledged for a lien or a mortgage.* If the proceeds from the sale of property do not fully satisfy the secured creditors' claims, the remaining balance owed them is treated as a general creditor claim. See Item 9.

2. *Trustee's costs to administer and operate the bankrupt firm.*

3. *Expenses incurred after an involuntary case has begun but before a trustee is appointed.*

4. *Wages due workers if earned within three months prior to the filing of the petition of bankruptcy.* The amount of wages is limited to $2,000 per person.

5. *Claims for unpaid contributions to employee benefit plans that were to have been paid within six months prior to filing.* However, these claims, plus wages in Item 4, are not to exceed the $2,000-per-employee limit.

6. *Unsecured claims for customer deposits, not to exceed a maximum of $900 per individual.*

7. *Taxes due a federal, state, county, or any other government agency.*

8. *Unfunded pension plan liabilities.* These have a claim above that of general creditors for an amount up to 30 percent of the common and preferred equity; any remaining unfunded pension claims rank with general creditors.

9. *General, or unsecured, creditors.* Holders of trade credit, unsecured loans, the unsatisfied portion of secured loans, and debenture bonds are classified as *general creditors.* Holders of subordinated debt also fall into this category, but they must turn over required amounts to the holders of senior debt.

10. *Preferred stockholders,* who can receive an amount up to the par value of the issue.

11. *Common stockholders,* who receive any remaining funds.

To illustrate how this priority of claims works out, consider the balance sheet of Panhandle Drilling, Inc., shown in Table 20A-1. Assets total $90 million. The claims are indicated on the right-hand side of the balance sheet. Note that the debentures are subordinated to the notes payable to banks. Panhandle has filed for reorganization under Chapter 11, but since no fair and feasible reorganization could be arranged, the trustee is liquidating the firm under Chapter 7.

Now assume that the assets are sold. The assets as reported in the balance sheet in Table 20A-1 are greatly overstated — they are, in fact, worth less than half of the $90 million at which they are carried. The following amounts are realized on liquidation:

Proceeds from sale of current assets	$28,000,000
Proceeds from sale of fixed assets	5,000,000
Total receipts	$33,000,000

The order of priority for payment of claims is shown in Table 20A-2. The first mortgage is paid from the net proceeds of $5 million from the sale of fixed property, leaving $28 million available to other creditors. Next come the fees and expenses of the trustee's administration, which are typically about 20 percent of gross proceeds; in this example they are assumed to be $6 million. Next in priority are wages due workers,

Table 20A-1 **Panhandle Drilling, Inc.: Balance Sheet**

Current assets	$80,000,000	Accounts payable	$20,000,000
Net fixed assets	10,000,000	Notes payable (due bank)	10,000,000
		Accrued wages, 1,400 at $500	700,000
		U.S. taxes	1,000,000
		State and local taxes	300,000
		Total current liabilities	$32,000,000
		First mortgage	6,000,000
		Second mortgage	1,000,000
		Subordinated debentures[a]	8,000,000
		Long-term debt	$15,000,000
		Preferred stock	2,000,000
		Common stock	26,000,000
		Paid-in capital	4,000,000
		Retained earnings	11,000,000
		Total equity	$43,000,000
Total assets	$90,000,000	Total liabilities and equity	$90,000,000

[a]Subordinated to $10 million of notes payable to the First National Bank.

Table 20A-2 **Panhandle Drilling, Inc.: Order of Priority of Claims**

Distribution of Proceeds on Liquidation

1. Proceeds from sale of assets	$33,000,000
2. First mortgage, paid from sale of fixed assets	5,000,000
3. Fees and expenses of administration of bankruptcy	6,000,000
4. Wages due workers earned within 3 months prior to filing of bankruptcy petition	700,000
5. Taxes	1,300,000
6. Available to general creditors	$20,000,000

Claims of General Creditors	Claim[a] (1)	Application of 50 Percent[b] (2)	After Subordination Adjustment[c] (3)	Percentage of Original Claims Received[d] (4)
Unsatisfied portion of first mortgage	$ 1,000,000	$ 500,000	$ 500,000	92
Unsatisfied portion of second mortgage	1,000,000	500,000	500,000	50
Notes payable	10,000,000	5,000,000	9,000,000	90
Accounts payable	20,000,000	10,000,000	10,000,000	50
Subordinated debentures	8,000,000	4,000,000	0	0
	$40,000,000	$20,000,000	$20,000,000	

[a]Column 1 is the claim of each class of general creditor. Total claims equal $40 million.
[b]From Line 6 in the upper section of the table, we see that $20 million is available for general creditors. This sum, divided by the $40 million of claims, indicates that general creditors will initially receive 50 percent of their claims. This is shown in Column 2.
[c]The debentures are subordinated to the notes payable, so $4 million is reallocated from debentures to notes payable in Column 3.
[d]Column 4 shows the results of dividing the amount in Column 3 by the original claim amount given in Column 1, except for the first mortgage, for which $5 million received from the sale of fixed assets is included.

which total $700,000. The total amount of taxes to be paid is $1.3 million. Thus far, the total of claims paid from the $33 million is $13 million, leaving $20 million for the general creditors.

The claims of the general creditors total $40 million. Since $20 million is available, claimants would each receive 50 percent of their claims before the subordination adjustment. This adjustment requires that the holders of subordinated debentures turn over to the holders of notes payable all amounts received until the notes are satisfied. In this situation the claim of the holders of the notes payable is $10 million, but only $5 million is available; the deficiency is therefore $5 million. After transfer of $4 million from the subordinated debentures, there remains a deficiency of $1 million on the notes. This amount will remain unsatisfied.

Note that 90 percent of the bank claim is satisfied, whereas a maximum of 50 percent of other unsecured claims will be satisfied. These figures illustrate the usefulness of the subordination provision to the security to which the subordination is made. Because no other funds remain, the claims of the holders of preferred and common stock are completely wiped out. Studies of bankruptcy liquidations indicate that unsecured creditors receive, on the average, about 15 cents on the dollar, whereas common stockholders generally receive nothing.

Social Issues in Bankruptcy Proceedings

An interesting social issue arose in connection with bankruptcy during the 1980s — the role of bankruptcy in settling labor disputes and product liability suits. Normally, bankruptcy proceedings originate after a company has become so financially weak that it cannot meet its current obligations. However, provisions in the Bankruptcy Act permit a company to file for protection under Chapter 11 if *financial forecasts* indicate that a continuation of business under current conditions will lead to insolvency. These provisions were applied by Frank Lorenzo, the principal stockholder of Continental Airlines, who demonstrated that if Continental continued to operate under its then-current union contract, it would become insolvent in a matter of months. The company then filed a plan of reorganization which included major changes in its union contract. The court found for Continental and allowed the company to abrogate its contract. The airline then reorganized as a nonunion carrier, and that reorganization turned the company from a money loser into a money maker. However, under pressure from labor, Congress changed the bankruptcy laws after the Continental affair to make it more difficult to use the laws to break union contracts.

The bankruptcy laws have also been used to bring about settlements in major product liability suits, the Manville asbestos case being the first, followed by the Dalkon Shield case. In both instances, the companies were being bombarded by literally thousands of lawsuits, and the very existence of such huge contingent liabilities made continued operations virtually impossible. Further, in both cases, it was relatively easy to prove (1) that if the plaintiffs won, the companies would be unable to pay off the full amounts claimed, (2) that a larger amount of funds would be available if the companies continued to operate than if they were liquidated, (3) that continued operations were possible only if the suits were brought to a conclusion, and (4) that a timely resolution of all the suits was impossible because of the number of suits and the different positions taken by different parties. At any rate, the bankruptcy statutes were used to consolidate all the suits and to reach a settlement under which all the plaintiffs obtained more money than they otherwise would have gotten, and the companies were able to stay in business. The stockholders did not do very well, because most of the companies' future cash flows were assigned to the plaintiffs, but, even so, the stockholders probably came out better than they would have if the individual suits had been carried through the jury system to a conclusion, because of the high costs of extended litigation.

We have no opinion about the use of the bankruptcy laws to settle social issues such as labor disputes and product liability suits. However, the examples do illustrate how financial projections can be used to demonstrate the effects of different legal decisions. Financial analysis is being used to an increasing extent in various types of legal work, from antitrust cases to suits against stockbrokers by disgruntled customers, and this trend is likely to continue.

PROBLEMS

20A-1   **Liquidation effects.** At the time it defaulted, Tapley Technologies had net current assets valued on the books at $30 million and net fixed assets valued at $37.5 million. At the time of final settlement its debts were as follows:

Current liabilities	$18.0 million
First-mortgage bonds	15.0 million
Second-mortgage bonds	7.5 million
Debentures	6.0 million

None of the current liabilities have preferences in liquidation as provided for in the bankruptcy laws, and none have been secured by the pledge of assets.

Assume that the amount shown for each of the four classes of liabilities includes all unpaid interest to the date of settlement. The fixed assets were pledged as security for the first mortgage bonds and repledged for the second mortgage bonds. Determine the appropriate distribution of the proceeds of liquidation under the following conditions:

a. Liquidation of current assets realizes $27 million, and $10.5 million is obtained from fixed assets.

b. Liquidation of current assets realizes $13.5 million, and $6 million is obtained from fixed assets.

■● 20A-2   **Liquidation effects.** Shome's Agricultural Tools, Inc. (SAT), is bankrupt and the firm's assets are to be sold to satisfy the claims of the firm's creditors. The firm's balance sheet follows.

Current assets	$2,520	Accounts payable	$ 540
Fixed assets	1,350	Notes payable (to bank)	270
		Accrued taxes	90
		Accrued wages	90
		Total current liabilities	$ 990
		First mortgage bonds	450
		Second mortgage bonds	450
		Total mortgage bonds	$ 900
		Subordinated debentures	540
		Total debt	$2,430
		Preferred stock	180
		Common stock	1,260
Total assets	$3,870	Total liabilities and equity	$3,870

The debentures are subordinated only to the notes payable. Suppose that $660 is received from the sale of the fixed assets, which were pledged as security for the first and second mortgage bonds, and $1,200 is obtained from the sale of current assets.

a. How much will each class of investors receive?

(Do Part b only if you are using the computerized problem diskette.)

b. How much would each class of investors receive if

1. $480 were received from the sale of fixed assets and $780 from the sale of current assets?

2. $840 were received from the sale of fixed assets and $1,620 from the sale of current assets?

Chapter 21

Determining the Dividend Policy

DECISION IN FINANCE

To Pay or Not to Pay Dividends

For 174 straight quarters, since it had gone public in 1946, Tucson Electric Power Company of Arizona had paid a dividend on its common stock. Then, in January 1990, the directors voted to omit the dividend. That decision followed months of upsetting announcements both from and about the utility company. In February 1989, Chief Financial Officer Joe Coykendall sold his 9,000 shares of stock for $48.25 per share. Then, Moody's downgraded the debt to below investment grade, blaming a trend toward harsh utilities regulation in Arizona. On June 20, 1989, Tucson Electric's vice president, Joseph B. Wilcox, sold 14,916 shares for about $34 each. On June 28, Coykendall resigned, and Einar Greve, chairman, president, and CEO, announced that he had sold two-thirds of his stock, 24,047 shares, at an average price of $32.29 each. The next day, J. Luther Davis, one of the utility's directors, announced that he had sold 5,203 shares at $32.00 each. Each of the sellers claimed personal reasons for divesting. Greve said he needed cash to pay off some loans, to pay taxes, and to offset some gains and

losses, and Wilcox said he sold for similar reasons and "absolutely not" because of concerns about the future of the utility. To make matters worse, the resignation and stock sales coincided with the filing of a $40 million lawsuit by an Arizona savings bank against a Tucson Electric subsidiary.

In early July, Greve sold the remainder of his holdings, and then he resigned under pressure from the board of directors, who told him his stock transactions had caused them to lose faith in him. After that meeting, the board warned stockholders that their dividends might have to be reduced, or even eliminated, because of a regulatory decision allowing Tucson Electric to recover only about $3.1 million of the approximately $70 million it had spent for fuel and purchased power. Its most recent dividend payment had been 97.5 cents per common share on June 26, 1989.

The board then elected John P. Schaefer as chairman and Thomas C. Weir as president and CEO. Schaefer, who had chaired an ad hoc committee of the board to investigate the insider stock sales, said he had met with Greve to review the committee's conclusions about the for-

See end of chapter for resolution.

779

mer CEO's sales. "Our findings were that, at [a] minimum, he exercised what we would call extremely poor judgment, [and] because of that, the board of directors lost confidence in his ability to lead."

The future continued to look dim, and directors were forced to deal with more bad news when, in October, Tucson Electric tried to sell $77 million of floating-rate, preferred stock but was unable to attract bids for the offering. Floating-rate preferred is sold at periodic auctions in a formal procedure that sets the rate for the next period—usually 49 days. If investors are concerned about the company's ability to service the preferred obligation, they simply will not bid for it, and the company will then have to pay off the issue, "ready or not." One other corporation's preferred stock had failed to

sell three times in the months preceding Tucson Electric's attempt. Failed auctions leave would-be sellers holding their stock until retirement financing can be arranged, or until a successful sale can be worked out, thus calling into question the liquidity of the securities. Liquidity is crucial for these securities because they were designed to be tax-favored securities held in liquid-asset portfolios.

As you read this chapter, consider Tucson Electric Power's situation, as well as the problems faced by its board of directors and its preferred stockholders. What options other than omission of the common stock dividend might they have considered? What effect is the dividend elimination likely to have on the utility's financial situation, on its reputation, and on its future ability to raise capital?

Dividend policy involves the decision to pay out earnings or to retain them for reinvestment in the firm. The basic stock price model, $\hat{P}_0 = D_1/(k_s - g)$, shows that if the firm adopts a policy of paying out more cash dividends, then D_1 will rise, which will tend to increase the price of the stock. However, if cash dividends are increased, then less money will be available for reinvestment, and plowing back less earnings into the business will lower the expected growth rate, which will depress the price of the stock. Thus, changing the dividend has two opposing effects. The **optimal dividend policy** *for a firm is the payout which strikes that balance between current dividends and future growth which maximizes the price of the firm's stock.*

A number of factors influence dividend policy, among them the investment opportunities available to the firm, alternative sources of capital, and stockholders' preferences for current versus future income. The primary goal of this chapter is to show how these and other factors interact to determine a firm's optimal dividend policy.

optimal dividend policy

The dividend payout policy which strikes that balance between current dividends and future growth which maximizes the firm's stock price.

RESIDUAL DIVIDEND POLICY

residual dividend policy

A policy in which dividends paid equal total earnings minus the amount of retained earnings necessary to finance the firm's optimal capital budget.

In the preceding chapters on capital budgeting and the cost of capital, we indicated that the marginal cost of capital and investment opportunity schedules must be combined before the cost of capital can be established. In other words, the optimal capital budget, the marginal cost of capital, and the marginal rate of return on investment are determined *simultaneously*. In this section we use this framework to develop what is called the **residual dividend**

policy, which states that a firm should follow these four steps when deciding on its payout ratio: (1) determine the optimal capital budget; (2) determine the amount of equity capital needed to finance that budget, given its target capital structure; (3) use retained earnings to supply the equity component to the greatest extent possible; and (4) pay dividends only if more earnings are available than are needed to support the optimal capital budget. The word *residual* means "left over," and the residual policy implies that dividends should be paid only out of leftover earnings.

The basis of the residual policy is the idea that *investors prefer to have the firm retain and reinvest earnings rather than pay them out in dividends if the rate of return the firm can earn on reinvested earnings exceeds the rate investors on average can themselves obtain on other investments of comparable risk.* For example, if the corporation can reinvest retained earnings at a 15 percent rate of return, whereas the best rate the average stockholder can obtain if the earnings are passed on in the form of dividends is 12 percent, then stockholders will prefer to have the firm retain the profits.

We saw in Chapter 19 that the cost of retained earnings is an *opportunity cost* that reflects rates of return available to equity investors. If a firm's stockholders can buy other stocks of equal risk and obtain a 14 percent dividend-plus-capital-gains yield, then 14 percent is the firm's cost of retained earnings. The cost of new outside equity raised by selling common stock will be higher than 14 percent because of the costs of floating the issue.

Because most firms have a target capital structure that calls for at least some debt, new financing is done partly with debt and partly with equity. As long as the firm finances with the optimal mix of debt and equity, and as long as it uses only internally generated equity (retained earnings), its marginal cost of each new dollar of capital will be minimized. Internally generated equity is available for financing a certain amount of new investment; beyond this amount the firm must turn to more expensive new common stock. At the point where new stock must be sold, the cost of equity, and consequently the marginal cost of capital, rises.

These concepts, which were developed in Chapter 19, are illustrated in Figure 21-1 with data from Georgia Paper Products (GPP). The firm has a marginal cost of capital of 12 percent as long as retained earnings are available, but the MCC begins to rise at the point where new stock must be sold. GPP has $60 million of net income and a 40 percent optimal debt ratio. Provided it does not pay cash dividends, GPP can make net investments (investments in addition to asset replacements financed from depreciation) of $100 million, consisting of $60 million from retained earnings plus $40 million of new debt supported by the retained earnings, at a 12 percent marginal cost of capital. Therefore, its marginal cost of capital is constant at 12 percent up to $100 million of capital. Beyond $100 million, the marginal cost of capital rises as the firm begins to use more expensive new common stock. Of course, if GPP does not retain all of its earnings, then its MCC will begin to rise before $100 million. For example, if GPP retained only $30 million, its MCC would begin to rise at $30 million retained earnings + $20 million debt = $50 million.

Figure 21-1 **Marginal Cost of Capital**

The marginal cost of capital is the weighted average of the costs of equity (k_s) and debt [$k_d(1 - t)$], as shown on the left. With a target debt ratio of 40 percent, the MCC will be 12 percent as long as GPP finances its equity needs through retained earnings. The right side of this figure shows that retaining earnings of $60 million will allow the firm to raise $100 million at an MCC of 12 percent. Beyond $100 million, new stock must be issued, which means an increase in the cost of equity and a resultant rise in the MCC.

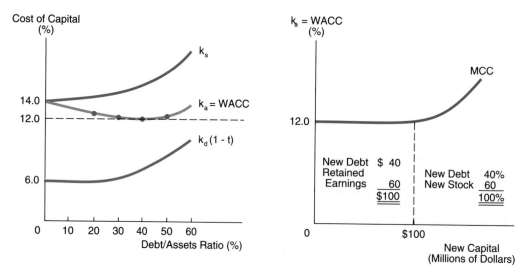

Next, suppose GPP's director of capital budgeting constructs investment opportunity schedules assuming three different economic conditions and plots them on a graph. The investment opportunity curves—one for a good economy (IOS_G), one for a normal economy (IOS_N), and one for a bad economy (IOS_B)—are shown in Figure 21-2. GPP can invest the most money, and earn the highest rates of return, when the investment opportunities are as given by IOS_G.

In Figure 21-3 the investment opportunity schedules are combined with the cost of capital schedule. The point where the IOS curve intersects the MCC curve defines the proper level of new investment. If investment opportunities are relatively bad (IOS_B), the optimal level of investment is $40 million; if opportunities are normal (IOS_N), $70 million should be invested; and if opportunities are relatively good (IOS_G), GPP should make new investments in the amount of $150 million.

Consider the situation in which IOS_G is the appropriate schedule. GPP has $60 million in earnings and a 40 percent target debt ratio. Thus, it can finance $100 million, consisting of $60 million of retained earnings plus $40 million of new debt, at a cost of 12 percent, if it retains all of its earnings. The remain-

Figure 21-2 **Investment Opportunity (or IRR) Schedules**

Investment opportunity schedules show which new investments are available to a firm at various rates of return. In this figure, IOS_G represents a good economy, IOS_N a normal economy, and IOS_B a bad economy. When investment opportunities are good, internal rates of return are higher and GPP can invest large amounts. When opportunities are poor, as in IOS_B, the firm will necessarily curtail its investment plans.

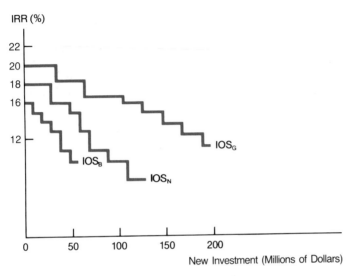

ing $50 million would include some external equity (new common stock) and thus would have a higher cost. If GPP paid out part of its earnings in dividends, it would have to begin using expensive new common stock earlier than need be, so its MCC curve would rise before it otherwise would. This suggests that under the conditions of IOS_G, GPP should retain all of its earnings. According to the residual policy, GPP's payout ratio should in this case be zero, and new common stock would have to be issued as well.

Under the conditions of IOS_N, however, GPP should invest only $70 million. How should this investment be financed? First, notice that if GPP retained all of its earnings, $60 million, it would need to sell only $10 million of new debt. However, if GPP retained $60 million and sold only $10 million of new debt, it would move away from its target capital structure. To stay on target, GPP must finance 60 percent of the required $70 million with equity (retained earnings) and 40 percent with debt. This means that it would retain only $42 million and sell $28 million of new debt. Since GPP would retain only $42 million of its $60 million total earnings, it would have to distribute the residual, $18 million, to its stockholders. Thus, its optimal payout ratio would be $18 million/$60 million = 30 percent, if IOS_N applied.

Figure 21-3 **Interrelations among Cost of Capital, Investment Opportunities, and New Investment**

A firm's optimal level of new investment can be determined by combining the MCC and IOS curves. In this figure GPP's IOS and MCC schedules are combined. The IOS_N curve is crossed by the MCC curve at an investment level of $70 million. Any investment beyond $70 million, in a normal year, would generate returns lower than the 12 percent marginal cost of capital and thus should not be undertaken.

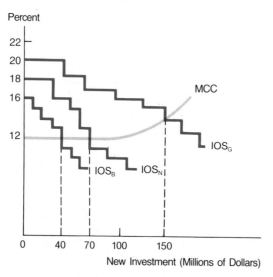

Under the conditions of IOS_B, GPP should invest only $40 million. Because it has $60 million in earnings, it could finance the entire $40 million out of retained earnings and still have $20 million available for dividends. Should this be done? Under our assumptions, this would not be a good decision, because this action would move GPP away from its optimal capital structure. To stay at the 40 percent target debt/assets ratio, GPP must retain $24 million of earnings and sell $16 million of debt. When the $24 million of retained earnings is subtracted from the $60 million in total earnings, GPP would be left with a residual of $36 million, the amount that should be paid out in dividends. Thus, under IOS_B, the payout ratio as prescribed by the residual policy would be $36 million/$60 million = 60 percent.

Since both the IOS schedule and the earnings level vary from year to year, strict adherence to the residual dividend policy would result in dividend variability—one year the firm might declare zero dividends because investment opportunities were good, but the next year it might pay a large dividend because investment opportunities were poor. Similarly, fluctuating earnings would also lead to variable dividends even if investment opportunities were stable over time. Thus, following the residual dividend policy would be optimal only if investors were not bothered by fluctuating dividends. However, if investors prefer stable, dependable dividends, k_s would be higher, and the stock price lower, if the firm followed the residual policy in a strict sense, rather than attempting to stabilize its dividends over time.

Self-Test

Explain the logic of the residual dividend policy.

List and describe the steps a firm would take to implement the residual policy.

If you owned stock in a company, would you want it to follow the residual policy? Would it matter if you relied on dividends to meet your living costs instead of simply saving any dividends received?

FACTORS THAT INFLUENCE DIVIDEND POLICY

The residual dividend policy is only a starting point in establishing the final dividend policy. Specific considerations that influence dividend policy may be grouped into four broad categories: (1) constraints on dividend payments, (2) investment opportunities, (3) availability and costs of alternative sources of capital, and (4) effects of dividend policy on the required rate of return, k_s. These categories and factors related to them are discussed in the following sections.

Constraints on Dividend Payments

1. Bond indentures. Debt contracts generally restrict dividend payments to earnings generated after the loan was granted. Also, debt contracts often stipulate that no dividends can be paid unless the current ratio, the times-interest-earned ratio, and other safety ratios exceed stated minimums.

2. Impairment of capital rule. Dividend payments cannot exceed the balance sheet item "retained earnings." This legal restriction, known as *the impairment of capital rule,* is designed to protect creditors. Without this rule, a company in trouble might distribute most of its assets to stockholders and leave its debtholders "out in the cold." (*Liquidating dividends* can be paid out of capital, but they must be indicated as such, and they must not reduce capital below the limits stated in the debt contracts.)

3. Availability of cash. Cash dividends can be paid only with cash. Thus, a shortage of cash in the bank can restrict dividend payments. Unused borrowing capacity can offset this factor, however.

4. Penalty tax on improperly accumulated earnings. To prevent wealthy individuals from using corporations to avoid personal taxes, the Tax Code provides for a special surtax on improperly accumulated income. Thus, if the IRS can demonstrate that a firm's dividend payout ratio is being deliberately held down to help its stockholders avoid personal taxes, the firm may be subject to heavy penalties. To date, this factor has been applied only to privately owned firms.

Investment Opportunities

1. **Location of the IOS schedule.** If a firm's "typical" IOS schedule, as shown in Figure 21-3, is far to the right, this will tend to produce a low target payout ratio, while if the IOS is far to the left, a large dividend payout is likely to result. The steeper the slope of the IOS, the more costly it is not to use the payout prescribed by the residual policy.

2. **Possibility of accelerating or delaying projects.** If the firm can accelerate or postpone projects, this will permit it more flexibility in its dividend policy.

Alternative Sources of Capital

1. **Cost of selling new stock.** If a firm needs to finance a given level of equity to help finance its capital budget, it can obtain this equity by retaining earnings or by selling new common stock. If flotation costs are high, k_e will be well above k_s, making it better to finance through retention rather than through sale of new common stock. On the other hand, if flotation costs are low, a high dividend payout ratio will be more feasible. Flotation costs differ among firms — for example, the flotation percentage is generally higher for small firms, so they tend to set low payout ratios. Hence, the importance of dividend policy and the optimal policy varies among firms.

2. **Control.** If management is concerned about maintaining control, it may be reluctant to sell new stock, and hence the company may retain more earnings than it otherwise would. However, if stockholders want higher dividends and a proxy fight looms, then the dividend will be increased.

3. **Capital structure flexibility.** A firm can finance a given level of investment with either debt or equity. If the firm can adjust its debt ratio without raising costs sharply, it can maintain a constant dollar dividend, even if earnings fluctuate, by using a variable debt ratio. The shape of the average cost of capital curve (left panel in Figure 21-1) determines the practical extent to which the debt ratio can be varied. If the average cost of capital curve is relatively flat over a wide range (which is normally the case), then a higher payout ratio will be more feasible than it would be if the curve had a V shape.

Effects of Dividend Policy on k_s

1. **Stockholders' desire for current versus future income.** Some stockholders desire current income; retired individuals and university endowment funds are examples. Other stockholders have no need for current investment

income, so they simply reinvest any dividends received, after first paying income taxes on the dividend income. If the firm retains and reinvests income rather than paying dividends, those stockholders who need current income will be disadvantaged. Although they will presumably receive capital gains, they will be forced to sell off some of their shares to obtain cash. This will involve brokerage costs, which are relatively high unless large sums are involved. Some institutional investors (or trustees for individuals) may be precluded from selling stock and then "spending capital." On the other hand, if high dividends are paid, then those stockholders who are saving rather than spending dividends will have to pay taxes and then incur brokerage costs to reinvest their dividends.

Investors can, of course, switch companies if they own stock in a firm whose dividend policy differs from the policy they desire; this is an example of what is called the **clientele effect.** However, there are costs associated with such changes (brokerage and capital gains taxes), and there may be a shortage of investors to replace those seeking to switch, in which case the stock price would fall.

clientele effect
The tendency of a firm to attract the type of investor who likes its dividend policy.

2. Riskiness of dividends versus riskiness of capital gains. It has been argued that investors regard returns coming in the form of dividends as being less risky than capital gains returns. Others disagree, arguing that if an investor receives dividends, then turns around and reinvests them in the same firm or one of similar risk, there is little difference in risk between this action and that of the company retaining and reinvesting the earnings in the first place. This question has been subjected to statistical studies, but without conclusive results.

3. Information content of dividends: signaling. It has been observed that an increase in the dividend (for example, the annual dividend per share is raised from $2 to $2.50) is often accompanied by an increase in the price of the stock, whereas an unexpected dividend cut generally leads to a stock price decline. This suggests to some observers that investors like dividends more than capital gains. However, others argue differently. They state that corporations are always reluctant to cut dividends, so firms do not raise dividends unless they anticipate higher, or at least stable, earnings in the future. Thus, a dividend increase is a signal to investors that the firm's management forecasts good future earnings. Conversely, a dividend reduction signals that management is forecasting poor earnings in the future. Therefore, the price changes following a change in dividend policy may not reflect investors' preference for either dividends or earnings growth, but simply may be a reflection of the important information regarding future earnings that is contained in the dividend announcement. As with many other controversies about dividend policy, empirical studies of the importance of the **information content (signaling) of dividends** have been inconclusive. There is clearly some information content in dividend announcements, but it may or may not

information content (signaling) of dividends
The theory that stock price changes following dividend announcements simply reflect the fact that investors regard dividend changes as signals of management's earnings forecasts.

completely explain the stock price changes that follow increases or decreases in dividends.

These points are considered by financial executives when they are establishing their firms' dividend policies, but the only real generalizations we can make are these:

1. The optimal dividend policy for a firm is influenced by many factors. Some factors suggest a higher payout than would be called for by the residual policy, whereas others suggest a lower optimal payout.

2. Much research has been done on dividend policy, but many points are still unresolved. Researchers are far from being able to specify a precise model for establishing corporate dividend policy.

Although no one has been able to construct a usable model for finding an optimal dividend policy, the residual policy does at least provide a good starting point, and we do have a good checklist of factors to consider before finalizing the dividend policy. Later in the chapter we return to the process of establishing a dividend policy, but first we must take up several other components of dividend policy.

Self-Test

Identify four broad categories of specific considerations that influence dividend policy.

What constraints affect dividend policy?

How do investment opportunities affect dividend policy?

How does the availability of outside capital affect dividend policy?

List the three factors that should be considered when assessing the effects of dividend policy on the cost of equity, k_s.

DIVIDEND PAYMENT POLICIES

Corporations tend to use one of three major dividend payment policies: (1) *constant, or steadily increasing, dividends,* (2) *constant payout ratio,* or (3) *low regular dividends plus extras.* These alternatives are discussed in this section.

Constant, or Steadily Increasing, Dividend per Share

Some firms set a specific annual cash dividend per share and then maintain it, increasing the annual dividend only if it seems clear that future earnings will be sufficient to allow the new dividend to be maintained. A corollary of the

Figure 21-4 **Shoal Creek Engineering:
Dividends and Earnings over Time**

Many firms use a stable dividend payment policy, maintaining a specific dividend amount and raising it only if earnings increase on an apparently permanent basis. As shown in this figure, Shoal Creek Engineering paid a dividend of $1.00 beginning in 1955 and maintained it for 10 years. Note that a temporary drop in earnings below the dividend level in 1970 did not affect the amount of dividend paid. In the 1990s, though, Shoal Creek expects earnings to grow steadily, and it plans to increase its dividend each year.

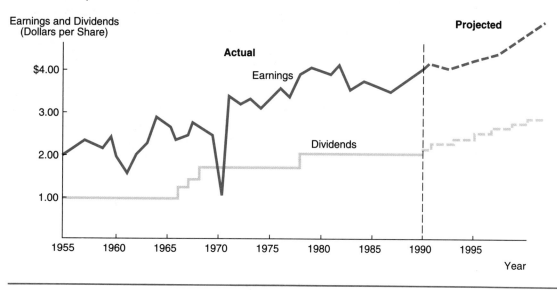

policy is this rule: *Avoid ever reducing the annual dividend.* The fact that most corporations do in fact follow, or attempt to follow, such a policy lends support to the information content (signaling) hypothesis described in the preceding section.

Figure 21-4, which illustrates a stable payment policy, presents data for Shoal Creek Engineering from 1955 to 1990 with earnings and dividends projected to 1995. Initially, earnings were $2 and dividends were $1 a share, so the payout ratio was 50 percent. Earnings rose for 4 years, while dividends remained constant; thus the payout ratio fell during this period. During 1960 and 1961 earnings fell substantially; however, the dividend was maintained, and the payout percentage rose. During the period between 1961 and 1965 earnings experienced a sustained rise. Dividends were held constant while management sought to determine whether the earnings increase would be permanent. By 1966, when it was apparent that the earnings gain would be maintained, dividends were raised in 3 steps to reestablish the target payout level. During 1970 a strike caused earnings to fall below the regular dividend. Expecting the earnings decline to be temporary, management maintained the dividend. Earnings fluctuated on a fairly high plateau from 1972 through 1977, during which time dividends remained constant. A new increase in earnings permitted management to raise the dividend in 1978 to reestablish the target payout level.

A variant of this policy is the "stable growth rate" policy. Here the firm sets a target growth rate for dividends (say, 5 percent per year) and strives to increase dividends by this amount each year. Obviously, earnings must be growing at a reasonably steady rate for this policy to be feasible. If Shoal Creek's earnings continue to grow as projected after 1990, the firm plans to adopt a constant growth rate dividend policy as illustrated in Figure 21-4 for the period following 1990.

There are several reasons for paying a stable, predictable dividend rather than exactly following the residual dividend policy. First, given the existence of the information content, or signaling, theory, a fluctuating payment policy would lead to greater uncertainty, hence to fluctuating stock prices, which in turn could lead to a higher k_s. Second, because stockholders who use dividends for current consumption want to be able to count on receiving dividends regularly, irregular dividends might lower demand for the stock, causing a decline in its price. Third, the optimal payout (in the residual policy sense) will almost certainly vary somewhat from year to year due to variations in earnings and in investment opportunities. However, it would probably be better to delay some investment projects, to depart from the target capital structure during a particular year, or even to sell new common stock rather than to cut the dividend or to reduce its growth rate. Finally, setting a steady dividend growth rate will confirm investors' estimates of g and thus enhance the price of the stock.

Constant Payout Ratio

Very few firms follow a policy of paying out a constant percentage of earnings. Because earnings surely will fluctuate, following this policy would necessarily mean that the dollar amount of dividends would vary. For reasons discussed in the preceding section, this policy is not likely to maximize a firm's stock price. However, before its bankruptcy, Penn Central Railroad did follow the policy of paying out one half its earnings: "A dollar for the stockholders and a dollar for the company," as one director put it. Logic like this could drive any company to bankruptcy!

Most companies conduct an analysis similar to our residual analysis for Georgia Paper as described earlier in the chapter and then establish a target payout based on that analysis. The target will not be met in every year, but over time the average payout will probably be close to the target level. Of

PENNZOIL COMPANY
A Natural Resources Company

DIVIDEND NOTICE

The following dividend has been declared:

75¢ per share on the Common Stock of the Company payable June 15, 1990 to stockholders of record at the close of business on May 31, 1990.

Linda F. Condit
Corporate Secretary

April 27, 1990

Pennzoil Company
Pennzoil Place
P.O. Box 2967
Houston, TX 77252-2967

Quarterly dividends paid for 66 consecutive years.

Dividend announcements are often reported in the business press. On April 27, 1990, Pennzoil's directors met and declared the regular quarterly dividend of $0.75 a share, payable to stockholders of record on May 31, 1990, with payment to be made on June 15, 1990. The announcement highlights that quarterly dividends have been paid for 66 consecutive years, further indicating the importance of not omitting dividends.

Source: *The Wall Street Journal*, May 1, 1990.

course, the target would change if fundamental changes in the company's position were to occur.

Low Regular Dividend plus Extras

The low regular dividend plus a year-end extra is a compromise policy. Such a policy gives the firm flexibility: investors can count on receiving a minimum dividend, but it will leave them somewhat uncertain about what their total dividend will be. Still, if a firm's earnings and cash flows are quite volatile, using **extra dividends** may well be the firm's best choice. The directors can set a relatively low regular dividend—low enough so that it can be maintained even in low-profit years or in years when a considerable amount of reinvestment is needed—and then supplement it with an extra dividend in years when excess funds are available. Ford, General Motors, and other auto companies, whose earnings fluctuate widely from year to year, formerly followed such a policy, but in recent years they have joined the crowd and now follow a stable dollar dividend policy.

extra dividend
A supplementary dividend paid in years when excess funds are available.

Self-Test

Describe the constant, or steadily increasing, dollar dividend policy, and give three reasons why a firm might follow such a policy.

Explain what a low-regular-dividend-plus-extras policy is, and tell why a firm might follow such a policy.

ACTUAL DIVIDEND PAYMENT PROCEDURES

Dividends are normally paid quarterly, and, if conditions permit, the dividend is increased once each year. For example, Pennzoil paid dividends of $3.00, $0.75 each quarter, during 1990. In common financial language, we say that Pennzoil's *regular quarterly dividend* is $0.75, and that its *annual dividend* is $3.00. The actual dividend payment procedure is as follows:

declaration date
Date on which a firm's directors issue a statement declaring a regular dividend.

1. Declaration date. On the **declaration date,** the directors of Pennzoil meet and declare the regular dividend. When they met on April 27, 1990, they issued a statement similar to the following: "On April 27, 1990, the directors of Pennzoil Company met and declared the regular quarterly dividend of $0.75 per share, payable to stockholders of record on May 31, payment to be made on June 15, 1990." For accounting purposes, the declared dividend becomes an actual liability on the declaration date, and if a balance sheet were constructed, the amount ($0.75) × (Number of shares outstanding) would appear as a current liability, and retained earnings would be reduced by a like amount.

holder-of-record date
If the company lists the stockholder as an owner on this date, then the stockholder receives the dividend.

2. Holder-of-record date. At the close of business on the **holder-of-record date,** May 31, the company closes its stock transfer books and makes up a list of the shareholders as of that date. If Pennzoil is notified of the sale and transfer of some stock before 5 P.M. on May 31, then the new owner receives the dividend. However, if notification is received on or after June 1, the previous owner of the stock gets the dividend check.

3. Ex-dividend date. Suppose Jean Buyer purchases 100 shares of Pennzoil stock from John Seller on May 29. Will the company be notified of the transfer in time to list Buyer as the new owner and thus pay the dividend to her? To avoid conflict, the securities industry has set up a convention of declaring that the right to the dividend remains with the stock until four business days prior to the holder-of-record date; on the fourth business day before the holder-of-record date, the right to the dividend no longer goes with the shares. The date when the right to the dividend leaves the stock is called the **ex-dividend date.** In this case, the ex-dividend date is four business days prior to May 31, or May 24:

ex-dividend date
The date on which the right to the current dividend no longer accompanies a stock; it is four working days prior to the holder-of-record date.

	. . . . .May 23
Ex-dividend date:	. . . . .May 24
	. . . . .May 25
Weekend:	. . . . .May 26 & 27
Holiday:	. . . . .May 28
	. . . . .May 29
	. . . . .May 30
Holder-of-record date:	. . . . .May 31

Therefore, if Buyer wishes to receive the dividend, she must buy the stock by May 23. If she buys it on May 24 or later, Seller will receive the dividend.

INDUSTRY PRACTICE

Corporate Get-Rich-Slowly Plans

For investors who do not need immediate cash income, more than 1,000 U.S. corporations offer a plan that is an almost guaranteed money-maker. It is a Dividend Reinvestment Plan (DRIP), which allows stockholders to use their dividends to buy more stock. Instead of receiving checks, they automatically get additional shares in the firm.

Reinvestors benefit whether the market moves up or down because a DRIP is a form of dollar-cost averaging—a proven way to lower the cost of investments. If dividends are reinvested regularly (and the payment period for most companies is 90 days), the same dividend buys more shares when the price is low and fewer when it is high. The result is a lower average cost per share.

The shareholder gets another important advantage—most DRIPs involve no brokerage fees. Although investors must own at least one share in a company to be eligible for its reinvestment plan, they pay a stockbroker only for that first purchase, and they do not need to work with a broker again. Regular purchases through a broker can cost from $35 to $100 or more for each transaction, so the savings in a reinvestment plan can be substantial.

The advantages to keeping shares for a long time are demonstrated by the profits enjoyed by a retired Texas engineer. In 25 years, his 700 shares of a utility stock, purchased for just

Sources: Daniel M. Kehrer, "Make Your Dividends Pay Again and Again," *Changing Times*, November 1988; "Buying Stocks—Without a Stockbroker," *Business Week*, November 7, 1988; Robert Guenther, "Chase Drops Parts of Dividend Plan Due to Stock Fall," *The Wall Street Journal*, February 16, 1990; "Chemical Banking Cuts Reinvestment Plan Following Stock Drop," *The Wall Street Journal*, February 23, 1990; "Chemical Banking Ends Discount on Stock Buys," *The Wall Street Journal*, March 29, 1990; "DRIPs Can Help Your Dividends Multiply," *Money*, May 1990.

under $10,000, grew to 5,000 shares, worth about $102,500, through dividend reinvestment alone—a 925 percent gain with no work involved. Under a shorter time frame, 100 shares of AT&T stock, purchased in 1985 for $1,950, would have grown to nearly 124 shares, worth $5,624 by mid-1990 if all dividends had been reinvested.

Still more can be amassed if a stockholder adds cash to the dividend reinvestments. Many companies allow this practice, with $3,000 being the typical maximum per quarter (however, in some cases, the maximum can be in the hundreds of thousands). In a few cases, even investors who do not already own stock in a firm can buy some directly from the company. Citibank and W.R. Grace both offer this service. "From the corporate point of view, it's a goodwill gesture," says the editor of a reinvestment-plan directory. "Most of those are consumer-oriented companies trying to attract long-term shareholders."

Corporations also benefit from DRIPs, because the plans strengthen shareholders' commitment to the company. Also, the plans can be used to raise capital when firms keep the cash and issue new shares. For example, NYNEX, which owns New York Telephone and New England Telephone, announced in 1990 that it would issue new shares under its DRIP, and it expected to raise approximately $250 million of equity per year to help fund its investment program.

As an additional lure to stockholders, some companies offer stock at a discount of from 3 to 5 percent below the market price. Two banks had to change their discount policies, however, when arbitragers figured out that they could sell shares short and then cover their positions by buying the stock at the 5 percent discount. This short selling caused the banks' stock prices to fluctuate. As a result, in February 1990, Chemical Bank lowered its discount for cash purchases from 5 percent to 2.5 percent, and then eliminated it altogether in March. Similarly, Chase Manhattan amended its cash option plan to 3 percent from 5 percent and reduced the maximum amount of stock a shareholder could buy from $250,000 a quarter to $40,000 a month. Arbitragers had not only been selling Chase shares short and covering this action with discount purchases, but they also avoided the $250,000 limit by buying the discounted shares under multiple names. Because of the practice, trading volume in Chase stock rose from an average of 590,000 shares per day in 1989 to more than 1.5 million shares in the first quarter of 1990, but the price of the stock dropped to a new low. Even so, neither Chase nor Chemical Bank is thinking of eliminating the DRIPs. Both banks need new equity, and Chase's plan raised $257 million in new equity in just two months, while Chemical's raised $106 million between November 1989 and February 1990.

Although investors continue to respond well to DRIPs, there are some drawbacks to them. For example, all reinvested dividends are taxable in the year they were paid, even though no cash goes directly to the shareholder. Obviously, the plans are inappropriate for those who need cash income for living expenses or for tax payments.

Despite the drawbacks, dividend reinvestment plans are an easy, low-risk way for shareholders to compound growth in a stock. A DRIP won't make anyone rich overnight, but as a long-term investment, it is hard to beat.

The dividend is $0.75 per share, so the ex-dividend date is important. Barring fluctuations in the stock market, we would normally expect the price of a stock to drop by approximately the amount of the dividend on the ex-dividend date. Thus, if Pennzoil closed at $76¼ on Wednesday, May 23, it would probably open at about $75½ on Thursday, May 24.

4. Payment date. The company actually mailed the checks to the holders of record on June 15, 1990, the **payment date.**

payment date
The date on which a firm actually mails dividend checks.

Self-Test

Briefly explain the steps in the dividend payment procedure.

DIVIDEND REINVESTMENT PLANS (DRIPs)

dividend reinvestment plan (DRIP)
A plan that enables a stockholder to automatically reinvest dividends received back into the stock of the paying firm.

During the 1970s most of the larger companies instituted **dividend reinvestment plans (DRIPs)**, whereby stockholders can automatically reinvest dividends received in the stock of the paying corporation.[1] There are two types of DRIPs: (1) plans which involve only "old" stock that is already outstanding, and (2) plans which involve newly issued stock. In either case, the stockholder

---

[1]See R. H. Pettway and R. P. Malone, "Automatic Dividend Reinvestment Plans," *Financial Management,* Winter 1973, pp. 11–18, for an excellent discussion of the topic.

must pay income taxes on the amount of the dividends, even though stock rather than cash is received.

Under the "old-stock" type of plan, the stockholder chooses between receiving dividend checks or having the company use the dividends to buy more stock in the corporation. If the stockholder elects reinvestment, a bank, acting as trustee, takes the total funds available for reinvestment (minus a fee), purchases the corporation's stock on the open market, and allocates the shares purchased to the participating stockholders' accounts on a pro rata basis. The transactions costs of buying shares (brokerage costs) are low because of volume purchases, so these plans benefit small stockholders who do not need cash dividends for current consumption.

The "new-stock" type of DRIP provides for dividends to be invested in newly issued stock; hence, these plans raise new capital for the firm. AT&T, Florida Power & Light, Union Carbide, and many other companies have had such plans in effect in recent years, using them to raise substantial amounts of new equity capital. No fees are charged to stockholders, and many companies offer stock at a discount of 5 percent below the actual market price. The companies absorb these costs as a tradeoff against the flotation costs that would have been incurred had they sold stock through investment bankers rather than through the dividend reinvestment plans.[2]

Self-Test

Describe the two different types of dividend reinvestment plans.

STOCK REPURCHASES

A recent *Fortune* article entitled "Beating the Market by Buying Back Stock" discussed the fact that during a one-year period, more than 600 major corporations had repurchased significant amounts of their own stock. It also gave illustrations of some specific companies' repurchase programs and their effects on stock prices. The article's conclusion was, ". . . buybacks have made a mint for shareholders who stay with the companies carrying them out." This section explains how **stock repurchases** are accomplished.

There are two principal types of repurchases: (1) situations in which the firm has cash available for distribution to its stockholders, and it distributes

stock repurchase
A transaction in which a firm buys back shares of its own stock, thereby decreasing shares outstanding, increasing EPS, and, often, increasing the price of the stock.

---

[2]One interesting aspect of DRIPs is that they are forcing corporations to reexamine their basic dividend policies. A high participation rate in a DRIP suggests that stockholders might be better off if the firm simply reduced cash dividends, as this would save stockholders some personal income taxes. Quite a few firms are surveying their stockholders to learn more about their preferences and to find out how they would react to a change in dividend policy. A more rational approach to basic dividend policy decisions may emerge from this research.

Also, it should be noted that companies either use or stop using new-stock DRIPs depending on their need for equity capital. Florida Power & Light recently stopped offering a new-stock DRIP with a 5 percent discount because its need for equity capital declined once it had completed a nuclear-powered generating plant.

this cash by repurchasing shares rather than by paying cash dividends; and (2) situations in which the firm concludes that its capital structure is too heavily weighted with equity, and it therefore sells debt and uses the proceeds to buy back its stock.

Until the 1980s, most repurchases amounted to a few million dollars, but in 1985 Phillips Petroleum announced plans for the largest repurchase on record — 81 million of its shares with a market value of $4.1 billion. Other large repurchases have been made by Atlantic Richfield, CBS, Coca-Cola, Goodyear, IBM, Teledyne, Texaco, and Xerox.

The repurchase of common stock raises the value of the firm's stock. Stock that has been repurchased by the issuing firm is called *treasury stock*. If some of the outstanding stock is repurchased, fewer shares remain outstanding. Assuming that the repurchase does not adversely affect the firm's earnings, the earnings per share on the remaining shares will increase, resulting in a higher market price per share. As a result, capital gains will have been substituted for dividends.

Several reasons exist for a firm to repurchase stock. First, the firm may wish to distribute cash to its shareholders in the form of a repurchase rather than a dividend. Prior to the 1986 Tax Act, capital gains were taxed at a lower rate than dividends, so wealthy individuals preferred selling stock to receiving dividends. Since dividends and capital gains are now taxed by the federal government at the same rate, it may seem that there is no advantage to the repurchase plan from an investor's point of view. However, profits earned on repurchases typically are not taxed until the stockholder sells the stock and receives a capital gain. Thus, a repurchase allows the stockholder to decide when to sell (or not sell), thereby allowing her or him to make optimal use of tax planning. On the other hand, the investor must accept dividend payments and pay taxes whenever dividends are issued. For years Teledyne, a $3 billion conglomerate earning $350 million annually, used repurchases as an alternative to dividends. Teledyne had not paid a dividend since its inception, and many analysts did not expect it to do so in the near future. However, in 1987 Teledyne declared and paid cash dividends of $4 per share, which it is still paying. *Value Line* predicts that Teledyne will follow a policy in the future of paying out a small percentage of earnings in dividends while continuing to repurchase its own stock.

A second reason that a firm might utilize a repurchase is to increase its debt ratio. A firm may conclude that its capital structure is too heavily weighted with equity and may then decide to sell debt, using the proceeds to buy back its stock. Consolidated Edison was confronted with a similar situation recently, so it repurchased $400 million of its common stock to affect changes in its capital structure. Had the firm changed its capital structure by financing all capital budgeting needs exclusively with debt, it would have taken years to reach the higher debt ratio. The repurchase program allowed Con Ed to reach its target capital structure quite rapidly. Goodyear and GenCorp have followed similar strategies lately.

A third reason that a firm uses a stock repurchase program is to fend off hostile takeovers. First, a firm with a high debt ratio is less attractive to an unwanted suitor. Second, by buying up excess shares, the firm reduces the ability of the suitor to purchase a controlling number of shares. For example, St. Joe Minerals held off a takeover bid by Seagram by borrowing heavily and using the funds to repurchase 7 million of its own shares at a cost of more than $400 million. Another type of takeover-related repurchase is represented by Disney's repurchase of its stock from Saul Steinberg and by Mobil's repurchase from T. Boone Pickens. These "raiders" had acquired stock in Disney and Mobil and had announced plans to take over the companies. Management bought them out, paying a premium price that is often called *greenmail.*

Stock repurchases are commonly made in one of three ways: (1) A publicly owned firm can simply buy its own stock through a broker on the open market. (2) The firm can make a *tender offer,* under which it permits stockholders to send in (that is, "tender") their shares to the firm in exchange for a specified price per share, generally at a premium over the current market price. When a firm makes a tender offer, it generally indicates that it will buy up to a specified number of shares within a particular time period (usually about two weeks). If more shares are tendered than the firm wishes to purchase, purchases are made on a pro rata basis. (3) The firm can purchase a block of shares from one large shareholder on a negotiated basis.

In conclusion, repurchase programs benefit investors by providing them with an opportunity to delay taxes on cash flows provided by the firm. Repurchases also can be especially valuable to the firm that wishes to make significant changes in its capital structure within a short period of time. However, repurchases on a regular, systematic basis may not be possible because of uncertainties about market price of the shares, how many shares would be tendered, and so forth.

Self-Test

Explain how repurchases can (1) help stockholders hold down taxes and (2) help firms change their capital structures.

What is treasury stock?

What are the three ways in which a firm can make repurchases?

STOCK DIVIDENDS AND STOCK SPLITS

Another aspect of dividend policy is the concept of stock dividends and stock splits. The rationale for stock dividends and splits can best be explained through an example; we will use United Chemical Company to illustrate.

As United Chemical continues to grow and retain earnings, its book value per share will also grow. More important, earnings per share and the market price per share will rise. The firm came into existence with only a few thousand shares outstanding. After some years of growth, each share had a very high EPS and DPS. When a "normal" P/E ratio was applied to the stock, the derived market price was so high that few people could afford to buy it. This limited demand for the stock, thus keeping the total market value of the firm below what it would have been if more shares, at a lower price, had been outstanding. The solution for United's dilemma was splitting the stock.

Although there is little empirical evidence to support the contention, there is nevertheless a widespread belief in financial circles that an *optimal price range* exists for stocks. Here *optimal* means that, if the price is within this range, the price/earnings ratio, and hence the value of the firm, will be maximized. Many observers, including United Chemical's management, believe that the best range for most stocks is from $20 to $80 per share. Accordingly, if at some future point the price of United's stock rose to $80, management would probably declare a 2-for-1 **stock split,** thus doubling the number of shares outstanding, halving the earnings and dividends per share, and thereby lowering the price of the stock. Each stockholder would have more shares, but each share would be worth less. If the post-split price were $40, United's stockholders would be exactly as well off as they were before the split. However, if the price of the stock were to stabilize above $40, stockholders would be better off. Stock splits can be of any size. For example, the stock could be split 2-for-1, 3-for-1, 1.5-for-1, or in any other way.[3]

Stock dividends are similar to stock splits in that they "divide the pie into smaller slices" without affecting the fundamental position of the current stockholders. With a 5 percent stock dividend, the holder of 100 shares would receive an additional 5 shares (without cost); with a 20 percent stock dividend, the same holder would receive 20 new shares; and so on. Because the total number of shares is increased, earnings, dividends, and the price per share all decline.

If a firm wants to reduce the price of its stock, should a stock split or a stock dividend be used? Stock splits are generally used after a sharp price run-up, when a large price reduction is sought. Stock dividends are frequently used on a regular annual basis to keep the stock price more or less constrained. For example, if a firm's earnings and dividends were growing at about 10 percent per year, the price would tend to go up at about that same rate, and it would soon be outside the desired trading range. A 10 percent annual stock dividend would maintain the stock price within the optimal trading range.

The economic effects of stock splits and stock dividends are virtually identical. Even so, the New York Stock Exchange has adopted a policy of calling a distribution of stock under 25 percent a *stock dividend* and a distribution

stock split

An action taken by a firm to increase the number of shares outstanding, such as doubling the number of shares outstanding by giving each stockholder two new shares for each one formerly held.

stock dividend

A dividend paid in the form of additional shares of stock rather than in cash.

---

[3]*Reverse splits,* which reduce the shares outstanding, can even be used. For example, a company whose stock sells for $5 might employ a 1-for-5 reverse split, exchanging 1 new share for 5 old shares, and presumably raising the value of the shares to about $25, which is within the optimal range. LTV Corporation did this after several years of losses had driven its stock price down below the optimal range.

Table 21-1 **United Chemical Company:**
Stockholders' Equity Accounts, Pro Forma
December 31, 1991

1. *Before a Stock Split or a Stock Dividend:*	
Common stock (60 million shares authorized, 50 million outstanding, $1 par)	$ 50,000,000
Paid-in capital	100,000,000
Retained earnings	1,850,000,000
Total common stockholders' equity	$2,000,000,000
Book value per share	$40.00
2. *After a 2-for-1 Stock Split:*	
Common stock (120 million shares authorized, 100 million outstanding, $0.50 par)	$ 50,000,000
Paid-in capital	100,000,000
Retained earnings	1,850,000,000
Total common stockholders' equity	$2,000,000,000
Book value per share	$20.00
3. *After a 20 Percent Stock Dividend:*	
Common stock (60 million shares authorized, 60 million outstanding, $1 par)[a]	$ 60,000,000
Paid-in capital[b]	890,000,000
Retained earnings	1,050,000,000
Total common stockholders' equity	$2,000,000,000
Book value per share	$33.33

Notes:
[a]Shares outstanding are increased by 20 percent, from 50 million to 60 million.
[b]A transfer equal to the market value of the new shares is made from the retained earnings account to the paid-in capital and common stock accounts:

$$\text{Transfer} = (50,000,000 \text{ shares})(0.2)(\$80) = \$800,000,000.$$

Of this $800 million, ($1 par)(10,000,000) = $10,000,000 goes to common stock and $790 million to paid-in capital.

greater than 25 percent a *split,* even if the issuing corporation calls its action something else.

Accountants also treat stock splits and stock dividends somewhat differently. Section 1 of Table 21-1 shows the equity portion of United Chemical Company's balance sheet before any action is taken on a stock dividend or split. In a 2-for-1 split, the shares outstanding are doubled and the par value is halved. This treatment is shown in Section 2 of the table, where the only accounting changes to United's 1991 stockholders' equity pro forma statement are the adjustments to the number of shares authorized and outstanding and to the par value of the stock. Had United decided to have a larger split, say a 5-for-1 split, we would have only had to divide the par value by 5 and to multiply the number of outstanding and authorized shares by 5 to reflect all necessary accounting changes. Since we can find the number of shares outstanding by dividing the common stock account by the par value of the stock, the new $0.20 par value and $50 million common stock account would indicate that the number of shares had grown fivefold, to 250 million shares.

Section 3 of Table 21-1 demonstrates the accounting changes that would occur in the equity section if United proceeded with a 20 percent stock dividend rather than the stock split. If United's common stock were selling at $80 per share, a 20 percent stock dividend would result in an $800 million transfer (or recapitalization) of funds from retained earnings to the common stock and paid-in capital accounts. The transfer from retained earnings is calculated as follows:

$$\begin{pmatrix} \text{Dollars} \\ \text{transferred from} \\ \text{retained} \\ \text{earnings} \end{pmatrix} = \begin{pmatrix} \text{Number} \\ \text{of shares} \\ \text{outstanding} \end{pmatrix} \begin{pmatrix} \text{Percentage} \\ \text{of the} \\ \text{stock dividend} \end{pmatrix} \begin{pmatrix} \text{Market} \\ \text{price of} \\ \text{the stock} \end{pmatrix}$$

$$= (50 \text{ million})(0.2)(\$80)$$

$$= \$800,000,000.$$

The common stock account would increase by the stock's par value ($1) per share for each of the 10 million new shares issued. The remaining $79 per share (price minus par value) would be added to paid-in capital.

Price Effects

Several empirical studies have examined the effects of stock splits and stock dividends on stock prices.[4] The findings of the Barker study, which are typical of those reported in the financial literature, are presented in Table 21-2. When a stock dividend was associated with a cash dividend increase, the value of the company's stock six months after the ex-dividend date had risen by 8 percent. On the other hand, when a stock dividend was not accompanied by a cash dividend increase, the stock value had fallen by 12 percent, which approximated the size of the average stock dividend, within six months.

These data suggest that investors see stock dividends for what they are — simply additional pieces of paper which do not represent true income. When they are accompanied by higher earnings and cash dividends, investors bid up the price of the stock. However, when stock dividends are not accompanied by increases in earnings and cash dividends, the dilution of earnings and dividends per share causes the price of the stock to drop by about the same percentage as the stock dividend. *Thus, the fundamental determinants of stock prices are the underlying earnings and dividends per share.*

---

[4]See C. A. Barker, "Evaluation of Stock Dividends," *Harvard Business Review,* July–August 1958, 99–144. Barker's study has been replicated several times in recent years, and his results are still valid; they have withstood the test of time. Another excellent study, using an entirely different methodology yet reaching similar conclusions, is that of E. Fama, L. Fisher, M. C. Jensen, and R. Roll, "The Adjustment of Stock Prices to New Information," *International Economic Review,* February 1969, 1–21.

Table 21-2 **Price Effects of Stock Dividends**

	Price at Selected Dates (in Percentages)		
	Six Months before Ex-Dividend Date	**At Ex-Dividend Date**	**Six Months after Ex-Dividend Date**
Cash dividend increase after stock dividend	$100	$109	$108
No cash dividend increase after stock dividend	100	99	88

Self-Test

What is the rationale for a stock split? What economic conditions might suggest that a series of stock dividends be used rather than a stock split?

Differentiate between the accounting treatments for stock splits and stock dividends.

What have been the results of studies concerning the effect of stock dividends on stock prices? What difference does it make if a cash dividend does or does not accompany the stock dividend?

ESTABLISHING A DIVIDEND POLICY: SOME ILLUSTRATIONS

Many factors interact to determine a firm's optimal dividend policy. Because these interactions are too complex to permit the development of a rigorous model for use as a guide to dividend policy, firms are forced to consider their dividend policies in a relatively subjective manner. Some illustrations of how dividend policies are actually set follow.

Shoal Creek Engineering

Shoal Creek Engineering analyzed its situation in terms of the residual policy, as shown earlier in Figure 21-3. The residual policy suggested a dividend of $2.08 per share during 1991, or about a 50 percent payout ratio. Shoal Creek's stock is widely held, and a number of tax-exempt institutions are important stockholders. A questionnaire to its stockholders revealed no strong preferences for dividends versus capital gains. Shoal Creek's long-range planning group projected a cost of capital and a set of investment opportunities during the next 3 to 5 years similar to those shown for this year.

On the basis of this information, Shoal Creek's treasurer recommended to the board of directors that it establish a dividend of $2.08 for 1991, payable 52 cents quarterly. The 1990 dividend was $1.98, so the $2.08 represented an increase of about 5 percent. The treasurer also reported to the board that, in the event of an unforeseen earnings downturn, the company could obtain additional debt to meet its capital expenditure requirements. The board accepted the treasurer's recommendation, and in December 1990 it declared a dividend of 52 cents per share, payable January 15, 1991. The board also announced its intention of maintaining this dividend for the balance of 1991.

Hytec Electronics

Hytec Electronics has a residual theory position that resembles IOS_G in Figure 21-3. This suggests that no dividend should be paid. Hytec has, in fact, paid no dividend since its inception in 1978, even though it has been continuously profitable and its earnings have recently been growing at a 25 percent rate. Informal conversations with the firm's major stockholders, all of whom are in high tax brackets, suggest that they neither expect nor want dividends; they would prefer to have the firm retain earnings, have good earnings growth, and provide capital gains, which are not taxed until the shares are sold. The stock now sells for $126 per share. Hytec's treasurer recommended a 3-for-1 split, no cash dividend, and a future policy of declaring an annual stock dividend geared to earnings for the year. The board of directors concurred.

Northwest Electric Company

Northwest Electric Company has an acute need for new equity capital. The company has a major expansion program under way and absolutely must come up with the money to meet construction payments. The debt ratio is high, and if the times-interest-earned ratio falls any lower, (1) the company's bonds will be downgraded and (2) it will be barred by bond indenture provisions from further debt issues. These facts suggest a cut in dividends from the $3.75 per share paid last year. However, the treasurer knows that many of the stockholders rely on dividends for current living expenses, so if dividends are cut, these stockholders may be forced to sell, thus driving down the price of the stock. This would be especially bad in view of the treasurer's forecast that there will be a need to sell new common stock during the coming year. (New outside equity would be needed even if the company totally eliminated the dividend.) The treasurer is aware that many other utilities face similar problems. Some have cut their dividends, and their stock prices invariably have fallen by amounts ranging from 30 to 70 percent.

Northwest's earnings were forecasted to increase from $5.00 to $5.26. The treasurer recommended that the dividend be raised by 4 percent, from $3.75 to $3.90, with the dividend increase being announced a few weeks before the company floated a new stock issue. The hope was that this action would cause the price of the stock to increase, after which the company could sell a new issue of common stock at a better price.

Pacific Industries

Pacific Industries' 1990 dividend was $3.80 per share, up from $3.57 in 1989. Both dividend figures represented about 50 percent of earnings, and this payout was consistent with a residual dividend policy analysis. The company's growth rate in EPS and DPS had been in the 5 to 10 percent range during the past few years, and management projected a continuation of this trend. The financial vice president foresaw a cash flow problem in 1991 — earnings were projected to increase in line with the historical average, but an especially large number of good investment opportunities (along with some unprofitable but required pollution-control expenditures) were expected. A preliminary analysis using the residual policy suggested that the dividend in 1991 should be cut back sharply, if not eliminated.

The financial vice president quickly rejected this cutback and recommended instead a 6 percent *increase* in the dividend, to $4.03, noting that the company could easily borrow funds during the coming year to meet its capital requirements. Even though the debt ratio would rise somewhat above the target, the firm's average cost of capital curve is relatively flat, and cash flows from 1991 investments should permit a reduction in the debt ratio over the next few years. The vice president thought that it was more important to maintain the steady growth in dividends than to adhere strictly to the target debt ratio.

SUMMARY

Dividend policy involves the decision to pay out earnings versus retaining them for reinvestment in the firm, and dividend policy decisions can have either favorable or unfavorable effects on the price of the firm's stock. The key factors influencing a firm's dividend policy are as follows:

- The **optimal dividend policy** is that policy which strikes the exact balance between current dividends and future growth that maximizes the price of the firm's stock.

- Two of many determining factors of dividend policy are the **information content (signaling) of dividends** and the **clientele effect.** The information content, or signaling, hypothesis states that investors regard dividend changes as a signal of management's forecast of future earnings. The clientele effect suggests that a firm will attract investors who like the firm's dividend policy.

- In practice, most firms try to follow a policy of paying a **constant, or steadily increasing, dollar dividend.** This policy provides investors with stable, dependable income, and, if the signaling theory is correct, it also gives investors information about management's expectations for earnings growth.

- Other dividend policies used include: (1) the **residual dividend policy,** in which dividends are paid out of earnings left over after the capital budget has been financed; (2) the **constant payout ratio policy,** in which a constant percentage of earnings is targeted to be paid out; and (3) the **low-regular-dividend-plus-extras policy,** in which the firm pays a constant, low dividend which can be maintained even in bad years, and then pays an extra dividend in good years.

- Other factors, such as **legal constraints, investment opportunities, availability and cost of funds from other sources,** and **taxes,** are considered by managers when they establish dividend policies.

- A **dividend reinvestment plan (DRIP)** allows stockholders to have the company automatically use their dividends to purchase additional shares of the firm's stock. DRIPs are popular with investors who do not need current income because the plans allow stockholders to acquire additional shares without incurring normal brokerage fees.

- Under a **stock repurchase plan,** a firm buys back some of its outstanding stock, thereby decreasing the number of shares, which in turn increases both EPS and the stock price. Repurchases are useful for making major changes in a firm's capital structure, as well as for allowing stockholders to delay paying taxes on their share of the firm's profits.

- A **stock split** is an action taken by a firm to increase the number of shares outstanding. Normally, splits reduce the price per share in proportion to the increase in shares because splits merely "divide the pie into smaller slices." A **stock dividend** is a dividend paid in additional shares of stock rather than in cash. Both stock dividends and splits are used to keep stock prices within an "optimal" range.

EQUATIONS

With a stock dividend, a transfer is made from retained earnings to both common stock and paid-in capital. The transfer from retained earnings is calculated as

$$
\begin{pmatrix} \text{Dollars} \\ \text{transferred from} \\ \text{retained} \\ \text{earnings} \end{pmatrix} = \begin{pmatrix} \text{Number} \\ \text{of shares} \\ \text{outstanding} \end{pmatrix} \begin{pmatrix} \text{Percentage} \\ \text{of the} \\ \text{stock dividend} \end{pmatrix} \begin{pmatrix} \text{Market} \\ \text{price of} \\ \text{the stock} \end{pmatrix}.
$$

RESOLUTION TO DECISION IN FINANCE

To Pay or Not to Pay Dividends

Tucson Electric's directors had already warned shareholders that their dividends might be cut or eliminated, and they tried the less difficult option first: In the third quarter of 1989, they reduced the dividend from 97.5 cents to 40 cents per share. This was not enough, though, and in early 1990, President/CEO Weir was forced to make this announcement: "Our negative cash flow mandates that the dividend be eliminated at this time. We will continue to monitor this closely, but there is little probability that a dividend can be paid for several years." He cited "excess generating capacity that will not be fully needed to serve our retail load for several years" as the primary problem. Growth in electricity needs had turned out

Sources: *The Wall Street Journal*, "Inside Track," July 12, 1989; Frederick Rose, "Tucson Electric's Chief, Greve, Quits Amid Stock Study," July 18, 1989; Frederick Rose, "Tucson Electric Preferred-Stock Auction Fails," October 2, 1989; Earl C. Gottschalk, Jr., "Tucson Electric Omits Dividend on Its Common," January 24, 1990.

to be slower than forecasted, and attempts to sell the excess capacity had failed because most other southwestern utility companies were experiencing the same problem.

Tucson's problems were aggravated because it had diversified into some nonutility businesses about which it knew little — real estate ventures and savings and loan institutions. The $40 million lawsuit filed by MeraBank Federal Savings Bank seeks recovery of a loan from one of the utility's subsidiaries, Sierrita Resources, Inc., which had invested in a Phoenix land development. Finally, the utility company was under investigation by the Securities and Exchange Commission for possible insider trading by the officers and directors who sold their stock.

As a result, Tucson Electric had a loss of $100.7 million, or $4.05 a share, in the third quarter of 1989, and as we write this in the fall of 1990, the stock is selling for $9.50, down from a high of $26.50 for the year.

QUESTIONS

21-1 As an investor, would you rather invest in a firm that has a policy of maintaining **(a)** a constant payout ratio, **(b)** a constant or steadily increasing dollar dividend per share, **(c)** a target dividend growth rate, or **(d)** a constant regular quarterly dividend plus a year-end extra when earnings are sufficiently high or corporate investment needs sufficiently low? Explain your answer, stating how these policies would affect your k_s. Discuss also how your answer might change if you were a 21-year-old student, a 48-year-old professional with peak earnings, or a retiree.

21-2 How would each of the following changes probably affect aggregate (that is, the average for all corporations) payout ratios, other things held constant? Explain your answers.

a. An increase in the personal income tax rate.

b. A liberalization of depreciation for federal income tax purposes; that is, faster tax write-offs.

c. A rise in interest rates.

    d. An increase in corporate profits.

    e. A decline in investment opportunities.

    f. Permission for corporations to deduct dividends for tax purposes as they now do interest charges.

    g. A change in the Tax Code so that both realized and unrealized capital gains in any year would be taxed at the same rate as dividends.

21-3   Discuss the pros and cons of having the directors formally announce what a firm's dividend policy will be in the future.

21-4   Most firms would like to have their stock selling at a high P/E ratio, and they would also like to have extensive public ownership (many different shareholders). Explain how stock dividends or stock splits may help achieve these goals.

21-5   What is the difference between a stock dividend and a stock split? As a stockholder, would you prefer to see your company declare a 100 percent stock dividend or a 2-for-1 split? Assume that either action is feasible.

21-6   "The cost of retained earnings is less than the cost of new outside equity capital. Consequently, it is totally irrational for a firm to sell a new issue of stock and to pay dividends during the same year." Discuss this statement.

21-7   Would it ever be rational for a firm to borrow money in order to pay dividends? Explain.

21-8   More NYSE companies had stock dividends and stock splits during the first 9 months of 1989 than during the whole 12 months of the previous record high year, 1985. Would you guess that the stock market was strong or weak in 1989? Explain the rationale that a financial vice president might give his or her board of directors to support a stock split/dividend recommendation.

21-9   One position expressed in the financial literature is that firms set their dividends as a residual after using income to support new investment.

    a. Explain what a residual dividend policy implies, illustrating your answer with a graph showing how different conditions could lead to different dividend payout ratios.

    b. Could the residual dividend policy be consistent with (1) a constant growth-rate policy, (2) a constant payout policy, and/or (3) a low-regular-dividend-plus-extras policy? Answer in terms of both short-term, year-to-year consistency and longer-term consistency.

    c. Think back to Chapter 20, in which we considered the relationship between capital structure and the cost of capital. If the k_a-versus-debt-ratio plot was shaped like a sharp V, would this have a different implication for the importance of setting dividends according to the residual policy than if the plot was shaped like a shallow bowl (or a flattened U)?

    d. Assume that Companies A and B both have IOS schedules that intersect their MCC schedules at a point which, under the residual policy, calls for a 30 percent payout. In both cases, a 30 percent payout would require a cut in the annual dividend from $3 to $1.50. One company cuts its dividend, whereas the other does not. One company has a relatively steep IOS curve, whereas the other has a relatively flat one. Explain which company probably has the steeper curve.

SELF-TEST PROBLEM

ST-1   Campos Aircraft Corporation (CAC) has an all-equity capital structure that includes no preferred stock. It has 500,000 shares of $2 par value common stock outstanding.

When CAC's founder and chief engineer, Jennifer Campos, retired suddenly in late 1990, CAC was left suddenly and permanently with materially lower growth expectations and relatively few attractive new investment opportunities. Unfortunately, there was no way to replace the founder's contributions to the firm. Previously, CAC had found it necessary to plow back most of its earnings to finance growth, which had averaged 12 percent per year. Future growth of 5 percent appears to be realistic, but that would call for an increase in the dividend payout. Further, it now appears that new investment projects with at least the 14 percent rate of return required by CAC's shareholders ($k_s = 14\%$) would amount to only $2,800,000 for 1991, in comparison to a projected $7 million of net income. If the existing 25 percent dividend payout were continued, retained earnings would be $5.25 million in 1991, but, as noted, investments that yield the 14 percent cost of capital amount to only $2.8 million.

The one encouraging thing is that the high earnings from existing assets are expected to continue, and net income of $7 million is still expected for 1991. Given the dramatically changed circumstances, CAC's management is reviewing the firm's dividend policy.

a. Assuming that the acceptable 1991 investment projects would be financed entirely by retained earnings during the year, calculate DPS in 1991, assuming that CAC uses the residual dividend policy.

b. What payout policy does this imply for 1991?

PROBLEMS

21-1   **Dividend payout.** Solimini Enterprises had net income for 1990 of $12 million.
a. What was the firm's payout ratio if it paid $7.5 million in dividends?
b. If the firm's payout was 25 percent, what was the dividend payment?
c. If the payout ratio was 40 percent, what was the retention rate?
d. In 1989 the firm's payout ratio was 60 percent, and $6.3 million was paid in dividends. What was Solimini's net income in 1989?

21-2   **Payout ratio.** Solectron Systems, Inc., expects net income of $600,000 for the next year. Its target, and current, capital structure is 40 percent debt and 60 percent common equity. The director of capital budgeting has determined that the optimal capital budget for next year is $900,000. If Selectron uses the residual dividend policy to determine next year's dividend payout, what is the expected payout ratio?

21-3   **External equity financing.** Tsetsekos, Inc., is expanding its productive capacity with a $9.6 million investment. The board of directors approved the expansion under the following conditions:
1. The firm would not exceed its current 40 percent debt/assets ratio.
2. The dividend payout ratio would remain at 30 percent.
If net earnings are expected to be $6 million this year, how much external equity must Tsetsekos seek during the year?

21-4 **Stock dividend.** Dimkoff Dress Boutiques, Inc., has the following common stock equity accounts on its balance sheet:

Common stock ($0.50 par)	$ 400,000
Paid-in capital	3,000,000
Retained earnings	8,000,000
Total equity	$11,400,000

The market price of the firm's stock is $20. Restate the equity accounts of Dimkoff to reflect a 20 percent stock dividend.

21-5 **Stock split.** Prestopino Publishing Company has just announced a 3-for-1 stock split. Prior to the split, dividends were $3.30 per share. The firm plans to pay a dividend of $1.20 per share after the split. What is the percentage increase in the cash dividend that occurs after the split?

21-6 **Stock split.** After a 5-for-1 split, Hoffmeister Corporation paid a dividend of $2.50 per new share, which represents a 10 percent increase in last year's pre-split dividend. What was last year's dividend per share?

21-7 **Cash and stock dividends.** Mathys Metals declared a 15 percent stock dividend and a cash dividend of $0.75 per share. The cash dividend is paid on both the old shares and the shares received in the stock dividend. Construct a pro forma balance sheet showing the effect of these actions; use one new balance sheet that incorporates both actions. The stock sells for $60 per share. A condensed version of Mathys's end-of-year balance sheet (before dividends) is given below (in millions of dollars):

Cash	$ 75	Debt	$1,500
Other assets	2,925	Common stock (30 million	75
		shares authorized, 25	
		million outstanding, $3 par)	
		Paid-in capital	300
		Retained earnings	1,125
Total assets	$3,000	Total liabilities and equity	$3,000

21-8 **Alternate dividend policies.** In 1989 Roussakis Equipment Company (REC) paid dividends of $3,125,000. The firm's net income for 1989 was $12.5 million. For the past 5 years REC's earnings and dividends have grown at a constant 8 percent rate. However, 1990 was an especially profitable year, with net income totaling $25 million. For 1991 REC has $20 million of profitable investment opportunities planned. Even so, the surge in earnings enjoyed in 1990 cannot last, and the firm's profits are expected to return to the previous 8 percent stable growth rate. Calculate the 1990 dividends for REC under each of the following dividend policies:
a. A stable and growing dividend payment.
b. Stable payout based on the 1989 payout ratio.
c. Residual dividend policy if the firm uses no debt to finance investment opportunities.
d. Residual dividend policy if the firm maintains a 40 percent debt/assets ratio.

21-9 **Dividend policy and capital structure.** North Carolina Tobacco, Inc. has for many years enjoyed a moderate but stable growth in sales and earnings. However, cigarette consumption and consequently North Carolina's sales have been falling recently, primarily because of an increasing awareness of the dangers of smoking to health. Anticipating further declines in tobacco sales in the future, North Carolina's management hopes eventually to move almost entirely out of the tobacco business and into a newly developed, diversified product line in growth-oriented industries. The company is especially interested in the prospects for pollution-control devices, because its research department has already done much work on the problems of filtering smoke. Right now the company estimates that an investment of $15 million is necessary to purchase new facilities and to begin operations on these products, but the investment could be earning a return of about 18 percent within a short time. The only other available investment opportunity totals $6 million, is expected to return about 10.8 percent, and is indivisible; that is, it must be accepted in its entirety or else be rejected.

The company is expected to pay a $1.50 dividend on its 6 million outstanding shares, the same as its dividend last year. The directors may change the dividend, however, if there are good reasons for doing so. Total earnings for the year are expected to be $14.25 million; the common stock is currently selling for $28⅛; the firm's target debt ratio (debt/assets ratio) is 45 percent; and its tax rate is 40 percent. The costs of various forms of financing are as follows:

New bonds, $k_d = 11\%$. This is a before-tax rate.

New common stock sold at $28⅛ per share will net $25⅝.

Required rate of return on retained earnings, $k_s = 15\%$.

a. Calculate North Carolina's expected payout ratio, the break point where the MCC rises, and its marginal cost of capital above and below the point of exhaustion of retained earnings at the current payout. (*Hint:* k_s is given, and D_1/P_0 can be found. Then, knowing k_s and D_1/P_0, g can be determined.)
b. How large should North Carolina's capital budget be for the year?
c. What is an appropriate dividend policy for North Carolina? How should the capital budget be financed?
d. How might risk factors influence North Carolina's cost of capital, capital structure, and dividend policy?
e. What assumptions, if any, do your answers to the preceding questions make about investors' preferences for dividends versus capital gains — that is, their preferences regarding the D_1/P_0 and g components of k_s?
(*Do Part f only if you are using the computerized problem diskette.*)
f. Assume that North Carolina's management is considering changing the company's capital structure to include more debt, and thus it would like to analyze the effects of an increase in the debt ratio to 60 percent. However, the treasurer believes that such a move would cause lenders to increase the required rate of return on new bonds to 12 percent before tax and that k_s would rise to 15.5 percent. How would this change affect the optimal capital budget? If k_s rose to 17 percent, would the low-return project be acceptable? Would the project selection be affected if the dividend were reduced to $0.94 from $1.50, still assuming $k_s = 17\%$?

SOLUTION TO SELF-TEST PROBLEM

ST-1   **a.** Projected net income $7,000,000
 Less: Projected capital investments 2,800,000
 Available residual $4,200,000

 Shares outstanding   500,000

$$DPS = \$4,200,000/500,000 \text{ shares} = \$8.40 = D_1.$$

b.

$$EPS = \$7,000,000/500,000 \text{ shares} = \$14.$$

$$\text{Payout ratio} = DPS/EPS = \$8.40/\$14 = 60\% \ or$$

$$\text{Total dividends/NI} = \$4,200,000/\$7,000,000 = 60\%.$$

Part VII

OTHER TOPICS IN FINANCIAL MANAGEMENT

Throughout this text we have been developing the basic framework for making financial decisions. At this point we still have two important topics to discuss: Chapter 22 deals with mergers and acquisitions, and Chapter 23 covers international finance. We deferred these final topics so that they could be analyzed on an integrated basis using analytical tools developed in earlier chapters.

Chapter 22

Mergers and Acquisitions

 DECISION IN FINANCE

Did Consolidated Freightways Take a Bad Flier?

Emery Air Freight qualified under federal standards as a "failing firm" when the nation's largest long-haul trucking company, Consolidated Freightways, paid $478 million to acquire it in April 1989. The Justice Department had originally opposed the move, because, when combined, the two companies controlled almost half of the U.S. heavy air cargo business. The Justice Department had been ordered to monitor any merger or acquisition that might result in higher consumer prices because of reduced competition. Such an acquisition, however, is legal if the acquired firm is failing and will probably not survive without the merger.

Why would Consolidated want to buy a failing firm that more than 20 other potential buyers had turned down? The company's CEO, Lary R. Scott, had never worried about other people's opinions, and his stubborn self-confidence and canny foresight had kept Consolidated profitable while other truckers were failing in the aftermath of deregulation and rate wars during

the 1980s. Now critics are wondering if he can keep Consolidated healthy during the 1990s after weighing down his company with Emery.

The reason for the purchase, says Scott, is that Consolidated needs to be an international air freight power. "This global thing is not a fad, [not] something that's going to go away. We want to leverage our North American operation [with the ability] to deliver goods to Asia and Europe."

Consolidated entered the air cargo business in 1985 under an agreement in which Eastern Airlines flew Consolidated's loads. It began operating its own airplane fleet in 1987 through its CF AirFreight subsidiary. Merging CF with Emery took longer than Scott and CF AirFreight President Donald Berger expected, but with the purchase they instantly gained 72 more airplanes (up from 26); a huge hub facility in Dayton, Ohio; terminal and landing rights in 78 more countries (up from 12); and 250 more foreign facilities (up from 22). Scott contended that this was more prudent than trying to expand CF AirFreight in competition with such big firms as Federal Express, which bought international freight specialist Flying Tiger Line in

See end of chapter for resolution.

813

mid-1989, and United Parcel Service, which has taken over several foreign shippers.

Scott had attempted to acquire Emery back in 1987, but he gave up after Emery's ill-conceived acquisition of Purolator Courier. Consolidated had acquired 9 percent of Emery's stock at the time but later sold it. Other big-money investors had bought Emery stock in early 1988, and they saw it almost double in price within a month. Unfortunately, Emery's service problems multiplied after the Purolator merger, and heavy debt diminished its cash flow. Emery was nearly bankrupt two years later, at which time Scott decided the acquisition was worth the risk.

True to Consolidated's reputation as a technological leader, it has thus far spent $38 million for new pickup and delivery equipment for Emery and another $35 million to upgrade Emery's outdated computerized freight tracking system. The company also inherited Emery's $236 million in debt, largely in high-interest junk bonds. On the positive side, since the takeover and Scott's improvements, Emery has been awarded a two-year U.S. Postal Service contract worth more than $170 million and a three-year, $125 million contract with IBM.

Emery lost $17.5 million in the second quarter of 1989 and $18 million in the third, but, in late 1989, Scott and Berger announced that they expected Emery to make a profit in 1990. However, when fourth-quarter results came in, Emery's operating loss had increased to $40 million, so the 1990 forecast had to be recalculated. Part of the problem was that, as Scott admitted, "We shot ourselves in the foot when we first took the company over." For instance, they tried to add a fuel surcharge of 4 to 7 percent to customers' bills and lost some business to competitors who did not raise their prices. They then closed down Emery's "retail" freight business, which was servicing consumers in competition with United Parcel Service, but they carelessly lost many small business customers, which they had wanted to keep.

As you read this chapter, consider Consolidated's problems in its efforts to make the merger with Emery successful despite the debt load and first-year setbacks. Was Scott right to acquire a company that was near bankruptcy, or should he have gone after a profitable company such as Federal Express? What actions do you think he and Berger might take to overcome some of their own mistakes in managing Emery?

merger
The combination of two firms to form a single firm.

Most corporate growth occurs through *internal expansion,* which takes place when the firm's existing divisions grow through normal capital budgeting activities. However, the most dramatic growth, and often the largest changes in firms' stock prices, are the results of **mergers.** Recently newspapers and business periodicals have reported a large number of business combinations, including those of Du Pont with Conoco, Getty Oil with Texaco, Marathon Oil with U.S. Steel, Electronics Data Systems (EDS) and Hughes Aircraft with General Motors, Burroughs with Sperry (to form Unisys), and many others. There are many important legal distinctions among the various means by which two or more economic units can combine. Our emphasis, however, is on the fundamental business and financial aspects of mergers and acquisitions.

THE ECONOMIC IMPLICATIONS OF MERGERS

The primary motivation for most mergers is to increase the value of the combined enterprise. If Companies A and B merge to form Company C, and if C's value exceeds that of A and B taken separately, then **synergy** is said to exist. Synergy has often been described as the "2 plus 2 equals 5 effect." Thus, when synergy exists, the new business entity is worth more than the simple sum of the merged firms. Such a merger is, of course, beneficial to both A's and B's stockholders. Synergistic effects can arise from four sources: (1) *operating economies* resulting from economies of scale in management, production, or distribution; (2) *financial economies,* which can include a higher P/E ratio, a lower cost of debt, or a greater debt capacity; (3) *differential management efficiency,* which implies that one firm's management is relatively inefficient, so the firm's profitability can be improved by merger; and (4) *increased market power* resulting from reduced competition. Operating and financial economies are socially desirable, as are mergers that increase managerial efficiency, but mergers that reduce competition are both undesirable and illegal.[1]

After the discussion of risk in Chapter 12, one may naturally assume that risk reduction would be an important economic implication in the combination of two firms. Indeed, managers often cite the stabilization of earnings and the resulting reduction of corporate risk as a prime motivation for mergers. Stabilization of the earnings stream through diversification should be beneficial to the firm's employees, customers, and suppliers, but is it beneficial to the firm's stockholders? After all, an investor can diversify more easily and cheaply than a firm. The shareholder can merge any combination of firms by purchasing shares of each stock. For example, if a merger of Delta and Holiday Inn would stabilize their earnings, an investor could purchase stock in each and efficiently create a merged firm at a much lower cost than would be possible if these firms merged in actuality. To achieve even greater diversification, individual investors can purchase shares of mutual funds. Therefore, for publicly held firms, diversification to reduce stockholder risk is not a valid motive for any merger.

Tax considerations have stimulated a number of mergers. For example, a firm which is highly profitable and in the highest corporate tax bracket could acquire a company with large accumulated tax losses, then use those losses to shelter its own income. (Mergers undertaken only to use accumulated tax losses would probably be challenged by the IRS. However, because many factors are present in any given merger, it is difficult to prove that a merger was motivated only, or even primarily, by tax considerations.)

synergy
The condition wherein the whole is greater than the sum of its parts; in a synergistic merger, the postmerger value exceeds the sum of the separate companies' premerger values.

---

[1] In the 1880s and 1890s, many mergers occurred in the United States, and some of them were clearly directed more toward gaining market power than toward increasing operating efficiency. As a result, Congress passed a series of acts designed to insure that mergers are not used as a method of reducing competition. The principal acts include the Sherman Act (1890), the Clayton Act (1914), and the Celler Act (1950). These acts make it illegal for firms to combine in any manner if the combination will tend to lessen competition. They are administered by the antitrust division of the Justice Department and by the Federal Trade Commission.

Sometimes a firm will become an acquisition candidate because the replacement value of its assets is considerably higher than its market value. For example, in the 1980s oil companies could acquire reserves with less expense by buying out other oil companies than by conducting exploratory drilling. This factor was a motive in Chevron's acquisition of Gulf Oil.

In recent years many *hostile mergers and takeovers* have occurred. The managers of the acquired companies generally lose their jobs, or at least their autonomy. Therefore, managers who own less than 51 percent of the stock in their firms look for devices to lessen the chances of their firm's being taken over. Mergers can serve as such a device. For example, when Enron was under attack, it arranged to buy Houston Natural Gas Company, paying for Houston primarily with debt. That merger made Enron much larger and hence harder for any potential acquirer to "digest." Also, the much higher debt level resulting from the merger made it hard for any acquiring company to use debt to buy Enron. Such **defensive mergers** are difficult to defend on economic grounds. The managers involved invariably argue that synergy, not a desire to protect their own jobs, motivated the acquisition, but there can be no question that many mergers today are designed more for the benefit of managers than for that of stockholders.

When two firms begin merger negotiations, or when one firm begins thinking about acquiring another, one of the first considerations is antitrust: Is the Justice Department likely to try to block the merger, and would it be able to do so? If the answer to either part of this question is yes, chances are high that the merger will be aborted because of the legal expenses involved in fighting the Justice Department. However, how the Justice Department will view the merger is often uncertain; this was especially true during the Reagan era, when mergers were constrained less than in some previous administrations. Occasionally, firms' managements believe that they will be allowed to merge and later find that they cannot. Southern-Pacific and Santa Fe railroads spent millions in the belief that their merger would be allowed, but after three years of deliberation, the Justice Department denied their merger.

defensive merger
A merger designed to make a company less vulnerable to a takeover.

Self-Test

What are the primary motives behind most mergers?

From what sources might synergistic effects arise?

Is diversification to reduce stockholder risk a valid motive for mergers? Explain.

TYPES OF MERGERS

horizontal merger
The combination of two firms that produce the same type of good or service.

Economists classify mergers into four groups: (1) *horizontal*, (2) *vertical*, (3) *congeneric*, and (4) *conglomerate*. A **horizontal merger** occurs when one firm combines with another in the same line of business—for example, the 1988 merger of Shearson Lehman and E. F. Hutton was a horizontal merger because both firms are brokerage houses. An example of a **vertical merger** is a steel producer's acquisition of an iron or coal mining firm, or a chemical producer's acquisition of a petroleum company that can supply it with a stream of raw materials. Du Pont's acquisition of Conoco was a vertical merger. Congeneric means "allied in nature or action"; hence, a **congeneric merger** involves related enterprises but not producers of the same product (horizontal) or firms in a producer-supplier relationship (vertical). Examples of congeneric mergers include Unilever's takeover of Chesebrough-Ponds, a toiletry maker, and Philip Morris's acquisition of General Foods. A **conglomerate merger** occurs when unrelated enterprises combine, as illustrated by Mobil Oil's acquisition of Montgomery Ward.

Operating economies (and also anticompetitive effects) are at least partially dependent on the type of merger involved. Vertical and horizontal mergers generally provide the greatest synergistic operating benefits, but they are also the ones most likely to be attacked by the U.S. Department of Justice. In any event, it is useful to think of these economic classifications when analyzing the feasibility of a prospective merger.

vertical merger
A merger between a firm and one of its suppliers or customers.

congeneric merger
A merger of firms in the same general industry, but for which no customer or supplier relationship exists.

conglomerate merger
A merger of companies in totally different industries.

Self-Test

Explain briefly the four economic classifications of mergers.

EXAMPLES OF MERGER ACTIVITY

Four major "merger waves" have occurred in the United States. The first was in the late 1800s, when consolidations occurred in the oil, steel, tobacco, and other basic industries. The second was in the 1920s, when the stock market boom helped financial promoters consolidate firms in a number of industries, including utilities, communications, and autos. The third was in the 1960s, when conglomerate mergers were the rage, while the fourth began in the early 1980s, and it is still going strong.

The current "merger mania" has been sparked by seven factors: (1) the depressed level of the dollar relative to Japanese and European currencies, which made U.S. companies look cheap to foreign buyers; (2) the unprecedented level of inflation that existed during the 1970s and early 1980s, which increased the replacement value of firms' assets even while a weak stock market reduced their market values; (3) the Reagan and Bush administrations' stated view that "bigness is not necessarily badness," which resulted in a more tolerant attitude toward large mergers; (4) the general belief among the major natural resource companies that it is cheaper to "buy reserves on Wall Street" through mergers than to explore and find them in the field; (5) attempts to ward off raiders by use of defensive mergers; (6) the development of the junk bond market, which made it possible to use far more debt in acquisitions than had been possible earlier; and (7) the increased globalization of business,

Table 22-1 **The Five Biggest Mergers (Billions of Dollars)**

Companies	Year	Value	Percent of Book Value	Type of Transaction
Time-Warner	1989	$14.0	350%	Acquisition for cash, stock, and debt
Chevron-Gulf	1984	13.3	136	Acquisition for cash
Philip Morris-Kraft	1988	12.9	609	Acquisition for stock
Bristol Myers-Squibb	1989	11.5	250	Acquisition for stock
Texaco-Getty	1984	10.1	191	Acquisition for cash and notes

Note: KKR's acquisition of RJR Nabisco exceeded $25 billion, but that transaction was an LBO, not a merger.

which has led to increased economies of scale and to the formation of world-wide corporations. Financial historians have not yet compiled the statistics and done the analysis necessary to compare the latest merger wave with the earlier ones, but it is virtually certain that the current wave will rank as the largest. Table 22-1 lists the top five mergers of all time, and they all occurred in the 1980s.

We present the highlights of six recent mergers to give you a flavor of how actual mergers occur.

1. Getty Oil, the fourteenth largest U.S. oil company, was acquired in 1984 by Texaco, the fourth largest, at a cost of $10.1 billion. Prior to the merger activity, Getty's shares were selling at around $65, and the descendants of J. Paul Getty, the founder, were complaining of inefficient management. Then the controlling trustees of the Sarah C. Getty Trust, together with Pennzoil, announced plans to take the firm private by buying the shares which they did not already control at a price of $112.50 per share. Texaco then jumped in with an offer of $125 per share.

The merger doubled Texaco's domestic oil and gas reserves, and, with Getty's retail outlets, gave Texaco a larger share of the gasoline market. Some analysts claimed that Texaco, with its sprawling network of refineries and its rapidly dwindling reserves, made the correct decision by acquiring Getty, with its large reserves and minimal refining operations. Other analysts contended that Texaco paid too much for Getty. Acquiring Getty's reserves may have been cheaper for Texaco than finding new oil, but the value of those reserves depends on the price of oil, which by 1988 was down by more than 40 percent but in 1990 rose again due to the crisis in the Middle East.

Two side issues arose at the end of the Getty merger. The first concerned the Bass Brothers of Texas, an immensely wealthy family that had acquired over $1 billion of Texaco stock during all the action. Texaco's management was afraid the Bass Brothers would try to take over Texaco, so they bought out the Bass interests at a premium of about 20 percent over the stock's market value. Some of Texaco's stockholders argued that the payment amounted to "greenmail," or a payoff made with stockholder's money just to insure that

Texaco's managers could keep their jobs. This situation, along with several similar ones, has led to the introduction of bills in Congress to limit the actions that a management group can take in its efforts to avoid being taken over. However, Congress has not actually passed such a law to date. The second side issue was a suit by Pennzoil, which charged that Texaco caused Getty to breach its contract with Pennzoil. Pennzoil won a $12 billion judgment, but Texaco appealed, and in 1988 Pennzoil settled for $3 billion, of which Pennzoil's lawyers got $400 million. Texaco was forced into bankruptcy. It appears that Texaco will survive, but that its top managers will lose their jobs.

2. Conoco, which had assets with a book value of $11 billion and which was, based on sales, the thirteenth largest company in the United States, was the target of three other giants: Mobil (the second largest U.S. corporation), Du Pont (the fifteenth largest U.S. corporation), and Seagram (a large Canadian company). This merger alone almost surpassed in dollar amount the previous record for all mergers in a single year (book value assets of $12 billion in 1968). Conoco's stock sold for about $50 just before the bidding started, but the bid price got up to over $100 per share before it was over, because Conoco's oil and coal reserves, plus its plant and equipment, were worth far more than the company's initial stock market value.

If Mobil had won, this would have been a horizontal merger. If Seagram had won, it would have been a conglomerate merger. Yet Du Pont won, and it was classified as a vertical merger because Du Pont uses petroleum in its production processes. The Justice Department would have fought a merger with Mobil, but it indicated that it would not do so in the case of Seagram or Du Pont. For this reason, even though Mobil made the highest bid of $115 per share, Du Pont ended up the winner with a bid of $98. Stockholders chose the Du Pont bid over that of Mobil because they were afraid a Mobil merger would be blocked, causing Conoco's stock to fall below the level of the Du Pont bid.

This was a *hostile merger* — Conoco's management would rather have had the company remain an independent entity. Obviously, though, that was not to be, and Conoco's top managers found themselves working for someone else (or out of a job). This is a good illustration of a point made in Chapter 1, namely, that managers have a strong motivation to operate in a manner that will maximize the value of their firms' stocks, for otherwise they can find themselves in the same boat as Conoco's managers.

3. Marathon Oil, a company only slightly smaller than Conoco, was the object of an attempted acquisition by Mobil after that company lost its bid for Conoco. Marathon's management resisted strongly, and again other bidders entered the picture. In the end, U.S. Steel picked up Marathon for about $6 billion, making this the fourth largest merger up to that time. U.S. Steel's bid for Marathon was unusual in that the firm offered to purchase only 51 percent of the stock and to exchange bonds for the remainder, with cash going

two-tier offer

A merger offer which provides different (better) terms to those who tender their stock earlier.

to those stockholders who agreed to the merger at an earlier date. This is called a **two-tier offer,** and it prompted many stockholders to tender their stock to U.S. Steel out of fear of having to accept bonds if they waited to see if the bid might go higher. Subsequently, Congress banned the use of two-tier offers.

4. Schlitz, once the largest U.S. brewer, had been losing both money and market share. By the 1980s it had become only the fourth largest brewer, with a market share of 8.5 percent, and it seemed to be on a collision course with bankruptcy. Schlitz's troubles arose from its poor marketing strategy, a problem that it was unable to conquer. G. Heileman, the sixth largest brewer, with a market share of 7.5 percent, was better managed, and its sales were growing rapidly. (Heileman's ROE was 27.3 percent; Schlitz's was negative.) Because of its successful marketing programs, Heileman needed more brewing capacity, whereas, because of its poor sales performance, Schlitz had 50 percent excess capacity. Heileman offered to buy Schlitz's common stock for $494 million. If the takeover attempt had been successful, Heileman would have acquired capacity at an effective cost of $19 per barrel versus a construction cost of about $50 per barrel. The merger would also have made Heileman the third largest in the nation. Although the Justice Department under the Reagan administration had previously taken the position that "bigness is not necessarily badness," it opposed this merger because in its judgment the resulting concentration would substantially reduce competition in the brewing industry. Therefore, Heileman abandoned the merger effort. However, Schlitz was still in trouble, and it was later acquired by Stroh Brewery, another good marketer, although smaller than G. Heileman.

5. General Motors recently acquired Electronics Data Systems (EDS), the world's largest data processing company, for $2.2 billion. GM had excess cash, and it wanted to diversify outside the auto industry to stabilize earnings. Also, its management believed that EDS could help GM set up better internal management control systems and help with the company's planned automation of manufacturing operations. Ross Perot, the founder and a 50 percent owner of EDS, was offered more than $1 billion, plus a seat on the GM board, for his stock, as well as a chance to continue running EDS. After the merger, Perot clashed with Roger Smith, GM's chairman, and GM bought Perot's stock at a substantial premium over the market price to get him off the board. In 1989, Perot started a new company which will compete with EDS.

6. Shortly after the EDS merger, GM also acquired Hughes Aircraft, a privately held company that was started by the late Howard Hughes in the 1930s, for $4.7 billion. Hughes was one of the largest defense contractors and was highly profitable, but what GM really wanted was its expertise in high-tech electronic controls. GM must utilize such technology in its design and manufacturing of autos if it is to compete effectively with the Japanese. Investment analysts believe that there are tremendous potential synergistic benefits to GM from both the Hughes and the EDS mergers, but at this point one can only wait to see if the $6.9 billion spent on the mergers will really pay off.

As we write this, the most recent merger wave is still alive and well.

Self-Test

What are the four major merger "waves" that have occurred in the United States?

What are the seven factors that sparked the most recent "merger mania"?

PROCEDURES FOR COMBINING FIRMS

In the vast majority of mergers, one firm (generally the larger of the two) simply decides to buy another company, negotiates a price for it, and then acquires the target company. Occasionally, the acquired firm will initiate the action, but it is much more common for a firm to seek acquisitions than to seek to be acquired. Following convention, we shall call a company that seeks to acquire another the **acquiring company** and the one which it seeks to acquire the **target company.**

    Once an acquiring company has identified a possible target, it must establish a suitable price, or range of prices, that it is willing to pay. With this in mind, the acquiring firm's managers must decide how to approach the target company's managers. If the acquiring firm has reason to believe that the target company's management will approve the merger, then it will simply propose a merger and try to work out suitable terms. If an agreement can be reached, the two management groups will issue statements to their stockholders recommending that they approve the merger. Assuming that the stockholders do approve, the acquiring firm will simply buy the target company's shares from its stockholders, paying for them either with its own shares (in which case the target company's stockholders become stockholders of the acquiring company), with cash, or with bonds. Situations in which the terms of the merger are approved by both management groups are called **friendly mergers.** Time's merger with Warner was an example of a friendly merger.

    Under other circumstances, the target company's management may resist the merger. Perhaps the managers believe that the price offered for the stock is too low, or perhaps the target firm's management simply wants to maintain its independence. In either case, the target firm's management is said to be *hostile*, rather than friendly, and, in a **hostile merger (takeover),** the acquiring firm must make a direct appeal to the target firm's stockholders. In hostile mergers, the acquiring company generally makes a **tender offer,** in which it asks the stockholders of the firm it is seeking to control to submit, or "tender," their shares in exchange for a specified price. The price is generally stated as so many dollars per share of the stock to be acquired, although it can be stated in terms of shares of stock in the acquiring firm. The tender offer is a direct

acquiring company
A company that seeks to acquire another.

target company
A firm that another company seeks to acquire.

friendly merger
A merger in which the terms are approved by the managements of both companies.

hostile merger (takeover)
A merger in which the target firm's management resists acquisition.

tender offer
The offer of one firm to buy the stock of another by going directly to the stockholders, frequently (but not always) over the opposition of the target company's management.

Announcements of *friendly mergers,* such as this advertisement in *The Wall Street Journal,* appear frequently in the business press. In this case, managements of both the acquiring company, Sony, and the target company, Columbia Pictures Entertainment, Inc., approved the terms of the merger. Allen & Company is the investment banking firm that handled the merger.

Columbia Pictures Entertainment, Inc.

has been acquired by

Sony Columbia Acquisition Corp.,

a Wholly Owned Subsidiary

of

Sony USA Inc.

The undersigned assisted in the negotiations and acted as financial advisor to Columbia Pictures Entertainment. Inc.

ALLEN & COMPANY
INCORPORATED

November 1989

Source: *Business Week,* December 25, 1989–January 1, 1990.

appeal to stockholders, so it need not be approved by the target firm's management. Tender offers are not new, but their frequency of use has increased greatly in recent years.

Self-Test

Differentiate between the acquiring company and the target company in a merger situation.

How do the acquiring company's actions in a hostile merger attempt differ from those in a friendly merger attempt?

FINANCIAL ANALYSIS OF A PROPOSED MERGER

In theory, merger analysis is quite simple. The acquiring firm simply performs a capital budgeting analysis to determine whether the present value of the cash flows expected to result from the merger exceeds the price that must be paid for the target company. If the net present value is positive, the acquiring firm should take steps to acquire the target firm. The target company's stockholders, on the other hand, should accept the proposal if the price offered exceeds the present value of the firm's expected future cash flows discounted at the cost of equity, assuming that the firm continues to operate independently. Theory aside, however, some difficult decisions are involved. First, the acquiring company must estimate the incremental cash flow benefits, including any synergistic effects, that will be obtained from the acquisition, and it must determine what effect, if any, the merger will have on its own required rate of return on equity. Then, the acquiring company must decide how to pay for the merger —with cash, with its own stock, or with some other type or package of securities. Finally, having estimated the benefits of the merger, it is necessary for the acquiring and target firms' managers and stockholders to bargain over how to share these benefits. The required analysis can be extremely complex.

Operating Mergers versus Financial Mergers

From the standpoint of financial analysis, there are two basic types of mergers: operating mergers and financial mergers.

1. An **operating merger** is one in which the operations of two companies are integrated with the expectation of obtaining synergistic effects. The Time-Warner deal is a good example of an operating merger.

2. A **financial merger** is one in which the merged companies will not be operated as a single unit and from which no significant operating economies are expected. Coca-Cola's acquisition of Columbia Pictures is an example of a financial merger.

Of course, a merger may actually be a combination of these two types. Thus, if Mobil had acquired either Conoco or Marathon, the merger would have

operating merger
A merger in which operations of the firms involved are integrated in hope of achieving synergistic benefits.

financial merger
A merger in which the firms involved will not be operated as a single unit and from which no operating economies of scale are expected.

been primarily an operating one. However, with Du Pont and U.S. Steel emerging as the victors in those acquisitions, the mergers were more financial than operating in nature.

Estimating Future Operating Income

In a financial merger, the postmerger cash flows are simply the sum of the expected cash flows of the two companies if they continued to operate independently. If the two firms' operations are to be integrated in order to achieve better financial results, however, then accurate predictions of future cash flows, which are difficult to obtain but absolutely essential to sound merger decisions, will be required.

The basic rationale for any operating merger is synergy. Del Monte Corporation provides a good example of a series of well-thought-out, successful operating mergers. Del Monte successfully merged and integrated numerous small canning companies into a highly efficient, profitable organization. It used standardized production techniques to increase the efficiency of all its plants, a national brand name and national advertising to develop customer brand loyalty, a consolidated distribution system, and a centralized purchasing office to obtain substantial discounts from volume purchases. Because of these economies of scale, Del Monte became the most efficient and profitable U.S. canning company, and its merger activities helped make possible the size that produced these economies. Consumers also benefited, because Del Monte's efficiency enabled the company to sell high-quality products at relatively low prices.

An example of poor pro forma analysis that resulted in a disastrous merger was the consolidation of the Pennsylvania and New York Central railroads. A premerger analysis suggested that large cost savings would result, but the analysis was grossly misleading. It failed to recognize that certain key elements in the two rail systems were incompatible and hence could not be meshed together. Thus, rather than gaining synergistic benefits, the combined system actually incurred additional overhead costs, and that led to bankruptcy.

In planning operating mergers, the development of accurate pro forma cash flows is the single most important aspect of the analysis. In fact, many firms that are actively engaged in mergers have acquisition departments which evaluate merger candidates, develop pro forma statements that forecast under varying assumptions the results of the mergers, and evaluate plans for making the projections materialize.

Terms of a Merger

The terms of a merger include two important questions: (1) Who will control the combined enterprise? (2) How much will the acquiring firm pay for the acquired company? These points are discussed next.

Postmerger Control. The employment/control situation is often of vital importance. Consider a situation in which a small, owner-managed firm sells out to a larger concern. The owner-manager may be anxious to retain a high-status position, and he or she also may have developed a camaraderie with the employees and thus be concerned about keeping operating control of the organization after the merger. If so, who keeps control is likely to be stressed during the merger negotiations. When a publicly owned firm, not controlled by its managers, is merged into another company, the acquired firm's management is also worried about its postmerger position. If the acquiring firm agrees to retain the old management, then management may be willing to support the merger and to recommend its acceptance to the stockholders. If the old management is to be removed, it probably will resist the merger.

The Price Paid. Another key element in a merger is the price to be paid for the target company—the cash or securities to be given in exchange for the firm. The analysis is similar to a regular capital budgeting analysis: the incremental cash flows are estimated; a discount rate is applied to find the present value of these cash flows; and, if the present value of the future incremental cash flows exceeds the price to be paid for the target firm, the merger is approved. If, because of operating economies or financial considerations, the target firm is worth more to the acquiring firm than its market value as a separate entity, the merger is feasible. Obviously, the acquiring firm tries to buy at as low a price as possible, whereas the target firm tries to sell out at the highest price possible. The final price is determined by negotiations, with the party that negotiates best capturing most of the incremental value. *The larger the synergistic benefits, the more room there is for bargaining, and the higher the probability that the merger actually will be consummated.*

There is the potential for a conflict of interest in most merger negotiations. If the target firm's management is offered highly paid jobs after the merger, or lucrative stock options, will it bargain as hard as possible over the price paid for the acquired firm's stock? Or, if competing offers are received, will management recommend the offer that is best for it or best for the target firm's stockholders? One solution to these problems is for a committee of the board of the target firm, consisting of outside (nonmanagement) directors, to do the negotiating. These outside directors must agree not to participate in any way with the surviving firm. Still, you should recognize that potential conflicts of interest are a real and a serious problem.

Self-Test

What, in theory, is involved in a merger analysis?

What is the essential difference between an operating merger and a financial merger?

In analyzing a proposed operating merger, what is the single most important factor?

When negotiating a friendly merger, what are the two most important considerations?

INDUSTRY PRACTICE

High-Tech Firms Get the Urge to Merge

Mergers are proliferating in the computer business as both hardware and software producers are joining forces to meet the increasing demands of customers and the stiffer competition within the industry. A group of small minicomputer makers, for instance, could hardly compete with IBM and Digital Equipment, which controlled about half the market in 1988. A wave of mergers was, therefore, predicted. "There's going to be an enormous amount of those deals," said Joe Henson, who was then CEO of Prime Computer, Inc. "It's the only viable route for many of these companies."

Henson went shopping himself after raising $375 million in early 1987. He bought Calma from General Electric and then acquired Computervision Corporation in a hostile takeover. These moves made Prime second in the computer-aided manufacturing market. Ironically, Henson's firm became a target itself 11 months after it acquired Computervision, when MAI Basic Four, Inc., made an unsolicited bid for it. Bennett S. LeBow of MAI said he wanted to link the maintenance, marketing, and manufacturing operations of the two companies in order to realize economies of scale.

Annual growth rates in the minicomputer market had slumped to just 5 percent in late 1988, from 15 percent in prior years. Hardware sales in the mainframe computer business were also slow, and the mainframe software market was soft as well. The result was a slew of mergers — from 1988 to 1990 there were 65, with a total value of $1.5 billion.

The biggest single merger during that period was the $425 million union of Duquesne Systems and Morino Corporation in 1989. Also, Computer Associates International bought three companies in the same year, bringing its total to more than 20 purchases since 1976. Its president, Anthony W. Wang, said, "Software companies see that there are economies of scale from joining forces, [and it is] especially [advantageous to merge] with a company that has a large sales organization."

The merger prognosticator from the minicomputer business, Joe Henson, is now up to his old tricks in the mainframe software industry. After retiring from Prime Computer, he became CEO at Legent Corporation, which was formed from the Duquesne-Morino merger. The heads of these united firms ran Legent jointly for a time, but they disagreed on how best to integrate the different corporate personalities of their former companies. Henson, who was a Legent director, then took over as chief executive. Combining the two firms has been "no piece of cake," he admits, and full integration took 14 months from the time of the merger.

When it was finally complete, Henson was ready to "shop" — he planned to buy at least 10 small software companies in 1990. In his seven years at Prime, he increased revenues fourfold, to $1.6 billion. Through mergers, he hopes to do the same at Legent. "I'd love to say I built both a billion-dollar hardware and a billion-dollar software company," he says. As of mid-1990, Legent was only a $125 million company, but analysts were predicting that its sales would grow 39 percent during the year, to $173 million, and that they would reach $460 million by 1994.

Sources: *Business Week,* Leslie Helm, "The Merger Wave Bearing Down on Minicomputer Makers" and Robert D. Hof, "Redrawing the Game Plan for Computer-aided Design," November 28, 1988; Judith H. Dobrzynski, "The Merger Go-round Is Coming Around Again," February 12, 1990; Walecia Konrad, Keith H. Hammonds, and Deidre A. Depke, "Survival of the Biggest," April 2, 1990; Keith H. Hammonds, Richard Brandt, and Sandra Atchison, "Overnight, Lotus Blossoms into No. 1," April 23, 1990; "Lotus Isn't Crying at the Altar," June 4, 1990.

In the meantime, in the software market for personal computers a proposed merger came close to creating a new giant. Lotus Development and Novell Inc. were prepared to join in a $1.5 billion stock deal in April 1990 that would have given them the financial and technical strength to challenge Microsoft, the industry leader. Combined sales for the merged firms were projected at $1.25 billion for 1990, surpassing Microsoft's $1.1 billion. The merger, negotiated by Lotus CEO Jim P. Manzi, was called "a brilliant move" before it fell apart just a month later, when Lotus refused the Novell directors' demands for more in the deal than originally requested by their chairman, Raymond J. Noorda. Now Lotus and Novell must continue to battle Microsoft as separate companies, without the size and product strength the merger would have created. The two executives still talk about some sort of future cooperation. "We hope that our relationship is not ended," says Noorda. More cautiously, Manzi says, "We're going to have to think twice about what that relationship is going to be."

One of the problems with many mergers, regardless of the industry, is a clash of individual corporate cultures and management styles. Had Novell and Lotus completed their merger, the very different life-styles in Provo, Utah, and Cambridge, Massachusetts, might have made the union difficult. To illustrate, when Mentor Graphics Corporation of Beaver, Oregon, acquired California Automated Design, the conservative former IBM employees in the acquired company had difficulty adjusting to the Mentor staff's informality. Similarly, in the mainframe software business, employees of McCormack & Dodge were accustomed to thinking of Management Science America's CEO John Imlay as an archenemy. Then the firms merged, and Imlay became their boss.

In addition to difficulty with staff adjustments, high-tech mergers may also be plagued with mismatched technology and widely dispersed plant locations. In spite of these problems, though, mergers often provide a better way to meet the competition than developing new product lines and service from scratch.

MERGER ANALYSIS

To illustrate how a merger may be analyzed, consider a proposed merger between Acquisition Technology and Target Industry, Inc. For Acquisition to determine the value of Target, two key items are needed: (1) a set of pro forma financial statements that develop Target's expected cash flows and (2) a discount rate, or cost of capital, to apply to these projected cash flows.

Pro Forma Income Statements

The merger team at Acquisition Technology, which includes people from finance, accounting, engineering, and marketing, has produced the projected income statements shown in Table 22-2. The data reflect all postmerger synergistic effects that may be expected in the merger of Acquisition Technology and Target Industry.

The accuracy of the projected cash flows is critical to a successful evaluation of Target, but they are extremely difficult to estimate. Because it is a friendly merger, Acquisition has sent part of the merger team, including dozens of financial analysts, accountants, engineers, and others, to Target's head-

Table 22-2 **Target Industry:**
Projected Postmerger Income Statement
(Millions of Dollars)

	1991	1992	1993	1994	1995
Net sales	$147	$176	$211	$244	$267
Cost of goods sold	112	132	155	178	192
Sales & administrative expenses	14	17	18	21	22
EBIT	$ 21	$ 27	$ 38	$ 45	$ 53
Interest	4	5	5	6	6
EBT	$ 17	$ 22	$ 33	$ 39	$ 47
Taxes	4	7	11	13	16
Net income	$ 13	$ 15	$ 22	$ 26	$ 31
Retained earnings	7	12	14	15	16
Annual cash flow to Acquisition Technology	$ 6	$ 3	$ 8	$ 11	$ 15
Terminal value					275
Net cash flow	$ 6	$ 3	$ 8	$ 11	$290

quarters to go over its books, to estimate required maintenance expenses and future fixed asset investments, to set values on patents and research and development projects, and the like.

The data in Table 22-2 reflect the incremental changes in Acquisition's cash flows that will result directly from its merger with Target. Some of the net income generated through the merger will be retained by Acquisition to finance its own asset growth, and some will be transferred to Target for investment in assets, for dividends, or for other purposes. The pro forma statement assumes that depreciation-generated funds will be used to replace worn-out and obsolete plant and equipment. The merger team projects that cash flows will grow at a constant rate of 10 percent after 1995. The value to Acquisition of all post-1995 cash flows as of December 31, 1995, is estimated by the constant growth model to be $275 million:

$$\text{Value in 1995} = CF_{1995}(1 + g)/(k_s - g)$$

$$= \$15(1.10)/(0.16 - 0.10)$$

$$= \$275 \text{ million.}$$

In the next section we discuss the determination of the appropriate discount rate.

Estimating the Discount Rate

Up to this point, our merger analysis has been quite similar to the analysis of capital budgeting projects, but an important difference exists between merger analysis and capital budgeting: In capital budgeting the cash flows are discounted by the cost of capital, but, in merger analysis, the cost of equity is the appropriate discount rate.

Note that the net cash flows shown at the bottom of Table 22-2 are equity cash flows, so they should be discounted at the cost of equity rather than at the overall cost of capital. The cost of equity used must reflect the riskiness of the net cash flows shown in the table. Also, the cost of equity that is used should be Target's cost of equity, not Acquisition's or that of the consolidated postmerger firm. Target currently uses 30 percent debt in its capital structure, but if the merger occurs, Acquisition will increase Target's debt ratio to 50 percent. Target's market-determined premerger beta was 1.15, which reflects the debt ratio of 30 percent. Acquisition's investment bankers estimate that Target's beta will rise to 1.4 if its debt ratio is increased to 50 percent.

The Security Market Line can be used to determine Target's new cost of equity capital. If the risk-free rate is 9 percent and the market risk premium is 5 percent, then Target's after-merger cost of equity, k_s, is estimated to be 16 percent:

$$k_s = k_{RF} + (k_M - k_{RF})b$$

$$= 9\% + (5\%)1.4$$

$$= 16\%.$$

This is the rate at which the cash flows shown in Table 22-2 should be discounted.

Determining the Acquisition's Value

Target's value to Acquisition in 1990 can be determined by discounting at 16 percent the cash flows that are expected to accrue to Acquisition:

Year	Cash Flow	PVIF at 16%	Discounted Cash Flow
1991	$ 6,000,000	0.8621	$ 5,172,600
1992	3,000,000	0.7432	2,229,600
1993	8,000,000	0.6407	5,125,600
1994	11,000,000	0.5523	6,075,300
1995	290,000,000	0.4761	138,069,000
			$156,672,100

Therefore, if Acquisition can acquire Target for $156,672,100 or less, the merger appears to be acceptable from Acquisition's point of view.

Self-Test

Explain how the cash flows required in a merger analysis are determined.

How is the discount rate that is used to evaluate the postmerger cash flows of the target firm obtained? Should this be an equity return or an overall cost of capital? Why?

THE ROLE OF INVESTMENT BANKERS

The investment banking community is involved with mergers in a number of ways. First, investment bankers help to arrange mergers. Also, because they are experts in arranging mergers, they have the expertise to help target companies *resist* mergers by developing and implementing defensive tactics. Finally, investment bankers help acquiring firms value target companies.

These merger-related activities have proved to be quite profitable to the investment banking community. For example, Paramount Communications incurred fees and related costs of about $50 million in its failed attempt to acquire Time, and Time's costs to fend off Paramount and to acquire Warner were over $100 million. No wonder investment banking houses are able to make top offers to finance graduates!

Arranging Mergers

The major investment banking firms have merger and acquisition groups that operate within their corporate finance departments. (Corporate finance departments sell advice to business firms. They are different from underwriting departments, which help firms issue new securities, and from brokerage departments, which trade outstanding securities.) Members of finance departments strive to identify firms with excess cash that might want to buy other firms, companies that might be willing to be bought, and firms that might be attractive to others for a number of reasons. If an oil company decided to expand into coal mining, it might enlist the aid of an investment banker's finance department to help it locate and then negotiate with a target coal company. Similarly, dissident stockholders of firms with poor track records may work with investment bankers to oust management by helping to arrange a merger. Drexel Burnham Lambert, the investment banking house that developed junk bond financing, offered financing packages to corporate raiders, with the package including both designing the securities used in tender offers and getting people and firms to buy the target firm's stock and then to tender it once the final offer was made.

Self-Test

How is the investment banking community involved with mergers?

MERGER DEFENSES

A target firm that does not want to be acquired usually enlists the help of an investment banking firm, along with a law firm that specializes in helping to block takeovers. Defenses include such tactics as (1) changing the firm's bylaws so that only one-third of the directors are elected each year and/or so that a 75 percent approval rate (a "supermajority"), rather than a simple majority, is required to approve a merger; (2) trying to convince the target firm's stockholders that the price being offered is too low; (3) raising antitrust issues in the hope that the Justice Department will intervene; (4) repurchasing stock in the open market in an effort to push the price above that being offered by the potential acquirer; (5) finding a **white knight** that is more acceptable to the target firm's management to compete with the potential acquirer; and (6) "taking a poison pill."

Some examples of **poison pills** — which really do amount to virtually committing suicide to avoid a takeover — involve such tactics as borrowing on terms that require immediate repayment of all loans if the firm is acquired, selling off at bargain prices the assets that originally made the firm a desirable target, granting such lucrative **golden parachutes** to the firm's executives that the cash drain from these payments would render the merger infeasible, and planning defensive mergers that would leave the firm with new assets of questionable value and a huge amount of debt to service. Companies have even given their stockholders the right to buy the stock of an acquiring firm at half-price should the company be acquired. The blatant use of poison pills is constrained by directors' awareness that such actions could trigger personal suits by stockholders against directors who voted for them. Perhaps in the near future, there will be laws that limit management's use of these tactics; in the meantime, investment bankers are busy thinking up new poison pill formulas, and others are just as actively trying to come up with "antidotes."

white knight
A company that is more acceptable to the management of a firm under attack in a hostile takeover attempt.

poison pill
An action which will seriously hurt a company if it is acquired by another.

golden parachutes
Large payments made to the managers of a firm if it is acquired.

Self-Test

List some defense tactics that can be used by target firms to block mergers.

List some examples of poison pills.

FAIR PRICE

If a friendly merger is being worked out between two firms' managements, it is important for them to be able to document that the agreed-upon price is a fair one; otherwise, the stockholders of either company may sue to block the merger. Therefore, in most large mergers, each side will engage an investment banking firm to evaluate the target company and to help establish the fair price. For example, General Electric employed Morgan Stanley to determine a fair price for Utah International, as did Royal Dutch to help establish the price it paid for Shell Oil. Even if the merger is not friendly, investment bankers may still be asked to help establish a price. If a surprise tender offer is to be made, the acquiring firm will want to know the lowest price at which it might be able to acquire the stock, while the target firm may seek help in proving that the price being offered is too low.

Self-Test

Why is it important to engage investment bankers in the determination of a fair price in an unfriendly merger?

CORPORATE ALLIANCES

corporate alliance
Any type of cooperative business arrangement between two or more companies.

joint venture
A corporate alliance in which two or more independent companies combine their resources to achieve a specific, limited objective.

Mergers are not the only way in which the resources of two firms can be combined. In fact, many companies are striking cooperative deals which fall far short of merging. Such cooperative deals are called **corporate alliances,** and they take many forms, from marketing agreements to joint ownership of world-scale operations. One form of corporate alliance is the **joint venture,** which involves the joining together of parts of two or more companies to accomplish a specific, limited objective. Joint ventures are controlled by the combined management of the two (or more) parent companies.

Joint ventures have been used often by U.S., Japanese, and European firms to share technology and marketing expertise. For example, in 1989, Whirlpool announced a joint venture with the Dutch electronics giant Philips under which it will produce appliances under the Philips brand names in five European countries. By joining with their foreign counterparts, U.S. firms can get a strong foothold in Europe before 1992, the year the European community will remove its trade barriers and become a unified market.

Self-Test

What is the difference between a merger and a joint venture?

DIVESTITURES

divestiture
The sale of some of a company's operating assets.

Although corporations do more buying than selling of operating assets, a good deal of selling also occurs. There are four types of **divestitures:** (1) sale of an operating unit to another firm; (2) sale of the unit being divested to the managers; (3) setting up the business to be divested as a separate corporation and then giving (or "spinning off") its stock on a pro rata basis to the divesting firm's stockholders; and (4) outright liquidation of assets.

Sale to another firm generally involves the sale of an entire division or unit, usually for cash but sometimes for the acquiring firm's stock. In a *managerial buyout,* the managers or employees of the division purchase the division themselves, usually for cash plus notes; then, as owner-managers, they reorganize the division as a closely held firm. In a *spin-off,* the firm's existing stockholders are given new stock representing separate ownership rights in the company that was divested. The new company establishes its own board of directors and officers, and it operates as a separate company. The stockholders end up owning shares of two firms instead of one, but no cash has been transferred. Finally, in a *liquidation,* the assets of a division are sold off piecemeal rather than as a single entity. We present some recent examples of the different types of divestitures in the next section.

Divestiture Illustrations

1. Esmark, Inc., a holding company which owned such consumer products companies as Swift meats and Playtex, sold off several of its nonconsumer-oriented divisions, including petroleum properties for which Mobil and some other oil companies paid $1.1 billion. Investors had generally thought of Es-mark as a meat packing and consumer products company, and its stock price had reflected this image rather than that of a company with huge holdings of valuable oil reserves carried at low balance sheet values. Thus, Esmark's stock was undervalued, according to its managers, and the company was in danger of a takeover bid. Selling the oil properties helped Esmark raise its stock price from $19 to $45.

2. ITT, in a move to streamline and rationalize its holdings, divested itself of 27 separate companies with a value of $1.2 billion. Some of these units were suffering losses and were holding down the parent company's earnings, while others simply no longer fitted into ITT's corporate strategy. Also, ITT had a debt ratio that many regarded as excessive, and it used some of the proceeds from the asset sales to reduce its debt.

3. International Paper (IP) recently sold its Canadian subsidiary to Canadian Pacific for $1.1 billion. IP planned to spend $4 billion to modernize its U.S. facilities, and the sale of the Canadian unit helped finance these expenditures.

4. IU International, a multimillion-dollar conglomerate listed on the NYSE, spun off three major subsidiaries—Gotaas-Larson, an ocean shipping company which owned Carnival Cruise Lines; Canadian Utilities, an electric utility; and Echo Bay Mining, a gold mining company. IU also owned (and retained) some major trucking companies (Ryder and PIE), several manufacturing businesses, and some large agribusiness operations. IU's management originally had acquired and combined highly cyclical businesses, such as ocean shipping and gold mining, with stable ones such as utilities, in order to gain overall corporate stability through diversification. The strategy worked reasonably well from an operating standpoint, but it failed in the financial markets. According to its management, IU's very diversity kept it from being assigned to any particular industrial classification, so security analysts tended not to follow the company and therefore did not understand it or recommend it to investors. (Analysts tend to concentrate on an industry, and they do not like to recommend—and investors do not like to invest in—a company they do not understand.) As a result, IU had a low P/E ratio and a low market price. After the spin-offs, IU's stock price plus those of the spun-off companies rose from $10 to over $75.

5. Paramount sold its finance division (The Associates) for about $4 billion. Paramount wants to concentrate on the media and entertainment businesses, and it plans to use the funds from the sale of The Associates to acquire a media or entertainment firm.

6. The managers of Beatrice Companies and some private investors borrowed $6.9 billion from a group of banks and used this money to buy all of the firm's stock. This type of debt-financed transaction is called a **leveraged buyout (LBO),** and Beatrice was said to have "gone private" because the public stockholders were bought out and all of the stock went into the hands of the management group. We will look at LBOs in more detail in a later section. The new Beatrice has been busily selling off divisions to raise money to reduce its bank loans; its loan agreements required it to sell off at least $1.45 billion in assets within a year, but Beatrice beat that schedule. The company sold Avis for $250 million just 12 days after it went private, and it later sold off its Coca-Cola bottling operations for about $1 billion. Beatrice also sold its refrigerated warehouse network, its Max Factor cosmetic line, its dairy products line, and other operations, raising another $2.4 billion in total.

7. In 1984 AT&T was broken up to settle a Justice Department antitrust suit filed in the 1970s. For almost 100 years AT&T had operated as a holding company which owned Western Electric (its manufacturing subsidiary), Bell Labs (its research arm), a huge long-distance network system, and 22 Bell operating companies, such as Pacific Telephone, New York Telephone, Southern Bell, and Southwestern Bell. AT&T was divided into eight separate companies: a slimmed-down AT&T, which kept Western Electric, Bell Labs, and all interstate long-distance operations, and seven new regional telephone holding companies (NYNEX, Bell Atlantic, BellSouth, Ameritech, US West, Southwestern Bell, and Pacific Telesis). The stock of the seven new telephone companies was then spun off to the old AT&T's stockholders. Thus, a person who held 100 shares of old AT&T stock owned, after the divestiture, 100 shares of the "new" AT&T plus 10 shares of each of the seven new operating companies. These 170 shares were backed by the same assets that had previously backed 100 shares of AT&T common.

The AT&T divestiture occurred as a result of a suit by the Justice Department, which wanted to break up the Bell System into a regulated monopoly segment (the seven regional telephone companies) and a manufacturing/long-distance segment which would be subjected to competition. The breakup was designed to strengthen competition in those parts of the telecommunications industry which are not natural monopolies.

The preceding examples illustrate the varied reasons for divestitures. Sometimes the market does not appear to properly recognize the value of a firm's assets when they are held as part of a conglomerate; the Esmark oil properties case was an example. Similarly, IU International had become so complex and diverse that analysts and investors did not understand it and consequently ignored it. Other companies need cash either to finance expansion in their primary business lines or to reduce a large debt burden, and divestitures can be used to raise this cash; the International Paper and Paramount

---

leveraged buyout
A situation in which a firm's managers or a group of outside investors borrow heavily against the firm's assets and purchase the company themselves.

examples illustrate this point. The ITT actions showed that running a business is a dynamic process — conditions change, corporate strategies change in response, and, as a result, firms alter their asset portfolios by acquisitions, divestitures, or both.

Self-Test

What are four ways of carrying out divestitures?

Differentiate among managerial buyouts, spin offs, and liquidations.

What are some reasons for divestitures?

HOLDING COMPANIES

Holding companies date from 1889, when New Jersey became the first state to pass a law permitting corporations to be formed for the sole purpose of owning the stocks of other companies. Any company that owns stock in another firm could be called a holding company. However, as the term is generally used, a holding company is a firm that holds large blocks of stock in other companies and exercises control over those firms. The holding company is often called the **parent company,** and the controlled companies are known as **subsidiaries** or **operating companies.** The parent can own 100 percent of a subsidiary's stock, but frequently control is exercised with less than that amount.

Many of the advantages and disadvantages of holding companies are identical to those of large-scale operations already discussed in connection with mergers and consolidations. Whether a company is organized on a divisional basis or with the operating units kept as separate companies does not affect the basic reasons for conducting a large-scale, multiproduct, multiplant operation. However, as discussed below, the holding company form has some advantages and disadvantages that differ from those of completely integrated, divisionalized operations.

Advantages of Holding Companies

Control with Fractional Ownership. Through a holding company operation a firm may buy 5, 10, 50, or any other percentage of another corporation's stock. Such fractional ownership may be sufficient to give the acquiring company effective working control or substantial influence over the operations of the company in which it has acquired stock ownership. Working control is usually considered to entail more than 25 percent of the common stock, but it can be as low as 10 percent if the stock is widely distributed. One financier noted that the attitude of management is more important than the number of shares owned, adding that "if they think you can control the company, then you do." In addition, a very slim margin of control can be held through friendship with large stockholders outside the holding company group.

holding company
A corporation that owns sufficient common stock of another firm to achieve working control of that firm.

parent company
A firm which controls another firm by owning a large block of its stock.

operating company (subsidiary)
A subsidiary of a holding company; a separate legal entity.

Isolation of Risks. Because the various operating companies in a holding company system are separate legal entities, the obligations of any one unit are separate from those of the other units. Therefore, catastrophic losses incurred by one unit of the holding company system might not be transmitted as claims on the assets of the other units.

Although this is the customary generalization on the nature of risk in a holding company system, it is not always valid. First, the parent company may feel obligated to make good on the subsidiary's debts, even though it is not legally bound to do so, to keep its good name and thus retain customers. Examples of this include American Express's payment of more than $100 million in connection with a swindle that was the responsibility of one of its subsidiaries, and United California Bank's coverage of a multimillion-dollar fraud loss incurred by its Swiss affiliate. Second, a parent company may feel obligated to supply capital to an affiliate to protect its initial investment; General Public Utilities' continued support of its subsidiaries' Three Mile Island nuclear plant is an example. Third, when lending to one of the units of a holding company system, an astute loan officer may require a guarantee or a claim on the assets of the parent or of other elements in the holding company system. Finally, an accident such as the one at Union Carbide's Bhopal, India, plant may be deemed the responsibility of the parent company, voiding the limited liability rules that would otherwise apply. To some degree, therefore, the assets in the holding company system are joined. Still, holding companies can at times prevent losses in one unit from bringing down other units in the system.

Legal Separation. Regulated companies such as financial institutions and utilities often find it easier to operate as holding companies than as divisional corporations. For example, Transamerica is a holding company that owns insurance companies, small loan companies, title companies, auto rental companies, and an airline. Similarly, Citicorp is a holding company that owns Citibank of New York, a leasing company, and a mortgage service company, among others.

Utilities also find the holding company format beneficial. All of the Bell telephone companies are parts of holding company systems. Southern Company, an electric utility that operates in and is regulated by several states, found it most practical to set up a holding company (Southern), which in turn owns a set of subsidiaries throughout several Southern states (Georgia Power, Alabama Power, Mississippi Power, Gulf Power, and Savannah Electric). However, even utilities that operate within a single state are finding it beneficial to operate as holding companies in order to separate those assets under the control of regulators from those not subject to utility commission regulation. Florida Power & Light recently reorganized and changed its corporate name to FPL Group, which owns a utility (Florida Power & Light) as well as subsidiaries engaged in insurance, real estate development, agriculture, and so on.

Disadvantages of Holding Companies

Partial Multiple Taxation. Provided that the holding company owns at least 80 percent of a subsidiary's voting stock, the Internal Revenue Service permits the filing of **consolidated returns,** in which case dividends received by the parent are not taxed. If less than 80 percent of the stock is owned, returns cannot be consolidated. However, 70 percent of the dividends received by the holding company are excluded from taxation, so only 30 percent of the dividends are taxable. With a tax rate of 34 percent and only 30 percent of the dividends subject to taxation, the effective intercorporate tax rate on dividends is 34% $\times$ 30% = 10.2%. This partial double taxation somewhat offsets the benefits of holding company control with limited ownership, but whether or not a penalty of 10.2 percent of dividends received is sufficient to offset other possible advantages is a matter that must be decided in individual situations.

consolidated return
An income tax return that combines the income statements of several affiliated firms.

Ease of Enforced Dissolution. It is relatively easy for the U.S. Department of Justice to require dissolution of a holding company operation it finds unacceptable. For instance, Du Pont was required to spin off its 23 percent stock interest in General Motors Corporation, acquired in the early 1920s. Because there was no fusion between the corporations, there were no difficulties, from an operating standpoint, in requiring the separation of the two companies. If complete amalgamation had taken place, however, it would have been much more difficult to break up the company after so many years, and the likelihood of forced divestiture would have been reduced.

Leverage in Holding Companies

The holding company vehicle has been used to obtain huge amounts of financial leverage. In the 1920s, several tiers of holding companies were established in the electric utility and other industries. In those days, an operating company at the bottom of the pyramid might have had $100 million of assets, financed by $50 million of debt and $50 million of equity. A first-tier holding company might have owned the stock of the operating firm as its only asset and then been financed with $25 million of debt and $25 million of equity. A second-tier holding company, which owned the $25 million of stock of the first-tier company as its only asset, might have been financed with $12.5 million of debt and $12.5 million of equity. The system could be extended to many more levels, but even with only two holding companies, we can see that $100 million of operating assets could be controlled at the top by only $12.5 million of second-tier equity, and $100 million of operating assets would have had to provide enough cash flow to support $87.5 million of debt. Such a holding company system is highly leveraged, even though the individual components each report 50 percent debt/assets ratios. Because of this *consolidated leverage,* even a small decline in profits at the operating company level could bring the whole system down "like a house of cards." In fact, many analysts regard the existence of highly leveraged holding companies as a major contributor to the severity of the stock market crash of 1929 and the resulting Great Depression of the 1930s.

Self-Test

Differentiate between holding companies and operating companies.

What are the major advantages and disadvantages of holding companies?

Explain how holding companies can be used to obtain high amounts of financial leverage.

LEVERAGED BUYOUTS (LBOs)

The 1980s witnessed a huge increase in the number and size of leveraged buyouts, or LBOs. This development occurred for the same reasons that other mergers and divestitures occurred — the existence of potential bargains, situations in which companies were using insufficient leverage, and the development of the junk bond market, which facilitated the use of leverage in takeovers.

LBOs can be initiated in one of two ways: (1) The firm's own managers can set up a new company whose equity comes from the managers themselves, plus some equity from pension funds and other institutions. This new company then arranges to borrow a large amount of money by selling junk bonds through an investment banking firm. With the financing arranged, the management group then makes an offer to purchase all the publicly owned shares through a tender offer. (2) A specialized LBO firm, such as Kohlberg Kravis Roberts (KKR), which is the largest and best known, will identify a potential target company, go to the management, and suggest that an LBO deal be done. KKR and other LBO firms have billions of dollars of equity, most put up by pension funds and other large investors, available for the equity portion of the deals, and they arrange junk bond financing just as a management-led group would do. Generally, the newly formed company will have at least 80 percent debt, and sometimes the debt ratio is as high as 98 percent. Thus, the term "leveraged" is most appropriate.

To illustrate an LBO, consider the $25 billion leveraged buyout of RJR Nabisco by Kohlberg Kravis Roberts (KKR). RJR, a leading producer of tobacco and food products, with brands such as Winston, Camel, Planters, Ritz, and Oreo, was trading at about $55 a share in October 1988. Then, F. Ross Johnson, the company's president and CEO, announced a $75 per share, or $17.6 billion, offer to take the firm private. The day after the announcement, RJR's stock price soared to $77.25, which indicated that investors thought that the final price would be even higher than Johnson's opening bid. A few days later, KKR offered $90 per share, or $20.6 billion, for the firm. The battle between the two bidders continued until late November, when RJR's board accepted KKR's revised bid of cash and securities worth about $106 per share, for a total value of about $25.1 billion.

Is RJR worth $25 billion, or did Henry Kravis and his partners let their egos govern their judgment? It will take several years before the answer is known, but at the time, analysts believed that the deal was workable — barely. To meet an estimated $2.5 billion in annual debt payments, KKR is expected to sell off a chunk of Nabisco's food businesses, lay off employees, cut advertising and marketing expenses, and slash spending on new plants. However, a recession or soaring interest rates could jeoparadize this strategy. In the highly leveraged world of LBOs, KKR insists that the structure of the buyout is relatively conservative. The new RJR owes banks and bondholders $22.8 billion, while stockholders' equity totals $7.4 billion. That's a 3-to-1 ratio, compared with the 9-to-1 ratio that is prevalent in other LBOs. Still, even the enormous annual cash flows produced by RJR's cigarettes and cookies probably will fall about $400 million short of meeting the annual interest payments over the next few years. On the plus side, RJR will no longer have to pay out $450 million annually in common dividends. Further, the new management team will be highly motivated to make a success of the venture.

Often, an LBO is an alternative to a merger. For example, in late 1988, Kraft Foods was approached by Philip Morris about a merger. Kraft's management resisted, and Philip Morris then announced that it would undertake a hostile tender offer, while Kraft's management announced that it would undertake an LBO to compete with Philip Morris. Philip Morris then raised its offer, and the merger, the third largest of all time, took place.

It is not clear whether LBOs are, on balance, a good or a bad idea. Some government officials, and others, have stated a belief that the leverage involved might destabilize the economy. On the other hand, LBOs have certainly stimulated some lethargic managements, and that is good. Good or bad, though, LBOs are helping to reshape the face of corporate America.

Self-Test

Identify and briefly explain the two ways in which an LBO may be initiated.

How has the development of the junk bond market affected the use of LBOs?

SMALL BUSINESS

Merging as a Means of Exiting a Closely Held Business

Imagine a small family-run business that has achieved some success. The entire family fortune may be tied up in the firm, as might be the case if a successful entrepreneur — say, Grandpa — started a business, brought his sons and daughters in as they reached adulthood, and continued to run the enterprise as it grew.

In such a situation, particularly if the firm is valued in the millions, the family's entire financial well-being may depend on the success of this business. As long as Grandpa is healthy and continues to run things, everything is fine. Grandpa may, in fact, be reluctant to sell the business; it gives him something to pass on to his family, and it provides a place for his children and grandchildren to work.

Closely held family businesses are fairly common in the United States. Yet, for several reasons, maintaining the business in its closely held form may not be in the family's best interests. First, there is the problem of succession. Because at some point Grandpa will retire or die, the issue of who will succeed him is important. Sometimes there is a clear choice for the successor, and everyone agrees with the choice. More often, however, even in families that are very close, the problem of succession can be an issue that splits the family apart. This problem is especially acute if Grandpa dies unexpectedly. At a highly emotional time, a key business decision needs to be made, and the choice is not a simple one. It is, therefore, essential that Grandpa and the other principals set up a plan of succession. If the issue is not resolvable, plans should be made for the outright sale of the business in the event of Grandpa's death.

A second problem is that the business represents the family's primary asset, but family members have no easy way to realize that value when they need cash: the business has no liquidity. Sometimes a plan will be made for someone to buy a family member's stock at a predetermined rate, such as at its book value per share. This enables the family member to obtain cash, but the price paid probably bears little relation to the market value of the shares. Thus, a family member gives up a valuable asset for the sake of liquidity, taking a potential loss in the process. An alternative, as discussed in Chapter 21, is to register the shares and take the company public so that family members can use their equity as they choose. A disadvantage to this approach is the potential loss of control as the number of shares held by the public increases.

A third problem is that as the firm grows, the family may be unable to provide the financial resources necessary to support that growth. If external funding is needed, it will generally be more difficult to obtain in a private, closely held business.

A perhaps even more serious problem is that, since the family's entire wealth is tied up in a single business, the family holds an *undiversified portfolio*. As was explained in earlier chapters, diversification through investment in a variety of securities reduces a portfolio's risk. Thus, the goals of maintaining control and reducing risk through diversification are in conflict. Again, a public offering would allow family members to sell some of their stock and to diversify their own personal portfolios.

Both the diversification motive and family members' liquidity needs indicate that the business's ownership structure should be changed. There is, however, another alternative besides going public — that of selling the business outright to another company or of merging it into a larger firm. This alternative is often overlooked by owners of closely held businesses, because it frequently means an immediate and complete loss of control. It deserves special consideration, however, because it can often be accomplished with far greater realization of value than can be achieved in a public offering.

With the sale of the business, the family gives up control, yet that control is what makes the firm more valuable in a merger than in a public offering. Merger premiums for public companies often range from 50 to 70 percent over the market price. Therefore, a company worth $10 million in the public market might be acquired for a price of $15 to $17 million in a merger. While mergers usually occur at higher prices than the stock would ordinarily command in market transactions, initial public offerings (IPOs) are normally made at below-market prices. Furthermore, if the owners sell a signifi-cant amount of their stock in the IPO, the market will take that as a signal that the company's future is dim, and the price will be depressed even more.

What are the disadvantages to a merger? An obvious disadvantage is the loss of control. Also, family members risk losing employment in the firm. In such a case, however, they will have additional wealth to sustain them while they seek other opportunities.

Owners of the closely held family business must consider the cost/benefit tradeoffs of continuing to be closely held versus going public or being acquired in a merger. Of the three alternatives, the acquisition alternative is likely to provide the most immediate wealth and security to the family members.

SUMMARY

In this chapter we discussed mergers, divestitures, holding companies, and LBOs. The key concepts covered are listed below:

- A **merger** occurs when two firms combine to form a single company. The primary motives for mergers are synergy, tax considerations, and the egos of the acquiring firms' managers.

- Mergers can provide economic benefits through **economies of scale** or through the **concentration of assets** in the hands of more efficient managers. However, mergers also have the potential for reducing competition, and for this reason they are carefully regulated by governmental agencies.

- In most mergers, one company **(the acquiring company)** initiates action to take over another **(the target company).**

- A **horizontal merger** occurs when two firms in the same line of business combine.

- A **vertical merger** is the combination of a firm with one of its customers or suppliers.

- A **congeneric merger** involves firms in related industries, but for which no customer-supplier relationship exists.

- A **conglomerate merger** occurs when firms in totally different industries combine.

- In a **friendly merger,** the managements of both firms approve the merger, while in a **hostile merger** the target firm's management opposes the merger.

- An **operating merger** is one in which the operations of the two firms are combined. A **financial merger** is one in which the firms continue to operate separately, and hence no operating economies are expected.

- In a **merger analysis,** (1) the price to be paid for the target firm and (2) the employment/control situation are the key issues to be resolved.

- To determine the **value of the target firm,** the acquiring firm must (1) forecast the cash flows that will result after the merger and (2) develop a discount rate to apply to the projected cash flows.

- **Poison pills** are actions a firm can take that will make the firm less valuable if it is acquired in a hostile takeover. **Golden parachutes** are large payments that are to be made to a firm's managers if it is acquired.

- A **joint venture** is a **corporate alliance** in which two or more companies combine some of their resources to achieve a specific, limited objective.

- A **divestiture** is the sale of some of a company's operating assets. A divestiture may involve (1) selling an operating unit to another firm, (2) selling a unit to that unit's managers, (3) **spinning off** a unit as a separate company, or (4) the outright **liquidation** of a unit's assets.

- The **reasons for divestitures** include antitrust, the clarification of what a company actually does, and the raising of capital needed to strengthen the corporation's core business.

- A **holding company** is a corporation which owns sufficient stock in another firm to achieve working control of it. The holding company is also known as the **parent company,** and the companies which it controls are called **subsidiaries,** or **operating companies.**

- Advantages to holding company operations are (1) that **control** can often be obtained for a smaller cash outlay, (2) that **risks may be segregated,** and (3) that regulated companies can **separate regulated from unregulated assets.**

- Disadvantages to holding company operations include (1) **tax penalties** and (2) the fact that incomplete ownership, if it exists, can lead to **control problems.**

- A **leveraged buyout (LBO)** is a transaction in which a firm's publicly owned stock is bought up in a primarily debt-financed tender offer, and a privately owned, highly leveraged firm results. Often, the firm's own management initiates the LBO.

- Maintaining a business as closely held may not be in the best interests of the owners for several reasons: (1) problems of succession, (2) valuation of the assets, (3) inability to provide financial resources to support growth, and (4) inadequate diversification.

RESOLUTION TO DECISION IN FINANCE

Did Consolidated Freightways Take a Bad Flier?

Emery lost 20 percent of its shipping volume in the third quarter of 1989, primarily in the delivery of small packages and envelopes that businesses send to each other, because of the mishandling of the consumer-division shutdown. "Our main focus," says Emery Vice-President Peter Boulais, "is getting back that business."

Because of Emery and its troubles, Consolidated's 1989 net income was only $12 million, compared with $113 million in 1988. Earnings dropped to about $1 per share from $3, and the price of the shares, $37 in January 1989, dropped to $26 in December and to approximately $14 in June 1990.

Consolidated is not accustomed to failure. In its 61-year history, it has had virtually nothing but success. Between 1982 and 1988, it doubled its tonnage shipped, increased revenues by 90 percent, and increased profits by 36 percent. Net income rose 8 percent in the first six months of 1988. With its stock trading at $33 that year, the same price it traded for in 1986, President Scott's main fear was a takeover. "We've not been approached," he said then. "But I'm sure someone has considered us."

Scott's worries in 1990 are quite different, but, he says, "We're over the worst of our problems." Not everyone agrees. Industrywide rate wars and high fuel prices have affected the trucking industry, and at least one analyst fears that this, in addition to Emery's problems, "could undermine the whole company."

New problems became evident in June 1990, when Consolidated suspended its common stock dividend (which had increased steadily for the last 18 years) because of continuing operating losses at Emery. This suspension — which will save $37 billion a year — was demanded by banks as a condition for lending Consolidated $860 million over the next five years.

Scott has been able to cut costs in other ways, and he hopes that Consolidated's goodwill, built over so many years, will see it through, especially since the company is putting more emphasis on customer service. Newly appointed Emery Vice-President Peter D. Boulais, transferred over from the trucking side, is a service specialist. His move may have been what a customer's logistics manager meant, among other things, when he said, "It's been a rough start [for Consolidated and Emery], but some moves they've made recently give us a lot of confidence." And the transportation manager of another customer, J.C. Penney, says, "We've got to be patient."

Scott's prescience may yet bring good results. He was also criticized in the 1970s when he forecasted deregulation for the trucking industry and spent $300 million to build the first national long-haul freight delivery system. People critized him again in the 1980s when he distributed regional operations around the country, specializing in next-day freight delivery. Both moves paid off for the company. If Scott is able to make Emery successful again, his detractors will be very surprised, but they may also be permanently silenced.

Postscript: Consolidated's board fired Scott on July 30, 1990. It is now clear that Scott made a major mistake when he acquired Emery. It was a "bet the company" decision, and Scott lost.

Sources: *Forbes,* Marc Beauchamp, "Skillful Driving," August 22, 1988, and " 'This Global Thing Is Not a Fad,' " December 11, 1989; "Emery's Failing Finances Spur Approval of Merger," *Aviation Week & Space Technology,* April 10, 1989; *Business Week,* Gene G. Marcial, "The Big Guns Aiming at Emery Air," February 1, 1988, Joan O'C. Hamilton, "Emery Is One Heavy Load for Consolidated Freightways," March 26, 1990, "Emery Delivers More Trouble for CF," July 2, 1990, and "Is Emery Too Heavy for Consolidated Freight?" August 13, 1990.

QUESTIONS

22-1   Four economic classifications of mergers are *horizontal, vertical, conglomerate,* and *congeneric.* Explain the significance of these terms in merger analysis with regard to **(a)** the likelihood of governmental intervention and **(b)** possibilities for operating synergy.

22-2   Firm A wants to acquire Firm B. Firm B's management agrees that the merger is a good idea. Might a tender offer be used?

22-3   Distinguish between operating mergers and financial mergers.

22-4   Two large, publicly owned firms are contemplating a merger. No operating synergy is expected, but returns on the two firms are not perfectly positively correlated, so σ_{EBIT} would be reduced for the combined corporation. One group of consultants argues that this risk reduction is sufficient grounds for the merger. Another group thinks that this type of risk reduction is irrelevant because stockholders can themselves hold the stock of both companies and thus gain the risk reduction benefits without all the hassles and expenses of the merger. Whose position is correct?

SELF-TEST PROBLEM

ST-1   Perrin-Stewart, a large conglomerate that has grown in the past through mergers, is analyzing its latest takeover target, Cleburne Pharmaceuticals (CP). Perrin-Stewart's financial analysts have made a projection of CP's cash flows for the next 4 years. The analysts have assumed that depreciation expense is negligible for this firm. They predict that Cleburne's market value in 1994 will equal 10 times that year's after-tax earnings. Their 4-year projection of CP's postmerger year-end cash flows (in millions of dollars) is reproduced in the following table:

	1991	1992	1993	1994
Sales	$300	$345	$375	$405
Cost of goods sold	195	210	220	225
Sales & administrative expenses	30	40	45	50
EBIT	$ 75	$ 95	$110	$130
Interest	15	18	20	21
EBT	$ 60	$ 77	$ 90	$109
Taxes (34%)	20	26	31	37
Net income	$ 40	$ 51	$ 59	$ 72
Retained earnings	20	26	24	22
Cash available to owners	$ 20	$ 25	$ 35	$ 50
Terminal value				$720
Net cash flow	$ 20	$ 25	$ 35	$770

Cleburne currently has a capital structure of 17 percent debt, but if Perrin-Stewart's merger plans are successful, CP's debt ratio will rise to 55 percent of assets. CP's marginal tax rate will remain at 34 percent after the merger. However, its market-determined beta will rise because of the large increase in debt from a premerger beta of 1.3 to an estimated beta of 1.8. The risk-free rate is 7 percent and the market risk premium, $k_M - k_{RF}$, is 5 percent.

     The estimated cash flows that were presented in the table include the additional interest payments required by the increase in leverage and asset expansion. Retained earnings will be used in addition to the new debt to finance required asset expansion. Therefore, the preceding estimated net cash flows are the flows that are expected to accrue to Perrin-Stewart's shareholders.

a. What is the appropriate discount rate for valuing the proposed acquisition?

b. What is Cleburne's value to Perrin-Stewart?

c. Cleburne Pharmaceuticals has 9 million shares outstanding, and its common stock currently sells for $39.75. What is the maximum price per share that Perrin-Stewart should offer for Cleburne's stock?

PROBLEMS

22-1 **Merger analysis.** Clouse Corporation wishes to acquire The Stanley Company for $2,000,000. Clouse expects the merger to provide incremental after-tax earnings of about $350,000 a year for 10 years. At the end of the 10-year period, the book and market value of Stanley will be zero. Management has calculated the marginal cost of equity capital for this investment to be 15 percent. Conduct a merger analysis for Clouse to determine whether or not it should purchase Stanley.

22-2 **Merger analysis.** Garcia Industries wishes to acquire Lupin Corporation for $1,500,000. Garcia expects the merger to provide incremental after-tax earnings of about $275,000 a year for 10 years. At the end of the 10-year period, the book value of Lupin will be $500,000, but its cash value will only be $200,000. Management has calculated the marginal cost of equity capital for this investment to be 12 percent. Conduct a merger analysis for Garcia to determine whether or not it should purchase Lupin Corporation. Garcia Industries has a 40% marginal tax rate.

22-3 **Merger analysis.** The Drake Corporation is contemplating the purchase of Tanning, Inc., a maker of tanning preparations and sun screens. Drake has determined that Tanning's after-tax cash flows, which are $3 million today, will grow at 12 percent annually for the next 3 years. The growth will slow to a constant 5 percent after that time. If Drake requires a 16 percent rate of return, what is the maximum price it should be willing to pay for Tanning?

22-4 **Merger analysis.** Donna's Designs has just purchased Gifts Galore, Inc., for $6 million. Donna's Designs' management has decided, however, that Gifts Galore is "worth more dead than alive," because the expected synergistic advantages of the merger are not possible. Therefore, Donna's Designs will sell Gifts Galore's assets, which have the following book and expected cash values:

Asset	Book Value	Cash Value
Cash	$ 375,000	$ 375,000
Accounts receivable	1,875,000	1,500,000
Inventory	3,750,000	2,250,000
Fixed assets	7,500,000	1,125,000
Total	$13,500,000	$5,250,000

Gifts Galore has a $375,000 short-term bank loan outstanding with the First National Bank. Donna's Designs' marginal tax rate is 40 percent, and its required rate of return is 15 percent.

a. If all divestitures can be accomplished in a 1-year period from the date of Gifts Galore's purchase, what is Donna's Designs' rate of return from the divestiture?

(*Hint:* Don't forget the tax writeoffs that occur when assets are sold at less than book value.)

b. If Donna's Designs' growth is largely dependent on acquisitions, what effect might this divestiture have on future growth?

22-5   **Merger analysis.** O'Brien Enterprises, a large conglomerate, is evaluating the possible acquisition of McCue Manufacturing Corporation (MMC). O'Brien's analysts project the following postmerger data for MMC (in thousands of dollars):

	1991	1992	1993	1994
Net sales	$250.00	$287.50	$312.50	$337.50
Selling and administrative expenses	25.00	31.25	37.50	40.00
Interest	12.50	15.00	16.25	17.50

Tax rate after merger: 40%
Cost of goods sold as a percentage of sales: 70%
Beta after merger: 1.50
Risk-free rate: 9%
Market risk premium: 6%
Terminal growth rate of cash flow available to O'Brien: 8%

If the acquisition is made, it will occur on January 1, 1991. All cash flows shown in the income statements are assumed to occur at the end of the year. MMC currently has a market value capital structure of 40 percent debt, but O'Brien would increase that to 50 percent if the acquisition were made. MMC, if independent, would pay taxes at a rate of 30 percent, but its income would be taxed at 40 percent if it were consolidated. MMC's current market-determined beta is 1.30, and its investment bankers think that its beta would rise to 1.50 if the debt ratio were increased to 50 percent. The cost of goods sold is expected to be 70 percent of sales, but it could vary somewhat. Depreciation-generated funds would be used to replace worn-out equipment, so they would not be available to O'Brien's shareholders. The risk-free rate is 9 percent, and the market risk premium is 6 percent.

a. What is the appropriate discount rate for valuing the acquisition?

b. What is the terminal value? What is MMC's value to O'Brien?

(Do Part c only if you are using the computerized problem diskette.)

c. 1. If sales in each year were $125 higher than the base case amounts, and if the cost of goods sold/sales ratio were 65 percent, what would MMC be worth to O'Brien?

2. With sales and the cost of goods sold ratio at the Part c-1 levels, what would MMC's value be if its beta were 1.8, k_{RF} rose to 10 percent, and RP_M rose to 7 percent?

3. Leaving all values at the Part c-2 levels, what would be the value of the acquisition if the terminal growth rate rose to 16 percent or dropped to 3 percent?

22-6   **Merger analysis.** Cowtown Computer Corporation is considering a merger with Mega Memory, Inc. Mega is a publicly traded company, and its current beta is 1.40. Mega has been barely profitable, so it has paid an average tax rate of only 25 percent during the last several years. It also uses little debt, having a market-value debt ratio of just 15 percent.

If the acquisition is made, Cowtown plans to operate Mega as a separate, wholly owned subsidiary. Cowtown would pay taxes on a consolidated basis, and thus the tax rate would increase to 34 percent. In addition, Cowtown would increase the debt capitalization in the Mega subsidiary on a market-value basis to 45 percent of assets, which would increase beta to 1.50. Cowtown's acquisition department estimates that Mega, if acquired, would provide the following net cash flows to Cowtown's shareholders (in millions of dollars):

Year	Net Cash Flow
1991	$1.60
1992	1.92
1993	2.25
1994	2.50
1995 and beyond	Constant growth at 6%

These cash flows include all acquisition effects. Cowtown's cost of equity is 12 percent, its beta is 1.0, and its cost of debt is 9.5 percent. The risk-free rate is 8 percent.

a. What discount rate should be used to discount the estimated cash flows? (*Hint:* Use Cowtown's k_s to determine the market risk premium.)

b. What is Mega's dollar value to Cowtown?

c. Mega has 1.5 million common shares outstanding. What is the maximum price per share that Cowtown should offer for Mega? If the tender offer were accepted at this price, what would happen to Cowtown's stock price?

SOLUTION TO SELF-TEST PROBLEM

ST-1   **a.** The appropriate discount rate, k_s, is determined as follows:

$$k_s = k_{RF} + (k_M - k_{RF})b$$

$$= 7\% + (5\%)1.8$$

$$= 7\% + 9\%$$

$$= 16\%.$$

b. Cleburne Pharmaceuticals' value to Perrin-Stewart is determined by discounting the cash flows that will be available to Perrin-Stewart if it acquires CP. Therefore:

Year	Cash Flow	$PVIF_{16\%}$	Present Value (Millions of Dollars)
1991	$ 20	0.8621	$ 17.2
1992	25	0.7432	18.6
1993	35	0.6407	22.4
1994	770	0.5523	425.3
			$483.5

c. The maximum price that Perrin-Stewart should offer for Cleburne's stock on a per-share basis is:

$$\$483.5 \text{ million}/9 \text{ million shares} = \$53.72.$$

Therefore, Perrin-Stewart should make its initial offer above the current market price of $39.75 but below its maximum offering price of $53.72.

Chapter 23

International
Financial Management

DECISION IN FINANCE

Philips Has the Weight of the World on Its Shoulders

Philips, the giant Dutch high-tech company which pioneered VCRs and invented the compact disc, collects millions each year in license fees from foreign manufacturers. Over the years it has also developed manufacturing capacity for a huge array of other products, ranging from saxophones to computer chips to stereos, and the $29 billion enterprise is Europe's top electronics firm. In addition, its wholly owned subsidiary, North American Philips Corporation, employs more than 50,000 people in the United States, where well-known Philips brands include Magnavox, Sylvania, and Norelco.

Originally "a federation of national organizations in 60 countries," according to one executive, Philips adjusted to the new global economy by taking away some of the national firms' autonomy and reorganizing according to worldwide product divisions. Gerrit Jeelof, vice chairman of the parent company's board of management and chairman/CEO of the North American division, says worldwide sales are necessary if

See end of chapter for resolution.

the company is to afford the large development costs of technologically advanced, competitive new products. For example, noting that pre-1950s telecommunications switching systems cost $10 million to develop and had a life of about 25 years, he said, "In the 1980s, when the first digital systems were developed, costs had risen to $1 billion and life expectancy had dropped to 8 to 12 years. Digital development costs of $1 billion require roughly 8 percent of the world market share just to recover costs." Since no single market in Europe has more than 6 percent of world market share, survival requires globalization. When making the move to a world market, Philips also consolidated two of its major product lines — telecommunications and computer technology — with the expectation that the two industries would steadily intertwine, merging into one global market.

Despite its size, its excellent reputation, and its efforts to adapt to a changed world, Philips disappointed investors during the first half of the 1980s with persistent low yields and meager profit margins. The turning point was supposed to be 1987, when profits were expected to be higher than in 1986. This forecast was, however, wrong—profits in 1987 sank below the previous year's mark. Announcing the slump, CEO Cornelis J. van der Klugt promised to take "drastic measures worldwide" to improve earnings by "lowering costs and strengthening the strategic power of the organization."

When he took control in 1985, Chairman van der Klugt found many problems in the giant corporation. Its management seemed to be somewhat complacent, its marketing was weak, and some of its products were "dowdy." As the company's current design chief puts it, "People knew about Philips from Mom and Dad. Market research showed that our image was gray." Consequently, Philips was losing market share to Japan and South Korea.

As you read this chapter, consider the steps van der Klugt might take to improve the company. What might he have done differently? How does the global financial picture differ from a national, or even multinational, one? What special problems does the global marketplace impose on managers? Why is the globalization of business stimulating mergers?

multinational corporation

A firm that operates in two or more countries.

The term **multinational corporation** is used to describe a firm that operates in two or more countries. During the period since World War II, a new and fundamentally different format for international commercial activity has developed, and it has greatly increased the degree of worldwide economic and political interdependence. The distinguishing characteristic between the new form of commercial transaction and earlier forms is that rather than merely buying resources from foreign concerns, firms now make direct investments in fully integrated operations, with worldwide entities controlling all phases of the production process—from extraction of raw materials, through the manufacturing process, to distribution to consumers throughout the world. Today, multinational corporate networks control a large and growing share of the world's technological, marketing, and productive resources.

The rapid expansion of foreign investment by U.S. companies has been caused, in large part, by lower overseas labor costs, which result in generally higher rates of return on foreign investments, especially in developing nations, as compared with equivalent-risk domestic projects. General Electric maintains production and assembly plants in Mexico, South Korea, and Singapore; many high-tech firms including IBM have computer hardware manufacturing and servicing subsidiaries in parts of Europe and the Far East; and Caterpillar produces tractors and farm equipment in the Middle East, Europe, the Far East, and Africa. U.S. executives frequently travel and live abroad, and U.S. multinational corporations have come to exert significant economic and political influence in many parts of the world. Similarly, foreign firms, especially Japanese and European firms, exert a significant influence within the United States.

Companies "go international" for a number of reasons. First, many U.S. multinational firms began their international operations because raw materials

This chapter was coauthored by Professor Roy L. Crum of the University of Florida.

were located abroad; this is true of oil, mining, and some food processing companies. Other firms expanded overseas to obtain an outlet for their finished products. Frequently, these firms first set up sales offices and then developed manufacturing plants when it became clear that the market would support such plants. Still other firms have moved their manufacturing facilities overseas to take advantage of low production costs in cheap labor areas — the electronics and textile industries are good examples. Finally, banks, accounting firms, and other service corporations have expanded overseas both to better serve their primary customers and to take advantage of new investment opportunities that are expected to be profitable.

The past decade has also seen an increasing amount of investment in the United States by foreign corporations. This "reverse" investment, which is of increasing concern to U.S. government officials, has actually been growing at a higher rate in the past few years than has U.S. investment abroad. The level of foreign investment in the United States has been concentrated in manufacturing operations, trading companies, and the petroleum industry. The fastest growth has been enjoyed by Japanese firms, such as Toyota in California and Honda in Tennessee, in the trade and manufacturing sectors.

These trends are important because of their implications for eroding the traditional doctrine of independence and self-reliance that has always been a hallmark of U.S. policy. Just as U.S. corporations with extensive overseas operations are said to use their economic power to exert substantial economic and political influence over host governments in many parts of the world, it is feared that foreign corporations are gaining similar sway over U.S. policy. These developments suggest an increasing degree of mutual influence and interdependence among business enterprises and nations, to which the United States is not immune.

In the past 12 months some dramatic international changes have taken place. These events have included a move toward a market economy in the Soviet Union and the collapse of communism in many Eastern European countries, which has been symbolized by the Soviet's policy of *perestroika* and the fall of the Berlin Wall. Future events will include the establishment of the European Economic Community with one Eurocurrency, the reunification of Germany, and the determination of how to help the cash-starved Eastern Bloc nations — all of which will have a tremendous impact on trade. Also, as we go to press, the situation in the Middle East has heated up, resulting in the United Nations' approving a trade embargo of Iraq. This too will certainly have an impact on the world economy.

Significant issues were discussed at the July 1990 Economic Summit, held in Houston, Texas. The "Group of Seven" (United States, Japan, Great Britain, France, Italy, Canada, and West Germany) discussed the major changes in East-West relations taking place, as well as ways to help the Soviet Union improve its economy. Discussions were also held regarding aiding in the reunification of Germany without triggering inflation. Of critical importance were the discussions of how to prepare for this "new world" where trade, rather than politics, will define relationships among nations, and of the General Agreement on Tariffs and Trade (GATT), the world's most comprehensive trade organization.

The participants of the 1990 Economic Summit issued a communiqué that (1) commended the movement toward democracy in Eastern Europe, and the movement toward more integration in Europe, (2) welcomed a unified Germany, (3) advocated discipline to stop trade-distorting export-credit subsidies, (4) praised the current system of international economic policy coordination, (5) endorsed current international debt strategy, and (6) commended the recently announced U.S. initiative to assist Latin American countries.

MULTINATIONAL VERSUS DOMESTIC FINANCIAL MANAGEMENT

In theory, the concepts and procedures discussed in various parts of the text are valid for both domestic and multinational operations. However, several problems uniquely associated with the international environment increase the complexity of the manager's task in a multinational corporation, and often they force the manager to alter the way alternative courses of action are evaluated and compared. Six major factors distinguish financial management as practiced by firms operating entirely in a single country from management by firms that operate in several different countries:

1. Different currency denominations. Cash flows in various parts of a multinational corporate system will be denominated in different currencies. Hence, an analysis of exchange rates, and the effects of changing currency values, must be included in all financial analyses.

2. Economic and legal ramifications. Each country in which the firm operates will have its own unique political and economic institutions, and institutional differences among countries can cause significant problems when the corporation tries to coordinate and control the worldwide operations of its subsidiaries. For example, differences in tax laws among countries can cause a given economic transaction to have strikingly dissimilar after-tax consequences, depending on where the transaction occurred. Similarly, differences in legal systems of host nations, such as the Common Law of Great Britain versus the French Civil Law, complicate many matters, from the simple recording of a business transaction to the role played by the judiciary in resolving conflicts. Such differences can restrict multinational corporations' flexibility to deploy resources as they wish, and can even make procedures illegal in one part of the company that are required in another part. These differences also make it difficult for executives trained in one country to operate effectively in another.

3. Languages. The ability to communicate is critical in all business transactions, and here U.S. citizens are often at a disadvantage because we are generally fluent only in English, while European and Japanese businesspeople are usually fluent in several languages, including English. Thus, they can invade our markets more easily than we can penetrate theirs.

4. Cultural differences. Even within geographic regions that have long been considered relatively homogeneous, different countries have unique cultural heritages that shape values and influence the role of business in the society. Multinational corporations find that such matters as defining the appropriate goals of the firm, attitudes toward risk taking, dealings with employees, the ability to curtail unprofitable operations, and so on, can vary dramatically from one country to the next.

5. Role of governments. Most traditional models in finance assume the existence of a competitive marketplace, in which the terms of competition are determined by the participants. The government, through its power to establish basic ground rules, is involved in this process, but its participation is minimal. Thus, the market provides both the primary barometer of success and the indicator of the actions that must be taken to remain competitive. This view of the process is reasonably correct for the United States and a few other major Western industrialized nations, but it does not accurately describe the situation in the majority of countries. Frequently, the terms under which companies compete, the actions that must be taken or avoided, and the terms of trade on various transactions are determined not in the marketplace, but by direct negotiation between the host government and the multinational corporation. This is essentially a political process, and it must be treated as such. Thus, our traditional financial models have to be recast to include political and other noneconomic facets of the decision.

6. Political risk. The distinguishing characteristic of a nation-state that differentiates it from a multinational corporation is that the nation-state exercises sovereignty over the people and property in its territory. Hence, a nation-state is free to place constraints on the transfer of corporate resources and even to expropriate without compensation the assets of the firm. This is a political risk, and it tends to be largely a given rather than a variable that can be changed by negotiation. Political risk varies from country to country, and it must be addressed explicitly in any financial analysis. Another aspect of political risk is terrorism against U.S. firms or executives abroad. For example, as we go to press, U.S. citizens, as well as citizens of other countries, are being held hostage in Iraq and Kuwait. Clearly, this is evidence of political risk.

These six factors complicate financial management within the multinational firm, and they increase the risks faced by the firms involved. However, higher prospects for profit often make it worthwhile for firms to accept these risks, and to learn how to minimize or at least live with them.

Self-Test

Identify and briefly explain six major factors that distinguish financial management as practiced by firms operating in a single country from management by firms that operate in several different countries.

INDUSTRY PRACTICE

Learning a New Vocabulary

Does your vocabulary include the word "globality"? How about "glocalism"? If neither word sounds familiar, you may be thinking "globaloney" and hoping the newspeak will somehow "glo" away. This, however, is unlikely. Many major companies realize that their very survival depends on their ability to see that "all the world is a stage" and to understand the "script" so well that they can "quickly step into the roles" that new opportunities offer them.

Currently, the traditional "triad" — the major markets of North America, Western Europe, and Japan — retains its world dominance. With only 15 percent of the world's population, the triad accounts for more than 50 percent of world output. Eastern Europe and the Third World countries of Indonesia, Mexico, Korea, and India are quickly growing, however, and together, the newly liberated countries of East Germany, Hungary, and Czechoslovakia have a higher gross national product (GNP) than does China. With their well-trained and low-paid workers ready to enter the European Community market, they could be Europe's challengers to the Asian giants.

Indonesia is eagerly seeking foreign investors, making life easier for foreigners by cutting out 67 percent of the previously required paperwork. The government of this fifth-most-populous nation approved more than $4 billion in new projects in 1988 and 1989. Mexico had only one-third as many state-owned industries in 1990 as it did in 1984, and it is also welcoming foreign corporations. India, where the government has loosened its grip on the economy, has 150,000,000 middle-class citizens shopping for consumer products, plus millions of additional poorer people.

One U.S. product that is popular around the world is soft drinks. PepsiCo has 70 bottling franchises in Eastern Europe alone, and its management thinks sales there can increase by another 50 percent by 1995.

Capital goods should also find a ready global market, since developing countries need new roads, bridges, electrical and telephone systems, and agricultural equipment. Many of these countries also need these goods to replace the infrastructure that is wearing out. The possibilities for worldwide sales of fiber-optic cable have impressed Corning Chairman James R. Houghton: "It's the only technology I know of that's even better for a developing country than for a developed one — because in a developing country you have no old copper to rip out."

Service industries may have even better opportunities, as evidenced by American Express, whose travel-related business in Eastern Europe rose 20 percent in 1989. American Express practices so-called "glocalism" — making global decisions on strategic questions about products, capital, and research, but letting local units decide tactical questions about packaging, marketing, and advertising. It hires local agencies to create ads for specific countries, even sometimes for specific cities, and this tactic has appealed to varying cultures so successfully that American Express's foreign customers provide 31 percent more revenue per card than its U.S. customers. As central planning gives way to capitalism in the Eastern Bloc, other opportunities are presenting themselves. A Washington consultant said, "With more investment in retail and wholesale trade, large improvements in efficiency — and consequently in profits — could be made."

If companies are profitable and growing already in their home areas, why should they take the difficult road to globalism? Says a Wharton School of Business professor, "Domestic markets have become too small. Even the biggest

Sources: *Fortune,* Jeremy Main, "How to Go Global — and Why," August 28, 1989, and "How to Manage in the New Era," January 15, 1990.

companies in the biggest countries cannot survive on their domestic markets if they are in global industries. They have to be in all major markets." A Wharton colleague identified 136 industries that must be world-class, including accounting, automobile manufacturing, banking, consumer electronics, entertainment, pharmaceuticals, publishing, travel services, and making washing machines.

Though no company is truly global yet, many have made huge strides in that direction. The key, say experts, is to visualize the world as a single market. Managers must set aside nationalism and go wherever necessary to raise capital, make products, buy supplies, and operate their headquarters. In a world without walls, a company without a country has an undeniable edge.

Another requirement for global success is to organize according to product lines rather than geography. Said one CEO, "For some products, you may find you need a plant on every continent, but not in every country." In global competition, market share is more important than short-term profits. When U.S. companies relied primarily on their large home markets, they could afford to be wary of foreign investment. Today, says the business dean at Columbia University, "When we walk away from a market, we're creating an opportunity for a European or Japanese company—and they then use that muscle to come into *our* market."

Global managers also have to think "alliance." Combining one company's product with another's distribution system, for instance, could bring new opportunities to both. Making alliances is often quicker than expanding a business overseas and cheaper than buying a new one.

The corporation that may be closest to the global ideal is Imperial Chemical Industries (ICI), formerly of Great Britain, with 49 major operations scattered from Canada to Argentina, Scotland to South Africa, and Malaysia to New Zealand. Some of the units are factories, some are division headquarters, and some are re-

search and development centers. ICI began going global in 1983, when it abandoned country-by-country organizations. The giant firm has annual sales of $21 billion in film, pharmaceuticals, explosives, agricultural chemicals, and other products. In moving toward globalization, ICI's management had to be tough. For example, 10,000 manufacturing jobs were abolished in Britain alone. "It's hard on people who have built national empires and [who] now don't have such freedom," says American Hugh Miller, head of ICI's advanced materials and electronics group. "We are asking people to be less nationalistic and more concerned with what happens outside their country." The advantage, says Miller, is better decision making. "Before, each territory would work up projects and you'd have warring factions competing in London for the same money. Now, with one person responsible for a global product line, it becomes immaterial where a project is located. The profits will be the same. When you start operating in this manner, it takes a lot of steam out of the defense of fiefdoms."

ICI also has an international board of directors—2 are Americans, 1 is Canadian, 1 is Japanese, 1 is German, and 11 are British. More than one-third of the company's 180 top executives are not British. Regardless of their nationalities, they may be assigned to work anywhere in the world.

One of the greatest hardships involved in going global is the idea of giving up preference for one's own nation and compatriots in making business and residency decisions. This doesn't always come easily—especially when workers in the home country must be laid off and factories must be closed to relocate production elsewhere. Aside from unhappiness among its people, companies attempting to become global also risk difficulty in overcoming the barriers in other countries of entrenched bureaucracies, hyperinflation, and currency exchange rates. Most knowledgeable observers, however, agree that the biggest risk lies in not being ready to move quickly as global opportunities arise.

EXCHANGE RATES AND THE INTERNATIONAL MONETARY SYSTEM

exchange rate
The number of units of a given currency that can be purchased for one unit of another currency.

An **exchange rate** specifies the number of units of a given currency that can be purchased for one unit of another currency. Exchange rates appear in the financial sections of newspapers each day. Selected rates from the July 20, 1990, issue of *The Wall Street Journal* are given in Table 23-1. The values shown in Column 1 are the number of U.S. dollars required to purchase one unit of foreign currency on July 19, 1990; this is called a *direct quotation*. Thus, the direct U.S. dollar quotation on July 19, 1990, for the German mark is $0.6094, because one German mark could be bought for 60.94 cents. The exchange rates given in Column 2 represent the number of units of foreign currency that can be purchased for one U.S. dollar on July 19, 1990; these are called *indirect quotations*. The indirect quotation for the German mark is DM1.6410. (The "DM" stands for *deutsche mark*; it is equivalent to the symbol "$.") Normal practice in the United States is to use indirect quotations (Column 2) for all currencies other than British pounds, for which direct quotations are given. Thus, we speak of the pound as "selling at $1.82" but of the German mark as "being at 1.64."

Table 23-1 **Illustrative Exchange Rates, July 19, 1990**

	Direct Quotation: U.S. Dollars Required to Buy One Unit of Foreign Currency (1)	Indirect Quotation: Number of Units of Foreign Currency per U.S. Dollar (2)
British pound	$1.8165	0.5505
Canadian dollar	0.8681	1.1520
Dutch guilder	0.5402	1.8510
French franc	0.18159	5.5070
German mark	0.6094	1.6410
Greek drachma	0.006223	160.70
Indian rupee	0.05727	17.46
Italian lira	0.0008313	1,203.01
Japanese yen	0.006764	147.85
Mexican peso	0.0003487	2,868.00
Norwegian krone	0.1587	6.2995
Saudi Arabian riyal	0.26681	3.7480
Singaporean dollar	0.5508	1.8157
South African rand	0.3817	2.6199
Spanish peseta	0.009940	100.60
Swedish krona	0.1681	5.9475
Swiss franc	0.7110	1.4065

Note: Column 2 equals 1.0 divided by Column 1.

Source: *The Wall Street Journal*, July 20, 1990.

It is also a universal convention on the world's foreign currency exchanges to state all exchange rates except British pounds on a "dollar basis" — that is, the foreign currency price of one U.S. dollar as reported in Table 23-1, Column 2. Thus, in all currency trading centers, whether in New York, Frankfurt, London, Tokyo, or anywhere else, the exchange rate for the German mark on July 19, 1990, would be displayed as DM1.6410. This convention eliminates confusion when comparing quotations from one trading center with those from another.

Let us use the rates in Table 23-1 to show how one figures exchange rates. Suppose a U.S. tourist on holiday flies from New York to London, then to Paris, then on to Munich, and finally back to New York. When she arrives at London's Heathrow Airport on July 19, 1990, she goes to the bank to check the foreign exchange listing. The rate she observes for U.S. dollars is $1.8165; this means that 1 pound will cost her $1.8165. Assume that she exchanges $2,000 for $2,000/$1.8165 = £1,101.02 and enjoys a week's vacation in London, spending £601.02 while there.

At the end of the week she travels to Dover to catch the Hovercraft to Calais on the coast of France and realizes that she needs to exchange her 500 remaining British pounds for French francs. However, what she sees on the board is the direct quotation between pounds and dollars ($1.8165) and the indirect quotation between francs and dollars (FF5.5070). (For our purposes, we assume that the exchange rates in effect on July 19 remain in effect throughout our example. This is very unrealistic for reasons explained later in this chapter.) The exchange rate between pounds and francs is called a *cross rate,* and it is computed as follows:

$$\text{Cross rate} = \frac{\text{Dollars}}{\text{Pound}} \times \frac{\text{Francs}}{\text{Dollar}} = \frac{\text{Francs}}{\text{Pound}}$$

$$= \$1.8165 \text{ dollars per pound} \times 5.5070 \text{ francs per dollar}$$

$$= 10.0035 \text{ francs per pound.}$$

Therefore, for every British pound she would receive 10.0035 French francs, so she would receive 10.0035 × 500 = 5,001.73 ≈ 5,002 francs.

When she finishes touring in France and arrives in Germany, the American tourist again needs to determine a cross rate, this time between French francs and German marks. The dollar-basis quotes she sees, as shown in Table 23-1, are FF5.5070 per dollar and DM1.6410 per dollar. To find the cross rate, she must divide the two dollar-basis rates:

$$\text{Cross rate} = \frac{\text{DM1.6410/\$}}{\text{FF5.5070/\$}} = \text{DM0.2980 marks per franc.}$$

Then, if she had FF3,000 remaining, she could exchange them for 0.2980 × 3,000 = DM894, or 894 marks.

Finally, when her vacation ends and she returns to New York, the quotation she sees is DM1.6410, which tells her that she can buy 1.6410 marks for a dollar. She now holds 50 marks, not dollars, however, so she wants to know how many U.S. dollars she will receive for her marks. First, she must find the reciprocal of the quoted indirect rate:

$$\frac{1}{DM1.6410} = \$0.6094,$$

which is the direct quote shown in Table 23-1, Column 1. Then she will end up with

$$\$0.6094 \times 50 = \$30.47.$$

In this example, we made two very strong and generally incorrect assumptions. First, we assumed that our traveler had to calculate the appropriate cross rates. For retail transactions, it is customary to display the cross rates directly instead of a series of dollar rates. Second, we assumed that exchange rates remain constant over time. Actually, exchange rates vary every day, often dramatically. During 1985, the dollar *strengthened,* or *appreciated,* against other currencies, so it took fewer dollars to buy one unit of those currencies in 1985 than it did in 1984. For instance, in 1984 the pound was selling for about $1.50, but in the spring of 1985 it was down to $1.10, a 27 percent decline. Thus it took fewer dollars to purchase a given number of pounds in 1985 than in 1984, and this strengthening, or appreciation, of the dollar (or cheapening of the pound) would have been of sufficient magnitude to introduce serious errors into financial decisions if it had not been anticipated.

For example, if a U.S. firm had invested $1 million in Great Britain in 1984, its pound investment would have been $1,000,000/1.5 = £666,667. If its pound investment appreciated by a healthy 15 percent, the pound value of the investment would be 1.15(£666,667) = £766,667. However, as we saw above, those pounds would now be worth only $1.10(766,667) = $843,333, down from the original $1,000,000. Although the U.S. firm's British investment was superficially profitable, the exchange rate differential turned its 15 percent profit into a substantial loss.

The situation reversed itself from 1985 to 1990, however. During this period the dollar generally *weakened,* or *depreciated,* so it took fewer yens, francs, pounds, and so forth, to buy a dollar.

As a result of all this, exchange rate fluctuations can have a considerable effect on the profitability of foreign investments. To understand what causes exchange rates to change over time, and thus to be able to predict exchange rates, it is necessary to look at the factors that affect currencies and the world monetary system.

Recent History of the World Monetary System

fixed exchange rate system
The world monetary system in existence after World War II until 1971, under which the value of the U.S. dollar was tied to gold, and the values of the other currencies were pegged to the U.S. dollar.

From the end of World War II until August 1971, the world was on a **fixed exchange rate system** administered by the International Monetary Fund (IMF). Under this system the U.S. dollar was linked to gold ($35 per ounce), and other currencies were then tied to the dollar. Exchange rates between other currencies and the dollar were controlled within narrow limits. For example, in 1964 the British pound was fixed at \$2.80 for 1 pound, with a 1 percent permissible fluctuation about this rate:

	Value of the Pound **(Exchange Rate in Dollars per Pound)**
Upper limit (+ 1%)	\$2.828
Official rate	2.800
Lower limit (− 1%)	2.772

Fluctuations in exchange rates tend to occur because of changes in the supply of and demand for dollars, pounds, and other currencies. These supply and demand changes have two primary sources. First, changes in the demand for currencies depend on changes in imports and exports of goods and services. For example, U.S. importers must buy British pounds to pay for British goods, whereas British importers must buy U.S. dollars to pay for U.S. goods. If U.S. imports from Great Britain were to exceed U.S. exports to Great Britain, there would be a greater demand for pounds than for dollars; this would drive up the price of the pound relative to that of the dollar. In terms of Table 23-1, the dollar cost of a pound might rise from \$1.8165 to \$2.0000. The U.S. dollar would be said to be *depreciating,* whereas the pound would be *appreciating.* In this example, the root cause of the change would be the U.S. **deficit trade balance** with Great Britain. Of course, if U.S. exports to Great Britain were greater than U.S. imports from Great Britain, Great Britain would have a deficit trade balance with the United States.[1]

deficit trade balance
A country's trade balance resulting from an excess of its imports over its exports.

Changes in the demand for a currency, and hence exchange rate fluctuations, also depend on capital movements. For example, suppose interest rates in Great Britain were higher than those in the United States. To take advantage of the high British interest rates, U.S. banks, corporations, and even sophisticated individuals would buy pounds with dollars and then use those pounds to purchase high-yielding British securities. These purchases would tend to drive up the price of pounds.[2]

---

[1]If the dollar value of the pound moved up from \$1.8165 to \$2.00, this increase in the value of the pound would mean that British goods would now be more expensive in the U.S. market. For example, a box of candy costing 1 pound in England would rise in price in the United States from \$1.8165 to \$2.00. Conversely, U.S. goods would be cheaper in England. For example, the British could now buy goods worth \$2.00 for 1 pound, whereas before the exchange rate change, 1 pound would buy merchandise worth only \$1.8165. These price changes would, of course, tend to *reduce* British exports and *increase* imports, and this, in turn, would lower the exchange rate, because people in the United States and other nations would be buying fewer pounds to pay for English goods. However, before 1971 the 1 percent limit severely constrained the market's ability to reach an equilibrium between trade balances and exchange rates.

[2]Such capital inflows would also tend to drive down British interest rates. If rates were high in the first place because of efforts by the British monetary authorities to curb inflation, the international currency flows would tend to thwart that effort. This is one of the reasons why domestic and international economics are so closely linked.

A good example of this occurred during the summer of 1981. In an effort to curb inflation, the Federal Reserve Board helped push U.S. interest rates to record levels. This, in turn, caused an outflow of capital from European nations to the United States. The Europeans were suffering from a severe recession and wanted to keep interest rates down in order to stimulate investment, but the U.S. policy made this difficult because of the ease of international capital flows.

Before August 1971 these fluctuations were kept within the narrow 1 percent limit by regular intervention of the British government in the market. When the value of the pound was falling, the Bank of England would step in and buy pounds, offering gold or foreign currencies in exchange. These government purchases would push up the pound rate. Conversely, when the pound rate was too high, the Bank of England would sell pounds. The central banks of other countries operated similarly. Of course, a central bank's ability to control its exchange rate was limited by its supply of gold and foreign currencies.

devaluation
The process of officially reducing the value of a country's currency relative to other currencies.

With the approval of the IMF, a country could **devalue** its currency—which means to officially lower its value relative to other currencies—if it experienced persistent difficulty over a long period in preventing its exchange rate from falling below the lower limit, and if its central bank was running out of the gold and other currencies that could be used to buy its own currency and thus prop up its price. For just these reasons the British pound was devalued from $2.80 per pound to $2.50 per pound in 1967. This lowered the price of British goods in the United States and elsewhere and raised the prices of foreign goods in Britain, thus stopping the British deficit trade balance that had been putting pressure on the pound in the first place. Conversely, a nation with an export surplus and a strong currency might **revalue** its currency upward, as West Germany did twice in the 1960s.

revaluation
The process of officially increasing the value of a country's currency relative to other currencies.

The Current Floating Exchange Rate System

Devaluations and revaluations occurred only rarely before 1971. They were usually accompanied by severe international financial repercussions, partly because nations tended to postpone these needed measures until economic pressures had built up to explosive proportions. For this and other reasons the old international monetary system came to a dramatic end in the early 1970s, when the U.S. dollar, the foundation upon which all other currencies were anchored, was cut loose from the gold standard and, in effect, allowed to "float."

floating exchange rates
System whereby exchange rates are for the most part not fixed by government policy but are allowed to float up or down in accordance with supply and demand.

The United States and the other major nations currently operate under a system of **floating exchange rates,** whereby currency prices are allowed to seek their own levels without much governmental intervention. The central bank of each country still does intervene in the foreign exchange market, buying and selling its currency to smooth out exchange rate fluctuations to some extent. There have also been agreements by groups of countries to keep the relative values of their currencies within a predetermined range. Such an agreement by the "Group of Seven" at the Seoul Economic Summit in October 1985 caused the U.S. dollar to fall substantially against most major currencies. This action was endorsed as appropriate at the Washington Economic Summit in September 1987. The "Group of Seven" was also responsible for helping to stabilize the falling dollar in early 1988. In 1990, Japan continues to increase its trade surplus, despite the fact that the yen continues to rise against the dollar. The rising yen makes Japanese goods more expensive for Americans while U.S. products are less expensive for the Japanese consumer. The United States and other nations have tried to increase the value of the yen in foreign exchange markets, and these actions have been successful. One of the topics of debate at the 1990 Economic Summit was the value of government intervention.

Each central bank also tries to keep its average exchange rate at a level deemed desirable by its government's economic policy. This is important, because exchange rates have a profound effect on the levels of imports and exports, which in turn influence the level of domestic employment. For example, if a country is having a problem with unemployment, its central bank might encourage a *decline* in the value of its currency. This would cause its goods to be cheaper in world markets and thus stimulate exports, production, and domestic employment. Conversely, the central bank of a country that is operating at full capacity and experiencing inflation might try to raise the value of its currency to reduce exports and increase imports. Under the current floating rate system, however, such intervention can affect the situation only temporarily, because market forces will prevail in the long run.

Figure 23-1 shows how German marks, Japanese yen, and British pounds moved in comparison to the dollar from 1960 to 1990. Until 1971, when the fixed rate system was terminated, rates were quite stable. The pound's fluctuations against the dollar were too small to even show up on the graph prior to 1967, when a devaluation of the British pound occurred. The mark was revalued in 1961 and again in 1969. The yen was stable until 1971, when the dollar was allowed to float. After 1971, economic forces became the major factor in setting relative currency values, and Figure 23-1 illustrates the volatility that has occurred since then. (Note that Figure 23-1 plots cumulative changes in relative value.) From the late 1970s until 1985, the German mark fell rapidly in value against the dollar, while the Japanese yen remained relatively stable during the period. The value of the British pound, on the other hand, generally drifted down from 1980 to 1985. Since early 1985 the dollar's value has fallen precipitously against all of these currencies, and it has generally continued to fall during the period from 1985 to 1990.

The inherent volatility of exchange rates under a floating system increases the uncertainty of the cash flows for a multinational corporation. Because these cash flows are generated in many parts of the world, they are denominated in numerous currency units. Since exchange rates change, the dollar-equivalent value of the consolidated cash flows is uncertain. This is known as **exchange rate risk,** and it is a major factor differentiating the multinational corporation from a purely domestic one. However, there are numerous ways for a multinational corporation to manage and limit its exchange rate risk, several of which are discussed in the next section.

exchange rate risk
The risk that the basic cash flows of a foreign project will be worth less in the parent company's home currency.

Figure 23-1 **Cumulative Changes in the Values of Marks, Yen, and Pounds Relative to the Value of the Dollar, 1960–1990**

Prior to 1971, world currencies were narrowly controlled, and changes in relative values were minimal. Since 1971, currencies have been allowed to float, resulting in marked fluctuations in values. As the figure shows, until 1985, the pound, relative to the dollar, had generally drifted down, whereas the yen had risen. The mark rose against the dollar until 1979, after which it fell in value until 1985. The dollar fell precipitously against all of these currencies beginning in early 1985. The dollar generally has continued to fall against all of these currencies (with some brief exceptions) during the period from 1985 to 1990.

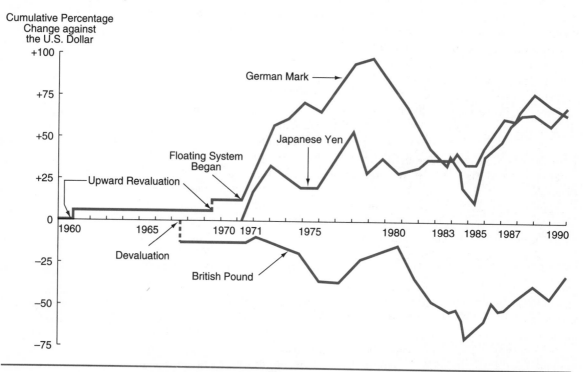

Self-Test

What is meant by the following statement: "It is a universal convention on the world's foreign currency exchanges to state all exchange rates except British pounds on a 'dollar basis'."

What is a cross rate?

Briefly explain the difference between a fixed exchange rate system and a floating rate system. Which system are most nations on now? Which system do you think is better? Explain.

What does it mean to say the dollar is appreciating with respect to the British pound? What does it mean for it to be depreciating?

TRADING IN FOREIGN EXCHANGE

Importers, exporters, and tourists, as well as governments, buy and sell currencies in the foreign exchange market. For example, when a U.S. trader imports automobiles from Germany, payment will probably be made in German marks. The importer buys marks (through its bank) in the foreign exchange market, much as one buys common stocks on the New York Stock Exchange or pork bellies on the Chicago Mercantile Exchange. However, whereas stock and commodity exchanges have organized trading floors, the foreign exchange market consists of a network of brokers and banks based in New York, London, Tokyo, and other financial centers. Most buy-and-sell orders are conducted by computer and telephone.[3]

Spot Rates and Forward Rates

spot rate
The effective exchange rate for a foreign currency for delivery on (approximately) the current day.

The exchange rates shown earlier in Table 23-1 are known as **spot rates,** which means the rate paid for delivery of the currency "on the spot" or, in reality, two days after the day of the trade. For most of the world's major currencies, it is also possible to buy (or sell) currency for delivery at some agreed-upon future date, usually 30, 90, or 180 days from the day the transaction is negotiated. This rate is known as the **forward exchange rate.** For example, if a U.S. firm must make payment to a Swiss firm in 90 days, the U.S. firm's treasurer can buy Swiss francs today for delivery in 90 days, paying the 90-day forward rate of $0.7096 per Swiss franc (which equals 1.4065 SF per dollar). Forward rates are exactly analogous to futures prices on commodity exchanges, where contracts are drawn up for wheat or corn to be delivered at agreed-upon prices at some future date. The contract is signed today, and the dollar cost of the Swiss francs is then known with certainty. Purchase of a forward contract is one technique for eliminating the volatility of future cash flows caused by fluctuations in exchange rates. This technique, which is called "hedging," will be discussed in more detail shortly.

forward exchange rate
An agreed-upon price at which two currencies are to be exchanged at some future date.

Forward rates for 30-, 90-, and 180-day delivery, along with the spot rates for July 19, 1990, for the more commonly traded currencies, are given in Table 23-2. If one can obtain *more* of the foreign currency for a dollar in the forward than in the spot market, the forward currency is less valuable than the spot currency, and the forward currency is said to be selling at a **discount.** Thus, because 1 dollar could buy 0.5505 British pounds in the spot market but 0.5682 pounds in the 180-day forward market, forward pounds sell at a discount as compared with spot pounds. Conversely, if a dollar will buy *fewer* units of a currency in the forward than in the spot market, the forward currency is worth more dollars than the spot currency, and the forward currency is said to be selling at a **premium.** Thus we see in Table 23-2 that on July 19,

discount on forward rate
The situation when the spot rate is less than the forward rate.

premium on forward rate
The situation when the spot rate is greater than the forward rate.

---

[3]For a more detailed explanation of exchange rate determination and operations of the foreign exchange market, see Steven Bell and Bryan Kettell, *Foreign Exchange Handbook* (Westport, Conn.: Quorum Books, 1983).

Table 23-2 **Selected Spot and Forward
Exchange Rates, July 19, 1990
(Number of Units of Foreign Currency per U.S. Dollar)**

	Spot Rate	Forward Rates			Spot Rate at a Premium or Discount
		30 Days	90 Days	180 Days	
British pound	0.5505	0.5536	0.5597	0.5682	Discount
French franc	5.5070	5.5147	5.5303	5.5570	Discount
Japanese yen	147.85	147.78	147.69	147.59	Premium
Swiss franc	1.4065	1.4074	1.4092	1.4115	Discount
German mark	1.6410	1.6411	1.6416	1.6433	Discount

Note: These are representative quotes as provided by a sample of New York banks. Forward rates for other currencies and for other lengths of time can often be negotiated.

Source: *The Wall Street Journal,* July 20, 1990.

1990, the forward pound, the French franc, the Swiss franc, and the German mark were selling at a discount but the forward yen was selling at a premium.

If the dollar is expected to *appreciate* against a particular foreign currency, then in the future $1 should buy *more* units of the foreign currency, and in that case, the forward rate will sell at a *discount* to the spot rate. Thus, based on Table 23-2, the dollar was, in July 1990, expected to appreciate against the British, French, Swiss, and German currencies, but to depreciate against the Japanese yen. These expectations, in turn, were influenced by trade balances, relative interest rates, and all the other factors which lead to changing exchange rates.

Hedging in the Foreign Exchange Markets

hedging exchange rate exposure
The process whereby a firm protects itself against loss due to future exchange rate fluctuations.

Individuals and corporations buy or sell forward currencies as a means of **hedging exchange rate exposure.** For example, suppose that on July 19, 1990, a U.S. firm buys televisions from a Japanese manufacturer for 100 million Japanese yen. Payment is to be made in Japanese yen 90 days after the goods are shipped, or on October 17, so the Japanese firm is extending trade credit for 90 days. The Japanese yen has been strong recently, and the U.S. company is apprehensive that the dollar will weaken because of large trade deficits. If the Japanese yen appreciates rapidly, more dollars will be required to buy the 100 million yen, and the profits on the television sets will be lost. Still, the U.S. firm does not want to forgo 90 days of free trade credit by paying cash. It can take the trade credit and protect itself by purchasing 100 million Japanese yen for delivery in 90 days. The 90-day rate is JY147.69, so the dollar cost is JY100,000,000/JY147.69 = $677,094. When payment comes due on October 17, 1990, regardless of the spot rate on that day, the U.S. firm can obtain the needed Japanese yen at the agreed-upon price of $677,094. The U.S. firm is said to have *covered* its trade payables with a *forward market hedge.*

Self-Test

Differentiate between spot and forward exchange rates.

Briefly explain what it means if a forward currency is selling at a discount, or at a premium.

What does "hedging exchange rate exposure" mean? Explain why a firm might wish to do this, and tell how it might be done.

INFLATION, INTEREST RATES, AND EXCHANGE RATES

Relative inflation rates, or the rates of inflation in foreign countries compared to that at home, have many implications for multinational financial decisions. Obviously, relative inflation rates will greatly influence production costs at home and abroad. Equally important, they have a dominant influence on relative interest rates as well as exchange rates. Both relative interest rates and exchange rates influence the methods chosen by multinational corporations for financing their foreign investments, and both of these factors have a notable effect on the profitability of foreign investments.

The currencies of countries with higher inflation rates than that of the United States tend over time to depreciate against the dollar. Some countries for which this has been the case include France, Italy, Mexico, and all the South American nations. On the other hand, the currencies of Germany, Switzerland, and Japan, which have had less inflation than the United States, have appreciated relative to the dollar. *In fact, a foreign currency will, on average, depreciate (or appreciate) at a percentage rate approximately equal to the amount by which its inflation rate exceeds (or is less than) our own.*

Relative inflation rates are also reflected in interest rates. The interest rate in any country is largely determined by its inflation rate; this point was discussed in Chapter 4. Therefore, countries currently experiencing higher rates of inflation than the United States also tend to have higher interest rates, whereas the reverse is true for countries with lower inflation rates.

It is tempting for the treasurer of a multinational corporation to borrow in the countries with the lowest interest rates. However, this is not always the best strategy. Suppose for example, that interest rates in Germany are lower than those in the United States because of Germany's lower inflation rate. A U.S. multinational firm could save interest by borrowing in Germany. However, the German exchange rate can be expected to appreciate in the future, causing annual interest and principal payments on this debt to cost an increasing number of dollars over time. Thus, *the lower interest rate could be more than offset by losses from currency appreciation.* Similarly, one should not expect multinational corporations to avoid borrowing in a country like Brazil, where interest rates are very high, because future depreciation of the Brazilian cruzeiro might well make such borrowing relatively inexpensive.

Self-Test

What implications do relative inflation rates have for multinational financial decisions?

What happens to the currencies of countries with higher inflation rates than that of the United States? What happens to those with lower inflation rates?

Why might a multinational corporation decide to borrow in a country like Brazil, where interest rates are high, rather than in a country like Germany, where interest rates are low?

INTERNATIONAL WORKING CAPITAL MANAGEMENT

International Cash Management

The objectives of cash management in a multinational corporation are similar to those in a purely domestic corporation — namely (1) to speed up collections and to slow down disbursements as much as is feasible, and hence to maximize net float; (2) to shift cash as rapidly as possible from those parts of the business where it is not needed to those parts where it is needed; and (3) to obtain the highest possible risk-adjusted rate of return on temporary cash balances. Multinational companies use the same general procedures for achieving these goals as domestic firms, but because of longer distances and more serious mail delays, lockbox systems and electronic funds transfers are especially important.

Although multinational and domestic corporations have the same objectives and use similar procedures, the multinational corporation faces a more complex task. As was mentioned earlier in our discussion of political risk, foreign governments often place restrictions on transfers of funds out of the country, so although IBM can transfer money from its Salt Lake City office to its New York concentration bank just by pressing a few buttons, a similar transfer from its Buenos Aires office is far more complex. Buenos Aires funds are denominated in australs (Argentina's equivalent of the dollar), so the australs must be converted to dollars before the transfer. If there is a shortage of dollars in Argentina, or if the Argentinean government wants to conserve the dollars in the country to use for the purchase of strategic materials, then conversion, and hence the transfer, may be blocked. Even if no dollar shortage exists in Argentina, the government may still restrict funds outflows if those funds represent profits or depreciation rather than payments for purchased materials or equipment, because many countries, especially the less developed countries, want profits reinvested in the country in order to stimulate economic growth.

Once it has been determined what funds can be transferred out of the various nations in which a multinational corporation operates, it is important to get those funds to locations where they will earn the highest returns. Whereas domestic corporations tend to think in terms of domestic securities, multinationals are more likely to be aware of investment opportunities all around the world. Most multinational corporations use one or more global concentration banks, located in money centers such as London, New York, Tokyo, Zurich, or Singapore, and their staffs in those cities, working with international bankers, know of and are able to take advantage of the best rates available anywhere in the world.

International Credit Management

Like most other aspects of finance, credit management in the multinational corporation is similar to but more complex than that in a purely domestic business. First, granting credit is more risky in an international context because, in addition to the normal risks of default, the multinational corporation must also worry about exchange rate changes between the time a sale is made and the time a receivable is collected. For example, if IBM sold a computer to a Japanese customer for 147.85 million yen when the exchange rate was 147.85 yen per \$1, IBM would obtain 147,850,000/147.85 = \$1,000,000 for the computer. However, if it sold the computer on terms of net/6 months, and if the yen fell against the dollar so that one dollar would now buy 184.8125 yen, IBM would end up realizing only 147,850,000/184.8125 = \$800,000 when it collected the receivable. Hedging can reduce this type of risk, but at a cost.

In addition to being riskier, credit policy is generally more important for a multinational than for a purely domestic firm for two reasons. First, much of the United States' trade is with poorer, less-developed nations, and in such situations granting credit is generally a necessary condition for doing business. Second, and in large part as a result of the first point, nations whose economic health depends upon exports often help their manufacturing firms compete internationally by granting credit to foreign countries. In Japan, for example, the major manufacturing firms have direct ownership ties with large "trading companies" engaged in international trade, as well as with giant commercial banks. In addition, a government agency, the Ministry of International Trade and Industry (MITI), helps Japanese firms identify potential export markets and helps potential customers arrange credit for purchases from Japanese firms. In effect, the huge Japanese trade surpluses are used to finance Japanese exports, thus helping to perpetuate their favorable trade balance. The United States has attempted to counter with the Export-Import Bank, which is funded by Congress, but the fact that the United States had a balance of payments deficit in 1989 of close to \$109 billion is clear evidence that we have been less successful than others in world markets in recent years.

The huge debt which countries such as Brazil, Mexico, and Argentina owe the international banks, including many U.S. banks, is well known, and this situation illustrates how credit policy (by banks in this case) can go astray. The banks face a particularly sticky problem with these loans, because if a sovereign nation defaults, the banks cannot lay claim to the assets of the country as they could if a corporate customer defaulted. Note too that although the banks' loans to foreign governments are getting most of the headlines, many multinational corporations are also in trouble as a result of granting credit to business customers in the same countries in which the banks' loans to the government are on shaky ground.

By pointing out the risks in granting credit internationally, we are not suggesting that such credit is bad. Quite the contrary, for the potential gains from international operations far outweigh the risks, at least for companies (and banks) that have the necessary expertise.

Inventory Management in the Multinational Corporation

As in most other aspects of finance, inventory management in a multinational setting is similar to but more complex than that in a purely domestic one. First, there is the matter of the physical location of inventories. For example, where should Exxon keep its stockpiles of crude oil and refined products? It has refineries and marketing centers located worldwide, and one alternative is to keep items concentrated in a few strategic spots, from which they can then be shipped to the locations where they will be used as needs arise. Such a strategy may minimize the total amount of inventories needed to operate the global business and thus may minimize the firm's total investment in inventories. Note, though, that consideration will have to be given to potential delays in getting goods from central storage locations to user locations all around the world. Both working stocks and safety stocks will have to be maintained at each user location, as well as at the strategic storage centers. Problems like the Iraqi occupation of Kuwait and the subsequent trade embargo, which brings with it the potential for a shutdown of production of about 25 percent of the world's oil supply, complicate matters even more.

Exchange rates also influence inventory policy. If a local currency, say the Danish krone, were expected to rise in value against the dollar, a U.S. company operating in Denmark would want to increase stocks of local products before the rise in the krone, and vice versa if the krone were expected to fall.

Another factor that must be considered is the possibility of import or export quotas or tariffs. For example, in 1988 Apple Computer Company was obtaining 256k memory chips from Japanese suppliers at bargain prices, but U.S. chipmakers had just charged the Japanese with dumping chips in the U.S. market at prices below cost and were seeking to force the Japanese to raise prices, so Apple decided to increase its chip inventory.[4] As an update to this

---

[4]The term "dumping" warrants explanation, because the practice is so potentially important in international markets. Suppose Japanese chipmakers have excess capacity. A particular chip has a variable cost of $25, and its "fully allocated cost," which is the $25 plus total fixed cost per unit of output, is $40. Now suppose the Japanese firm can sell chips in the United States at $35 per unit, but if it charges $40 it will not make any sales because U.S. chipmakers sell for $35.50. If the Japanese firm sells at $35, it will cover variable cost plus make a contribution to fixed overhead, so selling at $35 makes sense. Continuing, if the Japanese firm can sell in Japan at $40, but U.S. firms are excluded from Japanese markets by import duties or other barriers, the Japanese will have a huge advantage over U.S. manufacturers. This practice of selling goods at lower prices in foreign markets than at home is called "dumping." U.S. firms are required by antitrust laws to offer the same price to all customers and, therefore, cannot engage in dumping.

situation, U.S. chip supplies rose, computer sales slacked off, and Apple ended up having an oversupply of expensive computer chips. As a result, Apple's profits were hurt, and its stock price fell, demonstrating once more the importance of careful inventory management.

As mentioned earlier, another danger in certain countries is the threat of expropriation. If that threat is large, inventory holdings will be minimized, and goods will be brought in only as needed. Similarly, if the operation involves extraction of raw material such as oil or bauxite, processing plants may be moved offshore rather than located close to the production site.

Taxes must also be considered, and they have two effects on multinational inventory management. First, countries often impose property taxes on assets, including inventories, and when this is done, the tax is based on holdings as of a specific date, say January 1 or March 1. Such rules make it advantageous for a multinational firm (1) to schedule production so that inventories are low on the assessment date, and (2) if assessment dates vary among countries in a region, to hold safety stocks in different countries at different times during the year.

Finally, multinational firms may consider the possibility of at-sea storage. Oil, chemical, grain, and other companies that deal in a bulk commodity that must be stored in some type of tank can often buy tankers at a cost not much greater — or perhaps even less, considering land cost — than land-based facilities. Loaded tankers can then be kept at sea or at anchor in some strategic location. This eliminates the danger of expropriation, minimizes the property tax problem, and maximizes flexibility with regard to shipping to areas where needs are greatest or prices highest.

This discussion has only scratched the surface of inventory management in the multinational corporation. As we noted at the outset, the task is much more complex than for a purely domestic firm. However, the greater the degree of complexity, the greater the rewards from superior performance, so if you want challenge along with potentially high rewards, look to the international arena.

Self-Test

Why do managers of a multinational corporation face a more complex task of managing its cash than do those of a domestic corporation?

Why is granting credit more risky in an international context?

Why is credit policy generally more important for a multinational than for a purely domestic firm?

Why is inventory management in a multinational setting more complex than that in a purely domestic setting?

PROCEDURES FOR ANALYZING POTENTIAL FOREIGN INVESTMENTS

Although the same basic principles of capital budgeting analysis apply to both foreign and domestic operations, there are some key differences. First, cash flow estimation is generally much more complex for overseas investments. Most multinational firms set up a separate subsidiary in each foreign country in which they operate, and the relevant cash flows for these subsidiaries are the dividends and royalties repatriated to the parent company. Second, these cash flows must be converted to the currency of the parent company and thus are subject to future exchange rate changes. For example, General Motors' German subsidiary may make a profit of 100 million marks in 1989 and again in 1990, but the value of these profits to GM will depend on the dollar/mark exchange rate. How many *dollars* is 100 million marks worth?

repatriation of earnings
The process of sending cash flows from a foreign subsidiary to its parent company.

Third, dividends and royalties are normally taxed by both foreign and home-country governments. Furthermore, a foreign government may restrict the amount of the cash flows that may be **repatriated** to the parent company. For example, some governments place a ceiling, stated as a percentage of the company's net worth, on the amount of cash dividends that may be paid by a subsidiary to its parent company. Such restrictions are normally intended to force multinational firms to reinvest earnings in the foreign country, although restrictions are sometimes imposed to prevent large currency outflows, which might destabilize exchange rates.

Whatever the host country's motivation, the result is that the parent corporation cannot use cash flows blocked in the foreign country to pay current dividends to its shareholders, nor does it have the flexibility to reinvest cash flows elsewhere in the world, where expected returns may be higher. Hence, from the perspective of the parent organization, *the cash flows relevant for the analysis of a foreign investment are the financial cash flows that the subsidiary can legally send back to the parent.* The present value of these cash flows is found by applying an appropriate discount rate, and this present value is then compared to the parent's investment in the project to determine the project's NPV.

In addition to the complexities of the cash flow analysis, *the cost of capital may be different for a foreign project than for an equivalent domestic project because foreign projects may be more or less risky.* A higher risk could arise from two primary sources — (1) exchange rate risk and (2) sovereign risk — while a lower risk might result from international diversification.

Exchange rate risk reflects the inherent uncertainty about the home currency value of cash flows sent back to the parent. In other words, foreign projects have an added risk element that relates to what the basic cash flows will be worth in the parent company's home currency. The foreign currency cash flows to be turned over to the parent must be converted into U.S. dollar values by translating them at expected future exchange rates. Analyses should be conducted to ascertain the effects of exchange rate variations, and, on the basis of this analysis, an exchange rate risk premium should be added to the domestic cost of capital to reflect the *exchange rate risk* inherent in the investment. As we have seen, it is sometimes possible to hedge against exchange rate fluctuations, but it may not be possible to hedge completely, and, in addition, the costs of hedging must be subtracted from the project's cash flows.

Sovereign risk refers to any action (or the probability of an action) by a host government in exercising its political power, which reduces the value of a company's investment. It includes at one extreme the expropriation without compensation of the subsidiary's assets. Sovereign risk also includes less drastic actions that reduce the value of the parent firm's investment in the foreign subsidiary, including higher taxes, tighter repatriation or currency controls, and restrictions on prices or markets, among others. The risk of expropriation of U.S. assets abroad is small in traditionally friendly and stable countries such as Great Britain or Switzerland. However, in many parts of the developing world of Latin America, Africa, and the Far East, the risk may be substantial. Past expropriations include those of ITT and Anaconda Copper in Chile, Gulf Oil in Bolivia, Occidental Petroleum in Libya, Enron Corporation in Peru, and the assets of many companies in Iraq, Iran, and Cuba.

Generally, sovereign risk premiums are not added to the cost of capital to adjust for this risk. If a company's management has a serious concern that a given country might expropriate foreign assets, it simply will not make significant investments in that country. Expropriation is viewed as a catastrophic or ruinous event, and managers have been shown to be extraordinarily risk averse when faced with ruinous loss possibilities. However, companies can take steps to reduce the potential loss from expropriation in three major ways: (1) by financing the subsidiary with local sources of capital, (2) by structuring operations so that the subsidiary has value only as a part of the integrated corporate system, and (3) by obtaining insurance against economic losses from expropriation from a source such as the Overseas Private Investment Corporation (OPIC). In the latter case, insurance premiums would have to be added to the project's cost.

sovereign risk
The risk of expropriation of a foreign subsidiary's assets by the host country and of unanticipated restrictions on cash flows to the parent company.

Self-Test

List some key differences in the basic principles of capital budgeting analysis as they apply to foreign versus domestic operations.

What are the relevant cash flows which should be used in the analysis of an international investment? Explain.

Why might the cost of capital for a foreign project differ from that of an equivalent domestic project? Could it be lower? Explain?

What adjustments might be made to the domestic cost of capital for a foreign investment due to exchange rate risk and sovereign risk?

INTERNATIONAL CAPITAL MARKETS

Direct foreign investment by U.S. multinational corporations is one way for U.S. citizens to invest in world markets. Another way is to purchase stocks, bonds, or various money market instruments issued in foreign countries. U.S. citizens actually do invest substantial amounts in the stocks and bonds of large corporations headquartered in Europe and to a lesser extent in the Far East and South America. They also buy securities issued by foreign governments. Such investments in foreign capital markets are known as *portfolio investments,* and they are distinguished from *direct investments* in physical assets by U.S. corporations.

Eurodollars

Eurodollar
A U.S. dollar deposited in a bank outside the United States.

A **Eurodollar** is a U.S. dollar deposited in a bank outside the United States. (Although they are called Eurodollars because they originated in Europe, Eurodollars are really any dollars deposited in any part of the world, other than the United States.) The bank in which the deposit is made may be a host country institution, such as Barclay's Bank in London; the foreign branch of a U.S. bank, such as Citibank's Paris branch; or even a foreign branch of a third-country bank, such as Barclay's Munich branch. Most Eurodollar deposits are for $500,000 or more, and they have maturities ranging from overnight to about 5 years.

The major difference between Eurodollar deposits and regular U.S. time deposits is their geographic locations. The two types of deposits do not involve different currencies — in both cases, dollars are on deposit. However, Eurodollars are outside the direct control of the U.S. monetary authorities, so U.S. banking regulations, such as fractional reserves, interest rate ceilings, and FDIC insurance premiums, do not apply. The absence of these costs means that the interest rate paid on Eurodollar deposits tends to be higher than domestic U.S. rates on equivalent instruments.

Although the dollar is the leading international currency, German marks, Swiss francs, Japanese yen, and other currencies are also deposited outside their home countries; these *Eurocurrencies* are handled in exactly the same way as Eurodollars.

Eurodollars are borrowed by U.S. and foreign corporations and governments, which need dollars for various purposes, especially to pay for goods exported from the United States and to invest in the U.S. stock market. Also, U.S. dollars are used as an international currency, or international medium of exchange, and many Eurodollars are used for this purpose. It is interesting to note that Eurodollars were actually "invented" by the Soviets in 1946. International merchants did not trust the Soviets or their rubles, so the Soviets bought some dollars (for gold), deposited them in a Paris bank, and then used them to buy goods in the world markets. Others soon found it convenient to use dollars this same way, and soon the Eurodollar market was in full swing.

Eurodollar Interest Rates

Eurodollars are always held in interest-bearing accounts. The interest rate paid on these deposits depends (1) on the bank's lending rate, as the interest a bank earns on loans determines its willingness and ability to pay interest on deposits, and (2) on rates of return available on U.S. money market instruments. If rates in the United States were above Eurodollar deposit rates, these funds would be sent back and invested in the United States, whereas if Eurodollar deposit rates are significantly above U.S. rates, which is more often the case, more dollars will be sent out of the United States.

Interest rates on Eurodollar deposits (and loans) are tied to a standard rate known by the acronym *LIBOR,* which stands for *London InterBank Offer Rate.* LIBOR is the rate of interest offered by the largest and strongest London banks on deposits of other large banks of the highest credit standing. In July 1990, LIBOR rates were approximately four-tenths of a percentage point above domestic U.S. bank rates on time deposits of the same maturity — 7.7 percent for 3-month CDs versus 8.1 percent for LIBOR CDs. The Eurodollar market is essentially a short-term market; most loans and deposits are for less than one year.

International Bond Markets

Any bond sold outside the country of the borrower is called an **international bond;** however, there are two important types of international bonds: foreign bonds and Eurobonds. **Foreign bonds** are bonds sold by a foreign borrower but denominated in the currency of the country in which the issue is sold. For instance, Bell Canada may need U.S. dollars to finance the operations of its subsidiaries in the United States. If it decides to raise the needed capital in the domestic U.S. bond market, the bond will be underwritten by a syndicate of U.S. investment bankers, denominated in U.S. dollars, and sold to U.S. investors in accordance with SEC and applicable state regulations. Except for the foreign origin of the borrower (Canada), this bond will be indistinguishable from those issued by equivalent U.S. corporations. Since Bell Canada is a foreign corporation, however, the bond will be called a foreign bond.

The term **Eurobonds** is used to designate any bond sold in some country *other than* the one in whose currency the bond is denominated. Examples include a British firm's issue of pound bonds sold in France, a Ford Motor Company issue denominated in dollars and sold in Germany, or a German firm's sale of mark-denominated bonds in Switzerland. The institutional arrangements by which Eurobonds are marketed are different than those for most other bond issues, with the most important distinction being a far lower level of required disclosure than is usually found for bonds issued in domestic markets, particularly in the United States. Governments tend to apply regulations on securities denominated in foreign currencies less strictly than they apply them on home-currency securities because of the nature of the bonds'

international bond
Any bond sold outside the country of the borrower.

foreign bond
A bond sold by a foreign borrower but denominated in the currency of the country in which it is sold.

Eurobond
A bond sold in a country other than the one in whose currency the bond is denominated.

probable purchasers. This generally leads to lower total transaction costs for Eurobonds.

Eurobonds appeal to investors for several reasons. Generally, they are issued in bearer form rather than as registered bonds, so the names and nationalities of investors are not recorded. Individuals who desire anonymity, whether for privacy reasons or for tax avoidance, find Eurobonds to their liking. Similarly, most governments do not withhold taxes on interest payments associated with Eurobonds. If the investor requires an effective yield of 10 percent, a Eurobond that is exempt from tax withholding would need a coupon rate of 10 percent. Another type of bond—for instance, a domestic issue subject to a 30 percent withholding tax on interest paid to foreigners—would need a coupon rate of 14.3 percent to yield an after-withholding rate of 10 percent. Investors who desire secrecy would not want to file for a refund of the tax, so they would prefer to hold the Eurobond.

More than half of all Eurobonds are denominated in dollars; bonds in Japanese yen, German marks, and Dutch guilders account for most of the rest. Although centered in Europe, Eurobonds are truly international. Their underwriting syndicates include investment bankers from all parts of the world, and the bonds are sold to investors not only in Europe but also in such faraway places as Bahrain and Singapore. Up to a few years ago, Eurobonds were issued solely by multinational firms, by international financial institutions, or by national governments. Today, however, the Eurobond market is also being tapped by purely domestic U.S. firms such as electric utilities, which find that by borrowing overseas they can lower their debt costs.

Self-Test

Differentiate between foreign portfolio investments and direct foreign investments.

What are Eurodollars, and how are they different from Eurocurrencies?

On what two items does the interest rate paid on Eurodollars depend?

Differentiate among *international bonds, foreign bonds,* and *Eurobonds.*

For what reasons do Eurobonds appeal to investors?

INTERNATIONAL CAPITAL STRUCTURES

Significant differences have been observed in the capital structures of U.S. corporations in comparison to their German and Japanese counterparts. For example, the Organization for Economic Cooperation and Development (OECD) recently reported that, on average, Japanese firms use 85 percent debt to total assets (in book value terms), German firms use 64 percent, and U.S. firms use 55 percent. Of course, different countries use somewhat different accounting conventions with regard to (1) reporting assets on a historical versus a replacement cost basis, (2) the treatment of leased assets, (3) pension plan funding, and (4) capitalizing versus expensing R&D costs, and these differences make comparisons difficult. Still, even after adjusting for accounting differences, researchers find that Japanese and German firms use considerably more financial leverage than U.S. companies.

Why do international differences in financial leverage exist? Since taxes are thought to be a major reason for using debt, the effects of differential tax structures in the three countries have been examined. The interest on corporate debt is deductible in each country, and individuals must pay taxes on dividends and interest received. However, capital gains are not taxed in either Germany or Japan. The conclusions from this analysis are as follows: (1) From a tax standpoint, corporations should be equally inclined to use debt in all three countries. (2) Since capital gains are not taxed in Germany or Japan, but are taxed in the United States, and since capital gains are associated more with stocks than with bonds, investors in Germany and Japan should show a preference for stocks as compared with U.S. investors. (3) Investor preferences should lead to relatively low equity capital costs in Germany and Japan, and this, in turn, should cause German and Japanese firms to use more equity capital than their U.S. counterparts. Of course, this is exactly the opposite of the actual capital structures, so differential tax laws cannot explain the observed capital structure differences.

If tax rates cannot explain the different capital structures, what else might explain the observed differences? Another possibility relates to bankruptcy costs. Earlier, we saw that actual bankruptcy, and even the threat of potential bankruptcy, imposes a costly burden on firms with large amounts of debt. Note, though, that the threat of bankruptcy is dependent on the *probability* of bankruptcy. In the United States, equity monitoring costs are comparatively low—corporations produce quarterly reports, pay quarterly dividends, and must comply with relatively stringent audit requirements. These conditions are less prevalent in the other countries. Conversely, debt monitoring costs are probably lower in Germany and Japan than in the United States. In Germany and Japan, the bulk of corporate debt consists of bank loans as opposed to publicly issued bonds, but, more important, the banks are closely linked to the corporations which borrow from them. German and Japanese banks often (1) hold major equity positions in their debtor corporations, (2) vote the shares of individual shareholders for whom banks hold shares in trust, and (3) have bank officers sit on the boards of debtor corporations. Given these close relationships, the banks are much more directly involved with the debtor firms' affairs, and as a result they are also more accommodating in the event of financial distress than U.S. bondholders would be. This, in turn, suggests that a given amount of debt brings with it a lower threat of bankruptcy for a German or a Japanese firm than for a U.S. firm with the same amount of business risk. Thus, an analysis of both bankruptcy and equity reporting costs leads to the conclusion that U.S. firms ought to have more equity and less debt than firms in Japan and Germany.

We cannot state that one financial system is better or worse than another in the sense of making the firms in one country more efficient than those in another. However, as U.S. firms become increasingly involved in worldwide operations, they must become increasingly aware of worldwide conditions, and they must be prepared to adapt to conditions in the various countries in which they do business.

Self-Test

Why do international differences in financial leverage exist?

INTERNATIONAL MERGERS

The year 1988 was a banner one for mergers in the United States, with take-over deals totaling over $135 billion. One reason for the high level of merger activity was that foreign firms spent $40.6 billion buying American companies. For example, British Petroleum took over Standard Oil, Unilever acquired Chesebrough-Pond's, and Blue Arrow (a London employment agency) bought Manpower (another employment agency).

Foreign companies were interested in U.S. firms for several reasons. First, many of them wanted to gain a foothold in the U.S. market to avoid being shut out if Congress should pass protectionist legislation. Second, the purchase of an American firm can provide the overseas parent with a tax shelter. For example, the average Japanese firm pays 56 percent of its income in federal and local taxes. If that same firm operates in the United States, the income is generally subject to U.S. taxes of only 34 percent. Third, the decline in the value of the dollar relative to most foreign currencies has made U.S. firms more attractive to foreign purchasers. For example, in early 1988 British retailer Marks & Spencer PLC paid $750 million for American retailer Brooks Brothers. At the prevailing exchange rate of $1.86 per pound, the deal cost Marks & Spencer 403 million pounds. If the purchase had been made in 1985, when a pound was worth only $1.10, it would have cost Marks & Spencer 682 million pounds. Thus, the price of Brooks Brothers to a British company declined by 40.9 percent due to the decline in the value of the dollar. Similar exchange rate drops have occurred in the German mark, the Swiss franc, and the Japanese yen.

Investment analysts predicted at the beginning of 1988 that it would be a record year for foreign acquisition of U.S. firms. Indeed, foreign buyers were literally fighting over U.S. targets. For example, one highly publicized foreign takeover involved a fight between Japan's Bridgestone Corporation and Italy's Pirelli for ownership of Firestone Tire & Rubber Company. Bridgestone began the bidding at $1.25 billion. Then, Pirelli came in, aided by France's Michelin. In the end, Bridgestone won, paying $2.6 billion for Firestone, more than double its original offer. Jeffrey Rosen, head of the international mergers and acquisitions department at First Boston, was quoted in *Business Week* as saying, "1988 will be the year of the foreign acquirer." His prediction held true.

Self-Test

Why have foreign companies been interested in acquiring U.S. firms?

SUMMARY

This chapter discusses the differences between multinational and domestic financial management. Some of the key concepts are listed below.

- **International operations** are becoming increasingly important to individual firms and to the national economy. A **multinational corporation** is a firm that operates in two or more nations.

- Six major factors distinguish financial management as practiced by domestic firms from that of multinational corporations: (1) **different currency denominations**, (2) **economic and legal ramifications**, (3) **languages**, (4) **cultural differences**, (5) **role of governments,** and (6) **political risk.**

- The number of U.S. dollars required to purchase one unit of foreign currency is called a **direct quotation**, while the number of units of foreign currency that can be purchased for one U.S. dollar is an **indirect quotation.**

- Financial forecasting is especially difficult for multinational firms, because **exchange rate fluctuations** make it difficult to estimate the dollars that overseas operations will produce.

- Prior to August 1971, the world was on a **fixed exchange rate system** whereby the U.S. dollar was linked to gold, and other currencies were then tied to the dollar. After August 1971, the world monetary system changed to a **floating system** whereby major world currency rates float with market forces, largely unrestricted by any internationally agreed-upon limits. The central bank of each country does intervene in the foreign exchange market, buying and selling its currency to smooth out exchange rate fluctuations, but only to a limited extent.

- **Spot rates** are the rates paid for delivery of currency "on the spot," while the **forward exchange rate** is the rate paid for delivery of currency at some agreed-upon future date, usually 30, 90, or 180 days from the day the transaction is negotiated.

- If one can obtain *more* of the foreign currency for a dollar in the forward than in the spot market, the forward currency is said to be selling at a **discount.** If a dollar will buy *fewer* units of a currency in the forward than in the spot market, the forward currency is said to be selling at a **premium.**

- Granting credit is more risky in an international context because, in addition to the normal risks of default, the multinational firm must worry about **exchange rate changes** between the time a sale is made and the time a receivable is collected.

- Credit policy is especially important for a multinational firm for two reasons: (1) Much of the U.S. trade is with less-developed nations, and in such situations granting credit is a necessary condition for doing business. (2) The governments of nations such as Japan whose economic health depends upon exports often help their manufacturing firms compete internationally by granting credit to foreign customers.

- Foreign investments are similar to domestic investments, but sovereign risk and exchange rate risk must be considered. **Sovereign risk** is the risk that the foreign government will take some action which will decrease the value of the investment, while **exchange rate risk** is the risk of losses due to fluctuations in the value of the dollar relative to the values of foreign currencies.

- Investment in **international capital projects** is more risky than in purely domestic ones because of **exchange rate risk** and **sovereign risk.** The relevant cash flows in international capital budgeting are the dollar cash flows which can be turned over to the parent company.

- **Eurodollars** are U.S. dollars deposited in banks outside the United States. Interest rates on Eurodollars are tied to **LIBOR**, the London Inter-Bank Offer Rate.

- U.S. firms often find that they can raise long-term capital at a lower cost outside the United States by selling bonds in the **international capital markets.** International bonds may be either **foreign bonds,** which are exactly like regular domestic bonds except that the issuer is a foreign company, or **Eurobonds,** which are bonds sold in a foreign country but denominated in the currency of the issuing company's home country.

- Foreign firms have been acquiring U.S. firms at a record pace in recent years due to **the lower value of the dollar, foreigners' desire to gain a foothold in the U.S. market,** and the fact that U.S. **trade deficits** mean that foreigners have a great deal of U.S. funds.

RESOLUTION TO DECISION IN FINANCE

Philips Has the Weight of the World on Its Shoulders

Van der Klugt wielded a broad sword against his own company to strengthen it against the world. Over two years, he laid off 24,000 workers, despite angry protests at the affected plants. He reduced the home-country Dutch labor force by 30 percent, to about 70,000 employees, and he also reduced the number of headquarters staff at Eindhoven from 3,400 to 2,300. The telecommunications/computer systems merger put into place the year before van der Klugt became CEO was dissolved as of January 1, 1990. Officials said the expectations that led to the original merger had not come true, and separating the divisions again would help them respond more quickly to developments in their respective markets. They admitted that intense price competition had put the company's computer operations in the red.

The willingness to change to obtain greater efficiency and productivity led Philips to move its production of 14-inch television sets from the United States to Taiwan, and later to move it to Mexico. The company also found that some products formerly made in Singapore were now cheaper to produce in Belgium for the European market.

Van der Klugt also reorganized Philips's consumer electronics division to achieve "a considerable shortening of the time span between the conception of an idea for a new product and its marketing," according to a company spokesman. "The lines of decision making have to be shortened and internal communications enhanced." In the U.S. market, Philips's increased investment in televisions resulted in a challenge to Zenith for the Number 2 position. The company also began turning out new products like boom boxes to reach the changeable teenage market.

Van der Klugt raised cash by selling holdings, including all of Philips's U.S. defense operations, and he used the new capital primarily to compete with the Japanese. Major company spending included $1 billion invested in a five-year project with Siemens to produce submicron computer chips and $200 million to upgrade TV-tube plants. Van der Klugt also increased Philips's advertising budget from $6 million to $30 million. "We've been sacrificing profits to the tune of $250 million a year to restructure," he said. There have been some payoffs — Philips's share of the market in compact disc players rose from 8 percent to 12.5 percent in two years, while in televisions, it received its biggest order ever, $150 million for televisions, VCRs, and satellite dishes for a public school broadcasting system being set up by Whittle Communications.

Van der Klugt's least successful efforts involved divisions for semiconductors, where five years of huge investments failed to change the red ink to black, and for personal computers, where Philips concentrated on minicomputers while the world was moving to personal computers. Nevertheless, the CEO has persisted in trying to make Philips a major computer maker.

Van der Klugt streamlined his widespread operation and concentrated efforts and investment into four main divisions — consumer electronics, lighting, computers, and microchips. Net profits were expected to be up 38 percent in 1989, and a London analyst said in late 1988, "I think they've got the company turned around." Critics, however, said Philips was still spread too thin and that it would never be able to compete successfully in some markets.

Sources: *The Wall Street Journal,* "Philips Plans Restructuring in Consumer Electronics," June 13, 1988; "Global Manufacturing Is an Intricate Game," November 29, 1988; and "N. V. Philips to Reorganize Big Division," December 15, 1989; *Business Week,* Jonathan Kapstein, Thane Peterson, and Lois Therrien, "Look Out, World, Philips Is on a War Footing," January 15, 1990, and "A Would-Be World Beater Takes a Beating," July 16, 1990.

The critics turned out to be correct. In May 1990, when severe problems became evident, Philips's directors forced van der Klugt to resign. Philips will take a $718 million write-off on its unsold minicomputers and microchips. When Jan D. Timmer replaced van der Klugt as CEO, he stunned shareholders by forecasting a fiscal year loss of $1.06 billion — the largest loss ever. Timmer, the former head of Philips's still successful consumer electronics division, says he will cut more jobs and launch another restructuring. Investors doubted that his plans could turn the company around, and they sent the share price down 7 percent on the Amsterdam exchange.

To make matters worse, there are other problems that are beyond Timmer's control, or beyond the control of any other player in the global market. A major problem is the volatility of currency exchange rates. When money from Philips's 1987 worldwide sales was converted into Dutch guilders, an apparent 7 percent increase became a 2 percent decline, primarily because of a sharp drop in the U.S. dollar. A number of CEOs of European companies are pushing for a single European currency and a central European bank as a means of creating a more stable world monetary system, but those are both only in the idea stage at present.

Another major concern is the standardization of products. North American Philips Chairman/CEO Jeelof said, "When we came out with our compact disc, we decided right away we had to go for a world standard. The stand-alone character of many electronic products is disappearing. It is always interfaced with something, either with software, or the program, or the network. You can't just bring out something on its own. It always has to fit in somewhere, so the need for a standard is absolutely necessary."

Only the global community as a whole can solve the problems of currency exchange rates and product standardization. In the meantime, Timmer will be hard pressed to keep Philips in a starring role on the world stage.

QUESTIONS

23-1   Under the fixed exchange rate system, what was the currency against which all other currency values were defined?

23-2   Exchange rates fluctuate under both the fixed exchange rate and floating exchange rate systems. What, then, is the difference between the two systems?

23-3   If the French franc depreciates against the U.S. dollar, can a dollar buy more or fewer French francs as a result?

23-4   If the United States imports more goods from abroad than it exports, foreigners will tend to have a surplus of U.S. dollars. What will this do to the value of the dollar with respect to foreign currencies? What is the corresponding effect on foreign investments in the United States?

23-5   Why do U.S. corporations build manufacturing plants abroad when they could build them at home?

23-6   Most firms require higher rates of return on foreign projects than on identical projects located at home. Why?

23-7   What is a Eurodollar? If a French citizen deposits $10,000 in Chase Manhattan Bank in New York, have Eurodollars been created? What if the deposit is made in Barclay's Bank in London? Chase Manhattan's Paris branch?

PROBLEMS

23-1 **Exchange rate.** If British pounds sell for $1.82 (U.S.) per pound, what should dollars sell for in pounds per dollar?

23-2 **Currency appreciation.** Suppose that 1 French franc could be purchased in the foreign exchange market for 15 U.S. cents today. If the franc appreciated 10 percent tomorrow against the dollar, how many francs would a dollar buy tomorrow?

23-3 **Cross exchange rates.** Recently the exchange rate between U.S. dollars and the French franc was FF5.5 = $1, and the exchange rate between the dollar and the British pound was £1 = $1.82. What was the exchange rate between francs and pounds?

23-4 **Cross exchange rates.** Look up the 3 currencies in Problem 23-3 in the foreign exchange section of a current issue of *The Wall Street Journal.* What is the current exchange rate between francs and pounds?

23-5 **Exchange rates.** Table 23-1 lists foreign exchange rates for July 19, 1990. On that day how many dollars would be required to purchase 1,000 units of each of the following: Indian rupees, Italian lira, Japanese yen, Mexican pesos, and Saudi Arabian riyals?

23-6 **Exchange rates.** Look up the 5 currencies in Problem 23-5 in the foreign exchange section of a current issue of *The Wall Street Journal.*
a. What is the current exchange rate for changing dollars into 1,000 units of rupees, lira, yen, pesos, and riyals?
b. What is the percentage gain or loss between the July 19, 1990, exchange rate and the current exchange rate for each of the currencies in Part a?

23-7 **Results of exchange rate changes.** Early in September 1983, it took 245 Japanese yen to equal $1. Almost seven years later, in July 1990, that exchange rate had fallen to 148 yen to $1. Assume the price of a Japanese-manufactured automobile was $8,000 in September 1983 and that its price changes were in direct relation to exchange rates.
a. Has the price, in dollars, of the automobile increased or decreased during the 7-year period because of changes in the exchange rate?
b. What would the dollar price of the automobile be on July 19, 1990, again assuming that the car's price changes only with exchange rates?

23-8 **Hedging.** LaPage French Imports has agreed to purchase 15,000 cases of French wine for 16 million francs at today's spot rate. The firm's financial manager, Frank O'File, has noted the following current spot and forward rates:

	U.S. Dollar/Franc	**Franc/U.S. Dollar**
Spot	0.18159	5.5070
30-day forward	0.18133	5.5147
90-day forward	0.18082	5.5303
180-day forward	0.17995	5.5570

On the same day Mr. O'File agrees to purchase 15,000 more cases of wine in 3 months at the same price of 16 million francs.
a. What is the price of the wine, in U.S. dollars, if it is purchased at today's spot rate?
b. What is the cost, in dollars, of the second 15,000 cases if payment is made in 90 days and the spot rate at that time equals today's 90-day forward rate?
c. If Mr. O'File is concerned about the dollar losing value relative to the franc in the next 90 days, what can he do to reduce his exposure to exchange rate risk?

d. If he does not hedge his exposure to exchange rate risk, and the exchange rate for the French franc is 5.00 to $1 in 90 days, how much will he have to pay for the wine (in dollars)?

23-9   **Foreign investment analysis.** After all foreign and U.S. taxes, a U.S. corporation expects to receive 3 pounds of dividends per share from a British subsidiary this year. The exchange rate at the end of the year is expected to be $1.76 per pound, and the pound is expected to depreciate 5 percent against the dollar each year for an indefinite period. The dividend (in pounds) is expected to grow at 10 percent a year indefinitely. The parent U.S. corporation owns 10 million shares of the subsidiary. What is the present value of its equity ownership of the subsidiary? Assume a cost of equity capital of 14 percent for the subsidiary.

23-10   **Exchange gains and losses.** You are the vice president of International InfoXchange, headquartered in Chicago, Illinois. All shareholders of the firm live in the United States. Earlier this month you obtained a loan of 5 million Canadian dollars from a bank in Toronto to finance the construction of a new plant in Montreal. At the time the loan was received, the exchange rate was 87 U.S. cents to the Canadian dollar. By the end of the month it has unexpectedly dropped to 80 cents. Has your company made a gain or loss as a result, and by how much?

Appendix A

Mathematical Tables

Table A-1 **Present Value of $1 Due at the End of n Periods: $PVIF_{k,n} = 1/(1 + k)^n$**

Period	1%	2%	3%	4%	5%	6%	7%	8%	9%	10%
1	.9901	.9804	.9709	.9615	.9524	.9434	.9346	.9259	.9174	.9091
2	.9803	.9612	.9426	.9246	.9070	.8900	.8734	.8573	.8417	.8264
3	.9706	.9423	.9151	.8890	.8638	.8396	.8163	.7938	.7722	.7513
4	.9610	.9238	.8885	.8548	.8227	.7921	.7629	.7350	.7084	.6830
5	.9515	.9057	.8626	.8219	.7835	.7473	.7130	.6806	.6499	.6209
6	.9420	.8880	.8375	.7903	.7462	.7050	.6663	.6302	.5963	.5645
7	.9327	.8706	.8131	.7599	.7107	.6651	.6227	.5835	.5470	.5132
8	.9235	.8535	.7894	.7307	.6768	.6274	.5820	.5403	.5019	.4665
9	.9143	.8368	.7664	.7026	.6446	.5919	.5439	.5002	.4604	.4241
10	.9053	.8203	.7441	.6756	.6139	.5584	.5083	.4632	.4224	.3855
11	.8963	.8043	.7224	.6496	.5847	.5268	.4751	.4289	.3875	.3505
12	.8874	.7885	.7014	.6246	.5568	.4970	.4440	.3971	.3555	.3186
13	.8787	.7730	.6810	.6006	.5303	.4688	.4150	.3677	.3262	.2897
14	.8700	.7579	.6611	.5775	.5051	.4423	.3878	.3405	.2992	.2633
15	.8613	.7430	.6419	.5553	.4810	.4173	.3624	.3152	.2745	.2394
16	.8528	.7284	.6232	.5339	.4581	.3936	.3387	.2919	.2519	.2176
17	.8444	.7142	.6050	.5134	.4363	.3714	.3166	.2703	.2311	.1978
18	.8360	.7002	.5874	.4936	.4155	.3503	.2959	.2502	.2120	.1799
19	.8277	.6864	.5703	.4746	.3957	.3305	.2765	.2317	.1945	.1635
20	.8195	.6730	.5537	.4564	.3769	.3118	.2584	.2145	.1784	.1486
21	.8114	.6598	.5375	.4388	.3589	.2942	.2415	.1987	.1637	.1351
22	.8034	.6468	.5219	.4220	.3418	.2775	.2257	.1839	.1502	.1228
23	.7954	.6342	.5067	.4057	.3256	.2618	.2109	.1703	.1378	.1117
24	.7876	.6217	.4919	.3901	.3101	.2470	.1971	.1577	.1264	.1015
25	.7798	.6095	.4776	.3751	.2953	.2330	.1842	.1460	.1160	.0923
26	.7720	.5976	.4637	.3607	.2812	.2198	.1722	.1352	.1064	.0839
27	.7644	.5859	.4502	.3468	.2678	.2074	.1609	.1252	.0976	.0763
28	.7568	.5744	.4371	.3335	.2551	.1956	.1504	.1159	.0895	.0693
29	.7493	.5631	.4243	.3207	.2429	.1846	.1406	.1073	.0822	.0630
30	.7419	.5521	.4120	.3083	.2314	.1741	.1314	.0994	.0754	.0573
35	.7059	.5000	.3554	.2534	.1813	.1301	.0937	.0676	.0490	.0356
40	.6717	.4529	.3066	.2083	.1420	.0972	.0668	.0460	.0318	.0221
45	.6391	.4102	.2644	.1712	.1113	.0727	.0476	.0313	.0207	.0137
50	.6080	.3715	.2281	.1407	.0872	.0543	.0339	.0213	.0134	.0085
55	.5785	.3365	.1968	.1157	.0683	.0406	.0242	.0145	.0087	.0053

Period	12%	14%	15%	16%	18%	20%	24%	28%	32%	36%
1	.8929	.8772	.8696	.8621	.8475	.8333	.8065	.7813	.7576	.7353
2	.7972	.7695	.7561	.7432	.7182	.6944	.6504	.6104	.5739	.5407
3	.7118	.6750	.6575	.6407	.6086	.5787	.5245	.4768	.4348	.3975
4	.6355	.5921	.5718	.5523	.5158	.4823	.4230	.3725	.3294	.2923
5	.5674	.5194	.4972	.4761	.4371	.4019	.3411	.2910	.2495	.2149
6	.5066	.4556	.4323	.4104	.3704	.3349	.2751	.2274	.1890	.1580
7	.4523	.3996	.3759	.3538	.3139	.2791	.2218	.1776	.1432	.1162
8	.4039	.3506	.3269	.3050	.2660	.2326	.1789	.1388	.1085	.0854
9	.3606	.3075	.2843	.2630	.2255	.1938	.1443	.1084	.0822	.0628
10	.3220	.2697	.2472	.2267	.1911	.1615	.1164	.0847	.0623	.0462
11	.2875	.2366	.2149	.1954	.1619	.1346	.0938	.0662	.0472	.0340
12	.2567	.2076	.1869	.1685	.1372	.1122	.0757	.0517	.0357	.0250
13	.2292	.1821	.1625	.1452	.1163	.0935	.0610	.0404	.0271	.0184
14	.2046	.1597	.1413	.1252	.0985	.0779	.0492	.0316	.0205	.0135
15	.1827	.1401	.1229	.1079	.0835	.0649	.0397	.0247	.0155	.0099
16	.1631	.1229	.1069	.0930	.0708	.0541	.0320	.0193	.0118	.0073
17	.1456	.1078	.0929	.0802	.0600	.0451	.0258	.0150	.0089	.0054
18	.1300	.0946	.0808	.0691	.0508	.0376	.0208	.0118	.0068	.0039
19	.1161	.0829	.0703	.0596	.0431	.0313	.0168	.0092	.0051	.0029
20	.1037	.0728	.0611	.0514	.0365	.0261	.0135	.0072	.0039	.0021
21	.0926	.0638	.0531	.0443	.0309	.0217	.0109	.0056	.0029	.0016
22	.0826	.0560	.0462	.0382	.0262	.0181	.0088	.0044	.0022	.0012
23	.0738	.0491	.0402	.0329	.0222	.0151	.0071	.0034	.0017	.0008
24	.0659	.0431	.0349	.0284	.0188	.0126	.0057	.0027	.0013	.0006
25	.0588	.0378	.0304	.0245	.0160	.0105	.0046	.0021	.0010	.0005
26	.0525	.0331	.0264	.0211	.0135	.0087	.0037	.0016	.0007	.0003
27	.0469	.0291	.0230	.0182	.0115	.0073	.0030	.0013	.0006	.0002
28	.0419	.0255	.0200	.0157	.0097	.0061	.0024	.0010	.0004	.0002
29	.0374	.0224	.0174	.0135	.0082	.0051	.0020	.0008	.0003	.0001
30	.0334	.0196	.0151	.0116	.0070	.0042	.0016	.0006	.0002	.0001
35	.0189	.0102	.0075	.0055	.0030	.0017	.0005	.0002	.0001	*
40	.0107	.0053	.0037	.0026	.0013	.0007	.0002	.0001	*	*
45	.0061	.0027	.0019	.0013	.0006	.0003	.0001	*	*	*
50	.0035	.0014	.0009	.0006	.0003	.0001	*	*	*	*
55	.0020	.0007	.0005	.0003	.0001	*	*	*	*	*

*The factor is zero to four decimal places.

Appendix A Mathematical Tables

Table A-2 Present Value of an Annuity of $1 per Period for n Periods:

$$PVIFA_{k,n} = \sum_{t=1}^{n} \frac{1}{(1 + k)^t} = \frac{1 - \dfrac{1}{(1 + k)^n}}{k}$$

Number of Periods	1%	2%	3%	4%	5%	6%	7%	8%	9%
1	0.9901	0.9804	0.9709	0.9615	0.9524	0.9434	0.9346	0.9259	0.9174
2	1.9704	1.9416	1.9135	1.8861	1.8594	1.8334	1.8080	1.7833	1.7591
3	2.9410	2.8839	2.8286	2.7751	2.7232	2.6730	2.6243	2.5771	2.5313
4	3.9020	3.8077	3.7171	3.6299	3.5460	3.4651	3.3872	3.3121	3.2397
5	4.8534	4.7135	4.5797	4.4518	4.3295	4.2124	4.1002	3.9927	3.8897
6	5.7955	5.6014	5.4172	5.2421	5.0757	4.9173	4.7665	4.6229	4.4859
7	6.7282	6.4720	6.2303	6.0021	5.7864	5.5824	5.3893	5.2064	5.0330
8	7.6517	7.3255	7.0197	6.7327	6.4632	6.2098	5.9713	5.7466	5.5348
9	8.5660	8.1622	7.7861	7.4353	7.1078	6.8017	6.5152	6.2469	5.9952
10	9.4713	8.9826	8.5302	8.1109	7.7217	7.3601	7.0236	6.7101	6.4177
11	10.3676	9.7868	9.2526	8.7605	8.3064	7.8869	7.4987	7.1390	6.8052
12	11.2551	10.5753	9.9540	9.3851	8.8633	8.3838	7.9427	7.5361	7.1607
13	12.1337	11.3484	10.6350	9.9856	9.3936	8.8527	8.3577	7.9038	7.4869
14	13.0037	12.1062	11.2961	10.5631	9.8986	9.2950	8.7455	8.2442	7.7862
15	13.8651	12.8493	11.9379	11.1184	10.3797	9.7122	9.1079	8.5595	8.0607
16	14.7179	13.5777	12.5611	11.6523	10.8378	10.1059	9.4466	8.8514	8.3126
17	15.5623	14.2919	13.1661	12.1657	11.2741	10.4773	9.7632	9.1216	8.5436
18	16.3983	14.9920	13.7535	12.6593	11.6896	10.8276	10.0591	9.3719	8.7556
19	17.2260	15.6785	14.3238	13.1339	12.0853	11.1581	10.3356	9.6036	8.9501
20	18.0456	16.3514	14.8775	13.5903	12.4622	11.4699	10.5940	9.8181	9.1285
21	18.8570	17.0112	15.4150	14.0292	12.8212	11.7641	10.8355	10.0168	9.2922
22	19.6604	17.6580	15.9369	14.4511	13.1630	12.0416	11.0612	10.2007	9.4424
23	20.4558	18.2922	16.4436	14.8568	13.4886	12.3034	11.2722	10.3711	9.5802
24	21.2434	18.9139	16.9355	15.2470	13.7986	12.5504	11.4693	10.5288	9.7066
25	22.0232	19.5235	17.4131	15.6221	14.0939	12.7834	11.6536	10.6748	9.8226
26	22.7952	20.1210	17.8768	15.9828	14.3752	13.0032	11.8258	10.8100	9.9290
27	23.5596	20.7069	18.3270	16.3296	14.6430	13.2105	11.9867	10.9352	10.0266
28	24.3164	21.2813	18.7641	16.6631	14.8981	13.4062	12.1371	11.0511	10.1161
29	25.0658	21.8444	19.1885	16.9837	15.1411	13.5907	12.2777	11.1584	10.1983
30	25.8077	22.3965	19.6004	17.2920	15.3725	13.7648	12.4090	11.2578	10.2737
35	29.4086	24.9986	21.4872	18.6646	16.3742	14.4982	12.9477	11.6546	10.5668
40	32.8347	27.3555	23.1148	19.7928	17.1591	15.0463	13.3317	11.9246	10.7574
45	36.0945	29.4902	24.5187	20.7200	17.7741	15.4558	13.6055	12.1084	10.8812
50	39.1961	31.4236	25.7298	21.4822	18.2559	15.7619	13.8007	12.2335	10.9617
55	42.1472	33.1748	26.7744	22.1086	18.6335	15.9905	13.9399	12.3186	11.0140

Number of Periods	10%	12%	14%	15%	16%	18%	20%	24%	28%	32%
1	0.9091	0.8929	0.8772	0.8696	0.8621	0.8475	0.8333	0.8065	0.7813	0.7576
2	1.7355	1.6901	1.6467	1.6257	1.6052	1.5656	1.5278	1.4568	1.3916	1.3315
3	2.4869	2.4018	2.3216	2.2832	2.2459	2.1743	2.1065	1.9813	1.8684	1.7663
4	3.1699	3.0373	2.9137	2.8550	2.7982	2.6901	2.5887	2.4043	2.2410	2.0957
5	3.7908	3.6048	3.4331	3.3522	3.2743	3.1272	2.9906	2.7454	2.5320	2.3452
6	4.3553	4.1114	3.8887	3.7845	3.6847	3.4976	3.3255	3.0205	2.7594	2.5342
7	4.8684	4.5638	4.2883	4.1604	4.0386	3.8115	3.6046	3.2423	2.9370	2.6775
8	5.3349	4.9676	4.6389	4.4873	4.3436	4.0776	3.8372	3.4212	3.0758	2.7860
9	5.7590	5.3282	4.9464	4.7716	4.6065	4.3030	4.0310	3.5655	3.1842	2.8681
10	6.1446	5.6502	5.2161	5.0188	4.8332	4.4941	4.1925	3.6819	3.2689	2.9304
11	6.4951	5.9377	5.4527	5.2337	5.0286	4.6560	4.3271	3.7757	3.3351	2.9776
12	6.8137	6.1944	5.6603	5.4206	5.1971	4.7932	4.4392	3.8514	3.3868	3.0133
13	7.1034	6.4235	5.8424	5.5831	5.3423	4.9095	4.5327	3.9124	3.4272	3.0404
14	7.3667	6.6282	6.0021	5.7245	5.4675	5.0081	4.6106	3.9616	3.4587	3.0609
15	7.6061	6.8109	6.1422	5.8474	5.5755	5.0916	4.6755	4.0013	3.4834	3.0764
16	7.8237	6.9740	6.2651	5.9542	5.6685	5.1624	4.7296	4.0333	3.5026	3.0882
17	8.0216	7.1196	6.3729	6.0472	5.7487	5.2223	4.7746	4.0591	3.5177	3.0971
18	8.2014	7.2497	6.4674	6.1280	5.8178	5.2732	4.8122	4.0799	3.5294	3.1039
19	8.3649	7.3658	6.5504	6.1982	5.8775	5.3162	4.8435	4.0967	3.5386	3.1090
20	8.5136	7.4694	6.6231	6.2593	5.9288	5.3527	4.8696	4.1103	3.5458	3.1129
21	8.6487	7.5620	6.6870	6.3125	5.9731	5.3837	4.8913	4.1212	3.5514	3.1158
22	8.7715	7.6446	6.7429	6.3587	6.0113	5.4099	4.9094	4.1300	3.5558	3.1180
23	8.8832	7.7184	6.7921	6.3988	6.0442	5.4321	4.9245	4.1371	3.5592	3.1197
24	8.9847	7.7843	6.8351	6.4338	6.0726	5.4509	4.9371	4.1428	3.5619	3.1210
25	9.0770	7.8431	6.8729	6.4641	6.0971	5.4669	4.9476	4.1474	3.5640	3.1220
26	9.1609	7.8957	6.9061	6.4906	6.1182	5.4804	4.9563	4.1511	3.5656	3.1227
27	9.2372	7.9426	6.9352	6.5135	6.1364	5.4919	4.9636	4.1542	3.5669	3.1233
28	9.3066	7.9844	6.9607	6.5335	6.1520	5.5016	4.9697	4.1566	3.5679	3.1237
29	9.3696	8.0218	6.9830	6.5509	6.1656	5.5098	4.9747	4.1585	3.5687	3.1240
30	9.4269	8.0552	7.0027	6.5660	6.1772	5.5168	4.9789	4.1601	3.5693	3.1242
35	9.6442	8.1755	7.0700	6.6166	6.2153	5.5386	4.9915	4.1644	3.5708	3.1248
40	9.7791	8.2438	7.1050	6.6418	6.2335	5.5482	4.9966	4.1659	3.5712	3.1250
45	9.8628	8.2825	7.1232	6.6543	6.2421	5.5523	4.9986	4.1664	3.5714	3.1250
50	9.9148	8.3045	7.1327	6.6605	6.2463	5.5541	4.9995	4.1666	3.5714	3.1250
55	9.9471	8.3170	7.1376	6.6636	6.2482	5.5549	4.9998	4.1666	3.5714	3.1250

Appendix A Mathematical Tables

Compounding

Table A-3 Future Value of $1 at the End of n Periods: $FVIF_{k,n} = (1 + k)^n$

Period	1%	2%	3%	4%	5%	6%	7%	8%	9%	10%
1	1.0100	1.0200	1.0300	1.0400	1.0500	1.0600	1.0700	1.0800	1.0900	1.1000
2	1.0201	1.0404	1.0609	1.0816	1.1025	1.1236	1.1449	1.1664	1.1881	1.2100
3	1.0303	1.0612	1.0927	1.1249	1.1576	1.1910	1.2250	1.2597	1.2950	1.3310
4	1.0406	1.0824	1.1255	1.1699	1.2155	1.2625	1.3108	1.3605	1.4116	1.4641
5	1.0510	1.1041	1.1593	1.2167	1.2763	1.3382	1.4026	1.4693	1.5386	1.6105
6	1.0615	1.1262	1.1941	1.2653	1.3401	1.4185	1.5007	1.5869	1.6771	1.7716
7	1.0721	1.1487	1.2299	1.3159	1.4071	1.5036	1.6058	1.7138	1.8280	1.9487
8	1.0829	1.1717	1.2668	1.3686	1.4775	1.5938	1.7182	1.8509	1.9926	2.1436
9	1.0937	1.1951	1.3048	1.4233	1.5513	1.6895	1.8385	1.9990	2.1719	2.3579
10	1.1046	1.2190	1.3439	1.4802	1.6289	1.7908	1.9672	2.1589	2.3674	2.5937
11	1.1157	1.2434	1.3842	1.5395	1.7103	1.8983	2.1049	2.3316	2.5804	2.8531
12	1.1268	1.2682	1.4258	1.6010	1.7959	2.0122	2.2522	2.5182	2.8127	3.1384
13	1.1381	1.2936	1.4685	1.6651	1.8856	2.1329	2.4098	2.7196	3.0658	3.4523
14	1.1495	1.3195	1.5126	1.7317	1.9799	2.2609	2.5785	2.9372	3.3417	3.7975
15	1.1610	1.3459	1.5580	1.8009	2.0789	2.3966	2.7590	3.1722	3.6425	4.1772
16	1.1726	1.3728	1.6047	1.8730	2.1829	2.5404	2.9522	3.4259	3.9703	4.5950
17	1.1843	1.4002	1.6528	1.9479	2.2920	2.6928	3.1588	3.7000	4.3276	5.0545
18	1.1961	1.4282	1.7024	2.0258	2.4066	2.8543	3.3799	3.9960	4.7171	5.5599
19	1.2081	1.4568	1.7535	2.1068	2.5270	3.0256	3.6165	4.3157	5.1417	6.1159
20	1.2202	1.4859	1.8061	2.1911	2.6533	3.2071	3.8697	4.6610	5.6044	6.7275
21	1.2324	1.5157	1.8603	2.2788	2.7860	3.3996	4.1406	5.0338	6.1088	7.4002
22	1.2447	1.5460	1.9161	2.3699	2.9253	3.6035	4.4304	5.4365	6.6586	8.1403
23	1.2572	1.5769	1.9736	2.4647	3.0715	3.8197	4.7405	5.8715	7.2579	8.9543
24	1.2697	1.6084	2.0328	2.5633	3.2251	4.0489	5.0724	6.3412	7.9111	9.8497
25	1.2824	1.6406	2.0938	2.6658	3.3864	4.2919	5.4274	6.8485	8.6231	10.835
26	1.2953	1.6734	2.1566	2.7725	3.5557	4.5494	5.8074	7.3964	9.3992	11.918
27	1.3082	1.7069	2.2213	2.8834	3.7335	4.8223	6.2139	7.9881	10.245	13.110
28	1.3213	1.7410	2.2879	2.9987	3.9201	5.1117	6.6488	8.6271	11.167	14.421
29	1.3345	1.7758	2.3566	3.1187	4.1161	5.4184	7.1143	9.3173	12.172	15.863
30	1.3478	1.8114	2.4273	3.2434	4.3219	5.7435	7.6123	10.063	13.268	17.449
40	1.4889	2.2080	3.2620	4.8010	7.0400	10.286	14.974	21.725	31.409	45.259
50	1.6446	2.6916	4.3839	7.1067	11.467	18.420	29.457	46.902	74.358	117.39
60	1.8167	3.2810	5.8916	10.520	18.679	32.988	57.946	101.26	176.03	304.48

Period	12%	14%	15%	16%	18%	20%	24%	28%	32%	36%
1	1.1200	1.1400	1.1500	1.1600	1.1800	1.2000	1.2400	1.2800	1.3200	1.3600
2	1.2544	1.2996	1.3225	1.3456	1.3924	1.4400	1.5376	1.6384	1.7424	1.8496
3	1.4049	1.4815	1.5209	1.5609	1.6430	1.7280	1.9066	2.0972	2.3000	2.5155
4	1.5735	1.6890	1.7490	1.8106	1.9388	2.0736	2.3642	2.6844	3.0360	3.4210
5	1.7623	1.9254	2.0114	2.1003	2.2878	2.4883	2.9316	3.4360	4.0075	4.6526
6	1.9738	2.1950	2.3131	2.4364	2.6996	2.9860	3.6352	4.3980	5.2899	6.3275
7	2.2107	2.5023	2.6600	2.8262	3.1855	3.5832	4.5077	5.6295	6.9826	8.6054
8	2.4760	2.8526	3.0590	3.2784	3.7589	4.2998	5.5895	7.2058	9.2170	11.703
9	2.7731	3.2519	3.5179	3.8030	4.4355	5.1598	6.9310	9.2234	12.166	15.917
10	3.1058	3.7072	4.0456	4.4114	5.2338	6.1917	8.5944	11.806	16.060	21.647
11	3.4785	4.2262	4.6524	5.1173	6.1759	7.4301	10.657	15.112	21.199	29.439
12	3.8960	4.8179	5.3503	5.9360	7.2876	8.9161	13.215	19.343	27.983	40.037
13	4.3635	5.4924	6.1528	6.8858	8.5994	10.699	16.386	24.759	36.937	54.451
14	4.8871	6.2613	7.0757	7.9875	10.147	12.839	20.319	31.691	48.757	74.053
15	5.4736	7.1379	8.1371	9.2655	11.974	15.407	25.196	40.565	64.359	100.71
16	6.1304	8.1372	9.3576	10.748	14.129	18.488	31.243	51.923	84.954	136.97
17	6.8660	9.2765	10.761	12.468	16.672	22.186	38.741	66.461	112.14	186.28
18	7.6900	10.575	12.375	14.463	19.673	26.623	48.039	85.071	148.02	253.34
19	8.6128	12.056	14.232	16.777	23.214	31.948	59.568	108.89	195.39	344.54
20	9.6463	13.743	16.367	19.461	27.393	38.338	73.864	139.38	257.92	468.57
21	10.804	15.668	18.822	22.574	32.324	46.005	91.592	178.41	340.45	637.26
22	12.100	17.861	21.645	26.186	38.142	55.206	113.57	228.36	449.39	866.67
23	13.552	20.362	24.891	30.376	45.008	66.247	140.83	292.30	593.20	1178.7
24	15.179	23.212	28.625	35.236	53.109	79.497	174.63	374.14	783.02	1603.0
25	17.000	26.462	32.919	40.874	62.669	95.396	216.54	478.90	1033.6	2180.1
26	19.040	30.167	37.857	47.414	73.949	114.48	268.51	613.00	1364.3	2964.9
27	21.325	34.390	43.535	55.000	87.260	137.37	332.95	784.64	1800.9	4032.3
28	23.884	39.204	50.066	63.800	102.97	164.84	412.86	1004.3	2377.2	5483.9
29	26.750	44.693	57.575	74.009	121.50	197.81	511.95	1285.6	3137.9	7458.1
30	29.960	50.950	66.212	85.850	143.37	237.38	634.82	1645.5	4142.1	10143.
40	93.051	188.88	267.86	378.72	750.38	1469.8	5455.9	19427.	66521.	*
50	289.00	700.23	1083.7	1670.7	3927.4	9100.4	46890.	*	*	*
60	897.60	2595.9	4384.0	7370.2	20555.	56348.	*	*	*	*

*FVIF$_{k,n}$ > 99,999.

Appendix A Mathematical Tables

Table A-4 Future Value of an Annuity of $1 per Period for n Periods:

$$\text{FVIFA}_{k,n} = \sum_{t=1}^{n} (1 + k)^{n-t} = \frac{(1 + k)^n - 1}{k}$$

Number of Periods	1%	2%	3%	4%	5%	6%	7%	8%	9%	10%
1	1.0000	1.0000	1.0000	1.0000	1.0000	1.0000	1.0000	1.0000	1.0000	1.0000
2	2.0100	2.0200	2.0300	2.0400	2.0500	2.0600	2.0700	2.0800	2.0900	2.1000
3	3.0301	3.0604	3.0909	3.1216	3.1525	3.1836	3.2149	3.2464	3.2781	3.3100
4	4.0604	4.1216	4.1836	4.2465	4.3101	4.3746	4.4399	4.5061	4.5731	4.6410
5	5.1010	5.2040	5.3091	5.4163	5.5256	5.6371	5.7507	5.8666	5.9847	6.1051
6	6.1520	6.3081	6.4684	6.6330	6.8019	6.9753	7.1533	7.3359	7.5233	7.7156
7	7.2135	7.4343	7.6625	7.8983	8.1420	8.3938	8.6540	8.9228	9.2004	9.4872
8	8.2857	8.5830	8.8923	9.2142	9.5491	9.8975	10.260	10.637	11.028	11.436
9	9.3685	9.7546	10.159	10.583	11.027	11.491	11.978	12.488	13.021	13.579
10	10.462	10.950	11.464	12.006	12.578	13.181	13.816	14.487	15.193	15.937
11	11.567	12.169	12.808	13.486	14.207	14.972	15.784	16.645	17.560	18.531
12	12.683	13.412	14.192	15.026	15.917	16.870	17.888	18.977	20.141	21.384
13	13.809	14.680	15.618	16.627	17.713	18.882	20.141	21.495	22.953	24.523
14	14.947	15.974	17.086	18.292	19.599	21.015	22.550	24.215	26.019	27.975
15	16.097	17.293	18.599	20.024	21.579	23.276	25.129	27.152	29.361	31.772
16	17.258	18.639	20.157	21.825	23.657	25.673	27.888	30.324	33.003	35.950
17	18.430	20.012	21.762	23.698	25.840	28.213	30.840	33.750	36.974	40.545
18	19.615	21.412	23.414	25.645	28.132	30.906	33.999	37.450	41.301	45.599
19	20.811	22.841	25.117	27.671	30.539	33.760	37.379	41.446	46.018	51.159
20	22.019	24.297	26.870	29.778	33.066	36.786	40.995	45.762	51.160	57.275
21	23.239	25.783	28.676	31.969	35.719	39.993	44.865	50.423	56.765	64.002
22	24.472	27.299	30.537	34.248	38.505	43.392	49.006	55.457	62.873	71.403
23	25.716	28.845	32.453	36.618	41.430	46.996	53.436	60.893	69.532	79.543
24	26.973	30.422	34.426	39.083	44.502	50.816	58.177	66.765	76.790	88.497
25	28.243	32.030	36.459	41.646	47.727	54.865	63.249	73.106	84.701	98.347
26	29.526	33.671	38.553	44.312	51.113	59.156	68.676	79.954	93.324	109.18
27	30.821	35.344	40.710	47.084	54.669	63.706	74.484	87.351	102.72	121.10
28	32.129	37.051	42.931	49.968	58.403	68.528	80.698	95.339	112.97	134.21
29	33.450	38.792	45.219	52.966	62.323	73.640	87.347	103.97	124.14	148.63
30	34.785	40.568	47.575	56.085	66.439	79.058	94.461	113.28	136.31	164.49
40	48.886	60.402	75.401	95.026	120.80	154.76	199.64	259.06	337.88	442.59
50	64.463	84.579	112.80	152.67	209.35	290.34	406.53	573.77	815.08	1163.9
60	81.670	114.05	163.05	237.99	353.58	533.13	813.52	1253.2	1944.8	3034.8

Number of Periods	12%	14%	15%	16%	18%	20%	24%	28%	32%	36%
1	1.0000	1.0000	1.0000	1.0000	1.0000	1.0000	1.0000	1.0000	1.0000	1.0000
2	2.1200	2.1400	2.1500	2.1600	2.1800	2.2000	2.2400	2.2800	2.3200	2.3600
3	3.3744	3.4396	3.4725	3.5056	3.5724	3.6400	3.7776	3.9184	4.0624	4.2096
4	4.7793	4.9211	4.9934	5.0665	5.2154	5.3680	5.6842	6.0156	6.3624	6.7251
5	6.3528	6.6101	6.7424	6.8771	7.1542	7.4416	8.0484	8.6999	9.3983	10.146
6	8.1152	8.5355	8.7537	8.9775	9.4420	9.9299	10.980	12.136	13.406	14.799
7	10.089	10.730	11.067	11.414	12.142	12.916	14.615	16.534	18.696	21.126
8	12.300	13.233	13.727	14.240	15.327	16.499	19.123	22.163	25.678	29.732
9	14.776	16.085	16.786	17.519	19.086	20.799	24.712	29.369	34.895	41.435
10	17.549	19.337	20.304	21.321	23.521	25.959	31.643	38.593	47.062	57.352
11	20.655	23.045	24.349	25.733	28.755	32.150	40.238	50.398	63.122	78.998
12	24.133	27.271	29.002	30.850	34.931	39.581	50.895	65.510	84.320	108.44
13	28.029	32.089	34.352	36.786	42.219	48.497	64.110	84.853	112.30	148.47
14	32.393	37.581	40.505	43.672	50.818	59.196	80.496	109.61	149.24	202.93
15	37.280	43.842	47.580	51.660	60.965	72.035	100.82	141.30	198.00	276.98
16	42.753	50.980	55.717	60.925	72.939	87.442	126.01	181.87	262.36	377.69
17	48.884	59.118	65.075	71.673	87.068	105.93	157.25	233.79	347.31	514.66
18	55.750	68.394	75.836	84.141	103.74	128.12	195.99	300.25	459.45	700.94
19	63.440	78.969	88.212	98.603	123.41	154.74	244.03	385.32	607.47	954.28
20	72.052	91.025	102.44	115.38	146.63	186.69	303.60	494.21	802.86	1298.8
21	81.699	104.77	118.81	134.84	174.02	225.03	377.46	633.59	1060.8	1767.4
22	92.503	120.44	137.63	157.41	206.34	271.03	469.06	812.00	1401.2	2404.7
23	104.60	138.30	159.28	183.60	244.49	326.24	582.63	1040.4	1850.6	3271.3
24	118.16	158.66	184.17	213.98	289.49	392.48	723.46	1332.7	2443.8	4450.0
25	133.33	181.87	212.79	249.21	342.60	471.98	898.09	1706.8	3226.8	6053.0
26	150.33	208.33	245.71	290.09	405.27	567.38	1114.6	2185.7	4260.4	8233.1
27	169.37	238.50	283.57	337.50	479.22	681.85	1383.1	2798.7	5624.8	11198.0
28	190.70	272.89	327.10	392.50	566.48	819.22	1716.1	3583.3	7425.7	15230.3
29	214.58	312.09	377.17	456.30	669.45	984.07	2129.0	4587.7	9802.9	20714.2
30	241.33	356.79	434.75	530.31	790.95	1181.9	2640.9	5873.2	12941.	28172.3
40	767.09	1342.0	1779.1	2360.8	4163.2	7343.9	22729.	69377.	*	*
50	2400.0	4994.5	7217.7	10436.	21813.	45497.	*	*	*	*
60	7471.6	18535.	29220.	46058.	*	*	*	*	*	*

*$FVIFA_{k,n} > 99,999$.

Appendix B

Answers to Selected End-of-Chapter Problems

In this appendix we present some intermediate steps and final answers to selected end-of-chapter problems. Please note that your answer may differ slightly from ours due to rounding errors. Also, although we hope not, some of the problems may have more than one correct solution, depending on the assumptions made in working the problem. Finally, many of the problems involve some verbal discussion as well as numerical calculations; that verbal material is not presented here.

2-1 a. $41,750
     b. 27.83%
     c. 39%

2-2 a. $26,150
     b. $11,700
     c. $3,510

2-3 $22,400

2-4 a. $50,450
     b. $11,768
     c. 23.33%
     d. 33%

2-5 1990 refund = $180,000

2-6 a. $22,163
     b. Marginal rate = 33%; Average rate = 27%
     d. 18.2%

2-7 $53,000; $77,000; $34,000; $19,000; $11,000; $6,000

2-8 a. $33,000; $45,000; $15,000
     b. $5,250; $6,000; $32,000

3-1 b. $75,000,000

3-2 b. $60,000,000

4-1   **a.** $k_1 = 10.2\%$; $k_5 = 9.6\%$; $k_{20} = 9.9\%$

4-4 $IP_2 = 10\%$; k_1 in Year 2 = 13%

4-5   **a.** k_1 in Year 2 = 13%
          b. $IP_1 = 7\%$; $IP_2 = 10\%$

5-2 $2,555

5-3   **a.** $36,400

5-4   **a.** $300,000
          b. $375,000
          c. $500,000

5-6   **a.** $1.80
          b. $1.00
          c. $4,000

5-7   CS = $10,000,000; Paid-in capital = $14,400,000; Total equity = $66,800,000

5-8   **a.** $6.16
          b. $4.00
          c. RE = $53,200,000; Total equity = $77,600,000

5-9 $1,181,250

5-10 **a.** $0
          b. +$700,000
          c. +Profit
          d. +Profit
          e. −$200,000
          f. −$50,000

5-11 **a.** $790,000,000
          b. $3.00

5-12 −$60

5-13 −$400,000

5-14 $540

5-15 Total sources = $117 million

6-1   7.68%

6-2   24%

6-3   60%

6-4   3.02%

6-5   40 days

6-6   3×; 120 days

6-7   **a.** 43 days
          b. 47.78 days

6-8 $500,000; quick ratio = 1.2×

6-9 $1,250,000

6-10 2%; 40%

6-11 $2,880,000; DSO = 25 days

6-12   Fixed assets = $400,000; Total assets = $1,200,000; Current liabilities = $400,000; A/R = $250,000; Total debt = $480,000; R/E = $620,000

6-13   **a.** Current ratio 1.98; DSO = 75 days; Total assets turnover = 1.7; Debt ratio = 61.9%

6-14   **a.** TIE = 6.2×;
          S/TA = 1.6×;
          ROA = 3.7%

6-15   **a.** Inv. = $2,500;
          RE = $7,500;
          Int. = $2,500

6-16   **a.** 16%
          b. ROE = 20.99%

6-17   **a.** Quick ratio = 0.8; DSO = 37 days; ROE = 11.9%; Debt ratio = 56.3%

7-1   **a.** Total assets = $10.8 million
          b. $5,370,000

7-2   **a.** Total debt = $960,000
          b. $86,000

7-3   **a.** $370,000
          b. $81,000; $289,000
          c. 58.18%
          d. Current ratio = 1.66
          e. ROA = 5.45%

7-4   **a.** $220,000
          b. $81,000; $139,000
          c. 53.48%
          d. Current ratio = 1.95
          e. 6.07%

7-5   3.83%

7-6 $750,000

7-7 $2,250,000 excess funds

7-8   − $28,000 (surplus)

7-9 $600,000

7-10 $69,000,000

7-11 **a.** $16,325,000
          c. Current ratio = 1.87, ROE = 14.72%
          d. 1. $6,175,000 excess funds
          d. 3. Current ratio = 3.4, ROE = 11.37%

7-12 **b.** $1,080,000

7-13 **b.** 25% sales increase
          c. $5,400,000
          d. 10.64% ROE

7-14   **b.** $103,500
           d. 3.03%

7-15   **a.** AFN = $590,000

8-1   **a.** $1,800,000
         b. $1,220,000

8-2   **a.** 100 days
         b. $432,000
         c. 4 times

8-3   **a.** 45 days
         b. $405,000
         c. $45,000
         d. 42 days; $504,000

8-4   **a.** 10.08%; 11.52%
         b. 9.12%; 7.68%

8-5   **a.** Current ratio = 1.6; NWC = $3,750,000; ROE = 13.33%
         b. Current ratio = 2.4; NWC = $8,750,000; ROE = 11.2%

8-6   **a.** Plan 1: CR = 1.0; NWC = $0;
             D/TA = 0.48; ROE = 13.27%
             Plan 2: CR = 3.0; NWC = $3,000,000;
             D/TA = 0.48; ROE = 12.30%
             Plan 3: CR = 1.5; NWC = $1,500,000;
             D/TA = 0.24; ROE = 11.02%

8-7   **a.** Inventory turnover = 6.67
         b. Inventory turnover period = 54 days
         c. DSO = 70 days
         d. Cash cycle = 89 days
         e. ROA = 8.04%

8-8   **a.** $400,000
         b. $500,000
         c. 55 days
         d. ROA = 9.47%

8-9   **a.** 56 days
         b. 1.875; 11.25%
         c. 41 days; 2.03; 12.2%

8-10   **a.** ROE for: aggressive 15.58%; moderate 14.40%; conservative 12.35%

9-1   **b. 1.** $1,500,000
         b. 2. − $6,500,000

9-2   **a.** $2,700,000
         b. $270,000
         c. $22,500

9-3   Jan. $62,000; Feb. $67,200; Mar. $65,600

9-4   June $33,487.50; July $50,962.50; August $61,837.50

9-5   May $248,800,000; June $223,000,000; July $132,800,000

9-6   **a.** Dec. − $4,400; Jan. − $11,200; Feb. + $2,000
　　　　b. $164,400

9-7   Feb. − $1,580; Mar. + $2,840; Apr. + $1,160

9-8   **a.** July surplus cash = $33,875; October loans = $22,000

10-1   DSO = 85 days

10-2   **a.** DSO = 31 days
　　　　b. A/R = $62,000
　　　　c. DSO = 22 days; A/R = $44,000

10-3   **a.** DSO before = 26.5 days; after = 21 days
　　　　b. Before $662,500; after $525,000

10-4   **a.** DSO before = 25 days; after = 20 days
　　　　b. Discount costs are $19,600 before; $45,864 after change
　　　　c. $9,722.22 before; $10,111.11 after change
　　　　d. Bad debt loss is $40,000 before; $52,000 after change
　　　　e. $84,808

10-5 NI_3 = $46,811; NI_4 = $15,467; NI_5 = $8,539

10-6   No, ΔNI = − $2,010

10-7   **a.** NI_0 = $424,400; NI_N = $431,928

10-8   **a.** 600 pounds
　　　　b. 10 orders
　　　　c. 300 pounds

10-9   EOQ = 70 dozen boxes

10-10   **a.** 4,200 bags
　　　　b. 5,200 bags; $10,400
　　　　c. 3,100 bags; $6,200
　　　　d. 8.57 days

10-11   BT net benefit = $1,000

10-12   BT net benefit = $221

10-13   **a.** 90,000 square yards
　　　　b. $110,000
　　　　c. $40,000
　　　　d. 51,538 square yards

10-14   **a.** 21,000 units
　　　　b. 35 orders
　　　　c. 21,135 units

11-1   **a.** 18.18%
　　　　b. 24.24%
　　　　c. 36.73%
　　　　d. 29.39%
　　　　e. 7.27%
　　　　f. 22.27%
　　　　g. 111.34%

11-2   **a.** 27.84%

11-3   **a.** $138,889
    c. $416,667; 36.73%

11-4   **a.** $136.11
    b. Avg. w/Disc't = $1,361.11; w/o Disc't = $6,805.56;
       Free credit = $1,361.11; Costly credit = $5,444.45
    c. 18.4%

11-5   **a.** 12%
    b. 13.64%
    c. 24%

11-6   **a.** 14%
    b. 13.75%
    c. 13.92%
    d. 18%

11-7   **a.** 15%
    b. $112,500

11-8   15.625%

11-9   **a.** 18.37%
    b. 16.25%

11-10 15.29%

11-11 13.68%

11-12 **a.** (1) 55.67% (2) 18.56% (3) 24.09%

11-13 **b.** 12.58%
    c. 12.25%
    d. 12.06%
    e. 12.00%

11-14 **a.** Bank 11.11%; trade 14.69%

11-15 **a.** $150,000

11-16 **a.** 60 days
    b. 14.69%

11-17 **a. 1.** Trade 18.18%
    a. 2. Bank 12.68%

11-18 **a. 1.** $13,750
    a. 2. $20,417
    a. 3. $12,917
    a. 4. $16,167

11A-1 **a.** $Cost_L$ = $124,875;
        $Cost_F$ = $123,338

11A-2 $69,250

11A-3 **a.** $60,000

11A-4 **a.** $510,638
    b. Mos. cost = $10,638;
       Mos. savings = $11,213;
       Mos. net savings = $574

12-1 **a.** 7.5%
b. 6.42%

12-2 **a.** 15%
b. 27.73%
c. $CV_x = 1.46$; $CV_y = 1.18$

12-3 **a.** 11%
b. 13%
c. 17%

12-4 **a.** 14.4%

k_M	k_s

b. 1. 14%   16.4%
    2. 6% 10 12.4%
c. 1. $k_s = 17.6\%$
    2. $k_s = 11.2\%$

12-5 **a.** $10,000
d. 1. $1,800
    2. 18%

12-6 **a.** $k = 9\% + 0.96 (14\% - 9\%)$
b. 13.8%
c. 19%

12-7 **a.** Project A $4,500; Project B $5,100

12-8 **a.** $k_y = 11.30\%$; $k_z = 11.30\%$
b. $k_p = 11.30\%$
c. $\sigma_y = 20.79\%$; $\sigma_z = 20.78\%$; $\sigma_p = 20.13\%$
d. $CV_y = 1.84$; $CV_z = 1.84$; $CV_p = 1.78$

13-1 **a.** $1,060.00
b. $1,123.60
c. $943.40
d. $890.00

13-2 **a.** $1,628.90
b. $2,593.70
c. $613.90
d. $1,000.00

13-3 **a.** Between 14 and 15 years
b. Between 7 and 8 years
c. Between 4 and 5 years
d. 1 year

13-4 **a.** $13,181.00
b. $12,705.60
c. $5,000.00

13-5 **a.** $13,971.86
b. $14,230.27
c. $5,000.00

13-6   **a.** $7,360.10
    b. $7,209.60
    c. $5,000.00

13-7   **a.** $7,801.71
    b. $8,074.75
    c. $5,000.00

13-8   **a.** $PV_A = \$10,795.70$
       $PV_B = \$11,948.50$
    b. $15,000

13-9 $18,694.30

13-10 **a.** 15%

13-11 **a.** $11,733.20
    b. $12,671.80

13-12 **a.** 10%
    b. 10%
    c. 12%
    d. 9%

13-13 16%

13-14 20%

13-15 8%

13-16 10%

13-17 **a.** $50,808.00
    b. $39,364.56; $0.00

13-18 $620.90

13-19 **a.** $73,411.74
    b. $65,546.19

13-20 **a.** Year 1 $5.5 million; Year 5 $8,052,500

13-21 $2,500; $1,250

13-22 **a.** $3,950.55

13-23 $4,000

13-24 15 years

13-25 $1,757.05

13A-1 **a.** $786.75
    b. $786.90
    c. $802.35
    d. $563.40

13A-2 **a.** $313.70
    b. $311.60
    c. $443.70

13A-3 **a.** $1,979.50
    b. $2,512.22

13A-4 10.38% vs. 11%

14-1 **a.** 4½ years
      b. $108,300
      c. 18%

14-2 **a.** 3.6 years
      b. $167,400
      c. 12%

14-3 **a.** 2.3 years
      b. $48,120
      c. 14%

14-4 **a.** 3.13 years
      b. $0
      c. 14%

14-5 **a.** 3.17 years
      b. − $3,183.20

14-6 **a.** $3,612.70
      b. 14%

	NPV	IRR
14-7 Truck	$ 499.99	16.0%
Pulley	3,513.38	20.0%

	NPV	IRR
14-8 Elec.	$2,898.78	≈ 20%
Gas	2,411.14	≈ 20%

	X	Y
14-9 **a.**	2.17 years	2.86 years
b.	$5,301.00	$4,378.60
c.	18%	15%

14-10 **a.** $28,831.50
       b. 20%

14-11 $NPV_A = \$92,872$; $NPV_O = \$76,952$

	Year 1	Year 2	Year 3
14-12 **a.** $132,000		$142,800	$153,600
b. $30,337.68			

14-13 **a.** $286,410
       b. $54,037

	Year 1	Year 2	Year 3	Year 4	Year 5	Year 6
14-14 Cash flow	$39,000	$46,200	$38,400	$34,200	$33,600	$30,600

NPV = $5,287.56

14A-1 **a.** 0%: $NPV_s = \$12,000.00$; $NPV_L = \$21,600.00$
         6%: $NPV_s = \$8,001.60$; $NPV_L = \$11,206.08$
       c. $IRR_s = 21.53\%$; $IRR_L = 15.34\%$

14A-2 **a.** $Payback_M = 2\frac{1}{3}$ yrs; $Payback_O = 4\frac{1}{8}$ yrs
       b. 0%: $NPV_M = \$60,000$; $NPV_O = \$105,000$

6%: $NPV_M = \$33,331$; $NPV_O = \$47,717$
20%: $NPV_M = -\$11,533$; $NPV_O = -\$36,225$

14A-3   **b.** $IRR_A = 17.5\%$; $IRR_B = 24.0\%$

15-1   **a.** $34,200
        b. $4,912.02
        c. 15.80%

15-2 $59,043.64

15-3   NPV = $1,475.53

15-4   **a.** 14%
        b. $\approx\$0$
        c. 14%

15-5   **a.** 15%
        b. $12,723.20
        c. $\approx18\%$

15-6   **a.** $k_E = 14\%$; $k_F = 16\%$
        c. NPV_E @ 14% $= -\$23,538.66$;
          NPV_F @ 16% $= -\$10,090.60$

15-7   **a.** 18%
        b. $-$30,354

15-8 $NPV_A = \$4,000.01$;
       $NPV_B = \$5,731.58$

15-9   **a.** $-$790,000
        b. $\Delta Dep_1 = \$150,000$; $\Delta Dep_6 = \$10,000$
        c. Cash flow: Year 1 = $210,000; Year 6 = $154,000
        d. $45,000

15-10 $NPV_G = \$3,264.92$;
       $NPV_W = \$2,472.30$

15-11   **a.** $-$60,200
        b. $CF_1 = \$5,840$;
          $CF_3 = -\$2,800$
        c. $12,000
        d. NPV $= -\$43,747.38$

15-12   **a.** $-$172,000
        b. $CF_1 = \$87,200$; $CF_8 = \$68,000$
        c. $19,200
        d. NPV = $172,504.46

15-13   **a.** 16.5%
        b. Recap NPV = $8,682; Tire NPV $= -\$14,440$

16-1   **a.** $58.33

16-2   **a.** 14.13%
        b. 15%

16-3 $1,204.33

16-4 $1,206.46

16-5   **a. 1.** $1,081.15
      2. $1,000.00
      3. $926.41
   b. 1. $1,018.91
      2. $1,000.00
      3. $981.67

16-6   **a.** (1) 12.0%; (2) 6.0%

16-7   **a.** $844.47

16-8   **a.** $790,107.85
   b. $397,377.31
   c. $832,708.80
   d. $438,231.30

16-9   PMT = $388,033.06

	Year 1	Year 2	Year 3
16-10 a.	$295,623.14	$295,623.14	$595,623.14
b.	$698,112		

16-11 $43.53

16-12   **a.** YTM = 8.73%; YTC = 6.85%

17-1 $50.00

17-2 $53.00

17-3 $63.12

17-4 $26.67

17-5   **a.** 10%
   b. 17%

17-6   **a.** 6%
   b. $75.75

17-7 $35.71

17-8   **a.** D_1 = $2.10; D_2 = $2.205; D_3 = $2.3153
   b. $5.29
   c. $24.72
   d. $30.01
   e. $30.00

17-9   **a.** 8%
   b. 10%
   c. 18%

17-10   **a. 1.** $16.76
      2. $25.00
      3. $45.00
      4. $109.00
      5. $333.00
   b. 1. Undefined
      2. − $115.00

17-11 $20.00

17-12 **a.** $24.54

17-13 $24.41

17-14 $30.84

17-15 $10.54

17-16 **a.** $35.00
  b. $33.33
  c. $46.67
  d. $63.04

17-17 $108.85

17-18 **a.** No, new price = $29.44
  b. Beta = 0.70

17-19 **a.**

	1985	1990
EPS	$4,080	$ 6,000
DPS	$2,100	$ 3,000
Book value per share		$45,000

  d.

	1985	1990
EPS	$1.02	$ 1.50
DPS	$0.525	$ 0.75
Book value per share		$11.25

  g.

	ROE
Gemex	15.00%
Diamond Gallery	13.64%
Krauss	13.33%

  h.

	Debt Ratio
Gemex	42.86%
Diamond Gallery	36.59%
Krauss	55.00%

  i.

	P/E
Gemex	8.00×
Diamond Gallery	8.67×

  k.

Gemex	15.18%
Diamond Gallery	12.54%

17-20 **a.** P_0 = $47.60

18-1 $873,846

18-2 $766,538

18-4 PV_O = $2,760,627; PV_L = $2,667,429; NAL = $93,198; Lease

18-5 **a.** PV_O = $1,362,137; PV_L = $1,306,383; NAL = $55,754; Lease

18-6 **a.** −$2; $0; $3; $33
  d. 9%

18-8   **b.** Percent ownership: Original = 80%; Plan 1 = 53%; Plans 2 and 3 = 57%
     c. EPS_0 = $0.48; EPS_1 = $0.60; EPS_2 = $0.64; EPS_3 = $0.86
     d. D/A_1 = 13%; D/A_2 = 13%; D/A_3 = 48%

19-1   **a.** 11%
     b. 7.26%
     c. 6.6%
     d. 4.4%

19-2   7.5%

19-3   **a.** $863.79
     b. 12%

19-4   14.13%

19-5   **a.** 13.75%
     b. 13.75%

19-6   **a.** 8.82%
     b. 9%

19-7   17.7%

19-8   **a.** 9%
     b. $1.526
     c. 16.98% ≈ 17%

19-9   **a.** 15%
     b. 11.4%
     c. 13.0%

19-10   **a.** 14%
     b. 13.6%
     c. 13.5% − 15.5%; Avg = 14.5%
     d. 13.6% − 14.5%; ≈ 14%

19-11   **a.** 15%
     b. 7%
     c. 15.68%

19-12   **a.** 15%
     b. 6.75%
     c. 16.75%

19-13   **a.** DCF = 29%; CAPM = 16%; BY = 14–16%

19-14   **a.** $3,000,000
     b. $7,000,000
     c. $11,666,666.67
     d. $18,750,000; $31,250,000

19-15 $785,471

19-16   12.054%

19-17 $18,000,000

19-18   Projects A and B; $17,000

19-19   Projects B and C; $64,000

19-20   **a.** k_d = 7.2%; k_s = 16%
         b. 11.6%
         c. $7,800,000
         d. 17%

19-21   **a.** $15,000,000
         b. $9,000,000
         c. $3,000,000; $6,000,000
         d. k_s = 15%; k_e = 16.06%
         e. $5,000,000
         f. **1.** 11.64%
             2. 12.28%

19-22   **a.** 3
         c. 11.16%; 11.83%; 12.31%; 12.79%
         d. 16%; 14%

20-1   60%

20-2   **a.** 50,000 units
        b. $2,250,000
        c. 4.33
        d. −$112,500

20-3   **a.** 70,000 units
        b. $3,150,000
        c. 5.67
        d. −$225,000

20-4   **a.** $3,000,000
        b. 6
        c. $3,900,000
        e. $2,100,000

20-5   **a.**

Sales	Option 1	Option 2
$ 40,000	− 1.00	− 0.50
$120,000	3.00	∞
$360,000	1.29	1.50

20-6 $54

20-7 $150,000

20-8   **a.** DOL = 2.15
        b. DFL = 2.45
        c. DTL = 5.28

20-9   **a.** DOL = 3
        b. DFL = 2
        c. DTL = 6

20-10   **a.** DOL = 11
        b. DFL = − 5
        c. DTL = − 55

20-11 $330,000

20-12 $13.33 million

20-13 **a.** $3.99

20-14 **a.**

	DOL	
Sales	**LOL**	**HOL**
$1.2 million	3	∞
$1.6 million	2	4

b.

	DFL			
	LOL		**HOL**	
Sales	**No Debt**	**$900,000 Debt**	**No Debt**	**$900,000 Debt**
$1.2 million	1.00	10.00	1.00	0.00
$1.6 million	1.00	1.82	1.00	1.82

c.

	DTL	
Sales	**LOL**	**HOL**
$1.2 million	30.00	-6.67
$1.6 million	3.64	7.27

20-15 k_s, 0% Debt = 14.5%; k_s, 30% Debt = 16%

20-16 **a.**

	Debt Financing	**Stock Financing**
Expected EPS	$3.96	$3.67
σ_{EPS}	$0.70	$0.57
D/A	75.46%	58.80%
TIE	3.75 $\times$	6.00 $\times$

20A-1 **a.** Distribution: CL = $13,500,000; FA = $13,875,000
b. Distribution: 2nd Mtg. = $2,500,000; Deb. = $2,000,000

20A-2 **a.** Distribution: A/P = $346; 2nd Mtg. = $364; Subord. Deb. = $250

21-1 **a.** 62.5%
b. $3,000,000
c. 60%
d. $10,500,000

21-2 10%

21-3 $1,560,000

21-4 Total equity = $11,400,000; Paid-in capital = $6,120,000

21-5 9.09%

21-6 $11.3636

21-7 Paid-in capital = $513.75; Assets = $2,978.4375

21-8 **a.** $3,375,000
b. $6,250,000
c. $5,000,000
d. $13,000,000

21-9 **a.** Payout = 63.16%; Break point = $9,545,455; MCC_1 = 11.22%; MCC_2 = 11.51%
b. $15 million

22-1   − $243,420

22-2 $156,845

22-3 $34,170,539

22-4   **a.** 18.48%

22-5   **a.** 18%
              b. Terminal value = $283,500

22-6   **a.** 14%
              b. $25,493,273
              c. $17.00

23-1   0.5495 pounds per dollar

23-2   6.0606 francs per dollar

23-3   10.01 francs per pound

23-5

Dollars per 1,000 Units of				
Rupees	**Lira**	**Yen**	**Pesos**	**Riyals**
$57.27	$0.83	$6.76	$0.35	$266.81

23-7   **b.** $13,243.24

23-8   **a.** $2,905,393.14
              b. $2,893,152.27
              d. $3,200,000

23-9 $58.67

23-10 $350,000 gain

Appendix C

Selected Equations

Chapter 4

$$\text{Nominal interest rate} = k = k^* + IP + DRP + LP + MRP.$$

$$k = k_{RF} + DRP + LP + MRP.$$

$$k_{\text{T-bill}} = k_{RF} = k^* + IP.$$

Chapter 5

$$EPS = \frac{\text{Net income}}{\text{Shares outstanding}}.$$

$$DPS = \frac{\text{Dividends paid to common stockholders}}{\text{Shares outstanding}}.$$

$$\text{Assets} - \text{Liabilities} = \text{Stockholders' equity}.$$

Chapter 6

$$\frac{\text{Current}}{\text{ratio}} = \frac{\text{Current assets}}{\text{Current liabilities}}.$$

$$\frac{\text{Quick, or}}{\text{acid test,}}_{\text{ratio}} = \frac{\text{Current assets} - \text{Inventory}}{\text{Current liabilities}}.$$

$$\frac{\text{Inventory}}{\text{turnover}} = \frac{\text{Sales}}{\text{Inventory}}.$$

$$\frac{\text{Days sales}}{\text{outstanding}}_{\text{(DSO)}} = \frac{\text{Receivables}}{\text{Average sales}} = \frac{\text{Receivables}}{\text{Annual sales}/360}.$$

$$\frac{\text{Fixed assets}}{\text{turnover}} = \frac{\text{Sales}}{\text{Net fixed assets}}.$$

$$\frac{\text{Total assets}}{\text{turnover}} = \frac{\text{Sales}}{\text{Total assets}}.$$

$$\frac{\text{Debt}}{\text{ratio}} = \frac{\text{Total debt}}{\text{Total assets}}.$$

$$TIE = \frac{\text{EBIT}}{\text{Interest charges}}.$$

$$\text{Fixed charge coverage} = \frac{\text{EBIT} + \text{Lease payments}}{\text{Interest charges} + \text{Lease payments} + \left(\dfrac{\text{Sinking fund payment}}{1 - \text{Tax rate}}\right)}$$

$$\frac{\text{Profit}}{\text{margin}} = \frac{\text{Net income}}{\text{Sales}}$$

$$\text{Basic earning power (BEP) ratio} = \frac{\text{EBIT}}{\text{Total assets}}$$

$$\text{Return on total assets (ROA)} = \frac{\text{Net income}}{\text{Total assets}}$$

$$\text{Return on common equity (ROE)} = \frac{\text{Net income}}{\text{Common equity}}$$

$$\text{Price/earnings ratio} = \frac{\text{Market price per share}}{\text{Earnings per share}}$$

$$\text{Book value per share} = \frac{\text{Stockholders' equity}}{\text{Shares outstanding}}$$

$$\text{Market/book ratio} = \frac{\text{Market price per share}}{\text{Book value per share}}$$

$$\text{ROE} = \text{ROA} \times \frac{\text{Total assets}}{\text{Common equity}}$$

$$\text{ROA} = \frac{\text{Profit}}{\text{margin}} \times \frac{\text{Total assets}}{\text{turnover}}$$

Chapter 7

$$\text{AFN} = A^*/S(\Delta S) - L^*/S(\Delta S) - MS_1(1 - d).$$

$$\frac{\text{Full capacity sales}}{} = \frac{\text{Current sales}}{\% \text{ fixed assets operated}}$$

Chapter 8

$$\frac{\text{Inventory}}{\text{conversion period}} + \frac{\text{Receivables}}{\text{conversion period}} - \frac{\text{Payables}}{\text{deferral period}} = \frac{\text{Cash}}{\text{conversion cycle}}.$$

Chapter 9

$$\text{Net float} = \text{Disbursement float} - \text{Collection float}.$$

Chapter 10

$$\text{Cost of carrying receivables} = (\text{DSO})(\text{Sales}/360)\left(\frac{\text{Variable cost}}{\text{ratio}}\right)\left(\frac{\text{Cost of}}{\text{funds}}\right).$$

$$\text{Opportunity cost} = (\text{Old sales}/360)(\Delta\text{DSO})(1 - v)(k).$$

$$\text{EOQ} = \sqrt{\frac{(F)(S)}{(C)(P)}}.$$

$$\text{Reorder point} = (\text{Lead time} \times \text{Usage rate}) - \text{Goods in transit}.$$

Chapter 11

$$\text{Approximate percentage cost} = \frac{\text{Discount percent}}{100 - \left(\begin{array}{c}\text{Discount} \\ \text{percent}\end{array}\right)} \times \frac{360}{\left(\begin{array}{c}\text{Days credit is} \\ \text{outstanding}\end{array}\right) - \left(\begin{array}{c}\text{Discount} \\ \text{period}\end{array}\right)}.$$

$$\text{Effective rate}_{\text{Simple}} = \frac{\text{Interest}}{\text{Borrowed amount}}.$$

$$\text{Effective rate}_{\text{Discount}} = \frac{\text{Interest}}{\begin{array}{c}\text{Face} \\ \text{value}\end{array} - \text{Interest}}.$$

$$\text{Approximate effective rate}_{\text{Add-on}} = \frac{\text{Interest}}{(\text{Loan amount})/2}.$$

$$\text{Effective rate}_{\text{Simple/CB}} = \frac{\text{Stated interest rate (\%)}}{1.0 - \begin{array}{c}\text{Compensating} \\ \text{balance percentage}\end{array}}.$$

$$\text{Amount borrowed}_{\text{Simple/CB}} = \frac{\text{Funds needed}}{1 - \begin{array}{c}\text{Compensating balance} \\ \text{percentage}\end{array}}.$$

$$\text{Effective rate}_{\text{Discount/CB}} = \frac{\text{Stated interest rate (\%)}}{1.0 - \left(\begin{array}{c}\text{Compensating balance} \\ \text{percentage}\end{array}\right) - \left(\begin{array}{c}\text{Stated} \\ \text{interest} \\ \text{rate}\end{array}\right)}.$$

$$\text{Amount borrowed}_{\text{Discount/CB}} = \frac{\text{Funds needed}}{1 - \left(\begin{array}{c}\text{Compensating balance} \\ \text{percentage}\end{array}\right) - \left(\begin{array}{c}\text{Stated} \\ \text{interest} \\ \text{rate}\end{array}\right)}.$$

Chapter 12

$$\text{Expected rate of return} = \hat{k} = \sum_{i=1}^{n} P_i k_i.$$

$$\text{Variance} = \sigma^2 = \sum_{i=1}^{n} (k_i - \hat{k})^2 P_i.$$

$$\text{Standard deviation} = \sigma = \sqrt{\sum_{t=1}^{n} (k_i - \hat{k})^2 P_i}.$$

$$k = k_{RF} + (k_M - k_{RF})b.$$

Chapter 13

$FV_n = PV(FVIF_{k,n})$. $FVIF_{k,n} = (1 + k)^n$.

$PV = FV_n(PVIF_{k,n})$. $PVIF_{k,n} = [1/(1 + k)^n] = (1/FVIF_{k,n})$.

$FVA_n = PMT(FVIFA_{k,n})$. $FVIFA_{k,n} = \dfrac{(1 + k)^n - 1}{k}$. $PV(\text{perpetuity}) = \dfrac{PMT}{k}$.

$FVA_n(\text{Annuity due}) = PMT(FVIFA_{k,n})(1 + k)$.

$PVA_n = PMT(PVIFA_{k,n})$. $PVIFA_{k,n} = \dfrac{1 - \dfrac{1}{(1 + k)^n}}{k}$.

$PVA_n(\text{Annuity due}) = PMT(PVIFA_{k,n})(1 + k)$.

Appendix 13A

$$FV_n = PV\left(1 + \frac{k_{Nom}}{m}\right)^{mn}$$

$$\text{Effective annual rate} = \left(1 + \frac{k_{Nom}}{m}\right)^m - 1.0.$$

Chapter 14

$$\text{Net cash flow} = (\$REV - \$EXP)(1 - t) + (DEP)(t)$$

$$NPV = \sum_{t=1}^{n} \frac{CF_t}{(1 + k)^t} - C \qquad IRR = \sum_{t=1}^{n} \frac{CF_t}{(1 + IRR)^t} - C = 0$$

$$= \sum_{t=1}^{n} CF_t(PVIF) - C. \qquad = \sum_{t=1}^{n} CF_t(PVIF) - C = 0.$$

Chapter 15

$$k_{Project} = k_{RF} + (k_M - k_{RF})b_{Project}.$$

$$k_n = k_r + i.$$

$$NPV = \sum_{t=1}^{n} \frac{RCF_t}{(1 + k_r)^t} - Cost.$$

$$\text{Inflation-adjusted NPV} = \sum_{t=1}^{n} \frac{RCF_t(1 + i)^t}{(1 + k_n)^t} - Cost.$$

Chapter 16

$$\text{Value} = V = \sum_{t=1}^{n} I\frac{1}{(1 + k_d)^t} + M\frac{1}{(1 + k_d)^n}$$

$$= I(\text{PVIFA}_{k_d,n}) + M(\text{PVIF}_{k_d,n}).$$

$$V = \sum_{t=1}^{2n} \frac{I}{2}\left(\frac{1}{1 + \dfrac{k_d}{2}}\right)^t + M\left(\frac{1}{1 + \dfrac{k_d}{2}}\right)^{2n} = \frac{I}{2}(\text{PVIFA}_{k_d/2,2n}) + M(\text{PVIF}_{k_d/2,2n}).$$

$$\text{Approximate YTM} = \frac{I + (M - V)/n}{(M + V)/2}.$$

$$V_{ps} = \frac{D_{ps}}{k_{ps}}.$$

Chapter 17

$$\hat{P}_0 = \frac{D_1}{(1 + k_s)^1} + \frac{D_2}{(1 + k_s)^2} + \cdots + \frac{D_\infty}{(1 + k_s)^\infty}$$

$$= \sum_{t=1}^{\infty} \frac{D_t}{(1 + k_s)^t}.$$

$$\hat{P}_0 = \frac{D_1}{k_s - g}.$$

$$\hat{k}_s = \frac{D_1}{P_0} + g.$$

Chapter 18

$$\text{After-tax cost} = \text{Lease payment}(1 - \text{Tax rate}).$$

$$\text{Formula value} = \text{Current price of the stock} - \text{Striking price}.$$

$$\begin{matrix}\text{Pure debt} \\ \text{value}\end{matrix} = \sum_{t=1}^{n} \frac{I}{(1 + k_s)^t} + \frac{M}{(1 + k_s)^n}.$$

$$\begin{matrix}\text{Price paid for bond} \\ \text{with warrants}\end{matrix} = \begin{matrix}\text{Straight-bond} \\ \text{value}\end{matrix} + \begin{matrix}\text{Value of} \\ \text{warrants}\end{matrix}.$$

$$\text{Conversion price} = P_c = \frac{\text{Par value of bond}}{\text{CR}}.$$

$$\text{CR} = \frac{\text{Par value of bond}}{P_c}.$$

$$\begin{matrix}\text{Convertible's} \\ \text{initial price}\end{matrix} = \sum_{t=1}^{n} \frac{\text{Interest}}{(1 + k_c)^t} + \frac{\begin{matrix}\text{Conversion} \\ \text{value}\end{matrix}}{(1 + k_c)^n}.$$

Chapter 19

$$\text{After-tax } k_d = k_d (1 - t). \qquad k_e = \frac{D_1}{P_0(1 - F)} + g.$$

$$k_p = D_p/P_n. \qquad \text{WACC} = w_d k_d(1 - t) + w_p(k_p) + w_s(k_s \text{ or } k_e).$$

$$\text{Break point} = \frac{\text{Total amount of lower-cost capital of a given type}}{\text{Fraction of this type of capital in the capital structure}}.$$

Chapter 20

$$Q_{BE} = \frac{F}{P - V}. \qquad\qquad \text{DOL} = \frac{Q(P - V)}{Q(P - V) - F}.$$

$$\text{DOL} = \frac{S - VC}{S - VC - F}. \qquad\qquad \text{DFL} = \frac{EBIT}{EBIT - I}.$$

$$\text{DTL} = \frac{Q(P - V)}{Q(P - V) - F - I}. \qquad \text{DTL} = \text{DOL} \times \text{DFL}.$$

Chapter 21

$$P_0 = E_1(1 - b)/(k_s - br).$$

Glossary

ABC system A system used to categorize inventory items to insure that the most important ones are reviewed most often.

accounting profit A firm's net income, as reported on its income statement.

account receivable A balance due from a customer.

accruals Continually recurring short-term liabilities, especially accrued wages and accrued taxes.

acquiring company A company that seeks to acquire another.

additional funds needed (AFN) Funds that a firm must acquire through borrowing or by selling new stock.

add-on interest Interest calculated and added to funds received to determine the face amount of an installment loan.

after-tax cost of debt, $k_d(1 - t)$ The relevant cost of new debt financing, taking into account the tax deductibility of interest; used to calculate the WACC.

aging schedule A report showing how long accounts receivable have been outstanding; gives the percentage of receivables currently past due, and the percentages past due by specified periods.

amortization schedule A schedule showing precisely how a loan will be repaid. It gives the required payment on each specified date and a breakdown of the payment showing how much constitutes interest and how much constitutes repayment of principal.

amortize To liquidate on an installment basis; an amortized loan is one in which the principal amount of the loan is repaid in installments during the life of the loan.

amortized loan A loan that is repaid in equal payments over its life.

annual report A report issued annually by a corporation to its stockholders. It contains the basic financial statements, along with management's opinion of the past year's operations and of the firm's future prospects.

annuity A series of payments of an equal, or constant, amount for a specified number of periods.

annuity due An annuity on which payments occur at the beginning of each period.

arrearage An omitted dividend on preferred stock.

asked price The price at which a dealer in securities will sell shares of stock out of inventory.

asset management ratios A set of ratios which measures how effectively a firm is managing its assets.

assets All items which the firm owns.

average tax rate Taxes paid divided by taxable income.

balance sheet A statement of the firm's financial position at a specific point in time.

bank holding company (BHC) A corporation, which owns bank and nonbank subsidiaries, originally designed to circumvent bank regulation.

basic earning power ratio This ratio indicates the ability of the firm's assets to generate operating income; computed by dividing EBIT by total assets.

best efforts arrangement Agreement for the sale of securities in which the investment bank handling the transaction gives no guarantee that the securities will be sold.

beta coefficient, b A measure of the extent to which the returns on a given stock move with the stock market.

beta risk See *market, or beta, risk.*

bid price The price a dealer in securities will pay for a stock.

blue sky laws State laws that prevent the sale of securities having little or no asset backing.

Board of Governors of the Federal Reserve System Seven-member decision-making authority of the Fed.

bond A long-term debt instrument.

bond ratings Ratings assigned to bonds based on the probability of their default. Those bonds with the smallest default probability are rated Aaa and carry the lowest interest rates.

bracket creep A situation that occurs when progressive tax rates combine with inflation to cause a greater portion of each taxpayer's real income to be paid as taxes.

break, or jump, in the MCC schedule A change in the weighted average cost of capital that occurs when there is a change in a component cost of capital.

break point (BP) The dollar value of total new capital that can be raised before an increase occurs in the firm's weighted average cost of capital.

breakeven point The volume of sales at which total operating costs equal total revenues, and operating profits (EBIT) equal zero.

business risk The risk associated with future operating income; the risk that would exist even if the firm's operations were all equity financed.

bylaws A set of rules for governing the management of a company.

call option An option to buy, or "call," a share of stock at a certain price within a specified period.

call premium The amount in excess of par value that a company must pay when it calls a security.

call provision A provision in a bond or preferred stock contract that gives the issuer the right to redeem the securities under specified terms before the normal maturity date.

capital account The account that represents a bank's total assets minus its short-term liabilities.

Capital Asset Pricing Model (CAPM) A model based on the proposition that any stock's required rate of return is equal to the risk-free rate of return plus its risk premium, where its risk reduction reflects the effects of diversification.

capital budgeting The process of planning expenditures on assets the returns of which extend beyond one year.

capital component One of the types of capital used by firms to raise money.

capital gain The profit from the sale of a capital asset for more than its purchase price.

capital gains yield The capital gain (appreciation in price) during any one year divided by the beginning price.

capital intensity ratio The amount of assets required per dollar of sales (A*/S).

capital loss The loss from the sale of a capital asset for less than its purchase price.

capital markets The financial markets for stocks and for long-term debt (one year or longer).

capitalizing the lease Incorporating the lease provisions into the balance sheet by reporting the leased asset under fixed assets and reporting the present value of future lease payments as debt; required by FASB #13.

carrying costs The costs associated with carrying inventories, including storage, capital, and depreciation costs. Carrying costs generally increase in proportion to the average amount of inventory held.

cash The total of bank demand deposits plus currency.

cash account The account that represents a bank's vault cash, checks in process of collection, and funds required to be kept on deposit with the Federal Reserve.

cash budget A schedule showing cash flows (receipts, disbursements, and net cash) for a firm over a specified period.

cash conversion cycle The length of time from the payment for raw materials and labor to the collection of accounts receivable generated by the sale of the final product.

cash discount A reduction in the price of goods, given to encourage early payment.

cash flow The actual net cash, as opposed to accounting net income, that flows into (or out of) a firm during some specified period. It is equal to net income after taxes plus noncash expenses, including depreciation.

certificate of deposit (CD) A time deposit evidenced by a negotiable (for large-denomination CDs, generally $100,000 or more) or nonnegotiable (usually denominations under $100,000) receipt issued for funds deposited for a specified period of time; rates of interest generally depend on the amount of deposit, time to maturity, and the general level of interest rates.

change in net working capital The increased current assets required for a new project, minus the simultaneous increase in current liabilities.

Chapter 7 A chapter of the Bankruptcy Reform Act that governs liquidations, or selling of the firm's assets, due to bankruptcy.

Chapter 11 A chapter of the Bankruptcy Reform Act that governs reorganizations, or restructurings, due to bankruptcy.

charter A formal legal document that describes the scope and nature of a corporation and defines the rights and duties of its stockholders and managers.

check clearing The process of converting a check that has been written and mailed into cash in the payee's account.

classified stock Common stock that is given special designations, such as Class A, Class B, and so forth, to meet special needs of the company.

clientele effect The tendency of a firm to attract the type of investor who likes its dividend policy.

closely held corporation A corporation that is owned by a few individuals who are typically associated with the firm's management.

coefficient of variation Standardized measure of the risk per unit of return; calculated as the standard deviation divided by the expected return.

collateral Assets that are pledged to secure a loan.

collection float The amount of checks received but not yet credited to the account.

collection policy The procedures used to collect accounts receivable.

commercial finance companies Lending institutions that make both short- and long-term secured loans to businesses, generally at higher rates than commercial banks.

commercial paper Unsecured, short-term promissory notes of large, financially strong firms, usually issued in denominations of $100,000 or more and having an interest rate somewhat below the prime rate.

company-specific (diversifiable) risk That part of a security's risk associated with random events; it can be eliminated by proper diversification.

comparative ratio analysis An analysis based on a comparison of a firm's ratios with those of other firms in the same industry.

compensating balance (CB) A minimum checking account balance that a firm must maintain with a commercial bank to compensate the bank for services rendered, generally equal to 10 to 20 percent of the amount of the loans outstanding.

Competitive Equality in Banking Act (CEBA) An act passed in 1987 to stem the growth of banklike corporations.

compounding The arithmetic process of determining the final value of a payment or series of payments when compound interest is applied.

computerized inventory control system A system of inventory control in which computers are used to determine reorder points and to adjust inventory balances.

congeneric merger A merger of firms in the same general industry, but for which no customer or supplier relationship exists.

conglomerate merger A merger of companies in totally different industries.

consol A perpetual bond originally issued by the British government to consolidate past debts; in general, any perpetual bond.

consolidated return An income tax return that combines the income statements of several affiliated firms.

constant growth model Also called the Gordon Model; used to find the value of a constant growth stock.

conversion price, P_c The effective price paid for common stock obtained by converting a convertible security.

conversion ratio, CR The number of shares that are received when converting a convertible bond or share of convertible preferred stock.

conversion value, C_t The value of common stock obtained by converting a convertible security.

convertible bond A bond that is exchangeable, at the option of the holder, for common stock of the issuing firm.

convertible security A security, usually a bond or preferred stock, that is exchangeable at the option of the holder into shares of common stock.

corporate alliance Any type of cooperative business arrangement between two or more companies.

corporation A legal entity created by a state, separate and distinct from its owners and managers, having unlimited life, easy transferability of ownership, and limited liability.

cost of capital The discount rate that should be used in the capital budgeting process.

cost of new common equity, k_e The cost of external equity; based on the cost of retained earnings, but increased for flotation costs.

cost of preferred stock, k_p The preferred dividend, D_p, divided by the net issuing price, P_n. The rate of return investors require on the firm's preferred stock.

cost of retained earnings, k_s The rate of return required by stockholders on a firm's common stock.

costly trade credit Credit taken in excess of free trade credit, thereby necessitating a forfeit of the discount offered.

coupon interest rate The stated annual rate of interest on a bond.

coupon rate The stated, or nominal, rate of interest on a bond.

coverage The measure of a firm's ability to meet interest and principal payments; times interest earned (TIE) is the most common coverage ratio.

credit period The length of time for which credit is granted.

credit policy A set of decisions that includes a firm's credit period, discounts offered, credit standards, and collection policy.

credit standards Standards that stipulate the minimum financial strength that an applicant must demonstrate in order to be granted credit.

credit terms A statement of the credit period and any discounts offered — for example, 2/10, net 30.

cumulative dividends A protective feature on preferred stock that requires past preferred dividends to be paid before any common dividends can be paid.

current asset financial policy Basic policy decisions regarding target levels for each category of current assets, and regarding how current assets will be financed.

current asset management The administration, within policy guidelines, of current assets and the financing of those assets.

current ratio This ratio is computed by dividing current assets by current liabilities. It indicates the extent to which the claims of short-term creditors are covered by assets expected to be converted to cash in the near future.

current (interest) yield The annual interest payment on a bond divided by its current market price.

days sales outstanding (DSO) The ratio computed by dividing average *credit* sales per day into accounts receivable; indicates the average length of time the firm must wait after making a credit sale before receiving payment.

debenture A long-term debt instrument that is not secured by a mortgage on specific property.

debt ratio The ratio of total debt to total assets.

declaration date Date on which a firm's directors issue a statement declaring a regular dividend.

default risk The risk that a borrower will not pay the interest or principal on a loan.

default risk premium (DRP) The difference between the interest rate on a U.S. Treasury bond and a corporate bond of equal maturity and marketability.

defensive merger A merger designed to make a company less vulnerable to a takeover.

deficit trade balance A country's trade balance resulting from an excess of its imports over its exports.

degree of financial leverage (DFL) The percentage change in earnings available to common shareholders associated with a given percentage change in earnings before interest and taxes.

degree of operating leverage (DOL) The percentage change in EBIT resulting from a given percentage change in sales.

degree of total leverage (DTL) The percentage change in net income, EPS, and ROE brought about by a given percentage change in sales; DTL shows the effects of both operating leverage and financial leverage.

demand deposits Transaction deposits at commercial banks that are available on demand, usually through a check.

Depository Institutions Deregulation and Monetary Control Act (DIDMCA) An act that eliminated many of the distinctions between commercial banks and other depository institutions.

depreciable basis The portion of an asset's value which can be depreciated for tax purposes. The depreciable basis under MACRS is equal to the cost of the asset, including shipping and installation charges.

depreciation An annual noncash charge against income that reflects a rough estimate of the dollar cost of equipment used up in the production process.

detachable warrant A warrant that can be detached from a bond and traded separately.

devaluation The process of officially reducing the value of a country's currency relative to other currencies.

disbursement float The amount of checks that have been written but are still being processed and have not been deducted from the account balance by the bank.

discount bond A bond that sells below its par value; occurs when the going rate of interest is *higher* than the coupon rate.

discount interest Interest that is calculated on the face amount of a loan but is deducted in advance.

discount on forward rate The situation when the spot rate is less than the forward rate. The quotation is based on the number of units of foreign currency per U.S. dollar.

discount rate The interest rate used in the discounting process. Also, the interest rate charged by the Fed for loans of reserves to depository institutions.

discounted cash flow (DCF) techniques Methods of ranking investment proposals that employ time value of money concepts; two of these are the *net present value* and *internal rate of return* methods.

discounting The process of finding the present value of a payment or a series of future cash flows; the reverse of compounding.

divestiture The sale of some of a company's operating assets.

dividend policy decision The decision as to how much of current earnings to pay out as dividends rather than to retain for reinvestment in the firm.

dividend reinvestment plan (DRIP) A plan that enables a stockholder to automatically reinvest dividends received back into the stock of the paying firm.

dividend yield A stock's current dividend divided by the current price.

Du Pont chart A chart designed to show the relationships among return on investment, assets turnover, and the profit margin.

Du Pont equation A formula that finds the rate of return on assets by multiplying the profit margin by the total assets turnover.

earnings per share (EPS) The net income of the firm divided by the number of shares of common stock outstanding.

economic ordering quantity (EOQ) The optimal, or least-cost, quantity of inventory that should be ordered.

economic profit The amount left after all factors (labor and capital) have been paid.

effective annual rate The annual rate of interest actually being earned as opposed to the nominal or stated rate.

efficient capital market Market in which securities are fairly priced in the sense that the price reflects all publicly available information on each security.

EOQ model Formula for determining the ordering quantity that will minimize total inventory cost:

$$EOQ = \sqrt{\frac{2(F)(S)}{(C)(P)}}.$$

equilibrium price The price that will be low enough to induce investors to buy the stock, but not so low that it will rise sharply immediately after it is issued. Also, where $k_s = \hat{k}_s$.

equity Financing supplied by the firm's owners.

Eurobond A bond sold in a country other than the one in whose currency the bond is denominated.

Eurodollar A U.S. dollar deposited in a bank outside the United States.

ex-dividend date The date on which the right to the current dividend no longer accompanies a stock; it is four working days prior to the holder-of-record date.

excess capacity Capacity that exists when an asset is not being fully utilized.

excess reserves Reserves held by a commercial bank with a Federal Reserve bank in excess of the bank's required reserves.

exchange rate The number of units of a given currency that can be purchased for one unit of another currency.

exchange rate risk The risk that the basic cash flows of a foreign project will be worth less in the parent company's home currency.

expansion project A project that is intended to increase sales.

expectations theory The theory that the shape of the yield curve depends primarily on investors' expectations about future inflation rates.

expected dividend yield The expected dividend divided by the current price of a share of stock.

expected rate of return, $\hat{k}$ The rate of return expected to be realized from an investment; the mean value of the probability distribution of possible outcomes.

expected rate of return, $\hat{k}_s$ The rate of return on a common stock that a stockholder expects to receive.

expected total return The sum of the expected dividend yield and the expected capital gains yield on a share of stock.

externalities Effects of a project on cash flows in other parts of the firm.

extra dividend A supplementary dividend paid in years when excess funds are available.

factoring Outright sale of accounts receivable.

FASB #13 The statement of the Financial Accounting Standards Board that details the conditions and procedures for capitalizing leases.

Fed funds rate The interest rate, set by market forces, at which banks borrow in the Federal funds market.

Federal funds market The market in which banks lend reserve funds among themselves for short periods of time.

Federal Deposit Insurance Corporation (FDIC) An agency created by Congress in 1933 to protect depositors in insured banks from the effects of a bank failure.

Federal Open Market Committee (FOMC) Committee of the Federal Reserve System that makes decisions relating to open-market operations.

Federal Reserve (Fed) The central banking system in the United States; the chief regulator of the banking system.

Financial Institutions Reform, Recovery, and Enforcement Act (FIRREA) An act passed in 1989 that restructured the thrift industry.

financial intermediaries Specialized financial firms that facilitate the transfer of funds from savers to demanders of capital.

financial lease A lease that does not provide for maintenance services, is not cancelable, and is fully amortized over its life; also called a *capital lease.*

financial leverage The extent to which fixed-income securities (debt and preferred stock) are used in a firm's capital structure.

financial management The acquisition and utilization of funds to maximize the efficiency and value of an enterprise.

financial merger A merger in which the firms involved will not be operated as a single unit and from which no operating economies of scale are expected.

financial risk The portion of stockholders' risk, over and above the basic business risk, resulting from the use of financal leverage.

financial service corporations Institutions which offer a wide range of financial services, including investment banking, brokerage operations, insurance, and commercial banking.

five Cs of credit The factors used to evaluate credit risk: character, capacity, capital, collateral, and conditions.

fixed assets turnover ratio The ratio of sales to net fixed assets; also called the *fixed assets utilization ratio.*

fixed charge coverage ratio This ratio expands upon the TIE ratio to include the firm's annual long-term lease and sinking fund obligations.

fixed exchange rate system The world monetary system in existence after World War II until 1971, under which the value of the U.S. dollar was tied to gold, and the values of the other currencies were pegged to the U.S. dollar.

fixed operating costs Operating costs that do not vary directly with sales, that is, costs that would exist even if no sales were made. Examples include depreciation and lease payments.

floating exchange rates Exchange rates that for the most part are not fixed by government policy but are allowed to float up or down in accordance with supply and demand.

floating rate bond A bond whose interest rate fluctuates with shifts in the general level of interest rates.

floating rate preferred stock Preferred stock whose dividend rate fluctuates with changes in the general level of interest rates.

flotation cost, F The percentage cost of issuing new common stock.

flotation costs The costs of issuing new common stock, preferred stock, or bonds.

foreign bond A bond sold by a foreign borrower but denominated in the currency of the country in which it is sold.

formula value The value of an option security, calculated as the stock price minus the striking, or exercise, price.

forward exchange rate An agreed-upon price at which two currencies are to be exchanged at some future date.

founders' shares Stock owned by the firm's founders that has sole voting rights but has restricted dividends for a specified number of years.

free trade credit Credit received during the discount period and credit when no discount is offered for early payment, for example, net 30.

friendly merger A merger in which the terms are approved by the managements of both companies.

funded debt Long-term debt; "funding" means replacing short-term debt with longer maturity securities.

future value (FV$_n$) The amount to which a payment or series of payments will grow over a given future time period when compounded at a given interest rate.

future value interest factor (FVIF$_{k,n}$) The future value of $1 left in an account for n periods paying k percent per period, which is equal to $(1 + k)^n$.

FVA$_n$ The future value of an annuity over n periods.

FVIFA$_{k,n}$ The future value interest factor for an annuity of n periodic payments compounded at k percent.

Garn-St. Germain Act A thrift bailout act which allowed banks to buy failing thrifts.

going public The act of selling stock to the public at large by a closely held corporation or its principal stockholders.

golden parachutes Large payments made to the managers of a firm if it is acquired.

goods in transit Goods which have been ordered but have not been received.

growth rate, g The expected rate of growth in dividends per share.

half-year convention A feature of MACRS in which assets are assumed to be put into service at midyear and thus are allowed a half-year's depreciation regardless of when they actually go into service.

hedging exchange rate exposure The process whereby a firm protects itself against loss due to future exchange rate fluctuations.

holder-of-record date If the company lists the stockholder as an owner on this date, then the stockholder receives the dividend.

holding company A corporation that owns sufficient common stock of another firm to achieve working control of that firm.

horizontal merger The combination of two firms that produce the same type of good or service.

hostile merger (takeover) A merger in which the target firm's management resists acquisition.

hurdle rate The discount rate using the IRR method which determines whether a project should be accepted or rejected.

improper accumulation Retention of earnings by a corporation for the purpose of enabling stockholders to avoid personal income taxes.

income bond A bond that pays interest only if the interest is earned.

income statement A statement summarizing the firm's revenues and expenses over an accounting period.

incremental cash flow The net cash flow attributable to an investment project.

indenture A formal agreement between the issuer of a bond and the bondholders.

independent project A project whose cash flows are not affected by the acceptance or nonacceptance of some other project. The opposite of mutually exclusive.

indexed (purchasing power) bond A bond that has interest payments based on an inflation index so as to protect the holder from inflation.

inflation The tendency of prices to increase over time.

inflation premium (IP) A premium for expected inflation that investors add to the real risk-free rate of return.

inflation risk The risk that inflation will reduce the purchasing power of a given sum of money.

information content (signaling) of dividends The theory that stock price changes following dividend announcements simply reflect the fact that investors regard dividend changes as signals of management's earnings forecasts.

insiders Officers, directors, major stockholders, or others who may have access to information not available to the public about a company's operations.

interest rate The price paid to borrow money.

interest rate risk The risk of capital losses to which investors are exposed because of changing interest rates.

internal rate of return (IRR) method A method of ranking investment proposals using the rate of return on an asset investment, calculated by finding the discount rate that equates the present value of future cash inflows to the investment's cost.

international bond Any bond sold outside the country of the borrower.

inventory blanket lien A lending institution's claim on all of the borrower's inventories as security for a loan.

inventory management The balancing of a set of costs that increase with larger inventory holdings with a set of costs that decrease with larger order size.

inventory turnover ratio The ratio computed by dividing sales by inventories; also called the *inventory utilization ratio.*

inverted (abnormal) yield curve A downward-sloping yield curve.

investment banking house A financial institution that underwrites and distributes new investment securities and helps businesses obtain financing.

investment opportunity schedule (IOS) A graph of the firm's investment opportunities ranked in order of the projects' internal rates of return.

investment outlay Funds expended for fixed assets of a specified project (including delivery and installation) plus working capital funds expended as a result of the project's adoption.

investment tax credit (ITC) A specified percentage of the cost of new assets that businesses are *sometimes* allowed by law to deduct as a credit against their income taxes. ITCs were eliminated by the 1986 Tax Reform Act.

IRR The discount rate which forces the PV of a project's cash inflows to equal the PV of its costs.

joint venture A corporate alliance in which two or more independent companies combine their resources to achieve a specific, limited objective.

junk bond A high-risk, high-yield bond used to finance mergers, leveraged buyouts, and troubled companies.

just-in-time (JIT) system A system of inventory control in which a manufacturer coordinates production with suppliers so that raw materials and components arrive just as they are needed in the production process.

lead, or managing, underwriter The member of an underwriting syndicate that actually arranges a new securities issue.

lessee The party that uses, rather than the one who owns, the leased property.

lessor The owner of the leased property.

leveraged buyout A situation in which a firm's managers or a group of outside investors borrow heavily against the firm's assets and purchase the company themselves.

liabilities All the legal claims held against the firm by nonowners.

limited partnership An unincorporated business owned both by general partners having unlimited liability and by limited partners whose liability is limited to their investment in the firm.

line of credit An arrangement in which a financial institution commits itself to lend up to a specified maximum amount of funds during a designated period.

liquid asset An asset that can be readily converted to spendable cash.

liquidation The dissolution of a firm by selling off its assets.

liquidity The ability to sell an asset at a reasonable price on short notice.

liquidity (marketability) risk The risk that securities cannot be sold at close to the quoted price on short notice.

liquidity preference theory The theory that lenders prefer to make short-term loans rather than long-term loans; hence, they will lend short-term funds at lower rates than long-term funds.

liquidity premium (LP) A premium included in the equilibrium interest rate on a security if that security cannot be converted to cash on short notice.

liquidity ratios Ratios that show the relationship of a firm's cash and other current assets to its current liabilities.

lockbox plan A procedure used to speed up collections and reduce float through the use of post office boxes in payers' local areas.

lumpy assets Assets that cannot be acquired in small increments but must be obtained in large, discrete amounts.

margin requirement The minimum percentage of his or her own money that a purchaser must put up when buying a security.

marginal cost of capital (MCC) The cost of obtaining another dollar of new capital; the weighted average cost of the last dollar of new capital raised.

marginal cost of capital (MCC) schedule A graph that relates the firm's weighted average cost of each dollar of capital to the total amount of new capital raised.

marginal tax rate The tax applicable to the last unit of income.

market/book (M/B) ratio The ratio of a stock's market price to its book value.

market (beta or undiversifiable) risk That part of a security's risk that cannot be eliminated by diversification. It is measured by the security's beta coefficient.

market price, P_0 The price at which a stock sells in the market.

market risk premium, RP_M The additional return over the risk-free rate needed to compensate investors for assuming an average amount of risk.

market segmentation theory The theory that each borrower and lender has a preferred maturity and that the slope of the yield curve depends on the supply of and demand for funds in the long-term market relative to the short-term market.

market value ratios A set of ratios that relate the firm's stock price to its earnings and book value per share.

marketable securities Securities that can be sold on short notice for close to their quoted market prices.

maturity risk premium (MRP) A premium which compensates for interest rate risk.

measuring risk A common definition is that the tighter the probability distribution of expected future returns, the smaller the risk of a given investment.

merger The combination of two firms to form a single firm.

moderate current asset investment policy A policy that is between the two extremes of current asset investment policies: relaxed and restricted policies.

Modified Accelerated Cost Recovery System (MACRS) A depreciation system that allows businesses to write off the cost of an asset over a period much shorter than its operating life.

money markets The financial markets in which funds are borrowed or loaned for short periods (less than one year).

money market fund A mutual fund that invests in short-term, low-risk debt securities and allows investors to write checks against their accounts.

mortgage bond A bond backed by fixed assets. *First mortgage bonds* are senior in priority to claims of *second mortgage bonds*.

multinational corporation A firm that operates in two or more countries.

mutual fund A corporation that invests the pooled funds of savers, thus obtaining economies of scale in investing and reducing risk by diversification.

mutually exclusive projects A set of projects of which only one can be accepted.

National Association of Securities Dealers (NASD) An organization of securities dealers that works with the SEC to regulate operations in the over-the-counter market.

near-cash reserves Reserves that can be quickly and easily converted to cash.

net float The difference between a firm's checkbook balance and the balance shown on the bank's books, i.e., the difference between disbursement float and collection float.

net present value (NPV) method A method of ranking investment proposals using the NPV, which is equal to the present value of future net cash flows, discounted at the cost of capital.

net present value profile A curve showing the relationship between a project's NPV and the discount rate used.

net working capital Current assets minus current liabilities.

net worth See *stockholders' equity*.

New York Stock Exchange (NYSE); American Stock Exchange (AMEX) The two major U.S. security exchanges.

nominal (stated) interest rate The contracted, or stated, interest rate.

nominal risk-free rate, k_{RF} The rate of interest on a security that is free of all risk; k_{RF} is proxied by the T-bill rate or the T-bond rate. k_{RF} includes an inflation premium.

normal (constant) growth Growth which is expected to continue into the foreseeable future at about the same rate as that of the economy as a whole; g = a constant.

normal profits/rates of return Those profits and rates of return that are close to the average for all firms and are just sufficient to attract capital.

normal yield curve An upward-sloping yield curve.

NOW (negotiable order of withdrawal) account A form of savings account that allows withdrawal by check.

off-balance-sheet financing Financing in which the assets and liabilities under the lease contract do not appear on the firm's balance sheet.

offering price The price at which common stock is sold to the public.

open-market operations The purchase and sale of U.S. government securities by the Federal Reserve System.

operating company (subsidiary) A subsidiary of a holding company; a separate legal entity.

operating income Earnings before interest and taxes (EBIT).

operating lease A lease under which the lessor maintains and finances the property; also called a *service lease*.

operating leverage The extent to which fixed costs are used in a firm's operations.

operating merger A merger in which operations of the firms involved are integrated in hope of achieving synergistic benefits.

opportunity cost The return on the best alternative investment of equal risk available; the highest return that will *not* be earned if funds are reinvested in the firm.

optimal dividend policy The dividend payout policy which strikes that balance between current dividends and future growth which maximizes the firm's stock price.

option A contract that gives the option holder the right to buy or sell an asset at some predetermined price within a specified period of time.

ordering costs The costs of placing and receiving an order; this cost is fixed regardless of the average size of inventories.

ordinary (deferred) annuity An annuity on which payments occur at the end of each period.

organized security exchanges Formal organizations having tangible, physical locations that conduct auction markets in designated ("listed") securities.

out-sourcing The practice of purchasing components rather than making them in-house.

overdraft systems Systems whereby depositors may write checks in excess of their balances, with the banks automatically extending loans to cover the shortages.

over-the-counter market A large collection of brokers and dealers, connected electronically by telephones and computers, that provides for trading in unlisted securities.

paid-in capital Funds received in excess of par value when a firm sells stock.

par value The nominal or face value of a stock or bond.

parent company A firm which controls another firm by owning a large block of its stock.

partnership An unincorporated business owned by two or more persons.

payback period The length of time required for the net revenues of an investment to recover the cost of the investment.

payment date The date on which a firm actually mails dividend checks.

percentage of sales method A method of forecasting financial requirements by expressing various balance sheet items as a percentage of sales and then multiplying these percentages by expected future sales to construct pro forma balance sheets.

permanent current assets Current assets that are still on hand when business activity is at seasonal or cyclical lows.

perpetuity A stream of equal payments expected to continue forever.

pledging of accounts receivable Putting accounts receivable up as security for a loan.

poison pill An action which will seriously hurt a company if it is acquired by another.

post-audit A comparison of the actual and expected results for a given capital project.

precautionary balances Cash balances held in reserve for random, unforeseen fluctuations in cash inflows and outflows.

preemptive right A provision in the corporate charter or bylaws that gives common stockholders the right to purchase on a pro rata basis new issues of common stock (or securities convertible into common stock).

preferred stock A long-term equity security which pays a fixed dividend.

premium bond A bond that sells above its par value; occurs when the going rate of interest is lower than the coupon rate.

premium on forward rate The situation when the spot rate is greater than the forward rate. The quotation is based on the number of units of foreign currency per U.S. dollar.

present value (PV) The value today of a future payment or series of payments discounted at the appropriate discount rate.

present value interest factor ($PVIF_{k,n}$) The present value of $1 due n periods in the future discounted at k percent per period.

price/earnings (P/E) ratio The ratio of the price per share to earnings per share; shows how many times earnings investors will pay for the stock.

primary markets The markets in which newly issued securities are bought and sold for the first time.

prime rate A published rate of interest charged by commercial banks to very large, strong corporations.

pro forma financial statement A projected financial statement which shows how an actual statement will look if certain specified assumptions are realized.

probability distribution A listing of all possible outcomes, or events, with a probability (chance of occurrence) assigned to each outcome.

production opportunities The returns available within an economy from investment in productive investments.

profit margin on sales This ratio measures income per dollar of sales; it is computed by dividing net income by sales.

profit maximization The maximization of the firm's net income.

profitability ratios A group of ratios showing the combined effects of liquidity, asset management, and debt management on operating results.

progressive tax A tax that requires a higher percentage payment on higher incomes. The personal income tax in the United States, which goes from a rate of zero percent on the lowest increments of income to 33 percent and then back to 28 percent on the highest increments, is progressive.

promissory note A document specifying the terms and conditions of a loan, including the amount, interest rate, and repayment schedule.

prospectus A document describing a new security issue and the issuing company.

proxy A document giving one person the authority to act for another, typically the power to vote shares of common stock.

proxy fight An attempt by a person, group, or company to gain control of a firm by convincing stockholders that they should vote a new management team into office.

publicly owned corporation A corporation that is owned by a relatively large number of individuals who are not actively involved in its management.

put option An option to sell a share of stock at a certain price, within a specified period.

PVA_n The present value of an ordinary (deferred) annuity of n periods.

$PVIFA_{k,n}$ The present value interest factor for an annuity of n periodic payments discounted at k percent.

quick (acid test) ratio This ratio is computed by deducting inventories from current assets and dividing the remainder by current liabilities.

ranking methods Methods used to evaluate capital expenditure proposals.

rate of return (k) The rate of interest expected on an investment.

ratio analysis Analysis of the relationships among financial statement accounts.

real risk-free rate of interest, k* The rate of interest that would exist on short-term default-free U.S. Treasury securities if no inflation were expected.

recourse Situation in which the lender can require payment from the selling firm if an account receivable is uncollectible.

red-line method An inventory control procedure in which a red line is drawn around the inside of an inventory-stocked bin to indicate the reorder point level.

registration statement A statement of facts filed with the SEC about a company planning to issue securities.

Regulation Q A rule which, during 1933 through 1980, prohibited banks from paying interest on demand deposits.

reinvestment rate assumption The assumption that cash flows from a project can be reinvested (1) at the cost of capital, if using the NPV method, or (2) at the internal rate of return, if using the IRR method.

reinvestment rate risk The risk that a decline in interest rates will lead to lower income when securities mature and funds are reinvested.

relaxed current asset investment policy A policy under which relatively large amounts of cash, marketable securities, and inventories are carried and under which sales are stimulated by a liberal credit policy, resulting in a high level of receivables.

relevant cash flows The specific set of cash flows that should be considered in a capital budgeting decision.

relevant risk The risk of a security that cannot be diversified away, or market risk. This reflects a security's contribution to the risk of a portfolio.

reorder point That point at which stock on hand must be replenished.

reorganization The restructuring of debt and other claims against the firm.

repatriation of earnings The process of sending cash flows from a foreign subsidiary to its parent company.

replacement chain method A method of comparing projects of unequal lives which assumes that each project can be replicated as many times as necessary to reach a common life span; the NPVs over this life span are then compared, and the project with the higher common life NPV is chosen.

replacement decision The decision of whether or not to replace an existing asset that is still productive with a new one. Replacement projects are by definition mutually exclusive.

repurchase agreement (repo) A collateralized loan by one financial institution to another.

required rate of return, k_s The minimum expected rate of return on a common stock that a stockholder considers acceptable.

required reserves The minimum reserves that a bank must hold as vault cash or reserve deposits with the Federal Reserve.

reserve borrowing capacity Unused debt capacity that permits borrowing if a firm needs capital in troubled times.

residual dividend policy A policy in which dividends paid equal total earnings minus the amount of retained earnings necessary to finance the firm's optimal capital budget.

residual value The value of leased property at the end of the lease term.

restricted current asset investment policy A policy under which holdings of cash, securities, inventories, and receivables are minimized.

restrictive covenant A provision in a debt contract that constrains the actions of the borrower.

retention rate The percentage of its earnings retained by the firm after payment of dividends, which is equal to 1 minus the dividend payout ratio.

return on common equity (ROE) The ratio of net income to common equity; measures the rate of return on common stockholders' investment.

return on total assets (ROA) The ratio of net income to total assets.

revaluation The process of officially increasing the value of a country's currency relative to other currencies.

revolving credit agreement A formal line of credit extended to a firm by a bank or other financial institution.

risk The chance that some unfavorable event will occur. The probability that actual future earnings will be below the expected earnings. Also, in a money market context, the chance that a loan will not be repaid as promised.

risk-adjusted discount rate The discount rate that applies to a particular risky stream of cash flows; the firm's or division's cost of capital, WACC, plus a risk premium appropriate to the level of risk attached to a particular project's income stream.

risk aversion A dislike for risk. Risk averse investors demand higher rates of return on higher-risk investments.

risk premium, RP The difference between the expected rate of return on a given risky asset and that on a less risky asset.

S corporation A small corporation which under Subchapter S of the Internal Revenue Code elects to be taxed as a proprietorship or a partnership yet retains limited liability and other benefits of the corporate form of organization.

safety stocks Additional inventories carried to guard against increases in sales rates or production/shipping delays.

sale and leaseback An operation whereby a firm sells land, buildings, or equipment and simultaneously leases the property back for a specified period under specific terms.

sales (demand) forecast A forecast of a firm's unit and dollar sales for some future period, generally sales based on recent trends plus forecasts of the economic prospects for the nation, region, industry, and so forth.

salvage value The market price of a capital asset at the end of a specified period. In a capital budgeting decision, it is also the current market price of an asset being considered for replacement.

seasonal dating A procedure for inducing customers to buy early by not requiring payment until the customers' selling season, regardless of when the merchandise is shipped.

secondary markets The markets in which financial assets are traded among investors after they have been issued by corporations.

secured loan A loan backed by collateral, often inventories or receivables.

Securities and Exchange Commission (SEC) The U.S. government agency which regulates the issuance and trading of stocks and bonds.

Security Market Line (SML) The line that shows the relationship between risk as measured by beta and the required rate of return for individual securities.

selling group A group of stock brokerage firms formed for the purpose of distributing a new issue of securities.

shelf registration A procedure under which a large, well-established firm can sell new securities on very short notice.

simple interest Interest that is charged on the basis of the amount borrowed; it is paid when the loan matures rather than when it is taken out.

sinking fund A required annual payment designed to amortize a bond or preferred stock issue.

social responsibility The concept that businesses should be actively concerned about the welfare of society at large, even to the detriment of their stockholders.

sole proprietorship A business owned by one individual.

sovereign risk The risk of expropriation of a foreign subsidiary's assets by the host country and of unanticipated restrictions on cash flows to the parent company.

specialist banks Banks that act only as investment banks, concentrating on the organization, distribution, and trading of securities.

speculative balances Cash balances that are held to enable the firm to take advantage of any bargain purchases that might arise.

spontaneously generated funds Funds that are obtained automatically from routine business transactions.

spot rate The effective exchange rate for a foreign currency for delivery on (approximately) the current day.

spread The difference between the price a security dealer offers to pay for securities (the "bid" price) and the price at which the dealer offers to sell them (the "asked" price).

stand-alone risk The risk an asset has disregarding the facts that it is only one asset in the firm's portfolio of assets and that stockholders are also diversified it is measured by the variability of the asset's expected returns.

standard deviation, σ A statistical measurement of the variability of a set of observations.

statement of cash flows A statement reporting the impact of a firm's operating, investing, and financing activities on cash flows over an accounting period.

statement of retained earnings A statement reporting how much of the firm's earnings were not paid out in dividends. The figure for retained earnings that appears here is the sum of the annual retained earnings for each year of the firm's history.

stepped-up exercise price An exercise price that is specified to be higher if a warrant is exercised after a designated date.

stock dividend A dividend paid in the form of additional shares of stock rather than in cash.

stock repurchase A transaction in which a firm buys back shares of its own stock, thereby decreasing shares outstanding, increasing EPS, and, often, increasing the price of the stock.

stock split An action taken by a firm to increase the number of shares outstanding, such as doubling the number of shares outstanding by giving each stockholder two new shares for each one formerly held.

stockholder wealth maximization The appropriate goal for management decisions; considers the risk and timing associated with expected earnings per share in order to maximize the firm's stock price.

stockholders' equity (net worth) The capital supplied by stockholders — capital stock, paid-in capital, retained earnings, and, occasionally, certain reserves. *Common equity* is that part of total claims belonging to the common stockholders.

stretching accounts payable The practice of deliberately paying accounts payable late.

striking (exercise) price The price that must be paid for a share of common stock when it is bought by exercising an option.

subordinated debenture A bond having a claim on assets only after the senior debt has been paid off in the event of liquidation.

sunk cost A cash outlay that has already been incurred and which cannot be recovered regardless of whether the project is accepted or rejected.

supernormal (nonconstant) growth The part of the life cycle of a firm in which its growth is much faster than that of the economy as a whole.

synchronized cash flows A situation in which inflows coincide with outflows, thereby permitting a firm to hold transactions balances to a minimum.

synergy The condition wherein the whole is greater than the sum of its parts. In a synergistic merger, the postmerger value exceeds the sum of the separate companies' premerger values.

takeover An action whereby a person or group succeeds in ousting a firm's management and taking control of the company.

target (optimal) capital structure The percentages of debt, preferred stock, and common equity that will minimize the firm's weighted average cost of capital (WACC) and therefore maximize the price of the firm's stock.

target cash balance The minimum cash balance that a firm must maintain in order to conduct business.

target company A firm that another company seeks to acquire.

taxable income Gross income minus exemptions and allowable deductions as set forth in the Tax Code.

tax loss carry-back and carry-forward Losses that can be carried backward or forward in time to offset taxable income in a given year.

temporary current assets Current assets that fluctuate with seasonal or cyclical sales variations.

tender offer The offer of one firm to buy the stock of another by going directly to the stockholders, frequently over the opposition of the target company's management.

term loan A loan, generally obtained from a bank or insurance company, with a maturity greater than one year.

term structure of interest rates The relationship between yields and maturities of debt securities.

time preferences for consumption The preferences of consumers for current consumption as opposed to saving for future consumption.

times-interest-earned (TIE) ratio The ratio of earnings before interest and taxes (EBIT) to interest charges; measures the ability of the firm to meet its annual interest payments.

total assets turnover ratio The ratio computed by dividing sales by total assets; also called the *total assets utilization ratio*.

trade credit Inter-firm debt arising from credit sales and recorded as an account receivable by the seller and as an account payable by the buyer.

transactions balances Cash balances associated with payments and collections; those balances necessary to conduct day-to-day operations.

trend analysis An analysis of a firm's financial ratios over time; used to determine the improvement or deterioration of its financial situation.

trust receipt An instrument acknowledging that the borrower holds certain goods in trust for the lender.

trustee An official who insures that the bondholders' interests are protected and that the terms of the indenture are carried out.

two-bin method An inventory control procedure in which the reorder point is reached when one of two inventory-stocked bins is empty.

two tier offer A merger offer which provides different (better) terms to those who tender their stock early.

underwriting syndicate A syndicate of investment firms formed to spread the risk associated with the purchase and distribution of a new issue of securities.

underwritten arrangement Agreement for the sale of securities in which the investment bank guarantees the sale of the securities, thus agreeing to bear any risks involved in the transaction.

uneven payment stream A series of payments in which the amount varies from one period to the next.

Uniform Commercial Code A system of standards that simplifies and standardizes procedures for establishing loan security.

universal (global) banks Banks that offer both commercial and investment banking services to their customers.

variable operating costs Those operating costs of the firm that vary directly with sales. For example, selling and labor expenses.

variance, σ^2 The square of the standard deviation.

vertical merger A merger between a firm and one of its suppliers or customers.

warehouse receipt financing An arrangement under which the lending institution employs a third party to exercise control over the borrower's inventory and to act as the lender's agent.

warrant A long-term option to buy a stated number of shares of common stock at a specified price.

weighted average cost of capital, WACC = k_a A weighted average of the component costs of debt, preferred stock, and common equity.

white knight A company that is more acceptable to the management of a firm under attack in a hostile takeover attempt.

"window dressing" techniques Techniques employed by a firm to make its financial statements look better than they really are.

within-firm risk Risk not considering the effects of stockholders' diversification; it is measured by a project's effect on the firm's earnings variability. This risk is also called *corporate risk*.

working capital A firm's investment in short-term assets — cash, marketable securities, inventory, and accounts receivable.

yield curve A graph showing the relationship between yields and maturities of debt securities.

yield to maturity (YTM) The rate of return earned on a bond if it is held to maturity.

zero coupon bond (zeros) A bond that pays no annual interest but is sold at a discount below par, thus providing compensation to investors in the form of capital appreciation.

Index

ABC system of inventory control, **348**
Abnormal yield curve, **131**
Accelerated Cost Recovery System (ACRS), 157
Acid test, or quick, ratio, **184**–185
Accounting income vs. cash flow, 494–495
Accounting methods, 153–154(IP)
Accounting profit, **19**
Accounts payable, 157, 366–372. *See also* Trade credit
    stretching, 369
Accounts receivable, 157, **325**–338
    direct financing of, 383–384(SB), 395–398
    procedure for factoring, 396–397
    procedure for pledging, 395
Accounts receivable financing, 395–398
    cost of, 397
    evaluation of, 397
    future use, 398
Accruals, 157, **366**
Accrued federal income taxes, 157, 366
Accrued wages, 157, 366
Acid test ratio, **184**–185, 257
Acquiring company, **821**
Addison Products Company, 223–228, 258–263
Additional funds needed, **225**–230
Add-on interest, **378**
After-tax cost of debt, $k_d(1 - t)$, **694**
Aggressive current asset financing policy, 269
Aging schedule, **334**
American Express, 354(DIF)
American Stock Exchange, 62
Ames Department Stores, 219–220(DIF), 241(DIF)
Amortization schedule, 464–465
Amortize, **564**
Amortized loan, **464**–465
Annual percentage rate (APR), 482
Annual report, 150–**151**
Annuity, **454**–460
    deferred, 454–456
    future value of, 454–457
    ordinary, 454–456
    perpetuity, 460
    present value of, 457–460
Annuity due, **456**–457
Apex Corporation, 41–42
Arrearage, 592
Asked price, 63
Asset management ratios, **185**–187
    days sales outstanding (DSO), 186
    fixed assets turnover ratio, 187
    inventory turnover ratio, 185–186
    total assets turnover ratio, 187
Assets, **156**–157
    liquidity of, 13
Asset structure and capital structure decisions, 755
Atlas Industries, 418–420

AT&T, 834
Average tax rate, **36**

Balance sheet, 151, **156**–159
    assets, 156–157
    effect of leasing on, 650–652
    liabilities, 156, 157–158
    stockholders' equity, 158–159
Banker's acceptance, 311
Bankers Trust, 85–86(DIF), 115(DIF)
Bank funds sources and uses of, 90–94
Bank holding company, 90
Banking system, 88–97. *See also* Banks; Commercial banks, importance of, 88–90
Bank loans. *See* Short-term bank loans
Bankruptcy, 771–777
    federal laws, 771–772
    financial decisions in, 772–773
    liquidation procedures, 773–776
    social issues in proceedings, 776–777
Bankruptcy costs
    relationship with taxes and value of the firm, 750–752
Banks
    choice of, 372–374
    compensating balances for, 303–304
    importance of, 88–90
    overdraft systems used by, 304
Basic earning power ratio, 189, **192**
Beatrice Companies, 834
Berger, Donald, 813(DIF)
Berkshire Hathaway, 22(IP), 149(DIF), 170(DIF)
Best efforts arrangement, **630**
Beta coefficient, b, **423**–425
Beta risk, 421, **532**, 535–541, 729
Bid price, 63
Blue sky laws, 70
Board of Governors of the Federal Reserve System, **98**
Board Products, 28(SB)
Bond indentures affecting dividend policy, 785
Bond markets, 67–68
    international, 873–874
Bond prices, 68
Bond ratings, 128–129, 577–583
    bases for setting, 577–578
    changes in, 581–582
    coverage ratios, 582–583
    importance of, 578–581
    rates of return and, 578–581
Bonds, **564**–567, 570–590
    call provisions of, 566–567
    convertible, 571
    coupon interest rate, 565
    debentures, 570–571

    discount, 588
    Eurobonds, 873–874
    finding yield to maturity for, 589–590
    floating rate, 573-574
    foreign, 873
    income, 571
    indenture and trustee, 565
    indexed, or purchasing power, 572
    initial price, with warrants, 663–664
    international, 873
    investment grade, 577
    junk, 575–576
    mortgage, 570
    par value of, 565
    premium, 588
    ratings, 577–583
    recent innovations of, 572–576
    repayment provisions of, 565–567
    restrictive covenant provisions of, 567
    semiannual compounding for, 588–589
    sinking fund, 565–566
    subordinated debentures, 571
    types of, 570–572
    valuation of, 583–590
    warrants, 571
    zero coupon, 572–573
Bond-yield-plus-risk-premium approach, 699–700
Bottom line, 155
Boulais, Peter, 843(DIF)
Bracket creep, **36**
Break, or jump, in the MCC schedule, **704**–706
Breakeven point, **732**, 734
Break point (BP), **704**–706
Brittain, Alfred, 115(DIF)
Brokerage department, 63
Buffet, Warren, 22(IP), 149(DIF), 170(DIF)
Business activity affecting interest rates, 137
Business decisions and interest rates, 138–140
Business ethics, 23–24
Business organization, forms of
    corporation, 12–14
    partnership, 11–12
    sole proprietorship, 10–11
Business risk, **729**–738
    factors affecting, 730–731
    operating leverage and, 731–738
Bylaws, 13

Call option, **658**
Call premium, 566–567, **593**
Call provision, **566**–567
    for preferred stock, 593
Campeau Corporation, 272(IP), 406(DIF), 432(DIF)
Cancellation clause for an operating lease, 649
Candlish, Malcolm, 762(DIF), 767–768(DIF)

Note: Boldface terms in the index refer to key terms in the text, and the boldface number refers to the page on which the key term is defined. (DIF) refers to "Decision in Finance" and "Resolution to Decision in Finance," (SB) to "Small Business," and (IP) to "Industry Practice" sections.

Capital
  alternative sources of, 786
  cost of. *See* Cost of capital
Capital account, 92–93
Capital Asset Pricing Model (CAPM), 418, 535
  portfolio risk and, 418–425
  relationship between risk and rate of return and, 425–430
  used to find required rate of return on common equity, 698–699
Capital assets, 37
Capital budgeting, 488–513, 532–549
  comparing projects with unequal lives, 546–547
  evaluation of decision rules, 508–509
  illustrated, 509–512
  importance of, 489
  methods used to evaluate proposed projects, 498–508
  other topics, 541–547
  post-audit of, 512–513
  project proposals and classification, 490–491
  replacement decisions, 541–547
  risk analysis in, 532–541
Capital budgeting analysis effects of inflation on, 547–549
Capital components, 689–691
Capital formation process, 55
Capital gain, 37–38, 613
  ordinary income vs., 37–38
Capital gains yield, 586, 615
Capital in excess of par, 158
Capital intensity ratio, 231
Capitalizing the lease, 650–652
Capital lease, 649
Capital loss, 37–38
Capital markets, 51, 122
  efficient, 71–73
  international, 872–874
Capital requirements
  modifying forecast of, 235
  relationship with sales growth, 229–232
Capital spending, 531–532(DIF), 551(DIF)
  Japanese, 531–532(DIF), 551(DIF)
  United States, 531–532(DIF), 551(DIF)
Capital structure. *See also* Target capital structure
  additional problems and considerations, 752–753
  factors influencing decisions, 755–757
  flexibility affecting dividend policy, 786
  international, 874–876
  mergers and, 753–755
  optimal, determining, 738–739
  variations among firms, 757–758
Caprock Petroleum, 19
Carry-back and carry-forward of tax losses, 41–42
Carrying costs, 341
Carter Chemical Company, 151–152, 155–168, 183–199, 584–588
Cash, 157, **288**
  availability affecting dividend policy, 785
  marketable securities as substitute for, 305–306
  reasons for holding, 289–290
  where to stash, 313–314(IP)
Cash account, 93
Cash balances, 289–291, 293–295
Cash budget, 290–295
Cash conversion cycle, 258–260, 261–263
Cash discounts, 327–328
Cash dividends, 613
Cash flow, 19, **161, 492**
  accounting income vs., 494–495
  depreciation and, 164–165
  estimating, 492–497
  incremental, 495–497
  problems and bankruptcy, 272–273(IP)
  relevant, 493
  statement of, 163–168

Cash flow cycle, 160–163
Cash flow synchronization, 296
Cash management, 288–305
  bank relationships, 303–305
  cash budget, 290–295
  increasing efficiency of, 295–300
  international, 866–867
  matching the costs and benefits, 302–303
  in multidivisional firms, 302–303
  overdraft systems, 304
  reasons for holding cash, 289–290
  zero balance account, 304–305
Cash raising facilitated by going public, 627
Certificate of deposit (CD), 92
Change in net working capital, 497
Chapter 7, 772
Chapter 11, 772
Charter, 13
Chase Manhattan, 85(DIF)
Check clearing, 296–298
Chrysler Corporation, 77(DIF), 313(IP)
Citicorp, 85(DIF), 687–688(DIF), 715–716(DIF)
Clarke, Robert L., 273(IP)
Classified stock, 612–613
Class life, 45
Clientele effect, 787
Clough, Charles, 288(DIF)
Coca-Cola, 21–22(IP)
Coefficient of variation, 415–416
Collateral, 375
Collection, speeding of, 296–298
Collection float, 299–300
Collection policy, 333
Combining firms, procedures for, 821, 823
Commercial banks, 57, 85–86(DIF), 88–97, 115(DIF)
  choosing, 110–112(SB)
  competitor to investment banking, 85–86(DIF), 115(DIF)
  demand deposit creation, 94–97
  importance of, 88–90
  investment by, 93
  losses by, 92–93
  outcome of changing environment on, 108–109
  securities purchases by, 93
  as short-term credit source, 93–94
  sources and uses of funds for, 90–94
Commercial finance companies, 59
Commercial paper, 311–312, 380–381
  maturity and cost, 381
  use, 381
Common equity, 158–159
Common stock, 158
  advantages of financing using, 624–625
  buy-back, 287–288(DIF), 316(DIF)
  classified, 612–613
  disadvantages of financing using, 625–626
  evaluation of, as a source of funds, 624–625
  finding basic required rate of return on, 696–700
  founders' shares, 612
  issuance costs, 630–631
  issuance of, using investment banker, 629–633
  public ownership advantages, 626–627
  public ownership disadvantages, 627–628
  right to purchase, 611
  selling procedures for, 632
  setting offering price, 631–632
  social viewpoint of, 626
  types of, 612–613
  underwritten issues, 630
Common stock valuation, 613–624
  definition of terms, 614–615
  expected dividends as basis for, 615–616
  expected rate of return for a constant growth stock, 620–621

  "normal," or constant, growth, 617–619
  supernormal, or nonconstant, growth, 621–624
Communications Satellite Corporation (COMSAT), 165
Company-specific (diversifiable) risk, 421–423
Comparative ratio analysis, 199–201
Compensating balance, 289, 303–304, **375**–376
  effective interest rates and, 378–380
Competitive Equality in Banking Act (CEBA), 90
Competitive bid, 629
Compounding, 441
  compared with discounting, 449–451
  graphic view of, 445–446
Compounding periods, 482–484
Compound value, 441–445
Computerized financial planning models, 236
Computerized inventory control systems, 347
Computer use in financial management, 7
Congeneric merger, 816–817
Conglomerate merger, 816–817
Conservative current asset financing policy, 270
Consol, 460
Consolidated Edison, 796
Consolidated Freightways, 813–814(DIF), 843(DIF)
Consolidated leverage, 837
Consolidated returns, 43, 837
Constant dividend per share, 788–790
Constant growth model, 618
Constant (normal) growth, 617–619
Constant payout ratio for dividends, 790–791
Constraints on dividend payments, 785–786
Consumer credit markets, 51
Continuous probability distributions, 410–412
Controller, functions of, 14–15
Control of the firm, 610–611
  affecting dividend policy, 786
  capital structure decisions and, 756
  decreased by going public, 628
  by holding companies, 835
Conversion price (P$_c$), 666–667
Conversion ratio (CR), 666–667
Conversion value (C$_t$), 668
Convertibility, of preferred stock, 592
Convertible bonds, 571
Convertible securities, 665–672
  analysis, 668–671
  conversion ratio and conversion price, 666–667
  reporting earnings when outstanding, 672
  use of convertibles in financing, 671–672
Corporate alliance, 832
Corporate bonds, 67–68
Corporate income taxes, 38–43
  consolidation of tax returns, 43
  effect of interest and dividend paid out, 40–41
  effect of loss carry-back and carry-forward, 41–42
  improper accumulation, and 42
  on interest and dividend income received, 39–40
  taxation of capital gains, 41
Corporate risk, 534–535
Corporation, 12–14
Corporation bylaws, 13
Corporation charter, 13
Costly trade credit, 371
Cost of capital, 495, 688–711
  basic definitions for, 689–691
  capital components, 689–691
  changes in, 703–707
  conclusions on cost of equity, 700
  divisional costs, 710–711
  logic of the weighted average, 688–689
  marginal, 703–710
  minimum required return, 691–693
  punishment, 687–688(DIF), 715–716(DIF)
Cost of debt, k$_d$(1 − t), 693–695
Cost of external equity (k$_e$), 701–702

Cost of funds, 118–119
Cost of goods sold, 155
Cost of new common equity (k_e), 701–702
Cost of preferred stock (k_p) 695
Cost of reporting
    increased by going public, 627
Cost of retained earnings (k_s), 696
Cost of selling new stock affecting dividend policy, 786
Costs of running short, 340
Coupon (interest) rate, 68, 565
Coverage, 582–583
Coverage ratios, 582–583
Coykendall, Joe, 779(DIF)
Cray Research, Inc., 389(DIF)
Credit, five Cs of, 329
Credit associations, 329
Credit availability increasing by leasing, 657–658
Credit bureaus, 323–324(DIF), 354(DIF)
Credit information sources, 329–332
Credit management, international, 867–868
Credit period, 326–327
Credit policy, 326–338
    analyzing changes in policy variables, 335–338
    cash discounts, 327–328
    collection policy, 333
    credit period, 326–327
    credit standards, 328–332
    effectiveness of, 333–335
    profit from carrying charges, 333
Credit-reporting agencies, 330
Credit standards, 328–332
Credit terms, 326
Credit unions, 58
Credit Watch, 582
Cumulative dividends, 592
Current asset decisions
    combining with liability decisions, 274–275
Current asset financial policy, 257
Current asset financing policy, 266–274
Current asset investment policies, 263–266
Current asset management, 257
Current assets. *See also* Short-term financial planning
    effect on risk and return, 264–266
    financing policies, 266–274
    investment policies, 263–266
    management, 257
    permanent, 268
    temporary, 268
Current (interest) yield, 68, 586
Current ratio, 183–184, 257
Cyclical changes, 234

Davis, J. Luther, 779(DIF)
Days sales outstanding (DSO), 186, 333–337
Dayton Card Company, 291–295
Debentures, 157, 570–571
    subordinated, 571
Debt, cost of, 693–695
Debt crisis, 561–562(DIF), 603(DIF)
Debt management ratios, 188–191
    debt ratio, 190
    financial leverage and, 188–190
    fixed charge coverage, 190–191
    times interest earned (TIE), 190
Debt ratio, 190
Declaration date, 792
Default, 128
Default risk, 308
Default risk premium (DRP), 128–129
Defensive merger, 816
Deferred annuity, 454–456
Deficit trade balance, 859
Degree of financial leverage (DFL), 747–748
Degree of operating leverage (DOL), 736–738
Degree of total leverage (DTL), 748–750

Del Monte Corporation, 824
Demand deposits, 91
    creation of, 94–97
Demand forecast, 220–221
Demand variability, 730
Deposit expansion, 94–97
Depository Institutions Deregulation and Monetary Control Act, 90
Depreciable basis, 47
Depreciation, 44–48, 155, 157, **164**–165
    cash flow and, 164–165
Deregulation of financial institutions, 7
Detachable warrant, 664–665
Detector Electronics Corporation, 389(DIF)
Devaluation, 860
Direct transfers of capital, 55
Disbursement float, 299–300
Disbursements, slowing, 298–299
Disclosure
    required after going public, 627–628
Discount bond, 588
Discounted cash flow (DCF) techniques, 500
    used to find required rate of return on common equity, 697–698
Discount interest, 378
Discounting, 447–449
    compared with compounding, 449–451
    graphic view of, 448–449
Discount on forward rate, 863–864
Discount rate, 100–102, 501
    estimating for mergers, 828–829
    risk adjusted, 710
Diversifiable risk, 421–423
Diversification, to reduce risk, 539
Divestiture, 832–835
    illustrations of, 833–835
Dividend and interest income, taxation of, 36–37, 39–40
Dividend payment policies, 788–791
    constant, or steadily increasing, dividends per share, 788–790
    constant payout ratio, 790–791
    low regular, plus extras, 791
    residual, 780–785
Dividend payments, 792, 794
    constraints on, 785–786
Dividend policy, 780–803
    actual payment procedures, 792, 794
    dividend reinvestment plans (DRIPs), 793–794(IP), 794–795
    establishing, 801–803
    factors influencing, 785–788
    optimal, 780
    payment policies, 788–791
    stock dividends and stock splits, 797–801
    stock repurchases, 795–797
Dividend policy decision, 20
Dividend reinvestment plans (DRIPs), 793–794(IP), **794**–795
    tax consequences of, 794
Dividends
    information content of, 787–788
    stock repurchase as alternative to, 795–797
Dividend yield, 66
Divisional costs of capital, 710–711
Double taxation, 36
Drafts, 299
Drapkin, Donald C., 78(DIF)
Drexel Burnham Lambert, 60–61(IP), 575–576
Du Pont chart, 195–197, **198**–199
Du Pont equation, 196
Du Pont System, 195–199

E. F. Hutton, 300
Earnings
    reporting when warrants or convertibles are outstanding, 672

Earnings before interest and taxes, 155
Earnings per share (EPS), 19
    expected, effect of financial leverage on, 739–743
Eastern Communications, Inc., 408–415
Economic environment, 25–26
Economic ordering quantity (EOQ), 342
Economic profit, 19
Economies of scale, 232–234
Effective annual rate, 482
Efficient capital market, 71–73
Efficient financial markets, 51–52
Emery Air Freight, 813–814(DIF), 843(DIF)
Enforced dissolution, 837
Environmental projects, 491
EOQ model, 341, 342, 343, 347
Equifax, 323(DIF)
Equilibrium price, 631–632
Equity, 156
Equity multiplier, 197
Esmark, Inc., 833
Eurobonds, 873–874
Eurodollars, 314, 872–873
    interest rates on, 873
Eurodollar bank time deposits, 314
Ewing, Douglas, 219–220(DIF), 241(DIF)
Excess capacity, 230, 235
Excess reserves, 95–97
Exchange rate risk, 861–865, 870–871
Exchange rates, 856–866
    direct quotations for, 856–858
    fixed exchange rate system for, 858–860
    floating exchange rate system for, 860–862
    fluctuations in, 859–860
    forward, 863–864
    hedging exposure to, 864
    indirect quotations for, 856–858
    international monetary system and, 856–862
    relationship with inflation and interest rates, 865
    spot rates, 863–864
    trading in foreign exchange and, 863–865
Ex-dividend date, 792, 794
Exercise (striking) price, 658
Expansion, 491
Expansion project, 509
Expectations theory, 131, 133–134
Expected dividends as basis for stock values, 615–616
Expected dividend yield, 615
Expected earnings per share
    effect of financial leverage on, 739–743
Expected rate of return (k̂), 409–410, **614**
    for a constant growth stock, 620–621
Expected total return, 615
Externalities, 496
Extra dividend, 791

Factoring, 395–397, 383–384(SB)
    procedure for, 396–397
Fairness, standard of, 773
Fair price, in merger, 831
Fall Mills, Inc., 369–371
FASB #13, 650
Feasibility, standard of, 773
Federal deficits affecting interest rates, 136
Federal Deposit Insurance Corporation (FDIC), 90–91
Federal funds market, 92
Federal income tax system, 34–44. *See also* Taxes
    changes in, 34–35
    corporate income taxes, 38–43
    individual income taxes, 35–38
Federal Open Market Committee (FOMC), 99, 102–103
Federal Reserve Board, 117(DIF), 142(DIF)
    policy affecting interest rates, 135–136

Federal Reserve (Fed) System, 98–103, 120–121(IP)
  discount rate, 100–102
  open market operations of, 99, 102–103
  organization and structure of, 98–99
  reserve requirements of, 99–100
  tools of monetary policy used by, 99
Fed funds rate, 92
Field warehouse, 399–401
Finance
  areas within, 3
  changing emphasis in, 6–7
  place in business organization, 14–16
Financial Accounting Standards Board (FASB), 181–182(IP)
Financial asset markets, 50
Financial flexibility
  capital structure decisions and, 757
Financial institutions
  changing economic environment of, 107–109
  impact of globalization on, 109–110
  overview of, 87–88
Financial Institutions Reform, Recovery, and Enforcement Act (FIRREA), 90
Financial intermediaries, 54–59
  commercial banks, 57
  commercial finance companies, 59
  credit unions, 58
  financial service corporations, 59
  investment banking house, 55–57
  life insurance companies, 58
  mutual funds, 58–59
  mutual savings banks, 58
  pension funds, 58
  role of, 54–59
  savings and loan associations, 57–58
Financial lease, 649
Financial leverage, 188–190, **738**–747
  degree of, 747–748
  effect on expected earnings per share, 739–743
  effect on stock prices, 744–747
Financial management, 3, 6–**10**
  evolving role of, 6–7
  increasing importance of, 7–10
  international, 850–877
  multinational vs. domestic, 852–853
Financial manager
  primary activities, 5
Financial markets
  market efficiency, 51–52, 71–73
  role of, 48–54
  types of, 50–53
Financial merger, 823–824
Financial planning models
  computerized, 236
Financial risk, 729, 738–747
Financial service corporations, 59
Financial statements
  annual report, 150–151
  balance sheet, 151, 156–159
  effects of trade credit on, 369–370
  falsifying, 179(DIF), 205(DIF)
  forecasting, 220–237
  importance of, 180
  income statement, 151–152, 155
  interpreting. See Ratio analysis
  manipulating, 181–182(IP)
  projected, 226
  ratio effects of cash conversion cycle and, 262–263
  sources and uses of funds statement, 165–168
  statement of cash flows, 151, 163–168
  statement of retained earnings, 151, 159–160
Firm
  control of. See Control of the firm
  value of. See Value of the firm

First Boston Corporation, 727–728(DIF), 762(DIF)
First mortgage bonds, 157, 570
Five Cs of credit, 329
Fixed assets, 157
Fixed assets turnover ratio, 187
Fixed assets utilization ratio, 187
Fixed charge coverage ratio, 190–191
Fixed exchange rate system, 858–860
Fixed operating costs, 731
Float, using, 299–300
Floating exchange rates, 860–862
Floating rate bond, 573–**574**
Floating rate debt, 573–574
Floating rate preferred stock, 595
Flotation cost (F), 701
Flotation costs, 630–631
Forecasting financial requirements, 219–220(DIF), 221, 222–223(IP), 223–237, 241(DIF)
  computerized financial planning models, 236
  modifying forecast of additional funds needed, 235
  percentage of sales method, 221, 223–228
  when balance sheet ratios are subject to change, 232–235
Foreign bonds, 873
Foreign exchange, trading in, 863–865
Foreign investment and exchange risk, 870–871
  procedures for analyzing, 870–871
  repatriation of earnings and, 870–871
  sovereign risk and, 871
Formula value, 659–662
Forward exchange rate, 863–864
Forward market hedge, 864
Founders' shares, 612
Franchising, 237–239(SB)
Free trade credit, 371
Friendly merger, 821
Funded debt, 563
Futures markets, 50–51
Future value (FV), 441–445
  of an annuity (FVA$_n$), 454–457
  of an annuity due, 456–457
  present value vs., 449–451
Future value interest factor (FVIF$_{k,n}$), 444–445
FVA$_n$, 454
FVIFA$_{k,n}$, 455

Garn–St. Germain Act, 90
GCI of New Orleans, 541–545
General and administrative expenses, 155
General Electric, 287–288(DIF), 316(DIF)
General Motors, 181(IP), 313–314(IP), 487–488(DIF), 515(DIF)
General partners, 11
Georgia Paper Products (GPP), 781–785
Gibbons Green van Amerongen, 727–728(DIF), 762(DIF)
Global (universal) banks, 109–110
Globalism, 854–855(IP)
Globalization of financial institutions, 109–110
Goals of the firm, 16–17, 19–20, 22–26
  economic environment affecting, 25–26
  profit maximization, 19–20
  for small firms, 27–29(SB)
  social responsibility, 20, 22–23
  stockholder wealth maximization, 16–17
Going public, 626–629
  advantages of, 626–627
  conclusions on, 628–629
  considerations for small businesses, 633–635
  disadvantages of, 627–628
  real costs for small businesses, 711–712(SB)
Goizueta, Roberto C., 21(IP)
Golden parachutes, 831
Goods in transit, 345
Government securities, 311

Greenmail, 797
Greenspan, Alan, 117(DIF), 142(DIF), 273(IP)
Greve, Elinar, 779(DIF)
Gross working capital, 257
Growth, 445–446
  capital structure decisions and, 755
  financing in the small firm, 759–760(SB)
  normal, or constant, 617–619
  supernormal, or nonconstant, 621–624
  working capital needs and, 276–277(SB)
Growth rate (g), 614

Half-year convention, 46–47
Health Management Resources, Inc. (HMR), 222–223(IP)
Hedging exchange rate exposure, 864
Henson, Joe, 826(IP)
Hilton, Barron, 609(DIF)
Hilton Hotels Corporation, 609(DIF), 637(DIF)
Holder-of-record date, 792
Holding company, 835–838
  advantages of, 835–836
  disadvantages of, 837
  leverage in, 837–838
Hollis, Peter B., 219–220(DIF), 241(DIF)
Horizontal merger, 816–817
Hostile merger (takeover), 819, 821
Houston Trucking Company, 509–511, 541
Hurdle rate, 536
Hytec Electronics, 802

Impairment of capital rule and dividend policy, 785
Improper accumulation, 42
Income bonds, 571
Income statement, 151–152, 155
Income tax, 34–44. See also Taxes
  changes in, 34–35
  corporate, 38–43
  individual, 35–38
Incremental cash flow, 495–497
Indenture, 565
Independent projects, **501,** 523
Indexed, or purchasing power, bond, 572
Individual income taxes, 35–38
  average tax rate, 36
  bracket creep, 36
  capital gain vs. ordinary income, 37–38
  on dividend and interest income, 36–37
  marginal tax rate, 36
  taxable income for, 35–36
Inflation, 7, 118–119, 127–128
  effect on inventory management, 348
  effects on capital budgeting analysis, 547–549
  expected, 127–128
  impact on rate of return, 428
  relationship with exchange rates and interest rates, 865
  relationship with long-term interest rates, 124–125
Inflation-free rate of return, 428
Inflation premium (IP), 127–128, 428
Inflation risk, 309
Information content (signaling) of dividends, 787–788
  affecting dividend policy, 787–788
Ingersoll, Ralph, 562(DIF)
Input price variability, 730
Insiders, 69
Interest and dividend income
  taxation of, 36–37, 39–40
Interest, 49, 118–119, 121–140, 377–380
  business activity, 137
  business decisions and, 138–140
  changes in, over time, 123
  when compensating balances apply, 378–380

determinants of, 125–130
determining, 463–464
effective, 482
on Eurodollars, 873
federal deficits influencing, 136
Federal Reserve policy affecting, 135–136
foreign trade balance, 136–137
impact of supply and demand for savings on, 122
nominal risk-free rate (k_{RF}), 126–127
nominal (stated), 482
other factors that influence, 135–137
real risk-free rate of interest (k^*), 126
relationship with exchange rates and inflation, 865
relationship with inflation, 124–125
stock prices and, 138
term structure of, 123, 131–137
on term loans, 564
Interest rate risk, 129–130, **308–309**
Internal conditions of the firm
capital structure decisions and, 756–757
Internal rate of return (IRR) method, 501–508
conflicts with net present value method, 523–527
with constant cash inflows, 503
financial calculator and computer solutions, 507
graphic solution, 505–506
rationale and use of, 507–508
trial and error method, 503–505
International bond, 873
International bond markets, 873–874
International capital markets, 872–874
International capital structures, 874–876
International financial management, 850–877
exchange rates and international monetary system, 856–862
inflation, interest rates, and exchange rates, 865–866
international capital markets, 872–874
international capital structures, 874–876
international mergers, 876–877
international working capital management, 866–869
multinational vs. domestic, 852–853
procedures for analyzing potential foreign investment, 870–871
trading in foreign exchange, 863–865
International mergers, 876–877
International working capital management, 866–869
International Paper (IP), 833
Inventories, 157, 255–256(DIF), 279(DIF)
Inventory blanket lien, 398
Inventory control systems, 347–348
computerized, 347
Inventory conversion period, 260
Inventory costs, 340–341
Inventory financing, 398–401
Inventory management, 338, 339–351
determining inventory investment, 339–340
effects of inflation on, 348
goods in transit, 345
international, 868–869
inventory control systems, 347–348
inventory costs, 340–341
optimal ordering quantity, 341–343
other issues, 348, 349–350(IP), 351
safety stocks, 345–347
setting reorder point, 343–344
Inventory turnover ratio, 185–186
Inventory utilization ratio, 185–186
Inverted (abnormal) yield curve, 131
Investments, 3
by commercial banks, 93
foreign. See Foreign investment

Investment in the United States by foreigners, 850–852
Investment banking house, 55, 56–57
brokerage departments of, 63
role in mergers, 830
selection of, 630
Investment banking process, 629–633
company decisions prior to, 629–630
joint decisions, 630–632
maintenance of secondary market, 633
selling procedures, 632–633
Investment grade bonds, 577
Investment opportunities affecting dividend policy, 786
Investment opportunity schedule (IOS), 708–710
combining with marginal cost of capital (MCC), 707–710
location of, 786
marginal cost of capital and, 782–784
Investment outlay, 498
Investment overseas, 850–852
Investment tax credit (ITC), 47
IRR, 502
Issuance costs, 630–631
ITT, 354(DIF), 833, 835
IU International, 833

J. P. Morgan, 85(DIF)
Jim Walter Corporation, 603(DIF)
Johnson, Ross, 3–4(DIF), 30–31(DIF)
Joint venture, 832
Jump in the MCC schedule, 704–706
Junior mortgages, 570
Junk bond, 60–61(IP), **575**–576
Just-in-time (JIT) system, 348, 349–350(IP), 351

Keating, Charles H., Jr., 153(IP)
Kentucky Fried Chicken, 239(SB)
Kohlberg Kravis Roberts & Co. (KKR), 3–4(DIF), 30–31(DIF), 603(DIF)

Lead, or managing, underwriter, 632
Lease evaluation, 652–657
Lease payments, 155
Leases
cancellation clause for, 649
capital, 649
capitalizing, 650–652
estimating residual value of, 657
financial, or capital, 649
operating, 649
sale-and-leaseback, 648
service, 649
for small businesses, 673(SB)
Leaseway Transportation Corporation, 603(DIF)
Leasing, 648–658
evaluating, 652–657
factors affecting decisions, 657–658
financial statement effects of, 650–652
increasing credit availability, 657–658
types of, 648–649
Legal separation using holding companies, 836
Legent Corporation, 826(IP)
Lender attitudes
capital structure decisions and, 756
Lessee, 648
evaluation by, 652–657
Lessor, 648
Leverage. See Consolidated leverage; Financial leverage; Operating leverage
Leveraged buyouts (LBOs), 3–4(DIF), 30–31(DIF), **834,** 838–839
Levine, Dennis B., 60(IP)

Liabilities, 156, 157–158
Liability, 10–13
Liability decisions
combined with current asset decisions, 274–275
Life insurance companies, 58
Lifeline, 349(IP)
Limited liability, 12
Limited partnership, 11
Lincoln Savings and Loan, 153(IP)
Line of credit, 376
Liquid asset, 129
Liquidation, 772–776
Liquidity, 13
increased by going public, 627
Liquidity preference theory, 131, 133
Liquidity premium (LP), 129
Liquidity ratios, 183–185
Liquidity risk, 309
Local markets, 51
Lockbox plan, 297–298
Long-term, floating rate debt, 574
Long-term debt
compared with short-term debt, 273–274
Long-term gain or loss, 37–38
Lotus Development, 827(IP)
Low regular dividend plus extras, 791
Lumpy assets, 234

Management attitudes
capital structure decisions and, 756
Management by exception, 332
Managerial buyout, 832
Managing, or lead, underwriter, 632
Mandatory investments, 491
Manzi, Jim P., 827(IP)
Marginal cost of capital (MCC), 703–710
break point, 704–706
combining with investment opportunity schedule, 707–710
investment opportunity schedule and, 782–784
Marginal cost of capital (MCC) schedule, 704
break, or jump, in, 704–706
Marginal tax rate, 36
Margin requirement, 70
Marketability risk, 309
Marketable securities, 157, 305–312, 314
factors influencing the choice of, 308–310
reasons for holding, 305–306
returns on, 310
strategies for, 306–308
types of, 310–312, 314
Market/book ratio, 193
Market conditions
capital structure decisions and, 756
Market efficiency, 71–73
Market price (P_0), 614
Market (nondiversifiable) risk, 421–423, **532,** 535–541, 729. See also Beta risk
Market risk premium (RP_M), 426
Market segmentation theory, 131, 132–133
Market value ratios, 192–193
Maturity
of bank loans, 375
of preferred stock, 593
Maturity matching, 268–269
Maturity risk premium (MRP), 129–130, 574
Maxey, Keith, 255–256(DIF), 279(DIF)
Maxwell, Hamish, 21(IP)
McChesney, Dennis, 365(DIF)
McClintock, Fred, 349(IP)
MCC schedule, 704–706
break, or jump, in, 704–706
McDonnell, Sandy, 647(DIF), 676(DIF)
McDonnell Douglas Corporation, 647(DIF), 676(DIF)
Measuring risk, 412–416

Mergers, 814–832
advantages for small businesses, 840–841(SB)
analysis illustrated, 827–829
arranging, 830
capital structure and, 753–755
congeneric, 816–817
conglomerate, 816–817
defenses against, 830–831
defensive, 816
determining acquisition's value in, 829
economic implications of, 815–816
examples of, 817–821
fair price for, 831
financial, 823–824
financial analysis of proposed mergers, 823–825
friendly, 821
high-tech firms' urge to, 826–827(IP)
horizontal, 816–817
hostile, 819, 821
international, 876–877
motivation for, 815
operating, 823–824
price paid for target company, 825
procedures for combining firms, 821, 823
role of investment banker in, 830
terms of, 824–825
types of, 816–817
vertical, 816–817
Milken, Michael, 60–61(IP), 575
Minimum required return, 691–693
Mistele, Lloyd, 313–314(IP)
Moderate current asset investment policy, 264–266
Modified Accelerated Cost Recovery System (MACRS), 45–48
depreciable basis for computing, 46–47
half-year convention for computing, 46–47
illustration, 47–48
Modified DuPont chart, 195–199
Monetary policy, 99
Money and capital markets, 3
Money market funds, 59
Money market mutual funds, 312
Money markets, 51
Mortgage bonds, 570
Mortgage markets, 51
Multinational corporation, 850–852
Multinational financial management
cultural differences causing problems, 853
currency denominations causing problems, 852
domestic vs., 852–853
economic and legal ramifications of, 852
globalism, 854–855(IP)
languages causing problems, 852
political risk, 853
role of governments, 853
Multiple rates of return, 527
Mutual funds, 58–59
Mutually exclusive projects, **501,** 524
Mutual savings banks, 58

Nast Corporation, 572–573
National Association of Security Dealers (NASD), 64, 70
National markets, 51
Near-cash reserves, 311
Negotiable certificates of deposit, 312
Negotiated deal, 629
Net float, 300
Net present value (NPV) leasing analysis, 654–657
Net present value (NPV) method, 500–501
conflicts with internal rate of return method, 523–527
Net present value profile, 505–506
Net working capital, 257
changes in, 497

Net worth, 158–159
New York Stock Exchange, 62–63
bond trading on, 67–68
Nominal risk-free rate (k_{RF}), 126–127, 428
Nominal (stated) interest rate, 482
Nonconstant (supernormal) growth, 621–624
Nondiversifiable risk, 421–423
Nongovernment securities, 311
Non-revenue-producing projects, 491
Normal (constant) growth, 617–619
Normal profits, 20
Normal rates of return, 20
"Normal" yield curve, 131
Northwest Electric Company, 802
Northwestern National Bank, 365(DIF), 388–389(DIF)
Notes payable, 157
Novell Inc., 827(IP)
Novus Franchising, Inc., 238(SB)
NOW (Negotiable Order of Withdrawal) Account, 91

Off-balance-sheet financing, 650
Offering price, 631–632
Ohio Mattress Company, 727–728(DIF)
Olympia & York, 405–406(DIF), 432(DIF)
Open-market operations, 99, 102–103
Operating company (subsidiary), 835
Operating income, 729
estimating in mergers, 824
Operating lease, 649
Operating leverage, 731–738
affecting business risk, 732–738
capital structure decisions and, 755
control of, 737–738
degree of, 736–738
Operating merger, 823–824
Operating profits, 155
Opportunity cost, 446, 496, 696
Optimal capital structure, 702
determining, 738–739
Optimal dividend policy, 780
Optimal ordering quantity, 341–343
Options, 658–662
formula value vs. option price, 659–662
types and markets, 658–659
Ordering costs, 342
Ordinary annuity, 454–456
Ordinary income vs. capital gain, 37–38
Organized security exchanges, 62
Out-sourcing, 351
Overdraft systems, 304
Over-the-counter market, 63–64
Ownership interest transferability of, 12

Pacific Industries, 803
Paid-in capital, 158–159
Paramount, 833–834
Parent company, 835
Partial multiple taxation, 837
Participating preferred stock, 592
Partnership, 11–12
Par value, 158, 565
of preferred stock, 592
Payables deferral period, 260
Payback period, 498–500
Payment date, 794
Penalty tax on improperly accumulated earnings affecting dividend policy, 785–786
Pension funds, 58
PepsiCo, 179(DIF), 205(DIF)
Percentage of sales method, 221, 223–228
Perleman, Ronald O., 60(IP)
Permanent current assets, 268
Perot, H. Ross, 78(DIF)
Perpetuity, 460
Philip Morris, 21–22(IP)

Philips, 849–850(DIF), 879–880(DIF)
Phipps, Arthur, 349(IP)
Physical asset markets, 50
Pickens, T. Boone, 60(IP), 575
Pirie, Robert S., 77(DIF)
Pistner, Stephen, 241(DIF)
Pledging of accounts receivable, 383–384(SB), 395
Poison pill, 831
Portfolio risk, 418–423
beta coefficient and, 423–425
Capital Asset Pricing Model (CAPM) and, 418–425
company-specific, 421–423
market, 421–423
relevant, 422–423
Portfolio theory, 6
Post-audit, 512–513
Postmerger control, 824–825
Pre-authorized debits, 298
Precautionary balances, 289
Preemptive right, 611
Preferred stock, 591–597
advantages and disadvantages for investor, 593–594
advantages and disadvantages to issuer, 593
call provision of, 593
convertibility, 592
cost of, 695
cumulative dividends of, 592
evaluation of, 593–594
floating rate, 595
maturity of, 593
participating, 592
par value of, 592
provisions of issues, 591–593
recent innovations of, 594–595
sinking fund for, 593
valuation of, 595–597
voting rights, 592
Premium bond, 588
Premium on forward rate, 863–864
Present value (PV), 445, 446–449
of an annuity, 457–460
of an annuity due, 459–460
future value vs., 449–451
of an uneven series of receipts, 460–463
Present value interest factor ($PVIF_{k,n}$), 447–448
Price/earnings (P/E) ratio, 193
Primary markets, 51
Prime Computer, Inc., 826(IP)
Prime rate, 377
Priority in assets and earnings, 591
Private placement, 568–569(IP)
Probability distribution, 408–409
continuous, 410–412
Production opportunities, 118–119
Profitability
capital structure decisions and, 755
Profitability ratios, 191–192
Profit margin and need for external funds, 232
Profit margin on sales, 191, 195–196
Profit maximization, 19–20
Profits
social responsibility and, 20, 22–23
Pro forma balance sheet construction, 221, 223–228
Pro forma financial statements, 220
for mergers, 827–828
Progressive tax, 35
Project proposals
evaluation methods, 498–508
evaluation methods compared, 523–527
Project proposals and classification, 490–491
Project risk, 539–541
Projects with unequal lives
comparing, 546–547

Promissory note, 375
Prospectus, 69
Proxy, 610
Proxy fight, 17, 610
Public Service of Indiana (PSI), 8
Public warehouse, 399
Publicly owned corporation, 627
Put option, 659
PVA$_n$, 457
PVIFA$_{k,n}$, 457

Quick, or acid test, ratio, 184–185, 257

Ranking methods, 498
Rate of return, k, 441
   absolute vs. relative, 526
   impact of inflation on, 428
   multiple, 527
   normal, 20
   relationship with risk, 425–430
   social responsibility and, 20, 22–23
Rating agency attitudes
   capital structure decisions and, 756
Ratio analysis, 180, 183–202
   asset management ratios, 185–187
   debt management ratios, 188–191
   limitations of, 201–202
   liquidity ratios, 183–185
   market value ratios, 192–193
   profitability ratios, 191–192
   sources of comparative ratios, 199–201
   summary of, 193–195
   summary of Du Pont system, 195–199
   trend analysis, 195
   users of, 183
Real inflation-free rate of return (k*), 428
Real risk-free rate of interest (k*), 126
Receivables conversion period, 260
Recourse, 395
Recovery allowance percentages, 45–46
Recovery period, 45
Red-line method, 347
Refunding operation, 567
Regional markets, 51
Registration statement, 69
Regulation of securities markets, 69–71
Regulation Q, 91
Reichmann, Albert, 405–406(DIF), 432(DIF)
Reichmann, Paul, 405–406(DIF), 432(DIF)
Reinvestment rate assumption, 526–527
Reinvestment rate risk, 130
Relationship between growth in sales and capital
   requirements, 229–232
Relaxed current asset investment policy, 264–
   266
Relevant cash flows, 493
Relevant risk, 422–423
Remaining disbursements, 155
Reorder point, 343–344
Reorganization, 772
Repatriation of earnings, 870
Replacement, 491
Replacement chain method, 546–547
Replacement decisions, 541–547
   comparing projects with unequal lives, 546–547
Repurchase agreement (repo), 92
Required rate of return (k$_s$), 614
   finding, 696–700
   minimum, 691–693
   risk aversion and, 416–417
Required reserves, 99–100
Reserve borrowing capacity, 625
Residual dividend policy, 780–785
Residual value, 657
Resource poverty, 27–29(SB)
Restricted current asset investment policy,
   264–266

Restrictive covenant, 567
Retained earnings, 158
   cost of, 696
   improper accumulation of, 42
Retention rate, 229
Retirement, 439–440(DIF), 472–474(DIF)
Return on common equity (ROE), 192
Return on total assets (ROA), 192
Revaluation, 860
Revenues, 152
Revolving credit agreement, 376
Risk, 19, 118–119, 405–406(DIF), 407–408,
   432(DIF)
   beta, 532, 535–541, 729
   business, 729–738
   company-specific (diversifiable), 421–423
   conclusions on project, 539–541
   continuous probability distributions and, 410–
   412
   corporate, 534–535
   defining and measuring, 407–417
   diversifiable, 421–423
   diversification to reduce, 539
   exchange rate, 861–865, 870–871
   expected rate of return and, 409–410
   financial, 729, 738–747
   isolated by use of holding companies, 836
   market, 421–423, 532, 535–541, 729
   measuring, 412–416
   nondiversifiable, 421–423
   portfolio, 418–425
   probability distributions and, 408–409
   relationship with rate of return, 425–430
   relevant, 422–423
   sovereign, 871
   stand-alone, 532
   systematic, 421
   total, 729
   types of, 308–309, 729
   unsystematic, 421
   within-firm, 532, 729
Risk adjusted discount rate, 710–711
Risk and return
   effect of current assets on, 264–266
Risk aversion, 416–417
   changes in, 428
   required returns and, 416–417
Risk capital for small businesses, 598–599(SB)
Riskiness of dividends vs. riskiness of capital gains
   affecting dividend policy, 787
Risk premium (RP), 417
RJR Nabisco, 3–4(DIF), 30–31(DIF), 575
Roark Restaurant Supply Company, 335–338
Romantic Books, 342–347

Safety projects, 491
Safety stocks, 345–347
Sale-and-leaseback, 648
Sales forecasts, 220–221
Sales growth
   relationship with capital requirements, 229–232
Sales price adjustments for change in input prices,
   730
Sales price variability, 730
Sales revenues, 152
Sales stability
   capital structure decisions and, 755
Salvage value, 545
Samson, Solomon, 288(DIF)
Sanford, Charles S., Jr., 115(DIF)
Savings
   supply and demand for, 122
Savings and loan associations (S&Ls), 57–58
   crisis, 104–105(IP), 106–107
   proposed reforms, 106–107
Schaefer, John P., 779–780(DIF)
S corporations, 43–44

Scott, Lary R., 813–814(DIF), 843(DIF)
Sears, Roebuck financial service corporation, 59
Seasonal dating, 328
Secondary markets, 51
   maintenance of, 633
Secured loan, 382
Securities. See also Marketable securities
   emphasis on through 1920s, 6
   returns on, 310
   risks and returns on, 72–73
Securities and Exchange Commission, 69
   indentures approved by, 565
Security
   in short-term financing, 382–383, 395–401
Security agreement, 383
Security Market Line (SML), 425–430, 535–538
Security market regulation, 69–71
Seidman, William L., 154(IP)
Self-dealings
   exposed by going public, 628
Selling expenses, 155
Selling group, 632
Semiannual and other compounding periods, 482–
   484
Semiannual compounding for bonds, 588–589
Service lease, 649
Shelf registrations, 632–633
Shoal Creek Engineering, 801–802
Short-term assets, 257
Short-term bank loans, 372–380
   applying for, 374–375
   choosing a bank, 372–374
   cost of, 376–380
   features of, 375–376
   interest on, 377–380
Short-term credit
   advantages and disadvantages of, 270–271,
   273–274
   supplied by commercial banks, 93–94
Short-term debt
   compared with long-term debt, 273–274
Short-term financial operations, 259
Short-term financial planning, 255–279. See also
   Current assets
   aggressive approach, 269
   alternative financing policies, 266–274
   combining current asset and liability decisions,
   274–275
   conservative approach, 270
   investment policies, 263–266
   maturity matching, 268–269
   moderate investment policy, 264–266
   needed for growth, 276–277(SB)
   overview of cash conversion cycle, 258–262
   relaxed investment policy, 264–266
   restricted investment policy, 264–266
   short-term credit, 270–271, 273–274
   terminology, 256–258
Short-term financial policy, 268
Short-term financing
   use of security in, 382–383, 395–401
Short-term gain or loss, 37–38
Siemens, 314(IP)
Signaling of dividends, 787–788
Silent partners, 11
Simple interest, 377
Sinking fund, 157, 565–566
   for preferred stock, 593
Small businesses
   advantages of mergers for, 840–841(SB)
   choosing a banker, 110–112(SB)
   contracting with providers of risk capital, 598–
   599(SB)
   financing growth, 759–760(SB)
   financing receivables directly, 383–384(SB)
   franchises, 237–239(SB)
   goals in, 28–29(SB)

Small businesses, *continued*
  going public, 633–635(SB), 711–712(SB)
  growth and working capital needs, 276–277(SB)
  lease financing for, 673(SB)
  resource poverty, 27–28(SB)
  resources and goals in, 27–29(SB)
  venture capital financing and advice, 73–75(SB)
Smith, F. Alan, 487(DIF)
Smith, Roger, 488(DIF)
Social responsibility, 20, 22–23
Social welfare and stock price maximization, 24–25
Soifer, Raphael, 115(DIF)
Sole proprietorship, 10–11
Solving for time and interest rates, 451–453
Sommer, A. A., Jr., 170(DIF)
Sources and uses of funds statement, 165–168
Sovereign risk, 871
Specialist banks, 109
Speculative balances, 289
Spin-off, 832
Spontaneously generated funds, 224–225
Spot markets, 50
Spot rate, 863–864
Spread, 630
Stand-alone risk, 532
Standard deviation, 412–415
Standard of fairness, 773
Standard of feasibility, 773
Stated interest rate, 482
Statement of cash flows, 151, 163–168
  preparing, 165–168
  role of depreciation, 164–165
Statement of retained earnings, 151, 159–160
Stepped-up exercise price, 665
Stifler, Larry, 222–223(IP)
Stock. *See* Common stock and Preferred stock
Stock activity after going public, 628
Stock buy-back, 287–288(DIF), 316(DIF)
Stock dividends, 797, 798–801
  decision to use, 798
  effect on stock prices, 800–801
Stockholder control of the firm, 610–611
Stockholder diversification
  facilitated by going public, 626–627
Stockholders
  desire for current vs. future income affecting
    dividend policy, 786–787
  legal rights and privileges of, 610–613
Stockholders' equity (net worth), 158–159
Stockholder wealth maximization, 16–17, 614
  issues related to, 19–20, 22–26
  reasons for, 16–17
  social welfare and, 24–25
Stock market, 61–71
  bond markets, 67–68
  over-the-counter market, 63–64
  regulation of, 69–71
  reporting of, 64–66
  stock exchanges, 62–63
  trends in trading procedures, 64
Stock market reporting, 64–66
Stock-out costs, 340
Stock price maximization, 19–20, 24–25
Stock prices
  effect of financial leverage on, 744–747
  effect of stock dividends and stock splits on, 798

factors affecting, 25
  interest rate levels and, 138
Stock repurchase, 795–797
Stock splits, 797, 798–801
  decision to use, 798
  effect on stock prices, 800–801
Stretching accounts payable, 369
Striking (exercise) price, 658
Subordinated debentures, 571
Subsidiary, 835
Sunk cost, 496
Supernormal (nonconstant) growth, 621–624
Synchronized cash flows, 296
Synergy, 815–816, 824
Systematic risk, 421

T. J. Cinnamons, 238(SB)
Takeover, 610
Target (optimal) capital structure, 702, 728. *See
  also* Capital structure
Target cash balance, 291, 293–295
Target company, 821, 823
  determining value of, 829
  price paid for, 825
Taxable income, 36
Taxes. *See also* Federal income tax system
  capital structure decisions and, 756
  penalty tax on improperly accumulated earnings,
    42, 785–786
  relationship with value of the firm and
    bankruptcy costs, 750–752
Tax loss carry-back and carry-forward, 41–42
Temporary current assets, 268
Temporary investment, 306
Tender offer, 17, 797, 821, 823
Term loans, 563–564
  advantages of, 563–564
  amortization of, 564
  interest rate on, 564
Term structure of interest rates, 123, 131–137
  term structure theories, 131–134
Thompson, John, 28(SB)
Thrift crisis, 104–105(IP), 106–107
Time preferences for consumption, 118–119
Times interest earned (TIE) ratio, 190
Timmer, Jan. D., 880(DIF)
Total assets turnover ratio, 187
Total assets utilization ratio, 187
Total debt to total assets, 190
Total risk, 729
Toyota Motor Corporation, 313–314(IP)
Trade credit, 366–372
  costly, 371
  cost of, 367–369
  effect on financial statements, 369–372
  free, 371
Transactions balances, 289
Transferability of ownership interest, 12
Trans Union, 323(DIF)
Treasurer
  functions of, 14–15
Treasury stock, 796
Trend analysis, 195
Trump, Donald, 561–562(DIF), 603(DIF)
Trustee, 565
Trust receipt, 398–399
TRW, 323(DIF)

Tucson Electric Power Company, 779–780(DIF),
  805(DIF)
Turner, Ted, 575
Two-bin method, 347
Two-tier offer, 819–820

Underwriting syndicates, 632
Underwritten arrangement, 630
Underwritten issues, 630
Uneven payment streams, 461
  present value of, 460–463
Uniform Commercial Code, 382–383
  procedures under, 395–401
United Technologies, 182(IP)
Universal (global) banks, 109–110
Unsystematic risk, 421

Valuation of bonds, 583–590
Valuation of common stock, 613–624
Valuation of preferred stock, 595–597
Value of the firm
  established by going public, 627
  relationship with taxes and bankruptcy costs,
    750–752
Van der Klugt, Cornelis, 850(DIF), 879–880(DIF)
Variable operating costs, 732
Variance, 412
Venture capital, 73–75(SB), 598–599(SB)
Vertical merger, 816–817
Volcker, Paul A., 117(DIF)
Voting rights of stockholders, 592

Walker Products, 418–420
Wall Street crash of 1987, 33(DIF), 77–78(DIF)
Wall Street raider
  new definition of, 568–569(IP)
Warehouse receipt financing, 399–401
Warkocz, Reinhard, 314(IP)
Warrants, 571, 663–665
  detachable, 664
  initial market price of bonds with, 663–664
  reporting earning when outstanding, 672
  stepped-up exercise price of, 665
  use of in financing, 664–665
Weighted average cost of capital (WACC = k_a),
  702–703
  logic of, 688–689
Weir, Thomas C., 779(DIF), 805(DIF)
Welch, John F., 288(DIF)
White knight, 831
Wilcox, Joseph B., 779(DIF)
Window dressing techniques, 201
Within-firm risk, 532, 729
Working capital, 256–257
Working capital policy
  international, 866–869
World markets, 51
Wuliger, Ernest, 727(DIF)

Xerox, 349(IP)

Yield curve, 131–133
Yield to maturity (YTM), 589–590

Zero balance account, 304–305
Zero coupon bonds, 572–573
Zuckerman, Frederic, 77(DIF)